Formal and Practical Aspects of Domain-Specific Languages:

Recent Developments

Marjan Mernik
University of Maribor, Slovenia

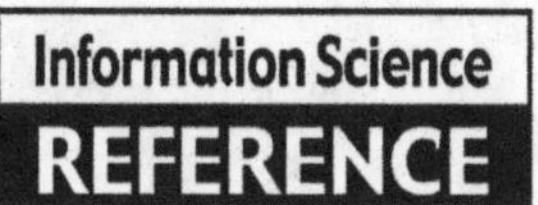

Managing Director: Lindsay Johnston
Editorial Director: Joel Gamon
Book Production Manager: Jennifer Romanchak
Publishing Systems Analyst: Adrienne Freeland
Development Editor: Hannah Abelbeck
Assistant Acquisitions Editor: Kayla Wolfe
Typesetter: Henry Ulrich
Cover Design: Nick Newcomer

Published in the United States of America by
Information Science Reference (an imprint of IGI Global)
701 E. Chocolate Avenue
Hershey PA 17033
Tel: 717-533-8845
Fax: 717-533-8661
E-mail: cust@igi-global.com
Web site: http://www.igi-global.com

Library of Congress Cataloging-in-Publication Data

Formal and practical aspects of domain-specific languages: recent developments / Marjan Mernik, editor.
p. cm.
Includes bibliographical references and index.
Summary: "This book presents current research on all aspects of domain-specific language for scholars and practitioners in the software engineering fields, providing new results and answers to open problems in DSL research"--Provided by publisher.
ISBN 978-1-4666-2092-6 (hardcover) -- ISBN 978-1-4666-2093-3 (ebook) -- ISBN 978-1-4666-2094-0 (print & perpetual access) 1. Domain-specific programming languages. I. Mernik, Marjan, 1964-
QA76.7.F655 2013
005.1'1--dc23

2012015755

British Cataloguing in Publication Data
A Cataloguing in Publication record for this book is available from the British Library.

Editorial Advisory Board

List of Reviewers

Table of Contents

Detailed Table of Contents

Out of a concern for focus and concision, domain-specific languages (DSLs) are usually very different from general purpose programming languages (GPLs), both at the syntactic and the semantic levels. One approach to DSL implementation is to write a full language infrastructure, including parser, interpreter, or even compiler. Another approach however, is to ground the DSL into an extensible GPL, giving you control over its own syntax and semantics. The DSL may then be designed merely as an extension to the original GPL, and its implementation may boil down to expressing only the differences with it. The task of DSL implementation is hence considerably eased. The purpose of this chapter is to provide a tour of the features that make a GPL extensible, and to demonstrate how, in this context, the distinction between DSL and GPL can blur, sometimes to the point of complete disappearance.

Domain specific language integration has to provide the right balance between the expressive power of the DSL and the implementation and maintenance cost of the applied integration techniques. External solutions may perform poorly as they depend on third party tools which should be implemented, tested and then maintained during the whole lifetime of the project. Ideally a self-contained solution can minimize third-party dependencies. The authors propose the use of C++ template metaprograms to develop a domain specific language integration library based on only the standard C++ language features. The code in the domain specific language is given as part of the C++ source code wrapped into C++ templates. When the C++ source is compiled, the C++ template metaprogram library implementing a full-featured parser infrastructure is executed. As the authors' approach does not require other tool than a standard C++ compiler, it is highly portable. To demonstrate their solution, the chapter implements a type-safe printf as a domain specific language. The library is fully implemented and downloadable as an open source project.

Convention dictates that the design of a language begins with its syntax. The authors of this chapter argue that early emphasis should be placed instead on the identification of general, compositional semantic domains, and that grounding the design process in semantics leads to languages with more consistent and more extensible syntax. They demonstrate this semantics-driven design process through the design and implementation of a DSL for defining and manipulating calendars, using Haskell as a metalanguage to support this discussion. The authors emphasize the importance of compositionality in semantics-driven language design, and describe a set of language operators that support an incremental and modular design process.

Domain-specific languages are often implemented by embedding them in general-purpose programming languages. The Kiama library used in this chapter for the Scala programming language contains a rewriting component that is an embedded implementation of the Stratego term rewriting language. The authors evaluate the trade-offs inherent in this approach and its practicality via a non-trivial case study. An existing Stratego implementation of a compiler for the Apply image processing language was translated into a Kiama implementation. The chapter examines the linguistic differences between the two versions of the Stratego domain-specific language, and compares the size, speed, and memory usage of the two Apply compiler implementations. The authors' experience shows that the embedded language implementation inflicts constraints that mean a precise duplication of Stratego is impossible, but the main flavor of the language is preserved. The implementation approach allows for writing code of similar size, but imposes a performance penalty. Nevertheless, the performance is still at a practically useful level and scales for large inputs in the same way as the Stratego implementation.

Domain Specific Languages (DSL) are becoming increasingly more important with the emergence of Model-Driven paradigms. Most literature on DSLs is focused on describing particular languages, and there is still a lack of works that compare different approaches or carry out empirical studies regarding the construction or usage of DSLs. Several design choices must be made when building a DSL, but one important question is whether the DSL will be external or internal, since this affects the other aspects of the language. This chapter aims to provide developers confronting the internal-external dichotomy with guidance, through a comparison of the RubyTL and Gra2MoL model transformations languages, which have been built as an internal DSL and an external DSL, respectively. Both languages will first be introduced, and certain implementation issues will be discussed. The two languages will then be compared, and the advantages and disadvantages of each approach will be shown. Finally, some of the lessons learned will be presented.

Internal DSLs are a special kind of DSLs that use an existing programming language as their host. In this chapter, the author explains an iterative development process for internal DSLs. The goals of this process are: (1) to give developers a familiar environment in which they can use known and proven development steps, techniques, tools, and host languages, (2) to provide a set of repeatable, iterative steps that support the continuous adaptation and evolution of the domain knowledge and the DSL implementation, and (3) to apply design principles that help to develop DSLs with essential properties and to use host language independent design patterns to plan and communicate the design and implementation of the DSL. The process consists of three development steps (analysis, language design, and language implementation) and applies four principles: open form, agile and test-driven development, design pattern knowledge, and design principle knowledge.

Internal DSLs are a special kind of DSLs that use an existing programming language as their host. To build them successfully, knowledge regarding how to modify the host language is essential. In this chapter, the author contributes six DSL design principles and 21 DSL design patterns. DSL Design principles provide guidelines that identify specific design goals to shape the syntax and semantic of a DSL. DSL design patterns express proven knowledge about recurring DSL design challenges, their solution, and their connection to each other – forming a rich vocabulary that developers can use to explain a DSL design and share their knowledge. The chapter presents design patterns grouped into foundation patterns (which provide the skeleton of the DSL consisting of objects and methods), notation patterns (which address syntactic variations of host language expressions), and abstraction patterns (which provide the domain-specific abstractions as extensions or even modifications of the host language semantics).

Domain Specific Languages (DSLs) are often defined in terms of metamodels capturing the abstract syntax of the language. For a complete definition of a DSL, both syntactic and semantic aspects of the language have to be specified. Metamodeling environments support syntactic definition issues, but they do not provide any help in defining the semantics of metamodels, which is usually given in natural language. In this chapter, the authors present an approach to formally define the semantics of metamodel-based languages. It is based on a translational technique that hooks to the language metamodel its precise and executable semantics expressed in terms of the Abstract State Machine formal method. The chapter also shows how different techniques can be used for formal analysis of models (i.e., instance of the language metamodel). The authors exemplify the use of their approach on a language for Petri nets.

Domain-specific languages (DSLs) provide developers with the ability to describe applications using language elements that directly represent concepts in the application problem domains. Unlike general-purpose languages, domain concepts are embedded in the semantics of a DSL. In this chapter, the authors present an interpreted domain-specific modeling language (i-DSML) whose models are used to specify user-defined communication services, and support the users' changing communication needs at runtime. These model changes are interpreted at runtime to produce events that are handled by the labeled transition system semantics of the i-DSML. Specifically, model changes are used to produce scripts that change the underlying communication structure. The script-producing process is called synthesis. The authors describe the semantics of the i-DSML called the Communication Modeling Language (CML) and its use in the runtime synthesis process, and briefly describe how the synthesis process is implemented in the Communication Virtual Machine (CVM), the execution engine for CML models.

This chapter contributes to the formal specification of Kermeta, a popular metamodelling framework useful for the design of DSL structure and semantics. The formal specification is tool-/tool syntax independent; it only uses classical mathematical instruments taught in usual computer science courses. This specification serves as a reference specification from which specialised implementation can be derived for execution, simulation, or formal analysis of DSLs. By providing such a specification, the chapter ensures that each and every DSL written in Kermeta, receives de facto a formal counterpart, making its definition fully formal. This radically contrasts with other approaches that require a new ad hoc semantics defined for every new DSL. The chapter briefly reports on two implementations conducted to demonstrate the feasibility of the approach.

XMF and XModeler are presented as technologies that have been specifically designed for Software Language Engineering. XMF provides a meta-circular, extensible platform for DSL definition based on syntax-classes that extend object-oriented classes with composable grammars. XModeler is a development environment built on top of XMF that provides an extensible client-based architecture for developing DSL tools.

An important challenge in software development is to have efficient tools for creating, debugging, and testing software components developed for specific business domains. This is more imperative if it is considered that a large number of users are not familiar with popular programming languages. Hence, Application Creation Environments (ACEs) based on specific Domain-Specific Languages (DSLs) can provide an efficient way for creating applications for a specific domain of interest. The provided ACEs should incorporate all the functionality needed by developers to build, debug, and test applications. In this chapter, the authors present their contribution in this domain based on the experience of the IPAC system. The IPAC system provides a middleware and an ACE for developing and using intelligent, context-aware services in mobile nodes. The chapter fully describes the ACE, which is a key part of the overall architecture. The ACE provides two editors (textual, visual), a wide functionality spectrum, as well as a debugger and an application emulator. The ACE is based on an Application Description Language (ADL) developed for IPAC. The ADL provides elements for the description of an application workflow for embedded systems. Through such functionality, developers are capable of efficiently creating and testing applications that will be deployed on mobile nodes.

In general, designing a domain-specific language (DSL) is a complicated process, requiring the cooperation of experts from both application domain and computer language development areas. One of the problems that may occur is a communication gap between a domain expert and a language engineer. Since domain experts are usually non-technical people, it might be difficult for them to express requirements on a DSL notation in a technical manner. Another compelling problem is that even though the majority of DSLs share the same notation style for representing the common language constructs, a language engineer has to formulate the specification for these constructs repeatedly for each new DSL being designed. The authors propose an innovative concept of computer language patterns to capture the well-known recurring notation style often seen in many computer languages. To address the communication problem, they aim for the way of proposing a DSL notation by providing program examples as they would have been written in a desired DSL. As a combination of these two ideas, the chapter presents a method for example-driven DSL notation specification (EDNS), which utilizes computer language patterns for semi-automated inference of a DSL notation specification from the provided program examples.

Domain-Specific Languages (DSLs) can be regarded as User Interfaces (UIs) because they bridge the gap between the domain experts and the computation platforms. Usability of DSLs by domain experts is a key factor for their successful adoption. The few reports supporting improvement claims are persuasive, but mostly anecdotal. Systematic literature reviews show that evidences on the effects of the introduction of DSLs are actually very scarce. In particular, the evaluation of usability is often skipped, relaxed, or at least omitted from papers reporting the development of DSLs. The few exceptions mostly take place at the end of the development process, when fixing problems is already too expensive. A systematic approach, based on techniques for the experimental evaluation of UIs, should be used to assess suitability of new DSLs. This chapter presents a general experimental evaluation model, tailored for DSLs' experimental evaluation, and instantiates it in several DSL's evaluation examples.

Chapter 15
Integrating DSLs into a Software Engineering Process: Application to Collaborative Construction of Telecom Services 408
Vanea Chiprianov, Telecom Bretagne, France
Yvon Kermarrec, Telecom Bretagne, France
Siegfried Rouvrais, Telecom Bretagne, France

The development of large and complex systems involves many people, stakeholders. Engineeringly speaking, one way to control this complexity is by designing and analyzing the system from different perspectives. For each perspective, stakeholders benefit from means, tools, languages, specific to their activity domain. A Domain Specific Language (DSL) per perspective is such a dedicated means. While DSLs are used for modeling, other means, tools, and languages are needed for other connected activities, like testing or collaborating. However, using such different types of tools together, integrating DSLs into stakeholders' software process is not straightforward. In this chapter, the authors advance an integration process of DSLs with other tools. The chapter proposes each stakeholder have their own DSL with associated graphical editor, operational semantics, and generation of scripts for off the shelf simulators, e.g., testing. Additionally to the integrated stakeholders' software process, the authors introduce a model driven process dedicated to the tool vendor which creates the DSLs and its associated tools. Due to the integration of DSLs into this process, they contend that stakeholders will significantly reduce system construction time. The chapter illustrates the two processes on Telecommunications service construction.

Section 4
Domain-Specific Language Examples

Chapter 16
Organizing the Aggregate: Languages for Spatial Computing 436
Jacob Beal, Raytheon BBN Technologies, USA
Stefan Dulman, Delft University, The Netherlands
Mirko Viroli, University of Bologna, Italy
Nikolaus Correll, University of Colorado Boulder, USA
Kyle Usbeck, Raytheon BBN Technologies, USA

As the number of computing devices embedded into engineered systems continues to rise, there is a widening gap between the needs of the user to control aggregates of devices and the complex technology of individual devices. Spatial computing attempts to bridge this gap for systems with local communication by exploiting the connection between physical locality and device connectivity. A large number of spatial computing domain specific languages (DSLs) have emerged across diverse domains, from biology

and reconfigurable computing, to sensor networks and agent-based systems. In this chapter, the authors develop a framework for analyzing and comparing spatial computing DSLs, survey the current state of the art, and provide a roadmap for future spatial computing DSL investigation.

Ivan Luković, University of Novi Sad, Serbia
Vladimir Ivančević, University of Novi Sad, Serbia
Slavica Aleksić, University of Novi Sad, Serbia
Milan Čeliković, University of Novi Sad, Serbia

In this chapter, the authors give an overview of the evolution of Information System (IS) development methods used in the last few decades and show how model driven approaches and Domain Specific Languages (DSLs) have managed to take an often essential role in the modern IS development process. To present an overall picture, the authors discuss significant breakthroughs, popular approaches, their strong and weak points, along with the examples of their practical use in the domain of IS development and generation of software applications. In order to further support the aforementioned points, the chapter offers a synopsis of Integrated Information Systems CASE Tool (IIS*Case), a model driven software development tool for IS modeling and prototype generation. A special attention is drawn to its evolution and position relative to some of the key changes in IS development approaches in recent history. The authors highlight the significance of DSLs in this context and present a DSL featured in the tool. The DSL was created to provide platform independent model (PIM) IS specifications which can be transformed into executable application prototypes through a chain of model-to-model and model-to-code transformations. Since the authors have developed both a textual DSL, and visual repository-based tools (visual DSLs) for this purpose, a discussion of pros and contras of textual vs. visual DSLs in the context of creating PIM specifications is also included. Furthermore, the chapter communicates practical experiences about creating meta-meta models of PIM concepts by means of attribute grammars and MOF meta-modeling language.

Ritu Arora, Texas Advanced Computing Center, USA
Purushotham Bangalore, University of Alabama at Birmingham, USA
Marjan Mernik, University of Maribor, Slovenia

There are several ongoing research efforts in the High Performance Computing (HPC) domain that are employing Domain-Specific Languages (DSLs) as the means of augmenting end-user productivity. A discussion on some of the research efforts that can positively impact the end-user productivity without negatively impacting the application performance is presented in this chapter. An overview of the process of developing a DSL for specifying parallel computations, called High-Level Parallelization Language (Hi-PaL), is presented along with the metrics for measuring its impact. A discussion on the future directions in which the DSL-based approaches can be applied in the HPC domain is also included.

Chapter 19
Design and Transformation of a Domain-Specific Language for Reconfigurable Conveyor Systems 553
Kyoungho An, Vanderbilt University, USA
Adam Trewyn, Vanderbilt University, USA
Aniruddha Gokhale, Vanderbilt University, USA
Shivakumar Sastry, The University of Akron, USA

Much of the existing literature on domain-specific modeling languages (DSMLs) focuses on either the DSML design and their use in developing complex software systems (e.g., in enterprise and web applications), or their use in physical systems (e.g., process control). With increasing focus on research and development of cyber-physical systems (CPS) such as autonomous automotive systems and process control systems, which are systems that tightly integrate cyber and physical artifacts, it becomes important to understand the need for and the roles played by DSMLs for such systems. One use of DSMLs for CPS systems is in the analysis and verification of different properties of the system. Many questions arise in this context: How are the cyber and physical artifacts represented in DSMLs? How can these DSMLs be used in analysis? This book chapter addresses these questions through a case study of reconfigurable conveyor systems used as a representative example.

Chapter 20
MoDSEL: Model-Driven Software Evolution Language 572
Ersin Er, Hacettepe University, Turkey
Bedir Tekinerdogan, Bilkent University, Turkey

Model-Driven Software Development (MDSD) aims to support the development and evolution of software intensive systems using the basic concepts of model, metamodel, and model transformation. In parallel with the ongoing academic research, MDSD is more and more applied in industrial practices. Like conventional non-MDSD practices, MDSD systems are also subject to changing requirements and have to cope with evolution. In this chapter, the authors provide a scenario-based approach for documenting and analyzing the impact of changes that apply to model-driven development systems. To model the composition and evolution of an MDSD system, they developed the so-called Model-Driven Software Evolution Language (MoDSEL) which is based on a megamodel for MDSD. MoDSEL includes explicit language abstractions to specify both the model elements of an MDSD system and the evolution scenarios that might apply to model elements. Based on MoDSEL specifications, an impact analysis is performed to assess the impact of evolution scenarios and the sensitivity of model elements. A case study is provided to show different kind of evolution scenarios and the required adaptations to model elements.

Compilation of References 595

About the Contributors 638

Index 648

Preface

Are you interested in new directions of software development? Would you like to have a detailed understanding of domain-specific languages? If you answered yes to either of these questions, then you should explore this book, which contains original academic work about current research in different areas of domain-specific languages. The book's mission is to give a comprehensive overview of the research in the field of domain-specific languages. Domain-specific languages represent an emerging technology, but their application is currently unduly limited by a lack of reliable knowledge available to potential domain-specific language developers. To remedy this situation, this book provides comprehensive material for anyone who would like to introduce domain-specific languages into their software engineering process. This book's ambition is to provide new results and answers to several open problems in domain-specific language research. The book is therefore indispensable for researchers and practitioners in the field of software engineering, as well as for educators who would like to introduce domain-specific languages into their curriculum.

There exist a plethora of computer languages. Some of them, such as Java and C#, are general-purpose programming languages that have many common features that can be used to write programs for a wide range of applications. These languages are the primary tools of the programmer. However, not all general-purpose computer languages are programming languages. For example, UML is a general-purpose modeling language for the abstract specification and documentation of many different kinds of software, and Z is a general-purpose formal specification language. Generality is a mixed blessing. Broad applicability often results in suboptimal expressiveness in any particular application domain, hence the motivation for domain-specific languages, which sacrifice generality in exchange for enhanced expressiveness in a particular domain. By providing notations and constructs tailored toward a particular application domain, domain-specific languages offer substantial gains in expressiveness and ease of use compared with general-purpose languages for the domain in question, with corresponding gains in productivity and reduced maintenance costs. By reducing the amount of domain and software development expertise needed, domain-specific languages expand their application to a larger group of software developers compared to general-purpose languages. These benefits have often been observed in practice and are supported by quantitative studies, although perhaps not as many as one would expect. The advantages of specialization are equally valid for programming, modeling, and specification languages.

Domain-specific languages have been around for a long time. BNF, for instance, dates back to the late 1950s, and represents an example of a domain-specific language that can be used to describe the syntax of a language. Although there are examples of many domain-specific languages from times past, it has only been recently that workshops and conferences emerged that have a focus on domain-specific languages. The development of domain-specific language is itself a significant software engineering task, requiring a considerable investment of time and resources. Without appropriate methodology and tools, the investment for domain-specific language support can exceed the savings that might be obtained from their usage. Hence, domain-specific language development should be based on strong software engineering principles with clearly identified phases (e.g., decision, analysis, design, implementation, deployment, maintenance) and artifacts. Despite the recent attention that domain-specific languages have attracted from researchers, many challenges still exist that need to be solved before domain-specific languages will become fully adopted by domain experts, end-users, and professional programmers. For example, general-purpose languages are often designed with great care and comply to language design principles. Unfortunately, this is not always the case for the design and development of domain-specific languages. Design and implementation of general-purpose languages may last several months, while development of domain-specific languages should be more cost effective. However, there is a serious threat that such cost-effectiveness will negatively impact language design and/or implementation. In this respect, some open problems are:

- How should results from domain analysis drive the language design process?
- Should a domain-specific language be designed by a domain expert, general-purpose language designer or software language engineer?
- How much domain analysis and language design is actually needed?
- Can we skip some initial domain-specific languages development phases? What are the consequences?
- Can we build tools that support earlier phases of domain-specific language development?

There are no straightforward answers to these questions, and actual decisions depend on many factors, such as domain-specific language end-users, project budget, time to market, and domain-specific language life span. After deciding to invest into domain-specific language development, a domain analysis should be performed with the aim to build the domain model, which is an explicit representation of the common and the variable properties of the system in a domain. The domain model should also describe the semantics of domain concepts and the dependencies between these concepts. Some typical domain analysis activities are analysis of similarity, analysis of variations, and analysis of combinations. Despite the existence of many domain analysis methods (e.g., FODA and FAST), they are rarely used in domain-specific language development. As a result, domain analysis is usually done informally and in an incomplete manner. There is an urgent need in domain-specific language research to identify the reasons for such informal development and possible solutions for improvement. An initial observation is that information gathered during domain analysis cannot be automatically used in the language design process. Another reason might be that complete domain analysis is often complex and may be outside of software engineers' capabilities.

Designing a language involves defining the constructs in the language and giving the semantics to the language, whether formal or informal. The semantics of the language describe the meaning of each construct in the language, but also some fixed behavior that it is not specified by the program. Designing a language is highly creative, but not an easy task. As stated before, information gathered in the domain analysis should be used along with additional constraints (e.g., capability to perform various analysis, readability). Of particular importance for domain-specific languages is the level of abstraction that can be represented in the language and the degree to which it may be analyzed. From previous experiences with programming language design and from criteria for programming language evaluation, researchers developed several criteria for good language design, such as readability, writeability, reliability, and cost. However, the criteria for language design are often contradicting (e.g., reliability vs. cost of execution, readability vs. writeability). Hence, language designers should find good trade-offs among these factors. To help language designers in this process, several rules of thumb have been proposed, such as:

- Don't include untried ideas - consolidation, not innovation.
- Simplicity is really the key - avoid complexity. Too many solutions make the language hard to understand.
- Avoid requiring something to be stated more than once.
- Automate mechanical, tedious, or error-prone activities by providing higher level features.
- Regular rules, without exceptions, are easier to learn, use, describe, and implement.

With respect to the language design phase, another important research question is whether domain-specific language design is radically different from general-purpose language design? The domain-specific language designer has to keep in mind the special characteristics of domain-specific languages, as well as the fact that users of the language may not be programmers. General-purpose languages are designed traditionally by computer scientists. The general-purpose language design process was driven by their personal aesthetics and theoretical judgments resulting in a computer language they would like to use. A domain-specific language for end-users should not be designed by such intuition because general-purpose language designers are not necessarily the targeted end-users. Therefore, domain-specific language design should be informed by empirical studies, involvement of end-users, or by psychology of programming research.

After a domain-specific language is designed, it should be implemented by building a domain-specific translator (e.g., compiler or interpreter). A vast array of implementation choices exists: interpreter/compiler, preprocessing, embedding, extensible compiler/interpreter, commercial of-the-shelf (COTS) components, or some hybrid variation. In the compiler/interpreter approach, standard compiler/interpreter techniques are used to implement a domain-specific language, such that a complete static semantic analysis is done on the program written in the domain-specific language. Using the preprocessing approach, the domain-specific language constructs are simply translated into constructs in a base language (e.g., Java or C++). In the preprocessing approach, static semantic analysis of a domain-specific program is limited to the capabilities available in the base language. There are important sub-patterns of the preprocessing approach (e.g., macro processing, source-to-source transformation, pipeline, and lexical processing). In the embedding approach, existing mechanisms in the host language (e.g., operator overloading, using functions as operators and vice versa) are used to build a library of domain-specific operations. The existing compiler/interpreter for the host language is completely reused, which means that a domain-specific program is also syntactically and semantically valid as a general-purpose program. In the extensible compiler/interpreter approach, the general-purpose compiler/interpreter is extended to be able to cover domain-specific constructs. In the COTS approach, existing tools and/or notations are applied to a specific domain (e.g., XML-based domain-specific languages). Blending particular implementation approaches is also possible and popular. Although various implementation approaches are beneficial, they bring another open research issue: which implementation approach is the most suitable from the point of implementers and from the point of language users? Finally, the differences and advantages/disadvantages in the implementation from the grammarware and modelware point of view have not yet been investigated deeply in the domain-specific language research community. Grammar-based domain-specific languages are those languages where structure (syntax) is defined by grammars, while structure of metamodel-based domain-specific languages is defined by metamodels. There is still lively debate among domain-specific language researchers about which syntax specification is the most appropriate.

A solution to the aforementioned problems would enable new horizons in domain-specific language and end-user development that would introduce a new paradigm shift in software development. The domain-specific language field is growing quickly, and it will take some time for stabilization of these issues. This book, comprised of 20 chapters, presents several recent developments in various aspects of domain-specific language development. The book is divided into the following cohesive sections, which can be read independently:

Section 1: Internal domain-specific languages (Chapters 1 – 7),
Section 2: Domain-specific language semantics (Chapters 8 – 10),
Section 3: Domain-specific language tools and processes (Chapters 11 – 15),
Section 4: Domain-specific language examples (Chapters 16 – 20).

The term "internal domain-specific language" is specifically related to the design and implementation phases of domain-specific language development. Approaches to domain-specific language design can be further characterized along two orthogonal (independent) dimensions:

- The formal nature of the design description
- The relationship between the domain-specific languages and existing languages

The first dimension is about informal versus formal language design. In an informal design, the specification is usually in some form of natural or computer language, which may include a set of illustrative domain-specific language programs. A formal design consists of a specification written using one of the available formal definition methods (e.g., regular expressions and grammars for syntax specifications, and attribute grammars, denotational semantics, operational semantics, or abstract state machines for semantic specification). The second dimension is about language exploitation versus language invention. In the former case, and often the easiest way, the design of a domain-specific language is based on an existing language, where the existing language is:

- **Partially Used:** Piggyback pattern (e.g., only Java statements are used)
- **Restricted:** Language specialization pattern
- **Extended:** Language extension pattern

One possible benefit of the language exploitation design pattern is familiarity for programmers. The implementation of the domain-specific language is also often easier with this pattern. If there is no relationship between the domain-specific language under development and an existing computer language, then a new language has to be invented. This requires the specification of the new language's syntax and semantics. Note that language exploitation vs. language invention is completely a design decision, and virtually any implementation pattern can be chosen after that to implement such a domain-specific language. For example, a new compiler or preprocessor can be implemented even when extending an existing language. Of course, such an extension would be in many cases easier to implement by embedding.

An internal domain-specific language is an extension of an existing computer language that is implemented by embedding. Hence, there is no need to write a compiler/interpreter for such a newly developed domain-specific language, because a host language compiler/interpreter is completely reused without any changes. An "external domain-specific language" refers to those domain-specific languages that require the construction of a new domain-specific language translator (usually requiring the implementation of a syntax and/or semantic analyzer). Note that if an existing computer language is only partially used or specialized, the existing host compiler/interpreter cannot be used without changes; such a domain-specific language is not internal. Hence, an internal domain-specific language is just a special case of the language exploitation design pattern (only for language extension pattern) with the requirement that such a domain-specific language can be implemented by embedding. An internal domain-specific language determines both the design and the implementation phase of a particular domain-specific language. On the other hand, an internal domain-specific language cannot be called an embedded domain-specific language because the term "embedding" has been mistakenly used in the domain-specific language community for two purposes and is a source of much confusion.

Firstly, domain-specific language embedding has been used as a synonym for a domain-specific language design phase where the domain-specific language is implemented by reusing existing language constructs by extension, specialization, or by a piggyback approach. Secondly, domain-specific language embedding was used originally as a synonym for a particular domain-specific language implementation approach where the domain-specific language is implemented by using the host language feature of function composition. This embedding is of the purest sense. It is clear that the term "embedding" is overloaded and should not cover both phases of design and implementation. To distinguish these two cases, two patterns emerged for the domain-specific language design phase: language exploitation versus language invention, while embedding in a pure sense is only one out of many different implementation approaches (compiler/interpreter, preprocessing, embedding, extensible compiler/interpreter, COTS, and hybrid). Hence, the terms "heterogeneous embedding" and "homogeneous embedding" have been also used to distinguish these two cases. The heterogeneous embedding indicates the case where a domain-specific language is designed by language exploitation (extension, specialization, piggyback) and not implemented by an embedding approach. As readers may notice, the terminology might be quite confusing - heterogeneous embedding uses the term "embedding" for the design phase and not for the implementation phase, where such a type of language is not implemented by embedding. On the other hand, 'homogeneously embedded domain-specific language' is a domain-specific language designed by language exploitation using only an extension sub-pattern and implemented by embedding (using macros, function composition, and libraries that provide domain-specific constructs) without changes in host compiler/interpreter. Hence, homogeneously embedded domain-specific languages is a synonym for internal domain-specific languages, while heterogeneous embedding is only one particular approach that can be used for external domain-specific languages, which covers also those domain-specific languages designed by the invention design pattern (Figure 1).

There are several benefits of internal domain-specific languages. Because the syntax and semantics are borrowed from a host language, there is less need to define such an internal domain-specific language formally. Hence, much less effort is needed to develop an internal domain-specific language. Many language features can be implemented with relative ease due to the reuse from a host language. Inherently, designing such an internal domain-specific language is less error prone. In general, it can be said that internal domain specific languages are well designed by default. Internal domain-specific languages may also reuse other language-based tools (e.g., editor, debugger) and/or whole integrated de-

Figure 1. Internal versus external domain-specific languages

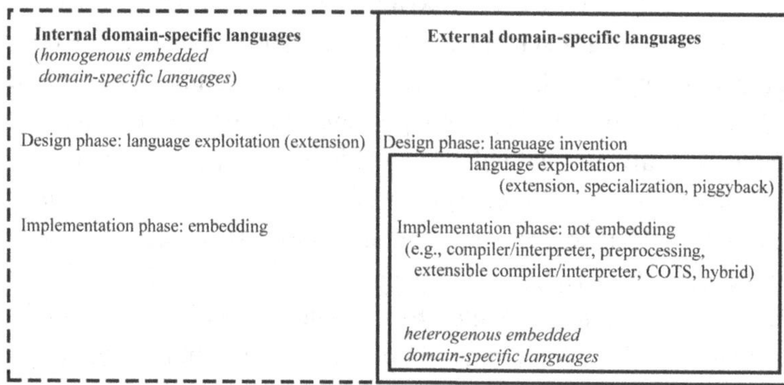

velopment environments of a host language. However, internal domain-specific languages may suffer from suitable domain notation and an inability to perform domain-specific analysis, verification, optimization, parallelization, and transformations (AVOPT). Appropriate or established domain-specific notations are usually beyond the limited user-definable notation offered by general-purpose languages. The importance of suitable notations should not be underestimated as they are directly related to the productivity improvement associated with the use of domain-specific languages. The degree to which internal domain-specific language can establish appropriate domain-specific notation depends on the flexibility of a host language. In this respect, general-purpose languages offer different possibilities.

The first four chapters of this book investigate appropriateness of different general-purpose programming languages (Lisp in Chapter 1, C++ in Chapter 2, Haskell in Chapter 3, and Scala in Chapter 4) as host languages for domain-specific notations. An additional goal of Chapter 3 is to show semantic-driven design where a language developer first concentrates on semantic domains and their operations, while an appropriate domain notation comes afterward. Appropriate or established domain-specific notation for anything more than a trivial domain-specific language is usually hard to achieve using the internal approach. One of the objectives of Chapter 4 is to experiment with a non-trivial domain-specific language to achieve an established notation using an internal domain-specific language. An appropriate or established domain-specific notation is much easier, and can often be achieved using an external domain-specific language because different syntax analyzers can be applied (e.g., generalized LR parser, backtracking parsers). The decision on whether to choose an internal or external domain-specific language has profound consequences on later phases. The final decision depends on many factors, and some are discussed in Chapter 5. The discussion on internal domain-specific languages concludes in Chapters 6 and 7, which discuss iterative development of internal domain-specific languages, and design principles/patterns for internal domain-specific languages. Despite their limitations, internal domain-specific languages are formidable competitors to external domain-specific languages. Even with improved domain-specific toolkits, it will remain the most cost-effective solution in many cases. Section 1 (Chapters 1 -7) of this book is unique in covering the details of internal domain-specific languages. Hopefully, the chapters in this book will become a standard source of knowledge for developing internal domain-specific languages.

The semantics of domain-specific languages are discussed in Section 2 (Chapters 8 – 10). Although formalizing domain-specific language semantics is often not needed for internal domain-specific languages, it is crucial for external domain-specific languages. With a formalization of a language, the meaning of domain-specific language constructs can be defined unambiguously. Also, other language-based tools can be constructed automatically from formal specifications (as with general-purpose languages). Although these benefits occur for grammar-based domain-specific languages where different semantic formalisms have been extensively used (e.g., attribute grammars, denotational semantics, operational semantics), the opposite is true for metamodel-based domain-specific languages, where syntax is formally specified, not by grammars, but metamodels. Chapters 8 and 9 discuss different aspects of formally defining the semantics of metamodel-based domain-specific languages. In Chapter 10, the formal semantics of Kermeta, a popular framework for metamodel-based domain-specific languages, is given. By providing such formal semantics, any domain-specific language developed with Kermeta is formally specified.

Domain-specific language tools and processes are discussed in Section 3 (Chapters 11 – 15). While using a dedicated domain-specific language, the tools for building domain-specific language translators are indispensable and expedite the domain-specific language development. However, there are very few such tools. To be productive, programmers need a domain-specific language translator and also other development tools (e.g., debugger, simulator, analyzer). Hence, Chapter 11 discusses domain-specific language development with the XMF notation in the XModeler tool and compares the tool with some other such available tools. The topic of constructing and using a particular domain-specific language debugger is the focus of Chapter 12. The development of a domain-specific language can be expedited by inferring the domain-specific notation, as presented in Chapter 13. Finally, after development, a newly developed domain-specific language should go through the process of verification and validation. Two key questions are related to this activity: Did we develop a domain-specific language that can solve the problems efficiently for which it was designed? Is the newly developed domain-specific language using a natural notation that is easy to use by end-users? Such questions should be answered during an evaluation of domain-specific languages. This topic is discussed in Chapter 14. Building a domain-specific language is generally not the only goal. A domain-specific language often must be integrated into an existing software engineering process through customization. This introduces several challenges, which are discussed in Chapter 15.

Finally, in Section 4 (Chapters 16 – 20) different examples of domain-specific languages are presented. In Chapter 16, domain-specific languages for spatial computing are discussed and systematically classified, and in Chapter 17 domain-specific languages for information system development are investigated. In Chapters 18 and 19, the domain-specific languages for high-level parallelization and for reconfigurable conveyor systems are presented, respectively. In Chapter 20, a domain-specific language for model-driven software evolution concludes the spectrum of different domain-specific languages.

There were 38 chapter proposals that were received in response to the call for chapters (CFC) issued in May 2011. Out of 38 two-page proposals, 30 were selected, and authors were invited to submit full chapters by October 2011. After the reviewing process, there were 20 chapters selected for inclusion into this book (thus, an overall 53% acceptance rate).

Marjan Mernik
University of Maribor, Slovenia & University of Alabama at Birmingham, USA
April 11, 2012

Acknowledgment

I would like to thank to all authors for submitting their valuable works, to reviewers for timely and critical review reports, and to members of the editorial advisory board for supervising the whole process. Finally, I would to thank Hannah Abelbeck, IGI Global Editorial Assistant, for her cooperation while preparing this book.

Section 1
Internal Domain-Specific Languages

Chapter 1
Extensible Languages:
Blurring the Distinction between DSL and GPL

Didier Verna
EPITA Research and Development Laboratory, France

ABSTRACT

Out of a concern for focus and concision, domain-specific languages (DSLs) are usually very different from general purpose programming languages (GPLs), both at the syntactic and the semantic levels. One approach to DSL implementation is to write a full language infrastructure, including parser, interpreter, or even compiler. Another approach however, is to ground the DSL into an extensible GPL, giving you control over its own syntax and semantics. The DSL may then be designed merely as an extension to the original GPL, and its implementation may boil down to expressing only the differences with it. The task of DSL implementation is hence considerably eased. The purpose of this chapter is to provide a tour of the features that make a GPL extensible, and to demonstrate how, in this context, the distinction between DSL and GPL can blur, sometimes to the point of complete disappearance.

INTRODUCTION

Domain-specific language (DSL) design and implementation is inherently a transverse activity (Ghosh, 2010; Fowler, 2010). It usually requires from the product team knowledge and expertise in both the application domain and language design and implementation, two completely orthogonal areas of expertise. From the programming language perspective, one additional complication is that being an expert developer in one specific programming language does not make you an expert in lan-

DOI: 10.4018/978-1-4666-2092-6.ch001

Figure 1. Taxonomy of DSLs

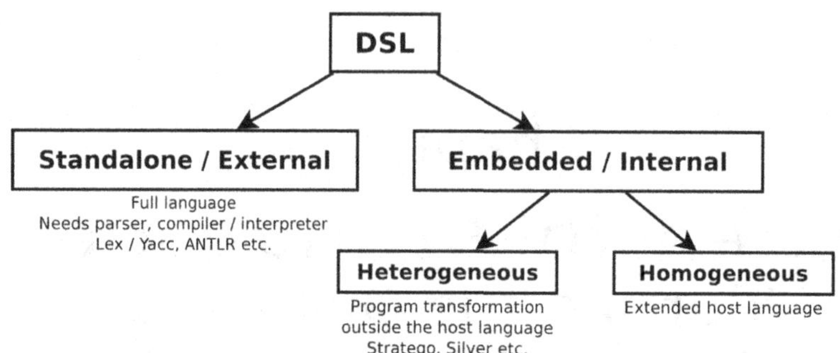

guage design and implementation - only in using one of them. DSLs, however, are most of the time completely different from the mainstream languages in which applications are written. A general-purpose programming language (GPL), suitable to write a large application, is generally not suited to domain specific modeling, precisely because it is too general. Using a GPL for domain-specific modeling would require too much expertise from the end-users and wouldn't be expressive enough for the very specific domain the application is supposed to focus on.

As a consequence, it is often taken for granted that when a DSL is part of a larger application, it has to be completely different from the application's GPL. But what if this assumption was wrong in the first place ?

Taxonomy of DSLs

Following Fowler (2005) and Tratt (2008, section 2), a taxonomy of DSLs is provided in Figure 1.

Standalone DSLs

A *standalone*, or *external* DSL is written from scratch, as a completely autonomous language. In such a case, a whole new compiler / interpreter chain needs to be implemented, presumably with tools like Lex, Yacc, ANTLR etc. As noted by Vasudevan and Tratt (2011):

Such an approach provides the DSL author with complete control over the DSL, from its syntax to its style of execution, but leads to high development costs as each implementation tends to be engineered from scratch.

In addition to that, the use of several languages in parallel, within the same application, may be regarded as a disadvantage (Ghosh, 2011):

Unless carefully controlled, this polyglot programming can lead to a language cacophony and result in bloated design.

Indeed, every time a standalone DSL needs to be extended, the whole language production chain may need to be modified in ways that were not anticipated.

Embedded DSLs

A second approach to DSL implementation consists in reusing the capabilities (both syntactic and semantic) of a host GPL, hence avoiding the need for rewriting a complete infrastructure. This approach leads to so-called *embedded* or *internal* DSLs, and idea which is probably at least 50 years old (Landin, 1966). In order to implement an embedded DSL, one needs to express it in terms of the differences from the host GPL. To that aim, two approaches currently exist.

1. **Embedded Heterogeneous DSLs:** The first approach consists in a two-steps process: first a DSL program is converted into a host GPL one by means of external program transformation tools such as Stratego/XT (Bravenboer et al., 2006) or Silver (Wyk et al., 2008). Then, the resulting transformed program is passed on to the original GPL's infrastructure.

The need for designing a DSL as a either standalone or embedded heterogeneous language often comes from the lack of extensibility of your GPL of choice. By imposing a rigid syntax, a set of predefined operators and data structures on you, the traditional GPL approach makes it practically impossible to "morph" the GPL into the requested DSL.

2. **Embedded Homogeneous DSLs:** An alternative view, however, is that some GPLs are flexible enough to let you implement a DSL merely as an extension to themselves. Here, "extension" means the ability to modify some aspects of the original GPL, in syntactic or even semantic terms.

Embedded DSLs in general offer the advantage of lightening the programming burden by making it possible to reuse software components from the host GPL. Embedded homogeneous DSLs are even more advantageous, particularly when the DSL is not supposed to produce standalone executables, but is instead part of a larger application (for example, a scripting, configuration or extension language).

In such a situation, the final application, as a whole, is written in a completely unified language. While the end-user does not have access to the whole backstage infrastructure and hence does not really see a difference with the other approaches, the gain for the developer is substantial. Since the DSL is now just another entry point for the same original GPL, there is essentially only one application written in only one language to maintain.

Moreover, no specific external language infrastructure (parser, interpreter, compiler, transformation tool etc.) is required for the DSL anymore, since it is simply expressed in terms of the original GPL. The already existing GPL infrastructure is all that is needed.

Objectives

This chapter focuses on embedded homogeneous DSL design and implementation through the use of extensible GPLs. Our purpose is actually twofold.

1. The first objective of this chapter is to provide a tour of what we think are the most important features that contribute to language extensibility. The next section provides such a survey.
2. The second objective of this chapter is to demonstrate how those features affect the process of DSL design and implementation.

The general message underlying the whole chapter is that with a truely extensible language, the separation between DSL and GPL can blur, sometimes to the point of complete disappearance. In order to demonstrate this, the remaining sections are devoted to incrementally building on a particular DSL example, introducing one interesting language feature at a time. The DSL in question is a simple one, yet it allows to demonstrate the use of many of the extensibility features mentioned in the next section, plus some others.

The example is developed using the Common Lisp (1994) language. The choice of Common Lisp is motivated by the following points.

1. Amongst all industrial-scale programming languages available today, Common Lisp is rarely talked about and somewhat forgotten. Lisp is nevertheless a family of languages that is worth knowing about.

2. As we will explain later on, the peculiar design of Lisp makes it extensible almost be definition. Despite being more that 50 years old, we still believe it to be the most extensible language in use today, which makes it a perfect candidate for illustrating our discourse.
3. Precisely in terms of extensibility, Lisp has many of the features exhibited in the next section, plus some others, less widely known, that nevertheless play a crucial role DSL design and implementation. These less conventional features will also be introduced in this chapter.

Note however that no prior knowledge of Lisp or any related dialect is required in order to understand the presented material.

EXTENSIBILITY AT A GLANCE

In this section, we provide a quick overview of the most important and / or widespread extensibility features that can be found in many programming languages. As the literature in this area is vast, providing an exhaustive survey is out of the scope of this chapter (such a work would probably require a whole chapter by itself). For more comprehensive or comparative studies, see for instance van Deursen et al. (2000), Vasudevan and Tratt (2011), Tratt (2008, section 2) and Elliott (1999, section 8).

Perhaps the first extensibility feature of a programming language is the support for user-defined data types and operations. This was already the case in the 70's with the Algol 68 algorithmic language (van Wijngaarden, 1981). At that time, that is, even before the term "Domain Specific Language" was grokked, some people thought of using its extension capabilities for domain-specific applications. For example, Denert et al. (1975) uses it to design a graphics sub-language making it easier to create objects (points, polygons etc.) and manipulate them (rotating, scaling etc.). Pagan (1979) also uses Algol 68, although this time, as a meta-language for denotational semantics. It is worth noting that by "user-defined operations" here, we mean infix operators, along with their respective priorities, a feature not so widespread even today (a more modern language allowing for defining new infix operators by way of their functional denotation is Haskell (Marlow, 2010).

Instead of extending the operators of a language by adding user-defined ones, it may also be possible to overload the existing ones with user-defined semantics. C++ (2011) is a language which provides this ability. By overloading the function application operator `()` for example, C++ objects can be made to behave like function calls. This technique is used, amongst others, by McNamara and Smaragdakis (2000) in order to provide a functional programming layer on top of classic C++.

Another important source of extensibility in C++ is its template system (Veldhuizen, 1996), also interesting in terms of performance as it is in fact a Turing-complete, purely functional language that executes at compile-time (Veldhuizen, 2003). For instance, techniques such as so-called *expression templates* along with many others (Abrahams and Gurtovoy, 2004) are used by Prud'homme (2006) in order to create a DSL for numerical projection, integration and other applications.

Forth (Moore, 1974) is an older language featuring operator-based extensibility as well as compile-time intercession. The programmer may not only define new operators ("words" in the Forth jargon) but also override the existing ones. Compile-time intercession is made possible precisely because the compiler appears to the programmer as a subset of the built-in words (which can therefore be modified). These features have been used for domain-specific purpose, for example by Ahson and Lamba (1985).

Compile-time meta-programming is considered a "hot" topic these days. Experimental languages such as Template Haskell (Sheard and

Figure 2. Highlighted output

```
Usage: advanced [-hd] [+d] [OPTIONS] cmd [OPTIONS]

Available commands: push pull.
Use 'cmd --help' to get command-specific help.
  -h, --help                 Print this help and exit.
  -(+)d, --debug[=on/off]    Turn debugging on or off.
                             Fallback: on
                             Environment: DEBUG
```

Jones, 2002) or MetaOCaml (Calcagno et al., 2003) extend their respective original language with compile-time intercession. A comparative study of their use for DSL production is given by Czarnecki et al. (2004). Compile-time meta-programming is not limited to statically typed languages. Dynamic languages such as MetaLua or Converge may also benefit from extensibility in this area (Tratt, 2005; Fleutot and Tratt, 2007). Nemerle is another such example (Skalski et al., 2004).

Functional languages such as ML (Milner et al., 1997) and Haskell (Marlow, 2010) are notoriously good at embedding DSLs, as demonstrated by Kamin (1998), Elliott (1999) and Hudak (1998). Crucial extensibility factors in functional languages are notably higher order functions, expressions (as opposed to instructions), polymorphism, and, for some of them, strong / static typing and laziness. It is worth mentioning that traditional languages are getting more and more functional features these days, pushing their extensibility limits farther away. For example, the latest C++ standard comes with additional facilities such as anonymous functions, range-based iterators and initializer lists which, in conjunction with older techniques such as operator overloading, makes it possible to implement a JavaScript engine, including much of its original syntax, on top of classic C++ (Chedeau and Verna, 2012).

Scala (Odersky et al., 2010) is a relatively recent language, also suitable for embedding DSLs. Features such as nominal and structural typing, virtual types, bounded and higher order polymorphism make for a high level of extensibility, including access to the compiler infrastructure. Scala is also used at the core of Delite (Rompf et al., 2011), a compiler framework and runtime for parallel embedded domain-specific languages. This also represents a new trend in DSL development putting the emphasis on reusable, language-oriented, software building block and IDEs (Fowler, 2005).

Finally, two notable examples of (more marginal) languages providing support for syntactic extension are the TeX typographic system by Donald E. Knuth (1984) and the M4 macro-expansion system (Kernighan and Ritchie, 1977; Turner, 1994). TeX has the notion of active characters that get specific semantics through their category code. The category code of any character may be changed at anytime with the `\catcode` built-in. M4 has the ability to modify its comment, quote and word syntax through the built-in `changequote`, `changecom` and `changeword` macros.

A CONCRETE EXAMPLE

In this section, we introduce the example that we are going to use as illustration in the whole chapter. This example is inspired from Clon (Verna, 2010), a library for command-line options management. Amongst its many features, Clon has the ability to automatically generate help strings, format them and display them on the terminal with ANSI coloring (SGR, 1991). A sample output is given in Figure 2.

The user of an application written with Clon has the ability to customize the highlighting process by creating theme files containing highlight specifications (hence the need for a DSL). Highlight specifications are based on two concepts: faces and properties. A face encompasses a block of text and describes the appearance of this block of text by means of properties. SGR-compatible terminals support Boolean properties such as `bold` or `underline` and other kind of properties like `foreground` or `background` colors (with values such as `white`, `black`, `cyan`, `yellow` etc.).

Clon provides a set of built-in faces which represent the various logical blocks of text in the help string. For instance, every option is encapsulated in a face called `option`. Faces can also be nested. The whole help string is encapsulated in a face called `toplevel`, a super-face of all other faces. The `option` face has 2 interesting sub-faces: one called `syntax`, corresponding to the left column in Figure 2, and one called `usage`, corresponding to the right column. Thanks to nesting, faces provide property inheritance: a property applies to a face and all its sub-faces, unless overridden deeper in the face tree.

Note that for the sake of clarity and concision, all code excerpts provided in this chapter are functional, but largely simplified. Only the points relevant to the chapter's focus are detailed, and in particular, everything related to error management has been omitted. A complete listing of the code presented here is available for download as a chapter companion: http://www.lrde.epita.fr/~didier/about/books.php. The original library, with actual production code can also be downloaded at the following address: http://www.lrde.epita.fr/~didier/software/lisp/clon.php.

IMPLEMENTING FACE SUPPORT

The first thing we need to do to in order to provide this highlighting model is to implement the support for faces in the library. A natural solution is to use CLOS, the Common Lisp Object System (Bobrow et al., 1988; Keene, 1989) and represent faces as objects of some `face` class.

The `face` Class

A simplified implementation of the face class would look like this:

```
(defclass face ()
  ((name :initarg :name)
   (bold :initarg :bold)
   (underline :initarg :underline)
   (foreground :initarg :foreground)
   (background :initarg :background)
   (subfaces :initarg :subfaces)))
```

Contrary to traditional object-oriented languages in which defining a class is done syntactically (e.g. `class Face {...};` in C++), Lisp does this through macro or function calls. The macro `defclass` defines a new class called `face`. The first, empty, pair of parenthesis denotes an empty list of super-classes for the `face` class. The rest of this call is the definition of class slots (class members in the Lisp terminology). We define some of the highlight properties mentioned earlier, and also the slot `name`, for storing the name of the face, and a slot `subfaces` for storing a list of sub-faces.

Note that no type information is provided for the class slots. Lisp is dynamically typed by default and performs type checking at runtime (it is however possible to provide static type information when available and suppress the dynamic type checks).

Once the `face` class is defined, we can create instances of it with the standard function `make-instance`. The following call literally means to create an instance of a class called `face`:

```
> (make-instance 'face)
=> #<FACE {B9656C9}>
```

Box 1.

```
> (make-instance 'face :name 'option :bold t :foreground 'cyan)
=> #<FACE {BA644E9}>
```

The quotation mark (`'`) prevents evaluation of the symbol `face`. Without it, `face` would be taken as a variable name, which, being unbound, would throw an error. The `#<...>` notation is used by Lisp to output a printed representation of something not normally printable (here, an instance of a particular class).

It is also possible to instantiate the class and provide initial values for slots at the same time. This is done with so-called *initialization arguments* and explains the `:initarg`'s in the call to `defclass`. An example of how you would create an `option` face displaying bold text in a cyan foreground is demonstrated in Box 1.

Thanks to the presence of `:initarg`'s in the class definition, make-instance knows that the value of `:name` (the symbol option) must be used to initialize the slot name, and so on. Also, note again that the initial values we provide for the `name` and `foreground` slots are the symbols `option` and `cyan` themselves (quoted to that purpose), not the values of hypothetical variables named `option` and `cyan`. The symbol `t`, on the other hand, is a special symbol standing for the truth value and needs not be quoted (in fact, `t` evaluates to itself).

A Crash-Course on Lisp Function Calls

Let us pause a minute here and consider the general topic of Lisp function calls. The fact that `make-instance`, in spite of being a standard function, automatically understands the `:initarg`'s for all classes we may create might be surprising. There is however no magic involved. It is just an ordinary function, but it makes use of a special feature of Lisp called *keywords*. Keywords are special symbols (prefixed with a colon) that, amongst other things, are used to implement support for named arguments in function calls. A function may define a set of accepted keywords and use them by name, like this:

```
(defun show-keys (&key key1 key2)
  (list key1 key2))

> (show-keys :key2 "test")
=> (NIL "test")
```

The `&key` construct means that the subsequent arguments are in fact keyword-named ones. A keyword argument not provided in the function call gets a default value, which itself defaults to `nil`. There is much more to Lisp function calls than just keywords. Let us also mention the fact that a Lisp function may get a fully reflexive access to its argument list by means of so-called *rest* arguments, introduced by the `&rest` keyword. A rest argument contains a list of all the arguments passed to a function, as illustrated in Box 2:

An Instantiation Wrapper

We can use the flexibility offered by Lisp function calls to produce a first refinement on our current face implementation. Using `make-instance` directly to create faces is not satisfactory for several reasons.

1. It exposes the actual name of the class, which can arguably be considered as an implementation detail.
2. Keyword arguments are intrinsically optional, so the programmer is not forced to provide them. This is not a problem for face

Box 2.

```
(defun show-args (&rest args &key key1 key2)
  (list key1 key2 args))

> (show-args :key2 "test")
=> (NIL "test" ( :KEY2 "test"))
```

Box 3.

```
(defun make-face (name &rest args &key &allow-other-keys)
  (apply #'make-instance 'face :name name args))
```

Box 4.

```
> (make-face 'option :bold t :foreground 'cyan)
=> #<FACE {C13AE99}>
```

properties, as they are all supposed to get default values, but this is a problem for face names, which should be mandatory.

In such situations, it is customary in Lisp to provide an *instantiation wrapper* so that the programmer avoids calling `make-instance` directly. Instead, a `make-face` function for creating new faces is provided in Box 3, which we can use as shown in Box 4.

Some details about `make-face` are in order here. First, note that the first argument, `name`, is mandatory. This ensures that every created face has a name. Next, we retrieve the full argument list in the rest argument called `args`. Finally, we stipulate that this function accepts keyword arguments (`&key`), but instead of naming them explicitly, we use a special marker, `&allow-other-keys`, to bypass the validity check for keywords. In essence, this means that `make-face` will silently accept any possible keyword argument whatsoever. The big advantage of this is that if at a later point, the face class evolves and gets new slots with new `:initarg`'s, we won't have to modify `make-face` to handle them. It is also worth mentioning that we loose nothing in terms of safety by accepting any possible keyword argument, because invalid initialization arguments are caught at a lower-level by the object system itself anyway. In other words, even if a wrong keyword argument escapes `make-face`, it won't escape `make-instance`.

Finally, let us explain how we go from calling `make-face` to calling `make-instance`. The key here is the standard function `apply`, which takes a function object, some arguments (the last one being in fact a list of arguments) and applies the function to the arguments. The hash-quote (`#'`) syntax literally means "the function object which is named `make-instance`". Next, we pass the relevant series of arguments to `make-instance`: the `face` class, the name of the new face after its corresponding initialization argument `:name`, and finally all the other initialization arguments as a list. The relevant steps in evaluating a call to `make-face` are presented in Box 5.

What is important to understand here is that in addition to reflexive access to argument lists, we also benefit from another language feature: the fact that Lisp is a functional language. Being

Box 5.

```
>  (make-face 'option :bold t :foreground 'cyan)
-> (apply #'make-instance 'face :name 'option '( :bold t :foreground cyan))
-> (make-instance 'face :name 'option :bold t :foreground 'cyan)
```

Box 6.

```
(setq default-theme
  (make-face 'toplevel :background 'black
    :subfaces (list (make-face 'option
                     :foreground 'white
                     :subfaces (list (make-face 'syntax
                                        :bold t
                                        :foreground 'cyan)
                                     (make-face 'usage
                                        :foreground 'yellow))))))
```

functional in this context means that functions are first-class objects that we can manipulate directly, for instance by constructing calls to them on the fly. The term "first-class object" (a.k.a. first-class citizen, first-order or higher-order etc.) was originally used by Christopher Strachey (Stoy and Strachey, 1972; Burstall, 2000) in order to informally reference programming languages entities that can be stored in variables, aggregated in structures, given as argument to functions or returned by them etc.

REFINING FACE SUPPORT

In our library, we probably want to provide a set of predefined themes, including a default one which would work in the absence of any user customization. Box 6 shows how we can programmatically create a default theme, in other words, a default face tree, in our current implementation.

This code in Box 6 is unsatisfactory in many respects:

1. We shouldn't need to create the toplevel face explicitly because we *know* that every theme starts with this face as the root object.
2. We need to explicitly create lists of subfaces to give to the `:subfaces` arguments. This is unfortunate because it exposes an implementation detail. What if, for instance, we decided one day to switch to arrays instead of lists? Besides, creating a list of faces explicitly is cumbersome when we have only one sub-face.
3. We need to explicitly call `make-face` to create each and every face. This redundancy shouldn't be needed because we know exactly how a `:subfaces` argument is to be constructed.
4. Finally, it is cumbersome to quote face names and color names, all of which are symbols. Note that in theory, everything should be quoted in a call to `make-face`. It just happens that keywords (starting with a colon) and the truth values `t` and `nil` are all self-evaluating: the value of `:foo` is `:foo` and the value of `t` is `t`. In the ideal case, we would want to get rid of all quoting.

Box 7.

```
(setq default-theme
  (make-theme
    :background 'black
    :subfaces (list (make-face 'option
                      :foreground 'white
                      :subfaces (list (make-face 'syntax
                                          :bold t
                                          :foreground 'cyan)
                                        (make-face 'usage
                                          :foreground 'yellow))))))
```

Problem #1 is easily solved. We can implement a function `make-theme` which wraps its arguments within a call to `make-face` in order to create the toplevel face implicitly:

```
(defun make-theme (&rest args)
  (apply #'make-face 'toplevel args))
```

Our default theme can now be created as shown in Box 7.

This solution only makes use of functionalities that we have already encountered (`apply`, first-class functions and reflexive manipulation of argument lists). Solving the three other issues will however require the introduction of new language features.

HIDING SUBFACES IMPLEMENTATION WITH THE MOP

In order to solve problem #2, we propose the following solution. Instead of using the `:subfaces` initialization argument directly, it would be more convenient to have a `:face` keyword argument, allowing us to specify one face at a time, but as many times as we like (including zero, or just one). The idea would be to collect all such faces and eventually create a list of them in order to initialize the `subfaces` slot. Creating a face with two subfaces would then look like this:

```
(make-face 'a-face
  :face (make-face 'subface-1)
  :face (make-face 'subface-2))
```

Given what we have learned so far, there is no technical challenge in implementing this feature: we already know how to manipulate argument lists. A more interesting question is where to implement it. `make-theme` is obviously not the right place because we want this feature to be available even without using themes (e.g. when manipulating faces individually). `make-face` would be a better choice, but still not the best one: the purpose of `make-face` was to both hide the actual face class name and make the face name argument mandatory. As such, it is not really involved the manipulation of initialization arguments. Besides, implementing the `:face` keyword argument at that level would introduce a semantic discrepancy between `make-face` and `make-instance` in terms of keyword handling. This means that ultimately, we would like `make-instance` itself to understand `:face` arguments, eventhough they are not actual initialization arguments.

Fortunately, there is a way to do so, which involves modifying CLOS, the Common Lisp Object System itself. Before going into the details, we first need to explain what makes CLOS special compared to traditional object systems.

Specificities of the Common Lisp Object System

- In CLOS, methods do not belong to classes (there is no privileged object receiving the messages). A polymorphic call appears in the code like an ordinary function call. Functions whose behavior is provided by such methods are called *generic functions*. A generic function's *method* is a specialization of that function for a specific set of argument classes. As a corollary, it is worth pointing out that CLOS methods are in fact *multi-methods*: the polymorphic dispatch is based on *any* number of arguments (not only the first one).
- CLOS itself is written on top of a Meta-Object Protocol, simply known as the CLOS MOP (Paepcke, 1993; Kiczales et al., 1991). Although not part of the Common Lisp ANSI specification (Common Lisp, 1994), the CLOS MOP is a de facto standard well supported by many Common Lisp implementations. In supporting implementations, the MOP layer allows for CLOS to be implemented in itself. For example, a CLOS class is a Lisp object of some class, called a *meta-class*. The MOP not only provides introspective access to the object system's state but also lets the programmer modify its behavior. This is what we are going to use now.

Extending the CLOS Object Initialization Process

Back to our original problem. Recall that we want to compute the `:subfaces` initialization argument automatically from the `:face` one(s). In the CLOS MOP, the object initialization phase, that is, the time when slots are initialized based on their corresponding initialization arguments, is performed by a generic function called `initialize-instance`. We can extend the standard behavior of CLOS by providing a new method for this function, as depicted in Box 8.

The first argument to initialize-instance (the list `(instance face)`) is a *specialization*. It is of the form `(var class)` and means that this method is only applicable for instance variables of the `face` class.

The purpose of this method is to dynamically construct a new function call with `apply` (we have done this before). Assume the existence of an `extract-faces` function which extracts all values for `:face` keywords from an argument list `args` and collects them into another list. As you can see, the arguments provided to the constructed function call are the instance we are initializing, a `:subfaces` keyword argument with all the faces collected from the original argument list, and finally the original argument list itself.

More interesting is `call-next-method`, the new function that we are calling. In CLOS, the set of applicable methods for a particular generic function call is sorted by order of specificity (explaining how it is done is beyond the scope of this chapter). Within the body of one method, `call-next-method` will invoke the next most specific one available. In our particular case, the

Box 8.

```
(defmethod initialize-instance ((instance face) &rest args)
  (apply #'call-next-method instance :subfaces (extract-faces args) args))
```

Box 9.

```
(setq default-theme
  (make-theme
    :background 'black
    :face (make-face 'option
            :foreground 'white
            :face (make-face 'syntax :bold t :foreground 'cyan)
            :face (make-face 'usage :foreground 'yellow))))
```

Box 10.

```
(defmethod initialize-instance ((instance face) &rest args &key face)
  (apply #'call-next-method instance :subfaces (extract-faces args) args))
```

method we provide is specific to `face` objects, and by using `call-next-method`, we are in fact invoking the standard initialization method provided by CLOS itself, only with a tweaked argument list. Given this small machinery, it is now possible to rewrite our default theme as shown in Box 9.

Here are two final remarks on `initialize-instance`.

1. You may have noticed that when we `call-next-method`, we not only provide a `:subfaces` argument, but also the original `:face` ones that remained in the original `args` list. To be really pedantic, we could clean up `args` so as to remove those spurious arguments, but this is in fact not necessary; they will simply be ignored by the initialization process because they don't correspond to any `:initarg`.
2. There is however a glitch in this policy. In CLOS, the instantiation process checks for the validity of keyword arguments and throws an error otherwise. Since `:face` is not a proper `:initarg`, we need to explicitly declare that it is nonetheless a valid initialization argument. Otherwise, the call to `make-instance` would break. There are several ways to do so. One we can use is to declare a `face` key in our `initialize-instance` method. CLOS will automatically register it as a valid `:initarg`. The new and final version of our `initialize-instance` method is presented in Box 10.

GETTING RID OF REDUNDANCY WITH NEW SYNTAX

Problem #3 is to get rid of the `make-face` verbosity. Recall that every time we see a `:face` keyword, we expect a subsequent call to `make-face`, so we shouldn't have to write it explicitly. In fact, only the list of arguments to the `make-face` call should be needed. We propose to solve this problem by extending the standard Lisp syntax with our own syntactic constructs.

A reader unfamiliar with Lisp so far may have noticed that the syntax of the language is very uniform: most of the code we wrote boils down to *prefix notation*, that is, a function name followed by its arguments, enclosed within a pair of parenthesis serving as list delimiters.

We have, however, also encountered small bits of specific syntax here and there. For instance, it is obvious that the parenthesis characters `()` are

Box 11.

```
(make-face 'syntax :bold t :foreground 'cyan)
```

Box 12.

```
(defun {-reader (stream char)
  (let ((make-face-arguments (read-delimited-list #\} stream t)))
    (push 'make-face make-face-arguments)))
```

treated in a special way. We have also already encountered the single quote character (`'`) that we used to prevent evaluation of a symbol, and the hash-quote (`#'`) construct which denotes a function object of some name.

It turns out that in Lisp, all of these syntactic bits are under the control of the programmer. The syntactic state of Lisp is described in a so-called *readtable*. A readtable lets you associate the desired characters with a specific syntactic behavior. Those characters are then called *macro characters* (although they have nothing to do with Lisp "macros"). All other characters are treated normally. The programmer has the ability to create, destroy or modify readtables at any time, and specify which one is to be used at which time. Also, it is important to understand that as their name suggests, readtables are used at *read-time*, that is, when some piece of Lisp code is actually parsed and read into the Lisp engine.

There are two kinds of macro characters in Lisp.

- Ordinary macro characters are like parenthesis or quote: single characters that get a specific syntactic meaning. Other notable standard examples are double-quotes (for denoting strings) and semicolons (for starting line comments). Note that the ampersand we encountered in `&rest` or `&key` is *not* a macro character by default. It simply is a valid character in symbol names.
- The second category contains so-called *dispatching* macro characters, which require a second, subsequent character to work. In standard Lisp syntax, the hash character (`#`) belongs to this category. We have already encountered the `#'` construct for denoting function objects. Other notable examples include `#A` for denoting arrays, `#S` for denoting structures and `#\` for denoting character objects. For instance, `#\{` means "the opening brace character".

For simplicity, we only consider the case of ordinary macro characters. A possible syntactic shortcut for the face instantiation expression is presented in Box 11, which can be achieved by using a dedicated brace notation:

```
{'syntax :bold t :foreground 'cyan}
```

The function `{-reader` below performs this transformation. Note that at this point, `{-reader` is a valid function name in Lisp because the brace character is not special yet, so it can appear literally in symbol names as shown in Box 12.

This function reads a list of tokens from a `stream`, this list being delimited by a closing brace character (`#\}`), and then pushes the symbol `make-face` on top of that list in order to construct the appropriate function call. In greater detail:

- The `char` argument is unused. It is bound to the macro character associated with this function, which we *know* is the opening

Box 13.

```
(set-macro-character #\{ #'{-reader)
(set-macro-character #\} (get-macro-character #\)))
```

Box 14.

```
(setq default-theme
  (make-theme
    :background 'black
    :face {'option :foreground 'white
                   :face {'syntax :bold t :foreground 'cyan}
                   :face {'usage :foreground 'yellow}}))
```

brace. This argument is useful when you use the same function for multiple macro characters.

- `Read-delimited-list` is the standard Lisp function that does all the job of parsing tokens until a closing brace is found (and consumed), and returning a list of them. Its last argument `t` deals with recursive calls to the Lisp reader (since faces have sub-faces, the Lisp reader may be called recursively).

The last thing we need to do is to actually hook this new syntax up into the Lisp reader itself. This is demonstrated in Box 13 by turning braces into ordinary macro characters.

From now on, the opening brace character has become special. Note that the second line makes the closing brace a special character as well and gives it the same meaning as a closing parenthesis (the end of a list). Macro characters defined in this way are said to be *terminating*: they have lexical semantics and terminate a token when the lexer eats input. This means for instance that it is not possible anymore to call a function `weird}name`, because that would be read as the symbol `weird`, the end of a list, and the symbol `name`. If you still want to do so, you need to escape the symbol name with pipes: `|weird}name|`. Making braces terminating macro characters is important because it ensures that they will always be used in the intended context only. Otherwise, the Lisp reader will throw an error.

Given this syntactic extension, it is now possible to rewrite our default theme as presented in Box 14.

One final remark: the way we have used `set-macro-character` is to modify the default readtable that is used throughout the whole application's code. It was done this way for simplicity but it is not a good idea in general. A better approach is to localize our syntactic extensions in a specific readtable and only activate it for the pieces of code we know are dealing with faces.

Wrap-Up

At this point, it is worth taking a step back and reconsider the state of our program. As a matter of fact, in only 5 lines of code, we have achieved something rather puzzling: we have extended the syntax of the original language with our own constructs, without having to write a full lexer or a parser.

Let us replay the different steps of a typical scenario involving ordinary macro characters (the scenario is almost the same for a dispatching macro character):

1. A Lisp program contains the following form: `{'option :foreground 'white}`
2. At read-time, that is, when the code is analyzed and parsed at the lexical and syntactic level, the brace character is read in and found to have a special semantics. Its reader function is invoked.
3. This function takes on parsing and calls `read-delimited-list`.
4. `read-delimited-list` continues parsing, eating tokens until the closing brace is found and returns a list of four elements: the quoted symbol `option`, the keyword `:foreground` and the quoted symbol `white`.
5. The reader function pushes the symbol `make-face` on top of that list, turning it into the list `(make-face 'option :foreground 'white)` and returns it.
6. The Lisp evaluator (which, as we will see later on, may involve a compilation step) receives this list as a piece of code, and executes it as a function call to `make-face` along with its arguments.

The key points in understanding the power of syntax extension here are the following:

- Macro characters and readtables let the programmer plug his own processing directly into the Lisp parser, that is, even before the code is evaluated.
- A reader function is just a Lisp function. This means that not only you have "write access" to the parsing phase, but the whole language is available to you at that time.
- The machinery that Lisp itself uses in its own reader is available to the programmer (notably `read` and `read-delimited-list`). That is precisely why you don't need to rewrite a parser in order to extend the original syntax, but only plug in the small bits you need. Those functions will perform the parsing of sub-expressions for you, possibly by recursively taking into account all currently installed extensions, and return unevaluated Lisp expressions, (lists of) tokens, that you can manipulate at will in order to provide the final expression.

Finally, note that the crucial aspect underlying everything here is Lisp's "code is data" philosophy. This is, in particular, what makes the transition between steps 5 and 6 a no-op in the above scenario. In step 5, you are manipulating a piece of your program's AST directly, and the internal representation of it is just a list of tokens (symbols most of the time); the very same list structure that you would use for data. In other words, your reader function manipulates a piece of data which is in fact a piece of code. Looking at `(+ 1 2)` from the data point of view, you would see a list containing the symbol + and the two numbers `1` and `2`. Looking at it from the code point of view, you would see a call to the function + with two arguments. The ability to manipulate code as data in its own internal representation is what makes Lisp so flexible.

GETTING RID OF QUOTING WITH MACROS

Problem #4 is to avoid the need for quoting every initialization argument when creating faces. For instance, when the initialization arguments are `('option :foreground 'white)`, we would prefer to write them down simply as `(option :foreground white)`. As in the previous section, this concern also rings the bell of code transformation.

In theory, it is possible to perform this transformation at read-time. We could for instance modify `{-reader` to not only push the symbol `make-face` on top of the argument list, but also add quotes where they are missing. This is however not a good idea for several reasons:

- The reader level should be concerned with syntax only. Adding syntactic sugar such as the `{}` construct for face creation is indeed a concern for the reader. Automatically quoting symbols, however, is not a syntactic concern. It's only another level of code transformation.
- Problem #4 is in fact completely orthogonal to syntax, so we might want to benefit from quotation avoidance even outside the `{}` construct. We could then combine both features, but only afterwards.

One elegant solution to this problem is hence to define a wrapper around `make-face` which does the job of quoting the arguments for us. The idea is to be able to write something like this:

```
(define-face option :foreground white)
```

That is the perfect job for a Lisp macro.

A Crash-Course on Lisp Macros

Lisp macros suffer from a great deal of confusion and lack of understanding, probably because in spite of what their name suggests, they bear no resemblance with conventional macro systems such as the C preprocessor which is merely a string expander.

The main characteristics of Lisp macros are the following.

- Just like a reader function, a Lisp macro works on chunks of code, that is, at the parser level.
- The purpose of a Lisp macro is to take Lisp expressions as input and transform them into a new expression which, in turn, will be evaluated.
- Just like a reader function, a Lisp macro is a Lisp function before anything else. This means that again, you have the full language at your disposal to perform code transformation.
- Contrary to ordinary functions, however, Lisp macros don't evaluate their arguments. This effectively gives you the ability to control what is evaluated and when, something that we are going to use soon. As a side note, this feature is also the key to implementing a lazy evaluation scheme in Lisp.
- Also contrary to ordinary functions, Lisp macros are executed at compile-time. It is only the result of their execution that is eventually compiled into machine code. This is very important because it shows that just as reader functions are hooks into the Lisp parser, macros are hooks into the Lisp compiler.

Let us take a simple example to illustrate those points. In Lisp, there is an `if` special operator that is used like this: `(if test then else)`. It is called "special operator" because contrary to ordinary function (but as one would expect), it only evaluates one of the `then` or `else` clause, according to the result of the test. For example:

```
> (if t 1 (error "ERROR!"))
=> 1
```

What would happen if you tried to define an `ifnot` function like this?

```
(defun ifnot (test then else)
  (if test else then))
```

It would not work, because Lisp operates in applicative rather than normal order (eager rather than lazy evaluation). Thus, the arguments of the function would be evaluated *before* the function were actually called, so you would get an error:

```
> (ifnot t (error "ERROR!") 1)
=> *** ERROR!
```

In order to compensate for this, we need to transform the `ifnot` expression into the corresponding `if` expression *before* it is evaluated. This means that `ifnot` needs to be a macro. Remember that the macro must not actually evaluate the `if` expression, only construct it and return it to whomever the caller might be (interpreter, compiler etc.). The `ifnot` macro is given below:

```
(defmacro ifnot (test then else)
  (list 'if test else then))
```

It constructs a list beginning with the `if` symbol and the 3 conditional clauses put back in order. Note that the `if` symbol is quoted. What we want is the symbol itself, not its value as a potential variable. On the other hand, we need to use the values of the `test`, `then` and `else` arguments, so they must not be quoted.

Let us check that this macro works as intended (see Box 15).

`macroexpand-1` is a standard function that prints the result of a macro expansion. It comes in very handy for debugging during macro development, and we see here that this macro works correctly. Again, what is important to notice is that the value of the `then` clause, that is, the call to the `error` function has not been evaluated.

We end this crash-course on Lisp macros with two very useful additional bits of syntactic sugar. When developing complicated macros expanding to a lot of nested function calls, you end up creating a lot of lists. This can render the macro code quite difficult to read. In order to make the macro code itself look closer to its actual output, you may use the backquote (`) operator instead of calls to the `list` function. Backquote is almost like quote: it prevents evaluation. The difference is that within a backquoted expression, you may still evaluate a sub-expression by prefixing it with a comma (`,`). Here is a new version of `ifnot`, using backquote, which is admittedly a bit more readable than the previous one:

```
(defmacro ifnot (test then else)
  `(if, test, else, then))
```

Finally, there is an important variation on comma: the `,@` construct. It works like comma in the sense that it permits evaluation within a backquoted expression, but in addition to that, the evaluation must produce a list, and this list will be "spliced" into the enclosing one. For instance, consider the difference between the two expressions below:

```
> `(1, (list 2 3) 4)
=> (1 (2 3) 4)

> `(1, @(list 2 3) 4)
=> (1 2 3 4)
```

The usefulness of backquote, comma and `,@` extends beyond their use in macros, as we will see later.

The `define-face` Macro

Back to our original problem. We want to insert quotes automatically to the values of keywords like `:foreground`, `:background` etc., but we must avoid doing so on `:face` (and even `:subfaces` if we want to be exhaustive). That is

Box 15

```
> (macroexpand-1 '(ifnot t (error "ERROR!") 1))
=> (IF T 1 (ERROR "ERROR!"))
```

Box 16.

```
(defmacro define-face (name &rest arguments)
  `(make-face ',name
    ,@(loop for key in arguments by #'cddr
            for val in (cdr arguments) by #'cddr
            collect key
            if (member key '( :face :subfaces))
              collect val
            else
              collect `',val)))
```

because an argument to the `:face` keyword is a call to `make-face` and hence must be evaluated. The idea is hence to create a macro which scans all its arguments and performs quoting only when required. The code provided in Box 16 does this, and is also a good opportunity for us to introduce an interesting standard macro: `loop`.

This macro creates a call to `make-face`: a list starting with the symbol `make-face` itself, followed by the face name, properly quoted. The interesting part is the loop over the other arguments, quoting them if needed. A call to `loop` almost reads as plain English:

1. We traverse the list of arguments with `key` bound to every i^{th} element and `val` bound to every $i+1^{th}$ element (`cdr` is the rest of a list, `cddr` is the rest of the rest of a list).
2. We `collect` the `key` itself (into a list).
3. If `key` is either `:face` or `:subfaces`, we `collect` its value directly. Otherwise, we collect the quoted value.

The result of this `loop`, the `collect`'ed list of potentially quoted arguments, is then spliced into to call to make-face with `,@`.

The loop macro is very pertinent for us because it is in fact a DSL for iteration in its own right. Interestingly enough, `loop` is controversial within in the Lisp community itself. Some people hate it because it is so unlispy: it has a complicated syntax with reserved keywords, and an infix notation which is in contradiction with the rest of the language. On the contrary, we think that `loop` is extremely lispy because it is the perfect example of the language's flexibility and extensibility. Within a simple macro call, you have the ability to implement a completely new and totally different language, and still be able to use it mixed within the original one.

As another example of `loop`, we provide in Box 17 the function `extract-faces` that we previously assumed to exist.

Let us now check that define-face works as intended as presented (see Box 18).

With a one-line modification to our reader function, we can also get rid of quoting in the { } construct. The reader function need only construct calls to `define-face` instead of `make-face` (see Box 19).

This allows us to rewrite the preceding expression as shown in Box 20.

Finally, remember that we had a `make-theme` function in charge of creating the `toplevel` face. If we want to avoid explicit quoting in `make-theme` as well, we need a `define-theme` macro instead. This macro must create the `toplevel` face using `define-face`, and that will be all:

```
(defmacro define-theme (&rest args)
  `(define-face toplevel, @args))
```

Box 17.

```
(defun extract-faces (keys)
  (loop for key in keys by #'cddr
        for val in (cdr keys) by #'cddr
        when (eq key :face)
        collect val))
```

Box 18.

```
> (macroexpand-1
    '(define-face option :foreground white
                         :face {'syntax :foreground 'yellow}))

-> (MAKE-FACE 'OPTION
     :FOREGROUND 'WHITE
     :FACE (MAKE-FACE 'SYNTAX :FOREGROUND 'YELLOW))
```

Box 19.

```
(defun {-reader (stream char)
  (let ((make-face-arguments (read-delimited-list #\} stream t)))
    (push 'define-face make-face-arguments)))
```

Box 20.

```
(define-face option :foreground white
                    :face {syntax :foreground yellow})
```

Box 21 presents how we can rewrite our default theme. Note that all the cumbersome quoting is gone now.

At this point, a Lisper will almost certainly find that the brace notation is unnecessary and prefer to switch back to plain parenthesis instead. This is in fact easily done: one just needs to adapt `define-face` by pushing the symbol `define-face` itself in front of the arguments to the `:face` keyword. In short, it needs to collect `(push 'define-face val)` instead of just collect `val`. It seems however that outside of the Lisp world, people are more accustomed to braces than to parenthesis, so for the sake of the exercise, we will stick to braces…

EXTERNALIZING THE DSL

With our recently designed macro `define-theme`, it seems that we have reached a point where, as programmers, we are rather satisfied with the code we need to write in order to create themes. But in fact, something even more interesting than that has happened in the process. If you look closely at what's inside a call

Box 21.

```
(setq default-theme
  (define-theme
    :background black
    :face {option :foreground white
                  :face {syntax :bold t :foreground cyan}
                  :face {usage :foreground yellow}}))
```

Box 22.

```
(defun read-user-theme ()
  (with-open-file
      (stream (merge-pathnames ".faces" (user-homedir-pathname)))
    (loop for expr = (read stream nil :eof)
          if (eql expr :eof)
            return exprs
          else
            collect expr into exprs)))
```

to `define-theme`, you will realize that it is in fact a DSL for theme creation. It is Lisp code, but it is also more than that. It's a purely declarative language for theme properties specification, with its own syntax and (evaluation) semantics.

This is an interesting point to make because especially in Lisp, it happens all the time. Given the flexibility of the language, Lisp programmers end up creating DSLs for such or such task constantly, and without even realizing it. Where a Lisp programmer merely sees a macro, an outsider will see a full blown DSL. Again, the `loop` macro is another typical example of this, although much more complicated to implement (because its syntax is so different from Lisp's original one). To quote John Foderaro (1991): "Lisp is a programmable programming language". What this means is what we are seeing in this chapter: whereas a programmer in a more conventional language often needs to adapt its desires to the constraints of the language, a Lisp programmer often adapts the language to his own desires. The language grows towards the application, not the other way around.

We are now going to implement support for user-level theme customization. In essence, our DSL is the contents of a call to `define-theme`. For simplicity, we assume that the application reads custom themes from a `.faces` file located in the user's home directory.

Reading User Themes

Box 22 presents the function `read-user-theme` that implements custom theme file reading.

`with-open-file` is a macro that does all the job of creating a `stream` from a file name, opening it for reading (in that case), and closing it afterwards. `merge-pathnames` constructs the full name of the `.faces` file under the user's home directory (`user-homedir-pathname`). Finally, the `loop` call reads expressions from the file `stream`, one at a time, until the end of the file is reached. The expressions are collected into an `exprs` list and the list is returned.

Box 23.

```
;;; My personal custom theme.
;;; Based on the default one, with some color changes.

:background blue
:face { option :foreground white
               :face { syntax :underline t :foreground red }
               :face { usage :foreground magenta }}
```

Box 24

```
(defun make-user-theme ()
  (eval '(define-theme, @(read-user-theme))))
```

Box 23 presents an example of a user theme file. Note that this file contains Lisp comment lines (starting with semicolons). Our DSL has implicitly inherited the Lisp comment syntax for free because `read` is in fact a Lisp *parser* accessible to the programmer. When it encounters a symbol, it returns it. When it encounters a parenthesis, it recursively calls itself to read a whole list and returns it. When it encounters a brace, given our extended syntax, it calls the associated reader function. When it encounters a semicolon, it discards the rest of the line and continues reading until the next Lisp expression is found. All of this is done for us already.

Creating User Themes

Now that we have read in a theme specification, we need to create an actual toplevel face out of it. In order to do so, we need to call `define-theme`, passing as arguments the output of `read-user-theme`. Here, we must pay attention to the fact that `define-theme` is a macro, not a function. This means that any explicit call to it in our code will be expanded at compile-time, which is not what we want. Instead, we want to dynamically evaluate a call to `define-theme`, with a properly computed argument list, at run-time. Box 24 presents the proper way to do so.

Obviously, `eval` is a standard function whose purpose is to evaluate one Lisp expression and return the result. Again, you see the importance of reflexivity here: the argument we provide `eval` with is a list starting with the symbol `define-theme` and continuing with the contents of the theme file. This list, which is a piece of data, is seen as code by eval. Just like `read` (and contrary to many other languages in which `eval` works on strings), `eval` directly manipulates abstract syntactic forms.

Optimizing Performance

Although in this very simple example, performance is certainly not an issue, a large application may suffer from efficiency problems when executing code written in an embedded DSL, especially if that DSL is interpreted. One is hence lead to implement a full blown compiler for it. In our specific case for instance, and assuming that eval is implemented as an interpreter (which, in fact, may not even be the case), creating the user theme could involve a lot of macro-expansion, which can be time consuming.

Box 25

```
(defun make-user-theme ()
  (eval '(funcall (compile nil (lambda ()
                                (define-theme, @(read-user-theme)))))))
```

Fortunately, there is a way out of this. The key point to remember is that although DSLs created in Lisp may be very different from the original language (recall the `loop` macro), a Lisp DSL program is in fact just a piece of Lisp code. As such, it can be compiled with a Lisp compiler, so there is no need to write a new one. What's more, it turns out that a Lisp compiler is available for free in every application written in Lisp, through the use of the `compile` function which is part of the standard. We can modify `make-user-theme` to benefit from compilation as presented in Box 25.

The first argument to `compile` is normally a function name, in which case the function's definition is compiled and replaces the former one, presumably interpreted. In this case however, `compile` works anonymously. We provide it with a so-called *lambda-expression*, that is, an anonymous function constructed on the fly. The body (definition) of this function is the same call to `define-theme` as the one we constructed in the previous version, but this time, `compile` creates and returns the compiled code for this lambda expression. The final step is to actually call the compiled function, which is the job of `funcall` (a variant of `apply`). Once this whole expression is created, `make-user-theme` `eval`'uates it.

Note that in many cases, this optimization step won't even be necessary. A frequent misunderstanding about `eval` is that it is an interpreter (the confusion is between *evaluation* and *interpretation*). As a matter of fact, many modern Common Lisp implementations don't have an interpreter at all. When you type expressions in the REPL (read-eval-print loop) for instance, the expressions are first compiled, and then evaluated. What this actually means is that the Lisp evaluator is in fact a JIT-compiler.

CONCLUSION

For a number of reasons, some of them historical, the vast majority of industrial languages like Java or C++ are pretty similar in terms of design or functionality. Because of that, the impact of the chosen GPL for DSL design and implementation is not very well known in the computer science community. It is only recently that other kinds of languages like functional, scripting or dynamic ones have regained some interest. The less conventional features that these languages bring to the picture must lead us to revise our view on DSL design and implementation.

One key aspect of a GPL that impacts DSL design and implementation is its extensibility. With the embedding approach, you don't need to create a brand new language from scratch anymore, but only express a *variant* of the original one. With a sufficiently extensible language, this variant can also be expressed directly in the original language, without the need for any external transformation tool. This is the embedded homogeneous approach.

In the cases where the DSL is part of a larger application, there are three main advantages in using an extensible GPL for creating an embedded homogeneous DSL: the first one is that the whole application ends up being written in a single, unified language, which makes it much easier in terms of maintainability. The second one is that the DSL layer is considerably smaller because instead of implementing a full language, you only need to implement the *differences* with the original one. Finally, when there is no more distinction between DSL and GPL code, a piece of DSL program can be used both externally and internally without any additional cost.

The second section provided a tour of many important language features for extensibility. The choice of Common Lisp for illustration purposes was justified by the fact that (apart from its striking lack of infix notation), a majority of those features are available in the language. More precisely, it is both functional and imperative, object-oriented, it has compile-time meta-programming facilities and its syntax can also be customized or extended. The whole interpreter / compiler chain, from source code parsing to actual execution is available to the programmer thanks to such functions as `read`, `eval` or `compile`. Lisp also contains less widespread extensibility features. The MOP allows the programmer to modify or extend the semantics of the object system. The macro layer, working directly on code segments, can be seen both as a code transformation and code generation facility.

DISCUSSION

In this section, we provide elements of discussion regarding the internal versus external approaches to DSL design and implementation, along with some considerations about the extensibility aspects that have been envisioned in this chapter.

Internal vs. External DSLs

Although this chapter was mostly devoted to exposing the virtues of extensibility, Kamin (1998) and Czarnecki et al. (2004) note several drawbacks to the embedding approach. We discuss two of them below.

1. **Suboptimal Syntax:** Since an embedded DSL is expressed in terms of differences from the original GPL, it may indeed be a lot of work to "bend" the original syntax sufficiently towards the desired one, if it is very different. In such a case, the amount of work could possibly turn out to be the same as in implementing a full parser.

It is true that most embedded homogeneous DSLs out there have a syntax very close to their host GPL, including the example developed throughout this chapter. In the specific case of Lisp, we have seen that the syntax is very minimalist. It boils down to symbols and S-Expressions (prefix notation for function calls). In particular, the absence of infix operators makes Lisp very well suited to syntax-poor languages such as XML and its derivatives, but less well suited to syntax-rich languages. Of course, anything is possible, including infix syntax, in a macro call, as demonstrated earlier by `loop`, but it requires more work. Note that the question of knowing whether it is desirable to design syntax-rich DSLs could be a matter of debate.

Still on the question of syntax, Martin Fowler (2010) draws an "important" distinction between internal and external DSLs:

Internal DSLs are particular ways of using a host language to give the host language the feel of a particular language. (. . .) External DSLs have their own custom syntax and you write a full parser to process them.

On the contrary, we think that when a DSL is grounded in a truly extensible GPL, this distinction is not really pertinent anymore (the "standalone" versus "embedded" terms are more accurate). Consider again the case of the `loop` macro. As a DSL for iteration the `loop` dialect is completely different from Lisp's original syntax, but you still don't need to "write a full parser" for it. At the time the macro is called, all its arguments (provided as a single `&rest` one) have already been properly parsed by the Lisp reader. In other words, when your DSL makes use of symbols, numbers, strings etc. (even lists), that is, Lisp's regular tokens, you can simply reuse the original lexer.

Previously, we have shown how straightforward it is to externalize a DSL. Because a DSL written in an extensible language is genuine GPL code, it can be used right in the middle of a regular program. In our case, because the `read` function is able to operate on files, strings or any kind of stream, it may take only a single line of code (`read -> eval`) to handle a DSL program stored externally. In the end, the DSL is neither internal, nor external. It is both.

Finally, we must also point out that we are in disagreement with Czarnecki et al. (2004), when they say that "a prerequisite for embedding is that the syntax for the new language be a subset of the syntax for the host language". As demonstrated in this chapter, embedding can also produce DSLs that are in fact *supersets* of the original GPL. In general, this is made possible when extensibility is available at the syntactic level. In the specific case of Lisp, we have also seen that the macro system makes it possible in theory to implement any kind of syntax on top of the original one, while remaining within the context of Lisp code.

As a side note, we also feel compelled to stress that the same disagreement exists at the semantic level. Both the existence of a MOP underlying the object-oriented infrastructure, and the macro level at which control over the evaluation scheme is available (Cf. section 11.2), a DSL can very well be defined as a *superset* of the semantic features of the underlying GPL.

2. **Poor Error Reporting:** As mentioned earlier, the code provided in this chapter doesn't tackle the problem of error management, out of a concern for simplicity. Error management is still an important aspect in the design and implementation of a DSL. However well designed your DSL is, it does not necessarily prevent the end-user from making syntactic or semantic mistakes. One problem with the embedding approach is that of poor, uninformative or even confusing error reporting. Indeed, in an embedded homogeneous DSL, the reported errors are related to the underlying host GPL instead of specifically those of the DSL, and may not make any sense for the end-user.

Research on better error reporting techniques for embedded DSLs is currently being pursued, for instance in the Converge language (Tratt, 2008). We are not aware of such equivalent research in the case of Lisp, and it certainly is a topic for future research. There is one additional extensibility feature that we didn't tackle in this chapter, although it surely helps in terms of error management: exception handling, also called the "condition system" in Lisp (Seibel, 2005, chapter 19). Extensible exception handling is widely spread today, including in mainstream languages such as C++ or Java, notably by letting the programmer define its own exception hierarchy. One way to support better error reporting for a DSL is to catch GPL errors and convert them into more pertinent user-defined ones. Note that at least in the case of Lisp, run-time errors may actually include compile-time ones when the JIT-compiler is used explicitly (Cf. section 9.3). The expected challenge is to provide the DSL user with pertinent information along with the error. It is not trivial to provide complete source code information, for instance when macro-expansion or already compiled code is involved (an area beyond the Common Lisp standard, in which every vendor has its own solution, or doesn't provide one). Also, the Common Lisp standard under-specifies the exact built-in errors that may be thrown in various situations, also leading into vendor-specific solutions or lack thereof.

On the other hand, the problem of debugging DSL code may be somewhat easier to tackle in Common Lisp, thanks to a specificity of its condition system. Indeed, you can not only signal errors and handle them, but also provide multiple *restarts*, which are points at which the application may resume its course. The programmer then has introspective access to all available restarts at any point in the program's execution *without unwinding the stack*, that is, without loosing the error context. This has two important implications with respect to DSL conception:

- First, introspecting the available restarts means that it is easy to dynamically provide the end-user with a human-readable set of recovery options, something very convenient when the end-user is not a computer scientist himself. Note that for more expert users, it is also possible to embed a complete Lisp debugger in your application.
- Second, since there is no mandatory stack unwinding, the condition system can not only be used for true error processing, but also to signal non-critical errors such as warnings or notices, letting the program continue normally.

Controversial Aspects of Extensibility

There are however two aspects of the language that may be somewhat controversial when it comes to DSL design and implementation. These are dynamic typing and strict evaluation.

1. **Dynamic Typing:** One feature that has been implicitly but constantly in use in this chapter is Lisp's dynamically typed nature. We regard this aspect of the language as an advantage for DSL design and implementation, although this view may not be shared by everyone.

We think that providing explicit, static type declarations in DSL code is rather undesirable, especially from the perspective of a non computer scientist end-user. If the underlying language is statically typed, one might need to build a complex machinery for providing the missing types and checking them in the DSL code, before it can actually be used. On the other hand, a DSL built on top of a dynamic language automatically inherits the dynamic typing, checking or even inference capabilities of the underlying language. The whole typing issue is hence completely delegated to the lower-level.

One drawback of this approach however, is that type errors will occur at run-time, hence affecting the end-user. It is a legitimate view to prefer avoiding such a situation altogether, at the expense of an explicitly typed DSL. This problem actually brings back the importance of proper error reporting and debugging mentioned in the previous section.

In the static camp, there is some research related to type checking a priori for a DSL, rather than a posteriori in the host language (Taha and Sheard, 1997). Another potential source for future research would be to consider languages that can freely mix dynamically and statically typed code, such as Racket (Tobin-Hochstadt et al., 2011) and C# (Hejlsberg et al., 2010, since version 4.0) . In the case of Common Lisp, it is in theory possible to implement a type inference system at the macro level, although it is certainly not straightforward.

One final note regarding performance: going for the purely dynamic solution will entail a performance cost. Depending on the target application, this cost may or may not be prohibitive, and hence may have an impact on the chosen solution. An intermediate solution may also be available in the case of Common Lisp. The language supports static type declarations which may be used by compilers in order to produce fully optimized code, achieving the same level of performance as equivalent C or C++ code, only at the expense of type safety (Verna, 2006, 2009). One could hence imagine compiling a fully optimized version of an otherwise dynamically typed DSL program after a testing phase.

2. **Strict Evaluation:** One particular aspect of functional languages that is known to help in DSL implementation is *laziness* (Elliott, 1999, section 8, Kiselyov and chieh Shan, 2009, section 5). A lazy (or "normal order") evaluation scheme means that the values of expressions, or parts of them, won't be calculated until they are actually needed. Laziness makes it straightforward to define infinite data structures because they will basically never be evaluated as a whole. Laziness also makes it easy to define new control primitives, such as conditional branches where selective evaluation is required. Finally, laziness helps in terms of memory management by reducing the amount of computation.

It should be noted that only "pure" functional languages such as Haskell can offer a normal order evaluation scheme. Because it is impossible to predict if or when a lazy expression is going to be evaluated, side effects must be prohibited (or at least contained, for example in Haskell's monads). Because Lisp provides imperative constructs, it cannot be based on a lazy evaluation scheme. Instead, it uses *strict* (or "applicative order") evaluation. Typically, operands are evaluated before applying the operator to them. Built-in control structures such as conditional branches that need to proceed in a lazy way are implemented differently from the rest of the language (these are called "special operators").

Implementing a lazy evaluation scheme is possible in Lisp at the macro level because a macro gives you control over the evaluation of its arguments. It is however not straightforward and certainly not as clean as using a lazy language right from the start. As we have already mentioned, working at the macro level comes with its own problems, for instance in terms of error reporting and debugging.

On the other hand, if the DSL needs imperative constructs and side effects, a purely functional language will get in the way, and "semi-functional" ones like Lisp, providing both higher order functions and imperative constructs may be a better alternative.

The Root of Extensibility

As we have seen early in this chapter, many languages besides Lisp have extensibility features today. Some others that we have not mentioned before are Ruby (Thomas et al., 2009) or Clojure (Halloway, 2009), which should come as no surprise since they explicitly acknowledge their Lisp heritage.

What makes the Lisp family special amongst extensible languages is its "code is data" philosophy. We have seen throughout the chapter the importance of reflection. A *reflexive* language gives the programmer the ability to examine and/or modify its own program at run-time. Reflection is usually decoupled into *introspection* (the ability to examine yourself) and *intercession* (the ability to modify yourself).

Reflection can be supported in two ways. A language can provide a specific API for introspection and / or intercession. With its "code is data" philosophy however, Lisp provides a more direct way to reflection than a specific API: since a piece of code is just a piece of data represented in a user-level data structure, no specific procedures are needed to access the program. This property of a programming language is known as *homoiconicity* (McIlroy, 1960; Kay, 1969).

Another important distinction in this notion is *structural* versus *behavioral* reflection (Maes, 1987; Smith, 1984). While structural reflection deals with providing a way to reify a program, behavioral reflection deals with accessing the language itself. Lisp is not the only language to provide full structural reflection. Prolog (1995), also homoiconic, and Smalltalk (1998) are two other notable examples.

Lisp, however, goes further by providing some level of behavioral reflection as well. Extending the Lisp syntax is a form of intercession at the parser level allowing to modify the language's syntax directly. Using Lisp macros is a form of intercession at the compiler level, allowing to program language modifications in the language itself (what Sheard (2001) calls a "homogeneous meta-programming system", as opposed to C++ templates for instance, which are heterogeneous: a different language). Using the CLOS MOP permits intercession at the object system level, allowing the programmer to modify the semantics of the object layer. Again, those features are made considerably easier to implement when the language is homoiconic. Because of this, Lisp was in fact ready for extensibility, both at the structural and behavioral levels, since its very birth, back in 1957. Practically all of the technical features that make Lisp suitable for being extended as a DSL come from this, and the ability to hook into the reader, the evaluator and the compiler.

REFERENCES

Abrahams, D., & Gurtovoy, A. (2004). *C++ template metaprogramming: Concepts, tools, and techniques from Boost and beyond*. Addison-Wesley Professional.

Ahson, S. I., & Lamba, S. S. (1985). The use of Forth language in process control. *Computer Languages, 10*(3), 179–187. doi:10.1016/0096-0551(85)90015-3

Bobrow, D. G., DeMichiel, L. G., Gabriel, R. P., Keene, S. E., Kiczales, G., & Moon, D. A. (1988). Common Lisp object system specification. *ACM SIGPLAN Notices, 23*(SI), 1-142.

Bravenboer, M., Kalleberg, K., Vermaas, R., & Visser, E. (2006). *Stratego/XT 0.16: Components for transformation systems*. Paper presented at the Workshop on Partial Evaluation and Program Manipulation, Charleston, SC.

Burstall, R. (2000). Christopher Strachey — Understanding programming languages. *Higher Order Symbolic Computation, 13*(1-2), 51–55. doi:10.1023/A:1010052305354

C++. (2011). *International standard: Programming language*. ISO/IEC 14882:2011 (E).

Calcagno, C., Taha, W., Huang, L., & Leroy, X. (2003). *Implementing multi-stage languages using ASTs, gensym, and reflection*. Paper presented at the of the Second International Conference on Generative Programming and Component Engineering, Erfurt, Germany.

Chedeau, C., & Verna, D. (2012). *JSPP: Morphing C++ into JavaScript*. Unpublished technical report 201201-TR, EPITA Research and Development Laboratory, France.

Common Lisp. (1994). *American national standard: Programming language*. ANSI X3.226:1994 (R1999).

Czarnecki, K. ODonnell, J., Striegnitz, J., & Taha, W. (2004). DSL implementation in MetaOCaml, Template Haskell, and C++. In C. Lengauer, D. Batory, C. Consel, & M. Odersky (Eds.), *Domain-Specific Program Generation: Vol. 3016. Lecture Notes in Computer Science* (pp. 51-72). Berlin, Germany: Springer Verlag.

Denert, E., Ernst, G., & Wetzel, H. (1975). GRAPHEX68 graphical language features in Algol 68. *Computers & Graphics, 1*(2-3), 195–202. doi:10.1016/0097-8493(75)90007-2

Deursen van, A., Klint, P., & Visser, J. (2000). Domain-specific languages: An annotated bibliography. *SIGPLAN Notices, 35*(6), 26-36.

Elliott, C. (1999). An embedded modeling language approach to interactive 3D and multimedia animation. *IEEE Transactions on Software Engineering, 25*(3), 291–308. doi:10.1109/32.798320

Fleutot, F., & Tratt, L. (2007). *Contrasting compile-time meta-programming in Metalua and Converge*. Paper presented at the workshop on Dynamic Languages and Applications, Berlin, Germany.

Foderaro, J. (1991). Lisp: Introduction. *Communications of the ACM - Special Issue on Lisp, 34*(9), 27-28.

Fowler, M. (2005). *Language workbenches: The killer-app for domain specific languages?* Retrieved April 2, 2012, from http://martinfowler.com/articles/languageWorkbench.html.

Fowler, M. (2010). *Domain specific languages*. Addison Wesley.

Ghosh, D. (2010). *DSLs in action*. Manning Publications.

Ghosh, D. (2011). DSL for the uninitiated - Domain-specific languages bridge the semantic gap in programming. *Communications of the ACM, 54*(7), 44–50. doi:10.1145/1965724.1965740

Graham, P. (1993a). *On Lisp*. Prentice Hall.

Graham, P. (1993b). *Programming bottom-up*. Retrieved April 2, 2012, from http://www.paulgraham.com/progbot. html.

Halloway, S. (2009). *Programming Clojure*. Pragmatic Bookshelf.

Hejlsberg, A., Torgersen, M., Wiltamuth, S., & Golde, P. (2010). *The C# programming language*. Addison Wesley.

Hudak, P. (1998). *Modular domain specific languages and tools*. Paper presented at the International Conference on Software Reuse, Washington, DC.

Kamin, S. N. (1998). Research on domain-specific embedded languages and program generators. *Electronic Notes in Theoretical Computer Science, 14*(1), 149–168. doi:10.1016/S1571-0661(05)80235-X

Kay, A. C. (1969). *The reactive engine*. Unpublished doctoral dissertation, University of Hamburg, Germany.

Keene, S. E. (1989). *Object-oriented programming in Common Lisp: A programmer's guide to CLOS*. Addison-Wesley.

Kernighan, B. W., & Ritchie, D. M. (1977). *The m4 macro processor*. Unpublished technical report, Bell Laboratories, NJ.

Kiczales, G. J., des Rivières, J., & Bobrow, D. G. (1991). *The art of the metaobject protocol*. Cambridge, MA: MIT Press.

Kiselyov, O., & Shan, C.-C. (2009). Embedded probabilistic programming. In Taha, W. (Ed.), *Domain-Specific Languages* (*Vol. 5658*, pp. 360–384). Lecture Notes in Computer Science Berlin, Germany: Springer Verlag. doi:10.1007/978-3-642-03034-5_17

Knuth, D. E. (1984). *The TeXbook*. Addison-Wesley.

Landin, P. J. (1966). The next 700 programming languages. *Communications of the ACM, 9*(3), 157–166. doi:10.1145/365230.365257

Maes, P. (1987). *Concepts and experiments in computational reflection*. Paper presented at the conference on Object-Oriented Programming Systems, Languages and Applications, Orlando, FL.

Marlow, S. (2010). *Haskell 2010 language report*. Retrieved April 2, 2012, from http://www.haskell.org/onlinereport/haskell2010

McIlroy, M. D. (1960). Macro instruction extensions of compiler languages. *Communications of the ACM, 3*(4), 214–220. doi:10.1145/367177.367223

McNamara, B., & Smaragdakis, Y. (2000). Functional programming in C++. *SIGPLAN Notices, 35*(9), 118-129.

Milner, R., Tofte, M., Harper, R., & MacQueen, D. (1997). *The definition of standard ML*. MIT Press.

Moore, C. H. (1974). Forth: A new way to program a mini computer. *Astronomy and Astrophysics Supplement*, *15*(3), 497–511.

Odersky, M., Spoon, L., & Venners, B. (2010). *Programming in Scala*. Artima.

Paepcke, A. (1993). User-level language crafting - Introducing the CLOS metaobject protocol. In Paepcke, A. (Ed.), *Object-oriented programming: The CLOS perspective* (pp. 65–99). Cambridge, MA: MIT Press.

Pagan, F. (1979). Algol 68 as a meta-language for denotational semantics. *The Computer Journal*, *22*(1), 63–66. doi:10.1093/comjnl/22.1.63

Prolog. (1995). *International standard: Programming language*. ISO/IEC 13211.1.

Prud'homme, C. (2006). A domain specific embedded language in C++ for automatic differentiation, projection, integration and variational formulations. *Journal of Scientific Programming*, *14*(2), 81–110.

Repenning, A., & Ioannidou, A. (2007). *X-expressions in XMLisp: S-expressions and extensible markup language unite*. Paper presented at the International Lisp Conference, Cambridge, MA.

Rompf, T., Sujeeth, A. K., Lee, H., Brown, K. J., Chafi, H., Odersky, M., & Olukotun, K. (2011). *Building-blocks for performance oriented DSLs*. Paper presented at the Working Conference on Domain-Specific Languages, Algarve, Portugal.

Seibel, P. (2005). *Practical Common Lisp*. Berkeley, CA: Apress. doi:10.1007/978-1-4302-0017-8

SGR. (1991). *International standard: Select graphic rendition*. ISO/IEC 6429 SGR / ECMA-48.

Sheard, T. (2001). Accomplishments and research challenges in meta-programming. In Taha, W. (Ed.), *Semantics, Applications, and Implementation of Program Generation* (*Vol. 2196*, pp. 2–44). Lecture Notes in Computer Science Berlin, Germany: Springer Verlag. doi:10.1007/3-540-44806-3_2

Sheard, T., & Jones, S. P. (2002). *Template metaprogramming for Haskell*. Paper presented at the Haskell Workshop, Pittsburgh, PA.

Skalski, K., Moskal, M., & Olszta, P. (2004). *Meta-programming in Nemerle*. Unpublished technical report, University of Wroclaw, Poland.

Smalltalk (1998). *American national standard: Programming language*. ANSI INCITS.319:1998 (R2002).

Smith, B. C. (1984). *Reflection and semantics in Lisp*. Paper presented at the Symposium on Principles of Programming Languages, Salt Lake City, UT.

Stoy, J., & Strachey, C. (1972). OS6 - An experimental operating system for a small computer. part 2: Input/output and filing system. *The Computer Journal*, *15*(3), 195–203. doi:10.1093/comjnl/15.3.195

Taha, W., & Sheard, T. (1997). *Multi-stage programming with explicit annotations*. Paper presented at the symposium on Partial Evaluation and Semantics-Based Program Manipulation, Amsterdam, Netherlands.

Thomas, D., Fowler, C., & Hunt, A. (2009). *Programming Ruby*. Pragmatic Bookshelf.

Tobin-Hochstadt, S., St-Amour, V., Culpepper, R., Flatt, M., & Felleisen, M. (2011). *Languages as libraries*. Paper presented at the Conference on Programming Language Design and Implementation, San Jose, CA.

Tratt, L. (2005). *Compile-time meta-programming in a dynamically typed OO language*. Paper presented at the symposium on Dynamic Languages, San Diego, CA.

Tratt, L. (2008). Domain specific language implementation via compile-time metaprogramming. *ACM Transactions on Programming Languages and Systems*, *30*(31), 131–140.

Turner, K. J. (1994). *Exploiting the m4 macro language*. Unpublished technical report, University of Stirling, Scotland.

van Wijngaarden, A. (1981). Revised report of the algorithmic language Algol 68. *ALGOL Bulletin*, *47*(Supplement), 1–119.

Vasudevan, N., & Tratt, L. (2011). Comparative study of DSL tools. *Electronic Notes in Theoretical Computer Science*, *264*(5), 103–121. doi:10.1016/j.entcs.2011.06.007

Veldhuizen, T. (1996). Using C++ template metaprograms. *C++ Report, 7*(4), 459-473.

Veldhuizen, T. L. (2003). *C++ templates are turing complete*. Unpublished technical report, University of Indiana, IN.

Verna, D. (2006). *Beating C in scientific computing applications*. Paper presented at the European Lisp Workshop, Nantes, France.

Verna, D. (2009). *Clos efficiency: Instantiation*. Paper presented at the International Lisp Conference, Cambridge, MA.

Verna, D. (2010). *Clon: The command-line options nuker library*. Retrieved April 2, 2012, from http://www.lrde.epita.fr/~didier/software/lisp/clon.php.

Wyk, E. V., Bodin, D., Krishnan, L., & Gao, J. (2008). Silver: An extensible attribute grammar system. *Electronic Notes in Theoretical Computer Science*, *203*(2), 103–116. doi:10.1016/j.entcs.2008.03.047

ADDITIONAL READING

Bourguignon, P. (2010). *OBJCL*. Retrieved April 2, 2012, from ftp://ftp.informatimago.com/users/pjb/lisp/objcl.tar.bz2.

Costanza, P. (2004). *Dynamic versus static typing - A pattern-based analysis*. Paper presented at the Workshop on Object-oriented Language Engineering for the Post-Java Era, Oslo, Norway.

Costanza, P., & D'Hondt, T. (2010). Embedding hygiene-compatible macros in an unhygienic macro system. *Journal of Universal Computer Science*, *16*(2), 271–295.

Gindling, J., Ioannidou, A., Loh, J., & Lokkebo, O. (1995). *LEGOsheets: A rule-based programming, simulation and manipulation environment for the LEGO programmable brick*. Paper presented at the international symposium on Visual Languages, Darmstadt, Germany.

Goodman, N. D., Mansinghka, V. K., Roy, D., Bonawitz, K., & Tenenbaum, J. B. (2008). *Church: A language for generative models*. Paper presented at the Conference on Uncertainty in Artificial Intelligence, Corvallis, OR.

Ioannidou, A., Repenning, A., & Webb, C. D. (2009). *Agentcubes: Incremental 3D enduser development*. Paper presented at the Symposium on Visual Languages and Human-Centric Computing, Orlando, FL.

MacCarthy, J. (1960). Recursive functions of symbolic expressions and their computation by machine, part I. *Communications of the ACM*, *3*(4), 184–195. doi:10.1145/367177.367199

Malenfant, J., Jacques, M., & Demers, F. N. (1996). *A tutorial on behavioral reflection and its implementation*. Retrieved April 2, 2012, from http://www2.parc.com/csl/groups/sda/projects/reflection96/docs/malenfant/ref96/ref96.html.

Repenning, A. (2007). *XMLisp*. Retrieved April 2, 2012, from http://code.google.com/p/xmlisp.

Rosenberg, K. M. (2006). *CL-SQL*. Retrieved April 2, 2012, from http://clsql.b9.com.

Weitz, E. (2008a). *CL-WHO*. Retrieved April 2, 2012 from http://weitz.de/cl-who.

Weitz, E. (2008b). *CL-INTERPOL*. Retrieved April 2, 2012, from http://weitz.de/cl-interpol.

Yoo, D. (2011). *Fudging up Racket*. Retrieved April 2, 2012, from http://hashcollision.org/brainfudge

KEY TERMS AND DEFINITIONS

CLOS: The Common Lisp Object System, part of the ANSI standard. CLOS is a class based object system with a non conventional design, featuring multiple inheritance, customizable dynamic dispatch and multi-methods.

Generic Function: Unlike conventional object systems, methods don't belong to classes in CLOS. Instead, CLOS provides generic functions, which look like, and are used like ordinary functions, except for the fact that their definition is polymorphic.

Macro: A Lisp function that takes expressions as arguments and returns a new expression. Lisp macros are usually executed at compile-time and can be seen as both code transformation / code generation tools. Contrary to ordinary functions, macros don't necessarily evaluate their arguments.

Macro Character: A character treated in a special way by the Lisp reader. Macro characters are associated with particular functions executed at read-time, giving the programmer access to the parsing phase of Lisp code. There are two categories of macro characters: ordinary ones such as (by default) parenthesis, quote and semi-colon, and dispatching ones such as (by default) # which start a sequence (e.g. `#'`, `#\` etc.).

Meta-Object Protocol: A de facto standard for a reflexive implementation for CLOS. The MOP defines CLOS in terms of itself: classes, as well as all other objects such as generic functions and methods, are instances of meta-classes. The programmer has access to the underlying infrastructure, allowing for making changes to the syntax and semantics of the object system.

Method: A method is the specialization of a particular generic function for a set of arguments. Arguments are specialized by class or by equality to some value (so-called "eql-specializers"). Unlike conventional object systems, a method may be specialized on more than one argument, providing for multiple dispatch (multi-methods).

Reader Macro: A function associated with a macro character. The name is misleading as reader macros are just ordinary functions. A reader macro is executed at read-time and must return an expression for subsequent potential macro-expansion and evaluation or compilation.

Readtable: A readtable stores the association between macro characters and reader macros. A programmer may implement syntax extensions / modifications by creating new readtables and (de) activating them either globally or locally.

Chapter 2
Domain-Specific Language Integration with C++ Template Metaprogramming

Ábel Sinkovics
Eötvös Loránd University, Hungary

Zoltán Porkoláb
Eötvös Loránd University, Hungary

ABSTRACT

Domain specific language integration has to provide the right balance between the expressive power of the DSL and the implementation and maintenance cost of the applied integration techniques. External solutions may perform poorly as they depend on third party tools which should be implemented, tested and then maintained during the whole lifetime of the project. Ideally a self-contained solution can minimize third-party dependencies. The authors propose the use of C++ template metaprograms to develop a domain specific language integration library based on only the standard C++ language features. The code in the domain specific language is given as part of the C++ source code wrapped into C++ templates. When the C++ source is compiled, the C++ template metaprogram library implementing a full-featured parser infrastructure is executed. As the authors' approach does not require other tool than a standard C++ compiler, it is highly portable. To demonstrate their solution, the chapter implements a type-safe printf as a domain specific language. The library is fully implemented and downloadable as an open source project.

INTRODUCTION

Although domain specific languages are indispensable in their domain, the vast majority of the programs execute most of their actions out of that domain. As an example, SQL might be a perfect solution for describing operations related to relational databases, but database servers will create threads, open network connections, communicate with the operating system in the means of a general purpose programming language. The usual solution is that the desired domain-specific

DOI: 10.4018/978-1-4666-2092-6.ch002

language or languages are used together with a general purpose programming language. In most cases the integration of these languages happens by embedding the DSL(s) into the general purpose language with or without some syntactical quotation. However, this integration should add minimal syntactical, semantic and maintenance overhead to the project.

Many strategies exist to provide smooth integration of the domain languages and the host language. Some of them apply external frameworks for integration; others are built on language extensions. Only a few solutions are based on standard programming language features like macros or generative language elements. External tools may introduce unwanted dependencies on third party software. There are only a few languages where language extensions do not require translators, precompilers or the modification of the compiler. The most manageable solution is based purely on standard language features.

In this chapter we would like to describe a DSL integration technique for the C++ programming language. The solution is based on compile-time parsing of the DSL code and a further development of the authors' earlier work (Porkolab, 2010). To eliminate the dependency on external tools we implemented a parser generator as a C++ template metaprogram library. Thus, the full parsing phase of the DSL is executed when the host program is compiled. The end result is an optimized, highly effective executable produced by the C++ compiler. The library uses standard C++ language elements only, thus our solution is extremely portable.

Defining new DSLs is a relatively simple task using our solution. Taking advantage of the declarative nature of C++ template metaprogramming the formal syntax of the DSL can be directly expressed in the source code. Thus, the grammatical rules of the DSL are presented explicitly with a minimal syntactical overhead. The result of this method is a highly self-documenting and maintainable C++ program. Our solution can be applied for a number of practical problems:

Most of the current C++ template metaprogramming code base suffers from unmaintenable syntax. The syntax of Boost.Xpressive and Boost. Proto as examples, are seriously restricted. With the help of our library it is possible to provide a clear syntax using the usual notions of the library domain. When this code is compiled our parser generator library takes effect first, and translates the new syntax to the old one without any user interaction or external tool other than the standard C++ compiler.

A further application area is to raise C++ template metaprogramming itself to a higher abstraction level using functional programming style script languages. Using our library it is possible to implement a Haskell-like syntax for template metaprogramming. Parsers based on our library are able to translate this syntax to template metaprograms as we know them now.

The structure of the chapter is the following. First we give a brief technical overview of C++ template metaprogramming. We explain how templates work and how they can be used to control the compilation process to execute algorithms. We define the basic building blocks of template metaprograms: template metafunctions and metafunction classes. Next we discuss some C++ specific examples of DSL embedding, especially those, that are connected to generative techniques. We mention the AraRat system implementing SQL embedding into C++ as the host language using expression templates, Boost.Xpressive, a regular expression library utilizing template metaprogramming for embedding. We also discuss Boost.Proto, a library which is designed for domain-specific language embedding. Then we introduce our solution, a parser generator library working with parser combinators implemented using template metaprogramming. As a real world example, we implement a type-safe printf library using DSL-based approach. This library type checks the printf arguments and reports type mismatches at compile-time. This section discusses the maintainability of our method. We evaluate the method from various performance points of view, such as compile- and run-time behavior, memory usage, etc. At the end of the chapter we discuss future research directions in the area and suggest further literature for the reader.

Our solution has been fully implemented and available as an open-source library (Sinkovics, 2011). The reader can download the source code in form of C++ header files and can apply it using any standard-compliant C++ compiler.

The chapter assumes basic knowledge of the C++ programming language and the templates. However, the reader is not expected to be a C++ expert to understand this chapter; we do our bests to explain all technical details.

C++ Template Metaprogramming

The C++ programming language is a popular general purpose programming language because its flexibility comprising both high-level and relatively low-level language features serves as an excellent tool for complex problems. C++ is a multi-paradigm programming language (Coplien, 1998) as it supports usual object-oriented features (like classes, inheritance, and virtual functions), functional paradigm and generic programming.

Templates are key language elements of C++ enabling algorithms and data structures to be parameterized by types or constants without performance penalties at run-time (Stroustrup, 2000). This abstraction is essential when using general algorithms, such as finding an element in a data structure, sorting, or defining data structures like vector or set. The generic features of these templates (like the behavior of the algorithms or the layout of the data structures) are the same, only the actual type parameter is different. The abstraction over the type parameter – often called parametric polymorphism – emphasizes that this variability is supported by compile-type template parameters. Reusable components – containers and algorithms – in C++ mostly use templates. The Standard Template Library (STL), an essential part of the C++ standard, is the most notable example (Josuttis, 1999).

Templates are code skeletons with placeholders for one or more type parameters. In order to use a template it has to be instantiated. This can be initiated either implicitly, when a template is referred to with actual type parameters or explicitly. During the instantiation the template parameters are substituted with the actual arguments and new code is generated. Thus, a different code segment is generated when a template is instantiated with different type parameters.

There are certain cases when a template with a specific type parameter requires a special behavior, which is different from the generic one. We may specify how to store values of the generic type parameter of a vector, but we may require a special implementation for vectors of boolean values. Also, we may specify an algorithm working fine for most of the data structures but requiring a different behavior in some specific cases. Such "exceptions" can be specified using template specializations. During the instantiation of a template the compiler uses the most specialized version of the template (Vandevoorde, 2002).

Templates can refer to other templates (even recursively) thus complex chains of template instantiations can be created. This mechanism enables us to write smart template codes affecting the compilation process. To demonstrate this capability of C++ templates Erwin Unruh wrote a program (Unruh, 1994) which was – in means of the C++ language terms – illegal and could not be compiled, but when someone tried to, the compiler emitted a list of prime numbers as part of the error messages. Unruh demonstrated that with cleverly designed templates it is possible to execute a desired algorithm at compilation time. This compile-time programming is called C++ Template Metaprogramming (TMP). A metaprogram is a program that manipulates other programs; for example compilers, partial evaluators, parser generators and so forth are metaprograms (Veldhuizen, 1995,1998; Czarnecki, 2000). Template metaprograms are special ones in the sense that they are self-contained: the program which manipulates the code is the C++ compiler itself and nothing, but a standard C++ compiler is required to execute them.

The following text book example, presented in Box 1, demonstrates how to compute the value of a factorial at compilation time.

We can see that the implementation uses recursion at compile-time. The enumeration value, `Factorial<5>::value` is referred to inside the main() function, thus the compiler is enforced to compute it. The instantiation process of the class `Factorial<5>` begins. Inside the Factorial template, `Factorial<N-1>::value` is referred to. The compiler is forced to instantiate `Factorial<4>`, then `Factorial<3>`, etc. The Factorial template class is instantiated several times recursively. The recursion stops when `Factorial<1>` is referred to, since there is a specialization for that. At the end, the compiler generates five classes and `Factorial<5>::value` gets calculated at compilation time.

Similarly, one can use control branches using template specialization. In the following example we declare the variable `i` to be of type `int` or long depending on whether the size of the `long` type is greater than the size of `int` as presented in Box 2.

The code snippet above works in the following way. In the `main` function the `if_` template is referred to, therefore its argument is evaluated as either true or false. In case the first template argument `(sizeof(int)<sizeof(long))` is true, the general case of the `if_` template is instantiated, thus `::value` is a `typedef` of `Then (long)`. Otherwise the specialization of the `if_` template is instantiated, thus `::value` is a `typedef` of `Else (int)`.

Box 1.

```
// compile-time recursion
template <int N>
struct Factorial
{
    enum { value = N * Factorial<N-1>::value };
}

template<>
struct Factorial<1>
{
    enum { value = 1 };
};

int main()
{
    int r = Factorial<5>::value;
    cout << r << endl;
    return 0;
}
```

Box 2.

```
template <bool condition, typename Then, typename Else>
struct if_
{
    typedef Then value;
};

template <typename Then, typename Else>
struct if_<false, Then, Else>
{
    typedef Else value;
};

int main()
{
    if_<sizeof(int)<sizeof(long), long, int>::value i;
    cout << sizeof(i) << endl;
    return 0;
}
```

As template metaprograms are "executed" by the compiler they fundamentally differ from usual run-time programs. Compilers among other actions evaluate constant values, deduce types and declare variables – all of these are immutable actions. Once a constant value has been computed, a type has been decided or a variable has been declared they remain the same. There is no such thing as assignment in template metaprograms. In this way C++ template metaprograms are similar to the pure functional programming languages where referential transparency is held. However, one can still write control-structures, using specializations. Loops are implemented using recursive templates, terminated by specializations. Control branches are based on partial or full specializations.

Having recursion and branching with pattern matching we have a complete programming language – executing programs at compilation time. Bohm and Jacopini (1966) proved that the implementation of a Turing machine is equivalent to the existence of conditional and looping control structures in a programming language. C++ template metaprograming forms a Turing complete programming language executed at compilation time (Bohm & Jacopini, 1966).

We can use data structures at compilation time (Alexandrescu, 2001). For example the list structure used by most functional programming languages can be implemented by a class, `NullType`, representing the empty list and a template class, `Typelist`, representing the list constructor. One can represent any list by using the constructor recursively. These classes can be implemented and used the following way as presented in Box 3.

Preprocessor macros make the use of typelists more handy as presented in Box 4.

The most commonly used data types are implemented by the Boost.MPL library in an efficient way and with an easy to use syntax, without having to use the preprocessor for creating lists. The above list can be defined using

Box 3.

```
class NullType {};

template <typename Head, typename Tail>
struct Typelist {};

typedef Typelist< char, Typelist<signed char, Typelist<unsigned char, NullType>
> > Charlist;
```

Box 4.

```
#define TYPELIST_1(x) Typelist< x, NullType>
#define TYPELIST_2(x, y) Typelist< x, TYPELIST_1(y)>
#define TYPELIST_3(x, y, z) Typelist< x, TYPELIST_2(y,z)>
#define TYPELIST_4(x, y, z, w) Typelist< x, TYPELIST_3(y,z,w)>
// ...
typedef TYPELIST_3(char, signed char, unsigned char) Charlist;
```

Box 5.

```
typedef boost::mpl::list<char, signed char, unsigned char> Charlist;
```

`boost::mpl::list` the following way as demonstrated in Box 5.

Sometimes ordinary values have to be stored in typelists. For this purpose they have to be encapsulated into types in a standard manner. Boxed values are provided by Boost.MPL:

```
template <int N>
struct int_
{
    static const int value;
    typedef int_<N> type;
};

template <int N>
const int int_<N>::value = N;

typedef int_<3> three;
```

The similarities between template metaprogramming and the functional paradigm are obvious. Static constants have the same role in template metaprograms as ordinary values in the run-time ones. Template metaprogramming uses symbolic names (typenames, typedefs) instead of variables. Specific classes are used to replace run-time functions.

To bring C++ metaprogramming from an adhoc approach to a more structured form, Czarnecki and Eisenecker defined the term template metafunction as a special template class (Czarnecki, 2000). The template metafunction is the unit to encapsulate compile time computations in a standard way. The arguments of the metafunction are the template parameters of the class, the value of the metafunction is a nested type of the template. The name of this nested type became a quasi-standard (Abrahams, 2004; Boost.mpl, 2011); it is called `type`. To evaluate a metafunction we provide actual parameters for the arguments and we use the nested type as the result of the function.

The following example is a simple metafunction converting a type `T` into a pointer to `T`.

```
template <typename T>
struct add_ptr
{
   typedef T* type;
};
```

This template metafunction can be evaluated by referring to the nested type.

Metafunctions – as we can expect in a functional programming language – are first class citizens in C++ template metaprogramming. However, a proper implementation is a bit tricky. Types can be parameters of templates – and template metafunctions – but the `add_ptr` metafunction above is not a type, it is a class template. A template metafunction can be turned into a type by wrapping it by a class. This is called a metafunction class.

```
struct add_ptr_f
{
   template <typename T>
   struct apply
   {
      typedef T* type;
   };
};
```

Again, Boost.MPL uses the name apply for the wrapped metafunction. `add_ptr` became a type and can be used as a parameter for or returned from template metafunctions. The possibility of writing compile-time metaprograms in C++ was not intentionally designed. Therefore C++ compilers are not focused on template metaprograms as primary targets. The syntax of the metaprograms are difficult, in most cases it is hard to understand. Debugging or profiling template metaprograms is rarely supported (Porkolab, 2006).

EARLIER APPROACHES FOR DSL INTEGRATION USING C++ TEMPLATE METAPROGRAMS

Two basic approaches exist when a DSL is about to be integrated into a host language. In one approach some external tool or framework can be used to identify, parse, syntactically and semantically check the domain specific language and generate the code integrated into the host language. As an alternative way one can use internal solutions, that do not require other tools than the infrastructure of the host language. Although many of the recent DSL integration approaches (Visser, 2004; Stratego, 2010; Icon, 2010; Katahdin, 2010; XMF, 2010) focus on the application of external tools, in the case of the C++ programming language there are vital examples for using the internal method. The primary candidate is template metaprogramming, in which one can define multi-staged compilation steps using only the C++ compiler. The Further Readings section discusses non-C++ internal solutions.

One of the oldest application areas of C++ template metaprogramming is expression templates (Veldhuizen, 2005). Expression templates is a technique for defining embedded mini-languages targeting specific problem domains. Originally this technique targeted high-speed mathematical libraries, in which memory and run-time effective execution of complex computations have to be accommodated with maintainable syntax. Since then expression templates have been used for various applications like defining regular expressions or embedding SQL queries. However, developing such libraries in an ad-hoc manner frequently leads to unmaintainable source codes.

The AraRat system makes type-safe SQL queries embeddable into C++ using expression templates, thus it demonstrates the integration of a relational algebra based DSL into C++ (Gil, 2007). The system works in multiple phases. First a lightweight tool is used to read the database schema and automatically generate C++ types reflecting the database schema and corresponding overloaded operators providing the fundamental action on the relational algebra: join, select, project, etc. These types and operations (including the generation of automatic conversions) are seamlessly connected and checked for consistency using template metaprogramming techniques. In the second step, the AraRat programmer simply creates queries using the pre-generated types and operators, which are compiled and type-checked using a standard C++ compiler. When the compilation is successful, the queries executed at run-time are guaranteed to be type-safe corresponding to the database schema. We have to mention, that the AraRat system as it was published targets only queries – no database updates are allowed. Also, when the database schema is modified, the generated types and operators become invalid. Still, AraRat is a great demonstration of the power of C++ template metaprograms for DSL integration.

Boost.Xpressive is an advanced, object-oriented regular expression library for C++ (Boost.Xpressive, 2011). Regular expressions are a commonly used domain specific language among modern generic purpose programming languages. They are used for a very special purpose, text manipulation, and have a specific, usually implementation-independent syntax. Regular expressions are usually implemented as libraries. Classical regular expression libraries, like `stl::regex` from the new C++ standard, are powerful and flexible. Patterns are represented as strings which can be specified at run-time. In this case a syntax error in the regular expression, such as unbalanced parenthesis, can be detected only at run-time. The Boost.Xpressive library, allows an alternative way: regular expressions can be defined using expression templates and thus they are checked at compilation time. Regular expressions can either be statically bound, hard-coded and syntax-checked by the compiler or dynamically bound and specified at run-time. These regular expressions can refer to each other recursively and match patterns in strings that ordinary regular expressions cannot.

While Boost.Xpressive integrates a domain-specific language at compile-time and performs syntax checks on it, its purpose is limited to a pre-defined domain: text manipulation. As a more generic approach, the Boost.Proto library takes one step further towards a framework for building generic embedded domain specific languages in C++.

Proto provides tools for constructing, type-checking, transforming and executing domain-specific languages based on expression templates (Boost.Proto, 2011). Data structures for representing the expressions and a mechanism for giving additional behaviors and members to them are given. Expression trees are built from the DSL expressions using the same operator overloading techniques we mentioned at AraRat. There are extendable utilities to transform and evaluate these expression trees. Boost.Proto is a general purpose DSL integration library for C++. However, it has some serious restrictions coming from the main characteristics that it has no parser of its own. Proto uses the C++ parser, therefore the syntax of the embedded DSL has to match the requirements of the C++ parser, among others no C++ keywords or new operator symbols can be used in the DSL. On the other hand no quotations are required to identify the DSL code.

COMPILE TIME PARSER GENERATOR LIBRARY

In this chapter, we present how to implement compile-time parsers in C++ Template Metaprogramming. We present how to construct parsers and how to prepare them for error-handling. Our approach is based on parser combinators (Andersson, 2001) and our implementation is built on top of Boost.MPL.

The parsers take some source text as input, which is a string. Since the parsers run at C++

Box 6.

```
vector_c<char, 'H','e','l','l','o',' ','W','o','r','l','d','!'>
```

Box 7.

```
template <int Len>
constexpr char nth(const char (&s)[Len], int n)
{
  return n >= Len ? 0: s[n];
}
```

compile-time, we have to be able to represent the input text as a template metaprogramming value. The text is a string, thus we need strings in template metaprogramming. Since the parsers need access to every character of the string, we need to represent them as character sequences. One way of creating such a character sequence is creating a compile-time list of characters using the containers provided by Boost.MPL as demonstrated in Box 6.

Using this approach makes the compile-time string difficult to read in the source code. Boost. MPL provides a string data-type, which offers a better way of constructing strings:

```
string<'Hell','o Wo','rld!'>
```

This approach lets the developer split the text into 4 character chunks instead of separating every character. This is based on the multicharacter-character constant feature. This approach is better, but it is still not ideal.

The major difficulty with using string literals as input is that the individual characters of the string literal need to be accessed at compile-time. Constexpr (Dos Reis, 2007), a new language feature introduced in C++11, made it possible. Constexpr functions are C++ functions with restrictions, that are evaluated at compile-time. Their results can be used as template arguments. Thus, one can create constexpr functions that return the nth character of a string literal as presented in Box 7.

Using this function a metaprogramming string can be constructed as demonstrated in in Box 8.

The value of the above code is a Boost.MPL string. This code can be automatically generated using the Boost Preprocessor Library. We don't present the details of this. An implementation of it can be found in the implementation of Metaparse (Sinkovics 2011). Using it, the above code can be generated from the following (or a similar) macro call:

```
_S("This is the string")
```

Now that we can provide the input, we present how to build parsers. A compiler has to be able to give good error messages to the developer when the text he compiles is invalid. To help the developer finding and fixing the bug, the error message should contain the location of the error in the invalid source code. We need to represent locations of the input text in our parsers.

A location is a pair of integers representing line and column number. In our implementation we have created a compile-time data-type for it, presented in Box 9.

Metafunctions for querying and updating these values are easy to implement. We have implemented the following ones:

Box 8.

```
#define S "This is the string"

boost::mpl::push_back<
  boost::mpl::push_back<
    // ...
      boost::mpl::push_back<
        boost::mpl::string<>,
        boost::mpl::char_<nth<sizeof(S)>(S, 0)>
      >::type,
    // ...
    boost::mpl::char_<nth<sizeof(S)>(S, 126)>
  >::type,
  boost::mpl::char_<nth<sizeof(S)>(S, 127)
>::type
```

Box 9.

```
template <typename Line, typename Col>
struct source_position;
```

- `get_col` queries the column information.
- `get_line` queries the line information.
- `next_char` returns a new source position pointing to the next character of the same line.
- `next_line` returns a new source position pointing to the first character of the next line.

Having all the metafunctions above, we can start implementing parsers. A parser is a template metafunction class taking the following arguments:

- The text to parse.
- Location information (line and column number) of the beginning of the input text in the entire input to parse. This argument is important, because the parser is given either the entire input text, or only a postfix of it.

For proper error reporting, the parser has to be aware of the exact location of the parsed chunk in the input text. The return value of the function is one of the following:

- A tuple of some resulting value, the remaining text and the location information of the beginning of the remaining text. This tuple is returned when the parser was successful. The first element of the tuple, the resulting value, can be any template metaprogramming value. It can be either a syntax tree, the result of the evaluation of the input text or anything else.
- A pair of some error description and a source location. This is returned when the parser failed to parse the input. The error description can be any template metaprogramming value.

We need to be able to differentiate the result of a successful parsing from a rejection. Boost.MPL assigns a class to every metaprogramming value. This class is called the tag of the class. Different types of values have different tags. Every class representing a value in Boost.MPL can have a nested type called `tag`, which is the tag associated to the value. We can use the same idea with the parsers. We can create two tags – one representing accept and one reject:

```
struct accept_tag;
struct error_tag;
```

The parsers have to tag their return values, so the user of the parser can tell by the tag if parsing was successful or not.

To parse some text, the text itself and source location pointing to the first character of the first line has to be passed to the parser. Since it is often used, this source position can get a custom name (in our implementation we called it `start`).

We implement three simple parsers:

- `return_`, a parser that always accepts its input and consumes nothing from the input text.
- `fail`, a parser that always fails to parse its input.
- `one_char`, a parser that consumes the first character of its input. It fails for empty input.

`return_` can be implemented the following way:

```
template < typename Result>
struct return_
{
  template <typename S, typename Pos>
  struct apply
  {
    struct type
    {
      typedef Result result;
      typedef S remaining;
      typedef Pos source_position;
    };
  };
};
```

`return_`<R> is a metafunction class, where `R` is the result the parser returns for any input. The metafunction takes two arguments:

- `S`, the input text.
- `Pos`, the source position of the beginning of the input text.

The rest of the simple parsers, `fail` and `one_char` can be implemented in a similar way.

Now that we have implemented the simple parsers, we can start building more complex ones. We do that by combining the simple ones together in many different ways. We implement functions taking parsers as arguments and building new parsers from them. These functions are called *parser combinators* (Andersson, 2001). As an example we implement a parser combinator that takes a parser and a predicate to build a new parser. The new parser accepts an input if and only if the original parser accepts it and the predicate returns true for the result of the parser. It can be implemented the following way as demonstrated in Box 10.

`Parser` is the parser to extend, `Pred` is the predicate to check the result with and `ErrorMsg` is a class representing a meaningful error message the new parser can return when the predicate returns false. `accept_when<Parser, Pred, ErrorMsg>` is the new parser. It applies `Parser` on the input first. To simplify the implementation, the name `result` is bound to the result of this. The new parser checks the result of applying `Parser` using the helper function `is_error`. The helper function checks the tag of the result, its implementation is straight forward. The `eval_if` structure of Boost.MPL is used to

Box 10.

```
template <typename Parser, typename Pred, typename ErrorMsg>
struct accept_when
{
  template <typename Result, typename S, typename Pos>
  struct impl:
    boost::mpl::eval_if<
      typename boost::mpl::apply<
        Pred,
        typename get_result<Result>::type
      >::type,
      Result,
      boost::mpl::apply<fail<ErrorMsg>, S, Pos>
    >
  {};

  template <typename S, typename Pos>
  struct apply
  {
    typedef boost::mpl::apply<Parser, S, Pos> result;
    typedef typename
      boost::mpl::eval_if<
        typename is_error<result>::type,
        result,
        impl<result, S, Pos>
      >::type
      type;
  };
};
```

forward the error when `Parser` rejects the input and proceed with applying the predicate otherwise. When the predicate returns true, the result of `Parser` is returned as it is. Otherwise an error with the message `ErrorMsg` is generated. The verification of the result using the predicate is implemented using `eval_if` as well. It had to be moved to a separate metafunction, `impl`, to avoid it being evaluated when `Parser` rejects the input. This helper function wouldn't be necessary if `eval_if` supported lazy evaluation of its predicate (Sinkovics, 2010).

The next parser combinator we present can be used to implement a parser that expects one specific character. When the first character of the input is the expected one, it accepts it, otherwise it rejects the input as presented in Box 11.

`C` is a boxed character, `lit<C>` is a parser accepting the input when its first character is `C`. `literal_expected` is a template class representing the error messages this parser can fail with. The parser is implemented using the `accept_when` parser combinator. It uses `one_`

Box 11.

```
template <typename C>
struct literal_expected {};
template <typename C>
struct lit:
  accept_when<
    one_char,
    typename boost::mpl::lambda<boost::mpl::equal_to<C, _1> >::type,
    literal_expected<C>
  >
{};
```

Box 12.

```
template <char C>
struct lit_c: lit<boost::mpl::char_<C> > {};

typedef
  one_of<
    lit_c<'0'>, lit_c<'1'>, lit_c<'2'>, lit_c<'3'>, lit_c<'4'>,
    lit_c<'5'>, lit_c<'6'>, lit_c<'7'>, lit_c<'8'>, lit_c<'9'>
  >
  digit;
```

`char` as the base parser and `equal_to<C, _1>` as the predicate.

Ordered choice can be implemented as a parser combinator as well. An ordered choice applies a number of parsers in order. The result is the result of the first parser that accepts the input. When all of the parsers reject the input, the combined parser rejects it as well. We don't present the implementation of this parser combinator here, it can be found as `one_of` in mpllibs (Sinkovics, 2011). Using this combinator a parser expecting a digit character can be implemented by combining a number of `lit` parsers as demonstrated in Box 12. We call this new parser `digit`.

We've defined `lit_c` to simplify the creation of `lit` parsers and combined `lit_c<'0'> ... lit_c<'9'>` with `one_of`. It accepts any character in the range `'0' - '9'` but nothing else.

Another example for parser combinators is one that combines a parser and a transformation function transforming the result of the parser into some other value. Its implementation can be found in the mpllibs source code (Sinkovics, 2011) it is the parser combinator called `transform`. Using it `digit` can be turned into a parser that returns the value of the digit as the result of parsing as demonstrated in Box 13.

This example defines a metafunction class, `char_to_int`, that converts a digit character into an integer value. The example builds a new parser, `digit_val` from `digit` using the parser combinator described above.

The Kleene star can be implemented as a parser combinator. It takes a parser as argument

Box 13.

```
struct char_to_int
{
  template <typename C>
  struct apply: boost::mpl::int_<C::type::value - '0'> {};
};
typedef transform<digit, char_to_int> digit_val;
```

Box 14.

```
using namespace boost;

typedef mpl::int_<0> int0;
typedef mpl::int_<10> int10;

struct calculate_int_value
{
  template <typename ListOfDigits>
  struct apply:
    mpl::fold<
      ListOfDigits,
      int0,
      mpl::plus<mpl::times<int10, mpl::_1>, mpl::_2>
    >
  {};
};

typedef transform<any1<digit_val>, calculate_int_value> int_;
```

and applies it repeatedly as long as it accepts the input text. The list of successful parser applications is the result of applying the combined parser. Its implementation can be found in mpllibs, it is called `any`.

When the underlying parser rejects the input for the first time, `any` still accepts it as zero matches. Another parser combinator, `any1`, is available that handles zero matches as a failure. Using it one can build a parser that accepts natural numbers as demonstrated in Box 14.

This combinator builds a list of integers by parsing the digits one by one. It calculates the value of the parsed integer number from the digits using `calculate_int_value`.

A parser combinator applying a list of parsers in order can be implemented as well. When any of them fails, the combined parser fails as well and skips the remaining parsers. When all of them succeed, the result of parsing is the list of results. This combinator is available in Metaparse as `sequence`.

We have shown parser combinators implementing sequences, choices and repetition. Using these tools, complex grammars can be constructed. In the next section we present how they can be used

Box 15.

```
safe::printf<_S("%d + %d = %d\n")>(11, 2, 13);
```

Figure 1. Mechanism of the library using safe::printf

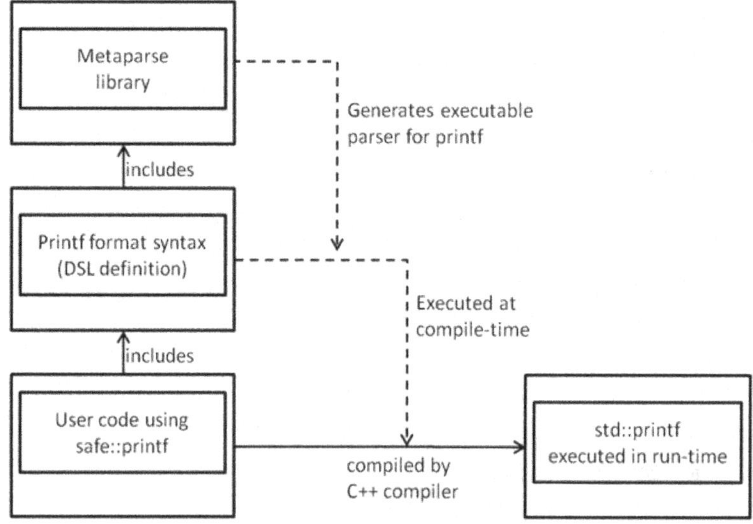

to implement a parser for a real domain specific language, the format string of `printf`.

A USE-CASE: IMPLEMENTING A TYPE-SAFE PRINTF AS DSL

The C standard library has a function, `printf` for outputting formatted text. Its first parameter is a format string specifying how to format the rest of its arguments. When the number or the types of the arguments are invalid according to the format string, the runtime behavior is undefined. In this chapter we present how to use our library to verify it at compile-time.

The syntax of the format string is an internal language inside C or C++. We can treat it as an embedded DSL and parse it using tools built for processing embedded DSLs. Using the original, non-type-safe version of printf looks like the following:

```
printf("%d + %d = %d\n", 11, 2, 13);
```

Using the type-safe printf presented in this chapter is similar to that as presented in Box 15.

The type-safe `printf` is a template function taking the format string as a template argument and the rest of `printf` 's arguments as runtime arguments. When the number or types of the arguments are invalid according to the format string, it generates a compilation error. It calls the original, unsafe version of `printf` otherwise.

In Figure 1, we describe the overall mechanism of using our library through `safe::printf` as an example. The application developer uses `safe::printf` in his code after including the DSL definition as a C++ header file. This definition contains the syntax of `safe::printf` in a DSL format. The header also includes the Metaparse library placed in separate header(s). When the user compiles his code, the C++ compiler executes the parser generator, which constructs the parser for `safe::printf`. This

Box 16.

```
template <typename FormatString, typename T1, typename T2>
int safe_printf(T1 t1_, T2 t2_)
{
  BOOST_STATIC_ASSERT(
        (valid_printf<FormatString, boost::mpl::list<T1, T2> >));
  return
    printf(boost::mpl::c_str<FormatString>::type::value, t1_, t2_);
}
```

parser is immediately used (in the same compilation phase) to type check the arguments of `safe::printf`. The result is either an executable code utilizing the standard `printf` or a compilation error reporting type mismatch.

We present how to implement this template function for a format string with two placeholders. The rest of the overloads can be implemented in a similar way and these things can be automatically generated using the Boost Preprocessor Library as demonstrated in Box 16 (Boost.preprocessor, 2011).

It uses `c_str` from Boost.MPL to convert the compile-time string into a runtime one that can be passed to the unsafe `printf`. The `BOOST_STATIC_ASSERT` is a macro taking a compile-time predicate as input and generating a compilation error when that predicates returns false. The predicate we use calls a template metafunction, `valid_printf`, and passes the format string and the list of argument types as arguments. `valid_printf` generates the list of expected argument types from the format string and compares it with the list of actual ones. When the two lists don't match, `valid_printf` returns false, thus the static assertion emits a compilation error.

An expected argument can be described by a three element list:

- A boolean value telling if a preceding integer argument describing the display length is expected.
- A boolean value telling if a preceding integer argument describing the precision is expected.
- The expected type of the argument. This is described by placeholder classes representing types. For example:

```
struct expect_character;
struct expect_string;
struct expect_double;
// ...
```

As an example here is a format string and the list of expected arguments we need presented in Box 17.

Only the placeholders are important. The rest of the format string can be ignored during type-checking.

`valid_printf` generates the list of expected argument types by parsing the format string. The parser can be built using the parser combinator library. It takes the format string as input and produces the list of expected types as the result of parsing. Here is the grammar of printf format strings based on (Printf, 2011) demonstrated in Box 18.

`CHARS` represents non-interpreted characters, `PARAM` represents one parameter to be substituted. Our parser has to skip all non-interpreted characters, determine the type required by the `PARAM` parts and build the list of these types.

Box 17.

```
// format string
"%d + %.*d = %*u"

// list of expected arguments
using namespace boost::mpl;

list<
  list<false_, false_, expect_signed_integer>,    // %d
  list<false_, true_,  expect_signed_integer>,    // %.*d
  list<true_,  false_, expect_unsigned_integer>   // %*u
>
```

Box 18.

```
S::= CHARS (PARAM CHARS)*
PARAM::= '%' FLAG* WIDTH PRECISION FORMAT
FORMAT::= 'h' FORMAT_HFLAG | 'l' FORMAT_LFLAG
           | 'L' FORMAT_LLFLAG | FORMAT_NO_FLAG
FORMAT_LLFLAG::= 'e' | 'E' | 'f' | 'g' | 'G'
FORMAT_LFLAG::= 'c' | 'd' | 'i' | 'o' | 's'
                 | 'u' | 'x' | 'X'
FORMAT_HFLAG::= 'd' | 'i' | 'o' | 'u' | 'x' | 'X'
FORMAT_NO_FLAG::= 'c' | 'd' | 'i' | 'e' | 'E'
                  | 'f' | 'g' | 'G' | 'o'
                  | 's' | 'u' | 'x' | 'X'
                  | 'p' | 'n' | '%'
PRECISION::= '.' WIDTH | NONE
WIDTH::= INTEGER | '*' | NONE
INTEGER::= DIGIT+
DIGIT::= '0' | '1' | '2' | '3' | '4'
          | '5' | '6' | '7' | '8' | '9'
FLAG::= '-' | '+' | ' ' | '#' | '0'
CHARS::= ('\' one_char | not ('%' | '\'))*
NONE::= epsilon
```

We can construct the parsers based on the grammar above. We can use `sequence` to implement |, `any` to implement *, `any1` to implement +, `except` to implement `not` and `return_` to implement `epsilon`. All of these combinators are part of our Metaparse library. Using them, a parser can easily be constructed from the grammar. By adding combinators manipulating the result of other parsers, we can create the parser we need. After adding those result manipulating combinators, it is still easy to reconstruct the grammar from the resulting parser.

Box 19.

```
typedef
  one_of<
    always<lit_c<'d'>, expect_short_signed_integer>,
    always<lit_c<'i'>, expect_short_signed_integer>,
    always<lit_c<'o'>, expect_short_signed_integer>,
    always<lit_c<'u'>, expect_short_unsigned_integer>,
    always<lit_c<'x'>, expect_short_unsigned_integer>,
    always<lit_c<'X'>, expect_short_unsigned_integer>
  >
  format_h_flag;
```

Box 20.

```
typedef
  one_of<
    last_of<lit_c<'h'>, format_h_flag>,
    last_of<lit_c<'l'>, format_l_flag>,
    last_of<lit_c<'L'>, format_capital_l_flag>,
    format_no_flag
  >
  format;
```

Parsing the `FORMAT_...` elements is simple. As an example, here is an implementation of `FORMAT_HFLAG` presented in Box 19.

The result of parsing such a formatting character is a placeholder for an expected type. `FORMAT_LFLAG`, `FORMAT_LLFLAG` and `FORMAT_NO_FLAG` can be implemented in a similar way. Using these parsers, we can build a parser for FORMAT, which parses a format character with a flag as demonstrated in Box 20.

It uses the appropriate format character parser based on the flag controlling the type of the `printf` argument. Every argument of `one_of` is a parser, which either succeeds completely or fails. `last_of` applies all of its arguments in sequence, expects all of them to succeed. The result of `last_of` is the result of the last sub-parser, thus the above implementation parses the format controlling flag (`'h'`, `'l'` or `'L'`), throws the result away and calls the appropriate `format_`... parser. The `lit_c` parsers act like guards. We can implement the parser for WIDTH the following way as demonstrated in Box 21.

The result of this parser is a boolean indicating if there should be an integer argument specifying the precision or not. Since we only care about type checking the runtime arguments of `printf`, when the precision is defined in the format string, we ignore its value. Using `WIDTH` we can implement `PRECISION`:

```
typedef
  one_of<
    last_of<it_c<'.'>, width>,
    return_<boost::mpl::false_>
  >
  precision;
```

Box 21.

```
typedef
  one_of<
    always<integer, boost::mpl::false_>,
    always<lit_c<'*'>, boost::mpl::true_>,
    return_<boost::mpl::false_>
  >
  width;
```

Box 22.

```
typedef
  one_of<lit_c<'-'>, lit_c<'+'>, lit_c<' '>, lit_c<'#'>, lit_c<'0'> >
  flag;
```

Box 23.

```
typedef
  last_of<
    lit_c<'%'>,
    any<flag>,
    sequence<width, precision, format>
  >
  param;
```

The result of this parser is a boolean similarly to `WIDTH`. `FLAG` parses a one character flag, its implementation is straightforward as presented in Box 22.

This parser returns the flag it has parsed. Since we're only interested in type-checking the arguments of `printf`, we can safely skip these flags. Having all these parsers, we can implement `PARAM` as well, as demonstrated in Box 23.

`param` parses the entire description of a placeholder. It expects a `%` character, then it parses the flags if there is any and the display length, the precision and the format character itself. It uses `sequence` to build a compile-time list of the results of the last three elements. This compile-time list is the result of this parser, thus this parser produces the elements we need at the end of parsing: the three element lists describing the expected arguments of `printf`.

In a format string the placeholders are separated by characters `printf` prints out as they are. We can ignore those characters. A sequence of those characters can be parsed by `CHARS` is presented in Box 24.

`except` is a parser combinator building a new parser that accepts everything the original one rejects. It is a look-ahead parser, since it doesn't consume any input. `any_one_of` is a combination of `any` and `one_of` to make parser definitions more compact.

Having all these parsers we can define the top-level parser of the `printf` grammar in Box 25.

It ignores normal characters and collects the parsed placeholders – the three element lists – into

Box 24.

```
typedef
  any_one_of<
    second_of<lit_c<'\\'>, one_char>,
    second_of<except<lit_c<'%'>, int>, one_char>
  >
  chars;
```

Box 25.

```
typedef last_of<chars, any<first_of<param, chars> > > S;
```

Box 26.

```
typedef build_parser<S> printf_parser;
```

Box 27.

```
printf_parser::apply<_S("%d + %d = %d\n")>::type
```

a list. This list is the result of parsing and can be used to validate the type of the runtime arguments.

To simplify the usage of the parsers, Metaparse provides a convenience metafunction taking care of applying a parser on an input and getting the end result. This is called `build_parser`. The top-level parser for the `printf` grammar can be constructed the following way as demonstrated in Box 26.

`printf_parser` is a metafunction class taking the input string as argument and returning the list of expected types. It can be used the following way as presented in Box 27.

We have shown a solution that validates the arguments of `printf` at compile time and generates a compilation error when they are invalid. The drawback of this solution is that the format string has to be available at compile-time, however, format strings are rarely constructed dynamically. Another drawback of this solution is its negative effect on compilation speed because everything happens at compile-time. However, this solution has no extra runtime cost.

FUTURE RESEARCH DIRECTIONS

The approach presented in this library makes it possible to provide an embedded DSL for implementing C++ template metaprograms. To implement such a DSL one has to develop template metaprograms. Applying the library on itself and developing a DSL for building parsers can significantly improve the usability of the library and embedded DSLs built with it. Following these ideas we're developing a DSL similar to the EBNF notation (Wirth 1977) for constructing parsers.

C++ template metaprogramming has a rapidly growing application area. It is used for implementing expression templates (Veldhuizen 1995), active libraries (Veldhuizen 1998, Juhász 2007), concepts (McNamara 2000, Siek 2000), etc. Unfortunately, supporting tools are a little behind. Debuggers, profiles are in experimental phase, thus tools maintaining template metaprograms require extra research efforts (Porkolab, 2006).

CONCLUSION

To minimize third-party dependencies at domain specific language integration a self-contained solution is proposed using only the standard C++ language features. The syntax of the domain specific language is arbitrary, the code is given in the form of compile time strings wrapped into C++ templates. This can be done with a minimal syntactical overhead. We created a C++ template metaprogram library which implements a full-featured parser infrastructure to parse the domain specific code and translate it to native C++. The parser is executed as a metaprogram during the compilation of the C++ source using no other tool than the standard C++ compiler. As our approach does not require external tools, it is highly portable. To demonstrate the solution we implemented a type-safe `printf` using a domain specific approach. Our library is fully implemented and downloadable as an open source project.

REFERENCES

Abrahams, D., & Gurtovoy, A. (2004). *C++ template metaprogramming: Concepts, tools, and techniques from Boost and beyond*. Boston, MA: Addison-Wesley.

Alexandrescu, A. (2001). *Modern C++ design: Generic programming and design patterns applied*. Addison-Wesley.

Andersson, L. (2001). *Parsing with Haskell*. Retrieved from http://www.cs.lth.se/eda120/assignment4/parser.pdf

Bennett, M., Borgen, R., & Havelund, K. Ingham, & M. Wagner, D. (2008). Development of a prototype domain-specific language for monitor and control systems. In *Proceedings of IEEE Aerospace Conference*.

Bohm, C., & Jacopini, G. (1966). Flow diagrams, Turing Machines and languages with only two formation rules. *Communications of the ACM*, *9*(5), 366–371. doi:10.1145/355592.365646

Boost.Mpl. (2011). *The Boost metaprogram libraries*. Retrieved from http://www.boost.org/doc/libs/1_46_0/libs/mpl/doc

Boost.Preprocessor. (2011). *The Boost preprocessor library*. Retrieved from http://www.boost.org/doc/libs/1_46_0/libs/preprocessor/doc

Boost.Proto. (2011). *The Boost proto library*. Retrieved from http://www.boost.org/doc/libs/1_46_0/doc/html/proto.html

Boost.Xpressive. (2011). *The Boost xpressive regular library*. Available at http://www.boost.org/doc/libs/1_46_0/doc/html/xpressive.html

Coplien, J. (1998). *Multi-paradigm design for C*. Addison-Wesley.

Czarnecki, K., & Eisenecker, U. W. (2000). *Generative programming: Methods, tools and applications*. Addison-Wesley.

Dos Reis, G. Stroustrup, & B. Maurer, J. (2007). *Generalized constant expressions -Revision 5*. N2235=07-0095. Retrieved from http://www.open-std.org/jtc1/sc22/wg21/docs/papers/2007/n2235.pdf

Gil, Y., & Lenz, K. (2007). Simple and Safe SQL queries with C++ templates. In C. Consel & J. L. Lawall (Eds.), *6th International Conference Generative Programming and Component Engineering (GPCE 2007)* (pp. 13-24).

Gregor, D., & Järvi, J. (2009). Variadic templates for C++. Symposium on Applied Computing, *Proceedings of the 2007 ACM Symposium on Applied computing* (pp. 1101-1108).

Icon. (2010). The Icon Programming Language http://www.cs.arizona.edu/icon

Josuttis, N. (1999). *The C++ standard library: A tutorial and reference*. Addison-Wesley.

Juhász, Z., Ádám Sipos, Á., & Porkoláb, Z. (2007). Implementation of a finite state machine with active libraries in C++. In R. Lammel, J. Visser, & J. Saraiva (Eds.), *Generative and Transformational Techniques in Software Engineering II, GTTSE 2007, Lecture Notes in Computer Science, Vol. 5235,* International Summer School, (pp. 474—488). Springer.

Karlsson, B. (205). *Beyond the C++ standard library: An introduction to Boost.* Addison-Wesley.

Katahdin. (2010). *The Katahdin project*. Retrieved from http://www.chrisseaton.com/katahdin

McNamara, B., & Smaragdakis, Y. (2000). Static interfaces in C. In *First C*. Template Programming Workshop.

Porkoláb, Z. (2010). Domain-specific language integration with compile-time parser generator library. In E. Visser & J. Järvi (Eds.), *9th International Conference Generative Programming and Component Engineering (GPCE 2010)* (pp. 137-146).

Porkoláb, Z., Mihalicza, J., & Sipos, A. (2006). Debugging C++ template metaprograms. In S. Jarzabek, D. C. Schmidt, & T. L. Veldhuizen (Eds.), *5th International Conference Generative Programming and Component Engineering (GPCE 2006)* (pp. 255—264).

Printf. (2011). *The printf grammar*. Retrieved from http://www.cplusplus.com/reference/clibrary/cstdio/printf

Siek, J., & Lumsdaine, A. (2000). Concept checking: Binding parametric polymorphism in C. In *First C*. Template Programming Workshop.

Sinkovics, Á. (2010). Functional extensions to the Boost metaprogram library. In P. Porkoláb (Ed.), *The 3rd Workshop on Generative Technologies (WGT 2010)* (pp. 56-66).

Sinkovics, Á. (2011). *The source code of mpllibs. metaparse.* Retrieved from http://github.com/sabel83/mpllibs

Sloane, A. M. (2008). *Experiences with domain-specific language embedding in Scala.* Retrieved from http://www.mendeley.com/research/experiences-domainspecific-language-embedding-scala/

Stratego (2010). The Stratego program transformation language. Retrieved from http://strategoxt.org/

Stroustrup, B. (2000). *The C++ programming language* (special edition). Addison-Wesley.

Stroustrup, B. (2010). *C++0x FAQ*. Retrieved from http://www.research.att.com/~bs/C++0xFAQ.html

Unruh, E. (1994). *Prime number computation.* ANSI X3J16-94-0075/ISO WG21-462.

Vandevoorde, D., & Josuttis, N. (2002). *C++ templates: The complete guide*. Addison-Wesley.

Veldhuizen, T. (1995). Using C++ template metaprograms. *C++ Report,* 7(4), 36-43.

Veldhuizen, T. (1995). Expression templates. *C++ Report,* 7(5), 26-31.

Veldhuizen, T., & Gannon, D. (1998). Active libraries: Rethinking the roles of compilers and libraries. In *Proceedings of the SIAM Workshop on Object Oriented Methods for Inter-operable Scientific and Engineering Computing (OO'98)* (pp. 21-23).

Visser, E. (2004). Program transformation with Stratego/XT: Rules, strategies, tools, and systems in StrategoXT-0.9. In Lengauer, C. (Eds.), *Domain-Specific Program Generation* (*Vol. 3016*, pp. 216–238). Lecture Notes in Computer Science. doi:10.1007/978-3-540-25935-0_13

Völter, M. (2011). MPS, the Meta Programming System. Retrieved from http://www.jetbrains.com/mps/

Wirth, N. (1977). What can we do about the unnecessary diversity of notation for syntactic definitions? *Communications of the ACM*, *20*(11), 822–823. doi:10.1145/359863.359883

XMF. (2010). *The XMF programming language*. Retrieved from http://itcentre.tvu.ac.uk/~clark/xmf.html

ADDITIONAL READING

Borók-Nagy, Z., Májer, V., Mihalicza, J., Pataki, P., & Porkoláb, Z. (2010). Visualization of C++ template metaprograms. *10th IEEE Working Conference on Source Code Analysis and Manipulation* (pp. 167-176).

Czarnecki, K., Eisenecker, U., Glück, R., Vandevoorde, D., & Veldhuizen, T. (1998). Generative programming and active libraries. In M. Jazayeri, R. Loos, & D. Musser (Eds.), *Selected Papers from the International Seminar on Generic Programming* (pp. 25-39). London, UK: Springer-Verlag.

Gregor, D., Järvi, J., Kulkarni, M., Lumsdaine, A., Musser, M., & Schupp, S. (2005). Generic programming and high-performance libraries. *International Journal of Parallel Programming*, *33*(2), 145–164. doi:10.1007/s10766-005-3580-8

Hudak, P. (1996). Building domain-specific embedded languages. *ACM Computing Surveys*, *28*(4). doi:10.1145/242224.242477

Musser, D., & Stepanov, A. (1994). Algorithm-oriented generic libraries. *Software, Practice & Experience*, *24*(7), 623–642. doi:10.1002/spe.4380240703

Sheard, T., Benaissa, Z., & Pasalic, E. (2000). DSL implementation using staging and monads. *ACM SIGPLAN Notices*, *35*(1), 81–94. doi:10.1145/331963.331975

Siek, G., & Lumsdaine, L. (2005). Essential language support for generic programming. *ACM SIGPLAN Notices*, *40*(6), 73–84. doi:10.1145/1064978.1065021

Sinkovics, Á. (2011). Nested lamda expressions with let expressions in C++ template metaprorgams. In P. Porkoláb, et al., (Eds.), *The 3rd Workshop on Generative Technologies*, Vol. III, (pp. 63-76).

Stroustrup, B. (2007). Evolving a language in and for the real world: C++ 1991-2006. In *Proceedings of the Third ACM SIGPLAN Conference on History of Programming Languages (HOPL III)* (pp. 1-59).

Szűgyi, Z., Sinkovics, Á., Pataki, N., & Porkoláb, Z. (2009). C++ metastring library and its applications. In M. Fernandes, J. Saraiva, R. Lammel, & J. Visser (Eds.), *Proceedings of the 3rd International Summer School Conference on Generative and Transformational Techniques in Software Engineering III (GTTSE'09)* (pp. 461-480).

Van Wyk, E., & Schwerdfeger, A. (2007). Context-aware scanning for parsing extensible languages. In *Proceedings of the 6th International Conference on Generative Programming and Component Engineering (GPCE '07)* (pp. 63-72).

Veldhuizen, T. (1999). C++ templates as partial evaluation. In O. Danvy (Ed.), *Proceedings of the 1999 ACM SIGPLAN Workshop on Partial Evaluation and Semantics-Based Program Manipulation* (pp. 13-18).

Veldhuizen, T. (2005). Software libraries and their reuse: Entropy, Kolmogorov complexity, and Zipf's law. In *OOPSLA 2005 Workshop on Library-Centric Software Design (LCSD'05)*.

Veldhuizen, T. (2006). Tradeoffs in metaprogramming. In *Proceedings of the 2006 ACM SIGPLAN Symposium on Partial Evaluation and Semantics-Based Program Manipulation (PEPM '06)* (pp. 150-159).

Veldhuizen, T. (2007). Parsimony principles for software components and metalanguages. In *Proceedings of the 6th international conference on Generative programming and component engineering (GPCE '07)* (pp. 115-122).

KEY TERMS AND DEFINITIONS

Boxed Value: As metaprograms work on types, constant values should be converted to types in a way that the original value is recoverable. Among other libraries, Boost.Mpl provides standard classes for this purpose.

Template Instantiation: The process when the C++ compiler generates new code from a given template definition. The compiler determines the actual parameters using parameter deduction and creates a new specialized function or class. Templates instantiated with at least one different parameter type are unrelated.

Template Metaprogram: A set of template definitions for the intention to control the compilation process and execute a desired algorithm as a side effect. Template metaprograms are executed at compilation time and may result either compilation errors or successful compilation.

Template Metafunction: Template metafunctions are the standard way to implement compile time actions in template metaprograms. They appear in the form of a template class which parameters represent the metafunction parameters. The return value of the metafunction is implemented using a public type member called `type`.

Template Metafunction Class: Metafunctions are first class citizens in C++ template metaprogramming. However, as only types and not templates can be used as template metafunction parameters they should be wraped by a class. A standard name `apply` is used to implement the metafunction inside the wrapper class.

Template Specialization: It is possible to give an alternative specification for function and class templates when certain template parameters are known. Class templates, unlike function templates can be partially specialized, i.e. an alternative version of the template is given when some of the template parameters are known, and others may remain generic.

Chapter 3
Semantics-Driven DSL Design

Martin Erwig
Oregon State University, USA

Eric Walkingshaw
Oregon State University, USA

ABSTRACT

Convention dictates that the design of a language begins with its syntax. The authors of this chapter argue that early emphasis should be placed instead on the identification of general, compositional semantic domains, and that grounding the design process in semantics leads to languages with more consistent and more extensible syntax. They demonstrate this semantics-driven design process through the design and implementation of a DSL for defining and manipulating calendars, using Haskell as a metalanguage to support this discussion. The authors emphasize the importance of compositionality in semantics-driven language design, and describe a set of language operators that support an incremental and modular design process.

INTRODUCTION

Despite the lengthy history and recent popularity of domain-specific languages, the task of actually *designing* DSLs remains a difficult and under-explored problem. This is evidenced by the admission of DSL guru Martin Fowler, in his recent book on DSLs, that he has no clear idea of how to design a good language (2010, p. 45). Instead, recent work has focused mainly on the *implementation* of DSLs and supporting tools, for example, through language workbenches (Pfeiffer & Pichler, 2008). This focus is understandable—implementing a language is a structured and well-defined problem with clear quality criteria, while language design is considered more of an art than an engineering task. Furthermore, since DSLs have limited scope and are often targeted at domain experts rather than professional programmers, general-purpose language design criteria may not always be applicable to the design of DSLs, complicating the task even further (Mernik et al., 2005).

DOI: 10.4018/978-1-4666-2092-6.ch003

Traditionally, the definition of a language proceeds from syntax to semantics. That is, first a syntax is defined, then a semantic model is decided upon, and finally the syntax is related to the semantic model. This widespread view is reflected in the rather categorical statement by Felleisen et al. that the specification of a programming language starts with its syntax (2009, p. 1). This view has been similarly echoed by Fowler, who lists defining the abstract syntax as the first step of developing a language (2005) (although he puts more emphasis on the role of a "semantic model" in his recent book (2010)).

In this chapter we argue for an inversion of this process for denotationally defined DSLs, where the semantic domain of the language is identified first, then syntax is added incrementally and mapped onto this domain. We argue that this *semantics-driven* approach to DSL design leads to more principled, consistent, and extensible languages. Initial ideas for semantics-driven DSL design were developed in our previous work (2011). This chapter expands these ideas and explains the process and the individual steps in detail.

Syntax-Driven Design

We begin by demonstrating the traditional syntax-driven approach, both for reference and to demonstrate how it can lead to a rigid and idiosyncratic language definition. Consider the design of a simple calendar DSL for creating and managing appointments. We first enumerate some operations that the DSL should support, such as adding, moving, and deleting appointments. It should also support basic queries like checking to see whether an appointment is scheduled at a particular time, or determining what time an appointment is scheduled for. One advantage of the syntax-driven approach is that it is easy to get off the ground; we simply invent syntax to represent each of the constructs we have identified. A syntax for the basic calendar operations is given below, where *Appt* represents appointment information (given by strings, say) and *Time* represents time values (Box 1).

The `add` ... `at` ... operation adds an appointment at the specified time, `move entry at` ... `to` ... reschedules the appointment at the first time to the second, and `delete` ... `entry` removes the appointment at the given time from the calendar. A program defining a calendar consists of a sequence of such operations.

Prog ::= *Op**

With an initial syntax for our calendar DSL in place, we turn our attention to defining its (denotational) semantics. This process consists of finding a semantic domain that we can map our syntax onto, then defining a valuation function that represents this mapping. Looking at our syntax, we can observe that an array-based representation of calendars will yield constant-time implementations of each of our basic operations. Therefore we choose *dynamic arrays* (Schmidt, 1986, Ch. 3) as a semantic domain. A dynamic array is a function that maps elements of a discrete domain to some element type that contains an error (or undefined) element, say ε. In our example, we use the type *Cal* as an instance of dynamic arrays in which the discrete domain is *Time*, and the element is appointment information *Appt*. The semantic domain of dynamic arrays is a semantic

Box 1.

```
Op  ::=  add Appt at Time
      |  move entry at Time to Time
      |  delete Time entry
```

algebra that offers operations for accessing and updating arrays. Accessing an element at position t in an array c means to apply the function that represents the array and is thus simply written as $c(t)$. The semantic *update* operation is defined as follows in Box 2.

The semantics of an operation *Op* is a function from one calendar array to another and is captured by a valuation function $[[\cdot]] : Op \rightarrow (Cal \rightarrow Cal)$, which is defined using the operations from the semantic algebra (Box 3).

The semantics of a calendar program is then defined as the accumulation of the effects of the individual calendar operations, applied to the initial array that is undefined everywhere, that is, $[[\cdot]] : Prog \rightarrow Cal$ (Box 4).

The array representation works very well as a semantic domain for the syntax we have defined. It also supports the queries we identified at the start: checking whether an appointment is scheduled at a particular time is just an index into the calendar array, and looking up the scheduled time of an appointment is a linear search. Its weaknesses only become apparent as we extend the language with new syntax and functionality.

First, we consider an extension of the language with a notion of appointment lengths, which will allow us to more accurately determine whether a particular time is available. To do this, we add an extra value to the add construct, an integer representing the number of time slots the appointment will last (Box 5).

The semantics of the modified `add` operation can then be defined by assigning the appointment to each time slot in the calendar that the appointment occupies (Box 6).

Box 2.

$$update : Time \times Appt \times Cal \rightarrow Cal$$
$$update(t, a, c) = c - \{(t, c(t))\} \cup \{(t, a)\}$$

Box 3.

$[[$`add` a `at` $t]]\ c = update(t, a, c)$

$[[$`move entry at` t `to` $t']]\ c = update\,(t', c\,(t), update\,(t, \varepsilon, c)\,)$

$[[$`delete` t `entry`$]]\ c = update\,(t, \varepsilon, c)$

Box 4.

$$[[o_1, o_2, \ldots, o_n]] = [[o_n]]\,(\ldots\,[[o_2]]\,([[o_1]]\ \{(t, \varepsilon) \mid t \in Time\})\ \ldots)$$

Box 5.

Op ::= `add` *Appt* `at` *Time* `with length` *Int*

| ...

Box 6.

$[[$`add` a `at` t `with length` $n]]\ c = update(t + n - 1, a, \ldots\ update(t + 1, a, update(t, a, c))\ \ldots)$

Note that although we have not changed the structure of our semantic domain, its use is now sufficiently changed that we have to redefine the valuation function of both other operations in our DSL as well since one appointment now will generally occupy several array slots. In other words, this extension is not modular, requiring a complete redefinition of our DSL's semantics.

As a second example, consider the extension of the DSL to support overlapping appointments. Note that this extension can be supported perfectly well by our existing syntax, but not by the flat appointment-array representation we have chosen as its semantic domain. We might update our semantic domain to support this feature by considering a calendar to be a time-indexed array of *lists* of appointments. Instead of directly assigning appointments to the array, our valuation function now adds and removes appointments from the list at each time slot. Again, this extension forces us to reconsider our semantics and completely redefine our valuation function.

That both of these seemingly minor extensions cannot be implemented in a modular way suggests that our initial calendar DSL was not very extensible. The problem lies mainly in our choice of semantic domain, which was chosen because it supported a nice and efficient implementation of our initial syntax. Ultimately, the semantic domain we choose has a profound impact on the quality of the language going forward—it gives terms in the language meaning, and so is the foundation on which the syntax is built. In the syntax-driven approach, this important decision is relegated to supporting an after-the-fact definition of some possibly idiosyncratic initial syntax.

Semantics-Driven Design

The semantics-driven approach begins instead with the identification of a small, compositional semantics core, then systematically equips it with syntax. We argue that considering the semantic domain of a language first leads to a more principled language design, in part, because it forces language designers to begin by carefully considering the *essence* of what their language represents. With the proper semantics basis, the language can be systematically extended with new syntax as new features are added.

It is of course still possible to identify a poor semantic domain when beginning with semantics, just as beginning with syntax does not doom one to a poor language design. The semantics-driven approach we describe in this chapter is not mechanical and still requires creativity and insight on the part of the DSL designer. It does, however, provide much-needed structure to the language design process, and emphasizes the importance of compositionality, reuse, and extensibility in DSL design.

Semantics-driven design is fundamentally incremental and domain-focused, while syntax-driven design is more monolithic and feature-focused. In the syntax-driven approach, designers begin by anticipating use cases and inventing syntax to implement corresponding features. This is problematic since it is difficult to foresee all cases, leading to an incomplete syntax and idiosyncratic semantics that must be extended in an ad hoc way. In the semantics-driven approach, designers begin by trying to identify a more general representation of the domain, then extend this in a structured way to support specific features.

Semantics-driven language design is also a mostly compositional process that leads naturally to compositional languages. That is, bigger languages can be defined by systematically composing or extending existing smaller languages. This supports the incremental development of DSLs and promotes the reuse of small DSLs in larger ones. Moreover, it supports the decomposition of a DSL's domain into simpler subdomains, making it easier to reason about and identify good semantics domains. Compositionality also makes semantics-driven design less ad hoc than the traditional approach. Compositional development produces a clear account of the individual components of the language and how they are related, making the design easier to reuse, extend, and maintain. This process also produces, as a byproduct, a library of smaller DSLs that can be reused in future language designs. Compositionality is especially important in the context of DSLs since the final language must often be integrated with other languages and tools.

Rest of this Chapter

Our research background is programming languages and functional programming, and we therefore approach and discuss the problem of DSL design from a different perspective than the majority of the chapters in this book. In the next section we take some time to describe the programming language view of DSLs and language design, and establish the terminology that will be used throughout the chapter. This will hopefully make the chapter accessible to as wide an audience as possible. We also introduce in this section the strongly-typed functional language Haskell (Peyton Jones, 2003) as a metalanguage for DSL design (Thompson, 2011).

In the third section we use these tools to describe semantics-driven DSL design in detail. We first present a high-level overview of the design process, then proceed by example, demonstrating the (re)design of the calendar DSL using the semantics-driven approach. We do this by first describing the process of decomposing and defining the semantic domain, which is followed by incrementally adding syntax.

The compositional nature of semantics-driven design leads to a view of the language design space in which languages are composed of smaller, mini-DSLs. The relationships of these mini-DSLs and the ways that they can be composed can be captured in *language operators*, which are discussed in the fourth section. The use of language operators supports a structured approach to language design and promotes language reuse.

In Related Work, we relate semantics-driven design to other language design strategies and also discuss other related work not discussed in the main body of the chapter. Conclusions will be presented in the final section.

BACKGROUND

Research on DSLs has been pursued mainly by two different communities: the modeling community and the programming languages (PL) community. Each brings a different background to the area and has developed its own specific views on DSLs. This often involves specialized terminology, a distinctive focus on particular goals, and consequently the use of different methods. Together these two approaches may provide deeper insights through a diversity of perspectives, but it also balkanizes the research area, making it harder for the different groups to talk to one another and potentially limiting progress in the field as a whole.

The purpose of this section is to explain the basic elements of the PL approach to DSLs and to acquaint the reader with the corresponding terminology and methods. This is necessary since the model-based view seems more dominant today—it is the view taken by Fowler (2010) and also the one found in most of the chapters in this book. This section will therefore explain the idiosyncrasies of the PL approach, in order to make this chapter accessible to a broader audience.

Language Structure of DSLs and the Role of Metalanguages

The two major aspects of any language are its *syntax* and *semantics*. (Language pragmatics is also an important aspect, but is probably less relevant in the design phase of languages.) In the PL approach, the syntax of a DSL is usually described by a context-free grammar, rather than by a metamodel. The semantics can be defined in several different ways. Two widely used methods are operational (Pierce, 2002) and denotational (Mitchell, 1998) semantics. A denotational semantics (which we focus on here) consists of two parts: (1) the *semantic domain*, which is a collection of semantic values and operations, and (2) the *valuation function* (or just *valuation*), which is a mapping from the syntax to the semantic domain (Schmidt, 1986). A semantic domain is, in principle, very similar to the notion of a *semantic model* as described in (Fowler, 2010).

Except for purely theoretical treatments of languages, the syntax and semantics of a DSL are commonly expressed in terms of a programming language that effectively acts as a metalanguage with respect to the defined DSL. In this case, the DSL syntax and semantics are defined using constructs of the metalanguage. Exactly how this is done and which constructs are used depends not only on the chosen metalanguage, but also on the implementation style of the DSL. An *external* DSL is a standalone language, which is parsed and interpreted by the metalanguage. In contrast, an *internal* DSL exists within the metalanguage itself, using metalanguage constructs as DSL syntax directly. Internal DSLs are also called domain-specific *embedded* languages (DSELs) (Hudak, 1998) and can be further classified into two embedding styles, *deep* or *shallow*. This will be described in detail later and is also explained in Chapter 19.3 of Simon Thompson's book (2011).

The purpose of this section is not to give a comprehensive overview and comparison of all possible variations on this theme, but only to provide the necessary background and context for the particular language-based approach employed in this chapter. We will therefore consider in the following only internal DSLs (DSELs) and their denotational semantics. Moreover, we will describe the perspective from the point of view of a typed, functional metalanguage.

For concreteness, we use Haskell (Peyton Jones, 2003) as our metalanguage; it has a long tradition as a metalanguage and has been used extensively and successfully to define a wide range of DSLs. We discuss some examples of these in the Related Work section, and many other examples are listed in the Additional Reading section at the end of this chapter. However, much of the discussion applies also to other languages.

Types as Semantic Domains

The values of the semantic domain are naturally given by values of the metalanguage. These values are elements of predefined or user-defined types or data types, and these types therefore define the semantic domain of the DSEL. The meaning of a type such as `Int` is obvious, but the meaning of a data type might not be so widely known. A data type consists of a set of constructors that each have a name and zero or more argument types. For example, the following definition introduces a data type with three constructors for representing pictures containing lines and circles.

```
type Point = (Int,Int)
data Pic = Line Point Point
         | Circle Point Int
         | Pic :+: Pic
```

The `type` definition simply introduces a new name `Point` for the type of integer pairs. This type is used as an argument type in two of the constructor definitions. Each of the shown constructors takes values as indicated by the argument types and builds a value of type `Pic`. For example, the first constructor `Line` builds a picture consisting of a single straight-line segment given by two endpoints. The second constructor `Circle` builds a picture consisting of a circle with the given point value as center and the integer value as its radius. Finally, the symbolic infix constructor `:+:` builds a `Pic` value by overlaying two other pictures.

A semantic domain, such as `Pic`, together with its operations (`Line`, `Circle`, `:+:`, and the pairing operation of points) forms a *semantic algebra* (Schmidt, 1986). Below is an example

Box 7.

```
ctr :: Point
ctr = (3,2)

pic :: Pic
pic = Line (1,0) (5,3) :+: Circle ctr 4 :+: Circle ctr 5
```

Box 8.

```
Cmd  ::=  line from Point to Point
       |  triangle at Point width Num height Num
       |  Cmd; Cmd
       |  ...
```

semantic value (a value of the `Pic` data type) that represents a picture consisting of two concentric circles and an intersecting line (Box 7).

The definition consists of two smaller definitions. First, a point value is bound to a variable `ctr`. Second, a picture value is bound to `pic`, using `ctr` as the center for the two circles in the picture. The first line of each variable definition is optional and indicates the type of the defined variable (if omitted, it will be inferred by the type checker). The second line provides the definition of the variable.

Built-in and user-defined types and data types are employed as semantic domains in the definition of DSELs. The semantics of the DSEL is then given by a valuation from the syntax to the semantics domain. What this syntax looks like, and how this mapping is realized, depends on the embedding style of the DSL.

An Embedding-Dependent Notion of Syntax

As mentioned above, internal DSLs can be either deeply or shallowly embedded (Thompson, 2011, Ch. 19.3). While semantic domains and semantic values are represented the same in either style of embedding, the representation of DSL syntax is quite different.

Deep Embedding

In a deep embedding, the (abstract) syntax of a DSEL is represented explicitly by a data type. Each constructor represents a grammar production (that is, an operation) of the language, and its argument types correspond to nonterminals that occur on the right-hand side of the production. Constructors without arguments represent terminal symbols, and constructors with basic type arguments (such as `Int`) form the link to the lexical syntax. The semantic domain of the represented language is captured by a separate (data) type, and some function `sem` acts as the valuation function, mapping syntactic values to semantic values.

Consider, for example, a DSL for describing pictures that contains commands for drawing lines and right triangles. The syntax for this DSL can be described by a context-free grammar. In the following, *Cmd* is the non-terminal ranging over drawing commands, while *Point* and *Num* range over points and integers, respectively (Box 8).

Box 9.

```
sem :: Cmd -> Pic
sem (Line' p1 p2)       = Line p1 p2
sem (Tri p@(x,y) w h) = Line p (x,y+h) :+: Line p (x+w,h) :+: Line (x,y+h) (x+w,y)
sem (Seq d d')          = sem d :+: sem d'
```

This grammar excerpt can be directly translated into the following data type.

```
data Cmd = Line' Point Point
         | Triangle Point Int Int
         | Seq Cmd Cmd
```

The constructor `Line'` represents a line between the given points,[1] the constructor `Triangle` represents the triangle, and the constructor `Seq` represents the sequential composition of commands. Note how the argument types of the constructors mirror the nonterminals in the corresponding grammar productions. A constructor name together with its the argument types distills the essential components of a grammar production and omits keywords such as `from` or `height`. In this way, data types represent the *abstract* syntax of languages, rather than the concrete syntax.

To define the semantics of the picture language, we employ the data type `Pic` as the semantic domain, then define a valuation function `sem`. We define `sem` by equation, using pattern matching. Each equation maps a case of the syntax (a constructor of `Cmd`) onto a corresponding semantic value (of type `Pic`) (Box 9).

The first equation is trivial, directly mapping a syntactic line onto a semantic one. In the second equation we have used a so-called "as-pattern" `p@(x,y)` that matches the complete point value to `p` and at the same time matches the components of the pair to the variables `x` and `y`. The valuation maps a triangle to three lines that are combined into one `Pic` value using the overlay constructor. Finally, a sequence of drawing commands is mapped to an overlay of the corresponding `Pic` values obtained for the two commands.

Shallow Embedding

In a shallow embedding, we do not define a data type for the syntax at all, but rather take the constructors of the semantic domain immediately as operations of the DSL. For example, in our picture-drawing DSEL we have as part of the semantic domain the constructor `Line`, which represents a semantic value and can thus be used directly as an operation of the DSL. If we are not satisfied with this syntax, we can always introduce a function definition to change the syntax.

Suppose we want the syntax to be closer to the concrete syntax given in the grammar, enforcing the use of keywords. We can define a function `line` that takes additional keyword arguments, as follows. First we define the keywords that we need as strings of the same name.

```
type KW = String
from = "from"
to = "to"
```

Then we extend the function definition for `line` to take additional `KW` arguments and check, using pattern matching, that the correct keywords have been used in a call of `line` (Box 10).

As illustrated in the function definition, it is very easy in this approach to extend the syntax on the fly, for example, with alternative orderings of arguments. (It is also easy to extend this definition to produce more elaborate error messages that report the incorrect keywords.) If we write a

Box 10.

```
line :: KW -> Point -> KW -> Point -> Pic
line "from" p "to" q = Line p q
line "to" p "from" q = Line q p
line _ _ _ _ = error "Incorrect keyword!"
```

Box 11.

```
triangle :: Point -> Int -> Int -> Pic
triangle p@(x,y) w h = Line p (x,y+h) :+: Line p (x+w,h) :+: Line (x,y+h) (x+w,y)
```

Figure 1. Summary of the language-based view of DSLs and the representation of internal DSLs within a typed, functional metalanguage

Language Aspect		Representation in Metalanguage			
		Deep Embedding		*Shallow Embedding*	
syntax	L	data type	`L`	function LHS	`f pat :: T`
program	$p \in L$	value	`p :: L`	expression	`p :: D`
semantic domain	D	(data) type	`D`	(data) type	`D`
semantic value	$v \in D$	value	`v :: D`	value	`v :: D`
valuation	$[[\cdot]] : L \to D$	function	`sem :: L -> D`	function RHS	`rhs :: D`
syntax + semantics	$(L, [[\cdot]])$	data type + function	`(L, sem)`	function	`f :: T -> D` `f pat = rhs`

command for drawing a line we have to use the keywords `from` and `to`. If we do, a semantic `Line` value is produced correctly, if we don't, the function reports a syntax error.

```
> line from (1,1) to ctr
Line (1,1) (3,2)
> line to p to ctr
*** Exception: Incorrect keyword!
```

In addition to the constructor names of the semantic domain (and potentially added syntactic sugar), we also introduce function definitions for those operations of the DSL that are not directly represented by constructors of the semantic domain. The operation for drawing triangles is such an example. The corresponding function definition is presented in Box 11.

As with the command for drawing lines, we could extend the above function definition by arguments representing keywords to enrich the concrete syntax.

The important observation here is that these function definitions are comprised of two parts that combine the definition of DSEL syntax *and* semantics. First, the function head, that is, the left-hand sides of the equations, with the name of the function and its argument patterns, defines the DSEL syntax. Second, the expressions on the right-hand sides of the equations define the semantics of that particular syntactic construct. Since we obtain different function definitions for different operations of the DSEL, the valuation function from syntactic elements to values in the semantic domain is spread across several function definitions.

A summary of the preceding discussion is presented in Figure 1.

Which Embedding for Semantics-Driven Design?

The semantics-driven design process can be used with either implementation strategy, although there are many trade-offs involved. The biggest trade-off between the two embedding styles is in the dimension of extensibility. Deep embeddings directly support the addition of new semantic interpretations of the language. For example, we might want to perform some static analyses on our language or generate a visualization of the program. A new semantic interpretation can be added by simply identifying the type of the new semantic domain, `D'`, and writing a new valuation function that maps values of `L` onto values of `D'`. However, extending a deep embedding with new syntactic constructs is relatively difficult—not only must we extend the `L` data type with new constructors, but we must extend the definition of every function that manipulates or interprets `L` as well.

Conversely, adding new syntax to a shallow embedding is very easy—we just add a new function that generates a value of the semantic domain `D`. Adding new semantic interpretations, on the other hand, is much more difficult in a shallow embedding (and is often incorrectly described as impossible). In order to add a new interpretation onto a type `D'`, we must first extend the semantics domain of the language from `D` to the product of `D` and `D'`, then extend every syntactic function to produce values of this new type. We can then obtain the desired semantic interpretation by simple projections.[2]

We will use the shallow embedding strategy in this chapter since it supports a more incremental style of language development and more closely matches the compositional process described here. Semantics-driven design forces us to carefully consider the semantic domain at the start, after which it remains relatively fixed while we incrementally extend the language with new syntax—this is exactly the strength of a shallow embedding. Syntactic flexibility is especially important during the early phases of semantics-driven design, while the language is evolving rapidly. Once the syntax is relatively stable, if a deep embedding is desired, it can be obtained from a shallow embedding by identifying a minimal set of core syntactic constructs (operations implemented as functions), replacing these by a corresponding data type `L`, and merging the original function bodies into a new function implementing the valuation from `L` to `D`. The remaining, non-core syntax functions remain as syntactic sugar that produce values of the abstract syntax `L`.

THE SEMANTICS-DRIVEN DESIGN PROCESS

In this section we will describe the semantics-driven design process in some detail. We will illustrate and discuss each step through the incremental development of a calendar DSL.

The semantics-driven design process consists of two major parts. The first part is concerned with the modeling of the semantic domain, which is based on the identification of basic semantic objects and their relationships. The second part consists of the design of the language's syntax, which is about finding good ways of constructing and combining elements of the semantic domain. Before delving into the details of semantics-driven design, however, we provide a high-level overview of the entire process. This will allow us to explain how concepts in the three involved realms—domain, language, and metalanguage—are related and combine to facilitate the semantics-driven design process (Figure 2).

Process Overview

Semantics-driven design leads from a problem domain to a domain-specific language that is described, or implemented, by a metalanguage.

Figure 2. Schematic illustration of the steps in the semantics-driven design process and their relationships. The two steps "Domain Decomposition" and "Domain Modeling" taken together comprise the Semantic Modeling part of the design process. The Syntactic Design step can be further distinguished as Inter- and Intra-DSL Syntax Design.

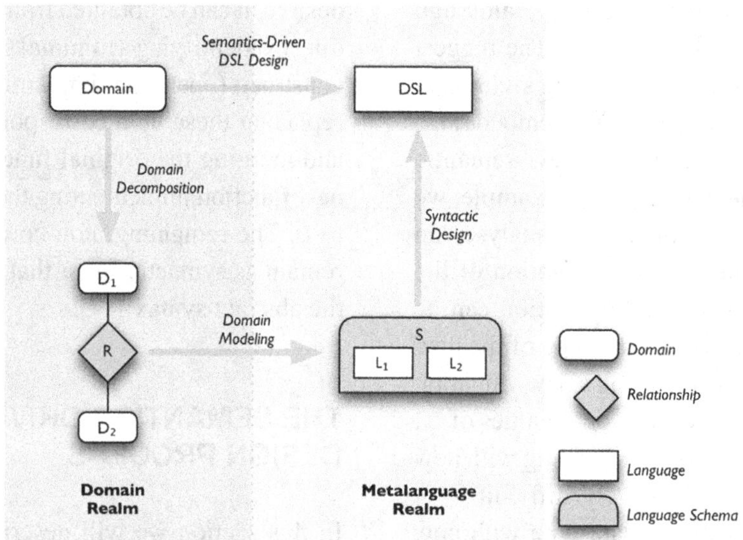

The process consists of three major steps, which are illustrated in Figure 2.

The first step decomposes the problem domain into smaller subdomains and identifies the relationships between them. In Figure 2 we find two subdomains D_1 and D_2 and a relationship R between them. This decomposition determines the semantic domain of our DSL. This step happens completely within the problem realm. No metalanguage concepts are invoked yet.

The second step concerns the modeling of the decomposed semantic domain in the metalanguage. Each subdomain forms the basis of (that is, is the semantic domain for) a little language called a *micro DSL*. The identified relationships between subdomains are modeled as *language schemas*. In Figure 2 we observe that each domain D_i is modeled as a micro DSL L_i and that the relationship R is modeled as language schema S. This step takes the DSL design from the problem realm into the metalanguage realm. In terms of Haskell, domain modeling means to define types to represent the semantics domains of languages and type constructors to represent the semantic domains of language schemas.

These first two steps taken together comprise the *semantic design* part of the DSL design process. All decisions regarding the semantics of the DSL happen in this part, which will be illustrated with the help of an example in the next subsection on "Semantic Design".

The third step in the design process is the design of the syntax of the DSL. This step can also be broken down into two parts. Specifically, we can distinguish between the syntactic design of each micro DSL and the design of syntax that spans several of these micro DSLs, leading to constructs that build relationships between these elementary objects. We have not specifically illustrated the separate parts of syntactic design in Figure 2 since this happens completely within the metalanguage. We will talk about this in detail in the subsection on "Syntactic Design" and also discuss how the design of syntax is guided by the already defined semantics.

Semantic Design

At the core of semantic design is the identification of the essential objects that the language must construct, refer to, and manipulate. This process consists of two parts: identifying and decomposing the semantic domain into smaller (sub)domains, then modeling each domain as a micro DSL within the metalanguage.

In the first part, each decomposition of a domain into subdomains can be described by an equation that shows the relationship between the decomposed domain and its subdomains. That is, a domain is modeled and decomposed by a set of equations of the following form.

$D_i = R_j(D_k, \ldots)$

In the second part, these equations are directly translated into a set of type definitions. Each such definition forms the semantic basis for a micro DSL, and the relationships between the DSLs is captured through the application of type constructors that implement language schemas.

```
type L_i = S_i L_k ...
```

In the following we will demonstrate and explain these two parts in detail.

Domain Identification and Decomposition

As an illustrative example, we consider again the design of a small calendar DSL. The existence of many competing calendar tools with different feature sets reveal that this is no trivial domain. That some calendar functionality is often performed by external tools (such as scheduling meetings with Doodle) suggests room for improvement.

To identify the domains involved in the language we first ask ourselves, what are the essential objects involved? The basic purpose of a calendar is to define (and remind of) appointments at particular times. We recognize two separate components in this description, "times" and "appointments". Each of these will be a subdomain of calendars, leading to two domain models and two micro DSLs in the subsequent steps.

Decomposing the calendar domain into these subdomains involves identifying the relationship between times and appointments in calendars. In this case, we observe that times are *mapped* to appointments. This mapping from the subdomain of times to that of appointments captures the essence of calendars. The mapping relationship corresponds on the language level to a language schema. A language schema represents a whole class of related languages and can be obtained from a language by parameterizing some of its parts. We can produce a language from a language schema by substituting languages for its parameters. The language schema for mapping one domain to another obviously has two parameters, representing the domain and range of the mapping.

In Haskell, we can represent the result of the domain identification and decomposition step with a simple type definition. In the following, the types `Time` and `Appointment` represent the subdomains we identified for the calendar application, while the two-parameter type constructor `Map` represents the language schema that relates them.

```
type Calendar = Map Time Appointment
```

The type `Calendar` represents the calendar DSL and is composed of the `Time` and `Appointment` micro DSLs.

Note that we can also leave some aspects of the domain parameterized, producing a class of related DSLs that can be instantiated for different subdomains; that is, we can define our DSL itself as a language schema. For example, suppose we want to define the semantic domain of a range of calendar DSLs that can work for many different types of appointments. We partially instantiate the `Map` language schema only with the subdomain for `Time`, defining a parameterized domain for calendars. This can be implemented in the metalanguage as follows.

```
type CalT a = Map Time a
```

We can produce the original `Calendar` semantics by instantiating this schema as `CalT Appointment`.

Having identified and decomposed the domain of calendars, we recursively consider the `Time` subdomain. We quickly realize that clock time alone is not sufficient since we want to also be able to define appointments on different dates. We might choose an abstract representation of time that incorporates this information, like seconds since January 1, 1970, but this is not very evocative from a language perspective. Instead, we choose a compositional representation based on the above description—we want to define appointments in terms of a date and (clock) time, so we will decompose the domain on the left-hand side of the calendar mapping further into the subdomains of Date and Time. The relationship between these domains can be captured by a language schema with two parameters that represents pairs. In the metalanguage, we will use Haskell's special syntax `(Date,Time)` to represent the application of the pairing schema to the `Date` and `Time` subdomains, and define a new calendar language schema as follows.

```
type CalDT a = Map (Date,Time) a
```

This decomposition results in semantic values that are quite redundant, however. Whenever we schedule appointments on the same date, the corresponding `Date` value will be repeated in the semantics. As a solution, we will reconsider the decomposition of our semantic domain in order to factor out the redundancy. We do this by creating a new language schema for date-only calendars, `CalD`, that maps dates to an arbitrary domain. Then we compose the `CalD` and `CalT` schemas to produce a date calendar of time calendars; that is, a mapping from dates to a nested mapping from times to some appointment domain.

```
type CalD a = Map Date a
type Cal  a = CalD (CalT a)
```

This example demonstrates the compositional power of language schemas. We will consider `Cal` to be the primary decomposition of the calendar semantics domain going forward, although we will sometimes also refer to other calendar domains by their name in the metalanguage.

Note that we could also have chosen to compose `CalD` and `CalT` in the opposite order, producing a mapping first from time and then to date. Rather than localizing all appointments on the same date, this semantics would localize appointments at the same time (but on different dates). This would also serve to reduce redundancy, but violates the natural hierarchical structure of dates and times, and so does not seem to accurately reflect the meaning of a calendar.

Language schemas also provide a simple solution to the problem posed in the Introduction, of extending the language to incorporate a notion of appointment length. We can simply add a `Time` value to each appointment by (partially) instantiating the `Cal` domain in the following way.

```
type CalL a = Cal (a,Time)
```

This defines a calendar domain in which each appointment is a pair of some arbitrary appointment value and a time value representing the length of the appointment. This extension is modular in the sense that the change to the semantic domain is localized, allowing us to directly reuse any syntax or operations that are polymorphic in the appointment subdomain (that is, that have types like `Cal a`). Recall that in the syntax-driven language from the Introduction, this extension led to an entirely new domain representation and forced changes to existing, unrelated parts of the language definition.

As the derivation of `Cal` demonstrates, identifying the best semantic domain is typically an iterative process. Although we present the steps linearly, often domain identification interacts with domain modeling, as the precise modeling of a semantic domain can lead to new insights about its decomposition.

Domain Modeling

Having identified the required domains and relationships for the calendar DSL, we can now start to model them, in detail, in our metalanguage. We begin with the `Map` language schema. Depending on the choice of metalanguage, generic language schemas might already exist in libraries.[3] Of course, if a required schema does not exist, or if we want more control over the representation, we have to define it ourselves. We employ the following definition. (Box 12) (Here and in the following we omit some Haskell-specific details, such as the definition of standard class instances).

This definition provides two infix constructors to build maps, one for building individual associations (`:->`), and one for composing two maps into a bigger map (`:&:`).

Next we consider the representation of our subdomains of `Date` and `Time`. A date consists of a month and a day, so we model the `Date` domain in the following straightforward way (Box 13).[4]

We model the `Time` domain in an equally obvious way.

```
type Hour = Int
type Minute = Int
data Time = T Hour Minute
```

That these definitions are so straightforward is a good thing. By simplifying the language design process through systematic decomposition, we make it less surprising and ad hoc and thus more comprehensible.

Note that we can consider both `Date` and `Time` to be composite domains. For example, we can decompose `Time` into the extremely simple domains of `Hour` and `Minute`. We combine these domains in Haskell within a data type, but if we wanted to make the decomposition explicit, we could instead use the pairing schema to model the domain as `(Hour,Minute)`. We choose the given data type representation of `Time` because it allows us to enforce syntactic constraints with the Haskell type system. That is, we can define operations that take `Time` values as arguments and ensure that they can only be applied to times and not to arbitrary pairs of integers (as the pair representation would allow). It is not uncommon for aspects of the metalanguage to influence minor design decisions in this way.

Finally, in order to instantiate the `Cal` language schema and write actual calendar programs, we need to identify and model an appointment domain. We can imagine several more or less complicated representations that vary depending on the context and kinds of information we need to track. To keep the discussion focused on more interesting aspects

Box 12.

```
data Map a b = a :-> b | Map a b :&: Map a b
```

Box 13.

```
data Month = Jan | Feb | Mar | Apr | May | Jun | Jul | Aug | Sep | Oct | Nov | Dec
type Day = Int
data Date = D Month Day
```

Box 14.

```
week52 :: Cal String
week52 = D Dec 30 :-> (T 8 0 :-> "Work") :&: D Dec 31 :-> (T 22 0 :-> "Party")
```

of the design, we assume appointments are given by plain strings and write our first program in the calendar DSL as follows (Box 14).

While we can express calendars by directly building semantic values in this way, it is not very convenient. The need to use the `D` and `T` constructors is annoying, and there is no way to directly express high-level concepts like repeating or relative appointments—entering such appointments manually is not only inconvenient but also error prone. Both of these shortcomings can be addressed by extending the DSL with new syntax.

Syntactic Design

Having realized a semantic core for our language, we now focus on building up its concrete syntax through the identification and implementation of new operations. Although we argue for designing the semantics first, this should not be misunderstood as devaluing the importance of syntax. On the contrary, the syntax of a language is extremely important. Good syntax has a significant impact on the usability of a language. Syntax can facilitate the expression of recurring patterns or templates, and be used to impose constraints on what can be expressed to help avoid erroneous programs.

Although each step of the semantics-driven design process provides feedback that may alter decisions made earlier, it is important that the design of syntax comes conceptually *after* the development of the semantics core. Adding new operations is an inherently ad hoc process since it is impossible to foresee all desired features and use cases. Building on a solid semantics core ensures that (1) these syntactic extensions are implemented in a consistent and principled way, and (2) the particular selection of operations does not fundamentally alter the expressiveness of the language. In a shallow embedding in Haskell, we can see that these two features are enforced by the fact that (1) all operations will be implemented as Haskell functions that produce values of the semantic domain, and (2) we can always build a value of the semantics domain directly, if a desired operation does not exist.

As we have seen in the previous section, given our choice of a shallow embedding in Haskell, the constructors of the data types `Map`, `Date`, and `Time`, which make up the semantic domain, serve directly as syntax in the DSL. Although these constructs are maximally expressive—they can obviously produce any calendar, date, or time captured by our semantic domain—they are also very nonspecific and low level. Through the addition of new operations, we can make the syntax more descriptive (and hence more usable and understandable) and raise the level of abstraction with new high-level operations that produce complex combinations of the low-level constructors.

One of the biggest advantages of the semantics-driven process is that it decomposes the difficult task of designing a DSL into several smaller and more manageable subproblems. At the level of semantic domains, as we saw in the previous sections, this process is completely modular: we identified the subdomains, decomposed the problem, and then tackled each one separately. We can perform a similar decomposition by subdomains at the syntactic level, developing syntax for the reusable micro DSLs for dates and times. However, we will also want syntax that spans and *integrates* multiple subdomains within the larger domain of calendars.

In the rest of this section, we will demonstrate the design and structured implementation of both syntactic levels. First, we develop the micro DSLs for dates and times. Then we develop syntax that integrates these languages into the larger calendar DSL.

Micro DSL Syntax

Syntax that is specific to a particular subdomain is modular in the sense that, combined with its semantic domain, it forms a micro DSL that can be reused in other, completely unrelated languages. Therefore, throughout the syntax development process, it is important to identify which subdomains new operations affect and associate the syntax accordingly. In Haskell, our new operations are implemented as functions, so determining the affected domains is as simple as examining their types.

When working with DSLs in Haskell, one of simplest, yet often tremendously useful syntactic extensions is the introduction of so-called *smart constructors*. These are values or functions that supply constructors of a data type with some or all of their arguments. For example, in the `Date` micro DSL, we can introduce a function for each month as follows in Box 15.

With these smart constructors we can now build dates more conveniently. For example, we can write more shortly `dec 31` for `D Dec 31`, hiding the `D` constructor of the `Date` data type. In addition, we can introduce all kinds of functions for constructing, say lists of individual dates (for example, the federal holidays) or ranges of dates. We can define addition or subtraction of dates or, if we had the year information, a weekday predicate or filter. The decision of which operations to define depends, of course, on the requirements of the concrete application.

For the `Time` DSL we define several similar operations as Haskell smart constructors. The `hours` operation *specializes* the more general `T` constructor and is used for producing times on the hour. The `am` and `pm` operations add support for 12-hour clocks by translating their arguments into 24-hour time.

```
hours h = T h 0
am h = hours h
pm h = hours (h+12)
```

Finally, we add operations `before` and `after` that support the definition of relative times by adding and subtracting times from each other.

```
before t t' = t'-t
after  t t' = t'+t
```

We also add another specializing operation `mins` that produces a `Time` value containing only minutes, useful for computing relatives times.

```
mins m = T 0 m
```

A nice feature of Haskell as a metalanguage is that it offers a fairly high degree of syntactic flexibility for the development of DSLs. As an example of this, the above operations for expressing relative times are intended to be used infix, such as `hours 3 'after' pm 2` which produces a time corresponding to three hours after 2pm, or `T 17 0`. Ideally we would refine this even further to make the `hours`, `mins`, `am`, and `pm` operations postfix. Okasaki (2002) demonstrates how such an effect can be achieved in Haskell.

The very small amount of subdomain-specific syntax provided here for our two micro DSLs is by no means comprehensive. But since the semantics-

Box 15.

```
[jan,feb,mar,apr,may,jun,jul,aug,sep,oct,nov,dec] = map D [Jan .. Dec]
```

driven approach and our shallow embedding in Haskell directly support the incremental and compositional extension of languages with new syntax, this is not a problem. We can just add new operations to the languages later, as needed. This syntax is also necessarily still quite low-level since the domains themselves are very constrained. In the next step we will encounter more complex operations by considering operations that integrate multiple semantic subdomains.

Domain Integration Syntax

Syntax that associates or combines multiple subdomains is necessarily less modular than the micro DSLs developed in the previous step. Domain integration syntax represents higher-level operations associated with larger DSLs that are made up of multiple subdomains. The compositional design of semantics-driven DSLs means that such syntax can also easily be developed for the solution of some particular problem.

For the purposes of this section it will be useful to separate the notion of *schedules* and *calendars*. In fact, we have already defined the corresponding semantic domain of schedules—mappings from clock times to appointments—as the `CalT` language schema. The `Cal` language schema can then be equivalently defined as a mapping from dates to schedules.

```
type Sched a = CalT a
type Cal   a = Map Date (Sched a)
```

The most fundamental example of domain integration syntax in the calendar DSL is the mapping operator `:->`. In the context of schedules, this operator integrates the domain of `Time` with the parameterized appointment domain `a`, bringing them into the domain of schedules. In the context of calendars, the operator integrates the `Date` and `Sched a` domains into calendars.

As a higher-level example, consider an operation `wakeAt` that captures the schedule of a morning routine. This is something we might want to add to a calendar regularly if we're either especially disciplined or forgetful. The argument to this operation is the time to wake up and the result is a schedule (Box 16).

So `wakeAt (hours 7)` would produce the following schedule (Box 17).

The type of the `wakeAt` function reveals that the operation integrates times into schedules. We can combine this schedule with a date to produce a calendar using the `:->` operator, for example `jan 1 :-> wakeAt (pm 1)`.

Now, suppose we want to define a schedule that repeats indefinitely. Since we represent calendar domains as explicit mappings, this may seem at first impossible. But this is another case where the specifics of our metalanguage can influence the design of our DSL. Lazy evaluation in Haskell allows us to define such an operation by enumerat-

Box 16.

```
wakeAt :: Time -> Sched String
wakeAt t = t :-> "Shower" :&: mins 20 `after` t :-> "Breakfast"
```

Box 17.

```
T 7 0 :-> "Shower" :&: T 7 20 :-> "Breakfast"
```

ing the infinite stream of dates and mapping each one to a schedule as follows.[5]

```
everyDay :: Date -> Sched a -> Cal a
everyDay d s = map (:-> s) [d..]
```

For example, if you join the military on October 10th, you might write:

```
oct 11 `everyDay` wakeAt (hours 4)
```

This very high-level operation demonstrates just how far you can get with a simple semantics core and a sufficiently powerful metalanguage.

So far all of our operations have concerned the construction of calendars and schedules. Of course, we can also define operations that modify them. Below is an operation `move f t` that reschedules any appointments from time `f` to time `t`. The first case propagates the move operation into subschedules, while the second changes the time of a mapping if it is scheduled for time `f` (Box 18).

To demonstrate, the following DSL program defines a schedule with two events, then reschedules one of them, resulting in the new calendar `T 12 0 :-> "Lunch" :&: T 14 0 :-> "Meeting"` (Box 19).

Note that we could reuse in the `move` operation the syntactic keyword trick demonstrated earlier. By including additional keywords, like `from` and `to`, we might make the operation's concrete syntax more evocative.

COMPOSITIONALITY AND LANGUAGE OPERATORS

The principle of compositionality says that the meaning of a sentence or expression is given by its structure and the meaning of its parts. This idea has a long tradition, and some of its roots can be traced back to Frege's context principle (1884). The notion of compositionality can be formalized, for example, by stipulating a homomorphism between the syntax of the language and its semantic domain (Montague, 1970).

The principle of compositionality is at work twice in the semantics-driven design process. First, the *decomposition* of domains into subdomains and their relationships *assumes* a compositional structure in the domain to be modeled. Second, the *composition* of a DSL out of several micro DSLs *exploits* the compositionality in the application of language schemas.

The second instance of compositionality brings us to the notion of *language operators*. A language operator takes one or more languages and produces a new language, either through the composition of several micro DSLs, or through the incremental addition of syntax. In terms of Haskell, a DSL is represented by a set of Haskell definitions (a Haskell program), so a language

Box 18.

```
move :: Time -> Time -> Sched a -> Sched a
move f t    (l :&: r) = move f t l :&: move f t r
move f t m@(u :-> a) = if f == u then t :-> a else m
```

Box 19.

```
busyDay   = T 12 0 :-> "Lunch" :&: T 13 0 :-> "Meeting"
longLunch = move (pm 1) (pm 2) busyDay
```

operator that transforms one DSL into another becomes effectively a Haskell metaprogram. Note that language operators usually cannot be expressed directly in the metalanguage. Instead they are given by high-level descriptions of changes to the DSL representation. In our previous work (2011) we have provided descriptions of language operators as transformation patterns of Haskell programs. This helps us understand the representation of DSLs in Haskell and also illustrates the concrete steps required to do semantics-driven DSL development in Haskell. In this section we will focus on the specific role that some of these operators play in the semantics-driven language design process.

Syntactic vs. Semantic Language Operators

In general, language operators can apply either to the syntax or the semantics of the involved languages. Since the syntax of a DSL is given in our approach through data constructors and function definitions, syntactic language operators will add, remove, or change these constructs. Likewise, semantic language operators will involve adding, removing, or changing type definitions.

In the previous section we saw several examples of syntactic extension through the addition of new function definitions. We can also extend the scope of existing operations in the DSL by applying another language operator that parameterizes an existing operation. For example, we could add a new parameter for minutes to the `pm` function. Other language operators include the inverse operations of removing function definitions to eliminate the corresponding syntax, and removing a parameter to reduce the scope of, or *specialize* an operation. The `hours` operation in the `Time` micro DSL is an example of a non-destructive specialization of the `T` operation for constructing times. Instead of removing the minutes parameter of `T` directly, we added a new function that hid it.

In general, the application of syntactic language operators, in the semantics-driven approach, is *guided* by the semantics. This is because the functions that implement specific syntax have to produce values of the semantic domain. Since, in Haskell, semantic domains are represented by types, the definition of new syntax is in some sense type directed. For example, the definition of the syntactic operation `wakeAt` has to employ the constructors of `Map` since it must build a value of type `Sched String`.

First-Order vs. Higher-Order Language Operators

In addition to the distinction between syntactic and semantic language operators, we can also distinguish between first- and higher-order language operators. A *first-order language operator* takes one or more languages and produces a new language, while a *higher-order language operator* takes other language operators as inputs or/and produces them as outputs.

First-order language operators directly change the representation of a DSL in the metalanguage. This can take quite different forms. For example, the addition of a function or data constructor extends the represented language by a new operation. Similarly, we can extend an existing language operation by adding a new argument to the function (or constructor) that represents that operation. We can also add whole languages by adding new data types; this is often a preparatory step to combine the language with others into a bigger language. And we can rename types, functions, and constructors. Each of these operators have natural inverse operations, for example, removing functions/constructors or their arguments, which amounts to the removal or restriction of the operation, respectively. We can similarly remove data types to eliminate whole micro DSLs. Renaming is its own inverse operation.

Most first-order operations can be composed to form other, more complicated language operations. For example, the merging of two languages `L` and `L'` into one involves adding (some of) the constructors from one data type, say `L'`, to the other one, `L`, plus changing the argument types of the added constructors from `L'` to `L`. Constructors in `L'` that represent operations already represented by constructors in `L` should be removed. The types of associated syntax functions must then also be changed from `L'` to `L`.

In contrast to first-order language operators that work directly on languages, a higher-order language operator takes other language operators as inputs or produces them as outputs. At this point it is important to recognize that a language schema is itself a language operator since it can produce, via instantiation, different languages. The higher-order language operators discussed below will produce and consume language schemas.

One important higher-order language operator is *language abstraction* that takes a language (or language schema) and produces a language schema by substituting a sublanguage by a parameter. In terms of Haskell this means to take a type (or type constructor), add a parameter to its definition, and replace some argument types of its constructors by this new parameter. For example, suppose we start with a calendar definition that does not use `Map` but that defines a monomorphic type with two similar constructors, fixing the argument types to `Date` and `Appointment`.

```
data Cal' = Has Date Appointment
          | Join Cal' Cal'
```

By abstracting from the `Date` and `Appointment` sublanguages represented in that type (and renaming the constructors), we can generalize the language `Cal'` into the language schema `Map`.

Dually, *language instantiation* takes a language schema and substitutes a language (or language schema) for one of its parameters, producing a language or a more specific language schema. For example, `CalD` was obtained from `Map` by substituting `Date` for `a`, and `Cal` was obtained from `CalD` by substituting `CalT a` for `a`.

As with first-order language operations, we can derive more elaborate higher-order language operators from abstraction and instantiation. A very powerful derived language operator is the *composition* of language schemas. The basic idea behind schema composition is to instantiate one schema with another. We have seen an example of this already in the definition of `Cal` by composing `CalD` and `CalT`. As another example, consider the following language schema `Access` for distinguishing between private and public information. Private information is protected by some kind of key, which we assume for simplicity to be represented by strings (Box 20).

We can compose the `CalD` language schema with the `Access` schema to obtain a calendar schema in which appointment information can be protected by this privacy micro DSL.

```
type CalDA a = CalD (Access a)
```

Unlike many other language operators, we can actually define an operator for language schema composition within Haskell quite easily.

```
type Compose s t a = s (t a)
```

This definition is analog to the definition of function composition, it just works on the level

Box 20.

```
type Key = String
data Access a = Protected Key a | Public a
```

of types. With this language operator we can give an alternative definition for `CalDA` that reflects the explicit application of the employed language operator.

```
type CalDA a = Compose CalD Access a
```

Higher-order language operators, such as language abstraction, instantiation, and composition, support the semantics-driven DSL design process by facilitating gradual changes to the overall structure of a language. These operators make it possible to employ language refactorings during the design process, supporting the incremental and iterative design of compositional languages.

RELATED WORK

Foundational and related work in the area of programming languages and functional programming has been discussed already in the background section (and elsewhere throughout the paper). In this section we briefly describe the relationship of syntax- and semantics-driven design to other theories about language design and software engineering. We also list a few examples of successful, real-world DSLs that exhibit the characteristics of semantics-driven design.

Languages centered around concrete syntax are often based on the non-compositional LL or LR parsing frameworks, an approach that imposes inherent limits on the composition of languages (Kats et al., 2010). The syntax-driven approach to language design is also indirectly promoted by the popular strategy of *user-centered design* (Norman & Draper, 1986). Since user-centered design asks users about how to solve specific tasks, there is the danger of focusing on too many details of too specific operations and losing the big picture. A critical view of user-centered design was provided by Don Norman himself (2005) where he instead argued for *activity-centered design*. Our proposal is to go one step further and focus directly on the domain with which tasks and activities are concerned.

The motivation for semantics-driven language design is similar to that for *model-driven engineering* (MDE) (Kent, 2002; Schmidt, 2006). MDE encourages that solutions be developed first from the perspective of the problem domain rather than from the solution domain. That is, the development of a software banking system would begin by abstractly modeling the concepts of accounts, customers, and transactions, and only then consider the translation of these concepts into a software implementation. The early emphasis on modeling attempts to manage complexity by decomposing the system into clearly defined abstractions before committing to a specific implementation. This is very similar to the early emphasis on domain identification and modeling in semantics-driven design, which leads to a more modular and compositional semantic basis before committing to a specific syntax.

Semantics-driven design is also closely related to the idea of *domain-driven design* promoted by Eric Evans (2003). An important aspect of domain-driven design is the development of a so-called *ubiquitous language*, to be used by software developers and domain experts alike. This ubiquitous language consists of terminology that closely reflects the key concepts of the domain to be modeled, which corresponds to the elements of the semantic domain in semantics-driven design. The main differences between the two approaches is that in domain-driven design, domain terminology is embedded into English when talking about language aspects, whereas semantics-driven design firmly grounds domain terminology in a metalanguage that is used to precisely and unambiguously define the semantic domain and the domain-specific language.

Finally, although in this chapter we name and provide structure to the semantics-driven design process, it reflects a philosophy that has long existed and proven very successful in the functional programming community. Many semantics-driven

Haskell DSELs have found success in the real-world. Examples include the PFP (Probabilistic Functional Programming) library for representing and computing with discrete probability distributions (Erwig & Kollmansberger, 2006) and the Pan language for creating and manipulating images (Elliott, 2003). Interestingly, semantic values in Pan are not ground values but functions. Pan syntax therefore consists of functions that manipulate and produce other functions. Such DSELs are called *combinator libraries* (Wallace & Runciman, 1999) and represent a simple but powerful extension of the basic process sketched in third section. Perhaps the most successful combinator library is Parsec, a widely-used DSEL for constructing recursive-descent parsers (Leijen & Meijer, 2001). Parsec's expressiveness and extensibility have led to it being ported to at least a dozen different host languages.

CONCLUSION

We advocate shifting the attention in the early phases of DSL design toward semantics. We argue that a semantics-driven and compositional approach to design leads to better DSL designs that are more general and reusable, and less ad hoc. The language development process is supported by one's choice of meta-language. We suggest Haskell as a good metalanguage for semantics-driven DSL design since it supports a clear interpretation of semantic domains as types, enables the incremental extension of syntax through function definition, in addition to other helpful features like a flexible syntax and lazy evaluation.

A beneficial side effect of compositional language design is that it also leads to compositional languages, in particular, when compared to syntax-driven language design. Compositionality is generally a highly valued feature of languages since it supports expressiveness with few language constructs. In a sense, compositional languages are more economical since they provide more expressiveness with fewer constructs.

ACKNOWLEDGMENT

This work is partially supported by the Air Force Office of Scientific Research under the grant FA9550-09-1-0229 and by the National Science Foundation under the grant CCF-0917092.

REFERENCES

Carette, J., Kiselyov, O., & Shan, C. C. (2009). Finally tagless, partially evaluated: Tagless staged interpreters for simpler typed languages. *Journal of Functional Programming*, *19*(5), 509–543. doi:10.1017/S0956796809007205

Elliott, C. (2003). Functional images. In Gibbons, J., & de Moor, O. (Eds.), *The fun of programming* (pp. 131–150). Palgrave MacMillan.

Erwig, M., & Kollmansberger, S. (2006). Probabilistic functional programming in Haskell. *Journal of Functional Programming*, *16*(1), 21–34. doi:10.1017/S0956796805005721

Erwig, M., & Walkingshaw, E. (2011). Semantics first! Rethinking the language design process. In *International Conference on Software Language Engineering*. To appear.

Evans, E. (2003). *Domain-driven design: Tackling complexity in the heart of software*. Addison-Wesley Professional.

Felleisen, M., Findler, R. B., & Flatt, M. (2009). *Semantics engineering with PLT Redex*. Cambridge, MA: MIT Press.

Fowler, M. (2005). Language workbenches: The killer-app for domain specific languages? Retrieved from www.martinfowler.com/articles/languageWorkbench.html

Fowler, M. (2010). *Domain-specific languages*. Addison-Wesley Professional.

Frege, G. (1884). *Die Grundlagen der Arithmetik: Eine logisch-mathematische Untersuchung über den Begriff der Zahl*. Breslau.

Hudak, P. (1998). Modular domain specific languages and tools. In *IEEE International Conference on Software Reuse* (pp. 134–142).

Kats, L. C. L., Visser, E., & Wachsmuth, G. (2010). Pure and declarative syntax definition: Paradise lost and regained. In *ACM International Conference on Object-Oriented Programming, Systems, Languages, and Applications* (pp. 918–932).

Kent, S. (2002). Model driven engineering. In *Integrated Formal Methods* (pp. 286–298).

Leijen, D., & Meijer, E. (2001). *Parsec: Direct style monadic parser combinators for the real world*. Technical Report UU-CS-2001-35, Department of Information and Computing Sciences, Utrecht University.

Mernik, M., Heering, J., & Sloane, A. M. (2005). When and how to develop domain-specific languages. *ACM Computing Surveys*, *37*(4), 316–344. doi:10.1145/1118890.1118892

Mitchell, J. C. (1998). *Foundations for programming languages*. Cambridge, MA: MIT Press.

Montague, R. (1970). Universal grammar. *Theoria*, *36*, 373–398. doi:10.1111/j.1755-2567.1970.tb00434.x

Norman, D. A. (2005). Human-centered design considered harmful. *Interactions (New York, N.Y.)*, *12*(4), 14–19. doi:10.1145/1070960.1070976

Norman, D. A., & Draper, S. W. (1986). *User-centered system design: New perspectives on human- computer interaction*. Erlbaum Associates.

Okasaki, C. (2002). Techniques for embedding postfix languages in Haskell. In *ACM SIGPLAN Workshop on Haskell* (pp. 105–113).

Peyton Jones, S. L. (2003). *Haskell 98 language and libraries: The revised report*. Cambridge, UK: Cambridge University Press.

Pfeiffer, M., & Pichler, J. (2008). A comparison of tool support for textual domain-specific languages. In *OOPSLA Workshop on Domain-Specific Modeling* (pp. 1–7).

Pierce, B. C. (2002). *Types and programming languages*. Cambridge, MA: MIT Press.

Schmidt, D. A. (1986). *Denotational semantics*. Newton, MA: Allyn and Bacon.

Schmidt, D. C. (2006). Model-driven engineering. *IEEE Computer*, *39*(2), 25–31. doi:10.1109/MC.2006.58

Thompson, S. (2011). *Haskell – The craft of functional programming* (3rd ed.). Harlow, UK: Addison-Wesley.

Walkingshaw, E., & Erwig, M. (2009). A domain-specific language for experimental game theory. *Journal of Functional Programming*, *19*(6), 645–661. doi:10.1017/S0956796809990220

Wallace, M., & Runciman, C. (1999). Haskell and XML: Generic combinators or type-based translation? In *4th ACM International Conference on Functional Programming* (pp. 148–159).

ADDITIONAL READING

Augustsson, L., Mansell, H., & Sittampalam, G. (2008). Paradise: A two-stage DSL embedded in Haskell. In *ACM SIGPLAN International Conference on Functional Programming* (pp. 225–228).

Bauer, T., & Erwig, M. (2009). Declarative scripting in Haskell. In *International Conference on Software Language Engineering, LNCS 5969*, (pp. 294–313).

Bauer, T., Erwig, M., Fern, A., & Pinto, J. (2011). Adaptation-based programming in Haskell. In *IFIP Working Conference on Domain-Specific Languages* (pp. 1–23).

Carette, J., Kiselyov, O., & Shan, C. (2009). Finally tagless, partially evaluated: Tagless staged interpreters for simpler typed languages. *Journal of Functional Programming, 19*(5), 509–543. doi:10.1017/S0956796809007205

Claessen, K., & Hughes, J. (2003). Specification-based testing with QuickCheck. In Gibbons, J., & de Moor, O. (Eds.), *The fun of programming* (pp. 17–39). Palgrave MacMillan.

Claessen, K., Sheeran, M., & Singh, S. (2003). Functional hardware description in Lava. In Gibbons, J., & de Moor, O. (Eds.), *The fun of programming* (pp. 151–176). Palgrave MacMillan.

Elliott, C., Finne, S., & de Moor, O. (2003). Compiling embedded languages. *Journal of Functional Programming, 13*(2), 9–26.

Erwig, M., & Walkingshaw, E. (2009). A DSL for explaining probabilistic reasoning. In *IFIP Working Conference on Domain-Specific Languages, LNCS 5658*, (pp. 335–359).

Erwig, M., & Walkingshaw, E. (2009). Visual explanations of probabilistic reasoning. In *IEEE International Symposium on Visual Languages and Human-Centric Computing* (pp. 23–27).

Holtzblatt, K., Burns Wendell, J., & Wood, S. (2005). *Rapid contextual design: A how-to guide to key techniques for user-centered design*. San Francisco, CA: Elsevier/Morgan Kaufmann.

Hudak, P. (1996). Building domain-specific embedded languages. *ACM Computing Surveys, 28*(4), 196–196. doi:10.1145/242224.242477

Hudak, P. (2003). Describing and interpreting music in Haskell. In Gibbons, J., & de Moor, O. (Eds.), *The fun of programming* (pp. 61–78). Palgrave MacMillan.

Hutton, G., & Meijer, E. (1998). Monadic parsing in Haskell. *Journal of Functional Programming, 8*(4), 437–444. doi:10.1017/S0956796898003050

Kiselyov, O., & Shan, C. (2009). Embedded probabilistic programming. In *IFIP Working Conference on Domain-Specific Languages, LNCS 5658*, (pp. 360–384).

Klint, P., Lammel, R., & Verhoef, C. (2005). Toward an engineering discipline for grammarware. *ACM Transactions on Software Engineering and Methodology, 14*, 331–380. doi:10.1145/1072997.1073000

Liang, S., Hudak, P., & Jones, M. (1995). Monad transformers and modular interpreters. In *ACM Symposium on Principles of Programming Languages* (pp. 333–343).

Merkle, B. (2010). Textual modeling tools: Overview and comparison of language workbenches. In *ACM International Conference on Object-Oriented Programming, Systems, Languages, and Applications*, (pp. 139–148).

Peyton Jones, S. L., & Eber, J. M. (2003). How to write a financial contract. In Gibbons, J., & de Moor, O. (Eds.), *The fun of programming* (pp. 105–129). Palgrave MacMillan.

Peyton Jones, S. L., Meijer, E., & Leijen, D. (1998). Scripting COM components in Haskell. In *International Conference on Software Reuse*, (pp. 224–233).

Pfenning, F., & Elliott, C. (1988). Higher-order abstract syntax. In *ACM SIGPLAN Conference on Programming Language Design and Implementation* (pp. 199–208).

Sheard, T. (2001). Accomplishments and research challenges in meta-programming. In *International Workshop on Semantics, Applications, and Implementation of Program Generation, LNCS 2196*, (pp. 2–44).

Tobin-Hochstadt, S., St-Amour, V., Culpepper, R., Flatt, M., & Felleisen, M. (2011). Languages as libraries. In *ACM SIGPLAN Conference on Programming Language Design and Implementation* (pp. 132–141).

Walkingshaw, E., & Erwig, E. (2011). A DSEL for studying and explaining causation. In *IFIP Working Conference on Domain-Specific Languages* (pp. 143–167).

KEY TERMS AND DEFINITIONS

Compositionality: The principle that an object can be defined and understood by considering its parts individually, then relating them in a systematic way. A desirable property of a language's design, its semantic domain, and the expressions it contains.

Domain Decomposition: The identification and separation of a semantic domain into its component subdomains and their relationships. Enables the domain to be modeled in a structured and modular way.

Domain Modeling: The representation of a (decomposed) semantic domain in a metalanguage with types and data types, forming a hierarchy of micro DSLs related by language schemas.

Domain-Specific Embedded Language (DSEL): A DSL defined within a metalanguage that uses metalanguage constructs directly as DSL syntax. Also called an internal DSL.

Deep Embedding: A technique for implementing DSELs where abstract syntax is represented by a data type and mapped onto the semantic domain by a valuation function.

Language Schema: A parameterized class of related languages, from which specific languages can be derived by instantiation.

Language Operator: An operation that produces a new language from one or more languages or language schemas (and possibly other arguments). Language operators are the mechanisms by which a language is incrementally extended and built from its component parts.

Semantics-Driven Design: A language design process that begins by identifying, decomposing, and modeling the semantic domain of a language, then systematically extending it with syntax.

Shallow Embedding: A technique for implementing DSELs where syntax is defined by functions that build semantic values directly.

Syntax-Driven Design: The traditional view that the design of a language begins by identifying its (abstract) syntax, and only later describing its semantics.

ENDNOTES

1 We cannot use the constructor name `Line` since it has been used already in the `Pic` data type.

2 Another strategy that is available in Haskell specifically is to overload functions using Haskell's type classes to produce different semantics (Carette et al., 2009).

3 For example, we could reuse `Data.Map` from the Haskell standard libraries.

4 We omit years from dates just for simplicity in this chapter.

5 Note that without an associated year value the stream of dates is actually cyclical.

Chapter 4
An Evaluation of a Pure Embedded Domain-Specific Language for Strategic Term Rewriting

Shirren Premaratne
Macquarie University, Australia

Anthony M. Sloane
Macquarie University, Australia

Leonard G. C. Hamey
Macquarie University, Australia

ABSTRACT

Domain-specific languages are often implemented by embedding them in general-purpose programming languages. The Kiama library used in this chapter for the Scala programming language contains a rewriting component that is an embedded implementation of the Stratego term rewriting language. The authors evaluate the trade-offs inherent in this approach and its practicality via a non-trivial case study. An existing Stratego implementation of a compiler for the Apply image processing language was translated into a Kiama implementation. The chapter examines the linguistic differences between the two versions of the Stratego domain-specific language, and compares the size, speed, and memory usage of the two Apply compiler implementations. The authors' experience shows that the embedded language implementation inflicts constraints that mean a precise duplication of Stratego is impossible, but the main flavor of the language is preserved. The implementation approach allows for writing code of similar size, but imposes a performance penalty. Nevertheless, the performance is still at a practically useful level and scales for large inputs in the same way as the Stratego implementation.

DOI: 10.4018/978-1-4666-2092-6.ch004

INTRODUCTION

One popular domain-specific language (DSL) implementation approach is to embed the DSL in a general-purpose *host language* to create an *internal language* (Mernik, 2005; Fowler, 2010; Ghosh, 2011). In this chapter we consider internal languages where the embedding consists only of pure DSL constructs that are written directly using the host language and an unchanged host language compiler performs the only compilation or translation step. In essence, the DSL is a host language library but the syntactic flexibility of the host language is exploited to implement the DSL syntax.

The embedding approach is attractive for a number of reasons, but has associated drawbacks. Reusing the host language compiler significantly simplifies implementation of the DSL compared to implementing a standalone version of the language – all host language tools can be reused. The main drawback is that the DSL syntax and semantics may not be directly realizable in the host language, resulting in compromises. Host language tools may not present a domain-specific view of programs, requiring the programmer to be aware of the way in which the DSL is implemented. Nevertheless, the pure embedding approach can be useful, particularly where the target users are developers who are familiar with the host language and where there is resistance to the adoption of new tools or build processes.

How can we evaluate the embedding approach beyond these generic high-level considerations? Our view is that real insight can only be gained through case studies of DSLs of varying styles and domains. In particular, if an external DSL has already been designed and a standalone implementation exists, then a side-by-side comparison with a new embedded version can be especially revealing. Evaluating how close the internal implementation gets to the existing external implementation provides a measure of the success of this approach. It is not our intention to undertake a full comparison of the implementation techniques, but to treat the existing external implementation as an ideal and to evaluate the ability of the embedded approach to reproduce that ideal.

Recently we have completed a project that studied an embedded implementation of a strategic term rewriting DSL and compared it to an existing implementation (Premaratne, 2011). (The code from the project is available at https://wiki.mq.edu.au/display/plrg/stragma.) The Kiama library (Sloane, 2011) contains term rewriting features inspired by an existing external language called Stratego (Visser, 2004). Kiama is embedded in the Scala general-purpose language (Odersky, 2008), which was chosen for its excellent support of pattern matching, flexible syntax and powerful static type system. When we developed the rewriting component of Kiama we adhered to the Stratego design as much as was possible and sensible, given the constraints and opportunities provided by Scala.

In this project, Stratego played the role of a well-established external DSL that is implemented by a compiler and Kiama played the role of an internal implementation of that DSL. We evaluated the two implementations using a non-trivial Stratego application that one of us had developed previously: a compiler for the Apply image processing language (Hamey, Webb & Wu, 1987; Hamey, 2007; Hamey & Goldrei, 2008). The Apply compiler translates Apply programs into C, conducting standard semantic analysis and non-trivial optimization along the way. We translated the existing Stratego implementation of the Apply compiler into Scala using the Kiama library. The two implementations perform the same analyses and translations and both run on the Java Virtual Machine. Since the focus of the comparison was the rewriting DSL, the two implementations of Apply share a common implementation of other passes such as parsing and pretty printing.

This chapter presents the results of the project with a focus on the trade-offs that the embedding approach imposes on the rewriting language and its implementation. We take the perspective that the Stratego language and compiler represent an ideal in the sense that the designer had full freedom to vary them as desired. A comparison with the Kiama version reveals the compromises from that ideal that a developer has to make when using an embedding approach. Therefore the comparison reveals important insights into embedding in general and, more specifically, explores Scala's suitability as a host language. As far as we are aware, this project is the first side-by-side comparison of two implementations of the same non-trivial DSL.

We do not consider other comparative dimensions, such as usability or social and training-based reasons for choosing one approach over the other, since we do not have data from users other than ourselves. Comparing the speed of development of the embedded DSL with Stratego was not possible since we do not have data from the Stratego development. Nor do we consider other alternatives for implementation of the DSL, such as embedding it in host languages other than Scala. We focus on the implementations that were actually used in the case study. All of these other aspects are interesting potential topics for future work.

Overall, we find that the embedding approach produces a language that is very similar to the Stratego language, but that compromises are required to fit Stratego's features into the Scala language in a natural way. Most notably, differences in the treatment of name binding and pattern matching mean that the rewrites in Kiama are expressed somewhat differently to the Stratego version. The performance of the two implementations is similar; the Kiama version incurs a penalty, but not one that limits practical use, particularly since the performance scales in the same way as the Stratego version as inputs grow large.

The structure of the rest of the chapter is as follows. We first discuss previous work that has evaluated pure embedding as an approach for building DSLs. Then we give an overview of strategic term rewriting, Stratego, and Kiama's rewriting library. Next we present the methodology we used in our comparison to ensure that the results were meaningful. Following that is an overview of the Apply language, a description of the Stratego Apply compiler implementation, and discussion of how the same compilation task was achieved using Kiama. The last two sections contain evaluation: first a discussion of the language-level differences between Stratego and Kiama's rewriting library due to the embedding approach and the characteristics of Scala, and then an analysis of the time and space performance of the two Apply compilers.

We conclude with a consideration of Future Research Directions, most notably to encourage other researchers to conduct similar experiments so that the research community can move towards a more comprehensive understanding of language embedding across a variety of domains and host languages. A secondary benefit of our study is that we have identified a number of areas where Kiama's version of strategy term rewriting is deficient when compared to Stratego, most notably support for concrete syntax, dynamic rules and congruence operations. The Future Research Directions section also contains a discussion of these aspects.

BACKGROUND

Much has been written about domain-specific languages and their implementation. Recent excellent examples are the books by Fowler and Parsons (2010) and Ghosh (2011) that together provide developers with a comprehensive introduction to the motivations for DSLs and survey modern implementation techniques, including comparisons with the pure embedded DSL approach that is evaluated in this chapter. However, since the purpose of these books is to introduce the DSL approach and they have a great deal of ground to cover, their examples and evaluations of any one technique are necessarily brief.

Many researchers have written about and evaluated particular embedded DSLs (van Deursen; 2000). In the vast majority of these cases the DSLs are designed from scratch to solve a particular problem. As such, the DSLs are evaluated for their ability to solve the problem for which they were designed, rather than for the suitability of the embedding approach itself. Usually the evaluation of the latter occurs in the form of high-level observations about how easy it was to develop the DSL but with little detailed comparison to alternative approaches.

Thus, it is rare to find a detailed, side-by-side comparison between pure embedding and other different DSL implementation techniques. The closest work of which we are aware is Kosar *et al*'s comparison between external DSLs and application programming interfaces (APIs) in a general-purpose language

(Kosar *et al*, 2010; Kosar *et al*, 2011). Their papers report relatively small empirical studies and show that DSLs do seem to confer a benefit in terms of program comprehension and understanding. We can get some insight into pure embedding from these studies if we regard the APIs as being embedded DSLs, but is not a clear insight. A closer comparison is performed in Kosar *et al* (2008) where a variety of DSL implementation approaches are compared along dimensions such as similarity to domain notation. As is common for this kind of study, the case considered is fairly simple, but it does point the way toward a more comprehensive evaluation of DSL implementations.

This chapter complements the earlier work by studying a bigger, pure embedded DSL and a non-trivial application that uses it. Unlike the empirical evaluations of Kosar *et al*, our example is a complete, complex program transformation language. This complexity constrains our study to be narrower because

it is not feasible to build many implementations of such a complex DSL. Also, rather than design a case-study DSL with the embedding approach assumed, as is done in much of the literature, we have built an embedded DSL to approximate an existing external DSL. Therefore, we are evaluating how well the embedding approach can solve a pre-defined problem. We are interested in the technical ways in which the embedded language and its implementation provide the same end-user capabilities as the existing external language and its implementation.

The rest of this section provides some background on the domain of program transformation that is addressed by the DSL.

Strategic Term Rewriting and Stratego

Strategic term rewriting is a formalism for specifying transformations that operate on tree-structured data (the terms) (Visser, 2005). In one common application, the terms are parse trees of programs, and the purpose of term rewriting is to transform those programs into other programs. Often the transformed programs are written in a language that is different from that used by the original programs. In this application, strategic term rewriting implements the core of a compiler for some other DSL. This chapter concerns a compiler for an image processing DSL.

Stratego is an external DSL for strategic term rewriting (Visser, 2004) and the Kiama library contains a version of Stratego as an internal Scala DSL. This section gives a brief overview of term rewriting in Stratego and describes how Kiama corresponds to Stratego.

Suppose that we want to simplify constant arithmetic expressions such as `(4 * 0) + 2`. We can write a term to represent this expression as follows:

```
Add(Mul(Int(4), Int(0)), Int(2))
```

A *strategy* in Stratego is a rewriter that can be applied to the subject term, either succeeding and producing a new subject term, or failing. The simplest kind of strategy is a rule that matches a pattern against the subject term. If the pattern matches the rule constructs a new term and succeeds otherwise the rule fails.

Suppose that we want to simplify our expressions by replacing multiplication of a term by zero with zero, and by replacing addition of zero to a term with that term. We can write these simplification rules `MulZero` and `AddZero` in Stratego as follows.

```
MulZero: Mul(x, Int(0)) -> Int(0)
AddZero: Add(Int(0), y) -> y
```

In this syntax, the identifier gives a name to the rule, the part before the arrow is the pattern to be matched to a subject term, and the part after the arrow is the replacement term.

The two rules `MulZero` and `AddZero` can be combined into a single simplification strategy `Simplify` as follows:

```
Simplify = try(MulZero + AddZero)
```

This strategy uses Stratego's `try` strategy and '+' operator to combine the individual rules. When this strategy is applied to the subject term, it will attempt to simplify the subject term using either the `MulZero` or `AddZero` rules. Stratego operators use the success or failure of strategies to control the rewriting process. The '+' operator combines two strategies so that the combination non-deterministically chooses one of the strategies to successfully apply to the subject term; if neither strategy succeeds, then the '+' operator itself fails.

The `try` strategy is a higher-order strategy that "swallows" failure. An expression `try(`*s*`)` (where *s* is itself a strategy or rule) *succeeds* with the result of *s* if *s* succeeds when it is applied to the subject term. If *s* fails when applied to the subject term then `try(`*s*`)` succeeds leaving the subject term unchanged. In fact, `try` is defined in terms of more primitive operations as follows:

```
try(s) = s <+ id
```

The operator '<+' represents deterministic choice. An expression s_1 <+ s_2 first tries strategy s_1 on the subject term; if it succeeds then its result is the new subject term. If s_1 fails, then s_2 is applied to the original subject term and its result (success or failure) is the result of the whole expression. Using '<+', `try` first tries *s*; if *s* fails, `try` uses the identity strategy `id` to succeed with the subject term unchanged.

`Simplify` by itself is no good to us for full simplification of a term, since it only applies its constituent rules at the root of the term. Stratego also provides higher-order generic traversal strategies that are the building blocks of programs that traverse into terms. For example, we may wish to apply our `Simplify` strategy in a bottom-up fashion to the whole term, so that simplifications are applied within sub-terms first and the results can then be exploited at higher levels. We can define a strategy to perform this whole term simplification as follows:

```
SimplifyAll = bottomup(Simplify)
```

Here, `bottomup` is a higher-order strategy that expresses the bottom-up traversal pattern without being specific about what is performed during the traversal. `bottomup` is defined as follows:

```
bottomup(s) = all(bottomup(s)); s
```

This implementation says to first recursively process all the sub-terms of the subject term, and then finally to apply the strategy argument *s* to the subject term itself. In detail, the semicolon operator is sequential composition. In 's_1; s_2', if s_1 succeeds, then its result is passed to s_2, otherwise the whole expression fails. The strategy `all(s)` is a generic traversal that applies *s* to all of the immediate sub-terms of the root of the subject term. If *s* succeeds on all of the sub-terms, the resulting new sub-terms are combined using the constructor that appears at the root of the original subject term and `all(s)` succeeds. If *s* fails on any of the children, then `all(s)` fails. This is where the `try` strategy in Simplify is important: the `AddZero` and `MulZero` rules do not match at all nodes in the tree, but `try` ensures that the `Simplify` strategy succeeds at the non-matching nodes, preserving them unchanged. This allows `SimplifyAll` to successfully process the entire tree.

This example touches on only a few of the library strategies that Stratego offers and only shows some of the power of this approach. The primitives such as deterministic and non-deterministic choice, sequencing, and generic traversals can be combined together to yield a vast array of complex rewriting processes. The Stratego language is a concise notation for these processes.

Kiama

The main goal of Kiama's rewriting library is to make the power of strategic term rewriting accessible to mainstream programmers. Using Stratego requires installation of a new toolset, conversion of data into the format that Stratego needs, and so on. In comparison, Kiama is a Scala library so any Scala program can use its facilities in a lightweight fashion with no new tools or data conversion being required.

When we developed Kiama's rewriting library, we tried to be faithful to the Stratego language as much as was possible and as much as was sensible. Kiama is constrained by Scala, so some things that Stratego offers are not possible due to clashes with Scala syntax and semantics. Others are not sensible because they conflict with the way that Scala programmers normally construct programs. We compare the languages in detail later in the chapter. For now, we illustrate Kiama by showing how the arithmetic simplification example above would be written in this embedded DSL.

The basic rules `MulZero` and `AddZero` can be written in Scala using Kiama's `rule` method. For example, `MulZero` would be

```
val MulZero =
    rule {
        case Mul(x, Int(0)) => Int(0)
    }
```

The only part of this rule definition that is specific to Kiama is the `rule` method; all other syntax and semantics is standard Scala. The argument to `rule` is a function literal, in this case standing for a partial function that performs the pattern match and, if the match is successful, returns the simplification. Kiama benefits greatly from the high level of support for pattern matching in Scala, but there are some consequences of using that support, which we discuss later.

In Kiama, strategies are implemented as functions that take the subject term and return a Scala *option* value to indicate success or failure. Option values come in two varieties: `None` that represents an optional value that is not present, and `Some(v)` that represents a value `v` that is present. A Kiama strategy that fails returns `None`, and one that succeeds returns `Some(v)` where `v` is the new value of the subject term.

`rule` lifts its partial function argument to this option encoding. If the partial function is defined on the current subject term, then it is applied and the function result is wrapped in a `Some` to indicate success and the new subject term. If the partial function is not defined on the subject term, then `None` is returned to indicate that the rule has failed.

Returning to the example, `Simplify` can be defined using Kiama in a similar way to the Stratego definition, except that `try` is a Scala keyword, so Kiama uses `attempt` instead as demonstrated in Box 1.

`attempt` is defined in a similar fashion to `try` in Stratego, except that more type information must be provided as presented in Box 2.

The argument `s` is passed by name (indicated by the prefix double arrow) to avoid premature evaluation of recursive strategies. `id` is the identity strategy as in Stratego. Thus, `attempt` returns a strategy that first tries `s` and, if that fails, leaves the subject term unchanged.

In these Kiama definitions we are using '+' and '<+' as if they were pre-defined operators, but they are actually methods of Kiama's Strategy class. Scala allows the period of a method call *o* . *m* (*a*) to be omitted when there is a single argument *a*, so it can be written *o m a*. Scala understands `s <+ id` to be `s.<+(id)`, invoking the '<+' method of the Strategy class.

The implementation of '<+' is straight-forward. It returns a strategy that first applies the left operand of '<+' to the subject term. If that application returns `Some(v)` for some value `v`, then the left operand has succeeded and that option becomes the result of the whole operation. If the application of the left operand returns `None`, then it has failed, so the strategy produced by '<+' then applies the right operand of '<+' to the subject term, returning whatever it produces. Similar approaches are used to define other primitive operations.

Box 1.

```
val Simplify = attempt(MulZero + AddZero)
```

Box 2.

```
def attempt(s: => Strategy): Strategy = s <+ id
```

Box 3.

```
val SimplifyAll = bottomup(Simplify)
def bottomup(s: => Strategy): Strategy =
   all(bottomup(s)) <* s
```

In the example, `SimplifyAll` and `bottomup` can be defined easily using Kiama as presented in Box 3.

In the `bottomup` definition, the Kiama method '<*' is used for sequential composition whereas ';' is used in Stratego. The syntactic change is necessary because Scala uses the semicolon character as a statement terminator and does not allow us to reuse it as a method name.

This simple example shows that the main aspects of the Stratego language and Stratego programs can be expressed in a natural way in Kiama and Scala. Some compromises are already evident: `attempt` replacing `try` and '<*' replacing ';', and additional type information must be provided for Kiama. We will compare the languages in more detail later in the chapter.

A major advantage of the embedding approach is the simplicity of the implementation of the rewriting language. The strategy libraries in Stratego and Kiama are of similar size since they use a similar syntax, but the core implementation of Kiama is smaller, only around 650 lines of mostly straightforward Scala code, excluding comments and blank lines. In contrast, Stratego has been bootstrapped so that its implementation consists of over 2000 lines of Stratego that produce Java output. (Note that the implementation language for the rewriting language (Scala or Java) is unrelated to the term language actually manipulated by a rewriting program.)

The differing implementation sizes are likely to have an impact on reliability, since we can expect that debugging and maintaining a small library is easier than doing the same for a non-trivial compiler. The Kiama implementation delegates a larger proportion of its functionality to the Scala compiler than the Stratego one does to the Java compiler. A comparison of reliability over a long period of time would be interesting but we do not have this data.

METHODOLOGY

The general question that we are investigating in this case study is whether embedding is a reasonable alternative to building an external domain-specific language implementation. Our methodology separates this question into two parts: one comparing the languages and one comparing their implementations. This section provides an overview of our approach to these sub-questions; we consider their answers in detail later in the chapter.

Our approach is to base our comparisons on a case study of a non-trivial application written in the domain-specific language: a compiler for the Apply image processing language designed and implemented in Stratego by one of us (Hamey, 2007; Hamey & Goldrei, 2008), which we will refer to as *Stratego-Apply*. Another of us translated Stratego-Apply into Kiama as far as was possible using a direct translation to produce *Kiama-Apply* (Premaratne, 2011).

Since we are only interested in comparing the rewriting language implementations, our comparison considers only the core phases of the Apply compilers that are implemented by Stratego and Kiama. Phases such as parsing the input text and pretty printing the output text are not implemented by the term rewriting DSL. These phases are shared between the two implementations and are not included in any measurements.

In both implementations, a parser that is generated from a specification developed for the original external implementation analyzes the input text. This parser produces an ATerm, a data representation specifically designed for term rewriting (van den Brand, 2000; van den Brand, 2007). The Kiama implementation further translates that ATerm into a native Scala data structure. In both versions, the core rewriting phases transform the term that represents the input text into a term that represents the target C program. Kiama-Apply then translates the Scala term back to ATerm format. Finally, both implementations used a shared pretty-printer to convert the final ATerm into the target code. We required that Kiama-Apply produce exactly the same target ATerms as Stratego-Apply for all available input texts, so that we can be confident that the same output text is produced by the two implementations.

A comparison of external and internal languages must consider both syntax and semantics, so we further sub-divide along those lines. The syntactic constructs that are possible in an external implementation are only limited by the imagination of the language designer and the parsing method being used. An internal implementation must reuse the syntax of the host language and take advantage of any available syntax extension facilities. Therefore an internal implementation of an existing external language is unlikely to be able to duplicate the external syntax exactly. The question becomes: how close can we get? We consider this question by examining the main language constructs as they are used in the Apply case study.

Similar to syntax, the semantics of an internal language is bound by the semantics of the host language. The semantics of an external language is unrestricted in the sense that the implementation is able to perform any interpretation or translation that is needed. The degree to which the internal language can faithfully reproduce the semantics of the existing external language depends on the similarity between the semantic models of the external language and host language. While in theory it is possible to reproduce the semantics of any external language in any Turing-complete host language, an awkward embedding due to widely differing semantic models is likely to be unsatisfactory. Again, we use the Apply case study code to examine these differences.

Assuming that a satisfactory syntactic and semantic correspondence can be achieved, it remains to compare the specific implementations of the Apply compiler. We consider the size of programs written in the rewriting DSL as a measure of implementation difficulty and the time-space performance of the implemented Apply compiler as a measure of usability. While a side-by-side comparison can only provide approximate estimates of these measures, it is sufficient to demonstrate the practicality or otherwise of the embedding approach. We expect that a custom external language implementation should outperform an internal one due to the opportunity for domain-specific optimization, particularly optimization of data representation. Somewhat balancing this advantage is the likelihood that the host language implementation will have been the focus of much more effort and general-purpose optimization than the implementation of the external language.

APPLY AND ITS COMPILERS

Apply is a language for expressing image processing operations. It has two main goals: efficient implementation and portability. Apply programs are portable across uniprocessor and parallel architectures and across different image data representations, while maintaining an efficiency that equals or exceeds good quality hand-written code (Hamey, 2007). This section provides a brief overview of Apply and its implementation sufficient to demonstrate the non-trivial nature of the domain and the processing performed by the Apply compiler. We skim over many details since they are not necessary to understand the rest of the chapter. A reader who wishes to learn more about image processing with Apply is directed to Hamey (2007) in the first instance.

Apply uses a processing model in which the programmer writes a computation for a single pixel location and the compiler generates code that performs the computation on all of the pixels in an image. This programming model allows the compiler to generate efficient code for a wide variety of architectures and to exploit parallelism since the pixel computations are independent.

As an example, consider the typical small Apply program in Figure 1 which implements part of a standard Sobel edge detector computation to identify boundaries between regions in an image. Syntactically, Apply is based on a 1980s version of the Ada programming language (Ada, 1982). This Sobel procedure considers a *window* into the image centered on a given pixel and extending one pixel outward in each direction (`from` argument in line 1). The output is a single byte that becomes the new intensity of the pixel under consideration (`to` argument in line 2). The algorithm combines the intensities of six of the neighbors of the pixel under consideration to get a new intensity for that pixel (lines 6 and 7). To keep the value in range it then takes the absolute value (line 8) and range limits it to fit into a byte (line 9). Finally, it returns the result (line 10). Of course, the pixels at the edge of the image do not have all of the six neighbors that are referenced by the procedure. The `border` keyword on the input image window (line 1) specifies what happens when the computation attempts to access a pixel that falls outside the input image bounds. In this example, the constant value `0` is used for any such pixel locations.

Apply programs are portable to different target environments, including different image data structures, alternative target languages and different parallel programming methodologies. To

Figure 1. A simple Apply program: Partial Sobel edge detection

```
procedure sobel(from: in window (-1..1, -1..1) of byte border 0,
                to: out window of byte)
is
  x : integer;
begin
  x := from(-1,-1) + 2 * from(-1,0) + from(-1,1)
     - from(1,-1) - 2 * from(1,0) - from(1,1);
  if x < 0 then x := -x; end if;
  if x > 255 then x := 255; end if;
  to := x;
end sobel;
```

provide this level of portability, the Stratego-Apply compiler is divided into phases (Figure 2). A specific intermediate phase (Environment) is used to adapt the Apply program to the target environment; replacing this phase with a different module will target the Apply compiler to a different environment. Similarly, the final compiler phases (C Language and Pretty-print) can be replaced to adapt the compiler to different target languages.

The Desugar phase is a small component of the compiler that performs some initial transformations to simplify the structure of the Abstract Syntax Tree (AST) for subsequent processing. For example, Desugar converts a list of declared variables that are associated with a single type declaration into a list of variables each of which has its own type declaration.

The Optimize phase is a significant component of the compiler that is responsible for a large portion of the transformation of the program. This phase performs both constant propagation optimizations, where expressions whose values are statically known to be constant are replaced by those constants, and constraint propagation optimizations, where statically known constraints on the values of variables are used to simplify code that uses those variables. The latter optimizations are particularly important for improving the generated code, particularly when constraints on loop indices are used to eliminate unnecessary bounds checks on image pixel accesses. These optimizations have a very significant effect on the execution speed of the generated code.

The Do-Apply phase prepares the Apply program for the Environment phase by inserting a placeholder for the image processing looping

Figure 2. The phases of the Apply compilers

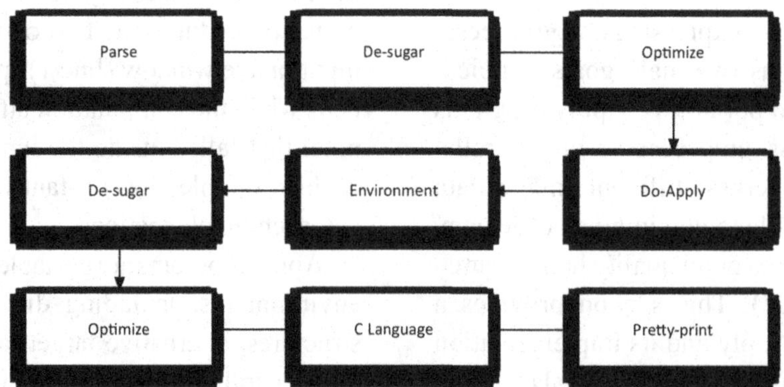

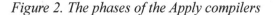

structure and associating more type information with variables. These transformations make it easier to write the Environment phase for different target environments.

The Environment phase uses the type information inserted by Do-Apply to generate the pixel accesses that are appropriate to the target environment, and to implement the image border handling (i.e., the special cases for pixels that occur at the border of an image and therefore do not have a full set of neighbors). Environment also inserts the loops that actually traverse the image. In the Apply compiler used in this paper, the Environment phase supports a uniprocessor implementation with images stored as matrices of pixels. Even in this simple target environment, Apply modules significantly outperform hand-written code because of the sophisticated looping structures and optimizations employed by the Apply compiler (Hamey, 2007).

Both of the Desugar and Optimize phases are performed first on the initial Apply program and then repeated after the Environment phase. This allows the Environment phase to be written with the full power and optimization capabilities of the Apply language. After the second optimization phase has run, the final two phases (C Language and Pretty Printing) translate the intermediate representation into an abstract syntax tree representing the generated C program, and print that tree to obtain the C program text, respectively.

To demonstrate an intermediate stage of program transformation and illustrate the complexity of the transformations, Figure 3 presents a pretty print of the AST for the Sobel program (Figure 1) after the Environment phase and before the second Optimize phase. (Some details have been omitted and the code has been reformatted slightly to keep Figure 3 as small as possible. See Hamey (2007) for a full description.) We use an extended concrete syntax to represent structures that are not part of the Apply language, allowing the compiler writer to express transformations using Stratego's concrete syntax capability. The extended syntax is identified by special tokens that commence with the '`@`' symbol. In Figure 3, the notation '`@:=`' represents a C-style assignment and '`@(...)`' represents array subscripting. In Apply, as in Ada, the same syntax is used for function calls and array subscripts, so the extended syntax is required to differentiate array subscripts from function calls.

The most obvious change in Figure 3 compared to Figure 1 is the expansion of the code. In particular, the Environment phase has embedded the Apply function body (lines 6-10 of Figure 1) into two loop blocks – the first loop block (lines 8-23 of Figure 3) processes pixels that are close to the edge of the image, explicitly modifying the `column` index variable to skip over the center of the image (lines 17-21). The second loop block (lines 24-32) processes the middle region of the image where the pixels that are being accessed fall entirely within the image. Border handling is required in the first loop block and implemented using inline if constructs (`@if` extended syntax) to compare the array subscripts against the image bounds and return the border value `0` for out-of-bound accesses (lines 12 and 13). The second loop block does not require border handling, but the Environment phase uses the same implementation code and relies on the subsequent Optimize phase to eliminate the unnecessary bounds checks using constraints on the loop index variables. This optimized two-loop structure greatly improves execution speed compared to a structure where a single loop block processes the entire image and the image bounds are checked for every pixel access.

Figure 3 also demonstrates the Apply assert statement which provides the constraints for optimization (lines 10, 11, 14, 15, 28 and 29). The `@cfor` loop (line 9) is extended syntax for a C-style `for` loop; the `assert` statements within it inform the compiler of the range constraints for the `row` and `column` loop index variables. The Optimize phase automatically generates similar constraints from Apply-language conditional and looping structures, and uses the constraints to optimize

Figure 3. Sobel Apply program after Environment stage

```
procedure sobel (from : @in array () of byte border 0,
                 to : @out array () of byte,
                 height, width : in integer)
is
  x : integer;
  row, column, app_index, app_size : integer;
begin
  for row in 0..height - 1 loop
    @cfor column @:= 0; column <= width - 1; loop
      assert column >= 0 and column <= width - 1;
      assert row >= 0 and row <= height - 1;
      x := @if (row >= - -1 and row < height - -1 and column >= - -1 and
                column < width - -1, from @((row + -1) * width + column + -1), 0) + …;
      if x < 0 then assert x < 0; x := - x; end if;
      if x > 255 then assert x > 255; x := 255; end if;
      to @(row * width + column) := x;
      if column = - -1 - 1 and row >= - -1 and row < height - 1 then
        column := column + width - 1 + -1 + 1;
      else
        column := column + 1;
      end if;
    end loop;
  end loop;
  for row in - -1..height - 1 - 1 loop
    for column in - -1..width - 1 - 1 loop
      x := @if (row >= - -1 and row < height - -1 and column >= - -1 and
                column < width - -1, from @((row + -1) * width + column + -1), 0) + …;
      if x < 0 then assert x < 0; x := - x; end if;
      if x > 255 then assert x > 255; x := 255; end if;
      to @(row * width + column) := x;
    end loop;
  end loop;
end sobel;
```

the code. In this example, the constraints generated from the second looping block are used later to eliminate the inline if constructs, resulting in efficient C code where the second looping block performs no bounds checks on pixel accesses.

Kiama-Apply

Each Stratego-Apply module was directly translated to a Scala class to construct Kiama-Apply.

The aim was to measure the effectiveness of the embedding method, not necessarily measure the best possible Scala implementation. Therefore, the strategies and rules were translated as directly as possible into equivalent Scala code that uses Kiama.

We will see in the Language Comparison section that some forms of binding through pattern matching in Stratego are hard to duplicate exactly in Scala since pattern matching cannot be separated from the actions carried out after a pattern matches. Therefore, in some cases, we used more idiomatic Scala rather than use a convoluted approach to mimic the Stratego code. For example, Stratego conditional choice expressions were often replaced with a sequence of pattern matching cases, and pattern guards were sometimes used to express constraints that would normally be handled in Stratego by side-conditions expressed using the `where` strategy.

Some Stratego library strategies that were used in Stratego-Apply but are not present in the

Kiama library were written and included in the Kiama-Apply support module. Also, the Environment stage of Stratego-Apply makes heavy use of concrete syntax to express patterns and terms, instead of writing them in prefix notation (Bravenboer, 2008). In some places, we developed new infix operators to make it easier to compose code fragments, in lieu of proper concrete syntax support.

We did not spend much time optimizing the Scala code to get the best performance. However, we did do some profiling to remove obvious hot spots. This approach is justified since we can assume that Stratego has had some basic performance optimization over its years of existence, but we have no reason to believe that its performance is as good as it can get. Of course, any performance measurements from this kind of comparison should be taken as indicative of the particular case being measured, and not necessarily representative of general performance. For this reason in the Implementation Comparison section we are mainly interested in trends that show performance changes as problem size increases, rather than in absolute numbers.

LANGUAGE COMPARISON

We now turn to a comparison of the two rewriting languages based on our experiences developing the two Apply compilers. As discussed earlier, we regard Stratego as an ideal and Kiama's rewriting library as an approximation to that ideal. The designer of Stratego had complete freedom when designing the syntax and semantics of the language. In Kiama we were constrained both by having Stratego as a target and by using Scala as the host language. What is the effect of this reduced flexibility? This section discusses the main differences between Stratego and Kiama's version of the DSL, identifying aspects of syntax, name binding, typing, and domain focus as key areas. We also identify specific features of Scala that enhance Kiama's ability to approximate Stratego, particularly its syntactic flexibility.

Expressions

Stratego has a rich expression language for describing strategies. As we saw in the arithmetic simplification example earlier, Kiama is able to closely approximate both the syntax and semantics of the strategy language. Scala is extremely helpful: the ability to use arbitrary characters in method names and to omit the period and parentheses in method calls means that Stratego's syntax can be duplicated almost exactly. Many general-purpose languages are less helpful, permitting only pre-defined operators to be overloaded or even restricting the library interface to conventional function-call syntax.

Even with this substantial help, one Stratego operator did require more thought. The ternary guarded deterministic choice operator, written $s_1 < s_2 + s_3$, is actually more primitive than the '<+' operator which we saw earlier. $s_1 < s_2 + s_3$ first applies s_1, and if s_1 succeeds, then applies s_2 to the result of s_1; if s_1 fails, s_3 is applied to the original subject term. s_1 <+ s_2 is therefore just syntactic sugar for s_1 < `id` + s_2.

Scala provides no direct assistance for ternary or higher-arity operators. Kiama's solution, conceived by our colleague Lennart Kats, is to define the '+' operator to play two roles. When the expression $s_2 + s_3$ is used as a strategy it has the expected non-deterministic choice semantics; when it is used as the second argument of the '<' binary operator (i.e., as s_1 `<` `(`s_2 `+` s_3`))` it simply acts as a tuple to hold the s_2 and s_3 strategies for use by the guarded choice. Scala defines '+' to have a higher precedence than '<', so the parentheses can be omitted.

The other main commonly used syntactic construct in Stratego expressions is the functional notation used in strategy definitions such as `bottomup`. This notation has a direct analog in Scala's method call syntax, as shown in earlier examples.

Kiama extends Stratego to some extent. For example, in Kiama, any term can be used as a strategy, with the meaning that the current subject term is discarded and replaced by the given term. This feature is the counterpart to Stratego's explicit exclamation mark build operator. Such a strategy always succeeds. Kiama implements this kind of conversion using Scala's user-defined implicit operations. If the Scala compiler determines that a value of type U is required in some context, but the value provided is of type T, then it will look for an operation of type $T \Rightarrow U$ that is marked with the `implicit` keyword. If such an operation is found, the compiler inserts a call to it to make the expression type correct. This facility means that the Scala type system can be extended with domain-specific conversions. Kiama terms can be used as strategies because there is an implicit operation that converts a term into a rule that matches anything and returns the term.

Binding Constructs

An important way in which external DSLs and internal DSLs often differ is in the way that they handle binding. Names are routinely bound to expressions and used elsewhere in a DSL program. External DSLs frequently have binding and scoping constructs that are non-standard, so it is not always possible to imitate them exactly in an internal language. The internal language must live with the binding constructs of the host language and the rules that govern their use.

Stratego has two main binding constructs: one for rules and one for strategies, as illustrated earlier in the Background section. Kiama uses Scala's value and method definition constructs to handle these two cases. Rules are typically defined as values; the availability of lazy values and the fact that Kiama's methods take their arguments by name enable recursive rules to be defined. Higher-order strategies are defined as methods that instantiate a strategy with arguments, with recursion coming for free.

A Stratego rule is syntactic sugar for a strategy that matches a pattern and, if the match succeeds, builds a new term, possibly using values that were bound during pattern matching. For example, a basic rule of the form *name* : p_1 -> p_2, is equivalent to the strategy definition *name* = ? p_1 ; ! p_2, where the question mark indicates a match of pattern p_1 and the exclamation mark indicates a build using pattern p_2. Implicit in the rule definition is that any free variables of p_1 are bound in a new local scope associated with the rule. This translation is generalized when the rule has arguments or when side conditions are placed on the matching process.

Kiama, on the other hand, reuses Scala's pattern matching facilities. Therefore a pattern match cannot be regarded as a primitive operation in the same way as in Stratego. A basic rule in Kiama is implemented by a value that is bound to the result of the rule method:

```
val name = rule { case p1 => p2 }
```

Therefore the match and the build are necessarily combined in Kiama. In practice, the same rules can be expressed, but the Kiama version is usually more verbose since there is no shorthand for matching.

Stratego's rule binding construct uses *implicit composition*: when presented with more than one rule definition with the same name, the rule bodies are combined using a deterministic choice operator to form a single rule definition that tries each body in turn until one succeeds or the rules are exhausted. More generally, implicit composition is when a name is used more than once to denote pieces of the definition of some entity, not different entities. It is frequently used in external DSLs to save the programmer from having to explicitly write out the composition operation. However, implicit composition is hard to realize in an internal language since general-purpose languages typically do not provide it as a primitive and there is no opportunity to collect the individual definitions.

A common problem with implicit composition is that the order of composition must be precisely defined, or it must be left undefined and cannot be relied upon by the programmer. Stratego chooses the latter approach which means that problems can occur if the patterns of the individual rules overlap. Scala does not have implicit composition for value or method definitions, so Kiama users must explicitly combine their rules, either in a single pattern-matching construct or by using an explicit choice operator.

Apart from pattern matching, Stratego's other binding facilities can be achieved in Kiama using normal Scala bindings. Stratego has an explicit scope operator, written using braces. New scopes can be introduced so that names bound outside are hidden. For example, the construct `{`*x*`:` *s*`}` introduces a scope that hides any existing binding of *x* during the application of the strategy *s*. Kiama uses normal Scala scoping mechanisms, including local blocks, so there is no need for another scoping construct. Local bindings in rule or strategy definitions take the place of Stratego's let construct. Stratego's strategy definitions syntactically differentiate between arguments that are terms and those that are strategies. No such distinction is needed in Kiama since the argument's type controls how it can be used. Finally, Stratego has a module system that is subsumed by Scala's extensive features for modularity and composition.

Semantics

As mentioned earlier, Stratego has a simple success or failure semantics for strategy application. The composition operations use the success or failure of component strategies to control subsequent strategy invocations. Kiama encodes success or failure as a simple option value, so it is easy to implement the composition operations.

Kiama distinguishes between rules and strategies more than Stratego, because of its use of Scala function literals to define the pattern matching inherent in the bodies of rules. Therefore, Kiama has additional constructs to enable rules and strategies to be combined in ways that are more natural in Stratego's unified approach. For example, Kiama provides a `rulefs` method that is analogous to `rule` but instead of the argument function returning a term, it returns a strategy.

The general form of Stratego's rule construct incorporates side-conditions expressed in a `where` clause. A rule p_1 `->` p_2 `where` *s* is equivalent to `?` p_1`;` `where(`*s*`);` `!`p_2, with `where(`*s*`)` being equivalent to `{`*x*`: ?`*x*`;` *s*`; !`*x*`}`, where *x* is free in *s*. By this definition, `where(`*s*`)` applies strategy *s* to the subject term, discarding any changes made by *s* to the subject term but retaining the success or failure and also retaining any variable bindings effected in *s*. Thus, *s* may be used to bind variables that can be used in p_2 (but not in p_1). The corresponding construct in Kiama is more limited since its bindings must obey the lexical nesting rules of Scala. Hence, in the Kiama version of a rule with a `where` clause the pattern matching in *s* must be moved so that it is nested within the right-hand side of the case that is executed after a successful match of p_1. In that position the bindings from *s* can be used by subsequent term construction in p_2.

Types

Stratego and Kiama differ significantly in the way that they approach typing issues. The types of the structures operated on by Stratego programs are expressed by signatures that specify the available constructors, their arities, and the types of their children. Stratego statically verifies that the arities are respected within rules and strategies, but does not require that the types of sub-terms match the types specified in the constructor definitions. The Stratego-Apply compiler takes advantage of this flexibility in a number of ways. For example, the signature of the term that represents the input text contains some anonymous constructors, which means that an implicit conversion of type may be performed when terms are built. Stratego-Apply also constructs terms that mix source and target constructs (e.g., Apply statements and C statements). In the Stratego/XT system, a separate program can be used to verify that a particular term matches a given signature.

In contrast, Kiama terms must be correctly typed at all times. Therefore the term signature is extended in Kiama-Apply to name anonymous constructors and to insert applications of them at appropriate places when the initial Scala value is constructed. Transformations that mix syntaxes require a common super type for the terms from the two languages that are to be mixed. As a result of these effects of stronger typing, the strategies are a bit longer in Kiama-Apply than in Stratego-Apply. However, in the Kiama version the Scala compiler is able to check that the terms being constructed are correctly typed, so Kiama is more statically type safe than Stratego.

Beyond their types, the representation of the terms is also a major difference. Stratego operates on terms implemented by the ATerm library. ATerms are designed specifically for term rewriting and are optimized to reduce duplication. Kiama terms are instances of Scala case classes (Odersky 2008, Chapter 15); in other words, they are standard Scala objects with some extra compiler-provided support for construction and pattern matching. Therefore, Kiama gains none of the benefits of using a representation designed for the rewriting domain, but Kiama terms can be used by other Scala code in a natural way.

Typing issues also arise for strategies. Stratego strategies are indistinguishable by type and Kiama follows this lead. This design limits the static checking that can be performed. For example, it is not possible to statically determine that s_1 ; s_2 will always fail by proving that the terms produced by s_1 are not acceptable to s_2. In both languages, such errors can only be detected through testing.

Breaking Out of the Domain

A major motivation for DSLs is to provide a restricted context in which a specific kind of problem can be solved. By keeping the number of constructs small, limiting the ways in which they can be combined, and defining a simple semantics, a DSL can enforce a discipline over development that helps to control application complexity and enables domain-specific optimizations. However, a DSL can also be seen as a straightjacket that forces all problems to be considered from its limited viewpoint (Mernik, 2005). Some problems may be impossible or inconvenient to solve using just the DSL.

Considering the Stratego DSL, we can ask whether it is natural to view all transformation problems or parts thereof as instances of the application of strategies to terms. For example, consider a problem that requires numeric data to be manipulated. The Stratego library provides strategies such as `add` which matches a tuple of values and adds them together if they are numbers. In effect, addition is lifted to the strategy domain. It is arguably more natural to just access two integers in a term, add them together and use the result to construct a new term. In a statically typed, internal DSL with access to host language arithmetic operations, this addition is easy and safe to use.

Another example of the power that can be achieved by an internal version of a DSL breaking out of the problem domain concerns complex data structures. In Stratego we can represent arbitrary data structures as terms, but it is common to want to reuse more standard ones such as lists, sets, or hash tables. Stratego provides syntactic sugar for list pattern matching and construction, but these operations still live in the rewriting world. Operations such as mapping over, filtering, or sorting a list are written as strategies. Sets are encoded as lists. Keeping within the strategic rewriting domain is attractive from a purity perspective, but is not a particularly natural way to think about these common data structures and operations on them. In fact, Stratego doesn't stay pure for all data structures; hash tables are provided as primitive values and their operations are defined outside the rewriting domain.

In contrast, Kiama's version of the DSL focuses entirely on the core rewriting problem domain and does not attempt to import data structures into that domain. Accordingly, the DSL is more lightweight and easier for a Scala programmer to pick up than if a new encoding of data structures had to be learned. For example, Scala collections can be intermixed freely with problem-specific terms. All rewriting operations are agnostic to the type of structure that is being processed. Operations such as sorting can be performed directly on the data structures rather than having to be expressed as rewrite rules. Data structures can also be used in rewriting operations without requiring them to be part of the subject term. For example, in the Apply context it could be useful to compute lookup tables that are accessed by rewrites during analysis and optimization.

Summary

Overall, Kiama's rewriting DSL syntax and semantics are quite close to Stratego's. Some Scala features, most notably pattern matching, user-defined infix operators and implicit conversion allow Kiama to closely approximate the syntax of Stratego rules and strategy definitions. The semantics of strategy evaluation was easily realized by the Kiama version and integrated nicely with Scala partial functions. The main semantic alteration was the inability to separate the build and match operations as in Stratego, since pattern matching in Scala is integrated with the specification of the action to take when a pattern matches. This change required some rephrasing of rewrites in the Kiama-Apply compiler. Scala's stronger typing also forced some changes, most notably by requiring terms to be properly typed. As expected, many features of Stratego, including definition syntax and modularity support, required little special treatment in Kiama since they come for free with Scala. The main exception was the inability of Kiama definitions to implicitly compose since Scala composition is explicit. The Kiama version was also able to avoid explicit support for auxiliary data structures such as lists and maps since these are available in Scala.

One aspect of language embedding that was not explicitly used in the Kiama-Apply compiler, but is worth mentioning, is the opportunity for language extension. It is easy for a programmer to add new primitives to the rewriting language since they are just normal Scala definitions. Extending Stratego would require adding new syntax definitions, semantic checks and translations to its compiler, a much bigger undertaking. On the other hand, perhaps the ability to extend the language is not desirable, since arbitrary extensions can obscure the meaning of a program.

IMPLEMENTATION COMPARISON

Having discussed linguistic differences, we now consider the two Apply compiler implementations. We discuss the size of the two implementations, as well as compare their run-time performance in terms of speed and memory usage.

It is important to realize that our aim is not to conduct a detailed low-level performance comparison of the two implementations. Such a comparison is largely meaningless for analyzing the practicality of embedding, since so much of the performance is influenced by the implementations of the Java and Scala compilers and the optimizations performed by the Java run-time. Also, while neither of the implementations exhibits major bottlenecks, both could be further optimized, and that would change any detailed measurements.

Instead, our study aims to determine whether the embedding approach is practical by comparing it with the external implementation on as level a playing field as possible. We are concerned with overall trends rather than low-level details. In particular, we are interested in scalability. Internal DSLs often perform well enough for small programs but cope less well with large ones, since they don't have the benefit of domain-specific optimization.

Experimental Setup

We compare the implementations running on the Java Virtual Machine (JVM) in byte-code interpretation mode. Table 1 summarizes the software and hardware versions used in the experiments.

Stratego has a native compiler (via C), but Scala's main implementation is for the JVM, so we use the Stratego to Java compiler, and the Java version of the ATerm library. The Java version of Stratego is younger than the native code implementation but it is used extensively in the Spoofax Language Workbench (Kats, 2010) so its performance is sufficiently optimized to provide a good baseline.

Performance metrics were captured using YourKit, a professional profiling tool (YourKit, 2011). This profiler supports accurate instrumentation through the use of the JVMTI API. Of the metrics captured, our interest is in the CPU processing time and memory requirements to complete a syntax tree rewrite. We report CPU time instead of wall clock time because CPU time measurements are usually more accurate.

Table 1. Software and hardware versions used in the experiments

Stratego/XT	0.17 (Java backend)
Kiama	1.2 with Scala 2.9.1
Java	1.6 (build 26, 64-bit)
YourKit	10.0.0
Experimental machine	Quad-Core Intel Xeon 2.66, 10GB memory, Mac OS X 10.7.1

Memory was measured by the program's consumption of the JVM heap; specifically, we calculated the retained size of the applications object graph with the class loader as the root object. The retained size is a measure of both strong references and weak references; unreachable objects and objects on the finalization queue are not included in the byte count.

Any good JVM implementation comes with various optimizations built in. Byte-code interpretation mode was invoked using the `-Xint` flag so that the measurements are not influenced by optimization opportunities or overhead of just-in-time compilation.

Any measurement will include some perturbation due to fluctuations in the measurement environment. To minimize the impact of such variations each test was run a few hundred times from which a statistical average was obtained. For brevity only the averages are presented.

Code Size

Table 2 shows that the programs of the Apply language compiler are not trivial by listing the non-blank, non-commented line counts for the individual compiler phases and other categories of code. The Support category includes code for tasks not directly related to rewriting, such as command-line processing. Most Kiama-Apply phases are larger than their Stratego-Apply counterparts. There are two to three lines of Scala code for each Stratego one line rule due mostly to the coding style, lack of concrete syntax, and extra code required to maintain strong typing guarantees. A small extra amount of code is present in the Kiama-Apply modules to provide interfaces for our test harness. The code size increase for Optimize is greater than for the other phases because this category aggregates a number of smaller optimization modules, each of which contributes code size increases as described.

Table 2. Non-blank, non-commented lines of code (LOC) in the Apply compiler phases and support categories

	Stratego-Apply (LOC)	Kiama-Apply (LOC)
De-sugar	30	53
Do-Apply	54	119
Optimize	588	985
Environment	416	467
C language	539	503
Support	222	311
Signatures	126	1737

The Support category includes code for tasks not directly related to rewriting, such as command-line processing. The Signatures category includes code that defines the term structures. Kiama-Apply is much larger in this category since we also include the code that translates ATerms into Scala values and vice-versa. A normal use of Kiama's rewriting library would not use ATerms at all, so this code would not be required.

A Typical Compilation

As discussed in the section Apply and Its Compilers, the Apply compilers are composed of a multi-phase pipeline (Figure 2). To begin our analysis, we present a scenario demonstrating how long a typical compilation takes in both Stratego-Apply and Kiama-Apply. In this example we consider the Apply implementation of the example Sobel edge detection algorithm.

Table 3 presents the timings for each transformation phase during the compilation of the Sobel module with both the Stratego-Apply and Kiama-Apply implementations. Our timings do not include measurements for parsing and the pretty printing phases because these phases are not primarily concerned with syntax tree rewrites.

Table 3. Compilation times and memory use when processing the Sobel edge detection algorithm

	Stratego-Apply		Kiama-Apply	
	Time (ms)	**Memory (MB)**	**Time (ms)**	**Memory (MB)**
De-sugar (1st time)	335	1.88	499	2.74
Optimize (1st time)	955	2.39	1175	2.96
Do-Apply	419	1.96	642	2.80
Environment	491	2.07	1054	2.83
De-sugar (2nd time)	380	1.93	572	2.77
Optimize (2nd time)	1401	2.46	3162	3.05
Total	≈ 4 seconds		≈ 7 seconds	

Each transformation phase is an independent module in Stratego-Apply and an independent class in Kiama-Apply. A phase reads in an ATerm, transforms it, and writes the transformed term out to disk to be used as input for the next phase. (The same ATerm library is used by the two implementations.) This approach is useful for compiler development and debugging. However in a production compiler, syntax trees would be passed internally from one phase to the next, with the input/output component only appearing at the start and end of the pipeline. For this reason, our measurements *exclude* the input and output components of the processing.

From this data we see that an end-to-end transformation in Stratego-Apply took approximately four seconds, whereas Kiama-Apply took approximately seven seconds. Thus the Kiama-Apply implementation is slower by a factor of approximately 40%. In addition the Kiama-Apply implementation consumes about 26% more memory. These performance measurements are typical of what we observed in other similar experiments and show that Kiama-Apply, while slower than Stratego-Apply, is still suitable for regular use. In the rest of this section we investigate how the performance scales as the input Apply program size varies and how it compares when rewriting is isolated from traversal.

Experimental Input

Due to a limited supply of large Apply programs, for the set of experiments investigating performance in more detail, we used a code generator to produce the input text of programs. The generator produces programs that perform image manipulations similar to the steps of the Sobel example shown earlier. Command-line options can be used to control the number of operations and the processing window size. Increasing the number of operations increases the width of the syntax tree, while increasing the window size increases the complexity of the processing statements and hence the depth of the tree. Thus, we can vary the input size to examine the effect of scale on the performance of the two implementations. The remaining experiments use test data generated by incrementing the window size in steps of two and operations in steps of five. In the experiments we report the syntax tree sizes in terms of number of nodes, which explains the non-obvious X-axis labels.

Experiment 1: Memory Use as Tree Size Varies

Recall that the "C Language" phase of the Apply compilers is responsible for translating the compiler's intermediate representation into an abstract syntax tree that represents the generated C program. For our first experiment we ran the C Language phases of the Stratego-Apply and Kiama-Apply compilers on a variety of syntax trees to measure their memory usage (Figure 4). The C Language phase was chosen because it exercises the rewriting machinery in a significant way, visiting all parts of the AST. The performance reported for this phase is also typical of the other phases. The syntax trees in this experiment are of increasing width, achieved by increasing the window size in the Apply code generator. As is to be expected, we observed that both compilers' memory consumption increased as the size of the syntax tree increased. The rate of memory consumption growth for Kiama-Apply was less than for Stratego-Apply. In addition, Stratego-Apply consumed less memory than Kiama-Apply for small to medium sized trees but more for large trees. The crossover point appears at around 50,000 tree nodes.

Our profiling results reveal that in the first data set from Figure 4 the ATerms occupied 9% of Stratego-Apply's memory usage compared to 45% for Kiama-Apply. However, for the last data set where the trees were at their largest the ATerms occupied close to 60% of the heap memory for both Stratego-Apply and Kiama-Apply. It is interesting to note that before the ATerms were read, the C Language phases in Stratego-Apply and Kiama-Apply occupied around the same amount of memory (approximately 1.7MB).

From this experiment we conclude that Kiama-Apply uses a reasonable amount of memory, particularly for large trees. We have not precisely identified the reason for the increasing memory overhead for Stratego-Apply. Preliminary analysis indicates that it may be due to the caching approach used by the ATerm library to avoid duplication.

Experiment 2: Execution Time when Varying the Width of the Tree

This experiment compares the CPU processing time for the C Language phase on syntax trees with fixed depth and varying widths (Figure 5). Increasing the number of operations for our code generator varied the widths of the trees.

Figure 5 shows that, for a fixed tree depth, the execution time is a linear function of the tree width for both Stratego-Apply and Kiama-Apply. We

Figure 4. C Language phase memory usage as tree size varies: X-axis: tree size in number of nodes; Y-axis: memory retained size in bytes

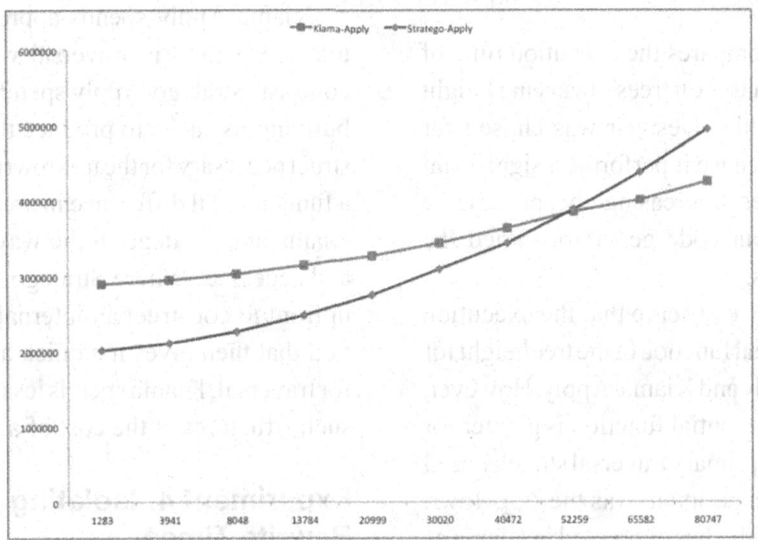

Figure 5. C Language phase CPU time as tree width varies: X-axis: tree width in nodes; Y-axis: CPU time in milliseconds

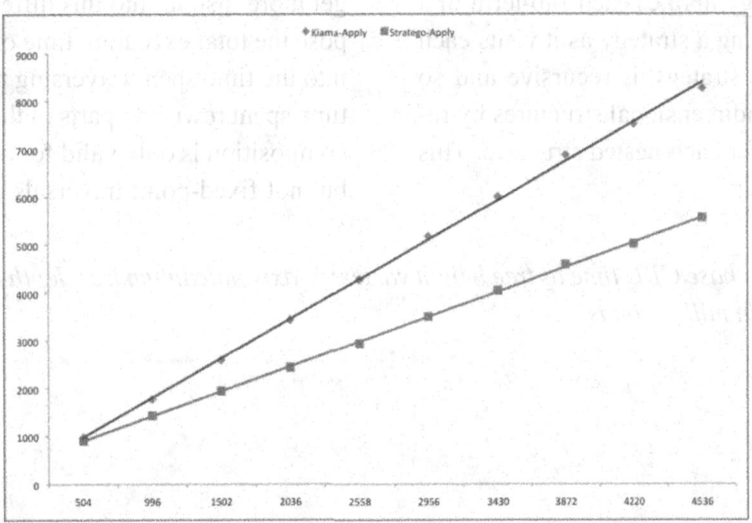

also observe that for trees with relatively small widths the performance of Stratego-Apply and Kiama-Apply was similar. However, as the width of the tree increased, Kiama-Apply's execution time increased more rapidly than Stratego-Apply's. In ATerms, these wider trees are represented by longer arrays at each node of the tree. A longer array represents more terms that undergo pattern matching and possible rewriting. From this we observe that pattern matching and term rewriting takes longer in the internal language. Overall, Kiama-apply is slower than Stratego-apply but scales in the same way.

Experiment 3: Execution Time when Varying the Height of the Tree

This experiment compares the execution time of the two Desugar phases on trees of varying height and consistent widths. Desugar was chosen for this experiment because it performs a significant number of rewrites. Increasing the processing window size for our code generator varied the heights of the trees.

From Figure 6 we observe that the execution time is an exponential function of the tree height for both Stratego-Apply and Kiama-Apply. However, the base of the exponential function is greater for Kiama-Apply. The primary traversal strategy used in this part of the experiment was the `topdown` traversal strategy, which is expressed in Kiama as

```
s <* all(topdown(s))
```

The `all` strategy iterates each sub-term of a subject term applying a strategy as it visits each subject term. This strategy is recursive and so navigates the multidimensional structures by repeating the `all` for each nested structure. This implementation explains the exponential results we see in Figure 6.

Kiama-Apply spends approximately 50% of total CPU time in traversal when rewriting. In contrast, Stratego-Apply spends much of its time building its cache to produce the optimized construct necessary for the tree rewrite. This highlights a fundamental difference in architecture between Kiama and Stratego in the way terms are stored and accessed. Where Stratego spends more time upfront to construct an internal term representation that then gives it a quick access mechanism for traversal, Kiama spends less time constructing such structures at the cost of a slower traversal.

Experiment 4: Isolating Rewrite Times

The previous experiment pointed to a difference in rewriting times in the two implementations. To get more insight into this difference, we decompose the total execution time of a transformation into the time spent traversing the tree (t) and the time spent rewriting parts of the tree (r). This decomposition is only valid for one-pass traversals but not fixed-point traversals (Visser, 2004). To

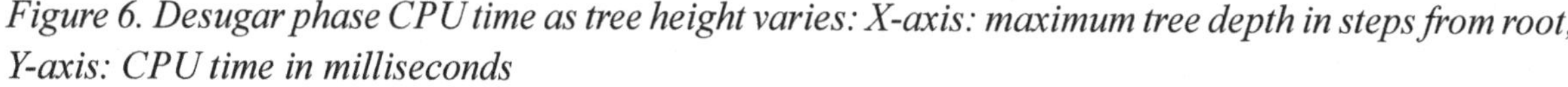

Figure 6. Desugar phase CPU time as tree height varies: X-axis: maximum tree depth in steps from root; Y-axis: CPU time in milliseconds

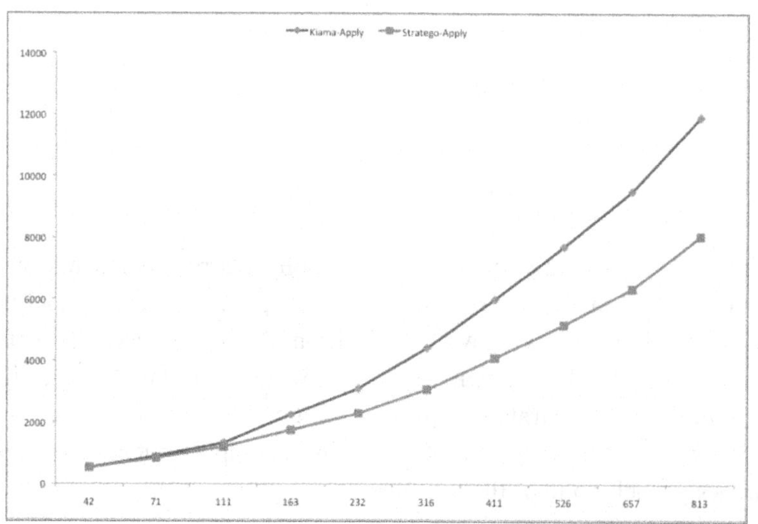

Figure 7. CPU time for rewrites as tree width varies: X-axis: tree width in nodes; Y-axis: CPU time in milliseconds

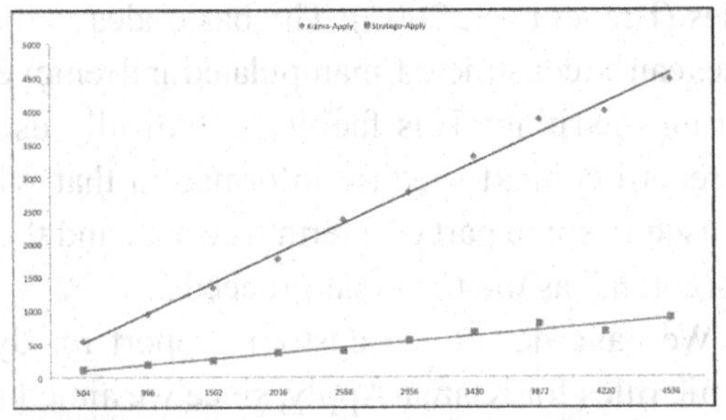

measure the transformation time (t) the rewrites in Desugar were temporarily disabled during this experiment. The results presented reveal that rewrite times in Stratego-Apply are quicker than that of Kiama-Apply by a factor of around five.

From Figure 7 we observe that as the width of the tree increases the rewrite times in both Stratego-Apply and Kiama-Apply increase linearly. We expected to see the implementation specifically designed for rewriting to out-perform one based on a general-purpose language without any special support for rewriting. Figure 7 does show this difference, since Kiama-Apply is quite a bit slower than Stratego-Apply. However, the Kiama-Apply performance is not unrealistic and we see a similar linear scaling pattern, so Kiama remains usable even at large tree sizes.

SUMMARY

As we expected, when a complete rewriting phase is measured Kiama-Apply is slower than Stratego-Apply and uses more memory. However, the performance is sufficiently good for most applications. Our more detailed experiments on synthetic input showed that the scaling behavior of the two implementations is similar. Therefore, we have confidence that Kiama's rewriting library is feasible even for large inputs. Performance of the library is likely to get better as the Scala compiler performs more optimization and the library is improved.

FUTURE RESEARCH DIRECTIONS

Future research directions flowing from the work presented in this chapter can be divided into two main topics: general research into DSL implementation via case studies similar to the one present here, and continued investigation of the term rewriting domain.

We strongly encourage other researchers to conduct side-by-side evaluations of the kind we have presented here. These evaluations can be time-consuming and may seem pointless to some degree, since an existing DSL is being duplicated. However, the true benefits and pitfalls of an implementation approach cannot really be appreciated until a proper evaluation is performed, so it is important that language researchers conduct them. Although we have focused on an embedding approach in this chapter, side-by-side comparison can be of benefit for any implementation method.

This chapter has presented an analysis of the two language implementations along various dimensions that made sense for this domain and implementation approach. It would be interesting to generalize these dimensions to develop a standard approach to language comparison that will help researchers structure their experiments. Further down the line, it is desirable to try to develop general criteria for assessing the suitability of different DSL implementation approaches, for which a starting point is presented in Kosar *et al* (2008). This task is non-trivial since the characteristics of DSLs and implementation approaches differ greatly. For example, even within the general embedding approach there are many different ways to implement a DSL, ranging from the pure approach used in this chapter to a more translation-based approach where an intermediate form is created. Capturing the advantages and disadvantages of all of these approaches in a succinct, comprehensible, general way is an important topic for future research.

In the rest of this section we outline some areas where the Kiama rewriting library could be extended, in some cases to remedy deficiencies compared to Stratego, and in others to go beyond. First and most simply, researchers have developed type systems for strategic rewriting (Lämmel, 2003). We expect that those systems could be instantiated in Scala's type system to provide more static assurances about the correctness of Kiama rewriting programs.

Concrete Syntax

Stratego provides an extremely useful facility for expressing patterns and term construction using the concrete syntax of the language(s) that are being processed (Bravenboer, 2008). Concrete syntax support means that verbose prefix constructor terms can be avoided, making the rules much easier to write and understand. Concrete syntax support is achieved in Stratego by a meta level of processing that combines the Stratego grammar with the grammar for the concrete syntax fragments. The resulting parser is able to process the input text to replace the concrete syntax with equivalent prefix term syntax.

Kiama does not have any support for concrete syntax at the moment. We plan to build a limited form of it as a plug-in for the Scala build tool. We will recognize concrete syntax fragments and pass them to a user-specified processor for parsing and pretty printing. The resulting code will be inserted into the Scala code for regular processing. Because the plug-in will not understand Scala syntax, the interaction between the code fragments and Scala code will be limited. Nevertheless, it should be sufficient for most purposes and keeping it separate from the rewriting library will mean that this facility can be used for other syntax tree matching and manipulation such as within tree decoration written using Kiama's attribute grammar library (Sloane, 2011).

Dynamic Rules

Stratego has extensive support for dynamic rewrite rules (Bravenboer, 2005). The basic idea is that rules can be constructed, manipulated and removed during rewriting. This facility is typically used to record context-specific information that will be used in some part of a term traversal and then "forgotten" as the traversal proceeds.

We have developed custom support for dynamic rules for Kiama-Apply, since we aimed to duplicate Stratego-Apply as closely as possible. We plan to revisit this code to see whether it can be usefully generalized and included in Kiama. At that time we will carefully consider whether applications of dynamic rules could more consistently be achieved using other mechanisms, such as by using Kiama's attribute grammar library to decorate terms with context-specific information. Nevertheless, we expect that having some form of dynamic rules will be useful.

Congruences

A Stratego congruence is a strategy that is named after a constructor. It provides a convenient syntactic sugar for matching on the constructor to extract the sub-terms, processing each sub-term with a potentially different strategy, and assembling the results. For example, if `Add` is a constructor with two sub-terms, then the congruence `Add` (s_1, s_2) first matches the subject term against the pattern `Add` (t_1, t_2), then applies s_1 to t_1 and s_2 to t_2. If both applications succeed then the results are combined as the sub-terms of a new `Add` term.

Kiama has some support for congruences but can't quite emulate the concise Stratego notation without some boilerplate. Since we are using a pure embedding, the patterns we need cannot be synthesized from the constructor definitions. Therefore we need boilerplate for each constructor that matches the term and extracts the sub-terms. The sub-terms are then passed to a generic Kiama routine that applies the individual strategies and constructs the new term, if appropriate. We do not currently use this congruence support in Kiama-Apply. Some strategies would be simplified if we did. We also don't have congruence support for data structures such as lists. It should be relatively easy to add using the high-level interfaces provided by Scala collections.

CONCLUSION

We have evaluated the effectiveness of an internal implementation of a domain-specific language by comparing it to an existing external implementation that performs the same task. A non-trivial compilation case study provided the context for a realistic comparison. We saw that the two languages were very similar, largely due to the power of the Scala host language, particularly its ability to define domain-specific operators. Differences in name binding resulted from our desire to reuse Scala's powerful pattern matching facilities. Scala's stronger type system required more discipline in the construction of terms.

A comparison of the two implementations of the case study compiler showed that their sizes were similar, but the internal version was slower and used more memory. This difference is to be expected, since the internal version is running on a generic run-time whereas the external one uses a run-time designed specifically for term rewriting. Nevertheless, the internal language is still practically useful since its performance is close enough to the external language and scales in the same way on large inputs. The performance deficiency is somewhat offset by a simpler implementation.

We hope that this study inspires other researchers to conduct similar evaluations. The methodology used here should translate into other settings without too much trouble. Issues such as expression syntax and binding constructs will be common to other DSLs, but will induce different solutions in different host languages. More case studies will allow the relative advantages of different host languages to be compared.

ACKNOWLEDGMENT

Much of the design and implementation work for Kiama's rewriting library was performed while Sloane was visiting the Delft University of Technology, supported by NWO project 040.11.001, Combining Attribute Grammars and Term Rewriting for Programming Abstractions. We thank Eelco Visser and Lennart Kats for providing their Stratego expertise. YourKit, LLC generously provided an open source license to their Java profiler.

REFERENCES

Ada. (1982). *Reference manual for the Ada programming language*. MIL-STD 1815 edition, U.S. Department of Defense.

Bravenboer, M. (2008). *Exercises in free syntax. Syntax definition, parsing, and assimilation of language conglomerates*. PhD. Thesis, Utrecht University.

Bravenboer, M., van Dam, A., Olmos, K., & Visser, E. (2005). Program transformation with scoped dynamic rewrite rules. *Fundamenta Informaticae, 69*, 1–56.

Fowler, M., & Parsons, R. (2010). *Domain specific languages*. Addison-Wesley Professional.

Ghosh, D. (2011). *DSLs in action*. Manning.

Hamey, L. G. C. (2007). Efficient image processing with the Apply language. *Proceedings of International Conference on Digital Image Computing: Techniques and Applications* (pp. 533-540). IEEE Computer Society Press.

Hamey, L. G. C., & Goldrei, S. N. (2008). Implementing a domain-specific language using Stratego/XT: An experience paper. *Electronic Notes in Theoretical Computer Science, 203*(2), 37–51. doi:10.1016/j.entcs.2008.03.043

Hamey, L. G. C., Webb, J. A., & Wu, I.-C. (1987). Low-level vision on Warp and the Apply programming model. In Kowalik, J. (Ed.), *Parallel computation and computers for artificial intelligence* (pp. 185–199). Kluwer Academic Publishers. doi:10.1007/978-1-4613-1989-4_10

Hamey, L. G. C., Webb, J. A., & Wu, I.-C. (1989). An architecture independent programming language for low-level vision. *Computer Vision Graphics and Image Processing, 48*, 246–264. doi:10.1016/S0734-189X(89)80040-4

Kats, L. C. L., & Visser, E. (2010). The Spoofax language workbench. *Proceedings of the 25th Annual ACM SIGPLAN Conference on Object-Oriented Programming, Systems, Languages, and Applications*, (pp. 444-463). ACM Press.

Kosar, T., Martínez López, P. E., Barrientos, P. A., & Mernik, M. (2008). A preliminary study on various implementation approaches of domain-specific language. *Information and Software Technology, 50*(5), 390–405. doi:10.1016/j.infsof.2007.04.002

Kosar, T., Mernik, M., & Carver, J. C. (2012). Program comprehension of domain-specific and general-purpose languages: Comparison using a family of experiments. *Empirical Software Engineering, 17*(3), 276–304. doi:10.1007/s10664-011-9172-x

Kosar, T., Oliveira, N., Mernik, M., Pereira Varanda, J. M., Črepinšek, M., Da Cruz, D., & Henriques, R. P. (2010). Comparing general-purpose and domain-specific languages: An empirical study. *Computer Science and Information Systems, 7*(2), 247–264. doi:10.2298/CSIS1002247K

Lämmel, R. (2003). Typed generic traversal with term rewriting strategies. *Journal of Logic and Algebraic Programming, 54*, 1–64. doi:10.1016/S1567-8326(02)00028-0

Mernik, M., Heering, J., & Sloane, A. M. (2005). When and how to develop domain-specific languages. *Computing Surveys, 37*(4), 316–344. doi:10.1145/1118890.1118892

Odersky, M., Spoon, L., & Venners, B. (2008). *Programming in Scala*. Artima Press.

Premaratne, S. (2011). *Strategic programming approaches to tree processing*. Master's thesis, Macquarie University.

Sloane, A. M. (2011). Lecture Notes in Computer Science: *Vol. 6491. Lightweight language processing in Kiama. Generative and Transformational Techniques in Software Engineering III* (pp. 408–425). Springer-Verlag. doi:10.1007/978-3-642-18023-1_12

Sloane, A. M., Kats, L., & Visser, E. (in press). A pure embedding of attribute grammars. *Science of Computer Programming*. doi:doi:10.1016/j.scico.2011.11.005

Sloane, A. M., Kats, L. C. L., & Visser, E. (2010). A pure object-oriented embedding of attribute grammars. *Electronic Notes in Theoretical Computer Science, 253*(7), 205–219. doi:10.1016/j.entcs.2010.08.043

van den Brand, M. G. J., de Jong, H. A., Klint, P., & Oliver, P. A. (2000). Efficient annotated terms. *Software, Practice & Experience, 30*(3), 259–291. doi:10.1002/(SICI)1097-024X(200003)30:3<259::AID-SPE298>3.0.CO;2-Y

van den Brand, M. G. J., & Klint, P. (2007). ATerms for manipulation and exchange of structured data: It's all about sharing. *Journal of Information and Software Technology, 49*(1), 55–64. doi:10.1016/j.infsof.2006.08.009

van Deursen, A., Klint, P., & Visser, J. (2000). Domain-specific languages: An annotated bibliography. *SIGPLAN Notices, 35*(6), 26–36. doi:10.1145/352029.352035

Visser, E. (2004). Program transformation with Stratego/XT: Rules, strategies, tools, and systems in StrategoXT-0.9. *Proceedings of the Domain-Specific Program Generation Workshop, Lecture Notes in Computer Science Vol. 3016,* (pp. 216-238). Springer-Verlag.

Visser, E. (2005). A survey of strategies in rule-based program transformation systems. *Journal of Symbolic Computation, 40*, 831–873. doi:10.1016/j.jsc.2004.12.011

Visser, E. (2006). Stratego/XT 0.16: components for transformation systems. *Proceedings of the 2006 ACM SIGPLAN Symposium on Partial Evaluation and Semantic-Based Program Manipulation* (pp. 95-99). ACM Press.

YourKit. (2011). Retrieved from http://www.yourkit.com/

ADDITIONAL READING

Baader, F., & Nipkow, T. (1998). *Term rewriting and all that*. Cambridge University Press.

Castleman, K. R. (1996). *Digital image processing*. Prentice-Hall.

Dubochet, G. (2006). On embedding domain-specific languages with user-friendly syntax. *Proceedings of the 1st ECOOP Workshop on Domain-Specific Program Development* (pp. 19-22).

Gonzales, R. C., & Woods, R. E. (2006). *Digital image processing*. Prentice-Hall.

Hofer, C., Ostermann, K., Rendel, T., & Moors, A. (2008). Polymorphic embedding of DSLs. *Proceedings of the 7th International Conference on Generative Programming and Component Engineering* (pp. 137-148). ACM Press.

Hudak, P. (1998). Modular domain specific languages and tools. *Proceedings of the 5th International Conference on Software Reuse* (pp. 134-142). IEEE Computer Society Press.

Jain, A. (1989). *Fundamentals of digital image processing*. Prentice-Hall.

Kats, L., Sloane, A. M., & Visser, E. (2009). Decorated attribute grammars: Attribute evaluation meets strategic programming. *Proceedings of the International Conference on Compiler Construction, Lecture Notes in Computer Science Vol. 5501,* (pp. 142-157). Springer-Verlag.

Kats, L., & Visser, E. (2010). The Spoofax language workbench: Rules for declarative specification of languages and IDEs. *Proceedings of the 2010 ACM SIGPLAN Conference on Object-Oriented Programming, Systems, Languages, and Applications,* (pp. 444-463).

Klint, P., van der Storm, T., & Vinju, J. (2011). Lecture Notes in Computer Science: *Vol. 6491. EASY meta-programming in Rascal. Generative and Transformational Techniques in Software Engineering III* (pp. 222–289). Springer-Verlag. doi:10.1007/978-3-642-18023-1_6

Martí-Oliet, N., & Meseguer, J. (2002). Rewriting logic: Roadmap and bibliography. *Theoretical Computer Science, 285*(2), 121–154. doi:10.1016/S0304-3975(01)00357-7

Moors, A., Rompf, T., Haller, P., & Odersky, M. (2012). Scala-virtualized. *Proceedings of the ACM SIGPLAN Workshop on Partial Evaluation and Program Manipulation* (pp. 117-120). ACM Press.

Sonka, M., Hlavac, V., & Boyle, R. (1998). *Image processing, analysis, and machine vision*. Brooks/Cole.

Ureche, V., Rompf, T., Sujeeth, A., Chafi, H., & Odersky, M. (2012). StagedSAC: A case study in performance-oriented DSL development. *Proceedings of the ACM SIGPLAN Workshop on Partial Evaluation and Program Manipulation* (pp. 73-82). ACM Press.

Visser, E. (2008). WebDSL: A case study in domain specific language engineering. In *Generative and Transformational Techniques in Software Engineering II* (*Vol. 5235*, pp. 291–376). Lecture Notes in Computer Science Springer-Verlag. doi:10.1007/978-3-540-88643-3_7

KEY TERMS AND DEFINITIONS

Apply: An image processing domain-specific language based on pixel-centered operations that are applied consistently across an image, automatically taking into account side conditions such as image edges. Implemented in Stratego as an optimizing compiler that produces C code.

Generic Traversal Strategy: A strategy that describes how to traverse to sub-terms of the term being rewritten, independently of the particular structure being traversed.

Internal DSL: A domain-specific language that is embedded as a library in a host general-purpose programming language.

Kiama: A language-processing library built by embedding various formalisms into the Scala programming language. Includes a strategic term rewriting component whose design is based on the Stratego language.

Language Embedding: An approach to language implementation where the syntax and semantics of another host general-purpose language are reused.

Name Binding: The association of a name with a program entity, such as in a definition of a value or method, or as a result of a successful pattern matching operation.

Pattern Matching: An operation that compares a pattern against a piece of data. A match either succeeds, possibly binding some names to parts of the data, or fails.

Pure Internal DSL: An internal DSL where the embedding is performed without any extra translation step. In other words, DSL programs are compiled and executed purely as host language programs.

Rewrite Rule: A rewriting specification that matches a pattern against the term being rewritten and either succeeds, constructing a new term, or fails.

Scala: A modern object-oriented and functional programming language whose main implementation targets the Java Virtual Machine.

Strategic Term Rewriting: A style of term rewriting where the application of rewrite rules is controlled by high-level strategies rather than by a fixed scheme.

Stratego/XT: A widely used strategic term rewriting language and associated tools. Stratego has both a compiler that produces native code via C, and a compiler that produces Java code.

Strategy: A rewriting specification that generalizes rewriting rules by allowing a combination of pattern matching, term construction, rules and choice. Rewriting is guided by the success or failure of the component operations.

Term Rewriting: A transformation process where tree-structured data (or terms) are rewritten by rules that pattern match on term structure.

Chapter 5
Comparison Between Internal and External DSLs via RubyTL and Gra2MoL

Jesús Sánchez Cuadrado
Universidad Autónoma de Madrid, Spain

Javier Luis Cánovas Izquierdo
École des Mines de Nantes – INRIA – LINA, France

Jesús García Molina
Universidad de Murcia, Spain

ABSTRACT

Domain Specific Languages (DSL) are becoming increasingly more important with the emergence of Model-Driven paradigms. Most literature on DSLs is focused on describing particular languages, and there is still a lack of works that compare different approaches or carry out empirical studies regarding the construction or usage of DSLs. Several design choices must be made when building a DSL, but one important question is whether the DSL will be external or internal, since this affects the other aspects of the language. This chapter aims to provide developers confronting the internal-external dichotomy with guidance, through a comparison of the RubyTL and Gra2MoL model transformations languages, which have been built as an internal DSL and an external DSL, respectively. Both languages will first be introduced, and certain implementation issues will be discussed. The two languages will then be compared, and the advantages and disadvantages of each approach will be shown. Finally, some of the lessons learned will be presented.

INTRODUCTION

Software applications are normally written for a particular activity area or problem domain. When building software, developers have to confront the semantic gap between the problem domain and the conceptual framework provided by the software language used to implement the solution. They must express a solution based on domain concepts using the constructs of a general purpose programming language (GPL), such as Java or C#, which typically leads to repetitive and error

DOI: 10.4018/978-1-4666-2092-6.ch005

prone code. This encoding task is considered to be "not very creative, and more or less waste or time", and existing code maintenance is difficult (Dmitriev, 2004). Since the early days of programming, domain-specific languages (DSLs) have therefore been created as an alternative to using GPLs.

DSLs allow solutions to be specified by using concepts of the problem domain, thus reducing the semantic gap between them, and thereby improving productivity and facilitating maintenance, as a number of studies and case studies report (Weiss & Lai, 1999; Ledeczi, Bakay, Maroti, Volgyesi, Nordstrom, Sprinkle & Karsai, 2001; Kelly & Tolvanen, 2008; Kosar, Mernik & Carver, 2011). DSLs are not new (Bentley, 1986), for instance SQL, Pic or Make are well-known examples, but the interest in them has increased considerably in the last decade with the emergence of *model-driven development* paradigms ("MDA Guide", 2001; Kelly & Tolvanen, 2008; Greenfield, Short, Cook & Kent, 2004; Voelter, 2008), which provide systematic frameworks for the building and use of DSLs, their core being meta-modeling.

Model-driven paradigms are based on three basic principles. Firstly, a software application is partially (or totally) described using models, which are high-level abstract specifications, rather than using solely a GPL. Secondly, these models are expressed with DSLs which are created by applying meta-modeling (i.e. the DSL abstract syntax is represented as a meta-model). Thirdly, automation is achieved by means of model transformations which are able to directly or indirectly transform models (e.g., DSL programs) into the final code of the application by creating intermediate models. Two kinds of model transformation languages are therefore needed (Czarnecki & Helsen, 2006): model-to-model transformation languages, which allow us to express how models are mapped into models, and model-to-text transformation languages, which allow us to express how models are mapped into text (e.g., GPL code). Model-based techniques can also be applied in software modernization tasks, and a third kind of model transformation with which to extract models from legacy software artifacts (e.g., GPL code or a XML document) is then involved, which is normally called text-to-model transformation.

A DSL normally consists of three basic elements: abstract syntax, concrete syntax, and semantics. The abstract syntax expresses the construction rules of the DSL without notational details, that is, the constructs of the DSL and their relationships. Meta-modeling provides a good foundation for this component, but other formalisms such as BNF have also been used over the years. The concrete syntax defines the notation of the DSL, which is normally textual or graphical (or a combination of both). There are several approaches for the semantics (Kleppe, 2008), but it is typically provided by building a translator to another language (i.e., a compiler) or an interpreter.

Several techniques have been proposed for the implementation of both textual DSLs (Fowler, 2010; Mernik, Heering & Sloane, 2005) and graphical DSLs (Kelly & Tolvanen, 2008; Cook, Jones, Kent & Wills, 2007). In this work we focus on textual DSLs, and particularly consider two kinds or styles according to the implementation technique used: external DSLs and internal DSLs. An external DSL is typically built by creating a parser that recognizes the language's concrete syntax, and then developing an execution infrastructure if necessary. An internal DSL, however, is implemented on top of a general purpose language (the host language), and reuses its infrastructure (e.g., concrete syntax, type system and run-time system), which is extended with domain specific constructs. The DSL is therefore defined using the abstractions provided by the host language itself. For instance, in an object-oriented language, method calls can be used to represent keywords of the language. Languages with a non-intrusive syntax (e.g., LISP, Smalltalk or Ruby) are well suited for use as host languages.

A number of design decisions must be made when building a DSL, such as those related to its concrete syntax, how the language semantics is going to be defined and in which form (interpreted or compiled), or whether there will be an underlying abstract syntax. However, deciding whether the DSL will be internal or external will have an impact on the other aspects of the language. Making an effective choice between these two options therefore requires a careful evaluation of the pros and cons of each alternative. Some important aspects that should be evaluated are the following, which are related to the three elements of a DSL: abstract and concrete syntaxes, and semantics (executability and optimizations), and to quality criteria (extensibility and efficiency) and DSL tooling (tools for developing DSL and tools for using DSL).

- **Concrete Syntax**: Does the DSL require a specialized syntax? Is the host language syntax suitable for the DSL? How much effort is needed to embed the DSL in comparison to building the DSL from scratch?
- **Abstract Syntax**: In which cases might an abstract syntax be necessary, and in which is it possible to manage without it? How different is it to support an abstract syntax in each case? This last issue is related to the following aspect.
- **Executability**: How much does the host language assist in the executability of the DSL? Do we need to adapt the (internal) DSL to facilitate its executability? In which cases is it most recommended to create an interpreted/compiled language?
- **Optimizations**: Can the execution process be optimized to improve the efficiency?
- **Language Extension**: How difficult is it to incorporate new constructs into the language?
- **Integration and Library Availability**: How can an internal/external language facilitate integration with other tools such as editors? Are the libraries required available in the chosen host language?
- **DSL Development Tools**: Are there tools that facilitate the creation of internal/external DSLs? How much freedom do they offer in the creation of the language? Do these tools support the aspects identified in this comparison?
- **Target Audience and Usability**: Does the target audience expect a language with a special syntax? Are they already used to the host language syntax?

Over the last few years we have gained some experience in developing DSLs for model-driven environments. Some of these have been built as internal DSLs (Sanchez Cuadrado & García Molina, 2007) and others as external DSLs (Diaz, Puente, Cánovas & García Molina, 2011; Cánovas & García Molina, 2009). Notably, we have developed RubyTL (Sánchez Cuadrado, García Molina & Menárguez, 2006) and Gra2MoL (Cánovas & García Molina, 2009) as internal and external DSLs, respectively. RubyTL is focused on model-to-model transformations, while Gra2MoL is intended to perform text-to-model transformations that are typically needed in modernization projects to obtain a model-based representation of source artifacts that are described by a grammar. Although each language is focused on addressing a specific MDE task, they share two characteristics: both are transformation languages (model-to-model and text-to-model, respectively), and both are inspired by the ATL transformation language (Jouault, Allilaire, Bézivin, & Kurtev, 2008) since both rely on rule and binding concepts as their main constructs, signifying that their execution mechanisms are alike. In addition, both languages have a navigation language, but of a different nature in each case.

As noted in (Mernik, Heering & Sloane, 2005) there is a shortage of guidelines and experience reports on DSL development. This chapter aims to provide guidance when confronting the external vs. internal dichotomy by discussing the design decisions involved in the creation of RubyTL and Gra2MoL. As both languages share similar features they provide a case study with which to compare both approaches, and what is more, to observe the results (benefits and drawbacks) of each approach. Both languages are first introduced, along with an explanation of their commonalities and differences, and some particular requirements that they have to satisfy. The aspects mentioned above are then discussed in the light of RubyTL and GraMoL, and finally some lessons learned are presented.

RUBYTL: AN INTERNAL DSL FOR MODEL-TO-MODEL TRANSFORMATION

RubyTL was created in 2005, as part of a project initiated to experiment with model transformation language features. To this end we planned to build an extensible model transformation language in order to gain some experience in model transformation languages and devise new features. A rapid and flexible implementation was therefore needed, and this was the main factor involved in our decision to implement this language as an internal DSL in Ruby.

During the first versions of RubyTL, several extensions were implemented, and their usefulness was tested by building transformations that put them in practice. The language later proved to be useful as a normal transformation language, and not only for experimentation purposes, so some of the extensions were selected and added to the stable version of the language. RubyTL will now be introduced by means of an example, and some implementation notes are then provided.

Language Description

RubyTL is a hybrid model-to-model transformation language, meaning that it provides both declarative and imperative constructs with which to write transformation definitions. The declarative part is inspired by ATL, which is based on the rule and binding concepts. Rules establish mappings between a source meta-model type and a target meta-model type, while a binding is a special kind of assignment that establishes a correspondence between a source type feature and a target type feature. As will be shown, a binding is resolved by a rule. Interestingly, the imperative part of RubyTL is reused from Ruby for free (i.e., any Ruby construct is valid in RubyTL) (Figure 1).

We shall illustrate the language by using an example that transforms Java code represented as a model into a UML model. Figure 1a shows the source Java meta-model, while Figure 1b shows an excerpt of the target UML meta-model. The source meta-model represents Java classes (`Class` metaclass) along with their methods (`methods` reference) and fields (`fields` reference), while the target meta-model represents UML classes (`Class` metaclass) and their properties (`ownedAttribute` reference). The piece of code listed in Figure 1c is the RubyTL model transformation for this example, in which every Java class is transformed into a UML class, and whenever such a class contains a `getInstance` method, it is considered as a singleton class. Java class fields are additionally transformed into UML class properties, and a property is marked as read-only when there is no method in the class, following the Java convention for setting attributes.

The transformation has two rules, `java-class2class` and `field2property`. As can be seen, a rule has a `from` part in which the source element metaclass is specified, a `to` part in which the target element metaclass is specified, and a `mapping` part in which the relationships between the source and target model elements are specified. These relationships are expressed either in a declarative style through of a set of bindings or in an imperative style using Ruby constructs. It is worth noting that both bindings and Ruby constructs can be mixed.

Figure 1. RubyTL Transformation example: (a) Source Java metamodel; (b) Excerpt of the UML metamodel considered in the example; (c) RubyTL transformation definition

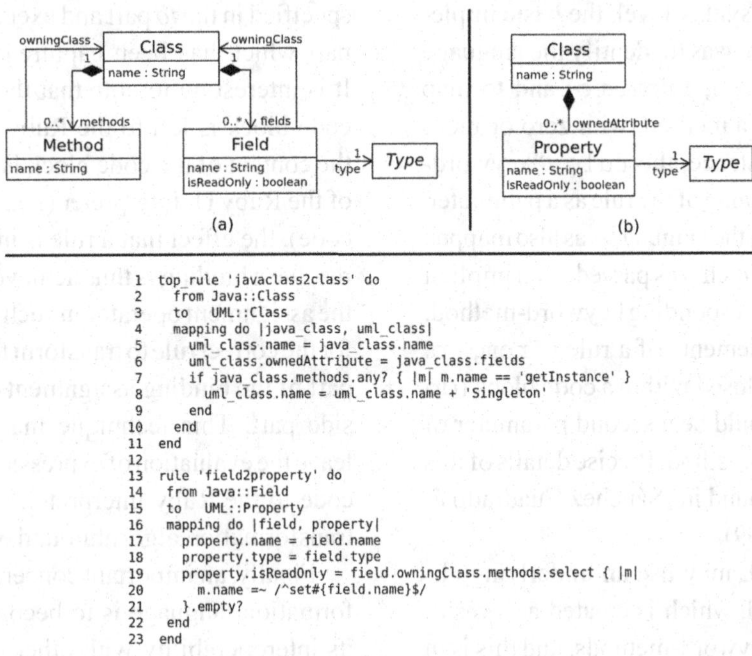

owningClass
Class
name : String
owningClass
1
1
0..* methods
0..* fields
Method
name : String
Field
name : String
isReadOnly : boolean
1
type
Type
(a)
Class
name : String
0..* ownedAttribute
Property
name : String
isReadOnly : boolean
1
type
Type
(b)
1 top_rule 'javaclass2class' do
2   from Java::Class
3   to   UML::Class
4   mapping do |java_class, uml_class|
5   uml_class.name = java_class.name
6   uml_class.ownedAttribute = java_class.fields
7   if java_class.methods.any? { |m| m.name == 'getInstance' }
8   uml_class.name = uml_class.name + 'Singleton'
9   end
10 end
11 end
12
13 rule 'field2property' do
14 from Java::Field
15 to   UML::Property
16 mapping do |field, property|
17   property.name = field.name
18   property.type = field.type
19   property.isReadOnly = field.owningClass.methods.select { |m|
20   m.name =~ /^set#{field.name}$/
21   }.empty?
22 end
23 end
(c)

In the example, the first rule is of "top" type, signifying that it is applied to each instance of `Java::Class`. Applying a rule means creating the target element metaclass and executing its mapping part. The second rule will be executed lazily, in the sense that it will be invoked only if it is needed to resolve a binding.

A binding is an assignment in the form *target. property = source-expression* where *source-expression* is a Ruby expression whose result is either an element or a collection of elements belonging to the source model. When a binding is evaluated, if the right-hand side type is different from the left-hand side type, a rule whose source type (`from` part) conforms to the right-hand type and whose target type (`to` part) conforms to the left-hand type is looked up. If found, the rule is applied using the right-hand side element of the binding as the source element, and the target element obtained is assigned to the target property. For example, the `uml_class.ownedAttribute = java_class.fields` (line 6) binding is resolved with the `field2property` rule.

As can be seen, it is possible to write imperative code in a rule (lines 7-9) using the regular Ruby syntax. In this respect, all of Ruby's features and libraries are available. For instance, lines 7 and 19 make use of the Ruby collection library to navigate models in an OCL-like style, and line 20 uses built-in regular expressions. It is worth noting that these features are provided free because RubyTL is a Ruby internal DSL, and provides developers with a means to tackle complex transformations when the declarative style is not sufficient.

Implementation Issues

The specific techniques used to implement an internal DSL depend on the paradigm the host language belongs to. In this case, as Ruby is a dynamic object-oriented language, the aspects commented on as follows are more amenable to be applicable to this kind of languages.

At the concrete syntax level, the basic implementation technique was to identify the language keywords (e.g., `rule`, `from`, `to`) and to map each keyword into a method, with zero or more parameters. For instance, the `rule` "keyword-method" takes the name of the rule as a parameter. A nested structure of the language was also mapped into a code block, which was passed as an implicit parameter to the corresponding keyword-method. For instance, the elements of a rule (`from`, `to`, `mapping`) are enclosed within a code block (`do - end`), which would be a second parameter of the `rule` keyword-method. Precise details of this technique can be found in (Sánchez Cuadrado & García Molina, 2009).

An internal DSL may use an underlying abstract syntax model, which is created as a result of evaluating the keyword-methods, and this is in some way evaluated afterwards. In (Fowler, 2010), the creation of this semantic model is considered essential if well-designed DSLs are to be obtained. The alternative would be to perform actions while the keyword-methods are evaluated (much in the style of syntax-directed translation (Aho & Ullman, 1977)). RubyTL uses a mixed approach, in which an abstract syntax model is obtained while keyword-methods are being evaluated, but with the distinguishing feature that, for the *mapping* keyword, the corresponding code block is captured to be executed later, as we shall explain below. This is done by allowing the abstract syntax of RubyTL point to the runtime Ruby object which represents the mapping code block.

With regard to the execution strategy, the transformation definition (represented by its abstract syntax model) is evaluated by the RubyTL interpreter. In fact, the classes that represent the abstract syntax include methods with which to perform the evaluation. For instance, in order to start the transformation, a method called `execute_at_top_level` is called for each top rule object. It applies the rule to all instances of the corresponding source type specified in its *from* part, thus creating an instance of the target type specified in the *to* part and executing the *mapping* part which has been captured as a code block. It is interesting to note that the execution of the code block is left to the Ruby interpreter. Since the content of the code block is out of the control of the RubyTL interpreter (i.e., it is regular Ruby code), the effect that a rule is invoked in order to resolve a binding is thus achieved by overloading the assignment operator in such a way as to search for the correct rule to transform the right-hand side part of the binding assignment into the left-hand side part. This technique makes it possible to leave the evaluation of expressions and imperative code to the Ruby interpreter, while keeping the transformation algorithm under control.

Finally, an important concern if a model transformation language is to become mainstream is its interoperability with other tools. At the time of developing RubyTL, Ecore/EMF was (and still is) the most frequently used meta-modeling framework, but it is written in Java, which hindered its use with RubyTL. Thus, when RubyTL began to be used by developers outside our team, interoperability became more important, and we therefore had to create an Ecore-compatible framework in Ruby. To this end we joined the RMOF project (http://rmof.rubyforge.org), and integrated RMOF with RubyTL to achieve interoperability with Ecore/EMF.

Gra2mol: An External DSL for Text-To-Model Transformation

In the context of a Struts-to-JSF migration project back in 2007, we needed to obtain models from some existing Java code in order to apply a model-driven modernization process. Extracting models from GPL source code requires establishing a mapping between elements of a grammar and elements of a target meta-model. Implementing this mapping involves intensive tree traversals in order to resolve references, that is, transforming the identifier-based implicit references between elements of the syntax tree into explicit references between model elements. Bearing in mind our previous experience, we decided to build a DSL, called Gra2MoL, which was tailored to the model extraction problem as an alternative to implementing ad-hoc parsers. The two main choices in the design of Gra2MoL were: providing a query language that was specially adapted to traverse and retrieve information from syntax trees, and allowing the grammar–meta-model bridge to be expressed in a RubyTL-style. Gra2MoL is in fact a text-to-model transformation language with which to extract models from any kind of artifact conforming to a grammar. To the best of our knowledge, Gra2MoL is the first language that uses a rule-based transformation approach for this type of problems.

From our experience in developing RubyTL, we decided to implement Gra2MoL as an external DSL owing to the complexity of the query language and scalability concerns, as will be commented on later. Gra2MoL and its query language will now be introduced by means of an example, and some implementation issues are then commented on.

Language Description

Gra2MoL is a rule-based transformation language in the style of RubyTL, but with two important differences: i) the source element of a rule is a grammar element rather than a meta-model element and ii) the navigation through the source code is expressed by a query language that is specific to syntax trees, rather than an OCL-like language (which would require writing complex and large navigation chains, since its objective is to traverse regular models) (Figure 2).

Throughout this section we shall use an example in order to illustrate the syntax and semantics of the language. The example could be part of model-driven modernization process of a Java system, where the first step would be to obtain Java models from Java source code. These Java models could later be the input of a model-to-model transformation, such as that presented previously for RubyTL.

Figure 2a shows an excerpt of the Java grammar considered in the example, whereas the Java meta-model has already been presented in Figure 1a. The grammar represents classes (`classDeclaration` rule) and their corresponding bodies (`classBody` rule), which can include several declarations (`memberDecl` rule). In this example we shall deal solely with method

Figure 2. Gra2MoL transformation example: (a) Excerpt of the Java grammar considered in this example; (b) Gra2MoL transformation definition

```
classDeclaration
 : 'class' ID (typeParams)? ('extends' type)?
   ('implements' typeList)? classBody
 ;
classBody
 : '{' classBodyDeclaration '}'
 ;
classBodyDeclaration
 : modifier* memberDecl
 | ...
 ;
memberDecl
 : methodDeclaration
 | ...
 ;
methodDeclaration
 : type ID methodDeclaratorRest
 ;
...
```

(a)

```
top_rule 'mapClass'
  from classDeclaration cd
  to   Class
  queries
    ms : /cd//#methodDeclaration
  mappings
    name    = cd.ID;
    methods = ms;
end_rule

rule 'mapMethod'
  from methodDeclaration md
  to   Method
  queries
  mappings
    name = md.ID;
end_rule
```

(b)

declarations (`methodDeclaration` rule). The corresponding Gra2MoL transformation in this example is composed of two rules, which are shown in Figure 2b.

As can be observed, a Gra2MoL rule has a structure which is very similar to that defined for RubyTL. A Gra2MoL rule is composed of `from`, `to`, `queries` and `mappings` parts. The `from` part specifies the source grammar element and declares a variable that will be bound to a syntax node element when the rule is applied. The `to` part specifies the target type. The `queries` part contains a set of query expressions that allow information to be retrieved from the syntax tree representing the source code. Finally, the `map-pings` part contains a set of bindings with which to initialize the features of the target meta-model element. Unlike RubyTL, in which Ruby imperative code can be written along with the bindings, in Gra2MoL only binding constructs can be used in this part.

Like the RubyTL example, the first rule of the example is of the "top" type, which means that it is executed for every element of its *from* type, and its bindings will yield the execution of other rules. The execution of a Gra2MoL transformation is therefore also driven by the bindings, whose syntax and semantics are similar to those previously explained for RubyTL. In Gra2MoL, the type of the source expression can be a literal value or one or more syntax tree elements. Like RubyTL, when a binding is evaluated, if the right-hand side type is different from the left-hand side type, a rule whose source type (`from` part) conforms to the right-hand type and whose target type (`to` part) conforms to the left-hand type is looked up. Whenever a rule is found, it is applied to the right-hand side element of the binding as a source element, and the target element obtained is assigned to the left-hand side property.

In the example, the `createClass` rule starts the transformation. This rule defines the mapping between the `classDeclaration` grammar element and the `Class` metaclass, that is, it creates an instance of the `Class` metaclass from every `classDeclaration` node in the syntax tree representing the source code. The `queries` part of the rule includes one query which collects all the method declarations of the class. The syntax and semantics of the query language will be explained in the following section. On the other hand, the mappings part of the `createClass` rule initializes the features of the target element. The first mapping sets the name attribute with the value obtained from accessing the `classId` leaf of the tree node matched by the rule (`cd` variable). The second binding, whose right-hand side part is the result of the `ms` query, is resolved by looking up and executing a conforming rule. In this case, the conforming rule is the `createMethod` rule, which is executed for each result node of the `ms` query, and it only assigns the `ID` (a leaf node with a string value) to the name of the method. The element created by the rule will be added to the `methods` reference.

The Query Language

One distinguishing feature of Gra2MoL is its structure-shy language inspired by XPath (XPath, 2011). It is tailored to navigate syntax trees in as simple manner, thus avoiding the need to define every navigation step by using XPath-like operators.

A query in Gra2MoL consists of a sequence of query operations, each of which includes four elements: an operator, a node type, a filter expression (optional) and an access expression (optional). There are three types of operators: /, // and ///. The / operator returns the immediate children of a node and is similar to dot-notation (e.g., in OCL). The // and /// operators permit the traversal of all the node children (direct and indirect), thus retrieving all nodes of a given type. The /// operator searches the syntax tree in a recursive manner, whereas the // operator only matches the nodes whose depth is less than or equal to the depth of the first matched node. These two operators allow us to ignore intermediate superfluous nodes, thus making the query definition easier, since it specifies what kind of node must be matched, but not how to reach it, in a structure-shy manner. The # operator is used to indicate the type of root nodes of the query result and must be associated with one and only one query operation.

As an example, the rule `createClass` uses the query `/cd//#methodDeclaration`, which collects all the `methodDeclaration`'s children (direct and indirect) of the node represented by the `cd` variable, which is a `classDeclaration` node. The same query expressed in the expression language provided by RubyTL (i.e., an OCL-like language) is as follows in Box 1:

It is worth noting how the clarity, legibility and conciseness are improved, because this query language is better suited to this domain (text-to-model transformation) than an OCL-like language (which is more general) like that provided by RubyTL.

Implementation Issues

As previously explained, although RubyTL and Gra2MoL have a similar syntax, the latter was implemented as an external DSL, principally to facilitate the implementation of the query language and to improve the scalability. The concrete syntax of the language was therefore defined with a grammar (from which we built the parser of the language), thus allowing us to tune the syntax more easily.

Gra2MoL uses abstract syntax models to represent transformation definitions. These models were initially obtained by using an ANTLR-based parser with annotations (i.e., actions) in the language grammar. Once a first prototype of the language had been obtained, we defined a kind of bootstrap process with which to obtain abstract syntax models from textual transformation definitions, since Gra2MoL can actually be used to extract models from any text conforming to a grammar. This process receives as inputs the grammar of the language, the abstract syntax meta-model, the transformation definition and the Gra2MoL transformation definition, and outputs are the abstract syntax model corresponding to the transformation definition of interest.

Regarding the language execution, the Gra2MoL engine executes transformation definitions in three phases. In the first phase, the source grammar is automatically annotated in order to generate a parser that is able to create a concrete syntax tree from the source code. This syntax tree is later used to execute the queries. In the second phase, the bootstrap process obtains the abstract syntax model from the textual transformation definition, as indicated above. This model is eventually used in the third phase by an interpreter that executes the transformation rules. While the rules are applied, the queries are also interpreted and executed through the use of the syntax tree obtained in the first phase. As a result of the transformation execution, the interpreter generates the

Box 1.

```
# Given a node "ClassDeclaration" namedncd
ifncd.classBody.classBodyDeclaration == nil
  []
else
  ncd.classBody.classBodyDeclaration.
    select { |decl| decl.kind_of?(MemberDcl) }.
    select {|member| member.kind_of?(MemberDeclaration) }
end
```

model extracted from the source code according to the transformation rules.

Besides the execution engine, we also developed an Eclipse plug-in that incorporates some development tools which facilitate the definition of new transformations (e.g., language-specific text editor with syntax highlighting and formatting, outline view, etc).

The language also incorporates an extension mechanism which allows new operators to be added to the rules, particularly in the queries and mappings parts. When developing new operators, it is necessary to provide both their functionality and a simple syntax. Since Gra2MoL has been developed in Java, the functionality of new operators must be implemented by using the extension framework provided by the language. With regard to the syntax for the new operators, in order to avoid having to modify the grammar of Gra2MoL for each new extension, the *ext* keyword allows the new operator to be referenced by name. For instance, if `digestName` is an extension that deals with string values, it is possible to write `name = ext digestName("some name")`.

COMPARISON OF RUBYTL AND GRA2MOL

Deciding whether to create a language as an internal or an external DSL is a key decision since it affects the other decisions involved in the process of creating the DSL, and more importantly, it may determine its success. This is for several reasons. First of all, the freedom to define the desired concrete syntax is very different in each case. Secondly, as we shall comment on later, the user perception of the DSL is typically different when it is internal or external. Finally, once the decision has been made, it is not easy to change to the other option since the implementation of most components of the languages is dependent on choice.

As mentioned previously, during the last few years we have gained some experience in developing both internal and external DSLs, learning a few lessons along the way. In this section we compare RubyTL and Gra2MoL with the series of aspects presented in the introductory section. These aspects should be taken into account in order to make an informed choice, based on the knowledge of the trade-offs of each approach with regard to the problem that is being addressed. The decisions made when building RubyTL and Gra2MoL are reviewed below in the light of these aspects and with the perspective of time.

Concrete Syntax

The concrete syntax required for the DSL is probably one of the main aspects that should be born in mind, because it is the front-end to the end-user. In this respect, if it must take on a certain shape (e.g., a well-known syntax for a certain target community) then the definition of an external DSL is generally recommended, since making the language internal will only be possible if the selected host language permits a suitable syntax. Languages with a non-intrusive syntax, such as Ruby, Smalltalk, Lisp or Haskell are therefore more likely to be used as host languages. However, the definition of an external DSL signifies that a grammar must be defined from scratch, which in most cases involves some extra work to define common language constructs such as expressions.

RubyTL did not require a very specialized syntax (beyond object-oriented manipulation in order to navigate models and write imperative code), or in other words, the host language syntax was suitable since the concrete syntax that we attained was sufficiently close to ATL and OCL, in the sense that only a few lexical variations were introduced (e.g., braces rather than parenthesis to denote the body of an iterator). However, in the case of Gra2MoL a concrete syntax close to XPath for the query language was required, as it was clear to us that an XPath-like syntax was suitable for the task that Gra2MoL was intended for. This kind of concrete syntax is in general difficult to achieve in an object-oriented language, and this was one of the reasons why we decided to implement Gra2MoL as an external DSL.

Abstract Syntax

Using an abstract syntax model as the internal representation is recommended when the compilation or evaluation of the DSL is not straightforward, and it is not possible to use syntax-directed evaluation. This was the case of both RubyTL and Gra2MoL in which the rule evaluation was sufficiently complex to require an abstract syntax to guide the interpreter. As explained previously, in RubyTL the abstract syntax model only covered the transformation-specific parts (e.g., rules), which refer at runtime to Ruby code blocks. This can be seen as interleaving the Ruby abstract syntax with a domain-specific abstract syntax. The Gra2MoL abstract syntax, however, was bigger and more complex as it had to cover all language features (e.g., rules and query expressions) in order for it to be later fully evaluated by the language interpreter.

Executability

The executability aspect is closely related to the decision to implement a compiler or an interpreter. In both cases it is possible to make the DSL internal, but in our experience the maximum gain is obtained by creating an interpreter since the runtime infrastructure of the host language can be reused. This is the case of RubyTL, in which the interpreter is very simple because it only deals with rule scheduling, while the rest of the execution is supported by Ruby itself. In this respect, there is a range of options when designing the language, from a so-called fluent API (Fowler, 2010) to more complex approaches like RubyTL. As regards Gra2MoL, there is no general-purpose language with built-in configurable support for XPath-like queries, and we could not therefore seek support from an existing execution infrastructure for Gra2MoL.

Optimizations

A typical limitation of internal DSLs is that it is difficult to implement domain-specific optimizations, and what is more, tweaking the host language to obtain certain syntax may involve performance penalties as is the case of RubyTL (e.g., meta-programming tricks which facilitate implementation at the cost of slowing down execution time). When fine-tuning is required, then an external DSL is the best option because developers can control the execution process. This is the case of Gra2MoL, in which we were able to boost the query execution performance. Related to this issue, a typical limitation of RubyTL transformations is that the abstract syntax model cannot be manipulated by another transformation (i.e., a higher-order transformation, also known as HOT) because it is a "mixed" abstract syntax model, as we have already explained. This has forced RubyTL users to move to ATL when they wish to use HOT techniques (including the developer of RubyTL himself).

When dealing with external DSLs, building an interpreter or a compiler requires a great implementation effort because developers must provide the execution semantics for each language construct. However, it allows developers to tune the execution process and to improve some features such as error control or performance. In our experience, the development of an interpreter is usually simpler than that of a compiler since developers do not have to define the translation to a low-level language, and the debugging and testing of the language is facilitated, although at the cost of a loss of performance.

Language Extensions

Incorporating language extensions as they are demanded by language users could be thought of as being easier in internal DSLs (particularly when the host language is a dynamic language) than in external DSLs, where an extension could imply making in-depth changes to the language. However, in our experience this largely depends on the kind of extension and what parts of the language must be changed (i.e., syntax or semantics). From a general point of view, external DSLs are usually easier to adapt to new concrete syntax requirements whereas internal DSLs greatly depend on how well the extension fits into the host language. As an example, Gra2MoL was extended to support a kind of rule called "skip" which has its correspondence in RubyTL in the form of *one-to-many* mappings. From an implementation point of view, the extension was easier to implement in RubyTL because it was easy to integrate it into the core of the language (i.e., the semantics), leaving most of the evaluation to the Ruby interpreter itself. Instead, in Gra2MoL parts of the interpreter had to be rewritten. However, we were forced to make the concrete syntax fit into Ruby, while the Gra2MoL designer had the opportunity to choose the most appropriate one.

Integration

Integration with other tools can be a decisive factor, depending on the purpose of the DSL. In our experience this issue is not, in general, influenced by the internal/external dichotomy, but by the availability of the libraries required in a given programming language. This issue is clearly illustrated in the case of RubyTL. In the first versions we used an early version of RMOF, a Ruby meta-modeling framework, in order to be able to read/write models in XMI format. However, as the language became more stable, some users required a better integration with Ecore/EMF (the widest used modeling framework). This forced us to practically re-implement RMOF to achieve a proper compatibility. Moreover, and despite our efforts, we never obtained a performance that was comparable to that of EMF in terms of execution time and memory consumption.

In some respects, the decision to implement Gra2MoL in Java was influenced by this experience, since it was clear that Gra2MoL should take advantage of the existing Eclipse modeling tools. In particular, Gra2MoL uses the EMF modeling framework to manage models and the CDO framework (CDO, 2012) to be able to store large models, since extracted models are normally large. Moreover, since it is written in Java (and probably as an external DSL) Gra2MoL has been proposed to become part of the MoDisco project (http://eclipse.org/MoDisco/). On the other hand, an alternative would have been to use JRuby (Ruby for the JVM), but at that time it was not as stable as it is now.

Another side of this aspect is integration with GPLs. In the case of an internal DSL, this is given by the very nature of the approach. In an external DSL, this functionality usually has to be created in an ad-hoc manner. As explained previously, Gra2MoL features a mechanism with which to add language extensions written in Java, which can be seen as a form of integration with a GPL. Some language workbenches, such as MPS, currently provide automatic support for this (Jetbrains, 2011).

Usability

Regarding usability, one important aspect to consider is IDE support. IDEs providing features such as syntax highlighting, code folding, autocompletion or cheat sheets are currently common for GPLs. An internal DSL not only inherits the host language's features, but it is also possible to take advantage of some features that are available in existing IDEs for the host language. For instance, features such as syntax highlighting and code folding are straightforward to reuse, while providing auto-completion based on the domain constructs is complicated to implement because it implies dealing with the whole grammar of the host language. On the other hand, external languages usually require the development of an IDE from scratch. However, it is currently possible to take advantage of tools such as such as xText (xText, 2011), TCS (Jouault et al., 2006) or Spoofax (Kats &Visser, 2010) to create IDEs for textual external languages including some advanced features (e.g., syntax highlighting, auto-completion and code folding).

RubyTL features an Eclipse-based IDE built on top of RDT (an extension of Eclipse for Ruby). We extended RDT with a functionality that was specific to RubyTL. Thus, with a limited effort we attained an editor with syntax highlighting, error and warning markers, program launchers, and a console with hyperlinks to navigate to source files when errors appeared. Figure 3 shows a screenshot of the RubyTL IDE. Building a similar environment for Gra2MoL proved too costly with similar resources since there were no mature tools to create IDEs at the moment of developing the IDE and everything had to be built from scratch. However, the Gra2MoL IDE does incorporate some language-specific features such as code completion, which would be too expensive to add to the RubyTL environment because it would require computing type information that is not statically available in a dynamic language like Ruby. Figure 4 shows a screenshot of the Gra2MoL IDE. The alternative would have been to alter the Ruby grammar to consider RubyTL specific constructs, but then it would no longer have been an internal DSL.

Target Audience

Another aspect of usability is the target audience. As we have already discussed, if the syntax expected by the users cannot be emulated by the host language, then an external DSL is the only choice. Another important aspect that must be considered before choosing the internal option is whether the target audience is used to the host language, and if not, whether they will reject the language because it implies learning a new general purpose language. In our experience, DSL users tend to perceive that an internal DSL is more complicated to learn because it implies learning

Figure 3. RubyTL IDE.

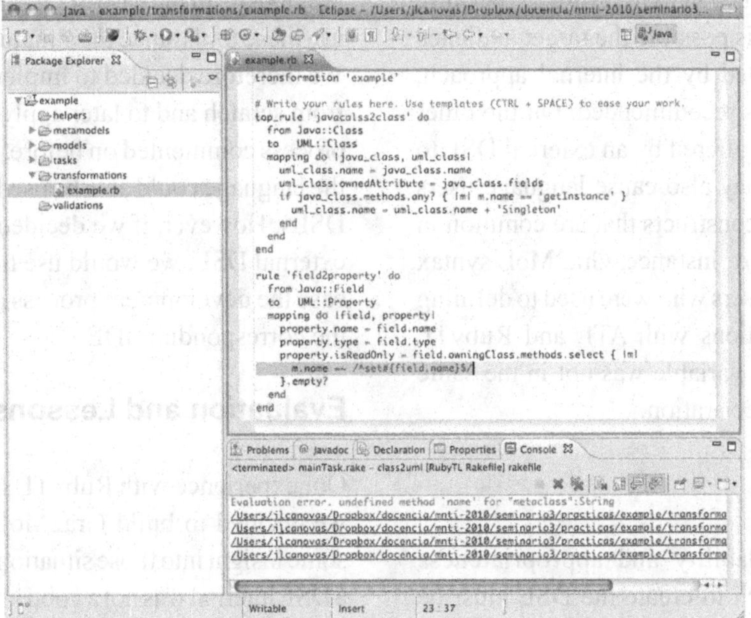

Figure 4. Gra2MoL IDE

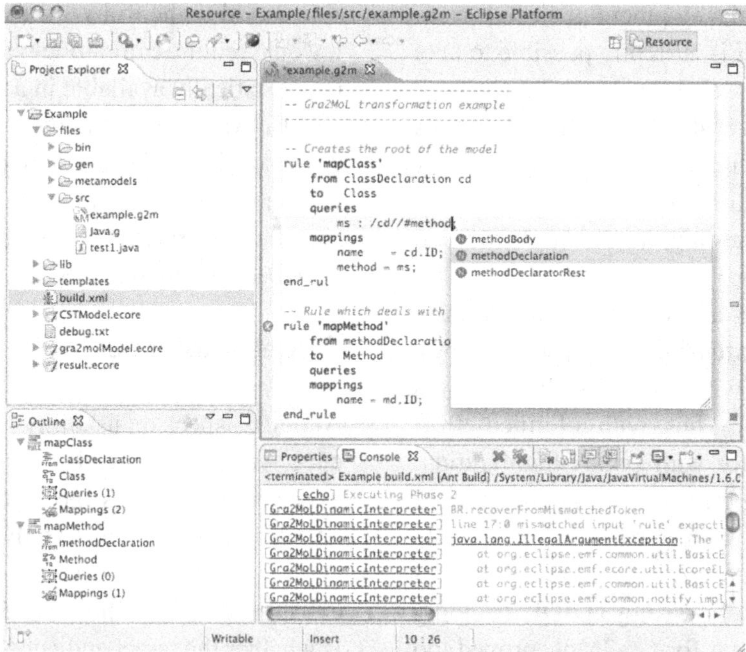

a new general purpose language, even when it is sufficient to learn only a part of the host language. For instance, in RubyTL it is not necessary to learn about Ruby classes, instance variables, etc., and it is sufficient to learn the Ruby collection library to navigate models. However, we have witnessed that users tend to be reluctant to use RubyTL because of this. Thus, if it is possible the target audience will feel intimidated by the internal approach, an external DSL is recommended. On the other hand, the freedom offered by an external DSL to shape its syntax may also cause language users to request certain constructs that are common in other languages. For instance, Gra2MoL syntax was criticized by users who were used to defining model transformations with ATL and RubyTL because the `from` variable was not in the same place in the rule declaration.

Tooling

Finally, the availability and appropriateness of tools with which to create the DSL must be considered. Regular editors or environments are sufficient for the development of an internal DSL. In the case of external DSLs, it is possible to seek support from tools like xText or Spoofax, which in turn incorporate tools with which to define the corresponding IDE, as commented on previously. In the case of Gra2MoL, we could not use these tools since their maturity level was low. We therefore decided to implement the language from scratch and to later apply the bootstrapping process commented on before, which proved that the language could also be used to define external DSLs. However, if we decided to develop a new external DSL, we would use this kind of tools to ease the development process and the creation of the corresponding IDE

Evaluation and Lessons Learned

Our experience with RubyTL signified that when we decided to build Gra2MoL, we already had some insight into those situations in which making a DSL internal was not a good idea. We had learned that in an internal DSL the concrete syntax was somewhat limited, but over all it was a must for Gra2MoL to use EMF to deal with large models, and this framework is only available in Java. The fact is that the libraries required for a given DSL are more likely to be available for mainstream programming languages (e.g., Java, C++) than for languages that are suitable for internal DSLs (e.g., Ruby, Smalltalk, LISP). This situation is currently changing with languages built on top of the JVM and CLR such as JRuby (JRuby, 2012), Clojure (Clojure 2012) or Scala (Scala, 2012).

The comparison above provides further insight into which is the best choice in each case. It would also be interesting to compare the implementation effort. We have made this comparison using two kinds of metrics. We have first applied a set of metrics to the grammars of RubyTL and Gra2MoL with the aim of understanding their characteristics. We have then measured the number of lines of code (LOCs) involved in the implementation of each language.

We shall measure the languages by using classical metrics (Power &Malloy, 2004), namely: `TERM`, `VAR`, `MCC` and `HAL`, which will allow us to obtain a brief description of the grammar complexity. We shall additionally use the `LRS`, `LTPS`, `LAT/LRS` and `SS` metrics proposed in (Črepinšek, Kosar, Mernik, Cervelle, Forax & Roussel, 2010), which will allow us to provide a better characterization of each language. For the sake of concreteness, we shall not detail each metric, but simply discuss their meaning with regard to RubyTL and Gra2MoL. Interestingly, there is no actual RubyTL grammar but as an internal DSL it programmatically inherits and "extends" the one from Ruby (i.e., grammar productions are not added by using "keyword-methods" as has been explained). Therefore, we have applied the metrics to Ruby, but for analysis purposes we have also manually enriched the Ruby grammar to consider RubyTL constructs.

Table 1 shows the results obtained, along with a brief explanation of each metric. The RubyTL column contains the values for the enriched Ruby grammar, and also indicates the variation regarding the Ruby values in a percentage. The results for Gra2MoL clearly denote its condition as a DSL: low values in `HAL`, `LRS` and `LTPS` metrics. On the other hand, the interpretation of the values for RubyTL is actually difficult because, as a Ruby internal DSL, the language inherits the characteristics from this host language. However, we can analyze how RubyTL alters the metric results. For instance, although the complexity of the Ruby grammar is slightly increased (see `HAL` and `LRS` values), the resulting internal language is actually easier to learn according to the `LAT/LRS` value. Upon considering the different nature of both DSLs, if both languages are compared, Gra2MoL is clearly simpler than RubyTL (see `HAL` and `LRS` values). However, the low value of `LAT/LRS`, along with a high verbosity (see `SS` value), denotes that RubyTL is easier to learn than Gra2MoL, whose query language format may influence this metric.

Table 2 summarizes the LOCs written to implement the concrete syntax, the core of the interpreter, and support libraries (e.g., integration with the modeling framework), and Figure 4 shows the percentage of implementation devoted to each of the components. Please bear in mind that it is expected that the same functionality in Ruby takes a few less LOCs (Figure 5).

As expected, the effort involved in defining the concrete syntax is less for RubyTL, and more so if we consider that the LOCs for RubyTL are just plain Ruby code, while for Gra2MoL it involves the grammar (194 LOCs) and the Gra2MoL bootstrapping transformation (587 LOCs). The interpreter is split into two parts: the rule engine and the expression evaluator. The rule engine has a similar complexity in both RubyTL and Gra2MoL (there are more LOCs for RubyTL because it includes a modularity mechanism that is not present in Gra2MoL (Sánchez Cuadrado & García Molina, 2010). The expression evaluator requires almost no code in RubyTL since it is an

Table 1. Metric results for Gra2MoL, Ruby, and RubyTL

Metric	Explanation	Gra2MoL	Ruby	RubyTL
TERM	Number of grammar terminals	71	88	108 (+23%)
VAR	Number of grammar non-terminals	32	83	99 (+19%)
MCC	Mcabe Cyclomatic Complexity: Effort for grammar testing and more potential parsing conflicts	3.4	2.61	2.37 (-9%)
HAL	Designer effort to understand the grammar	36.86	54.44	62.69 (+15%)
LRS	Grammar complexity independent of its size	5	13474	14.21 (+5%)
LTPS	Indicate language type. GPL > 1000	334	3200	3521 (+22%)
LAT/LRS	Facility to learn the language. Lower value is easier to learn.	0.28	0.26	0.21 (-19%)
SS	Verbosity of the language	1	1.47	1.8 (+22%)

internal DSL, only some tweaks to overload the assignment operator for bindings. However, it involves much more effort in Gra2MoL as it was developed from scratch. The model managers perform similar tasks in both cases, so they have similar LOCs.

As explained previously, RubyTL necessitated the creation of a modeling framework that was compatible with Ecore/EMF in Ruby, called RMOF. The effort of creating this framework is comparable to that of creating RubyTL itself. What is more, it could not be reused for Gra2MoL owing to the lack of efficiency with regard to EMF.

A first conclusion that can be drawn from these measures, is that the cost of building RubyTL is approximately half that of Gra2MoL, with the additional benefit that RubyTL has more features than Gra2MoL, in the sense that it provides the possibility of using Ruby features seamlessly (e.g., imperative constructs, regular expressions). However, if RMOF is taken into account then the total effort is similar. If we had realized sooner that libraries and integration were such important issues, then we would have probably chosen to implement RubyTL as an external DSL. On the other hand, it is true that we were able to modify and experiment with RubyTL really quickly, which provided benefits since it allowed us to devise new transformation mechanisms (Sánchez Cuadrado & García Molina, 2010).

Table 2. Lines of code (without comments and blank lines) involved in RubyTL and Gra2MoL

	RubyTL	Gra2MoL
Concrete syntax	331	781 (194 + 587)
Interpreter	1489	5133
Rule engine	1127	741
Expressions	362	4392
Model manager	737	933
Modeling framework	2187	–
Total	4744	6847

Another conclusion is that an internal approach makes more sense if the runtime infrastructure of the host language can be reused, as was the case of RubyTL. The cost of building an internal DSL that does not delegate on the host language for execution (i.e., building a complete abstract syntax model) would be equivalent to the external approach. As can be observed, the LOCs of both rule engines and model managers are alike, but the difference is that most of the implementation effort of Gra2MoL was in the query engine. The RubyTL interpreter was, in contrast, much simpler because it only dealt with the rule engine.

With regard to IDE support, if having domain-specific assistance in the DSL editor is important

Figure 5. LOC distribution for each DSL component between RubyTL and Gra2MoL

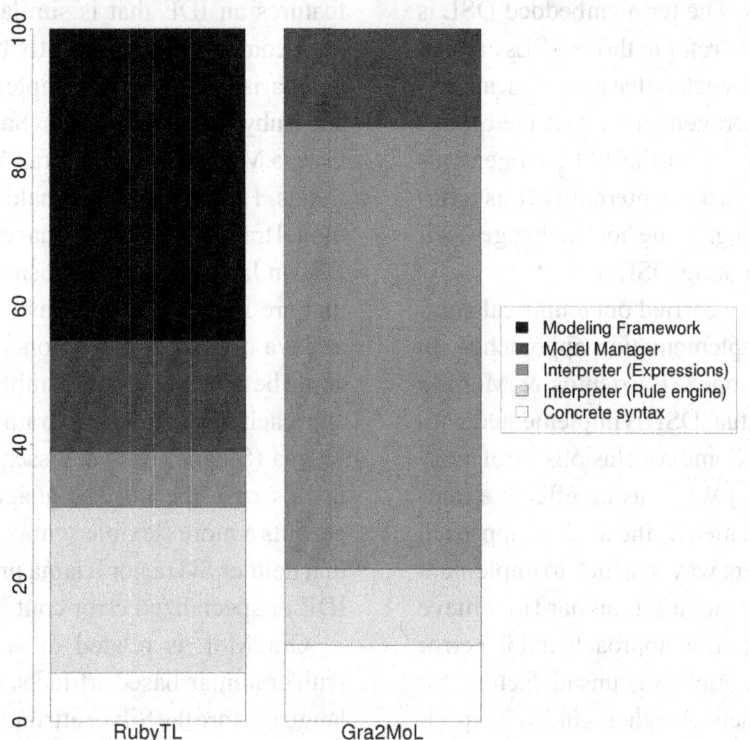

then the external DSL approach is the best choice, and more so when taking into account the existence of tools like xText, TCS or Spoofax.

Finally, regarding the target audience and the adoption of the language, it is our opinion that it is more difficult to engage users in an internal DSL than an external DSL when they do not already know the host language. This can be an insurmountable obstacle to the adoption of the language. Thus, if your target audience does not have some expertise in the host language, then it is better to choose the external approach.

RELATED WORK

The comparison presented in this chapter can be related to other works that report on DSL implementation and design techniques, in addition to works that describe DSLs for writing model transformations with similarities to RubyTL and Gra2MoL.

With regard to DSL techniques, Spinellis (Spinellis, 2001) identifies several design patterns that can be applied in the design and implementation of textual DSLs. These patterns tackle some recurrent problems that occur when dealing with DSLs, such as composition and specialization, and several DSL examples are given for each pattern. This work was extended in (Mernik, Heering & Sloane, 2005), in which the patterns are organized according to the phases in the DSL development process: decision, analysis, design and implementation. In (Czarnecki, Donnell & Taha, 2004) static meta-programming techniques applied to building internal DSLs in C++, OCaml, and Haskell are compared. In (Fowler, 2010) many topics related to the design and implementation of both internal and external DSLs are discussed. Finally, it is worth noting that in some works such as (Hudak, 1996) internal DSLs are referred to as embedded DSLs. The term embedded DSL is currently also used to refer to those DSLs created with language workbenches that provide seamless composition of heterogeneous DSLs (Jetbrains, 2011; Kats & Visser, 2010), that is, heterogeneous embedding. In contrast an internal DSL is a homogenous embedding, as the host language itself is used for implementing DSL.

Some works have carried out empirical studies for different implementation approaches. In (Kosar, Martinez-Lopez, Barrientos & Mernik, 2008), the same textual DSL is implemented with several approaches. Some conclusions are of interest to this chapter: i) When using effective lines of code (eLOC) as a metric, the internal approach was the most efficient way in which to implement DSLs; ii) the original notation was hard to achieve in the case of the internal approach and iii) error reporting and debugging was unsatisfactory for the internal approach. Another kind of experiment has been carried out in (Hermann, Pinzger & Deursen, 2009), in which the aim was to find the factors contributing to the success of a DSL, and the authors elaborated a survey to measure the success of the ACA-NET DSL amongst users of 30 projects all around the world. Factors such as usability, learnability, expressiveness, and reduction of the development costs are presented as factors for DSL success, and some lessons learned are discussed.

On the other hand, in the last few years several DSLs have been created for purposes similar to that of RubyTL and Gra2MoL. Some of these are reviewed as follows in order to highlight the variety of decisions that can be made. As acknowledged by (Czarnecki & Helsen, 2006) a diversity of model-transformation languages currently exists. In particular, ATL (Jouault, Allilaire, Bézivin & Kurtev, 2008) is the most similar to RubyTL with regard to its semantics. It is an external DSL, whose concrete syntax has been built with TCS (Jouault et al., 2006). The executability aspect is covered with a compiler from ATL to a dedicated virtual machine. It also features an IDE that is similar to RubyTL, but auto-completion has recently been added to it. A comparison between the implementations of ATL and RubyTL can be found in (Sanchez Cuadrado & García Molina, 2007). SiTra (Akehurst, Bordbar, Evans, Howells & McDonald-Maier, 2007) is a model transformation language built as an internal DSL in Java. It has mechanisms for defining rules that are implemented as Java classes. However, as Java does not have a non-intrusive syntax, it could be considered to be simply an API. A similar approach is taken for program transformation in Kiama (Sloane, Kats & Visser, 2011). However, in this case the host language is Scala, which permits a more flexible syntax. It is worth noting that neither SiTra nor Kiama provides an adapted IDE or specialized error control support.

Gra2MoL is related to languages that deal with grammar-based artifacts. Examples of those languages are the Silver attribute grammar system (Wyk, Bodin & Gao, 2010) and TXL (Cordy, 2006). In both cases, a command-line compiler is the tool front-end, and no IDE support is available. The LISA system is an example of grammar system that assists in generating DSLs as well as their associated IDEs (Henriques, et al., 2005). The Spoofax (Kats & Visser, 2010) environment is a language workbench for Eclipse that uses the Stratego program transformation system as its core. In addition to basic features such as syntax highlighting, it enables more complex features such as auto-completion.

CONCLUSION

In this chapter we have discussed the advantages and disadvantages of making a DSL internal or external, with the aim of providing developers who have to confront this question with guidance when beginning the development of a DSL. To this end, we have compared RubyTL and Gra2MoL, two transformation languages built using the internal and external approach respectively.

Both RubyTL and Gra2MoL have now been in use for several years, and some of the expectations of them have been satisfied, while others have not. We believe that choosing the internal or the external implementation technique has had a direct influence. To summarize the lessons learned during this time, an internal DSL is a good choice when the host language can support the DSL syntax seamlessly, there are no st.rong performance constraints, the host language runtime infrastructure can be heavily reused, and the target audience knows the host language or, at least, is not reluctant to learn it. In the other cases, we believe that an external DSL will be a better option.

ACKNOWLEDGMENT

This work has been supported by the Spanish government through the TIN2009-11555 project. We also thank the reviewers for their insightful comments.

REFERENCES

Aho, A. V., & Ullman, J. D. (1977). *Principles of compiler design*. Boston, MA: Addison-Wesley Longman Publishing Co., Inc.

Akehurst, D., Bordbar, B., Evans, M., Howells, W., & McDonald-Maier, K. (2007). SiTra: Simple transformations in Java. In *10th International Conference on Model Driven Engineering Languages and Systems, Lecture Notes in Computer Science, Vol. 4735*, (pp. 351-364). Springer.

Bentley, J. (1986). Programming pearls: Little languages. *Communications of the ACM, 29*(8), 711–721. doi:10.1145/6424.315691

Cánovas, J. L., & García-Molina, J. (2009). A domain specific language for extracting models in software modernization. In R. F. Paige, A. Hartman, & A. Rensink (Eds.), *5th European Conference on Model Driven Architecture - Foundations and Applications, Lecture Notes in Computer Science, Vol. 5562,* (pp. 82-97). Springer.

CDO. (2011). *CDO framework*. Retrieved March 23, 2012, from http://www.eclipse.org/cdo/

Clojure. (2012). *Clojure language*. Retrieved March 23, 2012, from http://www.clojure.org

Cook, S., Jones, G., Kent, S., & Wills, A. C. (2007). *Domain-specific development with visual studio DSL tools*. Boston, MA: Pearson Education, Inc.

Cordy, J. R. (2006). The TXL source transformation language. *Science of Computer Programming, 61*(3), 190–210. doi:10.1016/j.scico.2006.04.002

Črepinšek, M., Kosar, T., Mernik, M., Cervelle, J., Forax, R., & Roussel, G. (2010). On automata and language based grammar metrics. *Journal on Computer Science and Information Systems*, 7(2), 310–329.

Czarnecki, K., Donnell, J. O., & Taha, W. (2003). DSL implementation in MetaOCaml, Template Haskell, and C++. In C. Lengauer, D. S. Batory, C. Consel, & M. Odersky (Eds.), *International Seminar Domain-Specific Program Generation, Lecture Notes in Computer Science, Vol. 3016,* (pp. 1-22). Springer.

Czarnecki, K., & Helsen, S. (2006). Feature-based survey of model transformation approaches. *IBM Systems Journal*, *45*(3), 621–645. doi:10.1147/sj.453.0621

Diaz, O., Puente, G., Cánovas, J. L., & García Molina, J. (in press). Harvesting models from web 2.0 databases. *Software and Systems Modeling*, in press. DOI: 10.1007/s10270-011-0194-z

Dmitriev, S. (2004). *Language oriented programming: The next programming paradigm*. Retrieved October 5, 2011, from http://www.omg.org/cgi-bin/doc?omg/03-06-01

Fowler, M. (2010). *Domain-specific languages*. Boston, MA: Addison-Wesley Longman Publishing Co., Inc.

Greenfield, J., Short, K., Cook, S., & Kent, S. (2004). *Software factories: Assembling applications with patterns, models, frameworks, and tools*. Indianapolis, IN: Wiley Publishing.

Henriques, P. R., Varando Pereira, M. J., Mernik, M., Lenic, M., Gray, J., & Wu, H. (2005). Automatic generation of language-based tools using the LISA system. *Software IEE Proceedings, 152*(2), 54-69.

Hermans, F., Pinzger, M., & van Deursen, A. (2009). *Domain-specific languages in practice: A user study on the success factors*. Report TUD-SERG-2009-013. Delft University of Technology. Retrieved March, 28, 2012, from http://swerl.tudelft.nl/twiki/pub/Main/TechnicalReports/TUD-SERG-2009-013.pdf

Hudak, P. (1996). Building domain-specific embedded languages. *ACM Computing Surveys, 28*(4), 196. doi:10.1145/242224.242477

JetBrains. (2011). *MPS*. Retrieved March, 28, 2012, from http://www.jetbrains.com/mps

Jouault, F., Allilaire, F., Bézivin, J., & Kurtev, I. (2008). ATL: A model transformation tool. *Science of Computer Programming, 72*(1), 31–39. doi:10.1016/j.scico.2007.08.002

Jouault, F., Bézivin, J., & Kurtev, I. (2006). TCS: A DSL for the specification of textual concrete syntaxes in model engineering. In S. Jarzabek, D. C. Schmidt, & T. L. Veldhuizen (Eds.), *5th International Conference Generative Programming and Component Engineering* (pp. 249-254). ACM.

JRuby. (2012). *JRuby*. Retrieved March, 28, 2012, from http://www.jruby.com

Kats, C. L., & Visser, E. (2010). The spoofax language workbench: Rules for declarative specification of languages and IDEs. In W. R. Cook, S. Clarke, & M. C. Rinard (Eds.), *Proceedings of the 25th Annual ACM SIGPLAN Conference on Object-Oriented Programming, Systems, Languages, and Applications* (pp. 444-463). ACM.

Kelly, S., & Tolvanen, J. P. (2008). *Domain-Specific Modeling: Enabling full code generation*. Hoboken, NJ: John Wiley & Sons, Inc.

Kleppe, A. (2008). *Software language engineering*. Boston, MA: Addison-Wesley Longman Publishing Co., Inc.

Kosar, T., Martinez López, P. E., Barrientos, P. A., & Mernik, M. (2008). A preliminary study on various implementation approaches of domain-specific language. *Information and Software Technology, 50*(5), 390–405. doi:10.1016/j.infsof.2007.04.002

Kosar, T., Mernik, M., & Carver, J. (2012). Program comprehension of domain-specific and general-purpose languages: Comparison using a family of experiments. *Empirical Software Engineering, 17*(3), 276–304. doi:10.1007/s10664-011-9172-x

Ledeczi, A., Bakay, A., Maroti, M., Volgyesi, P., Nordstrom, G., Sprinkle, J., & Karsai, G. (2001). Composing domain-specific design environments. *Computer, 34*(11), 44–55. doi:10.1109/2.963443

Mernik, M., Heering, J., & Sloane, A. M. (2005). When and how to develop domain-specific languages. *ACM Computing Surveys, 37*(4), 316–344. doi:10.1145/1118890.1118892

Object Management Group. (2001). *MDA guide*. Retrieved October 5, 2011, from http://www.omg.org/cgi-bin/doc?omg/03-06-01

Power, J. F., & Malloy, J. F. (2004). A metrics suite for grammar-based software. *Journal of Software Maintenance and Evolution: Research and Practice, 16*(6), 405–426. doi:10.1002/smr.293

Sánchez Cuadrado, J., & García Molina, J. (2007). Building domain-specific languages for model-driven development. *IEEE Software, 24*(5), 48–56. doi:10.1109/MS.2007.135

Sánchez Cuadrado, J., & García Molina, J. (2009). A model-based approach to families of embedded domain specific languages. *IEEE Transactions on Software Engineering, 25*(6), 825–840. doi:10.1109/TSE.2009.14

Sánchez Cuadrado, J., & García Molina, J. (2010). Modularization of model transformations through a phasing mechanism. *Software & Systems Modeling, 8*(3), 325–345. doi:10.1007/s10270-008-0093-0

Sánchez Cuadrado, J., García Molina, J., & Menárguez, M. (2006). RubyTL: A practical, extensible transformation language. In A. Rensink & J. Warmer (Eds.), *Second European Conference Model Driven Architecture - Foundations and Applications, Lecture Notes in Computer Science, vol. 4066*, (pp. 158-172). Springer.

Scala. (2012). *Scala language*. Retrieved March, 28, 2012, from http://www.scala-lang.com

Sloane, A. M., Kats, L. C. L., & Visser, E. (in press). A pure embedding of attribute grammars. *Science of Computer Programming*, in press. Retrieved fromhttp://dx.doi.org/10.1016/j.scico.2011.11.005

Voelter, M. (2008). MD* best practices. *Journal of Object Technology, 8*(6), 79–102. doi:10.5381/jot.2009.8.6.c6

Weiss, D. M., & Lai, C. T. R. (1999). *Software product-line engineering: A family-based software development process*. Boston, MA: Addison-Wesley Longman Publishing Co., Inc.

Wyk, V. E., Bodin, D., & Gao, J. (2010). Silver: An extensible attribute grammar system. *Science of Computer Programming, 75*(2), 39–54. doi:10.1016/j.scico.2009.07.004

XPath. (2012). *XML path language (XPath) 2.0*. Retrieved March 28, 2012, from http://www.w3.org/TR/xpath20/

xText. (2011). *xText 2.0*. Retrieved March, 28, 2012, from http://www.xtext.org

ADDITIONAL READING

Aßmann, U., & Sloane, A. (Eds.). (2012). *Proceedings of the Fourth International Conference on Software Language Engineering, Lecture Notes in Computer Science, Vol. 6940*. Springer.

Batory, D. S., Johnson, C., MacDonald, B., & von Heeder, D. (2002). Achieving extensibility through product-lines and domain-specific languages: A case study. *ACM Transactions on Software Engineering and Methodology, 11*(2), 191–214. doi:10.1145/505145.505147

Bravenboer, M., de Groot, R., & Visser, E. (2006). MetaBorg in action: Examples of domain-specific language embedding and assimilation using Stratego/XT. In Lammel, R., Saraiva, J., & Visser, J. (Eds.), *International Summer School on Generative and Transformational Techniques in Software Engineering* (*Vol. 4143*, pp. 297–311). Lecture Notes in Computer Science Springer. doi:10.1007/11877028_10

Clark, T., Sammut, P., & Willans, J. (2004). *Applied metamodelling: A foundation for language driven development*. Retrieved October 5, 2011, from http://eprints.mdx.ac.uk/6060/1/Clark-Applied_Metamodelling_(Second_Edition)%5B1%5D.pdf

Cleaveland, J. C. (1988). Building application generators. *IEEE Software, 5*(4), 25–33. doi:10.1109/52.17799

Czarnecki, K., & Eisenecker, U. (2000). *Generative programming: Methods, techniques and applications*. Boston, MA: Addison-Wesley Co.

de Groot, R. (2005). *Implementation of the Java-Swul language a domain-speci□c language for the SWING API embedded in Java*. Retrieved March 28, 2012, from http://www.program-transformation.org/pub/Stratego/Java-Swul/swul-article.pdf

Deursen van, A., & Klint, P. (1998). Little languages: Little maintenance? *Journal of Software Maintenance: Research and Practice*, *10*(2), 75–92. doi:10.1002/(SICI)1096-908X(199803/04)10:2<75::AID-SMR168>3.0.CO;2-5

Favre, J. M., Gaševic, D., Lammel, R., & Winter, A. (Eds.). (2009). *IEEE Transactions on Software Engineering, Special Issue on Software Language Engineering, 35*(6).

Gaševic, D., Lämmel, R., & Van Wyk, E. (2009). *Proceedings of the First International Conference on Software Language Engineering, Lecture Notes in Computer Science, Vol. 5452*. Springer.

Ghosh, D. (2010). *DSLs in action*. Stamford, CT: Manning Publications Co.

Gronback, R. C. (2009). *Eclipse modeling project. A domain-specific language (DSL) toolkit*. Boston, MA: Pearson Education Inc.

Kelly, S., & Pohjonen, R. (2009). Worst practices for domain-specific modeling. *IEEE Software*, *26*(4), 22–29. doi:10.1109/MS.2009.109

Krueger, C. W. (1992). Software reuse. *ACM Computing Surveys*, *24*(2), 131–183. doi:10.1145/130844.130856

Kurtev, I., Bezivin, J., Jouault, F., & Valduriez, P. (2006). Model-based DSL frameworks. In P. L. Tarr & W. R. Cook (Eds.), *Proceedings of the 21th Annual ACM SIGPLAN Conference on Object-Oriented Programming, Systems, Languages, and Applications, OOPSLA* (pp. 602-616). ACM.

Malloy, B. A., Staab, S., & van den Brand, M. (Eds.). (2011). *Proceedings of the Third International Conference on Software Language Engineering, Lecture Notes in Computer Science, Vol. 6563*. Springer.

Parr, T. (2010). *Language implementation patterns: Create your own domain-specific and general programming languages*. Lewisville, TX: The Pragmatic Bookshelf.

Selic, B. (2008). Personal reflections on automation, programming culture, and model-based software engineering. *Automated Software Engineering*, *15*(3), 379–391. doi:10.1007/s10515-008-0035-7

Spinellis, D. (2001). Notable design patterns for domain speci□c languages. *Journal of Systems and Software*, *56*(1), 91–99. doi:10.1016/S0164-1212(00)00089-3

Steinberg, D., Budinsky, F., Paternostro, M., & Merks, E. (2008). *Eclipse modeling framework*. Boston, MA: Pearson Education Inc.

Thomas, D., & Hunt, A. (2000). *Programming Ruby: The pragmatic programmer's guide*. Boston, MA: Addison-Wesley Longman Publishing Co., Inc.

van den Brand, M., Gaševic, D., & Gray, J. (Eds.). (2010). *Proceedings of the Second International Conference on Software Language Engineering, Lecture Notes in Computer Science, Vol. 5969*. Springer.

van Deursen, A., Klint, P., & Visser, J. (2000). Domain-specific languages: An annotated bibliography. *ACM SIGPLAN Notices*, *35*(6), 26–36. doi:10.1145/352029.352035

Voelter, M. (2010). Embedded software development with projectional language workbenches. In D. C. Petriu, N. Rouquette, & Ø. Haugen (Eds.), *13th International Conference Model Driven Engineering Languages and Systems, Lecture Notes in Computer Science, Vol. 6394,* (pp. 32-46). Springer.

Wile. D. S., & Ramming, J. C. (Eds.). (1999). *IEEE Transactions on Software Engineering, Special Issue on Domain-Specific Languages, 25*(3).

KEY TERMS AND DEFINITIONS

Abstract Syntax: The construction rules of a language without taking notational details into account, that is, the valid constructs and their composition rules.

Concrete Syntax: The notation that the users of a language are provided with in order to develop programs or specifications.

Domain-Specific Language (DSL): A language specifically tailored to address a problem or a task in a particular application domain.

External DSL: An approach with which to implement a DSL, in which the language is built from scratch so that it has a custom made concrete syntax and a specific infrastructure.

Internal DSL: An approach with which to implement a DSL, in which the language is built on top of another language, the host language, reusing its infrastructure.

Meta-Modeling: Construction and support to the elements that allow models that represent a certain system or domain of interest to be described.

Model Transformation: The manipulation of model(s) that conform(s) to a particular meta-model. It includes, among others, in-place transformations, model-to-model transformations or text-to-model transformation.

Model-Driven Engineering: A family of software developing paradigms which promote the pervasive use of models in the software development cycle. Meta-modeling and model transformation are key elements of this approach.

Chapter 6
Iterative and Pattern-Based Development of Internal Domain-Specific Languages

Sebastian Günther
Vrije Universiteit Brussel, Belgium

ABSTRACT

Internal DSLs are a special kind of DSLs that use an existing programming language as their host. In this chapter, the author explains an iterative development process for internal DSLs. The goals of this process are: (1) to give developers a familiar environment in which they can use known and proven development steps, techniques, tools, and host languages, (2) to provide a set of repeatable, iterative steps that support the continuous adaptation and evolution of the domain knowledge and the DSL implementation, and (3) to apply design principles that help to develop DSLs with essential properties and to use host language independent design patterns to plan and communicate the design and implementation of the DSL. The process consists of three development steps (analysis, language design, and language implementation) and applies four principles: open form, agile and test-driven development, design pattern knowledge, and design principle knowledge.

INTRODUCTION

Domain-Specific Languages (DSLs) are languages specifically tailored to express the concepts and notations of a domain by embodying suitable abstractions and notations (van Deursen et al., 2000). Traditionally there are two kinds of DSLs. External DSLs allow the developer to freely choose the syntax and semantics of a DSL by writing a custom grammar, lexer, parser, and source code generators, often supported with dedicated development environments. Internal DSLs are built on top of an existing programming language by

DOI: 10.4018/978-1-4666-2092-6.ch006

leveraging the host constructs and exploiting syntactic variations. Internal DSLs also benefit from the fact that the existing language infrastructure – compiler/interpreter, IDE, debugger – can be reused. We focus our research efforts on internal DSL because they help developers to reuse their existing knowledge of the particular host language and they simplify the integration with other DSLs, frameworks, and libraries. From here on, if we speak of DSL, we mean internal DSLs.

Related work about DSL development can be broadly distinguished into general processes and processes specific for internal DSLs. General processes describe the DSL development as consisting of similar phases like they are used in software development: analysis, design, implementation, testing, deployment (Consel & Marlet, 1998; van Deursen et al., 2000; Mernik et. al, 2005). These phases need to be extended with precise advice how to provide the domain-specific notations and abstractions. Although several case studies for the development of internal DSLs exist, only a few of them explain the development process: In Dinkelaker & Mezini (2008), classes are created for all domain objects, in and Cunningham (2008) commonality/variability analysis is used for analyzing the domain, from which natural language expressions and finally statements and constructs of the DSL are retrieved. These approaches, however, explain host language specific mechanisms adapted for DSL implementation.

These and further related work show the diverse options available to developers of internal DSLs. In this chapter, we carefully review existing approaches, identify their challenges, and present a development process with three phases and four process principles.

In our process, the first phase, *domain analysis*, collects various domain material like handbooks, manuals, and expert knowledge, to define a domain model that details the concepts, attributes, and relationships of the domain. From this domain model, a set of valid host language expressions is developed during the *language design* phase. Finally, with the *language implementation* phase, the semantics behind these expressions are provided. These steps are tightly integrated and iterative in their nature. They allow designers to begin with a small excerpt of the domain: a few domain concepts and operations, for which sample expressions are defined, and implemented. Each step produces an executable DSL. Successive steps add to these expressions or refine existing ones, continuously growing the DSL expression by expression.

In addition to these steps, four principles are applied. The *open form principle* allows developers to use their known development steps (the three steps of the development process), their techniques (for requirements analysis, domain analysis, and domain modeling), and their host language tools (like the compiler/interpreter or the IDE) for the DSL development. This gives developers a familiar environment in which they can focus on understanding the domain and implementing the DSL. Through the *agile and test-driven development principle,* the tight integration between the development steps is enabled. The DSL is developed expression by expression, with the tests first, followed by the implementation. During iterations, a complete test suite for the DSL is created. This helps to continuously evolve the DSL and to use the DSL early on. Finally, *design pattern knowledge* and the *design principle knowledge* address the identified challenge to plan and communicate DSL designs. Host language independent patterns that document recurring design challenges and their solutions form a rich vocabulary to share DSL design knowledge. Each pattern provides a problem and generic solution, as well as explaining a host language specific application, therefore being also precise enough to be applied to a DSL. The DSL design principles identify essential properties of DSLs and suggest a specific design goal that can be achieved through applying the patterns.

The section "Background and related work" first discusses the background and related work to give a complete overview to other DSL development approaches. Then, the following section "Development Principles" presents the four development principles in detail. The section "Development Process" explains the development, which is followed by another section explaining a case study. Finally, the last section summarizes our chapter.

We use the following typeset to distinguish different concepts in this chapter: *keyword*, `source code`, PATTERN, and *subpattern*.

BACKGROUND AND RELATED WORK

We distinguish the existing work on DSL development into general processes, processes for external DSLs, and processes for internal DSLs. At the same tome, the background material id also regarded as related work from which our process is distinguished and as a source of reference about what needs to be considered in a development process.

General Development Processes

General development processes the same for developing internal and external DSLs. They provide a wide spectrum of design considerations to the DSL, even factors surrounding the DSL's deployment and application. We consider ideas described in Consel & Marlet (1998), van Deursen & Klint (1998), van Deursen et al. (2000), Mernik et al. (2005), Strembeck & Zdun (2009), and Čeh et al. (2011) as representative for general processes.

The first process has a strong focus on external DSLs – it regards a DSL as designating a member of a program family. Despite this strict focus, the process still provides useful insights. After the program family is identified, the *language analysis* phase identifies commonalities and variability of the domain and expresses this as objects and operations. In addition, language requirements and other language design elements are added and formalized. The next phase is *interface definition*, where the syntax and semantics of the language are formalized with respect to the analysis results. The process then continues to develop the static and dynamic semantics, formally designs, and finally implements an abstract machine that can execute the language (Consel & Marlet, 1998).

Another process consists of three phases that are close to software development phases. In the *analysis phase*, actions close to domain engineering (see Czarnecki & Eisenecker (2000)) are provided. Thereby, the domain is identified, the relevant domain knowledge collected (like handbooks, manuals, or expertise of professionals), and finally put in a domain model that provides the semantic notations and operations. Based on this model, a DSL is developed to describe applications in the domain. The *implementation phase* shows this process' focus on external DSLs: The semantics are implemented as a program library or by calling existing libraries, and the notations are translated by compiler to library calls. The final *use phase* is concerned with writing actual programs for the desired applications (van Deursen et al., 2000; van Deursen & Klint, 1998).

The next process consists of four different phases. At first, a *decision* is made if a DSL should be implemented at all. Important criteria to be considered in this decision are to measure the required investments that need to be made by the developers, the future reuse of the DSL, and the possible increase in productivity. If the decision is positive, then the following phases show a strong resemblance with other conventional software development phases. In the *analysis* phase, domain knowledge is collected, analyzed, and processed to form a domain model, which is either formal or informal in its description of the domain vocabulary. The domain model is used in the *design* phase: The syntax and semantic is defined. Dependent on whether the language is internal or external, one can either choose a suitable host language to "piggy-back" the DSL, or design the language freely. In both cases, the actual design is either formally specified or informally described. The *implementation* realizes the design, and the *deployment* considers the actual DSL usage and adjoining tasks like developer training (Mernik et. al, 2005).

The process in Strembeck & Zdun (2009) provides an overall framework of steps that can be customized to the individual DSL type, whether it is an embedded DSL, a DSL used for model-driven engineering, or a DSL on top of a library. The explained steps are (1) defining the DSL's core language model, (2) define the behavior of the DSL language elements, (3) define the DSL's core syntax, and (4) integrate DSL artifacts with the platform/infrastructure. In one example given for internal DSLs, it is suggested to develop the concrete syntax of the DSL first, driven by the domain terminology. From this, the DSL's concrete syntax and the semantics are defined. This is a useful consideration for our development process too.

Finally, Čeh et al. (2011) suggest a process with the same phases as Mernik et al. (2005): decision, domain analysis, design, implementation, testing, deployment, and – in addition – maintenance. The process suggests to use ontologies, formalized and structured representation of domain concepts, as the core document of domain analysis from which, with the help of an automated tool, a grammar description of the DSL can be created.

Processes for External DSLs

For external DSLs, development processes are often tightly coupled with specific *language development environments*. These environments provide tools like parser, pretty-printer, or syntax-directed editors for creating DSLs (Klein & Schürr, 1997; Bruce, 1997). Early development environments are PSG (Bahlke & Snelting, 1985; Bahlke & Snelting, 1986), Gandalf (Habermann & Notkin, 1986), Centaur (Borras et al., 1998), Graspin (Mannucci et al., 1989) and PAN (Ballance et. al, 1990). In PSG, developers describe the syntax, context conditions, and denotational semantics of the DSL. These formal specifications are used to define the DSL as well as to generate an integrated and interactive development environment for programs in this language (Bahlke & Snelting, 1985; Bahlke & Snelting, 1986). In PAN, developers use context-free grammars for the syntactical description and logical constraint grammar for the semantic description of their DSL. PAN allows for the integration of the DSL with other languages by using these formal descriptions (Ballance et. al, 1990).

In general, research about formalisms for syntax and semantics is a topic on its own – several formalisms are explained in the literature (Clark & Wilson, 2001; Sebesta, 1999; Watt, 1991; Pierce, 2002), and they influence the formalisms used in language development environments. While these formalisms are still important, more recent DSL development environments like Turnpike (Wada, 2005), Microsoft Visual Studio with DSL-Additions (Cook et al., 2007), and MetaGile (Buchwalder & Petitpierre, 2008) are moving towards simpler specification languages and give graphical support to describe a language.

Processes for Internal DSLs

In contrast to an external DSL development that is concerned with finding the right formal languages to describe the syntax and semantics, case studies of internal DSLs emphasize the importance of host language specific mechanisms that form the backbone of development (Agosta & Pelosi, 2007; Bennett et al., 2008; Cannon & Wohlstadter, 2007; Dinkelaker & Mezini, 2008; Havelund et al., 2010; Hudak, 1998; Plösch, 1997; Spiewak & Zhao, 2009; Wampler & Payne, 2009). One case study about a DSL for simulating rocket launches in Scala names the techniques of automatic closure construction, curried functions, and overloaded functions (Havelund et al., 2010). A DSL for making surveys in Ruby relies on the metaprogramming capabilities of its host, especially methods to execute strings containing code and sending messages to objects instead of calling them directly (Cunningham, 2008). Another case study develops an aspect-oriented DSL in Groovy, where an internal interpreter object is defined to receive and execute code blocks (Dinkelaker & Mezini, 2008). A DSL for design by contract in Python uses wrapper objects and method interception by using metaprogramming hooks in the language (Plösch, 1997). Two Python-based DSLs instead only use the extensible object model of Python to define domain-specific methods (Cannon & Wohlstadter, 2007; Agosta & Pelosi, 2007). Overall, these techniques are the essential semantic backbone to implement the DSLs inside their host languages.

These DSL development case studies rarely consider the overall design approach that they use. One process unusually uses a formal approach to define the language (Dinkelaker & Mezini, 2008). Here, the first step is to define the syntax of the language in a Backus-Naur form. Based on this, classes are created to represent the objects of the language, and the internal interpreter object defines the other literals of the language. Note that this approach can be used to process expressions of an external DSL as well as for the design of an internal DSL. In another approach where a Ruby-based survey DSL is developed, the process starts with a commonality/variability analysis of the domain. Results of this analysis are natural language expressions from which sample DSL expressions are derived. The DSL is then implemented by constructing an internal, AST-like representation of the input, checking this representation for errors, and then executed (Cunningham, 2008).

Another approach that leverages model-driven development techniques is explained by Cuadrado & Molina (2009). This work presents a framework implemented in Ruby that offers descriptive DSLs to define the metamodel, abstract syntax, and concrete syntax of a target DSL embedded in Ruby. The development process is "encoded" through using the descriptive DSL, but no overall design approach is given. Furthermore, the resulting DSL is not useable per se, but it requires a translational semantic description by mapping the expressions e.g. to another metamodel.

Section Summary

The spectrum of development processes for different types of DSLs may seem divergent, but in essence they follow a similar set of steps. The general processes showed that DSLs are developed with phases similar to conventional software application development: analysis, design, and implementation (van Deursen et al., 2000; Mernik et. al, 2005). These principal steps are enriched with methods of designing the syntax and semantics of the DSL.

Considering that our development process is about internal DSLs, we see three challenges when trying to reuse the explained existing approaches. First, most processes rely on formal methods to specify the syntax and semantics of the DSL. However, practitioners do not use formal methods for internal DSLs. Considered more specifically, the formal specification of a host language, followed by its extension with domain-specific concepts, appears cumbersome and tedious: The non-formal specification for Java has 596 pages (Gosling et al., 2005), and the specification of Ruby requires 285 pages (Information-technology Promotion Agency, 2009). Second, the processes are intended as top-down approaches, they emphasize the complete specification of the domain followed by the DSL implementation. This form is strict and rigid, it is difficult to cope with continuous developing domain knowledge and adaptations of the DSL. Third, the case studies about internal DSLs detail the host language constructs that they use, but do not help to generalize their findings in a way that is independent of the particular example that they provide or which can be used in another host language. It is difficult to use the constructs for communicating and planning a DSL and iIt is even more difficult to explain one DSL design to a developer that wants to use another host language.

Our development process and the development principles counter these challenges. The development principles are explained in the next section.

DEVELOPMENT PRINCIPLES

In this section, we explain the four essential principles of our development process: open form, agile and test-driven development, DSL design patterns knowledge, and DSL design principles knowledge.

Open Form Principle

The open form principle supports one of the most important goals of our development process: To allow developers to reuse their known development steps, techniques, and tools. Furthermore, this principle is also concerned to ensure that the process is independent of a particular domain and host language. We discuss these points in the next sections.

Development Process

Three steps are essential to the development of software: analysis, design, and implementation. Similar steps can be used to develop DSLs:

- **Analysis:** In common software development, analysis and specification provide the conceptual background material of the application: thorough domain knowledge improves the design quality. This is similarly important in DSLs where a clear description of the domain concepts, their attributes, and operations is essential. These results determine the concepts and keywords that belong to the DSLs syntax and explain the behavior of the operations. A graphical domain model is especially helpful because it facilitates to learn the structural dependencies of concepts.
- **Design:** For common software, application design means to create the application architecture, to provide the basic layout into systems, modules, and classes. Usually, these design considerations are manifested as diagrams. For example, the static structure of an application is described with deployment diagrams and class diagrams, while the dynamic structure (the applications' runtime behavior) is expressed through sequence and activity diagrams. For a DSL, class diagrams can be used to model the structure of the specific objects, derived from the domain model. Sequence diagrams can be used to illustrate how domain operations interact with the domain objects.
- **Implementation:** Implementation processes and techniques, especially agile development techniques that are used in software development, are also very helpful for developing DSLs. Agile techniques are especially important because they provide a convenient means to support continuous adaptation of the DSL towards its domain, and they help to explore the host language's capability when developing a DSL expression by expression.

Tool Support

Tool support for application development can be leveraged to be used for DSLs too:

- **Compiler/Interpreter:** The DSL uses the compiler or interpreter of the host language, it does not require to write a specific tool. Two challenges arise. First, if semantic changes to the host language are required, they should not be added by extending the host's compiler or interpreter, but by using the host's metaobject protocol or reflection facilities. Second, the evolution of the host language possibly needs to be reflected in the DSL itself. In most cases, slight patches to the compiler/interpreter or new language features tend to be downwards compatible and won't impact the DSL. But if host language modifications break the correct behavior of the DSL, we suggest to use the DSL's test suite – which is provided through the iterative and test-driven development principle (see below) – to pinpoint where the DSL behavior fails. The responsible implementation parts are fixed, the test suite updated when necessarily, and the DSL's correct behavior restored.

- **IDE:** An internal DSL is ultimately a very sophisticated program of the host language, and this program can be developed with conventional development environments of the host. For the DSLs implementation, this gives all the source code analysis, class browsing, refactoring, and syntax highlighting support. However, there is no specific support for the syntactic design or the implementation of domain-specific semantics.
- **Debugger:** The host languages' debugger can help to find bugs in the DSLs implementation, but it can not provide specific support for domain errors: developers need to be careful and rigorous in their implementation, ideally supported by an extensive test suite.

Overall, developing DSLs with the host's tools is possible, but a better treatment of the domain-specific requirements remains open.

Domain and Host Language Support

A domain is any area of knowledge on which a set of stakeholder share consensus to enable effective communication (Arango, 1989; Simos, 1997; Czarnecki & Eisenecker, 2000). Domains can be distinguished into horizontal and vertical domains (Czarnecki & Eisenecker, 2000). *Vertical domains* are complete business areas, for example e-commerce systems, factory management, or aviation control. *Horizontal domains* provide components of systems for the vertical domains, for example elements like a database system, a message queue, or a GUI. These domains can be subdivided: The GUI can be a desktop screen, a webpage, or a screen on a mobile device. Another type of domain are development concerns like specification, testing, and deployment. For each of these domains, DSLs have been developed too.

Our process is not focused on any specific domain or type of domain. It uses the same set of tools to analyze and model domains as the domain experts would use. The development steps are generic, and the (below suggested) patterns and principles are also independent of the domain. Similarly, we do not base the process on a specific host language. Instead, the patterns that govern the specific DSL design and the implementation are described in a host language independent way, explaining recurring design challenges and their solutions.

Agile and Test-Driven Development

This principle is important to enable the development process to cope with continuous evolution of the domain knowledge and its adaptation in the DSL. Furthermore, it provides a tight integration between the development steps, facilitating the iterations because tests are used to check the correct behavior of the DSL. We explain what agile and test-driven techniques are, and then detail how this is adapted to our process.

Agile practices are an important software development technique. To cope with the rapidly changing requirements of today's applications, agile software development techniques propose to develop software incrementally, in small steps, and to release the software often to get immediate feedback from the user (Beck & Andres, 2004; Sommerville, 2010). Through actively involving the user in the development process, the time difference between requirements and implementation are shortened. Conceptual as well as communicative errors are corrected before their consequences are too firmly fixed in the software to be easily removed.

Another important practice in modern software development approaches is test-driven development (Sommerville, 2010). This method emphasizes to produce automated tests first, followed by the source code to pass the tests (Chelimsky et al., 2010). Implementing a requirement starts with writing a small test, either a unit test for a dedicated part of the application, or a behavior test about the general response of the application. The test is executed to fail, and then the developer implements just enough code to pass it. Ideally, the existing code is now refactored, its structure straightened and simplified. Then the next requirement is implemented, until a complete feature runs and an accompanying test suite ensures the correct behavior.

The techniques of agile and test-driven development evolved independently from each other, but there are some advanced agile techniques, for example extreme programming, that recognize the importance of tests and suggests to use them actively (Beck & Andres, 2004; Sommerville, 2010). We also see these techniques as natural complements to each other. Agile development means to have small development steps with active involvement of the users. Test-driven development means to continuously produce tests first for these small steps. Putting both together improves the quality of the software even more.

Bringing these techniques to a DSL means to use small development steps where a new expression, a new domain concept or domain operation, is introduced – accompanied by a test suite to check that the DSL's behavior is correct. Tests are also important on the side of the host language and libraries as well, for being sure that the DSL does not break compatibility with them. Between each development step, we emphasize the importance of a clean and minimal code base: code refactorings should follow each step, with the goal to minimize the amount of code that is required for the DSL. Each iteration of the development steps result in an executable DSL. A minimal amount of code is better to maintain and better to extend in the immediate future. These techniques are incorporated in our development process.

DSL Design Patterns Knowledge

This principle provides the essential techniques to design and implement a DSL. It helps to identify the common design challenges and their solutions in a host language independent way. This enables developers to plan and communicate their DSL design.

Patterns are a known and accepted form to record mature and proven design structures (Coplien, 1999). The well known pattern book Gamma et al. (1997) did not only record these design structures, but as Fowler (2003) points out, patterns also help to establish a common vocabulary, a pattern language, to describe development problems and their solutions.

DSL design patterns share these characteristics. Three categories of patterns are important for DSLs: *Foundation patterns* that build the essentials of the DSL, its objects and the operations that are used in all DSL expressions, *notation patterns* that describe the syntactic options of a host language to simplify expressions for obtaining a domain-specific syntax, and *abstraction patterns* that provide advanced semantics for the DSL or carefully add and modify the semantics of the host language.

The patterns should be host language independent, as explained in the open form principle. In our experience, each pattern should ideally (1) identify a common problem in the DSL design, (2) provide a general and a host language specific solution, (3) identify further design goals of the patterns, (4) explain possible liabilities, and (5) explains the relationship to other patterns.

DSL Design Principles Knowledge

The final principle provides an additional design consideration that helps to shape the DSL according to specific design goals.

A principle is either a fundamental assumption that influences the perception of a concept, or it is a rule that can be applied to achieve a certain desired characteristic. DSLs have specific properties that set them apart form general purpose languages. We analyzed which properties are commonly mentioned for DSLs, and clustered them to this set of six principles (for more details, please see Chapter 7):

- **Abstraction:** Implement domain concepts as abstractions to deemphasize technical details.
- **Generalization:** Reduce the amount of concepts by replacing a group of more specific cases with a common case.
- **Optimization:** Implement algorithmic optimizations to improve the DSL's computational performance.
- **Notation:** Represent domain-specific concepts with suitable, clear distinguished entities.
- **Compression:** Remove tokens and keywords that have no meaning in the domain.
- **Absorption:** Absorb domain commonalities into the DSL expressions to facilitate DSL usage.

The design principles complement the design patterns by adding design goals to them. A design goal identifies to which purpose the pattern can be used to support a principle. For example, several patterns can be used to compress a DSL, by shortening expressions or by putting related domain operations together. By choosing a set of principles that the DSL should provide, the available patterns are determined and the specific utilization of these patterns is influenced.

Section Summary

The four process principles help to overcome the identified DSL development challenges. With the open form principle, developers can reuse their known development steps, techniques, and tools. The principle of iterative and test-driven development helps to evolve the DSL from a set of small expressions towards a complete representation of the domain – emphasizing tests and providing a complete test suite that ensures the correct behavior of the DSL. The DSL design pattern knowledge is crucial to plan and communicate a DSL design, by using proven and recurring design challenges and their solutions. Finally, the DSL design principle knowledge helps to shape DSLs by identifying specific design goals and guidelines how to apply the patterns.

DEVELOPMENT PROCESS

The DSL development process consists of four phases. The first phase, *domain analysis*, studies the different material from the domain to produce a domain model. This model is like a blueprint for the *language design* – the identified domain concepts, their attributes and their relationships are used to create expression by expression to develop the DSL's syntax. Also, the important choice of the DSL design principles is made here and appropriate notation patterns selected. Once a set of stable expressions is defined, objects and methods are provided in the *language implementation* phase. Thereby, abstraction patterns are used to provide domain-specific semantics, to extend or even to modify the semantics of the host language.

The process is highly iterative. In our experience, it is best to start with a small excerpt from the domain, only a few concepts and operations, for which sample DSL expressions are designed and implemented. These steps are repeated until the developers are satisfied with the domain coverage. Iterations can also occur between the phases, for example the close interaction between the design and implementation, when developers try and experiment with the host language.

During our research, we found 21 patterns (detailed in Chapter 7), that for simplicity are also used in the explanation of the DSL development steps. However, we strongly point out that these patterns are not required for the process per se, they just emphasize an important tool to communicate and plan DSL designs. Other patterns that explain how to shape the syntax and semantics of DSLs can be used too.

Each development phase is detailed in the following sections. For a graphical representation of the development process, see Figure 1.

Domain Analysis

The domain analysis phase identifies and documents the domain concepts, attributes, and relationships in the domain to produce a domain model. Employing the open form principle, the developers can use their known techniques and tools.

The first step to develop a DSL is to understand the domain. Therefore, developers *collect domain material*, for example handbooks, manuals, technical documentation, and more. Another knowledge source are domain experts. Creative techniques can be used to uncover their knowledge, such as brainstorming or questionnaires (Cuaresma & Koch, 2004). This material is thoroughly studied to *define the concept meaning and domain facts* in a dictionary. Contradicting meanings and facts are a good source of detecting profound domain knowledge – language defects like synonyms, homonyms and more (Lehmann, 2001) show where the domain experts need to agree on a common definition.

From the dictionary, the *domain model* is designed. This model contains the structural representation of all domain concepts, attributes, and relationships. True to the open form principle, different domain engineering techniques can be used to process this material. For uncovering the most important parts of a domain model, commonality and variability analysis is helpful (Coplien, 1999; Cunningham, 2008), which produce a dictionary of the most important terms of the domain. The domain model can be textual like in the dictionary, or it can be a detailed entity-relationship diagram (Kang. et. al, 1990) or a class diagram.

Language Design

The language design phase is concerned with developing the syntax of the DSL by creating one expression at a time in which the concepts and operations of the domain model are used. The design principle knowledge and design pattern knowledge are used to provide the essential DSL design knowledge how to shape the syntax and to select appropriate patterns.

In the first step, the applicable *design principles* are chosen. Based on the domain model that was defined during the domain analysis step, those principles are chosen which the developers want to emphasize in the DSL. The principle selection determines the applicable patterns because only some patterns can be supportive to the design goals that a principles expresses.

The next step is to create the *language expressions and apply patterns*. Dependent on the level of expertise that the developer has, the following three general approaches can be used:

1. **Language Games:** The concept of language games was developed in the philosophy of language by the philosopher Wittgenstein (Kutschera, 1975). Behind this concept is the motivation to find out whether a natural language expression complies with its grammar. The used mechanism is quite simple: The expression is just spoken out loudly, and if the speaker is not confused, then the expression is correct. We suggest to use this

Figure 1. DSL development process

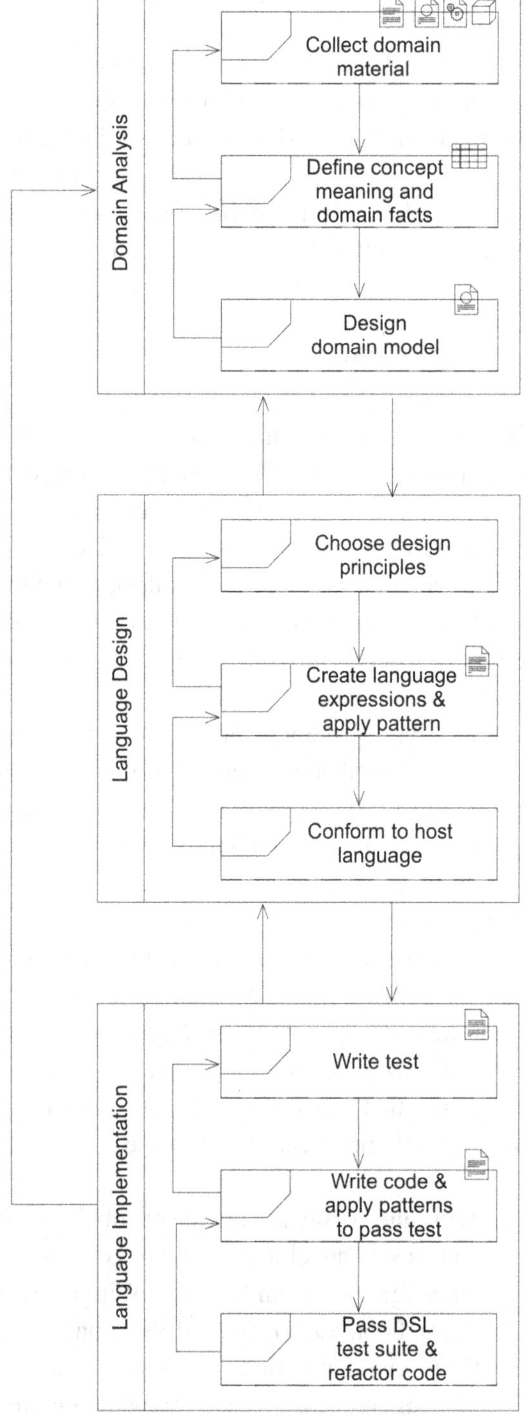

approach to design a DSL by inexperienced developers. Some host languages offer such a degree of syntactical options that "playing", trying out different expressions with the compiler/interpreter is a viable alternative to designing a DSL top-down.

2. **Expression Compression:** The second approach is possible for intermediate experienced developers. The basic assumption is that syntactically correct host language expressions are collected. Now the developers try to modify the expression, for example replacing complex algorithms with library calls, the elimination of tokens that have no meaning in the domain, such as parentheses or brackets, and improve the readability of method calls by reordering the arguments or constructing custom objects instead of parsing long argument lists. These refined expressions are then collected and exported to the next development step.
3. **Language Engineering:** The third approach is for experienced developers that have a firm grip on the embodied host language as well as DSL design patterns. Such developers can completely design the language by using the host's basic syntax and the patterns. With the right expertise, this approach is also the fastest to produce the DSL's syntax.

During the language design, two types of patterns can be used: Foundations patterns and notation patterns. Dependent on the choice of design principles, some pattern may be especially applicable to support the design goals behind the principles. In general, all of the following patterns are useable:

- **Foundation Patterns:** These patterns build the essentials of the DSL – its objects and the operations that are used in all DSL expressions.
  - **DOMAIN OBJECTS:** How to implement suitable abstractions and

  - representations of the domain entities and their relationships?
  - **DOMAIN OPERATIONS:** How to implement suitable representations of the domain operations?
- **Notation Patterns:** These patterns describe the syntactic options of a host language to simplify expressions for obtaining a domain-specific syntax. There are three groups of notation patterns:
- **Layout Patterns:** These patterns provide the overall layout of the DSL, which can be basically vertically aligned in blocks or horizontally in complex expressions.
  - **BLOCK SCOPE:** Has your DSL a flat scope where you mangle objects together, or is it difficult to express hierarchies of domain concepts that you create and combine to complex expressions?
  - **METHOD CHAINING:** Do you use too much command-like expressions that fail to represent the relation of different domain concepts or do not read fluently?
  - **KEYWORD ARGUMENTS:** Does your DSL suffer from passing too many arguments to functions, confusing the user in which order to pass arguments and what their meaning is?
- **Expression Patterns:** These patterns improve the notation of expressions by refining their intention towards a clear domain-specific representation.
  - **SEAMLESS CONSTRUCTOR:** How to avoid explicit object instantiation when this is not a domain concern?
  - **SUPERSCOPE:** How to refer to objects that exist in another scope without introducing cumbersome and cluttering variable references?
  - **ENTITY ALIAS:** How to rename built-in classes and external libraries to be consistent with the domain?
    - **Class/Module Alias:** Alias a class or module.
    - **Method Alias:** Provide an alias for a method.
  - **OPERATOR EXPRESSIONS:** How to use operators like +, *, & in DSL expressions?
- **Support Patterns:** Patterns that can be combined with most of the other patterns to provide further syntactic simplifications.
  - **CLEAN METHOD CALLS**: How to improve the readability of a DSL that is full of clutter from parentheses and other literals that are not helpful for the domain?
  - **CUSTOM RETURN OBJECTS**: How to overcome the limited vocabulary for accessing data in multiple structured objects?

After creating the expressions that *conform to the host language* through one of the mentioned approaches and by applying the patterns, these expressions are used as input to the language implementation phase.

Language Implementation

The language implementation phase provides the semantics for the expressions. The design principles knowledge and design patterns knowledge are used to determine which patterns are applicable to provide the domain-specific semantics. Furthermore, the agile and test-driven development principle shapes the steps in this development phase.

For each expression, the developer first *writes a test*, which can be as simple as the expression itself that needs to be executable, or a more complex test about the program state modification.

Then the developer *writes the code and applies patterns to pass the test*. The order in which the

DSL expressions are developed is not fixed. But in our experience, proceeding in the following order is beneficial to obtain a stable core of the DSL:

- **Core Expressions:** Expressions that occur frequently in the DSL provide most operations and concepts. These expressions should be used first to quickly define the DSL's "skeleton". Tests are rather simple at this stage: the very existence of methods and objects needs to be tested.
- **Domain Concepts:** Implementing the domain concepts and their collaboration is the next step. The first tests should check that setting and getting attribute values works as intended, followed by tests about specific behavior, like complex algorithms. When these tests are satisfied, finally the collaboration between the objects is tested and implemented.
- **Domain Operations:** The domain operations are the next target. Tests should specify the correct behavior of each operation, which can include complex conditions between created or modified domain concepts and even modified core behavior of the host language.
- **Auxiliary Expressions and Objects:** Now all other expressions of the DSL can be implemented, as well as three types of auxiliary objects. Helper objects provide background facilities or functionality that DSL users do not manipulate explicitly. Such entities perform complex calculations, monitor the program state, and provide additional validation. Another type of object are namespace objects, which provide a specific scope where domain operations are defined. Finally, adapter objects are used to encapsulate behavior that defines how a DSL interacts with another DSL, or a library, of the host language.
- **Language Features:** Finally, the DSL's other features can be implemented in a stepwise manner. Language features typically encompass whole sets of concepts and operations, as well as interactions or modifications of the core host language semantics. Therefore, accompanying tests suits should be very thoroughly provided.

During implementation, the developer applies patterns: those that are recommended through the chosen design patterns, or those that are necessary to fulfill the specified behavior. The following abstraction patterns are usable:

- **Abstraction Patterns:** Abstraction patterns provide advanced semantics for the DSL or carefully add and modify the semantics of the host language. Again, three different groups of patterns are defined.
- **Creation Patterns:** Their task is to provide objects with a custom, non-standard behavior from which other objects are created
- **BLANK SLATE:** How to provide objects with a minimal set of methods so that arbitrarily named methods can be added?
- **PROTOTYPE:** How to create new objects without using the instantiation process, for saving computational resources or for defining classes outside of the host language's rigid class structure?
- **HOOKS:** How to introduce more domain-specific behavior at predefined program execution places like class, method, and attribute declaration?
- **Composition Patterns:** Are concerned with the declaration and instantiation of new objects and thereby reuse functionality that is already available in the program.
- **TEMPLATE:** How to provide easily mutable code representations that facilitate runtime creation, modification, and execution for constant adaptation of the DSL?
    - **Scope Declaration Template:** Declaration of modules and classes.

   - **Method Declaration Template:** Declaration of method definitions.
   - **Method Call Template**: Declaration of method calls.
- **FUNCTION OBJECT:** How to represent the complete (defined) application behavior in one uniform form for arbitrary composition of new behavior?
- **Modification Patterns:** Are concerned with the modification of objects for providing more domain-specific behavior.
- **OPEN DECLARATION:** How to extend all built-in and application-specific classes at runtime?
- **META DECLARATION:** How to provide powerful customizations to modules, classes, and methods?
   - **Shared Scope:** Share the scope of multiple declarations between each other, providing access to local variables for including them in declarations.
   - **Scope Closure:** Conserve local variables in declarations, completely hiding the variables from any outside access.
- **EVAL:** How to execute any code representation at any scope of the program to modify it arbitrarily?
- **METHOD ALIAS:** How to transparently change the behavior of an existing method while preserving the old behavior?
   - **Alias Decorator:** Add functionality around an existing method.
   - **Alias Memoization**: Replace a method implementation with a fixed return value to save computational time.
- **METHOD MISSING:** Your DSL needs to react to method calls that are not defined at starting time, or it needs to dispatch the actual method call to a specific place in the system?
   - **Ghost Method:** Depending on the method's name, return a value to the caller that simulates a complete method call.
   - **Dynamic Proxy:** Forward the method call to another module or class.
   - **Missing Declaration:** Check the method name and define methods on the fly.

Once the expression-specific test passes, the complete *DSL test suite needs to be passed.* If tests fail, then the developer fixes his implementation until all tests are passed. Also, the code is *refactored* with the goal to provide as less code as possible to pass the expression-specific test. Refactoring includes all behavior-preserving modifications of the program, for example to reduce the lines of code for complex calculations, or to use other host language abstractions for providing domain-specific semantics.

Continuing in this manner, other DSL expressions are implemented. This iterative development continuously extends the DSL's test suite, which is the essential asset to ensure the DSL's correct behavior.

Section Summary

Our iterative DSL development process consists of three phases. First, in the domain analysis, all domain material is collected and processed to design a domain model. The domain models defines the domain concepts, attributes, and relationships. Second, the language design phase takes the domain model as a blueprint to provide a set of executable DSL expressions. Based on the expertise of the developer, he can either literally play with the compiler/interpreter of a host language or plan the syntax with the help of patterns. Third, the language implementation phase takes the designed expressions to stepwise implement them, accompanied by a test suite.

Figure 2. SPLL – domain model

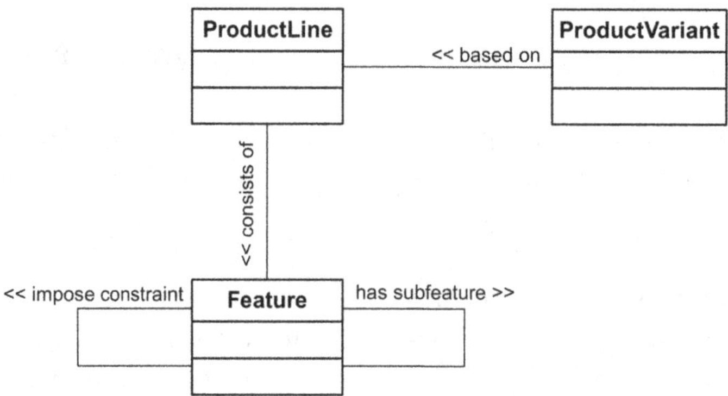

CASE STUDY

To illustrate our DSL development process, we design a Ruby-based DSL for modeling software product lines. Following subsections detail the domain analysis, language design, and language analysis.

Domain Analysis

For understanding what software product lines are, we analyze the related scientific literature. As Czarnecki & Eisenecker (2000) explain, product lines address the challenge to structure and systematically reuse software by defining a set of production assets. These assets are anything that adds functionality to the software, like source code, libraries, graphics, as well as additional material, like graphics, tutorials, and handbooks. All assets are structured, their variability with respect to the products addressed, and added to the product line.

The functional variability that a software product line provides is called feature (Whithey, 1996). To represent features, feature diagrams are used (Czarnecki & Eisenecker, 2000). These diagrams graphically model the relationships between the features, for example when the selection of a feature mandatory requires other features, or when features are optional.

The goal of our DSL, called Software Product Line Language (SPLL), is it to provide a textual language to define features and their relationships that are expressible in feature diagrams. We use Ruby as the implementation language. Based on the mentioned literature, we define the following domain concepts:

- **Feature:** A functionality of a software.
- **Feature Relationships:** Features can have hierarchical, parent-child relationships, where the child provides concrete properties of its parent. In a tree-like structure, hierarchies are represented through the position of the nodes (root, node, leaf).
- **Feature Constraints:** A feature may be dependent on another feature, so that the constraints in a feature composition need to be regarded in the software product line. We differentiate into optional, mandatory unique, and mandatory choice constraints.
- **Product Line:** A set of features, relationships, and constraints that provide a configuration space for individual product variants.
- **Product Variant:** A concrete product line configuration.

The domain entities and their relationships are shown as the domain model in Figure 2.

Language Design

During language design, we keep to the very same order of entities that we already provided in the domain analysis: features are put first, followed by their relationships, and finally their aggregation inside a product line and product variants. Each entity is explained in the following subsections. For illustration, we design a product line to configure cars, where options like the color and the transmission are used.

Representing Features

Feature is one of the main entities of our DSL, so we define it as a DOMAIN OBJECT in the form of a class from which instances are created to represent individual features. When a feature is created, we configure it, and therefore use `configure` as a DOMAIN OPERATION. In general, we want to have a vertical code layout: Properties of features should be configured one at a time. Using `configure`, we can supply a block of code that specifies the individual properties, for which we can use the BLOCK SCOPE notation pattern. This initial form of our DSL can be seen in the following listing:

```
Feature.configure do
#...
end
```

In this block, how to define the individual properties? For example, to specify the name of the feature, we could use the expressions `name = "Color"`. In our view, this expression is too host language specific, we want to use a more declarative style. The same meaning can also be expressed by `name("Color")` or as `name "Color"` (applying the CLEAN METHOD CALLS pattern) – this is our preferred solution. This addition leads our DSL look like shown in the following listing.

```
Feature.configure do
name "Color"
end
```

The combination of DOMAIN OPERATION and CLEAN METHOD CALLS results in declarative expressions that clearly show our intent. We kept this form and added all other properties likewise:

- To show the hierarchy between the features, we first designate the feature's position inside the feature tree by `root`, `node`, or `leaf`.
- To show parent-child relationships, we use, in the parent, the `subfeature` method that receives a list of this parent's children. To separate the real feature objects from their usage in declarative expressions, we use SUPERSCOPE to refer to features just by their name – the references are resolved to concrete feature objects during the execution of the DSL.
- To show constraints between features, we want to use a more complex expression. This expression has two parts. First, the keyword `requires` followed by the constraint-triggering feature. Second, an expression consisting of a constraint operator (`any`, `one`, `more`, `all`) and a list of other features – this part is a TEMPLATE string. To express that the first part implies the second part, we use the notation "=>", which can be achieved with the KEYWORD ARGUMENTS pattern. The semantics of the constraint operators are:

- `any` of the following features can be selected (optional features).
- `only` one feature can be selected (alternative features).
- at least `one` or `more` features must be selected (lower bound selection).
- `all` of the following features, or a single feature, needs to be selected (mandatory features).

We put all these considerations together in the following expression:

```
Feature.configure do
name "Color"
node
subfeatures:Red,:Blue
requires: Color => "one:Red,:Blue"
end
```

These declarations finish what we need to express for features. Now we continue to design the product line and product variant entities.

Representing Product Lines and Product Variants

As we defined, a product line is the aggregation of features from which individual variants can be composed. The basic design of this part of the language are the DOMAIN OBJECTS `ProductLine` and `ProductVariant` along with respective DOMAIN OPERATIONS for adding, removing, and activating features.

The `ProductLine` starts, as we used it for `Feature` too, with the `configure` keyword. A BLOCK SCOPE follows, where we use `description` to give a small explanation and then add defined `Feature` entities with the `add_feature` DOMAIN OPERATION. The result of this expression creates a new `ProductLine` element that is bound to a variable in the declaration scope. A `ProductLine` object remains modifiable after its creation: New features can be added and removed, even at runtime. This form is illustrated in the following listing, where the `color` variable is a pointer to the same-named feature that we explained above, and `car` describes a feature representing car configuration with their color, transmission, horse power and similar properties (Box 1).

Box 1.

```
CarPL = ProductLine.configure do
description "Simple Car Product Line"
add_feature car
add_feature color
end
```

Only the `ProductVariant` remains to be designed, but we have found the preferred form of the expression now. `ProductVariant` also start with `configure`. Inside their BLOCK SCOPE, they use the DOMAIN OPERATIONS `description` and `productline` to express to which `ProductLine` they belong. Also, the expression `activate_features`, followed by a list of features using SUPERSCOPE, is used. Similar to the `ProductLine` instances, `ProductVariant` instances are also bound to a local variable, and they are also modifiable after their creation. See the following listing for an example of these expressions (Box 2):

Language Implementation

Once we have gathered the set of language expressions that represent our DSL, we are implementing them step-by-step.

Core Expressions and Domain Operations

Our core expression is `configure`, called on one of the DOMAIN OBJECTS, and followed by a block of expressions that set individual properties. Since there are no namespace conflicts with

Box 2.

```
BlueCarVariant = ProductVariant.configure do
productline CarPL
description "A variant describing a blue car"
activate_features:Car,: Color,:Blue,: Transmission,: Automatic...
end
```

the built-in classes of Ruby, we can define our DOMAIN OBJECTS in the global namespace. The DOMAIN OBJECTS define the class method `configure`, followed by instance methods for the other DOMAIN OPERATIONS.

The Feature Domain Concept

For `Feature`, we define the DOMAIN OPERATIONS as follows:

- `name`: A method that receives a symbol which is used to internally identify this feature. This name is used in all other places where the SUPERSCOPE pattern is utilized.
- `root`, `node`, `leaf`: Methods without any arguments that just set an internal value for the feature object to represent its position in the feature tree.
- `subfeatures`: A method receiving a list of symbol arguments where the SUPERSCOPE pattern is applied again.
- `require`: The argument to this method is a KEYWORD ARGUMENTS, here implemented as a hash. The hash's key is the feature itself, and the hash's value is a string that is an implicit method call (represented with TEMPLATE pattern, executed with EVAL).

The `name` receives just a symbol representing another feature with the SUPERSCOPE pattern. To resolve this symbol to the actual feature object, we define an *auxiliary object* that stores all created features, which can then be queried for a specific feature. We also implement the *auxiliary function* `valid?`, which tests that all properties of the feature are set properly.

The ProductLine Domain Concept

All DOMAIN OPERATIONS of this entity are defined as methods in the scope of the entity:

- `description`: A method that receives a short explaining text.
- `add_feature`: A method that receives exactly one argument that is a `Feature`. Note that we need to pass objects, no SUPERSCOPE arguments here. Internally, all features are stored in the instance variable `@feature_tree`.
- `remove_feature`: A method that receives exactly one SUPERSCOPE argument and removes this feature from the internal feature tree.

`ProductLine` also defines the *auxiliary function* `valid?`. This function checks that (1) there is exactly one root feature in the feature tree, (2) the tree position of all features is correct (for example, a leaf cannot have children), (3) all features mentioned as subfeatures are actually included in the `ProductLine`, and (4) that all nodes of the feature tree are connected with each other.

Figure 3. SPLL – language entities

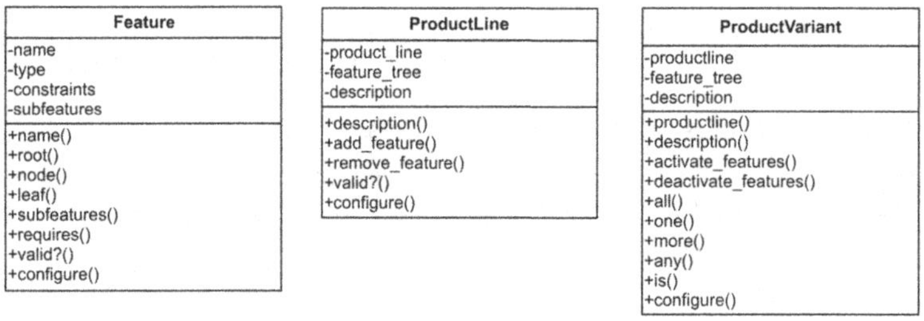

Feature
-name -type -constraints -subfeatures
+name() +root() +node() +leaf() +subfeatures() +requires() +valid?() +configure()

ProductLine
-product_line -feature_tree -description
+description() +add_feature() +remove_feature() +valid?() +configure()

ProductVariant
-productline -feature_tree -description
+productline() +description() +activate_features() +deactivate_features() +all() +one() +more() +any() +is() +configure()

The ProductVariant Domain Concept

We define these DOMAIN OPERATIONS:

- `productline`: A method with exactly one `ProductLine` argument for which this `ProductVariant` is built. Internally, the reference to the `ProductLine` is used to build a local copy of the feature tree in which all activated features are stored.
- `description`: This method receives exactly one string argument to describe this `ProductVariant`.
- `activate_features/deactivate_features`: Methods that receive a list of arguments as SUPERSCOPES, which then adds/removes the according Feature object to/from the local feature tree.
- `all, one, more, any, is` : Methods that represent the scope operators. They receive a list of arguments that are `Feature` objects represented as SUPERSCOPE.

Final Result and Object Relationships

The following Figure 3 shows all DOMAIN OBJECTS and DOMAIN OPERATIONS of our language.

Section Summary

In this section, we showed how our DSL development process can be used to develop a DSL for modeling software product lines. We explained all required steps. The language design phase analyzed the existing literature to define the main concepts in this domain, which are features, product lines, constraints etc. Then we designed the language, following the goal of a vertical block layout with expressions on each line that declares properties. Finally, we explained how each DOMAIN OBJECT and its' DOMAIN OPERATIONS are implemented.

CONCLUSION

Internal DSLs are a powerful form of abstraction that, when carefully used, help developers to express application concerns with concise language expressions. It is challenging to develop DSLs because many criteria have to be considered: conceptually defining and understanding the domain, defining the domain concepts, their properties and relationships, the DSL design to put the concepts in a language, and finally their implementation. Considering so many criteria during development is hard, so that a structured, stepwise DSL development process is necessary.

This chapter contributed with a perspective on DSL development processes. We gave an extensive background to existing DSL development approaches, and based on the found challenges, defined three important goals of our process: (1) to allow developers to use their known and proven development steps, techniques, and tools, (2) to base the process on iterative steps for continuous adaptation and evolution of the domain knowledge and the DSL implementation, and (3) to use host language independent design patterns to plan and communicate the design and implementation of the DSL.

Our process starts with the domain analysis where domain concepts, attributes, and relationships are identified and documented in a domain model. The language design phase takes this domain model and creates valid host language specific expressions that incorporate the concepts and operations of the domain model. Based on the developer's expertise, he can either just experiment with the interpreter/compiler of the language to explore possible notations, or he can select and apply design patterns. Finally, the language implementation phase stepwise implements the semantics of the expressions, focusing on the domain objects and domain operations first, followed by implementing auxiliary objects and methods that provide further behavior for the DSL in the background, such as interfacing with other libraries.

Four principles additionally substantiate the development process: (1) open form, which means that tools, analysis techniques, design techniques, and host languages of choice can be selected to work with the process, (2) agile and test-driven development, which means to develop a DSL stepwise with a complete test suite covering the DSL's behavior, (3) design pattern knowledge, documenting recurring design challenges and their solutions, as the essential knowledge how to form domain-specific notations and abstractions, and (4) design principle knowledge to provide further DSL design guidelines as principle-related design goals of each pattern.

We showed the applicability of our development process in a case study for designing a Ruby-based DSL to model software product lines. Furthermore, the development process was used to develop DSLs for feature-oriented programming (Günther & Sunkle, 2009; Günther & Sunkle, 2011), for cloud computing (Günther et al., 2010), and for database queries (Günther, 2011).

Although this process is explicitly created for internal DSLs, it provides value to external DSL development process too. Except for the open form principle, the other three principles are applicable and helpful. Small development steps support continuous evolution of the DSL. Tests are an asset assuring the correct behavior of the DSL. And as for the patterns, we assume that most of our notation patterns can be used in external DSLs as well, while the abstraction pattern would need to be substituted with semantics that are defined in the target programming language. The principles were derived from general work about DSLs – therefore they are valid for external DSLs too.

Future research can consist of more case studies that help us to refine the process, especially to learn more about the application of patterns in specific domains and possibly also the discovery of new patterns. Another future research track is to specifically adapt this process to the development of external DSLs.

REFERENCES

Agosta, G., & Pelosi, G. (2007). A domain specific language for cryptography. In *Proceedings of the Forum on specification and Design Languages (FDL)* (pp. 159–164). Gières, France: ECSI.

Arango, G. (1989). Domain analysis: From art form to engineering discipline. In *Proceedings of the 5th International Workshop on Software Specification and Design (WSSD)* (pp. 152–159). New York, NY: ACM.

Bahlke, R., & Snelting, G. (1985). The PSG - Programming system generator. *ACM SIGPLAN Notices, 20*(7), 28–33. doi:10.1145/17919.806824

Bahlke, R., & Snelting, G. (1986). The PSG system: From formal language definitions to interactive programming environments. *ACM Transactions on Programming Languages and Systems, 8*(4), 547–576. doi:10.1145/6465.20890

Ballance, R. A., Graham, S. L., & de Vanter, M. L. V. (1990). The pan language-based editing system for integrated development environments. *ACM SIGSOFT Software Engineering Notes, 15*(6), 77–93. doi:10.1145/99278.99286

Beck, K., & Andres, C. (2004). *Extreme programming explained: Embrace change* (2nd ed.). Boston, MA: Addison-Wesley Professional.

Bennett, M., Borgen, R., Havelund, K., Ingham, M., & Wagner, D. (2008). Development of a prototype domain-specific language for monitor and control systems. In *Aerospace Conference* (pp. 1–18). Washington, DC: IEEE Computer Society.

Borras, P., Clement, D., Despeyrouz, T., Incerpi, J., Kahn, G., Lang, B., & Pascual, V. (1989). Centaur: The system. In *Proceedings of the ACM SIGSOFT/SIGPLAN Software Engineering Symposium on Practical Software Development Environments (PSDE)*, Vol. 24, (pp. 14–24). New York, NY: ACM.

Bruce, D. (1997). What makes a good domain-specific language? APOSTLE, and its approach to parallel discrete event simulation. In S. Kamin (Ed.), *First ACM SIGPLAN Workshop on Domain-Specific Languages (DSL)* (pp. 17–35). University of Illinois.

Buchwalder, O., & Petitpierre, C. (2008). MEtaGile: A pragmatic domain-specific modeling environment. In *20th International Conference on Software Engineering and Knowledge Engineering (SEKE)* (pp. 764–768). Chicago, IL: Knowledge Systems Institute Graduate School.

Cannon, B., & Wohlstadter, E. (2007). Controlling access to resources within the Python Interpreter. In B. Cannon, J. Hilliker, M. N. Razavi, & R. Werlinge (Ed.), *Proceedings of the Second EECE 512 Mini-Conference on Computer Security* (pp. 1–8). Vancouver, Canada: University of British Columbia.

Čeh, I., Črepinšek, M., Kosar, T., & Mernik, M. (2011). Ontology driven development of domain-specific languages. *Computer Science and Information Systems, 8*(2), 317–342. doi:10.2298/CSIS101231019C

Chelimsky, D., Astels, D., Dennis, Z., Hellesoy, A., Helmkamp, B., & North, D. (2010). *The RSpec book: Behaviour driven development with RSpec, Cucumber, and friends*. Raleigh, NC: The Pragmatic Bookshelf.

Clark, R., & Wilson, L. (2001). *Comparative programming languages* (3rd ed.). Boston, MA: Addison-Wesley.

Consel, C., & Marlet, R. (1998). Architecturing software using a methodology for language development. *Lecture Notes in Computer Science: Vol. 1490, Proceedings of the 10th International Symposium on Programming Language Implementation and Logic Programming (PLILP)* (pp. 170–194). Berlin, Germany: Springer-Verlag.

Cook, S., Jones, G., Kent, S., & Wills, A. C. (2007). *Domain specific development with visual studio DSL tools*. Amsterdam, The Netherlands: Addison-Wesley Professional.

Coplien, J. O. (1999). *Multi-paradigm design for C*. Boston, MA: Addison-Wesley.

Cuadrado, J. S., & Molina, J. G. (2009). A model-based approach to families of embedded domain-specific languages. *IEEE Transactions on Software Engineering, 35*(6), 825–840. doi:10.1109/TSE.2009.14

Cuaresma, M. J. E., & Koch, N. (2004). Requirements engineering for Web applications - A comparative study. *Journal of Web Engineering*, *2*(3), 193–212.

Cunningham, H. C. (2008). A little language for surveys: Constructing an internal DSL in Ruby. In *Proceedings of the 46th Annual Southeast Regional Conference (ACM-SE)* (pp. 282–287). New York, NY: ACM.

Czarnecki, K., & Eisenecker, U. W. (2000). *Generative programming: Methods, tools, and applications*. Boston, MA: Addison-Wesley.

Deursen van, A., & Klint, P. (1998). Little languages: Little maintenance? *Journal of Software Maintenance: Research and Practice*, *10*(2), 75–92. doi:10.1002/(SICI)1096-908X(199803/04)10:2<75::AID-SMR168>3.0.CO;2-5

Deursen van, A., Klint, P., & Visser, J. (2000). Domain-specific languages: An annotated bibliography. *ACM SIGPLAN Notices, 35*(6), 26–36.

Dinkelaker, T., & Mezini, M. (2008). Dynamically linked domain-specific extensions for advice languages. In *Proceedings of the 2008 AOSD Workshop on Domain-Specific Aspect Languages (DSAL)* (pp. 1–7). New York, NY: ACM.

Fowler, M. (2003). *Patterns of enterprise application architecture*. Boston, MA: Addison-Wesley.

Gamma, E., Helm, R., Johnson, R., & Vlissides, J. (1997). *Design patterns - Elements of reusable object-oriented software* (10th ed.). Reading, UK: Addison-Wesley.

Gosling, J., Joy, B., Steele, G., & Bracha, G. (2005). *The Java language specification* (3rd ed.). Boston, MA: Addison-Wesley.

Günther, S. (2008). *Die Sprachbestandteile von Domänenspezifischen Sprachen: Eine Ableitung aus den sprachphilosophischen und linguistischen Wurzeln der Informatik.* Technical Report FIN-03-2008. Magdeburg, Germany: Otto-von-Guericke-Universität Magdeburg.

Günther, S. (2011, in press). PyQL: Introducing a SQL-like DSL for Python. In H.-K. Arndt & H. Krcmar (Ed.), *4th Workshop des Centers for Very Large Business Applications (CVLBA)*. Aachen, Germany: Shaker.

Günther, S., & Cleenewerck, T. (2010). Design principles for internal domain-specific languages: A pattern catalog illustrated by Ruby. In *Proceedings of the 7th Conference on Pattern Languages of Programs (PLoP)*.

Günther, S., Haupt, M., & Splieth, M. (2010). *Utilizing internal domain-specific languages for deployment and maintenance of IT infrastructures. Technical report (Internet) FIN-004-2010*. Magdeburg, Germany: Otto-von-Guericke-Universität Magdeburg.

Günther, S., & Sunkle, S. (2009). Feature-oriented programming with Ruby. In *Proceedings of the First International Workshop on Feature-Oriented Software Development (FOSD)* (pp. 11–18). New York, NY: ACM.

Günther, S., & Sunkle, S. (2011). rbFeatures: Feature-oriented programming with Ruby. *Science of Computer Programming, 77*(3), 52–173.

Habermann, A. N., & Notkin, D. (1986). Gandalf: Software development environments. *IEEE Transactions on Software Engineering, 12*(12), 1117–1127.

Havelund, K., Ingham, M., & Wagner, D. (2010). *A case study in DSL development – An experiment with Python and Scala*. In Scala Days. Lausanne, Switzerland: E'cole polytechnique fe'de'rale de Lausanne.

Hudak, P. (1998). Modular domain specific languages and tools. In P. Davenbu & J. Poulin (Eds.), *Proceedings of the Fifth International Conference on Software Reuse (ICSR)* (pp. 134–142). Washington, DC: IEEE.

Information-Technology Promotion Agency. (2009). *Programming languages – Ruby*. Retrieved March 16, 2011, http://ruby-std.netlab.jp/draft-spec/draft-ruby-spec-20091201.pdf

Kang, K., Cohen, S., Hess, J., Novak, W., & Peterson, A. (1990). *Feature-oriented domain analysis (FODA) feasibility study.* Technical Report CMU/SEI-90-TR-21. Pittsburgh, PA: Software Engineering Institute, Carnegie Mellon University.

Klein, P., & Schürr, A. (1997). Constructing SDEs with the IPSEN meta environment. In *Proceedings of the 8th International Conference on Software Engineering Environments (SEE)* (pp. 2–10).

Lehmann, P. (2001). *Meta-Datenmanagement in Data-Warehouse-Systemen - Rekonstruierte Fachbegriffe als Grundlage einer konstruktiven, konzeptionellen Modellierung*. Ph.D. thesis, Magdeburg, Germany: Otto-von-Guericke-Universität Magdeburg.

Mannucci, S., Mojana, B., Navazio, M. C., Romano, V., Terzi, M. C., & Torrigiani, P. (1989). Graspin: A structural development environment for analysis and design. *IEEE Software*, *6*(6), 35–43. doi:10.1109/52.41645

Mernik, M., Heering, J., & Sloane, A. M. (2005). When and how to develop domain-specific languages. *ACM Computing Surveys*, *37*(4), 316–344. doi:10.1145/1118890.1118892

Pierce, B. C. (2002). *Types and programming languages*. Cambridge, UK: MIT Press.

Pösch, R. (1997). Design by contract for Python. In *4th Asia-Pacific Software Engineering and International Computer Science Conference (APSEC)* (pp. 213–219). Washington, DC: IEEE Computer Society.

Sebesta, R. W. (1999). *Concepts of programming languages*. Reading, UK: Addison-Wesley.

Simos, M. (1997). Organization domain modeling and OO analysis and design: Distinctions, integration, new directions. In *Proceedings of the 3rd Conference on Smalltalk and Java in Industry and Education (STJA)* (pp. 126–132).

Sommerville, I. (2010). *Software engineering* (9th ed.). Boston, MA: Addison-Wesley.

Spiewak, D., & Zhao, T. (2009). ScalaQL: Language-integrated database queries for Scala. In M. van den Brand, D. Gasˇevic, & J. Gray (Eds.), *Lecture Notes in Computer Science: Vol. 5969. Proceedings of the 2nd International Conference on Software Language Engineering (SLE)* (pp. 154–163). Berlin, Germany: Springer-Verlag.

Strembeck, M., & Zdun, U. (2009). An approach for the systematic development of domain-specific languages. *Software, Practice & Experience*, *39*(15), 1253–1292. doi:10.1002/spe.936

von Kutschera, F. (1975). *Sprachphilosophie*. (2nd ed.). München, Germany: Wilhelm Fink Verlag.

Wada, H. (2005). Modeling turnpike: A model-driven framework for domain-specific software development. In *Companion to the 20th Annual ACM SIGPLAN Conference on Object-Oriented Programming, Systems, Languages, and Applications (OOPSLA)* (pp. 128–129). New York, NY: ACM

Wampler, D., & Payne, A. (2009). *Programming Scala*. Sebastopol, CA: O'Reilly Media.

Watt, D. A. (1991). *Programming languages syntax and semantics*. Cambridge, UK: Prentice Hall.

Withey, J. (1996). *Investment analysis of software assets for product lines*. Technical Report CMU/SEI96-TR-010. Pittsburgh, PA: Software Engineering Institute, Carnegie Mellon University.

ADDITIONAL READING

Consel, C. (2004). From a program family to a domain-specific language. In Lengauer, C., Batory, D., Consel, C., & Odersky, M. (Eds.), *Domain-Specific Program Generation* (*Vol. 3016*, pp. 19–29). Lecture Notes in Computer Science Berlin, Germany: Springer-Verlag. doi:10.1007/978-3-540-25935-0_2

Hessellund, A., Czarnecki, K., & Wąsowski, A. (2007). Guided development with multiple domain-specific languages. In Engels, G., Opdyke, B., Schmidt, D., & Weil, F. (Eds.), *Model Driven Engineering Languages and Systems* (*Vol. 4735*, pp. 46–60). Lecture Notes in Computer Science Berlin, Germany: Springer-Verlag. doi:10.1007/978-3-540-75209-7_4

Kosar, T., López, P. E. M., Barrientos, P. A., & Mernik, M. (2008). A preliminary study on various implementation approaches of domain-specific language. *Information and Software Technology*, *50*(5), 390–405. doi:10.1016/j.infsof.2007.04.002

KEY TERMS AND DEFINITIONS

Agile Development: A set of development techniques that emphasizes to use small, iterative development step to continuously progress in implementing a program.

Domain-Specific Language (DSL): A compiled or interpreted computer language that represents the concepts, attributes, and operations of a domain by implementing suitable abstractions and notations.

DSL Design Pattern: A structured description of common design challenges and their solutions that helps to communicate development knowledge and structure designs.

DSL Design Principle: A general guideline that expresses a design goal how to apply a design pattern.

DSL Process Principle: A general guideline that influences how the DSL development processes is designed.

Internal Domain-Specific Language: A DSL that uses an existing programming language as its host language, it uses the host's constructs and abstractions to define the domain-specific concepts, attributes, and operations. Also called embedded DSL.

Test-Driven Development: A software development approach to first write the test, followed by the implementation to achieve a specified behavior of a program.

Chapter 7
Design Patterns and Design Principles for Internal Domain-Specific Languages

Sebastian Günther
Vrije Universiteit Brussel, Belgium

ABSTRACT

Internal DSLs are a special kind of DSLs that use an existing programming language as their host. To build them successfully, knowledge regarding how to modify the host language is essential. In this chapter, the author contributes six DSL design principles and 21 DSL design patterns. DSL Design principles provide guidelines that identify specific design goals to shape the syntax and semantic of a DSL. DSL design patterns express proven knowledge about recurring DSL design challenges, their solution, and their connection to each other – forming a rich vocabulary that developers can use to explain a DSL design and share their knowledge. The chapter presents design patterns grouped into foundation patterns (which provide the skeleton of the DSL consisting of objects and methods), notation patterns (which address syntactic variations of host language expressions), and abstraction patterns (which provide the domain-specific abstractions as extensions or even modifications of the host language semantics).

INTRODUCTION

Domain-Specific Languages (DSLs) are languages specifically tailored to express the concepts and notations of a domain by embodying suitable abstractions and notations (van Deursen et al., 2000). Using DSLs increases the productivity, reduces errors, and allows to better focus on the problem space (Czarnecki & Eisenecker, 2000; Greenfield et al., 2004). DSLs are used for a wide spectrum of domains, for example in telephone services (Latry et al., 2007), for healthcare systems

DOI: 10.4018/978-1-4666-2092-6.ch007

(Munelly & Clarke, 2007), and for magnet tests at the Large Hadron Collider at CERN (Arpaia et al., 2009). This chapter focuses on one particular type of DSLs. Internal DSLs are based on an existing host language, they are built by carefully combining syntactic options of the host with well-scoped semantic modifications using the host's support for metaprogramming. In the remainder of this chapter, we mean internal DSLs whenever we talk of DSLs.

Considering existing open-source and research DSLs, which can be especially found in languages such as Ruby, Python, and Scala, we can study the applied syntactic and semantic modifications of the host. Although there are plenty examples of DSLs, two problems are apparent. First, it remains difficult for the individual developer to explain his particular design because the relation of used host language constructs and DSL design questions is not clear. Second, the host language constructs are language specific, so it is difficult to use designs from one host language in another one. Therefore, we think that only a common language to describe the syntactic and semantic modifications, as well as to understand how a modification affects the characteristic of a DSL, allows developers to communicate and plan DSL design. To achieve this goal, developers need to understand design principles and design patterns of DSLs.

Design principles are guidelines that provide design goals to shape the syntax and semantic of a DSL. The choice of principles influences how a DSL is developed, which results in DSLs that are distinguishable from each other and from host language code. In related work, two limitations become apparently. First, most case studies, including recent ones, do not consider them (Groote et al., 1995; Thibault et al., 1997; Barreto et al., 2002; Agosta & Pelosi, 2007; Dinkelaker & Mezini, 2008; Bennett et al., 2006; Havelund et al., 2010). And second because those DSL case studies that treat principles only define them, but do not show how to actually achieve them (Atkins et al., 1999; Oliveira et al., 2009; Bentley, 1986).

Design patterns are the essential way to provide a vocabulary for communicating and planning DSL designs. Although the implementation of a DSL is host language specific, a careful analysis of DSLs shows that there are language-independent techniques to form the syntax and semantics of a DSL. We refine these techniques to patterns, which identify a common DSL design challenge and a common solution that can be implemented by using host language specific mechanisms. Related work about DSL design patterns shows two limitations. One the one hand, case studies about internal DSL offer diverse techniques for design and implementation, ranging from modifications of a host language's metaobject protocol to object-oriented mechanisms (Agosta & Pelosi, 2007; Cannon & Wohlstadter, 2007; Cunningham, 2008; Dinkelaker & Mezini, 2008; Sloane, 2008). However, the explained techniques are not generalized outside the context of their DSL, which makes them hard to reuse for other case studies. And on the other hand, most existing work about DSL design patterns suggests very general patterns (Haase, 2007; Mernik et al., 2005; Spinellis, 2001; Zdun & Strembeck, 2009), which are not detailed enough for finer aspects of syntax and semantic design.

To overcome the mentioned limitations, we contribute with a set of 6 DSL design principles and an explanation of 21 DSL design patterns. We identify three design principles related to the syntax of a DSL (*notation*, *compression*, and *absorption*) and three principles related to the semantics (*abstraction*, *generalization*, and *optimization*). The patterns are grouped into *foundation patterns*, which provide the skeleton of the DSL consisting of objects and methods, *notation patterns*, which address syntactic variations by using host language expressions, and *abstraction patterns*, which provide the domain-specific abstractions as extensions or even modifications of the host language semantics. We show how to apply the principles by identifying individual design goals of the patterns – each goal giving the pattern a unique way of being applied. The patterns have been found and implemented in the context of languages with an object-oriented core and strong support for reflection, and therefore are especially applicable in similar programming languages. Furthermore, in the concluding section, we explain how programming languages with another core paradigm, for example functional languages, can benefit form these patterns.

In the course of the next sections, we first take a closer look at the background of DSL design and principles and refine our research questions. In the section "Design Principles" we define the principles of DSL design that we found. Section "Pattern Structure and Explanation" introduces the structure with which we explain the patterns, and the following sections explain the foundation, notation, and abstraction patterns. Section "Pattern Utilization" lists the known uses of each pattern, and section "Pattern Language" extends the pattern catalog to a pattern language. Finally, in the last section, we summarize our work and give an outlook to future research.

We use the following typesets to distinguish difference concepts in this chapter: *keyword*, `source code`, PATTERN, and *subpattern*.

BACKGROUND AND RELATED WORK

In this section, we define the term domain-specific language and come up with a definition that is driven by essential properties of such languages. Then, the second part considers the state of the art for patterns in domain-specific languages. Finally we explain the concept of DSL design principles.

Domain Specific Languages

The current definition of the term domain-specific language can be tracked through several stages in the early literature. We uncovered the following three definitions:

- **Specific Language:** Early during the design of the first mainstream programming languages, the fundamental concept to separate the appearance of a program from its representation was discovered. The first application of this concept led to compiler research and was necessary to start the implementation of Fortran (Pratt & Zelkowitz, 2000). Another application of this concept led to the idea of providing a family of languages that are based on the same internal program representation (Landin, 1967). Individual languages of this family were envisioned to be tailored towards their application areas, and were therefore called specific languages (Landin, 1967).
- **Domain Language:** The continued evolution of software engineering led to discover the importance of "domain" as a concept describing an area that is perceived as being important by a group of stakeholder (Srinivas, 1991). During designing software, a domain model is built that explains the most important concepts and operation of this domain. Neighbors (1980) had the idea to use the domain model terms in a declarative language to define system components. This language would then be transformed into other formats that further evolve the program to an executable form.
- **Little Language:** Related to the term specific languages, little languages again emphasize the provision of dedicated languages for specific application development problems (Bentley, 1986). Such languages consist of expressions that clearly represent the intent a developer wants to express. The design focus of a little language is the explicit focus on the user for whom appropriate notations need to be found. Typically, preprocessors are used to transform the expressions into an intermediate or executable form (Bentley, 1986).

The essential similarity between all these concepts is the goal to find a language that stands apart from full-blown general programming languages but gives enough capability to provide abstractions for a specific domain.

Finally, the term *domain-specific language* appeared. The initial definition of DSL is "[a] programming language tailored for a particular application domain" (Hudak, 1998, p. 1). According to Atkins et al. (1999), abstraction is one essential property of a DSL. Abstractions have to be chosen appropriately to provide "high-level entities and relationships that fit the domain closely" (Atkins et al., 1999, p. 1). Other authors acknowledge the role of abstractions as well: The DSL abstracts key concepts of a domain in the form of language constructs (Thibault et al., 1997), it captures the semantics of a domain precisely (Hudak, 1998). Of equal importance is the provision of domain-specific notations (Heering, 2000) that represent the abstractions (Thibault et al., 1997). The notations have to be appropriate to the domain and are usually restricted in their amount to be easily usable by the programmers (van Deursen et al., 2000).

DSLs can be either internal or external (Mernik et al., 2005). An internal DSL, also called embedded DSL, is based upon an existing programming language. This approach facilitates to reuse syntax and semantics of the host language (Hudak, 1998) as well as to use the existing language infrastructure of compiler, interpreter, and debugger (Mernik et al., 2005). In contrast to this, an external DSL is free in the design of its syntax and semantics, but the developers need to provide the language infrastructure or use a language development environment (Klint, 1993; Klein & Schürr, 1997).

Based on this material, we define a domain-specific language as follows:

A domain-specific language is a compiled or interpreted computer language that represents the concepts, attributes, and operations of a domain by implementing suitable notations and abstractions.

As explained, this paper focuses on internal DSLs, also called embedded DSLs, which we define as follows:

An internal DSL uses an existing programming language as its host, where domain-specific concepts, attributes, and operations are implemented through adaptions of the host's constructs and abstractions.

Design Patterns

Patterns are an accepted form to document recurring problems and their solutions in software development (Gamma et al., 1997). The nature of patterns is that they abstract from problems and describe a generalized solution, not an instruction how to achieve a certain goal (Greenfield et al., 2004).

It is essential t provide such patterns for DSLs because existing case studies are showing the diversity of language design and implementation techniques. For example, Cunningham (2008) talks of host language specific metaprogramming methods that are used for the DSL's semantics, while Dinkelaker & Mezini (2008) use the host language's metaobject protocol. In another case, internal interpreter objects (Dinkelaker & Mezini, 2008; Sloane, 2008) or object-oriented programming constructs, in particular methods (Cannon & Wohlstadter, 2007; Agosta & Pelosi, 2007), are used. Such techniques show the design space for DSLs, but to be able to discuss and plan a DSL implementation, we need a common vocabulary – and this common vocabulary can be provided by patterns.

However, the patterns that are discussed in related literature are not detailed enough to show how a DSL is actually implemented. Most research about design patterns in DSL focuses on general design decisions (Haase, 2007; Mernik et al., 2005; Spinellis, 2001; Zdun & Strembeck, 2009). For example, Spinellis (2001) presents eight patterns grouped into creational, structural, and behavioral. The creational patterns explain that restricting or specializing a host language can be used to approach DSL design, and structural patterns explain the relationship between a DSL and a system that uses the DSL. The patterns in Haase (2007) describe general forms of DSLs, such as a configuration language or expression language. In other works, patterns for the decision, analysis, design, implementation, and deployment of a DSL (Mernik et al., 2005), or for specific development steps (Zdun & Strembeck, 2009), are given.

During the author's research to find and document such patterns, two other research results were published. Perrotta (2010) explains several metaprogramming idioms in Ruby. The idioms are a general documentation of metaprogramming in Ruby, not specifically geared towards DSLs. However, Ruby-based DSLs use several of such idioms. Furthermore, when regarding the DSL design intent for which these idioms are used, we see that the same intent is expressed in DSLs based on Python or Scala – with similar host language techniques. Therefore, we say that some of the idioms in Perrotta (2010) could be refined to DSL design patterns that we explain in this chapter. When one of the DSL patterns is based on idioms of Perrotta (2010), it is documented to the beginning of the pattern.

Another work by Fowler (2010) provides a large number of patterns. One part of his work is concerned with the creation of external DSLs, and another one with internal DSLs. The patterns for internal DSLs are mostly focused on syntactic patterns that help to achieve a specific syntax of the language. Furthermore, Fowler (2010) uses a narrative style (the explanation of a pattern without a separation into problem, solution, and related pattern sections as we do) for the patterns, explains implementation mostly in Java and Ruby, and focuses on syntactic pattern. Comparing Fowler's work with our contribution, we see that some pattern share a similar intent, which we document in our patterns. However, we have an overall larger set of patterns for internal DSLs, we cover syntactic as well as semantic patterns, and we explain how design principles influence the application of a pattern to design DSLs with a specific focus on one or several chosen design principles.

To summarize, we clearly see the research need to provide a host language independent set of patterns for describing the notation and the abstraction of a DSL. Patterns are essential to communicate and plan DSL designs. Without DSL design patterns, there is a danger that DSL design knowledge is scattered across the different programming language communities, and as the knowledge evolves, it can become even more harder to communicate.

Design Principles

Design principles are the embodiment of properties that are put into the form of guidelines to be followed during the creation of a language. The most important property of a DSL is the provision of suitable notations and abstractions. We argue that principles enabling and affecting such properties need to be specifically formulated for being used in DSL development.

Observing how language design principles are explained and discussed in general, we see that there is insightful work on visual languages. Both Costagliola et al. (2002) and Moody (2009) explain the necessity of principles and define them to show several examples how following such principles leads to well designed languages. Taking this as an inspiration, we furthermore observe that design principles were discussed and applied during the design of the first mainstream programming languages such as Fortran and C (McKeeman, 1974; Hoare, 1973; Wirth, 1974; Cheatham, 1997). For example, Wirth (1974) explains features of Algol 60 and how they help to provide the simplicity of this language. Later work on principles and programming languages provided a perspective how language features can be used to satisfy principles (Butcher & Zedan, 1991; Booch, 1994; Finkel, 1996). The exceptional work of Booch (1994) details how principles like abstraction, encapsulation, and modularity are realized in the C++ programming language, which is very helpful to understand and apply these principles.

Specifically considering DSL, we see that most existing DSL case studies (Groote et al., 1995; Thibault et al., 1997; Barreto et al., 2002; Agosta & Pelosi, 2007; Dinkelaker & Mezini, 2008; Bennett et al., 2006; Havelund et al., 2010) do not discuss design properties or principles. Only some works (Atkins et al., 1999; Oliveira et al., 2009; Bentley, 1986) explicitly talk of principles: Atkins et al. (1999) names abstraction and restriction, Oliveira et. al (2009) names abstraction, high-level, and expressiveness, and Bentley (1986) considers similarity, extensibility, and openness. However, in these works, the principles are only defined, not explained how to achieve them.

We understand that principles are important guidelines to design and implement a DSL. Based on the existing work, we see the research need to clearly define DSL properties and refine them to principles that can be followed during designing the DSL.

Section Summary

A DSL provides domain-specific notations and abstractions. In order to implement a DSL on top of a host language, techniques must be applied that exploit syntactical variations of the host and provide a well-scoped declaration of its semantics. However, to communicate and plan the design of a DSL, host language independent patterns need to be defined. Each pattern identifies a common problem and solution, which can be implemented with host language specific techniques. Of equal importance is to regard the properties of a DSL and to formulate them as principles. Principles are guidelines that form the DSL development. We realize the application of principles in DSL design by identifying how each pattern contributes to a design goal that is related with a principle.

DESIGN PRINCIPLES

Design principles are guidelines how to develop a DSL. Each principle embodies one or several well-known characteristic of a DSL. To define our principles, this section begins with a listing of properties and principles that are mentioned in the related literature. We consider not only DSLs, but also work about programming languages because, as we defined, a DSL is a programming language too. We group and cluster these results to derive six essential principles.

DSL Properties and Principles

Existing literature has contributed a large number of properties and principles for programming languages as well as for domain specific languages. To show the diversity of definitions, we provide a list of explanations from the literature, and afterwards refine and consolidate this to six principles.

- **DSL Properties**
    - **Orthogonality:** Features of the language are unrelated of each other (Bentley, 1986)
    - **Generality:** Use one operation of the language for several purposes (Bentley, 1986)
    - **Parsimony/Small:** Delete unneeded operations from the language (Bentley, 1986); the language provides only essential features and concepts of the domain (Oliveira et al., 2009); "a restricted suite of notations and abstractions" (van Deursen et al., 2000, p. 2)
    - **Completeness:** The language should describe all objects of interest (Bentley, 1986)

    - **Similarity:** The language should be as suggestive as possible (Bentley, 1986)
    - **Extensibility:** The language should not be closed, but can grow in the future (Bentley, 1986)
    - **Openness:** The language should allow the user to escape into his known tools (Bentley, 1986)
    - DSL Principles
    - **Simplicity:** Keep your language simple and small to facilitate maintenance for developers and learnability for users (Bentley, 1986)
    - **Abstraction:** Define the objects and their operations according to the domain (Bentley, 1986); hide the operational semantics of the entities by providing high-level entities (Oliveira et al., 2009); provide "high-level entities and relationships that fit the domain closely" (Atkins et al., 1999, p. 1)
    - **Linguistic Structure:** Define your languages' syntax as a "trade-off between naturalness of expression and ease of implementation" (Bentley, 1986, p. 720)
    - **Restriction:** Restrict the language's expressiveness to aid automatic analysis (Atkins et al., 1999)
    - **Expressiveness:** The DSLs "notation helps the user to create mappings between the program and problem domain concepts" (Oliveira et al., 2009, p. 4)
- **Programming Language Properties**
    - **Abstraction:** "An abstraction denotes the essential characteristics of an object that distinguish it from all other kinds of objects and thus provides crisply defined conceptual boundaries, relative to the perspective of the viewer" (Booch, 1994, p. 38)
    - **Encapsulation:** "The process of compartmentalizing the elements of an abstraction that constitute its structure and behavior; encapsulation serves to separate the contractual interface of an abstraction and its implementation" (Booch, 1994, p.47)
    - **Modularity:** "The property of a system that has been decomposed into a set of cohesive and loosely coupled modules" (Booch, 1994, p. 54)
    - **Hierarchy:** "The ranking or ordering of abstractions" (Booch, 1994, p. 56)
    - **Typing:** "The enforcement of the class of an object, such, that objects of different types may not be interchanged, or at the most, they may be interchanged only in very restricted ways" (Booch, 1994, p. 63)
    - **Concurrency:** "The property that distinguishes an active object from one that is not active" (Booch, 1994, p. 71)
    - **Persistence:** "The property of an object through which its existence transcends time (i.e. the object continues to exist after its creator ceases to exist) and/or space (i.e. the objects location moves from the address space in which it was created)" (Booch, 1994, p. 74)
- **Programming Language Principles**
    - **Abstraction:** "Mechanisms should be available to allow recurring patterns in the code to be factored out" (Butcher & Zedan, 1991, p. 91); "There should be a way to factor out recurring patterns." (Finkel, 1996, p.4)
    - **Simplicity:** "The language should be based upon as few "basic concepts" as possible" (Butcher & Zedan, 1991,

p. 91); "there should be as few basic concepts as possible" (Finkel, 1996, p. 3)

- **Clarity:** "The mechanisms used by the language should be well defined, and the outcome of a particular section of code easily predicted" (Butcher & Zedan, 1991, p. 91); "Mechanisms should be well defined, and the outcome of code should be easily predictable "(Finkel, 1996)
- **Regularity/Uniformity:** "The basic concepts of the language should be applied consistently and universally" (Butcher & Zedan, 1991, p. 91); the languages' "basic concepts should be applied consistently", which means to use the concepts in different expression contexts without changing their form (Finkel, 1996, p. 3)
- **Orthogonality:** "Independent functions should be controlled by independent mechanisms" (Butcher & Zedan, 1991, p. 93); provide independent mechanisms for independent functions, do not mingle their workings (Finkel, 1996)

Discussion and Mapping

In Figure 1, we map and cluster all the mentioned properties and principles.

In our understanding, a property describes a desired characteristic of a concept. Whether the concept has the property or not can be measured by the existence of the desired characteristic. A principle is either a fundamental assumption that influences the perception of a concept, or it is a rule that can be applied to achieve a certain desired characteristic. With this understanding, we make

Figure 1. Mapping and clustering the principles and patterns

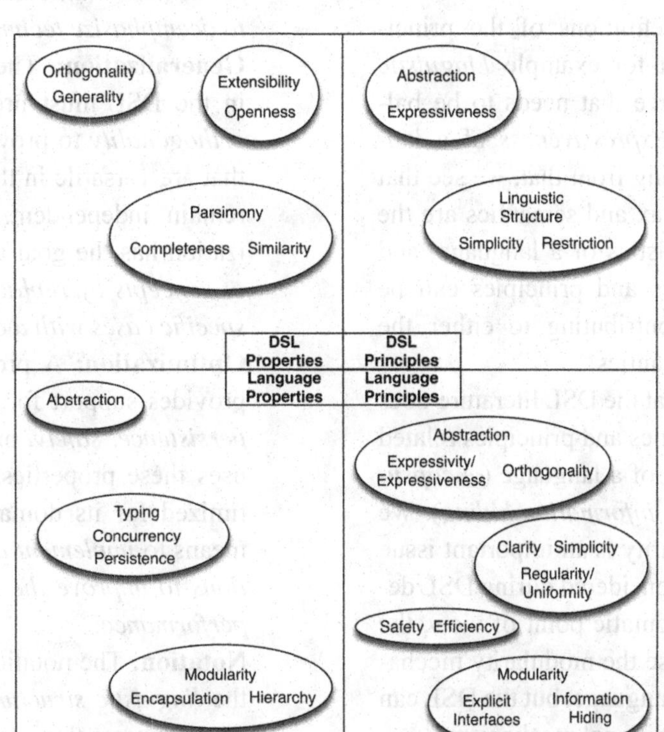

the following observations regarding the use of principles and patterns in the related work:

- There is a misconception between the understanding of properties and of principles. For example, *abstraction* is mentioned as a principle of DSLs and programming languages ("denotes the essential characteristics of an object" (Booch, 1994, p. 38)), as well as it is named as a property of programming languages (hide the details of basic concepts (Finkel, 1996)). Similarily, *modularity* is both a property and a principle of programming languages.
- The properties and principles are forming natural clusters. For example, the syntax of a DSL can be described with *Linguistic Structure*, *Simplicity*, *Restriction* on the principle side and with *Parsimony*, *Completeness*, and *Similarity* on the other side. Similarly, *Abstraction* provides *Expressivity/Expressiveness* and *Orthogonality*.
- Regarding the definitions of the principles, we see that for example *Linguistic Structure* is a force that needs to be balanced with the *Expressiveness* of a language. Generalizing from that, we see that a language's syntax and semantics are the driving characteristics of a language, and that all properties and principles can be considered as contributing to either the syntax or the semantics.
- It is interesting that the DSL literature does not define properties and principles related to the modularity of a language (*encapsulation, hierarchy, information hiding*). We think that modularity is an important issue that needs to be considered during DSL design. From a pragmatic point of view, the DSL can just reuse the modularity mechanisms of its host language, but the DSL can also introduce additional mechanisms.

In total, we identified 22 unique properties/principles. As we already showed in Figure 1, they naturally form cluster of similar concepts. However, in order to be useful for a DSL, we further need to restrict the amount of principles that developers need to remember. In psychological research it was discovered that, on average, humans can remember seven plus/minus two items at a time (Miller, 1956). Therefore, we strive for not more than seven principles. When we consider the meaning of the 22 unique properties/principles, we can group and consolidate them to the following six principles:

- **Abstraction:** *Abstractions* are entities that deemphasize technical details and represent a concept from the domain or from the programming language to be used. Abstractions need to be suitable to implement a wide range of programs and provide *expressiveness/expressivity*. Therefore, the abstraction principle defines the goal to *implement domain concepts as abstractions to deemphasize technical details*.
- **Generalization:** The available concepts in the DSL must provide *generality* and *orthogonality* to provide unique functions that are versatile in their combinations yet remain independent. Therefore, generalization has the goal to *reduce the amount of concepts by replacing a group of more specific cases with a common case*.
- **Optimization:** A programming language provides support for *typing*, *concurrency*, *persistence*, *safety*, and *efficiency*. A DSL uses these properties/principles to be optimized for its domain, which especially means to *implement algorithmic optimizations to improve the DSL's computational performance*.
- **Notation:** The notation of a DSL provides the *linguistic structure* with which developers express the intent of their programs. The notation should be designed for *par-*

simony/simplicity, *similarity* and *clarity*. Therefore, this principle's goal is to *represent domain-specific concepts with suitable, clear distinguished entities*.

- **Compression:** The expressions of a DSL need to provide *restriction* of essential notations and support *regularity/uniformity* to be used consistently in different usage context. Therefore, the goal of this principle is to *remove tokens and keywords that have no meaning in the domain*.
- **Absorption:** A DSL should not always require to make all expressions explicit. *Completeness* and *parsimony/simplicity* can be provided by implicitly assuming certain properties to be set in the DSL. Therefore, this principle's meaning is to *absorb domain commonalities into the DSL expressions to facilitate DSL usage*.

There is no fixed order, but we can define the relationships between these principles as follows: The DSL's syntax is built to express domain-specific *abstractions* with suitable *notations*. First, the necessary concepts are *generalized* out of similar concepts in the domain, and domain-specific *optimizations* are applied for their behavior. Then, the resulting language can be further *compressed* and obvious expressions *absorbed* into the DSL.

Formulating the DSL Design Principles

Based on our observations, we now define the principles and further describe their effects on DSLs.

Abstraction

Goal: Implement domain concepts as abstractions to deemphasize technical details.

DSLs provide two types of abstraction: They implement the relevant domain concepts and operations as entities that closely fit the domain (Atkins et al., 1999), and they provide the behavioral and structural abstractions of a programming language, like modules, classes, loops, or variables. A DSL can even extend the abstractions offered by its host language.

Generalization

Goal: Reduce the amount of concepts by replacing a group of more specific cases with a common case.

Generalization is a profound principle of any programming language because it gives the base abstractions the capability to be used in different, very specific contexts. Typically, such abstractions can be modeled as a hierarchy, for example in object-oriented languages, classes for representing numbers can be modeled in a hierarchy. The domain concepts naturally have a hierarchy too. According to this hierarchy, the most important concepts of the DSL should be generalized to retain the ability of representing more specific concepts. This also helps to achieve *Compression*.

Optimization

Goal: Implement algorithmic optimizations to improve the DSL's computational performance.

A DSL reuses its' host properties that support the optimization of its performance, such as concurrency and persistence. In addition, the DSL can provide domain optimizations by choosing suitable abstractions with respect to its host (Oliveira et al., 2009), such as data structures and efficient algorithms (Czarnecki & Eisenecker, 2000).

Notation

Goal: Represent domain-specific concepts with suitable, clear distinguished entities.

Clear, distinguishable entities and appropriate notations (van Deursen et al., 2000) define the notation of the DSL. An obvious limit is the syntactic variability of the host language. Some DSLs combine such variations to achieve a notation that does not any more represent it's host for providing the domain-specific constructs and keywords.

Compression

Goal: Remove keywords and tokens that have no meaning in the domain.

Simplifying expressions of the DSL or reducing the amount of keywords that needs to be used support compression. Also, the smaller the amount of concepts that needs to be included in the DSL, the smaller is the amount of needed constructs (Coplien, 1999). This restriction has several positive benefits. Programs written in the DSL can be better understood (Ladd & Ramming, 1994; Weinberg, 1971), and the constructs are better to maintain because the interactions between them are fewer. To further support compression, *Absorption* can be used too.

Absorption

Goal: Absorb domain commonalities into the DSL expressions to facilitate DSL usage.

A DSL provides a restricted amount of concepts and operations to express the developer's intent. In some cases, the explicit use of expressions to state the assumptions and concerns may not be necessary. By absorbing such assumptions and making them implicit in the expressions, developers can write more concise expressions without unneeded repetitions. This improves the implicit focused expressive power of a DSL (Tanter, 2008).

Section Summary

DSL design principles provide important guidelines to the development of DSLs. The extensive analysis on the related work on principles for programming languages and DSLs uncovered two important points. First, there is a misconception about the different of design principles and design properties. Second, among the 22 unique concepts, clusters of related concepts can be found. Based on such observations, we compressed the 22 principles/properties to 6 essential principles: Abstraction, generalization, and optimization, as well as Notation, Compression, and Absorptions.

In the next sections, we show how the principles are realized with the help of patterns

PATTERN STRUCTURE AND OVERVIEW

In this section, we explain the structure with which each pattern is presented, followed by a general overview to each pattern.

Pattern Structure

To facilitate learning our patterns, we provide a fixed structure that follows the conventional pattern structure (Gamma et al., 1997) as well as recent publications (Guerra et al., 2009; Correia et al., 2009; Zdun & Strembeck, 2009):

- **Name:** The name of the pattern.
- **Also Known As:** Lists a reference where a similar pattern, albeit not necessarily in the context of DSLs, is explained.
- **Problem:** Raises a question to the design of a DSL and explains the consequence of ignoring this problem.
- **Solution:** Explains the solution in one sentence, and for patterns adding to the syntax of the DSL, also shows an excerpt how this pattern's utilization looks like. Then, more details about the mechanisms behind applying this pattern are explained, and finally we give specific solution details and examples for the host languages Ruby, Python, and Scala.
- **Liabilities:** Explains potential pitfalls and tradeoffs when this pattern is applied.
- **Related Pattern:** Finally, a list of closely related patterns.

As we explained, it is important that the patterns are host language independent. Therefore, we explain the problem, the first part of the solution, and the liabilities independent of the host language. Host language specific implementation details for the three host languages Ruby, Python, and Scala are discussed in the second part of the solution. This further helps developers in such languages to immediately apply the pattern, as well as it gives developers who want to use another host language a point of reference from where they can learn and adapt the pattern implementation.

To illustrate the solution, we use a DSL that enables to declaratively express the setup and configuration of virtual servers in cloud computing environments (Günther et al., 2010). This DSL is implemented in Ruby, but for demonstration purposes, we also show how it could be implemented in Python and Scala. The following listing in Box 1 shows example expressions of this DSL.

These expressions have the following meaning:

- **Line 1–15:** To setup a machine, we use a constructor that sets the machine name and passes other configuration options in the form of a block.
- **Line 2–4:** Configures the type, owner, and the operating system of this machine.
- **Line 5–11:** A nested block that specifies the hypervisor-specific options, like the Amazon[1] machine image (ami) id and its source, the size, the security group (the security group determines the available services and the open ports of the machine, such as SSH on port 22), and the private key used to access this machine via SSH.

Box 1.

```
1 app_server = Machine "Application Server" do
2 type:ec2
3 owner "sebastian.guenther@vub .ac.be"
4 os:debian
5 hypervisor do
6 ami "ami dcf615b5"
7 source "alestic / debian -5.0 lenny -base -2009..."
8 size: m1_small
9 securitygroup "default"
10 private_key "ec2 -us east"
11 end
12 hostname "admantium.com"
13 monitor:cpu,:ram
14 bootstrap!
15 end
16
17 deploy "Apache" do
18 enroll " Server / Apache ",:on => app_server + aux_server do
19 #...
20 end
21 end
```

- **Line 12:** The hostname of the machine that is used inside the network.
- **Line 13:** Expresses to monitor the CPU and RAM usage of this machine.
- **Line 14:** Finally an expression to install basic software.
- **Line 17–21:** This expressions has the intention of deploying an Apache webserver on the newly created server.
- **Line 18:** This line provides additional configuration of the software packages, for example a choice between two libraries that provide the same capabilities. There are no such options for Apache, and that's why we just use an expression to insyall the Apache server on the application server as well as an auxiliary server for providing live backups.

Pattern Overview

We differentiate the patterns into foundation patterns, notation patterns, and abstraction patterns. Figure 2 gives a graphical overview to the patterns, Table 1 points to the page where the pattern is detailed, and the following subsections briefly list each pattern and the problem it addresses.

Figure 2. Pattern overview

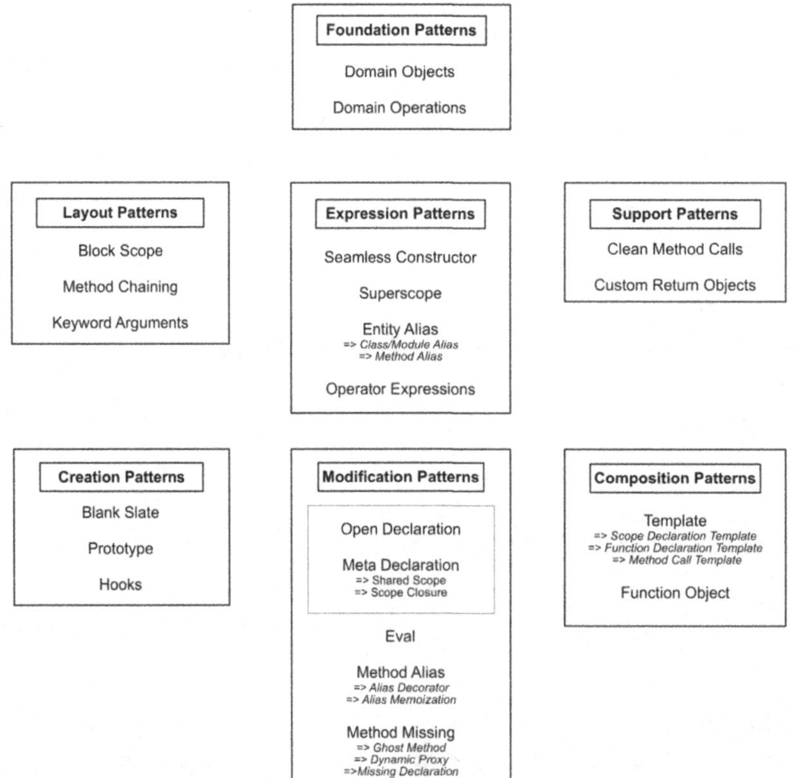

Table 1. Page references to the DSL design patterns

Pattern			Page
Foundation		Domain Objects	15
		Domain Operations	16
Notation	Layout	Block Scope	17
		Method Chaining	19
		Keyword Arguments	21
	Expression	Seamless Constructor	22
		Superscope	23
		Entity Alias	24
		Operator Expressions	26
	Support	Clean Method Calls	28
		Custom Return Objects	30
Abstraction	Creation	Blank Slate	31
		Prototype	33
		Hook	34
	Composition	Template	35
		Function Object	37
	Modification	Open Declaration	38
		Meta Declaration	39
		Eval	41
		Method Alias	42
		Method Missing	43

Foundation Patterns

Foundation patterns are the very first pattern to apply, they explain how the domain concepts, attributes, and operations are implemented as entities.

- **DOMAIN OBJECTS:** How to implement suitable abstractions and representations of the domain entities and their relationships?
- **DOMAIN OPERATIONS:** How to implement suitable representations of the domain operations?

Notation Patterns

The notation patterns structure the host's syntactic capabilities to form expressions that provide the domain-specific notations. They are structured into three groups.

- **Layout Patterns:** Provide the general layout of the DSL, either as vertical blocks or complex, horizontal expressions.
  - **BLOCK SCOPE:** Has your DSL a flat scope where you mangle objects together, or is it difficult to express hierarchies of domain concepts that you create and combine to complex expressions?
  - **METHOD CHAINING:** Do you use too much command-like expressions that fail to represent the relation of different domain concepts or do not read fluently?
  - **KEYWORD ARGUMENTS:** Does your DSL suffer from passing too many arguments to functions, confusing the user about the parameter's order and their meaning?
- **Expression Patterns:** These patterns target the representation of expressions. Their goal is to simplify and straighten the representation of DOMAIN OPERATIONS, or to rename built-in or library-added objects and methods so that they have a more domain-related name.
  - **SEAMLESS CONSTRUCTOR:** How to avoid explicit object instantiation when this is not a domain concern?
  - **SUPERSCOPE:** How to refer to objects that exist in another scope without introducing cumbersome and cluttering variable references?
  - **ENTITY ALIAS:** How to rename built-in classes and external libraries to be consistent with the domain?

        - *Class/Module Alias:* Alias a class or module.
        - *Method Alias:* Provide an alias for a method.
    - **OPERATOR EXPRESSIONS:** How to use operators like +, *, & in DSL expressions?
- **Support Patterns:** Further contribute to the efforts of the other patterns with unique effects to simplify expressions.
    - **CLEAN METHOD CALLS:** How to improve the readability of a DSL that is full of clutter from parentheses and other literals that are not helpful for the domain?
    - **CUSTOM RETURN OBJECTS:** How to overcome the limited vocabulary for accessing data in multiple structured objects?

Abstraction Patterns

Abstraction patterns help to implement and incorporate the DSL's semantics and abstractions into the host language. They are structured into three groups too.

- **Creation Patterns:** These patterns explain how to initially create new objects with properties that are different from common objects.
    - **BLANK SLATE:** How to provide objects with a minimal set of methods so that arbitrarily named methods can be added?
    - **PROTOTYPE:** How to create new objects without using the instantiation process, for saving computational resources or for defining classes outside of the host language's rigid class structure?
    - **HOOKS:** How to introduce more domain-specific behavior at predefined program execution places like class, method, and attribute declaration?
- **Composition Patterns:** Are concerned with the declaration and instantiation of new objects and thereby reuse functionality that is already available in the program.
    - **TEMPLATE:** How to provide easily mutable code representations that facilitate runtime creation, modification, and execution for constant adaptation of the DSL?
        - *Scope Declaration Template:* Declaration of modules and classes.
        - *Method Declaration Template:* Declaration of method definitions.
        - *Method Call Template:* Declaration of method calls.
    - **FUNCTION OBJECT:** How to represent the complete (defined) application behavior in one uniform form for arbitrary composition of new behavior?
- **Modification Patterns:** Are concerned with taking an existing object and modifying it to provide more domain-specific behavior.
    - **OPEN DECLARATION:** How to extend all built-in and application-specific classes at runtime?
    - **META DECLARATION:** How to provide powerful customizations to modules, classes, and methods?
        - *Shared Scope*: Share the scope of multiple declarations between each other, providing access to local variables for including them in declarations.
        - *Scope Closure*: Conserve local variables in declarations, completely hiding the variables from any outside access.

- **EVAL:** How to execute any code representation at any scope of the program to modify it arbitrarily?
- **METHOD ALIAS:** How to transparently change the behavior of an existing method while preserving the old behavior?
  - *Alias Decorator*: Add functionality around an existing method.
  - *Alias Memoization*: Replace a method implementation with a fixed return value to save computational time.
- **METHOD MISSING:** Your DSL needs to react to method calls that are not defined at starting time, or it needs to dispatch the actual method call to a specific place in the system?
  - *Ghost Method*: Depending on the method's name, return a value to the caller that simulates a complete method call.
  - *Dynamic Proxy*: Forward the method call to another module or class.
  - *Missing Declaration*: Check the method name and define methods on the fly.

FOUNDATION PATTERNS

The foundation of a DSL are its DOMAIN OBJECTS and DOMAIN OPERATIONS, they form the skeleton of a DSL that is then further substantiated through introducing the other patterns.

Pattern "Domain Objects"

Also known as Domain Model (Fowler, 2003) and Semantic Model (Fowler, 2010).

Problem

How to implement suitable abstractions and representation of the domain entities and their relationships?

Without these abstractions, there is no DSL.

Solution

Define well-scoped classes and constants that represent your domain concepts as demonstrated in Box 2.

Today's programming languages provide several means to define domain entities. The most suitable representation of domain concepts is to use classes. First, they form well-scoped entities in the program that define their own namespace. Second, inside this namespace, variables can be used to record state and behavior. Third, through explicitly or implicitly referring to other entities, the relationships can be represented conveniently. And finally, instances can be created from such classes with which the creation, modification, and eventually destruction of concepts can be represented.

Regarding the different host languages, textbooks about the specific programming languages provides the details about classes, attribute, and relationship definition. We do not need to repeat that here, but instead want to raise typical object-oriented design questions (Booch, 1994; Larman, 2003) that are also applicable to DOMAIN OBJECTS.

Box 2.

```
machine_record = ["Application Server"]
```

↓

```
Machine "Application Server" do
#...
end
```

- How to represent the domain concepts?
  - When several objects with the same data structures and behavior are needed, use classes.
  - When singletons are needed, use abstract classes or modules.
  - When similar objects with small structural differences are needed, then use class-based inheritance.
  - Define the objects at their respective namespace, either as globally visible entities or inside dedicated packages.
- How to represent attributes?
  - When the data needs to be accessed globally, use constants.
  - When several objects need to share some data, use class or module-based variables.
  - When objects need individual data, use instance variables.
  - Define all variables with a suitable data type, and use visibility modifiers to control which data is public accessible.
- How to represent relationships between the objects?
  - When the domain concepts have a natural hierarchy, use inheritance and subtyping.
  - When associations between structurally different entities are needed, store them as variables.

Design Goals

- **Abstraction:** Represent domain entities as objects by concentrating on their essential properties and provide the means to ensure their consistency.
- **Generalization:** Reduce the amount of entities and provide a clear hierarchical representation of the domain concepts through thoughtful inheritance relationships.
- **Notation:** Provide intuitive names, attributes, and methods that convey the original meaning of the domain concepts for the DSL's key objects.
- **Absorption:** Provide constructors and attribute setters that implicitly capture the essential properties, and provide optional setters for other properties.

Liabilities

- Depending on the used host language, the properties of classes or modules may be too restricted to adequately represent the concepts.

Related Patterns

- **DOMAIN OPERATIONS:** Depending on the DSL's syntax, implement some DOMAIN OPERATIONS in the DOMAIN OBJECTS.

Pattern "Domain Operations"

Problem

How to implement suitable representations of the domain operations?

Often, the operations are particularly required to give the DSL additional syntactic means to represent their conventions.

Solution

Define methods that set, read, or associate data to represent the domain operations as demonstrated in Box 3.

Following the declaration of DOMAIN OBJECTS, declaring the DOMAIN OPERATIONS is the next vital step. These operations closely interact with the DOMAIN OBJECTS and each other: They create or destroy objects, they set or read values, and they validate and optimize the

Box 3.

```
machine_record.set_attributes ("ec2", "sebastian.guenther@vub .ac.be")
↓
Machine "Application Server" do
type: ec2
  owner "sebastian.guenther@vub .ac.be"
  #...
end
```

objects. Some operations might even modify essential methods of the host language itself.

Despite the behavior, the scope where a method is declared is of equal importance. The scope can be *global*, *namespace-specific*, and *object-specific*. The choice which scope to take is based on its principal behavior: While the creation and modification of a large quantity of domain-objects is global, the modification of individual values is specific to the object. The global scope is especially helpful for methods that need to be closely integrated with the host language expressions. In our experience, it is difficult to find the correct scope for methods upfront, and modifications in the course of the DSL's evolution are very likely.

Design Goals

- **Abstraction:** Implement domain functions as operations that process and modify domain objects for representing domain behavior.
- **Generalization:** Overload methods to be useable in different variable contexts.
- **Optimization:** Implement domain-specific optimization algorithms.
- **Notation:** Provide clearly distinguished methods that represent the domain operations.
- **Absorption:** Express implicit behavior by absorbing domain commonalities into method execution.

Liabilities

- The intent of each operation needs to be clearly defined by its name, or the method may confuse DSL users.
- Methods should operate on well-defined properties of objects only, not on local variables that may have unexpected values.

Related Patterns

- DOMAIN OBJECTS: DOMAIN OPERATIONS are implemented in DOMAIN OBJECTS or in namespace entities.

Section Summary

The foundation patterns provide the essential building blocks of a DSL. DOMAIN OBJECTS represent the required domain concepts and implement their relationships as entities of a program. The DOMAIN OPERATIONS represent the behavior of status changes in the domain, which is the reason behind objects modifying each other to represent different states of a runtime domain representation. Now, the notation and the abstraction patterns help to define a clear syntax for forming expressions and provide the semantic details of implementing the behavior and integrating it with the behavior of the host language's built-in entities.

NOTATION PATTERNS

The notation of a DSL needs to reflect the domain clearly by offering a readable yet powerful syntax. To support these goals, we present several notation patterns that are grouped into three areas. First, the *layout patterns* provide the overall structure of the DSL. Second, the *expression patterns* provide syntactic alternatives for expressions, especially for method calls, in order for a more domain-specific notation. And finally, the *support patterns* further help to provide clearer expressions.

Layout Patterns

Layout patterns are providing the general layout of the DSLs. After applying these patterns, individual expressions are further designed with variation and support patterns.

Pattern "Block Scope"

Also known as Nested Closure (Fowler, 2010).

Problem

Has your DSL a flat scope where you mangle objects together, or is it difficult to express hierarchies of domain concepts that you create and combine to complex expressions?

A flat scope hides the context and natural connections between expressions, making it hard to spot what the expressions actually do.

Solution

Define one object that opens the block, and include all expressions that belong to the object's context as presented in Box 4.

A BLOCK SCOPE is defined by the visual arrangement of expressions in the form of an indented block. Semantically, the outer parts of the block provide a context in which the expressions of the inner part are executed. Therefore, the receiver of the inner expressions becomes clear, which allows to implicitly assume information that would otherwise need to be passed as additional arguments to isolated expressions. Putting such expressions inside a block provides both syntactic as well as semantic grouping. In the following listing in Box 5, we show example expressions for each host language.

In Ruby, blocks can be built with the `do...end` notation or curly braces. The code contained inside this block has two distinguishing properties. First, it encloses its surrounding scope and can serve as a closure for specific execution states. Second, it can be executed in another context, using the variables from the surrounding lexical scope.

Box 4.

```
machine = Machine.new("Admantium.com")
machine.owner("sebastian.guenther@vub .ac.be")
resource_bundle = Array.new(Resource.new("CPU"), Resource.new("RAM"))
machine.set_monitored_resources(resource_bundle)
```

↓

```
Machine "Admantium.com" do
owner "sebastian.guenther@vub .ac.be"
   monitor "CPU", "RAM"
end
```

Box 5.

```
# Ruby
Machine “Admantium.com” do
  owner “sebastian.guenther@vub .ac.be”
end

# Python
with Machine(“Admantium.com”) as machine:
  machine.owner(“sebastian.guenther@vub.ac.be”)

# Scala
Machine (“Admantium.com”) configure {
  owner(“sebastian.guenther@vub .ac.be”)
}
```

In Python, context managers can be used for introducing blocks with the notation `with... as`. Context managers are objects that define the special methods `__enter__` and `__exit__`, which are executed upon opening and exiting a block. Opposed to Ruby, fully-qualified method calls still have to be used inside the block.

In Scala, blocks are introduced with curly braces. They are used to group similar expressions, for example method declarations for classes. They can be applied in method calls too, where the return value of a block is passed as an argument to the function that "opens" the block. In the shown example, the result of `owner(“sebastian.guenther”)` is passed to `configure`.

Design Goals

- **Notation:** Group related expressions together for a vertical code layout and syntactically express the hierarchy of objects as indented blocks of code.
- **Absorption:** Absorb the most relevant execution information as a closure and use it later to infer contextual information.
- **Compression:** Remove fully-qualified method calls inside a block, and let the execution context be determined by the object or method receiving the block.
- **Abstraction:** Execute the expressions contained in a block in another location where they were defined in.

Liabilities

- Possibility of code injection: If the block object is dynamically constructed with input from the users, malicious users could exploit detailed knowledge of the application to read its data or perform file system operations. However, some programming language, such as Ruby, offer good support for safe levels as well as tainted and trusted objects (Thomas et al., 2007), which reduces this threat's potential.

Related Patterns

- **KEYWORD ARGUMENTS:** Alternatively to the vertical code layout provided with BLOCK SCOPE, code can be arranged hori-

Box 6.

```
app = application("Apache")
app.set_server("Admantium.com")
app.deploy
↓
deploy application Apache on server "Admantium.com"
```

zontally by suitable grouping and naming of arguments.

Pattern "Method Chaining"

Also known as Method Chaining (Fowler, 2010).

Problem

Do you use too much command-like expressions that fail to represent the relation of different domain concepts or do not read fluently?

Excessive command-like expressions make programs difficult to read and understand.

Solution

Combine repetitive methods in one sentence-like expression as demonstrated in Box 6.

Sentence-like expressions can be designed by chaining methods with appropriate names together in one line. This provides a tight coupling between the expression parts, thereby clarifying the meaning and enhancing readability. Along the chain, methods take up one of the following roles:

- **Context Provider:** Set the objects of the expression by storing them in one or several variables of the surrounding scope.
- **Referrer:** Methods that just refer to specific objects.
- **Glue:** Methods that only serve to syntactically ease the expression.

The methods are required to either operate on the same directly passed data or implicitly on data visible within the scope where the methods are executed.

Dependent on the host language, a method chain can take different forms. Because Ruby does not require fully-qualified method calls in the form of "receiver.method", the "." can be left out, allowing to chain method calls together that look like language keywords. In Python, chaining method calls both implies to use the dot notation between method calls and to use parentheses, such as in `method1().method2()`. In Scala, METHOD CHAINING requires a mix of class and method declarations to work. See the following listing in Box 7 for examples.

Box 7.

```
deploy Apache on server "Admantium.com"              # Ruby
deploy(Apache).on().server("Admantium.com")            # Python
deploy Apache on server("Admantium.com")              # Scala
```

Design Goals

- **Notation:** Express the domain in a more natural language like style by chaining method calls and their return values together, which also provides a horizontal code layout.
- **Compression:** Use chained methods to transform an input value step-by-step, adopting a more functional programming oriented style instead of imperative expressions.

Liabilities

- Requires adding several "glue" methods to the surrounding namespace, which possibly pollutes the namespace with empty methods.
- Limited options to check the correctness of the chain, and especially to check the correct order of called arguments.
- Limited applicability to modify existing libraries because of the required extensive modifications.
- If used with an existing library, requires changing method internals.
- The Law of Demeter (Lieberherr & Holland, 1989) states that methods should have a limited access to other methods and the object in which they are defined. A DSL that uses METHOD CHAINING requires a careful design choice to localize the method declarations in one scope (see DOMAIN OPERATIONS) and should not pollute the global namespace that would break the Law of Demeter.

Related Patterns

- **KEYWORD ARGUMENTS:** Both METHOD CHAINING and KEYWORD ARGUMENTS provide a horizontal code layout. KEYWORD ARGUMENTS are especially suitable when a complex expression can be refactored to nested subphrases. The additional benefit, as opposed to METHOD CHAINING, is that no "glue" methods are needed.
- **BLOCK SCOPE:** Instead of a horizontal code layout, BLOCK SCOPE provides a vertical layout that is especially useful to show hierarchies of objects. This pattern is recommended when very complex expressions need to be structured, where the block-like structure helps to disseminate the information. Of course, individual lines in BLOCK SCOPE expressions can be designed with METHOD CHAINING.

Pattern "Keyword Arguments"

Also known as Named Arguments (Perrotta, 2010) and Literal Map (Fowler, 2010).

Problem

Does your DSL suffer from passing too many arguments to functions, confusing the user about the parameter's order and their meaning?

If the order of arguments is not clear, hard to track bugs might occur that frustrate the user.

Solution

Define key-value pairs with the key as the argument's meaning and the value as the argument's value as demonstrated in Box 8.

The relationship between a key and a value can be used for different purposes in a DSL. When executing DOMAIN OPERATIONS, each pair can document a configuration option by explaining the meaning of each argument. This can be used to show for example how to execute an operation or to show the availability of additional arguments. Another use is to increase the

Box 8.

```
deploy_application("Apache", "Admantium", "default", "restart")
↓
deploy_application: application_name => "Apache",
        : server                   => "Admantium",
        : configuration           => "default",
        : server_action           => "restart"
```

Box 9.

```
weather:temperature => 17,:humidity => 25            # Ruby
weather(temperature =17, humidity=25)          # Python
weather("temperature" -> 17, "humidity" -> 25) # Scala
```

readability of the language, using additional terms of the domain that are added to the context of a method.

Multiple arguments can be passed by using hash expressions: The key denotes the argument's meaning and the value is the argument's value. In some languages, the key-value pairs can be expressed along several source code lines, and therefore provide a similar layout than BLOCK SCOPE.

The following listing shows different notations for KEYWORD ARGUMENTS in the analyzed host languages. Ruby hashes use the notation `key => value`, and they can be created as inline arguments to method calls. In Python, methods can be defined to receive `dict` (short for dictionary) objects. Such methods can be called with a hash like notation. In Scala, methods that receive tuples can be used, where the arguments form a sequence that can be parsed conveniently with case matchers as presented in Box 9.

Design Goals

- **Notation:** Avoid complex object interfaces with methods that receive more than two parameters, and avoid the ambiguity of putting long lists of arguments in the right order.
- **Notation:** Use keyword-value pairs as relationship declarations, to state mappings, or to declaratively express the desired system state.
- **Absorption:** From the list of passed arguments, infer implicit information for providing specialized behavior.
- **Compression:** Compress several singular method calls to a set of key-value pairs passed to one method.
- **Generalization:** By using multiple dispatch of arguments, the existing methods can serve as a focus point when adding new behavior.

Liabilities

- Complex combinations of parsing arguments and error checking can make the method declaration cumbersome.

Related Patterns

- **BLOCK SCOPE:** The horizontal code layout for key-value pairs can also be represented as a vertical stacking by using

Box 10.

```
machine = new Machine ("Admantium.com")
↓
machine = Machine "Admantium.com"
```

BLOCK SCOPE. Using a BLOCK SCOPE instead would mean to implement several additional methods to handle the argument passing.

- **METHOD CHAINING:** For an alternative horizontal code layout, represent the key-value pairs as methods inside a chain. However, likewise to BLOCK SCOPE, additional methods have to be implemented.

EXPRESSION PATTERNS

Expressions patterns target the representation of expressions. Their goal is to simplify and straighten the representation of DOMAIN OPERATIONS, or to rename built-in or library-added objects and methods so that they have a more domain-related name.

Pattern "Seamless Constructor"

Problem

How to avoid explicit object instantiation when this is not a domain concern?

In a DSL, using keywords that are too tight to the host language may not fit the domain: It is more desirable to automatically create instances, for example like the expression "42" that returns an integer object.

Solution

Use a custom method that receives the instance parameters to tarnish the object instantiation as demonstrated in Box 10.

Normally, keywords like `new` need to be used to create objects. In a DSL, the intention behind this keyword may conflict with the domain meaning. Therefore, we need a way to create objects yet removing the keyword from this operation.

The SEAMLESS CONSTRUCTOR can be implemented in two ways. First, by using a method with a similar, but not the same name, that receives instantiation values and returns an instance. Second, by using the very same symbol of the class where lexical scoping rules allow it.

Ruby allows to define objects and methods with the same name. Whether the method or the object is used depends on the context of the expression, especially in METHOD CHAINING.

In Python, object instantiation is always seamless: By combining the class symbol with (empty) parentheses, a new object is created. This can be simplified even more: A method call can be bound to any variable, so that even the parentheses can be removed in this case.

Scala provides two abstractions that can be used for the intent of the SEAMLESS CONSTRUCTOR. The first option is to use case classes. Such classes typically serve as data containers – instances are created without using any keyword, just by passing the instantiation parameters. The second option is to use the same symbol for the method and for the class. Scala's type system has no trouble to distinguish the two.

Design Goals

- **Notation:** Obtain a more fluently readable DSL by omitting the need for explicit keywords to create instances.
- **Absorption:** Avoid the technical details of creating new instances by absorbing this intention into the DSL.

Liabilities

- Lexical scoping determines whether the class or the method is meant when using the symbol.
- Method names written in capital letters violate naming conventions for example in Ruby and Python, which could lead to confusion if not properly explained.

Related Patterns

- **ENTITY ALIAS:** While SEAMLESS CONSTRUCTOR totally hides the intent to create instances, ENTITY ALIAS makes the intent visible, but allows to use a more domain-specific keyword.

Pattern "Superscope"

Problem

How to refer to objects that exist in another scope without introducing cumbersome and cluttering variable references?

Such references hamper the readability of the DSL and can confuse it's users with semantic details.

Solution

Use symbols or strings as references to objects, and implement the semantics to refer to the correct object in this method as presented in Box 11.

The correct scoping of DSL expressions depends on the level of integration between DSL and other host language code. Putting the DSL expressions inside a separate scope is usually the safest way of interoperability. However, explicitly stating scope-related information when accessing DOMAIN OBJECTS or DOMAIN OPERATIONS reduces the readability of those expressions. Therefore, we need a mechanism that allows the DSL to implicitly refer to other scopes.

Box 11.

```
deploy SoftwarePackage.fetch("Apache") do
#...
end
```

↓

```
deploy: Apache do
#...
end
```

This pattern essentially consists of two parts. The first part is to find a convenient type that is used to refer to objects. This can be a string, or – to save memory by not constantly creating new string objects – a fixed constant like a symbol in Ruby. The second part is the lookup mechanism that needs to be implemented. This mechanism needs to store in which namespace the actual objects reside, and it must prepare and manage erroneous references. These mechanisms are easy to implement in Ruby, Python, and Scala, and thus we refrain from giving more details.

The difference between SUPERSCOPE and a mere string argument is that a SUPERSCOPE represents a specific entity of the DSL which is not available in the current scope, while the latter may refer to entities that are not part of the DSL.

Design Goals

- **Notation:** Use indirect pointers instead of complex namespace-object expressions for better readability.
- **Compression:** Reduce long object reference strings by short and expressive ones.
- **Generalization:** Provide one declaration point in which the referred object can be replaced by another to facilitate the provision of specialized behavior.

Liabilities

- The lookup method needs to know the specific object references, which is a considerable factor in maintaining the DSL. Therefore, lookup methods should be defined in a global visible entity.
- When SUPERSCOPE arguments can be provided as external input to the DSL, they need to be checked carefully for preventing the access to prohibited resources.

Related Patterns

- **KEYWORD ARGUMENTS:** While the key provides the meaning, the value can be a SUPERSCOPE that refers to other entities.
- **METHOD CHAINING:** Some parts of the chain can be replaced by a SUPERSCOPE argument, which reduces the amount of required method declarations.
- **CUSTOM RETURN OBJECT:** The object that is referenced by a SUPERSCOPE can be further augmented for usage in yet another context.

Pattern "Entity Alias"

Problem

How to rename built-in classes and external libraries to be consistent with the domain?

For a tight integration of host language and DSL code, using appropriate names is crucial.

Solution

Declare modules, classes, and methods with domain-specific names that refer to the host language based type.

```
Machine("Admantium").eql? machine
↓
Machine("Admantium").should_be machine
```

Using domain-specific names for operation is an essential requirement that the DOMAIN OPERATIONS pattern emphasizes. When DSL and other host language code are integrated, the names of host language objects or operations may not express their domain intention. A mechanism to rename these objects and operation is required.

ENTITY ALIAS comes in three forms depending on what needs to be aliased: *Module Alias*, *Class Alias*, and *Method Alias* for the respective type. Such aliases can be used instead of their original name to better stay in the domain.

Aliases can be implemented with two principal solutions: By defining additional variables and constants that point to an object or method with a custom name, or by creating them with host language specific methods. All three analyzed host languages allow to build additional variables to point to entities. This is especially easy in Python because any class and method object can be referred from within the program. To implement a *Method Alias* in Ruby, the built-in method `alias` can be used.

Design Goals

- **Notation:** Change the name of existing modules, classes, and methods to a better, domain-specific name by providing an alias.
- **Abstraction**: Resolve name clashes when using multiple DSLs.

Liabilities

- Aliasing built-in methods can break compatibility with other libraries.
- Possible namespace conflict when executed globally.
- Sometimes, readability suffers if the used names are not obvious for other developers.

Box 12.

```
enroll "Webserver/Apache",:on => [app_server, aux_server]
↓
enroll "Webserver/Apache",:on => app_server + aux_server
```

Related Patterns

- **SEAMLESS CONSTRUCTOR:** If the intent to create instances should be completely hidden, then use SEAMLESS CONSTRUCTOR instead.
- **ALIAS METHOD:** This abstraction pattern is concerned with adding new behavior to built-in methods, but the same mechanism can be used for renaming functions.

Pattern "Operator Expressions"

Problem

How to use operators like +, *, & in DSL expressions?

For some DSLs, providing symbolic notations is essential to conform to the domain standards.

Solution

Define symbolic operators as method calls on objects as presented in Box 12.

Using common operator symbols in a DSL provides a convenient way to formulate short, concise expressions. Generic domains can benefit from operators to add, reduce, or filter a set of elements according to some criteria. Special domain can rely entirely on operations to express complex calculations, for example chemical formulas, interest rates for financial products, or an encryption algorithm. For these domains, OPERATOR EXPRESSIONS are an essential pattern.

In some common programming languages, operators are implemented as method calls on objects. In Ruby and Scala, method declarations that use the very symbol's name can be used, and Python uses special method names that refer to the symbol. Table 2, Table 3, and Table 4 list the available operator expressions of each language.

Design Goals

- **Notation:** Use intuitive symbols to express DSL behavior.
- **Compression:** Provide shorter alternatives for frequently used method keywords.
- **Generalization:** Provide different behavior for operator expressions by using multiple dispatch of arguments.

Liabilities

- Operator expressions are just normal method calls, so they need to take care of different argument types and more.

Table 2. Operator expressions – Available operators in Ruby (Flanagan & Matsumoto, 2008)

Operator	(Original) Operation
!	Boolean NOT
+ -	Unary plus and minus (defined with -@ or +@)
+ -	Addition (or concatenation), subtraction
**	Exponentiation
* / %	Multiplication, division, modulo
& | ^ ~	Bitwise AND, OR, XOR, and complement
<< >>	Bitwise shift-left (or append), bitwise shift-right
< <= >= >	Ordering
== === != =~ !~ <=>	Equality, pattern matching, comparison

Table 3. Operator expressions – available operators in Python (Lutz, 2009; Summerfield, 2010)

<table>
<tr><th>Operator</th><th>Method</th><th>(Original) Operation</th></tr>
<tr><td>+ -</td><td>__add__, __pos__, __sub__, __neg__</td><td>Addition, substraction (binary and unary</td></tr>
<tr><td>* **</td><td>__mul__, __pow__</td><td>Multiplication, power</td></tr>
<tr><td>%</td><td>__mod__</td><td>Modulo</td></tr>
<tr><td>// /</td><td>__floordiv__, __truediv__</td><td>Integer division and float division</td></tr>
<tr><td>& |</td><td>__and__, __or__</td><td>Logical “and” and “or”</td></tr>
<tr><td>< > <= >= == !=</td><td>__lt__, __gt__, __le__, __ge__, __eq__, __ne__</td><td>Comparison operators</td></tr>
<tr><td><< >> ~</td><td>__lshift__, __rshift__, __invert__</td><td>Bitwise shift and invert operations</td></tr>
</table>

Table 4. Operator expressions – available operators in Scala (Wampler & Payne, 2009)

<table>
<tr><th>Operator</th><th>(Original) Operation</th></tr>
<tr><td>= < ></td><td>Equality and comparison</td></tr>
<tr><td>+ - * /</td><td>Mathematical operators</td></tr>
<tr><td>\ |</td><td>Backslash and bar</td></tr>
<tr><td>! ? & :</td><td>Exclamation, question mark, ampersand and colon</td></tr>
<tr><td>% ^ @ # ~</td><td>Miscellaneous symbols</td></tr>
</table>

- Some operators are required to be defined in other applications or core library classes too.

Related Patterns

- **ENTITY ALIAS/METHOD ALIAS:** In some domains, OPERATOR EXPRESSION may seem inappropriate as part of the DSL. To obtain methods instead of the built-in operators, use an alias for defining the particular methods.

SUPPORT PATTERNS

Support patterns further contribute to the efforts of the other patterns with unique effects to simplify DSL expressions.

Pattern “Clean Method Calls”

Problem

How to improve the readability of a DSL that is full of clutter from parentheses and other literals that are not helpful for the domain?

By keeping the clutter in the DSL, the intent of expressions is veiled and too host language specific constructs make it difficult for domain expert to actually use the DSL.

Solution

Exploit ambiguous syntax of host languages to remove parentheses where it is possible.

```
Machine(“Application Server”) {
type(:ec2)
hypervisor() {
ami(“ami dcf615b5”)
}
}
```

↓

```
Machine “Application Server” do
type: ec2
hypervisor do
ami “ami-dcf615b5”
end
end
```

The clearer expressions are, the more easier it becomes for the writer to define and for the reader to understand DSL expressions. A common idiom in programming languages is the use of parentheses to denote method calls. Domain experts may not be accustomed to this syntax, so dropping them allows forming more readable domain expressions.

If and where parentheses can be dropped is very specific to a particular host language. In Ruby, most parentheses can be dropped from the expressions, except in some cases where lexical ambiguity forces the developer to use parentheses to distinguish method calls from variable/constant references. In Python, this pattern is only supported when OPERATOR EXPRESSIONS are used – they don't need parentheses to work. And in Scala, method call parentheses can be removed in two cases: When the method receives zero arguments, and in some cases when the argument passed to a method is used for calling a method on it again.

Despite parentheses, some host languages use other syntactic elements that can be removed or replaced. For example, Ruby allows closure objects to be defined either with the keywords `do...end` or with curly braces.

Design Goals

- **Notation:** Provide clear expressions that do not resemble their host language but look like DSL keywords.
- **Compression:** Remove parentheses, especially for nested method calls, to compress expressions.

Liabilities

- Sometimes, explicit knowledge about host language keywords and DSL keywords are more appropriate to understand the DSL completely.
- Lexical scoping determines the meaning of symbols, which may prevent certain forms of CLEAN METHOD.
- CALLS where using key-value pairs and blocks with curly parentheses could introduce syntactic errors.

Related Patterns

When available, CLEAN METHOD CALLS is often used and, being a support pattern, used in combination with all other patterns.

Pattern "Custom Return Objects"

Problem

How to overcome the limited vocabulary for accessing data in multiple structured objects?

Manually accessing array indexes is error-prone when the DSL changes and forces to use a syntax that may not be readable enough for the DSL.

Solution

Return objects with method-like accessors for their values to conveniently use them in expressions.

```
1 server("Admantium")["ip"]
↓
1 server("Admantium").ip
```

When a large amount of data is returned to the caller, manually filtering through the data and hampering with index values of an array is tedious and erroneous. Instead, return a custom object that implements getter methods to access the different data, which makes expressions more readable.

Suitable abstractions for such objects depend on the host language. One option is to return newly created classes. Another option is to use specific constructs, for example `Struct` classes in Ruby or case classes in Scala. Python again makes this modification simple because each object defines a private `dict` that defines all methods of the object – anything that is added to this structure can be accessed from within the program.

Figure 3. Notation patterns relationships

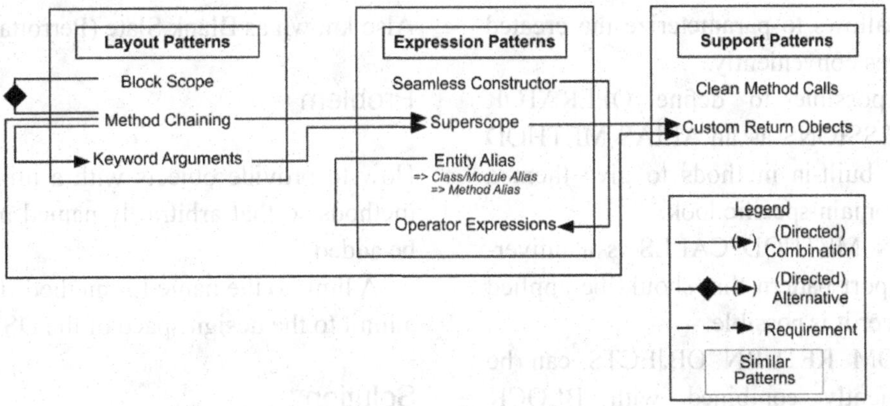

Design Goals

- **Notation:** Utilize keyword-based access to structured data instead of relying on array positions, providing better readability of data accesses.
- **Generalization:** Invoke specific semantics in the custom return objects without changing the original objects, which can be used to add specialized behavior.

Liabilities

- Named classes pollute the global symbol table – use anonymous Struct objects instead.
- The border between method calls and objects diminishes, which could make it hard to distinguish a custom object from "real" method calls.

Related Patterns

- **METHOD CHAINING:** When complex structured data is explicitly accessed, the implementation of methods becomes tightly coupled. Using a CUSTOM RETURN OBJECT relieves this tension because the data is accessed with "mnemonic" methods.

Section Summary

Overall, the notation patterns form an intrinsic network of relationships that reflects their close connection and that they are used together in various forms. All relationships that we found are shown in Figure 3.

We briefly give a summary of the relationships:

- BLOCK SCOPE provides an overall vertical code layout, where individual lines describe a desired property or operation of the DSL.
- Inside the BLOCK SCOPE, individual expressions can be built through METHOD CHAINING and KEYWORD ARGUMENTS. Thereby, METHOD CHAINING requires more tradeoffs because several glue methods need to be implemented.
- The SEAMLESS CONSTRUCTOR transparently hides the explicit creation of new instances. Combined with KEYWORD

ARGUMENTS, several more properties for the created instance can be added, which allows to parameterize the created instances conveniently.

- It is possible to define OPERATOR EXPRESSIONS as an ALIAS METHOD for the built-in methods to give them a more domain-specific look.
- CLEAN METHOD CALLS is a universal support pattern that should be applied whenever it is possible.
- CUSTOM RETURN OBJECTS can be conveniently combined with BLOCK SCOPE, METHOD CHAINING, and KEYWORD ARGUMENTS to simplify the access on multiple structured data and provide a convenient syntax thereby.

ABSTRACTION PATTERNS

Abstraction patterns provide both the domain-specific abstractions and the abstractions from the host language for obtaining a tight integration of the domain behavior with the host language. Abstraction patterns are structured into three groups. First, creation patterns provide objects with a base behavior that deviates from other standard objects of the host language. They are essential for very custom domain objects. Second, the composition patterns are concerned with providing behavior in various forms that can be composed and added to the program, also at runtime. Third, the modification patterns show how the host language's built-in objects and domain concepts can be modified to provide the domain-specific behavior.

Creation Patterns

The task of creation patterns is to provide objects with a custom, non-standard behavior from which other objects are created. With such objects, developers obtain a larger space for providing domain-specific methods or change the way how entities of the language are created.

Pattern "Blank Slate"

Also known as Blank Slate (Perrotta, 2010).

Problem

How to provide objects with a minimal set of methods so that arbitrarily named methods can be added?

A limit to the name for methods may impose a limit to the design space of the DSL too.

Solution

Either use pre-defined objects of the host language, or take the general common object and remove all methods to build your own BLANK SLATE as demonstrated in Box 13.

Appropriate DOMAIN OPERATIONS are crucial to communicate the intention of DSL users. In some languages, the available space to name such operations is limited because objects already implement, per default, several methods. BLANKSLATE provides objects that have a minimal set of methods, so that almost any DOMAIN OPERATION can be defined.

Object-oriented programming languages often have a generic object at the root of the class hierarchy. This object is the ancestor of all built-in as well as user-defined classes, and therefore provides the essential methods that each object needs to have. Either this object is already BLANKSLATE because it implements almost no methods, or its existing methods have to be removed.

Considering the individual host languages, we see that Ruby objects initially contain more than 200 methods. Utilizing `undef_method`, almost all initially defined methods can be removed. BLANKSLATE in Python is simple: All user-defined classes contain only the two fields `__doc__` and `__module__`, they are "blank" from the start. In Scala, classes are similarly minimal, they just define the methods passed from the `AnyRef` class.

Box 13.

```
class Parent
include BlankSlate
end

Parent.instance_methods # => ["__send__", "__id__"]
```

Design Goals

- **Abstraction:** Create objects that have no additional host-specific semantics expressed as methods, or use objects as pure empty namespaces.
- **Generalization:** Objects that offer a large room for naming methods can be used to generalize several domain concepts.
- **Optimization:** Create objects that require less computer memory.
- **Notation:** By removing built-in methods for an object, the amount of available notations is increased.

Liabilities

- To build valid BLANK SLATE objects, carefully select the methods that are to be removed (removing `__send__` from Ruby objects disables all method calls on this object!).
- Provide BLANK SLATE objects per application namespace to avoid removing methods that are needed by BLANK SLATE objects in other applications.

Related Patterns

- OPEN DECLARATION & META DECLARATION – Alternatively remove selected methods only by executing `undef_method` in class declarations or metaobjects (for Ruby).

Pattern "Prototype"

Also known as Prototype (Gamma et al., 1997).

Problem

How to create new objects without using the instantiation process, for saving computational resources or for defining classes outside of the host language's rigid class structure?

Manipulating the instantiation process provides powerful modifications of the objects that are the building blocks of the DSL.

Solution

Define a specialized class that is close to the host language's class hierarchy root, and manipulate the inheritance relationship and instantiation process of this class as presented in Box 14.

Inside a DSL, all DOMAIN OBJECTS are ultimately descendant's of the host language's core classes. Some DSL may require to change how new objects are instantiated. This intention is captured by PROTOTYPE, a specially designed object that instantiates objects outside the existing class structure. By using a class that is close to the root of the host language's core classes, the inheritance relationships are cut effectively. Then the conventional instantiation process of this class should be prohibited, and new instances are only returned via an appropriate named method, like `clone`. Changing the instantiation process is host language specific: In the easiest case, object cre-

Box 14.

```
class Parent
include Prototype
end

Parent.new # => RuntimeError: InstantiationError
Parent.clone => #< Class:0 x1005392a0 >
```

ation is governed by modifiable methods of the very object from which instances are created.

In Ruby, this modification is straight forward: Each object defines the `initialize` method that is executed when a new instance is created. We override this method, and can add a custom `clone` method instead.

In Python, this manipulation can be achieved similarly, but we need to use the class's `dict` object to change the methods. First, we modify the `__init__` method, which is executed during instantiation, to throw an error when being called. Then we add a custom clone method to the object that can be called instead of creating new instances.

In Scala, we can implement this behavior very similar to Python. We can create a Prototype class that is based on the built-in class `Clonable`, and override its `clone` method with the desired behavior. Note, however, that we cannot prevent conventional object instantiation in Scala.

Design Goals

- **Abstraction:** Remove the instantiation process for objects, yet retain the ability to create empty data structures with custom behavior.
- **Optimization:** Prevent the instantiation of objects to save some computational resources.

Liabilities

- Prototyped objects can't use inheritance to receive default behavior because of their creation mechanism.
- Independent prototyped objects can't be part of the "normal" class hierarchy, but can implement custom relationships and be extended with modules.

Related Patterns

- **BLANK SLATE:** Use objects with a minimal amount of methods to further boost the cloning process.

Pattern "Hooks"

Also known as Hook Method (Perrotta, 2010).

Problem

How to introduce more domain-specific behavior at predefined program execution places like class, method, and attribute declaration?

This modification is the key to provide very specific semantics to a DSL.

Solution

Use pre-defined hooks of the host language, like instantiating objects and field access, or define them on your own.

```
module IncludeHook
def self.included(Base)
print "Included the Hook"
end
end

class Test
include IncludeHook
end
# => "Included the Hook"
```

During program execution, several execution states are reached and special conditions achieved. DSLs that require monitoring the execution state and reacting upon them can use HOOKS to automatically execute required behavior.

In their own programs, developers can define arbitrary hooks in the control flow that check for a conditions and provide according behavior. This is a general design option that each developer has. On the other side, each host language offers a very specific set of hooks. We focus on such hooks in the following. Ruby and Python offer such hooks as methods that can be defined on objects. In Scala, hooks are not available as easily, but require to use a compiler plugin that however has disadvantages in portability and compatibility with extensions of the core Scala language, and therefore we do not cover this area.

In Ruby we find the following hooks (Thomas et al., 2007):

- **Adding and Removing Methods:** `method_added`, `method_removed`, `method_undefined`
- **Adding and Removing Singleton Methods:** `singleton_method_added`, `singleton_method_removed`, `singleton_method_undefined`
- **Using** `include`**, Called on the Module that is Included**: `append_features`, `included` (default behavior: adds the constants, variables, and methods of the included module as instance methods to the including object)
- **Using** `extend`**, Called on the Module that is Used for the Extension:** `extend_object`, `extended` (default behavior: adds the constants and methods of the module that is used for the extension as class methods to the extended object)
- **Calling an Undefined Method:** `method_missing`
- **Calling a Missing Constant:** `const_missing`
- **Inheriting from a Class (Called in the Superclass):** `inherited`

The following hooks are available in Python (Python Software Foundation, 2011):

- **Object Instantiation:** `__new__`, `__init__`, `__del__`
    - **Object Calling (Using "()" on Non-Class Objects):** `__call__`
- **Attribute Access**: `__getattr__`, `__setattr__`, `__delattr__`, `__getattribute__`
    - **Descriptor:** `__get__`, `__set__`, `__delete__`
    - **Container Access (Syntax** `object[key]`**):** `__getitem__`, `__setitem__`, `__delitem__`
    - **Context Manager (Syntax** `with Manager as manager`**):** `__enter__`, `__exit__`

Design Goals

- **Abstraction:** Provide domain-specific behavior that deviates from the common behavior.
- **Generalization:** Introduce specialized behavior at the predefined places.

Liabilities

- Modifications that deviate deeply from the common behavior should be properly documented and communicated to other DSL developers and DSL users.
- Global modifications may break compatibility with other frameworks and libraries, and therefore they should be avoided.

Related Patterns

- **METHOD MISSING:** A commonly used hook that serves to proxy method calls or defines methods on the fly.
- **OPEN DECLARATION & META DECLARATION:** Add hooks to built-in classes for powerful changes of the program.

Composition Patterns

Composition patterns are concerned with the declaration and instantiation of new objects and thereby reuse functionality that is already available in the program. This helps developers to effectuate program adaption and runtime extension.

Pattern "Template"

Also known as String of Code (Perrotta, 2010).

Problem

How to provide easily mutable code representations that facilitate runtime creation, modification, and execution for constant adaptation of the DSL?

When a DSL requires constant modifications to reflect the users input, or compute and memoize values, you need to quickly compose the necessary code.

Solution

Define string templates with placeholders for declaring entities and methods as demonstrated in Box 15.

Adaptive DSLs require mechanisms to define, add, or modify objects and behavior on the fly. For example, an open query language may allow its users to search for different criteria that they identify in one DOMAIN OPERATION, such as `find_by_package_and_type`. The DSL would parse the different parts of this query, and define a method on the fly. To define a method, it needs a TEMPLATE.

Some programming languages have the capability to execute code in the form of strings. In such languages, string templates can be defined to serve as placeholder for runtime code composition. A template has a basic structure and one or more anchors where code can be put. We distinguish into the following forms:

- *Scope Declaration Template*: Declaration of modules and classes. The anchors are the name of the class or module, the name of the subclass, and the body.
- *Method Declaration Template*: Declaration of method definitions. Anchors are the function name, parameters, and the body.
- *Method Call Template*: Declaration of method calls, with possible anchors of the method name and the parameters.

Defining such templates is only one side of using them. The capability to execute code contained in strings is language specific, we discuss it in more detail in the EVAL pattern. As we will see then, Ruby and Python support to execute such templates. Scala allows it too, but in a challenging way.

Box 15.

```
module Templates
def self.gen_method(name, params, body)
<<RUBY
def #{name}(#{params})
#{body}
end
RUBY
end
end

Templates.gen_method("test", "", "print 'Test Body'")
# => def test()
#          print 'Test Body '
#          end
```

Design Goals

- **Abstraction:** Create string representations of modules, classes, and methods that facilitate runtime modification and adaption, removing the need to provide all functionality upfront.
- **Abstraction:** Create string representations of method calls that can be conveniently altered before being executed.
- **Generalization**: Absorb several different object and method declarations into one template library, which can be used to quickly instantiate specific objects.

Liabilities

- In some languages, evaluating strings can be slow, which is the case in Ruby (Thomas et al., 2007).
- From a development perspective, strings are inferior to "normal" code because current IDEs do not support syntax highlighting or dedicated error checks.
- String code requires rigorous testing to protect against errors.

Related Patterns

- **EVAL:** Strictly required by TEMPLATE to actually execute the created code.
- **FUNCTION OBJECT:** Compose methods out of existing code objects using procs instead of strings.
- **OPEN DECLARATION & META DECLARATION**: Using stored templates to add objects and method to a DSL.

Pattern "Function Object"

Also known as Closure (Fowler, 2010).

Problem

How to represent the complete (defined) application behavior in one uniform form for arbitrary composition of new behavior?

Because so many different types of local and global methods exist, obtaining a common form is crucial.

Box 16.

```
Array.new.method:sort => #< Method: Array #sort >
```

Solution

Translate the program's method declarations into one common form, and compose new behavior out of this as demonstrated in Box 16.

FUNCTION OBJECT offers an alternative to TEMPLATE to define, add, or modify behavior at runtime. Instead of using mutable strings, this pattern uses the internal representation of methods, both from the DSL and built-in methods of core classes or other libraries. These representations can be composed into new behavior.

The first step is to create a uniform representations of behavior, which are global functions, class methods, or instance methods. We need to take them out of their original scope while retaining their semantics and the ability to pass parameters to them. The challenge is to ensure that dependent behavior is available during executing the detached method. Each host language offers different ways how to achieve this.

In Ruby, we can convert functions into `Proc` objects. Such objects can be called by using the method `call` or by one of the EVAL methods. Class methods and global functions can be cast to `Method` objects via `Object.method`, followed by a transformation to `Proc` objects with `Method#to_proc`. Instance methods can be transformed to `UnboundMethod` objects via `Object.instance_method`, and from this representation back to a `Proc` objects by binding the method to an instance of the originating class, and execute `Method#to_proc`.

In Python, global functions, class methods, and instance methods can be accessed for any built-in or application-specific class, which returns a `function`, `unbound method`, or `bound method` object respectively. Such objects have a `__code__` field that represents the binary code of the methods, which can be executed with one of the EVAL methods. Alternatively, `function` and `bound method` objects can be executed with the callable syntax "()", and `unbound methods` with the callable syntax "()" and by passing an instance of the originating class as the first argument.

In Scala, Method objects are created from classes and traits via `getMethod`. They are executed with invoke by passing – as the first argument – an instance of the originating class or an instance of a class that is extended with the originating trait.

Design Goals

- **Abstraction:** Provide an alternative to method declarations for implementing functionality by storing existing functionality in a non-method object. Additionally, gain the advantage to execute the code at another scope and copy those representations together in one form.
- **Optimization:** Store code in a language-internal form that is quicker to evaluate instead of using strings.

Liabilities

- Calling cloned functions that modify variables of the surrounding scope may provide unintended state changes.
- Since code objects are not readable in the source code, understanding their true semantics may be difficult.

Related Patterns

- **TEMPLATE:** Template functionality is not strictly predefined, we can combine several templates to create new methods.
- **OPEN DECLARATION & META DECLARATION**: Composed functions can also be used to modify existing functions at runtime.
- **EVAL:** Required to execute the FUNCTION OBJECT at an arbitrary scope in the program.
- **METHOD ALIAS:** Alternatively to copying a Function Object manually, use an alias for a simple 1:1 copy of a method.

Modification Patterns

The modification patterns are concerned with the modification of objects for providing more domain-specific behavior. Additionally, such patterns facilitate runtime adaptation of DSLs.

Pattern "Open Declaration"

Also known as Open Class, Monkeypatch (Perrotta, 2010).

Problem

How to extend all built-in and application-specific classes at runtime?

You need to add domain-specific behavior at runtime, or you need to frequently update all instances of the classes, and want to introduce this change just at one place.

Solution

Execute declarations in the context of the object, or manipulate the object's methods directly as demonstrated in Box 17.

Enhancing built-in classes with domain-specific operations increases the flexibility of the languages because native representations can be better incorporated into DSL expressions, and vice-versa. OPEN DECLARATON is a straightforward way to achieve this. The host languages offer different solutions, dependent on the language's mutability of built-in and library-added classes as well as the mechanism how to change such objects.

Ruby makes this modification especially simple: When a module or class declaration expression is executed, it does not replace the complete original one, but new declarations are added and existing declarations are overridden. Because instances just store a pointer to their defining class, such modifications are immediately available in all dependent objects.

In Python, one can access the private `dict` dictionary of user-defined classes where all methods are stored. The dictionary can be manipulated at will, for adding or overriding functions. Such

Box 17.

```
class Array
def sort_descending
print "Sorting..."
end
end

Array.new.sort_descending # => Sorting ...
```

changes are immediately available in all dependent objects.

Scala provides two options. First, new class declarations can be added, but instances of the "old" class will always point to the old class, while new instances will point to the "new" class. Second, dynamic class loading can be used to change class declarations at runtime: Java provides the metaobject `ClassLoader` that can be accessed and manipulated in a program (Liang & Bracha, 1998).

Design Goals

- **Abstraction**: View modules and classes as mutable providers of functionality – changing them also changes the behavior of other existing objects.
- **Optimization:** Gain the ability to modify application behavior in accordance with the runtime environment, providing optimization just-in-time.

Liabilities

- Modifying the behavior of built-in classes may lead to incompatibilities with other libraries, inexecutable programs, or even crashing a running application.
- Changing the visibility of methods may open them for unintended changes.

Related Patterns

- **META DECLARATION:** Modify classes and modules with additional options to reuse or enclose objects of the surrounding scope.
- **TEMPLATE & FUNCTION OBJECT:** Modify classes and modules by executing strings or procs that contain other module, class or method declarations.

Pattern "Meta Declaration"

Problem

How to provide powerful customizations to modules, classes, and methods?

You require that the basic building blocks of programs have non-standard, domain-specific semantics.

Solution

Provide custom modules, classes, and methods by using derivatives of their metaobjects as presented in Box 18.

Metaobjects are the programming language's core abstractions. They determine the base structure and behavior of all other objects in a language. The capability to modify these metaobjects or to create custom metaobjects allows powerful modifications for the creation of DSLs. META DECLARATIONS explain the mechanisms how to and which metaobjects can be created in strong object-oriented languages.

When metaobjects are available and manipulable for a host language, extensive modifications can be achieved. The amount of modifications are usually described as the metaobject protocol of the language (Kiczales et al., 1995).

META DECLARATION is not concerned with the complete manipulation of the metaobjects, but how to use their representation to create specialized modules, classes, and methods. Ruby provides all above-mentioned metaobjects with a constructor to return custom objects. Custom objects can be created like this: `Module.new`, `Class.new`, and `define_method`. The constructors receive a block argument that can access and capture elements of the surrounding scope. Through this capability, the following subpatterns are enabled:

- *Shared Scope:* Share the scope of multiple declarations between each other, providing

Box 18.

```
MyClass = Class.new do
def initialize
print "Custom Initialize"
end
end

MyClass.new # => Custom Initialize #<MyClass:0x100355830>
```

access to local variables for including them in declarations (Perrotta, 2010).
- *Scope Closure:* Conserve local variables in declarations, completely hiding the variables from any outside access.

The modification of the metaobjects is very different in Python. The `type` class, which is the metaclass of all classes, defines methods that govern the creation and initialization of new objects. Based on this class, custom metaclasses can be created that govern the creation of other similar entities. However, the basic mechanism of creating new objects from this representation is not modifiable.

Scala provides internal metaobjects, but like all built-in classes, they cannot be modified directly, and therefore this pattern is not available in Scala.

Design Goals

- **Abstraction:** Gain access to the metaobjects of a programming language that represent modules, classes, and methods for modifying existing entities.
- **Abstraction:** Share the scope of multiple declarations between each other using metaobjects, either to conserve local variables in a closure or to provide protected access to local variables to include them in declarations.
- **Optimization:** Deep-rooted modifications can be exploited to improve the runtime performance.

Liabilities

- Although some languages allow the modification of the built-in metaobjects, such changes should be used with great care and better be restricted to a smaller scope.
- When overriding existing methods, be careful about changing built-in methods because modifications could potentially break the compatibility with other libraries.
- In *Shared Scope*, one could use a local variable that unintentionally refers to variables in the surrounding scope.
- The *Scope Closure* is destroyed when the scope-containing method is overridden.

Related Patterns

- **OPEN DECLARATION**: Using common class or module declarations limits the availability of entities from the surrounding scope for modifications.
- **TEMPLATE & FUNCTION OBJECT**: Modify classes and modules by executing strings or procs that contain other module, class or method declarations.

Pattern "Eval"

Problem

How to execute any code representation at any scope of the program to modify it arbitrarily?

Box 19.

```
Array.class_eval("def sort_ascending; print 'Sorting ... '; end")

Array.new.sort_ascending # => Sorting ...
```

You need to declare, compose, and define behavior at runtime, and the scope of such definitions is not always the scope of the declaration.

Solution

Execute the code representation in any context with a host language specific command as demonstrated in Box 19.

The conventional way to execute code at a dedicated scope is to enter the appropriate lexical scope. However, it is not always desirable (need to explicitly construct) or manageable (created scope can not be reconstructed) to enter a specific scope. For these reasons, EVAL offers a convenient way to execute previously defined (or on the fly created) code at an arbitrary scope.

Before executing the code representation with a host language specific mechanism, the first step is to find a suitable representation. If a very mutable form is desirable, then TEMPLATE provides the solution, and if an internal form is better suited, than FUNCTION OBJECT should be used.

Ruby provides three distinct options to execute code: (1) `eval` for executing string objects, including declarations, (2) `instance_eval` for executing internal representations in the scope of any objects, and (3) `class_eval` that executes internal representations in an object's eigenclass.

Python provides several options too in order to support the various types of internal code objects that are available. First of all, when string representations are used, both the `eval` and the `exec` method can be used. However, `eval` only supports simple expressions, not declarations for which the `exec` method is needed. Furthermore, `exec` and `execfile` can also be used to access the file system and execute code contained in a file.

Scala does not support this pattern. Although string representations can be executed by using the internal Interpreter object, the compiled results reside in a separate execution space and cannot be accessed from the main namespace of the Scala interpreter.

Liabilities

- If parts of a code representation stem from user interactions, they should be carefully checked to not contain malicious code.
- In the scope where the code is executed, unintended modifications such as overriding values can occur, and therefore should be checked carefully.

Design Goals

- **Abstraction:** Gain the option to evaluate code that is specified in any scope to be executed in any other scope, including classes and modules.
- **Optimization:** Change existing behavior or provide new behavior to optimize the runtime behavior of a program.

Related Patterns

- **TEMPLATE & FUNCTION OBJECT**: To execute declarations contained in string or proc objects in any scope, EVAL is a strict necessity. On the contrary, EVAL can be used without an explicit template object, but just receive an inline expression.

Pattern "Method Alias"

Problem

How to transparently change the behavior of an existing method while preserving the old behavior?

You cannot remove the old behavior because you still need to use it, especially when you manipulate built-in methods, or you want to build yourself a chain of method calls that forward to each other.

Solution

Copy the old method to an aliased name, fully retaining scope and other information, and redefine the method with the same name as demonstrated in Box 20.

Modifying built-in methods is a powerful way to introduce domain-specific behavior. However, the risk to break compatibility with other programs or libraries is high, and therefore changes need to be introduced carefully. METHOD ALIAS provides a simple mechanism to overwrite yet retain an existing method, which can be used for the following subpatterns:

- *Alias Decorator:* Add functionality around an existing method. For example, enhance the original method's functionality by calling an additional logger or by augmenting the return value.
- *Alias Memoization:* Replace a method implementation with a fixed return value to save computational time. For example, complex computations that are based on static data waste computational resources when they are calculated each time. With *Alias Memoization*, the original method is replaced by a fixed return value. The alias checks, from time to time, whether changes in the data occurred, and updates its return value.

Ruby is very supportive for this pattern. The keyword `alias` is one of the few build-in operations of the Ruby language. Its first argument is the new name, and the second argument is the current name of the method. The same semantics provides `alias_method`, but it is a method itself that can be modified accordingly. It is possible to combine multiple method chains together.

Python does not provide a built-in function for aliasing, but the solution is to modify the `dict` dictionary field: it stores all fields and methods of an object. The limit with this modification is, however, that built-in classes cannot be modified this way.

Scala also has no dedicated method to support this modification, but the same effect can be achieved by following these steps: (1) define

Box 20.

```
class Array
alias old_shuffle shuffle
def shuffle()
print "New shuffling method"
end
end

Array.new.shuffle # => New shuffling method
```

a `Method` object of the aliased method, then (2) store this object in a local, generic function, and (3) redefine the original method. This modification cannot happen with built-in classes.

Design Goals

- **Abstraction:** Modify built-in or library-based methods to provide domain-specific behavior while preserving the existing functionality.
- **Generalization:** Specialize existing functions, but keep the ability to refer to the general behavior.
- **Optimization:** Replace a complex computation with a temporary memoized value.
- **Notation:** Provide more domain-specific names for built-in methods.

Liabilities

- *Alias Decorator* can change the behavior of an object, which may be confusing for DSL developers and DSL users if not properly documented and communicated.
- *Alias Memoization* requires a careful implementation because values stalled for too long can result in logic bugs.

Related Patterns

- **FUNCTION OBJECT:** Store an existing method declaration in an internal form to retain the original behavior. Then, redefine the method and optionally use the stored method for executing the unaltered behavior.
- **METHOD MISSING (Dynamic Proxy):** Instead of providing a fixed behavior, forward the call to a proxy that decides how to respond.

Pattern "Method Missing"

Also known as Dynamic Reception (Fowler, 2010).

Problem

Your DSL needs to react to method calls that are not defined at starting time, or it needs to dispatch the actual method call to a specific place in the system?

Since you cannot envision all possible calls, you need to manage undefined method calls flexible at program runtime.

Solution

Modify the method-call chain to fetch called methods, then define a method on the fly or dispatch the call to another part of the program as presented in Box 21.

Normally, the execution of non-defined methods leads to an error that potentially stops the program from running. This could irritate DSL uses that enter several expressions. On the other hand, allowing users to type in commands that have a meaning in the DSL which yet needs to be implemented is a powerful way to increase the DSL's versatility. Therefore, a mechanism to capture such method calls and treat them adequately is required.

When method calls are monitored and caught, then the following runtime adaptation effects can be achieved:

- **Ghost Method:** Depending on the method's name, a value is returned to the caller and a normal method call is simulated (Perrotta, 2010).
- **Dynamic Proxy:** Forward the method call to another module or class (or METHOD MISSING in another object) (Perrotta, 2010).

Box 21.

```
class Array
def method_missing (name,*args, &block)
if name.to_s =~ /^sort_/
print "Called undefined sorting method"
end
end
end

Array.new.sort_depth_first # => Called undefined sorting method
```

- **Missing Declaration:** Check the method name and define methods on the fly. For checking the method name, we can compare it to a fixed string or use regular expressions to check for certain parts of the method call (Perrotta, 2010).

Each host language defines its own method handling mechanisms. Some languages will try to call the method along the inheritance chain or included modules. If not successful, a generic method will be called to handle this exception. We call this method METHOD MISSING, which is a special case of HOOK so frequently occurring that we define it as a separate pattern.

In Ruby, the method responsible for handling method call exceptions is called `method_missing`. This method can be implemented anywhere along the method call chain, and receives as arguments the method name, the list of originally called arguments, and a block.

Python realizes this hook with the special method `__getattr__`. However, it only receives the name of the method that was called, other information is lost.

This pattern is not available in Scala because the compiler checks the method calls during compilation and will stop to compile a program that includes the obvious error of calling an undefined method.

Design Goals

- **Abstraction:** Abstract the convention that every response to a method call actually stems from a defined method.
- **Generalization:** Extend the known methods spectrum of an object as a convenient bundle in one method, not touching other parts of the object.

Liabilities

- Missing Declarations should be checked to not accidentally respond to an existing method.
- When Ghost Methods are explicitly defined as part of an object's interface, it is difficult to document them with tools that parse an application's source code.
- Ghost Methods are not supported by current IDEs in terms of syntax highlighting, error detection and more.

Related Patterns

- **TEMPLATE & FUNCTION OBJECT:** Define the called methods by executing a predefined string or internal form object.
- **METHOD ALIAS**: When one method can be accessed by different method names, define the missing ones by aliasing.

Figure 4. Abstraction patterns relationships

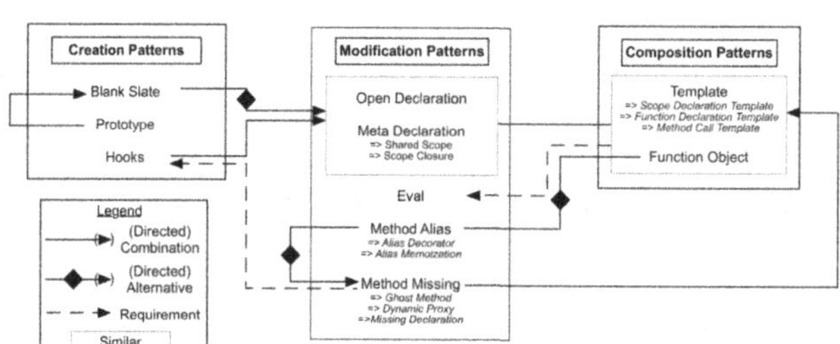

Section Summary

In Figure 4, we show the relationships between the abstraction patterns.

In supplement to the related patterns as explained above, we also see the following relationships:

- While PROTOTYPE relies on cloning to create new instances, BLANK SLATE should be used through subclassing. Both can be substantially enriched with custom HOOKS to gain flexibility in changing the status of such objects.
- TEMPLATE is a very powerful and mutable way to represent code, which results in costs to check their correct working, especially when processing user input to define functionality. FUNCTION OBJECT is easier to use and faster because it uses internal representations of code. Both need EVAL to be actually executed.
- The modification patterns OPEN DECLARATION, META DECLARATION, and EVAL synthesize parts of the same goal: To modify objects by either using the original objects, metaobjects, or executing code in the context of the objects. META DECLARATION is especially powerful, using Shared Scope or Scope Closure can provide entities with very custom behavior, OPEN DECLARATION and EVAL can be used to either add structure and behavior with names that are derived from the user input at runtime using TEMPLATE, and they can use FUNCTION OBJECTS to quickly provide behavior.
- METHOD ALIAS is concerned to transparently and reversibly add behavior around existing methods. It can be combined with FUNCTION OBJECT and TEMPLATE to use pre-defined behavior.
- METHOD MISSING is very versatile in treating method calls and define behavior at runtime. It can use EVAL together with FUNCTION OBJECTS and TEMPLATE to use pre-defined behavior too. It can also be used with METHOD ALIAS to hide existing functions, instead deciding on a case-per-case what to do with a particular method call.

PATTERN UTILIZATION

In order to show the applicability of our patterns and their utilization in existing DSLs, we briefly give a list of the analyzed DSLs and report when and where the patterns are used. The complete documentation can be found in Guenther (2011). Furthermore, we explain if and how the patterns can be used in other programming languages, specifically in functional programming languages.

Ruby

- **Rails (version 2.3.5):** A widely used web-application framework that provides many convenient expressions as a DSL for web applications. Rails is bundled together with ActiveSupport (version 2.3.5, adds helper classes), Actionpack (version 2.3.5, provides request and response objects), and Builder (version 2.1.2, provides objects representing XML-like data structures), which we analyzed separately (http://rubyonrails.com).
- **ActiveRecord (version 2.3.5):** A DSL that provides convenient database abstractions both for defining a schema and for queries (http://ar.rubyonrails.org/).
- **RSpec (version 1.3.0)**:Framework and DSL for behavior-driven development (http://rspec.info).
- **Sinatra (version 0.9.4):** Lightweight web framework and DSL that uses declarative expressions for specifying request handling (http://sinatrarb.com).

Python

- **Bottle (version 0.8.3):** Web framework that uses annotations and functions to conveniently define response handlers (http://bottle.paws.de/).
- **Should DSL (version 1.0, commit id 1725b62ad30195f578a4):** Supports simple behavior-driven testing by adding expressions like `should`, `be`, and `be_greater_than` as expressions for Python (http://github.com/hugobr/should-dsl).
- **Cryptlang:** A DSL for defining cryptographic algorithms and random number generators (Agosta & Pelosi, 2007).
- **LCS DSL:** The Constellation Launch Control System DSL is used to simulate flight and ground systems (Bennett et al., 2006).

Scala

- **Actors (version 2.7.7final):** Build into the Scala core library, this DSL facilitates asynchronous message passing and handling (http://www.scala-lang.org/api/current/scala/actors/package.html).
- **Specs (version 1.6.2.1):** DSL for behavior driven development similar to the block-like nature of RSpec (http://code.google.com/p/specs/).
- **Apache Camel (version 1.6.4):** DSL used in enterprise application architectures to describe how requests are routed (http://camel.apache.org/scala-dsl.html).
- **ScalaQL:** A DSL for formulating SQL queries (Spiewak & Zhao, 2009).

Analysis

Our goal is to show that the patterns are used in DSLs from the open-source community or from other researchers. In Table 5, Table 6, and Table 7 we document at least one occurrence of a pattern per host language and DSL if we found one (we did not check the availability of each pattern in each DSL).

As we can see in these tables, most of the patterns are used in the analyzed DSLs. At least in our analysis, there is no specific hint to see that one type of pattern is used more exclusively than another. However, we think that the current host languages provide powerful semantic abstractions so that the focus of the DSL is on finding creative ways to shape the domain-specific syntax.

Considering the overall usage of the individual patterns, we also see that some patterns are more often used than others. One interpretation is that some patterns provide a very specific role that is not needed in all DSLs. For example, the need to provide BLANK SLATE objects is obviously only

Table 5. Used patterns in Ruby-based DSLs

Pattern			Rails	Active Record	RSpec	Sinatra
Foundation		Domain Objects		X	X	
		Domain Operations		X		
Abstraction	Creation	Blank Slate	X			
		Prototype				
		Hooks		X	X	
	Composition	Template			X	X
		Function Object			X	
	Modification	Open Declaration			X	X
		Meta Declaration			X	
		Eval			X	X
		Method Alias	X		X	
		Method Missing	X	X		
Notation	Layout	Block Scope			X	X
		Method Chaining			X	
		Keyword Arguments		X		X
	Expression	Seamless Constructor				
		Superscope	X			
		Entity Alias				
		Operator Expressions		X		
	Support	Clean Method Calls			X	X
		Custom Return Objects		X		

important for one DSL. Another interpretation is that the knowledge about a pattern influences the amount of the utilization. This can be especially seen when comparing the host languages. For example, the METHOD ALIAS pattern is very helpful to safely modify methods and extend their behavior. In Ruby, this pattern is realized with a built-in function, while the same intent is possible in Python and Scala too, but not provided built-in. Therefore we conclude that this pattern is very often used in Ruby, but not in the other languages.

Pattern Utilization in Other Programming Languages

The explicit focus of the patterns is on programming languages that support object-oriented constructs. However, since the patterns themselves are host-language independent, they can be used with other programming languages as well when the solution can be adapted to the language-specific constructs. The essential requirements of any programming language in which the patterns are going to be used are (i) the creation of domain-specific data structures (DOMAIN OBJECTS) and functions (DOMAIN OPERATIONS), (ii) the modification of essential semantics via accessing the language's metaobject protocol, and (iii) creation of domain-specific syntax via using the notation patterns. We give a quick study of DSLs in functional programming languages and in C++/Java to see where the patterns are applied.

For Haskell, Leijen & Meijer (2001), Thielemann (2004), Augustsson et al. (2009), and Hudak

Table 6. Used patterns in Python-based DSLs

Pattern			Bottle	ShouldDSL	Cryptlang	LCS DSL
Foundation		Domain Objects	X		X	
		Domain Operations	X	X		
Abstraction	Creation	Blank Slate				
		Prototype				
		Hooks	X			
	Composition	Template	X			
		Function Object	X			
	Modification	Open Declaration				
		Meta Declaration	X			
		Eval	X			
		Method Alias				
		Method Missing				
Notation	Layout	Block Scope				
		Method Chaining			X	X
		Keyword Arguments	X			X
	Expression	Seamless Constructor		X		
		Superscope				X
		Entity Alias	X			
		Operator Expressions			X	
	Support	Clean Method Calls	X			
		Custom Return Objects				

(2004) present case studies in which mechanisms similar to our patterns are used. Especially the Haskore DSL for composing music is based on conventional lists and list operators, using DOMAIN OBJECTS, DOMAIN OPERATIONS, KEYWORD ARGUMENTS, and METHOD CHAINING (Hudak, 2004). For Scheme, Sadilek (2007) provides a stream-oriented DSL. This DSL uses S-expressions that represent DOMAIN OBJECTS and DOMAIN OPERATIONS to describe earthquake detection algorithms. Tobin-Hochstadt et al. (2011) describe Racket, based on Scheme, which provides very powerful support for implementing DSLs. It offers a reflection-based access to the language's static semantics. Syntactic extensions are done with macros, adding new keywords to the languages. Macros can be used to implement syntactic patterns such as METHOD CHAINING and SUPERSCOPE. Semantic extensions are defined by the evaluation of macros, and modules help to package language extensions conveniently.

Vanderbauwhede et al. (2010) describe a C++ DSL for special multimedia processors that increase the computation performance for audio/video processing tenfold. This DSL uses TEMPLATES and implements types for DOMAIN OBJECTS. Czarnecki et al. (2004) report their experiences about DSL implementations using staged interpreters and templates. Their implementation for the C++ programming language uses TEMPLATES to implement DSLs, similar as it was shown before by Czarnecki & Eisenecker (2000) for representing matrices. David (2009)

Table 7. Used patterns in Scala-based DSLs

Pattern			Actors	Spec	Apache Camel	Scala QL
Foundation		Domain Objects		X		
		Domain Operations	X			
Abstraction	Creation	Blank Slate				
		Prototype				
		Hooks				
	Composition	Template				
		Function Object				
	Modification	Open Declaration				X
		Meta Declaration			X	
		Eval				
		Method Alias		X		
		Method Missing				
Notation	Layout	Block Scope		X		
		Method Chaining		X		
		Keyword Arguments				
	Expression	Seamless Constructor				
		Superscope			X	
		Entity Alias		X		
		Operator Expressions	X			
	Support	Clean Method Calls		X	X	
		Custom Return Objects			X	

shows how to implement concepts – syntactic requirements on a set of types – as a C++ language extension again by using TEMPLATES. Tambe & Gokhale (2009) use template metaprogramming and operator overloading, similar to OPERATOR EXPRESSIONS, as the design techniques for an object-traversal language that allows to select objects from within a C++ programs. And for Java, Kabanov & Raudjärv (2008) explain their approach to implement type-safe DSLs for SQL-like querying and Java bytecode. Their approach is based on techniques such as static functions, metadata, closures (BLOCK SCOPE and EVAL), and Java Generics.

PATTERN LANGUAGE

The goal of a pattern language is to enrich the pattern catalog by providing detailed knowledge about the pattern relationships and general guidelines on the selection and application of patterns (Gamma et al., 1997; Avgeriou & Zdun, 2005). In this section, we start with a detailed relationship diagram that shows the various relationships between the patterns. This diagram can be used by developers for navigating along related patterns. The second part is a table that shows which principle is supported by which pattern, similarly helpful for developers that want to specifically use a selection of principles and appropriate patterns. Finally, we formulate a list of DSL design question and answers that explain in which development situations the pattern can also be used.

Pattern Relationships

The patterns have a rich set of relationships, as we already saw in the pattern relationship subsection for each pattern type. In addition to this perspective, we also want to show how patterns between the different groups can be used in combination. Such combinations help developers to learn about the pattern connections and navigate along the relationships. Specifically, we found the following relationships (which are also shown in Figure 5):

- The combination of DOMAIN OPERATIONS and KEYWORD ARGUMENTS supports the future evolution of the DSL because it provides a central point where new behavior can be introduced.
- To limit the amount of methods that needs to be defined when METHOD CHAINING is used, glue methods can be provided as "blind" METHOD MISSING that just forward the call to the next method.
- The expression patterns can be used with OPEN DECLARATION and META DECLARATION to modify the behavior of the built-in classes.
- CUSTOM RETURN OBJECTS can be built with the composition patterns
- We repeat the relationships diagrams for the abstraction patterns and the notation patterns, as well as adding a diagram that details the relationships between all patterns in Figure 5.

Design Principle Selection

When developers wish to focus upon a set of principles for their DSLs – in addition to the mandatory abstraction and notation principle – Table 8 helps them to quickly see which patterns are supported.

Design Questions

The patterns proposed in this chapter can be used effectively with the DSL development process explained in Chapter 6. This process consists of three steps. First, the domain model is designed by analyzing the available domain material. Second, the language is designed by providing a set of expressions that are executable for the host (by using the foundation and notation patterns). Third, the DSL's semantics are provided by using the abstraction patterns. Along these steps, the following design questions may arise:

- How to define the objects of my DSL?
    - Build DOMAIN OBJECTS and add appropriate setter/getter methods for accessing their values.
    - Put the DOMAIN OBJECTS into inheritance relationships that mirror the domain hierarchy.
- How to build the methods of my DSL?
    - First, implement the DOMAIN OPERATIONS that belong to the DOMAIN OBJECTS.
    - Second, implement the DOMAIN OPERATIONS that are part of the DSL itself, and dependent on the namespace in which the DSL expressions will be executed, put them either in the global or in a local namespace.
    - Third, embrace the change of the DSL's evolution by moving the DOMAIN OPERATIONS to more appropriate namespaces.
    - Finally, use BLOCK SCOPE to easily capture DSL expressions and execute them in the appropriate scope.
- What kinds of layouts can I use in my DSL?
    - A vertical code layout, where for example declarative expressions are stated from top to bottom, can be achieved with BLOCK SCOPE.

Figure 5. Relationships among the notation pattern, among the abstraction patterns, and among all patterns

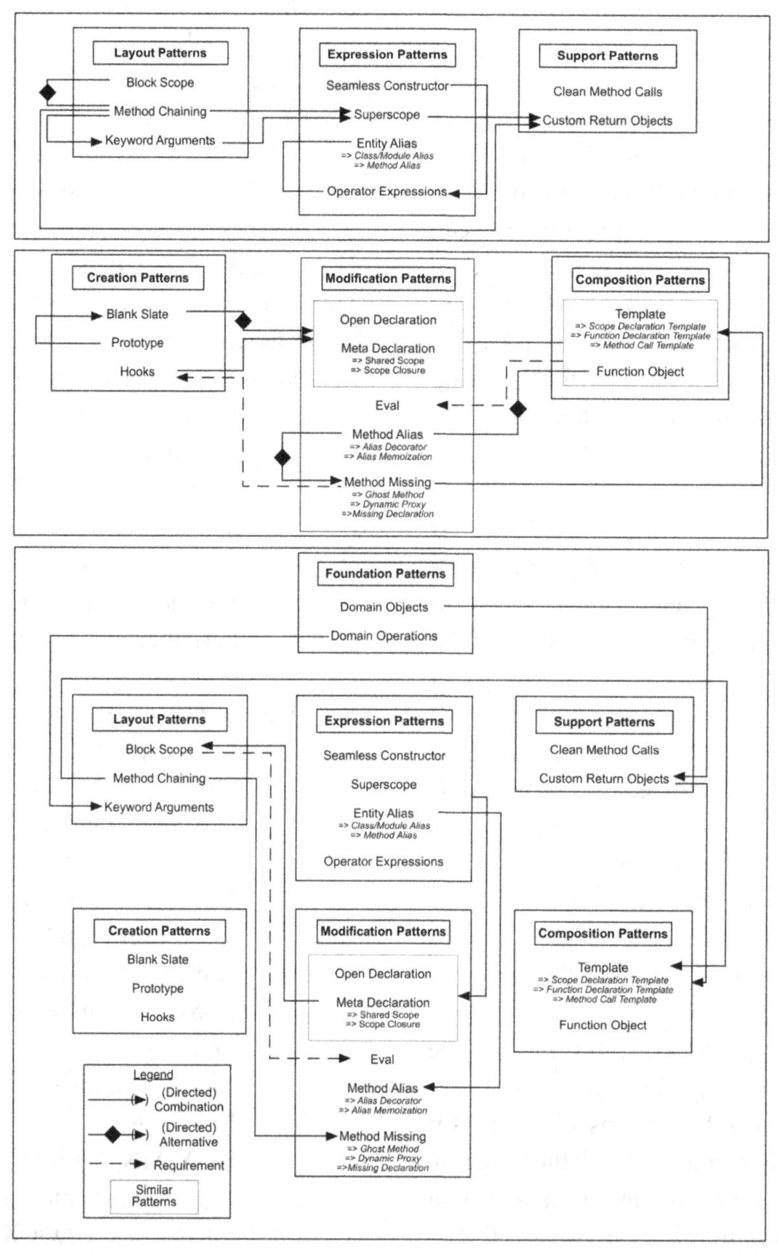

- A horizontal code layout, where complex and verbose expressions are used, can be achieved with METHOD CHAINING and KEYWORD ARGUMENTS.

- What are the options to modify the DSL expressions in such a way that they do not resemble their host language?
  - The combination of METHOD CHAINING and CLEAN METHOD

Table 8. How the patterns support the principles

Pattern			Abst.	Gene.	Opti.	Nota.	Comp.	Absorp.
Foundation		Domain Objects	X	X		X		X
		Domain Operations	X	X	X	X		X
Abstraction	Creation	Blank Slate	X	X	X	X		
		Prototype	X		X			
		Hook	X	X				
	Composition	Template	X	X				
		Function Object	X		X			
	Modification	Open Declaration	X		X			
		Meta Declaration	X		X			
		Eval	X		X			
		Method Alias	X	X	X	X		
		Method Missing	X	X				
Notation	Layout	Block Scope	X				X	X
		Method Chaining				X	X	
		Keyword Arguments	X			X	X	X
	Expression	Seamless Constructor				X		X
		Superscope		X		X	X	
		Entity Alias	X			X		
		Operator Expressions		X		X	X	
	Support	Clean Method Calls				X	X	
		Custom Return Objects		X		X		

CALLS can give the impression of a very free form, verbose language.

- ◦ CUSTOM RETURN OBJECTS can further strengthen the readability of METHOD CHAINING.
- ◦ SUPERSCOPE can remove the notation of explicit variable references.

- How to maximize the number of methods I can give my objects?
  - ◦ Start with a BLANK SLATE OBJECT that provides a large namespace for defining DOMAIN OPERATIONS.
  - ◦ Use ALIAS METHOD to hide built-in methods, than use their name appropriately.
- How to add new behavior at runtime?

- Define TEMPLATES, customize them at runtime, and then execute them with EVAL.
- Define FUNCTION OBJECT for the functionality that you want to reuse, and execute them with EVAL.

- How to defer the declaration and execution of my DSL expressions?
  - Instead of variables, use SUPER SCOPE to refer to entities for which the exact location will be given at runtime.
  - Put the expression in a BLOCK SCOPE, and execute the block where the methods are defined (for example DOMAIN OBJECTS or namespace objects).
- In complex expressions, how do I check the right order of expressions?
  - Store the execution order of method calls, and between the calls, check whether the order is correct.
  - Move explicit return values between the methods, and stop further evaluation if the method does not appear in the right order.
- How do I add methods to a built-in type?
  - When available, use OPEN DECLARATION or META DECLARATION to directly modify the type.
  - Alternatively, define a subclass of the built-in type and use it instead of the original one via ENTITY ALIAS.
- How to provide better domain-specific notations and abstractions for a library and my DSL?
  - The built-in modules, classes, and methods can get better domain-specific names by redefining them with ENTITY ALIAS respectively METHOD ALIAS.
  - Define additional methods in a custom object, and then use METHOD MISSING on the original object to refer undefined method calls to the custom objects.
- How to reduce the memory footprint of my DSL?
  - First, use the domain-specific representation of the concepts and their optimized algorithms for computations.
  - Second, use patterns such as BLANK SLATE and PROTOTYPE.
  - Third, if a large number of objects is usually created at runtime, strategically use DELETE CONSTANT to delete unneeded objects.
- How to package my DSL?
  - Use a specific namespace in which you define the DOMAIN OBJECTS and DOMAIN OPERATIONS.
  - Then, use the DSL within its namespace, or import the DSL into the global namespace.
- How can I integrate two DSLs?
  - Define generalized DOMAIN OBJECTS that provide a different representation in each DSL.
  - Implement meta-objects that collect the data of both domains and ensure the overall consistency.
  - Try to integrate the DSLs into each other by extending the objects and method of one DSL with the other through using METHOD MISSING, METHOD ALIAS, OPEN DECLARATION and META DECLARATION.
  - Introduce hooks at the most important program execution points, and use them to aggregate common data and check their consistency.

Section Summary

This section extended our pattern catalog to a pattern language. We provided several additional ways of learning, selecting, navigating among, and incorporating the patterns: Relationship diagrams, principle support diagrams, and a set of extensive DSL design questions. We now summarize our chapter.

CONCLUSION

The development of internal DSLs is a rewarding yet difficult challenge. The essential pitfall lies in understanding the available syntactic and semantic design options. Each host language is different, and the DSLs of each host language also vary in several ways. The danger behind this is that DSL design knowledge is scattered across the language communities, and as the knowledge evolves, it can become even more harder to communicate. Our answer to this danger is to provide a universal, host-independent set of design patterns and design principles.

The design patterns are our central contribution in this chapter. We explained 21 patterns that are grouped into foundation, notation, and abstraction patterns. The patterns explain the problem, generic solution, liabilities, and related patterns independent of a specific host language, and they detail how to implement the pattern in the host languages Ruby, Python, and Scala. We deepened this knowledge by providing a graphical overview to the manifold relationships among the patterns, such as useful combinations or clear alternatives to each other. Finally, we gave a list of design questions that can occur during the DSL design, and explained how to engage them by using the patterns.

Our design principles are an equally important contribution. Design principles are guidelines that provide design goals to shape the syntax and semantic of a DSL. We derived six principles that are aimed at the core task of a DSL: the provision of suitable domain-specific abstractions – by the principles abstraction, generalization, and optimization – and notations – by the principles notation, compression, and absorption. These principles are manifested by the design goals of each patterns, explaining a specific purpose how to apply this pattern. By using patterns related to a design principle, distinguished DSLs can be created.

Our work on DSL design patterns and design principles can be extended in several ways. An obvious extension is to specifically check the applicability of the patterns in other host languages. This is especially challenging since frequently new programming languages are appearing, which results in new notations and abstractions. Another extension is to analyze more existing DSLs, including those in other host languages, to define new notation and abstraction patterns. Finally it is also interesting to see whether the generic problem solution description of the patterns is applicable to the design of external DSLs as well.

REFERENCES

Agosta, G., & Pelosi, G. (2007). A domain specific language for cryptography. In *Proceedings of the Forum on Specification and Design Languages* (pp. 59–164). Gières, France: ECSI.

Arpaia, P., Buzio, M., Fiscarelli, L., Inglese, V., La Commara, G., & Walckiers, L. (2009). Measurement-domain specific language for magnetic test specifications at CERN. In *IEEE International Instrumentation and Measurement Technology Conference* (pp. 1716 –1720). Washington, DC: IEEE.

Atkins, D., Ball, T., Bruns, G., & Cox, K. (1999). Mawl: A domain-specific language for form-based services. *IEEE Transactions on Software Engineering*, *25*(3), 334–346. doi:10.1109/32.798323

Augustsson, L., Mansell, H., & Sittenpalam, G. (2008). Paradise: A two-stage DSL embedded in Haskell. *ACM SIGPLAN Notices*, *43*(9), 225–228. doi:10.1145/1411203.1411236

Avgeriou, P., & Zdun, U. (2005). Architectural patterns revisited - A pattern language. In A. Longshaw & U. Zdun (Ed.), *Proceedings of the 10th European Conference on Pattern Languages of Programs (EuroPLoP)* (pp. 431–469). Konstanz, Germany: Universitätsverlag Konstanz.

Barreto, L. P., Douence, R., Muller, G., & Südholt, M. (2002). Programming OS schedulers with domain-specific languages and aspects: New approaches for OS kernel engineering. In *Proceedings of the 1st AOSD Workshop on Aspects, Components, and Patterns for Infrastructure Software* (pp. 1–6). Vancouver, Canada: University of British Columbia.

Bennett, M., Borgen, R., Havelund, K., Ingham, M., & Wagner, D. (2008). Development of a prototype domain-specific language for monitor and control systems. In *Aerospace Conference* (pp. 1–18). Washington, DC: IEEE Computer Society.

Bentley, J. (1986). Programming pearls: Little languages. *Communications of the ACM, 29*(8), 711–721. doi:10.1145/6424.315691

Booch, G. A. (1994). *Object-oriented analysis and design with applications* (2nd ed.). Redwood City, CA: Addison-Wesley Longman.

Butcher, P., & Zedan, H. (1991). Lucinda – An overview. *ACM SIGPLAN Notices, 26*(8), 90–100. doi:10.1145/122598.122608

Cannon, B., & Wohlstadter, E. (2007). Controlling access to resources within the Python Interpreter. In B. Cannon, J. Hilliker, M. N. Razavi, & R. Werlinge (Eds.), *Proceedings of the Second EECE Mini-Conference on Computer Security* (pp. 1–8). Vancouver, Canada: University of British Columbia.

Cheatham, T. E. (1977). Programming language design issues. In J. H. Williams & D. A. Fisher (Eds.), *Lecture Notes in Computer Science: Vol. 54, Design and Implementation of Programming Languages – Proceedings of a DoD Sponsored Workshop* (pp. 399–435). Berlin, Germany: Springer-Verlag.

Coplien, J. O. (1999). *Multi-paradigm design for C*. Boston, MA: Addison-Wesley.

Correia, F. F., Ferreira, H. S., Flores, N., & Aguiar, A. (2009). Patterns for consistent software documentation. In *Proceedings of the 16th Conference for Pattern Languages of Programs*. New York, NY: ACM.

Costagliola, G., Delucia, A., Orefice, S., & Polese, G. (2002). A classification framework to support the design of visual languages. *Journal of Visual Languages and Computing, 13*(6), 573–600. doi:10.1006/jvlc.2002.0234

Cunningham, H. C. (2008). A little language for surveys: Constructing an internal DSL in Ruby. In *Proceedings of the 46th Annual Southeast Regional Conference* (pp. 282–287). New York, NY: ACM.

Czarnecki, K., & Eisenecker, U. W. (2000). *Generative programming: Methods, tools, and applications*. Boston, CA: Addison-Wesley.

Czarnecki, K., O'Donnell, J., Striegnitz, J., & Taha, W. (2007). DSL implementation in MetaOCaml, template Haskell, and C. In Lengauer, C., Batory, D., Consel, C., & Odersky, M. (Eds.), *Domain-Specific Program Generation* (*Vol. 3016*, pp. 51–72). Lecture Notes in Computer Science Berlin, Germany: Springer-Verlag. doi:10.1007/978-3-540-25935-0_4

David, V. (2009). *Language constructs for C++-like languages - Tools and extensions*. Ph.D. Thesis. Bergen, Norway: University of Bergen.

Dinkelaker, T., & Mezini, M. (2008). Dynamically linked domain-specific extensions for advice languages. In *Proceedings of the 2008 AOSD Workshop on Domain-Specific Aspect Languages* (pp. 1–7). New York, NY: ACM.

Finkel, R. A. (1996). *Advanced programming language design*. Menlo Park, CA: Addison-Wesley.

Flanagan, D., & Matsumoto, Y. (2008). *The Ruby programming language*. Sebastopol, CA, USA: O-Reilly Media.

Fowler, M. (2003). *Patterns of enterprise application architecture*. Boston, MA: Addison-Wesley.

Fowler, M. (2010). *Domain-specific languages*. Upper Saddle River, NJ: Addison-Wesley.

Gamma, E., Helm, R., Johnson, R., & Vlissides, J. (1997). *Design patterns - Elements of reusable object-oriented software* (10th ed.). Reading, MA: Addison-Wesley.

Greenfield, J., Short, K., Cook, S., & Kent, S. (2004). *Software factories - Assembling applications with patterns, models, frameworks, and tools*. Indianapolis, IN: Wiley Publishing.

Groote, J. F., Van Vlijmen, S. F. M., & Koorn, J. W. C. (1995). The safety guaranteeing system at station Hoorn-Kersenboogerd. In *Proceedings of the Tenth Annual Conference on Computer Assurance Systems Integrity, Software Safety and Process Security* (pp. 57–68). Washington, DC: IEEE.

Guerra, E., Souza, J., & Fernandes, C. (2009). A pattern language for metadata-based frameworks. In *Proceedings of the 16th Conference on Pattern Languages of Programs*. New York, NY: ACM.

Günther, S., Haupt, M., & Splieth, M. (2010). *Utilizing internal domain-specific languages for deployment and maintenance of IT infrastructures. Technical report (Internet) FIN-004-2010*. Magdeburg, Germany: Otto-von-Guericke-Universität.

Haase, A. (2007). Patterns for the definition of programming languages. In *Proceedings of 12th European Conference on Pattern Languages of Programs*.

Havelund, K., Ingham, M., & Wagner, D. (2010). A case study in DSL development – An experiment with Python and Scala. In *Scala Days*. Lausanne, Switzerland: Ecole polytechnique federale de Lausanne.

Heering, J. (2000). *Application software, domain-specific languages, and language design assistants. Technical report sen-r0010*. Amsterdam, Netherlands: Center for Mathematic and Computer Science, University of Amsterdam.

Hoare, C. A. R. (1973). *Hints on programming language design. Computer Science Department report no.stan-cs-73-403*. Stanford, CA: Stanford Artificial Intelligence Laboratory, Stanford University.

Hudak, P. (1998). Modular domain specific languages and tools. In P. Davenbu & J. Poulin (Ed.), *Proceedings of the Fifth International Conference on Software Reuse* (pp. 134–142). Washington, DC: IEEE.

Hudak, P. (2004). An algebraic theory of polymorphic temporal media. In Jayaraman, B. (Ed.), *Practical Aspects of Declarative Languages* (*Vol. 3057*, pp. 1–15). Lecture Notes in Computer Science Berlin, Germany: Springer-Verlag. doi:10.1007/978-3-540-24836-1_1

Kabanov, J., & Raudjärv, R. (2008). Embedded typesafe domain specific languages for Java. In *Proceedings of the 6th International Symposium on Principles and Practice of Programming in Java* (pp. 189–197). New York, NY: ACM.

Kiczales, G., Rivieres, J. d., & Bobrow, D. G. (1995). *The art of the metaobject protocol* (4th ed.). Cambridge, London, England: The MIT Press.

Klein, P., & Schürr, A. (1997). Constructing SDEs with the IPSEN meta environment. In J. Ebert & C. Lewerentz (Eds.), *Proceedings of the 8th International Conference on Software Engineering Environments* (pp. 2–10). Washington, DC: IEEE Computer Society.

Klint, P. (1993). A meta-environment for generating programming environments. *ACM Transactions on Software Engineering and Methodology, 2*(2), 176–201. doi:10.1145/151257.151260

Ladd, D. A., & Ramming, J. C. (1994). Two application languages in software production. In *Proceedings of the USENIX Very High Level Languages Symposium* (pp. 10–18). Berkeley, CA: USENIX Association.

Landin, P. J. (1966). The next 700 programming languages. *Communications of the ACM, 9*(3), 157–166. doi:10.1145/365230.365257

Larman, C. (2002). *Applying UML and patterns – An introduction to object-oriented analysis and design and the unified process* (2nd ed.). Upper-Saddle River, NJ: Prentice Hall.

Latry, F., Mercadal, J., & Consel, C. (2007). Staging telephony service creation: A language approach. In *Proceedings of the 1st International Conference on Principles, Systems and Applications of IP Telecommunications* (pp. 99–110). New York, NY: ACM.

Leijen, D., & Meijer, E. (2001). *Parsec: Direct style monadic parser combinators for the real world. Technical Report*. Utrecht, Netherlands: Utrecht University.

Liang, S., & Bracha, G. (1998). Dynamic class loading in the Java virtual machine. *ACM SIGPLAN Notices, 33*(10), 36–44. doi:10.1145/286942.286945

Lieberherr, K. J., & Holland, I. (1989). Formulations and benefits of the law of Demeter. *ACM SIGPLAN Notices, 24*(3), 67–78. doi:10.1145/66083.66089

Lutz, M. (2009). *Learning Python* (4th ed.). Sebastopol, CA: O'Reilly Media.

McKeeman, W. (1974). Programming language design. In F. L. Brauer, J. Eickel, F. L. D. Remer, M. Griffiths, U. Hill, J. J. Horning, … W. M. Waite (Eds.), *Lecture Notes in Computer Science: Vol. 21, Compiler Construction – An Advanced Course* (pp. 514–524). Berlin, Germany: Springer-Verlag.

Mernik, M., Heering, J., & Sloane, A. M. (2005). When and how to develop domain-specific languages. *ACM Computing Surveys, 37*(4), 316–344. doi:10.1145/1118890.1118892

Miller, G. (1956). The magical number seven, plus or minus two: Some limits on our capacity for processing information. *Psychological Review, 63*(2), 81–97. doi:10.1037/h0043158

Moody, D. L. (2009). The "physics" of notations: Toward a scientific basis for constructing visual notations in software engineering. *IEEE Transactions on Software Engineering, 35*(6), 756–779. doi:10.1109/TSE.2009.67

Munnelly, J., & Clarke, S. (2007). ALPH: A domain-specific language for crosscutting pervasive healthcare concerns. In *Proceedings of the 2nd Workshop on Domain Specific Aspect Languages*. New York, NY: ACM.

Neighbors, J. (1980). *Software construction using components*. Ph.D. thesis, University of California, Berkeley.

Oliveira, N., Pereira, M., Henriques, P., & Cruz, D. (2009). Domain specific languages: A theoretical survey. In *INFORUM Simposio de Informatica*. Lisboa, Portugal: University of Lisboa.

Perrotta, P. (2010). *Metaprogramming Ruby*. Raleigh, NC: The Pragmatic Bookshelf.

Pratt, T. W., & Zelkowitz, M. V. (2000). *Programming languages – Design and implementation*. Upper Saddle River, NJ: Prentice Hall.

Python Software Foundation. (2011). *Python reference documentation*. Retrieved March 16, 2011, from http://docs.python.org/release/2.6.6/

Sadilek, D. A. (2007). Prototyping domain-specific languages for wireless sensor networks. In *Proceedings of the 4th International Workshop on Software Language Engineering* (pp. 76–91).

Sloane, A. M. (2008). Experiences with domain-specific language embedding in Scala. In *2nd International Workshop on Domain-Specific Program Development*. Nashville, TN: ACM.

Spiewak, D., & Zhao, T. (2009). ScalaQL: Language-integrated database queries for Scala. In M. van den Brand, D. Gasěvic, & J. Gray (Eds.), *Lecture Notes in Computer Science: vol. 5966, Proceedings of the 2nd International Conference on Software Language Engineering* (pp. 154–163). Berlin, Germany: Springer-Verlag.

Spinellis, D. (2001). Notable design patterns for domain-specific languages. *Journal of Systems and Software, 56*(1), 91–99. doi:10.1016/S0164-1212(00)00089-3

Srinivas, Y. (1991). *Algebraic specification of domains. Domain Analysis and Software Systems Modeling* (pp. 90–124). New York, NY: IEEE.

Summerfield, M. (2010). *Programming in Python 3: A complete introduction to the Python Programming Language* (2nd ed.). Upper Saddle River, Boston, USA: Addison-Wesley.

Tambe, S., & Gokhale, A. (2009). LEESA: Embedding strategic and XPath-like object structure traversals in C. In Taha, W. (Ed.), *Domain-Specific Languages* (*Vol. 5658*, pp. 100–124). Lecture Notes in Computer Science Berlin, Germany: Springer-Verlag. doi:10.1007/978-3-642-03034-5_6

Tanter, E. (2008). Contextual values. In *Proceedings of the 2008 Symposium on Dynamic Languages*. Washington, DC, USA: IEEE.

Thibault, S., Marlet, R., & Consel, C. (1997). A domain-specific language for video device drivers: From design to implementation. In *Proceedings of the Conference on Domain-Specific* (pp. 11–26).

Thielemann, H. (2004). Audio processing using Haskell. In *Proceedings of the 7th International Conference on Digital Audio Processing* (pp. 201–206).

Thomas, D., Fowler, C., & Hunt, A. (2009). *Programming Ruby 1.9 - The pragmatic programmers' guide*. Raleigh, NC: The Pragmatic Bookshelf.

Tobin-Hochstadt, S., St-Amour, V., Culpepper, R., Flatt, M., & Felleisen, M. (2011). Languages as libraries. In *Proceedings of the 32nd ACM SIGPLAN Conference on Programming Language Design and Implementation* (pp. 132–141). New York, NY: ACM.

van Deursen, A., Klint, P., & Visser, J. (2000). Domain-specific languages: An annotated bibliography. *ACM SIGPLAN Notices, 35*(6), 26–36. doi:10.1145/352029.352035

Vanderbauwhede, W., Margala, M., Chalamalasetti, S. R., & Purohit, S. (2010). A C++-Embedded domain-specific language for programming the MORA soft processor array. In *Proceedings of the 21st IEEE International Conference on Application-Specific Systems Architectures and Processors* (pp. 141–148).

Wampler, D., & Payne, A. (2009). *Programming Scala*. Sebastopol, CA: O'Reilly Media.

Weinberg, G. M. (1971). *The philosophy of programming languages*. New York, NY: John Wiley & Sons.

Wirth, N. (1974). On the design of programming languages. In J. L. Rosenfeld (Ed.), *Proceedings of the 6th International Federation for Information Processing Congress* (pp. 386–393). Stockholm, Sweden: University of Stockholm.

Zdun, U., & Strembeck, M. (2009). Reusable architectural decisions for DSL design: Foundational decisions in DSL projects. In A. Kelly & M. Weiss (Eds.), *Proceedings of the 14th Annual European Conference on Pattern Languages of Programming*. Aachen, Germany: CEUR, RWTH Aachen.

ADDITIONAL READING

Karsai, G., Krahn, H., Pinkernell, C., Rumpe, B., Schindler, M., & Völkel, S. (2009). Design guidelines for domain specific languages. In M. Rossi, J. Sprinkle, J. Gray, & J.-P. Tolvanen (Eds.), *Proceedings of the 9th OOPSLA Workshop on Domain-Specific Modeling*. Aalto, Finland: HSE Publishing.

Kim, D.-K., France, R., & Ghosh, S. (2004). A UML-based language for specifying domain-specific patterns. *Journal of Visual Languages and Computing, 15*(3–4), 265–289. doi:10.1016/j.jvlc.2004.01.004

Parr, T. (2009). *Language implementation patterns: Create your own domain-specific and general programming languages*. Raleigh, NC: Pragmatic Bookshelf.

Schäfer, C., Kuhn, T., & Trapp, M. (2011). A pattern-based approach to DSL development. In *Proceedings of the Compilation of the Co-Located Workshops on DSM'11, TMC'11, AGERE!'11, AOOPES'11, NEAT'11, & VMIL'11* (pp. 39-46). New York, NY: ACM.

KEY TERMS AND DEFINITIONS

Domain-Specific Language (DSL): An artificially created, compiled or interpreted computer language that represents the concepts, attributes, and operations of a domain by implementing suitable abstractions and notations.

DSL Abstraction Patterns: Patterns that integrate the DSL's semantics and abstractions into the host language by using metaprogramming or reflection.

DSL Design Pattern: A structured description of common design challenges and their solutions that helps to communicate development knowledge and structure designs.

DSL Design Principle: A general guideline that expresses a design goal how to apply a design pattern.

DSL Foundation Patterns: Essential patterns that explain how the domain concepts, attributes, and operations are implemented as objects and methods of the DSL.

DSL Notation Patterns: Patterns that exploit syntactic variations of the host language to design the domain-specific notations of the DSL.

Internal Domain-Specific Language: An internal DSL uses an existing programming language as its host, where domain-specific concepts, attributes, and operations are implemented through adaptions of the host's constructs and abstractions. Also called embedded DSL.

ENDNOTES

1 http://aws.amazon.com

Section 2
Domain-Specific Language Semantics

Chapter 8
Formal Semantics for Metamodel-Based Domain Specific Languages

Paolo Arcaini
Università degli Studi di Milano, Italy

Angelo Gargantini
Università di Bergamo, Italy

Elvinia Riccobene
Università degli Studi di Milano, Italy

Patrizia Scandurra
Università di Bergamo, Italy

ABSTRACT

Domain Specific Languages (DSLs) are often defined in terms of metamodels capturing the abstract syntax of the language. For a complete definition of a DSL, both syntactic and semantic aspects of the language have to be specified. Metamodeling environments support syntactic definition issues, but they do not provide any help in defining the semantics of metamodels, which is usually given in natural language. In this chapter, the authors present an approach to formally define the semantics of metamodel-based languages. It is based on a translational technique that hooks to the language metamodel its precise and executable semantics expressed in terms of the Abstract State Machine formal method. The chapter also shows how different techniques can be used for formal analysis of models (i.e., instance of the language metamodel). The authors exemplify the use of their approach on a language for Petri nets.

INTRODUCTION

In the context of language and software development, *modeling* is beginning to take a more prominent role. Model-based approaches consider models as first-class entities that need to be maintained, analyzed, simulated and otherwise exercised, and mapped into programs and/or other models by automatic model transformations.

Domain Specific Languages (DSLs) themselves can be seen as artifacts of the model-based approach for language engineering. Indeed, in a

DOI: 10.4018/978-1-4666-2092-6.ch008

model-based language definition, the abstract syntax of a language is defined in terms of an object-oriented model, called *metamodel*, that characterizes syntax elements and their relationships, so separating the abstract syntax and semantics of the language constructs from their different concrete notations. Although a complete definition of a DSL requires both syntactic and semantic aspects of the language to be precisely specified, metamodeling environments (Eclipse/Ecore, GME/MetaGME, AMMA/KM3, XMF-Mosaic/Xcore, etc.) cope with most syntactic and transformation definition issues, but no standard and rigorous way exists for defining language semantics that is usually given in natural language. A rigorous approach to specify the semantics of metamodels is currently an open and crucial issue in the model-driven context.

In general, metamodel semantics can be given with different degrees of formality by a mapping to a sufficiently well-known domain or target platform (like the JVM). However, incomplete and informal specifications of a language make precise understanding of its syntax and semantics difficult. Moreover, the lack of formally specified language semantics can cause a semantic mismatch between design models and tools supporting the analysis of models of the language (Chen, Sztipanovits, & Neema, 2005). We believe these shortcomings can be avoided by integrating metamodeling techniques with formal methods providing the requested rigor and preciseness. Applying a formal method to a DSL defined in a metamodeling framework should have two main goals: (a) allowing the definition of the semantics of models conforming to the DSL and (b) providing several techniques and methods for the formal analysis (e.g., validation, property proving, model checking, etc.) of such models. Indeed, a semantics is essential to communicate the meaning of models or programs to stakeholders in the development process, and a formal definition of the semantics of a DSL is a key prerequisite for the verification of the correctness of models specified using such a DSL.

In (Gargantini, Riccobene, & Scandurra, 2009; Gargantini, Riccobene, & Scandurra, 2010), the feasibility and the advantages of integrating metamodeling techniques and formal methods in the context of the ASM (Abstract State Machine) formalism(Börger & Stärk, 2003) is analyzed. (Gargantini, Riccobene, & Scandurra, 2009) proposes different techniques to endow metamodel-based languages with precise and executable semantics. These techniques imply a different level of automation, user freedom, possible reuse, and user effort in defining semantics, but they all share a common unifying formal ASM framework.

In this chapter, we present the application of one of these techniques to express the semantics (possibly executable) of metamodel-based DSLs. We present the semantic *hooking* approach that allows designers to hook to the language metamodel an ASM, which contains all data structures modeling elements of the metamodel with their relationships, and all transition rules representing behavioral aspects of the language. Model-to-text transformations are used to map metamodel elements into corresponding ASM constructs. We exemplify the application of our approach on a language for Petri nets. This work extends (Gargantini, Riccobene, & Scandurra, 2009) by showing how different techniques, like simulation, scenario-based validation, model review, and model property checking, can be performed for formal analysis of DSL models.

The chapter is organized as follows:

- Section BACKGROUND provides an overview on the approaches existing in the literature for defining semantics of DSLs. It briefly introduces the Abstract State Machine formal method and the set of tools for model analysis the method supports. Furthermore, a very concise description of the two main formal analysis activities, *model validation* and *model verification,* is given.
- Section DSL CASE STUDY: PETRI NETS presents the abstract syntax of a language

for Petri nets used, throughout the chapter, as case study to exemplify the approach of semantic definition and model analysis.

- Section SEMANTIC FRAMEWORK FOR METAMODEL-BASED DSL presents an approach to endow language metamodels with precise executable semantics. It also shows the application of the approach on a language for Petri nets, endowing the language abstract syntax with an executable semantics in terms of the ASMs.
- Section FORMAL ANALYSIS OF DSL SEMANTICS discusses techniques for formal analysis, with particular emphasis on those supported by a set of tools for the ASMs, which can be used once ASM formal models are associated to language terminal models by automatic model transformation. Different techniques for model validation and verification are applied on Petri net models.
- Section ADVANTAGES AND LIMITATIONS OF THE ASM-BASED SEMANTIC APPROACH discusses the use of the ASMs in the context of the formal definition of DSL semantics.
- Section COMPARISON BETWEEN METAMODEL-BASED AND GRAMMAR-BASED DSLS discusses advantages and disadvantages of applying the proposed method for semantic definition on DSLs whose syntax is expressed in terms of a metamodel w.r.t. those having a grammar-based syntax.
- Section CONCLUSION AND FUTURE RESEARCH DIRECTIONS concludes the chapter and draws research future directions on the topic of DSL semantics definition.
- Suggestions for *additional readings* and definitions of a set of *keywords* are given at the end.

BACKGROUND

This section provides an overview on the approaches existing in the literature for defining language semantics. Particular emphasis is given to those concerning semantics of metamodel-based DSLs. It also briefly introduces the Abstract State Machine formal method, which is at the basis of the semantic framework in (Gargantini, Riccobene, & Scandurra, 2009), and the ASMETA tool set that has been developed for ASM models editing and analysis.

Existing Approaches for Defining Language Semantics

Language semantics describes the meaning of concepts in the language. There are many ways of describing that. They range from the use of a *natural language*, where semantics is a correlation or mapping between concepts in the language with thoughts and experiences of concepts in the world around us, to more *formal approaches* having a strong mathematical foundation, where this correlation or mapping has rigorous foundations and the target concepts have already a well-formed (i.e., clear and precise) definition. In both cases, a key requirement of semantics is that it should be of practical use in understanding the meaning of a language. However, a formal approach is desirable to avoid misinterpretation and developing tools proving contradictory implementations of the same semantics. Furthermore, if a DSL supports constructs for modeling behavior, it requires semantics able to describe how models or programs written in the language execute, and not all formal methods are suitable to this purpose.

In case of a metamodel-based DSL, the *abstract syntax* of the language defining the structure of the language is provided by means of a *metamodel*. It is an object-oriented model of the vocabulary of the language, which represents concepts provided by the language, the relationships existing among those concepts, and how they may be combined to create models. Precise guidelines exist (Strembeck & Zdun, 2009) to drive this modeling activity that leads to an instantiation of the chosen metamodeling framework for a specific domain of interest. This activity is, however, out of the scope of this chapter and we assume the reader is familiar with techniques to express the language abstract syntax in terms of a metamodel.

The abstract syntax is a prerequisite for defining semantics, as semantics adds a layer of meaning to the concepts defined in the abstract syntax. Semantics in this sense should also be distinguished from *static semantics*, consisting of rules dictating whether or not an expression of the language is well-formed. Static semantics rules are those employed by tools such as type checkers. Languages such as OCL (OMG. Object Constraint Language (OCL), v2.0 formal/2006-05-01, 2006) allow specifying structural semantics (static semantics) through invariants defined over the abstract syntax of the language. They are used to check whether a model conforms to its modeling language (i.e., it is well-formed) or not. The OCL is also often used to specify behavioral semantics through the definition of pre- and post-conditions on operations. However, being side-effect free, the OCL does not allow the change of a model state, though it allows describing it.

Different approaches have been introduced (Bryant, et al., 2011; Clark, Sammut, & Willans, 2008) to model the so-called *dynamic semantics*, and some recent works have addressed the problem of providing executability into current metamodeling environments. Proposed solutions may be classified into the following main categories, although the separation is not always well delimited:

- *Translational semantics*,
- *Operational semantics* through weaving behavior or rewriting rules,
- *Denotational semantics* with semantic domain modeling.

Translational Semantics

This approach consists in defining a mapping from the abstract syntax of the language to the concept of another language that has a precise semantics. The advantage of the translational approach is that it is possible to obtain an executable semantics for the language via the translation, under the existence of a machine that can execute the target language. The main disadvantage of the approach is that information might be lost during the transformation process and that it could not be obvious how the obtained primitives are related to the original language constructs. This translational semantics has been used, for example, in (Chen, Sztipanovits, & Neema, 2005). They propose a *semantic anchoring* to translate abstract syntax elements into well-established formal models of computation (such as FSMs, data flow, and discrete event systems), called *semantic units*, expressed in AsmL (an ASM dialect). Two main disadvantages can be detected in this approach: first, it requires well understood and safe behavioral language units and it is not clear how to specify the language semantics from scratch when these language units do not yet exist; second, in heterogeneous systems, specifying the language semantics as composition of some selected primary semantic units for basic behavioral categories (Chen, Sztipanovits, & Neema, 2007) is not always possible, since there may exist complex behaviors which are not easily reducible to a combination of existing ones. A translational approach was also proposed in (Di Ruscio, Jouault, Kurtev, Bézivin, & Pierantonio, 2006) to provide the dynamic semantics of the AMMA/ATL transformation language into XASM (Anlauff, 2000), an open source ASM dialect. A further recent result in (Sadilek, 2008) proposes ASMs, Prolog, and Scheme as description languages in a framework named EProvide 2.0 for prototyping the operational semantics of metamodel-based languages. Even if their approach belongs to the operational category, it can also be considered translational as it is based on three bridges: a physical, a logical, and a pragmatic bridge between grammarware language and modeling framework. The work presented in (Romero, Rivera, Durán, & Vallecillo, 2007) describes a translation semantics definition with Maude. The authors show how models, metamodels, and their dynamic behavior can be specified in Maude using rewriting logic. In (Rivera, Durán, & Vallecillo, 2009) they also show how analysis capabilities (like model checking, theorem proving, and so on) of a set of tools developed around Maude can be used to reason about models. The rewriting logic is also applied in (Stehr, Meseguer, & Ölveczky, 2001) as unifying framework for a wide range of Petri nets models. The logical and operational representation of Petri net models is used for formal verification and for the efficient execution and analysis using a rewriting engine such as Maude. A semantics definition approach, based on transition systems, is presented in (Sadilek & Wachsmuth, 2009): states are defined by metamodel instances and transitions are defined by model transformations. The Object-Z language, an object extension of the Z formal notation, is used in (Hahn, 2008) to define the semantics of agent-based systems in a visual manner. A semantic framework based on ASMs was introduced in (Gargantini, Riccobene, & Scandurra, 2009) to define the semantics of metamodel-based languages. They present three translational semantics techniques (semantic mapping, semantic hooking and semantic meta-hooking) usable at different levels of the metamodeling stack (meta-metamodel/metamodel/model) to translate the semantics into ASM models. Examples of application of these techniques can be found in (Gargantini, Riccobene, & Scandurra, 2010) where a complete integration of the semantic framework with the Eclipse Modeling Framework is presented, and in (Riccobene & Scandurra, 2010) where the complete semantics of the UML profile for the SystemC language is given.

Operational Semantics

Operational approaches aim at modeling operational behavior of language concepts. Different techniques fall within this category. The *weaving approach* consists of weaving behavior into metamodels, i.e., specifying an executable semantics directly on the abstract syntax of the language by promoting meta-languages for the semantics specification. Meta-programming languages like Kermeta (Muller, Fleurey, & Jezequel, 2005), xOCL (eXecutable OCL) of the XMFMosaic metamodeling framework (The Xactium XMF Mosaic, 2007), or also the approach in (Scheidgen & Fischer, 2007), are examples of the weaving technique. Inspired from the UML action semantics (Sunyé, Pennaneac'h, Ho, Le Guennec, & Jézéquel, 2001), they all use a minimal set of executable primitives to define the behavior of metamodels by attaching behavior to classes operations. Such action languages can be imperative or object-oriented. Although they aim to be pragmatic, extensible and modifiable, some of them suffer from the same shortcomings of traditional UML-based action languages, i.e., they are a simplified version of real programming languages, and therefore they are too platform-dependent and not always suitable to capture the model of computation of the underlying language. The adoption of more abstract action languages is desirable to reduce model complexity. Another effort toward this direction is presented in (Soden & Eichler, 2009) where the authors describe the M3Actions framework to support operational semantics for EMF models. In (Riccobene & Scandurra, 2009), a weaving approach is proposed to provide executability of Platform Independent Models (PIMs) by using the ASMs.

A different way to provide operational semantics is the *rewriting system* approach, where the system consists of rewrite rules and its execution is based on the repeated application of the rewrite rules to an existing configuration (i.e., a model). Typically, the existing approaches employ graph rewriting where the semantics can be specified in an operational fashion through the graphical definition given by graph grammars (Varró, 2002). Examples of this approach can be found in (Engels, Hausmann, Heckel, & Sauer, 2000) and in (Ermel, 2005) where graph transformations are used to give semantics of UML behavioral diagrams.

Denotational Semantics

It has the purpose of associating mathematical objects with concepts of the language. It requires the definition of a *semantic domain* where the concepts of the language can have meaning, and the definition of a *semantic mapping* to associate language constructs with elements of the semantic domain. Denotational descriptions of semantics tend to be static, i.e., they enumerate valid instances of concepts, but in a non-executable style. A denotational semantics can be defined in a metamodeling way by constructing a metamodel for the "semantic domain", and then using well-formedness OCL rules to map elements of the language metamodel into elements of the semantic domain metamodel. This approach is known as *semantic domain modeling*. It is used, for example, by the OMG task forces for the CMOF Abstract Semantics – see Chapter 15 in (OMG. Meta Object Facility (MOF), Core Specification v2.0, formal/2006-01-01, 2006) – and for the OCL (OMG. Object Constraint Language (OCL), v2.0 formal/2006-05-01, 2006). A similar technique, also used for the OCL semantics, involves set theory to formulate the semantic domain in terms of an object model (a formalization of UML class diagrams, not of the OCL metamodel) and system states for the evaluation of OCL expressions. This last was originally proposed in (Richters, 2001), and then used also in (Flake & Müller, 2004) where new components of the object model and system states have been introduced and the ASM formalism have been used to formalize the evaluation of OCL constraints.

For a specific category of metamodel-based languages, those DSLs whose metamodel is defined as a *profile*, i.e., a collection of stereotypes that can be viewed as sub-classes of UML or MOF model elements, an *extensional approach*, as also remarked in (Bryant, et al., 2011), can be used to define the semantics of the language. It is given as an extension of that of another language: modeling concepts in the new language inherit their semantics from concepts in the other language, and the user can add arbitrarily rich semantic extensions to the new concepts. This approach is quite orthogonal to the other techniques reported above. For example, if the extended language already has a denotational semantics, the semantics of languages defined with it can naturally follow this style. This approach requires a well-defined semantics of the original language. This is not the case for the UML.

Abstract State Machines

Abstract State Machines (Börger & Stärk, 2003) are an extension of Finite State Machines, where unstructured "internal" control states are replaced by states comprising arbitrary complex data. The *states* of an ASM are multi-sorted first-order structures, i.e., domains of objects with functions and predicates defined on them. The *transition relation* is specified by "rules" describing the modification of the functions from one state to the next. The basic form of a transition rule is the *guarded update*

```
if Condition then Updates
```

Functions are classified as *derived* functions, i.e., those coming with a specification or computation mechanism given in terms of other functions, and *basic* functions which can be *static* (never change during any run of the machine) or *dynamic* (may change as a consequence of agent actions or updates). Dynamic functions are further classified into: *monitored* (only read, as events provided by

Box 1. ASM tuple definition

```
ASM = (header, body, main rule, initialization)
```

the environment), *controlled* (read and write), *shared* and *output* (only write) functions.

These is a limited but powerful set of rule constructors to express simultaneous *parallel* actions (`par`), *sequential* actions (`seq`), *iterations* (`iterate`, `while`, `recwhile`), and *submachine invocations* returning values. Appropriate rule constructors also allow *non-determinism* (existential quantification `choose`) and unrestricted *synchronous parallelism* (universal quantification `forall`).

An *ASM M* is a finite set of rules for such guarded multiple function updates. State transitions of *M* may be influenced in two ways: internally through the transition rules, or externally through the modifications of the environment. A computation of *M* is a finite or infinite sequence $S_0, S_1, \ldots S_n$ of states of *M*, where S_0 is an initial state and each S_{i+1} is obtained from S_i by firing simultaneously all of the transition rules which are enabled in S_i.

Although the ASM method comes with a rigorous mathematical foundation, ASMs can be read as pseudocode on arbitrary data structures, and, in the sequel, we use its tuple definition as presented in Box 1.

The *header* contains the name of the ASM and its signature, namely all domain, function and predicate declarations. The *body* of an ASM consists of (static) domain and (static/derived) function definitions according to domain and function declarations in the signature of the ASM. It also contains declarations (definitions) of transition rules and definitions of invariants one wants to assume for domains and functions of the ASM. The (unique) *main rule* is a transition rule and represents the starting point of the machine program (i.e., it calls all the other ASM transition rules defined in the body). The main rule is closed (i.e., it does not have parameters) and since there are no free global variables in the rule declarations of an ASM, the notion of a move does not depend on a variable assignment, but only on the state of the machine. The *initialization* of an ASM is a characterization of the initial states. An initial state defines an initial value for domains and functions declared in the signature of the ASM. Executing an ASM means executing its main rule starting from a specified initial state.

The ASMETA toolset

The *ASMETA* (ASM mETAmodeling) toolset (Gargantini, Riccobene, & Scandurra, 2007; Arcaini, Gargantini, Riccobene, & Scandurra, 2011) is a set of tools around ASMs developed according to the model-driven development principles. The core of the toolset (see Figure 1) is the AsmM metamodel: a complete meta-level representation of ASMs concepts based on the meta-language EMF/Ecore.

In (Arcaini, Gargantini, Riccobene, & Scandurra, 2011) the model-driven process used to develop the ASMETA toolset is presented. This process builds a bridge from the AsmM to other technical frameworks. This allows the integration of external tools, to benefit from their features and the different analysis they perform.

Figure 1. The ASMETA tool set

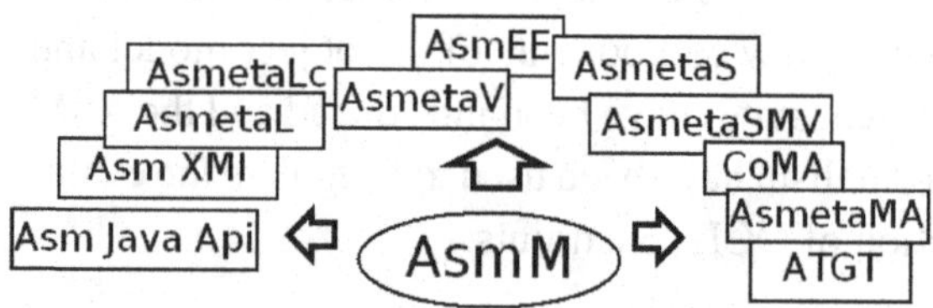

Currently, the ASMETA toolset includes, among other things,:

- A textual notation, *AsmetaL*, to write ASM models (conforming to the AsmM) in a textual and human-comprehensible form;
- A text-to-model compiler, *AsmetaLc*, and an OCL Checker to respectively parse AsmetaL models and check for their consistency w.r.t. the AsmM OCL constraints;
- An *XMI* (XML Metadata Interchange) interchange format for ASM models, *Java APIs* for the creation, storage, access and manipulation of ASM models;
- A simulator, *AsmetaS*, to execute ASM models;
- The Avalla language and the *AsmetaV* validator for scenario-based validation of ASM models;
- The *ATGT* tool for automatic test case generation from ASM models, which is based upon the SPIN model checker (Holzmann, 2004);
- An Eclipse plug-in called ASMEE (ASM Eclipse Environment) which acts as graphical front-end to edit, manipulate, and export ASM models by using all tools/artifacts listed above;
- The *AsmetaSMV* tool, a model checker for ASM models written in AsmetaL based on NuSMV. AsmetaSMV supports both the declaration of Computation Tree Logic (CTL) and Linear Temporal Logic (LTL) formulas;
- The *AsmetaMA* tool, to check that an AsmetaL model satisfies some quality properties (called *meta-properties*) that the model should assure.

Model Analysis Techniques

This section briefly sketches the main formal activities that can be performed on models specified by a DSL and that require a precise formal semantics of these models. Principal activities are: *model validation* and *model verification*.

Model Validation

Validation is intended as the process of investigating a model (intended as formal specification) with respect to its user perceptions, in order to ensure that the specification really reflects the user needs and statements about the application, and to detect faults in the specification as early as possible with limited effort. Techniques for validation include *scenarios generation*, when the user builds scenarios describing the behavior of a system by looking at the observable interactions between the system and its environment in specific situations; *simulation*, when the user provides certain input and observes

if the output is the expected one or not (it is similar to code debugging); *model-based testing*, when the specification is used as oracle to compute test cases for a given critical behavior of the system at the same level of the specification. These abstract test cases cannot be executed at code level since they are at a wrong level of abstraction. Executable test cases must be derived from the abstract ones and executed at code level to guarantee conformance between model and code.

Model Verification

Verification consists in applying more expensive and accurate analysis methods, like *requirements formal analysis* and *verification of properties*, that should be applied only when a designer has enough confidence that his/her model captures all informal requirements, thus after model validation. Formal verification has to be intended as the mathematical proof of system properties, which can be performed by hand or by the aid of *model checkers* (which are usable when the variable ranges are finite) or of *theorem provers* (which require strong user skills to drive the proof).

DSL CASE STUDY: PETRI NETS

This section presents the metamodel of a DSL used as case study in the chapter for modeling Petri nets. The metamodel is of manageable dimension and the Petri net semantics is well-known. We prefer the reader to concentrate on understanding our semantic technique rather than on comprehending a complex application case study.

The formal definition of Petri Nets, with weights, that can be found in (Murata, 1989), follows. An *infinite capacity Petri net* is a 5-tuple, $PN = (P, T, F, W, M_0)$

- $P = \{p_1, p_2, \ldots, p_m\}$ is the set of places
- $T = \{t_1, t_2, \ldots, t_n\}$ is the set of transitions
- $F \subseteq (P \times T) \cup (T \times P)$ is the set of arcs
- $W: F \rightarrow N^+$ is a weight function
- $M_0: P \rightarrow N$ is the initial marking
- $P \cup T \neq \varnothing$: a net has at least a place or a transition
- $P \cap T = \varnothing$: places and transitions are distinct

A *finite capacity Petri net* has the further parameter:

- $K: P \rightarrow N^+$ is the capacity function

Figure 2 shows an infinite capacity Petri net, while Figure 3 reports a finite capacity Petri net representing a producer and a consumer connected by a buffer of capacity 10.

Figure 4 shows the metamodel for the weighted infinite capacity Petri net formalism. It describes the static structure of a net consisting of places and transitions (the two classes *Place* and *Transition*), and of directed arcs represented by the *OutArc* class for arcs exiting from transitions and by the *InArc* class for arcs entering in transitions. Every arc has its weight and places keep track of the tokens in them. For Petri nets with capacity, the metamodel is the same, but the class *Place* has another attribute capacity representing the maximum number of tokens a place can contain.

Figure 2. Infinite capacity Petri Net

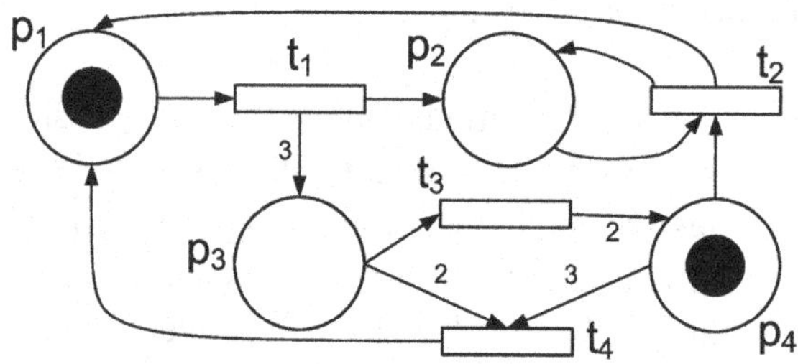

Figure 3. Finite capacity Petri net

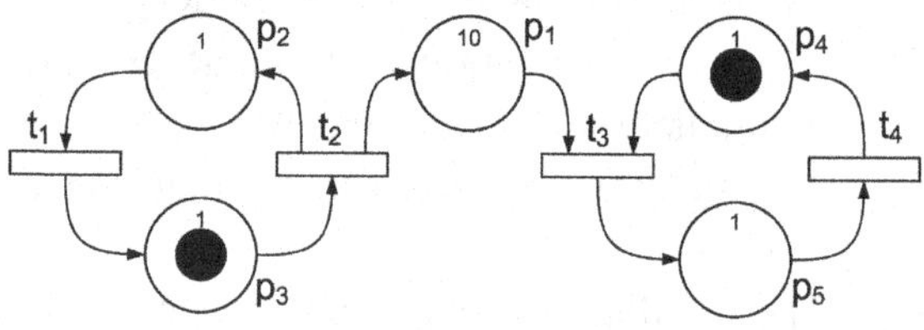

Figure 4. Infinite capacity Petri Nets metamodel

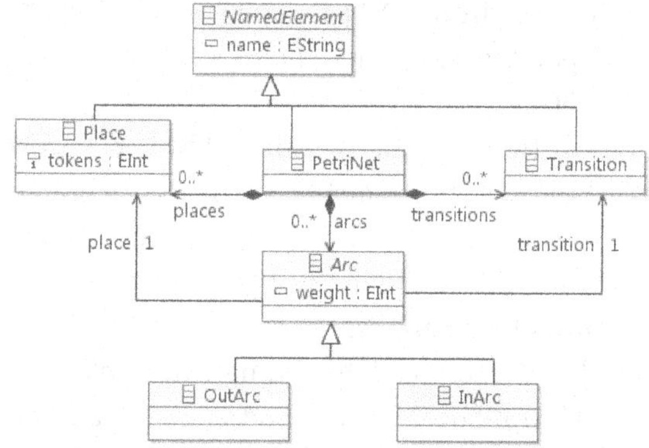

SEMANTIC FRAMEWORK FOR METAMODEL-BASED DSLS

This section presents the general ASM-based semantic framework, proposed in (Gargantini,

Riccobene, & Scandurra, 2009), to provide semantics of metamodel-based DSLs. Among the three semantic techniques there described, we here introduce *semantic hooking* that we believe can be of easier application. By using this technique, designers hook to the language metamodel A an abstract state machine M, which contains all data structures modeling elements of A with their relationships, and all transition rules representing behavioral aspects of the language. M does not contain the initialization of functions and domains, which will depend on the particular instance of A. In this way, semantics of a DSL is given by means of a unique ASM for any model conforming to A.

ASM-Based Language Semantics Definition

A metamodel-based language L has a well-defined semantics if a *semantic domain* S is identified and a *semantic mapping* M_S: $A \rightarrow S$ is provided (Harel & Rumpe, 2004) between the L's abstract syntax A (i.e., the metamodel of L) and S to give meaning to syntactic concepts of L in terms of the semantic domain elements.

Although the semantic domain S and the mapping M_S can be described with varying degrees of formality, from natural language to rigorous mathematics, to avoid mismatching and misunderstanding, both S and M_S should be defined in a precise, clear, and readable way.

The semantic domain S is usually defined in some formal, mathematical framework (transition systems, pomsets, traces, the set of natural numbers with its underlying properties, are examples of semantic domains). The semantic mapping M_S is not so often given in a formal and precise way, possibly leaving some doubts about the semantics of L. Thus, a precise and formal approach to define it is desirable. Sometimes, in order to give the semantics of a language L, another helper language L', whose semantics is clearly defined and well established, is introduced. Therefore, $M'_{S'}$ and S' should be already well-defined for L'.

L' can be exploited to define the semantics of L by:

1. Taking S' as semantic domain for L too, i.e., $S = S'$,
2. Introducing a building function $M: A \rightarrow A'$, being A' the abstract syntax of L', which associates an element of A' to every construct of A, and
3. Defining the semantic mapping M_S: $A \rightarrow S$ as $M_S = M'_S \circ M$

The function M *hooks* the semantics of A to the semantic domain S' of the language L'. The complexity of this approach depends on the complexity of building the function M. Note that the function M can be applied to terminal models m conforming to A in order to obtain models m' conforming to A', as shown in Figure 5 (note that ω is the conforming function).

In this way, the semantic mapping M_S: $A \rightarrow S$ associates a well-formed terminal model m conforming to A with its semantic model $M_S(m)$, by first translating m to m' conforming to A' by means of the M function, and then applying the mapping M'_S which is already well-defined.

Let us assume the ASMs as helper language. The semantic domain S_{AsmM} is the first-order logic extended with the logic for function updates and for transition rule constructors defined in (Börger & Stärk, 2003) and the semantic mapping M_S: $AsmM \rightarrow S_{AsmM}$ to relate syntactic concepts to those of the semantic domain is given in (Gargantini, Riccobene, & Scandurra, A Metamodel-based Language and a Simulation Engine for Abstract State Machines, 2008).

The semantics of a metamodel-based language is expressed in terms of ASM transition rules by providing the building function $M: A \rightarrow AsmM$. As already mentioned, the definition of the function M may be accomplished by different techniques

Figure 5. DSL semantics schema

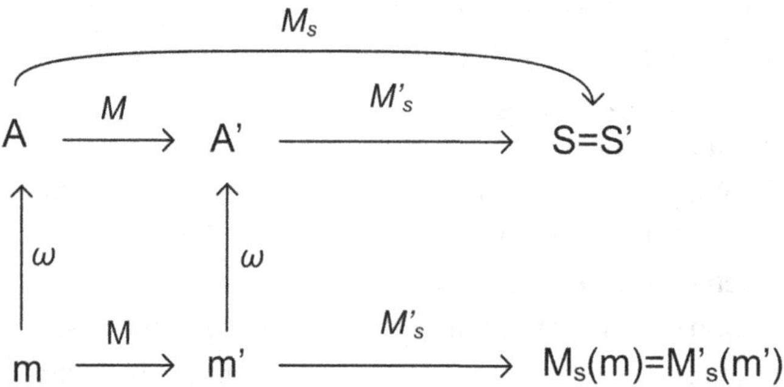

Box 2 Building function definition

$M(m) = \iota_A(\Gamma_A, m)$, for all m conforming to A

(see (Gargantini, Riccobene, & Scandurra, 2009)), which differ in the way a terminal model is mapped into an ASM. As example of such techniques, the *semantic hooking technique* is presented below. This technique is used in Section *Application of the Semantic Hooking to the DSL Case Study* to provide behavioral semantics of the language in our case study.

Semantic Hooking

By using this technique, the designer *hooks* to the language metamodel A an ASM Γ_A. Γ_A formalizes all modeling elements of A with their relationships, and contains all transition rules representing behavioral aspects of the language. Therefore, to use the semantic hooking, the language designer identifies the common concepts of all models conforming to A and builds an ASM Γ_A providing semantics to the structural elements of the language. The definition of Γ_A is manually obtained from A and a certain effort is required to capture the intended behavior of the metamodel concepts starting from their structure.

Γ_A is unique and it is common for all the terminal models of A. Γ_A does not contain the initialization of functions and domains, which will depend on the particular instance of A. This allows the language designer to reason about the language properties regardless the terminal models. The semantics of a particular model m is obtained from Γ_A by applying a function ι_A which provides initialization of domains and functions of Γ_A by taking information from m. Therefore, the final ASM depends on the particular terminal model only in its initialization part (initial elements of the domains, initial values for functions). Formally, the building function M is given as presented in Box 2.

Γ_A: *AsmM*, is an ASM which contains only declarations of functions and domains (the signature) and the behavioral semantics of L in terms of ASM transition rules.

ι_A: $AsmM \times A \rightarrow AsmM$, properly initializes the machine. ι_A is defined on an ASM a and a terminal model m instance of A; it navigates m and sets the initial values for the functions and the initial elements in the domains declared in the signature of a. It can add definitions for functions already declared in the signature of A. The ι_A function is applied to Γ_A and to the terminal model m for which it yields the final ASM.

Application of the Semantic Hooking to the DSL Case Study

The Γ_{PN} models the semantics for the Petri net language whose abstract syntax is given by the metamodel in Figure 4. In Γ_{PN} abstract domains for the transitions and the places must be defined. A controlled function *tokens* stores the number of tokens of each place; the number of tokens can change during the evolution of the Petri net.

The structure of the net is described by means of the static functions:

- *inArchWeight* contains the weights of the arcs between places and transitions; value 0 means that there is no arc between the place and the transition;
- *outArcWeight* contains the weights of the arcs between transitions and places; value 0 means that there is no arc between the transition and the place;
- *incidenceMatrix* contains the total number (positive or negative) of tokens that a place gains when a transition fires;
- *isInputPlace* states if there is an arc between a place and a transition.

The derived function *isEnabled* states if a transition is enabled to fire: its interpretation depends on the number of tokens contained in the places connected to the transition through input arcs (input places).

The behavior of a generic Petri net is given by the main rule that non-deterministically chooses a transition that is enabled and fires it with the macro call rule *r_fire*.

Code 1 reports the ASM model Γ_{PN}. It has been obtained using the Eclipse tool *Xpand*, a template-based engine which allows creating text output from EMF models.

The Γ_{PN} shown in Code 1 contains some placeholders (*iota_static_domain_elements*, *iota_static_function_definitions* and *iota_initialState*) that, in order to make the ASM model executable, must be filled by the function ι_{PN}. Code 2 shows the ι_{PN} built using the same Model to Text (M2T) technique of Γ_{PN}:

- In the *iota_static_domain_elements* section, a constant for each place and transition of the current PN is created;
- In the *iota_static_function_definitions* section, the *inArchWeight* and *outArchWeight* functions are defined using the correct weight if there is an arc between a place and a transition (or between a transition and a place), 0 otherwise;
- In the *iota_initialState* section, the initial marking is given assigning values to the *tokens* function.

Remark. Note that with the semantic hooking, the designer defines the whole building function *M.* Parts of *M*, namely the signature or part of it, could be derived automatically by using the meta-hooking approach (Gargantini, Riccobene, & Scandurra, 2009). By meta-hooking, each concept of the meta-metamodel is mapped to a concept of the ASM metamodel. For instance, any non-abstract class *C* is mapped to a static Abstract Domain in the AsmM. In the Petri Net case study, the four classes Place, Transition, InArc, and OurArc would be represented in *M* by four Abstract Domains with the same name. The building function obtained by this technique may be not as optimised as that generated manually by semantic-hooking.

FORMAL ANALYSIS OF DSL SEMANTICS

One of the main advantage of formal semantics is that it enables formal analysis. Therefore, besides the above stated requirements about the expressive power of a helper language *L'* as notation, it is important that formal analysis of models written in *L'* is supported by a set of tools for model

Code 1. Γ_{PN}.

```
«DEFINE gamma FOR PetriNet»
«FILE name + ".asm"»
// as generated for the net «name»
asm «name»
signature:
    abstract domain Place
    abstract domain Transition

    controlled tokens: Place -> Integer
    static inArcWeight: Prod(Place, Transition) -> Integer
    static outArcWeight: Prod(Transition, Place) -> Integer
    static incidenceMatrix: Prod(Place, Transition) -> Integer
    static isInputPlace: Prod(Place, Transition) -> Boolean
    derived isEnabled: Transition -> Boolean
    «EXPAND iota_static_domain_elements»

definitions:
  «EXPAND iota_static_function_definitions»
  function incidenceMatrix($p in Place, $t in Transition) =
        outArcWeight($t, $p) - inArcWeight($p, $t)
  function isInputPlace($p in Place, $t in Transition) = inArcWeight($p, $t) > 0

  function isEnabled ($t in Transition) =
  (forall $p in Place with isInputPlace($p, $t) implies tokens($p) >= inArcWeight($p, $t))

  rule r_fire($t in Transition) =
        forall $p in Place do
            tokens($p):= tokens($p) + incidenceMatrix($p, $t)

  invariant over tokens: (forall $p in Place with tokens($p) >= 0)

  main rule r_Main =   choose $t in Transition with isEnabled($t) do  r_fire[$t]

default init s0:
    «EXPAND iota_initialState»

«ENDFILE»
«ENDDEFINE»
```

execution, as simulation or testing, and for model verification. Indeed, the main goal of applying a formal notation to specify the semantics of a DSL *L* is to allow formal functional analysis of the models written in *L*, thus showing the consistency of the specified semantics with respect to the one intended by the DSL designers.

In Section Model Analysis Techniques, we already briefly described the two main formal analysis activities: *model validation* and *verification*. We here discuss how they can be performed on ASM models by using the ASMETA toolset.

Formal Analysis with the Asmeta Toolset

This section discusses techniques for formal analysis to be used once ASM models are associated to DSL terminal models. Indeed, a suitable set of models are selected as benchmark for language semantic analysis; these models are translated into ASM models by the hooking function *M*. These ASMs can then be functionally analyzed in different ways by exploiting the ASMETA toolset, thus providing increasing degrees of confidence in the semantics correctness. As main formal analysis activities, we present model validation

Code 2. ι_{PN}

```
// the signature
«DEFINE iota_static_domain_elements FOR PetriNet»
    «FOREACH places.typeSelect(Place) AS p»
    static «p.name»: Place
    «ENDFOREACH»
    «FOREACH transitions.typeSelect(Transition) AS t»
    static «t.name»: Transition
    «ENDFOREACH»
«ENDDEFINE»

// the definitions
«DEFINE iota_static_function_definitions FOR PetriNet»
    function inArcWeight($p in Place, $t in Transition) =
      switch($p, $t)
           «FOREACH this.arcs.typeSelect(InArc) AS arc»
           case («arc.place.name», «arc.transition.name»): «arc.weight»
           «ENDFOREACH»
           otherwise 0
         endswitch

    function outArcWeight($t in Transition, $p in Place) =
         switch($t, $p)
           «FOREACH arcs.typeSelect(OutArc) AS arc»
           case («arc.transition.name»,«arc.place.name»): «arc.weight»
           «ENDFOREACH»
           otherwise 0
         endswitch
«ENDDEFINE»

// the initial state
«DEFINE iota_initialState FOR PetriNet»
  function tokens($p in Place) = at({«FOREACH places.typeSelect(Place) AS p SEPARATOR ','»
                                   «p.name» -> «p.tokens»
                                «ENDFOREACH»}, $p)
«ENDDEFINE»
```

and property verification. Model validation can be performed by simulating ASM models of the DSL terminal models. Formal verification, intended as the mathematical proof of properties, can be performed by the use of a model checker for ASM models.

Model Validation

Simple model validation can be performed by *basic simulation* of ASM models with the ASM simulator AsmetaS. As key features for model validation, AsmetaS supports: *invariant checking* to check whether invariants expressed over the currently executed ASM model are satisfied or not, *consistent updates checking* for revealing inconsistent updates, *random simulation* where random values for monitored functions are provided by the environment, *interactive simulation* when required inputs are provided interactively during simulation, and configurable *logging facilities* to inspect the machine state. Invariant checking and random simulation allow the user to perform a draft system validation with minimal effort, while interactive simulation, although more accurate, requires the user interaction to provide the correct inputs and to judge the correctness of the observed behavior.

The most powerful validation approach is the *scenario-based validation* (Carioni, Gargantini, Riccobene, & Scandurra, 2008) by the ASM validator AsmetaV. AsmetaV is based on the simulator

AsmetaS and on the modeling language Avalla. This last provides constructs to express execution scenarios in an algorithmic way as interaction sequences consisting of actions committed by the user to set the environment (i.e., the values of monitored/shared functions), to check the machine state, to ask for the execution of certain transition rules, and to enforce the machine itself to make one *step* (or a sequence of steps by *step until*) as reaction of the actor actions. AsmetaV works as follows. It reads a user scenario written in Avalla, it builds the scenario as instance of the Avalla metamodel by means of a parser, it transforms the scenario and the AsmetaL specification which the scenario refers to, to an executable AsmM model. Then, AsmetaV invokes the AsmetaS interpreter to simulate the scenario. During simulation the user can pause the simulation and watch the current state and value of the update set at every step, through a watching window. During simulation, AsmetaV captures any check violation and if none occurs it finishes with a "PASS" verdict. Besides a "PASS"/"FAIL" verdict, during the scenario running AsmetaV collects in a final report some information about the coverage of the original model; this is useful to check which transition rules have been exercised. With this validation technique, therefore, in addition to the set of ASM models selected as benchmark for language semantic validation, a set of scenarios specifying the expected behavior of the models must be provided by the DSL designer and used for validation. These scenarios can be written from scratch in Avalla, or alternatively, if the considered DSL has already a simulator, these scenarios may be derived from the execution traces generated by such a simulator. This second approach is useful to check the conformance of the semantics implemented by the DSL simulator with respect to the semantics defined by the hooking function *M*.

Other powerful techniques for model validation are *model inspection and review*, which are able to identify defects early in the system development, by determining if a model satisfies several quality properties. Automatic model review can be performed for ASMs (Arcaini, Gargantini, & Riccobene, Automatic Review of Abstract State Machines by Meta Property Verification, 2010). An example of quality property for ASMs is: *No inconsistent update is ever performed.* An inconsistent update occurs when two updates clash, i.e., they refer to the same location but are distinct. This technique is useful for validating a DSL semantics: violation of quality properties of models can derive from imprecise or wrong transformations.

Model Checking

The ASMETA toolset provides support for temporal properties verification of ASM models by means of the model checker AsmetaSMV (Arcaini, Gargantini, & Riccobene, AsmetaSMV: A Way to Link High-Level ASM Models to Low-Level NuSMV, 2010), which takes in input ASM models written in AsmetaL and maps these models into specifications for the model checker NuSMV (Cimatti, et al., 2002). AsmetaSMV supports both the declaration of Computation Tree Logic (CTL) and Linear Temporal Logic (LTL) formulas. CTL/LTL properties to verify are declared directly into the ASM model in the form: `[CTLSPEC | LTLSPEC] p` where `p` is a CTL or a LTL formula. No knowledge of the NuSMV syntax is required to use AsmetaSMV.

Application of Formal Analysis to the Petri Nets Case Study

We here show analysis techniques for model validation and property verification of terminal models associated with the DSL case study.

Basic Simulation

Model validation of a Petri net can be initially performed by simply simulating the resulting ASM. The simulator itself chooses an enabled

Table 1. Simulation traces.

Simulation 1	**Simulation 2**	**Simulation 3**
<State 1 (controlled)>	<State 1 (controlled)>	<State 1 (controlled)>
tokens(p1)=0	tokens(p1)=0	tokens(p1)=0
tokens(p2)=1	tokens(p2)=1	tokens(p2)=1
tokens(p3)=3	tokens(p3)=3	tokens(p3)=3
tokens(p4)=1	tokens(p4)=1	tokens(p4)=1
</State 1 (controlled)>	</State 1 (controlled)>	</State 1 (controlled)>
<State 2 (controlled)>	<State 2 (controlled)>	<State 2 (controlled)>
tokens(p1)=0	tokens(p1)=0	tokens(p1)=1
tokens(p2)=1	tokens(p2)=1	tokens(p2)=1
tokens(p3)=2	tokens(p3)=2	tokens(p3)=3
tokens(p4)=3	tokens(p4)=3	tokens(p4)=0
</State 2 (controlled)>	</State 2 (controlled)>	</State 2 (controlled)>
<State 3 (controlled)>	<State 3 (controlled)>	<State 3 (controlled)>
tokens(p1)=1	tokens(p1)=1	tokens(p1)=0
tokens(p2)=1	tokens(p2)=1	tokens(p2)=2
tokens(p3)=2	tokens(p3)=0	tokens(p3)=6
tokens(p4)=2	tokens(p4)=0	tokens(p4)=0
</State 3 (controlled)>	</State 3 (controlled)>	</State 3 (controlled)>
<State 4 (controlled)>	<State 4 (controlled)>	<State 4 (controlled)>
tokens(p1)=2	tokens(p1)=0	tokens(p1)=0
tokens(p2)=1	tokens(p2)=2	tokens(p2)=2
tokens(p3)=2	tokens(p3)=3	tokens(p3)=5
tokens(p4)=1	tokens(p4)=0	tokens(p4)=2
</State 4 (controlled)>	</State 4 (controlled)>	</State 4 (controlled)>
...	...	...

Code 3. Example of scenario

```
scenario petriNet_scenario

load producerConsumer.asm

//A single token is always present in p2 and p3, but never in both.
//A single token is always present in p4 and p5, but never in both.
invariant tokensInv: (tokens(p2) + tokens(p3) = 1) and (tokens(p4) + tokens(p5) = 1);

//The machine is executed until the place p1 is full
step until tokens(p1) = 10;

//The machine is executed until the initial marking is reached again
step until tokens(p1) = 0 and tokens(p2) = 0 and tokens(p3) = 1 and tokens(p4) = 1 and tokens(p5) = 0;
```

transition and fires it. The user simply checks that the execution is as expected. The user can add invariants that are checked at every step of the simulation. Moreover, if the net reaches a deadlock, then the simulation quits and the user can inspect the behavior (as log). In Table 1 the first four steps of three different simulations of the Petri net shown in Figure 2 are reported; different simulations can produce different traces since, in each step, non-deterministically a transition is chosen to be fired.

Scenario-Based Validation

In scenario-based validation scenarios permit to automatize the execution of some simulations, checking if some properties are satisfied. In Code 3 a scenario for the Petri net shown in Figure 3 is reported.

Table 2. Scenario execution

```
<State 1 (controlled)>
tokens(p1)=1
tokens(p2)=1
tokens(p3)=0
tokens(p4)=1
tokens(p5)=0
</State 1 (controlled)>
...
<State 649 (controlled)>
tokens(p1)=9
tokens(p2)=0
tokens(p3)=1
tokens(p4)=0
tokens(p5)=1
</State 649 (controlled)>
<State 650 (controlled)>
tokens(p1)=10
tokens(p2)=1
tokens(p3)=0
tokens(p4)=0
tokens(p5)=1
</State 650 (controlled)>
```

```
...
<State 904 (controlled)>
tokens(p1)=0
tokens(p2)=0
tokens(p3)=1
tokens(p4)=0
tokens(p5)=1
</State 904 (controlled)>
<State 905 (controlled)>
step__=1
tokens(p1)=0
tokens(p2)=0
tokens(p3)=1
tokens(p4)=1
tokens(p5)=0
</State 905 (controlled)>
```

Code 4. Wrong implementation of r_fire rule

```
rule r_fire($t in Transition) =
    par
        forall $i in Place with isInputPlace($i, $t) do
               tokens($i) := tokens($i) - inEdgeWeight($i, $t)
        forall $o in Place with isOutputPlace($o, $t) do
               tokens($o) := tokens($o) + outEdgeWeight($t, $o)
    endpar
```

A scenario invariant checks that one token is always contained in *p2* or *p3*, but never in both; the invariant checks the same property also for *p4* and *p5*. The machine is executed until the place *p1* becomes full; then the machine is executed until the initial marking is reached again. In Table 2 a portion of the result of the simulation is shown: in this particular simulation, after 650 steps (that correspond to the firing of 650 transitions) the place *p1* has become full and, from that marking, after 255 steps the initial marking is reached.

Model Review

The model review and inspection, supported by the model advisor, can be used to find defects of the transformation itself, i.e., in the language semantics. For instance, assume that the language semantics was defined as in Code 4.

In this rule the update of the *tokens* controlled function is done by two parallel rules, one for subtracting the tokens taken by the fired transition, and the other adding the tokens produced by the transition. This ASM rule contains an inconsistent update in case the same place is input and output of the same transitions (called self-loop). Consider the net depicted in Figure 6. By running the *AsmetaMA* to the ASM produced for it, the user would find the violation reported in Box 3.

Note that the same error could have been found by simulation, but there is no guarantee. In this example the simulator could find the fault only after three steps and only if *t7* fires after *t3* and

Figure 6. Petri Net with self-loop (place p_4 and transition t_7)

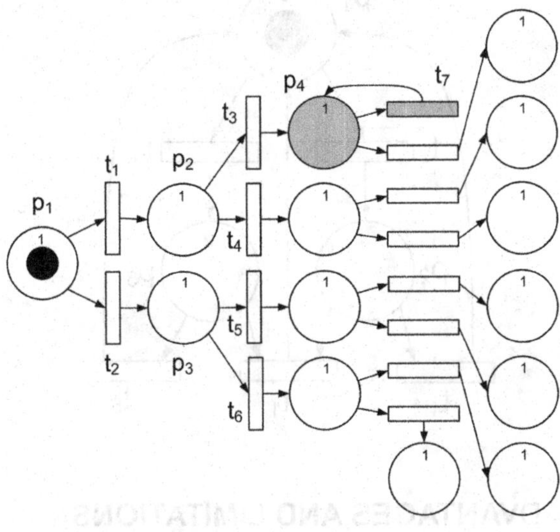

t2. In the 87,5% (7/8) of the runs it does not discover the inconsistency.

Model Checking

Model checking can be used to prove properties of the models. We experimented *AsmetaSMV* to prove the following properties:

- **Boundedness**: A net is said to be *k*-bounded if the number of tokens in each place does not exceed a finite number *k* for any marking reachable from the initial state. A net is said safe if it is 1-bounded. In CTL, this can be expressed as presented in Box 4.
- **Liveness**: A net is live, if it is always possible to eventually fire any transition by applying an existing firing sequence. Liveness guarantees deadlock free operation and is an ideal property for many systems. It can be expressed by the CTL property presented in Box 5.
- **Deadlock-Freeness**: A net has a potential deadlock if there is a firing sequence leading to a state where no transition can any longer fire (Figure 7). By definition nets with deadlock are not live. The absence of deadlocks can be proved by the CTL property reported in Box 6, stating that, in every state, there exists at least a transition which is enabled.
- **Reversibility**: A Petri net is said to be reversible if, for each marking *M* reachable

Box 3. Violation Found

Location `tokens(p4)` is updated to values `(tokens(p4) + outEdgeWeight(t7,p4))` and `(tokens(p4) - inEdgeWeight(p4,t7))` when are satisfied simultaneously the conditions `($t = t7 & isEnabled(t7) & isInputPlace(p4,t7))` and `($t = t7 & isEnabled(t7) & isOutputPlace(p4,t7))`.

Box 4. CTL property for boundedness

```
CTLSPEC ag((forall $p in Place with tokens($p) <= k))
```

Box 5. CTL property for liveness

```
CTLSPEC (forall $t in Transition with ag(ef(isEnabled($t)))
```

Figure 7. Non-reversible, not live, deadlocked net

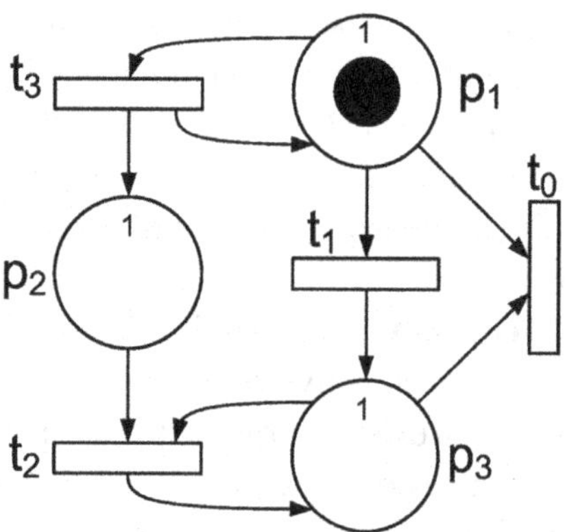

from M_0, M_0 is reachable from M (Figure 8). In order to check if a Petri net is reversible we must verify the property in Box 7.

We are able to check all the properties listed above for any Petri net by simply executing *AsmetaSMV* on the corresponding ASM. For instance, we found that:

- The net of Figure 3 is reversible, live and deadlock-free. We proved also that it is not 9-bound, since there exists a marking in which place *p1* becomes full.
- The net of Figure 7 is not reversible, not live and it is proved to have a deadlock.
- The net of Figure 8 is reversible and deadlock-free, but it is not live since *t1* is dead.

Figure 8. Reversible, deadlock-free, not live net

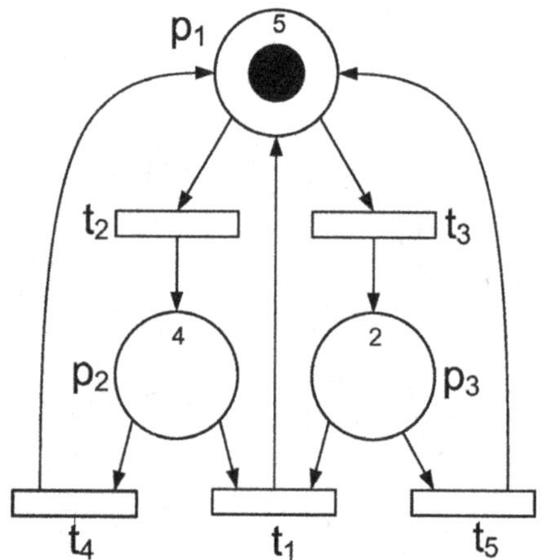

ADVANTAGES AND LIMITATIONS OF THE ASM-BASED SEMANTIC APPROACH

In a DSL engineering process, which mainly uses metamodeling capabilities, the semantics specification is a necessary step for making languages semantically precise and of practical use in tool chains. In a translational approach, to be a good candidate, a *specification language*, used to provide formal semantics of DSLs, should be (i) abstract and formal to rigorously define model behavior at different levels of abstraction, but without formal overkill; (ii) able to capture heterogeneous models of computation (MoC) in order to smoothly integrate different behavioral models; (iii) endowed with a model refinement mechanism leading to correct-by-construction

Box 6. CTL property for deadlock-freeness

```
CTLSPEC ag((exist $t in Transition with isEnabled($t)))
```

Box 7. CTL property for reversibility

```
CTLSPEC ag(ef(tokens(p1) = M0(p1) and … and tokens(pn) = M0(pn)))
```

system artifacts; (iv) executable, in order to be used for describing how DSL models behave without defining the implementation; and (v) supported by a set of tools for model analysis (like validation and verification). Furthermore, as MDE specific requirement, the specification language should be endowed with a metamodel-based definition in order to automatize the application of building function *M* by exploiting MDE techniques of automatic model transformation.

ASMs own all the characteristics we identified as the desirable properties a formal method should have in order to be used as specification language for DSL semantic definition: preciseness, abstraction, refinement, executability, tool analysis support, and metamodel-based definition. Furthermore, DSL models of computation are not restricted to imperative or object-oriented behaviors, and can transparently use distribute computation or concurrency, due to the ASM expressive power.

ASMs adopt an operational style while others formal notations are based on a declarative style, like Maude (Romero, Rivera, Durán, & Vallecillo, 2007). There has been an endless debate about which style fits better the designer needs: some argue that with an operational style the designers tend to insert implementation details in the abstract specifications, others observe that practitioners feel uncomfortable with declarative notations like temporal logics or rewriting rules. We believe that in general operational specifications are easier to write and understand especially for programmers. Moreover, working as virtual machine over abstract data type, an ASM can be used for model execution purposes instead of implementing code. Although direct encoding to programming languages is not supported yet, code implementation can be obtained in a correct way by a sequence of ASM refined models till a point where the reduction to code is straightforward (Börger & Stärk, 2003).

Up to now, our approach does not support back translation from ASMs to the DSL models. This would be needed in order to translate ASM states in DSL objects and their states, making possible to express ASM execution traces directly at the level of the modeler knowledge. Furthermore, although ASMs have been recently used for dealing with real-time and adaptive models, specifying DSLs in these contexts require further investigation.

COMPARISON BETWEEN METAMODEL-BASED AND GRAMMAR-BASED DSLS

Several works exist in literature aiming at defining transformation bridges to achieve interoperability between the *grammarware* and the *modelware* technical spaces (Wimmer & Kramler, 2005; Engelen & van den Brand, 2010), as both spaces share a common application field: the development of software. Most of these works focus on syntactical aspects and transformation tasks, such as processing the artifacts in the source technical space and transforming them into new artifacts that can be processed by tools from the target technical space. This section focuses mainly on comparing metamodel-based and grammar-based DSLs from the semantics formalization perspective.

In our work, we only considered metamodel-based DSLs, but the presented semantic framework and the analysis techniques are also applicable to DSLs defined in terms of a grammar, because the *conformity* relations existing in the metamodeling stack *meta-metamodel/metamodel/model* of the modelware technical space also exist in the 3-layer organization *EBNF/grammar/program* of the grammarware technical space – see (Bézivin, 2005; Kurtev, Bézivin, & Aksit, 2002). Several applications of the ASMs for the formalization of the operational semantics of programming languages and their associated compilers (Börger & Stärk, 2003) provide evidence of the validity and universality of the ASMs as a method for specifying the semantics of grammar-based DSLs. The only difference is (as better explained below) on how in concrete we define the building function *M* of the proposed framework by considering a *grammar* instead of a *metamodel*.

Basically, a metamodel is a graph composed of concepts and relationships between these concepts and they are more expressive than the textual representations typically used for grammar induction. Moreover, since a metamodel is an *ontology*, it provides a specific controlled vocabulary for a domain of interest and semantic intuitions as they are known by the DSL designer. The semantic definition process is, therefore, *inherently traceable* if the metamodel and the associated semantics specification in natural language are intended as requirement gathering documents. However, using grammars is the main formal approach to textual language definition. By using grammars, Abstract Syntax Trees (ASTs) (much more concise and easily manageable than Parse Trees) must be used for specifying the semantics in a syntax-driven way. An AST essentially relates terms in a controlled vocabulary via parent-child relationships, so its base mathematical structure is a tree. A corresponding semantics in ASM can be associated to an AST by visiting the tree nodes and varying the specification of the behavior of each node depending on the node type.

Metamodeling is the main practical approach to visual language definition, but at some extent. When the DSL has a mixed textual and visual notation, starting the semantics specification work from a metamodel perspective seems to be a good practice for coarse-grained concepts. However, when dealing, for example, with textual expressions of *surface action languages* or *action languages* (Engelen & van den Brand, 2010) at a low granularity level (such as the textual expressions, represented in terms of strings, of small atomic actions and of opaque actions in the UML metamodel), reasoning in terms of ASTs is preferable and judicious for fine-grained concepts. In this last scenario, a first semantics specification approach consists of dealing with the techniques related to grammars and the techniques related to metamodels separately, by converting textual models conforming to grammars into models conforming to metamodels and vice versa. An alternative is to combine both approaches. In the proposed ASM-based semantic framework, for example, both the techniques related to grammars and the techniques related to metamodels can be used in a freely mixed manner. We only recommend to investigate the level of integration of textual and graphical notation in the considered DSL to make explicit and clear in the semantics specification the points where parts of the model described in the metamodel can refer to elements described in terms of a grammar, in order to be able to exploit the benefits of both types of semantics specification means. In ASMs this is feasible by maintaining a unique signature of domains and functions symbols, and by defining appropriate functions to relate grammarware and modelware concepts to each other.

CONCLUSION AND FUTURE RESEARCH DIRECTIONS

A formal definition of the semantics of a DSL is a key prerequisite for the verification of the correctness of models specified using such a DSL. By prototyping the semantics of a DSL using an executable formal method, such as ASMs, DSL terminal models can be interpreted (executed), animated and debugged. Moreover, especially if the considered DSL has a rich dynamic semantics, advanced forms of formal analysis, such as the ones (model validation and verification) that we presented through ASMs, can also be carried out to validate and prove properties showing the consistency of the specified semantics with respect to the one intended by the DSL designers and users.

As future work, we would like to implement an environment for *prototyping the semantics* of metamodel-based DSLs according to the methodology of the proposed semantic framework and the principles of the offered techniques (with the associated model transformation chains). This toolkit would be linked to a conventional metamodeling environment (e.g., EMF) in order to handle within a unique environment as homogeneously as possible both the metamodeling editing and the definition of a reference semantics for a given DSL. This toolkit would also be used in synergy with the ASM ASMETA toolset for the model execution and formal analysis.

Investigating on the combined use of metamodeling and more advanced grammar parsing technology as a basis for prototyping the semantics of DSLs that are defined in terms of a metamodel but also embed a grammar (e.g., languages with a mixed graphical and textual concrete notation) is another promising direction for future research.

A further more complex task would be to deal with checking the behavioral equivalence with different translations from a given DSL to other similar semantics prototyping environments and techniques.

REFERENCES

Anlauff, M. (2000). XASM - An extensible, component-based ASM language. *Proceedings of the International Workshop on Abstract State Machines, Theory and Applications* (pp. 69-90). Springer-Verlag.

Arcaini, P., Gargantini, A., & Riccobene, E. (2010). AsmetaSMV: A way to link high-level ASM models to low-level NuSMV. In M. Frappier, U. Glässer, S. Khurshid, R. Laleau, & S. Reeves (Eds.), *Proceedings of the Second International Conference on Abstract State Machines, Alloy, B and Z (ABZ 2010). 5977*, (pp. 61-74). Berlin, Germany: Springer.

Arcaini, P., Gargantini, A., & Riccobene, E. (2010). Automatic review of abstract state machines by meta property verification. In C. A. Muñoz (Ed.), *Proceedings of the Second NASA Formal Methods Symposium (NFM 2010)* (pp. 4-13).

Arcaini, P., Gargantini, A., Riccobene, E., & Scandurra, P. (2011). A model-driven process for engineering a toolset for a formal method. *Software, Practice & Experience*, *41*(2), 155–166. doi:10.1002/spe.1019

Bézivin, J. (2005). On the unification power of models. [SoSym]. *Software & Systems Modeling*, *4*(2), 171–188. doi:10.1007/s10270-005-0079-0

Börger, E., & Stärk, R. (2003). *Abstract state machines: A method for high-level system design and analysis*. Springer Verlag. doi:10.1007/978-1-84882-736-3_3

Bryant, B., Gray, J., Mernik, M., Clarke, P., France, R., & Karsai, G. (2011). Challenges and directions in formalizing the semantics of modeling languages. *Computer Science and Information Systems*, *8*(2), 225–253. doi:10.2298/CSIS110114012B

Carioni, A., Gargantini, A., Riccobene, E., & Scandurra, P. (2008). A scenario-based validation language for ASMs. *Proceedings of the First International Conference on Abstract State Machines, B and Z (ABZ 2008)* (pp. 71-84): Springer-Verlag.

Chen, K., Sztipanovits, J., & Neema, S. (2005). Toward a semantic anchoring infrastructure for domain-specific modeling languages. *Proceedings of the 5th ACM International Conference on Embedded Software* (pp. 35-43). ACM.

Chen, K., Sztipanovits, J., & Neema, S. (2007). Compositional specification of behavioral semantics. *Proceedings of Design Automation and Test in Europe Conference (DATE 07)* (pp. 906-911). EDA Consortium.

Cimatti, A., Clarke, E., Giunchiglia, E., Giunchiglia, F., Pistore, M., Roveri, M., et al. (2002). Nusmv 2: An opensource tool for symbolic model checking. In E. Brinksma, & K. Larsen (Eds.), *Proceedings of the 14th International Conference on Computer Aided Verification* (pp. 359-364): Springer-Verlag.

Clark, T., Sammut, P., & Willans, J. (2008). *Applied Metamodelling: A Foundation For Language Driven Development* (2nd ed.). Ceteva.

Di Ruscio, D., Jouault, F., Kurtev, I., Bézivin, J., & Pierantonio, A. (2006). *Extending AMMA for supporting dynamic semantics specifications of DSLs. Laboratoire d'Informatique de Nantes-Atlantique*. LINA.

Engelen, L., & van den Brand, M. (2010). Integrating textual and graphical modelling languages. *Electronic Notes in Theoretical Computer Science, 253*(7), 105–120. doi:10.1016/j.entcs.2010.08.035

Engels, G., Hausmann, J. H., Heckel, R., & Sauer, S. (2000). Dynamic meta modeling: A graphical approach to the operational semantics of behavioral diagrams in UML. In A. Evans, S. Kent, & B. Selic (Eds.), *Proceedings of the Third International Conference on The Unified Modeling Language: advancing the standard (UML 2000)* (pp. 323-337). Springer-Verlag.

Ermel, C. H. (2005). Animated simulation of integrated UML behavioral models based on graph transformation. *Proceedings of the 2005 IEEE Symposium on Visual Languages and Human-Centric Computing* (pp. 125-133). IEEE Computer Society.

Flake, S., & Müller, W. (2004). An ASM definition of the dynamic OCL 2.0 semantics. In T. Baar, A. Strohmeier, A. Moreira, & S. Mellor (Ed.), *Proceedings of the Seventh International Conference on UML Modeling Languages and Applications (UML 2004).* (pp. 226-240). Springer.

Gargantini, A., Riccobene, E., & Scandurra, P. (2007). A metamodel-based simulator for ASMs. In A. Prinz (Ed.), *Proceedings of the 14th International ASM Workshop* (pp. 1-21).

Gargantini, A., Riccobene, E., & Scandurra, P. (2008). A metamodel-based language and a simulation engine for abstract state machines. *Journal of Universal Computer Science, 14*(12), 1949–1983.

Gargantini, A., Riccobene, E., & Scandurra, P. (2009). A semantic framework for metamodel-based languages. *Journal of Automated Software Engineering, 16*(3-4), 415–454. doi:10.1007/s10515-009-0053-0

Gargantini, A., Riccobene, E., & Scandurra, P. (2010). Combining formal methods and MDE techniques for model-driven system design and analysis. *International Journal on Advances in Software, 1&2*, 1-18.

Hahn, C. (2008). A domain specific modeling language for multiagent systems. *Proceedings of the 7th International Joint Conference on Autonomous Agents and Multiagent Systems (AAMAS 2008)* (pp. 233-240). International Foundation for Autonomous Agents and Multiagent Systems.

Harel, D., & Rumpe, B. (2004). Meaningful modeling: What's the semantics of "semantics"? *IEEE Computer, 37*(10), 64–72. doi:10.1109/MC.2004.172

Holzmann, G. J. (2004). *The SPIN model checker: Primer and reference manual*. Addison-Wesley.

Kurtev, I., Bézivin, J., & Aksit, M. (2002). Technological spaces: An initial appraisal. *Tenth International Conference on Cooperative Information Systems (CoopIS), International Symposium on Distributed Objects and Applications (DOA) - Federated Conferences, Industrial Track*, (pp. 1-6).

Muller, P.-A., Fleurey, F., & Jezequel, J.-M. (2005). Weaving executability into object-oriented meta-languages. *Proceedings of ACM/IEEE 8th International Conference on Model Driven Engineering Languages and Systems* (pp. 264-278). Berlin, Germany: Springer-Verlag.

Murata, T. (1989). Petri nets: Properties, analysis and applications. *Proceedings of the IEEE*, *77*(4), 541–580. doi:10.1109/5.24143

OMG Object Constraint Language (OCL), v2.0 formal/2006-05-01. (2006). *OMG. Object Constraint Language (OCL), v2.0 formal/2006-05-01*.

OMG Meta Object Facility (MOF), Core Specification v2.0, formal/2006-01-01. (2006). *OMG. Meta Object Facility (MOF), Core Specification v2.0, formal/2006-01-01*.

Riccobene, E., & Scandurra, P. (2009). Weaving executability into UML class models at PIM level. *Proceedings of the 1st Workshop on Behavior Modeling in Model-Driven Architecture (BM-MDA 2009)* (pp. 1-9). ACM.

Riccobene, E., & Scandurra, P. (2010). An executable semantics of the SystemC UML profile. In M. Frappier, U. Glässer, S. Khurshid, R. Laleau, & S. Reeves (Eds.), *Proceedings of the Second International Conference on Abstract State Machines, Alloy, B and Z (ABZ 2010)* (pp. 75-90). Berlin, Germany: Springer.

Richters, M. (2001). *A precise approach to validating UML models and OCL constraints*. PhD thesis, Universität Bremen, Germany.

Rivera, J. E., Durán, F., & Vallecillo, A. (2009). Formal specification and analysis of domain specific models using Maude. *Simulation*, *85*(11-12), 778–792. doi:10.1177/0037549709341635

Romero, J., Rivera, J., Durán, F., & Vallecillo, A. (2007). Formal and tool support for model driven engineering with Maude (J. Bézivin, & B. Meyer, Eds.). *Journal of Object Technology*, *6*(9), 187-207.

Sadilek, D. A. (2008). Prototyping domain-speci□c language semantics. *Companion to the 23rd ACM SIGPLAN conference on Object-oriented programming systems languages and applications* (pp. 895-896). Nashville, TN, USA: ACM.

Sadilek, D. A., & Wachsmuth, G. (2009). Using grammarware languages to define operational semantics of modelled languages. *47th International Conference Objects, Models, Components, Patterns (TOOLS Europe 2009)* (pp. 348-356).

Scheidgen, M., & Fischer, J. (2007). Human comprehensible and machine processable specifications of operational semantics. *Proceedings of the Third European Conference on Model Driven Architecture- Foundations and Applications (ECMDA-FA 2007)* (pp. 157-171). Haifa, Israel: Springer-Verlag.

Soden, M., & Eichler, H. (2009). Towards a model execution framework for Eclipse. *Proceedings of the First Workshop on Behavior Modeling in Model-Driven Architecture (BM-MDA 2009)* (pp. 1-7). ACM.

Stehr, M.-O., Meseguer, J., & Ölveczky, P. C. (2001). *Rewriting logic as a unifying framework for Petri nets. Unifying Petri Nets, Advances in Petri Nets* (pp. 250–303). Berlin, Germany: Springer-Verlag.

Strembeck, M., & Zdun, U. (2009). An approach for the systematic development of domain-specific languages. *Software, Practice & Experience*, *39*(15), 1253–1292. doi:10.1002/spe.936

Sunyé, G., Pennaneac'h, F., Ho, W.-M., Le Guennec, A., & Jézéquel, J.-M. (2001). Using UML action semantics for executable modeling and beyond. In K. R. Dittrich, A. Geppert, & M. C. Norrie (Ed.), *Proceedings of the 13th Conference on Advanced Information Systems Engineering (CAiSE 2001)* (pp. 433-447). Berlin, Germany: Springer.

The Xactium XMF Mosaic. (2007). *The Xactium XMF Mosaic*.

Varró, D. (2002). A formal semantics of UML statecharts by model transition systems. *Graph Transformation: First International Conference (ICGT 2002)* (pp. 378-392). Barcelona, Spain: Springer-Verlag.

Wimmer, M., & Kramler, G. (2005). Bridging grammarware and modelware. *MoDELS Satellite Events* (pp. 159-168).

ADDITIONAL READING

Álvarez, J. M., Evans, A., & Sammut, P. (2001). Mapping between levels in the metamodel architecture. *Proceedings of the 4th International Conference on The Unified Modeling Language, Modeling Languages, Concepts, and Tools* (pp. 34-46). London, UK: Springer-Verlag.

Balasubramanian, D., Narayanan, A., van Buskirk, C. P., & Karsai, G. (2006). The graph rewriting and transformation language: GReAT. *Electronic Communications of the EASST, 1*, 1–8.

Berard, B., Bidoit, M., Finkel, A., Petit, A., Laroussinie, F., Petrucci, L., & McKenzie, P. (2010). *Systems and software verification: Model-checking techniques and tools*. Springer-Verlag.

Börger, E. (2002). The origins and the development of the ASM method for high level system design and analysis. *Journal of Universal Computer Science (J.UCS), 8*(1), 2-74.

Börger, E. (2005). The ASM method for system design and analysis. a tutorial introduction. *5th International Conference on Frontiers of Combining Systems (FroCoS 2005)* (pp. 264-283). Berlin, Germany: Springer-Verlag.

Börger, E. (2010). The abstract state machines method for high-level system design and analysis. In Boca, P., Bowen, J., & Siddiqi, J. (Eds.), *Formal methods: State of the art and new directions* (pp. 79–116). Berlin, Germany: Springer-Verlag. doi:10.1007/978-1-84882-736-3_3

Börger, E., Gargantini, A., & Riccobene, E. (2006). ASM. In Habrias, H., & Frappier, M. (Eds.), *Software specification methods: An overview using a case study*. Hermes Science.

Chen, K., Sztipanovits, J., Abdelwalhed, S., & Jackson, E. (2005). Semantic anchoring with model transformations. *First European Conference on Modelling Foundations and Applications (ECMDA-FA 2005). 3748*, (pp. 115-129). Berlin, Germany: Springer.

Clarke, E. M., Grumberg, O., & Peled, D. A. (1999). *Model checking*. The MIT Press.

de Lara, J., Vangheluwe, H., & Alfonseca, M. (2004). Meta-modelling and graph grammars for multi-paradigm modelling in AToM3. *Software & Systems Modeling, 3*(3), 194–209. doi:10.1007/s10270-003-0047-5

Diaz, M. (2009). *Petri nets: Fundamental models, verification and applications*. Wiley.

Esser, R., & Janneck, J. W. (2001). *Moses - A tool suite for visual modeling of discrete-event systems* (pp. 272–279). Washington, DC: IEEE Computer Society. doi:10.1109/HCC.2001.995274

Fowler, M. (2010). *Domain-specific languages*. Addison-Wesley Professional.

Frankel, D. (2002). *Model driven architecture: Applying MDA to enterprise computing*. New York, NY: John Wiley & Sons, Inc.

Gargantini, A., Riccobene, E., & Scandurra, P. (2008). Model-driven language engineering: The ASMETA case study. In C. Dini, H. Mannaert, T. Ohta, & R. Pellerin (Ed.), *Proceedings of The Third International Conference on Software Engineering Advances (ICSEA 2008)* (pp. 373-378). IEEE Computer Society.

Gargantini, A., Riccobene, E., & Scandurra, P. (2009). Integrating formal methods with model-driven engineering. In K. Boness, J. Fernandes, J. Hall, R. Machado, & R. Oberhauser (Ed.), *Proceedings of The Fourth International Conference on Software Engineering Advances (ICSEA 2009)* (pp. 86-92). IEEE Computer Society.

Gargantini, A., Riccobene, E., & Scandurra, P. (2009). Ten reasons to metamodel ASMs. In Abrial, J.-R., & Glässer, U. (Eds.), *Rigorous Methods for Software Construction and Analysis, LNCS* (*Vol. 5115*, pp. 33–49). Berlin, Germany: Springer. doi:10.1007/978-3-642-11447-2_3

Gurevich, Y. (1995). Evolving algebras 1993: Lipari guide. In Börger, E. (Ed.), *Specification and validation methods* (pp. 9–36). New York, NY: Oxford University Press, Inc.

Guttman, M., & Parodi, J. (2007). *Real-life MDA: solving business problems with model driven architecture*. Morgan Kaufmann Publishers Inc.

Huth, M., & Ryan, M. (2004). *Logic in computer science: Modelling and reasoning about systems*. New York, NY: Cambridge University Press. doi:10.1017/CBO9780511810275

Kelly, S., & Tolvanen, J. (2008). *Domain-specific modeling: Enabling full code generation*. Wiley-Interscience.

Kleppe, A., Warmer, J., & Bast, W. (2003). *MDA explained: The model driven architecture: Practice and promise*. Addison-Wesley.

Moore, D. W. (2004). *Eclipse development using the graphical editing framework and the eclipse modeling framework*. Riverton, NJ: IBM Corporation.

Stahl, T., Voelter, M., & Czarnecki, K. (2006). *Model-driven software development: Technology, engineering, management*. John Wiley & Sons.

Steinberg, D., Budinsky, F., Paternostro, M., & Merks, E. (2009). *EMF: Eclipse modeling framework* (2nd ed.). Boston, MA: Addison-Wesley.

KEY TERMS AND DEFINITIONS

Metamodel: It is an object-oriented model of the vocabulary of the language, which represents concepts provided by the language, the relationships existing among those concepts, and how they may be combined to create models. Metamodel elements (or metaelements) provide a typing scheme for model elements expressed by the meta relation between a model element and its metaelement.

Metamodeling: It is the analysis, construction and development of the frames, rules, constraints, models and theories applicable and useful for modeling a predefined class of problems.

Model (or Terminal Model): It is a first class entity that conforms to a metamodel if and only if each of its elements has its metaelement defined within the metamodel.

Model Validation: It is the process of determining the degree to which a model is an accurate representation of the real world from the perspective of the intended uses of the model. It gives an answer to the question: Are we building the right model?

Model Verification: It is the process of determining that a model is correct and matches any agreed-upon specifications and assumptions. It gives an answer to the question: Are we building the model right?

Semantic Hooking: It is a semantic technique by which a designer hooks to the language metamodel *A* an abstract state machine *M*, which contains all data structures modeling elements of *A* with their relationships, and all transition rules representing behavioral aspects of the language.

UML Profile: It provides a generic extension mechanism for customizing models for particular domains and platforms. Extension mechanisms allow refining standard semantics in strictly additive manner, so that they cannot contradict standard semantics.

Chapter 9
Towards Dynamic Semantics for Synthesizing Interpreted DSMLs

Peter J. Clarke
Florida International University, USA

Yali Wu
University of Detroit Mercy, USA

Andrew A. Allen
Georgia Southern University, USA

Frank Hernandez
Florida International University, USA

Mark Allison
Florida International University, USA

Robert France
Colorado State University, USA

ABSTRACT

Domain-specific languages (DSLs) provide developers with the ability to describe applications using language elements that directly represent concepts in the application problem domains. Unlike general-purpose languages, domain concepts are embedded in the semantics of a DSL. In this chapter, the authors present an interpreted domain-specific modeling language (i-DSML) whose models are used to specify user-defined communication services, and support the users' changing communication needs at runtime. These model changes are interpreted at runtime to produce events that are handled by the labeled transition system semantics of the i-DSML. Specifically, model changes are used to produce scripts that change the underlying communication structure. The script-producing process is called synthesis. The authors describe the semantics of the i-DSML called the Communication Modeling Language (CML) and its use in the runtime synthesis process, and briefly describe how the synthesis process is implemented in the Communication Virtual Machine (CVM), the execution engine for CML models.

INTRODUCTION

Research in model-driven software development (MDD) (France & Rumpe, 2007; Hermans, Pinzger, & Deursen, 2009) and domain-specific modeling languages (DSMLs) (DSM Forum 2010, Sprinkle, Mernik, Tolvanen, & Spinellis, 2009) focuses on how models that provide good abstractions of complex software behaviors can be used to significantly improve software productivity and quality. In this work we differentiate between the two categories of domain-specific languages described in the literature; these are (1) text-based languages, referred to as DSLs (Mernik, Heering,

DOI: 10.4018/978-1-4666-2092-6.ch009

& Slone, 2005), and (2) graphical modeling languages, DSMLs. It should be noted that graphical languages are usually processed in an equivalent text representation, usually based on some form of XML. The use of DSMLs continues to grow in both academia and industry, resulting in a spectrum of DSMLs. This spectrum includes DSMLs that are used in the development of software artifacts which are then translated into a general-purpose high-level programming language, as well as DSMLs that are used to model the domain application and that are directly executed by a model execution engine. In this chapter we focus on the latter class of DSMLs, referred to as *interpreted DSMLs* (i-DSMLs), i.e., those that do not transformed models into the source code of another language. As we will demonstrate in this chapter, i-DSMLs are well-suited for creating and changing models at runtime.

Creating a DSML involves defining: a metamodel (abstract syntax and static semantics), one or more concrete syntaxes, and the dynamic semantics (Stahl et al., 2003). There are several tools that can be used to define the metamodel and concrete syntaxes for DSMLs, however there is little support for defining the dynamic semantics. Support for the definition of dynamic semantics for i-DSMLs is needed if they are to be used to produce models used at runtime to modify behavior, particularly in distributed runtime environments.

In this chapter, we describe an approach we used to develop the dynamic semantics of an i-DSML for the communication services domain, the *Communication Modeling Language* (CML) (Clarke, Hristidis, Wang, Prabakar, & Deng, 2006). The execution engine, the *Communication Virtual Machine* (CVM) (Deng et al., 2008), which is used to directly interpret CML models in a distributed environment, is also introduced. Although the communication services domain is the focus of this chapter, we are currently applying the approach to other domains, such as microgrid energy management (Allison, Allen, Yang, & Clarke, 2011). That is, we are in the process of developing the *Microgrid Modeling Language (MGridML)* and the *Microgrid Virtual Machine (MGridVM)* using the approach describe here. By applying our approach to multiple domains, we hope to eventually show how the approach can be generalized as a new way for defining semantics for i-DSMLs that can be directly executed by a virtual machine.

The main objective of this chapter is to describe the dynamic semantics to synthesis the i-DSML CML. CML model instances are used to synthesize control scripts (commands passed to the middleware of the execution engine – virtual machine) based on the state of the running system. Key aspects of the synthesis process are the identification of model changes and the interpretation of these changes at runtime. Using these model changes and the current state of the system, events are generated that trigger script generation tasks. The dynamic semantics of CML use labeled transition systems (LTSs) to describe how generated events are handled in the synthesis process. Details of the synthesis process in the CVM are provided, including details on how CML models are compared at runtime and how the model changes are used to execute negotiation and media transfer tasks, the two key aspects in user-defined communication. We will show how the LTS semantics for CML supports the synthesis process.

The chapter is organized as follows. The next section presents a literature review on DSMLs and the semantics of DSMLs. The following section motivates the need for i-DSMLs to support the use of models at runtime, introduces the abstract syntax for CML, the execution engine for CML, and defines a CML semantics that supports the use of CML model instances in the synthesis of control scripts. Some of the benefits, limitations and challenges of i-DSMLs are also presented in this section. Finally, we present future research directions and conclude the chapter.

BACKGROUND

In this section we introduce DSMLs and the various approaches used to describe DSML semantics. The work most closely related to the DMSL semantics approaches is also presented.

Domain-Specific Modeling Languages (DSMLs)

DSMLs may be defined as a five tuple consisting of a *concrete syntax*, *abstract syntax*, *semantic domain*, *syntactic mapping*, and *semantic mapping* (Chen, Sztipanovits, & Neema, 2005; Gargantini, Riccobene, & Scandurra, 2009). The abstract syntax defines the language concepts, their relationships and related constraints for the language. The concrete syntax, which may be graphical, textual or mixed, defines the specific notation used to express models. The semantics is defined based on some semantic domain which is used to describe the meaning of the models and is usually represented in some formal framework. Note that there is a distinction between the static semantics and behavioral semantics, where the static semantics define well-formed models and the behavioral semantics the meaning of the models. The syntactic mapping assigns syntactic constructs to elements in the abstract syntax. The abstract syntax and static semantics are both described in the metamodel for the DSML. The metamodel must be part of a metamodel architecture (Clark, Sammut, & Willans, 2008), where the language used to express the metamodel is defined by another metamodel (the meta-metamodel for the DSML). The semantic mapping relates the syntactic concepts to the semantic domain, thereby providing meaning to the instance models.

Unlike the specification of the abstract syntax that uses a metamodel, the specification of the semantic domain is more complicated since a single DSML may use several semantic domains and have several mappings associated with them (Chen et al., 2005). In addition to there being more than one semantic domain associated with a DSML, one question that faces language designers is how the semantics should be described. In the next subsection work done on semantics for DSMLs is presented.

Semantics for DSMLs

There are four main approaches to describing the semantics of languages: *translational* – translating from one language to another language with precise semantics; *operational* – modeling the operational behavior of language concepts; *extensional* – extending the semantics of existing language concepts; and *denotational* – modeling the mapping to semantic domain concepts. There are advantages and disadvantages of each approach (Clark et al., 2008). Although the semantics for traditional programming languages have been studied in some depth, there are few studies that report on the work done for DSMLs (Bryant et al., 2011). Gargantini, Riccobene, and Scandurra (2009) and Bryant et al. (2011) provide summaries of the recent approaches used to define semantics for DSMLs. These approaches include: *semantic anchoring* – reuses well-known models of computations (MoCs) to define the semantics for the DSML based on one or more MoCs; *weaving behavior* – incorporates the executable semantics into the abstract syntax of the DSML; *rewriting systems* – is a translational approach but tend to employ graph rewriting using graphical definitions and graphical grammars; and *semantics via an interpreter* – defines how the models are directly executed by an interpreter. The model interpreters in the literature usually refer to the automation of converting models in one language to models in another language (Edwards, Seo, & Medvidovic, 2008; Bryant et al., 2011) or the execution of a DSML model after it has been totally converted to a model in a lower-level language e.g., Abstract State Machine Language (AsmL) (Microsoft Research Team, 2012; Chen et al., 2005).

The approach presented in this chapter is an operational approach based on the semantics via an interpreter, where the semantics describe how models can be directly executed in the context of some environment. The formal definition of the interpreter approach is a mapping *i* that depends on the Model *M* and implements $i(M): I \times S(M) \rightarrow O \times S(M)$, where *I* is the input event alphabet, *O* is the output event alphabet, and *S* is the set of the internal states of the interpreter, also dependent on the model (Bryant et al., 2011). Our approach also requires the use of label transition systems to define abstract states in the system, based on user defined models, and the transition between these states. A *labeled transition system (LTS)* is a triple (L, S, →) consisting of a set L of labels, a set S of states (configurations), and a transition relation → ⊆ S x L x S (Fernando, 1993). The transitions in the labeled transition system can be labeled with annotations; we annotate the labels with events, guards and actions similar to the sate machines in UML (OMG, 2010). In this chapter we will use the term *execution engine* to refer to the artifact that executes a DSML model without first transforming the model completely into a lower-level language, e.g., AsmL, before the model is executed.

DYNAMIC SEMANTICS FOR SYNTHESIZING I-DSML MODEL INSTANCES

In this section we motivate the need for i-DSMLs, present the abstract syntax for CML, and the platform used to execute CML model instances, CVM. We also introduce a high-level description of the dynamic semantics to support the synthesis process for CML model instances. The synthesis process accepts models that are interpreted at runtime and produce scripts that are executed by a middleware. Unlike the traditional approaches of defining semantics for DSML models where a model is translated into a model of another language, the approach for CML requires the input of two instance models. These two models are compared and the resulting model changes along with the current state of the environment determine the control script that is generated. We will also introduce a second i-DSML and interpreter for the microgrid energy management domain, the Microgrid Modeling Language (MGridML), and the Microgrid Virtual Machine (MgridVM).

Motivation

During the Code Generation 2010 Conference[1] there was a "Birds of a Feather" session about code generation versus model interpretation. The discussion identified the advantages of both code generation and model interpretation. The advantages of code generation (Kelly & Tolvanen, 2008) are pretty well known and include targeting the customer's architecture, process is more iterative, and it allows for additional checking by the compiler, among others. The advantages of model interpretation include enabling faster changes to models (no need to regenerate or build code), enabling changes at runtime, and the ability to debug models at runtime, among others (den Haan, 2012). The interpretation of DSML models is appealing for those applications where end-users can create models, execute them and deploy changes to the executing model at runtime. Our research team has been working on an i-DSML for specifying and realizing user-driven communication applications for several years resulting in CML and CVM.

The initial version of CML and CVM were motivated in part by electronic communication problems that health professionals at the Miami Children's Hospital (MCH) experienced during their daily routine. One such problem is the dynamic nature of electronic communication needed between the health professionals, as illustrated in the *Fill Prescription* scenario below.

Fill Prescription Scenario

(1) After Dr. Burke (C - cardiologist) performs surgery on baby Jane he establishes an audio/video communication with Dr. Allen (P - pharmacist) to request medication for his patient. During the conversation, Dr. Burke composes the patient record for baby Jane and sends it to Dr. Allen as supporting documentation in order to fill the prescription. The patient record consists of a summary of patient's condition and prescription, *RecSum-Jane.txt* (non-stream file); and an x-Ray of the patient's heart, *xRay-Jane.jpg* (non-stream file). (2) After sending the package to Dr. Allen, Dr. Burke decides to contact Ms. Smith (NP – nurse practitioner) and Dr. Jones (AP – attending physician) to join the conversation with Dr. Allen to discuss the prescription and the recommended daily doses of the medication to be administered.

During the review of the current systems that were in place at MCH to support communication in healthcare, it was realized that all the tasks in the scenario could be performed with the existing technologies. However, this would require the cobbling together of different software applications and technologies, e.g., email, phone system (mobile of landline with conference capabilities), and access to database with patient records. In addition, it was not possible to automatically repeat these actions guided by some type of automated workflow.

Based on this scenario, CML was created to model an abstraction of the communication between the different actors and the various media accessed during their communication. The requirements of CML were that it should be simple and intuitive, be independent of underlying network and devices being used, and it would be able to model a majority of the communication scenarios we had identified at that time. After defining CML, there was the question of how to execute the CML models to realize the communication specified. The options were (1) to transform the models into a high-level language to be executed, or (2) develop a technique that would execute CML models directly. The second option was selected since it was important to dynamically change the executing model at runtime to incorporate new changes specified by the users. It is worth noting that CML and the execution strategy were developed with two types of end-users in mind, (1) *novice* - having little or no skill in programming and modeling e.g., doctor in the fulfill prescription scenario; and (2) *domain expert* - someone very familiar with the domain but not having extensive skills in programming or software modeling e.g., a medical IT specialist familiar with the work-flow processes and procedures in the medical domain. As a result the CVM was created with two modeling environments, one for the novice user e.g., doctor, and one for the expert user e.g., the medical IT specialist. We will describe these modeling environments later in the chapter.

We are currently investigating how the approach used to create CML and CVM can be used in other domains, such a microgrid energy management. We have developed a preliminary version of MgridML, used to specify energy management applications, and the respective virtual machine, MgridVM, to interpret models of these applications (Allison et al. 2011). One scenario we are currently working on is given below.

Energy Management Scenario

Dana is a customer in N.E. US where there are distinct seasonal changes in the weather. Dana's home contains a cooling system (AC), a heating system (heater), and a pool filtration system (pool), among other devices not relevant to the scenario. The home is connected to the local utility via a smartmeter, the primary energy source, and secondary energy source a storage device (battery). During winter time, the heating system in Dana's home is active and the cooling system and pool filtration system are turned off. The season has changed and it is now late spring, Dana wants to turn on the cooling system and the pool filtration

Figure 1. High-level structure of abstract syntax for i-DSMLs

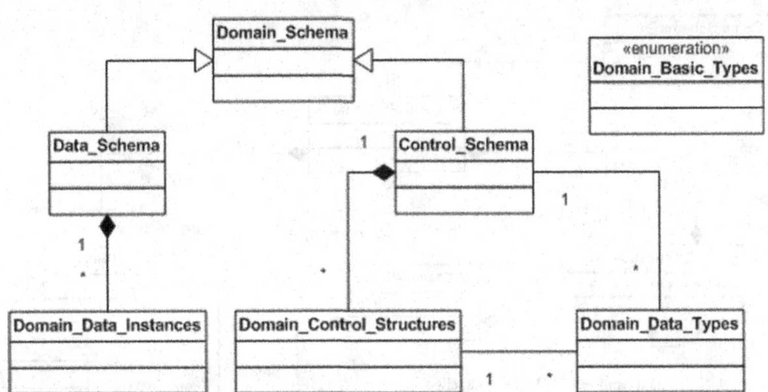

system, and turn off the heating system. At any time if there is a power interruption with the local utility, the energy for the home is provided by the storage device until it is depleted or the energy is restored by the local utility.

In the next subsection we describe the general structure of the abstract syntax for i-DSMLs and provide the specific abstract syntax for CML.

Abstract Syntax for CML

Based on our work with CML an i-DSML needs to generate two types of models one to represent the "program" (configurations, control structures) in the domain and the other to represent the "data" (entities) from the domain. We use the terms "program" and "data" to represent the traditional view of a computer system where the semantics are thought of as configurations as a mixture of syntactical objects, the *program* and *data* (Plotkin, 1981). Figure 1 shows the high-level structure of the abstract syntax for a domain schema, which may be a *control schema* or a *data schema*. The control schema represents the configuration of the user defined application, which consists of zero or more control structures and the data types from the domain. The data schema contains one or more data instances for the types defined in the control schema. There are also several specific basic types that can be defined for a given domain. The term *schema* is used in our context to represent an i-DSML model. We expect to have three concrete notations for each i-DSML including a graphical representation (expert user), an XML representation (machine readable) and a user interface representation (novice user). Examples for CML are presented later in this section.

As previously stated, CML is an i-DSML that is used to model user-driven communication services. CML is a two-tiered language, the first tier (basic CML) representing the basic communication service (Clarke et al., 2006) and the second tier (*WF-CML - workflow CML*) the coordination of basic communication services (Wu, Hernandez, France, & Clarke, 2011b). In this chapter we focus on basic CML, from here on referred to simply as CML. There are three concrete notations used to represent models in CML: the XML-based (X-CML), the graphical (G-CML) and the UI-based (UI-CML). Bi-directional model transformations between G-CML and X-CML, and UI-CML and X-CML have been defined and used in the current implementation of CVM. Three categories of communication models can be described using CML: *control schema* – specifies the configuration of a communication; *control instance* - fully instantiated control schema; and a *data instance* - specifies actual media (name or URLs/URIs) to be exchanged during a basic communication service. Figure 2

Figure 2. Abstract syntax for CML

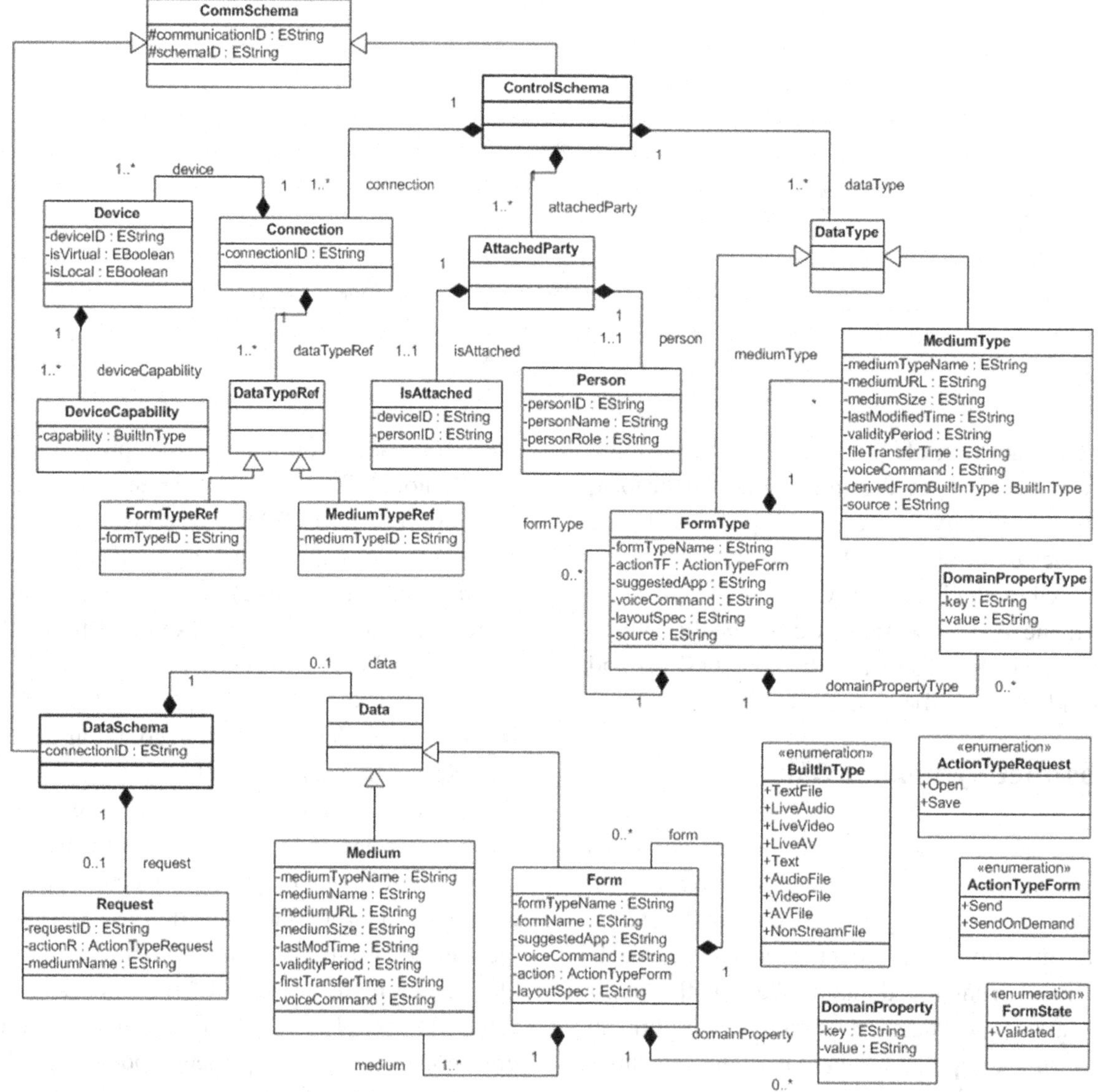

shows the abstract syntax for CML, the classes at the top of the figure shows the structure of the control schema and the classes at the bottom the data schema. The complete metamodel for CML can be found on the project's web page (http://cml.cs.fiu.edu/).

Figure 3 shows three of the G-CML models, equivalent to the X-CML models used by the CVM, during the realization of the fill prescription scenario. These models are presented for illustration purposes only since such models would not be created by the user at execution time. Figure 3(a) is the control instance for part one of the communication between Dr. Burke and Dr. Allen. Drs Burke and Allen are attached to devices with ids 001 and 002 respectively. Each device contains the capabilities required to transmit the media defined on the connection node. The connection node, shown as a diamond in the center of the figure, defines the following types - `LiveAudio`

Figure 3. CML for the fill prescription scenario: (a) Control instance, (b) First data instance, (c) Second data instance

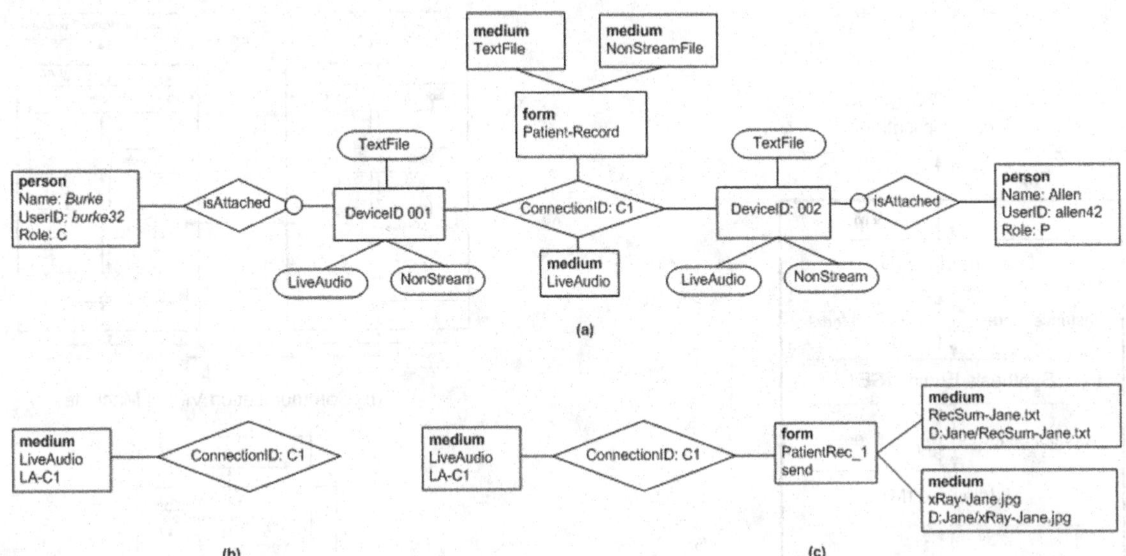

media type and `Patient_Record` a user-defined form type containing the media types `TextFile` and `NonStreamFile`. A *form* is a media structure that may contain other forms or basic media types. Figure 3(b) shows the G-CML model for the data instance that initiates the live audio-video stream during the communication. Figure 3(c) shows the model containing the patient record instance form sent to Dr. Allen during the communication with Dr. Burke.

CML Interpreter

The CVM prototype has provided us with some ideas for the structure of an i-DSML interpreter. Such an interpreter would take as input a set of models and execute them to realize some user-defined application in the appropriate domain. We continue to use the term "virtual machine" to refer to the i-DSML interpreter. For example, the CVM takes as input the models shown in Figure 3 and realizes part (1) of the fill prescription scenario. Figure 4(a) shows the layered architecture for a generic virtual machine used to execute i-DSML models. Figures 4 (b) and (c) show the specialization for the virtual machines in the domains of user-driven communication and microgrid energy management. The layers of the generic virtual machine are as follows:

1. **User Interface:** Allows users to declaratively specify their domain needs and requirements using the appropriate interfaces. The model for an application specified for a given domain can be loaded into the UI by a user or created on-the-fly. Before the model can be sent to the next layer in the interpreter it must be validated and converted to the XML-based representation.
2. **Synthesis Engine:** Accepts XML instances, both control and data, populates the control schemas with meta-data when necessary, and synthesizes the model instances resulting in the generation of the control scripts to be executed by the middleware layer.
3. **Middleware:** Executes the control scripts to manage and coordinate the delivery of domain services. These services may in-

Figure 4. (a) Layered architecture of the generic virtual machine, (b) Communication virtual machine (CVM), (c) Microgrid virtual machine (MGridVM)

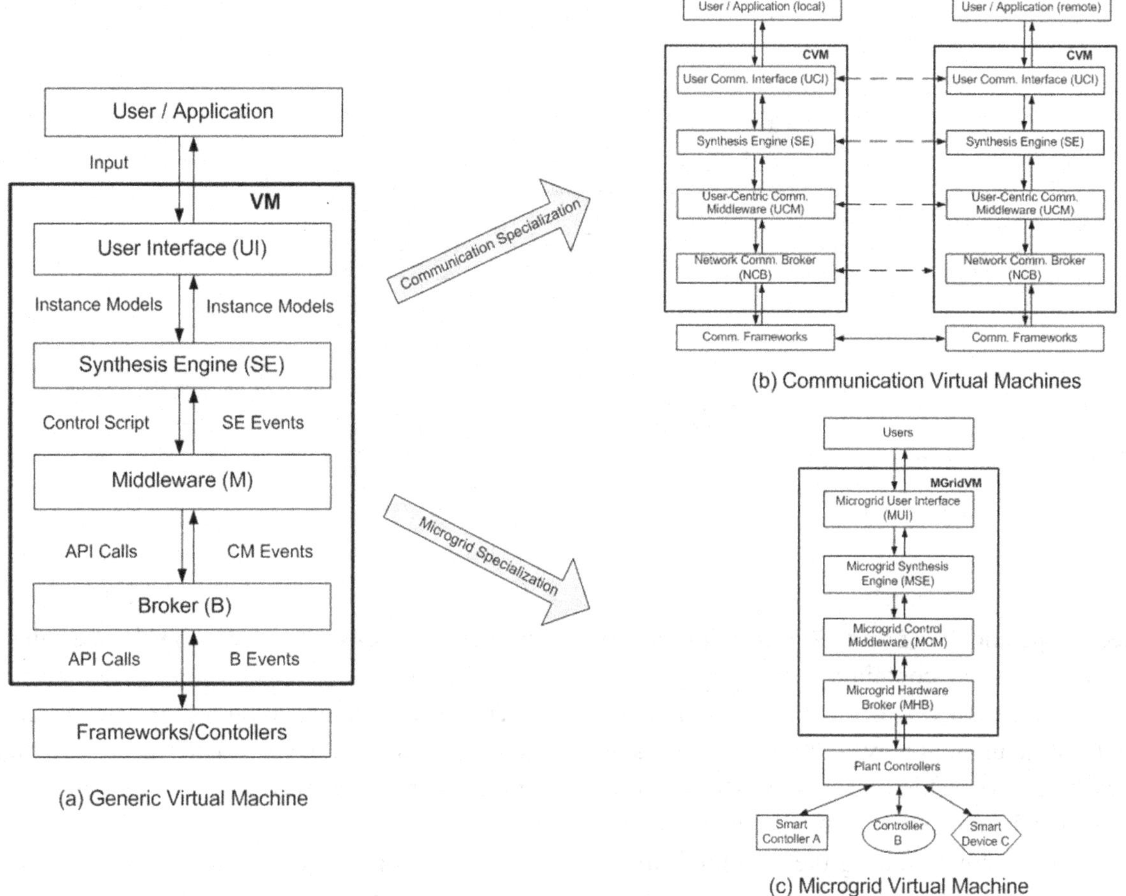

clude the application of domain-specific policies based on user-preferences or policies specified in the control schema. Based on the control scripts and policies received by the middleware, macros are loaded and executed.

4. **Broker:** Provides an independent API to the middleware and interfaces with the underlying frameworks and controllers to realize the services required. The broker removes the heterogeneity of the frameworks and controllers that provide the low-level services in the respective domains. The broker also interprets events from the underlying frameworks and controllers, and generates events and exceptions to be handled by the upper layers.

Table 1 shows the specifics associated with the CVM and MGridVM. The column labeled CVM describes concepts specific to user-driven communication and the MGridVM column concepts in the microgrid energy management domain. We are currently working on developing metamodels for the various layers of the generic virtual machine. It is our expectation that specific models for the layers in the VM for a given domain will be instantiated using these metamodels. The work by Nain, Daubert, Barais, and Jézéquel (2008)

Table 1. Functionality specific to the CVM and MGridVM

Layer	CVM	MGridVM
UI	Specifies communication requirements	Specifies microgrid management requirements
SE	Negotiates the control schemas with the parties in a connection and determines media transfer actions. Each person in a connection negotiates on a control schema that is the basis for receiving media during a communication.	Negotiates with the device controllers in the microgrid to determine if the device types and logical controller specified are adequate.
M	Responsible for delivery of communication services e.g., sending files to all parties in a connection, encrypting/decryption files and starting/stopping audio-video streams. Macros are written in Java.	Mapping groups of physical devices to logical controllers, executing energy management algorithms, and applying policies to various device configurations.
B	Provides a network independent API to the middleware and interfaces with the underlying networks or communication frameworks (e.g., Skype (Skype Limited, 2007) and Smack (Ignite Realtime, 2010)).	Provides a device independent API to the middleware and interfaces with the underlying device controllers (e.g., ZigBee Alliance (2012) enabled thermostats), and establishes a connection with these device controllers.

provide some insight on what the instantiated model for the MGridVM would look like.

Since we will be providing details on the synthesis process for CML model instances several core concepts in the user-defined communication domain are defined below:

- **(Re)negotiation:** Control schemas are negotiated between parties in a connection to establish if their devices have the capabilities to handle the media types defined in the control schema. For example, if the connection requires audio-video streams then all participants' devices must have the capability to display the audio-video stream. At anytime during the communication, a connection renegotiation may be required if new media types are introduced during the communication.
- **Media Transfer:** We use this term to refer to the process of starting/stopping a stream and sending/receiving a file and a form (media structure consisting of other media types).
- **Initiator:** Party that starts an action over the connection e.g., negotiation or a media transfer. During the synthesis process metadata is added to the control schema being negotiated to identify who is the *initiator* of the action in a connection.
- **Non-Initiator:** Party (participant) who is not the initiator of an action in a connection.
- **Local Party and Remote Party:** Used in the context of the CVM being described. For example, party A is local if the actions are being described in term of A's CVM. Note if A initiates an action but the action is being described in terms of B's CVM, then B is local and A is remote.

Figure 5 shows the UI representation of a CML model at runtime. The figure shows the interface for Dr. Allen's CVM, the receiver of the communication in part (1) of the fill prescription scenario, see rightmost box in Figure 3(a). The screen shot in the figure is just after Dr. Allen received the patient record for baby Jane, shown in the form component at the top of the figure. In this scenario Dr. Burke loads the control schema shown in Figure 3(a) and executes it. It should be noted that a user may either load a control schema from the dashboard and execute it, or create a new control schema on the fly and execute it. When using the interface in Figure 5, the user is not aware of the differences between the control and data schemas. Due to space limitation we do not show the G-CML modeling environment, the interested reader can see a picture of the environment in the article by Wu, Allen, Hernandez, France, and Clarke, (2011a).

Figure 5. The UI representation of CML at runtime

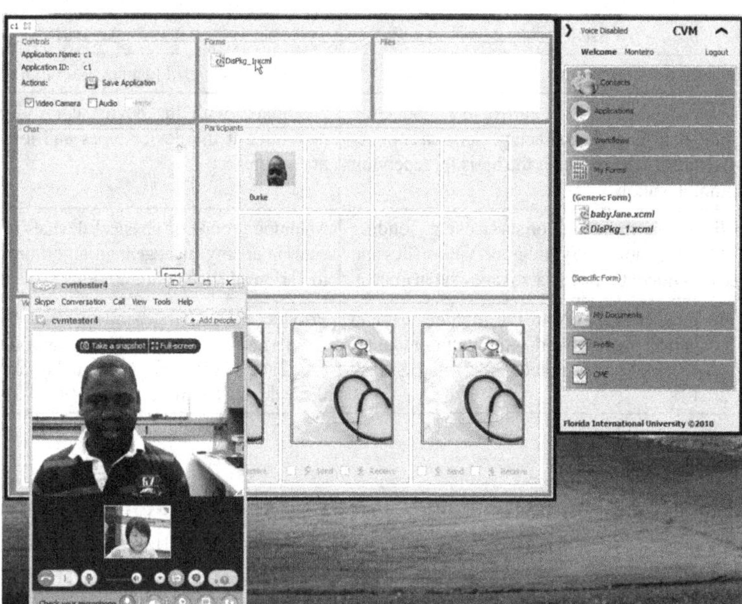

Figure 6 shows the syntax for the CVM control scripts using EBNF-like notation. Recall that the control scripts are generated during the synthesis process and executed by the UCM. Rule 1 states that a control script may consist of one or more commands. Rule 2 shows the commands that can be used in a control script, one of these commands being `createConnectionCmd`. Rule 3 defines the `createConnectionCmd` which creates a connection for the participants in the initial CML model. The subscript "A" associated with some terms represents the parameter for the command. For example, in rule 3 the create connection command has one parameter which is a unique connection identifier. An illustrative example is presented later in the chapter that shows how several of the control scripts are generated.

Semantics Based on Model Changes

The semantics for synthesizing i-DSML model instances can be defined by extending the interpreter approach presented in (Bryant et al. 2011). The synthesis process is defined as follows:

Figure 6. Partial list of the CVM control scripts commands using EBNF-like notation

1. *controlScript* := *command {command}*
2. *command* := *createConnectionCmd* | *closeConnectionCmd* | *addParticipantCmd* | *removeParticipantCmd* | *sendSchemaCmd* | *enableMediaInitiatorCmd* | *enableMediaReceiverCmd* | *disableMediaInitiatorCmd* | *disableMediaReceiverCmd* | *sendMediaCmd* | *sendFormCmd* | *declineConnectionCmd* | *requestFormCmd* | *requestMediaCmd* | *sendNegTokenCmd* | *requestNegTokenCmd*
3. *createConnectionCmd* := **createConnection** connectionID$_A$
4. *closeConnectionCmd* := **closeConnection** connectionID$_A$
5. *addParticipantCmd* := **addParticipant** connectionID$_A$ personID$_A$ {personID$_A$}
6. *removeParticipantCmd* := **removeParticipant** connectionID$_A$ personID$_A$ {personID$_A$ }
7. *sendSchemaCmd* := **sendSchema** connectionID$_A$ sender-personID$_A$ receiver-personID$_A$ {receiver-personID$_A$} schema$_A$
8. *enableMediaInitiatorCmd* := **enableInitiatorMedia** connectionID$_A$ mediaName$_A$
9. *enableMediaReceiverCmd* := **enableReceiverMedia** connectionID$_A$ mediaName$_A$
10. *disableMediaInitiatorCmd* := **disableInitiatorMedia** connectionID$_A$ mediaName$_A$
11. *disableMediaReceiverCmd* := **disableReceiverMedia** connectionID$_A$ mediaName$_A$
12. *sendMediaCmd* := **sendMedia** connectionID$_A$ mediaName$_A$ mediumURL$_A$
13. *sendFormCmd* := **sendForm** connectionID$_A$ formID$_A$ mediumURL$_A$ {mediumURL$_A$ } action$_A$

...

$$i(M_i, M_{i+1}): I \times S(M_i, M_{i+1}) \rightarrow O \times S(M_i, M_k) \quad (1)$$

where M_i represents the instance pair of the form (CI_i, DI_i), where, for i = 0… n, CI_i is a control instance and DI_i a data instance. M_i is the current model being executed (runtime model of the system). The initial instance pair (CI_0, DI_0) represents the initial state of the system with respect to the domain being modeled. M_{i+1} represents the instance pair received from the UI or Middleware; I is the input event alphabet; O is the output alphabet, containing the control script; S is the set of internal states of the execution engine, dependent on the communication models and labeled transition systems (LTSs) for the specific domain; M_k is a new instance pair generated during the synthesis process that may be equal to M_{i+1}. Note that during the next application of the synthesis process M_k becomes the new runtime model (M_i) of the control and data instances. We explicitly show M_i in Equation (1) which is internal to S to emphasis that two models are used to determine the dynamic semantics of the synthesis process.

The synthesis process described in Equation (1) can be mapped to CML model instances as follows:

- **M_{i+1} = (CI_{i+1}, DI_{i+1}):** New model containing the input control and data instances capturing a user's communication needs to be realized by the synthesis process.
- **M_i = (CI_i, DI_i):** Current model being executed in the synthesis process.
- **I:**events signifying that new models require synthesizing, as well as, the source of the model, e.g., initiator or non-initiator.
- **S:** On the left of (→), represents the current environment (state of the synthesis engine) including the runtime model, current control and data instances, M_i = (CI_i, DI_i), and the states of the domain LTSs described below.

The specific states for CML include the negotiation state, Neg_i, and media transfer state, MT_i. Negotiation and media transfer are domain specific processes that are defined using LTSs, respectively. We provide examples later in the chapter.

- **Neg_i:** Current state of a specific connection with respect to (re)negotiation. The negotiation environment contains the control instance (CI_{neg}) currently being negotiated on. CI_{neg} is initially CI_{i+1} but may change as the negotiation progresses. CI_{i+1} is the new control instance supplied by one of the parties in the connection to be negotiated on.
- **MT_i:** Current state of a specific connection process with respect to media transfer e.g., streaming audio or transferring files.
- **S:** On the right of (→), is similar to the description previously presented but represents the updated environment in the synthesis process.

M_k = (CI_k, DI_k) - updated control and data instances generated during the transition which may be different from (CI_{i+1}, DI_{i+1}). This model pair is stored in the current environment and used to update the user interface. M_k may not be the same as M_{i+1} after the operation since CI_{i+1} may change.

For example in the communication domain, if a party in the connection cannot satisfy an audio-video media type then the negotiation process may settle on an audio media type which is satisfied by all parties in the connection.

O includes the following events (1) the communication control scripts generated, e.g., (re) negotiation and media transfer scripts for CML, executed by the CVM middleware; and (2) (CI_k, DI_k) pair used to update the user interface.

Overview of Synthesis Process

An overview of the synthesis process for CML and MGridML are shown in Figure 7. The input to the synthesis process, shown on the left of the

Figure 7. Overview of synthesis process

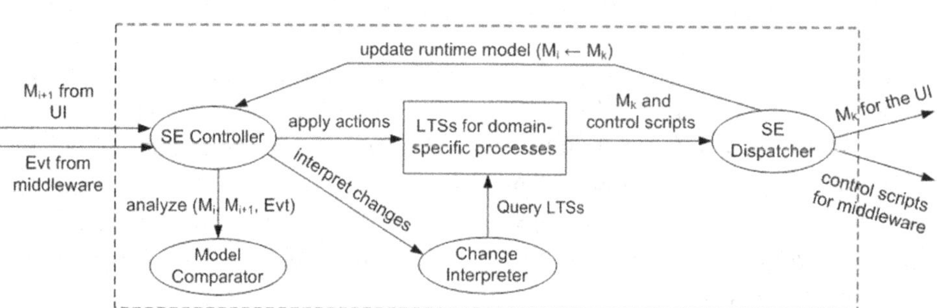

figure, includes the user-defined model (M_{i+1}) or an event from the middleware (Evt) which may contain M_{i+1}. The *SE Controller* calls the *Model Comparator* passing it the current runtime model of the control and data instances (M_i), $M_{(i+1)}$, and Evt. Note that either M_{i+1} or Evt may be null, but not both. Evt may contain a user-defined model based on the type of domain model being synthesized, e.g., (re)negotiation. The model comparator generates a list of changes by comparing M_i and M_{i+1}, which are then processed by the *Change Interpreter*. The change interpreter queries the LTSs for the respective domain-specific processes to obtain their current state, and generates a list of actions to be applied to the LTSs. Based on the actions applied to the LTSs, appropriate control scripts are generated and the runtime model for the control and data instances are updated. The *SE Dispatcher* updates the current runtime model, generates an event to send the updated control and data instances to the UI, and/or sends the control scripts to the middleware for processing.

Figure 8 shows a top-level UML state machine for the synthesis process of CML model instances. The state machine can be divided into three parts, these are: (1) *model analysis* (state 2, and submachines 3 and 4) - where communication models are received, changes are identified and the resulting changes are interpreted to determine the actions related to a connection; (2) *connection management* (submachines 5, 6 and 7) – these actions include the creation of a connection, managing negotiation and media transfer, and closing a connection; (3) *dispatching output* (submachine 8) - the control scripts are sent to the lower layer (UCM) in the CVM and the updated communication models sent to the upper layers (UCI). We claim that parts (1) and (3) of the state machine (state 2, and submachines 3, 4 and 8) are independent of the domain and the remaining parts are domain-specific. Note that the submachines 5, 6, and 7 are specific to the communication domain. Part 1 of the state machine is described as follows:

1. **Model Comparison:** The synthesis process starts when a new or updated CML model is received; see the transition between the *ready* and *modelReceived* states in Figure 8. The parameters to the *synthesize* action are: *CML_(i+1)* a CML model, consisting of a control instance (CI_{i+1}) and a data instance (DI_{i+1}), and *source*, identifying whether the CML model originated locally (from UI) or from a remote party (from UCM). The analysis of the incoming model and the currently executing model is performed in the submachine *modelComparator* where model changes are identified. The action *analyze* between state 2 and submachine 3 invokes the model comparator submachine and takes parameters *CML_(i+1), CML_i* – the currently executing model, and *source*. The models actually

Figure 8. State machine for the synthesis process

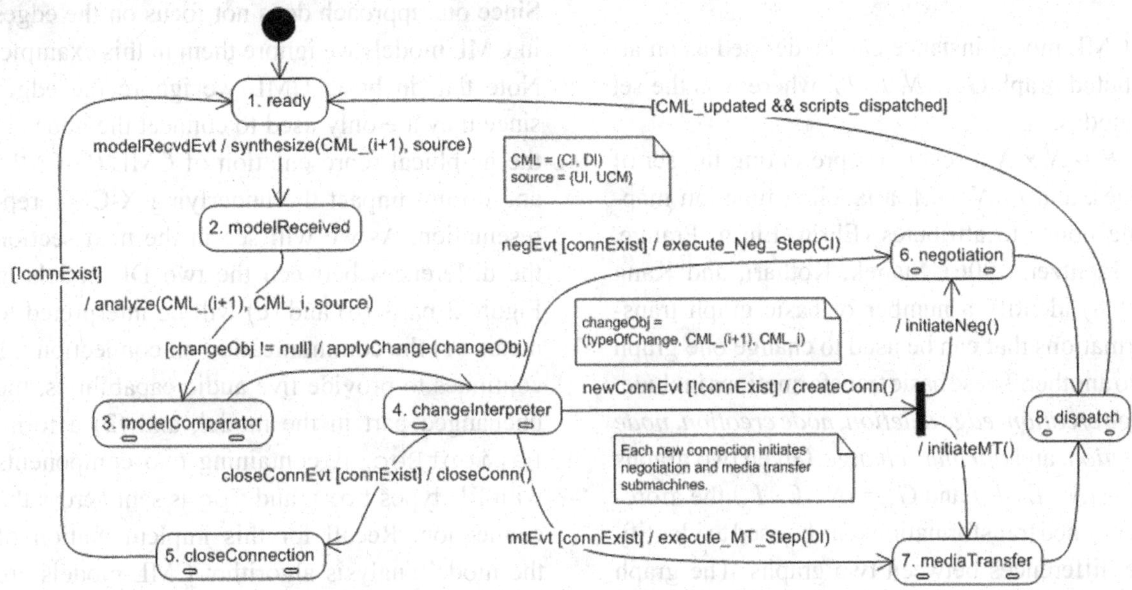

compared during analysis are the model pairs (CI_{i+1}, DI_{i+1}) and (CI_i, DI_i) shown in Figure 8 as the models *CML_(i+1)* and *CML_i*, respectively.

2. **Interpretation of Model Changes:** The model changes identified in the *modelComparator* submachine need to be converted into meaningful semantic actions in the communication domain, e.g., add a new party to an existing connection, or send a file to all parties in a connection. The submachine *changeInterpreter* uses the change information generated during model comparison and generates the appropriate event to either create a new connection, or perform transitions in the negotiation and media transfer submachines, as appropriate. The change information is passed as a parameter (*changeObj*) in the action *applyChange* on the transition between submachines 3 (*modelComparator*) and 4 (*changeInterpreter*). The parameter *changeObj* consists of *changeList* - a list of fine-grained changes, and the two CML models that were analyzed, *CML_(i+1)* and *CML_i*. Using the list of fine-grained changes a coarse-grained change is generated based on a set of patterns developed for the communication domain. Using the coarse-grained change the appropriate event is generated and sent to the corresponding submachine and the appropriate transition is executed.

We are currently defining the LTSs for the synthesis process in the microgrid energy management domain and the aforementioned approach seems feasible. One issue being addressed is how to represent manual actions to the devices in the microgrid plant. For example, if the user manually turns on a device in the microgrid plant how should this be reflected in the user-defined and runtime models for the control and data instances.

In the following subsections we describe the process of model comparison and model interpretation, for the communication domain, which are core aspects of the semantics for the synthesis process.

Model Comparison

A CML model instance can be defined as an attributed graph $G = (N, E, L)$, where N is the set of nodes,

$E = N \times N$ a relation representing the set of edges, and $L: N \rightarrow A$, a labeling function mapping nodes to attributes (Ehrig, Ehrig, Prange, & Taentzer, 2006). Stanek, Kothari, and Kang (2008) identify a number of basic graph transformations that can be used to change one graph into another. These basic transformations include: *edge creation*, *edge deletion*, *node creation*, *node deletion*, and *attribute change*. Given two graphs $G_1 = (N_1, E_1, L_1)$ and $G_2 = (N_2, E_2, L_2)$ the aforementioned transformations can be used to identify the differences between two graphs. The graph differencing problem is based on the well-known graph isomorphism problem which identifies the maximum common subgraph between G_1 and G_2. Once the maximal subgraph is found, the difference between G_1 and G_2 represents the extra nodes and/or edges in either G_1 or G_2. We can define graph differencing as a sequence of basic transformations that can be used to convert G_1 into G_2, written as $G_2 = T(G_1)$. Note that in general T does not produce a unique solution, however, there are restrictions that can be placed on the nodes and edges in a graph to provide a unique solution, e.g., uniquely identifying each node and edge (Lin, Gray, & Jouault, 2007). Altmanninger, Seidl, and Wimmer (2009) present a comprehensive survey of model changes, including the changes previously described. Our approach requires full model comparison since any addition or removal of nodes represents semantic actions in the domain.

We illustrate the changes to CML models by using the data instances (DIs) shown in Figure 3 parts (b) and (c). The changes required to go from the DI in part (b) to the DI in part(c) include adding the three nodes, on the right side of part (c), which is an instance of the form type `Patient-Record`. The nodes labeled Connection (`ConnectionID:C1`) and medium (`LiveAudio, LA-C1`) are left unchanged. Since our approach does not focus on the edges in CML models we ignore them in this example. Note that in basic CML we ignore the edges since they are only used to connect the nodes in the graphical representation of CML (G-CML) and do not impact the underlying X-CML representation. As we will see in the next section the differences between the two DI models in Figure 3 parts (b) and (c) will be interpreted to mean: (1) the communication on connection `C1` continues to provide live audio capabilities, the unchanged part in the model, and (2) a form, `PatientRec_1`, containing two components with file types `text` and `jpg` is sent across the connection. Recall for this implementation of the model analysis algorithm CML models are defined as labeled attributed graphs therefore we do not allow changes to labels. If during model analysis a label has changed, then we interpret that change to mean a node was removed and a new node added with the changed label.

Model Change Interpretation

Given the atomic changes generated by the differencing algorithm, we need to match these changes to patterns representing the semantic actions in the communication domain. We currently approach this problem by identifying patterns of model changes and mapping them to events used by the negotiation and media transfer LTSs shown in Figure 8, submachines labeled 6 and 7, respectively. Since the semantics for synthesis occurs in a distributed environment some model changes are interpreted in the context of whether the party is the initiator of the action or the receiver.

Table 2 shows the model changes and the events generated for the negotiation submachine (submachine 6 in Figure 8) and an explanation of the semantics associated with the changes. The table consists of four columns, which are from left to right, the assigned row number, the CI model changes between the executing model (CI_i) and

Table 2. Mapping model changes in CI to state machine events

No.	CI Models Changes (nodes)	Event	Explanation
Source of CI Model: **UCI** (updated model supplied by user)			
1	**added**: connection, device, isAttached (local), person, ...	intitiateNeg	initiates a new connection => negotiation of CI
2	**removed**: connection, device, isAttached (local), ...	removeSelf	if last connection => terminates all communication
3	**added**: connection, device, isAttached (remote), person	intitiateReNeg	initiates a new connection => re-negotiation of CI
4	**removed**: device, isAttached (local), person	intitiateReNeg	removes a connection, assuming there are no more remote parties on this connection, and there is still at least one other connection => re-negotiation of CI
5	**removed**: connection, device, isAttached (remote), person	intitiateReNeg	removes a connection, assuming there is still at least one other connection => re-negotiation of CI
6	**added**: device, isAttached (remote), person	intitiateReNeg	adds a new party to a connection => re-negotiation of CI
7	**removed**: device, isAttached (remote), person	intitiateReNeg	removes party from a connection, assuming there are other remote parties on the connection => re-negotiation of CI
8	**added**: medium capability (to device)	intitiateReNeg	if the new medium type is not a subtype of an existing medium => re-negotiation of CI
9	**added**: medium type (to connection)	intitiateReNeg	if the new medium type is not a subtype of an existing medium => re-negotiation of CI
10	**added**: form type (to connection)	intitiateReNeg	if the new form type is not a subtype of an existing medium => re-negotiation of CI
11	**removed**: medium capability (from device)	intitiateReNeg	if a medium type is removed from a device may impact capabilities => re-negotiation of CI
12	**removed**: medium type (from connection)	intitiateReNeg	if medium type is removed this restricts the types on the connection => re-negotiation of CI
13	**removed**: form type (from connection)	intitiateReNeg	if form type is removed this restricts the types on the connection => re-negotiation of CI
Source of CI Model: **UCM** (initiator of negotiation)			
14	**No Change**	localSameCI	no change to the CI during negotiation
15	**Any Change**	localChangeCI	remote party change CI restarts negotiation
Source of **new** CI Model: **UCM** (non-initiator of the negotiation and CI model **not** seen before from the initiator)			
16	**Change (see 6, 7 – 13)**	inviteNeg	invitation for negotiation from the non-initiator
Source of CI Model: **UCM** (non-initiator of negotiation and CI model seen before from the initiator)			
17	**No Change**	remoteSameCI	No change to the CI during negotiation
18	**Changes (see 6, 8 – 13)**	remoteChangeCI	Change to the CI indicates negotiator needs to restart negotiation.

incoming model ($CI_{(i+1)}$), the event generated for the negotiation state machine, and a brief explanation of the event, which may include some conditions required to generate the event.

The table is divided into four sections representing the context required to generate the event for the submachine. These sections are: (1) Rows 1-13 represent the model changes based on the executing model (CI_i) and the model from the local user ($CI_{(i+1)}$), (2) Rows 14-15 represent model changes between the executing model at the initiator's CVM and the model from the non-initiator, (3) Row 16 represents model changes between the executing model at the non-initiator's CVM and the model from the initiator ***not seen*** before, (4) Rows 17-18 represent model changes between the executing model at the non-initiator's CVM and the incoming model from the initiator, and the model was ***seen*** before.

Examples of how the events are generated from the model changes are as follows. In Row 3, the changes needed to transform CI_i (the executing model) to $CI_{(i+1)}$ (the new model received from the user) require adding the nodes *connection*, *device*, *isAttached (remote)* and *person*, these actions result in the event `initiateReNeg` being generated. The semantic action associated with these changes is the creation of a new connection in an existing communication. In Rows 14-15 and 17-18 the models being compared are versions of $CI_{(i+1)}$, the model to replace the currently executing model (CI_i). For example in Row 14 if the model $CI_{(i+1)}$ – the model from the non-initiator, is the same as CI_{neg} – the model that triggered the negotiation, at the initiator, then a `localSameCI` is generated taking the negotiation closer to completion. However, if there is a change in these models, Row 15, then a `local-ChangeCI` event is generated and negotiation has to be restarted. Since we use the three-phase negotiation protocol (Skeen, 1981) if there is no change in the model after the initiator receives it from the non-initiators then it is sent out one more time to the non-initiators. If the non-initiators receive the model with no change, Row 17, then a `remoteSameCI` event is generated and the negotiation is successful. Otherwise, Row 18 the negotiation fails and a `remoteChangeCI` event is generated.

Table 3 shows the model changes for the data instance (DI) and the events generated for the media transfer state machine (submachine 7 in Figure 8). Table 3 has a similar column structure to Table 2. Note however it is only divided into two sections. The first section, Row 1 through 6, represents the changes between the executing model (DI_i) and the new model containing the request from the user ($DI_{(i+1)}$), the initiator of media transfer action. The media transfer submachine is created when a connection is established between remote parties, as shown in Figure 8. Row 1 of Table 3 indicates that if a new medium stream is added to the connection node in the DI by the user then an `enableStream` event is generated, assuming that the medium type is defined in the CI. If the medium type does not exist in the CI then renegotiation is initiated implicitly by the synthesis engine controller, not currently shown in Figure 8.

The second section of Table 3, Rows 7 through 10, represents the changes between the executing data instance and the data instance received from the initiator of the media transfer action. If a DI model is received by the non-initiator of the medium request, Row 7, and there is a change with the medium stream added to the connection node, then the event `enableStreamRec` (enable stream receiver) is generated and sent to the media transfer submachine. It is worth noting that unlike streaming media where the medium remains on the connection until it is removed (disabled), non-streaming medium is sent immediately. This is the reason for no events being generated (`NA`) in Rows 5 and 6 of the table.

Illustrative Example

To illustrate how the dynamic synthesis process works using model analysis and change interpretation, we describe a simple example in this section using the fill prescription scenario presented in the Motivation section. Recall the CML models for the scenario are shown in Figure 3. To ensure the chapter is self-contained we described partial LTSs for the (re)negotiation and media transfer shown in Table 4 and Table 5, respectively. Complete LTSs for these processes may be found in

Table 3. Mapping model changes in DI to state machine events

No.	Models Changes (nodes)	Event	Explanation
Source of DI Model: **UCI** (updated model supplied by user - initiator)			
1	**added**: medium (stream) to connection	enableStream	if medium type exist in CI => start streaming medium; else start re-negotiation
2	**added**: medium (non-stream) to connection	sendNonStream	if medium type exist in CI => send non-stream medium; else start re-negotiation
3	**added**: form to connection	sendForm	if form type exist in CI => send form on connection; else start re-negotiation
4	**removed**: medium (stream) from connection	disableStream	stop streaming medium on connection
5	**removed**: medium (non-stream) from connection	NA	non-stream media is sent immediately
6	**removed**: form from connection	NA	form is sent immediately (from the point of view of synthesis)
Source of DI Model: **UCM** (model received by the non-initiator of the media request)			
7	**added**: medium (stream) to connection	enableStreamRec	receives stream
8	**added**: medium (non-stream) to connection	recNonStream	receives non-stream (e.g., file)
9	**added**: form to connection	recForm	receives form (e.g., discharge package)
10	**removed**: medium (stream) from connection	disableStreamRec	

Table 4. Partial state machine for (re)negotiation

T.	Source_State	Target_State	Event	Guard	Action
0	Initial	NegReady			
1	NegReady	NegInitiated	initiateNeg	hasNegToken	addNegBlock(CI_{neg}) genConnection_Script
2	NegReady	NegInitiated	initiateReNeg	hasNegToken	addNegBlock(CI_{neg})
3	NegInitiated	WaitingSameCI		#remoteParty != 0	genSendCS_Script
4	WaitingSameCI	WaitingSameCI	localSameCI	#responses < #remoteParty	
5	WaitingSameCI	NegComplete	localSameCI	#responses = = #remoteParty	genSendCS_Script
6	NegComplete	NegReady			$CI_{exe} \leftarrow CI_{neg}$ UCI.notify(CI_{exe})
	…	…	…	…	…
25	NegReady	SelfRemoved	removeSelf	hasNegToken	genRemoveSelf Script
	…	…	…	…	…

Wu et al. (2011a), as well as algorithms formally describing the synthesis process.

Table 4 shows several transitions from the LTS for the (re)negotiation process, submachine 6 in Figure 8. Columns 1 through 6 represent: number assigned to the transition, the sources state of the transition, the destination state, the event generated based on model analysis, the guard, and the

Table 5. Partial state machine for media transfer

T.	Source_State	Target_State	Event	Guard	Action
0	Initial	Ready	initiateNeg || intiateIn-viteNeg		
1	Ready	StreamEnabled	enableStream		genStreamEnable_Script
2	Ready	StreamEnabled	enableStreamRec		genStreamEnableRec_Script UCI.notify(DSi+1)
3	StreamEnabled	StreamEnabled	enableStream	!IsStreamEnabled	genStreamEnable_Script
4	StreamEnabled	StreamEnabled	disableStream	IsStreamEnabled && #streams > 1	genStreamDisable_Script
5	StreamEnabled	StreamEnabled	enableStreamRec	!IsStreamEnabled	genStreamEnableRec_Script UCI.notify(DSout)
6	StreamEnabled	StreamEnabled	disableStreamRec	IsStreamEnabled && #streams > 1	genStreamDisableRec_Script UCI.notify(DSout)
7	StreamEnabled	StreamEnabled	sendNonStream		genNonStreamSend_Script
8	StreamEnabled	StreamEnabled	sendForm		genSendForm_Script
	...	...	...	...	...

actions taken. For example, the transition labeled 1 starts in the *NegReady* state and moves to the *NegInitiated* state when an `initiateNeg` event is received, and the party's CVM has the negation token (*hasNegToken*). The negotiation token is necessary since negotiation is performed in a distributed environment and any party in the connection may start negotiation at any time. The party with the negotiation token is referred to as the *initiator*. After the transition is taken a negotiation block, containing additional information for negotiation, is added to the CI which is then sent to all parties in the connection. In addition, a control script to create the connection between the parties is generated (*genConnection_Script*) and sent to the UCM for execution. The control script to create a new connection is shown as Production 3 in Figure 6.

Table 5 shows several transitions from the LTS for the media transfer process, submachine 7 in Figure 8. Columns in Table 5 are labeled similar to those in Table 4. An example of a transition is shown in Row 1 where the machine is in the *Ready* state, an `enableStream` event is received, resulting in the machine moving to the *StreamEnabled* state and the stream enabled control script is generated (*genStreamEnable_Script*) and sent to the UCM for execution. The script to enable a stream is shown as the Production 8 in Figure 6.

Figure 9 shows a table containing several models used during the realization of the fill prescription scenario presented earlier in this section. Columns 1 and 2 contain the models for CML_i, the currently executing CML model, and $CML_{(i+1)}$ the input CML model, respectively. Recall that a CML model consists of a pair of models (CI, DI). Column 3 shows the changes identified by the differencing algorithm, Column 4 the event generated, and Column 5 the control scripts generated after the negotiation and media transfer LTSs are executed. The scenario starts when the control instance model shown in Figure

Figure 9. Changes made to the CML models at runtime

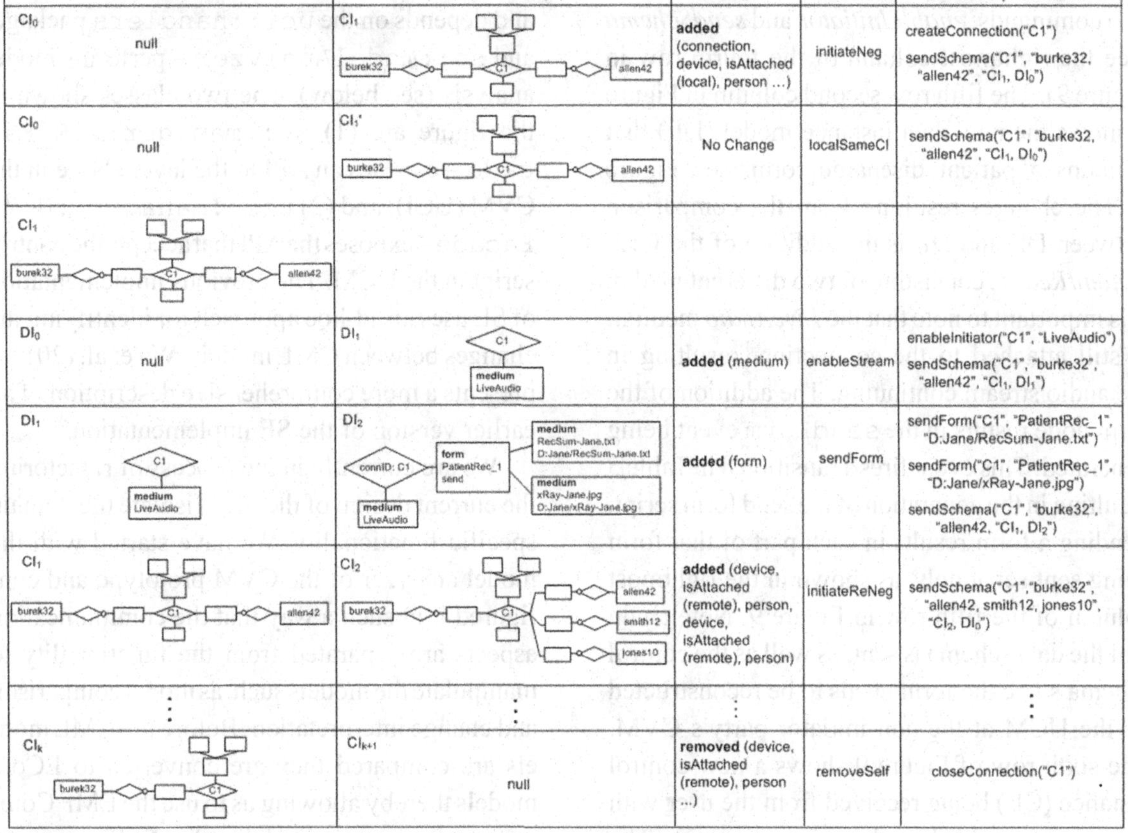

CML_i	$CML_{(i+1)}$	Changes	Event	Control Script Generated
CI_0 null	CI_1 burek32 C1 allen42	**added** (connection, device, isAttached (local), person …)	initiateNeg	createConnection("C1") sendSchema("C1", "burke32, "allen42", "CI_1, DI_0")
CI_0 null	CI_1' burke32 C1 allen42	No Change	localSameCI	sendSchema("C1", "burke32, "allen42", "CI_1, DI_0")
CI_1 burek32 C1 allen42				
DI_0 null	DI_1 C1 **medium** LiveAudio	**added** (medium)	enableStream	enableInitiator("C1", "LiveAudio") sendSchema("C1", "burke32", "allen42", "CI_1, DI_1")
DI_1 C1 **medium** LiveAudio	DI_2 connID: C1 **form** PatientRec_1 send **medium** RecSum-Jane.txt D:Jane/RecSum-Jane.txt **medium** xRay-Jane.jpg D:Jane/xRay-Jane.jpg **medium** LiveAudio	**added** (form)	sendForm	sendForm("C1", "PatientRec_1", "D:Jane/RecSum-Jane.txt") sendForm("C1", "PatientRec_1", "D:Jane/xRay-Jane.jpg") sendSchema("C1", "burke32", "allen42, "CI_1, DI_2")
CI_1 burek32 C1 allen42	CI_2 burek32 C1 allen42 smith12 jones10	**added** (device, isAttached (remote), person, device, isAttached (remote), person)	initiateReNeg	sendSchema("C1","burke32", "allen42, smith12, jones10", "CI_2, DI_0")
⋮	⋮	⋮		⋮
CI_k burek32 C1	CI_{k+1} null	**removed** (device, isAttached (remote), person …)	removeSelf	closeConnection("C1")

3(a) (CI_1) is received by the synthesis engine and compared to the initial model CI_0, as shown in the first row of Figure 9. We omit some of the nodes from the models shown in Figure 3 to improve readability. The results of the models CI_0 and CI_1 are similar to the changes identified in Row 1 of Table 2, resulting in the `initiateNeg` event being generated. This event starts the negotiation and media transfer state machines (see Transition 0 of both Table 4 and Table 5), generates the control script to create a connection (see Transition 1 of Table 4), and generates the script to send the control instance model (CI_1) to the non-initiator to be negotiated on (see Transition 3 of Table 4).

The second row of Figure 9 shows the same CI model being received from the non-initiator (remote) participant, labeled CI_1'. Since no change is detected a `localSameCI` event is generated and sent to the negotiation state machine. This event results in Transition 5 Table 4 being executed since there is only one other party in the communication. Transition 5 generates the control script to send CI_1 to the non-initiator party. This transition terminates negotiation and CI_1 becomes the control instance being executed (CML_i), see the third row of Figure 9.

Now that CI_1 is the currently executing control instance, data instances can now be realized in the synthesis engine. The fourth row of Figure 4 shows the first data instance generated by the user (DI_1) to be synthesized. The comparison between DI_0 and DI_1 results in the medium *LiveAudio* being added which generates an `enableStream` event. This event fires Transition 1 in Table 5, resulting in the generation of the stream enable script. Note that the generation of the stream enable script generates two commands, *enableInitiator* and *sendSchema* (see the rightmost column of the fourth row in Figure 9). The fifth row second column in Figure 9 shows the new data instance model (DI_2) that contains a patient discharge form, see Figure 9. The changes resulting from the comparison between DI_1 and DI_2 is the addition of the form *PatientRec_1*, consisting of two different media. It is important to note that the *LiveAudio* medium is still attached to the connection, resulting in the audio stream continuing. The addition of the form node results in the `sendForm` event being generated. This event fires Transition 8 in Table 5 resulting in the generation of the send form script. Sending a form results in each part of that form being sent separately, as shown in the rightmost column of the fifth row in Figure 9. Note again that the data schema is sent, as well as the control schema since the form needs to be reconstructed by the UCM at the non-initiator party's CVM. The sixth row of Figure 9 shows a new control instance (CI_2) being received from the user with a new party added to the connection C1. The changes resulting from CI_1 and CI_2 generate an initiate renegotiation event (`initiateReNeg`) which fires Transition 2 in Table 4. The last row of Figure 9 terminates the connection.

Synthesis Engine Implementation

The synthesis engine (SE) currently implemented in the CVM prototype accepts an X-CML instance (CI or DI), performs model analysis, negotiation, and media transfer, and generates executable control scripts. Figure 10 shows the main packages in the current implementation, including: `se::script` – responsible for generating control scripts; `se::conn` – implements the algorithms for the negotiation and media transfer submachines in Figure 8; `se::manager` – coordinates the activities of the SE; `se::handlers` – handles events from the lower layer in the CVM (UCM) and generates new events and exceptions and depends on the `uci::handlers` package; and `se::modelAnalyzer` – performs model analysis (see below). The two classes shown in the figure are (1) `se::manager::SE_Facade` – exposes an API to the layer above in the CVM (UCI), and (2) `ucm::manager::UCMFacade` – exposes the API that accepts the control script in the UCM. The previous implementation of SE uses an ad-hoc approach for identifying the changes between CML models. Wu et al. (2011a) presents a more comprehensive description of an earlier version of the SE implementation.

We are currently in the process of refactoring the current design of the SE to isolate the domain specific functionality. We have started with the model analyzer of the CVM prototype and configured it in such a way that the communication aspects are separated from the functionality to manipulate the models such, as model comparison and change interpretation. Before the CML models are compared they are converted to ECore models thereby allowing us to use the EMF Compare package provided by the EMF compare project (Brun, Goubet, Musset, & Eysholdt, 2011). We use a design in our class diagram that allows change patterns in a specific domain to be interpreted correctly. For example, each row in Table 2 and Table 3 are mapped to classes inherited from the change pattern for the control and data instances, respectively. We are currently using a similar approach to implement the model analyzer in the SE for the MGridVM.

Benefits, Limitations, and Challenges of the Approach

In this chapter we present an approach to defining CML and the semantics for synthesizing CML model instances, based on changes to model instances at runtime. These model instances represent both the control and configuration of the

Figure 10. Class diagram showing the main packages in synthesis engine

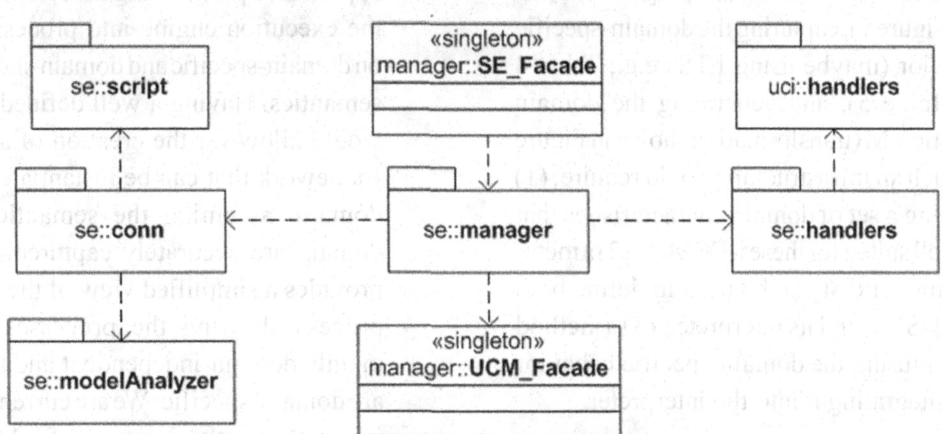

application, and the data required to realize the user's intent. We are currently working on applying this approach in the microgrid energy management domain as described earlier in the chapter. Recall that our approach is targeted to two types of users: (1) novice, having little or no skill in programming and modeling; and (2) expert, someone very familiar with the domain but not having extensive skills in programming or software modeling. There are few works in the models community that use such an approach to define the semantics for interpreted user-defined models.

The approach presented in this chapter has several benefits to the users of these systems and the developers for this class of i-DSMLs. Some of these benefits include:

1. **End-User Application Creation:** The structure of a DSML supports the use of several concrete syntaxes based on a common abstract syntax, which we exploit in our approach. The diagram in Figure 3(a), representing a control instance, shows a model that would be created by the expert user and used by novice to realize the *fill prescription* communication scenario, a specific communication task in the medical domain. The expert user most probably would create a control schema that would omit the specific parties involved in the communication, since they can be instantiated at runtime. The screenshot in Figure 5, on the other hand, shows the interface a novice would use to realize a communication scenario; this may be done by loading a control schema and executing it, or creating a control schema then executing it.
2. **User-Driven Dynamic Adaptation of Applications:** The user's ability to dynamically change the control instance at runtime allows for changes to be integrated into the control flow of the application during execution. Although there are some benefits for basic communication control schemas, similar to the one shown in Figure 3(a), the major benefits are realized for control schemas containing control structures such as *decision*, *forks*, and *loops* (Wu et al., 2011b). Unlike a traditional application where the program containing the control flow of the program is pretty much fixed at runtime, the user now has the ability to dynamically adapt the application by deploying a new version of the application containing control flow structures at runtime.
3. **Generalization of Approach:** The long-term goal of this research project is to generalize the approach on developing i-DSMLs. We expect to create an infrastructure that can

be used to assist with developing an i-DSML (see Figure 1), capturing the domain-specific behavior (maybe using LTSs e.g., Table 4 and Table 5), and generating the domain specific VM (transformation shown in Figure 4). Such an infrastructure would require: (1) defining a set of domain characteristics that are well suited for these i-DSMLs, (2) a meta-metamodel that can be used to define both the i-DSML and its interpreter, (3) a method for capturing the domain-specific behavior and integrating it into the interpreter.

Raising the level of abstraction in a specific domain provides users with the ability to specify the requirements for an application in the concepts and primitives most familiar to the user. However, providing this level of abstraction increases the semantic gap between the model and the implementation used to represent the application. Many of the limitations and challenges for traditional DSMLs are well known e.g., ability to capture all the main concepts in the domain by experts, changes in the domain due to paradigm shifts or legislative/regulatory changes, and DSML evolution, among others (Sprinkle, Gray, & Mernik, 2009; Bryant et al., 2011). The limitations and challenges specific to the approach presented in this chapter are as follows:

1. **i-DSML Evolution:** i-DSMLs have the same limitations as DSMLs but some limitations are exacerbated since each layer of the execution engine depends on a particular view of the domain semantics. Unlike other DSMLs, different views of the domain semantics for i-DSMLs are realized in the various layers of the respective interpreters. A change in the domain can have a cascading effect on the execution engine; however a solution the following challenge may alleviate this problem.
2. **Partitioning Functionality in Execution Engine:** One of the major challenges of our approach is partitioning the functionality of the execution engine into processes based on domain-specific and domain-independent semantics. Having a well defined partition would allow for the creation of a reusable framework that can be instantiated for any domain, assuming the semantics of the domain are accurately captured. Figure 7 provides a simplified view of the synthesis process showing the processes that are mainly domain-independent and those that are domain-specific. We are currently working on the synthesis process for MGridVM and the partition for the energy management domain appears to use a similar approach to that shown in Figure 7.

FUTURE RESEARCH DIRECTIONS

There are several areas of our approach that still need to be investigated and completed. These include (1) the granularity used to identify the initial changes, and (2) the order in which the changes are interpreted and applied to the executing CML model. From our preliminary investigation into the DSML for the microgrid energy management domain (*MGridML*) it appears that we will have to treat MGridML models as typed attributed graphs (Ehrig et al. 2006). This would mean that during the model comparison process we would have to treat some attribute changes as changing the value of an attribute in a node and not the replacement of the entire node. The second area that needs further investigation is the order in which the changes are interpreted and applied to the executing model; our intuition says that we should apply all the delete node changes first then the added nodes changes. However, the overhead encountered for some operations may prove otherwise, for example it may be more efficient to add a new non-initiator party to a connection before removing a non-initiator party, if the party to be removed is the only non-initiator party remaining in the connection.

In this chapter we focused our approach on models for basic configurations in a specific domain e.g., CML models for basic communication. We feel that applying our approach to model with more complex control flow constructs e.g. CML models with workflows (*WF-CML*) (Wu et al. 2011b), will raise some very interesting research questions. WF-CML models are defined in terms of nodes and edges since control structures such as forks, joins and loops need to be defined. In basic CML, we ignore the edges since they are only used to connect the nodes in the graphical representation of CML (G-CML) and do not impact the underlying X-CML representation. However, in WF-CML the X-CML must explicitly include the edges for the control structures. We may also have to model WF-CML models as typed attributed graphs (Ehrig et al. 2006). By explicitly using the edges in the WF-CML models, model comparison becomes more complex. The basic CML model is contained in an *atomic communication process node* in WF-CML model. Some of the other nodes used in a WF-CML model include: *composite communication process node, initial node, fork node, join node, decision node, merge node* and *final node*. One scenario we have been considering is that the currently executing WF-CML model contains a loop and the new model submitted by the user changes the termination node of the loop. We expect that the semantics for the model changes will be based on the currently executing node in the WF-CML model.

We also plan to define a workflow language for MGridML (*WF-MGridML*) using a similar approach to WF-CML. The energy management scenario described in the Motivation Section, where Dana wants to change over from using winter devices to spring devices, could be automated using a WF-MGridML model. Dana would just need to deploy the "Seasons Model" and based on the date or temperature reading the appropriate devices could be automatically turned on or off as needed.

CONCLUSION

In this chapter we presented an approach for developing a class of interpreted domain-specific modeling languages (i-DSMLs) whose instances are realized by an execution engine. Two i-DSMLs were introduced the Communication Modeling Language (CML) and the Microgrid Modeling Language (MGridML), and their respective execution engines, the Communication Virtual Machine (CVM) and the Microgrid Virtual Machine (MGridVM). The focus of the chapter was on the semantics of synthesizing i-DSML model instances based on changes to the instances at runtime. The semantic definition supports the direct execution of user-defined models thereby allowing these models to be causally connected to the user's requirements and the execution environment at all times. As a result of the causality between the models the execution environment can adapt the executing model when the user submits a new model at runtime. To show that the approach presented is feasible we provided a detailed description of how the synthesis process works for CML and CVM. We are currently working on the details for synthesizing MGridML model instances using MGridVM based on the approach presented. Our long term goal is to develop a methodology for developing i-DSMLs and their respective execution engines based on the semantics of the domain.

REFERENCES

Allison, M., Allen, A. A., Yang, Z., & Clarke, P. J. (2011). A software engineering approach to user-driven control of the microgrid. In *Proceedings of the 23rd International Conference on Software Engineering and Knowledge Engineering (SEKE 2011)* (pp. 59-64).

Altmanninger, K., Seidl, M., & Wimmer, M. (2009). A survey on model versioning approaches. *International Journal of Web Information Systems*, *5*(3), 271–304. doi:10.1108/17440080910983556

Brun, C., Goubet, L., Musset, J., & Eysholdt, M. (2011). *EMF compare project*. Retrieved from http://wiki.eclipse.org/EMF_Compare

Bryant, B., Gray, J., Mernik, M., Clarke, P., France, R., & Karsai, G. (2011). Challenges and directions in formalizing the semantics of modeling languages. *Computer Science and Information Systems*, *8*(2), 225–253. doi:10.2298/CSIS110114012B

Chen, K., Sztipanovits, J., & Neema, S. (2005). Toward a semantic anchoring infrastructure for domain-specific modeling languages. In *Proceedings of the 5th ACM International Conference on Embedded Software (EMSOFT '05)* (pp. 35-43). New York, NY: ACM.

Clark, T., Sammut, P., & Willans, J. (2008). *Applied metamodelling: A foundation for language driven development* (2nd ed.). Ceteva.

Clarke, P. J., Hristidis, V., Wang, Y., Prabakar, N., & Deng, Y. (2006). A declarative approach for specifying user-centric communication. In *Proceedings of the International Symposium on Collaborative Technologies and Systems (CTS '06)* (pp. 89-98). Washington, DC: IEEE Computer Society.

den Haan, J. (2012). *Model driven development: Code generation or model interpretation?* Retrieved February 1, 2012, from http://www.theenterprisearchitect.eu/archive/2010/06/28/model-driven-development-code-generation-or-model-interpretation

Deng, Y., Sadjadi, S. M., Clarke, P. J., Hristidis, V., Rangaswami, R., & Wang, Y. (2008). CVM - A communication virtual machine. *Journal of Systems and Software*, *81*(10), 1640–1662. doi:10.1016/j.jss.2008.02.020

Edwards, G., Seo, C., & Medvidovic, N. (2008). Model interpreter frameworks: A foundation for the analysis of domain-specific software architectures. *Journal of Universal Computer Science*, *14*(8), 1182–1206.

Ehrig, H., Ehrig, K., Prange, U., & Taentzer, G. (2006). *Fundamentals of algebraic graph transformation (Monographs in Theoretical Computer Science. an EATCS Series)*. Secaucus, NJ: Springer-Verlag New York, Inc.

Fernando, T. (1993). Comparative transition system semantics. In Börger, E., Jäger, G., Kleine Büning, H., Martini, S., & Richter, M. (Eds.), *Computer Science Logic* (*Vol. 702*, pp. 149–166). Lecture Notes in Computer Science Berlin, Germany: Springer. doi:10.1007/3-540-56992-8_11

Forum, D. S. M. (2010). *Domain-specific modeling*. Retrieved from http://www.dsmforum.org/

France, R., & Rumpe, B. (2007). Model-driven development of complex software: A research roadmap. In Briand, L., & Wolf, A. (Eds.), *Future of software engineering* (pp. 37–54). Washington, DC: IEEE Computer Society. doi:10.1109/FOSE.2007.14

Gargantini, A., Riccobene, E., & Scandurra, P. (2009). A semantic framework for metamodel-based languages. *Journal of Automated Software Engineering*, *16*(3-4), 415–454. doi:10.1007/s10515-009-0053-0

Hermans, F., Pinzger, M., & Deursen, A. (2009). Domain-specific languages in practice: A user study on the success factors. In *Proceedings of the 12th International Conference on Model Driven Engineering Languages and System (MODELS '09)* (pp. 423–437), Berlin, Germany, Springer-Verlag.

Ignite Realtime. (2010). *Smack API 3.1.0*. Retrieved from http://www.igniterealtime.org/

Kelly, S., & Tolvanen, J. P. (2008). *Domain-specific modeling: Enablingfull code generation*. Wiley-IEEE Computer Society Press.

Lin, Y., Gray, J., & Jouault, F. (2007). DSMDiff: A differentiation tool for domain-specific models. *European Journal of Information Systems. Special Issue on Model-Driven Systems Development*, *16*(4), 349–361.

Mernik, M., Heering, J., & Sloane, A. M. (2005). When and how to develop domain-specific languages. *ACM Computing Surveys*, *37*(4), 316–344. doi:10.1145/1118890.1118892

Microsoft Research Team. (2012). *AsmL: Abstract state machine language*. Retrieved from http://research.microsoft.com/en-us/projects/asml/

Nain, G., Daubert, E., Barais, O., & Jézéquel, J.-M. (2008). Using MDE to build a schizophrenic middleware for home/building automation. *Towards a Service-Based Internet. Lecture Notes in Computer Science*, *5377*, 49–61. doi:10.1007/978-3-540-89897-9_5

Object Management Group (OMG). (2010). *Unified modeling language: Superstructure*, version 2. Retrieved from http://www.omg.org/spec/UML/2.3

Plotkin, G. D. (1981). *A structural approach to operational semantics. DAIMI FN-19*. Computer Science Department, Aarhus University.

Skeen, D. (1981). Nonblocking commit protocols. In *Proceedings of the ACM SIGMOD International Conference on Management of Data (SIGMOD '81)* (pp. 133-142). New York, NY: ACM.

Skype Limited. (2007). *Skype developer zone*. Retrieved from https://developer.skype.com/

Sprinkle, J., Gray, J., & Mernik, M. (2009). *Fundamental limitations in domain-specific language evolution*. (Report No. TR-090831). Electrical and Computer Engineering, University of Arizona.

Sprinkle, J., Mernik, M., Tolvanen, J.-P., & Spinellis, D. (2009). Guest editors' introduction: What kinds of nails need a domain-specific hammer? *IEEE Software*, *26*(4), 15–18. doi:10.1109/MS.2009.92

Stahl, T., Volter, M., Bettin, J., Haase, A., Helsen, S., & Czarnecki, K. (2003). *Model-driven software development: Technology, engineering, management*. John Wiley & Sons.

Stanek, J., Kothari, S., & Kang, G. (2008). Method of comparing graph differencing algorithms for software differencing. In *Proceedings of the Electro/Information Technology (EIT 2008)* (pp.482-487).

Wu, Y., Allen, A. A., Hernandez, F., France, R., & Clarke, P. J. (2011a). A domain-specific modeling approach to realizing user-centric communication. *Journal of Software Practice and Experience*, *42*(3), 357–390. doi:10.1002/spe.1081

Wu, Y., Hernandez, F., France, R., & Clarke, P. J. (2011b). A DSML for coordinating user-centric communication services. In *Proceedings of the 35th IEEE International Computer Software and Applications Conference (COMPSAC 11)* (pp. 93-102). IEEE Computer Society.

ZigBee Alliance. (2012). *ZigBee smart energy overview*. Retrieved from http://www.zigbee.org/Standards/ZigBeeSmartEnergy /Overview.aspx

ADDITIONAL READING

Balasubramanian, K., Gokhale, A., Karsai, G., Sztipanovits, J., & Neema, S. (2006). Developing applications using model-driven design environments. *Computer*, *39*(2), 33–40. doi:10.1109/MC.2006.54

Burke, R. P., & White, J. A. (2004). Internet rounds: A congenital heart surgeon's web log. *Seminars in Thoracic and Cardiovascular Surgery*, *16*(3), 283–292. doi:10.1053/j.semtcvs.2004.08.012

Consel, C., & Réveillère, L. (2004). *A DSL paradigm for domains of services: A study of communication services.* International Seminar on Domain-Specific Program Generation, Dagstuhl.

Deursen van, A., & Klint, P. (2002). Domain-specific language design requires feature descriptions. *Journal of Computing and Information Technology*, *10*(1), 12–14.

Fowler, M. (2010). *Domain-specific languages*. Addison-Wesley Professional.

Harel, D., & Rumpe, B. (2004). Meaningful modeling: What's the semantics of "semantics"? *Computer*, *37*(10), 64–72. doi:10.1109/MC.2004.172

Heckel, R., & Voigt, H. (2004). Model-based development of executable business processes for web services. *Lecture Notes in Computer Science*, *3098*, 559–584. doi:10.1007/978-3-540-27755-2_16

Jackson, E. K., & Sztipanovits, J. (2009). Formalizing the structural semantics of domain-specific modeling languages. *Software & Systems Modeling*, *8*(4), 451–478. doi:10.1007/s10270-008-0105-0

Karsai, G., Agrawal, A., Shi, F., & Sprinkle, J. (2003). On the use of graph transformation in the formal specification of model interpreters. *Journal of Universal Computer Science*, *9*(11), 1296–1321.

Kirshin, A., Dotan, D., & Hartman, A. (2006). A UML simulator based on a generic model execution engine. In T. Kühne (Ed.). In *Proceedings of the 2006 International Conference on Models in Software Engineering* (MoDELS'06) (pp. 324-326). Berlin, Germany: Springer-Verlag.

Kleppe, A. (2008). *Software language engineering: Creating domain-specific languages using metamodels*. Addison-Wesley Professional.

Rangaswami, R., Sadjadi, S. M., Prabakar, N., & Deng, Y. (2007). Automatic generation of user-centric multimedia communication services. In *Proceedings of the IEEE International Performance Computing and Communications Conference (IPCCC)* (pp. 324-331). IEEE Computer Society.

Schmidt, D. C. (2006). Guest editor's introduction: Model-driven engineering. *Computer*, *39*(2), 25–31. doi:10.1109/MC.2006.58

Wu, Y., Hernandez, F., Ortega, F., Clarke, P. J., & France, R. (2010). Measuring the effort for creating and using domain-specific models. In *Proceedings of the 10th Workshop on Domain-Specific Modeling (DSM'10) in conjunction with SPLASH 2010*, article 14. New York, NY: ACM.

Yelmo, J. C., del lamo, J. M., Trapero, R., & Martn, Y.-S. (2011). A user-centric approach to service creation and delivery over next generation networks. *Computer Communications*, *34*(2), 209–222. doi:10.1016/j.comcom.2010.04.002

Zhang, C., Sadjadi, S., Sun, W., Rangaswami, R., & Deng, Y. (2010). A user-centric network communication broker for multimedia collaborative computing. *Multimedia Tools and Applications*, *50*(2), 335–357. doi:10.1007/s11042-009-0385-6

KEY TERMS AND DEFINITIONS

Communication Modeling Language (CML): A DSML for specifying user-defined communication services.

Communication Virtual Machine (CVM): A model execution engine for CML that provides users with the ability to specify and realize communication services.

Control Schema: A model used to specify the configuration of the user defined application, which consists of zero or more control structures and the data types from the domain.

Data Schema: A model that specifies one or more data instances for the types defined in the control schema.

Domain-Specific Modeling Language (DSML): A graphical-based modeling language that provides users with the ability to specify applications in a given domain.

Interpreted DSML (i-DSML): A DSML whose model instances are directly executed by a model execution engine without first converting these instances into representations in another language.

Synthesis: Generation of domain-specific scripts based on the changes to user-defined models at runtime.

ENDNOTES

1 http://www.codegeneration.net/cg2010/

Chapter 10
A Formal Semantics of Kermeta

Moussa Amrani
University of Luxembourg, Luxembourg

ABSTRACT

This chapter contributes to the formal specification of Kermeta, a popular metamodelling framework useful for the design of DSL structure and semantics. The formal specification is tool-/tool syntax independent; it only uses classical mathematical instruments taught in usual computer science courses. This specification serves as a reference specification from which specialised implementation can be derived for execution, simulation, or formal analysis of DSLs. By providing such a specification, the chapter ensures that each and every DSL written in Kermeta, receives de facto a formal counterpart, making its definition fully formal. This radically contrasts with other approaches that require a new ad hoc semantics defined for every new DSL. The chapter briefly reports on two implementations conducted to demonstrate the feasibility of the approach.

INTRODUCTION

Model-Driven Engineering (MDE) is a novel approach to Software Development. This approach elects models as first-class artifacts during all phases of development while having as main concern to improve and maximise the productivity in short and long term. Domain-Specific Modeling Languages (DSMLs) use the MDE methodology, but focus on a particular expertise domain. DSMLs take the opposite philosophy of what is intended with General-Purpose Languages: by focusing on a particular domain, they discard by nature the possibility of reuse in areas that go beyond their domain of interest. However, thanks to this restriction, DSMLs allow domain experts to achieve a better degree of automation when getting the final result without knowing low level details.

However, from a theoretical point of view, DSMLs are still languages: it should be possible

DOI: 10.4018/978-1-4666-2092-6.ch010

to study their essence with the classical tools available from research and practice on formal languages. We propose to study the theoretical implications of the definition of DSMLs, by mathematically characterising what a DSML is, and providing a formal description of its components. This task is helpful in several concerns: it provides a common ground for comparing, evaluating and engineering DSMLs; and offers a practical and manipulable knowledge about DSMLs that serves the construction of associated tools accompanying DSMLs. The study focuses on Kermeta DSMLs (Drey, Faucher, Fleurey, Mahé & Vojtisek, 2009; Muller, Fleurey & Jézéquel, 2005; http://www.kermeta.org) for precise reasons:

1. It covers all aspects of DSML definition;
2. It is based on two Object Management Group's (OMG) standard languages, MOF (Object Management Group, 2006) and OCL (Object Management Group, 2010), and deals with transformation through an object-oriented action language which makes it easy to use;
3. It is involved in a joint effort to bring MDE technology into the industrial field, making it effectively used for industrial cases (http://www.topcased.com); and
4. It has gained maturity, stability, and is backed up by an important user community.

The core contribution of this chapter is the full formal specification of the semantics of a consequent subset of the Kermeta language. The proposed formalisation does not rely on any tool-oriented syntax or formalism, relieving the reader from learning other formalisms in order to understand the specification, but rather uses classical computer science tools: *set theory* captures the meaning of the structures involved in metamodels; and *rewriting rules* expressing a structural operational semantics capture the dynamics of the Action Language. The approach and the notions discussed in this chapter go beyond Kermeta: they provide to the readers, either researchers and practitioners, or lecturers and students, a strong background in semantics specification techniques that can be reused for building semantics specifications of other non-trivial languages.

The chapter is organised as follows. First, a proper motivation for addressing the formalisation of Kermeta is given, and the contribution is positioned within the plethora of already existing works on formal specification of DSLs and metamodeling frameworks. Then, background on Kermeta and basic mathematical notations is provided, together with a small running example used to illustrate the semantics constructions. The formal specification is then presented in two parts: Kermeta's Structural and Action Languages. Finally, the practical applications of semantics specification are discussed before ending with concluding remarks.

MOTIVATION

Domain-Specific Modeling (DSM) realises the MDE approach by systematically using Domain-Specific Languages (DSLs) for capturing the knowledge of an expertise domain: they provide higher levels of abstractions instead of constraining to think at implementation level; and they are specific in the sense that they directly reflect notions of an expertise domain instead of using general-purpose languages or models (like UML). Being more focused, they naturally discard reuse in completely different domains, but gain accurate analysis and automation capabilities.

However, from a theoretical point of view, a DSL is still a language and should possess the two core components of every language (Harel & Rumpe, 2004): several syntaxes, among which one is abstract and describes the concepts and their links, as well as the consistency rules governing them, that emanate from the expertise domain, and others that are concrete, serving as interfaces with the experts; and a semantics, explaining the intended meaning of the DSL in terms of a semantic domain.

Historically however, DSMLs' behavioural aspects were not addressed at the beginning, but received proper attention only lately. In particular, formalising the behaviour always pursues further goals: providing a complete specification that can serve as a reference for the language; disambiguating the DSL behaviour for harmonising the tools working with them; or enabling formal analysis and verification. This is especially true in embedded and critical applications, where ambiguities result in failures with enormous human, ecological or financial costs. In this contribution, we aim at the same goals, but within the context of Kermeta. In order to supply for the lack of formal verification techniques, a first step to achieve is the formalisation of the Kermeta framework. This chapter contributes with a significant advance: it addresses Kermeta's Structural Language and a relevant subset of its Action Language. To be more precise, this formalisation aims at three goals:

- First, it provides a formal description of Kermeta's semantics that can serve as a reference semantics independent of its current implementations (historically in Java, in the near future in Scala), so that users can "play" and reason with it independently of the execution platform, and propose more advanced analysis tools without being forced to deal with the entire platform.
- Second, it will offer for free a lightweight executable framework to any implementation of this work if the target platform beneficiates from execution features.
- Third, by choosing an adequate implementation platform, it is possible to directly take advantage of existing analysis tools, helping covering the various necessary formal analysis. By disposing of a common reference formal description, it is easier to precisely identify the key difficulties and to select a core subset to handle, when wanting to address a precise formal analysis technique. For example, performing shape or escape analysis will focus on operation calls sites whereas seeking for model-checking capabilities requires to represent as precisely as possible the data structures manipulated by Kermeta's transformations.

Several interesting properties can then be verified using adequate techniques, but all have as a prerequisite the existence of a formal specification of the involved features: general properties such as termination of the DSL execution, or properties characterising the execution, such as the preservation of structures of interest during the execution (for example, the fact that a link between a provider and a client is never lost), or dynamic properties targeting safety properties (e.g., a client command is always honoured). A deeper discussion on a classification of properties for model transformation in general, and DSML semantics in particular, can be found in Amrani et al. (2012).

Several approaches exist for equipping a DSL with a behavioural semantics: an interesting and recent review has been proposed by Bryant et al. (2011); the differences between these aspects are nevertheless not always clearly delimited. The *translational semantics* is by far the most popular approach. It consists in translating the DSL metamodel and behaviour in terms of another metamodel with formal foundations. This approach presents the advantage of beneficiating directly from the already existing verification machineries defined for the target frameworks, but has the drawback to impose DSL designers to learn the target language. Furthermore, as every translational approach, the potential difference of abstraction level between the metamodelling language and the target framework makes difficult the expression of analysis results back into the original concepts. Depending on what is considered formal or not, there exist several semantic targets represented in the literature. Abstract State Machines (ASMs) is an important formalism (Börger & Stärk, 2003) that proposes two different approaches: semantic anchoring (Chen, Sztipanovits, Abdelwahed & Jackson, 2005) and semantic mapping, hooking and meta-hooking (Gargantini, Riccobene & Scandurra, 2009), which is the topic of chapter 8. Petri Nets are another target formalism that deal very well with state-based DSL semantics, which is exemplified by deLara and Vangheluwe (2010). Rewriting is another popular technique. Graph-Based Transformations and Rewriting Logics share common verification capabilities like reachability analysis and model-checking. Among others, Riveira and Vallecillo (2007), later extended with real-time behaviours by Riveira (2010), formalise DSL behaviour using Maude (Clavel et al., 2007); whereas Arendt, Biermann, Jurack, Krause and Taentzer (2010) with Henshin on the one hand and de Lara and Vangheluwe (2002) with Atom[3] on the other hand, are popular tools based on graph transformations enabling the definition of DSL semantics in a visual manner.

Another approach is based on *operational semantics* that consists in enriching the metamodels by executable statements inside operations bodies. Clearly, Kermeta belongs to this approach. We refer the reader to the work of Combemale, Crégut, Garoche and Thirioux (2009) that provides a comprehensive review of the different trends existing within this approach and our *Related Work* discussion within the *Action Language* Section (Figure 1).

Our approach radically contrast with the previous ones in several dimensions. Because Kermeta embeds directly an Action Language suitable for expressing transformations, it can be directly used for expressing DSML behaviour. This requires to formalise the Action Language itself, which is more complicated, but presents an interesting advantage: it induces a formal semantics for any DSL specified within Kermeta, instead of having to build *ad hoc* specifications for each new DSL. Of course, it means that only DSLs whose behaviour fits into Kermeta's model of computation can be expressed. Finally, the semantics we propose is agnostic of any tool, being defined with mathematical frameworks: it is then possible

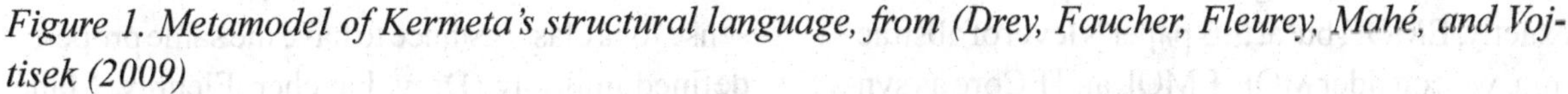

Figure 1. Metamodel of Kermeta's structural language, from (Drey, Faucher, Fleurey, Mahé, and Vojtisek (2009)

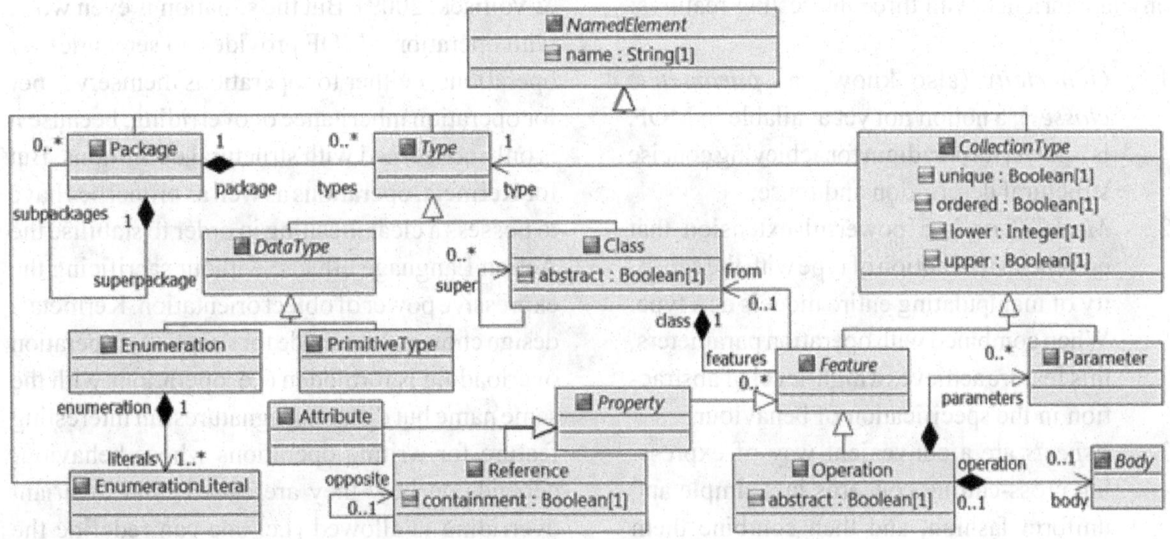

to derive from this specification semantics implementations that take advantage of any tool specificities. The last Section, namely *Perspectives And Future Research Directions*, reports our own experience about two possible implementations.

BACKGROUND

This Section provides basic knowledge about Kermeta for explaining the design choices of the semantics, presents a small running example used for illustrating the mathematical constructions, and ends by setting basic notations used throughout the document.

Kermeta

Kermeta is a well-known metamodelling framework that emerged around 2006. It covers all steps required for building DSLs: syntax and associated constraints definition, as well as behaviour. One of the first requirements in Kermeta design was to respect standards: Kermeta's Structural Language is a conservative extension of the OMG standard MOF (Object Management Group, 2006) (more exactly, EMOF, but at this paper's level of abstraction, we consider MOF, EMOF and ECore as synonyms) enriched with three interesting features:

1. *Genericity* (also known as *parametric classes*), a notion not yet available in MOF, is a powerful paradigm for achieving concise structural description and reuse;
2. *Model Type* is a powerful extension that enriches MOF notion of type with the capacity of manipulating entire models as a type. When combined with operation parameters, this feature achieves a high-level of abstraction in the specification of behaviour.
3. *Aspects* are a convenient way of expressing cross-cutting concerns in a simple and uniform fashion, and then combine them properly. This feature introduces modularity in the metamodelisation process.

These features are already known from the design of object-oriented languages (apart maybe for model types) but their formal grounds are still open research questions (e.g., Castagna and Xu (2011) discuss integration of genericity with imperative constructions). For this reason, they are left for future work.

Kermeta Action Language supports several features: model navigation, instance creation, basic iterative constructs (conditionals, assignments and loops), operation calls, exception handling, and the possibility of interfacing with native Java methods for high performance algorithmic computations or for communications with external engines like databases or internet servers.

Multiple inheritance raises well-known issues when combined with object-orientation: a feature appearing in several inheritance paths causes conflicts (Meyer, 1997). Sometimes seen as not desirable, multiple inheritance is a reality for very big metamodels that rely on library or reuse already existing and immutable metamodels. The situation has to be discarded for properties, since from a metamodeling point of view, it does not make sense for a class instance to have the same property defined multiply (Drey, Faucher, Fleurey, Mahé & Vojtisek, 2009). But the situation is even worst with operations: MOF provides no semantics for operations, neither for operations themselves nor for operation inheritance or overriding, because it is only concerned with structural definitions. But for Kermeta, operations as well as properties have to possess a clear meaning in order to stabilise the Action Language effects, without sacrificing the expressive power of object orientation. Kermeta's design choices were made for simplicity: operation overloading is forbidden (i.e. operations with the same name but different signatures, an interesting feature for writing operations whose behaviour depends on how they are called), but invariant overriding is allowed (i.e. one can redefine the behaviour of a superclass operation, but without specialising parameter or return types). The classical techniques for handling the object dynamic dispatch will be adapted for this case.

Resolving conflicts due to multiple inheritance has been widely studied in the literature (Meyers, 1997; Abadi & Cardelli, 1996). Kermeta chooses to "include a minimal selection mechanism that allows the user to explicitly select the inherited method to override" (Drey et al., 2009, §2.9.5.4) through the form of a *disambiguation clause* introduced by the keyword from. It allows for a multiply defined operation to select one of its implementation among those inherited from superclasses. But it is equally needed for properties in order for the Action Language to be fully statically type-checkable. For this purpose, we introduced the same feature for properties, leading to the introduction of an extra class *Feature* in the Kermeta metamodel presented in Figure 1.

Kermeta goes beyond a simple language: it is a complete metamodelling platform, with advanced features for the management and the manipulation of metamodels. Moreover, it is involved in several industrial projects, making it mature and robust enough to play a central role in the future of MDE. Contributing to formally specifying Kermeta's semantics will play a central role when the need of formal verification will appear.

Running Example: The FSM Example

Figure 2 depicts a simple example modelling a Finite State Machine (FSM). FSM models are required to possess exactly one initial state and one final state. Unfortunately, these conditions cannot be described through a metamodel, but requires a constraint language like OCL (Object Management Group, 2010), which is beyond the scope of this chapter.

The FSM metamodel includes one package named FSM, which is not represented with the usual MOF notation (because it encloses the metamodel classes). It contains four classes: Label, FSM, State and Transition; and one enumeration Kind. All classes inherit from Label: it represents the FSM and state name, and the transition label. The FSM class has an attribute alphabet as a (non-empty) set of Strings, representing the FSM's possible actions. A FSM contains a (non-empty) sequence of States (through the reference states) and a sequence of Transitions (through the reference transitions) where each element is unique: both inherit a label that represents the name of the State and the action of the Transition. Furthermore, a State has a kind attribute that determines its nature: either a START or a STOP (i.e. final) state, or a NORMAL state; whereas a Transition is attached to a source

Figure 2. The FSM example: Metamodel (top) and model (bottom)

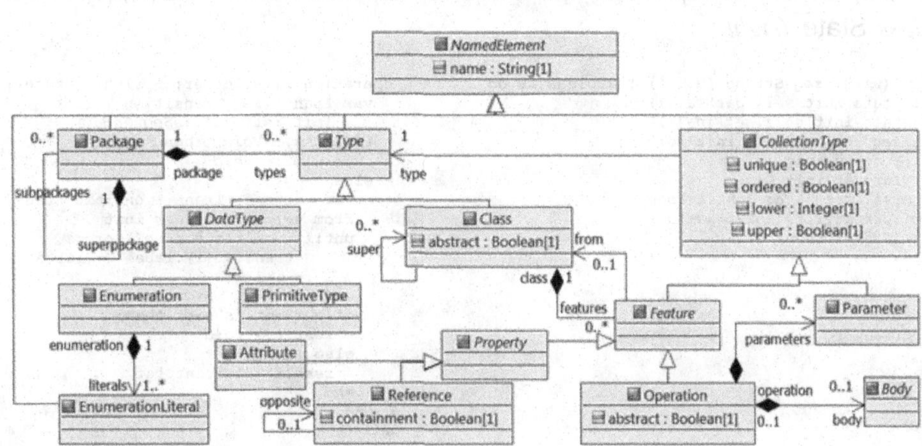

and a target State (corresponding to the src and tgt references, respectively). Notice that in the MOF visual representation, the fact that a property is unique or ordered is not directly visible (one has to check the property panel in Eclipse, for example) whereas in the Kermeta editor, it is possible to associate keywords for attributes (cf. the alphabet attribute in FSM). Figure 2 depicts a conformant FSM with three states and three transitions on the given alphabet (using the classical concrete notation).

The classes FSM and State declare operations whose body can be defined using the Kermeta's Action Language. In particular, it is possible to accept a word, given as a sequence of Strings, that can be recognized by the FSM: if, starting from the START state and consuming each letter of the word by firing the corresponding transition, one finishes in a FINAL state, the word is said to be accepted. The accept operation makes use of the fire operation in the State class: fire takes as parameter a letter and returns the state reachable from the current one through a transition that carries the same action as the letter. Figure 3 gives the Kermeta code for these operations.

Mathematical Background

The sign $\stackrel{\triangle}{=}$ denotes a set definition. The Boolean set is noted $\mathbb{B} \stackrel{\triangle}{=} \{\top, \bot\}$ with truth values true and false, respectively. The Natural, Integer, Real and String sets are noted $\mathbb{N}$, $\mathbb{Z}$, $\mathbb{R}$, $\mathbb{S}$ respectively; and we introduce $\mathbb{N}^\star \stackrel{\triangle}{=} \mathbb{N} \setminus \{0\}$. If S is a set, we note $S_\bot \stackrel{\triangle}{=} S \cup \{\bot\}$ with $S \cap \bot = \varnothing$.

Our mathematical framework extensively uses functions and collections of values. *Total*, respectively *partial*, functions are noted $f : S \rightarrow S'$ and $f : S \nrightarrow S'$; the domain is noted $Dom(f)$. Partial functions are right-associative: $g : S \nrightarrow S' \nrightarrow S''$ means $g : S \nrightarrow (S' \nrightarrow S'')$ and we abbreviate $(g(s))(s')$ into $g(s)(s')$. Substituting f by $(s_1, s_2) \in S \times S'$, noted $f[s_1 \mapsto s_2]$, results in a function f' where forall $s \neq s_2, f'(s) = f(s)$ and $f'(s_1) = s_2$. If $h : S \rightarrow S' \times S''$, we sometimes write $h(s) = (\_, s'')$ or $h(s) = (s', \_)$ when the first or second element is not relevant in context, and use the same notation for substitution.

We only introduce the necessary notations for abstract datatypes, since they are classic in computer science, and widely studied through, e.g., algebraic specification (Ehrig & Mahr, 1985) or

Figure 3. FSM operations example: The operation accept *from class* FSM *(left) and the operation* fire *from class* State *(right)*

```
operation accept(word: seq String [0..*]) : Boolean is do
  var current: State init self.getStart()
  var final : State init self.getFinal()
  var toEval : seq String[0..*] init word
  var isNull : Boolean init false
  from var i : Integer init 0
  until i == toEval.size() or isNull loop
    current := current.fire(toEval.at(i))
    if(current.isVoid) then
      isNull := true
    end
      i := i+1
  end
  result := (current == final)
end
```

```
operation fire(letter: String): State [0..1] is do
  var trans: seq Transition [0..*]
      init self.out.asSequence()
  if(trans.isVoid) then
    result := void
  else
    var current: Transition init trans.at(0)
    from var i : Integer init 0
    until i == trans.size() or
         trans.at(i).label == letter loop
      i := i+1
    end
    if(current.isVoid) then
      result:= void
    else
      result:= current.tgt
    end
  end
end
```

set-theory (Spivey, 1992). Consider values $t_1, \ldots, t_n \in T$ of an arbitrary set T. Collections possess two orthogonal dimensions: uniqueness, i.e. whether a collection admits the repetition of elements (in our case, all t_i are different) or not; and *ordering*, i.e. whether the order of these elements matter or not. In MDE, four kinds of collections are used:

- *Bags* (also known as *multisets*) are collections of arbitrary values, possibly repeated, and noted $[t_1, \ldots, t_n] \in [T]$ (and $[\,]$ stands for the empty bag)
- *Sets* are of course collections of values without repeated elements, and traditionally noted $\{t_1, \ldots, t_n\} \in \wp(T)$ (and $\varnothing$ stands for the empty set)
- *Sequences* are collections where order matters. We distinguish between sequences admitting repetitions (the usual meaning of "sequence" in Computer Science), noted $\langle t_1, \ldots, t_n \rangle \in \langle T \rangle$ (or $\langle\rangle$ if it is empty) from sequences that do not (usually called *ordered sets*[a] in MDE), noted $\langle\langle t_1, \ldots, t_n \rangle\rangle \in \langle\langle T \rangle\rangle$ (and $\langle\rangle$ and $\langle\langle\rangle\rangle$ stand respectively for the empty sequence and the empty ordered sequence) (Figure 4).

If C is one of these collections of values of type T, we note $\sharp(C)$ the number of elements in C; and $t \oplus C$ and $t \ominus C$ respectively adding/removing an element t from C: adding/removing in a bag modifies the number of repetitions of t, and adds an element in top (or beginning) of a sequence. If C is a non-empty sequence, it can be decomposed in $t :: C'$ where t is the *top* (or *head*) element and C' the *rest* of (or *tail*) the sequence. If operations to remove repeated elements in a collection, or choose an arbitrary order between unordered elements, are available on collections, it is possible to convert any collection to any other one.

STRUCTURAL LANGUAGE

Kermeta's Structural Language (SL) is used by DSL designers to specify their DSL metamodels and models, as we did in Figure 2. In Kermeta, metamodels can be created graphically by using the dedicated Kermeta editor (the one we used for the FSM example), or by using another visual tool and then export into Kermeta: among others, UML and EMF/ECore tools. Metamodels, as well as models, can also be created textually: we provide the full code for the FSM example in Appendix A, which illustrates this point. This Section fully formalises Kermeta's SL but since it is aligned on

Figure 4. Overview of the construction of the SL semantics

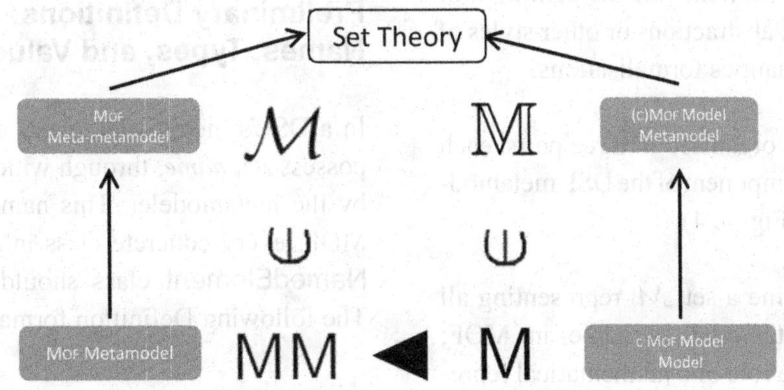

the OMG EMOF standard (Object Management Group, 2006) [b], this formalisation encompasses also the OMG MOF standard. Therefore, this Section can be seen as one of the standard formalisations of the core notions of metamodelling: the pair metamodels / models and the underlying conformance relationship.

Structural Semantics Overview

The semantics for Kermeta's SL is designed with two important goals in mind that are necessary to understand:

- First, it is designed with *reuse* in mind: as already stated, since Kermeta's SL is fully aligned with the OMG MOF standard, any MOF-compliant tool can easily exchange DSL metamodels / models with Kermeta. For that purpose, we did not formalise the extra features available in Kermeta (namely, genericity model typing and aspects) not already present in MOF at the time being. This makes our formalisation sustainable beyond Kermeta, by establishing a reference mathematical formalisation independent of any tool, which helps comparing actual implementations.
- Second, this formalisation is entirely expressed in Set Theory which provides an interesting basis for further developments. One of them is naturally the definition of Kermeta's AL, but it can be directly used for other applications like the definition of composition, abstractions or other styles of dynamic semantics formalisations.

This Section is organised in three parts, each formalising one component of the DSL metamodeling process (cf. Figure 4):

- First, we define a set $\mathcal{M}$ representing all possible metamodels writable in MOF; $\mathcal{M}$ plays the role of a mathematical representation for the MOF meta-metamodel itself. To remain general, we base our construction on MOF's graphical representation, which is widely understood because it uses an UML-based visual syntax.
- Second, we define a set $\mathbb{M}$ representing all possible models that can be written accordingly to CMOF, or using Kermeta's textual syntax.
- Third, we define a binary predicate that relates a model $\mathsf{M} \in \mathbb{M}$ and a metamodel $\mathsf{MM} \in \mathcal{M}$: it expresses that M conforms to MM, and is noted $\mathsf{M} \blacktriangleright \mathsf{MM}$. When defining a DSL metamodel, one actually induces a (generally infinite) set of models $\mathsf{M}_1, \ldots, \mathsf{M}_n, \ldots \in \mathbb{M}$, and the conformance ensures that a particular model M is actually one of those: formally speaking, there exists i such that $\mathsf{M} = \mathsf{M}_i$.

Before jumping to these formal definitions, we need to capture the meaning of central artefacts at the core of these sets: *names* identify artefacts both in metamodels and models, and should be distinguished from the notion of identifiers, which is an implementation-specific concept (that is not perceived by the DSL metamodeler); *types* are used in metamodels for declaring named artefacts; and values are used in models for representing actual DSL instances. Each notion is illustrated over the FSM running example.

Preliminary Definitions: Names, Types, and Values

In a DSL's metamodel, every concrete element possesses a *name*, through which it is perceived by the metamodeler. This name is required by MOF: every concrete class inheriting from the NamedElement class should have a name[c]. The following Definition formally defines these

Box 1.

$$\mathsf{Element} \stackrel{\Delta}{=} \{\mathsf{Pkg}, \mathsf{Class}, \mathsf{Enum}, \mathsf{Attr}, \mathsf{Ref}, \mathsf{Op}, \mathsf{Param}\}$$
$$\mathsf{Name} \stackrel{\Delta}{=} (\mathsf{Name}_e)_{e \in \mathsf{Element}}$$

concrete elements and associated names as presented in Box 1.

Sorted names adequately reflect ontologically different artefacts carrying the same name. Moreover, sorts establish a direct correspondence between the mathematical representation of names and their "position" in the visual notation. We introduce, accordingly to the MOF vocabulary, the notions of property (name), i.e. either attribute or reference (name), and *feature (name),* i.e. either property or operation (names).

$$\mathsf{PropN} \stackrel{\Delta}{=} \mathsf{AttrN} \cup \mathsf{RefN}$$
$$\mathsf{FeatN} \stackrel{\Delta}{=} \mathsf{PropN} \cup \mathsf{OpN}$$

Example 1: In Figure 2, the name of the main package would be represented as $\mathsf{FSM} \in \mathsf{PkgN}$. Class names correspond to the following list: $\mathsf{Label}, \mathsf{FSM}, \mathsf{State}, \mathsf{Transition} \in \mathsf{ClassN}$. Notice how the sorts Pkg and Class help distinguishing between the package and the class with the same name. ■

Each MOF artefact is declared along with a *syntactic type*. For example, each time a class or a class property is defined, it has a type that determines its possible values within a model. According to the MOF type hierarchy (located under the abstract Type class), a type (sometimes called *basic* type) is either a *primitive type*, a *class name* or an *enumeration*, both declared in the scope of a given package. Each basic type is then combined with two other information: a *collection kind* Collection, which leads to a collection type CType; and a *multiplicity,* which leads to a multiple type MType^d, which constitutes our notion of syntactic type as presented in Box 2.

Following the previous shortcut notations, we introduce shortcuts for class and enumerations declared within the scope of a package. The set DataType, borrowed from MOF, is constituted by the set of primitive types and enumerations. Moreover, user-defined types, i.e. enumerations or classes, are always considered within their enclosing package, constituting the sets PClassN and PEnumN.

$$\mathsf{DataType} \stackrel{\Delta}{=} \mathsf{PEnumN} \cup \mathsf{PrimType}$$
$$\mathsf{PClassN} \stackrel{\Delta}{=} \mathsf{PkgN} \times \mathsf{ClassN}$$
$$\mathsf{PEnumN} \stackrel{\Delta}{=} \mathsf{PkgN} \times \mathsf{EnumN}$$

An ordering relation, built inductively, is introduced for comparing syntactic types: primitive types and collections are ordered with $\preceq_{\mathsf{Prim}}$ and $\preceq_{\mathsf{Coll}}$ respectively, as depicted in the previous Hasse Diagram; enumerations are not ordered; and ordering over classes, which corresponds to the notion of subclasses, is addressed later.

Example 2: The FSM example contains only one enumeration named Kind, which is represented as $(FSM, Kind) \in PEnumN$; but contains several classes represented as: $(FSM, Label), (FSM, FSM), \ldots, \in PClassN$.
Look now at the FSM class, more particularly at the alphabet attribute: it has a collection type $(\mathsf{Set}, \mathsf{String}) \in \mathsf{CType}$ and a multiple type

Box 2.

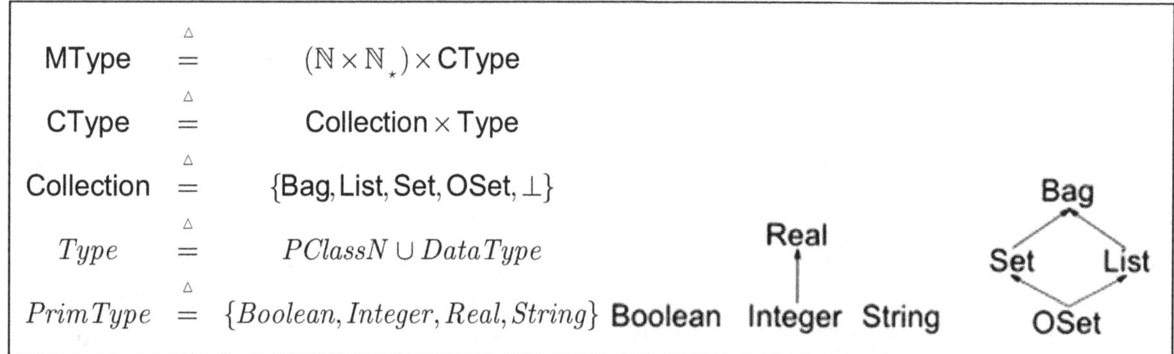

$$\mathsf{MType} \stackrel{\triangle}{=} (\mathbb{N} \times \mathbb{N}_{\star}) \times \mathsf{CType}$$

$$\mathsf{CType} \stackrel{\triangle}{=} \mathsf{Collection} \times \mathsf{Type}$$

$$\mathsf{Collection} \stackrel{\triangle}{=} \{\mathsf{Bag}, \mathsf{List}, \mathsf{Set}, \mathsf{OSet}, \perp\}$$

$$Type \stackrel{\triangle}{=} PClassN \cup DataType$$

$$PrimType \stackrel{\triangle}{=} \{Boolean, Integer, Real, String\}$$

$((1,\star),(\mathsf{Set},\mathsf{String})) \in \mathsf{MType}$. Similarly, the transitions reference as a multiple type $((0,\star),(\mathsf{Set},\mathsf{Transition})) \in \mathsf{MType}$. In the sequel, we always flatten multiple types: e.g. for transitions, we note
$(0,\star,\mathsf{Set},\mathsf{Transition}) \in \mathsf{MType}$. ■

After having defined types, corresponding sets of value naturally need to be specified. These values will allow modelers to define models by precisely relating values in models with types in metamodels. In MOF, it corresponds to the underspecified definitions found in Complete MOF (Object Management Group, 2006, §15.2). The set of values $\mathbb{V}$ is built by union of the primitive values (booleans, integers, reals and strings), the set of all possible enumeration literals $\mathbb{E}$ and the set of objects $\mathbb{O}$ that plays the role of values for the class type. Then, they are combined with all possible collections (bags, sets and sequences) as presented in Box 3.

Example 3: In Figure 2, the model shows values that correspond to the declarations of the corresponding metamodel. Some values are explicit: for example, the attribute alphabet has for value a set constituted of three strings "a", "b", "c" (simply denoted by their letter); three objects correspond to the class type
$(\mathsf{FSM},\mathsf{State}) \in \mathsf{PClassN}$ are simply denoted by their corresponding labels "1", "2", "3". Some values are implicit if they are embedded within a visual syntax: for example, the arrow in state "1" denotes that the attribute kind in class State is actually set to $\mathsf{START} \in \mathbb{E}$. ■

Metamodels

When defining a DSL metamodel, a metamodeller actually defines its abstract syntax: from the expertise domain perspective, the metamodel represents in an abstract fashion "the concepts of the domain, the relationships between them, and the structuring rules that constrain the model elements and their combinations in order to respect the domain rules" (Rivera and Vallecillo, 2007). Take for instance the metamodel presented in Figure 2: it adequately represents the State and Transition concepts necessary to manipulate FSMs, and the fact that these concepts are related: a transition always stands between an source (src) and a target (tgt) state, and all transitions attached to a particular source (resp. target) state are out going (resp. in going) transitions. Of course, a metamodel is itself written in a particular metamodel, called meta-metamodel: in our case, it is MOF used with its usual UML-based visual syntax.

A metamodel consists basically in declarations: MOF elements (through their name) are bind to (syntactic) types and other information, w.r.t. a particular topology defined by its meta-metamodel.

Box 3.

$$\mathbb{V} \stackrel{\triangle}{=} \begin{array}{cccccccccccc} \mathbb{B} & \uplus & \mathbb{Z} & \uplus & \mathbb{R} & \uplus & \mathbb{S} & \uplus & \mathbb{E} & \uplus & \mathbb{O} & \uplus \\ [\mathbb{B}] & \uplus & [\mathbb{Z}] & \uplus & [\mathbb{R}] & \uplus & [\mathbb{S}] & \uplus & [\mathbb{E}] & \uplus & [\mathbb{O}] & \uplus \\ \wp(\mathbb{B}) & \uplus & \wp(\mathbb{Z}) & \uplus & \wp(\mathbb{R}) & \uplus & \wp(\mathbb{S}) & \uplus & \wp(\mathbb{E}) & \uplus & \wp(\mathbb{O}) & \uplus \\ \langle\mathbb{B}\rangle & \uplus & \langle\mathbb{Z}\rangle & \uplus & \langle\mathbb{R}\rangle & \uplus & \langle\mathbb{S}\rangle & \uplus & \langle\mathbb{E}\rangle & \uplus & \langle\mathbb{O}\rangle & \uplus \\ \langle\langle\mathbb{B}\rangle\rangle & \uplus & \langle\langle\mathbb{Z}\rangle\rangle & \uplus & \langle\langle\mathbb{R}\rangle\rangle & \uplus & \langle\langle\mathbb{S}\rangle\rangle & \uplus & \langle\langle\mathbb{E}\rangle\rangle & \uplus & \langle\langle\mathbb{O}\rangle\rangle & \uplus \end{array}$$

The formalisation proceeds as follows: for each MOF concrete concept (namely, the classes corresponding to *packages*, *enumerations*, *classes*, *properties* and *operations*), a partial function captures its meaning by mapping the concept's names with the information required by the meta-metamodel of Figure 2. These partial functions are then gathered together to build the notion of metamodel, which is the purpose of the following definition. For further details, with particular insight on the way we extract this information from the MOF visual syntax, and all the mathematical details for the careful construction of these functions, the reader should refer to (Amrani, 2012).

Definition 1 (Metamodels $\mathcal{M}$): *A metamodel* $\mathsf{MM} \in \mathcal{M}$ *is a tuple* $\mathsf{MM} = (p, c, e, prop, o)$ *where:*

- $p : PkgN \nrightarrow \wp(PkgN) \times \wp(ClassN) \times \wp(EnumN) \in \mathcal{P}$ is a package function $p \in \mathcal{P}$ that maps packages that are part of a metamodel to their subpackages, and nested classes and enumerations. p is correct if no package contains itself;
- $e : PkgN \nrightarrow EnumN \nrightarrow \langle\langle\mathbb{E}\rangle\rangle \in \mathcal{E}$ is an enumeration function $e : \mathcal{E}$ that maps enumerations declared inside a package to an ordered set of enumeration literals;
- $c : PkgN \nrightarrow ClassN \nrightarrow \mathbb{B} \times \wp(ClassN)$ is a class function that represents classes declarations: such a function $c \in C$ maps classes declared inside a package to a boolean indicating if they are abstract, and the set of their superclasses; it is *correct* if no class inherits from itself, and if the inheritance hierarchy is acyclic;
- $prop : PkgN \nrightarrow ClassN \nrightarrow PropN \nrightarrow \mathbb{B} \times ClassN_{\perp} \times MType \times RefN_{\perp}$ is a property function that represents properties declarations: such a function $p \in \mathcal{Prop}$ maps each class property to a Boolean indicating if it is contained, an optional class used for the from clause, the multiplicity type of the property and its optional opposite reference;
- $o : PkgN \nrightarrow ClassN \nrightarrow OpN \nrightarrow \mathbb{B} \times ClassN_{\perp} \times \langle\langle \mathcal{P}\mathsf{aram} \rangle\rangle \times MType_{\perp} \times Body$ is an operation function that represents operations declarations: such a function $o \in \mathcal{O}$ maps each class operation to a boolean indicating if it is abstract, an optional class used for the *from* clause, a multiplicity type representing the return type (where corresponds to *void*), an (ordered) sequence of parameters together with their types, and the definition of the body; and o is correct if every operation defined as abstract does not contain a body. Here, $\mathcal{P}aram$ is defined as a pair containing the parameter name and its multiplicity type: $\mathcal{P}\mathsf{aram} \stackrel{\triangle}{=} \mathsf{ParamN} \times \mathsf{MType}$.

MM is valid if all classes declared inside a package also appear in the domains of *c*, *prop* and *o* under the same package, and every class containing an abstract operation is also declared abstract[e]. ■

We can now define the *subclass relation* $\prec_{\mathsf{Class}} \subseteq \mathsf{PClassN} \times \mathsf{PClassN}$ (also called the *specialisation relation*) over classes defined in MM: $(\mathsf{pkg}, \mathsf{c}) \prec_{\mathsf{Class}} (\mathsf{pkg}, \mathsf{c}')$ if, of course, c and c' are defined within the same package pkg and c directly inherits from c'. The previous definition required that $\prec_{\mathsf{Class}}$ is not reflexive and that its transitive closure $\prec^{+}_{\mathsf{Class}}$ is acyclic. By combining orders over classes and primitive types, we obtain an order $\prec_{\mathsf{Type}} \subset \mathsf{Type} \times \mathsf{Type}$ on Type, which is then combined with the order over collections to obtain an ordering $\prec \subset \mathsf{CType} \times \mathsf{CType}$ on CType.

This long definition is now illustrated on some artefacts from our running example: for space reasons, and because it is easily inferred from the given elements, we only present characteristic elements of the metamodel.

Example 4: Let us call $\mathsf{MM}_{\mathsf{FSM}} \in \mathcal{M}$ the mathematical representation of the metamodel depicted in Figure 2. First, we have to precise the domains of all partial functions:
$\mathrm{Dom}(p) = \mathrm{Dom}(c) = \mathrm{Dom}(prop) = \mathrm{Dom}(o) = \{FSM\}$
because the metamodel only contains one package. Then, we have
$Dom(c(FSM)) = Dom(prop(FSM)) = Dom(o(FSM)) = C_{FSM}$
with $C_{FSM} = \{\mathsf{Label}, \mathsf{FSM}, \mathsf{State}, \mathsf{Transition}\}$, i.e. the classes contained inside the **FSM** package; and $Dom(e(FSM)) = E_{FSM}$ with $E_{FSM} = \{\mathsf{Kind}\}$, which is the unique enumeration declared in the metamodel. The domains of *prop* and *o* are built by gathering all properties and operations names respectively. For example, we have:

- In class **Label**, $Dom(prop(FSM)(Label)) = \{label\}$ and $Dom(o(FSM)(Label)) = \varnothing$ because no operation is declared;
- In class **FSM**, $Dom(prop(FSM)(FSM)) = \{alphabet, states, transitions\}$ for the three properties declared and $\mathrm{Dom}(o(FSM)(FSM)) = \{getStart, getFinal, accept\}$ for the operations.

We now must define the all component functions of the metamodel. The package function p makes use of the previously defined sets of classes and functions; the enumeration function just collects the enumeration literals (see Box 4).
All classes except Label are similarly defined, because they are concrete and inherit from `Label`.

InstExp ::= self | lhs

$$c(FSM)(Label) = (\top, \varnothing)$$
$$c(FSM)(FSM) = (\bot, \{Label\})$$

We provide in Box 5 the definition of the property function for the **Label** and **FSM** classes, which cover the main variations encountered in metamodels. ■

With this example, it becomes clearer how a MOF metamodel is translated into our mathematical structure representing metamodels. We first introduce the notion of *qualified names*: a qualified name is intuitively a *valid* feature name captured within a model, qualified by its enclosing class and package (operations, respectively, features, qualified names are defined accordingly) as presented in Box 6.

Example 5: In $\mathsf{MM}_{\mathsf{FSM}}$, within the class FSM, the qualified property names of $\mathsf{alphabet}$ and states are $(\mathsf{FSM}, \mathsf{FSM}, \mathsf{alphabet}) \in \mathsf{QPropN}$ and $(\mathsf{FSM}, \mathsf{FSM}, \mathsf{states}) \in \mathsf{QPropN}$ respec-

Box 4.

$$
\begin{array}{lcl}
p(FSM) & = & (\varnothing, C_{FSM}, E_{FSM}) \\
e(FSM)(Kind) & = & \langle\langle NORMAL, STOP, START \rangle\rangle
\end{array}
$$

Box 5.

$$prop(\mathsf{FSM})(\mathsf{Label})(\mathsf{label}) = (\top, \bot, (1, 1, \bot, \mathsf{String}), \bot)$$
$$o(\mathsf{FSM})(\mathsf{FSM})(\mathsf{accept}) = (\bot, \bot, \langle\langle(\mathsf{word}, (0, \star, \mathsf{List}, \mathsf{String}))\rangle\rangle, (1, 1, \bot, \mathsf{Boolean}), b_{accept})$$

$$
\begin{array}{lcl}
prop(\mathsf{FSM})(\mathsf{FSM})(\mathsf{alphabet}) & = & (\top, \bot, (1, \star, \mathsf{Set}, \mathsf{String}), \bot) \\
prop(\mathsf{FSM})(\mathsf{FSM})(\mathsf{states}) & = & (\top, \bot, (1, \star, \mathsf{OSet}, \mathsf{State}), \bot) \\
prop(\mathsf{FSM})(\mathsf{FSM})(\mathsf{transitions}) & = & (\top, \bot, (1, \star, \mathsf{OSet}, \mathsf{Transition}), \bot)
\end{array}
$$

$$
\begin{array}{lcl}
o(\mathsf{FSM})(\mathsf{FSM})(\mathsf{getStart}) & = & (\bot, \bot, \langle\langle\cdot\rangle\rangle, (1, 1, \bot, \mathsf{State}), b_{\mathsf{getStart}}) \\
o(\mathsf{FSM})(\mathsf{FSM})(\mathsf{getFinal}) & = & (\bot, \bot, \langle\langle\rangle\rangle, (1, 1, \bot, \mathsf{State}), b_{getFinal})
\end{array}
$$

tively; and the qualified operation name of accept is $(\mathsf{FSM}, \mathsf{FSM}, \mathsf{accept}) \in \mathsf{QOpN}$. ■

For facilitating the definition of the Action Language's semantics, we now introduce a number of functions that allow the manipulation of a particular metamodel's information. These functions act like projectors, i.e. they select particular elements from the images of the functions constituting the metamodel as presented in Box 7.

The choices for function names are kept as natural as possible given the role of each of them. We only illustrate how the function $super$ is formally built, the reader can easily infer the other functions' constructions (or can refer to Amrani (2012)). Let $(\mathsf{pkg}, \mathsf{c}) \in \mathsf{PClassN}$ such that $\mathsf{c} \in Dom(c(\mathsf{pkg}))$, $super$ represents $(\mathsf{pkg}, \mathsf{c})$'s superclasses as follows:

$$super_{MM}(pkg, c) = C \overset{\Delta}{\Leftrightarrow} c_{MM}(pkg)(c) = (\_, C)$$

Similarly, abs indicates if a class or an operation is abstract; *from* retrieves the disambiguation class (if any) of a feature; and $type$ the multiplicity type of a feature (which can be $\bot$, i.e. **void**, in the case of an operation); and $partype$ and $parnames$ retrieve the ordered list of respectively the collection types and the names of an operation's parameters.

Example 6: Let us focus on class FSM, which is almost completely defined in Example 3. From the definition of the class function $c(\mathsf{FSM})(\mathsf{FSM})$, we deduce that $abs(\mathsf{FSM})(\mathsf{FSM}) = \bot$ and $super(\mathsf{FSM})(\mathsf{FSM}) = \{\mathsf{Label}\}$, meaning that the FSM class is not abstract and inherits from Label. From the definition of the operation function $op(\mathsf{FSM})(\mathsf{FSM})(\mathsf{accept})$ for the accept operation, we deduce

$abs(\mathsf{FSM}, \mathsf{FSM}, \mathsf{accept}) = \bot$,

$type(\mathsf{FSM}, \mathsf{FSM}, \mathsf{accept}) = \mathsf{Boolean}$,

$from(\mathsf{FSM}, \mathsf{FSM}, \mathsf{accept}) = \bot$ and

Box 6.

$$\mathsf{QPropN}_{\mathsf{MM}} \stackrel{\triangle}{=} \begin{array}{l}\{(\mathsf{pkg},\mathsf{c},\mathsf{p}) \in \mathsf{PkgN} \times \mathsf{ClassN} \times \mathsf{PropN} \mid \\ \mathsf{pkg} \in Dom(prop) \wedge \mathsf{c} \in Dom(prop(\mathsf{pkg})) \wedge \mathsf{p} \in Dom(prop(\mathsf{pkg})(\mathsf{c}))\}\end{array}$$

Box 7.

$$\begin{array}{lcl} from_{\mathsf{MM}} & : & \mathsf{QFeatN} \rightarrow \mathsf{ClassN}_{\perp} \\ type_{\mathsf{MM}} & : & \mathsf{QFeatN} \rightarrow \mathsf{MType}_{\perp} \\ parnames_{\mathsf{MM}} & : & \mathsf{QOpN} \rightarrow \langle\langle \mathsf{ParamN} \rangle\rangle \end{array} \qquad \begin{array}{lcl} super_{\mathsf{MM}} & : & \mathsf{PClassN} \rightarrow \wp(\mathsf{ClassN}) \\ abs_{\mathsf{MM}} & : & \mathsf{QOpN} \cup \mathsf{PClassN} \rightarrow \boxtimes \\ partypes_{\mathsf{MM}} & : & \mathsf{QOpN} \rightarrow \langle\langle \mathsf{CType} \rangle\rangle \end{array}$$

$partypes(\mathsf{FSM},\mathsf{FSM},\mathsf{accept}) = \langle\langle String \rangle\rangle$, meaning that acccept is not abstract, returns a Boolean value, is not ambiguous and has only one parameter of type String. ■

Models

When defining a DSL model, a modeller actually represents a concrete element from its expertise domain. This model is supposed to be valid regarding the expertise domain, which is captured by the fact that the model actually obeys the rules captured by the metamodel. In Figure 2, we showed a concrete FSM constituted of three states and three transitions in the usual concrete syntax.

A model consists basically in a collection of objects (or equivalently called instances). Each object has a type, i.e. a class of a metamodel, and maintains a state. An object's state is intuitively a mapping between property names and values, in such a way that the involved names correspond to the declared names for the object's type.

Definition 2 (Models $\mathbb{M}$***):*** *A* model $M \in \mathbb{M}$ *is a function that associates objects to their type and state.*

$$\begin{array}{lcl} \mathbb{S}tate & \stackrel{\triangle}{=} & \{\sigma : PropN \not\rightarrow \mathbb{V}\} \\ \mathbb{M} & \stackrel{\triangle}{=} & \{M : \mathbb{O} \not\rightarrow PClassN \times \mathbb{S}tate\} \end{array}$$

■

Given a model $M \in \mathbb{M}$, we note σ_M^o the state of the object $o \in \mathbb{O}$ if $o \in Dom(M)$ and $type_M(o)$ its type (subscripts are omitted if clear from context).

Example 7: Let us call $M_{abc} \in \mathbb{M}$ the representation of the FSM model depicted in Figure 2. Using the states names and transitions labels as object identifiers, we have $Dom(M_{abc}) = \{abc, 1, 2, 3, a, b, c\}$ with the following types: $\sigma(abc) = (FSM, FSM)$, $\sigma(1) = \sigma(2) = \sigma(3) = (FSM, State)$ and $\sigma(a) = \sigma(b) = \sigma(c) = (FSM, Transition)$. For the purpose of future usage, we only describe the state of the FSM object *abc* together with one state object and two transitions as presented in Box 8. ■

In the presence of inheritance (and *a fortiori* multiple inheritance), referring to features by their names might be ambiguous because names can be repeated throughout the inheritance hierarchy. In fact, in Kermeta, for a given object, all prop-

Box 8.

$$\sigma^{abc}(\text{label}) = \text{"(ab) + c"} \qquad \sigma^{a}(\text{label}) = \text{"a"}$$
$$\sigma^{abc}(\text{alphabet}) = \{\text{"a"},\text{"b"},\text{"c"}\} \qquad \sigma^{a}(\text{src}) = 1$$
$$\sigma^{abc}(\text{states}) = \langle\langle 1,2,3\rangle\rangle \qquad \sigma^{a}(\text{tgt}) = 2$$
$$\sigma^{abc}(\text{transitions}) = \langle\langle a,b,c\rangle\rangle \qquad \sigma^{a}(\text{fsm}) = abc$$

$$\sigma^{1}(\text{label}) = \text{"1"} \qquad \sigma^{b}(\text{label}) = \text{"b"}$$
$$\sigma^{1}(\text{kind}) = \text{START} \qquad \sigma^{b}(\text{src}) = 2$$
$$\sigma^{1}(\text{in}) = \langle\langle b\rangle\rangle \qquad \sigma^{b}(\text{tgt}) = 1$$
$$\sigma^{1}(\text{out}) = \langle\langle a\rangle\rangle \qquad \sigma^{b}(\text{fsm}) = abc$$
$$\sigma^{1}(\text{fsm}) = abc$$

erty names of objects are unique with respect to the disambiguation clause. Suppose now a model $M \in \mathbb{M}$ of a metamodel $MM \in \mathcal{M}$, and an object o of type $(pkg, c) \in PClassN$. To be correctly defined, o's state should associate a value to all accessible property declared in MM, i.e. these properties defined in the inheritance scope of C: either directly declared in C, or inherited from C's superclasses. Similarly, O's accessible operations are these operations that are either defined directly in C or inherited from superclasses. We must ensure that *each accessible property for* o has an unique name and *each operation call on* o resolves to an unique operation. Why these two facts hold come from different reasons, we only sketch the proofs for each of them.

First, as already mentioned, direct feature names are unique (for operations, overloading is not allowed in Kermeta). Second, in a single inheritance path, feature names are unique: properties cannot be overridden because "*it simply does not make sense from a structural point of view*" (Drey et al., 2009, §2.9.5); and Kermeta allows only invariant overriding, so that an operation call always resolves to the closest operation name up to the inheritance hierarchy. Finally, in case of multiple inheritance, uniqueness must be enforced by using the *from* disambiguation clause (Drey, Faucher, Fleurey, Mahé & Vojtisek, 2009, §2.9.5.4).

As operations rely on dynamic lookup, i.e. the chosen operation's body for a call depends on the dynamic type of the object, it is not possible to define a similar function. The decision will be made dynamically (cf. Section Semantics).

We introduce two functions π_{MM} and ω_{MM} over a metamodel $\text{MM} \in \mathcal{M}$ that recursively compute the information relative to accessible properties and operations, respectively, presented in Box 9.

Conformance

Once a modeller has defined its models, it will be certainly helpful to check if they are *conform* to their metamodel, i.e. if they belong to the set of models effectively induced by the metamodel's definition. Usually, *structural* conformance, involving only the model, is distinguished from *constrained* conformance, which extends the latter notion with structural constraints satisfaction (otherwise referred to as metamodels' *static semantics* or *well-formedness* rules, see e.g. (Bo-

Box 9.

$$\pi_{\mathsf{MM}} : \mathsf{PkgN} \nrightarrow \mathsf{ClassN} \nrightarrow \mathsf{PropN} \nrightarrow \mathbb{B} \times \mathsf{MType} \times \mathsf{RefN}_{\perp}$$
$$\omega_{\mathsf{MM}} : \mathsf{PkgN} \nrightarrow \mathsf{ClassN} \nrightarrow \mathsf{OpN} \nrightarrow \mathbb{B} \times \langle\langle \mathcal{P}\mathsf{aram} \rangle\rangle \times \mathsf{MType} \times \mathsf{Body}$$

ronat, 2007)). Nowadays, this property is well understood and automatically checked within modelling frameworks.

Let $\mathsf{M} \in \mathbb{M}$ be a model and $\mathsf{MM} \in \mathcal{M}$ a metamodel: M *conforms to* MM, noted $\mathsf{M} \blacktriangleright \mathsf{MM}$, if all objects contained in M (i.e. for all $o \in Dom(\mathsf{M})$) respect the following conditions:

1. o's type is declared in MM and all accessible property from this type has a value;

$$type(o) = (\mathsf{pkg}, \mathsf{c}) \Rightarrow \begin{cases} \mathsf{p} \in Dom(p) \\ p(\mathsf{pkg}) = (P, C, E) \Rightarrow \mathsf{c} \in C \\ Dom(\sigma^o) = Dom(\pi(\mathsf{pkg})(\mathsf{c})) \\ \forall \mathsf{p} \in Dom(\sigma^o), \sigma^o(\mathsf{p}) \in \mathbb{V} \end{cases}.$$

2. For each property $p \in PropN$ that is accessible from o (i.e. $p \in Dom(\sigma^o)$) and that has value $v \in \mathbb{V}$ and type $mt = (low, up, C, t) \in MType$ then (i) v's type specialises (C, t); and (ii) v's size respects p's declared bounds.

$$\text{(i)} \quad type(v) \preceq (\mathsf{C}, \mathsf{t})$$
$$\text{(ii)} \quad low \leq |v| \leq up$$

3. Furthemore, if v is a collection containing the (internal) values $v_1, \ldots, v_n$ (i.e. $C \neq \perp$) then each of these v_i has a type that specialises t (remember that collection values are always well-formed)

$$\forall i, type(v_i) \preceq t$$

4. Finally, if the property p is a reference with an opposite property opp (*i.e.* $p \in RefN$ such that $opp(pkg, c, p) \neq \perp$), then opp's value is either an object v itself, or a collection of (internal) objects $v'_1, \ldots, v'_n$; in this case, the original object o must be included between *opp*'s (internal) value(s).

$$opp \neq \perp \Rightarrow \forall I, o \subseteq \sigma^{v_i}(opp)$$

Example 8: In Example 4 and 7, we defined respectively the metamodel $\mathsf{MM}_{FSM} \in \mathcal{M}$ and the model $\mathsf{M}_{abc} \in \mathbb{M}$ of Figure 2. We now prove the conformance, i.e. $\mathsf{M}_{abc} \blacktriangleright \mathsf{MM}_{FSM}$.

Condition 1 is simply checked from the definition of M_{abc} itself: the objects abc, 1, 2, 3, a, b, c have types appearing in MM_{FSM} and each accessible property possesses a value. It then remains to prove that each accessible property has a *valid* value regarding the declared property type, and so for opposites. The proofs are very similar for objects of the same type, therefore we only provide the proofs for one state and one transition objects. The reader can easily infer the other proofs.

- A State instance has five accessible properties: $\mathsf{label}, \mathsf{kind}, \mathsf{in}, \mathsf{out}, \mathsf{fsm}$. Properties in and out only differ for their opposite, therefore we only consider in.

- label: Remember that $\sigma^1(label) = "1"$ and $prop(\text{FSM})(\text{Label})(\text{label}) = (\top, \bot, (1, 1, \bot, \text{String}), \bot)$.
  - Since $type("1") = (\bot, \text{String})$, it implies that Condition 2.i holds;
  - Since $|"1"| = 1$, it implies that Condition 2.ii holds;
  - label has no collection value and does not declare an opposite so the last check is irrelevant, so Conditions 3 and 4 are irrelevant.
- kind: We have $\sigma^1(\text{kind}) = \text{START}$ and $prop(\text{FSM})(\text{State})(\text{Kind}) = (\top, \bot, (1, 1, \bot, \text{Kind}), \bot)$.
  - Since $type(\text{START}) = (\bot, \text{Kind})$, it implies that Condition 2.i holds;
  - Since $|START| = 1$, it implies that Condition 2.ii holds;
  - kind has no collection value and does not declare an opposite so the last check is irrelevant, so Conditions 3 and 4 are irrelevant.
- in: We have $\sigma^1(\text{in}) = \langle\langle b \rangle\rangle$ and $prop(\text{FSM})(\text{State})(\text{in}) = (\bot, \bot, (0, \star, \text{List}, \text{Transition}), tgt)$
  - Since $type(\langle\langle b \rangle\rangle) = (\text{OSet}, \text{Transition})$, it implies that Condition 2.i holds;
  - Since $|\langle\langle b \rangle\rangle| = 1$, it implies that Condition 2.ii holds;
  - We have $\sigma^b(\text{tgt}) = 1$ and $prop(\text{FSM})(\text{Transition})(\text{tgt}) = (\bot, \bot, (1, 1, \bot, \text{State}), \text{in})$, so effectively, $1 \in \sigma^b(\text{tgt})$ which makes Condition 3 holding.
  - A transition instance has four accessible properties: label, src, tgt, fsm. The property label is similar to the State's property label and is therefore not presented; the properties src and tgt only differ for their opposite, so we only consider tgt (as the opposite of property in for type State).
- tgt We have $\sigma^b(\text{tgt}) = 1$ with $prop(\text{FSM})(\text{Transition})(\text{tgt}) = (\bot, \bot, (1, 1, \bot, \text{State}), \text{in})$.
  - Since $type(1) = (\bot, (\text{FSM}, \text{State}))$, it implies that Condition 2.i holds;
  - Since $|"b"| = 1$, it implies that Condition 2.ii holds;
  - We already saw that $\sigma^1(in) = \langle\langle b \rangle\rangle$ with $prop(\text{FSM})(\text{State})(\text{in}) = (\bot, \bot, (0, \star, \text{List}, \text{Transition}), \text{tgt})$
  - So effectively, we have $b \in \sigma^1(in)$ and Condition 3 and 4 hold. ■

Related Works

We discuss here contributions addressing specifically DSML structural specifications; contributions more directly related to DSML transformations and behaviour are postponed to the next Section.

Historically, most formalisations focused on structural aspects, which is an understandable and natural first step. Several formal frameworks were used, but accordingly to our initial motivation, they contrast with our work by the fact that they are expressed in the syntax of a particular tool. Moreover, some of them are incomplete regarding MOF.

As already mentioned, Algebraic Specifications were used to formalise MOF in (Boronat & Meseguer, 2008) together with its reflection capabilities, using Maude. Abstract State Machines (ASM) serve both as formal foundations for MOF (Gargantini, Riccobene, & Scandurra, 2009) and as a metamodeling framework for ASM (Gargantini, Riccobene, & Scandurra, 2008), thus providing bridges between MDE and ASM tools. Song, He, Liang, and Liu (2005) used Z language but do not cover packages, and stay very general for attributes/references by not taking into consideration collection/multiplicity types, despite the fact that Z offers these concepts natively.

Category Theory is another important framework: Constructive Type Theory was used by Poernomo (2006) to formalise MOF in the context of the "proofs-as-programs" concept, but without an explicit notion of containment/opposite references; besides, he does not provide a clear mechanism to transform MOF specifications into Constructive Type Theory. Graph-Based formalisations are used to achieve both formalisation of MOF and transformations (Rozenberg, 1997; Biermann, Ermel & Taentzer, 2008), but usual MOF constructions like containment and inheritance were not addressed until recently (Jurack and Taentzer, 2010).

Numerous contributions try to formalise UML diagrams (and in particular, as expected, UML Class Diagrams) by translating them into languages with well-defined semantics. As a general remark, these contributions always address specific parts or small subsets of UML Diagrams. Among many other formalisms, we already mentioned Z (Song et al., 2005), but also Object-Z (Soon-Kyeong & Carrington, 1999), the algebraic language Casl (Reggio, Cerioli & Astesiano, 2001) where the behaviour is expressed with transition systems that naturally flow from algebraic specifications, and the theorem-prover Pvs by abstracting Diagrams into state predicates in (Krishnan, 2000).

ACTION LANGUAGE

Kermeta's Action Language (AL) allows DSL designers to specify the semantics of their metamodels, as we did for our running example in Figure 2 and Figure 3 (the complete specification of the FSM DSL is given in Appendix A): practically, designers fill the operations' bodies of their DSL metamodel to specify the behaviour. They can manipulate their model's elements, such as class instances, features' values and so on, textually using statements defined by the AL. What we propose in this Section is to provide the formal semantics of the AL itself. Notice here that this work should be distinguished from the definition of the DSL semantics (Bryant et. al., 2011). Defining the semantics of the AL has an obvious advantage: because Kermeta's AL can serve as a language for defining DSL semantics, formally specifying it provides a natural formal counterpart to every DSL semantics.

Dynamic Semantics Overview

The AL expresses dynamic changes over the structures defined through the DSL metamodel. Capturing the AL semantics requires using the mathematical techniques designed to capture dynamic behaviour. In nature, such a semantics is always defined with the help of three components (Harel & Rumpe, 2004): a *semantic domain*, more or less close to the language being defined, captures the language's concepts by providing an interpretation for each of them in terms of mathematical objects; and a *semantic mapping* between the abstract constructions provided by the language's metamodel into the semantic mapping. Researchers classically distinguish three approaches given the nature of these objects and the way the mapping is expressed (Winskel, 1993):

- The *denotational* approach uses domain theory for representing concepts and functions combined with compositions, fixpoints and functors, for representing computations; it generally leads to semantic definitions that are difficult to implement;
- The *axiomatic* approach uses logic formulae to capture the meaning of concepts and formal calculus to describe their evolution (one of the most popular is Hoare logics); it is mainly used for proving assertions over executions;

- The *operational* approach, the one we choose, uses set theory and rewriting rules to define the semantics under the form of a transition system. This approach describes the language's execution by means of the execution of an abstract machine, which can then be implemented with the help of a language that possess the required features.

What we expect from this formalisation is a certified Kermeta interpreter, which should help designers to formally execute, test, and analyse their models' transformations. This Section explains the core parts of Kermeta's dynamic semantics by following the traditional approach for the definition of a structural operational semantics:

- First, the AL receives a clean *Definition* in the subsequent Section. Considering the original Kermeta's AL, we define a Bnf grammar for a Core AL that focus on relevant statements for the definition of DSL semantics. The restrictions are motivated, and illustrated on our running example to help understand how bridging both languages can easily be performed.
- Second, we define a *Type-Checking System* that ensures the grammar sentences, appearing within a DSL operations' bodies, are *well-formed*, i.e. do not violate the structural declarations in the DSL's metamodel.
- Third, we define the abstract machine's execution in Section *Semantics* in two steps: we first define the semantic domain, and then the necessary rewriting rules.

This Section ends with some *Related Works* on the complete formalisation of transformation languages.

Since the Core AL is large, we only present in this chapter the relevant parts of the semantics that are specific to Kermeta: other parts follow already explored techniques relative to object-oriented programming languages such as Java (Stärk, Börger & Schmidt, 2001; Pollet, 2004), which largely inspired us. The full and complete definition is available in (Amrani & Amàlio, 2011), as well as a deeper discussion about choices and possible variations on the chosen language.

Definition

The Core AL is built from Kermeta's AL by removing two kinds of constructions: first, constructions related to elements already discarded at the SL level (namely, genericity and model typing and functionals); and second, the constructions we choose to not deal with in this study (namely, exceptions, aspects and Java native calls). All other constructions are part of the Core AL, and try to reflect Kermeta's concrete textual syntax (cf. Figure 5 for the full Kermeta's metamodel).

In (Muller, Fleurey & Jézéquel, 2005; Drey, Faucher, Fleurey, Mahé & Vojtisek, 2009), authors explain how the Kermeta's AL is weaved into the SL by extending the class Operation with a Body (cf. Figure 1) that consists in a sequence of (unique) statements. From a mathematical point of view, the Bnf grammar in Figure 6 defined a top-level non-terminal Body that is attached to the corresponding element set within the operation functions (cf. Definition 1 and Example 4).

The Core AL's grammar is divided in two syntactic groups: expressions Exp are side-effect free and simply evaluate to a value; they are used inside statements Stm that actually alter the model under execution. This simplification is not new (Aho, Sethi & Ullman, 1986) and is convenient to clarify the semantics of OO languages without loss of generality.

Expressions are of four kinds: the null expression; *scalar expressions* ScalarExp ; *instance expressions* InstExp ; or *collection expressions*. A scalar expression is either a literal Literal or an instanceof expression. The terminal Literal

Figure 5. Kermeta's Action Language from Drey et al. (2009, §3.3)

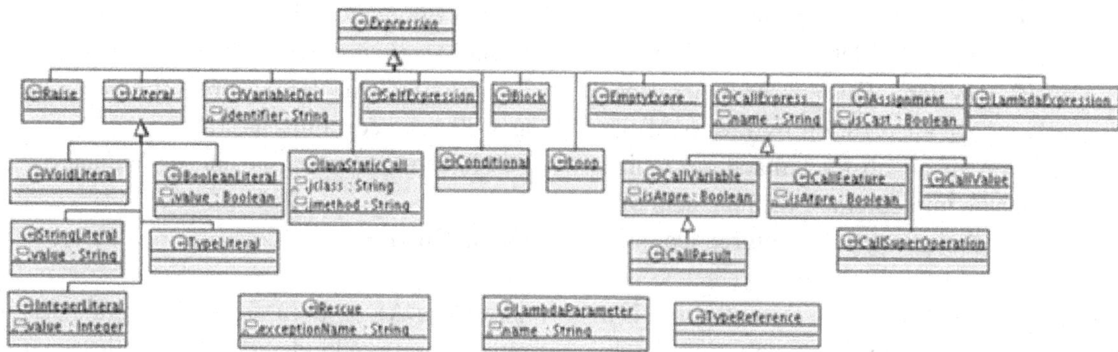

Figure 6. Core action language: Expressions (left) and statements (right)

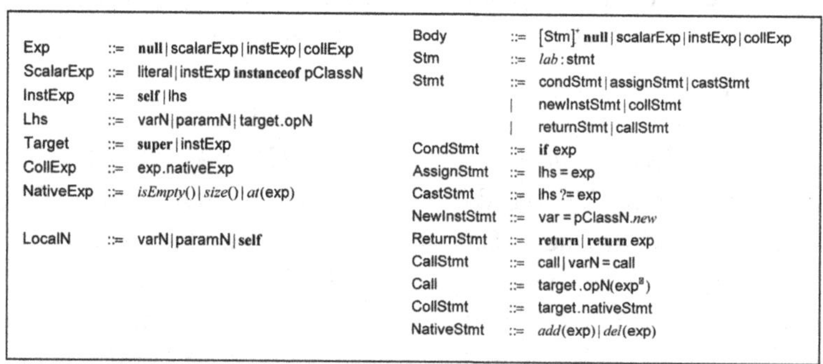

```
Exp         ::= null | scalarExp | instExp | collExp
ScalarExp   ::= literal | instExp instanceof pClassN
InstExp     ::= self | lhs
Lhs         ::= varN | paramN | target.opN
Target      ::= super | instExp
CollExp     ::= exp.nativeExp
NativeExp   ::= isEmpty() | size() | at(exp)

LocalN      ::= varN | paramN | self
```

```
Body        ::= [Stm]+ null | scalarExp | instExp | collExp
Stm         ::= lab : stmt
Stmt        ::= condStmt | assignStmt | castStmt
              | newInstStmt | collStmt
              | returnStmt | callStmt
CondStmt    ::= if exp
AssignStmt  ::= lhs = exp
CastStmt    ::= lhs ?= exp
NewInstStmt ::= var = pClassN.new
ReturnStmt  ::= return | return exp
CallStmt    ::= call | varN = call
Call        ::= target .opN(exp*)
CollStmt    ::= target.nativeStmt
NativeStmt  ::= add(exp) | del(exp)
```

abstracts from the actual representation of literal and associated operations. An *instanceof* expression consists of an instance expression and a declared class in the form of a package name and a class name, thus reflecting in the grammar the definition of PClassN. Instance expressions have values that designate "assignable" entities: either self, or a left-hand side expression. Left-hand side expressions Lhs are either a variable / parameter access, or a property access at the level of the superclass or by navigating through an instance. Collection expressions consists in an instance expression that designates a collection, and a native expression, which is one of the following: size() that returns the size of a collection; isEmpty() that returns true iff a collection is empty; or at() that returns an element in an ordered collection at the position given by the expression. An extra syntactic set LocalN is defined, which is not strictly part of the grammar definition, but usefully collects local names inside an operation's body for easing the semantics' formalisation.

Statements are of five kinds: *conditional*, *cast* and *assignment*, *instance creation*, *operation call management*, and *collection statements*. A conditional CondStmt is reduced to a conditional branching statement. An assignment AssignStmt assigns an expression to a left-hand side expression. A cast CastStmt casts an expression to a variable. An instance creation NewInstStmt assigns to a variable a fresh instance of a specified class, again through the form of a PClassN. A return ReturnStmt is either the simple keyword return, or this keyword used with a return expression. An operation call CallStmt is either a simple call, or it can return a value which is assigned to a variable. A collection statement

Figure 7. The fire operation's body. At the left, declarations and associated initialisations are shifted at the beginning and loop and result statements are transformed; in the middle, statements are flattened according to Table 1; the control flow is explicated at the right.

```
    var trans: oset Transition [0..*]
    var current: Transition
    var i: Integer
01: trans := self.out
02: current := trans.at(0)
03: i := 0
04: if(trans == null){
05:   return null
    }else{
06:   while(i == trans.size() or
        trans.at(i).label == letter){
07:     i := i+1
      }
08:   if(current == null){
09:     return null
      }else{
10:     return current.tgt
      }
    }
```

```
    var trans: oset Transition [0..*]
    var current: Transition
    var i: Integer
01: trans := self.out
02: current := trans.at(0)
03: i := 0
04: if(trans == null){
05: return null

06: while(i == trans.size() or
        trans.at(i).label == letter){
07: i := i+1

08: if(current == null){
09: return null

10: return current.tgt
```

L_{fire}	nxt
01	$(02,\bot)$
02	$(03,\bot)$
03	$(04,\bot)$
04	$(05,06)$
05	$(\bot,\bot)$
06	$(07,08)$
07	$(06,\bot)$
08	$(09,10)$
09	$(\bot,\bot)$
10	$(\bot,\bot)$

CollStmt consists in a call expression, place before the "." that designates a collection, on which one of the following native statement is applied: add(exp) or del(exp) respectively adds or removes an element given by the parameter expression (between parenthesis).

Three particularities characterise the Core AL: there is no explicit variable declaration; every statement is labelled; and there is only one branching statement (namely, CondStmt). These simplifications do not change the behaviour of an operation: they provide an adequate refactoring of operations' bodies that will simplify the formal specification of the semantics of the statements by focusing on the relevant dynamic aspects and by using a minimal set of statements in which all other statements can be expressed (Aho et al., 1986). We now explain these simplifications with the help of the fire operation's body in class State (cf. Appendix A for the original code and Figure 7 for the refactored code).

Local variable declarations are all shifted at the beginning of the body, before any other statement (variables can always be renamed consistently to avoid name clashes), and scope to the entire body. Nevertheless, the typing information related to these local declarations are needed to ensure a correct execution of statements, and is mathematically captured in a *local type environment*.

Definition 3 (Local Type Environment): *A local type environment λ_{MM} attached to a metamodel $MM \in \mathcal{M}$ is a function that associates to each operation in* MM *a function mapping local declarations to their types. λ_{MM} is correct if an abstract operation does not declare variables.*

$$\lambda_{MM} : QOpN \nrightarrow LocalN \nrightarrow MType$$

$$\forall \mathsf{qop} \in \mathsf{QOpN}, abs_{MM}(\mathsf{qop}) \Rightarrow Dom(\lambda_{MM}(\mathsf{qop})) = \varnothing$$ ■

Example 9: The fire operation in Figure 7 declares three local variables: trans, current, and i. Therefore

$Dom(\lambda_{FSM}(FSM)(State)(fire)) = \{trans, current, \mathbf{self}, i\}$.

According to the declarations, we obtain the fol-

Box 10.

$$\begin{aligned}
\lambda(\mathsf{FSM}, \mathsf{State}, \mathsf{fire})(\mathsf{trans}) &= (0, \star, \mathsf{OSet}, \mathsf{Transition}) \\
\lambda(\mathsf{FSM}, \mathsf{State}, \mathsf{fire})(\mathsf{current}) &= (1, 1, \bot, \mathsf{Transition}) \\
\lambda(\mathsf{FSM}, \mathsf{State}, \mathsf{fire})(\mathsf{i}) &= (1, 1, \bot, \mathsf{Integer}) \\
\lambda(\mathsf{FSM}, \mathsf{State}, \mathsf{fire})(\mathsf{letter}) &= (0, 1, \bot, \mathsf{String}) \\
\lambda(\mathsf{FSM}, \mathsf{State}, \mathsf{fire})(\mathbf{self}) &= (1, 1, \bot, \mathsf{State})
\end{aligned}$$

Box 11.

$$\begin{aligned}
\mathsf{labs}_{\mathsf{FSM}}(\mathsf{FSM}, \mathsf{State}, \mathsf{fire}) &= \mathsf{L}_{\mathsf{fire}} \\
\forall \mathsf{lab} \in \mathsf{L}_{\mathsf{fire}}, \mathsf{op}_{\mathsf{FSM}}(\mathsf{lab}) &= (\mathsf{FSM}, \mathsf{State}, \mathsf{fire})
\end{aligned}$$

lowing definition for $\lambda(\mathsf{FSM}, \mathsf{State}, \mathsf{fire})$ as presented in Box 10. ■

Using labels allow to represent the control flow between statements in a very efficient manner: instead of relying on the statement itself, we can completely identify statements with their label, if we ensure that they are unique throughout the metamodel.

Definition 4 (*Labelling*): *Let* Lab *be a set of statements. A* label encloser function op_{MM} *associates a label to its enclosing operation in a metamodel; its reverse function* lab_{MM} *retrieves all labels within an operation.*

$$\begin{aligned}
labs_{\mathsf{MM}} &: \mathsf{QOpN} \nrightarrow \langle\langle \mathsf{Lab} \rangle\rangle \\
op_{\mathsf{MM}} &: \mathsf{Lab} \nrightarrow \mathsf{QOpN}
\end{aligned}$$ ■

Example 10: Let $\mathsf{L}_{\mathsf{fire}} = \langle\langle 01, 02, \ldots, 09, 10 \rangle\rangle$ be the integer labels from 01 to 10. From the fire operation's body in Figure 7, we easily deduce the following (as presented in Box 11). ■

Using a single conditional branching statement (namely, CondStmt) avoid well-studied issues that traditionally occur when using imperative constructions like iterative (while, do, for) or conditional (**if-then-else**) statements (Aho, Sethi & Ullman, 1986; Stärk, Börger & Schmid, 2001; Pollet, 2004), such as variable scopes and nested control flows. Instead, statements contained in such constructions are flattened. Combined with the labelling process, it provides a convenient way for expressing the control flow within an operation's body.

***Definition 5* (*Control Flow*):** *The* control flow *function* $\mathsf{nxt}_{\mathsf{MM}}$ *attached to a metamodel* $\mathsf{MM} \in \mathcal{M}$ *is a function that associates to each label within* MM *the next labels to proceed.*

$$\mathsf{nxt}_{\mathsf{MM}} : \mathsf{Lab} \rightarrow \mathsf{Lab} \times \mathsf{Lab}_{\bot}$$ ■

Consider a labeled statement $\mathsf{lab} : \mathsf{stmt} \in \mathsf{Stm}$. Most statements have exactly one following statement, the following one in the declaration order: in such case, $nxt(\mathsf{lab}) = (\mathsf{lab}', \bot)$, where lab' is the next label in the operation's body. If $\mathsf{stmt} \in \mathsf{ReturnStmt}$ is a return statement, the control flow escapes from the operation and no following statement is expected: $nxt(\mathsf{lab}) = (\bot, \bot)$.

If $\mathsf{stmt} \in \mathsf{CondStmt}$ is a conditional statement, there is two possible following statements, depending on the value of the conditional: $nxt(\mathsf{lab}) = (\mathsf{lab}', \mathsf{lab}'')$, where lab' (resp. lab'') is the statement to which to proceed if evaluated to true (resp., false).

Table 1 shows how our single branching statement CondStmt acts as a normal form for the classical `while` and `if-then-else`: they have a common representation but differ only in the definition of their associated control flow function nxt (columns CF showing $nxt(\mathsf{lab})$, whith lab is given in first column). Other iterative statements like `do` or `for` can syntactically be reduced to a `while` (Aho et al., 1986).

Example 11: At the right of Figure 7 is a table showing the definition of the function nxt for the fire operation's body. ■

Type-Checking System

Before executing a DSL transformation, one must ensure that all statements are used correctly with respect to the metamodel's declarations and variables declared within operations' bodies. For example, consider a simple assignment between two variables: v := o.p where v is a local variable and o an object of class C possessing a property p. If v and p have incompatible types, this assignment will fail during all possible execution of a transformation.

The goal of a type-checking system (Cardelli, 2004) is to detect situations where inconsistencies within statements (and their constituting expressions) occur based on the DSL metamodel and local variables declarations, by precisely defining when these statements are valid. Building a sound type-checking system is usually not trivial, but it allows DSL designers to detect defects in their transformations early in the design process. Since Kermeta's AL is based on classical imperative programming and object-oriented constructions,

Table 1. Common representation of traditional `while/if-then-else` *statements with* CondStmt

Lab	While		Flattened Representation	If-Then-Else	
	C.F	Original		Original	C.F
0	$(1, n+1)$	while(...){	if(...){	if(...){	$(1, n+1)$
1	$(2, \perp)$	stm_1	stm_1	stm_1	$(2, \perp)$
		...			
N	$(0, \perp)$	stm_n	stm_n	stm_n	$(n+m+1, \perp)$
		}		}else{	
n+1	$(n+1, \perp)$	stm_{n+1}	stm_{n+1}	stm_{n+1}	$(n+2, \perp)$
		...	...	...	
n+m	$(n+m+1, \perp)$	stm_{n+m}	stm_{n+m}	stm_{n+m}	$(n+m+1, \perp)$
		...		}	
N+m+1		stm_{n+m+1}	stm_{n+m+1}	stm_{n+m+1}	

Box 12.

$$\mathsf{Exp} ::= \mathbf{null} \mid \mathsf{scalarExp} \mid \mathsf{instExp} \mid \mathsf{collExp}$$

$$\frac{}{\lambda \bullet \mathsf{qop} \vdash_{\mathsf{Expr}} \mathbf{null} \rhd (\bot, \mathbf{Null})}$$

$$\frac{\lambda \bullet \mathsf{qop} \vdash_{\mathsf{Expr}} \mathsf{scalarExp} \rhd (\bot, \mathsf{t}) \quad \mathsf{t} \in \mathsf{DataType}}{\lambda \bullet \mathsf{qop} \vdash_{\mathsf{Expr}} \mathsf{scalarExp} \rhd (\bot, \mathsf{t})} \qquad \frac{\lambda \bullet \mathsf{qop} \vdash_{\mathsf{Expr}} \mathsf{scalarExp} \rhd \mathsf{ct} \quad \mathsf{ct} \in \mathsf{CType}}{\lambda \bullet \mathsf{qop} \vdash_{\mathsf{Expr}} \mathsf{instExp} \rhd \mathsf{ct}} \qquad \frac{\lambda \bullet \mathsf{qop} \vdash_{\mathsf{Expr}} \mathsf{collExp} \rhd \mathsf{ct} \quad \mathsf{ct} \in \mathsf{CType}}{\lambda \bullet \mathsf{qop} \vdash_{\mathsf{Expr}} \mathsf{collExp} \rhd \mathsf{ct}}$$

we propose to set the necessary framework for building the entire type-system, but only deal with the specific constructions of Kermeta. Imperative constructions mainly follow those presented in (Winskel, 1993); object-oriented ones follows those in (Drossopoulou, Eisenbach & Khurshid, 1999).

The type-checking system is built by structural induction, following the AL definition of Figure 6. For ***expressions***, we introduce a judgement $\lambda_{\mathsf{MM}} \bullet \mathsf{qop} \vdash^{\mathsf{MM}}_{\mathsf{Expr}} \mathsf{exp} \rhd \mathsf{t}$. It means that in $\mathsf{MM} \in \mathcal{M}$, the expression $\mathsf{exp} \in \mathsf{Exp}$ appears in the body of operation $\mathsf{qop} = (\mathsf{pkg}, \mathsf{c}, \mathsf{op}) \in \mathsf{QOpN}$ and is of type $\mathsf{t} \in \mathsf{CType}$. We first define rules that just transfer the computation to specific rules for each kind of expressions: scalar expressions should be typed by a $\mathsf{DataType}$; instance expressions should be typed by a class $\mathsf{PClassN}$. The null expression has obviously the type **Null**. We skip the scalar expressions, because their type-checking is classic and deal directly with instance and collection expressions as presented in Box 12.

Instance Expressions: The type of **self** is the declared type in the local environment of op's scope. The type of a left-hand side expression is computed by a specific judgment $\vdash^{\mathsf{MM}}_{\mathsf{Lhs}}$. The type of a variable/parameter access is also the declared type in the local environment of op's scope.

The type of a property access depends on the target expression. First, the class c' corresponding to the target is computed. Then, it depends of the fact that propN is ambiguous or not in the context of c' (given by from value). If not, then there must be a class c'' in the inheritance hierarchy of c that has propN in its scope, i.e either declares it or inherits it (which fact is encapsulated in π). If it is ambiguous, then there must exist a disambiguation class c'' from which the property declaration is retrieved (also through π).

Collection Expressions. Let $\mathsf{instExp.nativeExp} \in \mathsf{CollExp}$. First, instExp must have a collection type with an actual collection. Then, the type of $isEmpty()$ is Boolean, the type of $size()$ is Integer. The type of at is instExp 's basic type if the associated expression's type is Integer and instExp collection kind specialises List (i.e. must be ordered to enable indexed access)

For statements, we introduce a judgement $\lambda_{\mathsf{MM}} \bullet \mathsf{qop} \vdash^{\mathsf{MM}}_{\mathsf{Stm}} \mathsf{stm}$. It means that the statement $\mathsf{stm} \in \mathsf{Stm}$ appears within the body of operation $\mathsf{qop} \in \mathsf{QopN}$ and is well-formed. A stm is well-formed if its inner statement stmt is well-formed and its labels are consistent, i.e. stm 's execution proceeds to statements within the same operation's body. As a consequence, we introduce a new judgement $\vdash_{\mathsf{Stmt}}$ also defined by induction. We skip the classical imperative and object oriented constructions (conditional, instance creation, assignment, casting, and **return**) to present only the rules specific to Kermeta's AL, namely the operation calls and the collection statements.

An Operation Call statement is typed in two steps. The first step assumes another judgement $\vdash_{\mathsf{Call}}$ explained hereafter. A call without assignment is well-typed if the call expression is well-typed and the operation has no return type; and a call with assignment is well-typed if the call expression is well-typed and the return type of the operation specialises the type.

The following set of rules deals with the call itself (for $\vdash_{\mathsf{Call}}$). First, the type of the target expression should denote a class (which is obviously the case for **super**). Second, all expressions for effective parameters are also well-typed. Third, the type-checking follows the same schema as for property access because it depends on the target and the possible multiply inherited method name: if the method name is ambiguous, then the method call is well-typed if there exists a method with the same name in the inheritance hierarchy of the disambiguated class; if it is not, then the method call is well-typed if there exists one class in the inheritance hierarchy that declares a method with the same name. The class from which the method name is looked for depends on the target: if the target is **super**, then the method name is looked for from the superclass; otherwise, it is looked from the class to which the instance target is typed. Finally, the types of the effective parameters expressions must specialise the formal parameters' types (in order).

The two collection statements are typed the same way. They are well-formed if their application expression's type has an actual collection kind, and if their parameter expression's basic type specialises the application expression's one.

Example 12: Let us check that the test $\mathsf{i == trans.size()}$, appearing inside the the loop within fire 's body, is correctly typed as $\mathsf{Boolean}$. In this case, we have $\mathsf{qop} = (\mathsf{FSM}, \mathsf{State}, \mathsf{fire})$. Recalling the definition of $\lambda_{\mathsf{FSM}}(\mathsf{FSM})(\mathsf{State})(\mathsf{fire})$ in Example 9, we first deduce that that the collection expression trans is typed as $(\mathsf{OSet}, \mathsf{Transition})$, which makes the premises hold (because then, trans ' collection type is not empty, i.e. $\mathsf{OSet} \neq \perp$). From the rule for collection expressions, we deduce that $\mathsf{trans.size()}$ has type $(\perp, \mathsf{Integer})$. Second, we deduce from λ_{FSM} that i is also typed as $(\perp, \mathsf{Integer})$. Because $\mathsf{==}$ is a Boolean comparison operator between to comparable types, we conclude that this expression is correctly typed to $(\perp, \mathsf{Boolean})$ (As presented in Box13, Box 14, Box 15, and Box 16). ■

Semantics

Once the type-checking system is defined, we can proceed with the execution semantics of the AL statements, i.e. explaining the effects of each statements by means of modifications of the semantic domain. We choose an Sos approach because we need a directly executable semantics in order to perform formal analysis of DSL models and transformations. An Sos specification is based on three elements:

1. A *semantic domain* mathematically captures the meaning of the data structures behind the DSL metamodel; it is generally equipped with several *semantic operations* that facilitate its formal manipulation;
2. A *state*, or *configuration*, built on top of the semantic domain, encloses all necessary information for describing the execution machinery;
3. A *set of (rewriting) rules*, expressed between a source and target configuration,

Box 13.

$$\mathsf{InstExp} ::= \mathbf{self} \mid \mathsf{lhs}$$

$$\frac{(\_,\mathsf{ct}) = \lambda(\mathsf{qop})(\mathbf{self})}{\lambda \bullet \mathsf{qop} \vdash_{\mathsf{Stmt}} \mathbf{self} \rhd \mathsf{ct}} \qquad \frac{\lambda \bullet \mathsf{qop} \vdash_{\mathsf{Lhs}} \mathsf{lhs} \rhd \mathsf{ct}}{\lambda \bullet \mathsf{qop} \vdash_{\mathsf{Stmt}} \mathsf{lhs} \rhd \mathsf{ct}}$$

$$\frac{\begin{array}{ccc} \mathit{from}(\mathsf{pkg},\mathsf{c},\mathsf{propN}) & = & \bot \\ \mathsf{c}' & \in & \mathit{super}(\mathsf{pkg},\mathsf{c}) \\ \mathsf{propN} & \in & \mathit{Dom}(\pi(\mathsf{pkg})(\mathsf{c}')) \\ (\_,\_,(\_,\mathsf{ct}),\_) & = & \pi(\mathsf{pkg})(\mathsf{c}')(\mathsf{propN}) \end{array}}{\lambda \bullet (\mathsf{pkg},\mathsf{c},\mathsf{op}) \vdash_{\mathsf{Inst}} \mathbf{super}.\mathsf{propN} \rhd \mathsf{ct}} \qquad \frac{\begin{array}{ccc} \lambda \bullet (\mathsf{pkg},\mathsf{c},\mathsf{op}) & \vdash_{\mathsf{Inst}} & \mathsf{instExp} \rhd \mathsf{c}' \\ \mathit{from}(\mathsf{pkg})(\mathsf{c})(\mathsf{propN}) & = & \bot \\ \mathsf{c}'' & \in & \mathit{super}(\mathsf{pkg},\mathsf{c}) \\ \mathsf{propN} & \in & \mathit{Dom}(\pi(\mathsf{pkg})(\mathsf{c}'')) \\ (\_,\_,(\_,\mathsf{ct}),\_) & = & \pi(\mathsf{pkg})(\mathsf{c}'')(\mathsf{propN}) \end{array}}{\lambda \bullet (\mathsf{pkg},\mathsf{c},\mathsf{op}) \vdash_{\mathsf{Lhs}} \mathsf{instExp}.\mathsf{propN} \rhd \mathsf{ct}}$$

$$\frac{\begin{array}{ccc} \mathit{from}(\mathsf{pkg},\mathsf{c},\mathsf{propN}) & = & \mathsf{c}' \\ (\_,\_,(\_,\mathsf{ct}),\_) & = & \pi(\mathsf{pkg})(\mathsf{c}')(\mathsf{propN}) \end{array}}{\lambda \bullet (\mathsf{pkg},\mathsf{c},\mathsf{op}) \vdash_{\mathsf{Call}} \mathbf{super}.\mathsf{propN} \rhd \mathsf{ct}} \qquad \frac{\begin{array}{ccc} \lambda \bullet (\mathsf{pkg},\mathsf{c},\mathsf{op}) & \vdash_{\mathsf{Inst}} & \mathsf{instExp} \rhd \mathsf{c}' \\ \mathit{from}(\mathsf{pkg})(\mathsf{c})(\mathsf{propN}) & = & \mathsf{c}'' \\ (\_,\_,(\_,\mathsf{ct}),\_) & = & \pi(\mathsf{pkg})(\mathsf{c}'')(\mathsf{propN}) \end{array}}{\lambda \bullet (\mathsf{pkg},\mathsf{c},\mathsf{op}) \vdash_{\mathsf{Lhs}} \mathsf{instExp}.\mathsf{propN} \rhd \mathsf{ct}}$$

Box 14.

$$\mathsf{CollExp} ::= \mathsf{exp}.\mathit{isEmpty}() \mid \mathsf{exp}.\mathit{size}() \mid \mathsf{exp}.\mathit{at}(\mathsf{exp})$$

$$\frac{\begin{array}{ccc} \lambda \bullet \mathsf{qop} & \vdash_{\mathsf{Expr}} & \mathsf{exp} \rhd (\mathsf{C},\_) \\ \mathsf{C} & \neq & \bot \end{array}}{\lambda \bullet \mathsf{qop} \vdash_{\mathsf{Expr}} \mathsf{exp}.\mathit{isEmpty}() \rhd (\bot,\mathsf{Boolean})} \qquad \frac{\begin{array}{ccc} \lambda \bullet \mathsf{qop} & \vdash_{\mathsf{Expr}} & \mathsf{exp} \rhd \mathsf{C} \\ \mathsf{C} & \neq & \bot \end{array}}{\lambda \bullet \mathsf{qop} \vdash_{\mathsf{Expr}} \mathsf{exp}.\mathit{size}() \rhd (\bot,\mathsf{Integer})} \qquad \frac{\begin{array}{ccc} \lambda \bullet \mathsf{qop} & \vdash_{\mathsf{Expr}} & \mathsf{exp}' \rhd (\bot,\mathit{integer}) \\ \mathsf{C} & \neq & \bot \\ \mathsf{C} & \preceq_{\mathsf{Coll}} & \mathsf{List} \end{array}}{\lambda \bullet \mathsf{qop} \vdash_{\mathsf{Expr}} \mathsf{exp}.\mathit{at}(\mathsf{exp}') \rhd (\bot,t)}$$

$$\mathsf{CallStmt} ::= \mathsf{target}.\mathsf{opN}(\mathsf{exp}^*) \qquad \mathsf{CallStmt} ::= \mathsf{varN} = \mathsf{target}.\mathsf{opN}(\mathsf{exp}^*)$$

$$\frac{\begin{array}{ccc} \lambda \bullet \mathsf{qop} & \vdash_{\mathsf{Call}} & \mathsf{target}.\mathsf{opN}(\mathsf{exp}^*) \\ \mathit{type}(\mathsf{qop}) & \neq & \bot \end{array}}{\lambda \bullet \mathsf{qop} \vdash_{\mathsf{Stmt}} \mathsf{target}.\mathsf{opN}(\mathsf{exp}^*)} \qquad \frac{\begin{array}{ccc} \lambda \bullet \mathsf{qop} & \vdash_{\mathsf{Call}} & \mathsf{target}.\mathsf{opN}(\mathsf{exp}^*) \\ \lambda \bullet \mathsf{qop} & \vdash_{\mathsf{Expr}} & \mathsf{varN} \rhd \mathsf{t} \\ \mathit{type}(\mathsf{qop}) & \preceq & \mathsf{t} \end{array}}{\lambda \bullet \mathsf{qop} \vdash_{\mathsf{Stmt}} \mathsf{varN} = \mathsf{target}.\mathsf{opN}(\mathsf{exp}^*)}$$

describes inductively the effect of each statement of the AL.

We first define the necessary component for the rewriting rules (namely, the semantic domain and the configuration) as well as associated notations. Then, we proceed with three rules that are

Box 15.

$$\mathsf{Call} ::= \mathsf{instExp.opN}(\mathsf{exp}^*)$$

$$\begin{array}{c}
\begin{array}{ccc}
\forall i, \lambda \bullet (\mathsf{pkg},\mathsf{c},\mathsf{op}) & \vdash_{\mathsf{Expr}} & \mathsf{exp}_i \rhd \mathsf{ct}_i \\
\lambda \bullet (\mathsf{pkg},\mathsf{c},\mathsf{op}) & \vdash_{\mathsf{Expr}} & \mathsf{instExp} \rhd \mathsf{c}' \\
\mathit{from}(\mathsf{pkg},\mathsf{c}',\mathsf{op}) & = & \bot \\
\mathsf{opN} & \in & \mathit{Dom}(\omega(\mathsf{pkg})(\mathsf{c}')) \\
\mathit{partypes}(\mathsf{pkg},\mathsf{c}',\mathsf{op}) & = & \langle\!\langle(_,_,\mathsf{ct}_1),\ldots,(_,_,\mathsf{ct}_n)\rangle\!\rangle \\
\forall i, \mathsf{ct}_i & \preceq & \mathsf{ct}_i'
\end{array} \\
\hline
\lambda \bullet (\mathsf{pkg},\mathsf{c},\mathsf{op}) \vdash_{\mathsf{Call}} \mathsf{instExp.opN}(\mathsf{exp}_1,\ldots,\mathsf{exp}_n)
\end{array}
\qquad
\begin{array}{c}
\begin{array}{ccc}
\forall i, \lambda \bullet (\mathsf{pkg},\mathsf{c},\mathsf{op}) & \vdash_{\mathsf{Expr}} & \mathsf{exp}_i \rhd \mathsf{ct}_i \\
\lambda \bullet (\mathsf{pkg},\mathsf{c},\mathsf{op}) & \vdash_{\mathsf{Expr}} & \mathsf{instExp} \rhd \mathsf{c}' \\
\mathit{from}(\mathsf{pkg},\mathsf{c}',\mathsf{op}) & = & \mathsf{c}'' \\
\mathsf{opN} & \in & \mathit{Dom}(\omega(\mathsf{pkg})(\mathsf{c}'')) \\
\mathit{partypes}(\mathsf{pkg},\mathsf{c}'',\mathsf{op}) & = & \langle\!\langle(_,_,\mathsf{ct}'_1),\ldots,(_,_,\mathsf{ct}'_n)\rangle\!\rangle \\
\forall i, \mathsf{ct}_i & \preceq & \mathsf{ct}_i'
\end{array} \\
\hline
\lambda \bullet (\mathsf{pkg},\mathsf{c},\mathsf{op}) \vdash_{\mathsf{Call}} \mathsf{instExp.opN}(\mathsf{exp}_1,\ldots,\mathsf{exp}_n)
\end{array}$$

Box 16.

$$\mathsf{Call} ::= \mathbf{super}.\mathsf{opN}(\mathsf{exp}^*)$$

$$\begin{array}{c}
\begin{array}{ccc}
\forall i, \lambda \bullet (\mathsf{pkg},\mathsf{c},\mathsf{op}) & \vdash_{\mathsf{Expr}} & \mathsf{exp}_i \rhd \mathsf{ct}_i \\
\mathsf{c}' & \in & \mathit{super}(\mathsf{pkg},\mathsf{c}) \\
\mathit{from}(\mathsf{pkg},\mathsf{c},\mathsf{op}) & = & \bot \\
\mathsf{opN} & \in & \mathit{Dom}(\omega(\mathsf{pkg})(\mathsf{c}')) \\
\mathit{partypes}(\mathsf{pkg},\mathsf{c}',\mathsf{op}) & = & \langle\!\langle(_,_,\mathsf{ct}_1),\ldots,(_,_,\mathsf{ct}_n)\rangle\!\rangle \\
\forall i, \mathsf{ct}_i & \preceq & \mathsf{ct}_i'
\end{array} \\
\hline
\lambda \bullet (\mathsf{pkg},\mathsf{c},\mathsf{op}) \vdash_{\mathsf{Call}} \mathbf{super}.\mathsf{opN}(\mathsf{exp}_1,\ldots,\mathsf{exp}_n)
\end{array}
\qquad
\begin{array}{c}
\begin{array}{ccc}
\forall i, \lambda \bullet (\mathsf{pkg},\mathsf{c},\mathsf{op}) & \vdash_{\mathsf{Expr}} & \mathsf{exp}_i \rhd \mathsf{ct}_i \\
\mathit{from}(\mathsf{pkg},\mathsf{c},\mathsf{op}) & = & \mathsf{c}' \\
\mathsf{opN} & \in & \mathit{Dom}(\omega(\mathsf{pkg})(\mathsf{c}')) \\
\mathit{partypes}(\mathsf{pkg},\mathsf{c}',\mathsf{op}) & = & \langle\!\langle(_,_,\mathsf{ct}_1),\ldots,(_,_,\mathsf{ct}_n)\rangle\!\rangle \\
\forall i, \mathsf{ct}_i & \preceq & \mathsf{ct}_i'
\end{array} \\
\hline
\lambda \bullet (\mathsf{pkg},\mathsf{c},\mathsf{op}) \vdash_{\mathsf{Call}} \mathbf{super}.\mathsf{opN}(\mathsf{exp}_1,\ldots,\mathsf{exp}_n)
\end{array}$$

$$\mathsf{CollStmt} ::= \mathsf{exp.add}(\mathsf{exp}') \mid \mathsf{exp.del}(\mathsf{exp}')$$

$$\begin{array}{c}
\begin{array}{ccc}
\lambda \bullet \mathsf{qop} & \vdash_{\mathsf{Expr}} & \mathsf{exp}(\mathsf{C},\mathsf{t}) \\
\lambda \bullet \mathsf{qop} & \vdash_{\mathsf{Expr}} & \mathsf{exp}'(\mathsf{C},\mathsf{t}') \\
\mathsf{C} & \neq & \bot \\
\mathsf{t}' & \preceq & \mathsf{t}
\end{array} \\
\hline
\lambda \bullet \mathsf{qop} \vdash_{\mathsf{Stmt}} \mathsf{exp}.___(\mathsf{exp}')
\end{array}$$

Kermeta-specific and illustrative of a semantics definition process.

Kermeta's AL manipulates models by keeping local information through variables. The definition of the semantic domain just reflect this fact.

Definition 6 (*Semantic Domain – Target*): *The semantic domain* $\mathbb{D}$ *is a pair consisting of a model and a local (store) environment. A local store environment* $\mathbb{L}$ *is a function mapping local names to values. A target* $t \in \mathbb{T}$ *designates an element that carries a value: either a local name stored in the local environment; or a property within an object, stored inside a model.*

$$\mathbb{L} \stackrel{\triangle}{=} \mathsf{LocalN} \not\rightarrow \mathbb{V}$$
$$\mathbb{D} \stackrel{\triangle}{=} \mathbb{M} \times \mathbb{L}$$
$$\mathbb{T} \stackrel{\triangle}{=} \mathsf{LocalN} \cup (\mathbb{O} \times \mathsf{PropN})$$ ■

We will manipulate domains and targets functionally: if $d = (m, l) \in \mathbb{D}$ is a domain element, we note $d(t)$ the value stored in t, i.e. $d(t) \stackrel{\triangle}{=} l(t)$ if $t \in \mathsf{LocalN}$ denotes a local name, and $d(t) \stackrel{\triangle}{=} m(o, \mathsf{p})$ if $t = (o, \mathsf{p}) \in \mathbb{O} \times \mathsf{PropN}$ denotes a model property. We extend this notation for update: we note $d[t \mapsto v]$ the updating of t by v in d i.e. $d[t \mapsto v] \stackrel{\triangle}{=} l[t \mapsto v]$ and $d[t \mapsto v] \stackrel{\triangle}{=} l[t \mapsto v]$ respectively.

The set of configurations Γ consists in the label denoting the statement under execution, a stack storing the information between operation calls, and the semantic domain. A stack is a sequence whose elements comprise the label where to resume after completing the execution of a call, the local environment of the call, and eventually the variable to which the result of the call need to be assigned.

Definition 7 (*Configuration*): *A* configuration *is a triplet* $(\mathsf{lab}, S, d) \in \mathsf{Lab} \times \langle \mathbb{E}nv \rangle \times \mathbb{D}$, *where* $\mathbb{E}nv \stackrel{\triangle}{=} (\mathsf{Lab} \times \mathbb{L}) \cup (\mathsf{Lab} \times \mathbb{L} \times \mathsf{VarN})$. ■

Example 13: The configuration obtained at the beginning of our running example's execution, after the initialisation statements (remember that **init** is in fact expanded into assignment statements at the beginning), within accept's body, consists of the following: lab is the label associated to the first statement in accept's body; $S = \varnothing$ because no operation has been called yet; and $d = (m, l)$ where $m \in \mathbb{M}$ is defined accordingly to Example 7, and $l \in \mathbb{L}$ maps local variables to their values (w is the String sequence given in parameter):

$$l \begin{bmatrix} \mathsf{current} & \mapsto & 1 \\ \mathsf{final} & \mapsto & 3 \\ \mathsf{isNull} & \mapsto & \mathsf{false} \\ \mathsf{toEval} & \mapsto & w \end{bmatrix}$$ ■

The rewriting system takes the form of a rule $\gamma \xrightarrow{\mathsf{stm}} \gamma'$ meaning that the configuration $\gamma \in \Gamma$ is rewritten in γ' when executing the statement $\mathsf{stm} \in \mathsf{Stm}$ under some conditions. All operations that occur in a rule are considered atomic. Notice that inside the rules, we explicitly recall the label to bind the statement with the control flow. We provide the definitions of the rules for three statements: the conditional statement, which only manipulates labels; the return statement, which manipulates the environment in a simple manner; and the assignment statement, which requires the definition of a semantic operation.

A conditional statement CondStmt only changes the label to the adequate one, according to the boolean value of its expression.

$$\frac{\begin{array}{rcl} v & = & [\![\mathsf{exp}]\!](d) \\ (\mathsf{lab}', \mathsf{lab}'') & = & nxt(\mathsf{lab}) \\ v & \Rightarrow & \mathsf{lab}_{\mathsf{res}} = \mathsf{lab}' \\ \neg v & \Rightarrow & \mathsf{lab}_{\mathsf{res}} = \mathsf{lab}'' \end{array}}{(\mathsf{lab}, S, d) \xrightarrow{\mathsf{lab:\ if\ exp}} (\mathsf{lab}_{\mathsf{res}}, S, d)}$$

A return statement ReturnStmt proceeds to the label stored in the top element of the stack and changes the current local environment with the stored one, then removes the top element. If the return statement has an expression, it is evaluated in the context of the stored local environment and assigned to the variable stored in the top element.

An assignment AssignStmt execution just call a semantic operation designed to take care of the assignment, then proceeds to the next label as demonstrated in Box 17.

Box 17.

$$\frac{s = (\mathsf{lab}', l')}{(\mathsf{lab}, s :: S, (m, l')) \xrightarrow{\text{lab:return}} (\mathsf{lab}', S, (m', l'))} \qquad \frac{\begin{array}{rcl} S & = & (\mathsf{lab}', l', \mathsf{var}) \\ (m', l'') & = & [\![\mathsf{var}, \mathsf{exp}]\!](m, l') \end{array}}{(\mathsf{lab}, s :: S, (m, l)) \xrightarrow{\text{lab: return exp}} (\mathsf{lab}', S, (m', l''))}$$

$$\frac{\begin{array}{rcl} (m', l') & = & [\![\mathsf{lhs}, \mathsf{exp}]\!](m, l) \\ (\mathsf{lab}', \_) & = & nxt(\mathsf{lab}) \end{array}}{(\mathsf{lab}, S, (m, l)) \xrightarrow{\text{lab: lhs = exp}} (\mathsf{lab}', S, (m', l'))}$$

The assignment statement is crucial to the behaviour of the AL: it ensures that object integrity is preserved during updating. Since assignments can transparently update a variable, a reference, an association or a containment, its behaviour must ensure the global consistency and the containment uniqueness property of models. Suppose an assignment statement lhs = exp evaluated in a domain $d \in \mathbb{D}$, for which expression exp evaluates to the value $v \in \mathbb{V}$, and left-hand side (LHS) lhs refers to the target $t \in \mathbb{T}$ whose type is $\mathsf{t} \in \mathsf{CType}$. The effect of the assignment depends on both the type and the nature of the LHS involved (Fleurey, 2006, Appendix A).

1. If the target's type is a DataType, it does not deal with containment and t's value is simply replaced by v after properly converting it in case of numerical values.
2. If it is not a DataType, then t represents an object o and there is two cases:
   a. $t \in \mathsf{LocalN}$ either t refers to a local name and the assignment has the usual effect of replacing the current object's value by the object denoted by v;
   b. $t = (o, \mathsf{p}) \in \mathbb{O} \times \mathsf{PropN}$ is a property access and it depends on the collection nature of p. The case without collection is depicted in Figure 8: in this case, v is assigned to t, the container of the previous object $x \overset{\Delta}{=} d(t)$ pointed by o is reset; and in case of bidirectional reference, the opposite property q is set to o to preserve consistency. If there is a collection, then this process is repeated to all objects within the collection.

The definition of the assignment function $[\![\bullet, \bullet]\!]$ reflects these remarks and addresses the situation with collection values: here, the update is done on each target object t' of all objects contained within the collection value v, i.e. $t' \overset{\Delta}{=} (o', opp(\mathsf{p})) \forall o' \in objs(v)$ where the function $objs_{\mathsf{MM}} : \mathbb{V} \to \wp(\mathbb{O})$ retrieves all objects contained in a collection value and $[\![t, v]\!]_{Conv}$ adequately converts numerical values if necessary.

$$[\![\bullet, \bullet]\!] : \mathsf{Lhs} \times \mathsf{Exp} \to \mathbb{D} \to \mathbb{D}$$

$$(\mathsf{lhs}, \mathsf{exp})(d) \mapsto \begin{cases} d[t \mapsto [\![t, v]\!]_{Conv}] & \text{if (1)} \\ d[t \mapsto (v)] & \text{if (a)} \\ d\left[\begin{array}{l|l} t & v \\ t' & (\_, o) \\ x & (\_, \bot) \end{array}\right] & \text{if (b)} \end{cases}$$

Figure 8. Assignment of objects in a reference (Dashed/plain arrows represent the situation before/after assignment)

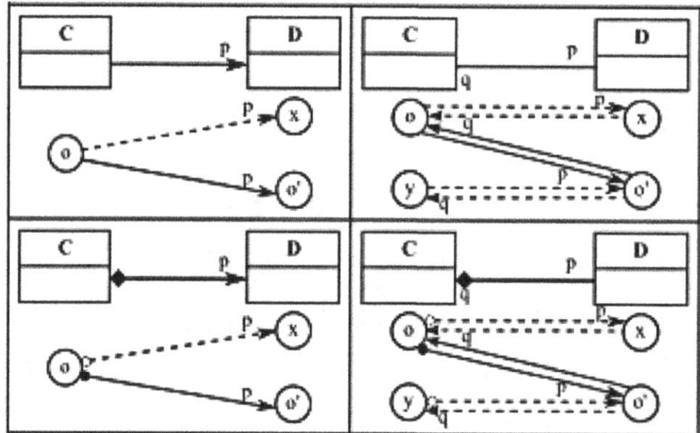

Related Works

We review here contributions addressing the formal specification of transformation languages, with similar or different approaches than Kermeta's AL. For techniques and methodologies concerning DSL semantics specification, we refer the reader to the *Motivation* Section.

A first level of work concerns the formalisation of Kermeta. Fleurey (2006) outlined in his pioneering work about Kermeta almost the same AL subset as ours. Nevertheless, his work is questionable in several outcomes: the structuring concepts used for the AL lacks a formal counterpart; he uses a big-step semantics, which is not directly executable; and his AL subset lacks a formal type system.

A second level relates other metamodelling frameworks that use the weaving technique for enriching a structural language with transformation capabilities. For example, the MOF Action Language (Paige, Kolovos & Polack, 2006) equips MOF with an Action Semantics that shares some constructions with Kermeta, but uses an event-based mechanism, which is more general that operation calls. Similarly, XOCL (Clark, Evans, Sammut & Willans, 2008) enriches OCL with executability facilities, coming up with a convenient framework for expressing several kinds of transformations, among which DSL semantics. Several Action Languages are available for UML (which is now considered as a MOF metamodel by the OMG), among which the best known are the Action Specification Language (ASL) (Kennedy Carter Ltd, 2000) and the Specification and Description Language (SDL) (International Telecommunication Union, 1999). Semantics for this kind of languages also frequently uses Action Semantics and State Machines, they are reviewed by Yang, Michaelson, and Pooley (2008), which also provide their own semantics.

A last level concerns the use of external formalisms for expressing transformations, and *a fortiori* DSL semantics. Usually, these formalisms are already executable, and they directly benefit from previously developed verifications capabilities that can be easily adapted for analysing DSLs and their behaviour. Without being exhaustive because it is impossible, we refer, as a witness, to some contributions within each tendency. Graph-Based Transformations beneficiate of solid formal foundations based on Category Theory (Rozenberg, 1997), allow a natural expression of behavioural DSL semantics, usually written in the same concrete syntax used for specifying models. It is possible to perform model-checking and reachability analysis, as well as ensuring basic properties of transformations, such as confluence and termination. Nevertheless, some usual metamodelling features, such as containment and inheritance, were addressed only recently (Jurack & Taentzer, 2010). We already mentioned the work of deLara and Vangheluwe (2010) about Petri Nets. Abstract State Machines (ASMs), with foundations in algebraic specifications, is another major trend: it covers the whole metamodelling engineering process, and open various possibilities of analysis, such as model and scenario validation, and model-checking. An overview is given in chapter 8. An overview of techniques and analysis possibilities are surveyed by Combemale, Crégut, Garoche, and Thirioux (2009), who propose to validate DSL semantics with respect to a reference DSL semantics on which simulation proofs are established using the Coq theorem-prover.

PERSPECTIVES AND FUTURE RESEARCH DIRECTIONS

The formal specification presented in this chapter can serve as a reference documentation for engineers, researchers and more generally any Kermeta user, as well as a reference to compare different implementations. When specifying such a semantics, one always has to deal with ambiguities and under-specifications in official documentation. Many discussions with members of the Triskell team as well as several experiments conducted on the platform itself helped us to apprehend and gain insight about Kermeta's languages. For example, extending the from clause already used for operations was a discussed natural simple choice required in order to have a full static type-checking.

To further enforce our confidence in the structural part's specification, which can serve for any MOF-like language, and is the basis for the Action Language, we implemented it very early in Z (Spivey, 1992), together with a small example that covers all syntactic constructs. It took approximatively one week for an expert to read, understand and implement the specification and the example, and three days to fully achieve the conformance proof (Amrani & Amàlio, 2011). Several lessons were learned. First, selecting Z was a natural choice regarding the gap between its language and the fully mathematical specification. Second, as expected, implementing some parts of the specification described with classical computer science formalisms irremediably suffer from the accidental complexity of the chosen tool: Z lacks a proper specification for strings and we therefore used named identifiers, with the extra burden of adding constraints to ensure names' unicity over the different name sorts; the type algebra (corresponding to MType) required the use of free types, which are difficult to manipulate when writing the example by hand. Some structural components, like coupled opposite references, were better represented in a way that does not strictly follow the specification to take advantage of Z relation definitions as well as to overcome the well-formedness constraints specific to attributes and references. This point actually illustrates perfectly the purpose of this work: the specification is tool-agnostic, but it can be sometimes clever to take advantage of built-in or slightly different representations. Finally, Z/EVE, the associated prover we used, does not offer specialised proof tactics and strategies that are a key point for the conformance proof that heavily relies on definition expansions; we think we can benefit from more specialised theorem-provers.

We are now investigating the full implementation of this specification in Maude (Clavel et al., 2007). Maude is already used in several projects and initiatives in the MDE arena (Boronat & Meseguer, 2008; Rivera, 2010) but not specifically for Kermeta. The idea of formalising complete languages is not new: it already exists for several languages, among which Java, CSS, Prolog (Clavel et al., 2007) and more recently, C (Ellison & Rosu, 2011). Using Maude offers several substantial advantages. First, it is directly executable from the specification itself. Second, Maude permits several kinds of analysis: reachability and model-checking, as well as theorem-proving. Since we explicitly target model-checking of behavioural properties, it is an ideal candidate.

CONCLUSION

DSMLs is at the core of the Model-Driven Engineering approach, by advocating an intensive use of DSLs for targeting a given expertise domain. Since this approach gains importance and tends to be used even for safety critical and embedded applications, ensuring the correct specification of DSLs semantics becomes a natural challenge for ensuring adequate communication between different modelling tools and enabling the formal verification of such applications.

In this chapter, we contribute with the formal specification of Kermeta, a popular metamodelling framework. Two languages compose Kermeta: a Structural Language, aligned on the OMG standard MOF, used for defining the DSL's metamodel, i.e. the concepts and their relationships as well as the underlying business rules governing them; and an Action Language, based on object-orientation, a popular and powerful paradigm, used for defining transformations, and in the context of DSLs, their semantics. The formal specification is tool/syntax independent, it only uses classical mathematical instruments taught in usual computer science courses: set theory and rewriting rules in Sos style. This specification serves as a reference specification from which specialised implementation can be derived, and for which proper abstractions and optimisations can be derived, depending on a particular use, for achieving various analysis. By providing a formal specification of Kermeta, we ensure that each and every DSL written in Kermeta, using our core AL, receives *de facto* a formal counterpart, making its definition fully formal. This radically contrasts with other approaches, where each new DSL requires the definition of a new *ad hoc* semantics, often written in a third-party formal language.

We sketched the potential benefits of such a contribution, among which the possibility to consider this work as a reference implementation that encompasses every MOF-like structural language (thus covering a relevant part of the UML class diagrams language) and for many action languages weaved into the structural language to allow transformations. We briefly reviewed two possible implementations. First, a Z implementation, conducted to ensure our specification was correct and well-formed. We provided simple example of the fact that a tool-independent formalisation avoids tackling essential complexity from the tool itself. Second, we are currently implementing a more ambitious implementation in Maude. Since Maude offers natively model-checking and theorem-proving capabilities, we plan to use this framework for addressing formal verification analyses of behavioural properties.

ACKNOWLEDGMENT

This work is partially supported by the Luxemburgish Fonds National de la Recherche (Fnr). The author thanks Nuno Amàlio for reading an early draft of this work. The author would like to warmly thank the Triskell team, and especially Benoît Combemale for early very helpful discussions, and Didier Vojtisek for answering technical questions about Kermeta's languages; and we are grateful to Yves Le Traon for useful comments that led to a better presentation of the technical material.

REFERENCES

Abadi, M., & Cardelli, L. (1996). *A theory of objects*. New-York, NY: Springer. doi:10.1007/978-1-4419-8598-9

Aho, A., Sethi, R., & Ullman, J. (1986). *Compilers: Principles, techniques & tools*. Boston, MA: Addison-Wesley.

Amrani, M. (2012). *A Formal Semantics of Kermeta*. Technical Report. Luxembourg: University of Luxembourg.

Amrani, M., & Amàlio, N. (2011). *A set-theoretic formal specification of the semantics of Kermeta (Technical Report No. Tr-Lassy-11-03)*. Luxembourg: University of Luxembourg.

Amrani, M., & Lúcio, L. Selim. G., Combemale, B., Dingel, J., Vangheluwe, H., Le Traon, Y., & Cordy, J. (2012). A tridimensional approach for studying the formal verification of model transformations. In *Proceedings of the First Workshop on Verification and Validation of Model Transformations* (Volt). (to appear)

Arendt, T., Biermann, E., Jurack, S., Krause, C., & Taentzer, G. (2010). Henshin: Advanced concepts and tools for in-place EMF model transformations. In Petriu, D. C., Rouquette, N., & Haugen, Ø. (Eds.), *Model Driven Engineering Languages and Systems (MoDELS)* (*Vol. 6394*, pp. 121–135). Lecture Notes in Computer Science Berlin, Germany: Springer. doi:10.1007/978-3-642-16145-2_9

Biermann, E., Ermel, C., & Taentzer, G. (2008). Precise semantics of EMF model transformations by graph transformation. In Czarnecki, K., Ober, I., Bruel, J.-M., Uhl, A., & Völter, M. (Eds.), *Model Driven Engineering Languages and Systems (MoDELS)* (*Vol. 5301*, pp. 53–67). Lecture Notes in Computer Science Berlin, Germany: Springer-Verlag. doi:10.1007/978-3-540-87875-9_4

Börger, E., & Stärk, R. (2003). *Abstract state machines: A method for high-level system design and analysis*. Berlin, Germany: Springer-Verlag. doi:10.1007/978-1-84882-736-3_3

Boronat, A. (2007). *MoMent: A formal framework for MOdel manageMENT* (Ph.D. Doctoral Dissertation), University of Valencia, Spain.

Boronat, A., & Meseguer, J. (2008). An algebraic semantics for MOF. In Fiadeiro, J. L., & Inverardi, P. (Eds.), *Fundamental Approaches to Software Engineering (Fase)* (*Vol. 4961*, pp. 377–391). Lecture Notes in Computer Science Berlin, Germany: Springer-Verlag. doi:10.1007/978-3-540-78743-3_28

Bryant, B., Gray, J., Mernik, M., Clarke, P., France, R., & Karsai, G. (2011). Challenges and directions in formalizing the semantics of modeling languages. *Journal of Computer Science and Information Systems*, *8*(2), 225–253. doi:10.2298/CSIS110114012B

Cardelli, L. (2004). Type systems. In Tucker, A. B. (Ed.), *The computer science and engineering handbook*. Boca Raton, FL: CRC Press.

Castagna, G., & Xu, Z. (2011). *Set-theoretic foundation of parametric polymorphism and subtyping*. In 16th ACM SigPlan International Conference on Functional Programming. Tokyo, Japan.

Chen, K., Sztipanovits, J., Abdelwahed, S., & Jackson, E. (2005). Semantic anchoring with model transformation. In *Proceedings of Model-Driven Architecture* (*Vol. 3748*, pp. 115–129). Nuremberg, Germany: Foundations and Applications.

Clark, T., Evans, A., Sammut, P., & Willans, J. (2008). *Applied metamodelling – A foundation for language-driven development*. Sheffield, UK: Ceteva.

Clavel, M., Duran, F., Eker, S., Lincoln, P., Marti-Oliet, N., & Meseguer, J. (2007). *All about Maude. A high-performance logical framework*. Berlin, Germany: Springer.

Combemale, B., Crégut, X., Garoche, P.-L., & Thirioux, X. (2009, November). Essay on semantics definition in MDE: An instrumented approach for model verification. *Journal of Software*, *4*(9), 943–958. doi:10.4304/jsw.4.9.943-958

de Lara, J., & Vangheluwe, H. (2010). Automating the transformation-based analysis of visual languages. *Formal Aspects of Computing*, *22*(3–4), 297–326. doi:10.1007/s00165-009-0114-y

de Lara, J., & Vangheluwe, H. (2002). Using Atom^3 as a meta-case tool. In *Proceedings of Fourth International Conference on Enterprise Information Systems* (Iceis): Vol. 2. (pp. 642 – 649). Berlin, Germany: Springer.

Drey, Z., Faucher, C., Fleurey, F., Mahé, V., & Vojtisek, D. (2009). *The Kermeta language — Reference manual*. (Technical Report) University of Rennes, France. Retrieved from http://kermeta.org/documents/user_doc/manual/

Drossopoulou, S., Eisenbach, S., & Khurshid, S. (1999). Is the Java type system sound? *Journal of Theory and Practice of Object Systems (Tapos)*, *5*(1), 3–24. doi:10.1002/(SICI)1096-9942(199901/03)5:1<3::AID-TAPO2>3.0.CO;2-T

Ehrig, H., & Mahr, B. (1985). Fundamentals of algebraic specifications. In Brauer, W., Rozenberg, G., & Salomaa, A. (Eds.), *Monographs in Theoretical Computer Science: An EATCS Series* (*Vol. 6*). Berlin, Germany: Springer-Verlag.

Ellison, C. M., & Rosu, G. (2012). An Executable Formal Semantics of C with Applications. In J. Field & M. Hicks (Eds.), *Proceedings of the 39th Acm Sigplan-Sigact Symposium on Principles of Programming Languages (POPL)* (pp. 533–544). New York, NY: Association for Computing Machinery.

Fleurey, F. (2006). *Langage et methode pour une ingenierie des modeles fiable* [Language and Method for Trustable Modelling Engineering]. (Ph.D. Doctoral Dissertation) University of Rennes, France.

Gargantini, A., Riccobene, E., & Scandurra, P. (2008). Model-driven language engineering: The ASMETA case study. In *Proceedings of the Third International Conference on Software Engineering Advances* (*ICSEA*) (pp. 373–378). Washington, DC: IEEE Computer Society.

Gargantini, A., Riccobene, E., & Scandurra, P. (2009). A semantic framework for metamodel-based languages. *Automated Software Engineering*, *16*(3–4), 415–454. doi:10.1007/s10515-009-0053-0

Harel, D., & Rumpe, B. (2004). Meaningful modelling: What's the semantics of "semantics"? *IEEE Computer*, *37*(1), 64–72. doi:10.1109/MC.2004.172

International Telecommunication Union. (1999). *Specification and description language*. (Technical Report No. Z-100). Geneva, Switzerland: International Telecommunication Union.

Jurack, S., & Taentzer, G. (2010). A component concept for typed graphs with inheritance and containment structures. In Ehrig, H., Rensink, A., Rozenberg, G., & Schürr, A. (Eds.), *Graph Transformations (ICGT)* (*Vol. 6372*, pp. 187–202). Lecture Notes in Computer Science Berlin, Germany: Springer. doi:10.1007/978-3-642-15928-2_13

Kennedy Carter Ltd. (2000). *UML ASL reference guide, ASL language level 2.5" manual. Guilford*. UK: Kennedy Carter.

Krishnan, P. (2000). Consistency checks for UML. In *Proceedings of the Seventh Asia-Pacific Software Engineering Conference (APSEC)* (pp. 162–171). Washington, DC: IEEE Computer Society.

Meyer, B. (1997). *Object-oriented software construction* (2nd ed.). Upper Saddle River, NJ: Prentice Hall.

Muller, P.-A., Fleurey, F., & Jézéquel, J.-M. (2005). Weaving executability into object-oriented meta-languages. In Briand, L. C., & Williams, C. (Eds.), *Model Driven Engineering Languages and Systems (MoDELS)* (*Vol. 3713*, pp. 264–278). Lecture Notes in Computer Science Berlin, Germany: Springer. doi:10.1007/11557432_19

Object Management Group. (2006). *Meta-object facility (MOF) v2.0 core specification. (OMG Document No. formal/2006-01-01)*. Object Management Group.

Object Management Group. (2010). *Object constraint language (OCL) v2.0 specification. (OMG Document No. formal/2006-05-01)*. Object Management Group.

Paige, R., Kolovos, D., & Polack, F. (2006). An action semantics for MOF 2.0. In H. Haddad (Ed.), *ACM Symposium on Applied Computing* (SAC) (pp. 1304–1305). New York, NY: Association for Computing Machinery.

Poernomo, I. (2006). The meta-object facility (MOF) typed. In H. Haddad (Ed.), *Proceedings of the ACM Symposium on Applied Computing* (SAC) (pp. 1845–1849). New York, NY: Association for Computing Machinery.

Pollet, I. (2004). *Towards a generic framework for the abstract interpretation of Java*. (Ph.D. Doctoral Dissertation), Catholic University of Louvain, Belgium.

Reggio, G., Cerioli, M., & Astesiano, E. (2001). Towards a rigorous semantics of UML supporting its multiview approach. In Hußmann, H. (Ed.), *Fundamental Approaches to Software Engineering (FASE)* (*Vol. 2029*, pp. 171–186). Lecture Notes in Computer Science Berlin, Germany: Springer-Verlag. doi:10.1007/3-540-45314-8_13

Rivera, J. E. (2010). *On the semantics of real-time domain-specific modeling of languages*. (Ph.D. Doctoral Dissertation). University of Malaga, Spain.

Rivera, J. E., & Vallecillo, A. (2007). Adding behavioral semantics to models. In *Proceedings of the Eleven IEEE International Enterprise Distributed Object Computing Conference* (EDOC) (pp. 169–180). Washington, DC: Ieee Computer Society.

Rozenberg, G. (Ed.). (1997). Handbook of graph grammars and computing by graph transformation: *Vol. I. Foundations*. River Edge, NJ: World Scientific Publications.

Song, D., He, K., Liang, P., & Liu, W. (2005). A formal language for model transformation specification. In C. S. Chen, J. Filipe, I. Seruca, & J. Cordeiro (Eds.), *Proceedings of Seventh International Conference on Enterprise Information Systems* (ICEIS): Vol. 3, (pp. 429–433). Berlin, Germany: Springer.

Soon-Kyeong, K., & Carrington, D. (1999). Formalizing the UML class diagram using object-Z. In R. France & B. Rumpe (Eds.), *Lecture Notes in Computer Science: Vol. 1723, Second Conference on the Unified Modelling Language: Beyond the Standard* (pp. 83–98). Berlin, Germany: Springer-Verlag.

Spivey, J. M. (1992). *The Z notation: A reference manual*. Upper Saddle River, NJ: Prentice-Hall.

Stark, R. F., Borger, E., & Schmid, J. (2001). *Java and the Java virtual machine: Definition, verification, validation*. Berlin, Germany: Springer-Verlag.

Steinberg, D., Budinsky, F., Paternostro, M., & Merks, E. (2009). *EMF: Eclipse modeling framework 2.0*. Upper Saddle River, NJ: Addison-Wesley.

Winskel, G. (1993). *The formal semantics of programming languages: An introduction*. Cambridge, MA: Mit Press.

Yang, M., Michaelson, G., & Pooley, R. (2008). Formal action semantics for a UML action language. *Journal of Universal Computer Science*, *14*(21), 3608–3624.

ADDITIONAL READING

Baader, F., & Nipkow, T. (1998). *Term rewriting and all that*. New-York, NY: Cambridge University Press.

Baier, C., & Katoen, J.-P. (2008). *Principles of model-checking*. The MIT Press.

Cousot, P. (1998). Semantic foundations of program analysis. In Muchnick, S. S., & Jones, N. D. (Eds.), *Program flow analysis: Theory and applications* (pp. 303–342). Englewood Cliffs, NJ: Prentice Hall.

Cousot, P. (2002). Constructive design of a hierarchy of semantics of a transition system by abstract interpretation. *Journal of Theoretical Computer Science*, *277*(1-2), 47–103. doi:10.1016/S0304-3975(00)00313-3

Grumberg, O., & Veith, H. (Eds.). (2008). 25 years of model-checking – History, achievements, perspectives. In *Lecture Notes in Computer Science: Vol. 5000, Theoretical Computer Science and General Issues*. Berlin, Germany: Springer.

Jézéquel, J.-M., Combemale, B., & Guy, C. (2012). Model transformation reuse with model typing. In Lano, K., & Zschaler, S. (Eds.), *Composition and evolution of model transformations*. Berlin, Germany: Springer.

Kleppe, A. (2009). *Software language engineering: Creating domain-specific languages using metamodels*. Upper Saddle River, NJ: Addison-Wesley.

Nielson, F., Nielson, H. R., & Hankin, C. (1999). *Principles ofprogram analysis*. Berlin, Germany: Springer-Verlag.

Nielson, H. R., & Nielson, F. (1992). *Semantics with applications: A formal introduction*. Wiley Professional Computing.

Rodriguez-Priego, E., García-Izquierdo, F. J., & Luis Rubio, A. (2010). Modeling issues: A survival guide for a non-expert modeler. In Petriu, D. C., Rouquette, N., & Haugen, Ø. (Eds.), *Model Driven Engineering Languages and Systems (MoDELS)* (*Vol. 6395*, pp. 361–375). Lecture Notes in Computer Science Berlin, Germany: Springer. doi:10.1007/978-3-642-16129-2_26

Rusu, V. (2012). Embedding domain-specific modeling languages into Maude specifications. *Journal of Software and Systems Modeling* (SoSyM). (Preprint). Doi:10.1007/s10270-012-0232-5

KEY TERMS AND DEFINITIONS

BNF: Backus-Naur Form. A classical notation for describing language syntaxes in textual format. Strictly less powerful than the usual notation in MDE, metamodels.

DS(M)L: Domain-Specific (Modeling) Language. A concrete incarnation of the MDE approach. It favours high level abstraction and focuses on an expertise domain to achieve efficient automation.

Kermeta: A metamodeling framework allowing expressing model transformation through the use of an object-oriented Language, and based on the OMG standard MOF.

MDE: Model-Driven Engineering. A novel approach for software engineering advocating the use of models and model transformations in software development. Domain-Specific Modelling and Model-Driven Architecture are two incarnations of this approach.

(Meta-)Model: Model is at the centre of the MDE Approach. Metamodels are the *de facto* artefact in MDE for capturing abstract syntax of models. Metamodels are strictly more expressive than Bnf grammars. Models have to respect metamodel's definitions to be *conform*.

OMG: Object Management Group. Consortium of academics, engineers and industrial focused on the standardisation of languages and methodologies in favour of interoperability.

Rewriting System: System manipulating basic objects called *terms*, through the application of transformation rules that manipulate terms syntactically. Logical systems or operational semantics are common example of such systems.

Semantics: Meaning of a language traditionally expressed by means of a semantic domain. It always exists, at least in the language designer's mind, but has to be mathematically described for avoiding ambiguities. Three traditional techniques exist: axiomatic, operational or denotational.

Set-Theory: Branch of mathematics studying sets and their relationships, forming an universal language used in several computer science fields.

ENDNOTES

a The term usually used in MDE is ordered set, which is quite confusing: in set theory, an ordered set is a set equipped with an order on the element (i.e. a binary relation); whereas in the MDE vocabulary, an ordered set is a set where the elements are stored, or are accessible, in a certain order (which is not a traditional notion of set theory, since it is not usually concerned with computations over sets). This is why in this background, the more precise term "*sequence with unique representative*" is preferred.

b The MOF Specification (Object Management Group, 2006) comprises two parts: EMOF, (or Essential MOF) and CMOF (or Complete MOF). EMOF describes metamodels' syntax, making it a *meta-metamodel*. CMOF extends EMOF by explicitly defining what the OMG calls the "CMOF abstract semantics" (Object Management Group, 2006, §15), i.e. a language (always as a model) that describes models' syntax.

c For a discussion on how MOF actually deals with names, elements identifiers and constraints over names in a metamodel, the reader can refer to Specification Document (Object Management Group, 2006, §10, §12.4 and §12.5). For our concern, we strictly identify elements with their names, as Kermeta does. From now on, unless clearly specified, we will not distinguish between a metamodel's element and its name.

d The set $\mathbb{N}_\star$ is defined as $\mathbb{N}_\star \stackrel{\Delta}{=} \mathbb{N} \cup \{\star\}$ and equipped with the ordering relation $\leq$ defined by $\forall n, n' \in \mathbb{N}_\star, n \leq n' \Leftrightarrow (n' = \star) \vee (n \leq_{\mathbb{N}} n')$.

e Strictly speaking, this last constraint comes from Kermeta: "*Kermeta requires that every class that contains an abstract operation must be declared as an abstract class.*" (Drey et al., 2009, §2.8.2).

APPENDIX: Complete KERMETA Code for the FSM Example

```
package FSM;
  require kermeta
  using kermeta::standard
  enumeration Kind {NORMAL;START;STOP;}

  class Label{
     attribute label: String
  }

  // FSM assumes there is only one START and one FINAL State
  class FSM inherits Label{
    attribute alphabet: set String [1..*]
    reference states: seq State [1..*] #fsm
    reference transitions: seq Transition [0..*]#fsm

    operation getStart(): State is do
      var i : Integer init 0
      from i := 0 until i == states.size() or states.at(i).kind == Kind.START
loop
        i := i+1
      end
      if i == states.size() then
        result := void
      else
        result := self.states.at(i)
      end
    end

    operation getFinal(): State is do
      var i : Integer init 0
      from i := 0 until i == states.size() or states.at(i).kind == Kind.STOP
loop
        i := i+1
      end
      if i == states.size() then
        result := void
      else
        result := self.states.at(i)
      end
    end
```

```
    operation accept(word: seq String [0..*]) : Boolean is do
      var current: State init self.getStart()
      var final : State init self.getFinal()
      var toEval : seq String[0..*] init word
      var isNull : Boolean init false
      from var i : Integer init 0 until i == toEval.size() or isNull loop
        current := current.fire(toEval.at(i))
        if(current.isVoid) then
          isNull := true
        end
        i := i+1
      end
      result := (current == final)
    end
  }

  class State inherits Label{
    attribute kind: Kind
    reference fsm: FSM #states
    reference in: Transition [0..*] #tgt
    reference out: Transition [0..*] #src
    operation fire(letter: String): State [0..1] is do
      var trans: seq Transition [0..*] init self.out.asSequence()
      if(trans.isVoid) then
        result := void
      else
        var current: Transition init trans.at(0)
        from var i : Integer init 0 until i == trans.size() or trans.at(i).
label == letter loop
          i := i+1
        end
        if(current.isVoid) then
          result:= void
        else
          result:= current.tgt
        end
      end
    end
  }

class Transition inherits Label{
   reference fsm: FSM # transitions
   reference tgt: State [1..1] #in
   reference src: State [1..1] #out
}
```

Section 3
Domain-Specific Language Tools and Processes

Chapter 11
Software Language Engineering with XMF and XModeler

Tony Clark
Middlesex University, UK

James Willans
HSBC, UK

ABSTRACT

XMF and XModeler are presented as technologies that have been specifically designed for Software Language Engineering. XMF provides a meta-circular, extensible platform for DSL definition based on syntax-classes that extend object-oriented classes with composable grammars. XModeler is a development environment built on top of XMF that provides an extensible client-based architecture for developing DSL tools.

INTRODUCTION

Software Engineering is different from other Engineering disciplines, such as Civil, Electrical and Chemical. Traditional Engineering disciplines are based on a collection of well-understood, fixed rules that are the same for each new system. There is a single *formal system* that describes the elements of each discipline and how they work together to build systems. A Software Engineer is free to design a formal system for each new application. For example, a financial application executes in terms of elements and rules that are different from a telecom system or a car engine controller. Each new formal system leads to a *domain specific language* (DSL) that can represent a family of related systems.

Conventional software development requires that systems are implemented in a *general purpose language* (GPL) such as C or Java. A *language engineering approach* requires that the DSL is embedded in a GPL. Fortunately, even a minimal programming language has a surprising property that allows programs to be expressed as data to be

DOI: 10.4018/978-1-4666-2092-6.ch011

processed and executed by another program. This meta-ability that allows programs to be represented as data and *vice versa*, both differentiates Software Engineering from other Engineering disciplines and makes it possible for programming languages to process other programming languages.

The process of building languages is termed *Software Language Engineering* and requires a meta-technology that can build and process languages. A DSL can be *internal* if it is assimilated as part of the host language and *external* if it is stand-alone. Languages that support *Language Oriented Programming* (LOP) allow DSLs to be defined and to be integrated with the host language execution engine (whether external or internal). Languages for LOP offer a range of features that can process syntax from *concrete* to *abstract* and can embed new language structures into the execution cycle of the host language either by *desugaring* to the host language structures or by producing data that is subsequently processed by an interpreter written in the host language.

XMF and XModeler are tools that have been designed for Software Language Engineering. XMF is a programming language for LOP and XModeler is an IDE written in XMF on Eclipse for building XMF applications and domain specific modelling tools. XMF is bootstrapped and XModeler is constructed by using XMF-defined languages to control a small number of tool primitives for graphics, tree-browsing, property editing, menus and text editors.

XMF is bootstrapped using a self-describing meta-model that supports an arbitrary number of meta-class instances. The XMF meta-model includes higher-order functions (closures) that are extensively used to process syntax structures and provides a basic language based on an extension of the Object Constraint Language (OCL) that conveniently supports a range of list processing operations. The basic language provided by XMF can be changed by replacing the default grammar. Finally, the meta-model for XMF allows classes to be associated with extensible grammars to form *syntax-classes*.

A syntax-class defines how to transform delimited text (concrete syntax) into abstract syntax that is subsequently processed by the XMF execution engine. Once defined, a syntax-class can be used in any XMF program. It can be embedded as an internal language construct in expressions or included via an external file. Unlike many systems, grammars can refer to each other and new language constructs can refer to the host language thereby allowing the new construct to be interleaved with the host.

XMF and XModeler were developed as commercial products and successfully used on a range of customer projects including those for BAES, Citi-Group, Artisan Software and BT (Georgalas et al., 2004, 2005). They are both open-source[1] and form the basis of language engineering examples described in the widely cited e-books (Clark et al., 2008). These tools were independently evaluated (Helsen Ryman & Spinelli, 2008) as providing the highest-level of support for systems abstraction compared to other tools for software engineering and is regularly included in comparative studies of language engineering tools.

XMF and XModeler provide key technical solutions when implementing languages for SLE and LOP. XMF has been the basis for a number of DSL developments (Clark & Tratt, 2010; Clark & Tratt, 2009; Clark et al., 2008; Clark et al., 2004; Petrascu & Chiorean, 2010). The key contribution that these technologies make to DSL development is to apply a uniform, reflective approach to language engineering. The meta-level architecture of XMF is completely open and extensible, and data at all levels (values, types, syntax, meta-types, operations) is represented using a simple single meta-circular representation. This leads to a uniquely uniform software language engineering technology that is described in this chapter.

SOFTWARE LANGUAGE ENGINEERING WITH XMF

Our proposition is that Software Engineering is predominantly a Language Engineering based discipline. The definition of any new system involves the comprehension of several domains, including the problem and solution domains, and the ability to control one or more technology platforms so that they support a collection of desired computations.

The control of a technology platform involves the use of interfaces together associated data formats. The trade-off and interplay between interfaces and data allows data to be translated into operation calls and vice-versa. A language emerges when control occurs predominantly in terms of data rather than interface. A domain specific language occurs when a language is expressed in terms of the problem domain rather than the solution domain, leading to interesting translation issues.

Assuming that SLE is a viable approach, what constitutes a language? Figure 1 shows the key features of a language. Our claim is that XMF and XModeler provide a suitable platform for engineering these features; this section provides an overview of the features and describes how they are supported by XMF.

A language has *syntax* features for its human-centric and computer-centric representations. The *concrete* syntax of a textual language is defined using grammars; however, standard grammar technology tends to be used once whereas SLE requires the ability to construct modular language fragments that can be composed. The *abstract* syntax of a language is a model of its representation. A language has a *semantics*. The different types of semantics are described in more detail in (Clark et al., 2008), however a language must have a semantic *domain* that is a model of the things it denotes or computes. This chapter presents a language with an *operational* semantics, meaning that the language can be executed. A language may have a *graphical* representation in which case its abstract syntax must be mapped to graphical components that allow it to be rendered on the screen. Finally, a language must support interoperability through a *serialization* format, typically XML.

XMF and XModeler have been designed to support the features shown in Figure 1. XMF supports XCore that is an extensible meta-meta-model suitable for representing and manipulating languages. XCore is class-based and therefore supports abstract syntax models and allows concrete syntax to be defined by extending classes with modular extensible grammars to become *syntax-classes*. Semantic domains are created by using and extending the basic XCore classes. XMF provides a declarative extensible language called XOCL that can be used to add operational semantics to language features. XMF provides de-

Figure 1. Language features

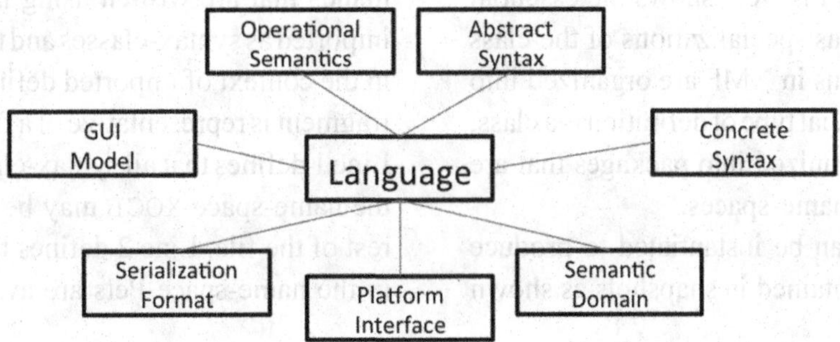

clarative mechanisms for producing and consuming a serialization formal of a language in XML.

XModeler provides a suite of extensible tool models that can be used as the basis of GUI models for languages. XModeler is also a rich technology platform and can be used to support a wide variety of language types either via its built-in libraries (HTML as shown in this chapter) or via a Java interface.

The rest of this section provides an overview of the key features of XMF that will be used to construct a simple language. The following section uses the features to construct a simple language and then XModeler is described and used to complete the language definition.

XMF consists of a collection of basic building blocks called XCore, a default extensible programming language called XOCL, and language definition features: syntax-classes, and XML processing. These features are described in the following subsections. XMF includes libraries for monitoring object state changes, data walkers, input-output, processing collections, generating documentation and Java integration, however these are beyond the scope of this chapter.

The XCore Meta-Model

XMF is built on a collection of concepts, called XCore, that are used to build languages and executable models. XMF and XCore are designed to be extensible and to support the development of tools; therefore XCore is meta-circular and is based on systems such as ObjVLisp (Cointe, 1987) and Smalltalk where there is a single unifying data type. Figure 2 shows the essential features of XCore as specializations of the class Element. Definitions in XMF are organized into name-spaces; a special type of definition is a class, and classes are organized into packages that are specializations of name-spaces.

XMF classes can be instantiated to produce objects that are contained in snapshots as shown in Figure 2. Classes contain operations as shown in Figure 3. The body of an operation is an instance of the abstract XCore class `Performable` that defines operations to both interpret and compile abstract syntax (Figure 4). The origins of XMF are in the UML 2.0 standardization process and its default programming language is an extension of the Object Constraint Language (OCL). When a message is sent to an XMF object, the operation with the message-name is found via the type of the object and its body (whether compiled or interpreted) is evaluated. XMF raises exceptions when errors occur and is multi-threaded. Threads are used in the implementation of GUI clients, as described in the section below on XModeler.

XMF provides support for language engineering via *syntax-classes*. A syntax-class is a normal class that contains a grammar. The grammar is used when the class is encountered as a language construct in source code as described in the next section. Figure 4 shows the structure of syntax classes in XCore. A grammar contains parse-rules called clauses each of which has a recognizer; sub-classes of recognizer form a regular-expression style language. Syntax-class grammars synthesize XCore elements as the parse progresses. Typically, a syntax-class will synthesize an instance of `Performable`.

The XOCL Programming Language

The previous section has provided an overview of the XCore element types that form part of the abstract-syntax of XOCL. XMF is file-based. Each file contains a collection of definitions and commands that are written using languages that are imported as syntax-classes and that are performed in the context of imported definitions. The code-fragment is representative of a file of XOCL code. Line 1 defines that all syntax-classes contained in the name-space `XOCL` may be referenced in the rest of the file. Line 2 defines that all definitions in the name-space Pets are available in the rest

Figure 2. The kernel of XCore

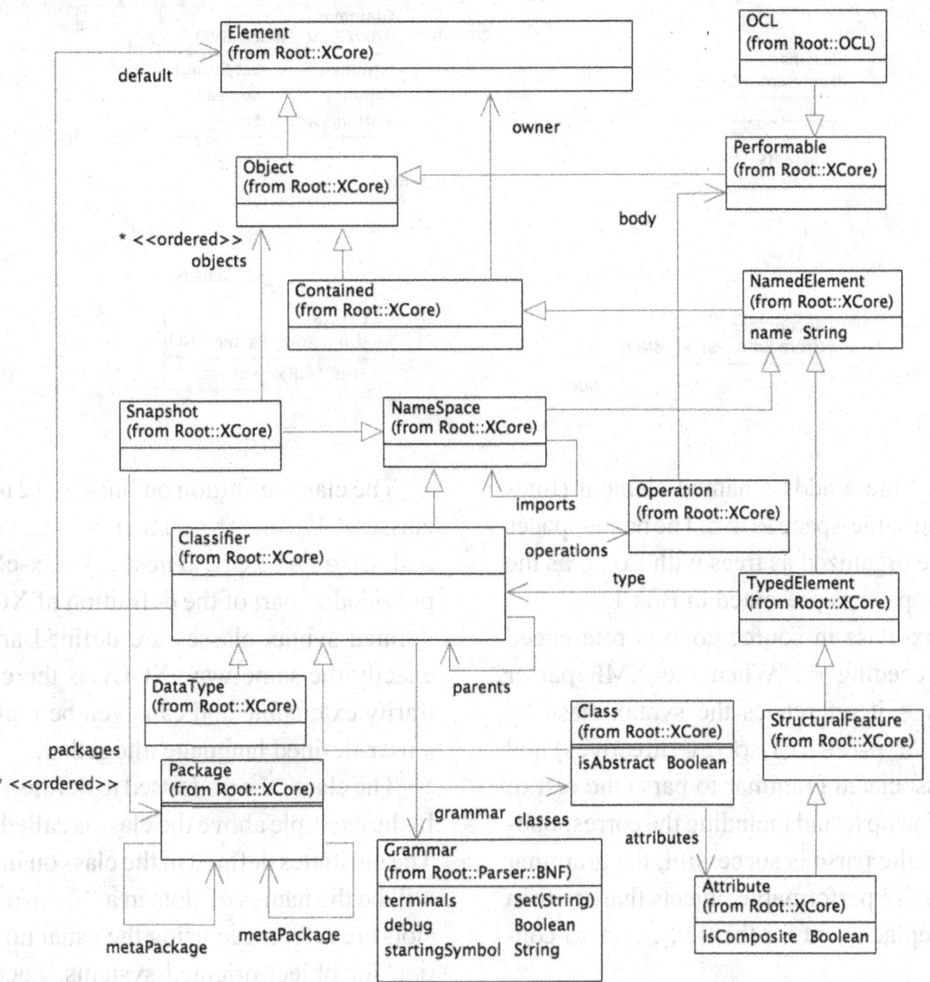

Figure 3. XCore behaviour

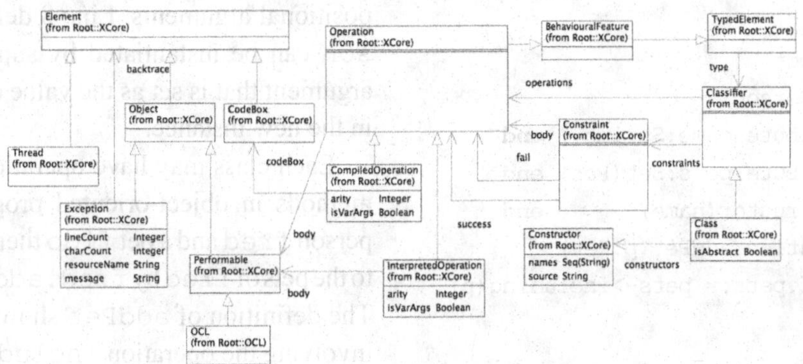

Figure 4. XCore syntax classes

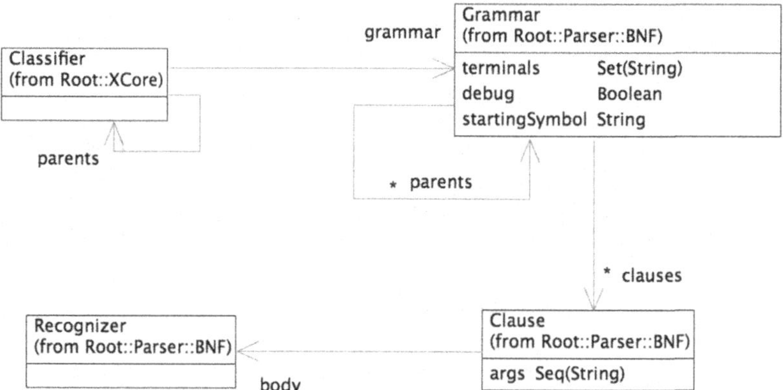

of the file. Line 4 adds a named-element (lines 5--12) to the name-space `Root`. The name-spaces in XMF are organized as trees with `Root` as the root-name-space as presented in Box 1.

A syntax-class in source code is referenced using a preceding `@`. When the XMF parser encounters `@` it references the syntax-class by name (via the `parserImport` directives) and uses the associated grammar to parse the rest of the definition up to and including the corresponding `end`. If the parse is successful, the grammar will synthesize performable objects that are then used as a replacement for the `@ ... end` construct.

Box 1.

```
(1)  parserImport XOCL;
(2)  import Pets;
(3)
(4)  context Root
(5)    @Class Person
(6)      @Attribute name:String      end
(7)      @Attribute pets:Set(Pet)    end
(8)      @Constructor(name)          end
(9)      @Operation addPet(p:Pet)
(10)       self.pets:= pets->including(p)
(11)     end
(12)   end
```

The class definition on lines 5--12 use syntax-classes `Class`, `Attribute`, `Constructor` and `Operation`. These syntax-classes are provided as part of the definition of XOCL. User defined syntax-classes are defined and used in exactly the same way. XOCL is therefore, arbitrarily extensible and can even be replaced with a user-defined language altogether.

The class `Class` is used to define a new class. In the example above the class is called `Person`. The attributes defined in the class on lines 6 and 7 will be the names of slots in a `Person`-instance; slots are referenced using the usual infix '.' notation for object-oriented systems. Each attribute has a type that indicates the XCore data type of the slot-values.

Classes are instantiated by using them as operators as in `Person("Fred")`. Slot initialization is performed by finding a constructor in the class definition with the same number of positional arguments. Line 8 defines that `Person` can be instantiated by supplying a single argument that is set as the value of the name slot in the new instance.

Each class may have operations that act like methods in object-oriented programs. Given a person `fred` and a pet `fido` then `fido` is added to the pets of `fred` by `fred.addPet(fido)`. The definition of `addPet` shows an expression involving the operation `including`. This is an

Figure 5. Definition of NotNull syntax class

```
parserImport XOCL, Parser::BNF;

import OCL, XOCL;

context XOCL
  @Class NotNull extends Sugar
    @Attribute exp          : String (?,!)        end
    @Attribute name         : String (?,!)        end
    @Attribute isMessage    : Boolean (?,!)       end
    @Attribute args         : Seq(Performable)    end
    @Attribute alt          : Performable (?,!) end
    @Constructor(exp,name,alt) end
    @Constructor(exp,name,args,alt) self.isMessage := true end
    @Grammar extends OCL
      NotNull ::= '[' e = Exp ']' '.' n = Name NotNullTail^(e,n).
      NotNullTail(e,n) ::=
        '(' as = NotNullArgs ')' x = NotNullElse { NotNull(e,n,as,x) }
      | x = NotNullElse { NotNull(e,n,x) }.
      NotNullArgs ::= e = Exp es = (',' Exp)* { Seq{e|es} } | { Seq{} }.
      NotNullElse ::= 'else' Exp | { [| null |] }.
    end
    @Operation desugar():Performable
      [| let notNullValue = <exp>
         in if notNullValue = null
            then <alt>
            else <if isMessage
                  then Send([| notNullValue |],name,args)
                  else [| notNullValue.<name> |]
                  end>
            end
         end
      |]
    end
  end
```

example a built-in collection operation provided by XMF. All of the OCL operations are provided in addition to many more defined as syntax-classes (see below), see the book (Clark et al., Superlanguages, 2008) for more detail.

Class definitions include a number of optional modifiers in XMF. For example the use of ? and ! in an attribute definition automatically generates operations for querying and setting slots in instances of the class.

Classes are collected together into packages. These technologies are used to construct abstract syntax and semantic domains. Since XMF is meta-circular via XCore (classes such as `Person` are objects just like `fred` and `fido`) it is possible to use XCore as the semantic domain of both a language and of language-engineering.

Syntax Classes

XMF allows any class to be extended with a grammar. The class then defines a new syntax construct that is completely integrated into the base language of XMF. Any number of classes can be added in this way and new syntax-classes can build on existing syntax classes.

A grammar is added to a class by providing the grammar definition in-line with the class definition or by adding the grammar to the class using a `context` definition. The concrete syntax for a grammar definition is based on BNF and is introduced by examples below. The grammar of a syntax-class must synthesize code. This can be achieved using the constructors of sub-classes of `Performable`, however this rapidly gets very complex. XMF provides quasi-quotes [| and |] as

Box 2.

```
If(BinExp(Var("x"),"=",Int(10)),Dot(Var("o"),"a"),Dot(Var("o"),"b")))
```

Box 3.

```
[| if x = 10 then o.a else o.b end |]
@Operation mkref(test:Performable,object:Performable,field1:String,field2:String)
  If(test,Dot(object,field1),Dot(object,field2))
end
```

Box 4.

```
@Operation mkref(test:Performable,object:Performable,field1:String,field2:String)
  [| if <test> then <object>.<field1> else <object>.<field2> end |]
end
```

an alternative syntax construction mechanism. For example, if we want to construct the expression `if x = 10 then o.a else o.b end` then we can use constructors for XOCL classes as presented in Box 2.

If the XOCL expression is typed into a running XMF system, it returns a value of type `Performable` which is another XOCL expression. Since XMF provides a complete model of the XOCL syntax (extended each time a new syntax-class is added) then program expressions and definitions are also program values. The same expression can be constructed by typing the following expression using quasi-quotes as presented in Box 3:

The utility of quasi-quotes becomes apparent when constructing non-literal expressions using drop-quotes < and >. For example suppose we want an operation that constructs a conditional expression to perform a field reference on the same object as demonstrated in Box 4.

Compared to using nested drop-quotes inside quasi-quotes as presented in Box 5.

Quasi-quotes make code-templates such as `mkref` more readable, especially when the code becomes large. Quasi-quotes and drop-quotes can be nested arbitrarily with the expected meaning. Quasi-quotes are especially useful when defining syntax-classes. A syntax-class includes a grammar definition that describes how to process a concrete syntax occurrence of the language feature. Support we want to implement a new class that doubles the value of an expression `@Double e end`. A syntax class can be defined as presented in Box 6.

The grammar extends XOCL and thereby provides access to the rule named `exp` that parses all XOCL expressions. A grammar consists of a collection of parse-rules and a syntax-class must define a parse-rule with the same name as the class. The rule `Double` processes an exp that it will refer to using the name `e` and then expects to find the keyword `end` in the input stream (since there is no more required input). Each parse-rule synthesizes a value using an expression delimited by braces. The `Double` rule synthesizes a binary expression. The equivalent definition using quasi-quotes is:

As you can see, the expression within the quasi-quotes looks familiar with the exception of the drop-quotes surrounding e because we want

Box 5.

```
@Class Double
  @Grammar extends OCL
    Double::= e=exp { BinExp(e,"*",IntExp(2)) }.
  end
```

Box 6.

```
@Class Double
  @Grammar extends OCL
    Double::= e=exp { [| <e> * 2 |] }.
  end
```

to *drop* the expression that is the value of e *into* the binary expression.

The following is a more realistic example of a syntax-class that implements a simple guarded expression:

```
@NotNull [e1].m(e2,e3,e4)
 else e5
end
```

Where e1 evaluates to produce an object to which we want to send the message m with args e2, e3 and e4. However, e1 might produce null in which case we don't want to send the message, we want to do e5 instead. This language construct is implemented in Figure 5.

NotNull extends Sugar which itself is a sub-class of Performable. Therefore an instance of NotNull is syntax and must implement the performable interface required by the XMF interpreter and compiler. Sugar is a convenience class that redirects the performable interface via desugar. The implementation of desugar in NotNull returns code using quasi-quotes that checks whether the object is null before sending the message or referencing the field. The grammar definition in NotNull extends the OCL grammar and thereby imports all of the basic grammar-rule definitions. This provides the rule for Exp which is the top-level rule for all language constructs.

The syntax-class TableGet is another example where:

```
@TableGet x=t[k] do e
  else a
end
```

Table t is checked to see if it contains the key k. If so then variable x is bound to the value of the key in the table before performing expression e, otherwise expression a is performed.

```
@Operation desugar()
  self.lift()
end
```

Every element e in XCore provides the operation lift that returns an expression; when the expression is evaluated it will recreate the element e (including all the elements it contains). The class Syntax is a sub-class of Sugar that implements desugar as shown in Box 7.

Sub-classes of Syntax are constants when they are synthesized by a grammar. A sub-class of Syntax is Exp which is a wrapper for an arbitrary expression. Typically an expression will contain variables that must be associated with values before the expression can be evaluated. The class Exp provides an operation keyApply that is supplied with an environment of variable-value pairs and returns the value of the expression for example the following produces the value 2:

This brief overview has shown how class definitions can be extended with grammars.

Box 7.

```
Exp([| x + 1 |]).keyApply(Seq{Seq{"x" | 1}})
```

Grammars can synthesize syntax because XMF provides access to the model of XOCL. Since, the XOCL model is extensible, new language features can be added and new functionality can be added to existing syntax classes. Therefore, XMF provides support for engineering both concrete and abstract syntax.

XML Processing

DSLs are often implemented in XML because, although it is verbose, it provides a universal extensible concrete syntax that does not require sophisticated parsing engines. An XML document is a tree consisting of nested elements of the form: `<TAG ATT=VAL ...> CHILD ... </TAG>`. Each element has a tag that determines its type; several attribute-value pairs and can contain any number of child elements.

XML-implemented DSLs are attractive because the concrete and abstract syntax representations for element of a language are in one-to-one correspondence. Whilst this is verbose and difficult to read for a human, it is perfect for machine processing. Therefore, XMF provides support for languages represented in XML by providing XOCL language constructs for producing and consuming XML. The language construct `@XML` defined in the package `XML::PrintXML` is used to generate XML:

```
parserImport XML::PrintXML;
@XML(out)
  <person name=p.name>
    @For c in p.children do
      @XML(out)
        <child name=c/>
      end
    end
  </person>
end
```

XML is consumed using a grammar that parses and synthesizes XML from an input channel. The grammar language closely resembles standard BNF where terminals are XML tags and attribute names. For example to process a document containing a person that was generated by the code fragment as demonstrated in Box 8.

Comparison with SLE Technologies

The previous sections have described the key features of XMF that can be used for text-based Software Language Engineering, and the features of XModeler that support graphical SLE.

There is a long history of technologies that support language engineering. These include parser generators such as YACC and JavaCC, Lisp macros, and meta-CASE tools developed in the 1980s such as the Ipsys Tool Builder. More recently there has been interest in DSLs and meta-modelling tools; this section reviews the key technologies and compares them to XMF and XModeler.

EMF is part of the Eclipse Modelling Project and provides a standard reflective interface over Java data to support model interchange and to place monitors on state changes. The meta-model for EMF, called ECore, is very similar to XCore except that XCore include behavioural aspects that are not present in EMF (although at the time of writing this is being added to EMF) and XCore is fully reflective. GMF is a similar technology for generating graphical tools from EMF models and provides similar features to XModeler although behavioural features must be programmed in Java.

Box 8.

```
parserImport XML::parser;
let grammar =
      @Grammar
         Person::= <person n=name> cs=Child* </person> { Person(n,cs) }.
         Child ::= <child n=name/> { n }.
      end then
    sin = StringInputChannel("<person name='fred'><child name='pebbles'/></
person>") then
    xml_in = ParserChannel(sin,grammar)
in xml_in.parse("Person")
end
```

MetaEdit+ is a CASE tool from MetaCase that allows the user to produce graphical modelling tools from tool models. The features of MetaEdit+ are more extensive than those of XModeler, however there is not equivalent of XMF for textual language engineering. It is unclear whether a purely graphical approach is sufficient for most applications.

The tool frameworks Visual Studio and Eclipse have similar aims to XModeler although their features are much more extensive and their aims are wider. Eclipse allows tools to be plugged in via a standard meta-interface that is supplied as a mixture of XML and Java. The Software Factories initiative from Microsoft aims to allow tools to be constructed using XML descriptions although it is unclear how successful this has been. The textual DSL initiative called Oslo from Microsoft aims to integrate DSLs with databases but development seems to have stopped. In all cases, frameworks provide much lower-level support for SLE and therefore place the burden of work on the developer whereas XMF and XModeler aim to provide dedicated technologies for SLE.

A number of technologies for textual Domain Specific Languages have emerged in recent years. These include MontiCore, XText, Stratego/XT and Spoofax. XText is representative of these technologies and provides a means for generating a language editor from a grammar definition. Editor support includes keyword highlighting and semantic processing such as type checking. These technologies are more advanced than XMF in terms of the language tools they produce, however none of them are integrated into a programming language in the way that XMF is into XOCL and within a tool set in the way that XModeler supports XMF. We believe that providing language tools integrated into a suitable programming framework is the correct architecture for SLE since this provides recourse to sophisticated language processing where required and also allows new tool support to be developed within the framework. An obvious development step for XMF would be to provide tool support for languages such as that provided by XText.

In conclusion, XMF and XModeler have been designed as a complete and tightly integrated set of technologies for SLE. Other technologies for SLE provide more sophisticated solutions for parts of the SLE process but are incomplete in terms of the language features shown in Figure 1. XMF and XModeler provide a useful reference for SLE technologies including XCore, XOCL, syntax-classes, XML grammars, tool modelling.

CASE STUDY

XMF is a platform for textual language engineering. Previous sections have described *XCore* which is the meta-circular kernel of XMF, *syntax classes*, that are used to transform classes into language features, the *XOCL language* that is used to define processing over XCore, and XML processing that is used as a *lingua franca* to implement languages that can interoperate with other systems.

The thesis proposed by this chapter is that Software Engineering is fundamentally a language engineering based discipline and that both XMF and its tool environment XModeler provide a suitable toolset for SLE. In order to show we will use a case study to establish our proposal. The language is not entirely new since parts of it have been described elsewhere, e.g. (Clark et al., Superlanguages, 2008), however, this chapter extends the existing descriptions of the case study by placing it into the context of SLE and including a description of language serialization and its tool support via XModeler.

The case study language consists of the following SLE features (definitions appearing elsewhere are noted with (E) and a brief overview is given in this chapter): concrete syntax (E); abstract syntax (E); semantics (E); XML processing; HTML processing; graphical tooling. This section reviews the existing material and subsequent sections complete the language definition.

The case study description is taken from (Clark et al., Superlanguages, 2008): An increasing number of interactive applications can be downloaded onto devices such as mobile phones, web-browsers and TV set-top boxes. The applications involve presenting the user with information, options, menus and buttons. The user typically enters information by typing text and choosing amongst alternatives. The user clicking a button or selecting from a menu generates an event. Once an event is generated an engine that services the interactive application processes the event, updates its internal state and then produces a new dialog to present to the user. We will investigate a specific type of such an application: a quiz.

```
@Model Quiz
  score: Integer;
  screen START()
   vertical
     text
       Welcome to the Quiz.
       Click the button to Start
     end
     button Start
      go Question1()
     end
   end
end
```

The case study involves a collection of possible languages. Firstly we need a language that will allow us to define how to logically present information to the user. Secondly we need a language of interaction between the user and the application. Thirdly, we need a language that can be used by the application to communicate with the system that renders the application on a screen. Finally, we need a low-level language that can be used to drive the basic technology platform that hosts the application. This section deals with the first two languages. XModeler is used as the host for the application and therefore the second two languages are described in the rest of the chapter.

A fragment of the concrete syntax for the proposed DSL is shown on the right. It is defined using a single syntax-class (as seen by the use of `@`). The definition includes a state variable (`score`) and a screen definition that describes the logical layout of some text and a button. When the button is pressed, control passed to the screen named `Question1` as presented in Box 9.

A question involves a number of options as shown on the right that sets the value of a variable (`Choice`) that can be referenced within the screen definition. If the user chooses the correct option then the global state variable score is updated.

Box 9.

```
screen Question1()
  vertical
    text Score: $score end
    text What is the capital of England? end
    options Choice
      option London;
      option Paris;
      option Madrid;
    end
   horizontal
    button Next
      if Choice = "London"
      then
        display
          text Well Done end
          button Next
            score:= score + 1;
            go Question2()
          end
        end
      else
        display
          text Wrong! Answer is London. end
          button Next go Question2() end
        end
       end
    end
    button Quit go Quit() end
  end
end
```

The case-study language must have a concrete and an abstract syntax. The abstract syntax models are defined as XMF classes as described in (Clark et al., Superlanguages, 2008), the concrete syntax is defined as an XMF grammar as shown in Figure 6. Notice that the language definition is layered by defining several different syntax-classes that extend each other. This feature of XMF allows languages to be modular, to be developed incrementally and to be reused.

The semantics of the interaction language is defined in XOCL by attaching operations to the abstract syntax classes. This is described in detail in (Clark et al., Superlanguages, 2008) and will not be considered further except to note that the definition of a new language feature `NotNull` that is given earlier in this chapter is used when making a transition between screens as presented in Box 10.

Our language currently bound to XMF because, although the definitions are given in text, the

Figure 6. Concrete syntax definition

```
context Action
  @Grammar extends OCL
    Action ::= UpdateProperty | IfAction | Go | DisplayScreen.
    UpdateProperty ::= n = Name ':=' e = LogicalExp ';' { Update(n,Exp(e,e.FV()->asSeq,null)) }.
    Go ::= 'go' n = Name '(' as = GoArgs ')' { Go(n,as) }.
    GoArgs ::= e = GoArg es = (',' GoArg)* { Seq{e|es} } | { Seq{} }.
    GoArg ::= e = LogicalExp { Exp(e) }.
    IfAction ::= 'if' e = LogicalExp 'then' d1 = Action 'else' d2 = Action 'end' {
      If(Exp(e,e.FV()->asSeq,null),d1,d2)
    }.
  end

context Display
  @Grammar extends Action, OCL
    Display ::= Text | Button | Options | Horizontal | Vertical.
    DisplayScreen ::= 'display' ms = Menu* ds = Display* 'end' { DisplayScreen(ms,ds) }.
    Text ::= 'text' t = (Not('end') Char)* 'end' { Text(Exp(t.asString().lift())) }.
    Button ::= 'button' n = ComputedName as = Action* 'end' { Button(n,as) }.
    ComputedName ::= n = Name { Exp(n.lift()) } | e = LogicalExp { Exp(e) }.
    Options ::= 'options' n = ComputedName os = Option* 'end' { Options(n,os) }.
    Option ::= 'option' n = Name ';' { n }.
    Horizontal ::= 'horizontal' ds = Display* 'end' { Horizontal(ds) }.
    Vertical ::= 'vertical' ds = Display* 'end' { Vertical(ds) }.
  end

context Screen
  @Grammar extends Display
    Screen ::= 'screen' n = Name '(' as = ScreenArgs ')' ds = Display* 'end' {
      Screen(n,as,DisplayScreen(ds))
    }.
    ScreenArgs ::= a = Name as = (',' Name)* { Seq{a|as} } | { Seq{} }.
  end

context Property
  @Grammar extends OCL
    Property ::= n = Name ':' e = Exp ';' { Property(n,e) }.
  end
```

format of the definitions is specific to the XMF technology. When defining a language, it must be possible to make the definitions written in the language interoperable using a suitable format. XML is an ideal candidate technology for interoperability and XMF provides a number of declarative mechanisms for working with XML. For example, the definitions of `display` above are attached to abstract syntax classes and specify how their instances are translated to XML. The text example shows how variables are substituted into the text. The button example shows how operations are registered in a table called `engine` that can be processed when an event with the associated ID is received (Figure 6).

The final language considered by this section is the language of events. When a user interacts with a GUI that has been produced from the application language, the event is encoded using a specific language definition. The *event-statements* include an identifier that can be decoded by the application and associated with a handler that has been registered in the engine (for example see the `Button` example above). The following is an example of an event-statement: `?Choice=London&BUTTON=Next` that is processed by XMF using the following grammar and associated operation presented in Box 11.

Box 10.

```
@Operation go(screen:String,args:Seq(Element),engine:Engine,out:OutputChannel)
  @NotNull [model.indexScreensByName(screen,null)].
display(self,args,engine,out)
    else self.error("No screen called " + screen)
  end
end
context Text
  @Operation display(instance,env,engine,out)
    @XML(out)
      <Text text=self.substRefs(exp.keyApply(env),instance)/>
    end
  end
context Button
  @Operation display(instance,env,engine,out)
    let id = exp.keyApply(env)
    in engine.registerActions(id,instance,env,actions);
      @XML(out)
        <Button name=id/>
      end
    end
  end
```

Box 11.

```
context Engine
  @Grammar
    EventString::= '?' e=Binding es=('&' Binding)* EOF {Seq{e|es}}.
    Binding::= n = Name '=' v = Name { Seq{n|v} }.
  end
context Engine
  @Operation getDisplay(event:String)
    let env = Engine.grammar.parseString(event,"EventString",Seq{}) then
        name = env->lookup("BUTTON")
    in @TableGet handler = idTable[name] do
         idTable.clear();
         handler(env)
       else self.error("No handler for " + name + " handlers = " + idTable.keys())
       end
    end
  end
```

Figure 7. Client architecture

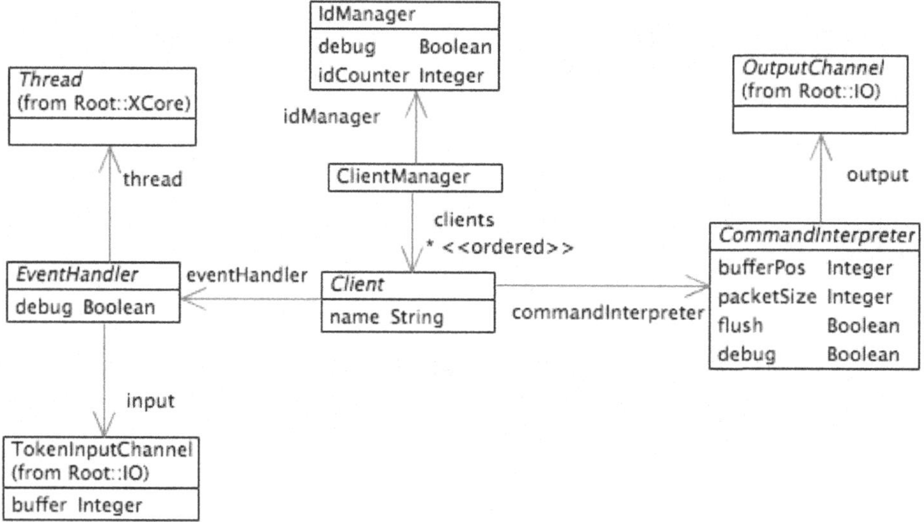

TOOL ENGINEERING WITH XMODELER

Previous sections have described XMF, its language system XOCL, how they support language engineering together with a case study for an interactive TV DSL that is implemented in XMF. XModeler is a platform that is layered on XMF to provide a collection of extensible tools for language engineering. XModeler is built using Eclipse in terms of a small collection of primitive libraries that support diagrams, form-based editors, tree browsers and text editors. Access to the libraries is provided to user code through the XOCL compiler, and used to construct a extensible tools as XOCL programs. This section describes the architecture of XModeler, provides an overview of the tools, and shows a specialization of a tool for the Interactive TV case study.

An Extensible Architecture

XModeler implements a collection of extensible clients, each of which is an interface to a fixed library that is implemented by Eclipse. A client is a two-way communication mechanism between XMF and the underlying Eclipse platform. Outgoing communication is performed using *commands* and incoming communication is implemented as *events*. Both commands and events are implemented as string encoded messages; each message has a name and contains a sequence of simple argument values. Commands cause the underlying platform to perform an action; events are mapped to messages sent to a handler that is registered with an appropriate client object in XMF.

Figure 7 shows the general client architecture. XMF manages a single instance of the class `ClientManager` that contains a collection of named clients; each client maps to a specific XModeler tool or service. The client manager also references an `IdManager` that holds a table associating XMF objects with unique identifiers that are allocated by the underlying Eclipse libraries. The identifiers allow both sides of the XModeler platform to keep in sync.

Each client implements a command interpreter and an event handler. The command interpreter receives commands from XMF code and delivers them to the underlying platform via an output channel. This is managed efficiently in terms of a shared buffer. The event handler runs

Figure 8. XModeler clients

Client	Commands	Events
Diagrams	delete, move, newBox, newDiagram, showDiagram, newEdge, newEdgeText,newNode, newPort, newRightClickMenu, newText, resize, setEdgeSource, setEdgeTarget, setText	delete, diagramOpen, edgeDeselected, edgeSelected, edgeSourceReconnected, edgeTargetReconnected, moveEdgeText, move, newEdge, newNode, nodeDeselected, nodeSelected, resizeNode, rightClickMenuSelected,textChanged, diagramClosed, focusGained, focusLost, textDimension, selected
Forms	newForm, addItem, addTableRow, addRule, changesMade, clear, clearForm, closeForm, delete, disable, enable, forceFocus, newButton, newCheckBox, newComboBox, newList, newTextBox, newText, setText, setEditable	buttonPressed, formClosed, focusGained, focusLost, lockForm, browseHistory, clearHistory, nextInHistory,previousInHistory, textChanged, resetText, getEditableText, setBoolean, deselected, selected, doubleSelected, expanded, rightClickMenuSelected, comboBoxSelection
ModelBrowser	deselectNode, expandNode, removeNode, newModelBrowser, addNode, addMenuItem, closeModelBrowser, removeNode, selectNode, setFocus, setNodeIcon, setToolTipText	modelBrowserClosed, focusGained, focusLost, textChanged, deselected, selected, doubleSelected, expanded,rightClickMenuSelected
TextEditor	addLineHighlight, addMultilineRule, addWordRule, delete, clearHighlights, getCursorPosition, getText, getTextAt, newBrowser, newRightClickMenu, newOleEditor, newTextEditor, saveAs, setCursorPosition, setClean, setFocus, setName, setText, setTextAt, setUrl, showLine, setDirty	rightClickMenuSelected, urlRequest, editorText, textClosed, textDirty, focusGained, focusLost, saveText, oleClosed

Figure 9. Diagram elements

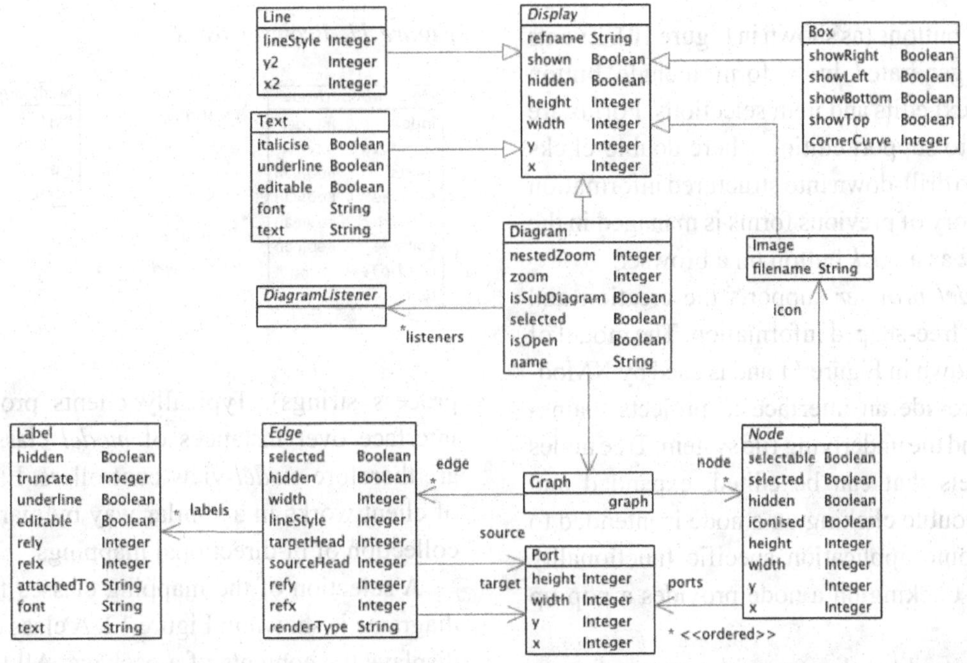

in its own XMF thread and waits to receive events from the underlying platform. When the event is received on an input channel, the handler dispatches to an appropriate XMF operation.

Figure 8 shows commands and events that are processed by the four main XModeler tool clients. The diagrams client manages graphs whose nodes are associated with display elements including boxes and text (shown in Figure 9), and whose edges are labelled lines with way-points. Nodes contain ports that are connection points for edges. A diagram exists in selection or creation modes, where creation mode generates `newEdge` or `newNode` events that contain edge and node type information based on a palette of types that are displayed as part of the diagram.

A *form* is a property editor that presents text fields, pull-down selections, lists of selectable

Figure 10. Forms

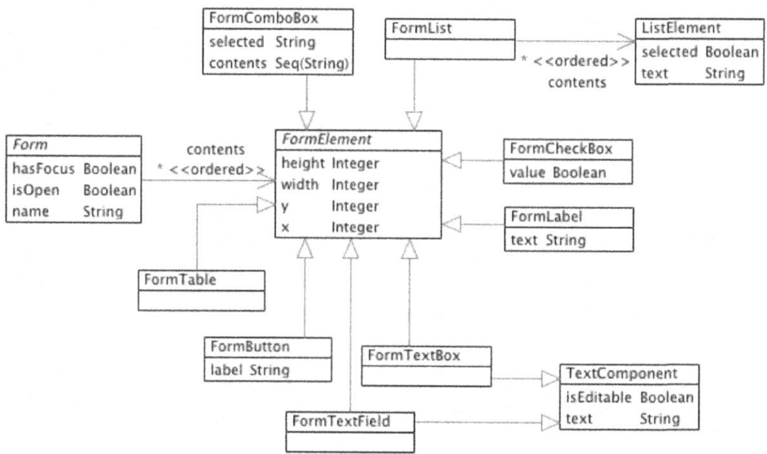

items and buttons (as shown in Figure 10). Events that are generated by a form include button presses, text edits and item selections. Forms are intended to support editing where double-clicks are used to drill-down into structured information and a history of previous forms is managed in the same way as a *back* button on a browser.

A *model browser* supports the creation and editing of tree-shaped information. The model of trees is shown in Figure 11 and is used by XModeler to provide an interface to projects, namespaces, and the underlying file system. Tree nodes have labels that can be edited, expanded and closed. Double clicking on a node is intended to invoke some application specific functionality and right clicking on a node provides a pop-up menu.

The text-editor client provides an interface to the Eclipse text editor, to Windows applications through an OLE bridge and to a web-browser. Events are raised when text changes, when a save request is made and when a URL is requested. The editor provides commands to control the text and to change the browser contents.

Each client can be specialized and used in an application specific way. Client commands process instances of the *view* classes shown in figures Figure 9 - Figure 11 (text editing commands just

Figure 11. Browser trees

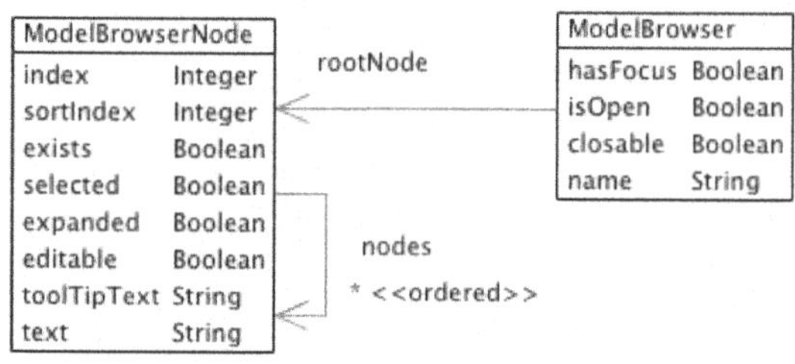

process strings). Typically clients provide an interface over instances of *model* classes, and are therefore *model*-view controllers. Each type of client works in a similar way by managing a collection of bi-directional mappings.

A selection of the mapping classes for class diagrams is shown in Figure 12. A class diagram displays the contents of a package. All the class diagrams in this chapter have been exported from XModeler and are XMF packages that are managed by the XModeler diagrams client using the classes shown in Figure 12 (including itself).

The class `ElementXDiagram` is a general purpose mapping that associates a diagram with an XMF element. It is specialized to produce `PackageXClassDiagram` in order to implement the appropriate operations that propagate changes on the diagram to the package and vice

Figure 12. Model-view-controller architecture

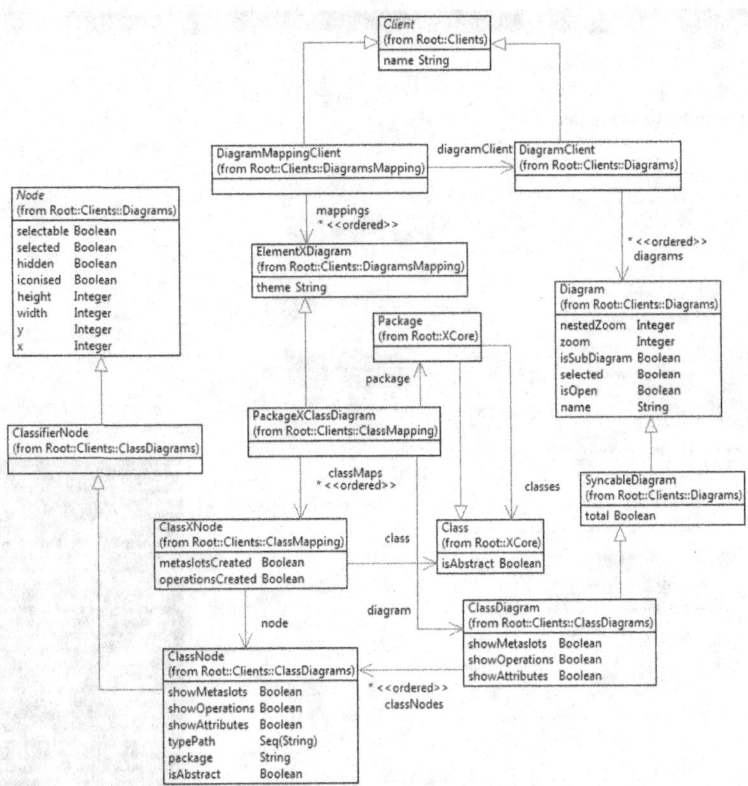

versa. Both the package and the class diagram associated with `PackageXClassDiagram` are monitored by daemons so that any change to either element raises an event. Changes on the diagram are produced by the client when client-events occur and cause the package to be updated. Changes to the package generate events that are transformed in turn to client-commands that update the diagram.

The mapping structure follows the structure of the model, therefore `PackageXClassDiagram` contains a collection of `ClassXNode` mappings that maintain consistency between classes in the package and the nodes on the diagram. Mappings lower down the structure (such as operations and attributes) are not shown in Figure 12.

Development Tools

XModeler implements a number of development tools using the clients described above. Model browsers are used to provide an interface to the file-system where XMF source code is created. Applications are defined, compiled and loaded through special files called *manifests* that contain a language construct similar to Unix makefiles.

Once compiled and loaded, the resulting packages of definitions can be browsed using a model browser and displayed on class diagrams. XModeler also supports a development method whereby packages of classes are created using class diagrams and then exported as source code to the file system.

Packages and their contents can be edited using a property editor that is defined using the forms client. The XCore meta-model defines all elements to be instances of `Object` and therefore a single

Figure 13. XModeler development tools

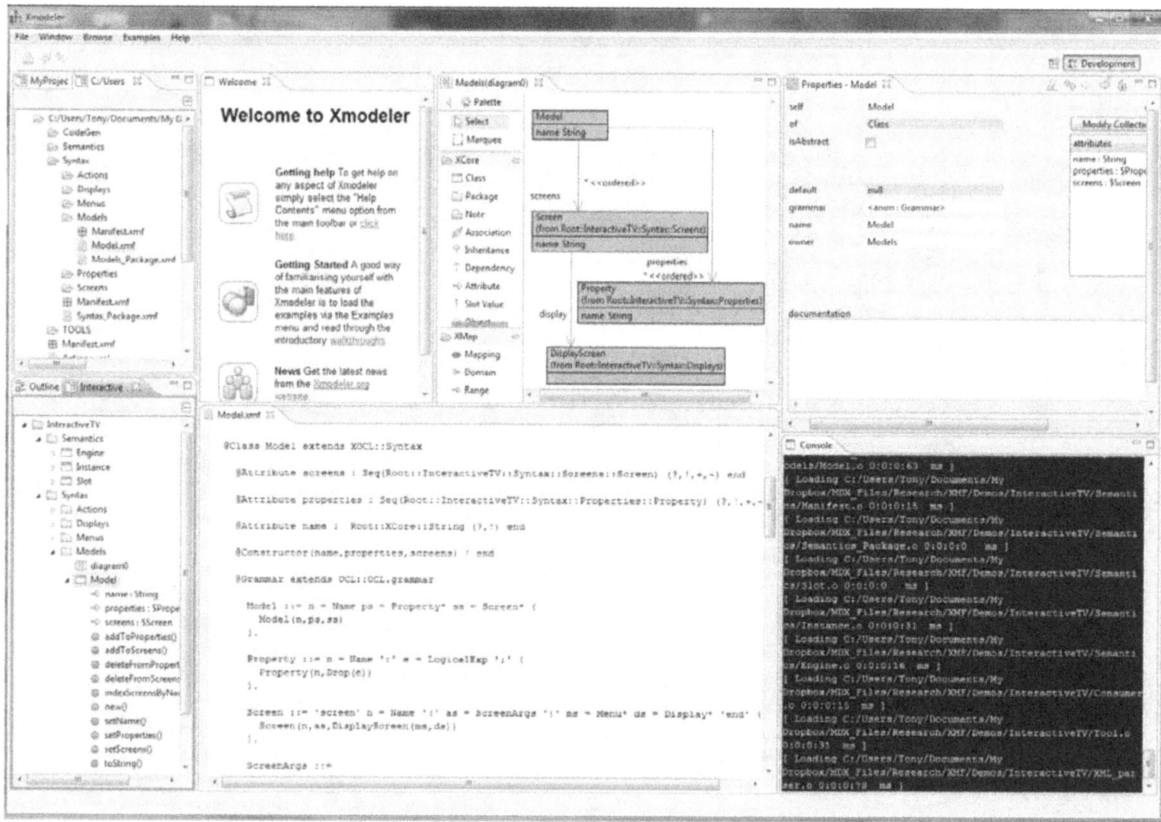

general-purpose property editor can be used to inspect and edit all types of object whether they are classes or instances of classes.

XModeler provides a console (implemented as a client) that implements an interactive command interpreter. The console is used to interact with data, for example by instantiating classes and sending the resulting instances messages to start an application.

Figure 13 shows a screen-shot of XModeler after loading the Interactive TV case study. It shows how the browser provides access to the case study source code and the packages that have been created after loading the code. The editor window shows the contents of a source file, and the welcome page is shown in a browser. A class diagram shows the definition of the class `Model` that is edited via a form. The console shows output that was produced when the files were loaded.

The top-left of the screen-shot shows a number of menus. XModeler supports extensible menus in a similar way to the extension points of Eclipse. The user can tailor most standard element types to add new menu items in order to support application specific functionality via the XModeler GUI. Of course, all of the standard clients can be extended (as described for class diagrams) to implement application specific tools. The events and messages are, however, fixed without modifying the XModeler source code and rebuilding.

Case Study Implementation

We have described how XModeler provides an extensible tool environment for language devel-

Figure 14. XML to HTML transformation

```
parserImport XOCL, XML::Parser;

import XML::Parser, IO;

context Root
  @Operation fold(ss) ss->iterate(x s="" | s + x) end
context Root
  @Operation rows(ss) fold(ss ->collect(s | "<TR><TD>" + s + "</TD></TR>")) end
context Root
  @Operation cols(ss) "<TR>" + fold(ss ->collect(s | "<TD>" + s + "</TD>")) + "</TR>" end

context Root
  @Grammar Screen_Grammar
    Screen ::= <Screen> d=Display* </Screen> {
      "<HTML><FORM ACTION='http://quiz' METHOD='PUT'>" + fold(d) + "</FORM></HTML>"
    }.
    Display ::= Vertical | Horizontal | Text | Button | Options.
    Vertical ::= <Vertical> d=Display* </Vertical> { "<TABLE>" + rows(d) + "<TABLE>" }.
    Horizontal ::= <Horizontal> d=Display* </Horizontal> { "<TABLE>" + cols(d) + "<TABLE>" }.
    Text ::= <Text t=text/> { t }.
    Options ::= <Options n=name> o=Option* </Options> {
      "<SELECT NAME='" + n + "'>" + fold(o) + "</SELECT>"
    }.
    Option ::= <Option n=name/> { "<OPTION>" + n + "</OPTION>" }.
    Button ::= <Button n=name> </Button> {
      "<INPUT TYPE='SUBMIT' NAME='BUTTON' VALUE='"+n+"'/>"
    }.
  end

context Root
  @Operation toHTML(screen:String)
    let sin = StringInputChannel(screen) then
        xin = ParserChannel(sin,Screen_Grammar)
    in xin.parse("Screen");
       xin.values->head
    end
  end
```

opment via a client architecture and have given an overview of the key XModeler tools and how they are used to develop the Interactive TV case study. This section completes the case study by showing how the text-editor client is extended to support a user-interface.

We have shown how a DSL for the Interactive TV case study is implemented in XMF. The language allows interactive applications to be easily represented and defines how individual screens are produced as XML. The application loops as follows. A screen is produced in XML and the engine waits for a user-generated event. When the event is received, it is processed and the engine produces the next screen in XML, and so on.

As defined earlier, the engine does not define a screen renderer. Any implementation must provide a translation from the XML screen representation to a library that drives the TV screen. In order to check that the model works correctly, we will implement a renderer in XModeler based on a web-browser by extending the text-editor client `HTMLViewer`.

Figure 14 shows an XML grammar defined using the XML syntax-class technology that was introduced earlier. It translates from the screen language to a string containing HTML. A screen is translated into an HTML form so that choice and button events are handled by the `HTMLViewer` client. Horizontal and vertical layout in a screen is translated to HTML tables.

The operation `toHTML` maps a string containing an XML representation of a screen (as produced by an instance of the class Engine) to a string

Figure 15. Extension of the HTMLViewer tool

```
parserImport XOCL;

import IO;
import Clients::TextEditor;
import InteractiveTV::Semantics;

context Root
  @Class Tool extends HTMLViewer
    @Attribute engine : Engine end
    @Constructor(name,model)
      self.engine := Engine(model.new());
      xmf.textClient().newBrowser(self)
    end
    @Operation display(event)
      let xml = engine.getDisplay(event)
      in self.setURL(toHTML(xml))
      end
    end
    @Operation requestURL(url:String)
      self.display(url)
    end
  end
```

containing the equivalent HTML. Figure 15 shows an extension to the HTMLViewer client that will display screens generated by an engine. A new tool is created by supplying a name and a model. The model is instantiated by sending it a `new` message and is then supplied to a new engine. When the text client is supplied with the new HTML viewer, a browser window appears in XModeler.

The `Tool` operations `display` and `requestURL` implement the application loop. Firstly `display` is called with a dummy event to initiate the loop. The `Engine` operation `getDisplay` processes the event and returns a string containing a screen encoded as XML. The XML is translated to HTML using `toHTML` and then the client-command `setURL` is used to update the browser window.

A user-generated event in a browser window is processed as the client-event `requestURL`. When the URL is received by the tool, it simply passes it back to the `display` operation for processing by the engine. The following operation presented in Box 12 can be used to test the application.

Figure 16, Figure 17, Figure 18, and Figure 19 show four screen-shots of XModeler after calling test.

RESEARCH DIRECTIONS IN SOFTWARE LANGUAGE ENGINEERING

There is increasing interest in *Software Language Engineering* (SLE) where new languages are defined as part of the system engineering process. In particular Domain Specific Language (DSL) Engineering (Fowler, 2010; Mernik, Heering & Sloane, 2005) is an approach whereby a new language is defined or an existing language is extended; in both cases DSLs involve constructing abstractions that directly support the elements of a single problem domain. This is to be contrasted with *General Purpose Languages* (GPLs) that have features that can be used to represent elements from multiple problem domains.

There are a large number of technologies that are currently used to perform SLE. These include: *grammarware* that are traditionally used to process syntax; *macros* that are used to extend a language with rewrite rules; language IDEs such as XText (Eysholdt & Behrens, 2010) and MPS (Voelter & Solomatov, 2010) that can be

Box 12.

```
context Root
  @Operation test()
    Tool("http://quiz/",quiz_model).display("?BUTTON=START")
  end
```

Figure 16. Start the quiz

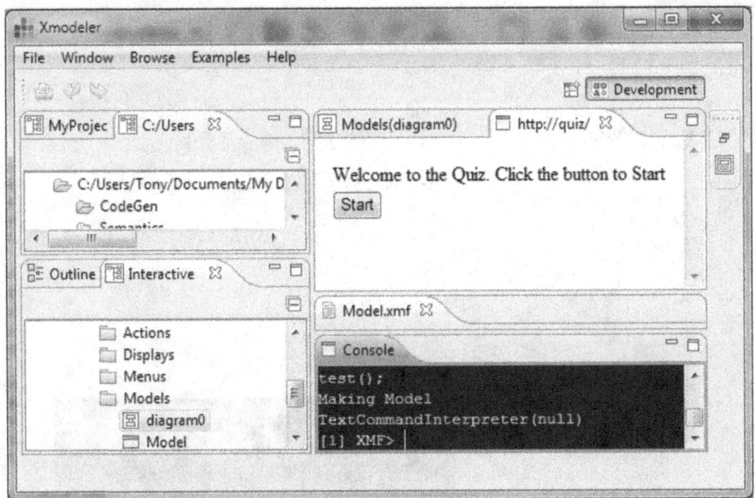

Figure 17. First question

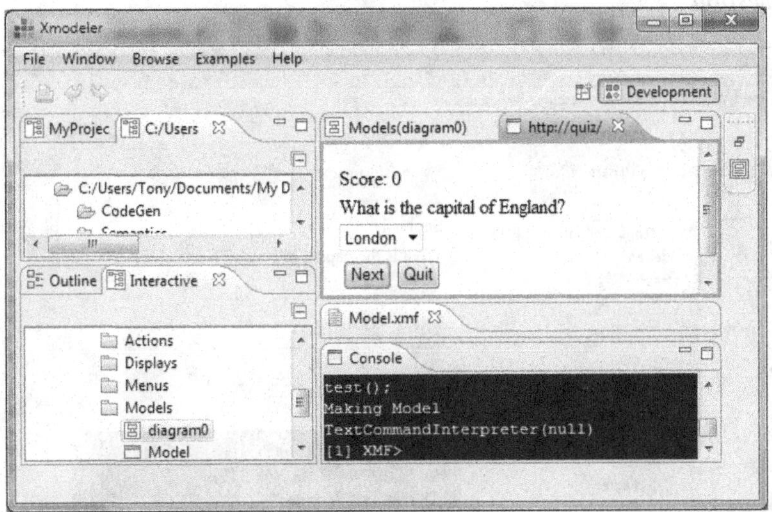

used to generate language-specific tooling; TXL and Stratego/XT (Bravenboer et al., 2008) that are based on language rewriting. XMF supports grammarware in terms of syntax-classes where extensible grammars are attached to classes that manage the expansion of the abstract syntax trees. The extensibility of this approach is similar to the features of LISA (Mernik et al., 2000; Mernik & Zumer, 2005) which uses attribute grammars with inheritance to declare extensible languages. Unlike LISA, XMF embeds a full programming language (XOCL) within the grammars that makes them less declarative but more expressive in terms of parse-time processing.

Some of these technologies have been available in languages that were designed many years ago. For example Common Lisp, designed in the 1980's contains an extensive macro system. Some of the technologies are very new such as MPS and Stratego/XT. Emerging languages such as Fortress (Allen et al., 2005) include language extension mechanisms.

Figure 18. Correct answer

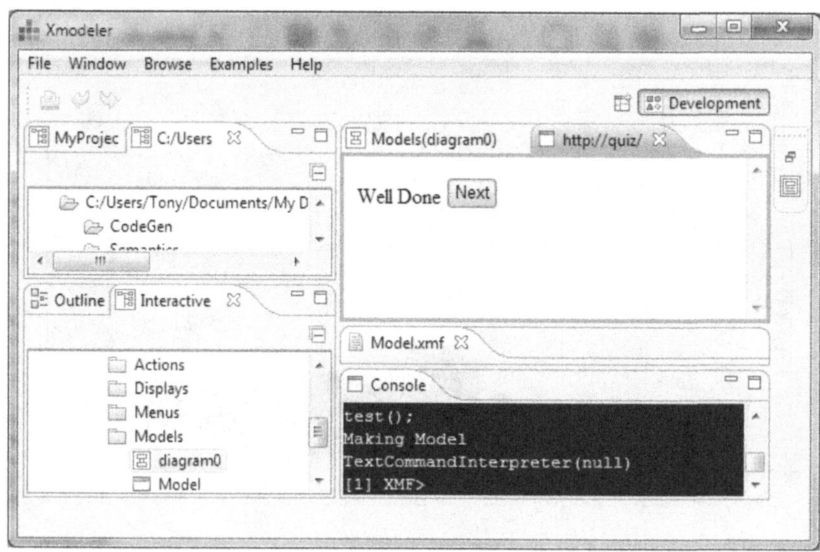

Figure 19. Next question

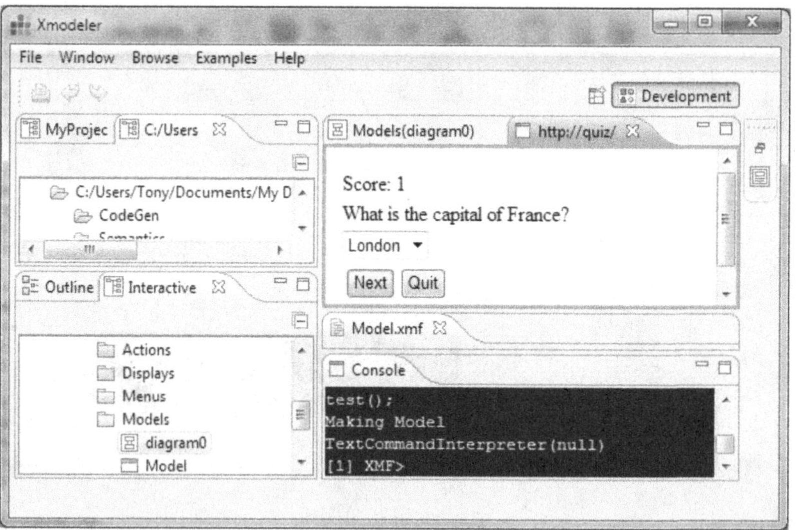

Although there are many different technologies that support SLE, they have many similar features. Many provide mechanisms for transforming text to syntax structures that are subsequently processed either in terms of evaluation or translation to other languages. Furthermore, many of these technologies allow new language features to be embedded in an existing language, effectively incrementally extending the host language.

Languages can be defined using traditional compiler technologies such as Lex, Yacc, ANTLR (Parr & Quong, 1994), JavaCC (Kodaganallur, 2004), and more recent technologies such as XText (Behrens, 2010). These technologies provide mechanisms for defining grammars. A grammar defines the syntax of a language; grammar translations produce tools for language processing such as parsers and editors. However, these technologies do not provide mechanisms for language integration or defining the dynamic semantics of a language (although some provide technology for a limited form of static semantics). Pre-processor languages such as Awk and A* (Ladd & Ramming, 1995) can be used to implement new language features, however typically, a pre-processor has very limited knowledge of the underlying language structure and cannot access contextual information.

Template Haskell (Sheard & Peyton-Jones, 2002) introduced a number of features for constructing and manipulating programs within a functional programming language context. In particular, Template Haskell uses quasi-quotes to construct programs using concrete syntax while *drop* and *splice* are used to turn concrete syntax into patterns, or *templates*, by defining holes where syntax values can be inserted. In addition, Template Haskell uses monads to achieve hygiene and, since Haskell is statically typed, code manipulation is checked at compile-time. The limitations of the approach are that the Haskell concrete syntax cannot be extended in any way and compile-time meta-programming is limited to a single stage (i.e. cannot be nested). Similar languages include MetaML (Moggi et al., 1999) and MetaOCaml (Calcagno et al., 2003), which differ from Template Haskell in that they provide a lisp-like *run* operation for executing code at run-time.

The approach described in (Braband & Schwartzbach, 2002) reviews a number of languages that provide macros: the C pre-processor CPP; C++ templates; M4; Tex; Dylan; the Jakarta Tool Suite JTS; Scheme; the Meta Syntactic Macros System MS2 Pre-processors, such as M4 and CPP, are described as being limited due to having no knowledge of the underlying syntax structure. The authors make a distinction between languages with one-pass and multi-pass macro systems and those with macro binding scopes. A distinction is made between macro calls within a macro definition that lazily expand (on each invocation) and those that eagerly expand (once at definition time). Macro systems differ in terms of the amount of error handling they provide, particularly in terms of trailing back from an error to the original syntax. The authors go on to define a macro language that allows new language constructs to be added to the host language in terms of syntax and metamorphism (syntax translation rule) definitions.

In (Lammel & Verhoef, 2001) the authors propose a solution to what they term the *500 Language Problem* by which they mean the proliferation, and problems arising as a result, of the huge number of languages, public and proprietary, used in commercial software systems. The proposal is to base system engineering around a generic core and to use a grammar-based approach to provide interoperable technology for *language renovation*. The term grammarware is coined in (Klint et al., 2005) to describe an approach to Software Engineering in terms of the construction, tooling and maintenance of grammars, and by implication of a language driven approach to engineering software systems.

Language Oriented Programming (Ward, 1994) often involves extending an existing language with a macro system. Maya (Baker & Hsieh, 2002) is a system that supports language extensions to Java. New language constructs are added to the current Java language by defining Mayans that define grammar rules and how the rules synthesize language constructs. Each Mayan is defined in terms of pattern matching over existing Java language constructs. Maya provides access to the Java abstract syntax so that each Mayan can return an abstract syntax tree that is inserted into the surrounding tree. Maya supports hygiene by detecting variable binding and generating new variable names for locally bound variables in Mayans. OpenJava (Tatsubori et al., 2000) is another example where meta-classes that inherit from OJClass implement a `translateDefinition()` method to expand occurrences of their instances (class definitions). OpenJava provides a limited form of syntax extension occurring at predefined positions in the Java grammar. Nemerle (Skalski, Moskal & Olszta, 2004) is a language defined on the .NET platform that includes a macro definition system. Nemerle macros use quasi-quotes and drop-quotes, can be defined to be hygienic, can construct syntax and can extend the base language by defining new constructs in terms of existing constructs interleaved with newly defined keywords.

The Lisp family of languages provides macros for defining new language constructs. Lisp has an advantage when defining new syntax constructs because of the conflation of program and data into a single structure: the list. Common Lisp (Guy L. Steele, 1990) macros are top-level definitions that use backquote (`), comma (,) and comma-at (,@) to construct abstract syntax. The Scheme dialect of Lisp (Sperber et al., 2009) provides similar features, however it goes further by providing syntax pattern-matching, hygiene and local syntax definitions.

Grammar composition can be used to define new languages in terms of old. The AHEAD approach (Batory et al., 2004) allows grammars to be refined by viewing them as being defined in terms of data members (tokens) and methods (syntax productions). Grammar composition in AHEAD produces the union of two grammars in terms of the sets of data members and methods where overlapping productions are controlled via a *run-super* mechanism. Grammar composition operators are described in (Luca Cardelli, Ma & Abadi, 1993) that allow an existing grammar to be extended with new productions, updates existing productions with new alternatives, and replaces an existing production so that all references are updated accordingly, and includes an early use of quasi-quotes for syntax construction. Attribute grammars can also be used to define extensible languages as described in (Van Wyk et al., 2008). A number of authors, including (Schwerdfeger & Van Wyk, 2009) and (Bravenboer & Visser, 2008), describe formal properties of grammars that allow grammars to be compiled separately and the resulting combination of the parse tables do not lead to ambiguous languages.

New language constructs are often implemented in terms of a base language. Quasi-quotes are often used for this, but term rewriting is also used in systems such as Phobos (Granicz & Hickey, 2003) (which also uses inheritance between modular language definitions), Stratego/XT and ASD/SDF. An approach to grammar composition and evolution is described in (Kats, Visser & Wachsmuth, 2010).

As discussed in (Wende et al., 2010) language engineering can benefit from a modular approach in terms of reuse and maintenance providing that the modules are self-contained. It is also argued that the composition of languages must occur at both the syntax and the semantics level. The authors go further: *to realize self contained and reusable components it is vital to decouple reusable semantics of a component and semantics interconnection.*

There have been several attempts to develop approaches and technologies for modular language development. Many of the approaches are syntactic and therefore fall exclusively into the category of grammarware (Klint et al., 2005). These include mechanisms such as Generalized-LR (Tomita, 1985), Early parsing (Earley, 1970) and Packrat parsers (Grimm, 2006) all of which aim to allow languages to be composed at the syntax level.

The MontiCore language (Krahn et al., 2008) is designed to support the modular development of languages. This is achieved by having a language of grammars that can be composed in terms of multiple-extension. The semantics of the languages are defined in terms of the effects of the extension operators on class models of the synthesized abstract syntax structures.

Software libraries are argued to be language components in (Bravenboer & Visser, 2008) where each library is given a DSL syntax front-end. This approach provides a useful mechanism for developing existing libraries as embedded DSLs but does not address the issue of semantics or composition. The authors do, however, raise an interesting issue of the scope of language embedding and define a number of different categories of scope.

All aspects of language components are discussed in (Cazzola & Speziale, 2009) including syntax, type-checking, and operational features. The authors describe a system called Hive for expressing all these features which is similar to the Language Factories approach defined in (Clark & Tratt, 2009), however neither of these systems give a precise definition of the composition mechanisms.

CONCLUSION

XMF and XModeler were designed to support modular Software Language Engineering both in terms of the construction of DSLs and in terms of their associated toolsets. In particular XMF provides a collection of features that we believe are necessary for SLE: meta-circularity; open-architecture; modular syntax-classes; XML support. XModeler extends these features with: daemons (necessary for MVC tooling) and an extensible client architecture together with some standard tooling. We believe that these technologies are necessary for universal SLE and represent the most integrated SLE tool-set to date. Other approaches to tool generation from language definitions includes XText, EMF and LISA (Henriques et al., 2005) and whilst these approaches can fully generate tools from declarative language definitions, they are limited in terms of tool expressivity. XModeler includes a tool model language (not described here) that aims to provide a rich tool description that is separate from the language definition, although this too suffers from a limited expressivity. Ultimately, XMF tools are created as a mixture of models and XOCL code using the general tool architecture provided by XModeler.

There are, however, features missing from XMF/XModeler. Whilst the XOCL language allows types to be included in programs, there is no static type checking. Since XMF is both dynamic and meta-circular, static type checking turns out to be a very challenging problem. In particular the issue of how to integrate a type system with syntax classes is not clear.

XOCL syntax-classes are not hygienic. This means that variables used in the code generated by a syntax-class can be captured by an enclosing scope leading to unintended errors. It is possible to define an extension of syntax classes that enforce hygiene, however this is not provided by default. The software that implements the case study is available at: http://www.eis.mdx.ac.uk/staffpages/tonyclark/Software/InteractiveTV.zip.

REFERENCES

Allen, E., Chase, D., Hallett, J., Luchangco, V., Maessen, J., Ryu, S., … Eastlund C. (2005). *The Fortress language specification*. Sun Microsystems.

Bakern, J., & Hsieh, W. (2002). Maya: Multiple-dispatch syntax extension in Java. *Proceedings of the ACM SIGPLAN 2002 Conference on Programming Language Design and Implementation* (pp. 270-281).

Batory, D., Sarvela, J., & Rauschmayer, A. (2003). Scaling step-wise refinement. *Proceedings of the 25th International Conference on Software Engineering (ICSE 2003)* (pp. 187-197).

Brabrand, C., & Schwartzbach, M. (2002). Growing languages with metamorphic syntax macros. *SIGPLAN Workshop on Partial Evaluation and Semantics-Based Program Manipulation,* (pp. 31-40).

Bravenboer, M., Kalleberg, K., Vermaas, R., & Visser, E. (2008). Stratego/XT 0.17. A language and toolset for program transformation. *Science of Computer Programming, 72*(1-2), 52–70. doi:10.1016/j.scico.2007.11.003

Bravenboer, M., & Visser, E. (2008). Designing syntax embeddings and assimilations. In *Models in Software Engineering* (pp. 34-46).

Bravenboer, M., & Visser, E. (2008). Parse table composition. In *Software Language Engineering* (pp. 74-94).

Calcagno, C., Taha, W., Huang, L., & Leroy, X. (2003). *Implementing multi-stage languages using asts, gensym, and reflection. Generative Programming and Component Engineering* (pp. 57–76). GPCE.

Cardelli, L., Ma, F., & Abadi, M. (1993). Extensible grammars for language specialization. In *Proceedings of the Fourth International Workshop on Database Programming Languages* (pp. 11-31).

Cazzola, W., & Speziale, I. (2009). Sectional domain specific languages. *In Proceedings of the Fourth Workshop on Domain-Specific Aspect Languages* (pp. 11-14).

Clark, T., Evans, A., Sammut, P., & Willans, J. (2004). *Transformation language design: A metamodelling foundation* (pp. 223–226). Graph Transformations.

Clark, T., Sammut, P., & Willans, J. (2008). *Applied Metamodelling: A foundation for language driven development*. Retrieved from http://bit.ly/He29h7

Clark, T., Sammut, P., & Willans, J. (2008). Beyond annotations: A proposal for extensible Java (XJ). In *Proceedings of the 8th IEEE International Working Conference on Source Code Analysis and Manipulation* (pp. 229-238).

Clark, T., Sammut, P., & Willans, J. (2008). *Superlanguages: Developing languages and applications with XMF*. Retrieved from http://bit.ly/HiTOKp

Clark, T., & Tratt, L. (2009). Language factories. *SIGPLAN Conference Companion on Object Oriented Programming Systems Languages and Applications* (pp. 949-955).

Clark, T., & Tratt, L. (2010). Formalizing homogeneous language embeddings. *Electronic Notes in Theoretical Computer Science*, *253*(7), 75–88. doi:10.1016/j.entcs.2010.08.033

Cointe, P. (1987). Metaclasses are first class: The ObjVlisp model. *SIGPLAN Notices*, *22*(12), 156–162. doi:10.1145/38807.38822

Earley, J. (1970). An efficient context-free parsing algorithm. *Communications of the ACM*, *13*(2), 94–102. doi:10.1145/362007.362035

Eysholdt, M., & Behrens, H. (2010). XText: Implement your language faster than the quick and dirty way. *SIGPLAN Conference Companion on Object Oriented Programming Systems Languages and Applications* (pp. 307-309).

Fowler, M., & Parsons, R. (2010). *Domain specific languages*. Addison-Wesley Professional.

Georgalas, N., Azmoodeh, M., Clark, T., Evans, A., Sammut, P., & Willans, J. (2004). MDA-driven development of standard-compliant OSS components: The OSS/J inventory case-study. *In Proceedings of the Second European Workshop on Model Driven Architecture (MDA)*.

Georgalas, N., Azmoodeh, M., & Ou, S. (2005). *Model driven integration of standard based OSS components.* EURESCOM Summit 2005-Ubiquitous Services and Applications.

Granicz, A., & Hickey, J. (2003). Phobos: A front-end approach to extensible compilers. *In Proceedings of the 36th Annual Hawaii International Conference on System Sciences.*

Grimm, R. (2006). Better extensibility through modular syntax. *ACM SIGPLAN Conference on Programming Language Design and Implementation* (pp. 38-51).

Helsen, S., Ryman, A., & Spinellis, D. (2008). Where's my jetpack? *IEEE Software*, *25*(5), 18–21. doi:10.1109/MS.2008.138

Henriques, P., Varando, P., Maria, J., Mernik, M., Lenič, M., Gray, J., & Wu, H. (2005). Automatic generation of language-based tools using the LISA system. *IEE Proceedings. Software, 152*(2), 54–69. doi:10.1049/ip-sen:20041317

Kats, L., Visser, E., & Wachsmuth, G. (2010). Pure and declarative syntax definition: Paradise lost and regained. *ACM SIGPLAN Notices, 45*(10), 918–932. doi:10.1145/1932682.1869535

Klint, P., Laemmel, R., & Verhoef, C. (2005). Toward an engineering discipline for grammarware. *ACM Transactions on Software Engineering and Methodology, 14*(3), 331–380. doi:10.1145/1072997.1073000

Kodaganallur, V. (2004). Incorporating language processing into java applications: A JavaCC tutorial. *IEEE Software, 21*(4), 70–77. doi:10.1109/MS.2004.16

Krahn, H., Rumpe, B., & Voelkel, S. (2008). Monticore: Modular development of textual domain specific languages. *In Proceedings of the 30th International Conference on Software Engineering* (pp. 925-926).

Ladd, D., & Ramming, J. (1995). A*: A language for implementing language processors. *IEEE Transactions on Software Engineering, 21*(11), 894–901. doi:10.1109/32.473218

Lämmel, R., & Verhoef, C. (2001). Cracking the 500-language problem. *IEEE Software, 18*(6), 78–88. doi:10.1109/52.965809

Mernik, M., Lenič, M., Avdičauševič, E., & Žumer, V. (2000). Multiple attribute grammar inheritance. *Informatica, 24*(2), 319–328.

Mernik, M., & Žumer, V. (2005). Incremental programming language development. [Elsevier.]. *Computer Languages, Systems & Structures, 31*(1), 1–16. doi:10.1016/j.cl.2004.02.001

Moggi, E., Taha, W., Benaissa, Z., & Sheard, T. (1999). An idealized MetaML: Simpler, and more expressive. In *Proceedings of the 8th European Symposium on Programming Languages and Systems* (pp. 640-641).

Parr, T., & Quong, R. (1994). Antlr: A predicated-ll(k) parser generator. *Software, Practice & Experience, 25*(7), 789–810. doi:10.1002/spe.4380250705

Petrascu, V., & Chiorean, D. (2010). Towards improving the static semantics of XCore. *Studia Universitatis Babes-Bolyai. Informatica, 55*(3), 61–70.

Schwerdfeger, A., & Van Wyk, E. (2009). Verifiable composition of deterministic grammars. *ACM SIGPLAN Conference on Programming Language Design and Implementation* (pp. 199-210).

Sheard, T., & Peyton-Jones, S. (2002). Template meta-programming for Haskell. *SIGPLAN Notices, 37*(12), 60–75. doi:10.1145/636517.636528

Skalski, K., Moskal, M., & Olszta, P. (2004). *Meta-programming in Nemerle*. Retrieved from http://www.nemerle.org/

Sperber, M., Dybvig, R., Flatt, M., Straaten, A., Findler, R., & Matthews, J. (2009). Revised report on the algorithmic language Scheme. *Functional Programming, 19*, 1–301. doi:10.1017/S0956796809990074

Steele, G. Jr. (1990). *Common LISP: The language* (2nd ed.). Digital Press.

Tatsubori, M., Chiba, S., Killijian, M., & Itano, K. (2000). OpenJava: A class-based macro system for Java. In *Proceedings of the 1st OOPSLA Workshop in Reflection and Software Engineering: Reflection* (pp. 117-133).

Tomita, M. (1985). *Efficient parsing for natural language: A fast algorithm for practical systems*. Kluwer Academic Publishing.

Van Wyk, E., Bodin, D., Gao, J., & Krishnan, L. (2008). Silver: An extensible attribute grammar system. *Electronic Notes in Theoretical Computer Science*, *203*(12), 103–116. doi:10.1016/j.entcs.2008.03.047

Voelter, M., & Solomatov, K. (2010). Language modularization and composition with projectional language workbenches illustrated with MPS. In *Proceedings of the 3rd International Conference on Software Language Engineering*.

Ward, M. (1994). Language-oriented programming. *Software — Concepts and Tools, 15*(4), 147-161.

Wende, C., Thieme, N., & Zschaler, S. (2010). A role-based approach towards modular language engineering. In *Proceedings of the 3rd International Conference on Software Language Engineering* (pp. 254-273).

ADDITIONAL READING

Kohlbecker, E., Fridman, D., Felleisen, M., & Duba, B. (1986). *Hygienic macro expansion: LISP and functional programming* (pp. 151-161).

Landin, P. (1966). The next 700 programming languages. *Communications of the ACM, 9*(6), 157–166. doi:10.1145/365230.365257

Mernik, M., Heering, J., & Sloane, A. (2005). When and how to develop domain-specific languages. *ACM Computing Surveys, 37*(4), 316–344. doi:10.1145/1118890.1118892

Steele, G. (1999). Growing a language. *Higher-Order and Symbolic Computation, 12*(3), 221–236. doi:10.1023/A:1010085415024

Tolvanen, J., & Kelly, S. (2008). *Domain-specific modeling: Enabling full code generation*. Wiley-IEEE Society Press.

KEY TERMS AND DEFINITIONS

Abstract Syntax: A computer oriented representation of a language. Can often be thought of as defining a data structure representation, called an *abstract syntax tree*, for a language.

Concrete Syntax: A human oriented representation of a language; how the language will look on the screen or page.

Domain Specific Language: A Language that is defined to support abstractions in a particular subject area.

Grammar: Rules that can be used to recognize and process a language. Grammar rules usually consist of patterns that recognize concrete syntax and may include actions that build, or *synthesize*, data. A parser takes a grammar and uses it to process concrete syntax and often to synthesize abstract syntax.

Macro: A collection of definitions used to translate from a source language fragment to a target language fragment.

Meta-Model: A model whose instances are models. Often expressed as a collection of classes with well-formedness rules expressed in natural language or in the Object Constraint Language (OCL). A met-model is often referred to as a *language definition*.

Model View Controller: A synchronized mapping between a model and some data (the view).

Parsing: The act of recognizing a language by processing concrete syntax and synthesizing a result (usually abstract syntax).

Software Language Engineering: Tasks related to designing, constructing, analyzing or using a computer based language.

Software Tool: A software artifact used to perform or support a task.

ENDNOTES

1 http://www.eis.mdx.ac.uk/staffpages/tonyclark/Software/Systems and www.xmodeler.org

Chapter 12
Creating, Debugging, and Testing Mobile Applications with the IPAC Application Creation Environment

Kostas Kolomvatsos
National & Kapodistrian University of Athens, Greece

George Valkanas
National & Kapodistrian University of Athens, Greece

Petros Patelis
National & Kapodistrian University of Athens, Greece

Stathes Hadjiefthymiades
National & Kapodistrian University of Athens, Greece

ABSTRACT

An important challenge in software development is to have efficient tools for creating, debugging, and testing software components developed for specific business domains. This is more imperative if it is considered that a large number of users are not familiar with popular programming languages. Hence, Application Creation Environments (ACEs) based on specific Domain-Specific Languages (DSLs) can provide an efficient way for creating applications for a specific domain of interest. The provided ACEs should incorporate all the functionality needed by developers to build, debug, and test applications. In this chapter, the authors present their contribution in this domain based on the experience of the IPAC system. The IPAC system provides a middleware and an ACE for developing and using intelligent, context-aware services in mobile nodes. The chapter fully describes the ACE, which is a key part of the overall architecture. The ACE provides two editors (textual, visual), a wide functionality spectrum, as well as a debugger and an application emulator. The ACE is based on an Application Description Language (ADL) developed for IPAC. The ADL provides elements for the description of an application workflow for embedded systems. Through such functionality, developers are capable of efficiently creating and testing applications that will be deployed on mobile nodes.

DOI: 10.4018/978-1-4666-2092-6.ch012

INTRODUCTION

In Computer Science applications, software components should be developed in order to provide more intelligence in the produced systems. However, users, lacking experience with programming languages are not able to write productive software components.

In such cases, *Application Creation Environments* (ACEs) play a critical role in building and testing software components. With these tools, developers can efficiently design software components as they can utilize a number of editing facilities without the need of using a conventional programming language. In general, ACEs contain: a) a source code editor, b) a debugger, and c) application building automation tools. Software components are developed for a specific domain. Therefore, the vast majority of programming languages do not provide an efficient solution. In this case, *Model-Driven Engineering (MDE)* (Schmidt, 2006) can provide a number of advantages. MDE is a software development methodology, aiming to increase efficiency in developing applications for a specific domain, through the creation of appropriate models. *Domain-Specific Languages (DSLs)* (Mernik et al., 2005) follow the principles of MDE development and can provide a number of advantages in cases of limited programming knowledge. A DSL is a language designed to solve problems that arise in a particular field of application, targeting more specific tasks than classic programming languages. DSLs provide the means for describing parameters for a domain of interest having a concrete syntax. Several semantic models are used for the description of the problem. These semantics lead to the automatic generation of specific tools used for the creation of the final code, which could be in a general purpose programming language (e.g. Java). In DSL tools, there are specific methodologies for the definition of the semantics of each language. Compared to general-purpose languages they offer better expressiveness in their specific focus domain. The most significant advantage of DSLs is that they provide users with the capability to write domain specific programs more easily. These programs are independent of the underlying platform, which is another advantage.

However, developing applications with a DSL also presents some disadvantages. The most important is that there are not any commonly used debuggers for DSLs. A primary reason for this fact is that DSLs are oriented to specific domains and generic debuggers cannot be used. Hence, the development of debugging facilities for DSLs is necessary. Based on such tools, users will be capable of debugging the source code of their applications. The debugger should be DSL-oriented, covering all of the language elements. Another disadvantage is that applications developed for embedded systems should be emulated prior to final deployment. Through emulation, developers can identify possible errors, as well as performance issues. However, as in the case of debuggers, there are not any generic emulators that can be adapted to every DSL.

In this chapter, we present our system for creating and testing applications developed with a DSL, fully integrated into ACE functionalities. The *Integrated Platform for Autonomic Computing* (IPAC) (Tsetsos et al., 2010) ACE provides two editors: a textual, and a visual editor. Each of them provides a number of functionalities for the application creation process. Such applications are created for deployment in mobile nodes. The provided ACE aims not only to experienced developers but also to non – experienced programmers. The IPAC ACE depends on an *Application Description Language* (ADL) created in the framework of the IPAC project. The ADL is the basis for the creation of a number of s/w productivity tools. We describe the code generation component responsible for producing the target code in a certain language (e.g., Java). We developed the IPAC *Debugger,* responsible for accepting logging messages that follow a pre-defined format and present them in a user friendly interface. Such logging messages also encode useful information so that the debugger is capable of mapping lines from the initial source code (DSL code) to lines in the target code. Our proposal is simple but efficient as it requires little experience and effort in the developer's side. Furthermore, our debugging model can easily be adapted to cover other DSLs, as its main component is the mapping process. Finally, the IPAC *Emulator* is used for emulating each application before final deployment. The Emulator "replays" scenarios generating values from hypothetical sensors in specific time instances. Therefore, we are capable of emulating how the application reacts to specific sensor input. In the majority of cases, sensor values trigger events in the application workflow. To summarize, the core contributions of our framework are the following:

- We provide an ACE for creating applications based on a DSL. Developers can use either the textual or the visual editor (suitable for non-experienced developers). The provided DSL is appropriate for creating intelligent, context – aware applications for mobile nodes.
- We provide a Debugger for the discussed DSL. The debugging process is based on a simple yet efficient process through mapping DSL code lines to general purpose programming language commands (e.g. Java). Through the provided GUI, the developer is capable of controlling variables values.
- We provide an Emulator for emulating the application execution in the IPAC framework. The Emulator is based on specific scenarios defined by developers.

The paper is organized as follows. Section II is devoted to the discussion on related work. We present research efforts in defining ACEs and DLSs. Accordingly, in Section III, we briefly describe the IPAC system. Section IV describes the discussed ACE. We present the ADL for IPAC applications. We describe the textual and the visual editor as well as their functionalities. In addition, we focus on the code generation component that produces the target code (Java). In Section V, we describe peripheral components of the IPAC ACE. Such components include the *Application Profile Editor* (APE), *the Graphical User Interface (GUI) Creator*, the IPAC *Debugger* and the application *Emulator*. Finally, a case study for an example application is presented in Section VI, describing (step by step) the creation, the debugging and the emulation process. We conclude this paper in Section VII.

Related Work

A number of interesting efforts related to the definition of ACEs can be found in the literature. The Oracle *Business Process Execution Language (BPEL) Process Manager* (Oracle Corporation, 2011) is provided as a member of the Oracle Fusion Middleware family of products. It is used for designing, deploying and managing BPEL processes. It also provides a GUI for building such processes. The BPEL Designer provides a graphical and user-friendly way to build BPEL processes and it is available as a module/plug-in for JDeveloper and Eclipse. Moreover, it enables developers to view and modify the BPEL source at any time.

PoLoS *Service Creation Environment* (SCE) assists the service creator in developing new Location-Based Services (LBS) and deploying them in the PoLoS platform (Ioannidis et al., 2003). Each service is defined through a script written in a new service specification language, which is based on XML and is capable of supporting the description of the functionality pertaining to each LBS. This language is flexible and easy to use in order to allow for the specification and easy deployment of any type of LBS without too much effort and cost from the service provider.

The *RapidFLEXACE* from Pactolus (Pactolus, 2011) is a Windows-based software, that allows users to productively create multimedia communication services. The RapidFLEX ACE enables fine-grain control of *Session Initiation Protocol* (SIP) signalling and control over database, web and IP media server resources. This gives developers the power to create sophisticated enhanced services.

WIT-CASE SCE (Braem et al., 2006) is a high-level, visual SCE for Web service-based applications that provides service composition templates, verification of compatibility and guidelines, and advanced separation of concerns through aspect-oriented software development. The software guides users in creating correct compositions by verifying correctness throughout the steps of the process.

In such environments, specific languages were defined in order to describe the main elements of each application in a higher level than conventional programming languages. DSLs attracted a lot of attention due to the fact that they provide abstraction in the definition of applications for specific research fields. In (Wu & Gray, 2005), the authors demonstrate a framework to automate the generation of DSL testing tools. The presented framework adopts Eclipse plug-ins for defining DSLs as well as a set of tools. The aim is to present the feasibility and applicability of debugging and testing information derived from a DSL in a friendly programming environment.

A program transformation engine supporting the debugging process of DSL code is described in (Wu et al., 2004; Wu et al., 2005; Wu et al., 2006). The discussed approach concerns the methodology of generating a set of tools needed to use a DSL. Such tools are: the editor, the compiler and the debugger. This research effort focuses on issues regarding the debugging support for a DSL development environment. The debugger is automatically generated by a language specification. Authors describe two approaches for the debugger in conjunction with the *DSL Debugging Framework (DDF)* plug-in. The first approach is applicable when the aspect weaver is available for the generated GPL while the second approach involves the *Design Maintenance System (DMS)* transformation and is applied when the aspect weaver is not available.

In (Sadilek & Wachsmuth, 2008), the authors describe a prototyping methodology for *Domain-Specific Modeling Languages (DSMLs)* on an independent level of the MDE architecture. They argue that the prototyping method should describe the DSML semantics in an operational manner. For this, they use standard modeling techniques such as *Meta Object Facility* (MOF) (OMG MOF Specification, 2011) and *Query/View/Transformations* (QVT) Relations (OMG QVT Specification, 2011). By combining the discussed approach with existing, metamodel-based, editor creation technologies, they enable the inexpensive prototyping of visual interpreters and debuggers. The authors rely on the use of *Eclipse Modeling Framework (EMF)* which is similar to MOF and using the Ecore metamodel of a DSML they can generate the language plug-in with EMF. The generated plug-in is the basis to create, access, modify, and store models that are instances of the DSML.

A logic programming based framework for specification and automatic verification of domain specific languages is presented in (Gupta & Pontelli, 2002). Their proposal is based on Horn logic and specific constraints to define semantics of DSLs. The semantic specification serves as an interpreter but more efficient implementations of the DSL, such as a compiler, can be automatically derived by partial evaluation. The executable specification can be used for automatic or semi-automatic verification of DSL programs as well as for automatically obtaining conventional debuggers and profilers. The syntax and semantics of the DSL are expressed through Horn logic. The authors also provide evidence of the efficiency of the discussed methodology.

THE IPAC FRAMEWORK

The IPAC system provides a middleware and an ACE for developing intelligent, context-aware services in mobile nodes. The main focus of the system is the development of an embedded middleware platform. The lightweight and flexible IPAC middleware provides all the required services for the deployment and the execution of diverse applications in mobile ad hoc networks. These middleware services are supported by novel knowledge which deals with interoperability, integration and re-configuration issues that can be met in embedded platforms. Being context-aware, the IPAC relies on advanced sensing components providing innovative application architecture. Figure 1 shows the IPAC system architecture.

An important component of the IPAC framework is the ACE. This environment is based on Eclipse and provides a friendly user interface to developers. At the core of the implementation is the Eclipse platform which integrates projects such as the *Eclipse Modeling Framework (EMF)* (Eclipse EMF Project, 2011), the *openArchitectureWare (oAW) – Eclipse Modeling Project* (Eclipse Modelling Project, 2011) and the *Graphical Modeling Framework (GMF)* (Eclipse GMF Framework, 2011) frameworks.

Figure 1. The IPAC system architecture

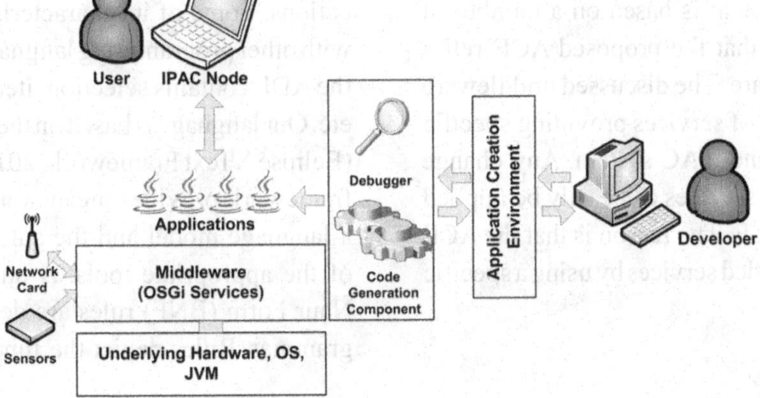

Based on this component, developers are capable of creating applications that will be uploaded to the IPAC nodes. The developer uses the ACE to compose applications and exploit the services provided by the middleware. Applications use the capabilities and resources of the sensing elements and network interfaces, wireless ad hoc networking facilities and pervasive sharing of information according to their needs.

The ACE provides two editors: the *textual* and the *visual*. In addition, the ACE provides debugging and emulating facilities in order to help developers to debug their applications prior to their final deployment. The workflows produced by the editors comply with the *Application Description Language (ADL)* grammar. The ADL is a high-level language created especially for IPAC. A short description of the ADL is provided in the following Section.

APPLICATION CREATION ENVIRONMENT

The high level architecture of the ACE is described in Figure 2. The basic components are a) the *Application Description Language* (ADL), b) the *Textual Editor*, c) the *Visual Editor* and d) the *Code Generation Component.* Additionally,

Figure 2. The ACE architecture

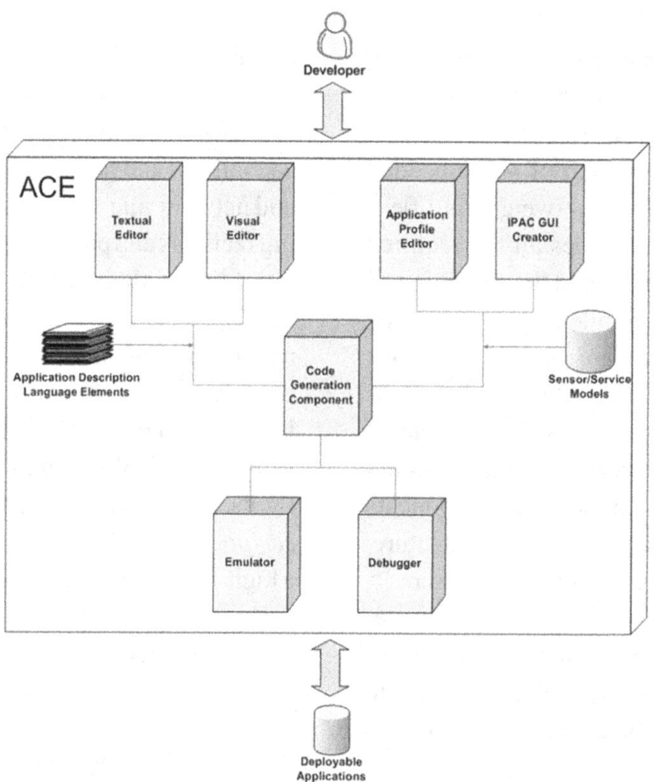

there are some peripheral components, such as: a) the *Application Profile Editor* (APE), b) the *GUI Creator*, c) the *Debugger* and, d) the *Emulator*. The ACE is based on the Eclipse platform and each module is developed as a separate plug-in that extends the core functionality of the environment. The provided editors are based on the ADL meta-model and, thus, any change in the ADL model affects them. The proposed ACE could be adapted to any framework that is based on a number of services meaning that the proposed ACE relies on top of middleware. The discussed middleware involves a number of services providing specific functionalities to the IPAC system. Any change to the middleware services can easily be applied to the proposed ACE. The reason is that the ACE identifies the provided services by using a specific service model.

Application Description Language (ADL)

The IPAC ADL consists of the basic component of the ACE. The ADL provides the necessary model elements for the creation of an application. The syntax of a command expressed in ADL terms is simple, however, covering all the necessary functionality for the development of IPAC applications. Some of its characteristics are common with other programming languages. For example, the ADL contains selection, iteration commands, etc. Our language is based on the *XText framework* (Eclipse XText Framework, 2011). The discussed framework provides means for the definition of a language model and the automatic generation of the appropriate tools. A number of Backus-Naur Form (BNF) rules are defined in the ADL grammar. Rules depict the functionality of each

Table 1. The reserved words of the IPAC ADL

application	int
as	invoke
blocked	listen
body	method
boolean	nonBlocked
break	onFault
case	set
const	string
default	switch
double	true
else	value
entry	var
event	vector
false	wait
if	while

element which is a combination of static and dynamic parts. In Table 1, we provide a list with the reserved words. Some of them are used for declarations, statements, or middleware service invocations. Declarations can be used for constants or variables while statements involve assignments, selection or iteration commands. As an example, in Box 1 and Box 2, we can see two BNF rules of the ADL concerning variable declarations and the '*if*' selection command.

The ADL is based on the Ecore model which is created by the *XText generator* (Eclipse XText Framework, 2011). The provided editors are based on this model. Apart from the Ecore model, the generator produces a number of components such as the parser and the serializer. In Figure 3, we can see a part of the Ecore model produced by the XText generator. For more information about the IPAC ADL, the interested reader can refer to (Nomikos & Kolomvatsos, 2009).

Finally, some extension mechanisms are defined in order to enhance the ADL semantics. These extensions can be used to provide more facilities such as a checking mechanism. Extension mechanisms are responsible for the dynamic validation of models written in ADL. Validation can be performed in three ways: a) the parser can automatically validate the syntactical correctness of any input, b) the parser automatically checks for broken crosslinks, and, c) extensions to the basic Ecore model can be provided by defining additional constraints. For instance, according to the dynamic semantics of the ADL,

Box 1. Rule for variable declarations

```
VariableDeclaration:
"var" name=ID "as" type=TypeName ("value" cValue=ConstantValue)?;
```

Box 2. Rule for simple selection commands

```
IfStatement:
              "if""(" ifExpression=Expression ")" "{"
                              (ifStatements+=Statement)*
                    "}"
         ("else" "{"
                    (elseStatements+=Statement)*
                    "}")?;
```

Figure 3. A part of the Ecore model

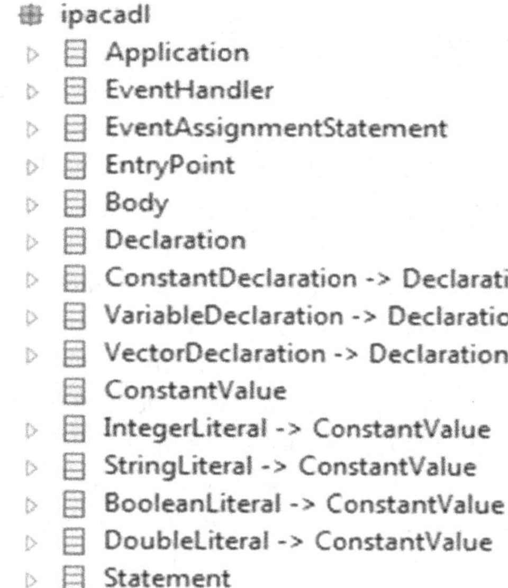

the application name cannot be a reserved word or begin with a digit. Such constraints are defined in a specific file by means of a specific check language provided by the framework. Within this file, we can define conditions that should be fulfilled when the application workflow is defined. Such conditions are checked by the editor and in the case of error, a warning message is issued for the developer. There are two types of checks (producing two kinds of messages respectively): *Errors* and *Warnings*.

Apart from the checking language, the XText framework can provide a mechanism for expanding our model. A specific file is used for expanding the main model. In this file, both the interface of each method extending our model and the connection with the class containing these methods are defined. Therefore, problems that might have been extremely difficult to be covered by our initial model can be resolved easily.

Textual Editor

The Textual Editor of the ACE is a fundamental component. It provides all of the common text editing facilities. As already mentioned, the XText framework provides efficient means for the creation of such editors. The editor can be either integrated into the Eclipse workbench or deployed as a stand-alone application. Rich editing facilities are supported and both a checking as well as a content assist mechanism are used for more effective definition of applications. Moreover, a set of extensions are used in order to provide additional functionality in the development procedure.

The textual editor supports all the features provided by modern *Integrated Development Environment* (IDEs). Actually, the ACE textual editor integrates into the workbench and inherits the built-in Eclipse editing mechanisms. Syntax highlighting, outline view, hyperlinks, etc, can facilitate the navigation process, while content assist, template completion, constraints, code folding, code formatting or searching functionality can provide efficiency in the definition of new IPAC applications. Colors and fonts can be customized according to the meaning of each element or the developer's preferences. Figure 4 shows a snapshot of the generated editor for the ADL. The ADL keywords are highlighted with different color while the minus sign (-) at the left part of the editor indicates the code folding functionality.

Visual Editor

The IPAC Visual Editor is a component of the ACE which provides facilities for developing applications by using a graphical editor. Thus, the developer is not writing directly, code in the ADL language as is the case with the textual editor. The graphical environment is provided by the *Graphical Editing Framework* (GEF) (Eclipse GMF Framework, 2011). The design of the visual editor is strongly coupled with the design of the textual editor.

The most important feature of the Visual Editor is its customized toolbar which consists of the following categories (Figure 5):

Figure 4. Syntax highlighting and code folding functionalities of the textual editor

```
DummyApp.adl
application DummyApp {
    body {
        var threshold as int
        vector resultSet as double
    }
}
```

- **Workflow Patterns:** contains all the available creation tools which will create visual elements representing each ADL declaration and statement.
- **Services:** Contains all the creation tools which represent all of the available IPAC middleware services.
- **Applications:** Contains all the creation tools that correspond to the already created applications.

The developer can choose a tool from the palette and insert it in the main area. Each workflow pattern can be connected with the rest through a '*connection*' element. The '*connection*' element defines the sequence of the main workflow patterns in the application code. Finally, specific property values for each element can be defined in a properties window.

In addition, the Visual Editor provides a checking mechanism. This mechanism recognizes workflow inconsistencies during the application creation. It is available through a button in the main menu toolbar and by clicking on it, the workflow is validated and elements with inconsistencies are visually marked with an appropriate icon (i.e.).

It should be noted that both editors are fully synchronized. This way, the developer can switch between editors making the most of the facilities provided by our ACE. The synchronization between the two editors is achieved by using specific extensions that are based on the common application model.

Code Generation Component

The code generation component is also based on the XText framework. It is created utilizing the Eclipse plug-in technology and interfaces with the textual and the visual editor. It utilizes a number of predefined templates in order to produce the final code. There are two templates available, depending on whether we want to use the debugger's functionality or not. The first is a debugger-enabled template, used when the developer wishes to debug an application. The second template does not contain any debugging symbols, and is appropriate for actual deployments. Note the resemblance of this approach with similar functionality of general purpose compilers, adding appropriate debugging symbols when compiling in *debug* mode. The developer can choose from these two templates. The produced code is in the form of a general purpose programming language such as Java. We can easily adapt the code generation component to other programming languages. The final code is generated using the semantics of the ADL and the predefined template files. The input is the application workflow and the output is the target code. The basic concept is that when the developer uses the editors for the definition of an application, an *Abstract Syntax Tree (AST)* is generated according to the defined ADL rules.

Figure 5. The visual editor palette

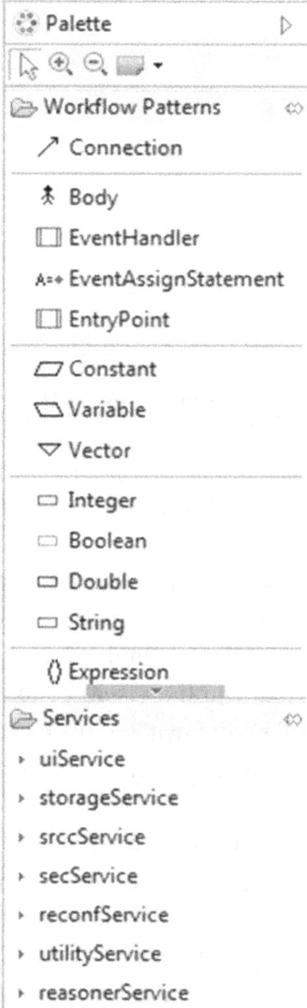

The *XPand template language* (Eclipse XText Framework, 2011) provides all the necessary functionality in order to produce the target code. In our framework, we use two kinds of templates: the first is used for the generation of the target code that will be uploaded on a mobile node, while the second is used for debugging purposes. An example template for the main body code of an application is depicted in Figure 6.

The debug template files contain specific commands in order to define the required information for the debugger. These commands consist of a static and a dynamic part. The static part is related to the Java code lines we want to insert in the target code while the dynamic part is related to commands that will produce result when the code runs in the developer's node.

As mentioned, the output of the code generator is the actual code of an application ready to be deployed in the IPAC system. The application is then packed as an *Open Service Gateway initiative* (OSGi) *bundle* (OSGi Alliance, 2011). Our ACE provides an automatic mechanism that creates the final application file that will be deployed to the mobile nodes.

Peripheral Components

Application Profile Editor

When the developer creates a new application, he/she should first define the application profile, which encodes basic information regarding the application. The *Application Profile Editor* (APE) provides the means to create such an application profile in an easy way. For example, information in the application profile is used by the reasoner service of the IPAC system to decide whether the application can be uploaded on a specific mobile node taking into account the node's characteristics, thus, ensuring some minimum requirements. The APE provides a table-like form to the developer to define generic information as well as information related to application events. Figure 7 shows a snapshot of the APE window.

As we can see in Figure 7, the developer using the APE is capable of defining generic application characteristics at the upper part of the window and properties related to events (events are triggered by sensor values) in the lower part of the window. The developer can insert several events and for each one specifies the conditions that should be met in order to trigger an event. When an event is triggered while the application is executed, it (the application) should react to provide the expected functionality.

Figure 6. An example template of the application main body

```
public class «firstUpperCase(splitAppName(appName))» extends Thread {

    public String appName;
    «EXPAND declaration FOREACH declarations-»

    public «firstUpperCase(splitAppName(appName))»() {
        start();
    }

    public void run () {
        while(!Thread.interrupted() ) {
            «EXPAND body(this.appName) FOR body»
        }
    }

    public void pauseThread() {
        suspend();
    }

    public void resumeThread() {
        resume();
    }

    public void stopThread() {
        interrupt();
    }
```

Figure 7. The main window of the APE

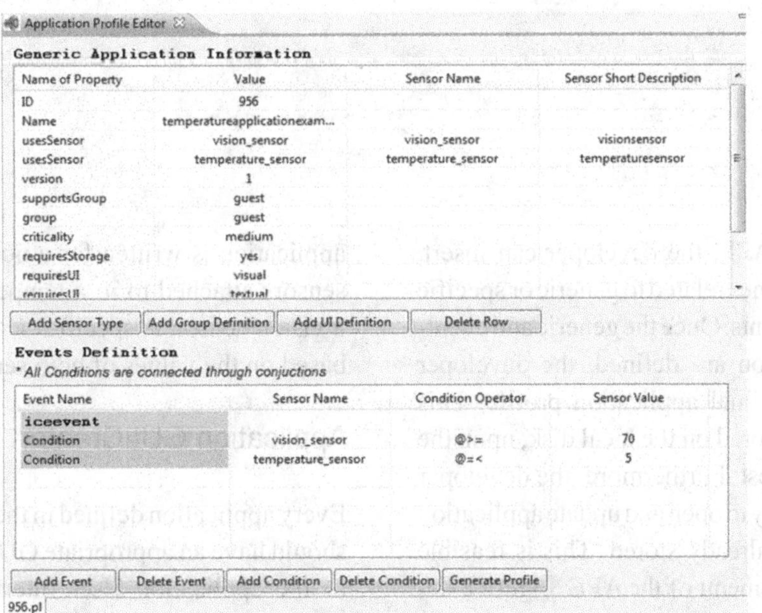

Figure 8. An application profile example

```
hasName(956, temperatureapplicationexample).
usesSensor(956, vision_sensor).
type(vision_sensor, vision_sensor).
hasDescription(vision_sensor, "visionsensor").
usesSensor(956, temperature_sensor).
type(temperature_sensor, temperature_sensor).
hasDescription(temperature_sensor, "temperaturesensor").
version(956, 1).
supportsGroup(956, guest).
group(956, guest).
criticality(956, medium).
requiresStorage(956, yes).
requiresUI(956, visual).
requiresUI(956, textual).
requiresCommRange(956, 500).
reportingPeriod(956, 10).
event(iceevent) :- vision sensor@>=70 ,temperature sensor@=<5.
```

Figure 9. The GUI creator environment

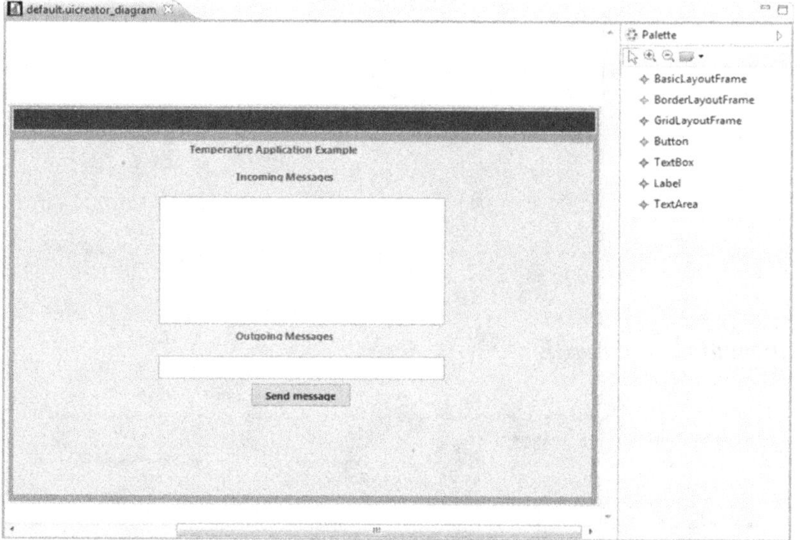

Through the APE, the developer can insert, update or delete lines related to generic or specific application elements. Once the generic and event-related information are defined, the developer can produce the final application profile. This file can then be stored on the local disk, upon the developer's request. Furthermore, the developer has the opportunity to open and update application profiles that are already stored. This is feasible through the main menu of the APE. Figure 8 depicts an application profile example that is defined in Prolog-like form. We can see that the specific application is written for a node which has two sensors attached to it: a temperature sensor and a vision sensor. A specific '*ice event*' is defined based on the values of both sensors.

Application GUI Creator

Every application defined in the IPAC framework should have an appropriate GUI. For the creation of the application User Interface (UI), a GUI creator is defined (Figure 9). A UI that meets the requirements and provides full functionality of any application greatly enhances the potential of adopting it. The creation of an application UI is an offline process. A list of available components is provided and the user is allowed to select from, all of which are lightweight to ensure minimized resource consumption. A main window frame is used to display the created UI, which is automatically updated as the user inserts/removes components in/from it.

Due to the limited resources of IPAC nodes (mobile nodes), UIs are as simplistic as possible, made of lightweight components, because in such a way they require less memory and update rapidly. Therefore, the developer is able to build the application UI in a specific layout, having two main choices: a *BorderLayout* and a *GridLayout.* Basic components that the user is allowed to use include labels and scrollable text areas for displaying text, text boxes to be used as user input (and possibly as output based on the circumstances), buttons as the default way of creating and sending a new message to the middleware and drop-down lists (combo boxes) for selection from multiple choices. All of the above components will be available from a list of options, allowing the user to select any of them (at the right of the environment). The user adds the selected components to the main window, constructing step by step the desired UI.

Debugger

When using DSLs, the main problem in the debugging process is that we want to debug the initial code of each application. However, this is very difficult due to the fact that there are not already defined debuggers, for all the DSLs. Moreover, it is very difficult to define a high-level debugger that is appropriate for every DSL.

In this Section, we provide the basic characteristics of the IPAC Debugger. For more information, the interested reader should refer to (Kolomvatsos et al., 2012). In our case, the code generation component produces a number of Java classes corresponding to the initial application code. For the definition of a debugger, we propose a solution that utilizes a logging process based on the known *Apache log4j library* (Apache Software Foundation, 2011). The rationale is to insert specific logging commands in the produced Java code and to create an OSGi logging service that will accept the log messages when the final Java code runs.

A first stage of debugging in IPAC is performed during application development, where the code is actually written, through incorrect syntax highlighting, cross-checking and code validation. A second stage of debugging is required when the produced Java code is ready for integration and execution. Apart from syntax errors, or fatal errors which will be obvious, both of which will be displayed on screen and logged to files, the challenging task is to locate all logical errors that will produce incorrect results. Therefore, logging messages provide an insight into the variables' values and a powerful trace of execution flow can assist in error recognition and correction. In Figure 10, we can see the architecture of the proposed debugger.

Our approach is implemented on top of *Apache* log4j, which only plays the role of the communication medium. IPAC nodes may run multiple applications at any given time. Moreover, each application may use a number of variables to provide the desired functionality. Hence, a key requirement is to simultaneously support an arbitrary number of applications along with their variables. A notable particularity of the IPAC framework and its associated debugger is that they operate on top of a wireless sensor network. The interesting part about this setting is that the debugger may not run on the same node as the application being debugged, and hence the variables involved in a possible error are not known in advance. Moreover, even if they were, IPAC is targeted towards autonomic computing, which means that events may be triggered at any moment during execution (i.e. sensor values) and from a

Figure 10. The architecture of the IPAC debugger

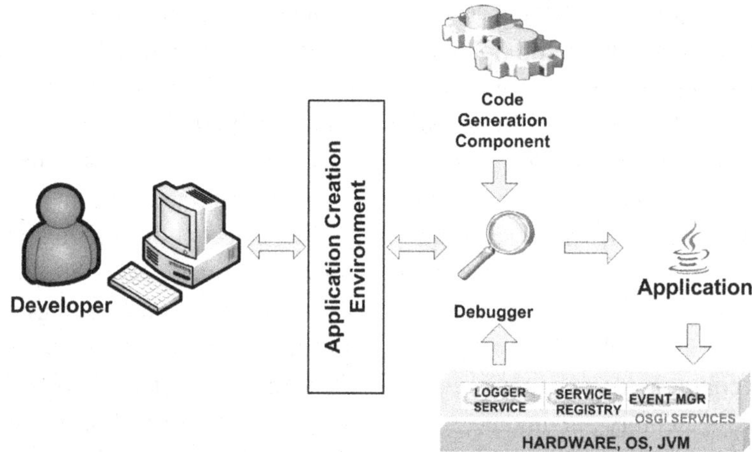

node other than the one running the application, due to collaborative context-awareness.

We create specific code generation templates. The template specifies the insertion of predefined logging events in specific commands of our application final code. We insert such commands when we deal with the modification of variable values. Such modifications are held in assignment statements. For the definition of a logging event we define a custom format including:

1. The application ID. The ID is used for the identification of the application sending the logging message. This way, the debugger can simultaneously support a number of applications.
2. The line in the Java code where the specific command is located.
3. The line in the application workflow written in terms of our DSL.
4. The variable name that is affected by the command.
5. The value of the specific variable.

The specified message is transmitted over a TCP connection that can be either local or remote. The debugger listens for connections on a predefined port. When we need to debug an application in the IPAC framework, a connection is established between the application and the debugger. At first, the application sends a predefined message 'DEBUGGER UP' accompanied by the location of the application jar file and the break points file path. Once the connection has been established, we register the new application for debugging, by sending a 'START <appId>' message to the debugger. We can use a similar message to stop debugging an application (STOP <appId>), which is useful to release resources. When it comes to variables, though, we are interested in more information other than its value. We need to know where this variable was used, for example, the line where it was referenced in the application. Since the application is written in DSL, i.e. a higher level language, then a variable reference is associated with one or more lines of a lower level language. The mapping between the two languages is handled in the code generation component. Both language references are used in the debugger, to allow for better manipulation and overview of the code by the programmer.

Prior to executing the IPAC application in debug mode, the programmer may add breakpoints in lines of interest, to control the program flow. In our setting, adding breakpoints is only possible before starting executing the application. In order

Figure 11. Emulator XML file format

```
<?xml version="1.0" encoding="UTF-8"?>
<!DOCTYPE EmulationConfiguration SYSTEM "schema5.dtd">
<EmulationConfiguration>
    <SensingElement SensorType="" SensorID="" Value="">
    </SensingElement>
</EmulationConfiguration>
```

to add breakpoints in the code, a specific ADL command is used for their definition (BREAKPOINT command) in the application workflow. During the target code generation, a file containing only the ADL and target code lines of the breakpoints is created on the local disk. As previously mentioned, the path of the final jar file and the breakpoints file are sent to the debugger logging service through a pre-defined message.

Apart from the underlying methodology, we have also developed a GUI for the debugger, where debugged variable information is displayed. To address simultaneous applications, we have followed a tabbed approach, where each application is accommodated in its own tab. Each tab contains a table where rows represent variables and columns are time units of updating. Therefore, a table cell contains the value of the variable for that time unit. Upon clicking on the cell, the rest of the information about the variable is displayed, including where it was referenced in the DSL and the low-level language. The case study presented in Section VI describes the debugging process of an example application.

Emulator

The IPAC Emulator is another important component of the IPAC ACE based on which application can be tested under a certain scenario. The purpose of developing an emulator is to give developers the opportunity to check and verify whether or not the overall functionality of the IPAC platform meets its specifications. Actually, the emulator handles scenarios describing sensor values. Therefore, the emulator manages configurable scenarios that provide testing capabilities which are similar to real time execution of an IPAC application. Instead of actual sensors, the emulator uses user-defined XML files containing information and measurements. The format of such a file is presented in Figure 11.

The XML file contains all the appropriate information needed by the emulator in order to work properly. The sensor type and the sensor id define which sensor is going to be used in an application and the value is the measurement taken at a specific time instance.

Figure 12 describes the flow of the IPAC emulator. The emulator can be considered as a black box and its functionality can be divided in two parts: the file processing and the interaction part. To begin with, the developer must select a certain scenario for a specific application. The selection is materialized via a UI which appears to the user just after the emulator starts. After the scenario's selection, the emulator parses the XML file in order to define the available sensor and its measurements. The interaction with other services is the next step. The emulator sends the processed data to the storage and distributes them, wherever they are needed, to other services.

During emulations, a "lightweight" version of the IPAC platform is used. This lightweight version has the full operability of the real middleware, but there is no physical equipment (sensors, nodes, wireless cards, etc) present, and therefore all actions that would be performed by nodes and sensors are just logged on a file or displayed on the screen. The emulator is implemented in Java. It has two main operation modes:

Figure 12. IPAC emulator architecture

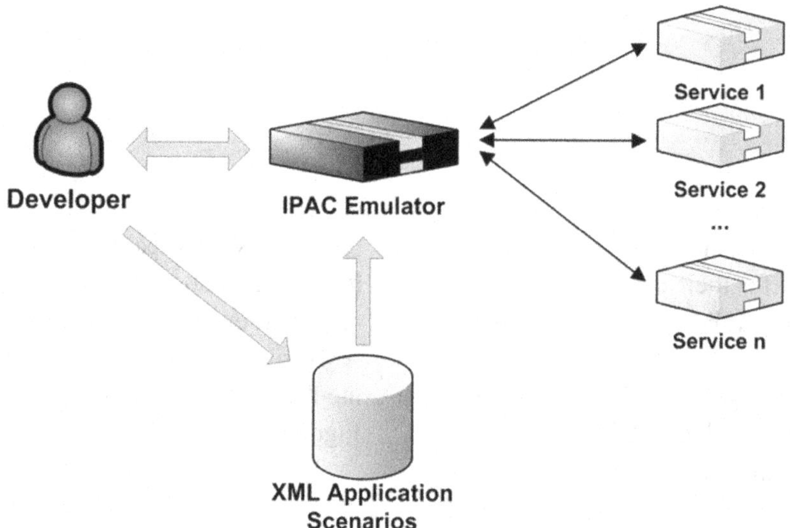

- The "static" mode will use pre-defined values (stored in specific files) of all sensors and activity that will be emulated, so during runtime, the application will read values from files and send them to the IPAC platform as real data. This will require almost no human intervention, as all actions of the emulator will be already defined and specified within files.
- In the "dynamic" mode, the emulator can either produce random values (within specified bounds), or can let a human, through an appropriate simple interface, to send specific values to the IPAC platform, or simply change some parameters of the emulation model, and watch the platform's reaction.

These modes are not mutually exclusive and may be combined, depending on the emulation scenario used. The sensing data and the network messages are generated from two respective components which are configurable through XML files. The network message generator component generates messages and forwards them to the appropriate middleware service using the appropriate exposed interface. Both the network message generator component and the sensing data generator component are configurable in terms of what data/message are to be generated and the relative time at which this information is to be sent to the middleware. Relative time is understood as the time in seconds after the emulation begins.

Advantages and Limitations

IPAC is targeted towards autonomic computing, which means that sensor events may be triggered at any moment during execution (i.e. sensor values) and from a node other than the one running the debugger application, due to collaborative context-awareness. In such cases, the proposed framework provides efficiency, as it can help developers to define applications that react to sensor events. Furthermore, the provided Debugger and Emulator could be proved useful in the identification of execution errors. The debugger viewer is very efficient when we deal with a large number of applications running in the IPAC framework.

Improvements include increased efficiency and effectiveness of the provided debugger functionality. For example, we can enhance the debugger

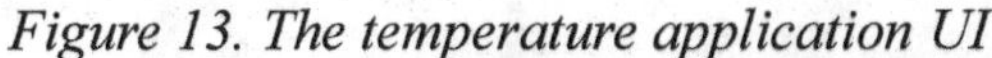

Figure 13. The temperature application UI

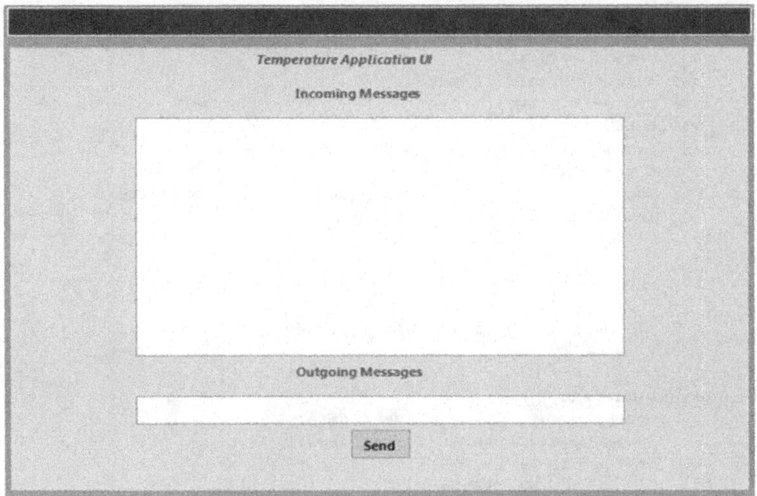

viewer with more complex windows, to provide more information to developers. Finally, the manipulation of break points could be enhanced. For this, real time communication between the OSGi environment with the Eclipse framework is needed. The discussed improvements are future extensions to the current research effort.

Case Study: Creating and Testing a Temperature Application

In this Section, we describe the steps required by the creation, the debugging and the emulation process of an example application. We start by describing the application business logic and accordingly we describe step by step the rest of the process.

Application Short Description

The application we choose to describe is a very simple application based on sensor values. We consider a mobile node that has a temperature and a vision sensor attached to it. In this application, we have defined a specific UI that the end user can utilize in order to send or see messages sent by other mobile nodes or produced by the application. For this, in the application workflow, we define a UI event responsible to define actions taken when a UI event is triggered. For example, when the user wants to send a message, he/she enters the information in the correct text box and presses a 'send' button. Figure 13 presents the UI of the discussed application. The UI screen is created by using the IPAC ACE as well as the UI generated code.

Moreover, based on values taken by the temperature and the vision sensor, we define an ice event. The application profile is depicted in Figure 7 and Figure 8. In case of an ice event, a specific message is presented on the screen, containing the temperature value. This value is presented on the appropriate place in the application UI ('*Incoming Messages*' area).

Application Code

In Figure 14, we depict the sample application ADL code. The main workflow indicates that the application runs an endless loop. We have defined two events: an ice and a UI event. The ice event is triggered when the temperature retrieved by the sensor is lower than 5° C and the vision sensor indicates possibility of ice (sensor value

Figure 14. The application ADL code

```
application temperatureapplicationexample_956 {
    // Variable Declarations
    var data as String
    var sensor_value as String
    var msg as String
    var evtID as int
    // EventHandler Declarations
    event iceevent {
        property sensor_value value iceevent.sensor_value
        invoke uiService {
            method displayContent ( 3, "Ice Event !!!! \n")
        }
        set msg = "The temperature is : " + sensor_value + "\n"
        invoke uiService {
            method displayContent ( 3, msg)
        }
    }
    event uievent {
        property data value uievent.data
        property evtID value uievent.evtID
        if ( evtID == 6) {
            invoke srccService {
                method disseminateAppInfo ( 956, data, "High", 12, 7)
            }
        }
    }
    // Application Logic
    body {
        while (true) {
            wait 5
        }
    }
}
```

Figure 15. The main body workflow

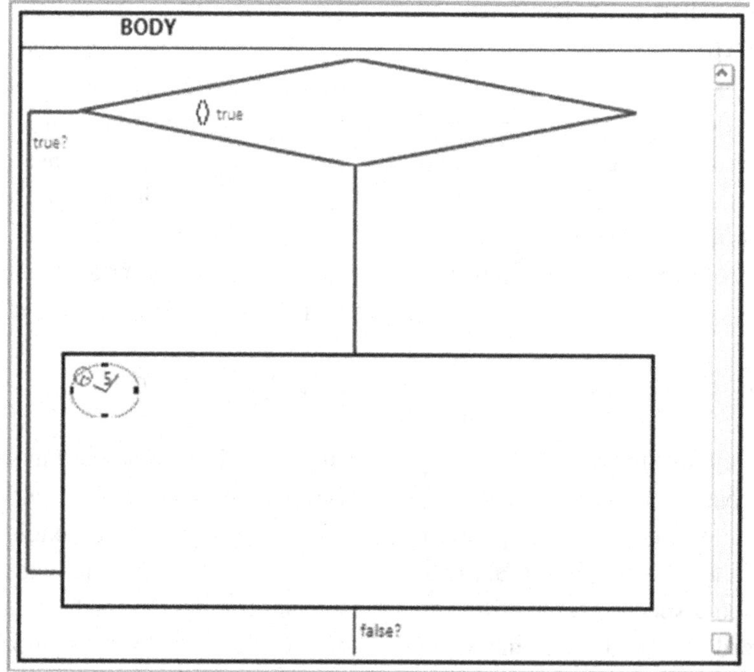

Figure 16. The ice event workflow

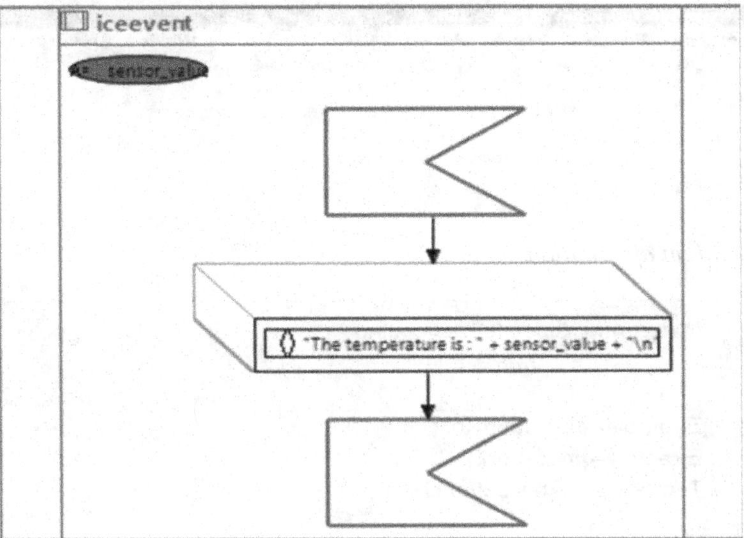

Figure 17. The UIevent workflow

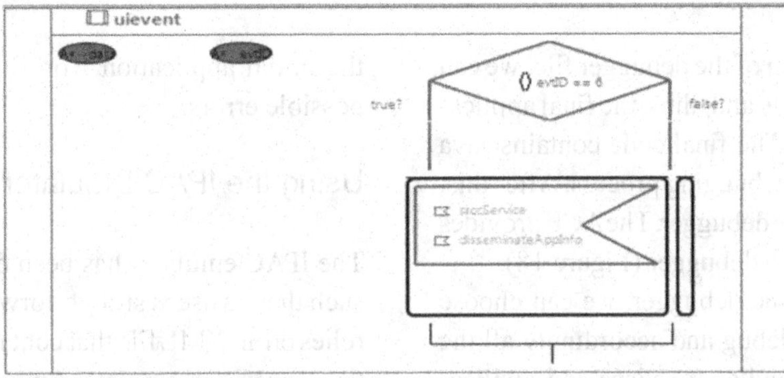

greater than 70). In this case, the application displays a warning message in the UI together with the temperature retrieved by the sensor. The UI event is triggered when the user presses the '*Send*' button in the application UI. In this case, the application retrieves the text message defined by the user and sends it to the network. In Figure 15, Figure 16, and Figure 17, we see the visual editor diagrams for the main body, the ice and the UI event respectively.

Using the IPAC Debugger

As mentioned, the application workflow is defined by using the IPAC ACE tool. The ACE also provides functionalities related to the debugging process. After the creation of the application workflow, the first step in the debugging process is the creation of a specific debugger file. This can be done through the special Eclipse wizard created for such purposes. The aim of the new file is the invocation of the debugger templates in the code generation component as explained in previous sections.

Figure 18. Eclipse toolbar and menu for the debugger invocation

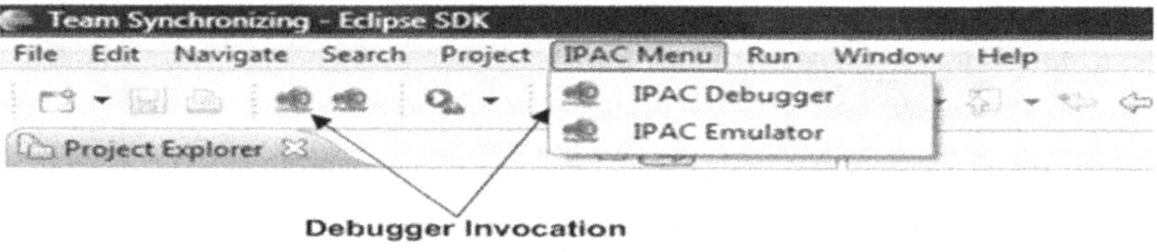

Figure 19. Selection of an application

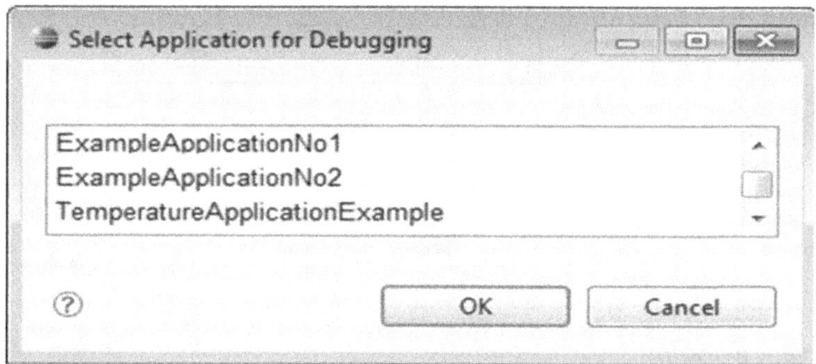

After the creation of the debugger file, we can run the mapping code and, thus, the final application code is ready. The final code contains Java lines related to the debugging process. After this, we are able to call the debugger. The ACE provides specific hooks to the debugger (Figure 18).

After invoking the debugger, we can choose the application to debug and accordingly all the necessary OSGi bundles (services and applications) are automatically uploaded in the OSGi environment(Figure 19). This is done only if necessary.

The most important aspect in this process is that we can debug an application either by using real sensor values or by using the IPAC emulator. After completing the steps described above, the developer is able to see the application messages in the debugger viewer. Figure 20 shows the results for the discussed temperature application. By clicking on a specific row, the developer can see the lines of the initial application workflow and the Java file that produced the specific variable value. This way, he/she is capable of managing the initial application workflow and correcting possible errors.

Using the IPAC Emulator

The IPAC emulator has been designed in a way, such that its use is straightforward. The emulator relies on an XML file that contains information of the scenario to emulate. An example of such an XML scenario file is shown in Figure 21. In this scenario, we describe time instances where sensor values are retrieved. We define values for two sensors: a vision sensor and a temperature sensor. When the emulator starts, the user is prompted to choose a scenario file. After selecting the scenario to run, the user can run the actual application for testing purposes. In Figure 22, we present the UI of the application described above. The values located in the scenario file trigger the ice event, resulting in a warning message appearing on the screen.

Figure 20. A snapshot of the debugger viewer

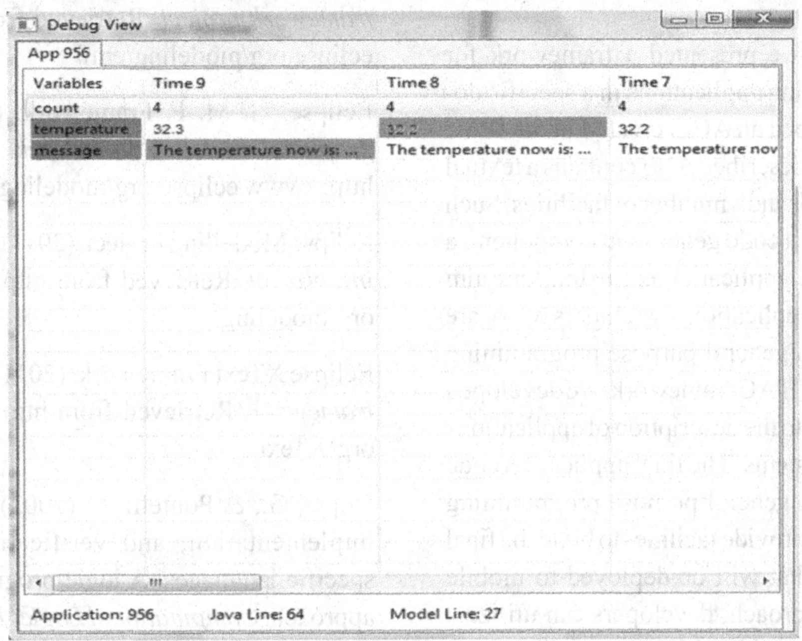

Figure 21. An emulator scenario example


```
<?xml version="1.0" encoding="UTF-8"?>
<!DOCTYPE DOCType SYSTEM "schema5.dtd">
<EmulationConfiguration>
        <SensingElement SensorType="vision_sensor" SensorID="FFFFFFFFFF0000000000_6"
              Value="77"/>
        <SensingElement SensorType="vision_sensor" SensorID="FFFFFFFFFF0000000000_6"
              Value="73"/>
        <SensingElement SensorType="vision_sensor" SensorID="FFFFFFFFFF0000000000_6"
              Value="63"/>
        <SensingElement SensorType="temperature_sensor" SensorID="5B18C1F5EB4AB2897D1D_1"
              Value="2"/>
        <SensingElement SensorType="temperature_sensor" SensorID="5B18C1F5EB4AB2897D1D_1"
              Value="3"/>
        <SensingElement SensorType="temperature_sensor" SensorID="5B18C1F5EB4AB2897D1D_1"
              Value="4"/>
</EmulationConfiguration>
```


Figure 22. The APPLICATION UI

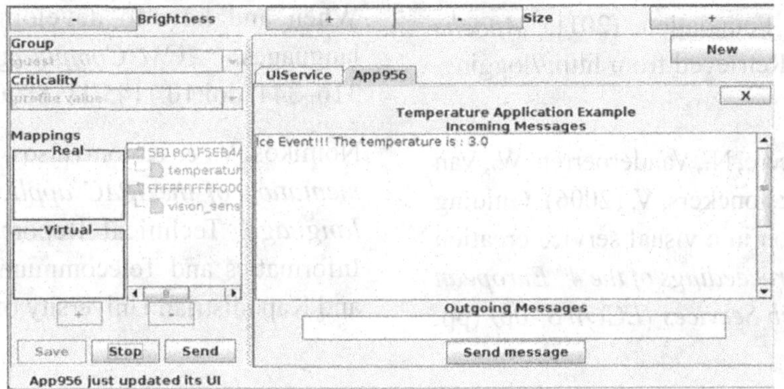

CONCLUSION

In this chapter, we presented a framework for building and testing applications in a specific domain. We described an ACE, created in the IPAC framework. The described ACE contains a textual and a visual editor and a number of facilities. Such facilities include a code generation component, a debugger and an application emulator. Our aim is to facilitate application developers who are not familiar with general purpose programming languages. In the IPAC framework, we developed an ADL oriented to the description of applications for embedded systems. The final application code is translated to a general purpose programming language and we provide facilities to build the final executable file that will be deployed to mobile nodes. In our approach, developers can utilize a number of functionalities. Moreover, our ACE can be adapted to every system that utilizes a number of middleware services.

ACKNOWLEDGMENT

This work was partially supported by the European Commission through the FP7 ICT Programme in the scope of the project IPAC (Integrated Platform for Autonomic Computing), contact FP7-ICT-224395.

REFERENCES

Apache Software Foundation. (2011). *Apache logging services*. Retrieved from http://logging.apache.org/

Braem, M., Joncheere, N., Vanderperren, W., Van der Straeten, R., & Jonckers, V. (2006). Guiding service composition in a visual service creation environment. *In Proceedings of the 4th European Conference on Web Services (ECOWS '06)* (pp. 13-22).

Eclipse, E. M. F. Project. (2011). *Eclipse modeling framework project*. Retrieved from http://www.eclipse.org/modeling/emf/

Eclipse, G. M. F. Framework. (2011). *Eclipse graphical modeling framework*. Retrieved from http://www.eclipse.org/modeling/gmp/

Eclipse Modelling Project. (2011). *Eclipse modeling project*. Retrieved from http://www.eclipse.org/modeling/

Eclipse XText Framework. (2011). *Eclipse XText framework*. Retrieved from http://www.eclipse.org/XText/

Gupta, G., & Pontelli, E. (2002). Specification, implementation, and verification of domain specific languages: A logic programming-based approach. *Computational Logic: Logic Programming and Beyond, Essays in Honour of Robert A. Kowalski, Part I,* (pp. 211 – 239).

Ioannidis, A., Priggouris, I., Marias, I., Hadjiefthymiades, S., Faist-Kassapoglou, C., Hernandez, J., & Merakos, L. (2003). PoLoS: Integrated platform for location-based services. In *Proceedings of the IST Mobile & Wireless Communications Summit,* Portugal.

Kolomvatsos, K., Valkanas, G., & Hadjiefthymiades, S. (2012). Debugging applications created by a domain specific language: The IPAC case. *Journal of Systems and Software*, *85*(4), 932–943. doi:10.1016/j.jss.2011.11.1009

Mernik, M., Heering, J., & Sloane, A. (2005). When and how to develop domain-specific languages. *ACM Computing Surveys, 37*(4), 316–344. doi:10.1145/1118890.1118892

Nomikos, V., & Kolomvatsos, K. (2009). *Documentation of the IPAC application description language.* Technical Report, Department of Informatics and Telecommunications, National and Kapodistrian University of Athens.

OMG MOF Specification. (2011). *Meta object facility specification*. Retrieved September 9th, 2011, from http://www.omg.org/spec/MOF/2.0/PDF/

OMG QVT Specification. (2011). *Query/view/transformation specification*. Retrieved September 9th, 2011, from http://www.omg.org/spec/QVT/1.1/PDF/

Oracle Corp. (2011). *BPEL process manager*. Retrieved from http://www.oracle.com/technology/products/ias/ bpel/index.html

OSGi Alliance. (2011). *OSGi service platform specification*. Retrieved from http://www.osgi.org/Release4/Download

Pactolus. (2011). *Guide to the RapidFLEX service creation environment*: *Product manual*. Retrieved September 9th, 2011 from http://radisys.custhelp.com/ci/fattach/get/128/

Sadilek, D. A., & Wachsmuth, G. (2008). Prototyping visual interpreters and debuggers for domain-specific modelling languages. *In Proceedings of the 4th European Conference on Model Driven Architecture: Foundations and Applications* (pp. 63 – 78). Berlin, Germany.

Schmidt, D. (2006). Model-driven engineering. *IEEE Computer*, *39*(2), 25–31. doi:10.1109/MC.2006.58

Tsetsos, V., Papataxiarhis, V., Kontos, T., Seneclauze, M., Hadjiefthymiades, S., & Fytros, E. (2010). An advanced sensor platform for autonomic computing: The IPAC approach. In *7th European Conference on Wireless Sensor Networks (EWSN),* Coimbra, Portugal.

Wu, H., & Gray, J. (2005). Testing domain-specific languages in Eclipse. In *Proceedings of the Conference on Object Oriented Programming Systems Languages and Applications, Companion to the 20th Annual ACM SIGPLAN Conference on Object-Oriented Programming, Systems, Languages and Applications* (pp. 173-174). San Diego, USA.

Wu, H., Gray, J., & Mernik, M. (2004). *Debugging domain-specific languages*. In Object Oriented Programming Systems, Languages, and Applications, Eclipse Technology Poster Session, Vancouver, Canada.

Wu, H., Gray, J., & Mernik, M. (2008). Grammar-driven generation of domain-specific language debuggers. *Software, Practice & Experience*, *38*(10), 1073–1103. doi:10.1002/spe.863

Wu, H., Gray, J., Roychoudhury, S., & Mernik, M. (2005). Weaving a debugging aspect into domain-specific language grammars. In *Proceedings of the 2005 ACM Symposium on Applied Computing* (pp. 1370 – 1374). Santa Fe, New Mexico.

ADDITIONAL READING

Dunlavey, M. R. (1994). *Building better applications: A theory of efficient software development*. International Thomson Publishing.

Heitmeyer, C. (1998). Using the SCR toolset to specify software requirements. In *Proceedings of the Second IEEE Workshop on Industrial Strength Formal Specification Techniques*.

Kelly, S., & Pohjonen, R. (2009). Worst practices for domain-specific modeling. *IEEE Software*, *26*(4), 22–29. doi:10.1109/MS.2009.109

Kelly, S., & Tolvanen, J. P. (2008). *Domain-specific modeling: Enabling full code generation*. John Wiley and Sons.

Kos, T., Kosar, T., & Mernik, M. (2012). Development of data acquisition systems by using a domain-specific modeling language. *Computers in Industry*, *63*(3), 181–192. doi:10.1016/j.compind.2011.09.004

Kos, T., Kosar, T., Mernik, M., & Knez, J. (2011). *Ladybird: Debugging support in the sequencer. Applications of Mathematics and Computer Engineering* (pp. 135–139). WSEAS Press.

Larus, J. (2009). Spending Moore's dividend. *Communications of the ACM, 52*(5), 62–69. doi:10.1145/1506409.1506425

McLennan, B. (1999). *Principles of programming languages: Design, evaluation and implementation*. Oxford University Press.

Roberts, D., & Johnson, R. (1996). Evolve frameworks into domain-specific languages. In *Proceedings of the 3rd International Conference on Pattern Languages*.

Spinellis, D. (2001). Notable design patterns for domain specific languages. *Journal of Systems and Software, 56*(1), 91–99. doi:10.1016/S0164-1212(00)00089-3

van Deursen, A., Klint, P., & Visser, J. (2000). Domain-specific languages: An annotated bibliography. *ACM Sigplan Notices, 35*(6), 26–36. doi:10.1145/352029.352035

KEY TERMS AND DEFINITIONS

Application Creation Environment: Environment providing enhanced functionalities for creating and testing applications for a specific domain.

Application Description Language: Language designed for creating applications in the IPAC system.

Application Profile Editor: Software providing functionalities for defining an application profile in the IPAC system.

Debugger: Software providing functionalities for debugging an application.

Domain Specific Language: Language designed for a specific field of applications.

Emulator: Software providing functionalities for emulating an application.

Model Driven Engineering: Methodology for developing software components for a specific domain based on a specific model.

Chapter 13
Abstraction of Computer Language Patterns:
The Inference of Textual Notation for a DSL

Jaroslav Porubän
Technical University of Košice, Slovakia

Ján Kollár
Technical University of Košice, Slovakia

Miroslav Sabo
Technical University of Košice, Slovakia

ABSTRACT

In general, designing a domain-specific language (DSL) is a complicated process, requiring the cooperation of experts from both application domain and computer language development areas. One of the problems that may occur is a communication gap between a domain expert and a language engineer. Since domain experts are usually non-technical people, it might be difficult for them to express requirements on a DSL notation in a technical manner. Another compelling problem is that even though the majority of DSLs share the same notation style for representing the common language constructs, a language engineer has to formulate the specification for these constructs repeatedly for each new DSL being designed. The authors propose an innovative concept of computer language patterns to capture the well-known recurring notation style often seen in many computer languages. To address the communication problem, they aim for the way of proposing a DSL notation by providing program examples as they would have been written in a desired DSL. As a combination of these two ideas, the chapter presents a method for example-driven DSL notation specification (EDNS), which utilizes computer language patterns for semi-automated inference of a DSL notation specification from the provided program examples.

DOI: 10.4018/978-1-4666-2092-6.ch013

INTRODUCTION

Designing computer languages is hard, and designing domain-specific computer languages is even harder. The notation of a language must be defined to suit a specific domain but at the same time it has to be processable by a computer. What we often see in the notation of various computer languages is the recurrence of some particular patterns. These notation patterns are used to represent general language constructs found in many computer languages. They help users understand programs written in such languages by basing the notation on their prior experience. People who are familiar with such patterns are able to immediately comprehend a rough idea of a program without having to learn the language first. Since the human usability is one of the main features of DSLs, the notation of these languages is naturally full of such recurring language patterns. From the perspective of the language design, these patterns must be identified and translated into the grammar rules repeatedly for each new DSL. Although for experienced language engineers, this is a simple yet menial and repetitive task, for new ones it may present a serious assignment. To address the problems of both cases we propose to capture the knowledge of a language engineer as computer language patterns. Each language pattern systematically names, explains and captures the recurring notation and provides the means to reflect this notation in a language design. Our ultimate goal is to capture the knowledge of the language design in a form that people can use effectively.

MOTIVATION

Scenario 1: Communication with Domain Experts

Anna works as a developer for a global market company. Until now, the goods between stores and warehouses have been ordered and delivered according to handwritten enquiries. To improve this process, the company decided to go for automation. However, as the style used for writing the enquiries has been retained over the years and many employees are used to it, the company wants to keep it in the electronic version as well.

The task that Anna has been assigned is to develop a language with the well-known structure and notation defined by existing enquiries. The approach to specifying a language notation by providing example documents is also very convenient even if documents do not exist and have to be created at first. This is very common in development of vertical DSLs[1] since for the non-technical domain experts, writing down the examples is often the best way of communicating their thoughts on the look and feel of a language being designed.

Scenario 2: Analyzers of Generated Textual Output

An SMS or email notification is a service commonly provided by many companies. Bob has subscribed to an online auctioning site and now he receives emails every time some important events happen (e.g. somebody bids on an item he is interested in). To increase his chances in the auction, he decided to track the biddings of each participant and analyze them for predictions of their future behavior. Since the only source of such information is emails with well formatted messages, Bob has to extract the desired data from them. Messages can be of a variable length and different content depending on the type and number of events they report therefore using regular expressions would not suffice for this purpose.

This scenario describes a situation where a parser for existing formatted documents has to be created. Software systems generate a lot of textual output, either as a main product of their execution or for other purposes such as logging or reporting. If the output is intended for information transfer and further processing by another system, its structure must be explicitly defined (e.g. XML and XSD), so that the receiving system is able to transform the textual content into an appropriate structural representation. On the other hand, if the output is intended for a human recipient, the structure of the textual content is often not defined explicitly but it is rather hidden in its human-usable notation. In most of these cases, the explicit specification of a structure is not even necessary, as the primary purpose of such textual output is to store the information in a form which is easily comprehensible to human users just by reading it. However, what sometimes happens is that the textual output originally intended for people has to be processed by a computer (e.g. to perform an analysis). Since explicit specification of its structure does not exist, it has to be defined first.

Considering the generative origin and a human-usable notation, we think of such a textual output as of documents written in some DSL. From this perspective, the task of specifying a structure can be formulated as a problem of the DSL notation specification. The straightforward option is to examine the source code of the system that generates the output and construct the grammar of a DSL accordingly. Besides the complexity of such task, the developer requires original source code, which might be not accessible. That leaves us with option to specify the language notation by inferring it from the provided documents.

Scenario 3: Language-Specific Tool Support

Charles works for a company that sells a complex software product which, moreover, is extensible with a wide set of various modules. The versions of the product and particular modules may vary among customers, and configuration of the extension modules may be different for each customer as well. Since the beginning of the product's lifecycle, the release management has been built on a properties configuration file that defines the extensions, versioning, integration commands, dependencies and other information necessary for a successful deployment of the patch, hot fix or a regular release. With the growing number of customers and modules, the writing of such configurations by hand has become an error-prone and time-consuming task. To enhance this process, the company has assigned Charles with developing an in-house textual editor to support the writing of the configuration files. The editor should provide all the language-specific support features, such as syntax highlighting, code completion or outline view.

This is a very common situation often seen in many companies. Configuration files that were designed at the beginning of the product's lifecycle become unmaintainable as the product matures and expands. Due to legacy reasons or preservation of backward compatibility, the way of how configuration is handled cannot be changed. Considering the high costs of automating the creation of configuration files, another viable solution is to develop a supporting tool that would facilitate the writing of them. With the existence of frameworks and workbenches capable of generating such tools from the given language specification, the solution for a problem described in this scenario can be again formulated as an inference of a DSL specification from the existing files.

BACKGROUND

In this section we will briefly introduce the areas which have already been implied in the scenarios above. In essence, the work tackles three areas. Computer language development is the central theme of the work. To narrow down the scope, we focus on the development of domain-specific languages. We are particularly interested in the notation of a language. Since we aim to infer it from the existing documents that represent the programs written in such a DSL, approach to example-driven DSL notation specification is addressed in the work as well.

Domain-Specific Language Development

Domain-Specific Languages (DSLs) are often used to improve the productivity and quality of software engineering in a particular application domain. They are characterized by high level of expressiveness in a particular domain, narrowing the scope of their usability to the domain at the same time. The specificity of a language, which on one hand brings all of the benefits, is at the same time a cause of the biggest cost connected with using a DSL, and that is the cost of developing it first. In this work, we discuss different approaches to development of DSLs. We compare the traditional approach to specification of a computer language using the grammars with model-driven approach that is based on metamodeling. Of particular interest to us is the way of how both approaches address the specification of two related parts of a computer language – abstract and concrete syntaxes.

Notation of Domain-Specific Languages

Since one of the most important features of a DSL is its domain-specific notation, we put a special emphasis on the specification of the concrete syntax of a language. From the motivation scenarios, it is apparent that we are concerned with situations where the requirements on the notation of a DSL are given in a form of example documents. We consider them to be the program instances written in such language. In this work, we are concerned with the inference of a notation specification from these examples. By analyzing many programs written in both kinds of computer languages, general-purpose and domain-specific, we have observed some recurring patterns in the style of their notation. Hence, we decided to exploit this knowledge to achieve automation of the notation inference process.

Specification by Examples

Scenarios above illustrated various situations when providing examples is the most convenient approach to expressing the requirements on a DSL notation. While in the first scenario the motivating factor was the bridging of communication gap between non-technical domain expert and technical language engineer, the other two scenarios were motivated by the existence of a precise definition of the DSL notation, however, not expressed in the form of grammar rules. According to these cases, we consider the possibility to specify a DSL notation by providing examples an idea worth exploring. In this work, we address it with the proposal of the method for example-driven DSL notation specification.

PROBLEM STATEMENT

The current adoption of the domain-specific approach to software development naturally leads to an increased demand for the development of domain-specific languages. Despite the well-known benefits of DSLs, they have not been used in the past due to high costs of their implementation. This has changed lately with the appearance of several frameworks (EMFText, Xtext) that enable generation of a full language implementation given just the language specification. Although parser generators are not a new idea, the major difference these frameworks bring is that besides the language itself they are capable of generating a tooling support in a form of fully-fledged language-specific Integrated Development Environments (IDEs) as well. This completely changes the view on the process of developing a DSL, since the main task now switches from an actual implementation (that is automated) to writing of language specification. We decided to go a step further and automate the writing of the language specification as well. These are the problems that motivated us to make such a decision.

Communication Gap between Language Engineers and Domain Experts

When developing a vertical DSL (i.e. a computer language intended for use in a non-technical application domain such as finance or medicine), one has to pay a special attention to the definition of its notation. High requirements on the notation are just natural, as it might often happen that programs written in such DSL should be reviewed, validated or signed-off by a domain expert. Sometimes, it should even be possible for domain experts to create such documents. As in such cases experts represent the main users of a language, its notation must be designed appropriately for them to understand it without any difficulties. Therefore it is considered a good practice to design the notation by following requirements given directly by experts. However, the problem that often has to be dealt with is that domain experts are not able to express their thoughts in a technical manner. In this work, we will try to address this problem of the communication gap between domain experts and language engineers.

Required Knowledge of a Language Design

Development of DSLs is hard, requiring expertise in both application domain and computer language construction areas (Mernik, Heering & Sloane, 2005). The requirements on the knowledge of a language design and implementation have been lowered with the introduction of frameworks capable of generating a full implementation from language's specification. However, these frameworks place a different burden on language designers, and that is to learn a custom language for specifying a DSL. All frameworks provide their own languages, and even though they are all grammar-based and share some similarities, one has to invest the resources and time to learn them before being able to write a DSL specification. The issue of custom specification languages becomes apparent as well as when trying to reuse the existing specification in a different framework.

Repetitive Specification of the Same Notation Style

When observing programs written in various computer languages, one can easily observe some recurring patterns in a notation style. This is more evident with DSLs which are the languages aiming for a better human usability and understandability. Generally, when writing documents, a human inherently uses particular notations for expressing particular language constructs. This is a reason why people are able to comprehend the meaning of DSL programs, even though they are not familiar with the DSL at all. Drawing from this experience, to specify any DSL notation, language designer often has to define the same style repeatedly for each new DSL. In the field of external computer language design, there is no such concept of patterns for language notation as it is in the field of object-oriented software development for design patterns (Gamma, Helm, Johnson & Vlissides, 1994). We consider this an important area worth to improve, therefore we address the problem of recurring specification in this work.

COMPUTER LANGUAGE PATTERNS

What is a Language Pattern?

Likewise to design patterns, where design structures are expressed in terms of objects and interfaces, language patterns use terms of metamodeling. However, the meaning of these structures is completely different. While structures in design patterns prescribe how the object-oriented design should be carried out, structures in language patterns capture the abstract syntax that is represented by a well-known recurring notation in computer and even natural languages. This fact also differs computer language patterns from design patterns for DSL (Spinellis, 2001) oriented to the field of DSLs implementation and partially even from design patterns for internal domain-specific languages described in Chapter 6 and Chapters 7 of this book. Our language patterns resemble the most notation patterns from these chapters but are intended for external languages.

To illustrate the concept of computer language patterns, let's have a look at the following excerpts of the programs written in various computer languages (Figure 1):

Without knowing the syntax of any of these languages, one can easily comprehend that tokens 10, 20 and 30 are somehow related (the same applies for triplets "Saab", "Volvo", "BMW" and Ian, Sean, Phil). We are able to deduce this because we understand that these tokens represent the items of a list. But how do we know that what we see are individual items? The key parts of the notation that has led us to this conclusion are delimiter marks (e.g. comma, semicolon) that separate these individual items from each other.

Since using delimiter marks is a well-known recurring style for representing the lists, we consider this a language pattern (the Separator language pattern). In a traditional approach to computer language development, every occurrence of such a language construct would have been formulated in a language design using the same set of grammar rules. Language patterns remove this necessity to write the same rules over and over again, and raise the task of a language design to higher level of abstraction. It is apparent that language patterns are natural for the humans since they simplifies the comprehension of a program and represents the reusability in the form of understanding. In our research we are concentrating on general notation and abstract syntax language patterns which are occurring even in the natural language not only in DSLs. However, one can deduce that there are many language patterns connected to a programing paradigm or a domain. These patterns are usually reused in various languages for a paradigm.

How to Use a Language Pattern

As concept of language patterns operates in terms of abstract and concrete syntaxes, it has been designed for the application in the abstract syntax driven computer language development. To recall the rationale of this approach, language design starts with identification of language concepts and relations between them. Both should be contained in the output of domain analysis that includes terminology, concepts, their common and variable properties, and interdependencies between them. After concepts and relations are formalized in a form of domain models that represent the abstract syntax of a language, language designer can proceed with definition of concrete syntax and semantics. Although semantics is not in the focus of this work, the results of our research in this area can be found in our earlier work (Porubän, Sabo, Kollár & Mernik, 2010). The regular approach to concrete syntax definition is to formulate the rules of a grammar using the concepts from the abstract syntax as non-terminals. Even though the abstract and concrete syntaxes are clearly separated, using a grammar to define the notation of language results in the same situation of

Figure 1. Excerpts of programs written in three different programming languages

```
Java:          int[] array = {10, 20, 30}
JavaScript:    var myCars = ["Saab", "Volvo", "BMW"]
DSL:           Department Management: Ian, Sean, Mary
```

repetitive writing the same set of rules, as it is in traditional approach.

The concept of language patterns takes advantage of having the abstract syntax already defined. Since the patterns encapsulate the recurring notation and corresponding structures of the abstract syntax, we look at concrete syntax definition as a process of application of language patterns on the domain model representing the abstract syntax of a language (Figure 2).

In our original approach 10 notation patterns were identified and supported by YAJCo parser generator (Porubän, Forgáč, Sabo & Běhálek, 2010):

- Patterns *Optional* and *Range* were used to mark the optionality and multiplicity of a relation between two domain concepts.
- Token patterns *Before*, *After*, and *Separator* for marking a concept instance in a sentence and the *Token* pattern for the binding value of lexical units to an abstract syntax of a domain concept.
- Common language patterns for specification of operators with their priority and associativity called *Operator* and *Parentheses* and two patterns for concept instance identification and referencing in a sentence called *Identifier* and *References*.

The abstract syntax of a language was defined using the conceptual class diagrams. Notation patterns were used to annotate conceptual class diagrams representing the abstract syntax of the language and defines mapping from the abstract syntax to the concrete syntax of the language. Language patterns were implemented as a standard Java annotation types in YAJCo parser generator. During the phase of concrete syntax definition the parser generator assists a developer with suggestions and hints for making the concrete syntax unambiguous. Each class represented some language domain concept and 'is-a' and 'has-a' relations between classes represented relations between domain concepts. Therefore, the definition of a language was based on metamodeling. Later on we decided to switch from the class diagrams to EMF Ecore Metamodels (Sabo, 2011). In a similar way, Kleppe argues for concentrating on the abstract syntax and metamodels when designing a computer language (Kleppe, 2007).

Figure 2. Incremental language design process

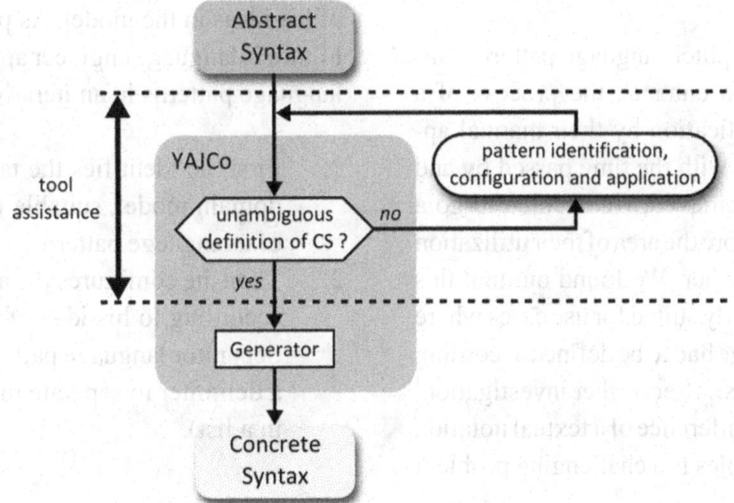

The actual process of applying a language pattern is very simple. However, it is preceded by pattern identification. The process of the pattern identification is performed manually by searching a domain model for the structure prescribed by the target of a pattern. If such a structure is found, the pattern can be applied on it. The pattern application itself consists of marking the elements of the identified structure with special annotations prescribed by the pattern. If a pattern contains some variable properties, they are configured through annotations as well. Once the identified structure is annotated, we call it a pattern instance.

As seen in the Figure 2, concrete syntax definition is an incremental process consisting of iterative identification and application of language patterns. This process is performed manually by a language designer who has to decide whether the notation is defined unambiguously. However, in making such decision, he is aided by tool assistance (Porubän, Forgáč, Sabo & Běhálek, 2010). Once the positive decision is made, annotated domain model is transformed into the concrete syntax specification written in a particular formalism in an automated manner. This is performed by utilizing the YAJCo Generator tool (Lakatoš, Porubän & Sabo, 2011).

Language Patterns and Inference of a Textual Notation

The concept of computer language patterns was initially proposed to enhance the process of a DSL notation specification by their manual application. However, with the time passed by and successful results achieved, we decided to go a step further and explore the area of their utilization in an automated manner. We found out that this approach was perfectly suited for use cases where notation of a language had to be defined according to program examples. After further investigation, we realized that the inference of a textual notation from existing examples is a challenging problem worth exploring.

Generally, the task of notation inference using the concept of language patterns can be divided into two stages:

1. Recognition of language patterns in provided examples, and
2. Inference of notation specification according to the identified pattern instances.

Since the second stage has already been successfully addressed in our earlier research (Porubän, Forgáč, Sabo & Běhálek, 2010; Porubän, Sabo, Kollár & Mernik, 2010; Lakatoš, Porubän & Sabo, 2011), in this work we elaborate on the problem of recognizing the language patterns in existing textual documents.

Original Approach

The initial proposition of the concept of language patterns was designed with the intention to alleviate the problem of repetitive writing of the same grammar rules. Language engineer who has a clear idea of how the notation of a DSL should look like is given a domain model that represents the abstract syntax of a language (Figure 3). His task is to transfer the image of a notation from his mind into the domain model. To perform this transfer, he uses language patterns as conveyors specifically designed for the seamless formulation of his ideas in the model. As presented earlier in Figure 2, language engineer applies the particular language patterns in an iterative manner:

1. First, he identifies the target structure in a domain model, suitable for the application of a language pattern.
2. Then, he configures the appropriate pattern according to his idea of a notation (e.g. in Separator language pattern, use "," mark as a delimiter to separate the individual items in a list).

Figure 3. Original approach to notation definition using language patterns

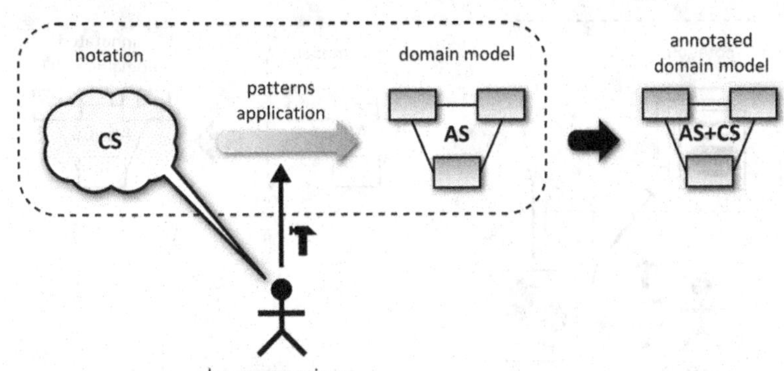

3. Finally, he applies the configured pattern in a domain model by annotating the appropriate structure.

This cycle is repeated until the idea of a notation is fully reflected in the domain model.

This approach can also be used in the case when the language engineer has no idea about how the notation of a language should look like. Given just the plain domain model, he can use a tool assistance feature of YAJCo tool to check whether the unambiguous notation specification can be generated from the model (Porubän, Forgáč, Sabo & Běhálek, 2010). If not, the advices of which patterns should be applied to remove such ambiguities are given to the engineer. After the application of the suggested patterns, the tool assistance can be run again for another check. In such manner, the engineer can be guided in an incremental design of the unambiguous notation for a language.

Inference Approach

Inference approach, that is in the focus of this work, differs from the original approach in two main points:

1. The proposal of the notation is given explicitly as concrete examples of programs, rather than as ideas in mind of a designer.
2. The machinery around pattern application is automated rather than performed manually by a designer.

Even though the patterns are applied automatically, the process follows the same identify/configure/apply design (Figure 4), as described in the original approach. The automation of identifying target structures suitable for application of the language patterns is straightforward. The language patterns prescribe these structures as their target property and a domain model is given as an EMF Ecore model. The identification therefore boils down to the model matching task that can be easily automated.

Configuration of identified patterns presents the first major difference when compared to the original approach. Since variable properties of the patterns should be configured according to the proposed notation, these properties must be retrieved from the provided examples at first. Considering that notation is given informally as plain textual documents, to be able to recognize the notation of particular language patterns, a first step is to formalize these documents. For this purpose, a simple ProgXample modeling formalism has been proposed to represent the textual content in a tree-like form (Sabo, 2011). ProgXample is a compositional modeling language for tree representation of textual content.

Figure 4. Inference approach to notation definition using language patterns

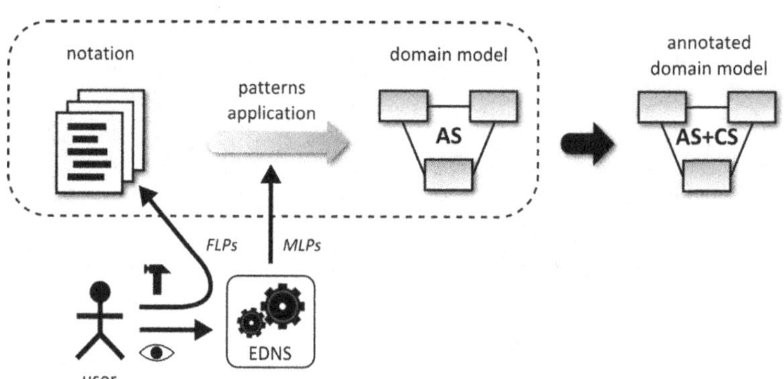

The automated process of building tree models is driven by Formatting Language Patterns (FLPs), a special instance of the concept of language patterns[2]. Once the example documents are formalized, variable properties of the identified patterns can be automatically retrieved. This is performed by recognition of the recurring notation of an identified pattern in tree models. The elements of a model that represent the notation are automatically identified according to the structure template prescribed by the newly introduced ProgXample Target property of a pattern. Finally, after the identified pattern has successfully been configured with properties from the examples provided, it can be automatically applied in the domain model.

We call the overall process of notation inference an Example-Driven DSL Notation Specification and the method that implements it is called an EDNS method. Since all stages of patterns application are automated, the role of a user has radically changed. Recalling the stages from end to beginning, pattern application and configuration are fully in the competence of the EDNS method, so the user does not have to deal with the implementation tasks at all. However, to control the process of a notation inference, the user can manage the configuration of identified patterns indirectly by amending the program examples (Figure 5). For this purpose the EDNS method provides visualizers for the domain model and tree models that represent the program examples. In this way, a user can review the application of each pattern, and in cases when needed (e.g. incorrect notation recognition or incorrect identification of a target structure), he is able to perform the appropriate amendments through GUI. User interface can also be used for a manual identification of language patterns by marking the appropriate structures of the domain model and tree models in the visualizers.

Summary

Both approaches to using language patterns, original and inference, bring some contributions when compared to the traditional approach to computer language design. The original approach removes the necessity of repetitive writing of the same sets of rules for each new designed language. Moreover, the language is designed on a higher level of abstraction, since the language patterns hide the implementation details and are applicable as the reusable notation components. On the other hand, the process of defining the notation must be performed by a person experienced in language design, as he must be able to identify the language patterns first. The knowledge of metamodeling and annotations is another requirement induced by the process of pattern application that is carried out manually by annotating the domain model.

Figure 5. Incremental language design process using the EDNS method

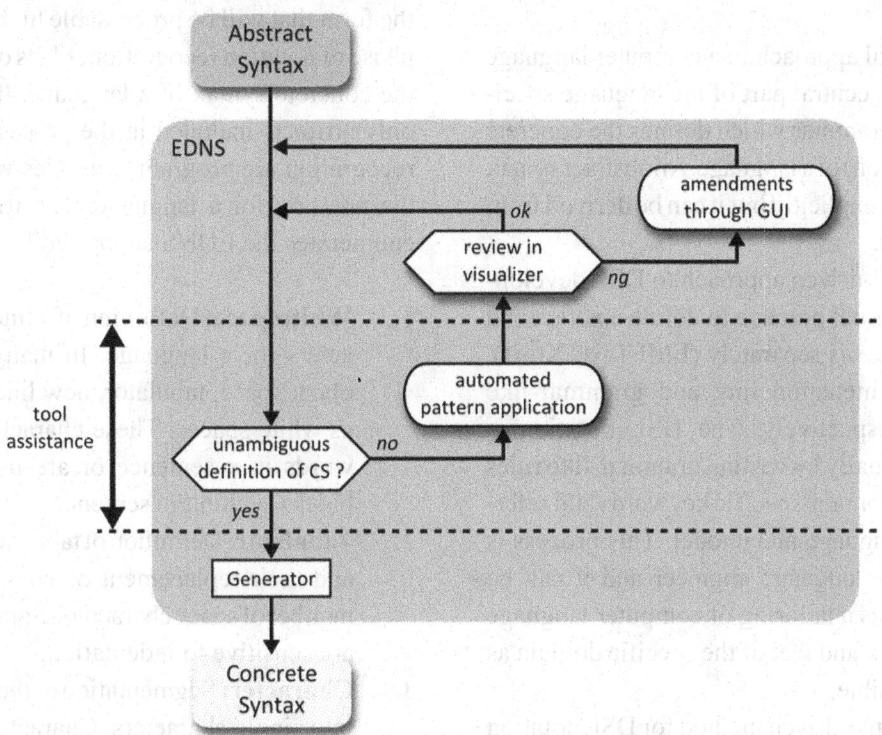

The inference approach is aimed towards better usability of the language patterns. The technical details of their identification, configuration and application are hidden in the proposed EDNS method. All stages are fully automated and a user serves as a reviewer of the overall process. He manages the identification of particular patterns interactively through the provided GUI. Since all implementation details are hidden behind the graphical interface, the requirements imposed upon technical skills of a user are significantly lowered. He only interacts with the visualizers of a domain model and program examples, and in cases when needed, he amends the patterns identified in these artifacts by marking/unmarking the corresponding structures, or parts of the text respectively. Therefore, this role is manageable even by a domain expert with limited technical background.

EXAMPLE-DRIVEN DSL NOTATION SPECIFICATION

Although syntax recognition is a well-established area of research and multiple approaches to grammar inference have already been implemented (Ahonen, Mannila & Nikunen, 1994; Črepinšek et al., 2005b; Mernik & Žumer, 2005; Dupont, 1994), in our work we propose a method for Example-Driven DSL Notation Specification (EDNS) based on language patterns. The automated identification of such patterns in provided program examples eliminates the necessity to specify the same notations manually and repeatedly for each designed language. Besides the recognition of recurring notation, the EDNS method can also assist in checking whether the recognized notation satisfies the conditions of a machine-processable computer language (e.g. unambiguity).

The EDNS Method

In a traditional approach to a computer language development, central part of the language specification is a grammar which defines the concrete syntax (notation) of a language. An abstract syntax is not defined explicitly but it can be derived from that grammar.

In a model-driven approach to DSL development, it is a usual practice to define abstract and concrete syntaxes separately (EMFText, Xtext), using some metamodeling and grammar-like languages respectively. The DSL notation is specified formally by writing grammar-like rules that contain domain-specific keywords and references to a language metamodel. This process is performed by language engineer and it can be looked upon as a tailoring of computer language to suit the look and feel of the specific domain as much as possible.

The example-driven method for DSL notation specification (EDNS) takes the opposite direction and starts with the ideal domain-specific notation proposed informally by a domain expert through examples of programs as they would have been written in a desired DSL (Figure 6). The formal computer-processable specification is then inferred from the examples using the concept of the language patterns. The method consists of three consecutive phases – construction of models of program examples, DSL notation recognition and generation of language specification.

The Identified and Supported Patterns

Till today we have identified and formalized more than ten language patterns (Sabo, 2011). According to their utilization in the EDNS, they come in two flavors as formatting language patterns or mapping language patterns. The formatting language patterns (FLPs) are used in the early phase of the EDNS method when ProgXample models are being created. Their purpose is to formalize the plain text of an example file into the form that will be processable in the following phase of notation recognition. FLPs only concern the concrete syntax of a language, therefore the only artifacts included in the process of pattern recognition are program examples which define the notation for a language. The following list enumerates the EDNS supported FLPs.

1. **Whitespace:** Definition of whitespace characters for a language. In many languages blank space, tabulator, new line are treated as white spaces. These characters separate words in a sentence or are used to mark blocks within the sentence.
2. **Tabulator:** Definition of tabulator characters and their replacement of with appropriate number of space characters. Some languages are sensitive to indentation.
3. **Character:** Segmentation of the input string into single characters. Characters are separated by whitespaces and are merged into large units called words.
4. **Special:** Definition of special characters for a language. These characters usually form operators.
5. **Word:** Tokenizing text string words delimited by whitespaces and merging of consecutive characters into a word.
6. **Block:** Dividing the sequence of elements into blocks and identification of the sentence block structure. Blocks are defined using indentation, special characters or words (e.g. begin, end, {, }) and forms tree structures.

The mapping language patterns (MLPs) are used in the main phase of EDNS method when the actual process of DSL notation recognition happens. Their purpose is to infer the concrete human-usable notation for a language from the provided program examples. The inferred notation is then defined as a mapping between abstract and concrete syntaxes. Since MLPs concern both syntaxes of a language, the artifacts involved in the

Figure 6. Overview of the method for example-driven DSL notation specification

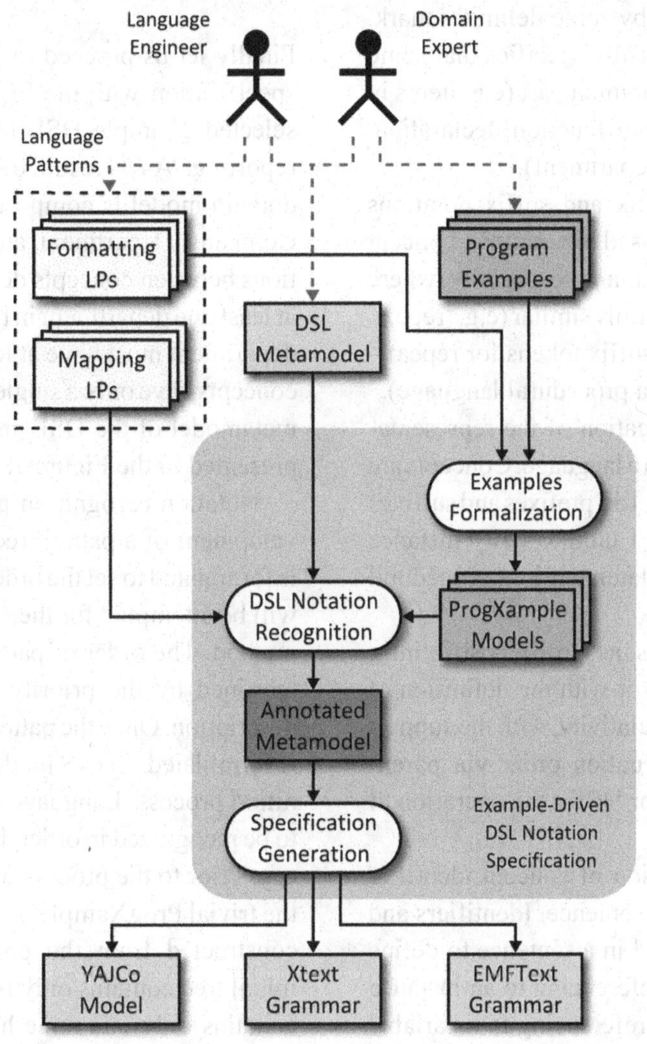

process of inference include both, DSL metamodel representing the abstract syntax and ProgXample models (formalized program examples) representing the concrete syntax. MLPs are similar to FLPs in a way that they capture the widely known and accepted notation, however MLPs are concerned with the notation in a connection to the abstract syntax of a language. They address the recurring notation of common language constructs defined in abstract syntax, rather than individual markings which are independent of the abstract syntax of a language. The following MLPs are supported in the ENDS.

1. **Keyword:** Keywords in DSLs are often defined as names of concepts used in the abstract syntax of a language (domain model) or their abbreviation and are used to recognize concept instance in a sentence (e.g. 'department' keyword if the concept Department exists in a language).

2. **Separator:** In the notation of list, items are usually separated by some delimiter mark. Separator semantically specifies that some concepts shares common part (e.g. items in a list, parameters in function declaration, and persons in a department).
3. **Before/after:** Prefix and suffix notations of concepts are used for simple concept recognition by humans, especially where are concept structurally similar (e.g. 'repeat' prefix and 'until' suffix tokens for repeat – until statement in a procedural language).
4. **Concept:** Identification of the representations of concepts in a language. Concepts are marked with keywords, prefixes and suffixes (e.g. 'repeat x:=x+1 until(x < 10)' instance of repeat – until statement in a procedural language).
5. **Operator:** Comes as prefix/postfix/infix well known operator with the definition of a priority and associativity, with the support for changing evaluation order via parenthesis (e.g. operator '+' for the operation of addition).
6. **Reference:** Notation of concept identifier and reference in a sentence. Identifiers and references are used in a sentence to define graph structures referencing to an instance of a concept (e.g. referencing to a variable in procedural language).

The EDNS Example

Finally let us proceed to the example of a DSL specification with the EDNS method. We have selected a simple DSL for company personnel reporting. As a result of a domain analysis a domain model is composed of three concepts – Company, Department, and Employee. The relations between concepts define that there must be at least one department in the company, and every department must have at least one employee. All concepts have only a single property, a name. The metamodel of the DSL and notation example is presented in the Figure 7.

Notation recognition process starts with development of a pattern recognition strategy that is formulated to set the order in which the patterns will be attempted for their recognition by EDNS method. The order of patterns application is determined by the priority property of a pattern description. Once the pattern recognition strategy is formulated, EDNS method can start the recognition process. Language patterns are attempted to be recognized in order determined by the strategy. Prior to the process of notation recognition, the trivial ProgXample models are automatically constructed from the program examples. The initial tree contains only root with one node that contains only one node holding the whole textual content of an example. The tree model is then iteratively compared against language patterns and if the structure prescribed by its ProgXample

Figure 7. Metamodel and notation example of the DSL for a company personnel reporting

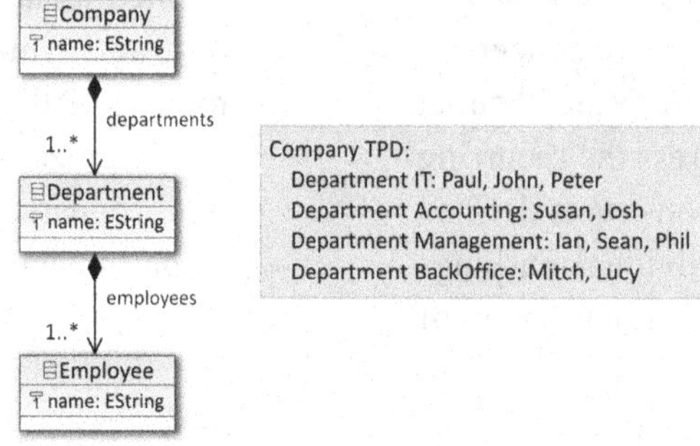

Target property is identified in the model, the pattern is applied on the ProgXample model which results in its modification that reflects the recognized pattern.

Besides tree restructuralization, the modification may also include the addition of nodes of a new kind to express the specific nature of the text that the nodes hold. However, for a tree model to conform to a ProgXample metamodel, the metamodel must contain the appropriate metaclasses. This is achieved by composability feature which enables the core metamodel to be extended with other elements. The application of the Separator language pattern on the fragment of a ProgXample model will look like the one in the Figure 8. The tree nodes in the ProgXample model corresponds to the applied patterns: C – Concept, K – Keyword, WS – whitespace, S – separator, W – word, B – Block.

Finally, once the notation recognition process is finished, annotated DSL metamodel is transformed into YAJCo model from which the DSL on context-free grammar parser and other language tools are generated.

Related Approaches

Considering the main contribution of the EDNS method to be the innovative approach of how the notation recognition problem is addressed, it is difficult to find a proper set of related works to compare it against. The problem of syntax recognition from existing resources has been specifically addressed by the grammar inference research community. Successful results have been achieved in inferring regular languages using various algorithms like EDSM (Lang, Pearlmutter & Price, 1998) and RPNI (Oncina & Garcia, 1991). Genetic-programming approach was used for inferring regular grammars (Dupont, 1994). The methodologies of context-free grammars induction for domain-specific languages are the aim

Figure 8. Fragment of the input sentence formalized as ProgXample

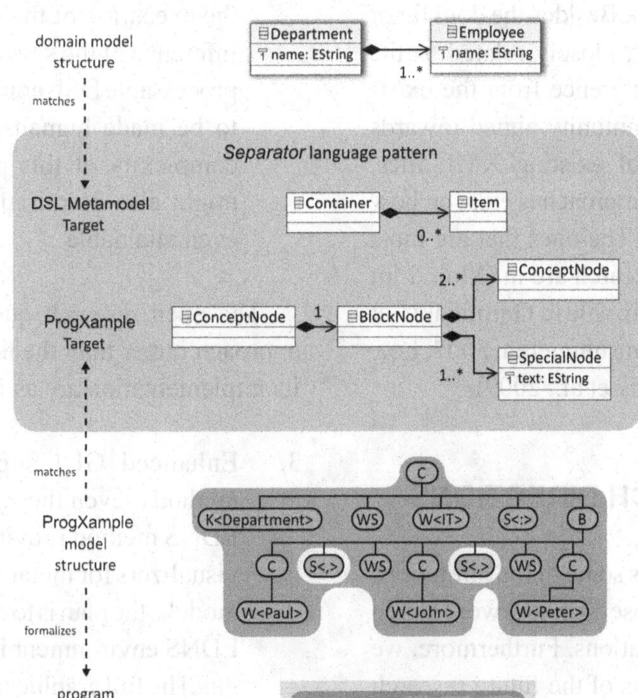

of GenParseProject research group. Their initial research of genetic approach resulted in the successful induction of small grammars (Črepinšek et al., 2005c), however their current focus is on incremental grammar learning (Črepinšek et al., 2005a; Javed et al., 2008a, 2008b) and memetic algorithm working with false negative samples, (Hrnčič et al., 2011, 2012) which should allow for bigger DSLs to be inferred as well.

Although yet another various approaches either automatic (Henriques et al., 2005) or semi-automatic (Javed et al., 2008a; Lämmel & Verhoef, 2001) exist, they are all targeted towards the language design based on concrete syntax which is recognized solely from artifacts represented as sentences/programs written in an unknown language. Similar approach to pattern instance recognition in programs that is inspired by works in the area of design pattern recovery is described by Ablonskis and Nemuraite (2010).

The aim of our research is, however, on the language development based on the abstract syntax since we advocate that structure of a language with separated abstract and concrete syntaxes is more suitable for a DSL design. Besides the domain of a language development, closely related to the problem of a notation inference from the existing examples, is the community aimed towards inferring the structure of existing XML files. There, as well, multiple approaches exist on how to address this problem. The ones that are most closely related to our research are in (Moh, Lim & Ng, 2000; Chidlovskii, 2001; Garofalakis et al., 2003; Bex, Neven, Vansummeren, 2007; Lee, Kim & Lee, 2007; Mernik et al., 2009).

FUTURE RESEARCH DIRECTIONS

In this section, we discuss some of the limitations of our approach and propose the future work aimed at alleviating these limitations. Furthermore, we introduce some directions of the future research that build upon the work presented in this chapter.

In the future work, we plan to address the technical limitations of our research prototype. We recall the most important ones below:

1. Validation of a recognized concrete syntax – although the final output of the EDNS method is a DSL specification file, written in a notation specific for the chosen language framework, the method cannot ensure that the specification is valid. It may happen that the minor amendments to the file have to be done manually. Even though this is a major flaw that compromises the benefit of automation presented in this work, at the same time, it is a great source of cases which expose the limits of currently used language patterns. Hence, ironically, such cases help us to explore the new computer language patterns.
2. Uncertainty of halting the iterative recognition process – this problem is similar to the previous one. Currently, in the EDNS method, we cannot automatically determine if the patterns recognized until some point in the execution of the process suffice for the inference of the specification of a machine-processable DSL notation. This decision has to be made human user. Considering the complexity of this problem, the question might also be raised whether such task is even attainable.

The open research questions related to our approach rather than the technical limitations of its implementation are as follows:

3. Enhanced GUI support for the EDNS method – even though the prototype of the EDNS method provides a simple GUI with visualizers for metamodel and ProgXample models, the plan is to develop a fully-fledged EDNS environment in form of Eclipse plugin. The full graphical user interface support for the EDNS method will enable the further

enhancements to achieve even higher user-friendliness of the method.

4. Identification and formalization of other language patterns – the success of notation inference is directly influenced by a number of language patterns that are to be looked for. Indeed, the ones listed in this work certainly do not encompass all of the patterns that can be observed in the computer languages. Since the language patterns are still the subject of ongoing research, we expect to identify and formalize more of them in the future.

CONCLUSION

Capturing the recurring notation style of common language constructs and its formalization in a form of computer language patterns is an unexplored topic in the area of computer language design. In this work, we have elaborated on this novel idea and have discussed its application in the context of model-driven language development. The proposed method for Example-Driven DSL Notation Specification (EDNS) has been introduced. The work has presented in detail the concept of formatting and mapping the language patterns and its application in the EDNS method.

The language patterns open new possibilities in the construction of computer languages. They can be utilized in both directions to creating a language specification, analytical and synthetic. Although synthetic approach was not among the objectives of this article, more details on this subject can be found in our earlier work (Porubän, Forgáč, Sabo & Běhálek, 2010). This article presented the analytical approach, set up in the context of the proposed EDNS method. We believe that by using it, there is a potential for speeding up the process of a language creation since a DSL notation is inferred from the program examples automatically and the only part of a DSL specification that must be performed manually by a language engineer boils down to the construction of a DSL metamodel. Besides the cases where the program examples are provided as an output generated by the software, the examples can be created manually as well. This gives a possibility to define a DSL notation even for a person not versed in the language construction, however, most competent for such task – a domain expert. Since having a domain expert as a direct author of DSL notation can significantly increase the quality and usability of developed DSL, we consider this an important benefit contributed by the EDNS method. Although our research on the computer language patterns can still be considered in its early stage, the initial results of case the studies indicate that our approach is worth further exploration.

REFERENCES

Ablonskis, L., & Nemuraite, L. (2010). Discovery of complex model implementation patterns in source code. *Information Technology and Control, 39*(4), 291–300.

Ahonen, H., Mannila, H., & Nikunen, E. (1994). Forming grammars for structured documents: An application of grammatical inference. *Proceedings of the Second International Colloquium on Grammatical Inference and Applications* (pp. 153-167). Springer-Verlag.

Bex, G. J., Neven, F., & Vansummeren, S. (2007). Inferring XML schema definitions from XML data. *Proceedings of the 33rd International Conference on Very Large Data Bases* (pp. 998-1009). VLDB Endowment.

Chidlovskii, B. (2001). Schema extraction from XML data: A grammatical inference approach. *Proceedings of the Eighth International Workshop on Knowledge Representation Meets Databases, CEUR Workshop Proceedings*.

Črepinšek, M., Mernik, M., Bryant, B. R., Javed, F., & Sprague, A. (2005a). Inferring context-free grammars for domain-specific languages. *Electronic Notes in Theoretical Computer Science*, *141*, 99–116. doi:10.1016/j.entcs.2005.02.055

Črepinšek, M., Mernik, M., Javed, F., Bryant, B. R., & Sprague, A. (2005b). Extracting grammar from programs: Evolutionary approach. *ACM SIGPLAN Notices*, *40*(4), 39–46.

Črepinšek, M., Mernik, M., & Žumer, V. (2005c). Extracting grammar from programs: Brute force approach. *ACM SIGPLAN Notices*, *40*(4), 29–38.

Dupont, P. (1994). Regular grammatical inference from positive and negative samples by genetic search: The GIG method. *Proceedings of the Second International Colloquium on Grammatical Inference and Applications* (pp. 236-245). Springer-Verlag.

Gamma, E., Helm, R., Johnson, R., & Vlissides, J. M. (1994). *Design patterns: Elements of reusable object-oriented software*. Addison-Wesley Professional.

Garofalakis, M., Gionis, A., Rastogi, R., Seshadri, S., & Shim, K. (2003). XTRACT: Learning document type descriptors from XML document collections. *Data Mining and Knowledge Discovery*, *7*, 23–56. doi:10.1023/A:1021560618289

Henriques, P. R., Varando Pereira, M. J., Mernik, M., Lenič, M., Gray, J. G., & Wu, H. (2005). Automatic generation of language-based tools using the LISA system. *IEE Proceedings. Software*, *152*(2), 54–69. doi:10.1049/ip-sen:20041317

Hrnčič, D., Mernik, M., & Bryant, B. R. (2011). Embedding DSLS into GPLS: A grammatical inference approach. *Information Technology and Control*, *40*(4), 307–315. doi:10.5755/j01.itc.40.4.980

Hrnčič, D., Mernik, M., Bryant, B. R., & Javed, F. (2012). A memetic grammar inference algorithm for language learning. *Applied Soft Computing*, *12*(3), 1006–1020. doi:10.1016/j.asoc.2011.11.024

Javed, F., Mernik, M., Bryant, B. R., & Sprague, A. (2008b). An unsupervised incremental learning algorithm for domain-specific language development. *Applied Artificial Intelligence*, *22*(7), 707–729. doi:10.1080/08839510802164127

Javed, F., Mernik, M., Gray, J., & Bryant, B. R. (2008a). MARS: A metamodel recovery system using grammar inference. *Information and Software Technology*, *50*(9-10), 948–968. doi:10.1016/j.infsof.2007.08.003

Kleppe, A. (2007). Towards the generation of a text-based IDE from a language metamodel. *Proceedings of the 3rd European Conference on Model Driven Architecture-Foundations and Applications* (pp. 114-129). Springer-Verlag.

Lakatoš, D., Porubän, J., & Sabo, M. (2011). Assisted software language creation using internal model. *Proceedings of the International Conference on Engineering of Modern Electric Systems* (pp. 1-5). ACM.

Lämmel, R., & Verhoef, C. (2001). Semi-automatic grammar recovery. *Software, Practice & Experience*, *31*(15), 1395–1448. doi:10.1002/spe.423

Lang, K. J., Pearlmutter, B. A., & Price, R. A. (1998). Results of the Abbadingo One DFA learning competition and a new evidence-driven state merging algorithm. *Proceedings of the 4th International Colloquium on Grammatical Inference* (pp. 1-12). Springer-Verlag.

Lee, M.-H., Kim, Y.-S., & Lee, K.-H. (2007). Logical structure analysis: From HTML to XML. *Computer Standards & Interfaces*, *29*(1), 109–124. doi:10.1016/j.csi.2006.02.001

Mernik, M., Heering, J., & Sloane, A. M. (2005). When and how to develop domain-specific languages. *ACM Computing Surveys*, *37*(4), 316–344. doi:10.1145/1118890.1118892

Mernik, M., Hrnčič, D., Bryant, B., Sprague, A., Gray, J., Liu, Q., & Javed, F. (2009). *Grammar inference algorithms and applications in software engineering. ICAT 2009 Information* (pp. 1–7). Communication and Automation Technologies.

Moh, C. H., Lim, E. P., & Ng, W. K. (2000). Re-engineering structures from Web documents. *Proceedings of the Fifth ACM Conference on Digital Libraries* (pp. 67-76). New York, NY: ACM.

Oncina, J., & Garcia, P. (1992). Inferring regular languages in polynomial update time. [World Scientific Publishing.]. *Pattern Recognition and Image Analysis*, 49–61. doi:10.1142/9789812797902_0004

Porubän, J., Forgáč, M., Sabo, M., & Běhálek, M. (2010). Annotation Based Parser Generator. *Computer Science and Information Systems*, *7*(2), 291–307. doi:10.2298/CSIS1002291P

Porubän, J., Sabo, M., Kollár, J., & Mernik, M. (2010). Abstract syntax driven language development: Defining language semantics through aspects. *Proceedings of the International Workshop on Formalization of Modeling Languages* (pp. 21-25). ACM.

Sabo, M. (2011). *Computer language patterns: The inference of textual notation for domain-specific languages.* Ph.D. Dissertation, Technical University of Košice.

Spinellis, D. (2001). Notable design patterns for domain-specific languages. *Journal of Systems and Software*, *56*(1), 91–99. doi:10.1016/S0164-1212(00)00089-3

ADDITIONAL READING

Appeltauer, M., & Kniesel, G. (2008). Towards concrete syntax patterns for logic-based transformation rules. *Electronic Notes in Theoretical Computer Science*, *219*, 113–132. doi:10.1016/j.entcs.2008.10.038

Atkinson, D. C., & Griswold, W. G. (2006). Towards effective pattern matching of source code using abstract syntax patterns. *Software, Practice & Experience*, *36*(4), 413–447. doi:10.1002/spe.704

Bézivin, J. (2004). In search of a basic principle for model driven engineering. *Upgrade*, *5*(2), 21–24.

Bryant, B. R., Mernik, M., Hrnčič, D., Javed, F., Liu, Q., & Sprague, A. (2010). Grammar inference technology applications in software engineering. *Proceedings of the 10th International Colloquium Conference on Grammatical Inference: Theoretical Results and Applications* (pp. 276-279). Springer-Verlag.

Cook, S., Jones, G., Kent, S., & Willis, A. C. (2007). *Domain-specific development with visual studio DSL tools*. Addison-Wesley Professional.

Deursen van, A., Klint, P., & Visser, J. (2000). Domain-specific languages: An annotated bibliography. *ACM SIGPLAN Notices*, *35*(6), 26-36.

Djurič, D., Gaševič, D., & Davedžič, V. (2006). The Tao of modeling spaces. *Journal of Object Technology*, *5*(8), 125–147. doi:10.5381/jot.2006.5.8.a4

Dubey, A., Pankaj, J., & Sanjeev, K. A. (2008). The learning context free grammar rules from a set of programs. *IET Software*, *2*(3), 223–240. doi:10.1049/iet-sen:20070061

Fondement, F., & Baar, T. (2005). Making metamodels aware of concrete syntax. *Proceedings of the 1st European Conference on Model Driven Architecture® Foundations and Applications* (pp. 190-204). Springer-Verlag.

Gold, E. M. (1976). Language identification in the limit. *Information and Control*, *10*(5), 447–474. doi:10.1016/S0019-9958(67)91165-5

Jouault, F., Bézivin, J., & Kurtev, I. (2006). TCS: A DSL for the specification of textual concrete syntaxes in model engineering. *Proceedings of the 5th International Conference on Generative Programming and Component Engineering* (pp. 249-254). ACM.

Karsai, G., Krahn, H., Pinkernell, C., Rumpe, B., Schneider, M., & Völkel, S. (2009). Design guidelines for domain specific languages. *Proceedings of the 9th OOPSLA Workshop on Domain-Specific Modeling* (pp. 7-13).

Kelly, S., & Tolvanen, J. P. (2008). *Domain-specific modeling*. Wiley-Blackwell.

Kleppe, A. (2007). A language description is more than a metamodel. *Proceedings of the 4th International Workshop on Software Language Engineering* (pp. 1-9).

Kleppe, A. (2008). *Software language engineering: Creating domain-specific languages using metamodels*. Addison-Wesley Professional.

Kunnert, A. (2008). Semi-automatic generation of metamodels and models from grammars and programs. *Electronic Notes in Theoretical Computer Science*, *211*, 111–119. doi:10.1016/j.entcs.2008.04.034

Kurtev, I., Bézivin, J., Jouault, F., & Valduriez, P. (2006). Model-based DSL frameworks. *Proceedings of the Companion to the 21st ACM SIGPLAN Symposium on Object-Oriented Programming Systems, Languages, and Applications* (pp. 602-616). ACM.

Mernik, M., Gerlič, G., Žumer, V., & Bryant, B. R. (2003). Can a parser be generated from examples? *Proceedings of the 2003 ACM Symposium on Applied Computing* (pp. 1063-1067): ACM.

Parr, T. (2007). *The definitive Antlr reference: Building domain-specific languages*. Pragmatic Bookshelf.

Parr, T. (2010). *Language implementation patterns: Create your own domain-specific and general programming languages*. Pragmatic Bookshelf.

Pfeiffer, M., & Pichler, J. (2008). A comparison of tool support for textual domain-specific languages. *Proceedings of the 8th OOPSLA Workshop on Domain-Specific Modeling* (pp. 1-7).

Porubän, J., Václavík, P., & Sabo, M. (2009). *The role of abstraction in computer language engineering. Computer Science and Technology Research Survey* (pp. 37–44). Department of Computer and Informatics, Technical University of Košice.

Sabo, M. (2010). Abstract syntax driven concrete syntax recognition. *Journal of Information. Control and Management Systems*, *8*(4), 393–402.

Sakakibara, Y. (1992). Efficient learning of context-free grammars from positive structural examples. *Information and Computation*, *97*(1), 23–60. doi:10.1016/0890-5401(92)90003-X

KEY TERMS AND DEFINITIONS

Abstract Syntax: Characterizes the essential concepts and structure of expressions in a language. The structure is defined by the relations between the concepts. The two most common ways of how to define the abstract syntax are context-free grammars and metamodels.

Concrete Syntax: Defines how the concepts from abstract syntax and combinations thereof are rendered in a concrete notation, so that they can be interpreted and produced by users of a language.

Domain-Specific Language (DSL): Is a computer language with high level of expressiveness in a particular domain, which is achieved at the cost of narrowing the scope of usability of a language to this domain.

DSL Metamodel: Is a central part of the computer language specification as it defines the abstract syntax of a language. It is composed of domain concepts, their properties and relations between the concepts.

Language Pattern: Is knowledge of recurring well-known notation of a computer language, captured as a mapping between abstract and concrete syntax of a language.

ENDNOTES

1. Vertical DSLs focus on narrow non-technical application domains (e.g. finance, insurance, market, e-health), while horizontal DSLs address technical domains (e.g. user interface, workflow, configuration, data manipulation, security) and are more likely to be used throughout applications addressing various domains.
2. To reflect the differences between formatting and regular language patterns in the naming terminology as well, regular language patterns have been renamed to Mapping Language Patterns (MLPs), as they capture the mapping between abstract and concrete syntaxes.

Chapter 14
Evaluating the Usability of Domain-Specific Languages

Ankica Barišić
Universidade Nova de Lisboa, Portugal

Vasco Amaral
Universidade Nova de Lisboa, Portugal

Miguel Goulão
Universidade Nova de Lisboa, Portugal

Bruno Barroca
Universidade Nova de Lisboa, Portugal

ABSTRACT

Domain-Specific Languages (DSLs) can be regarded as User Interfaces (UIs) because they bridge the gap between the domain experts and the computation platforms. Usability of DSLs by domain experts is a key factor for their successful adoption. The few reports supporting improvement claims are persuasive, but mostly anecdotal. Systematic literature reviews show that evidences on the effects of the introduction of DSLs are actually very scarce. In particular, the evaluation of usability is often skipped, relaxed, or at least omitted from papers reporting the development of DSLs. The few exceptions mostly take place at the end of the development process, when fixing problems is already too expensive. A systematic approach, based on techniques for the experimental evaluation of UIs, should be used to assess suitability of new DSLs. This chapter presents a general experimental evaluation model, tailored for DSLs' experimental evaluation, and instantiates it in several DSL's evaluation examples.

INTRODUCTION

Software Languages Engineering (SLE) is becoming a mature and systematic activity, building upon the collective experience of a growing community, and the increasing availability of supporting tools (Kleppe, 2009). A typical SLE process starts with the domain engineering phase, in order to elicit the domain concepts. The next phase consists in the actual design of the language, by capturing the referred concepts and their relationships. This is followed by its implementation, evaluation,

DOI: 10.4018/978-1-4666-2092-6.ch014

deployment, evolution, and finally its retirement. Although this process is becoming streamlined, it still presents a serious gap in what should be a crucial phase - *language evaluation,* which includes acceptance testing. A good DSL is hard to build because it requires domain knowledge and language development expertise, and few people have both (Mernik, Heering & Sloane, 2005). We should evaluate claims such as *"our new language brings efficiency to the process"*, or that *"our new language is usable and effective"*, with an unbiased and objective process.

DSLs are meant to close the gap between the Domain Experts and the computation-platforms. As such, DSLs can be used as a structured/comprehensive means to achieve Human/Computer (H/C) Interaction. Most of the requirements concerning the evaluation of User Interfaces (UI) are actually associated with a qualitative software characteristic called *Usability*, which is defined by the quality standards in terms of achieving the Quality in Use (ISO, 2001a).

Usability evaluation involves a phase of acceptance testing with actual users, which is typically a very costly process. A poorly conceived evaluation process can ultimately undermine the conclusions about the quality of the UI under analysis. This generic UI problem also applies to the realm of DSL's construction.

In our opinion, usability can be fostered from the beginning of the DSL development cycle by adopting user centered methods. The objective is to ensure that the developed DSLs can be used by real people (the domain experts) to perform their tasks in the real world. This requires not only intuitive UIs, but also the appropriate functionality and support for the activities and workflows that are to be specified with the DSLs.

In this chapter, we discuss how user-centered design can be adapted to the context of DSL's development. In general, working with languages involves not only physical and perceptual activities, but also cognitive activities such as learning, understanding and remembering. Experimenters in human factors have developed a list of tasks to capture those particular aspects. The process is complex and must be tailored case-by-case (Reisner, 1988). We will further discuss these issues, and show how they fit into the DSL's development process. Following that, we will define a general model for the DSL's experimental evaluation. This model will help us planning and designing the DSL's evaluation processes, as well as conducting post-mortem analysis of other DSL's evaluation efforts in a systematic way, thus fostering the aggregation of several DSL's evaluation results. As discussed in (Basili, 2007), a single study outside the context of a larger set of studies has limited value, but combined, they can be a valuable increment to the existing body of knowledge.

The usage of our model is illustrated through the systematic analysis of several evaluations of DSLs found in the literature. Our comparative analysis will help identifying the commonalities, differences, strengths and weaknesses of the compared studies. The usage of our model in future replications of this comparative study to other DSL evaluations has the potential for fostering meta-analysis, leading to sound increments of the body of knowledge in DSLs and their evaluation.

BACKGROUND

In general, the software industry does not report investment on the usability evaluation of DSLs, as shown in a recent systematic literature review (Gabriel, Goulão & Amaral, 2010). This conveys a perception that there is an insufficient understanding of the SLE process which, in our opinion, must include the evaluation of the produced DSLs. Many language engineers may perceive the investment in usability evaluation as an unnecessary cost and prefer to risk providing a solution which has not been properly validated, namely with respect to its usability, by the end users. This apparent state of practice contrasts with the return of investment on usability reported for other software products (Nielsen & Gilutz, 2003). In general, these benefits span from a reduction of development and maintenance costs, to increased revenues brought by an improved effectiveness by the end users (Marcus, 2004).

Software Language Evaluation

Comparing the impact of different languages in the software development process has some tradition in the context of General Purpose Languages (GPLs) (*e.g.*, (Prechelt, 2000)), namely concerning their impact on developer's productivity. Typically, the popularity (see, for an instance of a popularity index, http://lang-index.sourceforge.net/) of a language is used as a surrogate for its usability. The rationale for this informal assessment is that, if there are so many people using a particular GPL, then that must say something about its usability. Naturally, usability is only one of several factors that make a language popular. Historic reasons, for instance, also play a major role. In any case, this kind of indirect usability assessment is not adequate to be applied to DSLs as they are often intended for a small number of users, and it is generally not easy to know neither the size of the community that is actually using a DSL nor the potential size of that community (*i.e.* other domain experts that might use the DSL in the future). In any case, it would only make sense to use community size for comparing DSLs within the same domain.

Other sorts of evaluations on GPLs include benchmarks, feature-based comparisons and heuristic-based evaluations (Prechelt, 2000). These language comparisons are done on different versions of the same language or on different languages, focusing on a subset of characteristics that indicate the suitability of languages to a specific intended Context of Use. There are also Heuristic-based evaluations that provide guidelines for evaluating syntax of visual languages based on the studies of cognitive effectiveness (Moody, 2009). Because the end users of the GPLs are the people who are usually close to computation concepts, while the ones of DSLs are closer to domain concepts of the context of use, these methods are not appropriate for DSLs in all cases. However, it is necessary to take in consideration these methods and adapt them for DSLs.

When usability problems are identified too late, a common approach to mitigate them is to build tool support that minimizes their effect on users' productivity (Bellamy, John, Richards & Thomas, 2010; Phang, Foster, Hicks & Sazawal, 2009). There is an increasing awareness to the usability of languages, fostered by the competition of language providers. Better usability is a competitive advantage, although evaluating it remains challenging: it is hard to interpret existing metrics in a fair, unbiased way, which is resistant to external validity threats concerning the broad user groups, or internal ones – it is very easy to end up comparing apples with oranges, when evaluating competing languages.

The increased productivity achieved by using DSLs, when compared to using GPLs, is one of the strongest claims by the DSL community. With anecdotal reports of 3-10 times productivity improvements of DSLs, (Kelly & Tolvanen, 2000; MetaCase, 2007b; Weiss & Lai, 1999), or *"clearly boosted development speeds"* (MetaCase, 2007a) in industrial settings, why bother with their validation?

The problem, of course, is that those anecdotal reports on improvements lack external validity. Other reports, such as (Batory, Johnson, MacDonald & Von Heeder, 2002), present maintainability and extensibility improvements brought by a combination of DSLs and Software Product Lines (SPL), but it is unclear which share of the merits belongs to DSLs and which should be credited to SPLs. The usage of DSLs has been favorably compared to the usage of templates in code generation, with respect to flexibility, reliability and usability (Kieburtz, McKinney, Bell, Hook, Kotov, Lewis, Oliva, Sheard, Smith

& Walton, 1996). Another success story can be found in (Hermans, Pinzger & Deursen, 2009), where a survey conducted with users of a particular DSL clearly reports on noticeable improvements in terms of reliability, development costs, and time-to-market. The usability of that particular DSL and its toolset are among the most important success factors of DSL introduction in that context. But are these improvements typical, or exceptional? The honest answer can only be one: we do not know. Comparisons can also be made among competing DSLs: for instance, (Murray, Paton, Goble & Bryce, 2000) compare a visual DSL against the textual language for which it is a front-end.

The incremental nature of a typical DSL life cycle may give to the language engineers an erroneous feeling that their language is being validated through the interaction with the domain experts that are helping to build the language. The problem is that these domain experts are not necessarily the language's end users, so they may introduce biases in the perception of the language's usability.

Domain-Specific Languages as User Interfaces

Intuitively, a language is a means for communication between peers. For instance, two persons can communicate with each other by exchanging sentences. These sentences are composed by signs in a particular order. According to the context of a conversation, these sentences can have different interpretations. If the context is not clear, we call these different interpretations ambiguous. Here, we focus our attention in the communication between humans and computers. We only consider languages that are used as communication interfaces between humans and machines *i.e.* UIs. Human-human languages (*e.g.*, natural languages) and machine-machine languages (*e.g.*, communication protocols) are not discussed this chapter. Examples of UIs range from compilers, to command shells and sophisticated graphical applications. In each of those examples we can deduce the (H/C) language that is being used to perform that communication: in compilers we may have a programming language; in a graphical application, we may have an application specific language with some visual syntax, and so on. Moreover, we argue that any UI is a realization of a language. This view is in line with that of a growing community, built around the PLATEAU workshop series (http://ecs.victoria.ac.nz/Events/PLATEAU/WebHome), that aims to bridge the gap between language engineers and UIs experts, so that the former can build languages that are easier to use, leading to increased productivity by their users. In this perspective, we define DSLs as being languages that reduce the use of computation domain concepts and focus on the domain concepts of the contexts of use's problem.

Usability is a key characteristic for evaluating the Quality of UIs. Since we defined H/C languages as UIs, in our perspective, we should also use it for evaluating the Quality of this family of languages. The difference between usability and the other software qualities is that to achieve it, one has to concentrate not only on system features but specifically on user-system interaction characteristics. The term usability is overloaded and has been given several interpretations and definitions. The need for a generally accepted usability definition is discussed in several references (Bevan, 1999, 2009; Petrie & Bevan, 2009).

ISO 9241-11 provides the definition of usability that is used in subsequent related ergonomic standards (ISO, 2001b). ISO 9126 (ISO, 2001a) extends that definition by introducing the notion of *Quality in Use*, *i.e.*, the quality as perceived by the user during actual utilization of a product in a real Context of Use. Quality in Use is measured in terms of the result of using the software, rather than on properties of the software itself. The ISO standard states that achievement of Quality in Use can be assured by achieving internal and external Quality. These two types of Quality provide us metrics that can be used early in software development process.

The complete Quality model for achieving Quality in Use is given by ISO IEC CD 25010.3 (Petrie & Bevan, 2009) and is discussed in the context of DSL evaluation in (Barišić, Amaral, Goulão & Barroca, 2011a). This model provides us with a complete structure of quality, but we cannot take general conclusions about which characteristics will lead us to final usability, as they are dependent on the DSLs intended context of use.

EVALUATING A DSL

Evaluation with users, also known as Empirical Evaluation, is recommended (Nielsen & Molich, 1990) at all stages of development, if possible, or at least in the final stage of development. *Formative methods* focus on understanding the user's behavior, intentions and expectations in order to understand any problems encountered, and typically employ a 'think-aloud' protocol. *Summative methods* measure the product usability, and can be used to establish and test user requirements. Testing may be based on the principles of standards and measure a range of usability components. Each type of measure is usually regarded as a separate factor with a relative importance that depends on the Context of Use (Barišić, Amaral, Goulão & Barroca, 2011c). Iterative testing with small numbers of participants is usually preferable, starting early in design and development process.

Iterative User Centered Evaluation Practices

User Centered Design can reduce development and support costs, increase sales, and reduce staff cost for employers by allowing significant changes to correct deficiencies along the development process instead of just evaluating at the end of it, when it might be too late (Catarci, 2000). The essential activities required to implement User Centered Design are described in ISO 13407 (Bevan, 2005).

Usability has two complementary roles in design: as an attribute that must be designed into the product, and as the highest level quality objective, which should be the overall objective of design. In the first phase it is important to study existing style guidelines, or standards for a particular type of system. Interviewing current or potential users about the current approach they are using to accomplish their tasks, can also help identifying its strengths and weaknesses, and their expectations for a new or re-designed system. It is also important to assess the Context of Use of a particular situation. All these contribute to an initial understanding of what the system should do for the users and how it should be designed. Initial design ideas can then be explored, considering alternative designs and how they meet user's needs. After developing potential designs it is time to build the prototypes that should be obviously simple and unfinished, as that allows people involved in evaluations to realize that it is acceptable to criticize them. In contrast, a prototype very close to the final product is likely to inhibit evaluators from openly criticizing it, which might lead to a loss of valuable feedback from those evaluators. It is important to explore particular design problems before considerable effort is put into full implementation and integration of components of the system. A number of iterations of evaluation, designing and prototyping may be required before acceptable levels of Usability are reached. Once the design of various components of the system has reached acceptable levels, the integration of components and final implementation of the interactive system may be required. Finally, once the system is released to users, an evaluation of its use in real contexts may be highly beneficial (Petrie & Bevan, 2009). This kind of iterative evaluation approach should be merged with the DSL development cycle (Barišić, Amaral, Goulão & Barroca, 2011a).

Cognitive Factors Involved

In order to know the users we should identify the characteristics of the target user population. For several kinds of end users we should analyze these characteristics using techniques like questionnaires, interviews and observations. Understanding *"how"* and *"why"* should give us a deeper knowledge about the tasks. Performing task analysis by studying the way people perform tasks with existing systems, or by having a high level abstraction study of cognitive processes, we should identify what are the individual tasks that the language should enable to perform. From this, we can model the desired cognitive model for the language context based on user-task scenarios. For each task we should identify: *Goal, Pre-conditions, Dependencies, User background* and *Sub tasks.*

The cognitive activities that should be analyzed in the study of cognitive processes are:

- *Learning* both syntax and semantics;
- *Composition* of the syntax required to perform a function;
- *Comprehension* of function syntax composed by someone else;
- *Debugging* of syntax or semantics written by ourselves or others;
- *Modification* of a function written by ourselves or others.

Experimenters in human factors have developed a list of tasks to capture these particular aspects (Reisner, 1988): *Sentence writing, Sentence reading, Sentence interpretation, Comprehension, Memorization* and *Problem solving.* To evaluate these tasks, we can use tests like: *Final exams, Immediate Comprehension, Reviews, Productivity, Retention* and *Re-learning.*

Testing different tasks in the language usage is interesting, but to perform an exhaustive evaluation of all of them would be very expensive. Therefore, the evaluation usually concerns only the most critical activities.

Evaluation Process Experiments

We argue that the quality in use of a DSL should be assessed experimentally. In Software Engineering, a controlled experiment can be defined as *"a randomized experiment or quasi-experiment in which individuals or teams (the experimental units) conduct one or more Software Engineering tasks for the sake of comparing different populations, processes, methods, techniques, languages or tools (the treatments)."* (Sjøberg, Hannay, Hansen, Kampenes, Karahasanovic, Liborg & Rekdal, 2005). For our purposes, this can be instantiated with developers typically conducting software construction, or evolution tasks, for the sake of comparing different languages – including the DSL under evaluation and any existing baseline alternatives to that DSL.

Experiment Activity Model

Figure 1 outlines the activities needed to perform an experimental evaluation of a software engineering claim, following the scientific method. During *requirements definition*, the problem statement (*i.e.* research questions), experimental objectives and context are defined. The next step is to perform *design planning*, where context parameters and hypotheses are refined, subjects are identified, a grouping strategy for subjects is selected, and a sequence and synchronization of observations and treatments for each of the experimental groups is planned. The sequencing and synchronization of such interventions, their nature (observations or treatments) and the group definition policy, define the *experimental design*. The data collection activities plan is also set during design planning. This is followed with *data collection,* which often includes a pilot session, to correct any remaining issues, and the evaluation itself, following the designed plan. This step is followed with *data analysis* where data is described in the form of statistical tables and graphs, and, if necessary, the data set is reduced. Hypotheses are then tested.

Figure 1. Experiment activity model overview

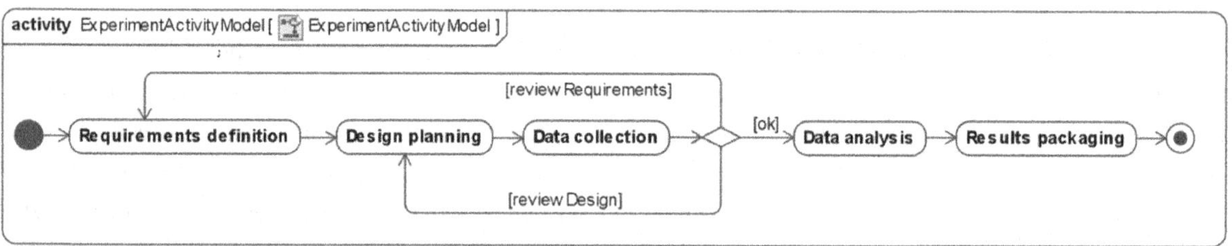

Finally, during *results packaging*, the results are interpreted and possible validity threats and lessons learned are identified. A detailed discussion on how this process can be followed in a software engineering experimentation context can be found in (Goulão, 2008; Goulão & Abreu, 2007). Experimental reporting guidelines, generally followed by the experimental software engineering community, are also available (Jedlitschka, Ciolkowski & Pfahl, 2008). By reporting a given language's quality in use, and the evaluations adhering to such guidelines, the overall ability to make study replications (for independent validation and validity threats mitigation) and its meta-analysis (for building a body of knowledge supported by the evidence collected in different contexts) is expected to increase.

Experiment Design Model

In order to contrast the selected DSL experimental validations, we start by modeling their relevant information. This is captured in the class diagrams, adapted and extended from (Goulão, 2008). In a nutshell, this model partially captures some of the essential information of an experimental language evaluation, namely the details on evaluation requirements and planning.

Before conducting an experimental language evaluation, one should start by clearly defining the problem that the evaluation will address as modeled in *Figure 2*. This includes identifying where this problem can be observed (*i.e.*, its context, typically where the language will be used), and by whom (*i.e.*, the stakeholder who is affected by the problem – *e.g.*, the language user). It is also important to state how solving the identified problem is expected to impact on those who observe it, and which quality attributes will be affected. The class QualityAttribute can take values that are defined in Quality model from ISO Standards (Barišić, Amaral, Goulão & Barroca, 2011a).

Figure 2. Problem statement design model

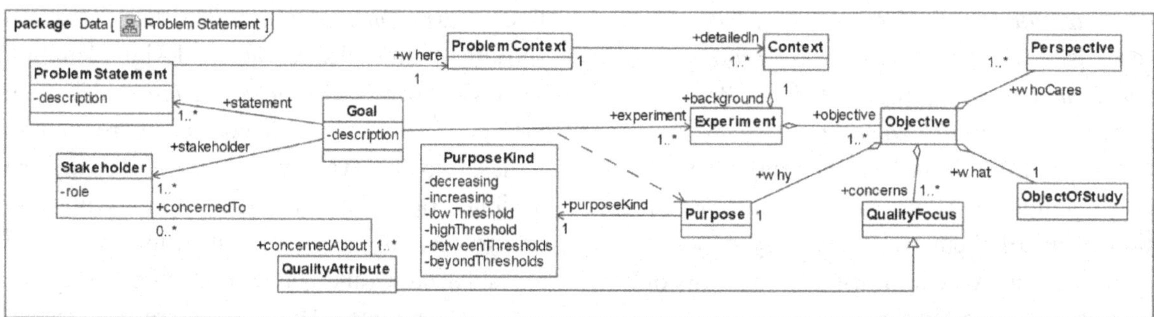

When conducting language evaluation experiments, one should clearly define the experiments' objectives. Building upon Basili's earlier work (Basili, 1996), Wohlin *et al.* proposed a framework to guide the experiment definition (Wohlin, Runeson, Höst, Ohlsson, Regnell & Wesslén, 1999). The framework is to be mapped into a template with the following elements: the *object of study* under analysis, the *purpose* of the experiment, its *quality focus*, the *perspective* from which the experiment results are being interpreted, and the *context* under which the experiment is run.

While the experiment definition expresses something about why a particular language evaluation was performed, the experiment planning expresses something about how it will be performed. Before starting the experiment, decisions have to be made concerning the *context* of the experiment, the *hypotheses* under study, the set of *independent* and *dependent variables* that will be used to evaluate the hypotheses, the selection of *subjects* participating in the experiment, the experiment's *design* and *instrumentation*, and also an evaluation of the experiment's validity. Only after all these details are sorted out should the experiment be performed. The outcome of planning is the *experimental language evaluation design*, which should encompass enough details in order to be independently replicable.

Figure 3 includes information on the *context*, including where the experimental language evaluation will take place. The context of an experiment determines our ability to generalize from the experimental results to a wider context. Experiments can be conducted in different contexts, each of them with their own benefits, costs, and risks. These constraints have to be made explicit, in order to ensure the comparability among different studies, and to allow practitioners to evaluate the extent to which the results obtained in a study, or set of studies, are applicable to their own particular needs. Throughout the experiment, there are a number of context parameters that remain stable and their value is the same for all the subjects in the experiment during the whole process. Therefore, we can safely assume that differences observed in the results cannot be attributed to these parameters, while the actual parameters to be reported may vary (Wohlin, Runeson, Höst, Ohlsson, Regnell & Wesslén, 1999). Concerning their integration within the language development process, experiments can be conducted either *online*, or *offline*. The former, carried as part of the software process in a professional environment, involve an element of risk, since experiments may become intrusive in the underlying development activity. This intrusiveness may even manifest itself through resources and time overheads on a real project. A common alternative is to carry out the experiment offline.

An experimental language evaluation design prescribes the division of our sample into a set of groups, according to a given strategy. Each of those groups receives a set of *interventions*, which may be either *observations* where data is col-

Figure 3. Context design model

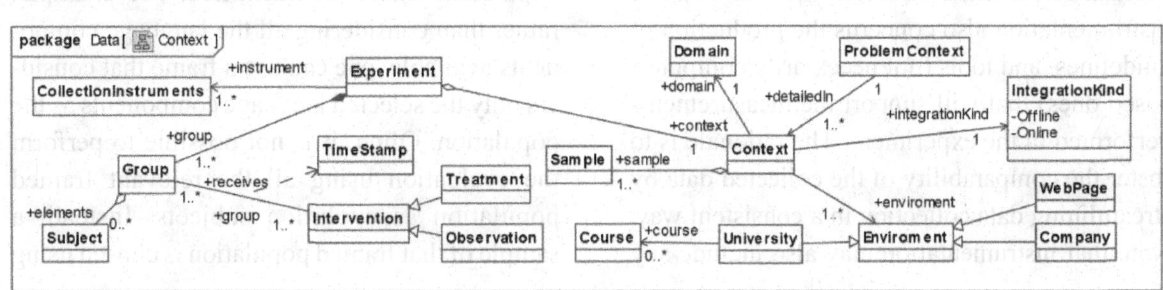

Figure 4. Instrument design model

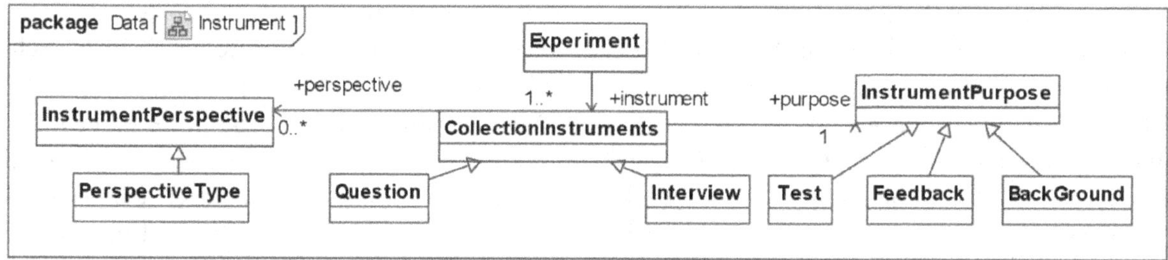

lected, or *treatments*, where the groups receive some sort of input (*e.g.*, training in using a language). The association class with the time stamp allows this data to be ordered in time, so that a sequence of observations and treatments can be established. The sequencing and synchronization of such interventions, their nature, and the group definition policy, define the *experimental design*.

The *instrument* design presented in *Figure 4* includes the definition of the artifacts that will be used in the experiment. For instance, in a language evaluation experiment, the syntactical problem instantiation specified with a language can be used as an artifact that will then be changed by the evaluation participants. These changes could be monitored, using a collection instruments such as those depicted in *Figure 4* – *e.g.*, a combination of a test with a post-test questionnaire. This kind of evaluation allows addressing the instrument perspectives as cognitive activities that are fundamental to assessing the usability of a language, and the quality of instantiation, especially during modification (see, for instance the usage of cognitive dimensions in (Kosar, Mernik & Carver, 2012; Kosar, Oliveira, Mernik, Pereira, Črepinšek, Cruz & Henriques, 2010). The instrumentation also concerns the production of guidelines, and tools (not necessarily computer-based ones) that will support the measurements performed in the experiment. The rationale is to foster the comparability of the collected data by streamlining data collection in a consistent way. Note that instrumentation may also include any training material distributed to the participants, before their participation in the experiment.

In *Figure 5*, we can see the *sample* design model that includes the participants' profile and the artifacts used in the language evaluation. An orthogonal classification of context concerns the people involved in the language evaluation. One may choose among performing the language evaluation with professional practitioners, or with surrogates for those practitioners (*e.g.*, students). The first option leads to results that are more easily comparable to others obtained in a professional context, but care must be taken to reduce potential overheads to practitioners' activities. Using students as surrogates for professional practitioners is less expensive, but makes the experimental results harder to extrapolate for a professional community. In order to reduce this gap between the students and the practitioners, the researcher should prefer using graduate students, whose expertise is closer to that of novice practitioners.

It is common to use a frame of the population, if it is not feasible to identify all the population's members. In contrast, all members of the chosen population frame are identified. For example, rather than considering all the language components available, one can use a frame that considers only the selected language components as the population. Often, it is not possible to perform the evaluation using all the relevant framed population as evolution subjects. Instead, a sample of that framed population is chosen using

Figure 5. Sample design model

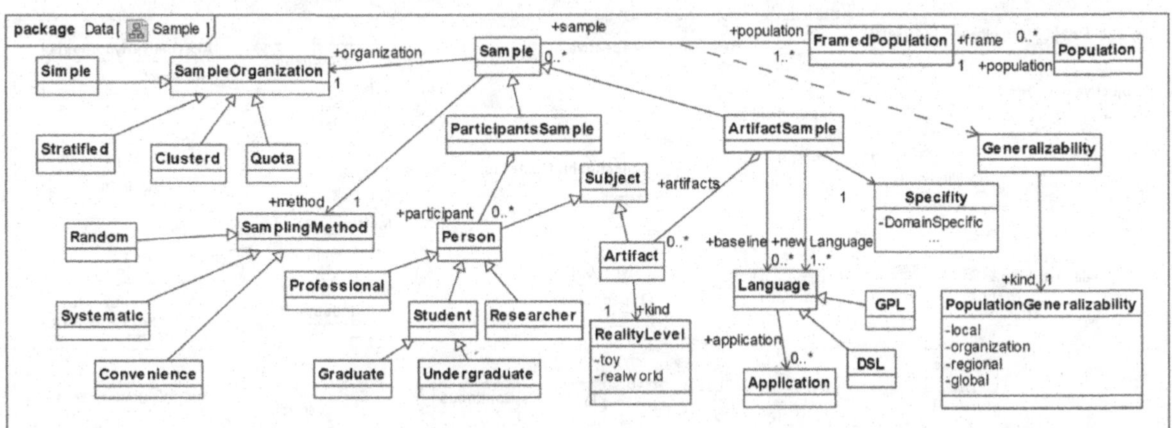

a selected sampling technique, with the objective of being as much representative of the framed population as possible, considering the available resources of the experimenter.

Yet another dimension constraining the language evaluation is the usage of *toy* vs. *real* problems. There are at least two issues that motivate the usage of toy problems: the resources available for the language evaluation and the risks concerned with the outcome of the evaluation. The former results from the often very limited amount of time that the subjects can devote to the evaluation. The latter relates to the potential harm caused by the outcome of the evaluation (*e.g.* while experimenting with using different languages on a real problem, a language that leads to worse productivity can lead to additional costs to a customer). The question, here, is whether the results obtained with a toy problem will scale up to real problems, or not. Toy problems are often used in early evaluations, as their usage is less expensive. If the results of evaluations conducted with toy examples are satisfactory, the risk of scaling up the problem to a real one may be mitigated to a certain extent, although it will not be completely eradicated.

The artifacts used in these evaluations can be *generic* or *domain-specific*. When comparing programming languages it is common for these artifacts to be domain-specific, regardless of the original language they were built with. This means, that we can use this model, taking in the consideration this attribute specification, to compare GPLs, DSLs, or GPLs vs. DSLs.

Figure 6 includes the *hypotheses tested* and the *variables* used with their characteristics, such as *type*, *scale*, and *level*. The hypothesis formulation should be stated as clearly as possible and presented in the context of the theoretical background it is derived from. The *null hypothesis* states that there is no observable pattern in the experimental evaluation setting, so any variations found are resulting from coincidence. This is the hypothesis that the researcher is trying to reject. The alternative is that the variations observed are not resulting from coincidence. When the null hypothesis is rejected, we can conclude that the null hypothesis is false. However, if we cannot reject the null hypothesis, we can only say that there is no statistical evidence to reject it. Conversely, if we reject the null hypothesis, we can accept its alternative. If we cannot reject the null hypothesis, we cannot accept the alternative.

Hypothesis testing always assumes a given level of significance denoted by *alpha*, which represents a fixed probability of wrongly rejecting the null hypothesis, if it is in fact true. The probability value (*p-value*) of a statistical hypothesis

Figure 6. Hypothesis and variables design model

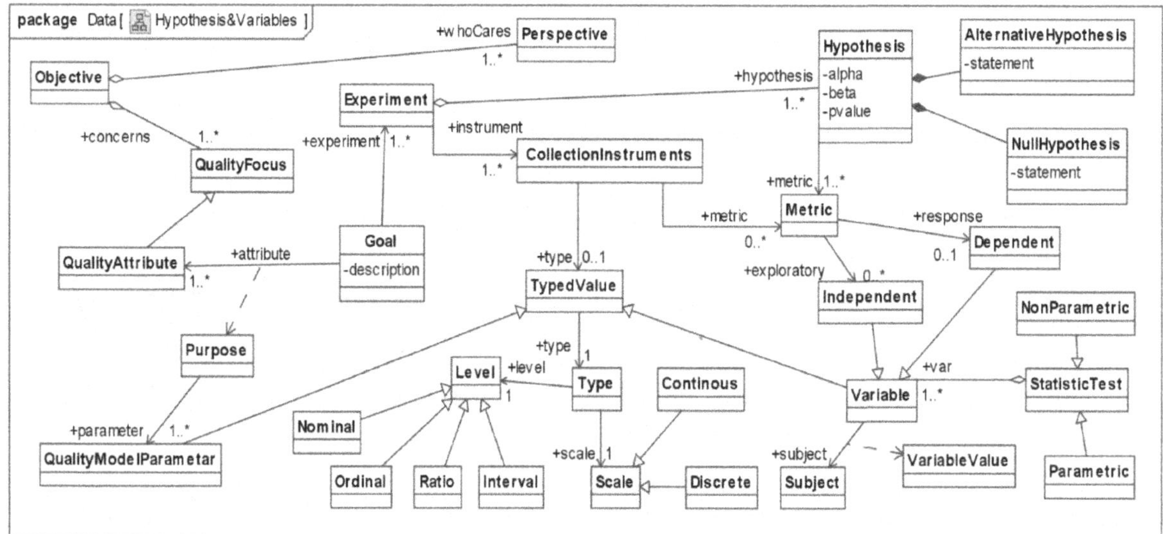

test is the probability of getting a value of the test statistic as extreme as or more extreme than that observed by chance alone, if the null hypothesis is true. *Figure 6* presents the relationships between the main concepts involved in hypotheses definitions, starting from the overall objectives of the research, through the specific goals of the experiment, and the questions that will allow assessing the achievement of the goals. The hypotheses are then assessed using metrics.

The language evaluator selects both *dependent* and *independent* variables. Dependent variables should be explicitly tied to the research goals (in the context of this chapter, these typically involve evaluating DSLs), and chosen for their relevance with respect to those goals. When it is not feasible to collect direct measures of the level of achievement of the research goals, surrogates can be used, although such replacement is to be avoided, when possible, and clearly justified. When not – *e.g.* when assessing the usability of a DSL – we may use *effectiveness* in specifying a system with it as a surrogate for the DSL's usability. Similarly, independent variables are chosen according to their relevance to the research goals.

The analysis techniques chosen for the language evaluation experiment depend on the adopted language evaluation design, the variables defined earlier, and the research hypotheses being tested. More than one technique may be assigned to each of the research hypotheses, if necessary, so that the analysis results can be cross-checked later. Furthermore, each of the hypotheses may be analyzed with a different technique. This may be required if the set of variables involved in that hypothesis differs from the set being used in the other hypotheses under tested. Discussions relating statistical tests (in particular, *parametric* vs. *non-parametric* ones) with variable types can be found in statistics text books, such as (Maroco, 2003).

By capturing a rich set of data of an language evaluation, we can pave the way for further analysis, where the information collected in several independently conducted language evaluations can be combined. To do so, the next step is to instantiate this model. In *Figure 7*, we illustrate a partial instantiation of this model, using information collected from the family of language evaluation experiments described (Kosar, Mernik & Carver, 2012). This particular example is chosen for illustration because that family of evaluation

Figure 7. Experiment design model instantiation, built from info in (Kosar, 2012)

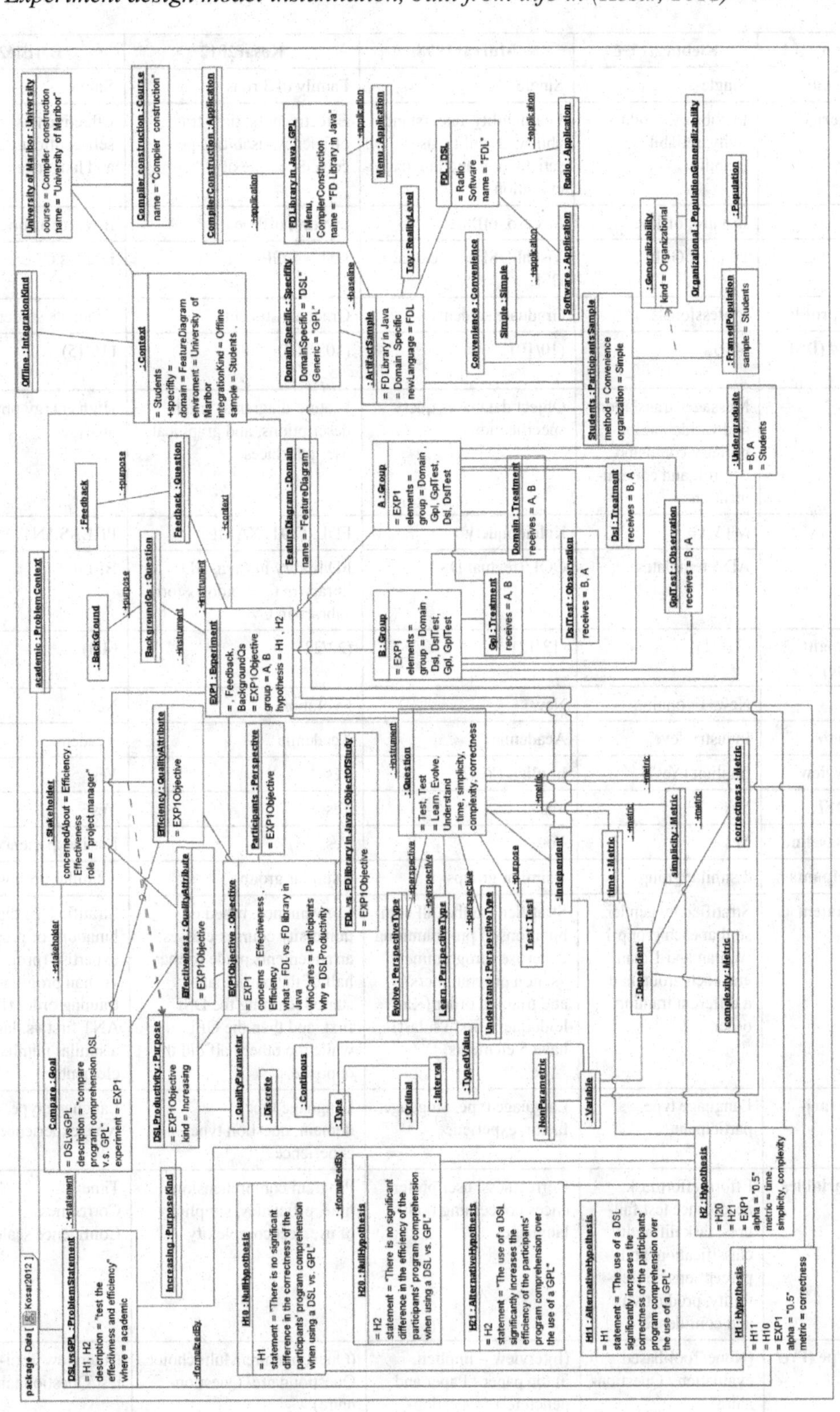

Table 1. Experiments overview

Criteria	Kieburzt1996	Murray1998	Kosar2012	Barišić2011
Experiment runs	Single	Single	Family of 3 runs	Single
Quality concerns	Flexibility, productivity, reliability, usability	Learnability, understandability, usability, user satisfaction and language evolution	Effectiveness, time frame, efficiency, usability, perceived complexity	Effectiveness, efficiency, self-confidence in results and language evolution
Context	In-vitro, offline	In-vitro, offline	In-vitro, offline	In-vitro, offline
Comparison	DSL vs. GPL	Visual DSL vs. Textual DSL	DSL vs. GPL	DSL vs.GPL
Participants profile	Professionals	Graduate students?	Graduate students	Graduate students
Participants # (DSL/ Baseline)	(4/4)	(10/10)	(108/107)	(15/15)
Domain(s)	Messages translation and validation for military command, control, and communications	Object databases query specification	Feature diagrams, graph descriptions, and graphical user interfaces	High energy physics analysis
DSL	MTV-G	Kaleidoquery	FDL, DOT, XAML	PHEASANT
Baseline	ADA templates	OQL (textual DSL)	FD library in Java, GD library in C, Windows form Library in C#	BEE/C++
Tasks/Participant (DSL/Baseline)	(31/31)	(12/12)	(22/22)	(4/4)
Tasks kind	New+Evolution	New	Evolution	New
Materials origin	Industry-level	Academic	Academic	Academic
Pre-test/Interview	Implicit (Yes?)	Implicit (Yes?)	Yes	Yes
Training in DSL	Yes	Yes	Yes	Yes
Training in Baseline	Yes	Yes	Yes	For inexperienced users
Group participants	2 similar groups	4 similar groups	6 similar groups	4 similar groups
Group assignment	Stratified by gender, so that each group 1 woman and 1 man, and each group had a different training order.	Stratified, so that all combinations of programming expertise (programmers vs. non programmers) and training order (Kaleidoquery first vs. last) have 5 elements.	Convenience, based on university courses classes; arrangements made so that half of the participants started learning the DSL first, and then the GPL, while the other half did the opposite.	Stratified, so that all combinations of programming expertise (programmers vs. non programmers) and training order (PHEASANT first vs. last) have a similar number of elements
Independent variables	Language type, participant	Language type, language factor, experience	Language type, domain, question type, experience	Language type, question type, experience
Dependent variables	Effort, effort/task, acceptance test failures, task difficulty classification, and perceptions on flexibility, productivity and confidence.	Correctness, user preferences concerning both languages	Program comprehension, time, efficiency, simplicity of use, test complexity	Time Correctness Confidence scale
Evaluation type (Pre/ Eval/Post)	(None/Tool-based evaluation / Questionnaire)	(Interview – implicit, in the paper / Paper and pencil test / Questionnaire)	(Questionnaire/Multi choice Questionnaire/ Questionnaire)	(Interview/Tool-based test/Questionnaire)

continued on following page

Table 1. Continued

Criteria	Kieburzt1996	Murray1998	Kosar2012	Barišić2011
Analysis	ANOVA	Paired sample T-test, independent samples T-Test	Wilcoxon Signed Ranks Test	Wilcoxon Signed Ranks Test, Sign Test
Results summary	Increased productivity, reliability, flexibility, with MTV-G. Users preferred its usability to the alternative baseline.	Increased effectiveness and self confidence in results with Kaleidoquery for non-programmers, who clearly preferred Kaleidoquery. No significant difference with programmers, who generally outperformed non-programmers	Increased effectiveness and efficiency of programs written in DSLs when compared to baseline GPL	Increased effectiveness, efficiency, self-confidence in results with PHEASANT, when compared to the baseline C++/BEE. Experts generally outperformed non-experts.

experiments is an excellent example of how DSL properties validation can be performed in a sound way. The instantiation is only partial, as the whole instantiation would be extremely cluttered.

Experiments Overview

The main point in streamlining the evaluation of DSLs and making information available in a common framework is that we can build upon that framework an evidence-based body of knowledge on DSLs and their properties with respect to their usability. To illustrate this, we present a systematic comparison of four language evaluation experiments. As noted earlier in this chapter, these evaluations are currently exceptional in the realm of DSLs and are chosen precisely for that: they are examples of best practices in languages evaluation with a concern on usability, from which we can perform some meta-analysis, leading not only to a collection of lessons learned "from the trenches", but also to the identification of opportunities to further improve existing validation efforts. Table 1 outlines our comparison. The selected studies are (Barišić, Amaral, Goulão & Barroca, 2011b; Kieburtz, McKinney, Bell, Hook, Kotov, Lewis, Oliva, Sheard, Smith & Walton, 1996; Kosar, Mernik & Carver, 2012; Murray, Paton, Goble & Bryce, 2000). In this table, the first column represents a specific criterion that we will use in our comparative overview of these studies. The four remaining columns provide information on each of the selected studies. Kosar *et al.* conducted a family of three experiments, while the remaining selected studies are single experiments. The generic lack of families of experiments, rather than single experiments is a long identified shortcoming in the experimental validation of software engineering claims, so this should be highlighted as a very strong point in this work. Families of experiments help mitigating validity threats that occur in single experiments. In this particular case, the fact that the tested hypotheses have consistent results in all the three experiments in the experiment family increases the confidence in the soundness of the obtained results. Ideally, there should also be experiments within the family run by completely separate research groups, so that any biases by the experiment team that might exist would also be removed. Independent replication of experiments is a standard practice in other domains. For example, the Cochrane Collaboration (http://www.cochrane.org/) supports a common repository for health care evidence, which is fed by independently run families of experiments.

Back in 1997, Brooks advocated that meta-analysis should be used to combine the results of independent study replications in Software Engineering (Brooks, 1997). Miller attempted to perform meta-analysis on a set of independent defect detection experiments, but found serious difficulties concerning the diversity of the experiments and heterogeneity of their data sets, and was unable to derive a consistent view on the overall results (Miller, 2000). A noticeable feature in the quality concerns row is that, either directly or indirectly, all these studies are concerned with the quality in use of a DSL, including perspectives such as its effect on the productivity of practitioners, which is sometimes indirectly assessed through the effectiveness and efficiency of the language usage. This is, of course, not surprising, as these examples were chosen precisely because they illustrate how such evaluation can be performed, in different contexts. Kosar *et al.*'s work is an independent evaluation of several DSLs, and is mostly concerned with program comprehension correctness and efficiency while using the DSLs, when compared with using GPLs. A detailed analysis of their data could be used to identify opportunities for improving the tested DSLs. Kieburtz *et al.*'s experiment addresses DSL evolution as part of the concern with flexibility, while the remaining two experiments explicitly look for opportunities for improving the respective DSLs under scrutiny.

The four studies are run *in vitro* (*i.e.*, in the laboratory, under controlled conditions), *off-line*. This context is particularly interesting in that the researchers can better control extraneous factors that would otherwise bring validity threats to each of the experiment. Being off-line, the risks for the organizations where the studies are conducted are also mitigated, in the sense that if anything goes wrong with the experimentation, this will have no visible effect to external stakeholders (*e.g.*, clients that were considering using a DSL). The downside for this is that there are validity threats concerning the realism of an assessment performed in vitro, as well as that of conducting the experiment off-line. Clearly, there are interesting research opportunities to mitigate these threats, by evaluating the same DSLs in a real-world, uncontrolled environment, to strengthen the external validity of the obtained results. The same holds for selection of participants in the experiment, where, whenever possible, real users of the DSL should be involved (as it happened, for instance, with the experienced participants in the PHEASANT experiment).

The number of participants is also an issue, due to the relatively high costs of engaging real users in the validation of languages. Concerning this, we would highlight Kieburtz's experiment as it shows how a meaningful assessment can be performed, even with a very low number of participants (only 4). Of course, for statistical soundness, larger numbers of subjects should be used, but, as noted by usability experts, a small number of users can still detect a high number of usability improvement opportunities in a product (Nielsen, 1993). Using a small number of participants is an interesting option in early evaluations aimed at identifying defects of the language, to reduce costs. In order to draw more definitive conclusions (with high reliability and validity) that state if the language is better than the previous baseline it is necessary to use a larger number of participants. For instance, in Kieburtz's experiment, the conclusions were sound with respect to the participants, but had a threat with respect to their external validity: with only 4 participants, it was not possible to rule out the possibility of their individual skills playing a role in how the competing languages were evaluated. A similar comment might be made for the evaluation experiments described by Murray and Barišić, with 10 and 15 participants, respectively. In isolation, each of these experiments has its own external validity threats. Interestingly, if we combine the results in all these experiments, a consistent pattern of DSL success starts to emerge. Last, but not the least, several of these evaluation experiments uses academic examples for validation, rather than "real-world" problems. This is, of course, a convenience constraint which entails the obvious

Figure 8. Experiments design: Observations and treatments

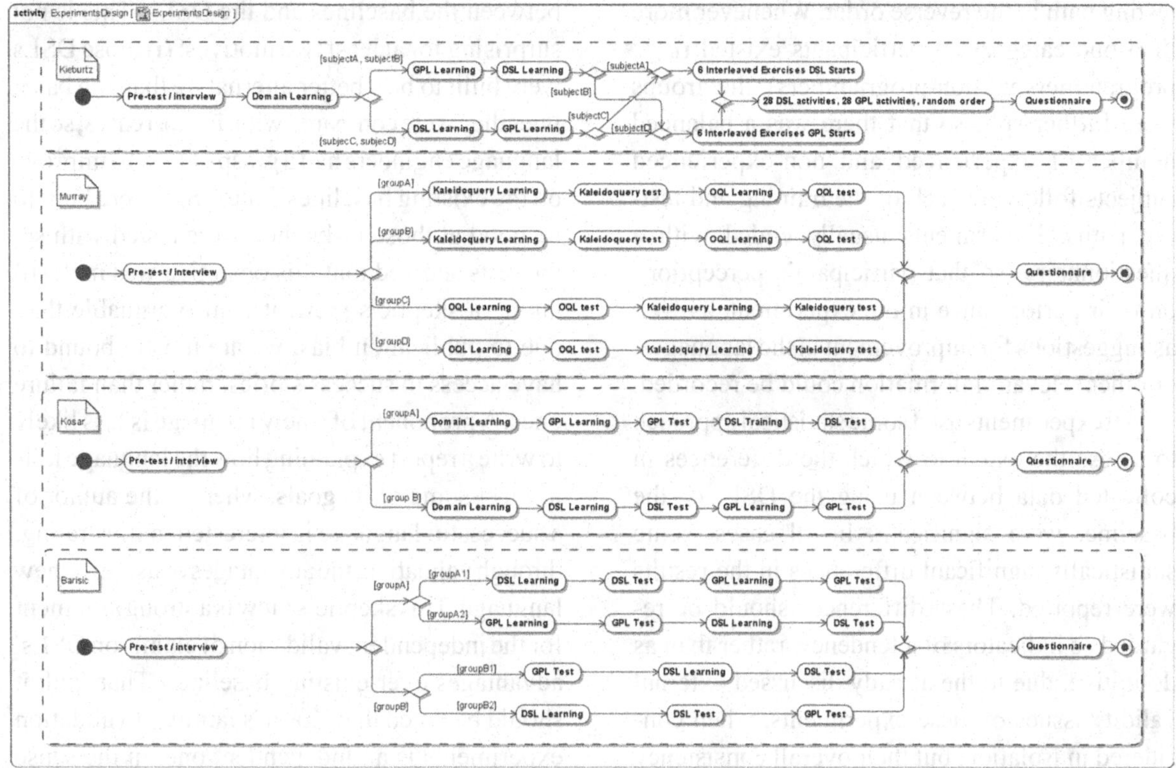

threat of external validity, if the examples are not representative of the actual tasks real users will have to perform with the DSLs. Even with real-world examples, the (lack of) coverage of the DSL language with those examples is also a common threat.

In all these DSLs, there is a high variability of domains and techniques to build DSLs, suggesting that the lessons learned from this collection of language evaluation experiments should, in principle, apply to DSLs from other domains. All the selected studies compare DSLs with an existing baseline which is, in most cases, a GPL-based solution. The noticeable exception is Murray's experiment, where a graphical DSL is contrasted with the textual notation it is built upon. This illustrates how, in most reported cases, the usability evaluation of DSLs is performed once. In a user-centered design process, this should not be the case. As such, we would expect to find DSL usability assessments covering several versions of the same language, thus supporting the language evolution. Language evolution is covered in some of these studies, usually in the final questionnaire that is prepared for participants, in the end of the evaluation. This feedback can be valuable for language engineers, but the effect of implementing the changes suggested by participants' feedback should ideally also be assessed by a new replica of the experiment, to run with the new version of the DSL.

Concerning the experimental designs (see *Figure 8*), whether implicitly or explicitly, they all report collecting some background information. In some of them, domain training was necessary, while in others, it was not. One of the common concerns in all experiments was to cancel possible learning effects, by splitting participants into at least a couple of groups, so that one of the groups would learn the baseline first and then the DSL, while the other group would have its training and testing path in the reverse order. Whenever more than one category of participants existed (*e.g.*, programmers *vs.* non-programmers), the groups were further split so that there was a balanced number of experienced and non-experienced subjects following each of the training and testing paths. Experiments usually ended with a questionnaire, so that participant's perceptions on their performance in the experiment, as well as suggestions for improvement in the languages, or other relevant information could be recorded.

All experiments used some statistical approach to assess the extent to which the differences in collected data between using the DSL, or the baseline, were significant. In all cases, some statistically significant differences in the results were reported. These differences should be regarded as indicators of a tendency, rather than as definitive, due to the already discussed external validity issues of these experiments, when considered in isolation, but their overall consistency gives us some trust on the observed trends. In all experiments, the quality impacts of using DSLs *vs.* using the existing baselines are noticeable, and strengthen the claims concerning a stronger usability using DSLs, when compared to their baselines, with an impact on the productivity of professionals using them, in these tests. We also note how, whenever there is a separation among experienced and non-experienced test participants, the improvement effects are more noticeable in the non-experienced participants. The overall feedback, usually collected through a mix of Likert-scale questionnaires (*e.g.*, each answer is encoded in a symmetric scale expressing the level of agreement with a given statement, ranging from a strong agreement to a strong disagreement), and open questions is, in general, favorable to DSLs, or indifferent, but only rarely favorable to the baseline.

The obvious conclusion of all these studies is that, in general, the analyzed DSLs outperformed their baselines, confirming the anecdotal stories on the benefits of DSLs, with varying differences between the baselines and the DSLs. This is not surprising for at least two motives: (i) those DSLs were built to be a better alternative than the baselines they were compared with, in most cases, so the language engineers had a grasp of how to improve on the existing baselines – the DSLs were built to be good at those tasks they were tested with so, the tests showed that this objective was met; (ii) taking a skeptic's view, it is also arguable that, due to publication bias, we are mostly bound to have access to success stories, rather than failure ones. A proponent of a new language is less likely to write a report explaining how the language fails to meet some of its goals, whereas the author of a successful language is interested in illustrating, through validation, the advantages of using the new language. This skeptic's view is a strong argument for the independent validation of claims on DSLs' advantages over existing baselines. That said, it should be noted that Kosar's family of validation experiments is an independent one, in the sense that the evaluators are not simultaneously the developers of the solutions under comparison.

FUTURE RESEARCH DIRECTIONS

The research focus on the problem of Evaluating the Quality of DSLs, so far, has only been scratched very superficially. Although we have presented a way to systematize the evaluation process, so that we could fight its complexity, we need to go further and derive an integrated and effective set of tools to support this phase in a cost effective way. Further research is also required to prove that the user centered design process is a good way to reduce costs in DSL development – we need to organize case studies so that we collect more experimental evidences supporting that claim. We foresee new developments and an emerging community in this area in the near future.

CONCLUSION

Under the perspective of a Software Language Engineer, in order to experimentally evaluate a DSL, we need to know what are the criteria involved, understand the notion of Quality, and understand the evaluation process itself. This is usually complex, and a challenge with respect to reuse, because this is tailored to the specificity of the language under evaluation and its context.

In this chapter, we covered all the aspects mentioned before, and we brought some light to the systematic approach to do so. With general models of DSL's experimental evaluation such as the one we presented in this chapter, the Software Language Engineer is able to effectively reason about his experimental process and eventually detect flaws before it is applied and analyzed.

REFERENCES

Atkinson, C., & Kühne, T. (2003). Model-driven development: A metamodeling foundation. *IEEE Software*, *20*(5), 36–41. doi:10.1109/MS.2003.1231149

Barišić, A., Amaral, V., Goulão, M., & Barroca, B. (2011). Quality in use of domain specific languages: A case study. In *3rd ACM SIGPLAN Workshop on Evaluation and Usability of Programming Languages and Tools (PLATEAU2011)* (pp. 65-72). Portland, USA.

Barišić, A., Amaral, V., Goulão, M., & Barroca, B. (2011a). *How to reach a usable DSL? Moving toward a systematic evaluation. Electronic Communications of the EASST*. MPM.

Barišić, A., Amaral, V., Goulão, M., & Barroca, B. (2011c). Quality in use of DSLs: Current evaluation methods. In *3rd INForum - Simpósio de Informática (INForum2011)*, Coimbra, Portugal.

Basili, V. R. (1996). The role of experimentation in software engineering: past, current, and future. In *18th International Conference on Software Engineering (ICSE 1996)* (pp. 442-449).

Basili, V. R. (2007). The role of controlled experiments in software engineering research. In V. R. Basili, D. Rombach, K. Schneider, B. Kitchenham, D. Pfahl, & R. Selby (Eds.), *Empirical software engineering issues: Critical assessment and future directions* (pp. 33-37). Berlin, Germany: Springer.

Batory, D., Johnson, C., MacDonald, B., & Von Heeder, D. (2002). Achieving extensibility through product-lines and domain-specific languages: A case study. [TOSEM]. *ACM Transactions on Software Engineering and Methodology*, *11*(2), 191–214. doi:10.1145/505145.505147

Bellamy, R., John, B., Richards, J., & Thomas, J. (2010). *Using CogTool to model programming tasks*. In *2nd ACM SIGPLAN Workshop on Evaluation and Usability of Programming Languages and Tools (PLATEAU2010)*, Reno, Nevada, USA.

Bevan, N. (1999). Quality in use: Meeting user needs for quality. *Journal of Systems and Software*, *49*(1), 89–96. doi:10.1016/S0164-1212(99)00070-9

Bevan, N. (2005). Cost benefits framework and case studies. In *Cost-justifying usability: An update for the internet age*. Morgan Kaufmann. doi:10.1016/B978-012095811-5/50020-1

Bevan, N. (2009). Extending quality in use to provide a framework for usability measurement. *Human Centered Design*, 13-22.

Brooks, A. (1997). Meta analysis - A silver bullet for meta-analysts. *Empirical Software Engineering*, *2*(4), 333–338. doi:10.1023/A:1009793700999

Catarci, T. (2000). What happened when database researchers met usability. *Information Systems*, *25*(3), 177–212. doi:10.1016/S0306-4379(00)00015-6

Gabriel, P., Goulão, M., & Amaral, V. (2010). Do software languages engineers evaluate their languages? In *XIII Congreso Iberoamericano en "Software Engineering" (CIbSE'2010)* (pp. 149-162). Cuenca, Ecuador.

Goulão, M. (2008). *Component-based software engineering: A quantitative approach.* PhD Dissertation, Faculdade de Ciências e Tecnologia, Universidade Nova de Lisboa, Lisboa, Portugal.

Goulão, M., & Abreu, F. B. (2007). Modeling the experimental software engineering process. In *6th International Conference on the Quality of Information and Communications Technology (QUATIC'2007)* (pp. 77-90). Lisbon, Portugal.

Hermans, F., Pinzger, M., & Deursen, A. V. (2009). Domain-specific languages in practice: A user study on the success factors. In *12th International Conference on Model Driven Engineering Languages and Systems* (pp. 423-437). Denver, Colorado, USA.

ISO9126. (2001). *ISO/IEC 9126: Information technology - Software product evaluation - Software quality characteristics and metrics*. Geneva, Switzerland: International Organization for Standardization.

ISO. (2001a). *ISO/IEC 9126-1 Quality model.*

ISO. (2001b). *ISO/IEC 9241-11 Ergonomic requirements for office work with visual display terminals (VDTs) -- Part 11: Guidance on usability.*

Jedlitschka, A., Ciolkowski, M., & Pfahl, D. (2008). Reporting experiments in software engineering. In F. Shull, J. Singer, & D. I. K. Sjøberg (Eds.), *Guide to advanced empirical software engineering, Vol. 5971.* London, UK: Springer-Verlag.

Kelly, S., & Tolvanen, J.-P. (2000). *Visual domain-specific modelling: benefits and experiences of using metaCASE tools*. In International Workshop on Model Engineering, at ECOOP'2000.

Kieburtz, R. B., McKinney, L., Bell, J. M., Hook, J., Kotov, A., & Lewis, J. ... Walton, L. (1996). A software engineering experiment in software component generation. In *18th International Conference on Software Engineering (ICSE'1996)* (pp. 542-552). Berlin, Germany.

Kleppe, A. G. (2009). *Software language engineering: Creating domain-specific languages using metamodels*. Addison-Wesley.

Kosar, T., Mernik, M., & Carver, J. (2012). Program comprehension of domain-specific and general-purpose languages: Comparison using a family of experiments. *Empirical Software Engineering, 17*(3), 276–304. doi:10.1007/s10664-011-9172-x

Kosar, T., Oliveira, N., Mernik, M., Pereira, M. J. V., Črepinšek, M., Cruz, D., & Henriques, P. R. (2010). Comparing general-purpose and domain-specific languages: An empirical study. *Computer Science and Information Systems*, *7*(2), 247–264. doi:10.2298/CSIS1002247K

Marcus, A. (2004). The ROI of usability. In R. G. Bias & D. J. Mayhew (Eds.), *Cost-justifying usability*. North- Holland: Elsevier.

Maroco, J. (2003). *Análise Estatística - Com Utilização do SPSS* (2nd ed.). Lisbon, Portugal: Edições Sílabo.

Mernik, M., Heering, J., & Sloane, A. M. (2005). When and how to develop domain-specific languages. *ACM Computing Surveys, 37*(4), 316–344. doi:10.1145/1118890.1118892

MetaCase. (2007a). EADS case study. Retrieved from http://www.metacase.com/papers/MetaEditinEADS.pdf.

MetaCase. (2007b). Nokia case study. Retrieved from http://www.metacase.com/papers/MetaEditinNokia.pdf

Miller, J. (2000). Applying meta-analytical procedures to software engineering experiments. *Journal of Systems and Software, 54*(11), 29–39. doi:10.1016/S0164-1212(00)00024-8

Moody, D. L. (2009). The "physics" of notations: Toward a scientific basis for constructing visual notations in software engineering. *IEEE Transactions on Software Engineering, 35*(6), 756–779. doi:10.1109/TSE.2009.67

Murray, N. S., Paton, N. W., Goble, C. A., & Bryce, J. (2000). Kaleidoquery--A flow-based visual language and its evaluation. *Journal of Visual Languages and Computing, 11*(2), 151–189. doi:10.1006/jvlc.1999.0150

Nielsen, J. (1993). *Usability engineering*. Academic Press.

Nielsen, J., & Gilutz, S. (2003). *Usability return on investment* (4th ed.). Nielsen Norman Group.

Nielsen, J., & Molich, R. (1990). Heuristic evaluation of user interfaces. In *SIGCHI Conference on Human Factors in Computing Systems: Empowering People (CHI'90)* (pp. 249-256). Seattle, WA, USA.

Petrie, H., & Bevan, N. (2009). The evaluation of accessibility, usability and user experience. In Stephanidis, C. (Ed.), *The universal access handbook*. CRC Press. doi:10.1201/9781420064995-c20

Phang, K. Y., Foster, J. S., Hicks, M., & Sazawal, V. (2009). Triaging checklists: A substitute for a PhD in static analysis. In *1st ACM SIGPLAN Workshop on Evaluation and Usability of Programming Languages and Tools (PLATEAU 2009)*.

Prechelt, L. (2000). An empirical comparison of seven programming languages. *IEEE Computer, 33*(10), 23–29. doi:10.1109/2.876288

Reisner, P. (1988). Query languages. In *Handbook of human-computer interaction* (pp. 257–280). Amsterdam, The Netherlands: North-Holland.

Sjøberg, D. I. K., Hannay, J. E., Hansen, O., Kampenes, V. B., Karahasanovic, A., Liborg, N.-K., & Rekdal, A. (2005). A survey of controlled experiments in software engineering. *IEEE Transactions on Software Engineering, 31*(9), 733–753. doi:10.1109/TSE.2005.97

Weiss, D. M., & Lai, C. T. R. (1999). *Software product-line engineering: A family-based software development process*. Addison Wesley Longman, Inc.

Wohlin, C., Runeson, P., Höst, M., Ohlsson, M. C., Regnell, B., & Wesslén, A. (1999). *Experimentation in software engineering: An introduction* (*Vol. 6*). Kluwer Academic Publishers.

ADDITIONAL READING

Benestad, H. C., Arisholm, E., & Sjøberg, D. I. K. (2005). *How to recruit professionals as subjects in software engineering experiments*. Paper presented at the Information Systems Research in Scandinavia (IRIS), Kristiansand, Norway.

Cao, L., Ramesh, B., & Rossi, M. (2009). Are domain-specific models easier to maintain than UML models? *IEEE Software, 26*(4), 19–21. doi:10.1109/MS.2009.87

Cook, S., Jones, G., Kent, S., & Wils, A. C. (2007). *Domain-specific development with visual studio DSL tools*. Addison-Wesley Professional.

Deursen, A., van, Klint, P., & Visser, J. (2000). Domain-specific languages: An annotated bibliography. *ACM SIGPLAN Notices, 35*(6), 26-36.

Deursen, A. V., & Klint, P. (1998). Little languages: Little maintenance? *Journal of Software Maintenance: Research and Practice, 10*(2), 75–92. doi:10.1002/(SICI)1096-908X(199803/04)10:2<75::AID-SMR168>3.0.CO;2-5

GME. (2007). *GME: Generic modeling environment*. Vanderbilt University.

Gray, J., Rossi, M., & Tolvanen, J.-P. (2004). Preface. *Journal of Visual Languages and Computing, 15*, 207–209. doi:10.1016/j.jvlc.2004.03.001

Guizzardi, G., Ferreira Pires, L., & van Sinderen, M. (2005). *An ontology-based approach for evaluating the domain appropriateness and comprehensibility appropriateness of modeling languages. Model Driven Engineering Languages and Systems (MoDELS'2005)* (pp. 691–705). Jamaica: Montego Bay.

Johnson, P. (1992). *Human computer interaction: Psychology, task analysis, and software engineering*. McGraw-Hill.

Kelly, S., Lyytinen, K., & Rossi, M. (1996). *MetaEdit+: A fully configurable multi-user and multi-tool CASE and CAME environment.* Paper presented at the 8th International Conference on Advanced Information Systems Engineering, CAiSE'96.

Kelly, S., & Pohjonen, R. (2009). Worst practices for domain-specific modeling. *IEEE Software, 26*(4), 22–29. doi:10.1109/MS.2009.109

Kitchenham, B. A. (2007). *Guidelines for performing systematic literature reviews in software engineering.* Keele University and Durham University Joint Report.

Kitchenham, B. A., Al-Khilidar, H., Babar, M. A., Berry, M., Cox, K., & Keung, J. (2008). Evaluating guidelines for reporting empirical software engineering studies. *Empirical Software Engineering, 13*(1), 97–121. doi:10.1007/s10664-007-9053-5

Kitchenham, B. A., Dybå, T., & Jørgensen, M. (2004). Evidence-based software engineering. *26th International Conference on Software Engineering* (ICSE 2004) (pp.273-281). Edinburgh, Scotland.

Kosar, T., Martínez López, P. E., Barrientos, P. A., & Mernik, M. (2008). A preliminary study on various implementation approaches of domain-specific language. *Information and Software Technology, 50*(5), 390–405. doi:10.1016/j.infsof.2007.04.002

Luoma, J., Kelly, S., & Tolvanen, J.-P. (2004). *Defining domain-specific modeling languages: Collected experiences.* In OOPSLA Workshop on Domain-Specific Modeling, Vancouver, British Columbia, Canada.

Moore, W., Dean, D., Gerber, A., Wagenknecht, G., & Vanderheyden, P. (2004). *Eclipse development using the graphical editing framework and the Eclipse modeling framework.* IBM Redbooks.

Seffah, A., Donyaee, M., Kline, R. B., & Padda, H. K. (2006). Usability measurement and metrics: A consolidated model. *Software Quality Journal, 14*(2), 159–178. doi:10.1007/s11219-006-7600-8

Smolander, K., Tahvanainen, V.-P., & Marttiin, P. (1991). *MetaEdit - A flexible graphical environment for methodology modelling.* In International Conference on Advanced Information Systems Engineering, CAISE'91.

White, J., Hill, J. H., Tambe, S., Gokhale, A., & Schmidt, D. C. (2009). Improving domain-specific language reuse with software product line techniques. *IEEE Software, 26*(4), 47–53. doi:10.1109/MS.2009.95

KEY TERMS AND DEFINITIONS

Contexts of Use: The set of users, tasks, equipment (hardware, software and materials), and the physical and social environments in which a product is used' (ISO, 2001a). It is one of the characteristics that we can use to evaluate a product's usability. In fact, we can use this characteristic to pragmatically distinguish between different products: in DSLs, different languages may have different Contexts of Use (Atkinson & Kühne, 2003). Moreover, if they have different Contexts of Use, then we can infer that the users of those languages (the humans) most likely will have different knowledge sets, each one with a minimum amount of ontological concepts required in order to actually be able to use each language.

Effectiveness: Usability characteristic that determines the accuracy with which a developer completes language sentences.

Efficiency: Usability characteristic which tells us what level of effectiveness is achieved at the expense of various resources, such as mental and physical effort, time or financial cost, commonly measured in the sense of time spent to complete a sentence.

Language: A theoretical object (a model) that describes the allowed terms and how to compose them into the sentences involved in a given communication.

Satisfaction: Usability characteristic which captures freedom from inconveniences and positive attitude towards the use of a product (in the context of DSLs, the use of a language).

Semantics: Defines the meaning of the sentences of a language. In the case of DSLs, we are interested in languages which have computational meaning, where its semantics is specified by stating how the sentences in such kind of languages can be logically interpreted by a machine.

Semiotics: The study of the structure and meaning of languages. It is a part of linguistics that studies the dependencies and influences among the following parts: Pragmatics, Syntax, and Semantics.

Syntax: Defines what signs can be used in a language, and how those signs can be composed to form sentences.

Usability: The extent to which a product can be used by specified users to achieve specified goals – "Goal Quality". It has to be evaluated through the Quality in Use that is perceived by the user during actual utilization of a product in real Context of Use. Achieving Quality in Use is dependent on achieving the necessary External quality, which in turn is dependent on achieving the necessary Internal quality (ISO9126, 2001).

Chapter 15
Integrating DSLs into a Software Engineering Process:
Application to Collaborative Construction of Telecom Services

Vanea Chiprianov
Telecom Bretagne, France

Yvon Kermarrec
Telecom Bretagne, France

Siegfried Rouvrais
Telecom Bretagne, France

ABSTRACT

The development of large and complex systems involves many people, stakeholders. Engineeringly speaking, one way to control this complexity is by designing and analyzing the system from different perspectives. For each perspective, stakeholders benefit from means, tools, languages, specific to their activity domain. A Domain Specific Language (DSL) per perspective is such a dedicated means. While DSLs are used for modeling, other means, tools, and languages are needed for other connected activities, like testing or collaborating. However, using such different types of tools together, integrating DSLs into stakeholders' software process is not straightforward. In this chapter, the authors advance an integration process of DSLs with other tools. The chapter proposes each stakeholder have their own DSL with associated graphical editor, operational semantics, and generation of scripts for off the shelf simulators, e.g., testing. Additionally to the integrated stakeholders' software process, the authors introduce a model driven process dedicated to the tool vendor which creates the DSLs and its associated tools. Due to the integration of DSLs into this process, they contend that stakeholders will significantly reduce system construction time. The chapter illustrates the two processes on Telecommunications service construction.

DOI: 10.4018/978-1-4666-2092-6.ch015

INTRODUCTION

The development of large and complex systems involves many people, stakeholders, each with their own perspective, viewpoint. To document, understand and master this complexity, models are an important means. Another manner is by separation of concerns, i.e. distributed definition of specifications, of models, from multiple perspectives, viewpoints. In ISO/IEC 42010 (2007), a viewpoint is defined as a ''work product establishing the conventions for the construction, interpretation and use of architecture views to frame specific system concerns''. According to the same standard, a view is defined as a ''work product expressing the architecture of a system from the perspective of specific system concerns''. Within the same standard, a concern is an ''interest in a system relevant to one or more stakeholders'', where a stakeholder is an ''individual, team, organization, or classes thereof, having an interest in a system''.

One approach that handles system complexity is *Model Driven Engineering (MDE)*. The main artifact of MDE is the model. *Models* are representations of the reality for a given purpose. One way to manage complexity of a system is to describe it from different perspectives, using a Domain Specific Language (DSL) for each viewpoint as a modeling means. MDE also proposes a *meta-modeling approach for language definition* (Clark et al., 2001), targeted to languages that allow specifying models. It is frequently used to define graphical DSLs. As such, a *Domain Specific Language (DSL)* is ''a language that offers, through appropriate notations and abstractions, expressive power focused on, and usually restricted to, a particular problem domain'' (Deursen, Klint & Visser, 2000). DSLs can enhance quality, productivity, reliability, maintainability, re-usability, flexibility (Baker, Loh & Weil, 2005) (Kieburtz et al., 1996). Hence, it is advantageous they were used.

Although DSLs are numerous and their numbers are increasing, they address only part of modeler's activities. We consider here modelers to be system and software architects and designers. In practice, there are legacy or mature, domain specific, off the shelf (i.e. software that other software projects can reuse and integrate into their own products) tools that are used regularly by modelers (e.g., for testing purposes, for communication and collaboration). Therefore, DSLs should be conceived as part of the larger activities of a modeler and integrated into his/her process of work. A first question that needs addressing is: *How do DSLs integrate with other tools used by modelers in their regular activities?* Moreover, the tool vendors need to integrate the DSL development process into their tool building process. As such, *How do they integrate the DSL development process into their tool building process?* As they are focused on specific, narrow domains, it is expected more than one DSL be used at one time. How about composing several DSLs? There can be made a distinction between system/product DSLs, used to describe the product under construction, and transversal DSLs, that are not specific to the domain, but rather to connected activities (e.g., describing decision rationale, model versioning).

One example of complex systems are telecom services. They have a long life-cycle, with many stakeholders intervening at its different phases. Recent challenges (e.g. convergence with the Internet, the telecom market deregulation) have determined former national telecom providers to investigate ways to reduce the creation time of new services, while affecting non-negatively other parameters like cost, quality of service. Modeling telecom services using MDE and DSLs constitute a promising investigation path for reducing this time. However, telecom stakeholders already have a wealth of tools specific to their domain. To be successful, to increase their chances of being accepted by professionals, DSLs must integrate as seemingly as possible with these tools. This integration is at two levels: the one of usage, but also the level of development.

The next section presents our answer to the issue of DSL integration with other tools. It proposes a process of integrating the use of DSLs in modeling, together with the use of off the shelf simulation tools for verifying the models, with a DSL for describing decision rationale to enhance collaboration, and with DSL interoperability (i.e. the ability of two or more tools to exchange models so as to use them in order to operate effectively together) activities. We propose to do the verification activity after modeling and before implementation. This way, any necessary changes that are detected can be handled early in the system life-cycle. The models produced using the DSLs are fed as input to simulation tools. The translation between the DSLs and respectively the internal format of the simulator is of course automatized. The simulation results are then used in the modeling activity to make adjustments.

To reduce the time alloted to seeking information, we propose capturing and formalizing decision rationale with a DSL which is integrated with the system modeling DSLs. This rationale DSL is transversal to all DSLs intended for roles, is independent of them, and in general, of the domain. It can be used for any domain that implies decisions and requires their capture. This is expected to reduce the rationale capture intrusiveness.

Because interoperability is a complex problem, there are numerous proposals of decomposing it into levels. One particularly suitable for our approach makes a distinction between syntactic (between the syntaxes of DSLs) and semantic (between the semantics of DSLs) interoperability. Approaches to ensure syntactic interoperability between different DSLs have been proposed; they are powerful and mature. *S*emantic interoperability is still a research topic, and we have proposed a solution for ensuring it.

The section after that starts from existing generic processes of DSL development and of the shelf components integration, which we adjust to the practical needs of tool vendors and integrate into one overall tool building process. We exemplify the processes in the section after that, by building tools for telecommunications service construction and showing how to use them on a conference service example. We finish by indicating perspectives on the proposed processes.

GENERIC INTEGRATION OF DSLS INTO MODELERS' PROCESS

The waterfall model is a sequential development approach, in which development is seen as flowing downwards through the phases of requirements analysis, design, implementation, testing (validation), and maintenance. Such a process still reflects current practices of some industries (e.g. telecommunications) in which a system/product is defined using a block approach, without going back to a previous phase, and in isolation from other systems. It is therefore expected to be easily accepted by practitioners. Stakeholders are sometimes called actors; they may be attached to roles. A role (The Open Group, 2009) is a ''named specific behavior of an actor participating in a particular context''. In a waterfall-like process, a role converses only with the roles immediately upstream and immediately downstream it in the system life-cycle. It consists of the same activities each role does, after which the model goes downstream, to the next role, which will perform the same set of activities.

Modelers are considered here to be: system architects (i.e. the high-level designer of a system to be implemented), system designers (i.e. somebody working under the direction of a systems architect, designing, developing and implementing the clearly defined requirements of a new information system), software architects (i.e. the high-level, coarse grain designer of a software to be implemented), software designers (i.e. usually an engineer doing low-level, fine grain component and algorithm implementation). The responsibilities of a modeler (Kruchten, 2008) are:

- **Define the Architecture/Design of the System:** A modeler abstracts the complexity of a system into a manageable model that describes the essence of a system by exposing important details and significant constraints. This comprises technical activities like: extracting architecturally significant requirements, translating business strategy into technical vision, exploring alternatives, making choices (e.g. technology selection), synthesizing a solution, validating them, defining the major modules of the system, etc.
- **Maintain the Architectural Integrity of the System:** This is done through regular reviews, writing guidelines, and presenting the architecture/design/model to various parties, at different levels of abstraction and technical depth.
- **Participate in Project Planning:** This is done by assessing technical risks and working out mitigation strategies/approaches, or by proposing order and content of development activities.
- **Discuss with Implementation, Integration, Product Marketing Teams:** Due to their technical expertise, modelers are involved into problem-solving activities that are beyond solving strictly modeling issues. They have insights into what is feasible, and influence business strategy accordingly.

Some of these responsibilities are engineering, others are related to management, organizational politics, business strategy. From all modeler responsibilities, we focus on the following modeling activities (*MA*), for modelers of all roles:

1. **MA 1 Model:** Modeling the service from their perspective. Each stakeholder/role describes the system from his/her perspective, according to his/her concerns.
2. **MA 2 Test:** Testing/verifying the system modeled from their perspective. Early validation, verification or simulation permit to identify errors (more costly to repair later) or performance/dimensioning issues.
3. **MA3 Collaborate:** Collaborating with other modelers from the same role. Of course, in each role there are several professionals working together. They interact with each other and with professionals from other roles.
4. **MA 4 Inter-operate:** Inter-operating with the software used by modelers from other roles. Professionals also import/integrate/compose their models. The most important challenge introduced by this process is the interoperability of models developed in different views.

Obviously, the *MA 1 Model* can be done with the help of a DSL. However, other modeling activities like *MA 2 Test*, *MA 4 Inter-operate*, require different software tools. These activities and the tools used with them have to be integrated into a coherent process.

In the process we propose (Figure 1), the modeler begins by importing an existing model (if there exists one) (cf. Modeler, and the ''(I) Imports ...'' activity in (Figure 1)). He/She adds information to this model according to his/her concerns, from his/her perspective (cf. the ''(D) Describes ...'' activity in (Figure 1)). His/Her modeling may be influenced by constraints coming from other viewpoints downstream in the process (cf. ''(I) Integrate ...'' activity in (Figure 1)). These constraints may either result from previous projects and so be integrated in the tool he/she is using, or may result from (in)formal discussions with modelers from other roles. After developing a first version of the model, he/she may check it for conformance or simulate to find e.g. performance issues (cf. the ''(V) Tests ...'' activity in (Figure 1)). According to the obtained results, he/she may change the model, then test it again. So, there are a number of iterations between these two activities. While

Figure 1. Generic integration of DSLs into modelers' process

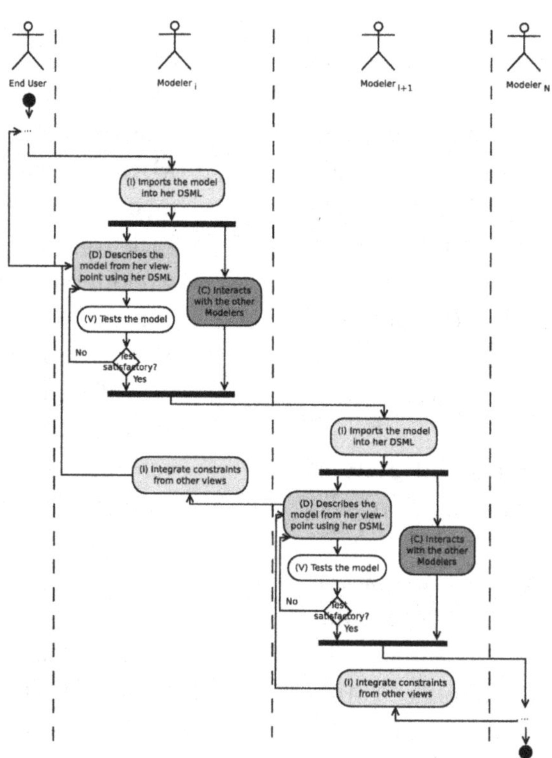

describing and testing the model, the modeler is not the only one doing this. Most often, he/she is part of a team, and as such collaborates with other modelers during the entire duration of the description and test activities (cf. the ''(C) Interacts ...'' activity in (Figure 1)). When the model reaches a satisfactory state (according to the modeler's experience), it is transfered to modelers of the next role downstream.

The same kind of activities are done by the modelers of all roles. The four activities can be viewed as a pattern, which is repeated for each role (Figure 1). The entire process is started by the end user, whose needs are captured in a first model. At the end of the process, the new system has been constructed and is ready to enter the deployment phase.

Modeling a Viewpoint

Modeling is the process of generating abstract, conceptual, graphical and/or mathematical models[1]. The *MA 1 Model* comprises technical activities that correspond to the *Define the architecture/design of the system* responsibility of the modeler. To support these activities, modeling languages are an important means. A *Modeling Language (ML)* is, ''a graphical language for visualizing, specifying, constructing, and documenting the artifacts of a software-intensive system'' (Booch, Rumbaugh & Jacobson, 2005).

An important aspect of modeling languages is their generality. General Purpose Languages (GPLs) (e.g. UML) are intended to be used in any domain. They can promote common understanding across different domains. However, because of their generality, the solution to a specific problem may be unnecessarily difficult to express and hard to understand. In contrast, a *Domain Specific Language (DSL)* is ''a language that offers, through appropriate notations and abstractions, expressive power focused on, and usually restricted to, a particular problem domain'' (Deursen, Klint & Visser, 2000). DSLs promise productivity increase based on the conciseness of produced models. The main disadvantages of DSLs are the additional cost of designing, implementing and maintaining it. DSL development is hard, requiring both domain and language development expertise, which few people have (Mernik, Heering & Sloane, 2005). So it is important to balance the return, the benefits a DSL generates, with the investment in its development, before deciding to create it. Empirical studies (Kosar et al., 2010) show that programmers' success rate is around 15% better for DSLs than GPLs, concerning learning, perception and evolution.

A *Domain Specific Modeling Language (DSML)* is taken in this chapter to be a graphical language that offers, through appropriate notations and abstractions, expressive power focused on a particular problem domain, to visualize, specify, construct and document the artifacts of a software-intensive system. DSMLs allow experts in general to express, validate, modify solutions and achieve tasks specific to their domain. A DSML requires less cognitive effort from experts than a more general purpose language, as it offers a higher closeness of mapping between the problem world and the solution world. Empirical studies conform that DSLs are superior to GPLs in all cognitive dimensions (Kosar et al., 2010).

DSMLs, by their definition, have reduced dimensions. So, when they describe large domains, or different viewpoints for a domain, it is natural to define several DSMLs. While they are similar, they do differ by syntax and semantics. A *family of languages* is ''a set of related languages that offer similar functionality at an equivalent level of abstraction'' (Ober et al., 2008). Their main advantage is the systematic reuse of member languages. Their main issue is their interoperability, addressed in the subsection after the next. As we propose to define a DSML for each role, we will also have a family of languages. Our proposal for the modeling activity is to integrate DSMLs, one for each viewpoint, into the process of system creation.

Testing through Simulation

Testing is the process of executing a software or system with the intent of finding errors (Myers & Sandler, 2004). This *MA 2 Test* involves any activity aimed at evaluating an attribute or capability of a system and determining that it meets its required results. A means of evaluating a capability of a system is through simulation.

Testing may be seen as a generic activity that is applied throughout the whole life cycle (e.g. CMMI). However, we focus here on testing models, and on doing so by using simulation. In the context of this focus, we consider testing through simulation as a phase.

By testing models, any necessary changes that are detected can be handled early in the system life-cycle. As such powerful software tools already exist for simulation, we leverage them by ensuring the interoperability between the DSMLs used for the *MA 1 Model* and a simulator, which is used for the *MA 2 Test*. In this way, the models produced using the DSMLs are fed as input to simulation tools. The interoperability/translation between DSMLs and respectively the internal format of the simulator is of course automatized (e.g. using MT approaches - see next section). The simulation results are then used in the modeling activity to make adjustments.

Collaboration inside a Role

An important and common issue of collaboration is information seeking, which consumes much of software engineers' time (e.g. 31,90% according to (Goncalves, Souza & Gonzalez, 2009)). Collaboration is a process where two or more stakeholders (persons or organizations) work jointly or together to create or achieve the same thing/aim, by sharing knowledge, learning and building consensus (Merriam-Webster), (Cambridge Advanced Learner). The most absent information in collocated software development teams is about design and program behavior (Ko, DeLine & Venolia, 2007). Design Rationale (DR) is the justification behind decisions, the reasoning that goes into determining the design of the artifact (Dutoit et al., 2006). So, capturing DR and enabling its retrieval would reduce significantly the information seeking time, increasing the performance of collaboration. DR supports collaboration also by (Dutoit et al., 2006): promoting coordination in design teams, exposing differing points of view, facilitating participation and collaboration, building consensus.

The main activities involving DR are:

- **Capture:** The process of eliciting rationale from designers (e.g., directly from designers themselves, or through an automatic manner) and recording it. Designers may be quite reluctant about capturing rationale (Dutoit et al., 2006). One of the most important factors of this resistance seems to be the intrusiveness of the capture process (e.g., the actual work required for capture, the disruption in designers' thinking). To solve the capture problem, one direction explores reducing its intrusiveness. Proposals include finding when rationale is elicited naturally as part of design communication and capturing at that moment, and integrating rationale artifacts with the system models (Wolf, 2008), thus ingraining the communication channels in the system models, thus reducing the participants' reluctance to communicate and to capture raising issues.
- **Formalization:** The process of transforming rationale into the desired representation form. There are many ways in which DR argumentation may be structured. One branch of thought uses a group of DR schemas having IBIS, DRL, Questions Options Criteria (QOC) (MacLean et al., 1991) among its most prominent members.
- **Retrieval:** The process of getting recorded rationale to the people who need it, providing access to it. Knowledge is thus capitalized upon and transmitted between projects. The most common approach to accessing DR is through use of a system that lets users browse a hyper document containing the rationale. Conventional information retrieval search techniques can also be used.

To address the DR capture problem, we propose formalizing the rationale with a DSML which is integrated with the system modeling DSMLs. This DR DSML is transversal to all DSMLs intended for roles, is independent of them, and in general, of the domain. It can be used for any domain that implies decisions and requires their capture. The DR DSML is based on argumentative formalization of DR, and contains concepts and constructs from the representation schema. One or a combination of schemas like IBIS, QOC, DRL can be used. Modelers use it during the *MA 1 Model*, at the moment which is natural to them. This is expected to reduce the DR capture intrusiveness. For DR retrieval, existing navigation or query-based systems can be integrated with the DSMLs framework.

Towards Automatic Semantic Interoperability of Modeling Languages

Our process proposes to model a system using DSMLs for the different viewpoints that characterize the roles involved. While this makes complexity manageable, it introduces the difficult issue of interoperability. The modelers from different roles exchange models with the modelers from adjacent roles (i.e. just upstream and downstream of them). For these models to be exchanged, their format/schema must be understood by the tools of the adjacent role downstream. We propose to ensure this understanding, interoperability, in an automatic manner, so the only activity of the modeler be ''Imports the model into her DSML'' (Figure 1).

For our purposes, and following (Peristeras & Tarabanis, 2006), we consider interoperability to be the ability of two or more tools to exchange models so as to use them in order to operate effectively together. Considering this definition, to operate together, tools for adjacent role DSMLs need to exchange models. Considering that models are conformant with (the syntax of) DSMLs, the issue of tools exchanging models written in different DSMLs becomes an interoperability issue between DSMLs. So, to ensure interoperability between models, one must address interoperability between DSMLs.

Because interoperability is a complex problem, there are numerous proposals of decomposing it into levels. One particularly suitable for our approach is the C4IF (Connection, Communication, Consolidation, Collaboration Interoperability Framework) (Peristeras & Tarabanis, 2006). C4IF proposes four levels of interoperability: Connection, Communication, Consolidation, Collaboration. We consider the C4IF *Connection* level as being implemented by existing communication and signaling media in computers. *Communication*, syntactic interoperability, between DSML tools, is the level of interoperability between the syntaxes of DSMLs. Approaches to ensure syntactic interoperability between different DSMLs have been proposed, like combining them (Vallecillo, 2010): extension, merge, embedding, weaving or hybrid approaches. These are powerful and mature approaches. *Consolidation*, semantic interoperability, between DSML tools, is the level of interoperability between the semantics of DSMLs. Semantic interoperability is still a research topic, and we have proposed a solution for ensuring it (cf. Section *Using ontologies for ensuring semantic interoperability*). We do not yet address *Collaboration* (i.e. the ability of systems to act together), as we consider, in conformance with their (strict) linearity property (i.e. to reach an upper level of interoperability, all the previous levels must have been successfully addressed) (Peristeras & Tarabanis, 2006), that the Consolidation level must be ensured first.

Discussion

Although we propose a four modeling activity process, there are other activities of the modeler that have not been addressed in this chapter (e.g., project planning, discussing with other teams).

Our proposal for *MA 1 Model*, defining a DSML for each role, while promising increased expressive power and thus higher modeler performance, it is a hard and costly task. It would be beneficial if some of these disadvantages could be reduced. One manner is by defining DSMLs as extensions to existing modeling languages.

We tackle *MA 2 Test* by proposing integration with existing widely used software tools, simulators. However, round-trip testing (i.e. integrating automatically the test results into the model) would be highly useful. Also, integration with many other testing tools, capable of analyzing different aspects of models, is needed.

Like testing, *MA 3 Collaborate* is a vast subject. We tackle one of the most important issue, the lack of rationale behind modeling decisions. We built on DR research to propose a DSML based on schemas and integrated with the system DSMLs. This integration is expected to reduce the capture intrusiveness problem and determine modelers to use the DR DSML. More collaboration software tools and devices (e.g.; multi-writer, real-time, distributed collaborative editors that also include chat, white-board, and screen sharing functionality; multi-touch table; interactive white-boards) should be integrated.

To help the modeler in his/her *MA 4 Interoperate*, we propose to ensure DSML interoperability automatically, at the syntactic and semantic levels. However, this does not address the flow of information upstream, and it is the modeler's responsibility to integrate constraints that may come from other views, roles (cf. activity "(I) Integrate constraints from other views" from (Figure 1)).

While numerous DSLs have been proposed, and numerous approaches for the other tasks of MA 2 Test, MA 3 Collaborate and MA 4 Interoperate exist, as far as we know there have been no attempts to use together DSLs with other software tools. Until now, the major focus has been on using DSLs in isolation, without considering how they may integrate with other tools.

The system construction process proposes the same set of activities to modelers of all roles. The advantage is that tool vendors can re-use the same tool building process (cf. next section), for all roles. The disadvantage is that, being based on a waterfall model, the process lacks the flexibility of iterative and agile processes for example. However, the waterfall model can be considered the basis of one iteration in an iterative process. In the future, such an iterative process is very probable to surpass, replacing by integrating it, the waterfall-like process proposed here. This will probably have a negligible effect, if any, on DSMLs, and will emphasize their generative benefits even more. However, having several development iterations requires an even higher degree of interoperability and integration between DSMLs, to reduce interoperability/translation time. Therefore, the introduction of of an iterative process will increase the interoperability challenge. In the proposed waterfall-like process, although there is some information that goes upstream, this is rather reduced; once a role has finished its activities, there is no going back upstream. The process proposed in this section illustrates the integration of DSMLs into the software engineering process for creating systems, and the interaction of the *MA 1 Model* with other modelers' activities.

GENERIC INTEGRATION OF DSL DEVELOPMENT INTO A VENDOR'S TOOL BUILDING PROCESS

To build the software tools to implement the proposed process, define the modeling and collaboration DSMLs, build their software tools, generate configuration files to existing simulation tools, as well as ensure automatic interoperability, we elaborate a tool building process, targeted at tool vendors (Figure 2). The tasks for defining DSMLs are inspired from the meta-modeling approach for modeling language definition, an instantiation of a general DSML process, focused on tool vendors' practical needs (cf. tasks marked with 'D' in (Figure 2)). Enabling testing through simulation is based on code generation approaches (cf. tasks marked with 'V' in (Figure 2)). The integration of the collaboration DSML (cf. tasks marked with 'C' in (Figure 2)) and viewpoint-specific DSMLs is based on model combination. Ensuring interoperability is done through lifting of the MMs into ontologies, followed by their alignment, and generation of model transformations (cf. tasks marked with 'I' in (Figure 2)).

Integrating DSMLs into software engineering processes, in addition to the language development process to be followed, introduce issues like: leveraging Off the Shelf (OTS) components, combining several DSMLs, ensuring interoperability between DSML-associated tools.

DSML Development Process

DSML development approaches propose processes with several phases. For example (Čeh et al., 2011) introduce a seven phase process:

1. **Decision:** Characteristics of problems deserving a DSML approach include: well

Figure 2. Generic integration of DSL development into a vendor's tool building process

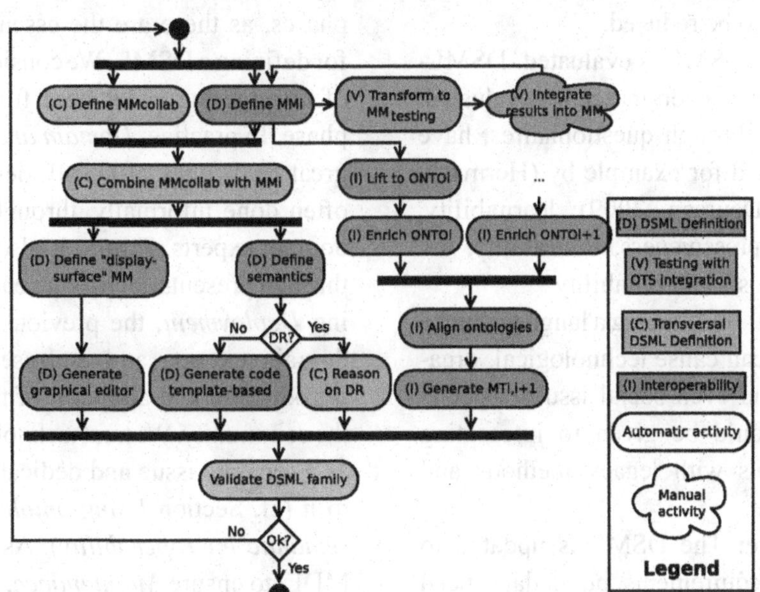

defined domain, domain with repetitive elements (e.g. multiple products, features), a growing developer community, intended use by a domain expert (Sprinkle et al., 2009).

2. **Domain Analysis:** The goal of this phase is to select and define the domain of focus and collect appropriate domain information and integrate it into a coherent domain model. Although various formal methodologies exist (e.g., FODA, FAST (Coplien, Hoffman & Weiss, 1998)), domain analysis is still done informally most of the time. A possible solution may be Semi-automated Domain Modeling (Reinhartz-Berger, 2010), an approach which matches, merges and generalizes multiple application models in a domain, considering syntactic, semantic and structural aspects.
3. **Design:** In this phase, the syntax and semantics of the language are defined. The main definition methods (Mernik, Heering & Sloane, 2005) are: inventing a new language from scratch, and starting from an existing language. There are three main ways of re-using a base language: by piggybacking (partially reusing it), specializing (restricting it), extending (adding new features or constructs). The syntax and semantics can be described with a formal (e.g.; BNF, MMs for syntax; grammars, denotational semantics for semantics) or informal method (e.g. natural language and illustrative DSML models).
4. **Implementation:** Consists in building the language tools that describe the execution semantics. Approaches include: compiler/interpreter, source-to-source transformation, embedding (new abstract data types and operators are defined on top of those of a base language), compiler generator, extensible compiler, etc. A comparison of ten such implementation approaches is presented by (Kosar et al., 2008). It shows that the implementation effort and the end-user effort of using the DSML are almost inversely proportional (first approach according to one of the measures ranked penultimate according to the other). As end-user effort should be

kept as low as possible, the implementation effort needs to be reduced.

5. **Testing:** The DSML is evaluated. DSML-specific success factors that can be evaluated, for example through questionnaires, have been identified for example by (Hermans, Pinzger & Deursen, 2009): learnability, usability, expressiveness, re-usability, development costs and reliability.
6. **Deployment:** Introducing a language into a community can cause technological, organizational and even social issues. Special attention should be given to integrating the new tools with legacy methods and infrastructure.
7. **Maintenance:** The DSML is updated to reflect new requirements, but updates need to maintain consistency and continuity between versions of language and associated tools. A framework for the evolution of modeling languages is introduced by (Meyers & Vangheluwe, 2011). It co-evolves the syntax, semantics and transformations through migration operators.

Most language developers seem to focus on *Design* and *Implementation* phases. The least known and least examined is *Domain analysis* (Čeh et al., 2011). *Testing* is often skipped or relaxed by language developers (Gabriel, Goulao & Amaral, 2010).

Applied DSML Definition Process

The process we propose to tool vendors is an instantiation of the general DSML process presented in the previous section, focused on their practical needs. As DSMLs are graphical, and because we want to take advantage of meta-tools, we focus on model driven approaches. The general accepted meaning of a *meta-tool* is a tool that allows specification and generation of another tool. Meta-tools reduce significantly the time, effort and cost of constructing language-associated tools. We also concentrate on the *Design* and *Implementation* phases, as these are the essential initial phases for defining a DSML. We consider *Decision* more of a triggering event born from a need, than a phase. In practice, *Domain analysis* is one of the great challenges of DSML development, and is often done informally, through discussion with domain experts. *Testing* is also done informally, through presentations to the end-users. Concerning *Deployment*, the previous discussions with domain experts and end-users facilitates the introduction and adoption of the new DSML in the community. We treat technological integration as a separate issue and dedicate another process to it (cf. Section *Using ontologies for ensuring semantic interoperability*). As our process uses MDE, to ensure *Maintenance*, operators derived from model differencing, comparison, evolution (at present hot research topics) can be leveraged, as proposals like (Meyers & Vangheluwe, 2011) begin doing.

In MDE, models are conformant to *meta-models (MM)*, much like a program is conformant to the grammar of the programming language. MMs are models also, that are more abstract and general than regular models. Besides describing models, model transformations are the focus of MDE. A *model transformation (MT)* (Kleppe, Warmer & Bast, 2003) is the automatic generation of a target model from a source model, according to a set of transformation rules. A transformation rule is a description of how one or more constructs in the source language can be transformed into one or more constructs in the target language.

MDE also proposes a *meta-modeling approach for language definition* (Clark et al., 2001), in which abstract and concrete syntax are described through MMs, and their mappings through MTs. Similarly to the traditional compiler method for implementing programming languages, the meta-modeling approach uses meta-tools. When language definition evolves, it impacts the MMs describing the syntax and the semantics. Due to meta-tools, language-specific tools can be regenerated to include the new language features, with limited modifications, fast and inexpensive.

The process we propose for MM-based DSMLs (cf. activities marked with a (D), from (Figure 2)), focused on the *Decision* and *Implementation* phases, is based on the meta-modeling approach for language definition. It has at its center the MM used to describe the abstract syntax (cf. activity ''(D) Define MM_i'' from (Figure 2)). For the concepts present in this MM, another MM which describes the concrete syntax is defined (cf. activity ''(D) Define display-surface MM'' from (Figure 2)). The link between the two can be described with model transformations or implemented in the programming language into which the MMs are translated. The MM describing the concrete syntax is used as input to a semi-automated process of generating the editor (cf. activity ''(D) Generate graphical editor'' from (Figure 2)). Starting from the MM describing the abstract syntax again (which justifies the claim that this MM is at the center of the process), DSML semantics is described. We propose to implement DSMLs through template-based code generation techniques (cf. activity ''(D) Generate code template-based'' from (Figure 2)). This process can be employed for DSMLs of all roles, resulting in a family of DSMLs. This family has to be tested, validated by end-users, which usually involves iterations (cf. task ''Validate DSML family'' and decision block ''Ok?'' from (Figure 2)).

Process for the Integration of Off the Shelf Components

We start by presenting a generic process for the integration of components off the shelf, which we then adjust for the practical needs of tool vendors.

Generic Process for the Integration of Components Off the Shelf

The term *Off the Shelf (OTS)* component is very generic; it can refer to many different types and levels of software. We adopt the definition as stated by (Torchiano & Morisio, 2004): ''a commercially available or open source piece of software that other software projects can reuse and integrate into their own products''. It includes both components/services acquired for a fee (known as Commercial OTS - COTS) and from Open Source communities (known as Open Source Software – OSS).

Advantages of components OTS include: savings in development resources; increased potential for improved quality, enhanced reliability, availability, maintenance (Sedigh-Ali, Ghafoor & Paul, 2001). However, there are also caveats when using OTS components: integration effort; difficulty of selection (Ayala et al., 2011).

The particular nature of components OTS requires a particular process of using them. One such process for vendors is proposed by (Morisio et al., 2002). It consists of four phases, in which OTS specific activities are combined with non-OTS activities. The four phases, with the OTS-specific activities, are:

1. **Requirements:** The tools/components/packages are identified/evaluated/selected. As underlined in the disadvantages, this is a major issue;
2. **Design:** The glue-ware and interfaces are identified;
3. **Coding:** The glue-ware and interfaces are written/implemented;
4. **Integration:** the components are integrated between themselves and with the system. The system is tested. The acceptance system test is the final activity.

There are also two review activities, after the *Requirements* and the *Design* phases, and the customer should be involved in the *Requirements* phase.

Process for the Integration of Components Off the Shelf Applied to Leveraging Simulators

Due to the fact that there are numerous mature simulation and testing tools, we propose leveraging them as OTS tools. We do not discuss the arduous activity of OTS selection, considering it the appanage of domain experts. We focus instead on the *Design* and *Coding* phases (cf. activity "(V) Transform to $MM_{testing}$" from (Figure 2)). As a consequence of our proposal to use model transformations for the *Coding* phase, *Integration* of information from the main system to the OTS components is no longer a problem. However, the flow backwards still is an issue (cf. activity "(V) Integrate results into MM_i" from (Figure 2)).

The *Design* phase of our process consists in constructing a MM that captures the data used by the tool OTS to be integrated. The *Coding* phase consists in writing a MT between the MM of the DSML and the MM of the tool OTS produced in the *Design* phase. In this way, the flow of information, represented by the models obtained with the DSML and inputed in the OTS tool, is automated. This solves the *Integration* issue between the main system, the DSML, and the OTS tools. However, as many of the results of the OTS tools have a visual nature, they can be accessed only by their end-users, not by programmatic means. Therefore, it is their activity to interpret the results and modify the model accordingly.

Leveraging OTS tools is conceivable for other modeling activities than testing. For example, existing tools for communication (e.g., chat, VoIP) could be integrated using the process proposed here, helping the *MA 3 Collaborate*.

Towards Collaboration through Combination of System DSMLs with a DR DSML

From the large field of collaboration, we have decided to focus on DR and build a DSML for its capture. The process of defining the DR DSML is the same with that for the system DSMLs (cf. Section *Applied DSML Definition Process*). The MM describing the abstract syntax, based on schema structured argumentation formalization approaches (e.g., IBIS, QOC, DRL), is defined (cf. activity "(C) Define MM_{collab}" from (Figure 2)). However, the DR DSML is transversal to system DSMLs. To be used by modelers from all roles, it has to be combined with each of the system DSMLs. There are many DSML combination approaches, reviewed for example by (Vallecillo, 2010). As they are both based on MMs, their combination becomes a combination of MMs (through e.g., MM extension, MM merge).

For the DR DSML, the concrete syntax (cf. activity "(D) Define display-surface MM" from (Figure 2)) and graphical editor (cf. activity "(D) Generate graphical editor" from (Figure 2)) are defined and respectively generated, just like for any other DSML. Of course, starting again from the MM describing the abstract syntax, the semantics of the DR DSML is implemented. Here is the most specific point in defining this language compared with the system ones. The interest in DR is not to execute it, like with the system models, but to do inferences and queries on it, so that modelers can retrieve it at a later date (cf. activity "(C) Reason on DR" from (Figure 2)). Existing tools for DR retrieval can be integrated using the component OTS integration process (cf. previous section).

Other DSMLs transversal on system DSMLs (e.g. for model versioning, for SPLs of models) can be conceived using the same process. The central issue of the proposed process is the MM combination operation. While it could be automatized using model (vs. MM) combination approaches, MMs describing language syntax have a low number of components. Accordingly, an expert-driven approach to extending MMs is both practicable and preferable to an automatic one, which has a higher level of inaccuracy.

Using Ontologies for Ensuring Semantic Interoperability

Ensuring automatic syntactic and semantic interoperability between DSMLs is dependent of DSML implementation choices. As we chose a meta-modeling approach, the (abstract) syntax of DSMLs is described by a MM. Therefore, ensuring *syntactic interoperability* between two DSMLs means describing the common concepts of the two MMs. Approaches to ensure syntactic interoperability between different DSMLs have been proposed, like combining them (Vallecillo, 2010): extension, merge, embedding, weaving or hybrid approaches. However, we strongly recognize that the most flexible way to describe relations between two MMs, is through MTs. Using MTs, one can describe the similarity relations between two MMs and capture the intersection between the concepts of their respective DSMLs. Nevertheless, MMs describe only the syntaxes of DSMLs. So MTs, or other combination approaches between MMs, can describe interoperability only at a syntactic level. We focus in what follows on semantic interoperability.

The common thread in defining *ontology* (Welty, 2003) is that it is a *formal description* of a domain, intended for *sharing* among different applications, and expressed in a language that can be used for reasoning. We propose to use ontologies for: describing the static semantics of DSMLs (i.e. model enrichment) and discovering a common reference ontology (i.e. semi-automatic identification of mappings between MMs). A common ontology will ensure semantic interoperability and coherence between two adjacent role DSMLs. It can be discovered by determining the mapping between two ontologies, each describing the semantics of one DSML. For this, we promote this approach:

1. **Lift:** It transforms each MM into an ontology (cf. activity ''(I) Lift to $ONTO_i$'' from (Figure 2)). We implement it through a MT between the meta-MM describing the modeling technical space (e.g. Ecore[2]) and the meta-MM describing the ontology space (e.g. OWL DL[3]). OWL DL is particularly suited for our approach, as its definition is already given in the form of a MM.
2. **Enrich:** The lifted MMs are enriched by applying patterns (cf. activity ''(I) Enrich $ONTO_i$'' and ''(I) Enrich $ONTO_{i+1}$'' from (Figure 2)). Finding correspondences between relationships of different MMs can be addressed this way. Patterns similar to that of ''Association Class Introduction'' (Kappel et al., 2006) can be used. A new class is introduced in the ontology similarly to an association class in UML, thus transforming relationships from MMs into concepts in ontologies. We implement it through an endogenous MT, with input and output the meta-MM describing the ontology space.
3. **Align:** In the ontology technical space we apply ontology-specific techniques (e.g. alignment) on the lifted and enriched MMs of two adjacent roles, thus discovering their intersection (cf. activity ''(I) Align ontologies'' from (Figure 2)). Because the lifted and enriched MMs describe semantics of DSMLs, the discovered *shared ontologies* represent in fact the semantics of the model transformations between the original MMs. Rediscovering these shared ontologies each time the (lifted and enriched) MMs describing static semantics of DSMLs evolve, is what we mean by ensuring (static) semantic interoperability between two DSMLs.
4. **Generate:** Model transformations which have as input and/or as output other model transformations are called *Higher Order Transformations (HOTs)*. We use shared ontologies as input for HOTs between the meta-MM describing the ontology technical space and the meta-MM describing the MT space (e.g. QVT[4]), which generate model transformations between the original MMs

(cf. activity ''(I) Generate $MT_{i,i+1}$'' from (Figure 2)).

Consequently, we can automatically generate and evolve model transformations for a family of DSMLs, through their connections with shared ontologies, thus ensuring their syntactic and static semantic interoperability. The whole process can be automatized and thus enables a high rate of reuse and faster iterations on evolving MMs.

Discussion

The tool building process proposed in this section ((Figure 2) in its totality) builds on processes for DSML development, DSML combination approaches, component OTS integration, ontology generation and alignment. The proposed DSML development process has advantages:

- Clear separation between abstract syntax, concrete syntax, semantics;
- Easy evolution of both language design and tools;
- Easy composition of several languages;
- Partial generation of language-associated tools from MMs;
- Semi-automatic interoperability between tools associated to different languages from the family; but also disadvantages, which could limit its practical usability by tool vendors:
- Even informally done, domain analysis is long and difficult. Domain analysis methodologies, knowledge capture and representation approaches, tool support, that are suitable for DSL development are needed;
- The choice of concepts (abstract syntax) and of the representation of concepts (concrete syntax) requires several iterations and direct involvement of domain experts and end-users.

The process for DR DSML definition reuses the DSML development process, may reuse model combination approaches transfered to MMs, and may reuse the tool OTS integration process. The MM combination effort is the only overhead for integrating the DR DSML with a system DSML. No extra effort is needed to integrate the concrete syntaxes or the semantics of the two languages.

The main advantage of the proposed off the shelf tools integration process is the leverage of components OTS. This results in massive re-use of existing formalisms and tools. The use of MTs allows easy building of bridges between DSMLs and OTS tools and enables their model-based evolution. The difficulty of this process lies in constructing the MM describing the data format used by the OTS tool. This is especially poignant when dealing with commercial tools which do not provide many details about the format of the files they use, or with tools poorly documented. Moreover, the flow backwards, integrating results (i.e. round-tripping) from the OTS tools into the model described with the DSML, is currently done manually, with the investigation of (semi-) automatic solutions being one direction of our current work.

Using a meta-modeling approach combined with ontologies for ensuring syntactic and semantic interoperability of DSMLs has the advantage of co-evolving the syntactic and semantic bridges. However, this co-evolution depends greatly on the shared ontology between roles. If this would be poor or even empty, the interoperability bridge would be narrow. Consequently, in order for the proposed approach to be effective one should first make sure that the vocabularies for different viewpoints have a fair amount of concepts in common. This supports the idea that such an approach would be beneficial especially in the case of families of modeling languages. The proposal presented in this section can also be found in our article (Chiprianov, Kermarrec & Rouvrais, 2011c).

Similarly to the fact that the use of DSLs together with other tools has not been tackled yet, to the best of our knowledge, the development of DSLs together with other tools have not been addressed yet, to the best of our knowledge. There are processes to guide the development of DSLs, like (Čeh et al., 2011), but no work on how this process may integrate and benefit a larger software development process.

The tool building process proposed in this section adjusts these general processes to the practical needs of tool vendors. It also combines them into one overall process, showing the integration of the DSML definition process into a larger vendor process which tackles not only modeling tools, but also testing, collaboration and interoperability. As part of this overall process, a new sub-process based on MTs, HOTs and ontologies is proposed to ensure DSML interoperability.

Noteworthy is the fact that the MM describing the abstract syntax of a DSML is an input to all sub-process (Figure 2). Its importance is therefore central, crucial even, to the entire process. As it is the result of the *Domain analysis* phase, the importance of this phase becomes evident. Applying formal methods of carrying out this phase could be very helpful in evolving the MM.

APPLYING THE TOOL VENDOR BUILDING PROCESS AND THE MODELERS' PROCESS TO TELECOM SERVICE CONSTRUCTION

To better answer telecom-specific modeling requirements, we decided to implement the system DSMLs as extensions of an Enterprise Architecture (EA) modeling language. The proposal, together with the choice of ArchiMate (Open Group, 2009) as EA modeling language, has been extensively argued (Chiprianov et al., 2011). ArchiMate defines three layers: Business, Application, and Technology. We considered each layer as a DSML target at different stakeholders, and defined a family of three DSMLs.

Applying the Tool Vendor Building Process

We extended each of these three DSMLs with telecom-specific concepts. Therefore, the result of the ''(D) Define MM_i'' activity (Figure 2) is in this case an extension of the ArchiMate MM for one of the layers. The three MMs have been presented in detail (Chiprianov, Kermarrec & Rouvrais, 2011b), (Chiprianov, Kermarrec & Rouvrais, 2012) (Chiprianov, Kermarrec & Rouvrais, 2011), together with the extension process (Chiprianov, Kermarrec & Rouvrais, 2011b). We present here for exemplification the MM of the Telecom extension at the ArchiMate Application layer (Figure 3). Three Telecom specific concepts (marked with the superscript T) have been introduced in the ArchiMate MM.

The ''display-surface'' MMs of the three DSMLs (cf. ''Define display-surface MM'' activity) have been defined taking in consideration both proximity to the extended language, and specificity to the telecom domain. An example for the ''display-surface'' MM of the Telecom extension at the ArchiMate Application layer is presented here (Figure 4). In this figure, the display representations for the three concepts introduced at the Application layer (Figure 3) can be observed. One integrated graphical editor has been (partially) generated (cf. activity ''(D) Generate graphical editor'' from (Figure 2)) for all three DSMLs using Eclipse Modeling Framework (EMF). The generated stubs have been further developed with Eclipse Graphical Editing Framework (GEF). The editor was developed by reusing an existing open source project for ArchiMate, Archi, an Eclipse plug-in. The process of developing the telecom specific editor as a plug-in extension of Archi has been presented in detail (Chiprianov, Kermarrec & Rouvrais, 2011a).

Figure 3. ArchiMate application MM extended by a telecom profile (superscript T)

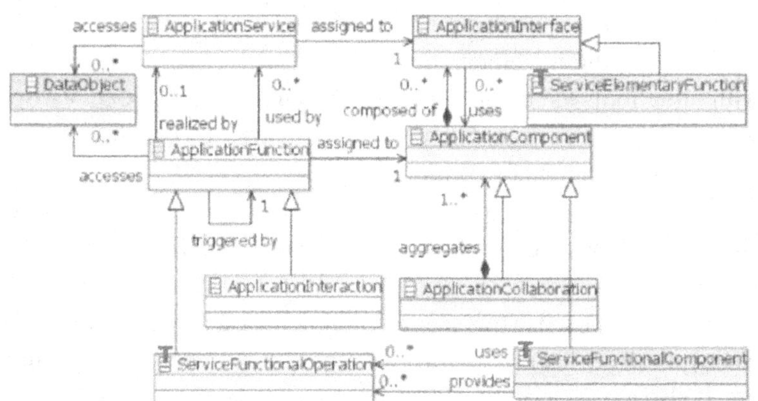

Figure 4. ArchiMate business and application concrete syntaxes extended for telecom

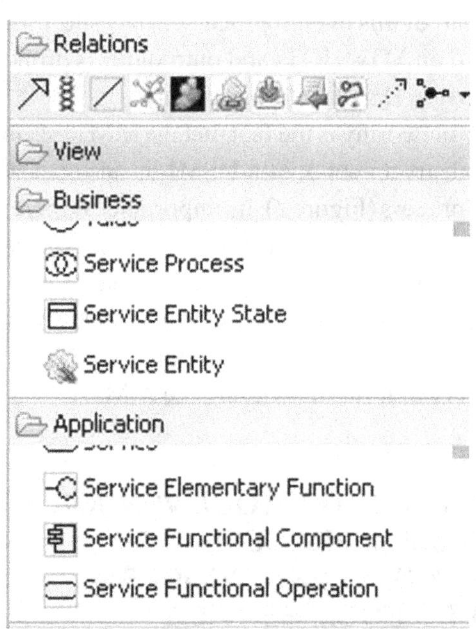

To define the semantics of the three DSMLs (cf. activity ''(D) Define semantics" from (Figure 2)), we defined template-base code generation rules (Chiprianov, Kermarrec & Rouvrais, 2012) to describe the model transformations from the MMs describing the abstract syntax to the Java grammar. We present here an excerpt of the code generation rules for one concept at the Application layer (Figure 5).

For testing through simulation, we chose a telecom-specific, powerful, mature tool, OPNET. The *Design* and *Coding* of the glue-ware needed to integrate the OTS tool (cf. ''(V) Transform to $MM_{testing}$" activity from (Figure 2)) have been done using template-based code generation rules (reference removed for refeering) that describe the model transformations from the MMs of the three system DSMLs to the internal format of OPNET. We present here (Figure 6) an example of the code generation rules that describe the transformation of three concepts at the Technology layer of ArchiMate Telecom (PCSCF, SCSCF and ICSCF) into an OPNET-specific concept (Linux_Server).

To define the DSML for collaboration, we defined a MM for formalizing DR. The MM is inspired from the DR schema QOC and has been presented elsewhere. We present here the concrete syntax of the DR DSML (Figure 7). The DR MM has been manually composed, using the approach presented in (Chiprianov, Kermarrec & Rouvrais, 2011b), with the MMs of the three system DSMLs. To implement the DR DSML semantics, OTS tools for DR retrieval can be integrated. To insure interoperability between the three system DSMLs, the proposed process could be used. OTS tools for ontology alignment could be integrated. However, the decision of extending ArchiMate impacts the interoperability issue as well. ArchiMate

Figure 5. Excerpt of template-based code generation rules for ArchiMate telecom application layer

```
<<DEFINE  javaClass (String FolderName, String PackageName) FOR model::
    ApplicationComponent>>

<<FILE  FolderName+"\\"+PackageName+"\\"+this.name.replaceAll("[:]","_").replaceAll
    ("[ ]+","")+".java">>
<<EXPAND AddJavaHeader(this,name,FolderName,PackageName) FOR Void->>
  public class <<this.name.replaceAll("[:]","_").replaceAll("[ ]+","")->>
    <<EXPAND CheckApplicationAggregation(this,name) FOR Void->>
    <<EXPAND CheckSpecialisation(this,name) FOR Void->>
    <<EXPAND CheckRealisation(this,name) FOR Void->>
    {
      <<FOREACH this.properties AS prop>>
        <<prop.metaType.name>> <<prop.key>> = <<prop.value>>;
      <<ENDFOREACH>>
    ...
    }
<<ENDDEFINE>>
```

Figure 6. Excerpt of template-based code generation rules for transforming ArchiMate telecom concepts at the technology layer into OPNET concepts

```
<<DEFINE GenerateTopologyXMLOPNET (ArchimateModel type,String FolderName, String
    PackageName,List LinkedToRouter,List DirectLinks,List Ports,List Ports_Router)
    FOR model::Node->>
...
<<IF model::PCSCF.isInstance(this.metaType.newInstance()) || model::SCSCF.
    isInstance(this.metaType.newInstance()) || model::ICSCF.isInstance(this.
    metaType.newInstance())->>
  <<DestPrefApp.add("Video Conference").toString().replaceAll(".*","")->>
  <<EXPAND Tech_NodeXMLOPNET(L,this.name,'Linux_Server','dell_pe8450','Linux Server
      ','14:08:46 Mar 17 2011',DestPrefApp,DestPrefSymb,DestPrefAct,SelectedWeights
      ,SupProfiles) FOR Void->>
<<ENDIF->>
...
<<ENDDEFINE>>
```

defines the relations possible between concepts of its three different layers. So this addresses the interoperability issue between our three DSMLs.

Our applying the proposed Tool Vendor Building process to Telecom service construction has had both negative and positive experiences. Negative ones include:

- The code generation capabilities for e.g. generating the graphical editor, are not 100% complete; additional code has to be written (and manually maintained).
- Extending open-source software tools may be difficult: additions are usually not enough, modifications of the provided code are needed as well. We argue therefore for an approach in which certain categories of tools are designed from the start for extensibility. One common way may be to provide plug-ins with extension points, thus ensuring that additions are sufficient,

Figure 7. The concrete syntax of the DR DSML

and no modifications of provided code is necessary (Chiprianov, Kermarrec & Rouvrais, 2011a).

- (Commercial) OTS components do not provide documentation about the data format they use. This makes it difficult to construct a MM for them. This MM is needed as target for MTs, to integrate them into software processes that use multiple tools.
- Evolving MMs implies changes also in the manually written code, which becomes difficult to maintain.

Positive experiences include:

- Code generation capabilities, though they do not generate the entire needed code, are great and reduce significantly development effort.
- Many OTS and open-source tools can be reused, which also greatly reduces development time.
- An MDE process like the one we propose, with a good automation, allows the main focus to be on modeling the domain, while much less concern is dedicated to developing tools.
- Having a process to guide the development, conferred a clearer view at any moment of the advancement and allowed to better manage risks. Moreover, the process can be followed in several ways, therefore confering much flexibility.

We have finished the first iteration in defining the DSML family, so validation by end-users is the next step. The proposed processes can and should be improved, for example by applying software process improvement approaches like CMMI (SEI, 2010).

Applying the Modelers' Process

The tools build for telecommunications service construction have been used according to the process proposed in Section *Generic integration of DSLs into modelers' process*, on a conferencing service. The conference example has been presented in detail (Chiprianov, Kermarrec & Rouvrais, 2012). We are presenting here the main components of this example.

A conferencing service is a virtual meeting, done with the help of a set of telecommunications technologies (e.g. telephone, video, web), which allows for two or more geographically remote locations to interact in real-time via two-way video and/or audio and/or text transmissions simultaneously. It has been the subject of a significant amount of research.

We modeled the conferencing service using the modelers' process (Figure 1), with the three DSMLs. At first, there was no model, therefore there is nothing to import (cf. the ''(I) Imports ...'' activity in (Figure 1)). We than described the model from the Business point of view. Excerpts of the models at the Business, Application and Technology layers have been presented elsewhere (Chiprianov, Kermarrec & Rouvrais, 2012). We present here an excerpt at the Application layer (Figure 8).

We than executed the activity ''(V) Tests ...'' (Figure 1). We present here an excerpt of the model for the simulation with OPNET at the Technology layer (Figure 9). After executing the simulation model, if the results were not satisfactory, we would change the model and re-simulate it.

During modeling, we had to take certain decisions, to make choices (cf. the ''(I) Interacts ...'' activity from (Figure 1)). For example, in the model for the ArchiMate Telecom Application layer (Figure 8), the issue of displaying an error had to be considered. The proposals, criteria used and the argumentation to reach a resolution were

Figure 8. Excerpt of the conferencing service model at the ArchiMate telecom application layer

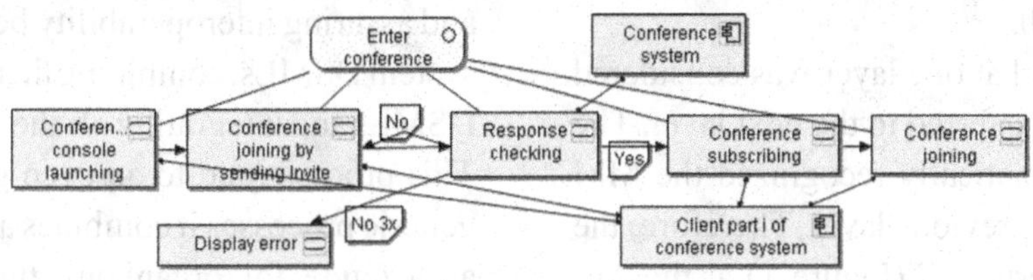

Figure 9. Excerpt of the conferencing service model for testing through simulation with OPNET

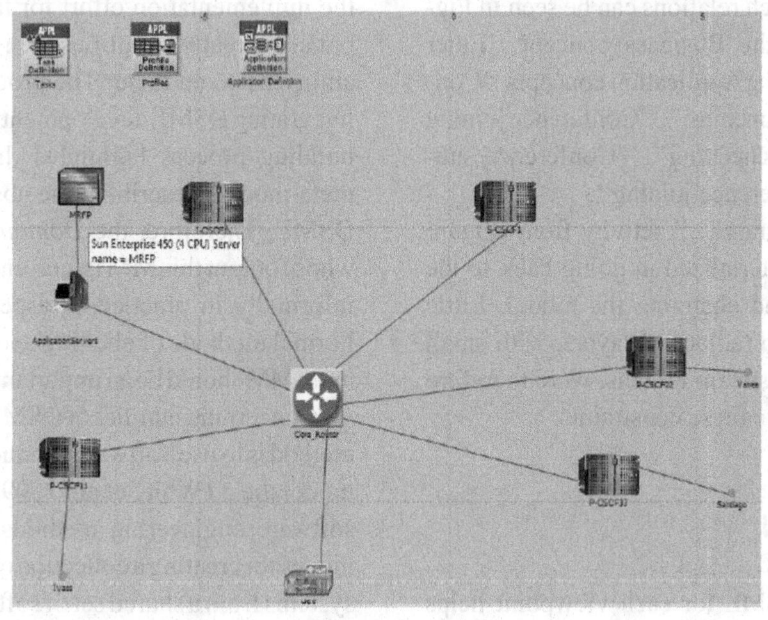

Figure 10. Excerpt of DR recorded for the conferencing service model at the ArchiMate telecom application layer

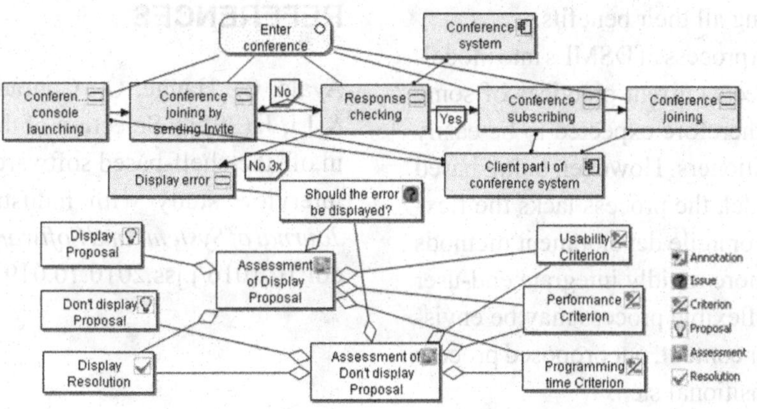

recorded with the DR DSML. An excerpt is presented in Figure 10.

When the model at one layer was considered finished, it was transferred to the next layer. The DSML tools automatically recognized the MM concepts from the previous layer. Therefore, the activity ''(I) Imports ...'' (Figure 1) at the Application and respectively Technology layers was mainly automatic. Because of the specific use of ArchiMate, it did involve the manual definition of relations between concepts of different layers. An example of such relations can be seen in Figure 8, between the Business concept ''Enter conference'' and the Application concepts ''Conference console launching'', ''Conference joining ...'', ''Response checking'', ''Conference subscribing'', ''Conference joining''.

The ''(I) Integrate ...'' activity from (Figure 1) has mainly materialized in going back to the previous layer and changing the model. Little iterations between (adjacent) layers, with small changes in the upstream models, were therefore needed to integrate these constraints.

CONCLUSION

Developing a DSML for each viewpoint helps managing high complexity. DSMLs capture domain and concern specific information, thus enabling its reuse. They also increase modeler productivity and product quality. Therefore, succeeding in integrating DSMLs in modeler's activities allows enjoying all their benefits.

The integration process of DSMLs into modelers' activities reflects current practices of some industries and is therefore expected to be easily accepted by practitioners. However, being based on a waterfall model, the process lacks the flexibility of iterative or agile development methods for example. To more rapidly integrate end-user feedback, a more flexible process may be envisaged; in this bigger context, our proposed process is a necessary transitional step.

We have proposed a process for developing and assuring interoperability between a family of system DSMLs, combining them with transversal DSMLs and integrating off the shelf components. This process (and to an even greater extend the generic processes it combines and adjusts) serves as a guide for organizing the main activities. However, in practice, decisions taken during one activity may impact another. For example, our choice of implementing the system DSMLs as EA modeling language extensions not only reduces the implementation effort for the three DSMLs, but also greatly simplifies the issue of interoperability between them. The process proposed for integrating DSML development into tool vendors' building process highlights the importance of meta-models describing the abstract syntax of a DSML. Therefore, the *Domain analysis* phase, whose output this MM is, currently treated mainly informally in practice, is especially important. Formal methods of eliciting and evolving the domain MM should be an important research subject.

Concerning families of DSMLs, one promising method is to use Software Product Lines (SPLs) to model them (White et al., 2009). SPLs comprise software engineering methods, tools and techniques for creating a collection of similar software systems from a shared set of software assets using a common means of production. SPLs use feature models, which can describe commonalities and variabilities between DSMLs.

REFERENCES

Ayala, C., Hauge, O., Conradi, R., Franch, X., & Li, J. (2011). Selection of third party software in off-the-shelf-based software development-An interview study with industrial practitioners. *Journal of Systems and Software*, *84*(4), 620–637. doi:10.1016/j.jss.2010.10.019

Baker, P., Loh, S., & Weil, F. (2005). Model-driven engineering in a large industrial context - Motorola case study. In Briand, L., & Williams, C. (Eds.), *Model Driven Engineering Languages and Systems* (*Vol. 3713*, pp. 476–491). Lecture Notes in Computer Science. doi:10.1007/11557432_36

Booch, G., Rumbaugh, J., & Jacobson, I. (2005). *Unified modeling language user guide*. Reading, MA, USA: Addison-Wesley Professional Object Technology Series.

Čeh, I., Črepinšek, M., Kosar, T., & Mernik, M. (2011). Ontology driven development of domain-specific languages. *Computer Science and Information System*, *8*(2), 317–342. doi:10.2298/CSIS101231019C

Chiprianov, V., Alloush, I., Kermarrec, Y., & Rouvrais, S. (2011). Telecommunications service creation: Towards extensions for enterprise architecture modeling languages. In *Proceedings of the 6th International Conference on Software and Data Technologies* (pp. 23–29). Seville, Spain.

Chiprianov, V., Kermarrec, Y., & Rouvrais, S. (2011a). On the extensibility of plug-ins. In *Proceedings of the 6th International Conference on Software Engineering Advances* (pp. 557–562), Barcelona, Spain.

Chiprianov, V., Kermarrec, Y., & Rouvrais, S. (2011b). Practical model extension for modeling language profiles: An enterprise architecture modeling language extension for telecommunications service creation. In *Proceedings of Journées nationales Ingénierie Dirigée par les Modèles, Conférence francophone sur les Architectures Logicielles, et du Groupe De Recherche Génie de la Programmation et du Logiciel* (pp. 85–91). Lille, France.

Chiprianov, V., Kermarrec, Y., & Rouvrais, S. (2011c). Towards semantic interoperability of graphical domain specific modeling languages for telecommunications service design. In *Proceedings of the 2nd International Conference on Models and Ontology-based Design of Protocols, Architectures and Services* (pp. 21–24). Budapest, Hungary.

Chiprianov, V., Kermarrec, Y., & Rouvrais, S. (2012). Extending enterprise architecture modeling languages: Application to telecommunications service creation. In *Proceedings of the 27th Symposium on Applied Computing* (pp. 810–816). Trento, Italy.

Clark, T., Evans, A., Kent, S., & Sammut, P. (2001). *The MMF approach to engineering object-oriented design languages*. Paper presented at Workshop on Language Descriptions, Tools and Applications.

Coplien, J., Hoffman, D., & Weiss, D. (1998). Commonality and variability in software engineering. *IEEE Software*, *15*(6), 37–45. doi:10.1109/52.730836

Dutoit, A. H., McCall, R., Mistrík, I., & Paech, B. (2006). Rationale management in software engineering: Concepts and techniques. In *Rationale Management in Software Engineering* (pp. 1–48). Springer. doi:10.1007/978-3-540-30998-7_1

Gabriel, P., Goulao, M., & Amaral, V. (2010). Do software languages engineers evaluate their languages. In Proceedings of the *XIII Congreso Iberoamericano en Software Engineering* (pp. 149–162). Cuenca, Ecuador.

Goncalves, M. K., de Souza, C. R. B., & Gonzalez, V. M. (2009). Initial findings from an observational study of software engineers. In *Proceedings of the 13th International Conference on Computer Supported Cooperative Work in Design* (pp. 498–503).

Hermans, F., Pinzger, M., & van Deursen, A. (2009). Domain-speci□c languages in practice: A user study on the success factors. In *Proceedings of the 12th International Conference on Model Driven Engineering Languages and Systems* (pp. 423–437).

ISO/IEC 42010. (2007). *Systems and software engineering – Architecture description*.

Kappel, G., Kapsammer, E., Kargl, H., Kramler, G., Reiter, T., Retschitzegger, W., & Wimmer, M. (2006). Lifting meta-models to ontologies - A step to the semantic integration of modeling languages. In *Proceedings of the ACM/IEEE 9th International Conference on Model Driven Engineering Languages and Systems* (pp. 528–542).

Kieburtz, R. B., McKinney, L., Bell, J. M., Hook, J., Kotov, A., & Lewis, J. ... Walton, L. (1996). A software engineering experiment in software component generation. In *Proceedings of the 18th International Conference on Software Engineering* (pp. 542–552).

Kleppe, A. G., Warmer, J., & Bast, W. (2003). *MDA explained: The model driven architecture: Practice and promise*. Boston, MA: Addison-Wesley Longman Publishing Co., Inc.

Ko, A. J., DeLine, R., & Venolia, G. (2007). Information needs in collocated software development teams. In *Proceedings of the 29th International Conference on Software Engineering* (pp. 344–353).

Kosar, T., Lopez Martinez, P. E., Barrientos, P. A., & Mernik, M. (2008). A preliminary study on various implementation approaches of domain-specific language. *Information and Software Technology*, *50*(5), 390–405. doi:10.1016/j.infsof.2007.04.002

Kruchten, P. (2008). Controversy corner: What do software architects really do? *Journal of Systems and Software*, *81*(12), 2413–2416. doi:10.1016/j.jss.2008.08.025

MacLean, A., Young, R. M., Bellotti, V. M. E., & Moran, T. P. (1991). Questions, options, and criteria: Elements of design space analysis. *Human-Computer Interaction*, *6*(3), 201–250. doi:10.1207/s15327051hci0603&4_2

Meyers, B., & Vangheluwe, H. (2011). A framework for evolution of modelling languages. *Science of Computer Programming, Special Issue on Software Evolution. Adaptability and Variability*, *76*(12), 1223–1246.

Morisio, M., Seaman, C. B., Basili, V. R., Parra, A. T., Kraft, S. E., & Condon, S. E. (2002). COTS-based software development: processes and open issues. *Journal of Systems and Software*, *61*(3), 189–200. doi:10.1016/S0164-1212(01)00147-9

Myers, G. J., & Sandler, C. (2004). *The art of software testing* (2nd ed.). Hoboken, NJ: John Wiley & Sons, Inc.

Ober, I., Dib, A. A., Féraud, L., & Percebois, C. (2008). Towards interoperability in component based development with a family of DSLs. In *Proceedings of the 2nd European Conference on Software Architecture* (pp. 148–163). Paphos, Cyprus.

Open Group. (2009). *ArchiMate 1.0 specification*.

Peristeras, V., & Tarabanis, K. (2006). The connection, communication, consolidation, collaboration interoperability framework (C4IF) for information systems interoperability. *International Journal of Interoperability in Business Information Systems*, *1*(1), 61–72.

Reinhartz-Berger, I. (2010). Towards automatization of domain modeling. *Data & Knowledge Engineering*, *69*(5), 491–515. doi:10.1016/j.datak.2010.01.002

Sedigh-Ali, S., Ghafoor, A., & Paul, R. A. (2001). Software engineering metrics for COTS-based systems. *Computer*, *34*(5), 44–50. doi:10.1109/2.920611

SEI. (2010). *CMMI for development*, version 1.3. Retrieved October 10, 2011, from http://www.sei.cmu.edu/library/abstracts/reports/10tr033.cfm

Sprinkle, J., Mernik, M., Tolvanen, J.-P., & Spinellis, D. (2009). Guest editors' introduction: What kinds of nails need a domain-specific hammer? *IEEE Software*, *26*(4), 15–18. doi:10.1109/MS.2009.92

Torchiano, M., & Morisio, M. (2004). Overlooked aspects of COTS-based development. *IEEE Software*, *21*(2), 88–93. doi:10.1109/MS.2004.1270770

Vallecillo, A. (2010). On the combination of domain specific modeling languages. In *Proceedings of the 6th European Conference on Modelling Foundations and Applications, Lecture Notes in Computer Science 6138,* Paris, France (pp. 305–320).

van Deursen, A., Klint, P., & Visser, J. (2000). Domain-specific languages: An annotated bibliography. *SIGPLAN Notices*, *35*(6), 26–36. doi:10.1145/352029.352035

Welty, C. (2003). Ontology research. *AI Magazine*, *24*(3), 11–12.

White, J., Hill, J. H., Gray, J., Tambe, S., Gokhale, A. S., & Schmidt, D. C. (2009). Improving domain-specific language reuse with software product line techniques. *IEEE Software*, *26*(4), 47–53. doi:10.1109/MS.2009.95

Wolf, T. (2007). *Rationale-based unified software engineering model*. PhD thesis, TU Munchen, Germany.

ADDITIONAL READING

Achilleos, A., Yang, K., & Georgalas, N. (2008). A model driven approach to generate service creation environments. In *Global Telecommunications Conference IEEE Globecom* (pp. 1-6). New Orleans, LA, USA.

Bryant, B. R., Gray, J., Mernik, M., Clarke, P. J., France, R. B., & Karsai, G. (2011). Challenges and directions in formalizing the semantics of modeling languages. *Computer Science and Information Systems*, *8*(2), 225–253. doi:10.2298/CSIS110114012B

Choi, N., Song, I. Y., & Han, H. (2006). A survey on ontology mapping. *ACM Sigmod*, *35*(3), 34–41. doi:10.1145/1168092.1168097

Czarnecki, K., & Helsen, S. (2006). Feature-based survey of model transformation approaches. *IBM Systems Journal*, *45*(3), 621–645. doi:10.1147/sj.453.0621

Egyed, A., & Balzer, R. (2001). Unfriendly COTS integration instrumentation and interfaces for improved plugability. In *Proceedings of the 16th IEEE International Conference on Automated Software Engineering*, (pp. 223-231). Washington, DC, USA.

Euzenat, J., Ferrara, A., Meilicke, C., Pane, J., Scharffe, F., & Shvaiko, P. … Trojahn dos Santos, C. (2010). First results of the Ontology Alignment Evaluation Initiative 2010. In *Proceedings of the 5th International Workshop on Ontology Matching*, with the *9th International Semantic Web Conference*, Shanghai, China. Retrieved from http://ceur-ws.org/Vol-689/oaei10_paper0.pdf

Evans, A., Maskeri, G., Sammut, P., & Willans, J. S. (2002). *Building families of languages for model-driven system development.* Paper presented at the 2nd Workshop in Software Model Engineering, San Francisco, CA, USA.

Green, T. R. G., & Petre, M. (1996). Usability analysis of visual programming environments: A 'cognitive dimensions' framework. *Journal of Visual Languages and Computing, 7*(2), 131–174. doi:10.1006/jvlc.1996.0009

Hetzel, W. C., & Hetzel, B. (1991). *The complete guide to software testing* (2nd ed.). New York, NY: John Wiley & Sons, Inc.

Jean-Mary, Y. R., Shironoshita, E. P., & Kabuka, M. R. (2009). Ontology matching with semantic verification. *Web Semantics: Science. Services and Agents on the World Wide Web, 7*(3), 235–251. doi:10.1016/j.websem.2009.04.001

Kang, K. C., Cohen, S. G., Hess, J. A., Novak, W. E., & Peterson, A. S. (1990). *Feature-oriented domain analysis (FODA) feasibility study. Technical report.* Carnegie-Mellon University Software Engineering Institute.

Kunz, W., Rittel, H. W. J., Messrs, W., Dehlinger, H., Mann, T., & Protzen, J. J. (1970). *Issues as elements of information systems.* Technical report.

Kurtev, I., Bézivin, J., Jouault, F., & Valduriez, P. (2006). Model-based DSL frameworks. In Companion to the *21st ACM SIGPLAN Symposium on Object-Oriented Programming Systems, Languages, and Applications* (pp. 602–616).

Ladd, D. A., & Ramming, J. C. (1994). Two application languages in software production. In *Proceedings of the USENIX 1994 Very High Level Languages Symposium Proceedings on USENIX* (pp. 10–10), Berkeley, CA, USA.

Land, R., Blankers, L., Chaudron, M., & Crnković, I. (2008). COTS selection best practices in literature and in industry. In *Proceedings of the 10th International Conference on Software Reuse: High Confidence Software Reuse in Large Systems* (pp. 100–111).

Land, R., Sundmark, D., Lüders, F., Krasteva, I., & Causevic, A. (2009). Reuse with software components - a survey of industrial state of practice. In *Proceedings of the 11th International Conference on Software Reuse: Formal Foundations of Reuse and Domain Engineering* (pp. 150–159).

Law, A. M., & Kelton, D. W. (2007). *Simulation modeling and analysis.* McGraw-Hill Series in Industrial Engineering and Management Science.

Lee, J. (1991). Extending the Potts and Bruns model for recording design rationale. In *Proceedings of the 13th International Conference on Software Engineering* (pp. 114–125). Los Alamitos, CA, USA.

Li, J., Conradi, R., Slyngstad, O. P., Torchiano, M., Morisio, M., & Bunse, C. (2008). A state-of-the-practice survey of risk management in development with off-the-shelf software components. *IEEE Transactions on Software Engineering, 34*(2), 271–286. doi:10.1109/TSE.2008.14

Li, W. D., & Qiu, Z. M. (2006). State-of-the-art technologies and methodologies for collaborative product development systems. *International Journal of Production Research, 44*(13), 2525–2559. doi:10.1080/00207540500422080

Mannadiar, R., & Vangheluwe, H. (2011). Debugging in domain-speci□c modelling. In *Proceedings of the Third International Conference on Software Language Engineering* (pp. 276–285).

Mens, T., Czarnecki, K., & van Gorp, P. (2006). A taxonomy of model transformation. *Electronic Notes in Theoretical Computer Science, 152,* 125–142. doi:10.1016/j.entcs.2005.10.021

Prechelt, L., & Beecher, K. (2011). Four generic issues for tools-as-plugins illustrated by the distributed editor Saros. In *Proceedings of the 1st Workshop on Developing Tools as Plug-ins* (pp. 9-11).

Ramsin, R., & Paige, R. F. (2008). Process-centered review of object oriented software development methodologies. *ACM Computing Surveys, 40*(3), 1–89. doi:10.1145/1322432.1322435

Renger, M., Kolfschoten, G. L., & Vreede, G.-J. (2008a). Challenges in collaborative modeling: A literature review. In Aalst, W., Mylopoulos, J., Rosemann, M., Shaw, M. J., Szyperski, C., & Dietz, J. L. G. (Eds.), *Advances in Enterprise Engineering I, Lecture Notes in Business Information Processing 10* (pp. 61–77). doi:10.1007/978-3-540-68644-6_5

Renger, M., Kolfschoten, G. L., & Vreede, G.-J. (2008b). Using interactive whiteboard technology to support collaborative modeling. In *Groupware: Design, implementation, and use* (pp. 356–363). Springer.

Rothenberg, J. (1989). The nature of modeling. In William, L. E., Loparo, K. A., & Nelson, N. R. (Eds.), *Artificial intelligence, simulation, and modeling* (pp. 75–92). New York, NY: John Wiley and Sons, Inc.

Safa, L. (2007). *The making of user-interface designer: A proprietary DSM tool*. Paper presented at the 7th OOPSLA Workshop Domain-Specific Modeling.

Schobbens, P.-Y., Heymans, P., & Trigaux, J.-C. (2006). Feature diagrams: A survey and a formal semantics. In *Proceedings of the 14th IEEE International Conference on Requirements Engineering* (pp. 136–145). Minneapolis, USA.

Shen, W. M., Hao, Q., & Li, W. D. (2008). Computer supported collaborative design: Retrospective and perspective. *Computers in Industry, 59*(9), 855–862. doi:10.1016/j.compind.2008.07.001

Spinellis, D. (2001). Notable design patterns for domain-specific languages. *Journal of Systems and Software, 56*(1), 91–99. doi:10.1016/S0164-1212(00)00089-3

Strembeck, M., & Zdun, U. (2009). An approach for the systematic development of domain-specific languages. *Software, Practice & Experience, 39*(15), 1253–1292. doi:10.1002/spe.936

van Deursen, A., & Klint, P. (1998). Little languages: little maintenance. *Journal of Software Maintenance, 10*(2), 75–92. doi:10.1002/(SICI)1096-908X(199803/04)10:2<75::AID-SMR168>3.0.CO;2-5

Weiss, D. M., & Lai, C. T. R. (1999). *Software product-line engineering: A family-based software development process*. Boston, MA: Addison-Wesley Longman Publishing Co., Inc.

Wu, H., Gray, J., & Mernik, M. (2009). Unit testing for domain-specific languages. In *Proceedings of the IFIP TC 2 Working Conference on Domain-Specific Languages* (pp. 125–147).

Zhang, Y., & Xu, B. (2004). A survey of semantic description frameworks for programming languages. *ACM SIGPLAN Notices, 39*(3), 14–30. doi:10.1145/981009.981013

KEY TERMS AND DEFINITIONS

Collaboration: A process where two or more stakeholders (persons or organizations) work jointly or together to create or achieve the same thing/aim, by sharing knowledge, learning and building consensus.

Conferencing Service: A virtual meeting, done with the help of a set of telecommunications technologies (e.g. telephone, video, web), which allows for two or more geographically remote locations to interact in real-time via two-way video and/or audio and/or text transmissions simultaneously.

Design Rationale (DR): The justification behind decisions, the reasoning that goes into determining the design of the artifact.

Domain Specific Language (DSL): A language that offers, through appropriate notations and abstractions, expressive power focused on, and usually restricted to, a particular problem domain.

Family of Languages: A set of related languages that offer similar functionality at an equivalent level of abstraction.

Interoperability: The ability of two or more tools to exchange models so as to use them in order to operate effectively together.

Model Driven Engineering (MDE): A software development method which focuses on creating and exploiting domain models. It allows the exploitation of models to simulate, estimate, understand, communicate and produce code.

Off the Shelf Component: A commercially available or open source piece of software that other software projects can reuse and integrate into their own products.

Ontology: A formal description of a domain, intended for sharing among different applications, and expressed in a language that can be used for reasoning.

Process: Provides guidance as to the order of the activities, specifies what artifacts should be developed and directs the tasks of individuals and the team as a whole.

Telecommunications Service: The offering of telecommunications (i.e. the transmission of information over significant distances) for a fee directly to the public, or to such classes of users as to be effectively available directly to the public, regardless of the facilities used.

Testing: The process of executing a software or system with the intent of finding errors.

ENDNOTES

1 http://en.wikipedia.org/wiki/Scientific_modelling, accessed on 10.10.2011

2 http://www.eclipse.org/modeling/emf, accessed on 10.10.2011

3 http://www.omg.org/spec/ODM/1.0/, accessed on 10.10.2011

4 http://www.omg.org/spec/QVT/1.0/, accessed on 10.10.2011

Section 4
Domain-Specific Language Examples

Chapter 16
Organizing the Aggregate: Languages for Spatial Computing

Jacob Beal
Raytheon BBN Technologies, USA

Mirko Viroli
University of Bologna, Italy

Stefan Dulman
Delft University, The Netherlands

Nikolaus Correll
University of Colorado Boulder, USA

Kyle Usbeck
Raytheon BBN Technologies, USA

ABSTRACT

As the number of computing devices embedded into engineered systems continues to rise, there is a widening gap between the needs of the user to control aggregates of devices and the complex technology of individual devices. Spatial computing attempts to bridge this gap for systems with local communication by exploiting the connection between physical locality and device connectivity. A large number of spatial computing domain specific languages (DSLs) have emerged across diverse domains, from biology and reconfigurable computing, to sensor networks and agent-based systems. In this chapter, the authors develop a framework for analyzing and comparing spatial computing DSLs, survey the current state of the art, and provide a roadmap for future spatial computing DSL investigation.

INTRODUCTION

Computation has become cheap enough and powerful enough that large numbers of computing devices can be embedded into nearly any aspect of our environment. A widening gap, however, exists between the potential users of embedded systems (biologists, architects, emergency response teams, etc.), and the increasingly complex technology available. Typically, the users know what they want from the aggregate of devices, but the programming or design interfaces that they are presented with operate mainly at the level of individual devices and their interactions. Thus, biologists who want to monitor wildlife with mesh-networked sensors end up having to debug real-time code for parallel algorithms in order to minimize Joules-per-packet, and architects who want to create responsive buildings end up worrying about how to create distributed algorithms

DOI: 10.4018/978-1-4666-2092-6.ch016

Figure 1. A widening gap exists between the application needs of users and the implementation details of those applications on increasingly complex systems of interacting computing devices. This gap must be crossed by global-to-local compilation: the transformation of specifications of aggregate behavior to actions of individual devices.

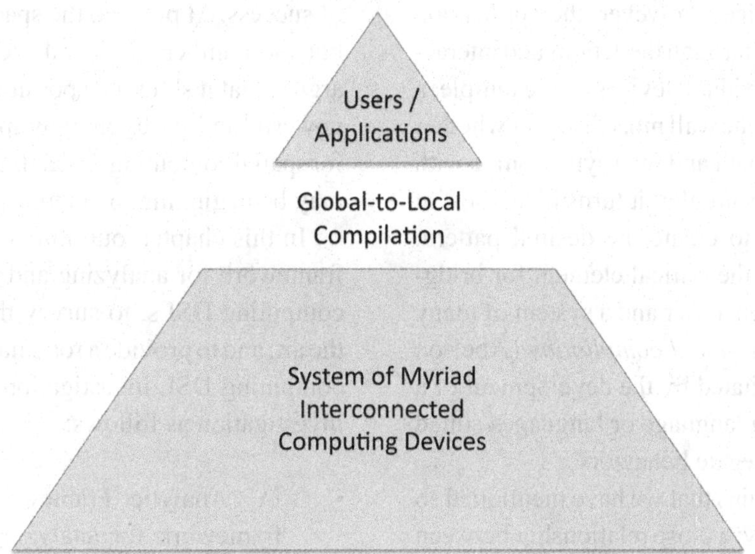

to ensure correct time-synchronization across the application modules.

Similar gaps are found in many other areas besides embedded systems. For example:

- Robots are becoming cheaper and more reliable, such that teams of robots can now be used in many more applications. For instance, search-and-rescue workers might use a group of unmanned aerial vehicles to search a wilderness area. These search-and-rescue workers should be able to specify aggregate behaviors like sweep patterns, rather than worry about how to share localization and progress data in order to keep those sweep patterns consistent between robots. Modular and reconfigurable robotic systems have similar issues.
- Reconfigurable computing devices like Field Programmable Gate Arrays (FPGAs) can solve complex problems extremely quickly. Programming and code reuse are difficult, however, because subprograms need to be tuned for their layout on each particular model chip and their context of use relative to other subprograms. Similar issues are likely to emerge in multi-core systems as the number of cores continues to rise.
- In synthetic biology, it will soon be desirable to program engineered biological organisms in terms of the structure of tissues or colonies, and of their interaction patterns, rather than by selecting particular trans-membrane proteins and adjusting their signal dynamics and metabolic interactions. Emerging chemical and nanotechnological computing platforms are likely to face similar issues.

Fundamentally, this gap lies between programming the aggregate and programming the individual (Figure 1). For the users, the application is often best specified in terms of collective behaviors of aggregates of devices. For example, an architect may wish to use sweeping patterns of light on the floor and walls to guide visitors through a building. When implemented on a system of computing devices, however, the application must be carried out through the actions and interactions of many individual devices. For example, a particular LED on the wall must discover whether it is on a visitor's path and then synchronize with its neighbors to ensure that it turns on and off at the correct times to create the desired pattern. Thus, we see that the critical element for bridging the gap between a user and a system of many devices is *global-to-local compilation* (Abelson et al., 2000), facilitated by the development of a new programming language or languages suited to describing aggregate behaviors.

All of the domains that we have mentioned so far share a property: a close relationship between the computation and the arrangement of the computing devices in space. These systems thus fit the definition of *spatial computers*-collections of local computational devices distributed through a physical space, in which:

- The difficulty of moving information between any two devices is strongly dependent on the distance between them, and
- The "functional goals" of the system are generally defined in terms of the system's spatial structure.

This correlation between location and computation can be exploited to help bridge the gap between aggregate and individual. Geometry and topology include many "intermediate" aggregate concepts, such as regions, neighborhoods, and flows, that can be used as building blocks for programming applications and automatically mapped to the behavior of individual devices.

Across many different communities, researchers have built domain specific languages (DSLs) that use spatial abstractions to simplify the problem of programming aggregates. These DSLs take a wide variety of different approaches, often blending together generally applicable spatial concepts with specific requirements of a target sub-domain or application, and have met with varying degrees of success. At present, the space is quite chaotic, but the number of shared ideas between DSLs argues that it should be possible to develop more powerful and more generally applicable languages for spatial computing. Indeed, as we will see, some may be beginning to emerge.

In this chapter, our aim is to develop a clear framework for analyzing and comparing spatial computing DSLs, to survey the current state of the art, and to provide a roadmap for future spatial computing DSL investigation. We organize our investigation as follows:

- In "Analytic Framework," we define a framework for analyzing spatial computing DSLs, separating more abstract spatial concerns from the pragmatic needs of particular implementations or application domains.
- Following in "Survey of Existing Spatial DSLs," we survey existing spatial computing DSLs across a number of domains and summarize their key attributes. To aid in comparison, we encode a reference example in representative languages.
- We then analyze the relationship between languages in "Analysis," identifying common themes and gaps in the existing space of languages.
- Finally, in "Conclusions and Future Research Directions," we summarize our results and propose a roadmap for the future development of spatial computing DSLs.

ANALYTIC FRAMEWORK

In this section, we develop a framework for analyzing spatial computing domain specific languages. We begin by defining the scope of work that will be considered in this chapter. We then organize our analytic framework in terms of a generic aggregate programming architecture, which separates aggregate and space-focused aspects of a system from underlying lower level details. Finally, for each layer in this architecture we define the attributes that will be examined as part of this survey.

Chapter Scope

For purposes of this review, we will define a spatial computing DSL as any system construction mechanism that:

- is targeted at programming some class of spatial computers,
- includes explicitly geometric or topological constructs that implicitly operate over aggregates of computing devices, and
- allows an unbounded combination of systems to be specified.

Our aim is to develop both a survey and a roadmap for spatial computing domain specific languages, however, we will also include two classes of systems that do not fit these properties: We will discuss some aggregate programming languages that are designed for spatial computers, but where no constructs are explicitly geometric or topological. These languages typically attempt to abolish space in some way, and comparison with these languages will help to illuminate the benefits and costs involved in incorporating spatial constructs in a DSL for aggregate programming. We will also discuss some systems that are not explicitly languages, but that still can serve as toolkits for general system specification. These are included in the case where they include significant spatial constructs for aggregate programming, and can therefore help define the known design space for spatial computing DSLs or reveal thinking relative to spatial DSLs in an application domain.

The classes of spatial computers that we consider in this chapter are roughly: amorphous computers, natural and engineered biological organisms, multi-agent systems, wireless sensor networks, pervasive computing, swarm and modular robotic systems, parallel computers, reconfigurable computers, cellular automata, and formal calculi. The boundaries of these fields are, of course, fuzzy and in many cases overlapping. We also acknowledge that, although we have tried to be thorough, this is by no means an exhaustive list of all classes of spatial computers, and due to the wide variety of terminology used across fields, we may have missed some significant examples of spatial computing DSLs. Our belief, however, is that this survey has been sufficiently broad to provide a clear map of the known design space for spatial computing DSLs.

Generic Aggregate Programming Architecture

Different spatial computing DSLs operate at different levels of abstraction and address different types of concern. To aid us in better understanding their relationship, we refine the simple "gap" diagram in Figure 1 into a generic aggregate programming architecture comprised of five layers. We illustrate this architecture as a pyramid in Figure 2, the wider base representing more detail in implementation. The lower three layers deal only with individual devices and their local interactions. From lowest to highest, these are:

- The *physical platform* layer at the base is the medium upon which computation will ultimately occur. This could be anything from a smart phone or an unmanned aerial vehicle to a living biological cell. It may also be a virtual device, as is the case for simulations.
- The *system management* layer is where the operating system and whatever services are built into the platform live. For example,

Figure 2. Spatial computing fills an architectural gap between individual computation devices and users wishing to control aggregate behavior.

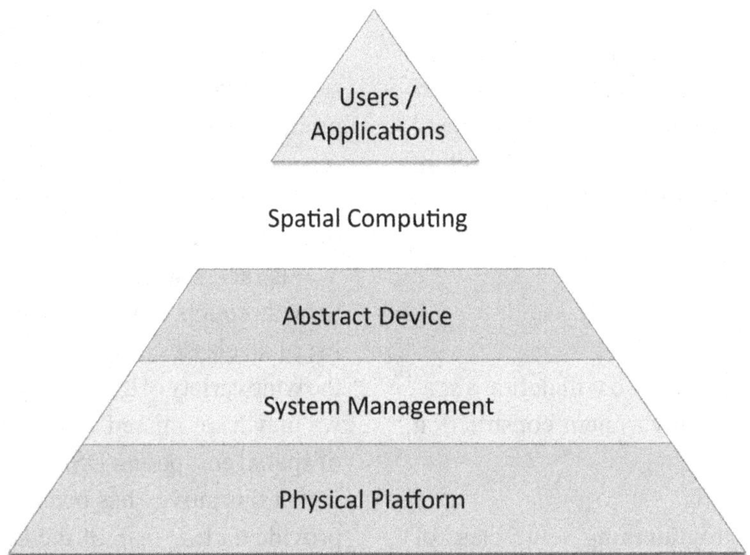

on an embedded device, this layer is likely to include real-time process management, sensor and actuator drivers, and low-level networking.

- The *abstract device* layer hides details of the device, presenting a simplified interface to other devices with which it interacts. For example, a complex embedded computing platform might be abstracted as a graph node that periodically executes rounds of computation over its edges.

Above the abstract device is the gap that we have previously discussed, between the interface for programming individual devices and the aggregate-level needs and desires of users. We consider the *spatial computing* abstractions and models that can connect between individual devices and aggregates. While there may be other things besides spatial computing that help in bridging this gap, they are out of scope of our discussion in this chapter.

Finally, the top of the pyramid consists of *users and applications* that wish to deal, not with individual devices, but with behaviors of the aggregate.

Spatial DSL Properties

This aggregate programming architecture forms the basis of our analytic framework. For each spatial computing DSL that we consider, we will analyze that DSL in terms of which layers it focuses on and what properties it has with respect to each layer.

As we shall see, different languages have different priorities, and no system spans the whole range of considerations. This is by no means a bad thing: in a similar case, the OSI stack (Zimmermann, 1980), which factors networking into seven different abstraction layers, has been a powerful enabling tool for allowing the interconnection of many different specialized tools to form the modern Internet. This does mean, however, that for nearly every property that we consider, there will be at least some DSLs for which the language property is not present or not applicable, since said property is out of scope of that particular DSL (Figure 3).

Figure 3. DSL design patterns describe the relation of the new DSL to existing languages: an extension contains the existing language, a restriction is contained within it, piggyback languages both extend and restrict, and invented languages are created from scratch.

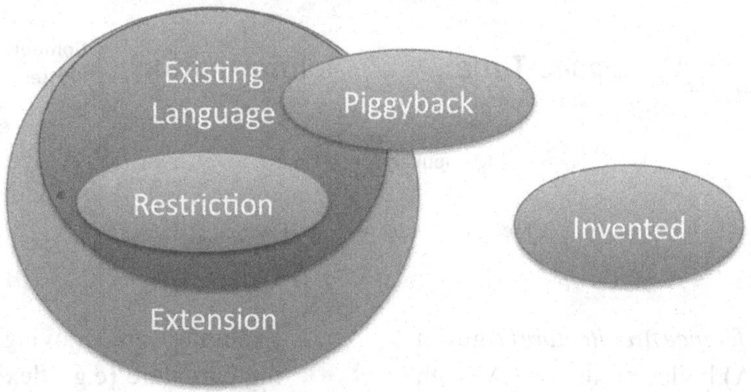

The top-level properties we analyze for each spatial computing DSL categorize the language itself and define the general scope that the language covers:

- *What type of programming language is the DSL?* Common types include functional, imperative, and declarative.
- *What is the design pattern for this DSL?* This property reflects the degree to which the language is related to an existing conventional language, and is defined as in (Mernik et al., 2005). DSLs may be based on existing languages in three ways: it may be a *restriction,* meaning that it removes some language features problematic for the domain, an *extension*, meaning that it adds new features, or a *piggyback* that adds some and removes others. A DSL may also be *invented*, which means that a whole language has been created from scratch, with its own syntax and interpreter or compiler.
- *For what physical platforms is the language primarily/originally intended?* Although spatial DSLs may have relevance across a number of different domains, their representational framework typically shows strong traces of their "home" platform. This choice also typically regulates whether computing devices are assumed to be universal or not.
- *On which intermediate layers does the language focus?* The previous questions dealt with the top and bottom layers of the pyramid. Most DSLs of interest to this review focus on one or two of the middle layers: spatial computing, abstract device, and/or system management.

For the spatial computing and abstract device layers, we elaborate our framework to include a set of key properties focused on that layer. For the spatial computing layer, we consider what space-spanning abstractions are supported by each DSL. For the abstract device layer, we consider how devices are related to space, and how information moves through the system.

We will not directly address the system management layer in this document, as decisions at this layer are largely disconnected from spatial considerations in current systems. A useful framework for analyzing system management properties, however, has already been developed by the agent community. The *Agent System Reference Model* (Regli et al., 2009) (ASRM) defines functional concepts that are typical in agent frameworks, and

Figure 4. The basic duality of space-time and information in a spatial computer implies four general classes of operations, plus meta-operations that manipulate computations.

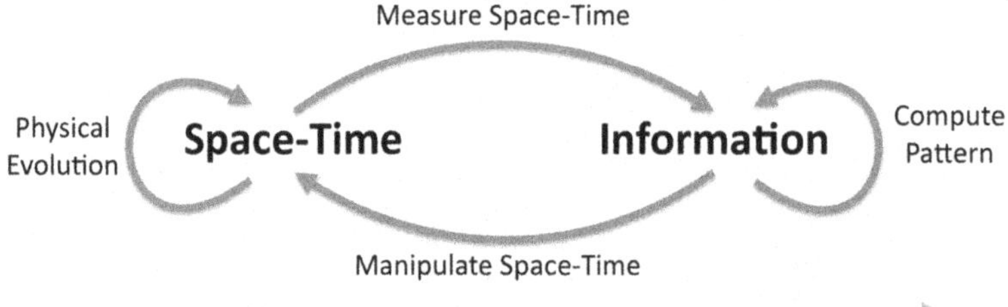

the *Agent System Reference Architecture* (Nguyen et al., 2010) (ASRA) builds on the ASRM with architectural paradigms for these functional concepts. As the ASRM and ASRA address pragmatic concerns that are shared across a wide spectrum of distributed systems, they could be applied to analyze any of the DSLs that we survey.

Types of Space-Time Operations

Figure 4 shows the two base elements of a spatial computer and the relations between them. At a basic level, a spatial computer is a dual entity: on the one hand, we have the volume of space-time spanned by the computer and on the other hand, the information that is associated with locations in that volume of space-time.

From this duality, we may derive four classes of operations (partially based on the universal basis set of space-time operators proposed in (Beal, 2010)):

- **Measure Space-Time:** These are operators that take geometric properties of the space-time volume and translate them into information. Examples are measures of distance, angle, time duration, area, density, and curvature.
- **Manipulate Space-Time:** These operators are the converse of measurement, being actuators that take information and modify the properties of the space-time volume. Examples are moving devices, changing curvature (e.g., flexing a surface), expanding or contracting space locally (e.g., changing the size of cells in a tissue), or changing local physical properties such as stiffness that will directly affect the physical evolution of the system.
- **Compute Pattern:** Operations that stay purely in the informational world may be viewed at a high level of abstraction as computing patterns over space-time. For example, stripes are a pattern over space, a timer is a pattern over time, and a propagating sine wave is a pattern over space-time. This category includes not just computation, but most communication and any "pointwise" sensor or actuator that does not interact directly with geometry, such as a light or sound sensor or an LED actuator.
- **Physical Evolution:** Many physically instantiated systems have inherent dynamics that cause the shape of the space to change over time even without the use of actuators to manipulate space-time. Examples include inertial motion of robots or the adhesive forces shaping a colony of cells. By their nature, these operations are not directly part of programs, but languages may assume such dynamics are in operation or have operations that are targeted at controlling them.

Any spatial computation can be described in terms of these four classes of operations. We are speaking of languages, however, so we also need to consider the meta-operations that can be used to combine and modulate spatial computations. We identify two such classes of meta-operation: *Abstraction and Composition* operations hide the implementation details of spatial computations, and allow them to be combined together and to have multiple instances of a computation executed. *Restriction* operations modulate a spatial computation by selecting a particular subspace on which the computation should be executed.

These categories of operations are of primary interest for our survey, as the innovations of a DSL pertinent to spatial computing will generally be closely linked to a set of space-time operations. For each DSL we consider, we will thus report what significant operators are provided for each category.

Abstract Device Model

The abstract device model relates computing devices to the space that they occupy and specifies the ways in which devices can communicate with one another. The *Discretization* of devices with respect to space falls into three general types: *discrete* models that assume a set of non-space-filling devices, as is typical of sensor network systems, *cellular* models that assume discrete devices that do fill space, as is typical of modular robotic systems and cellular automata, and *continuous* models that assume an infinite continuum of devices that will then be approximated by actual available hardware.

We identify three key properties of communication that describe the information flows between devices:

- **Communication Region:** This is the relationship between a device's communication partners and space. The most common types we will encounter are a distance-limited *neighborhood* (though not necessarily regular) and *global* communication.
- **Transmission Granularity:** Do devices *broadcast* the same thing to all neighbors, *unicast* a potentially different value to each neighbor, or *multicast* to groups of neighbors?
- **Mobility of Code:** Do devices have the same *uniform* program (which may execute differently depending on state and conditions), do devices have *heterogeneous* (but fixed) programs, or is code *mobile* and able to shift from device to device?

Reference Example: "T-Program"

As a means of evaluating and demonstrating the space-time operators which are supported by classes of languages, we derive a *reference example* and implement portions of the example in representative languages considered during the survey. For the example, which we refer to as the "T-Program," to be completely implemented requires the ability to perform each of the three basic families of space-time operators described in Types of Space-Time Operations: measurement of space-time, pattern computation, and manipulation of space-time.

The three stages of the "T-program" are illustrated in Figure 5:

- Cooperatively create a local coordinate system (Figure 5(a)). This requires measurement of space-time.
- Move or grow devices to create a T-shaped structure (Figure 5(b)). This requires manipulation of space-time.
- Compute the T's center of gravity and draw a ring pattern around it (Figure 5(c)). This requires measurement of space-time and pattern computation.

For purposes of this example, these may happen in any order, including concurrently.

Figure 5. The "T program" reference example exercises the three main classes of space-time operations: measurement of space-time to organize local coordinates (a) and compute the center of gravity (c), manipulation of space-time to move devices into a T-shaped structure (b), and pattern computation to make a ring around the center of gravity (c).

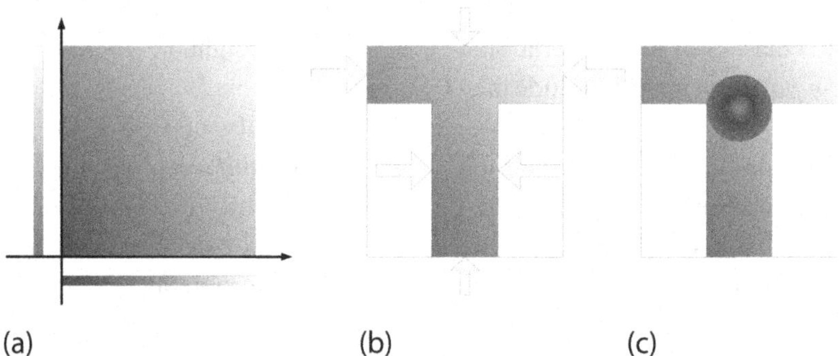

This simple challenge will show how various exemplary languages approach the three basic categories of space-time operations in programs. Meta-operations are not required, but we will either illustrate or discuss them as well.

SURVEY OF EXISTING SPATIAL DSLS

We now apply our analytic framework in a survey of spatial computing DSLs, organizing our survey roughly by major domains. Note that the boundaries of domains are somewhat fuzzy, and in some cases we have placed a language in one domain or another somewhat arbitrarily.

We begin with two domains where the goals are often explicitly spatial: amorphous computing and biological modeling and design. We then discuss the more general area of agent-based models, followed by four application domains that are being driven towards an embrace of spatiality by the nature of their problems: wireless sensor networks, pervasive systems, swarm and modular robotics, and parallel and reconfigurable computing. Finally, we survey a few additional computing formalisms that deal with space explicitly. A theme that we will see emerge throughout this discussion is that DSLs throughout these domains are often torn between addressing aggregate programming with space-time operators and addressing other domain-specific concerns, particularly so in the four application domains surveyed.

To better enable an overall view of the field and comparison of languages, we have collected the characteristics of the most significant DSLs or classes of DSLs in three tables, as derived from our analytic framework. Table 1 identifies the general properties of the DSL, Table 2 identifies the classes of space-time operations that each DSL uses to raise its abstraction level from individual devices toward aggregates, and Table 3 identifies how each DSL abstracts devices and communication. Note that for purposes of clarity, many of the languages discussed are not listed in these tables, only those that we feel are necessary in order to understand the current range and capabilities of spatial computing DSLs.

Amorphous Computing

Amorphous computing is the study of computing systems composed of irregular arrangements of vast numbers of unreliable, locally communicating simple computational devices. The aim of this research area is to deliberately weaken many of

Table 1. DSL characteristics of spatial computing languages

DSL	Type	Pattern	Platform	Layers
Amorphous Computing				
Proto	Functional	Invention	Any	SC,AD
PyMorphous	Imperative	Extension	Any Network	SC,AD
ProtoVM	Imperative	Invention	Any Network	AD,SM
Growing Point Language	Declarative	Invention	Any Network	SC
Origami Shape Language	Imperative	Invention	2D Mesh Network	SC
Biological				
L-systems	Functional	Invention	Simulation	SC
MGS	Declarative	Invention	Simulation	SC,AD
Gro	Imperative	Invention	Simulation	AD
GEC	Functional	Invention	Biological cells	AD
Proto BioCompiler	Functional	Piggyback	Biological cells	AD
Agent-Based				
Graphical Agent Modeling Language	Graphical	Extension	Conceptual	AD
Agent Framework	Imperative*	Extension	Any Network	AD,SM
Multi-agent Modeling and Simulation Toolkit	Any	Any	Any	SC,AD,SM
* JESS, being declarative, is a notable exception in this group				
Wireless Sensor Networks				
Regions based DSLs*	Imperative	Extension	Wireless Network	AD
Data-flow based DSLs	Imperative	Invention	Wireless Network	AD,SM
Database-like DSLs	Declarative	Piggyback	Wireless Network	SC
Centralized-view DSLs	Imperative	Piggyback	Wireless Network	AD
Agent-based DSLs	Imperative	Extension	Wireless Network	AD
* Regiment, an invented functional language is a notable exception in this group				
Pervasive Computing				
TOTA	Imperative	Extension	Wireless/Wired Network	AD,SM
Chemical reaction model	Declarative	Invented	Wireless/Wired Network	AD,SM
Spatially-Scoped Tuples	Imperative	Extension	Wireless/Wired Network	AD,SM
Swarm & Modular Robotics				
Bitmap Language	Descriptive	Invented	Swarms and Modular Robots	SC
Graph Grammars	Functional	Invented	Robot Swarms	SC,AD
PRISM	Declarative	Invented	Robot Swarms	AD
Meld	Declarative	Extension	Modular Robots	SC,AD
DynaRole/M3L	Imperative/Declarative	Invention	Modular Robots	SC,AD
ASE	Imperative	Extension	Modular Robots	SC,AD,SM

continued on following page

Table 1. Continued

DSL	Type	Pattern	Platform	Layers
Parallel & Reconfigurable				
Dataflow DSLs	Any	Any	Parallel Hardware	SM,AD
MPI	Imperative	Extension	Parallel Hardware	SC,AD,SM
Erlang	Functional	Invented	Parallel Hardware	SC,AD,SM
X10/Chapel/Fortress	Imperative	Invented	Parallel Hardware	SC,AD,SM
GraphStep	Imperative	Invented	Parallel Hardware	SC,AD,SM
StarLisp	Functional	Piggyback	Parallel Hardware	SC,AD
Grid Libraries	Imperative	Extension	Parallel Hardware	SC,AD,SM
Cellular Automata	Declarative	Invented	Simulation	SC,AD
Formal Calculi				
3π	Process Calculus	Extension	Abstract geometric space	PP,AD
Mobile ambients	Process Calculus	Extension	Abstract nested compartments	PP,AD

the assumptions upon which computer science has typically relied, and to search for engineering principles like those exploited by natural systems. Amorphous computing languages fall into two general categories: pattern languages and manifold programming languages.

Pattern Languages

The majority of the languages that have emerged from amorphous computing have been focused on the formation of robust patterns. The most well known of these are Coore's Growing Point Language (GPL) (Coore, 1999) and Nagpal's Origami Shape Language (OSL) (Nagpal, 2001). The Growing Point Language is based on a botanical metaphor and expresses a topological structure in terms of "growing points" that build a pattern by incrementally passing activity through space and "tropisms" that attract or repel the motion of growing points through simulated chemical signals. The combination of these two primitives allows the programmer to specify a graph and its order of development. GPL is capable of creating arbitrarily large and complex topological patterns (Gayle & Coore, 2006), and has been used for general geometric constructions as well (D'Hondt & D'Hondt, 2001b; D'Hondt & D'Hondt, 2001a).

The Origami Shape Language is the complement, for geometric rather than topological patterns. In OSL, the programmer imperatively specifies a sequence of folds, with the catalog of possible folds taken from Huzita's axioms for origami (Huzita & Scimemi, 1989). These are then compiled into local programs such that, given an initial identification of edges, the local interactions will compute the desired fold lines, eventually producing the specified shape. Like GPL, OSL is tolerant of changes in its conditions of execution, with distorted initial conditions producing a similarly distorted final pattern.

A third similar language, the Microbial Colony Language (MCL) (Weiss, 2001), is a rule-based pattern language that includes chemical signals that diffuse over space to produce patterns: the programmer specifies the range of propagation and the length of time that the signal will persist. Its level of abstraction is significantly lower than OSL or GPL, for the reason that it was intended to hew more closely to biological realizability.

Closely related, though more a matter of cellular automata than spatial computing, was the

Table 2. Spatial computing operators of spatial computing languages

DSL	Measure	Manipulate	Pattern	Evolve	Meta
Amorphous Computing					
Proto	Duration, Local Coordinates, Density, Curvature	Vector Flow, Frequency, Density, Curvature	Neighborhood, Feedback	Modular	Functional, Domain Restriction
PyMorphous	Duration, Local Coordinates	Vector flow	Neighborhood	-	Procedural
ProtoVM	Duration, Local Coordinates, Density, Curvature	Vector Flow, Frequency, Density, Curvature	Neighborhood, Feedback	Modular	Procedural
Growing Point Language	-	-	Line growth, tropisms	-	-
Origami Shape Language	-	Fold	Huzita's axioms	-	-
Biological					
L-systems	-	Local Rewrite	-	-	-
MGS	Topological Relations, Local Coordinates	Topological Rewrite, Geometric Location	Neighborhood	-	Functional
Gro	Duration, Volume	Frequency, Growth	Rates	Growth, Diffusion, Reactions	-
GEC	-	-	Diffusion	-	Functional
Proto BioCompiler	Duration,Density	Frequency	Diffusion, Feedback	Modular	Functional
Agent-Based					
Graphical Agent Modeling Language	-	-	-	-	-
Agent Framework	-	-	-	-	-
Multi-agent Modeling and Simulation Toolkit	Distance,Time	Physical Movement	Diffuse	-	-
Wireless Sensor Networks					
Region-based DSLs	Distance	-	Regions	-	- *
Data-flow based DSLs	-	-	-	-	-
Database-like DSLs	Distance, Time	-	Surfaces, Time Intervals	-	-
Centralized-view DSLs	-	-	-	-	-
Agent-based DSLs	-	-	-	-	-
* Being a functional language, Regiment offers functional composition and abstraction					
Pervasive Computing					
TOTA	-	-	Neighborhood	-	-
Chemical reaction model	Transfer rate	-	Neighbor diffusion	-	-
Spatially-Scoped Tuples	Movement	-	Neighborhood Geometry	-	-

continued on following page

Table 2. Continued

DSL	Measure	Manipulate	Pattern	Evolve	Meta
Swarm & Modular Robotics					
Bitmap Language	-	Physical Movement, Shape	-	-	-
Graph Grammars	-	Shape	-	-	-
PRISM	Time	-	-	-	Grouping of states
Meld	Time	Physical Movement, Shape	-	-	-
DynaRole/M3L	Angles,Time	Physical Movement, Shape, Angles	-	Kinematics	-
ASE	-	Physical Movement, Shape	Broadcast, gossip, gradient, consensus, synchronization	-	-
Parallel & Reconfigurable					
Dataflow Languages	-	-	Array *	-	Procedural
MPI	-	-	-	-	Procedural
Erlang	-	-	-	-	Functional
X10/Chapel/Fortress	-	Locality	Locality	-	Procedural, Locality
GraphStep	-	-	Neighborhood	-	-
StarLisp	-	-	Shifts	-	Functional
Grid Libraries	-	-	Neighborhood	-	Procedural
Cellular Automata	-	-	Neighborhood	-	-
* Huckleberry also offers "split patterns"					
Formal Calculi					
3π	Geometric position	Translation, Rotation, Scaling	-	Force fields	-
Mobile ambients	-	Compartment Change, Motion	Neighbor diffusion	-	-

pattern language established by Yamins (Yamins, 2007). Investigating what types of patterns could be achieved with local communication and finite state, he was able to establish a constructive proof system that, for any pattern, either generates a self-stabilizing program for generating that pattern or proves the pattern is impossible to create with finite state. While the pattern elements were not assembled into a full language, they have a sufficiently broad collection of primitives, possess a means of composition, and serve as a de facto language in (Yamins, 2007).

For the languages mentioned thus far, the behavior is restricted to the patterning of a pre-existing medium. Kondacs (Kondacs, 2003) extended this concept with a "bitmap language" that takes a two-dimensional shape and decomposes it into a covering network of overlapping circles. The shape can then grow from any fragment: as they grow, the circles establish overlapping coordinate systems that link to form the shape as a whole.

Separating the formation of the pattern from the actuation, Werfel has created a number of systems for collective construction of two- and three-dimensional structures (Werfel et al.,

Table 3. Abstract device characteristics of spatial computing languages

DSL	Discretization	Comm. Region	Granularity	Code Mobility
Amorphous Computing				
Proto	Continuous	Neighborhood	Broadcast	Uniform
PyMorphous	Discrete	Neighborhood	Broadcast	Uniform
ProtoVM	Discrete	Neighborhood	Broadcast	Uniform
Growing Point Language	Discrete	Neighborhood	Broadcast	Uniform
Origami Shape Language	Continuous	Neighborhood	Broadcast	Uniform
Biological				
L-systems	Cellular	Local Pattern	N/A	Uniform
MGS	Cellular	Local Pattern	Multicast	Uniform
Gro	Cellular	Chemical Diffusion	Broadcast	Uniform
GEC	N/A	Chemical Diffusion	Broadcast	Heterogeneous
Proto BioCompiler	Cellular	Chemical Diffusion	Broadcast	Uniform
Agent-Based				
Graphical Agent Modeling Language	Discrete	Global	Unicast	-
Agent Framework	Discrete	Global	Unicast	Mobile
Multi-agent Modeling and Simulation Toolkit	Discrete, Cellular	Global, Neighborhood	Unicast, Multicast	Uniform
Wireless Sensor Networks				
Region-based DSLs	Mixed	Region	Multicast	Uniform
Data-flow based DSLs	Discrete	Neighborhood	Unicast	Uniform
Database-like DSLs	Continuous	-	-	Uniform
Region-based DSLs	Discrete	-	-	Uniform
Agent-based DSLs	Mixed	Neighborhood	Unicast	Mobile
Pervasive Computing				
TOTA	Discrete	Global, Neighborhood	Multicast	Uniform
Chemical reaction model	Discrete	Neighborhood	Unicast	Uniform
Spatially-Scoped Tuples	Discrete	Neighborhood	Unicast	Uniform
Swarm & Modular Robotics				
Bitmap Language	Discrete	-	-	Uniform
Graph Grammars	Discrete	Neighborhood	Broadcast	Uniform
Meld	Discrete	Neighborhood	Broadcast	Uniform
DynaRole/M3L	Discrete	Neighborhood	Multicast	Uniform
ASE	Discrete	Neighborhood	Multicast	Uniform
Parallel & Reconfigurable				
Dataflow Languages	Discrete	Graph	Unicast	Heterogeneous
MPI	Discrete	Global	Unicast	Heterogeneous
Erlang	Discrete	Global	Unicast	Heterogeneous
X10/Chapel/Fortress	Discrete	Global	Unicast	Heterogeneous

continued on following page

Table 3. Continued

DSL	Discretization	Comm. Region	Granularity	Code Mobility
GraphStep	Discrete	Neighborhood	Broadcast	Uniform
StarLisp	Cellular	Shift	Unicast	Uniform
Grid Libraries	Cellular	Neighborhood	Unicast	Uniform
Cellular Automata	Cellular	Neighborhood	Broadcast	Uniform
Formal Calculi				
3π	Discrete	Global	Unicast	Mobile
Mobile ambients	Discrete	Neighborhood	Unicast	Mobile

2005;Werfel, 2006). These systems use mixtures of local rules and reaction to environmental state to enable a group of robots to effectively collaborate in construction, and have been implemented with real hardware. While the initial forms were all "bitmap languages," based on regular grids, some recent work has generalized to include a constraint programming system that generates adaptive patterns on the fly (Werfel & Nagpal, 2007). Bitmap languages are frequently found in modular robotics as well, and to a lesser extent in swarm robotics (see section on Swarm and Modular Robotics below).

A notably different approach is taken by Butera's paintable computing (Butera, 2002), which is also often applied to pattern formation (e.g., self-organizing text and graphics display (Butera, 2007)). The programming model is considerably lower-level, however, uses general computation over shared neighbor data and viral propagation of code and data, and thus has the potential to be used for general parallel computing.

Manifold Programming Languages

On the opposite end of the spectrum, amorphous computing has also given birth to more general languages for spatial computing. Chief among these is Proto (Beal & Bachrach, 2006;MIT Proto, 2010), a purely functional language with a LISP-like syntax. Proto uses a continuous space abstraction called the amorphous medium (Beal, 2004) to view any spatial computer as an approximation of a space-time manifold with a computing device at every point. Information flows through this manifold at with a bounded velocity, and each device has access to the recent past state of other devices within a nearby neighborhood. Proto primitives are mathematical operations on fields (functions that associate each point in space-time with a value) and come in four types: pointwise "ordinary" computations (e.g., addition), neighborhood operations that imply communication, feedback operations that establish state variables, and restriction operations that modulate a computation by changing its domain. Proto programs interact with their environment through sensors and actuators that measure and manipulate the space occupied by devices: for example, Proto has been applied to swarm robotics by computing vectors fields, which are then fed to a movement actuator that interprets them as continuous mass flow and moves devices to approximate (Bachrach et al., 2010).

Two derivatives have since forked off of the Proto project, Gas (Bachrach, 2009) and PyMorphous (Dietrich, 2011). Gas is very closely related to Proto, mostly just changing its syntax and adding some new sensors and actuators. PyMorphous is a relatively new and more ambitious project, aimed at producing an imperative language equivalent of Proto, piggybacked onto Python as a library. Besides these, the compilation target for Proto is itself a domain specific language, an assembly

Figure 6. Creating a local coordinate system, moving into a "T" shape, and finding its center of mass in Proto (Figure 7 shows the same program running in three-dimensional space)

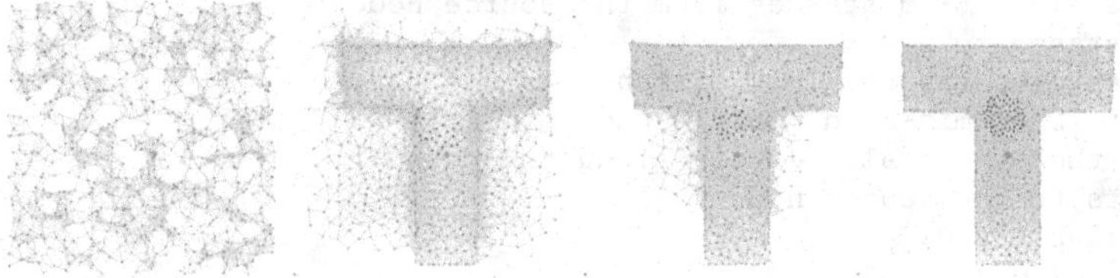

Box 1.

```
(def t-demo (origin)
        (let* (
                ;; establish local coordinates
                (c (abscoord origin))
;; find center-of gravity
                (cg (compute-cg origin c))
                ;; compute distance to center-of-gravity
                (dist-to-cg (vlen (- c cg))))
        ;; make nodes move...
        (mov (mux origin (tup 0 0 0) ;; origin does not move
                (+ (vmul 0.2 (disperse)) ;; move away from each other
                        (normalize (make-t (vmul -0.005 c)))))) ;; make "T"
        ;; turn on "bullseye" pattern
        (red (< dist-to-cg 10))
        (blue (and
                (> dist-to-cg 10)
                (< dist-to-cg 20)))))
```

language for a stack-based virtual machine model (Bachrach & Beal, 2007) that serves as a common reference point for platform-specific implementations of the amorphous medium model.

Reference Example: Proto

Proto works by compiling a high-level program (written in the Proto programming language) into a local program that is executed by every node in the network. The local program is executed in the Proto Virtual Machine (VM) which runs on a variety of platforms, including a simulator (shown in Figure 6).

The high-level Proto program for our "T" reference example can be launched with the command `(t-demo (sense 1))`. This allows the user to select, via a generic "test" sensor, the node to select as the origin of the coordinate system. The origin selection is largely inconsequential as any node can be selected as the origin, however selecting a node close to the center of the space requires less overall node movement. The `t-demo` function makes use of several other functions, however their separation is useful for code reuse and general abstraction purposes as presented in Box 1.

One useful sub-function is `abscoord`, which establishes a local coordinate system around an origin node. This is accomplished by finding the vector from every node to the origin node using the `vec-to` function. This implementation for finding the vector distance from one node to another uses a self-healing distance computation

Box 2.

```
(def vec-to (src)
     ;; establish a field of distances from the source nodes
     (let* ((d (distance-to src))
            ;; parent has the smallest distance to the source
            (parent (2nd (min-hood (nbr (tup d (mid)))))))
       ;; value is the sum of all vectors along the path
       ;; of parents to the source node
       (rep value (tup 0 0 0)
            (mux src (tup 0 0 0)
                 (sum-hood (mux (= (nbr (mid)) parent)
                                (+ (nbr-vec) (nbr value))
                                (tup 0 0 0)))))))
 (def abscoord (origin)
     (vec-to origin))
```

Box 3.

```
(def tree-aggregate (root value default-val)
     ;; establish a field of distances from the source nodes
     (let* ((d (distance-to root))
            ;; parent has the smallest distance to the source
            (parent (2nd (min-hood (nbr (tup d (mid)))))))
       ;; sumval is the sum of all values along the path
       ;; of parents to the root node
       (rep sumval value
            (+ value (sum-hood (mux (and
                                     (not (nbr root))
                                     (= (mid) (nbr parent)))
                                    (nbr sumval)
                                    default-val))))))
 (def compute-cg (root coordinates)
     ;; center-of-gravity = sum of coordinate / number of devices
     (broadcast root (vmul
                      (/ 1 (tree-aggregate root 1 0))
                      (tree-aggregate root
                                      coordinates
                                      (tup 0 0 0)))))
```

(part of the core library of Proto functions) in aggregating the vector values between all the nodes along the path between the source (origin) and the destination (node seeking to find its coordinates relative to the origin).

This portion of the program utilizes a common paradigm in Proto, embedding a neighborhood operation (e.g., `sum-hood`) inside a feedback operation (e.g., `rep`). This paradigm allows data to be shared over multiple network hops rather than just direct network neighbors (as neighborhood operations allow) as presented in Box 2..

The method used to compute the center of mass also makes use of the feedback-neighborhood paradigm. The `tree-aggregate` function constructs a tree from the node passed-in as the *root* argument. It then traverses the tree, aggregating the *value* parameter along the path. The `compute-cg` function broadcasts the sum of all agents' coordinates (in each dimension) by the total number of agents in the network, both of which are calculated using the `tree-aggregate` function as presented in Box 3.

The `make-t` function is used to move the nodes into a "T" shape. By applying the spatial constraints, as done in `x-constraints`, `y-constraints`, and `z-constraints`; the sum of the vectors returned by each function defines the direction (and speed) in which each node moves.

```
(def x-constraints (x y z)
     ;; skinny part of T
     (if (< y 0.20)
       (if (< x -0.15)
          (tup 1 0 0)
          (if (> x 0.15)
             (tup -1 0 0)
             (brownian)))
       ;; top part of T
       (if (< x -0.50)
          (tup 1 0 0)
          (if (> x 0.50)
             (tup -1 0 0)
             (brownian)))))

(def y-constraints (x y z)
     (if (< y -0.50)
       (tup 0 1 0)
       (if (> y 0.50)
          (tup 0 -1 0)
          (brownian))))

(def z-constraints (x y z)
     (if (< z -0.50)
       (tup 0 0 1)
       (if (> z 0.50)
          (tup 0 0 -1)
          (brownian))))

(def make-t (pos)
  (let ((x (1st pos))
   (y (2nd pos))
          (z (3rd pos)))
    (+ (x-constraints x y z)
       (y-constraints x y z)
          (z-constraints x y z))))
```

There are a few desirable properties of this Proto program. Like most other Proto programs, in addition to running in two-dimensional space, it also runs in three-dimensional space with no additional code (as shown in Figure 7). Additionally, all Proto programs are first compiled to local programs that execute in a portable Proto VM. Thus, Proto offers a straightforward path to execution on a real distributed network platform. Finally, there are several tools in Proto's core library that help in designing and constructing self-healing distributed algorithms. For example, by simply using the naturally self-healing `distance-to` function in the implementation of the reference example, our "T" program inherits this desirable property.

Figure 7. The Proto reference example "T" program running in three-dimensional space.

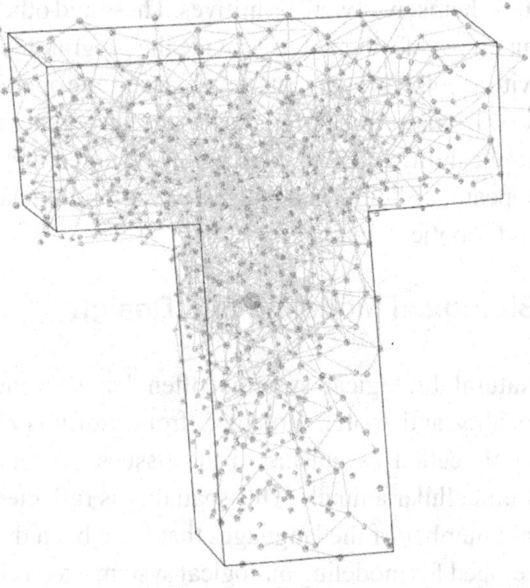

Analysis

The characteristics of key amorphous computing DSLs are summarized in Table 1, Table 2, and Table 3, based on the taxonomy proposed in Section 2.

Given the goals of amorphous computing, it is unsurprising that we find that nearly all of the languages in this domain address the challenges of global-to-local compilation and producing predictable aggregate behaviors from the actions of individual devices. The pattern formation languages use a wide variety of high-level representations, but are ultimately limited in scope: different types of patterns are difficult to mix together and cannot be generally be cleanly composed.

Proto and its derivatives do not inherently provide the programmer with quite as high a level of abstraction: the primitive operations of Proto only deal with local neighborhoods in space-time. Because Proto has a functional semantics defined in terms of aggregate operations, however, standard library functions like `distance-to` and `broadcast` can fill that gap, acting as though they themselves were primitives. These and other functions like them thus provide the programmer with a toolkit of aggregate-level space-time operators. This is a critical ingredient in the fairly general applicability of Proto, which may be noted in its appearance below in the discussion of biological and robotic domains.

Biological Modeling and Design

Natural biological systems often have strong locality and spatial structure, from biofilms of single-celled organisms to the tissues of large multicellular animals. This spatiality is reflected in a number of the languages that have been developed for modeling biological systems, as well as some of the new languages that are beginning to emerge in synthetic biology for the design of new biological organisms.

Modeling Languages

A number of biological modeling languages have been developed, such as Antimony (Smith et al., 2009), ProMoT (Mirschel et al., 2009), iBioSim (Myers et al., 2009), and little b (Mallavarapu et al., 2009), which allow the bio-molecular reactions of cells to be described at a somewhat higher level of abstraction. These generally include some spatial operations as well, in the form of compartments through which chemicals can pass (which can include movement from cell to cell). These notions have been further generalized and formalized as with P-systems and the Brane calculus (discussed below in the section on formal calculi). The space in these cases, however, is generally extremely abstract.

More explicitly spatial are L-systems (Prusinkiewicz & Lindenmayer, 1990) and MGS (Giavitto et al., 2002; Giavitto et al., 2004). L-systems are a graph-rewriting model used to model the growth and structure of plants, and are specified in terms of rules for modification of local geometric structures. MGS has a somewhat similar approach, but allows fully general rule-based computation on the much more spatially general structure of topological complexes-it has actually been applied much more widely than biological modeling, but biology has been both an important inspiration and application area for MGS. MGS programs operate both by manipulating values locally and by topological surgery to modify the local structures. Coupled with a physics model that adjusts the geometry, this has allowed MGS to express complex models of biological phenomena with elegant simplicity.

Another recent addition is Gro (The Klavins Lab, 2012), a Python-like language designed for stochastic simulation of genetic regulatory networks in a growing colony of E. coli. Gro includes built-in notions of chemical reaction rates, diffusive communication, and cell growth, and allows the programmer to construct arbitrary chemical models to control them.

Synthetic Biology Languages

More recently, the field of synthetic biology has been applying computer science approaches to the design of engineered biological organisms. Of the few high-level languages that have so far emerged, only two include spatial operations.

GEC (Pedersen & Phillips, 2009) is a logical programming language where the programmer describes a biological circuit in terms of design constraints. The spatial aspects of this language are extremely minimal: as with most modeling languages, they only deal with motion of molecules from compartment to compartment.

A biology-focused version of Proto (Beal et al., 2011), the Proto BioCompiler, has been applied in this space as well, using a chemical diffusion model of communication rather than local message passing. Here, an extension to the language associates Proto primitives with genetic regulatory network motifs, allowing Proto programs to be

Box 4.

```
//*****************************************************************
// Basic growth model

record Cell = { cpt1, cpt2 } ;;
record FGP = cell + { cpt1 != 0 } ;;
record SGP = cell + { cpt1 = 0, cpt2 != 0 } ;;
record Empty = { ~cpt1, ~cpt2 } ;;
fun NextFGP (c:FGP) = c + { cpt1 = c.cpt1-1 } ;;
fun NextSGP (c:SGP) = c + { cpt2 = c.cpt2-1 } ;;

let seed = { cpt1 = 5, cpt2 = 3 } ;;
```

compiled into genetic regulatory network designs instead of virtual machine code. The range of Proto constructs that can be mapped to biological constructs at present, however, is fairly limited.

Other high-level biological design languages, however, such as Eugene (Berkeley Software 2009 iGem Team, 2010) and GenoCAD (Czar et al., 2009), do not currently have any spatial language constructs at all.

Reference Example: MGS

MGS is a biological modeling language that allows general rule-based computation on topological complexes. In this example, we illustrate MGS's spatial approach to creating a "T" shape for our reference example "T-Program."

The following code segment describes the local state of an entity. This entity will interact with the other entities in its neighborhood. Interactions are specified using *transformations*, a kind of "rewriting" of the spatial structure, which is composed of the local state of all the entities. The "T" shape grows starting from one (or few) entities in two successive phases. In the first growth phase (`FGP`), the growth process follows a "vertical" direction. In the second growth phase (`SGP`), the two horizontal segments of the "T" grow in parallel. The functions `NextFGP` and `NextSGP` are used to evolve the `Cell` type's counters `cpt1` and `cpt2`. We start from an initial state called `seed` as demonstrated in Box 4.

The spatial structure underlying this object is a cellular complex: a space built by aggregating elementary cells. We use three types of cells in this example:

- *0-cells* are vertices.
- *1-cells* are edges. An edge is bound by two vertices.
- *2-cells* are surfaces. Here the surfaces are parallelograms bound by 4 edges.

The `letcell` construct introduces a recursive definition of cell relationships. The collection specification builds a collection using the cells introduced by the `let` (and other cells if needed). A collection associates a value to a cell as demonstrated in Box 5.

A record of positions x and y is associated to the vertices. The edges are labeled by symbols distinguishing three kinds of edges (Apical, Basil, and Lateral), illustrated in Figure 8. The idea is that the growth takes place on the "Apical" side during the first growth phase (FGP) and along the "Lateral" sides during the second growth phase (SGP).

Next, we specify the transformation used to compute the mechanics of the systems. For the sake of simplicity, we use a very simple mass-spring system and Aristotelian mechanics (that is, the speed is proportional to force, not acceleration). Each edge is a spring with a length of `L0` (at rest) and a strength of `k`.

Box 5.

```
//***************************************************************
// Chain implementation
// Spatial specification
let init =
  letcell v1  = new_vertex ()
  and     v2  = new_vertex ()
  and     v3  = new_vertex ()
  and     v4  = new_vertex ()
  and     e12 = new_edge v1 v2
  and     e23 = new_edge v2 v3
  and     e34 = new_edge v3 v4
  and     e41 = new_edge v4 v1
  and     f   = new_acell 2 (e12,e23,e34,e41) in
    { x = ..., y = ... } * v1 + { x = ..., y = ... } * v2 +
    { x = ..., y = ... } * v3 + { x = ..., y = ... } * v4 +
    `Basal * e12 + `Lateral * e23 + `Apical * e34 + `Lateral * e41 + seed * f
;;
```

Figure 8. Labeled sides of an MGS cell. During the first growth phase, growth occurs along the "Apical" side; during the second growth phase, growth occurs along the "Lateral" sides.

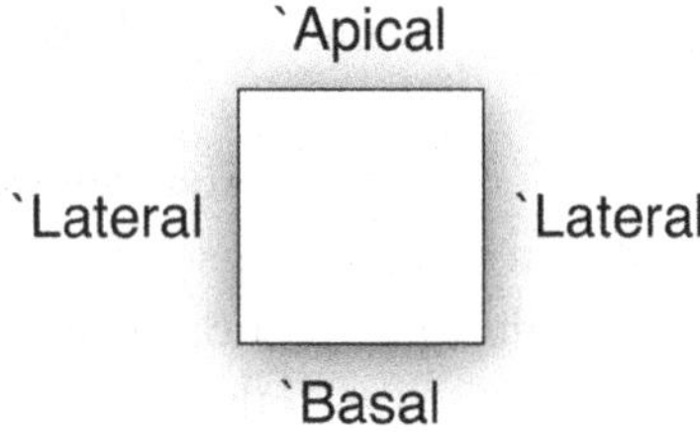

The transformation matches only "2-cells" (due to the <2> after the `trans` keyword). Then, for each cell, we compute the number of "0-cells" on its border. The primitive `icellsfold` is used to iterate over the "0-cells" on each cell's border as presented in Box 6.

The next transformation integrates the forces and updates the position of the vertexes accordingly. The qualifier `<0,1>` means that we focus on "0-cells" and that the neighborhood considered in the `neighborsfold` operation meets the following criteria: two "0-cells" are neighbors if they border a common "1-cell" (i.e., vertices are neighbors if they are linked by an edge) as demonstrated in Box 7.

There is one additional transformation to compute the growth of the "T" shape. The first evolution rule specifies the "Apical" growth during the first phase. The second evolution rule describes the growth along the "Lateral" edges for the second phase. When the rule fires, it builds several new cells, replaces edge `e12` with `'e12` and updates the neighborhood relationships of the remaining cells. What is finally built (in both phases) is a new parallelogram (i.e., a new face `f'`). Figure 9 shows the evaluation of these rules in the MGS simulator as presented in Box 8.

The computation of a center of mass can then be implemented directly using a `fold` operator (there is a fold on any kind of collection in MGS). This *fold* is very similar to the `fold` operator in LISP or other functional languages: it iterates over all the elements of a collection and propagates an accumulator using a binary reduction function.

Implementing a ring around the center-of-mass is straightforward once the center-of-mass is discovered. This point can diffuse some substance that degrades over distance. The ring can be selected by the nodes that have a level of substance in a given interval. Implementing this kind of diffusion is straightforward. The procedure is similar to the computation of the sum of forces that acts on a node (Giavitto & Spicher, 2008) describes a fully generic diffusion operator (valid for all kind

Box 6.

```
trans <2> MecaFace[k,L0,dt] = {
  f => (
    let n = icellssize f 0 in
    let g = icellsfold (fun acc v -> { x = acc.x + v.x, y = acc.y + v.y }) { x = 0.0, y = 0.0 } f 0
    in
      f + { x = g.x/n, y = g.y/n }
  )
} ;;
```

Box 7.

```
trans <0,1> MecaVertex[k,L0,dt] = {
  v => (
    let Fspring = neighborsfold (fun acc v' ->
                                  let d = sqrt((v'.x - v.x)*(v'.x - v.x) + (v'.y - v.y)*(v'.y - v.y))
in
                                  let f = k * (d - L0) / d in
                                    { x = acc.x + f*(v'.x-v.x), y = acc.y + f*(v'.y-v.y) }
                                ){ x = 0.0, y = 0.0 } v
    in
    let Ftot = icellsfold (fun acc g ->
                            let d = sqrt((g.x - v.x)*(g.x - v.x) + (g.y - v.y)*(g.y - v.y)) in
                            let f = k * (d - sqrt(2.0)*L0) / d in
                              { x = acc.x + f*(g.x-v.x), y = acc.y + f*(g.y-v.y) }
                          )Fspring v 2
    in
      v + { x = v.x + dt*Ftot.x, y = v.y + dt*Ftot.y }
  )
} ;;

fun Meca(ch) = MecaVertex(MecaFace(ch)) ;;
```

of spaces of all dimensionality) by implementing a generic Lagrangian operator.

Analysis

The characteristics of biological DSLs with significant spatial operations are summarized in Table 1, Table 2, and Table 3, based on the taxonomy proposed in Section 2. Although many of the languages for this space are focused on individual agents, those languages that do raise their abstraction level toward the aggregate provide a rich variety of space-time operations. MGS in particular provides an extremely powerful modeling language, capable of manipulating space both geometrically and topologically, and also of succinct functional abstraction and composition of such programs.

The design languages are much more limited at present, though this is largely due to the current sharp limits on the ability to engineer organisms, and will likely change as synthetic biology continues to progress.

Agent-Based Models

Agent-based models explained by Macal and North (Macal & North, 2010) are capable of describing any or all of three elements:

- A set of *agents*, their attributes, and their behavior(s);
- The *relationships* between agents and methods of interaction; and
- The *environment* in which the agents interact.

Figure 9. Construction of a "T" shape in MGS, beginning with an initial cell and using spring forces to distribute cells as they are created by topological surgery

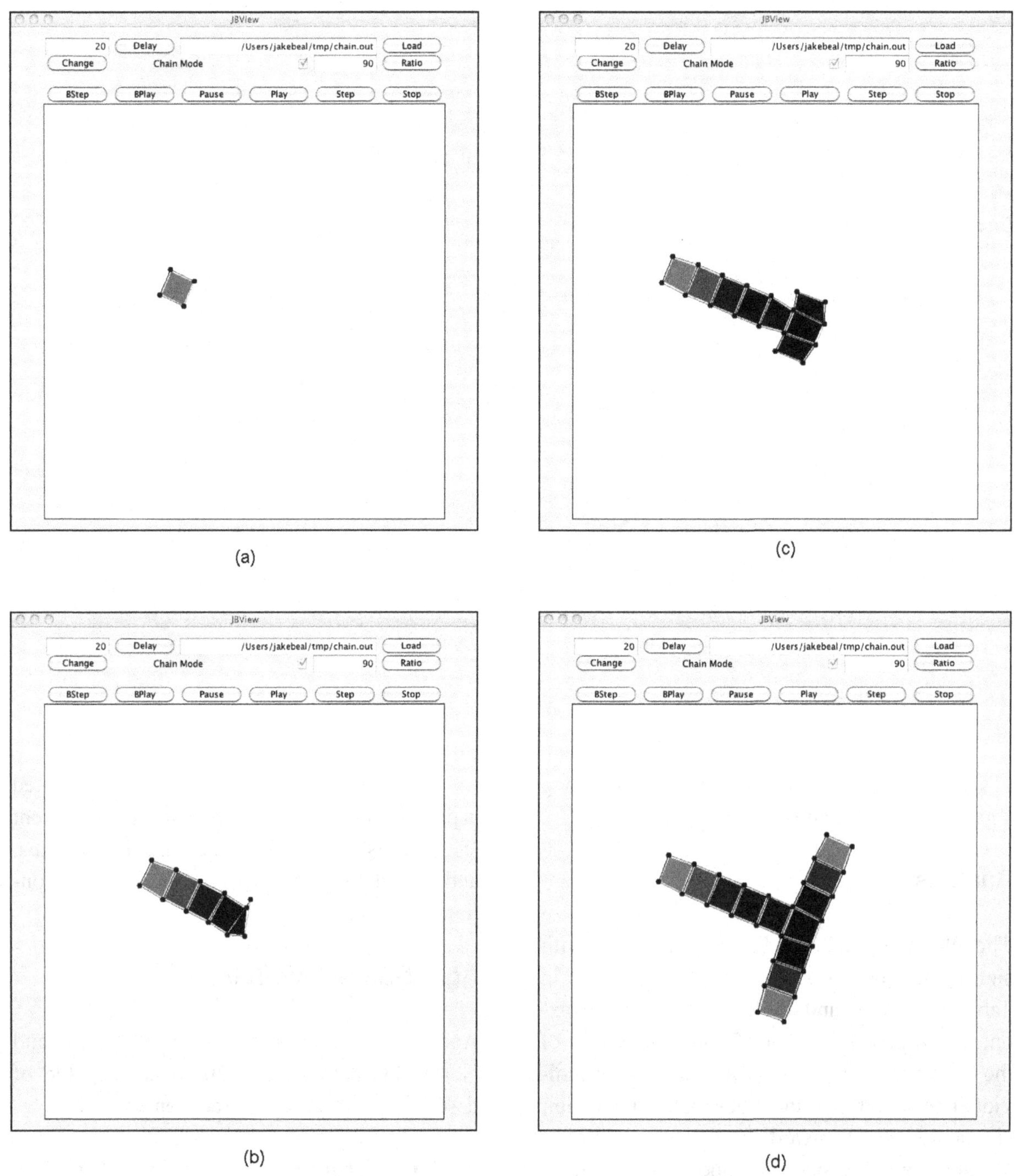

Behavioral models, such as the Belief-Desire-Intent (BDI) agent model (Rao & Georgeff, 1995), implemented in frameworks such as Jadex (Pokahr et al., 2003), describe the internals of agents. The agent internals can usually be reduced to Russel and Norvig's conceptual view of agents (Russell

Box 8.

```
// Evolution rules
patch Rules = {
  ~v1 < e12 < ~f:[dim=2, FGP(f)] > e12 > ~v2 / (e12 == `Apical) => (
    letcell v3   = new_vertex ()
    and     v4   = new_vertex ()
    and     e23  = new_edge v2 v3
    and     e34  = new_edge v3 v4
    and     e41  = new_edge v4 v1
    and     e12' = new_edge v1 v2
    and     f'   = new_acell 2 (e12,e23,e34,e41) in
      (v2 + { x = v2.x + (v2.x-f.x) * random(0.1), y = v2.y + (v2.y-f.y) * random(0.1) }) * v3 +
      (v1 + { x = v1.x + (v1.x-f.x) * random(0.1), y = v1.y + (v1.y-f.y) * random(0.1) }) * v4 +
      `Internal * e12' + `Lateral * e23 + `Apical * e34 + `Lateral * e41 + (NextFGP f) * f'
  );

  ~v1 < e12 < ~f:[dim=2, SGP(f)] > e12 > ~v2 / (e12 == `Lateral) => (
    letcell v3   = new_vertex ()
    and     v4   = new_vertex ()
    and     e23  = new_edge v2 v3
    and     e34  = new_edge v3 v4
    and     e41  = new_edge v4 v1
    and     e12' = new_edge v1 v2
    and     f'   = new_acell 2 (e12,e23,e34,e41) in
      (v2 + { x = v2.x + (v2.x-f.x) * random(0.1), y = v2.y + (v2.y-f.y) * random(0.1) }) * v3 +
      (v1 + { x = v1.x + (v1.x-f.x) * random(0.1), y = v1.y + (v1.y-f.y) * random(0.1) }) * v4 +
      `Internal * e12' + `Basal * e23 + `Lateral * e34 + `Basal * e41 + (Next SGP f) * f'
  );
} ;;

fun Step ch = Rules(Meca* ch) ;;
```

et al., 1995) with *sensors* (that read from the environment), *effectors* or *actuators* (that change the environment), and *behavioral mappings* between the sensors and effectors. Relationships between agents are typically encoded as topologies. Macal and North also explain that "In some applications, agents interact according to multiple topologies" (Macal & North, 2010). For example, a network topology may offer low-level agent communication relationships and simultaneously a social overlay network may guide the necessity for inter-agent messaging. Agent environmental modeling can vary widely based on the purpose of the modeling effort, from simple geospatial models to complex biologic models. Often, environmental information (such as global location) is *sensed* by an agent. Likewise, *actuators* modify the environmental model, which in turn serves as a blackboard for agents (i.e., stigmergy).

In this section, we categorize the agent-oriented DSLs as one of the following:

- **Graphical Agent Modeling Language:** These languages usually extend or piggy-back some form of UML. They focus on modeling the internals of agents and (sometimes) their interaction patterns using graphical tools rather than formal languages.
- **Agent Framework:** These languages are extensions of general-purpose languages, usually libraries, that impose common structure on agent specifications. By conforming to this common structure, programmers can utilize tools provided by the framework (i.e., agent administration, logging, simulation).
- **Multi-Agent Modeling and Simulation Toolkit:** These languages focus on model-

ing and simulating inter-agent interactions and environmental interactions in agent systems.

After categorizing the agent-oriented DSL, we give a brief description of each DSL. Then, we show and describe an implementation of the reference example "T" program in a representative multi-agent-based DSL.

Graphical Agent Modeling Languages

(Huget, 2005) cites MAS modeling languages Agent UML (Odell et al., 1999;Bauer et al., 2001) and the Agent Modeling Language (AML) (Trencansky & Cervenka, 2005). These largely-graphical languages aim to extend traditional UML documents with agent and multi-agent system concepts. Other graphical agent modeling languages (e.g., Agent-DSL (Kulesza et al., 2005;Kulesza et al., 2004) and DSML4MAS (Hahn, 2008)) further enhance usability by embedding the languages in development and simulation environments.

Agent Frameworks

While there are very many agent frameworks (sometimes labeled as "architectures"), we do not intend to specify all, but simply give a list of a few representative, popular examples.

Jade (Telecom Italia Lab, 2011) extends Java with a library for producing FIPA-compliant (IEEE Computer Society, 2011) agents and managing their interactions. AGLOBE (Czech Technical Institute Agent Technology Center, 2011) also extends Java with a small, lightweight library for implementing goal-oriented agents. The Cognitive Agent Architecture (Cougaar) (Helsinger et al., 2004;BBN Technologies, 2011) is another Java extension library for a highly-configurable, QoS-adaptive intelligent agent framework. JESS (Ernest Friedman-Hill, 2008), although written for use in Java, is an example of a *declarative* rule engine and scripting environment to provide "reasoning" skills to agent systems.

Multi-Agent Modeling and Simulation Toolkits

ASCAPE (Inchiosa & Parker, 2002;ASCAPE, 2011) is a Java extension for simplification of agent model composition and agent behavior execution using topological abstraction and rule-based execution respectively. NetLogo (Sklar, 2007;Wilensky, 2011) and StarLogo (Resnick, 1996;MIT Media Lab & Schellar Teacher Education Program, 2011) are extensions to the Logo language for "turtle" sensing operations and simultaneous control of multiple agents. Repast (North et al., 2007;Repast Team, 2011) is a multi-language (with extensions to Java and Logo) toolkit for modeling and simulating MAS, with additional tools for running in high-performance computing environments (Collier & North, 2011). MASON (Luke et al., 2004;George Mason University Evolutionary Computation Laboratory & Center for Social Complexity, 2011) is a discrete-event multi-agent simulation toolkit that aims to weakly-couple the MAS model from its visualization and scale to millions of agents.

The Strictly Declarative Modeling Language (SDML) (Moss et al., 1998;Centre for Policy Modelling, 2011) represents multi-agent systems using declarative rules where each agent's beliefs are transcribed to databases. Inter-agent communication occurs by reading and writing directly to an agent's database or a shared container.

Swarm (Minar et al., 1996;University of Michigan Center for the Study of Complex Systems, 2011) is a platform and tool suite for agent-based modeling and simulation of complex adaptive systems. MAML (Gulyás et al., 1999;Gulyás et al., 2011) is an Objective-C extension language and compiler (`xmc`) for helping non-programmers create Swarm applications. Echo (Forrest & Jones, 1994;Jones & Forrest, 2011) extends genetic algorithms with location, resource competition, and agent interactions. Echo is intended to capture important properties of ecological systems toward the goal of modeling and simulating complex adaptive systems.

Echo is also an example of a system that conducts modeling and simulation of Cellular Automata (CA). CA are also a topic of research in distributed systems and parallel computing, and will be discussed further in Parallel and Reconfigurable Computing.

Distributed Systems

We include distributed systems DSLs within agent-based DSLs due to their high degree of overlap. Distributed system DSLs fall into two categories: 1) distributed system modeling languages, and 2) information movement languages. An example of distributed system modeling languages is the Ψ Calculus (Kinny, 2002), a formal modeling language for abstract plan execution agents with a sense-compute-act computation cycle. On the other hand, information movement languages aim to abstract the process of moving information to the points in space-time where/when they are needed. For example, the Knowledge Query and Manipulation Language (KQML) (Finin et al., 1994) focuses on agent communication for managing distributed collaboration.

Reference Example: NetLogo

This section shows and explains an implementation of the reference example "T-Program" (described in Section 2.4) in NetLogo (Wilensky, 2011)-a language that we have chosen as being representative of Multi-Agent System DSLs. The purpose of this exercise is to demonstrate how NetLogo supports the basis set of spatial operations described above in Types of Space-Time Operations.

The implementation starts with "global" values that are shared (and constant) between all agents in the system. Note that NetLogo, because of its roots in Logo, uses the terminology `turtle` to mean "agent." Thus the position of the `origin-turtle` (i.e., the agent elected as the origin of the local coordinate system) is shared between all agents.

```
globals [ origin-turtle ]
```

NetLogo also allows agents to track their own "local" values. By default, agents track their global position in local variables `xcor` and `ycor`, however, under the constraints of our reference example, we cannot make use of global coordinates. Thus, we define `xpos` and `ypos` as our local coordinate values. Further, we add a state variable `is-origin` as a convenient way for an agent to determine if it has been designated as the origin of the local coordinate system.

```
turtles-own [ xpos ypos is-origin ]
```

The `setup` method resets the state of the world and randomly distributes and rotates a certain number of turtles. The variables `numturtles` and `screensize` are configuration values which are set at configuration time and have global scope (Figure 10). Figure 10(a) shows a simulation of the execution of the `setup` method as presented in Box 9.

To establish a local coordinate system, we make use of each agents' ability to determine the direction and distance to an "origin" node, selected in the `coordinatize` function. The notion of the network is abstracted and it is assumed that any agent can determine the vector (i.e., direction and distance) to any other agent (via the function `compute-vec-to`). We then use the function `polar-to-cartesian` to convert distance (*r*) and direction (*theta*) into Cartesian coordinates as demonstrated in Box 10.

The next section of the program, the `make-t` function, selects nodes that fall within ranges of the coordinate space and moves them to create a "T" shape around the origin. Note that the `mov`

Figure 10. NetLogo execution of the "T program" reference example

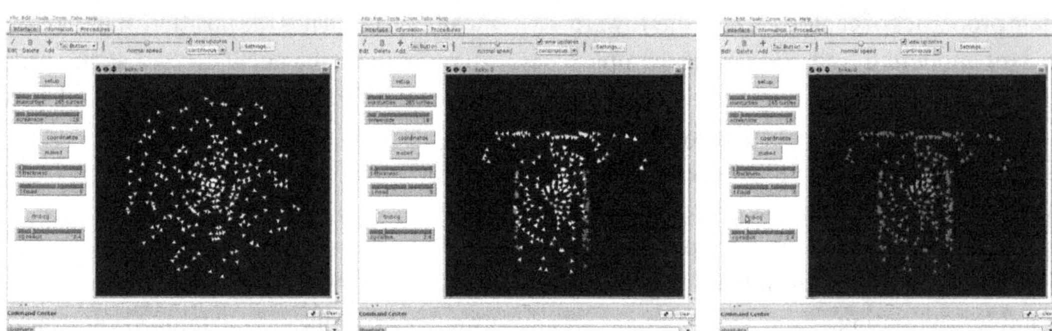

Box 9.

```
to setup
  clear-all        ;; clear the world
  crt numturtles   ;; make new turtles
  ask turtles
    [
      set color white        ;; all turtles turn white
      fd random screensize   ;; ...move forward one step
      rt random 360          ;; ...and turn a random amount
      set is-origin false    ;; default all to non-origin
    ]
end
```

command first ensures that an agent is facing a given direction, then proceeds forward for a given number of steps as presented in Box 11.

The center-of-gravity is computed by dividing the sum of all agents' positions in each dimension by the number of agents. This approach assumes that every node is weighted equally and every node is connected. Finally, if agents fall within a certain radius from the center-of-gravity, they are colored orange as demonstrated in Box 12.

Analysis

The characteristics of the DSL classes are summarized in Table 1, 2, and 3, based on the taxonomy proposed in Section 2. Table 1 shows the *linguistic* properties for each class of agent-based DSL. Table 2 similarly depicts each class's *spatial* properties, and Table 3 summarizes each class's *abstract device* properties.

First we discuss the linguistic properties of the agent-based DSLs (summarized in Table 1). Graphical Agent Modeling Languages typically target end-users with a graphical UI. Often, these languages are simply graphical representations (or extensions) of other agent modeling languages (e.g., UML), paradigms (e.g., Belief-Desire-Intent (BDI) (Rao & Georgeff, 1995)), or meta-models (e.g., FAML (Beydoun et al., 2009)). Graphical Agent Modeling Languages function at a conceptual level-mapping actions or behaviors to the components of the agent system. Agent Frameworks, whose functions and designs are analyzed thoroughly in the Agent System Reference Model (ASRM) (Regli et al., 2009) and Agent System Reference Architecture (ASRA) (Nguyen et al., 2010), are often extensions of general-purpose languages that provide common tools to agent system designers and developers. The Foundation for Intelligent Physical Agents (FIPA) (IEEE Computer Society, 2011) provides specifications for which

Box 10.

```
to-report polar-to-cartesian [theta r]
  let x (r * cos(theta))
  let y (r * sin(theta))
  report list x y
end

to compute-vec-to [agent]
  ifelse is-origin = true
  [
    set xpos 0
    set ypos 0
  ]
  [
    let cartesian polar-to-cartesian towards agent distance agent
    set xpos item 1 cartesian
    set ypos (-1 * item 0 cartesian)
    face agent
  ]
end

to coordinatize
  if is-turtle? origin-turtle
  [ ask origin-turtle
    [
      set is-origin false
      set color white
    ]
  ]
  set origin-turtle one-of turtles
  ask origin-turtle
  [
    set is-origin true
    set color green
  ]
  ask turtles
  [ compute-vec-to origin-turtle ]
end
```

these language extensions can be implemented and interchangeably utilized. Most often, these libraries extend imperative languages (as was the case for Jade (Telecom Italia Lab, 2011), Cougaar (Helsinger et al., 2004), and AGLOBE (Czech Technical Institute Agent Technology Center, 2011)), but there are also some declarative agent frameworks (e.g., JESS (Ernest Friedman-Hill, 2008)). The platform scope of agent frameworks, however, varies widely. Multi-Agent Modeling and Simulation Toolkits, which focus on modeling and simulating inter-agent and environmental interactions, have a broad scope in terms of their DSL design. Their types and patterns vary from LOGO-based scripting and simulation environments (e.g., NetLogo (Sklar, 2007), StarLogo (Resnick, 1996)) to full tool-suites designed for use by non-programmers (e.g., Swarm (Minar et al., 1996), MAML (Gulyás et al., 1999)).

As shown in Table 2, the only class of Agent-Based DSLs that exhibit spatial properties are the Multi-Agent Modeling and Simulation Toolkits. This fact is likely due to tight integration between the language and simulation environments, allowing the toolkit to expose language features that are unavailable in many distributed systems (e.g., distance, movement).

Box 11.

```
to mov [head dist]
  set heading head
  fd dist
  compute-vec-to origin-turtle
end

to make-t
  ;; right side of the lower part of the T
  ask turtles with [(xpos > t-thickness) and (ypos < t-head)]
    [
      set color red
      ;; move into the body of the T
      while [ xpos > t-thickness ]
        [mov 90 1]
    ]
  ;; left side of the lower part of the T
  ask turtles with [(xpos < (-1 * t-thickness)) and (ypos < t-head)]
    [
      set color blue
      ;; move into the body of the T
      while [ xpos < (-1 * t-thickness) ]
        [mov 270 1]
    ]
  ;; top of the T
  ask turtles with [ypos > (t-head + t-thickness)]
    [
      set color yellow
      ;; move into the body of the T
      while [ypos > (t-head + t-thickness)]
        [mov 180 1]
    ]
end
```

Box 12.

```
to find-cg
  ;; center-of-gravity = sum of coordinate / number of devices
  ask turtles
  [
    ifelse (abs(xpos - (sum [ xpos ] of turtles / numturtles)) < cg-radius)
    [
      ifelse (abs(ypos - (sum [ ypos ] of turtles / numturtles)) < cg-radius)
      [set color orange]
      [set color violet]
    ]
    [set color violet]
  ]
end
```

Abstract device properties of agent-based DSLs are shown in Table 3. Agent-based DSLs typically offer discrete modalities for interacting with agents, although some (e.g., Echo (Forrest & Jones, 1994)) offer cellular discretization. Similarly, most agent-based DSLs attempt to abstract the notion of the network from the programmer, offering global communication ranges. Notable exceptions are in the Multi-Agent Modeling and Simulation Toolkit class, where first-class notions of network topology and network links allow the programmers to *simulate* the restriction of agent communication. The granularity of communication is typically unicast (i.e., agent to agent), however some Multi-Agent Modeling and Simulation Toolkits allow communication to occur in a multicast style (i.e., to a set of agents). This is ideally demonstrated by the *ask* feature of NetLogo in the reference example in Section 3.3.5. NetLogo allows unicast communication by specifying a single turtle (e.g., *ask origin-turtle*) or multicast communication by specifying a set of turtles (e.g., *ask turtles*). Finally, mobile code is a feature of some agent-based DSLs because it is a useful mechanism for distributed algorithms. Modeling and simulation languages and toolkits typically execute a single, uniform program, whereas agent frameworks tend to provide features for facilitating agent (code) mobility (Usbeck & Beal, 2011).

WIRELESS SENSOR NETWORKS

Wireless sensor networks are a field of research concerned with the development of large networks made up of devices performing primarily a sensing function. The devices in the network (*nodes* or *motes*) are usually built using off-the-shelf-components and include a processor, a wireless communication interface and one or more sensors. As they are autonomous devices, the amount of energy they can use is often limited (by the battery on board or energy scavenging device) - hence the main design restriction targets *energy efficiency*. In order to optimize for this, common practice includes duty-cycling (having the mote alternate between long power-down modes and short bursts of activity), trade-offs between "expensive" wireless communication and "cheap" local processing, multi-hop communication and distributed algorithms.

The main goal of wireless sensor networks is efficient data collection and delivery to a gateway linked to infrastructure (i.e., Internet). Exceptions exist in the form of wireless sensor networks employing actuators, networks with multiple (mobile) gateways, etc. We will focus on the "traditional" sensor network made up of a collection of homogeneous or heterogeneous static devices. Collecting data at a single gateway from a large network is a non-scalable process (limited bandwidth being the major constraint). Thus, techniques such as data aggregation, selection of a subset of data to be gathered, filtering of data and in-network processing are common operations the designer faces in most of the deployments. These techniques are usually gathered under the saying "the network is the tool" reflecting the fact that a network delivering pre-processed data or synthesized events is often desired.

Data collection and dissemination is heavily linked to the network topology under which it operates. For example, organizing the network as a graph (a tree) is a common technique that allows simple algorithms to be employed on resource-poor devices. Aspects such as communication patterns (short or long transmission ranges, broadcast or unicast type, group based or device based, etc.) are a key building block of the final application and are usually dictated by the underlying hardware platform.

In order to implement data dissemination on top of the distributed platform, each device must be capable of supporting the execution of its local algorithm. In order to do this, operating systems such as TinyOS (Levis et al., 2005) and Contiki (Dunkels et al., 2004) are employed, providing common functionality such as hardware abstraction layers, scheduling mechanisms for tasks, execution parallelism, etc. It is common to see virtual machines implemented on top of these systems, in order to extend the basic functionality offered.

This brief introduction already outlines the main concerns faced by designers of applications for wireless sensor networks. They are basically driving factors for developing DSLs for the wireless sensor network platforms. Automating and abstracting some of the following mechanisms is the logical step to take:

- *Hardware and software platform* is usually specific to each deployed application. Usual operations that can be automated are the control of the hardware components via a hardware abstraction layer, providing common programming support in the form of an operating system, etc. The possibility of turning on and off components (radio, sensors, processing routines) reacting to the event-driven programming paradigm is an important feature.
- *Communication and topology control* is being performed in virtually all sensor networks applications. Primitives abstracting the communication protocols needed for discovering, creating and maintaining a topology need to be provided. This is the key goal of several DSLs in the region-based DSLs category (presented below) while completely abstracted in all other categories. The basic ingredients for this are neighborhood discovery, routing algorithms, and transport protocols.
- *Data dissemination* being the main goal of the sensor networks applications must be supported with high level primitives for querying the network for specific items (for example, in the form of a SQL-like language). This is achieved by combining networking algorithms with transport protocol, ensuring data delivery over optimal paths. The maintenance of these paths is done without the involvement of the user.
- *Energy efficiency constraints* lead to the need of predefining or automatically tuning the trade-off between communication and local processing. Estimation of quality of service metrics at runtime is a common mechanism through which this is achieved. The collection and processing of data for deriving the metrics (e.g., the radio link quality between two devices) is performed in the background.

A large number of DSLs have been built already, addressing combinations of the previous concerns (see (Sugihara & Gupta, 2008;Mottola & Picco, 2011) for recent surveys). Taking note of the previous work, we would like to extend the analysis in (Mottola & Picco, 2011) in order to bring into focus the aspect of spatial computing. We propose an extension of the original taxonomy, looking at the basic mechanisms used in programming the network. We have identified five classes, as follows.

Region-Based DSLs

By far, the largest number of DSLs targeting wireless sensor networks is found in the category of region-based DSLs, showing the programmer's need for expressing operations at the level of regions (i.e., neighborhoods, sets, etc.) rather than individual devices. For example, *Abstract Regions* (Welsh & Mainland, 2004) offers a family of spatial operators that allows addressing of regions of the network. Additional characteristics include information about the trade-off communication-computation resources and extension of the underlying TinyOS operating system with a thread-like concurrency mechanism called fibers. A similar DSL is *Hood* (Whitehouse et al., 2004), which offers functionality for defining one-hop neighborhoods and sharing data between nodes (these mechanisms being transparent to the programmer).

Logical Neighborhoods (Mottola & Picco, 2006) is somewhat more general in the sense that the definition of neighborhood is relaxed, not being restricted to physical proximity anymore. Nodes sharing the same characteristics can be addressed together, even if they are spread throughout the network. A direct extension is *Virtual Nodes* (Ciciriello et al., 2006), in which each neighborhood is seen as a single virtual sensor. The language adds further optimization to the compiler and network level.

Several other DSLs are built upon the same concept of addressing local neighborhoods, *Pieces* (Liu et al., 2003) and *TeenyLime* (Costa et al., 2006) being a few examples. The neighborhood information can be addressed in several manners: *EnviroSuite* (Abdelzaher et al., 2004) provides a programming interface aimed at tracking applications which creates objects for physical entities.

Snlog (Chu et al., 2006) is a rule-based approach, similar to logic programming, where rules are executed using a one-hop abstraction. It follows the foundation laid by NDLog (Loo et al., 2006) and actually belongs to a larger suite of languages including Dedalus (Alvaro, 2009) and DAHL (Lopes et al., 2010). In this group, the closest to the spatial languages comes Netlog (Grumbach & Wang, 2010) whose semantics allow moving of facts to neighbors and to any routable device with a known ID.

Regiment (Newton et al., 2007) presents itself as a functional language, allowing easy access to data streams (called signals). Low level details (such as one-hop communication, parallelism, etc.) are achieved from successive translations of the initial program into different languages stacked on top of each other (four translations are necessary to obtain final code). It is the closest language to spatial computing in the wireless sensor network domain. This is due to the combination between the flexibility with which users can specify regions (both hop-based and distance-based - similar to Abstract Regions), and the functional interface it offers.

The concept of *region* comprises several representations of the space. The region can be defined geometrically, as the distance from a certain point (as done in Regiment and Abstract Regions), the set of nodes within a number of hop counts from a node (as done in Hood) or a set of nodes complying to some predicates (as done in Logical Neighborhoods).

Dataflow Based DSLs

Dataflow based DSLs are one level of abstraction higher. Although their execution uses neighborhoods as part of the implementation, the user does not need to access them directly. Instead, the applications can be specified as a dataflow graph, in which the user specifies how the software components are linked by data. The location of the software, the communication between devices, locating and transferring the data in the neighborhoods, etc. are built into the languages. The simplest example in this category is *Active Messages* (Gay et al., 2003) in which software components are expressed in the nesC programming language. Active Messages is a mechanism allowing asynchronous communication between components via interfaces that provide commands and events. The resulting system is similar to a socket system, having the advantage of allowing modularity and enabling event-driven computation.

As a conceptual extension, *Abstract Task Graph* (ATAG) (Pathak et al., 2007) allows the user to express data transformations in a distributed system independent of the architecture. Abstract tasks run on individual devices communicating via abstract data, accessible via abstract channels. The user specifies the code for the tasks and the way in which they interact with data. Low-level operations, such as task deployment and physical communication, are abstracted away. *MiLAN* (Heinzelman et al., 2004) provides automatic selection of sensors and groups of nodes based on the quality of service of the collected data. The user specifies the execution as a state machine with quality of service requirements for each transition. Milan selects the appropriate sensors to collect the data. Networking layers functionality is provided by the network plug-in system and a service discovery is employed as well.

This class of DSLs presents almost no common characteristics with the spatial programming approaches. The focus of these languages is on providing functionality by linking the right software components, spatial features are to be implemented on top, as part of the components themselves.

Database-Like DSLs

Database-like DSLs treat the wireless sensor network as a real database. They abstract low-level communication functionality, focusing exclusively on data collection and aggregation. As example, *DSWare* (Li et al., 2004) is a SQL-based approach built on top of an extended event concept. Paths are established in the network, linking the subscriptions for specific data at the gateway with the nodes actually producing the events. The user benefits from the functionality of optimizations at network level, both in the network paths creation and maintenance, and the data aggregation in the network.

TinyDB (Madden et al., 2002) is one of the first high-level DSLs proposed and follows the database approach, hiding the necessary networking mechanisms from the user (e.g., the queries emitted in the network define the routing tree). Users are not involved in the low level aspects of data aggregation. Closely related, *Cougar* (Yao & Gehrke, 2002) (not to be confused with the agent language Cougaar (Helsinger et al., 2004)) allows the user to write queries over the data in the database and the system optimizes the dissemination of the queries and the aggregation of the results. A notable example of DSL in this category is *SINA* (Shen et al., 2001) which differs due to a mechanism which allows easy addition of new data operators, extending the original set of SQL commands. The authors of (Duckham et al., 2005) propose a database-like approach as well, with the difference that the querying mechanism is built upon a qualitative representation of *dynamic fields*. The authors identify two basic entities used in accessing the network, mainly the *continuants* (e.g., regions that endure time) and *occurents* (e.g., transitory events).

This class of DSLs has two characteristics in common with those of amorphous computing. First, the computation pattern relies on a continuous representation of space, where users specify areas of interest and time intervals. Second, the high level description of the queries are basically operators over the space/time continuum.

Centralized-View DSLs

Centralized-view DSLs are basically a set of high-level languages that approach wireless sensor networks from a different perspective than the dataflow-based DSLs. The main differences lie in the fact that the data collection and aggregation functionality is not predefined. These languages allow the user to define the application functionality *for the whole network* with a single program. For example, *Pleiades* (Kothari et al., 2007) allows sequential execution over the whole sensor network. The network is seen as a central object, a container of nodes, and users can write a "for" loop which iterates through all the nodes. Parallel execution of the basic "for" instruction can be specified and the compiler transforms the initial program into a collection of distributed algorithms that emulate sequentially over the distributed system.

Kairos (Gummadi et al., 2005) is similar to Pleiades, offering a centralized view of the whole network. It presents itself as an extension of the Python language. Somewhat different, *MacroLab* (Hnat et al., 2008) is a programming approach similar to Matlab - the network being represented as a matrix. Each row in the matrix represents one sensor node, each column a data type. Operations such as dot product are allowed over the whole matrix and the language abstracts the networking part.

None of the languages in this class have common points with the spatial computing approach. The effort is on providing the user with a discrete representation of the space, where data on each device can be addressed individually, using sequential programming.

Agent-Based DSLs

Agent-based DSLs are a special subset of DSLs for wireless sensor networks, making the transition to more powerful system, such as mobile ad-hoc networks. The basic idea is that software agents contain the needed functionality to process data and to perform local aggregation while, for example, following a certain physical event through the network. These languages also build upon the region information, but they allow more complex applications than data collection and dissemination.

As notable examples in this category, we mention *Agilla* (Fok et al., 2005) which is an agent framework built on top of TinyOs. Agents travel across the nodes together with their state. Each node maintains a tuple space allowing interaction between the agents and are addressed by location rather than network address. Basic functionality offered to the programmer includes the list of neighbors, information on the tuple space at neighboring nodes, migration of agents. Agilla supplies an agent manager and implements memory management and a virtual machine. *SensorWare* (Boulis et al., 2007) is similar to Agilla, only that the code is expressed in Tcl. The state of the agents is not maintained, thus code re-initializes each time the agent moves to a different node. *Spatial Programming* (Borcea et al., 2004) combines a light agent-based approach, in which scripts can migrate, with a unique addressing of space involving geographical areas. The addressing of space is translated automatically to the real network deployment. The migration of the agents is provided automatically by all these frameworks. Due to the unreliability of radio communication, there is always a chance that the transfer of agents fails, the effort of ensuring safe relocation of the agents being a distinguishing factor between these three approaches.

With the exception of the last presented DSL, the languages in this class have little in common with spatial computing. As in the dataflow-based category, the focus is on specifying the functionality of the building blocks (agents) in close relationship to the available events/data rather than to space/time.

Reference Example: Regiment

Most of the "T-Program" example cannot be implemented by wireless sensor network DSLs, since they only gather data and do not have the ability to actuate. Most also do not have the ability to measure space that is needed for computing coordinates, but depend on global coordinates to be provided. Computing an aggregate property like the center of gravity, however, is a task for which these DSLs are typically well-suited.

The following Regiment program (adapted from (Newton et al., 2007)) computes the X-coordinate of the center of gravity by averaging of the X values of all members of a network of sensors. The program uses the constructs *rmap* to obtain readings of an assumed global X coordinate from all devices and *rfold* to fold them into a single signal. The aggregation is realized via the *dosum* function which uses a tuple (total value, counter) to represent the collected data. After computing the average, the result is directed towards the base. The example shows the great flexibility offered by the in-network aggregation, achieved in an elegant manner and with relatively small amount of code as presented in Box 13.

Analysis

The characteristics of the five DSL classes are summarized in Table 1, 2, and 3, based on the taxonomy proposed in Section 2. Table 1 shows that only the dataflow-based DSLs fall under the category of language inventions (according to the taxonomy proposed in (Mernik et al., 2005)). The predominant type of programming is imperative,

Box 13.

```
dosum:: float, (float, int) -> (float, int)
fun dosum(X, (sumX, count)) {
  (sumX+X, count+1)
}

Xreg = rmap(fun(nd){sense("X",nd)}, world);
sumsig = rfold(dosum, (0,0), Xreg);
avgsig = smap(fun((sum,cnt)) {sum / cnt}, sumsig);

BASE <- avgsig
```

the database-like DSLs being the exception. As far as layers in Figure 2 are concerned, the results vary widely. From the perspective of the need of a spatial description of the languages, only the database-like DSLs come close. Unfortunately, these DSLs are very limited in their functionality, being specifically designed for the data dissemination application. As far as the platform is concerned, three out of the five categories address the network as a whole, offering a balanced alternative (taking into account also the number of DSLs in each category).

Regarding the spatial characteristics of the surveyed DSLs, Table 2 gives a clear argument against the suitability of the wireless sensor network DSLs for filling the gap between designers and embedded systems platforms. The only two categories having entries in this table are the region-based DSLs and database-like DSLs. Even for these two, most of the columns contain no entries. One of the reasons for which wireless sensor network DSLs do not meet the spatial computing requirements is that the application which primarily drove their development (data dissemination) is restrictive in itself regarding the needed functionality. Additionally, we note that the large majority of setups include static topologies with a single data-collection point (mobile networks and multiple-gateway setups are seen as exceptions).

As far as the abstract device taxonomy is concerned, the results are presented in Table 3. Inspecting this data, it follows that there is a balance between the categories of DSLs from the spatial and communication perspective. The main design constraint of static networks for monitoring applications is reflected in the last column where with the exception of the agent-based DSLs, the code is mainly stationary. It is worth noticing that the agent-based DSLs are a somewhat exceptional case in the wireless sensor networks world, requiring powerful hardware that is at the boundary of what is called a resource-poor device.

As a conclusion to this section, we note that a large collection of DSLs exists for the field of wireless sensor networks. This study surveyed only the ones which allow writing general applications for the sensor network platform - several other DSLs exist targeting specific sub-problems (such as cluster formation (Frank & Romer, 2005), efficient code dissemination (Levis & Culler, 2002), etc.). We noticed also that languages are often stacked, to combine the complementary features they offer. From the spatial computing perspective, two categories of languages share a few characteristics (region-based DSLs and database-like DSLs), being nonetheless extremely limited.

PERVASIVE COMPUTING

Pervasive computing is the scenario in which people, immersed in their typical environment, are able to automatically interact with sensors and actuators spread throughout in order to consume information of interest based on their preferences and situation, and to produce information for other people. Due to the intrinsic complexity of such systems, metaphors inspired by nature are typically adopted for their design and implementation (Zambonelli & Viroli, 2011).

The computational network over which pervasive computing applications typically run, very much resembles a WSN: it hosts mobile nodes (e.g., smartphones, sensors on cars, etc.) and it heavily relies upon wireless technologies because devices spread throughout the environment are rarely networked by wires. On the other hand, some differences from WSNs are worth noting: pervasive computing *(i)* appears to handle a wider set of networking scenarios, which can possibly include global communications, *(ii)* is much less constrained by limitations in energy or computational power, and *(iii)* is intrinsically more "open" to handle a heterogeneous set of devices and content (data, knowledge, media) (Zambonelli & Viroli, 2011). Accordingly, in pervasive computing the interactions of devices typically require both techniques of self-organization to make global properties emerge, and expressive means to elaborate information (e.g., semantic matching, or application-specific programmed matching).

There are relatively few examples of pervasive computing DSLs with spatial operators: most, like the LINDA coordination language (Gelernter & Carriero, 1992) and other tuple-space languages, largely seek to abstract the network from the programmer entirely. Thus, each of the following sections describe a particular language or model. *Tuples on the Air (TOTA)* is a middleware for sharing data in the form of tuples (i.e., lists) efficiently throughout a network. Next, the *Chemical Reaction Model* draws on inspiration from chemical reactions to shape how data spreads throughout the network. Finally, Zones-of-Influence (ZoI) from the Peer-It system models the pervasive devices that can influence or interact with each other.

Tuples on the Air (TOTA)

The main example of a programming framework for pervasive computing incorporating ideas related to spatial computing is Tuples On the Air (TOTA) (Mamei & Zambonelli, 2008) TOTA is a tuple-based middleware supporting field-based coordination: each node hosts a tuple space, from which tuples can diffuse in the network through neighbors, creating spatial fields. In TOTA each tuple, when inserted into a node of the network, is equipped with content (the tuple data), a diffusion rule (the policy by which the tuple is to be cloned and diffused), and a maintenance rule (the policy whereby the tuple should evolve due to events or elapsed time). Hence, it carries the behavior needed to identify its region of influence. These behaviors are written in Java, making TOTA an extension DSL.

The only spatial operator directly supported by TOTA is the *neighbor* concept. Other concepts are possible like GPS absolute/relative position, but they must be programmed on top of the TOTA API. Using such concepts allows for more advanced spatial mechanisms, which would not otherwise be supported natively in TOTA.

Chemical Reaction Model

Following the idea of TOTA, the work in (Viroli et al., 2011a) aims to create a DSL for the coordination of pervasive computing applications-as in TOTA, it addresses management of agent interaction, not of agent behavior. This is a biochemical-inspired language of semantic reactions: each reaction dictates how the population of tuples, spread through the network, should evolve and diffuse. Evolution is meant to exactly mimic chemistry, in that a "concentration value" is carried in each tuple and is updated using stochastic chemical models after the fashion of (Gillespie, 1977). Most importantly here, diffusion is achieved by reactions producing so-called "firing" tuples, which schedule them for relocation to a neighboring device. The destination is selected probabilistically, taking into account a transfer rate characterizing each node-to-node interaction channel. The proposed language actually abstracts the details of semantic matching, which is however recognized as a key ingredient of DSLs for pervasive computing. A preliminary DSL including semantic and spatial aspects into a chemical-inspired framework is presented in (Viroli et al., 2011b). There, spatial aspects are handled as any other semantic information: the existence (and relative position, distance, and orientation) are treated as a tuple, and relocation

Box 14.

```
⟨gradient, Source, Dist ⟩→ ⟨gradient, Source, Dist ⟩, +⟨gradient, Source, Dist+#D ⟩
⟨gradient, Source, Dist ⟩, ⟨gradient, Source, Dist2 ⟩→ ⟨gradient, Source, min(Dist,Dist2) ⟩
```

of a tuple is achieved by modifying a specific `location` property of it.

This work is an extension of the work in (Montagna et al., 2011), in which the syntax of chemical reactions is directly applied to specify pattern rules for local processing of tuples. A pattern can be prepended by symbol + meaning that the tuple is to be searched in a neighbour r of the node n in which the reaction is fired. Additionally, variable #D can be used to mean the estimated distance of r from n, and #T is the time at which the reaction is fired. As an example, the reactions used to create a gradient structure of tuples would be as presented in Box 14.

The former propagates a clone of the gradient tuple in any neighbour, properly replacing the distance value; the latter takes two gradients tuples for the same source and retains the one with shortest distance from the source.

Spatially Scoped Tuples

An alternate approach is to explicitly encode spatial scope into tuples, using relative or global coordinates, and then use localization of devices to determine their distribution.

Geo-Linda (Pauty et al., 2007) is an example of such a DSL. Derived from the earlier SPREAD system (Couderc & Banatre, 2003), it combines the tuple manipulation of LINDA with the geometric addressing concepts of SPREAD. In Geo-Linda, tuples are read and published over an assortment of geometric primitives, such as boxes, spheres, cylinders, and cones, all defined relative to a device. The language also introduces primitives to detect coarse movement of devices through the appearance or disappearance of tuples.

Another example is the Peer-It system (Ferscha et al., 2008; Holzmann & Ferscha, 2010), in which a "Zone-of-Influence" (ZoI) model is introduced to describe whether a pervasive device may or may not influence the activity of another one depending on their relative position in space.

Technically, a ZoI represents a spatial region (numerical position, direction and spatial extent), but qualitative abstractions can be used including concepts like: being in front or behind an object, near/medium/far from an object, being in similar/opposite/left/right direction, and covering disjoint/overlapping/equal areas.

Though this work does not form a complete programming language, it does present a markup language to express such ZoIs which could be used as the basis for specifications of behavior in another pervasive DSL.

Reference Example: TOTA

The lack of primitives for measuring or manipulating space means that TOTA cannot implement most of the reference "T-Program" example. Assuming a center of gravity has been calculated, however, the following code shows how a ring pattern can be computed in TOTA by means of a gradient tuple, spreading from the center of gravity and keeping track of the estimated distance from that source. (activation will then happen to tuples whose distances from the source falls within a given range) as presented in Box 15.

A gradient tuple always spreads in all neighbors because of the implementation of method `decidePropagate()`. As it is received in a neighbor, method `decideEnter()` is executed to decide whether this tuple (`this`) is to be stored or not, which in this case is true if no gradient tuple is already there (`prev`) or if this tuple has a lesser `hop` counter. If the tuple is to be stored, method `changeTupleContent` increments

Box 15.

```
class RingTuple extends FieldTuple{
 ...
  protected boolean decideEnter() {
    RingTuple prev = (RingTuple)tota.keyrd(this);
    return prev == null ||
           prev.hop > (this.hop + 1);
  }
  protected void changeTupleContent() {
    hop++;
    if (hop <= RingTuple.RING_MAX &&
       hop >= RingTuple.RING_MIN) {
      this.ring_activation=true;
    }
  }
  protected void decidePropagate() {
    return true;
  }
}
```

the hop counter by one, which sets a flag stopping the run if the counter is in the desired range.

Analysis

The characteristics of the Pervasive Computing DSL classes are summarized in Table 1, 2, and 3, based on the taxonomy proposed in Section 2.

As summarized in Table 1, TOTA, a Java library, is an imperative language extension designed for wired and wireless multi-hop networks. The chemical reaction model, although targeted at the same types of networks as TOTA, has an invented syntax with rule-based semantics, while the spatially-scoped tuple approaches tend to be extensions.

Table 2 shows the spatial properties of pervasive computing DSLs. TOTA, like the LINDA coordination language (Gelernter & Carriero, 1992) and other tuple-space languages, largely seeks to abstract spatial properties of the network from the programmer. Thus, TOTA has very few spatial properties-with the exception of neighborhood propagation. The chemical reaction model, on the other hand, makes use of a spatial gradient for *diffusing* information to network neighbors. Spatially scoped tuples, on the other hand, offer explicit patterns over communication neighborhoods.

As far as the abstract device model summarized in Table 3, all pervasive computing DSLs utilize an immobile (i.e., uniform) program targeted for discrete devices, though the devices might be moved by external agents, such as humans carrying or operating them. The difference in frameworks comes from their communication modalities. TOTA uses a distributed publish-subscribe mechanism for global, multicast communication and has a neighborhood communication range. The chemical reaction model and spatially-scoped tuples also use a neighborhood communication range, however, they can also direct messages to individual users (i.e., unicast granularity).

SWARM AND MODULAR ROBOTICS

Multi-robot systems tend to be spatial both due to the locality of their communication and the physical interactions of the robots. In swarm robotics, the robots are typically not in physical contact and may be spread fairly broadly through space: goals are typically specified in terms of sensing and actuation interactions with the external environment, such as mapping or search and rescue. In modular robotics, on the other hand, the robots are typically in contact and working together to form a desired physical shape. There is a great deal of similarity in the control problems encountered in these fields, however, and some recent projects (e.g., (Christensen et al., 2007)) bridge the two domains.

Swarm Robotics

Swarm robotics emphasizes multi-robot systems with large number of agents, individual simplicity, and local interactions. One of the promises of swarm robotics is robust and scalable operation with applications such as environmental monitoring, search and rescue using swarms of aerial vehicles, or oil spill clean-up - applications that take advantage of the ability of a swarm to cover large amounts of space in parallel. Efficient algorithms to these problems usually require the individual swarm members to localize themselves either globally or locally with respect to each other. These physical capabilities also lend themselves directly to measuring and manipulating space-time such as they are facilitated by the Proto (Bachrach et al., 2010) DSL, which has been demonstrated on robot swarms with local range and bearing capabilities. The typical approach to swarm control with Proto has been to compute vector fields over the swarm, computing with them and combining them to produce a commanded velocity for each robot.

In order to control the shape of a swarm, e.g., to implement the reference example "T-Program," a robot would need the following capabilities:

- The ability to *localize* to resolve a coordinate system (possibly indirectly, e.g., by inference from change of neighbors).
- The ability to *communicate* either locally or globally to exchange state information, and
- The existence of *unique identification numbers* to identify other robots' communication messages.

With these abilities, the swarm could be either programmed using a multi-agent framework such as NetLogo using the code in the Agent-Based Models example or a manifold language such as Proto using the code in the Amorphous Computing example. Here it is worth noting that the choice of language might heavily bias the performance of the implementation: for example, the NetLogo construct *ask turtles* is implemented as a loop whose execution time scales linearly with the number of robots (and scales quadratically with respect to the total number of messages exchanged in the swarm), as each robot queries every other robot's coordinates. The Proto implementation's *sum-hood* operator instead implies a broadcast operation that scales more favorably (but whose reliable implementation in a congested communication environment is dependent on its low-level implementation). However, using a language such as NetLogo limits execution to simulation (hence the linear behavior of *ask turtles*), whereas Proto compiles to local behavior, thus allowing the program to run on a real network of robots.

An additional class of swarms are those whose individual members do not have access to global and/or local localization. This is the case for bacteria assembling structures at the microscale (Martel & Mohammadi, 2010) or miniature robots imitating the capabilities of social insects whose capabilities to localize are also limited to exploitation of gradient fields (pheromones, e.g.) or crude global bearing estimates based on sun, wind or magnetic field. Robotic instances of such systems include collaborative manipulation (Martinoli et al., 2004), aggregation (Correll & Martinoli, 2011), and clustering (Martinoli et al., 1999). The behavior of the individual units in these kind of swarms can usually be described using a Finite State Machine (FSM), which has both deterministic and probabilistic transitions, where transition probabilities reflect the uncertainty of sensing and actuation on a miniature robot. As localization is usually not assumed, space is abstracted by assuming an average spatial distribution of the swarm. This distribution can be uniform and constant, leading to constant probabilities for robots to encounter objects and each other in the environment, or arbitrarily parameterized, leading to a time and space-dependent encountering probability (Prorok et al., 2011). A DSL targeted to this class of systems is MDL2ε, which allows the description of states and state transitions using an XML-based language and compiles to bytecode for a virtual machine JaMOS (Szymanski & Woern, 2007). JaMOS/MDL2ε is helpful to the programmer in abstracting the hardware interfaces of a specific platform and facilitates programming of the platform as only byte code needs to be transferred. It does provide only little conceptional benefits, however.

In contrast, the PRISM language (Kwiatkowska et al., 2011) is a state-based language, based on the Reactive Modules formalism (Alur & Henzinger, 1999) targeted at probabilistic model checking of stochastic communication networks, biological reaction networks and potentially robotic swarms that can be described as probabilistic automata such as those encoded by MDL2ε or those hand-coded for systems like (Martinoli et al., 2004;Correll & Martinoli, 2011;Martinoli et al., 1999). After defining a probabilistic automaton, Markov chain, or Markov Decision process, PRISM compiles differential equations that model the average number of agents in a certain state if possible, or uses Gillespie simulation (Gillespie, 1977) otherwise. This allows the designer to quickly understand the average stochastic dynamics that emerge from a specific set of rules.

Graph grammars are another important approach to specifying swarm formations. Graph grammars, or graph rewriting systems, are rule sets that transform one graph into another. In a self-assembly context, e.g., for assembling the T-shape, a desired assembly can be represented as a graph. The assembly process becomes a sequence of (labeled graph) transformations of an edgeless graph into the target graph, known as Graph Rewriting Systems on Induced Subgraphs (Litovsky et al., 1992;Klavins et al., 2006). This graph rewriting system takes one subgraph as input and has another subgraph as output (in the process removing or adding edges and changing the labels). Here, nodes represent individual robots, the rewriting represents reconfiguration of these robots, and the labels represent robot states. Rewriting rules are of the form:

$$\phi_{fi}: X \quad A \Rightarrow Y - Z$$

For executing a rule the labels of the two modules constituting the subgraph are compared to the LHS (left-hand side) of the graph grammar rule ϕ_{fi}. If these subgraphs match, they are replaced by the subgraph shown on the RHS of the ϕ_{fi}. This replacement indicates that the states of the original modules *X* and *A* are replaced by *Y* and *Z* respectively. The actual physical connection between robots is indicated by the existence or absence of edges '−' between the nodes of the subgraph on either side of the rule ϕ_i. We therefore refer to ϕ_{fi} as a *construction rule*. In order to break up a connection, we can define a *reversal rule*

$$\phi_{ri}: Y - Z \Rightarrow X \quad A$$

Thus, connections can be made or broken between modules, depending on whether the LHS of the rule is satisfied, which itself might depend on the existing connection between modules represented by the subgraph. Reversal rules, can be executed by the environment or by active decisions of the modules themselves, which then need to exchange their states and initiate a disconnect sequence when either one detects a valid LHS. In this paper, we use the convention that atomic modules that are not part of a structure are in state *A*.

Modular Robotics

Modular robots are reconfigurable robots that are constructed from modules that have the ability to autonomously attach and/or detach from each other to re-arrange themselves into different shapes (Yim et al., 2007). There also exist modular robot systems that require manual assembly and disassembly. The promise of modular robotic systems is increased versatility, due to their ability to reconfigure into robots with different functions, and robustness due to their potential to self-repair. As modular robotic systems consist of tens to hundreds of actuators and distributed computation, they pose deep challenges to DSLs for global-to-local programming. We explicitly consider two specific problems: generating local rules for module re-configuration from global descriptions of a desired shape, and generating local rules for motion generation from global descriptions of a desired spatio-temporal pattern.

- **Pattern Formation:** A DSL created for modular robotic systems is Meld (Ashley-Rollman et al., 2007;Ashley-Rollman et al., 2009), a declarative logic programming language. The goal of Meld is to simplify programming of modular robots, mainly with respect to expressiveness and size of the resulting code, as well as enable proofs of correctness based on the formal definition of the language. Meld is indeed able to express spatial computing algorithms such as gradient dissemination, shortest-path routing, and localization. These are important primitives for expressing morphology changes, and Meld has been used to implement morphological changes of large-scale distributed modular robotic systems in simulation. Meld does not provide primitives for solving the global-to-local programming problems for generating arbitrary patterns, however. Such patterns are commonly defined in the form of a 3D matrix using arbitrary graphical interfaces or directly using data structures provided the high-level programming language that implements the algorithm for local rule generation. For example, a T-shape such as the one used in our running example could be defined as computer-aided design (CAD) model, which can then be used to generate motion plans and local rules.

These algorithms operate at the *abstract device* layer. A common abstraction is the assumption that modules are *unit-compressible*, that is they can contract and extend their faces to move other modules within the structure and make room for other modules (Rus & Vona, 2001). Other abstractions include modules that are capable of linear motion on a plane of modules as well as convex and concave transitions into another plane (Rus et al., 2002;Stoy & Nagpal, 2004), modular robots that have the ability to disassemble as their sole mode of actuation (Gilpin et al., 2008), or simply modules that can be created or disappear anywhere in a 3D lattice (Dewey et al., 2008), among others. Finally, modular robots are dual to robot swarms when they are able to move in free-space (e.g., fly, swim, or roll). In this case, graph grammars as described in the previous section can be derived from a desired target-graph such as the T-shape example in a 1-to-1 mapping. As graph grammars only encode the result of two interactions, however, they are limited to systems in which the generation of individual robot trajectories is trivial and can be achieved by local sensing, e.g., random walk with mutual attraction of matching pairs.

As such, the specification of desired shapes can be understood as a primitive form of a *declarative* DSL, in which the compiler essentially solves a path-planning problem (Walter et al., 2004). These compilers then generate a sequence of (event-driven) actuations that can be executed by the individual modules, often via a primitive virtual machine.

Once modular robots are assembled into a static shape, they become targets for any spatial computing programming approach, which then allows a programmer to implement algorithms such as the center-of-gravity example on a T-shape. Few works, however, are concerned with spatial computing aspects that go beyond the pattern formation problem.

- **Motion Generation:** The problem of motion generation can be expressed as a manipulation of space-time based on computed patterns. For example, motion of an inchworm-like structure can be generated by activating its actuators in a sinusoidal pattern. The resulting physical evolution will lead to the equivalent of a traveling sine wave. Most often, this is done by means of centralized control, but a number of spatial languages have emerged as well.

A DSL that we have already encountered that can be readily applied to this purpose is Proto (Beal & Bachrach, 2006). The actuations used are different than for moving swarm robots, since the devices typically remain fixed with respect to one another. Instead, the programmer manipulates shape with operations such as adjusting the curvature of space (corresponding to joint actuation), scaling space (corresponding to linear actuation), or adjusting its density (omnidirectional expansion or contraction of a robot). These continuous representation are more indirect, but abstract the choice of specific platform.

There are also specialized motion generation DSLs for modular robotics. One particularly powerful example is the DynaRole language (Schultz et al., 2007), which dynamically assigns behaviors to modules using code that migrates from a seed over the graph of connected modules, and has recently been extended to include gossip-based synchronization and automatic reversibility of behaviors (Bordignon et al., 2011b). This was made more spatial with the addition of directional labels (Schultz et al., 2008), and coupled with Modular Mechatronics Modelling Language (M3L) (Bordignon et al., 2011a), a DSL for high-level kinematic specification of modular robots. Together, these allow a behavior to be specified abstractly using labels, then to be automatically mapped onto the spatial realization of any compatible platform's actuators, either in automatically generated simulations or on physical robots.

A related effort (as well as one of the targets supported by DynaRole) is ASE (Christensen et al., 2011), constructed as a C library that provides a wide variety of aggregate space-time operations, including broadcast, gossip, distance-measuring gradient, consensus, and synch-quite similar to the aggregate operators in Proto's library. Another approach uses models of diffusing hormones to organize motion: this has been investigated in both (Shen et al., 2004) and (Hamann et al., 2010).

Reference Example: Graph Grammars

For our reference "T-Program" example, in order to construct a T-Shape consisting of 6 robots that has a width of 3 robots and a height of 4 robots, we could define the following rules that can be implemented by a finite automata and require only local communication and orientation:

```
X X  -> A-B
B0 X -> B-C
C0 X -> C-D
D1 X -> D-F
D3 X -> D-E
```

This program assumes that each robot is in state `X` initially. As soon as two `X` meet, they begin constructing the T-shape from the bottom, up. The notation `B0` indiciates the port of the robot at which another robot can dock. In this example, we choose a 4-neighborhood, labeling the ports from 0 to 3 in clockwise order, with 0 being at the "top" of a robot. The robots will therefore assemble a column `ABCD` and then adding an `E` to the left and an `F` to the right, forming a simple T-shape as shown in Figure 11.

As soon as the shape is assembled, a coordinate system can be established in a multi-hop fashion enabling a spatial computing approach such as

Figure 11. Construction of T-shape using a graph grammar

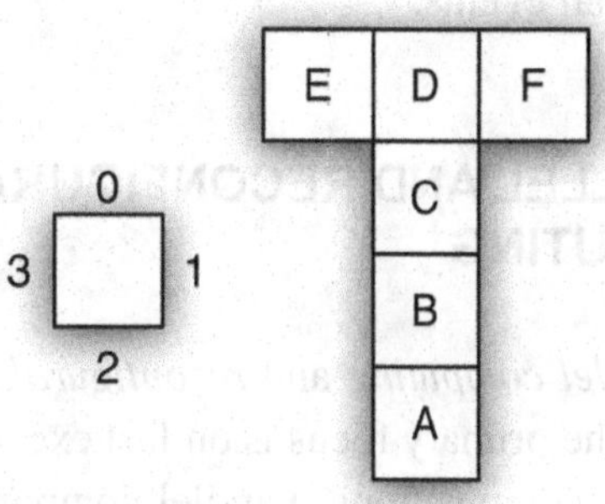

Proto to compute the center-of-gravity and produce the ring pattern.

Analysis

The characteristics of robotics DSL classes are summarized in Table 1, 2, and 3, based on the taxonomy proposed in Section 2. By and large these DSLs focus on the manipulation of space. For swarm robotics, the amorphous and agent languages already encountered provide the most spatial approach to aggregate control, but require that robots can obtain at least some local coordinate information. For modular robotics, in addition to Proto, which we have already encountered, ASE gives a large toolkit of aggregate space-time programming abstractions. One concern with ASE, however, is that to date it seems to have been tested only on small numbers of devices and so its scalability is not yet well established.

One of other notable things that appears in this domain are languages with an explicit connection to formal verifiability: in particular, Meld is both a spatial language and a predicate logic language, and work has been done on proving correctness of Meld programs. It is unclear, however, how well this actually translates to modular robotics, due to uncertainties in sensing, actuation, and communication. Thus, despite the advantages shown by Meld and ASE, it is not yet clear whether there is a general DSL for a large modular robotic system that allows to efficiently maintain dynamic state and specify the behavior of a large modular robotic system across both shape reconfiguration and locomotion in response to external events.

PARALLEL AND RECONFIGURABLE COMPUTING

In *parallel computing* and *reconfigurable computing*, the primary focus is on fast execution of complex computations. Parallel computing has tended to focus on architectures with many processors, while reconfigurable computing has tended to focus on single chips with many configurable processing elements. In both cases, however, the extremely high speed at which computations are executed mean that time delays from communication between computing devices are a dominant concern, whether those devices are individual transistors or entire processors. In high performance systems, the computing devices are tightly packed together in 2D or 3D space, and thus the communication cost is typically strongly-correlated with the distance between devices.

Parallel and reconfigurable architectures have thus long embraced spatiality. Notable examples include cellular automata machines (Toffoli & Margolus, 1987) such as the CAM-8 (Margolus, 1993), processor grids such as the Connection Machines (Palmer & G.L. Steele, 1992), tiled architectures such as RAW (Taylor et al., 2002) and Warp (Annaratone et al., 1987), reconfigurable fabrics like Tartan (Mishra et al., 2006) and WaveScalar (Swanson et al., 2007), and massively multicore systems like SVM/Microgrid (Jesshope et al., 2009). Indeed, DeHon's papers on the likely future evolution of such architectures (DeHon & Wawrzynek, 1999;DeHon, 2002) are one of the origins of the term "spatial computing."

The computation to be executed, however, often does not have a structure with an obvious mapping to such spatial architectures. As a result, programming languages for parallel and reconfigurable systems have embraced spatiality to a much lesser degree than the architectures that they target. With regards to spatial computing, we classify languages for parallel and reconfigurable computing into three categories: dataflow languages, topological languages, and field languages.

Dataflow Languages

Most DSLs for parallel and reconfigurable computing are what we will categorize as "dataflow languages:" languages that attempt to accelerate computations by identifying dependencies, so that independent operations can be executed in parallel. In effect, these languages conceive of a computation as a partial order, yielding one dimension of parallelism and one dimension of order or time. The job of the compiler is then to pack this dataflow graph as effectively as possible into the two- or three-dimensional space of hardware available.

The vast majority of these DSLs are either minor variants that extend or piggyback on C (e.g. Cilk (Blumofe et al., 1995)), FORTRAN (e.g. HPF (HPF, 1997)), or MATLAB or else are circuit specification languages like VHDL. Many are implemented simply through pre-processor macros or library calls that encourage a programmer to code in a way that makes it easier to extract parallelism. A thorough discussion of such approaches for reconfigurable computing can be found in (Mucci et al., 2007) and (Jozwiak et al., 2010); a similar survey for parallel computing can be found in (Barney, 2012).

A more sophisticated approach is taken by languages for systolic arrays or streaming. These languages make the dataflow model explicit. Systolic array languages, such as SDEF (Engstrom & Cappello, 1989) and ReLaCS (Raimbault & Lavenier, 1993), are the older technology and typically assume a highly regular structure onto which the program must be decomposed. Streaming languages such as StreamIT (Thies et al., 2001) and SCORE (Caspi et al., 2000) operate conversely, allocating resources to balance the needs of the computation. Most recently, APIs like OpenCL (OpenCL, 2011) take advantage of modern GPU hardware, which is often laid out in a stream-friendly manner: one dimension of parallelism by one dimension of pipeline sequence, curled to fit on a rectilinear chip.

Despite the strong spatial concerns in utilization of resources, however, the languages themselves do not contain any spatial operations. Rather, the programmer is expressing constraints, which imply things about spatial structure, but often fairly indirectly. One recent and intriguing exception is Huckleberry (Collins, 2011), which provides "split patterns" that explicitly manipulate the spatial relations between stages of a recursive computation, with patterns like 1D mixing and 1D or 2D partitions.

Topological Languages

In the cluster of DSLs that we shall call "topological languages," spatial locality is explicit, but abstracted from the two or three dimensions of actual hardware on which a computation will be executed. Topological languages differ from dataflow languages in that the computation is viewed in terms of information exchange amongst a collection of processes, rather than a unidirectional flow. These types of languages have been formalized with the π-calculus and its relatives (discussed below in the section on formal calculi).

The classic example of the topological approach is MPI (Gropp et al., 1994), a library extension to C and Fortran in which a computation is specified as a collection of processes that interact by passing messages through shared memory. MPI is widely used for supercomputing applications, and this continues to be the case for its descendants, OpenMP (OpenMP, 2011) and MPI-2 (MPI2, 2009). Erlang is another widely used topological language. Although initially declarative, over time it has evolved into a functional language in which processes interact by asynchronous message passing (Erlang, 2011;Armstrong, 2007). More recently, major efforts have been undertaken to build concurrent programming languages that scale well and support modern approaches to safety and object oriented programming: X10 (Saraswat et al., 2012) at IBM, Chapel (Chapel, 2011) at Cray, and Fortress (Allen et al., 2008) at Sun. All of these include explicit statements of locality ("places," "locales," and "regions," respectively) that constrain interaction and can be combined hierarchically into aggregate locations.

The GraphStep language (deLorimier et al., 2011) takes a different approach, trading generality for efficiency. In GraphStep, a computation is expressed as a distributed graph processing algorithm, where at each step every graph node receives messages from its neighbors, computes over those messages, and then sends an update message along the edges to its neighbors. Given a computation and a dataset, GraphStep maps the graph onto available hardware, decomposing complex nodes and arranging nodes to balance the communication cost. Similar ideas have been developed for embedding Markov Random Field (Chen et al., 2003) and Bayes net computations (Rejimon & Bhanja, 2005) in reconfigurable hardware, but these have not been as well developed.

Field Languages

Finally, "field languages" are those DSLs that make an explicit connection between the structure space-filling hardware and computation with arrays of two or more dimensions. These languages thus tend to be the most spatial of the parallel and reconfigurable computing DSLs.

The driver for field languages tends to be the recognition that many high-performance computing applications are based on physical phenomena that are themselves highly spatial, such as atmospheric simulation, machine vision, VLSI design, and biological tissue simulation.

A major early example is StarLisp (Lasser et al., 1988), a functional programming language for the Connection Machine. In StarLisp, the programmer manipulates "pvars" (parallel variables), which were arrays with anywhere between 1 and 16 dimensions. Each element of a pvar was mapped to a different processor on the Connection Machine, taking advantage of its hypercubic architecture to allow efficient manipulation of these fields of data, including shifts along any combination of dimensions, using either a grid (boundaries) or torus (wrapping) topology.

StarLisp faded along with the Connection Machines, however, and field languages have remained a niche in high-performance computing, primarily supported through libraries like FLIC (Michalakes, 1997) or RSL (Michalakes, 1994). The most interesting of these from a spatial computing perspective are the Scalable Modeling System (SMS) (Govett et al., 2003), which exposed spatial communication structure to the programmer through the notion of manipulations on grids partitioned into per-processor chunks, each of which interacts with its neighbors through a cached "data halo," and PyNSol (Tobis, 2005), which attempts to raise the level of abstraction through a Python front-end where a programmer manipulates objects with spatial types like "torus" and "grid." There is a growing recognition of the need for field languages in the high-performance community, as evidenced by the recent "rediscovery" of spatial computing put forth in (Yang et al., 2011).

The other direction from which field languages have been developed is cellular automata. A number languages have been developed to allow succinct specification of cellular automata: examples include the CAM-8 assembly language (Margolus, 1993), ALPACA (Pressey, 2012), CANL (Calidonna & Furnari, 2004), CAOS (Grelck et al., 2007), CARPET (Spezzano & Talia, 1997), CELLANG (Eckart, 1997), JCASim (Freiwald & Weimar, 2002), and Trend/jTrend (Chou et al., 2002), as well as Echo (Forrest & Jones, 1994) and NetLogo (Sklar, 2007) already discussed in previous sections. Because they are all describing the same computational model, these languages are all fairly similar: essentially declarative specifications of the neighborhood structure and rules for the evolution of cells. Their differences are mostly in syntax: ALPACA uses pseudo-english, CANL has lisp-like syntax, CARPET's syntax is C-like, and JCASim is hosted in Java, and so on. Some languages allow only 2D cellular automata, while others support 1D or 3D as well, and CAOS supports arbitrary dimensions. An interesting generalization is suggested by MacLennan's continuous spatial automata (MacLennan, 1990), which generalize the concept of CAs to continuous space using differential equations, but this has not yet been implemented in any DSL.

Analysis

For this section, we do not provide a reference example, as it is not particularly suitable for the languages of this domain: no parallel or reconfigurable computing DSL supports measurement or manipulation of space and only cellular automata (themselves at the edge the domain) can create patterns.

This fact reflects a long-standing assumption of the domain: that hardware is essentially static with respect to programs. The programmer then lives in an idealized rectilinear environment and the connection between computation and hardware thus becomes entirely the job of the compiler and system management services. This assumption may not last, however, as the continued evolution of computing hardware brings issues of power density and variable performance to greater prominence.

The characteristics of the DSL classes are summarized in Table 1, 2, and 3, based on the taxonomy proposed in the Analytic Framework section. At present, amongst the three classes of DSL that we have discussed, the predominant languages of the domain are dataflow and topological languages, which have minimal spatial operations and focus heavily on the lower layers of our taxonomy. The field languages are explicitly spatial, but support only a very narrow range of operations on rectilinear grids. What the languages of this domain do have, however, that is likely to be of interest for future development of spatial DSLs, is a wide variety of models for how to specify program control flow in a distributed environment.

FORMAL CALCULI FOR CONCURRENCY AND DISTRIBUTION

A special form of DSL is the formal calculus, a primitive language used to describe in an abstract way, certain features and behaviors of a system of interest, in order to reason about its properties and possibly guide compliant implementations. Examples include process algebras (Milner, 1999;Priami, 1995;Pierro et al., 2005;Cardelli & Gordon, 2000), used to model distributed system of communicating processes, membrane computing models (Paun, 2002), used to reason about chemical-inspired computing systems, and core languages of programming languages (Igarashi et al., 2001), used to formally ground application code. In this section we review the formal calculi that are more related to spatial computing-that is, those with first-class concepts of space. It is worth noting that most of them are extensions of the archetype process algebra π-calculus (Milner, 1999), which intentionally abstracts from topological issues of the computational network, modeling the overall system as a flat composition of processes that interact through channels-a sort of "space" accessible to all processes that know its name.

3π Process Algebra

3π was developed as an extension of π-calculus with the idea of modeling the space where processes execute as a 3-dimensional geometric space (Cardelli & Gardner, 2010). In 3π, each process has a position and an orientation in space (a *basis*), encoded in a so-called geometric data. Other than accessing it (symbolically), a process can also send or receive geometric data through channels and can evolve to new processes located elsewhere (i.e., movement). The interesting point of this approach is that geometric data are manipulated in an abstract way, namely, only by *frame shift* operations (translation, rotation, and scaling). For a process p to move towards process q, q must communicate its position to p, p should perform a subtraction operation between its position and q's obtaining a frame shift f, and then p should evolve to a new process to which frame shift f is applied. So, although there is indeed a unique coordinate system in the space, processes do not know their position in it, but can just compare their position/orientation with respect to others. In analogous ways, one can model a force field as a process communicating to (the processes of) mobile agents a frame shift they should apply to themselves (e.g., a translation in a given direction), or a developmental-like creation of "matter" can be modeled by processes being spawned incrementally to form 3D structures as observed in nature-e.g., lung development in mice as described in (Cardelli & Gardner, 2010). The main motivation of the proposed approach is to describe and reason about systems of developmental biology, where the evolution of biological matter over time might be considered as a fabric for computing.

Another significant fact is that 3π has no embedded notion of time. Processes just execute in each node and synchronize by the exchange of messages (both sending and receiving are blocking operations). A notion of time could be achieved by a global process sending a "tick" message to all others-an approach that would hardly result in a meaningful implementation. Similarly, processes form a flat set, with no notion of communication by proximity. Like in π-calculus, a process can send a message to another only if it holds the other's unique name, and independently of its position. Any notion of geometrically local communication must be encoded on top of the model, resulting in specifications where both writing and reasoning are difficult.

Ambient Calculus

A different approach than 3π is taken in the Ambient calculus (Cardelli & Gordon, 2000) and its derivatives - like Brane Calculi (Cardelli, 2005) and P-systems (Gheorghe & Paun, 2000) - in which processes execute in a spatial system of hierarchically nested compartments. Each process is a located in a compartment, and can execute a number of space-aware operations such as destroying the membrane of the compartment to which it belongs, moving outside the current compartment, entering a nested compartment, creating a new compartment, and so on. Communication is not a primitive in the ambient calculus, but must be implemented through interactions such as the diffusion of "messenger processes" in and out of compartments. Although based on a more primitive notion of space than the work in 3π, ambient-related approaches are interesting for their reliance upon an unconventional notion of space. This is more often the norm, however, when considering the computations carried-out in biochemical systems of cells and tissues of cells.

Reference Example: 3π

In order to illustrate programming in 3π, we exploit a concrete version of the 3π process algebra-a somewhat straightforward variation of it which we devised for the sake of clarity, playing the same role that, e.g., PICT (Pierce & Turner, 2000) would do for π-calculus (Milner, 1999). Considering the reference example used in this chapter, we can create a T-shaped structure (on the XY-plane, centered in the origin) by a force field, namely by a process `t-force` that communicates to all interested processes (`device`) the affine transformation they should apply to themselves (moving to x-axis if their y-coordinate is positive, and moving to y-axis otherwise) as shown in Figure 12. This can be achieved by the specification presented in Box 16.

Note that an affine map is represented by a 3x3 matrix and a translation vector, hence the map `affinemap((x-axis,0,0),0)` would, e.g., actually represent ⟨((1,0,0),(0,0,0),(0,0,0)),(0,0,0)⟩, which when applied to a position (x,y,z) yields the new position (x,0,0).

The implementation of other spatial computations, like identification of center of gravity and

Figure 12. Creation of T-shape with 3π

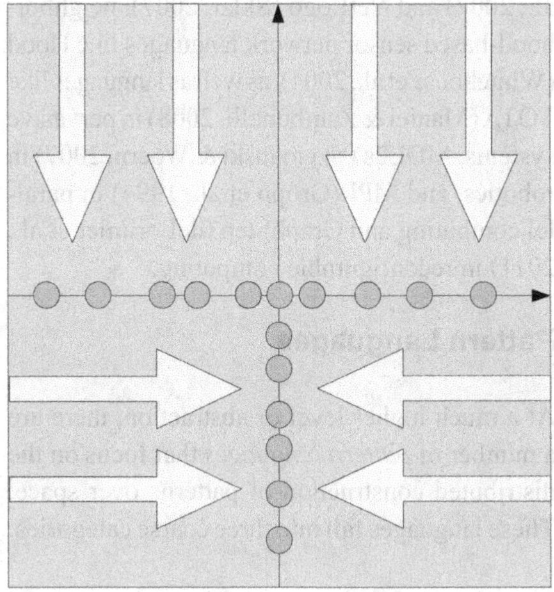

drawing a ring around it, is not shown here for the sake of brevity: the details depend very much on how the various devices (namely, processes) are actually connected, which requires also developing a representation of local communication. An example approach would amount to let the process `T-force` also *(i)* initially create a new process `CG`, *(ii)* incrementally compute the average of all device positions it receives (which as time passes tends to the center of gravity of all available devices), and *(iii)* communicate to `CG` to move towards that average. This would make `CG` move from the origin towards the actual center of gravity. Drawing a ring can then be similarly achieved by letting `CG` create a new set of processes forming the ring.

Analysis

The characteristics of the Formal Calculi DSL classes are summarized in Table 1, 2, and 3, based on the taxonomy proposed in the Analytic Framework section.

As summarized in Table 1, both formal calculi analyzed, 3π and Mobile Ambients, are types of process algebras that extend the π-calculus for defining independent processes that communicate through message-passing channels. However, whereas 3π processes are aware of their position in space relative to other processes, ambient calculus processes are aware of their spatial container.

Table 2 summarizes the spatial properties of the formal calculi DSLs. 3π is capable of measuring geometric space relative to other processes, and space is manipulated by specifying transformations on location and orientation of processes. The computation patterns for 3π processes are essentially global-allowing execution of any named process. Mobile ambients, on the other hand, can manipulate their containers (e.g., destroying the container's membrane) and communicate via patterns like diffusion through container neighborhoods.

The abstract device characteristics of formal calculi DSLs are listed in Table 3. Both process

Box 16.

```
process T-force(ForceChannel) is
    ForceChannel.receive(Device-id,Device-position);        % receiving device info
    if (scalarproduct(y-axis,Device-position) >=0)          % checking device position
        then Device-id.send(affinemap([x-axis,0,0],0))      % moving to x-axis
        else Device-id.send(affinemap([0,y-axis,0],0));     % moving to y-axis
    call T-force(ForceChannel)                              % recursive call

process Device(ForceChannel) is
    generate Device-Id;                                     % generating a new channel
    ForceChannel.send(Device-id,myposition);                % sending device information
    Device-id.receive(Map);                                 % receiving a map
    applymap Map;                                           % moving
```

algebras focus on mobile processes that operate on discrete devices and can address specific devices. They vary, however, in their communication range. Where 3π can address processes globally throughout the system, ambient processes communicate with processes near their current container.

ANALYSIS

As we have seen in the previous section, there are a plethora of domain-specific languages (and DSL-like frameworks) that have been designed to address spatial computing problems. Although these span many different domains, these DSLs nevertheless cluster into just a few cross-cutting groups-a convergence that may be due to the constraints imposed by space-time itself. Ignoring borderline cases, we find there to be four rough groups of spatial computing DSLs: device abstraction languages, pattern languages, information movement languages, and general purpose spatial languages.

Device Abstraction Languages

The vast majority of DSLs for spatial computers are not particularly spatial at all. Instead, these *device abstraction languages* attempt to simplify the aggregate programming problem by simplifying other complicating details from the programmer's perspective. Therefore, these languages tend to provide the most system management services. They typically provide a great deal of control over how a program is implemented locally but little (or nothing) in the way of spatial operations over aggregates-leaving that as a problem for the programmer. To support distributed algorithm construction, however, these languages frequently provide strong abstractions of local communication, which do greatly simplify the specification of distributed algorithms.

Device abstraction languages are found throughout all spatial computing domains: for example, the agent languages Repast (North et al., 2007) and NetLogo (Sklar, 2007), neighborhood-based sensor network languages like Hood (Whitehouse et al., 2004), as well as languages like TOTA (Mamei & Zambonelli, 2008) in pervasive systems, MDL2ε (Szymanski & Woern, 2007) in robotics, and MPI (Gropp et al., 1994) in parallel computing and GraphStep (deLorimier et al., 2011) in reconfigurable computing.

Pattern Languages

At a much higher level of abstraction, there are a number of *pattern languages* that focus on the distributed construction of patterns over space. These languages fall into three coarse categories:

- *Bitmap* languages specify a pattern to be formed using a regular pattern of pixels or voxels. These languages tend to be fairly rigid, and it is arguable whether they are properly languages at all. These are found often in swarm and modular robotics, e.g., (Werfel, 2006) or (Stoy & Nagpal, 2004)
- *Geometric* languages specify the pattern as an arrangement of geometric constructs. Frequently these include simple solids such as spheres and rectangles or Euclidean constructions such as lines and bisectors. L-systems (Prusinkiewicz & Lindenmayer, 1990) applied to biological modeling are an example of a geometric language. When the constructions are tolerant of distortion, the patterns may be adaptive, as in the case of the OSL (Nagpal, 2001) amorphous language.
- *Topological* languages specify the pattern in terms of connectivity and hierarchical relationships between elements, which then need to be satisfied as best as possible by the arrangement of these elements in space. Examples include the GPL (Coore, 1999) amorphous computing language and

the ASCAPE (Inchiosa & Parker, 2002) agent language.

In all of these cases, the pattern is specified without reference to the process that will create it, except that the language will often be constrained to certain classes of design. The actual implementation of how the pattern is computed then varies wildly from language to language, as well as from domain to domain, including generating a pattern on an existing surface (e.g., GPL (Coore, 1999) in amorphous languages and Yamins' self-stabilizing pattern language (Yamins, 2007) in cellular automata), arranging swarm or modular robots into a pattern (Ashley-Rollman et al., 2007), or collective construction of a pattern by autonomous robots (Werfel, 2006).

Information Movement Languages

The *information movement languages* focus on gathering information sampled from regions of space-time and delivering it to other regions of space-time. As in the case of pattern languages, the programmer typically specifies what information to gather and where it needs to go (either in a push model or a pull model), but not how to go about doing so or the degree of distribution / centralization of collection points. While many of these languages do not include spatial relations, there is a significant subclass that explicitly allow spatial constructs, which tend to be based on space and time measuring operators.

Sensor networks include a large group of information movement languages focused on data gathering, including languages like TinyDB (Madden et al., 2002) and Regiment (Newton & Welsh, 2004). Although a few languages in other domains are also focused on data, such as the distributed system language KQML (Finin et al., 1994), the information movement languages of other domains tend to be more general, such as the agent frameworks described above in the Agent-Based Models section.

General Purpose Spatial Languages

Finally, we have a small but significant group of *General Purpose Spatial Languages* (GPSL). These languages are still domain-specific languages, in that they are specialized for spatial computers, but are general in the sense that they have applicability across a wide range of domains. At their best, these languages combine the strong spatial abstractions of pattern formation and information movement languages with the abstract device languages' ability to control implementation dynamics. Unlike abstract device languages, however, GPSLs permit a spatial aggregate view that allows abstraction of individual devices.

The two currently most significant GPSLs that we have identified are Proto (Beal & Bachrach, 2006) and MGS (Giavitto et al., 2002). Both of these are relatively mature languages, have been applied successfully to a number of different domains, and offer a wide range of spatial operators, including meta-operators.

Comparison of Languages

At present, each group of spatial computing DSLs has significant strengths and weaknesses.

- Device abstraction languages do little to cover the gap between device and aggregate, yet many of the important problems at the system management level are simply ignored by languages in the other three groups. Device abstraction languages are currently the best approach for handling issues such as resource management, conflict management, logging, and security.
- Pattern languages and information movement languages are typically excellent at carrying out a narrow set of tasks under a particular set of assumptions. Their abstractions typically dissociate the programmer so far from the implementation, however, that it is impossible for the system to

be reconfigured to combine tasks of different types or to operate under different assumptions. For example, a sensor network language aimed at data gathering may drop the rate of sampling when the network is overloaded, although the user may prefer to keep the rate the same but sample from fewer devices.

- GPSLs combine the spatial aggregate abstractions lacking from device abstraction languages with the composibility and configurability lacking from pattern and information movement languages. Their generality, however, means that the more specialized capabilities of these other languages are not built into GPSLs, and need to be implemented in libraries for the language. While this is not ultimately a limitation, at these languages present state of maturity these libraries are often not available and must be implemented by the programmer.

It is worth noting as well that every group contains a mixture of different types of languages: imperative, functional, and declarative languages exist in all groups. Likewise, every group of languages cuts across many different domains. We take this to be a confirmatory sign that, in fact, the spatial nature of a DSL is an orthogonal attribute to the type of language.

The DSLs that we have examined can also be divided into languages that are proficient at measuring/manipulating space-time and those that are proficient at maintaining dynamic state. For example, the functional language Proto lends itself to spatial computing with space-time operators like restriction, which can modulate programs by changing the space-time region where they execute. Programs with dynamic state or state transitions, however, are cumbersome in Proto. On the other hand, a language such as MDL2ε, which deals naturally with dynamic state and state transitions, has no aggregate space-time operators, making it cumbersome of write complex spatial programs. At present, there seem to be no languages that adequately address the problem of both maintaining dynamic state and also efficiently describing global spatio-temporal system behavior.

This lack may be due to a fundamental tension between asynchronous parallel execution and state transitions. In general, it is impossible to guarantee that these three statements always hold:

- Every device in the spatial computer makes the same state transition.
- Decisions are made in parallel at separate devices.
- State transitions occur more frequently than the time to send a message across the diameter of the spatial computer.

To understand why this is, consider the following: assume two devices, A and B, have a choice between two state transitions, and that the decision will depend on the value of a piece of information that has just appeared at A. If B is always to decide the same way as A, then it must get A's information. Device A, however, might be as far away as the whole diameter of the spatial computer. Thus, we are always left with a choice of which property to weaken: parallelism, speed, or coherence.

There are many reasonable ways to approach this problem, and different languages have made different choices. Different spatial computing languages choose different ways to make this trade-off. For example, both Proto and MDL2ε weaken coherence, but in different ways: Proto chooses to keep the aggregate model coherent, at the cost of making state transitions cumbersome, while MDL2ε keeps state transitions simple at the cost of having no operations that span regions of space-time. OSL, on the other hand, weakens speed, executing a sequence of space-time operators by inserting synchronization barriers where the program waits for long enough to ensure that the last set of state transitions have completed. There are, however, many cases where a programmer would want to have a mixture of strategies, such as programming a sequence of swarm behaviors. At present, there is no language that allows a programmer to elegantly make trade-offs between the different options.

Another limitation of the current spatial DSLs is that almost none of them provide any benefits beyond a concise description of the desired global behavior. This is in contrast to formal languages that provide correctness guarantees and to probabilistic modeling tools such as PRISM, which can automatically generate the expected (i.e., average) spatio-temporal trajectories of a swarming system defined as a probabilistic FSM.

In sum, therefore, what is currently lacking are spatial computing DSLs that:

- Allow general combination of aggregate programming and state-based programming schemes,
- Have the ability to warn about programs that use functionality that go beyond the physical or hardware capabilities of a specific platform, e.g., localization capabilities to perform space-time measurements or the maneuvering capabilities of a robot, and
- Both generate executables for an actual platform and also generate models for tool-assisted formal verification.

Whereas the first item can likely be achieved by combining existing approaches, we expect the other two to pose deep research issues. This is due to the fact that physical assumptions and correctness conditions are often not explicitly defined in code, but result implicitly from environment interaction. One possibility is to design a DSL so that the programmer needs to supply goal and assumption information; another is to cross-compile a DSL to an embodied simulator that would use transitions extracted from past experimental data using system identification to predict the behavior of new programs. Likely, these challenges are areas where the connection to particular domains will continue to play a major role.

CONCLUSION AND FUTURE RESEARCH DIRECTIONS

As we have seen, there are a large number of spatial computing DSLs that attempt to bridge the gap between the aggregate programming needs of users and the execution of programs on individual devices. These languages have emerged across a number of different application domains, yet share broad commonalities likely due to the fact that all are dealing with spatial constraints.

Looking forward, the increasing complexity of engineered systems is likely to favor the increased development of GPSLs: device abstraction languages do not offer enough leverage on the aggregate programming problem, while pattern and information movement languages tend to be too specialized for practical use in large-scale systems. Besides the pragmatic questions of language and library development, we see four key research directions that are critical to the future development of GPSLs:

- Although a major focus of GPSLs is robustness to problems and failures, no GPSL currently exposes error handling or quality of service (QoS) information to the programmer. Addressing error handling and QoS scalably for a distributed aggregate is an open research question.
- The pragmatic issues of the system management layer are largely unaddressed by current GPSLs, sharply limiting their usability in deployed systems. Resolving this is likely to involve building on top of device abstraction languages that do address issues such as security and logging: the key question is how to best expose these

issues to the programmer in an aggregate abstraction.

- No GPSL currently offers full support for first class functions. A key reason for this is that, although there are many ways in which distributed function calls have been implemented, yet no language resolves some of the fundamental problems of identity (Beal, 2009) and scope (Beal & Usbeck, 2011) in functions that are defined at run-time.
- Finally, there are a number of common programming paradigms, such as publish/subscribe, observer/controller, and first order logical inference, that are difficult or impossible to implement on current GPSLs. It is unclear whether the problem is due to limitations in existing GPSLs, or whether it is due to scalability problems or hidden assumptions in how these paradigms are currently implemented. Future research on spatial computing DSLs needs to find ways to bridge this gap, so that the benefits of these programming paradigms can be adapted for the aggregate environment.

In addition to GPSLs, we expect that there will be a continued role for more specialized spatial computing DSLs, as they can directly address domain- and application-specific issues that GPSLs cannot, as well as taking advantage of assumptions that come from a more restricted scope. An important research direction for future work on specialized spatial computing DSLs, however, will be to determine whether they can be implemented in terms of existing GPSLs, whether as libraries or as variations of the language. Doing so will allow a new spatial computing DSL to bootstrap its space-time operators from the theory, software, and system management resources of its base GPSL, rather than needing to build up from scratch. This will also benefit GPSLs, by pushing their boundaries and driving them to support the needs to the DSLs they come to host.

It is our hope that such future research directions will be aided by a clearer understanding of the properties and relationships of spatial computing DSLs, such as that offered by the framework, survey, and analysis in this chapter.

ACKNOWLEDGEMENT

Work partially sponsored by DARPA; the views and conclusions contained in this document are those of the authors and not DARPA or the U.S. Government.

REFERENCES

Abdelzaher, T., Blum, B., Cao, Q., Chen, Y., Evans, D., & George, J. … Krishnamurthy, S. (2004). Envirotrack: Towards an environmental computing paradigm for distributed sensor networks. In *Proceedings of the 24th International Conference on Distributed Computing Systems* (pp. 582-589). IEEE.

Abelson, H., Allen, D., Coore, D., Hanson, C., Homsy, G., & Knight, T. Jr (2000). Amorphous computing. *Communications of the ACM, 43*(5), 74–82. doi:10.1145/332833.332842

Allen, E., Chase, D., Hallett, J., Luchangco, V., Maessen, J.-W., Ryu, S., Jr., G. L. S., … Tobin-Hochstadt, S. (2008). *The Fortress language specification version 1.0*. Sun Microsystems.

Alur, R., & Henzinger, T. (1999). Reactive modules. *Formal Methods in System Design, 15*(1), 7–48. doi:10.1023/A:1008739929481

Alvaro, P. (2009). *Dedalus: Datalog in time and space. Technical report*. DTIC Document.

Annaratone, M., Arnould, E., Gross, T., Kung, H. T., Lam, M., Menzilcioglu, O., & Webb, J. A. (1987). The warp computer: Architecture, implementation, and performance. *IEEE Transactions on Computers C, 36*(12), 1523–1538. doi:10.1109/TC.1987.5009502

Armstrong, J. (2007). A history of Erlang. In *HOPL III Proceedings of the Third ACM SIGPLAN Conference on History of Programming Languages* (pp. 6-1 - 6-26).

ASCAPE. (2011). *Ascape guide*. Retrieved from http://ascape.sourceforge.net/

Ashley-Rollman, M., Goldstein, S., Lee, P., Mowry, T., & Pillai, P. (2007). Meld: A declarative approach to programming ensembles. In *Proceedings of the IEEE/RSJ International Conference on Intelligent Robots and Systems* (pp. 2794-2800).

Ashley-Rollman, M. P., Lee, P., Goldstein, S. C., Pillai, P., & Campbell, J. D. (2009). Language for large ensembles of independently executing nodes. In *Proceedings of the International Conference on Logic Programming (ICLP '09)* (pp. 265-280).

Bachrach, J. (2009). *Programming chained robotics in the gas programming language. Technical report*. Makani Power.

Bachrach, J., & Beal, J. (2007). *Building spatial computers*. Technical Report MIT-CSAIL-TR-2007-017, MIT.

Bachrach, J., Beal, J., & McLurkin, J. (2010). Composable continuous space programs for robotic swarms. *Neural Computing & Applications, 19*(6), 825–847. doi:10.1007/s00521-010-0382-8

Barney, B. (Retrieved Feb. 20, 2012). *Introduction to parallel computing*. Retrieved from https://computing.llnl.gov/tutorials/parallel_comp/

Bauer, B., Müller, J., & Odell, J. (2001). Agent UML: A formalism for specifying multiagent interaction. In *Agent-Oriented Software Engineering, Volume 1957*, (pp. 91-103).

Technologies, B. B. N. (2011). *Cougaar: The cognitive agent architecture*. Retrieved from http://cougaar.org

Beal, J. (2004). Programming an amorphous computational medium. In *Unconventional Programming Paradigms International Workshop, volume 3566 of Lecture Notes in Computer Science*, (pp. 121-136). Springer Berlin.

Beal, J. (2009). Dynamically defined processes for spatial computers. In *Spatial Computing Workshop* (pp. 206-211).

Beal, J. (2010). A basis set of operators for space-time computations. In *Spatial Computing Workshop* (pp. 91-97).

Beal, J., & Bachrach, J. (2006). Infrastructure for engineered emergence on sensor/actuator networks. *IEEE Intelligent Systems, 21*(2), 10–19. doi:10.1109/MIS.2006.29

Beal, J., Lu, T., & Weiss, R. (2011). Automatic compilation from high-level languages to genetic regulatory networks. *PLoS ONE, 6*(8), E22490. doi:10.1371/journal.pone.0022490

Beal, J., & Usbeck, K. (2011). On the evaluation of space-time functions. In *Self-Organizing Self-Adaptive Spatial Computing Workshop* (pp. 49-54).

Berkeley Software 2009 iGem Team (October 2009, Retrieved May 10, 2010.). *Eugene*. Retrieved from http://2009.igem.org/Team:Berkeley_Software/Eugene.

Beydoun, G., Low, G., Henderson-Sellers, B., Mouratidis, H., Gomez-Sanz, J., Pavon, J., & Gonzalez-Perez, C. (2009). FAML: A generic metamodel for MAS development. *IEEE Transactions on Software Engineering, 35*(6), 841–863. doi:10.1109/TSE.2009.34

Blumofe, R. D., Joerg, C. F., Kuszmaul, B. C., Leiserson, C. E., Randall, K. H., & Zhou, Y. (1995). CILK: An efficient multithreaded runtime system. In *Proceedings of the Fifth ACM SIGPLAN Symposium on Principles and Practice of Parallel Programming (PPoPP)* (pp. 207-216).

Borcea, C., Intanagonwiwat, C., Kang, P., Kremer, U., & Iftode, L. (2004). Spatial programming using smart messages: Design and implementation. In *Proceedings of 24th International Conference on Distributed Computing Systems* (pp. 690-699). IEEE.

Bordignon, M., Stoy, K., & Schultz, U. P. (2011a). Generalized programming of modular robots through kinematic configurations. In *2011 IEEE/RSJ International Conference on Intelligent Robots and Systems (IROS)* (pp. 3659-3666).

Bordignon, M., Stoy, K., & Schultz, U. P. (2011b). Robust and reversible execution of self-reconfiguration sequences. *Robotica, 29*(1), 35–57. doi:10.1017/S0263574710000664

Boulis, A., Han, C., Shea, R., & Srivastava, M. (2007). Sensorware: Programming sensor networks beyond code update and querying. *Pervasive and Mobile Computing, 3*(4), 386–412. doi:10.1016/j.pmcj.2007.04.007

Butera, W. (2002). *Programming a paintable computer*. PhD thesis, MIT, Cambridge, MA, USA.

Butera, W. (2007). Text display and graphics control on a paintable computer. In *International Conference on Self-Adaptive and Self-Organizing Systems* (pp. 45-54).

Calidonna, C., & Furnari, M. (2004). The cellular automata network compiler system: Modules and features. In *International Conference on Parallel Computing in Electrical Engineering* (pp. 271-276).

Cardelli, L. (2005). Brane calculi. In V. Danos & V. Schächter (Eds.), *International Conference on Computational Methods in Systems Biology (CMSB 2004), Revised Selected Papers, volume 3082 of Lecture Notes in Computer Science*, (pp. 257-278). Springer.

Cardelli, L., & Gardner, P. (2010). Processes in space. In F. Ferreira, B. Löwe, E. Mayordomo, & L. M. Gomes (Eds.), *Programs, Proofs, Processes, 6th Conference on Computability in Europe, CiE 2010, volume 6158 of Lecture Notes in Computer Science*, (pp. 78-87). Springer.

Cardelli, L., & Gordon, A. D. (2000). Mobile ambients. *Theoretical Computer Science, 240*(1), 177–213. doi:10.1016/S0304-3975(99)00231-5

Caspi, E., Chu, M., Huang, R., Yeh, J., Wawrzynek, J., & DeHon, A. (2000). Stream computations organized for reconfigurable execution (score). In *Conference on Field Programmable Logic and Applications (FPL)*, (pp. 605-614).

Centre for Policy Modelling. (2011). *Strictly declarative modelling language*. Retrieved from http://cfpm.org/sdml/

Chapel. (2011). *Chapel language specification version 0.82*. Cray, Inc.

Chen, J., Mundy, J., Bai, Y., Chan, S.-M. C., Petrica, P., & Bahar, R. I. (2003). A probabilistic approach to nano-computing. In *Workshop on Non-Silicon Computation*, (pp. 1-8).

Chou, H.-H., Huang, W., & Reggia, J. A. (2002). The trend cellular automata programming environment. *Simulation, 78*(2), 59–75. doi:10.1177/0037549702078002204

Christensen, A., O'Grady, R., & Dorigo, M. (2007). Morphology control in a multirobot system. *IEEE Robotics & Automation Magazine, 14*(4), 18–25. doi:10.1109/M-RA.2007.908970

Christensen, D. J., Schultz, U. P., & Moghadam, M. (2011). The assemble and animate control framework for modular reconfigurable robots. In *IROS Workshop on Reconfigurable Modular Robotics* (pp. 1-6).

Chu, D., Tavakoli, A., Popa, L., & Hellerstein, J. (2006). Entirely declarative sensor network systems. In *Proceedings of the 32nd International Conference on Very Large Data Bases*, (pp.1203-1206). VLDB Endowment.

Ciciriello, P., Mottola, L., & Picco, G. (2006). Building virtual sensors and actuators over logical neighborhoods. In *Proceedings of the International Workshop on Middleware for Sensor Networks*, (pp. 19-24). ACM.

Collier, N., & North, M. (2011). Repast SC++: A platform for large-scale agent-based modeling. *Large-Scale Computing Techniques for Complex System Simulations*, *80*, 81–109.

Collins, R. L. (2011). *Data-driven programming abstractions and optimization for multi-core platforms*. PhD thesis, Columbia University.

Coore, D. (1999). *Botanical computing: A developmental approach to generating interconnect topologies on an amorphous computer*. PhD thesis, MIT.

Correll, N., & Martinoli, A. (2011). Modeling self-organized aggregation in a swarm of miniature robots. *The International Journal of Robotics Research. Special Issue on Stochasticity in Robotics and Biological Systems*, *30*(5), 615–626.

Costa, P., Mottola, L., Murphy, A., & Picco, G. (2006). Teenylime: Transiently shared tuple space middleware for wireless sensor networks. In *Proceedings of the International Workshop on Middleware for Sensor Networks* (pp. 43-48). ACM.

Couderc, P., & Banatre, M. (2003). Ambient computing applications: an experience with the spread approach. In *Hawaii International Conference on System Sciences (HICSS' 03)* (pp. 9-17).

Czar, M., Cai, Y., & Peccoud, J. (2009). Writing DNA with genocad. *Nucleic Acids Research, 37*(W), W40-W47.

Czech Technical Institute Agent Technology Center. (2011). *Aglobe*. Retrieved from http://agents.felk.cvut.cz/aglobe/

DeHon, A. (2002). Very large scale spatial computing. In *Unconventional Models of Computation*. In *Lecture Notes in Computer Science* (*Vol. 2509*, pp. 27–37). Springer.

DeHon, A., & Wawrzynek, J. (1999). Reconfigurable computing: What, why, and implications for design automation. In *Design Automation Conference (DAC)*, (pp. 610-615).

deLorimier, M., Kapre, N., Mehta, N., & DeHon, A. (2011). Spatial hardware implementation for sparse graph algorithms in graphstep. *ACM Transactions on Autonomous and Adaptive Systems, 6*(3), 17:1-17:20.

Dewey, D., Ashley-Rollman, M., Rosa, M. D., Goldstein, S., Mowry, T., & Srinivasa, S. … Campbell, J. (2008). Generalizing metamodules to simplify planning in modular robotic systems. In *Proceedings of the IEEE/RSJ International Conference on Intelligent Robots and Systems*, (pp. 1338-1345).

D'Hondt, E., & D'Hondt, T. (2001a). Amorphous geometry. In *European Conference on Artificial Life 2001*, (pp. 645-648).

D'Hondt, E., & D'Hondt, T. (2001b). Experiments in amorphous geometry. In *2001 International Conference on Artificial Intelligence* (pp. 285-290).

Dietrich, C. (2011). *Pymorphous: Python language extensions for spatial computing*. Retrieved from http://pymorphous.googlecode.com

Duckham, M., Nittel, S., & Worboys, M. (2005). Monitoring dynamic spatial fields using responsive geosensor networks. In *Proceedings of the 13th Annual ACM International Workshop on Geographic Information Systems (GIS '05)* (pp. 51-60). New York, NY: ACM.

Dunkels, A., Gronvall, B., & Voigt, T. (2004). Contiki-a lightweight and flexible operating system for tiny networked sensors. In *29th Annual IEEE International Conference on Local Computer Networks*, (pp. 455-462). IEEE.

Eckart, J. D. (1997). *Cellang: Language reference manual*. Radford University.

Engstrom, B. R., & Cappello, P. R. (1989). The SDEF programming system. *Journal of Parallel and Distributed Computing*, *7*(2), 201–231. doi:10.1016/0743-7315(89)90018-X

Erlang. (2011). *Erlang reference manual user's guide version 5.9*. Ericsson AB.

Ferscha, A., Hechinger, M., Riener, A., dos Santos Rocha, M., Zeidler, A., Franz, M., & Mayrhofer, R. (2008). Peer-it: Stick-on solutions for networks of things. *Pervasive and Mobile Computing*, *4*(3), 448–479. doi:10.1016/j.pmcj.2008.01.003

Finin, T., Fritzson, R., McKay, D., & McEntire, R. (1994). Kqml as an agent communication language. In *Proceedings of the Third International Conference on Information and Knowledge Management (CIKM '94)* (pp. 456-463). New York, NY: ACM.

Fok, C., Roman, G., & Lu, C. (2005). Rapid development and flexible deployment of adaptive wireless sensor network applications. In *Proceedings of the 25th IEEE International Conference on Distributed Computing Systems*, (pp. 653-662). IEEE.

Forrest, S., & Jones, T. (1994). Modeling complex adaptive systems with echo. *Complex systems: Mechanisms of adaptation* (pp. 3-21).

Frank, C., & Romer, K. (2005). Algorithms for generic role assignment in wireless sensor networks. In *Proceedings of the 3rd International Conference on Embedded Networked Sensor Systems* (pp. 230-242). ACM.

Friedman-Hill, E. (2008). *JESS, the rule engine for the Java platform*. Retrieved from http://herzberg.ca.sandia.gov/jess/

Freiwald, U., & Weimar, J. (2002). The java based cellular automata simulation system Jcasim. *Future Generation Computer Systems*, *18*, 995–1004. doi:10.1016/S0167-739X(02)00078-X

Gay, D., Levis, P., Von Behren, R., Welsh, M., Brewer, E., & Culler, D. (2003). The NesC language: A holistic approach to networked embedded systems. *ACM Sigplan Notices*, *38*(5), 1–11. doi:10.1145/780822.781133

Gayle, O., & Coore, D. (2006). Self-organizing text in an amorphous environment. In *International Conference on Complex Systems,* (pp. 1-10).

Gelernter, D., & Carriero, N. (1992). Coordination languages and their significance. *Communications of the ACM*, *35*(2), 97–107. doi:10.1145/129630.129635

George Mason University Evolutionary Computation Laboratory and Center for Social Complexity. (2011). *MASON multiagent simulation*. Retrieved from http://cs.gmu.edu/~eclab/projects/mason/

Giavitto, J.-L., Godin, C., Michel, O., & Zemyslaw Prusinkiewicz, P. (2002). *Computational models for integrative and developmental biology*. Technical Report 72-2002, Univerite d'Evry, LaMI.

Giavitto, J.-L., Michel, O., Cohen, J., & Spicher, A. (2004). *Computation in space and space in computation.* Technical Report 103-2004, Univerite d'Evry, LaMI.

Giavitto, J.-L., & Spicher, A. (2008). Topological rewriting and the geometrization of programming. *Physica D. Nonlinear Phenomena*, *237*(9), 1302–1314. doi:10.1016/j.physd.2008.03.039

Gillespie, D. T. (1977). Exact stochastic simulation of coupled chemical reactions. *Journal of Physical Chemistry*, *81*(25), 2340–2361. doi:10.1021/j100540a008

Gilpin, K., Kotay, K., Rus, D., & Vasilescu, I. (2008). Miche: Modular shape formation by self-disassembly. *The International Journal of Robotics Research*, *27*, 345–372. doi:10.1177/0278364907085557

Govett, M., Middlecoff, J., Hart, L., Henderson, T., & Schaffer, D. (2003). The scalable modeling system: Directive-based code parallelization for distributed and shared memory computers. *Parallel Computing*, *29*(8), 995–1020. doi:10.1016/S0167-8191(03)00084-X

Grelck, C., Penczek, F., & Trojahner, K. (2007). Caos: A domain-specific language for the parallel simulation of cellular automata. In *Parallel Computing Technologies, 9th International Conference (PaCT'07)* (pp. 410-417). Springer-Verlag.

Gropp, W., Lusk, E., & Skjellum, A. (1994). *Using MPI: Portable parallel programming with the message passing interface*. Cambridge, MA: MIT Press.

Grumbach, S., & Wang, F. (2010). *Netlog, a rule-based language for distributed programming* (pp. 88–103). Practical Aspects of Declarative Languages. doi:10.1007/978-3-642-11503-5_9

Gulyás, L., Kozsik, T., & Corliss, J. (1999). The multi-agent modelling language and the model design interface. *Journal of Artificial Societies and Social Simulation*, *2*(3), 8.

Gulyás, L., Kozsik, T., & Fazekas, S. (2011). *Multi-agent modeling language MAML*. Retrieved from http://www.maml.hu/

Gummadi, R., Gnawali, O., & Govindan, R. (2005). *Macro-programming wireless sensor networks using kairos* (pp. 466–466). Distributed Computing in Sensor Systems.

Hahn, C. (2008). A domain specific modeling language for multiagent systems. In *Proceedings of the 7th International Joint Conference on Autonomous Agents and Multiagent Systems-Volume 1* (pp. 233-240). International Foundation for Autonomous Agents and Multiagent Systems.

Hamann, H., Stradner, J., Schmickl, T., & Crailsheim, K. (2010). A hormone-based controller for evolutionary multi-modular robotics: from single modules to gait learning. In *IEEE Congress on Evolutionary Computation (CEC'10)* (pp. 244-251).

Heinzelman, W., Murphy, A., Carvalho, H., & Perillo, M. (2004). Middleware to support sensor network applications. *IEEE Network*, *18*(1), 6–14. doi:10.1109/MNET.2004.1265828

Helsinger, A., Thome, M., & Wright, T. (2004). Cougaar: A scalable, distributed multi-agent architecture. In *IEEE International Conference on Systems, Man and Cybernetics, Volume 2*, (pp. 1910-1917). IEEE.

Hnat, T., Sookoor, T., Hooimeijer, P., Weimer, W., & Whitehouse, K. (2008). Macrolab: A vector-based macroprogramming framework for cyber-physical systems. In *Proceedings of the 6th ACM Conference on Embedded Network Sensor Systems* (pp. 225-238). ACM.

Holzmann, C., & Ferscha, A. (2010). A framework for utilizing qualitative spatial relations between networked embedded systems. *Pervasive and Mobile Computing*, *6*(3), 362–381. doi:10.1016/j.pmcj.2010.03.001

HPF. (1997). *High performance Fortran language specification, Version 2.0*. High Performance Fortran Forum.

Huget, M. (2005). Modeling languages for multiagent systems. *Agent-Oriented Software Engineering (AOSE-2005)* (pp. 1-12).

Huzita, H., & Scimemi, B. (1989). The algebra of paper-folding. In *First International Meeting of Origami Science and Technology* (pp. 215-222).

IEEE. Computer Society. (2011). *Foundation for intelligent physical agents*. Retrieved from http://www.fipa.org/

Igarashi, A., Pierce, B. C., & Wadler, P. (2001). Featherweight Java: A minimal core calculus for Java and GJ. *ACM Transactions on Programming Languages and Systems, 23*(3), 396–450. doi:10.1145/503502.503505

Inchiosa, M., & Parker, M. (2002). Overcoming design and development challenges in agent-based modeling using ASCAPE. *Proceedings of the National Academy of Sciences of the United States of America, 99*(Suppl 3), 7304–7310. doi:10.1073/pnas.082081199

Jesshope, C., Lankamp, M., & Zhang, L. (2009). Evaluating cmps and their memory architecture. In *Proceedings the 22nd International Conference on Architecture of Computing Systems ARCS 2009, LNCS 5455*, (pp. 246-257).

Jones, T., & Forrest, S. (2011). *An introduction to SFI echo*. Retrieved from http://tuvalu.santafe.edu/ pth/echo/how-to/how-to.html

Jozwiak, L., Nedjah, N., & Figueroa, M. (2010). Modern development methods and tools for embedded reconfigurable systems: A survey. *Integration, the VLSI Journal, 43*(1), 1-33.

Kinny, D. (2002). The ψ calculus: An algebraic agent language. In J.-J. Meyer & M. Tambe (Eds.), *Intelligent Agents VIII, volume 2333 of Lecture Notes in Computer Science*, (pp. 32-50). Berlin, Germany: Springer.

Klavins, E., Ghrist, R., & Lipsky, D. (2006). A grammatical approach to self-organizing robotic systems. *IEEE Transactions on Automatic Control, 51*(6), 949–962. doi:10.1109/TAC.2006.876950

Kondacs, A. (2003). Biologically-inspired self-assembly of 2D shapes, using global-to-local compilation. In *International Joint Conference on Artificial Intelligence*, (pp. 633-638).

Kothari, N., Gummadi, R., Millstein, T., & Govindan, R. (2007). Reliable and efficient programming abstractions for wireless sensor networks. In *Proceedings of the 2007 ACM SIGPLAN Conference on Programming Language Design and Implementation*, (pp. 200-210). ACM.

Kulesza, U., Garcia, A., & Lucena, C. (2004). An aspect-oriented generative approach. In *Companion to the 19th Annual ACM SIGPLAN Conference on Object-Oriented Programming Systems, Languages, and Applications (OOPSLA '04)* (pp. 166-167). New York, NY: ACM.

Kulesza, U., Garcia, A., Lucena, C., & Alencar, P. (2005). A generative approach for multi-agent system development. *Software Engineering for Multi-Agent Systems, III*, 52–69. doi:10.1007/978-3-540-31846-0_4

Kwiatkowska, M., Norman, G., & Parker, D. (2011). PRISM 4.0: Verification of probabilistic real-time systems. In G. Gopalakrishnan & S. Qadeer (Eds.), *Proc. 23rd International Conference on Computer Aided Verification (CAV'11), volume 6806 of LNCS*, (pp. 585-591). Springer.

Lasser, C., Massar, J., Miney, J., & Dayton, L. (1988). *Starlisp reference manual*. Thinking Machines Corporation.

Levis, P., & Culler, D. (2002). Mate: a tiny virtual machine for sensor networks. In *ACM Sigplan Notices, 37*(10), 85-95.

Levis, P., Madden, S., Polastre, J., Szewczyk, R., Whitehouse, K., & Woo, A. … Brewer, E. (2005). Tinyos: An operating system for sensor networks. In *Ambient Intelligence*, (pp. 115-148).

Li, S., Lin, Y., Son, S., Stankovic, J., & Wei, Y. (2004). Event detection services using data service middleware in distributed sensor networks. *Telecommunication Systems*, *26*(2), 351–368. doi:10.1023/B:TELS.0000029046.79337.8f

Litovsky, I., Métivier, Y., & Zielonka, W. (1992). The power and the limitations of local computations on graphs. In *Workshop on Graph-Theoretic Concepts in Computer Science* (pp. 333-345).

Liu, J., Chu, M., Liu, J., Reich, J., & Zhao, F. (2003). State-centric programming for sensor-actuator network systems. *IEEE Pervasive Computing / IEEE Computer Society [and] IEEE Communications Society*, *2*(4), 50–62. doi:10.1109/MPRV.2003.1251169

Loo, B., Condie, T., Garofalakis, M., Gay, D., Hellerstein, J., & Maniatis, P. … Stoica, I. (2006). Declarative networking: Language, execution and optimization. In *Proceedings of the 2006 ACM SIGMOD International Conference on Management of Data* (pp. 97-108). ACM.

Lopes, N., Navarro, J., Rybalchenko, A., & Singh, A. (2010). Applying prolog to develop distributed systems. *Theory and Practice of Logic Programming*, *10*(4-6), 691–707. doi:10.1017/S1471068410000360

Luke, S., Cioffi-Revilla, C., Panait, L., & Sullivan, K. (2004). Mason: A new multi-agent simulation toolkit. In *Proceedings of the 2004 SwarmFest Workshop* (pp. 1-8).

Macal, C., & North, M. (2010). Tutorial on agent-based modelling and simulation. *Journal of Simulation*, *4*(3), 151–162. doi:10.1057/jos.2010.3

MacLennan, B. (1990). *Continuous spatial automata.* Technical Report Department of Computer Science Technical Report CS-90-121, University of Tennessee, Knoxville.

Madden, S. R., Szewczyk, R., Franklin, M. J., & Culler, D. (2002). Supporting aggregate queries over ad-hoc wireless sensor networks. In *Workshop on Mobile Computing and Systems Applications*, (pp. 49 – 58).

Mallavarapu, A., Thomson, M., Ullian, B., & Gunawardena, J. (2009). Programming with models: Modularity and abstraction provide powerful capabilities for systems biology. *Journal of the Royal Society, Interface*, *6*(32), 257–270. doi:10.1098/rsif.2008.0205

Mamei, M., & Zambonelli, F. (2008). Programming pervasive and mobile computing applications: The TOTA approach. *ACM Transactions on Software Engineering and Methodology, 18*(4), 15:1-15:56.

Margolus, N. (1993). CAM-8: A computer architecture based on cellular automata. In *American Mathematical Society, 6*(1) 167-187.

Martel, S., & Mohammadi, M. (2010). Using a swarm of self-propelled natural microrobots in the form of flagellated bacteria to perform complex micro-assembly tasks. In *Proceedings of the International Conference on Robotics and Automation (ICRA)* (pp. 500-505).

Martinoli, A., Easton, K., & Agassounon, W. (2004). Modeling of swarm robotic systems: A case study in collaborative distributed manipulation. *The International Journal of Robotics Research, 23*(4), 415–436. doi:10.1177/0278364904042197

Martinoli, A., Ijspeert, A. J., & Mondada, F. (1999). Understanding collective aggregation mechanisms: From probabilistic modelling to experiments with real robots. *Robotics & Autonomous Systems. Special Issue on Distributed Autonomous Robotic Systems, 29*, 51–63. doi:10.1016/S0921-8890(99)00038-X

Mernik, M., Heering, J., & Sloane, A. (2005). When and how to develop domain-specific languages. *ACM Computing Surveys, 37*(4), 316–344. doi:10.1145/1118890.1118892

Michalakes, J. (1994). *RSL: A parallel runtime system library for regular grid finite difference models using multiple nests.* Technical Report ANL/MCS-TM-197, Argonne National Laboratory.

Michalakes, J. (1997). *FLIC: A translator for same-source parallel implementation of regular grid applications*. Technical Report ANL/MCS-TM-223, Argonne National Laboratory.

Milner, R. (1999). *Communicating and mobile systems: The Pi-calculus*. Cambridge University Press.

Minar, N., Burkhart, R., Langton, C., & Askenazi, M. (1996). *The swarm simulation system, a toolkit for building multi-agent simulations.* Technical Report Working Paper 96-06-042, Santa Fe Institute.

Mirschel, S., Steinmetz, K., Rempel, M., Ginkel, M., & Gilles, E. D. (2009). Promot: Modular modeling for systems biology. *Bioinformatics (Oxford, England), 25*(5), 687–689. doi:10.1093/bioinformatics/btp029

Mishra, M., Callahan, T., Chelcea, T., Venkataramani, G., Budiu, M., & Goldstein, S. (2006). Tartan: Evaluating spatial computation for whole program execution. In *Proceedings of 12th ACM International Conference on Architecture Support for Programming Languages and Operating Systems (ASPLOS 2006)* (pp. 163-174).

MIT Media Lab and Schellar Teacher Education Program. (2011). *Starlogo*. Retrieved from http://education.mit.edu/starlogo/

Proto, M. I. T. (Retrieved November 22, 2010). *MIT Proto*. Retrieved from http://proto.bbn.com/

Montagna, S., Viroli, M., Risoldi, M., Pianini, D., & Di Marzo Serugendo, G. (2011). Self-organising pervasive ecosystems: A crowd evacuation example. In *3rd International Workshop on Software Engineering for Resilient Systems, volume 6968 of Lecture Notes in Computer Science*, (pp. 115-129). Springer.

Moss, S., Gaylard, H., Wallis, S., & Edmonds, B. (1998). SDML: A multi-agent language for organizational modelling. *Computational & Mathematical Organization Theory, 4*, 43–69. doi:10.1023/A:1009600530279

Mottola, L., & Picco, G. (2006). *Logical neighborhoods: A programming abstraction for wireless sensor networks* (pp. 150–168). Distributed Computing in Sensor Systems. doi:10.1007/11776178_10

Mottola, L., & Picco, G. (2011). Programming wireless sensor networks: Fundamental concepts and state of the art. *ACM Computing Surveys, 43*(3), 19–75. doi:10.1145/1922649.1922656

MPI2. (2009). *MPI: A message-passing interface standard version 2.2*. Message Passing Interface Forum.

Mucci, C., Campi, F., Brunelli, C., & Nurmi, J. (2007). Programming tools for reconfigurable processors. In Nurmi, J. (Ed.), *System-On-Chip Computing for ASICs and FPGAs on Processor Design* (pp. 427–446). Springer.

Myers, C., Barker, N., Jones, K., Kuwahara, H., Madsen, C., & Nguyen, N. (2009). iBioSim: A tool for the analysis and design of genetic circuits. *Bioinformatics (Oxford, England), 25*, 2848–2849. doi:10.1093/bioinformatics/btp457

Nagpal, R. (2001). *Programmable self-assembly: Constructing global shape using biologically-inspired local interactions and origami mathematics*. PhD thesis, MIT.

Newton, R., Morrisett, G., & Welsh, M. (2007). The regiment macroprogramming system. In *Proceedings of the 6th International Conference on Information Processing in Sensor Networks* (pp. 489-498). ACM.

Newton, R., & Welsh, M. (2004). Region streams: Functional macroprogramming for sensor networks. In *First International Workshop on Data Management for Sensor Networks (DMSN)* (pp. 78-87).

Nguyen, D. N., Usbeck, K., Mongan, W. M., Cannon, C. T., Lass, R. N., Salvage, J., & Regli, W. C. (2010). A methodology for developing an agent systems reference architecture. In *11th International Workshop on Agent-Oriented Software Engineering* (pp. 177-188).

North, M., Howe, T., Collier, N., & Vos, J. (2007). A declarative model assembly infrastructure for verification and validation. In *The First World Congress on Advancing Social Simulation* (pp. 129-140). Springer Japan.

Odell, J., Parunak, H., & Bauer, B. (1999). Extending UML for agents. In *Agent-Oriented Systems Workshop at the 17th National Conference on Artificial Intelligence* (pp. 3-17). AAAI Press.

Open, C. L. (2011). *The OpenCL specification, version 1.2*. Khronos OpenCL Working Group.

Open, M. P. (2011). *OpenMP application program interface version 3.1*. OpenMP Architecture Review Board.

Palmer, J., & Steele, J. G. L. (1992). Connection machine model cm-5 system overview. In *Fourth Symposium on the Frontiers of Massively Parallel Computation* (pp. 474-483). IEEE Press.

Pathak, A., Mottola, L., Bakshi, A., Prasanna, V., & Picco, G. (2007). Expressing sensor network interaction patterns using data-driven macroprogramming. In *Proceedings of the Fifth IEEE International Conference on Pervasive Computing and Communications Workshops* (pp. 255-260). IEEE Computer Society.

Paun, G. (2000). Computing with membranes. *Journal of Computer and System Sciences*, *61*(1), 108–143. doi:10.1006/jcss.1999.1693

Paun, G. (2002). *Membrane computing: An introduction*. Springer.

Pauty, J., Couderc, P., Banatre, M., & Berbers, Y. (2007). Geo-linda: a geometry aware distributed tuple space. In *IEEE 21st International Conference on Advanced Networking and Applications (AINA '07)* (pp. 370-377).

Pedersen, M., & Phillips, A. (2009). Towards programming languages for genetic engineering of living cells. *Journal of the Royal Society, Interface*, *6*, S437–S450. doi:10.1098/rsif.2008.0516.focus

Pierce, B. C., & Turner, D. N. (2000). Pict: a programming language based on the pi-calculus. In Plotkin, G. D., Stirling, C., & Tofte, M. (Eds.), *Proof, language, and interaction, essays in honour of Robin Milner* (pp. 455–494). The MIT Press.

Pierro, A. D., Hankin, C., & Wiklicky, H. (2005). Continuous-time probabilistic klaim. *Electronic Notes in Theoretical Computer Science*, *128*(5), 27–38. doi:10.1016/j.entcs.2004.11.040

Pokahr, A., Braubach, L., & Lamersdorf, W. (2003). Jadex: Implementing a BDI-infrastructure for jade agents. *EXP-in Search of Innovation*, *3*(3), 76–85.

Pressey, C. (Retrieved Feb 20, 2012). *The alpaca meta-language*. Retrieved from http://catseye.tc/projects/alpaca/

Priami, C. (1995). Stochastic pi-calculus. *The Computer Journal, 38*(7), 578–589. doi:10.1093/comjnl/38.7.578

Prorok, A., Correll, N., & Martinoli, A. (2011). Multi-level spatial models for swarm-robotic systems. *The International Journal of Robotics Research. Special Issue on Stochasticity in Robotics and Biological Systems, 30*(5), 574–589.

Prusinkiewicz, P., & Lindenmayer, A. (1990). *The algorithmic beauty of plants*. New York, NY: Springer-Verlag. doi:10.1007/978-1-4613-8476-2

Raimbault, F., & Lavenier, D. (1993). Relacs for systolic programming. In *International Conference on Application-Specific Array Processors* (pp. 132-135).

Rao, A., & Georgeff, M. (1995). BDI agents: From theory to practice. In *Proceedings of the First International Conference on Multi-Agent Systems (ICMAS-95)* (pp. 312-319).

Regli, W. C., Mayk, I., Dugan, C. J., Kopena, J. B., Lass, R. N., & Modi, P. J. (2009). Development and specification of a reference model for agent-based systems. *Transactions on Systems Man and Cybernetics, 39*(Part C), 572–596. doi:10.1109/TSMCC.2009.2020507

Rejimon, T., & Bhanja, S. (2005). Scalable probabilistic computing models using bayesian networks. In *48th Midwest Symposium on Circuits and Systems* (pp. 712-715).

Repast Team. (2011). *The repast suite*. Retrieved from http://repast.sourceforge.net/index.html

Resnick, M. (1996). Starlogo: An environment for decentralized modeling and decentralized thinking. In *Conference Companion on Human Factors in Computing Systems: Common Ground* (pp. 11-12). ACM.

Rus, D., Butler, Z. J., Kotay, K., & Vona, M. (2002). Self-reconfiguring robots. *Communications of the ACM, 45*(3), 39–45. doi:10.1145/504729.504752

Rus, D., & Vona, M. (2001). Crystalline robots: Self-reconfiguration with compressible unit modules. *Autonomous Robots, 10*(1), 107–124. doi:10.1023/A:1026504804984

Russell, S., Norvig, P., Canny, J., Malik, J., & Edwards, D. (1995). *Artificial intelligence: A modern approach*. Englewood Cliffs, NJ: Prentice Hall.

Saraswat, V., Bloom, B., Peshansky, I., Tardieu, O., & Grove, D. (2012). *X10 language specification version 2.2*. Yorktown Heights, NY: IBM.

Schultz, U., Bordignon, M., Christensen, D., & Stoy, K. (2008). Spatial computing with labels. In *Spatial Computing Workshop* (pp. 326 – 331).

Schultz, U. P., Christensen, D. J., & Stoy, K. (2007). A domain-specific language for programming self-reconfigurable robots. In *Workshop on Automatic Program Generation for Embedded Systems (APGES)* (pp. 28-36).

Shen, C., Srisathapornphat, C., & Jaikaeo, C. (2001). Sensor information networking architecture and applications. *IEEE Personal Communications, 8*(4), 52–59. doi:10.1109/98.944004

Shen, W.-M., Will, P., Galstyan, A., & Chuong, C. (2004). Hormone-inspired self-organization and distributed control of robotic swarms. *Autonomous Robots, 17*(1), 93–105. doi:10.1023/B:AURO.0000032940.08116.f1

Sklar, E. (2007). Netlogo, a multi-agent simulation environment. *Artificial Life, 13*(3), 303–311. doi:10.1162/artl.2007.13.3.303

Smith, L. P., Bergmann, F. T., Chandran, D., & Sauro, H. M. (2009). Antimony: A modular model definition language. *Bioinformatics (Oxford, England), 25*(18), 2452–2454. doi:10.1093/bioinformatics/btp401

Spezzano, G., & Talia, D. (1997). A high-level cellular programming model for massively parallel processing. In *2nd Int'l Workshop on High-Level Programming Models and Supportive Environments (HIPS'97)* (pp. 55-63).

Stoy, K., & Nagpal, R. (2004). Self-repair through scale independent self-reconfiguration. In *Proceedings of the IEEE/RSJ International Conference on Intelligent Robots and Systems* (pp. 2062-2067).

Sugihara, R., & Gupta, R. (2008). Programming models for sensor networks: A survey. *ACM Transactions on Sensor Networks, 4*(2), 8:1-8:29.

Swanson, S., Schwerin, A., Mercaldi, M., Petersen, A., Putnam, A., Michelson, K., … Eggers, S. J. (2007). The wavescalar architecture. *ACM Transactions on Computing Systems, 25*(2), 4:1-4:54.

Szymanski, M., & Woern, H. (2007). JaMOS - A MDL2ε based operating system for swarm micro robotics. In *Proceedings of the 2007 IEEE Swarm Intelligence Symposium* (pp. 324 – 331).

Taylor, M. B., Kim, J., Miller, J., Wentzlaff, D., Ghodrat, F., & Greenwald, B. (2002). The raw microprocessor: A computational fabric for software circuits and general purpose programs. *IEEE Micro, 22*(2), 25–35. doi:10.1109/MM.2002.997877

Telecom Italia Lab. (2011). *JADE - Java Agent DEvelopment framework*. Retrieved from http://jade.tilab.com/

The Klavins Lab. (2012). *Gro: The cell programming language*. University of Washington. Retrieved from http://depts.washington.edu/soslab/gro/

Thies, W., Karczmarek, M., Gordon, M., Maze, D., Wong, J., Hoffmann, H., & Brown, M. (2001). *Streamit: A compiler for streaming applications*. Technical Report MIT-LCS Technical Memo TM-622, Massachusetts Institute of Technology.

Tobis, M. (2005). Pynsol: Objects as scaffolding. *Computing in Science & Engineering, 7*(4), 84–91. doi:10.1109/MCSE.2005.78

Toffoli, T., & Margolus, N. (1987). *Cellular Automata Machines: A new environment for modeling*. MIT Press.

Trencansky, I., & Cervenka, R. (2005). Agent modeling language (AML): A comprehensive approach to modeling MAS. *Informatica Ljubljana, 29*(4), 391.

University of Michigan Center for the Study of Complex Systems. (2011). *Swarm development wiki.* Retrieved from http://www.swarm.org/index.php/Main_Page

Usbeck, K., & Beal, J. (2011). An agent framework for agent societies. In *Proceedings of the Compilation of the Co-Located Workshops on DSM'11, TMC'11, AGERE!'11 at Systems, Programming, Languages and Applications: Software for Humanity* (pp. 201-212).

Viroli, M., Casadei, M., Montagna, S., & Zambonelli, F. (2011a). Spatial coordination of pervasive services through chemical-inspired tuple spaces. *ACM Transactions on Autonomous and Adaptive Systems, 6*(2), 14:1 - 14:24.

Viroli, M., Nardini, E., Castelli, G., Mamei, M., & Zambonelli, F. (2011b). A coordination approach to spatially-situated pervasive service ecosystems. In G. Fortino, A. Garro, L. Palopoli, W. Russo, & G. Spezzano (Eds.), *WOA 2011 - XII Workshop Nazionale "Dagli Oggetti agli Agenti", volume 741 of CEUR Workshop Proceedings*, (pp. 19-27). Sun SITE Central Europe, RWTH Aachen University.

Walter, J., Welch, J., & Amato, N. (2004). Distributed reconfiguration of metamorphic robot chains. *Distributed Computing, 17*, 171–189. doi:10.1007/s00446-003-0103-y

Weiss, R. (2001). *Cellular computation and communications using engineered genetic regular networks*. PhD thesis, MIT.

Welsh, M., & Mainland, G. (2004). Programming sensor networks using abstract regions. In *Proceedings of the First USENIX/ACM Symposium on Networked Systems Design and Implementation (NSDI '04)* (pp. 3-17).

Werfel, J. (2006). *Anthills built to order: Automating construction with artificial swarms*. PhD thesis. Cambridge, MA: MIT Press.

Werfel, J., Bar-Yam, Y., & Nagpal, R. (2005). Building patterned structures with robot swarms. In *International Joint Conference on Artificial Intelligence* (pp. 1495—1502).

Werfel, J., & Nagpal, R. (2007). Collective construction of environmentally-adaptive structures. In *2007 IEEE/RSJ International Conference on Intelligent Robots and Systems (IROS 2007)* (pp. 2345 – 2352). IEEE.

Whitehouse, K., Sharp, C., Brewer, E., & Culler, D. (2004). Hood: A neighborhood abstraction for sensor networks. In *Proceedings of the 2nd International Conference on Mobile Systems, Applications, and Services* (pp. 99-110). ACM Press.

Wilensky, U. (2011). *Netlogo*. Retrieved from http://ccl.northwestern.edu/netlogo/

Yamins, D. (2007). *A theory of local-to-global algorithms for one-dimensional spatial multi-agent systems*. PhD thesis, Harvard, Cambridge, MA, USA.

Yang, C., Wu, H., Huang, Q., Li, Z., & Li, J. (2011). Using spatial principles to optimize distributed computing for enabling the physical science discoveries. [PNAS]. *Proceedings of the National Academy of Sciences of the United States of America, 108*(14), 5498–5503. doi:10.1073/pnas.0909315108

Yao, Y., & Gehrke, J. (2002). The cougar approach to in-network query processing in sensor networks. *SIGMOD Record, 31*(3), 9–18. doi:10.1145/601858.601861

Yim, M., Shen, W., Salemi, B., Rus, D., Moll, M., & Lipson, H. (2007). Modular self-reconfigurable robot systems: Grand challenges of robotics. *Robotics & Automation Magazine, IEEE, 14*(1), 43–52. doi:10.1109/MRA.2007.339623

Zambonelli, F., & Viroli, M. (2011). A survey on nature-inspired metaphors for pervasive service ecosystems. *International Journal of Pervasive Computing and Communications, 7*(3), 186–204. doi:10.1108/17427371111172997

Zimmermann, H. (1980). OSI reference model-the ISO model of architecture for open systems interconnection. *IEEE Transactions on Communications, 28*(4), 425–432. doi:10.1109/TCOM.1980.1094702

ADDITIONAL READING

Beal, J., Phillips, A., Densmore, D., & Cai, Y. (2011b). High-level programming languages for bio-molecular systems. In Koeppl, H., Densmore, D., di Bernardo, M., & Setti, G. (Eds.), *Design and analysis of bio-molecular circuits* (pp. 225–252). Springer. doi:10.1007/978-1-4419-6766-4_11

KEY TERMS AND DEFINITIONS

Abstract Device Layer: Abstraction that hides details of the device where a program is executing.

Device Abstraction Languages: Spatial computing DSLs that simplify aggregate programming by hiding details but without much power in the way of spatial abstractions.

General Purpose Spatial Languages: Languages that provide a wide range of powerful spatial abstractions for aggregate programming, but typically require more work to apply to any particular domain.

Global-to-Local Compilation: Transformation of a program for an aggregate of devices into a program that can execute on individual devices.

Information Movement Languages: Spatial computing DSLs that focus on gathering information in one region of space-time and delivering it to another region, typically at the expense of more general computation.

Pattern Languages: Spatial computing DSLs that focus on construction of patterns over space, typically at the expense of more general computation.

Physical Platform: The actual computing device where a program is executed.

Space-Time Operations: Aggregate programming abstractions falling into one of five categories: measurement of space-time, computation of patterns over space-time, manipulation of space-time, physical evolution, and meta-operations.

Spatial Computer: A collection of local computational devices distributed through a physical space, in which the difficulty of moving information between any two devices is strongly dependent on the distance between them, and the "functional goals" of the system are generally defined in terms of the system's spatial structure.

System Management Layer: Mechanisms that provide low-level "operating system" services, such as real-time process management, sensor and actuator drivers, or low-level networking.

Chapter 17
DSLs in Action with Model Based Approaches to Information System Development

Ivan Luković
University of Novi Sad, Serbia

Slavica Aleksić
University of Novi Sad, Serbia

Vladimir Ivančević
University of Novi Sad, Serbia

Milan Čeliković
University of Novi Sad, Serbia

ABSTRACT

*In this chapter, the authors give an overview of the evolution of Information System (IS) development methods used in the last few decades and show how model driven approaches and Domain Specific Languages (DSLs) have managed to take an often essential role in the modern IS development process. To present an overall picture, the authors discuss significant breakthroughs, popular approaches, their strong and weak points, along with the examples of their practical use in the domain of IS development and generation of software applications. In order to further support the aforementioned points, the chapter offers a synopsis of Integrated Information Systems CASE Tool (IIS*Case), a model driven software development tool for IS modeling and prototype generation. A special attention is drawn to its evolution and position relative to some of the key changes in IS development approaches in recent history. The authors highlight the significance of DSLs in this context and present a DSL featured in the tool. The DSL was created to provide platform independent model (PIM) IS specifications which can be transformed into executable application prototypes through a chain of model-to-model and model-to-code transformations. Since the authors have developed both a textual DSL, and visual repository-based tools (visual DSLs) for this purpose, a discussion of pros and contras of textual vs. visual DSLs in the context of creating PIM specifications is also included. Furthermore, the chapter communicates practical experiences about creating meta-meta models of PIM concepts by means of attribute grammars and MOF meta-modeling language.*

DOI: 10.4018/978-1-4666-2092-6.ch017

INTRODUCTION

As the information technology constantly grows and evolves, new possibilities for its incorporation in ISs continue to appear. Although this enriches those systems with novel capabilities, "optimal" methods and techniques to develop an IS are still far from obvious. There are many ways and approaches that may be deployed to improve the process of IS development. Our focus is on the usage of DSLs based on model driven approaches. Through our research, we have created a textual language aimed at modeling PIM specifications of an IS. Our research goals are to couple it with Integrated Information Systems CASE Tool (IIS*Case). IIS*Case is a model driven software development tool that provides IS modeling and prototype generation. At the level of PIM specifications, IIS*Case provides conceptual modeling of database schemas and business applications. Starting from such PIM models as a source, a chain of model-to-model and model-to-code transformations is performed in IIS*Case to obtain executable program code of software applications and database scripts for a selected target platform.

One of the main motives for developing IIS*Case is in the following. For many years, the most favorable conceptual data model is widely-used Entity-Relationship (ER) data model. A typical scenario of a database schema design process provided by majority of existing CASE tools is to create an ER database schema first and then transform it into the relational database schema. Such a scenario has many advantages, but also there are serious disadvantages (Luković, 2009). Deploying IS design methodologies based on the techniques such as ER modeling or general purpose family of languages UML, and even the relational data model and an appropriate CASE tool, requires advanced knowledge, skills, and high perception power. Failing to find an appropriate number of designers that possess these properties may lead to a risk of designing poor quality ISs (Kosar et al., 2010). Besides, these methods and techniques are often incomprehensible to end-users. In practice, that may lead to problems in communication and to misunderstanding between designers and end-users. As a rule, misunderstanding results in a poorly-designed database schema or a software application, because support of all the specified user requirements is not ensured. Usually, both designers and end-users become aware of that too late, when the database schema or a software application is already implemented.

To overcome these disadvantages, we created an alternative approach and related techniques that were mainly based on the usage of model driven software development (MDSD) (Bézivin, 2004) and DSL paradigms (Deursen et al., 2000; Mernik et al., 2005). The main idea was to provide the necessary PIM meta-level concepts to IS designers, so that they can easily model semantics in an application domain. Afterward, they may utilize a number of formal methods and complex algorithms to produce database schema specifications and IS executable code, without any considerable expert knowledge.

In order to provide design of various PIM models by IIS*Case, we created a number of modeling, meta-level concepts and formal rules that are used in the design process. In the following text we name all these concepts and rules as IIS*Case Meta-model. In early stages of our research, we formally specified IIS*Case Meta-model by means of predicate calculus formulas, and additionally described its semantics in a form of free text (Mogin et al., 1994). Later on, we also developed and embedded into IIS*Case visual and repository based tools (visual DSLs) that fully apply IIS*Case Meta-model. They assisted designers in creating formally valid models and their storing as repository definitions in a guided way.

Apart from having IIS*Case Meta-model represented as repository definitions, there is a strong need to have its equivalent representation given in a platform independent way. By this, it becomes fully independent of repository definitions that typically may include some implementation details. Our current research is based on two related approaches to formally describe IIS*Case Meta-model. One of them is based on Meta-Object Facility (MOF) ("MOF," 2011), as it is discussed in Čeliković et al. (2011), and the other one on a textual DSL (Luković et al., 2011). A benefit of introducing a MOF based representation of IIS*Case Meta-model is providing software documentation in formal way. Besides, created meta-model can be used for the IIS*Case tool verification in EMF environment. Finally, and even more important, is that it also represents a domain analysis specification necessary to create IIS*CDesLang – a textual DSL representation of IIS*Case Meta-model. IIS*CDesLang is also aimed at creating PIM project specifications that may be later transformed into the other specifications, and finally to programs.

In this book chapter, we first summarize significant breakthroughs in recent IS development approaches with a special attention given to MDA and the role which DSLs have in such a context. This review attempts to show how ideas typical for different periods managed to supplement each other and how they present a single thread continuing to the present. A motivation to create such an extensive overview of various IS development approaches is to better recognize a scope of our research, as well as related research works, and locate them in a long-lasting evolution of a diverse of IS development processes and approaches. Although we found a lot of references different in its nature about the history of IS development process, MDSD approaches and applications of DSLs in various problem domains, we could not find much about a systematic overview of MDSD and DSL applications specific just to the IS development process. On the other hand, we believe that the existence of such an overview coupled with a short presentation of history of various approaches may be helpful for researchers in positioning their recent researches in this area, as well as for practitioners in recognizing the current trends in IS development process.

Furthermore, we describe how IIS*Case evolved in such circumstances and present in brief both a MOF based specification of IIS*Case Meta-model, and IIS*CDesLang. On the basis of such a presentation, our goal is to present in the two concluding sections what our future research plans are. In that way, this chapter may be seen as a manifesto of wider future trends and directions of our approach, IIS*Case tool, IIS*Case Meta-model, and IIS*CDesLang.

TOWARD IS DEVELOPMENT BASED ON MDA AND DSLS

Numerous IS development approaches have been formulated in the last few decades. Nowadays, however, it is not uncommon for many updated versions of the old methods to be still in use. The community has embraced new ideas while keeping its favorite techniques from the past. In spite of the paradigm shifts brought by MDA and the recent popularity of DSLs, IS designers still spend much of their time conceptually modeling a real system, only managing to speed up the development of an IS by relying on code generation and use of more specialized languages, albeit with certain trade-offs. In the rest of this section, we divide the recent evolution of IS development into three historical phases according to the important transitions which happened in software engineering and were caused by the general acceptance of fundamental principles of MDA and DSLs. In addition to the description of approaches typical for these periods, there is a summary of advantages and disadvantages of their representative methods. It is further shown that the aforementioned changes although radical in some aspects are primarily evolutional and usually fit well into approaches and frameworks created prior to their emergence. The greatest attention is given to DSLs, as the most recent set of ideas which often attempt to utilize the previously popular methods and the benefits these might offer. Although the notion of DSL is of a relatively recent origin, languages which could be put into this category have existed for a long time, especially in the IS domain. However, we do not attempt to reduce the term to the confines of a language and its development process, but strive to exemplify how DSLs can influence software engineering and IS development in a broader sense.

Traditional IS Development

Issues of IS development do not revolve solely around the technology used – there are also numerous problems related to business, organizational, and sociological aspects of such a venture. Taking into account a broad view of an IS, Hirschheim & Klein (1989) identified IS development paradigms defined by the four possible combinations between the dimensions of: (i) order-conflict, emphasizing the stability or change of the social world, and (ii) objectivist-subjectivist, emphasizing the possibility or impossibility of studying the social world using objective methods of natural science. Although the IIS*Case tool might appear to favor the functionalist view (order and objectivist), which presumes that a system models reality, it is not restricted to a single paradigm because it supports prototyping and does not require expert users. These capabilities allow an easy generation of revised system while future users may participate in the construction process if needed.

Problems encountered in IS development, together with their solutions, motivated formulation of a discipline on the engineering of IS development methods and tools known as method engineering (Brinkkemper, 1996). Nowadays, almost all of the widely used methods in IS development are model-based. One of the particularly prominent phases in a typical IS development is conceptual modeling (CM) which is expected to produce a representation of a real world system using selected PIM concepts. In the research on CM, four important elements were identified by Wand & Weber (2002): CM grammars (sets of constructs and associated combination rules), CM methods (application of grammars), CM scripts (modeling products), and the modeling context. An interesting twist in this kind of modeling was the creation of an ontological model of an IS, also done by Wand & Weber (1990). Instead of representing real world entities which an IS should model, they built a formal IS model comprised of states, events, systems, subsystems, and other concepts. Similarly, for IIS*Case there is a metamodel featuring IS concepts essential for the IS perspective offered by the tool.

One taxonomy of IS modeling techniques was proposed by Giaglis (2001). He reviewed some of the popular IS modeling techniques (data flow diagramming, ER diagramming, state transition diagramming, IDEF1x, and UML) and categorized them according to their breadth (modeling goals and objectives) and depth (offered perspectives). Since data are essential for any IS, there are a vast number of data and database specification notations. As these notations deal with a domain of data modeling, they can be regarded as domain specific modeling languages (DSMLs). Some of the well-known methods include the use of hierarchical model, ER model proposed by Chen (1976) with its subsequent extended versions, relational data model (Codd, 1970), and object-oriented models.

The increased dependence on CM in IS development has added various benefits, but at the same time it has brought up new issues. One of the advantages of CM is that it makes the collaboration between developers and users smoother since this approach allows the creation of an environment where end-users can better understand the system being developed and even contribute by doing some of the modeling themselves. Although this kind of modeling makes the initial development phases more open and understandable to an average user, expert modelers should not be excluded from the design process. For example, in a study done by Shanks (1997), it was concluded that "data models built by expert data modelers are more correct, complete, innovative, flexible and better understood than those built by novices" (p. 71). Furthermore, conceptual modeling is considered to be difficult in practice and, for that reason, it should be aided with the reuse of conceptual models (vom Brocke & Buddendick, 2006) in addition to the reliance on expert modelers. Some of the general recommendations on modeling collected in the Guidelines of Modeling (GoM) by Schuette & Rotthowe (1998) are concerned with the suitability of the language used to create models, model clarity, and comparability.

Emergence of MDA and MDE

An important event in the history of software development methods was the introduction of Model Driven Architecture (MDA) by the Object Management Group (OMG). MDA can be regarded as a software development framework focused on the creation of PIMs, which are unaware of implementation technology. Through automated transformation procedures, Platform Specific Models (PSMs) are generated from PIMs. A PSM is closely linked to a particular technology and used as a basis for the generation of a matching program code. In this manner, a complete software application can be generated using a chain of model transformations which starts from a single PIM. Therefore, a developer is expected to build just a PIM, while the rest of the creation process is done by the available transformation procedures.

Vara et al. (2009) proposed a model driven approach for automatic development of object-relational (OR) database schemas. Starting from a PIM in the form of a UML class diagram, a PSM (OR model) is created through a model transformation and finally SQL code is generated in a model-text transformation from the PSM. Gudas & Lopata (2007) demonstrated how knowledge-based IS development may support use case modeling by leveraging knowledge present in enterprise meta-model and enterprise model of a particular domain. By relying on mappings of enterprise meta-model elements to elements of various use case meta-models, use case models can be generated from particular elements of an enterprise model. An included benefit of the method is that it verifies user requirements specifications against the domain knowledge. Another example of an approach that follows a logic similar to the one presented in MDA is the OO-Method for IS modeling and development (Pastor et al., 2001). It is an object-oriented (OO) approach which starts from a set of system requirements defined in three different types of conceptual models: object, dynamic, and functional. These models are automatically transformed into a formal OO specification which is further mapped into an implementation in one of the OO programming languages, thus creating an IS in accordance with the requirements. Similarly, in IIS*Case, a system development starts from a PIM which represents a base for system generation done through model transformations and code generation. Final products include executable code and associated database scripts for the selected platform (Luković et al., 2007; Luković et al., 2008).

A term often coupled with MDA is Model Driven Engineering (MDE). It is described as a "promising approach to address platform complexity—and the inability of third-generation languages to alleviate this complexity and express domain concepts effectively" (Schmidt, 2006, pp. 26-27) which combines DSMLs with corresponding transformation engines and generators. According to this vision, MDE should include more of the higher abstractions and help make the software process easier. It is a broad term which includes MDA but is not restricted only to that.

The benefits of utilizing the MDA approach should include improved developer productivity, portability of generated software, cross-platform interoperability, and the facilitation of software documenting and maintenance (Kleppe et al., 2003). Nevertheless, MDA is also criticized for its allegedly overambitious, if not unattainable, objectives. Some of the fundamental difficulties include the issue of support for PSMs targeted at complex platforms, necessity of constant updating to the latest platform version, and battling the complexity of modern multilayered applications (Thomas, 2004). One possible solution to these problems could be a greater reliance on domain oriented programming (DOP) languages which "allow the domain developer to map domain abstractions into DOP abstractions" (Thomas & Barry, 2003, p. 2) and serve as a base for DSL implementation. In the similar manner, Kelly (2005) argued that the main focus in MDA is on UML which does not capture the important domain expertise usually already present in organizations. He stated that a key to the further improvement of developer productivity lies in the application of domain specific modeling (DSM) which could produce models to be used as starting points for automatic code generation. MDA proponents consider the capabilities of UML profiles powerful enough for effective domain (or platform) customization of UML (Fuentes-Fernández & Vallecillo-Moreno, 2004). In addition to that, it is possible to create completely new meta-models using MOF if required. One of the implementations of such approach is presented in Perišić et al. (2011).

Ideas and practical solutions presented in the previous paragraph clearly illustrate that even with the value added by employing MDA, complexity issues continue to arise, thus requiring the application of DSLs to battle these problems through a better inclusion of domain knowledge in software process. Such a union of two paradigms is not only mutually beneficial, but it also represents the next logical step in the evolution of IS development methods.

DSLs in IS Development

There are many examples of DSLs being used in different software development phases and contexts relevant to IS development: specification and generation of software connectors between software components (Bureš et al., 2008), integration of heterogeneous systems (Frantz et al., 2008; Milanović et al., 2009), communication between heterogeneous health information systems (Menezes et al., 2010), specification and generation of data mappings (Grundy et al., 2004), specification of the structure of database applications (Dejanović et al., 2010a), etc. Software architecture is another domain for which many DSLs exist. Some of the architecture description languages (ADLs) are AADL, Acme, Aesop, Darwin, and Wright. Djukić et al. (2011) introduced DSLs in the process of document formal specification and rendering in directory publishing. They have developed four languages for modeling: a) small advertisements, b) appropriate documents, c) workflow control, and d) layout patterns. They developed an integrated meta-model of four DSLs named DVDocLang. The presented DSLs were developed by means of MetaEdit+ language workbench. For the development of kiosk applications, a Kiosk Specification Language (KSL) was developed by Živanov et al. (2008). It is a textual DSL which attempts to hide all the redundant implementation details of touch-screen kiosk applications and hence make the process less error-prone. From a textual specification in KSL, a kiosk application is generated using a template application for a particular platform. In this approach, new target platforms can be made available by adding corresponding templates.

Besides being employed for conceptual modeling, DSLs have additional roles in ISs operating in various domains. For instance, they can be used in enterprise information systems (EIS). Freudenthal (2010b) pointed out that an EIS is usually "shallow but wide" which entails the need for the inclusion of different DSLs and one general-purpose language so the EIS could possess required functionality. However, he noted that this approach requires dealing with the issues of DSL versioning and deployment of DSL programs in the context of an EIS. A conducted evaluation of available DSL tools demonstrated that, at the moment, there is no such set of DSL tools that could support all the requirements for the process of DSL integration into an EIS. In a like manner, a DSL can be used in a customs IS for specifying document verification rules (Freudenthal, 2010a). In the domain of hospital information systems (HISs), there is the Revised Three-layer Graph-based Meta Model (3LGM^2) and the associated tool (Wendt et al., 2004; Winter et al., 2003). The meta-model was created using UML to support three interconnected layers: domain, logical tool, and physical tool layer. Using the tool, information managers can create HIS model in compliance with the 3LGM^2.

Integration of MDA and DSLs in a single approach has been repeatedly proved worthwhile. One example of this kind of a combination is the development of repository-based Eclipse plugins (Sivonen, 2008). These plugins can be described using a specially developed DSML which supports all the concepts essential for this particular domain. Actual plugins are generated from models created in this DSML and represent products of a specially written code generator. Therefore, in order to obtain a plugin, a developer only has to build a model of that plugin. Similarly, Bicevskis et al. (2011) created a DSML for business process modeling (BPM) in which a model consists of three types of diagrams: business process (BP), information system, and customer service diagrams. IS diagrams are primarily intended to be used by IS developers, and, therefore, have more graphical symbols than BP diagrams. A higher level of detail in IS diagrams is needed for the automatic translation of models into executable code.

In IS development, greater reliance on DSLs in MDE approach could even be considered a necessity. For example, model transformation languages are essential for model based IS development. Some of the numerous languages belonging to the aforementioned group include: ATL Transformation Language (ATL), Query/View/Transformation (QVT), Kermeta – meta-model engineering language which supports model transformations, Tefkat, etc. Although they support model transforming, there are efforts to create even more specific languages that would be restricted to the transformation of models belonging to a particular domain. These languages are known as domain specific transformation languages (DSTLs). Irazábal et al. (2010) suggested that their implementation should be done using regular transformation languages, while Reiter et al. (2006) proposed a generic framework for domain specific model transformation languages (DSMTLs).

A feature that is especially relevant to IIS*Case, as well as model based IS development in general, is the DSL text-model interoperability which makes it possible for developers to convert a textual specification to its model equivalent and vice-versa so these could be used interchangeably. One such solution for DSLs defined using ATLAS Model Management Architecture (AMMA), a MDE framework, is the Textual Concrete Syntax (TCS) DSL which allows the creation of concrete syntax specifications (mappings of a meta-model to syntactic representations) for a particular meta-model (Jouault et al., 2006). Once there is such a specification, the translators between Modelware and Grammarware can be created. Therefore, TCS specifications are bidirectional and generate an annotated grammar in ANTLR together with a pair of translators. However, the structural difference between a TCS model and a meta-model should not be too big if the mapping is to be properly done.

Another issue of importance for modern IS development is an effective development of required DSLs. There are a number of meta-modeling approaches and tools suitable for the purpose of creating DSLs that are generally based on their own meta-meta-model specifications. One of them is Generic Modeling Environment (GME) ("GME," 2008), a configurable toolkit for domain specific modeling and program synthesis based on

UML meta-models. MetaEdit+ ("MetaCaseMetaEdit+," n.d.) allows the creation of meta-models in a graphical editor using the Object-Property-Role-Relationship data model. The Eclipse Modeling Framework (EMF) ("Eclipse Modeling Framework," n.d.) is also a commonly used meta-modeling framework, where meta-meta-model named Ecore is used to create meta-models, or to import them from UML tools or textual notations. Ecore is the Eclipse implementation of MOF 2.0 in Java programming language. There are various Eclipse plugins suitable for creating DSLs. All of them are based on Ecore meta-meta-model and EMF. EMFText and Xtext are suitable for the creation of textual DSLs. On the other hand, there is Graphical Modeling Framework (GMF) which is used for the implementation of graphical DSLs. XText framework generates not only the parser, but also the abstract syntax model and Eclipse editor. In our research, we also used EMF to create a MOF 2.0 representation of IIS*Case Meta-model (Čeliković et al., 2011).

In this section, we summarized important advances in IS development approaches including both traditional and model based efforts. Special attention was given to DSLs, with a particular focus on the purpose and examples of their use in the IS context. Our goal was to demonstrate how IS development methods evolved to the current state of fully embracing the power of DSLs. An interesting view on the evolution of software engineering, not unlike the one presented herein, is given by Kurtev et al. (2006) who stated that MDE is a generalization of MDA, while DSL engineering, which is "positioned at a more abstract level, using different technical solutions like MDE (sometimes called Modelware), Grammarware, XML solutions, etc." (p. 602) is a generalization of MDE. One direction of the evolution of MDE includes the production of Domain Specific Application Development Environments (DSADEs) which support creation and evolution of different applications belonging to one application family (France & Rumpe, 2007). One such example is the HyperDe environment for the rapid prototyping of web applications (Nunes & Schwabe, 2006). It combines an application specification DSL with the model driven development approach and primarily supports the creation of small but complex web applications. In the same way, the IIS*Case tool also provides a DSL for PIM modeling and a model driven approach to the development of applications in the domain of ISs which is based on rapid prototyping. Therefore, in addition to being a MDSD tool, IIS*Case can be also regarded as a DSADE.

IIS*CASE AND ITS EVOLUTION

We created IIS*Case as a model driven tool for assisting in IS design and generating executable application prototypes. Apart from the tool, we also defined a methodological approach to the application of IIS*Case in the software development process. It is presented in Luković et al. (2006) and Luković et al. (2007). By this approach, the software development process provided by IIS*Case is, in general, evolutive and incremental. It enables an efficient and continuous development of an IS, as well as an early delivery of software prototypes that can be easily upgraded or amended according to the new or changed users' requirements. In our approach we strictly differentiate between the specification of a system and its implementation on a particular platform. Detailed information about IIS*Case may be found in several authors' references. A case study illustrating main features of IIS*Case and the methodological aspects of its usage is given in Luković et al. (2007). IIS*Case currently provides the following functionalities:

- Conceptual modeling of database schemas, transaction programs, and business applications of an IS;
- Automated design of relational database subschemas in the 3rd normal form (3NF);

- Automated integration of subschemas into a unified database schema in the 3NF;
- Automated generation of SQL/DDL code for various database management systems (DBMSs);
- Conceptual design of common user-interface (UI) models; and
- Automated generation of executable prototypes of business applications.

At the abstraction level of PIMs, IIS*Case provides conceptual modeling of database schemas that include specifications of various database constraints, such as domain, not null, check, key and unique constraints, as well as various kinds of inclusion dependencies. Such a model is automatically transformed into a model of relational database schema, which is still technology independent specification. It is an example of model-to-model transformations provided by IIS*Case (Luković et al., 2008; Luković, 2009).

A Brief History of IIS*Case Development

Even in early stages of the development of IIS*Case in late 1980s, we recognized a need for some new meta-level concepts suitable to provide conceptual modeling of database schemas. In that time, as well as in many recent years, ER data model was typically used for conceptual database schema design. Implementation database schema, often expressed in relational data model, was obtained by applying transformation rules and algorithms onto a previously created ER database schema. Many CASE tools provided such approach. However, one of the principal problems of such approach was in that there was no guarantee that the same structure of ER database schema with different semantics assigned, would result in the same relational database schema structure. As a consequence, average skilled designers felt difficulties in reaching a required quality of relational database schema being created.

On the other hand side, we recognized a well-known Beeri & Bernstein synthesis algorithm not only as a theoretical tool for relational database schema design, but also as a powerful mechanism that may be deployed in practice of database design process so as to overcome the aforementioned problem. However, there were two main problems blocking its direct practical application: (i) direct creating sets of all attributes and functional dependencies as the input specifications was practically impossible and (ii) functional dependencies and keys are not the only constraints to be considered in database schema design. By this, it follows that synthesis algorithm could not be put as a sole tool into the practice application. We discussed these issues in more details in Luković (2009).

To raise the synthesis algorithm to the level of its practical usage, during the years, we (i) developed new meta-level concepts providing conceptual database schema design and (ii) improved the synthesis algorithm so as to process not only functional dependencies and generate relation scheme keys only, but also other kind of relational database constraints.

The first meta-level concepts that we developed were: attribute, form type, component type, form instance and component instance. Similar concepts were also presented in other research works, such as in Choobineh, J. et al. (1988), but with a different purpose – not to deploy synthesis algorithm, but to generate ER database schema specifications from a set of form types being created. However, in both research works the principal idea was the same – to create a new meta-level model providing conceptual database schema design and relying on concepts the end-users are familiar with.

The approach was to borrow meta-level concepts from a business domain, formalize them, but keep them well-recognizable by the end-users. In this way, for example, the form type concept was borrowed from a business domain as a generalization of a business document. Keeping in mind that the end-users are not supposed to care about "more technical" ER data model concepts such as entity type, relationship type, cardinality, as well as the principle of normalization, we were convinced that the form type concept was much more comprehensible by average end-users and also designers in their perception of the conceptual data model. By this, we provided a better assistance to the database designers and end-users in their intensive communication during the requirements specification and conceptual database design process. On the other hand side, we deployed the improved synthesis algorithm as a powerful database design technique to provide transformations of conceptual database models into relational database schemas. Designers are not supposed to know details how the transformation algorithm works in deep and use it as a "black-box". In this way, its high complexity is hidden from the designers. Designers are supposed just to validate the generated results and analyze them in the context of their initial conceptual specifications. In this way, a better quality of designed database schemas may be reached.

The application of IIS*Case in a number of small and large industry projects during 1990s proved these our initial suppositions. Even fairly inexperienced designers supported by an expert and using the approach and IIS*Case were capable of producing an integrated database schema of a high quality in a reasonably short time. Designers found that the form type concept was easy to understand and convenient for communicating with end-users. Generating a relational database schema was an easy task. Designers did not find any problems in reviewing the resulting database schema, detecting semantic errors, and finding their causes in the form types. Database schema integration was performed through sessions with designers. It was the hardest task at the start, because it was often hard to persuade designers to make necessary changes in the form types. However, as soon as designers realized that the changes were justified, and how they propagate from their source form types to relation schemes, they became able to anticipate the appropriate solutions in advance and avoid future model inconsistencies. More details about our practical experiences in the application of IIS*Case in industry projects may be found in Luković et al. (2007).

In that way, the roots of our IIS*Case Meta-model were created in late 1980s, and the improved synthesis algorithm was the first transformation tool deployed to provide automatic generation of relational database schema specifications from the conceptual database schema model expressed by form types. From that time IIS*Case Meta-model is continuously developing. Till the mid of 2000s, we worked on continuous improvements of the synthesis algorithm and its implementation into the IIS*Case tool. From the present perspective, we may say that it was the hardest and most complex task in the development of IIS*Case. By the implementation of the improved synthesis algorithm in IIS*Case, we finally completed a core of IIS*Case and established a sound base for its effective further improvements. In parallel, we developed a methodological approach to the application of IIS*Case. During that time, IIS*Case Meta-model was specified by means of predicate calculus formulas, and additionally described its semantics in a form of free text. Development of IIS*Case Meta-model has been followed by the development of the IIS*Case tool with its repository implemented as a relational database. The repository provides all IIS*Case Meta-model concepts. Therefore the repository database schema specification becomes another form of IIS*Case Meta-model specification, at the same time.

IIS*Case also comprises visual repository-based tools that provide building formally correct IS models by means of IIS*Case Meta-model concepts. Therefore, it follows that IIS*Case also provides visual DSLs for IS development, for many years. In conclusion, we may say that we coupled a MDE and DSL paradigms in the IS development process and deployed them even in early stages of our research and the development of our approach and IIS*Case. Besides, we may observe our semi-formal specification of IIS*Case Meta-model given in a form of predicate calculus formulas and additionally described in a form of free text as the main result of a domain oriented analysis – an early step in developing a new DSL. Also, the specification of IIS*Case Meta-model given in a form of a repository database schema specification may be observed as an abstract syntax specification of the same DSL. The language itself with the first version of correctness checker of models being created was implemented "by hand" through IIS*Case repository-based visual tools.

From the second half of 2000s till present, we are investing additional research efforts to create a stronger relationship between IIS*Case Meta-model and IIS*Case tool, at one side, and DSL paradigm involved in MDE and DSM principles, at the other side. Our current research efforts are directed to coverage of all life-cycle steps in a DSL development process, as well as exploiting different approaches and modern tools that may be deployed to target this goal in a most suitable way.

Advanced Functionalities of IIS*Case

In the case of large systems being developed by the incremental approach, a system is decomposed into several subsystems that are modeled independently and usually by different designers. The process of independent design of subsystems and their database schemas may lead to collisions in expressing the real world constraints and business rules. Therefore, in our approach, the process of system integration is not just a mere unifying of its subsystems. It is based on detecting and resolving all the formal constraint collisions. In (Ristić et al., 2003; Luković et al., 2003) we proved that, at the level of relational data model, it is possible to automatically detect formal collisions of database constraints embedded into different subschemas, where each subschema represents a database schema of a sole IS subsystem. If collisions are detected, at least one subschema is formally not consistent with the current version of a database schema of a whole system. Programs made over inconsistent subschemas do not guarantee logically correct database updates. Therefore, we created and embedded into IIS*Case algorithms for detecting formal constraint collisions for the most often used constraint types at the level of relational data model. Besides, we embedded into IIS*Case a number of collision reports that assist designers in their resolving. By this, the database schema integration process based on the approach of a gradual integration of subschemas into a unified database schema is supported by IIS*Case in a large extent.

In Aleksić et al. (2007) and Aleksić et al. (2011) we presented features of SQL Generator that is implemented into IIS*Case, as well as aspects of its application. We also presented selected methods for implementation of database constraints, using mechanisms provided by a relational DBMS. It is an example of model-to-code transformations provided by IIS*Case.

At the abstraction level of PIMs, IIS*Case also provides conceptual modeling of common UI models, as well as business applications that include specifications of: (i) UI, (ii) structures of transaction programs aimed to execute over a database, and (iii) basic application functionality that includes the following "standard" data operations: read, insert, update, and delete. A PIM model of business applications is combined with a selected common UI model and then automatically transformed into the program code. In this way, fully executable application prototypes are generated. Such a generator is also an example of model-to-code transformations provided by IIS*Case (Banović, 2010; Ristić et al., 2011).

IIS*CASE PIM CONCEPTS

IIS*Case Meta-model contains an extensive number of meta-level concepts, their properties, relationships and rules. It is beyond the scope of this chapter and even impossible to present all of them here in detail. A reader may find these details in several authors' references that are all accessible upon request. A selection of 15 such references is also given in the References section of this chapter. IIS*Case Meta-model provides formal specifications of all the concepts embedded into IIS*Case repository definitions. Just to illustrate the main idea, here we focus on the selected PIM meta-level concepts only. By this, we give a brief overview of the following concepts: project, application system, form type, component type, application, call type, as well as fundamental concepts: attribute and domain. We present the concepts here with very basic details about their associated semantics. Good starting points to collect additional and detailed information are references Luković et al., (2006) and Luković et al., (2007). Also, in Ristić et al., (2007) and Ristić et al., (2011) we presented a more practitioner's approach to the usage of IIS*Case Meta-model and IIS*Case.

A work in IIS*Case is organized through projects. Everything that exists in the IIS*Case repository is always stored in the context of a project. One project is one IS specification and has a structure represented by the project tree. Each project has its (i) name, (ii) fundamental concepts or fundamentals for short, and (iii) application systems. A designer may also define various types of application systems – application types for short, and introduce a classification of application systems by associating each application system to a selected application type. At the level of a project there is a possibility to generate various reports that present the current state of the IIS*Case repository.

Application systems are organizational parts, i.e. segments or subsystems of a project. A motivation to introduce the application system concept is to provide a mechanism for decomposing large projects into manageable project segments. We suppose that each application system is normally sized to be designed by one designer, but more designers may also be engaged. Fundamental concepts are formally independent of any application system. They are common for a project as a whole. They are created at the level of a project and may be used in various application systems. Fundamental concepts are: domains, attributes, inclusion dependencies and program units. Here we focus on domains, attributes, and functions as a category of program units.

In the following text, we use a notion of domain with a meaning that is common in the area of databases. It denotes a specification of allowed values of some database attributes. We classify domains as (i) primitive and (ii) user defined. Primitive domains exist "per se", like primitive data types in various formal languages. We have a small set of primitive domains already defined, but we allow a designer to create his or her own primitive domains, according to the project needs. User defined domains are created by referencing primitive or previously created user defined domains. Domains are referenced later from attribute specifications. A list of all project attributes created in IIS*Case belongs to fundamentals. Attributes are used in various form type specifications of an application system.

A concept of a function is used to specify any complex functionality that may be used in other project specifications. A complex functionality typically includes a series of various database operations and calculations. It is not just a sole query, insert, update, or delete operation over a database relation. Each function has its name, a list of formal parameters and a return value type. Besides, it encompasses a formal specification of function body that is created by the *Function Editor* tool of IIS*Case.

Domains and Attributes

A user defined domain specification includes a default value, domain type, and check condition. We distinguish the following domain types: (i) domains created by the inheritance rule and (ii) complex domains that may be created by the: a) tuple rule, b) choice rule or c) set rule. Inheritance rule means that a domain specification is created by inheriting a specification of a superordinated domain – a primitive domain or previously defined user defined domain. It may be stronger, but not weaker than the superordinated domain specification. A domain created by the tuple rule is called a tuple domain. It represents a tuple (record) of values. Choice domain is the same as choice type of XML Schema Language. A set domain represents sets (collections) of values over a selected domain. Check condition, or the domain check expression is a regular expression that further constrains possible values of a domain. We have a formal syntax developed and the *Expression Editor* tool that assists in creating such expressions. We also have a parser for checking the syntax correctness. Currently we do not have a possibility to define allowed operators over a domain in IIS*Case repository. It is a matter of our future work.

Each attribute in an IIS*Case project is identified only by its name. Therefore, we obey to the Universal Relation Scheme Assumption (URSA) (Luković, 2009), well known in the relational data model for many years. The same assumption is also applicable in many other data models. We also specify if an attribute is included into database schema, derived, or renamed.

Most of the project attributes are to be included into the future database schema. However, we may have attributes that will present some calculated values in reports or screen forms that are not included into database schema. They derive their values on the basis of other attributes by some function, representing a calculation. Therefore, we classify attributes in IIS*Case as a) included or b) non-included in database schema. Also we introduce another classification of attributes, by which we may have: a) elementary or non-derived and b) derived attributes. If an attribute is specified as non-derived, it obtains its values directly by the end-users. Otherwise, values are derived by a function that may represent a calculation formula or any algorithm. Any attribute specified as non-included in database schema must be declared as derived one. A renamed attribute references a previously defined attribute and has to be included in the database schema. It has its origin in the referenced attribute, but with a slightly different semantics. Renaming is a concept that is analogous to the renaming that is applied in mapping ER database schemas into relational data model. If a designer specifies that an attribute A1 is renamed from A, actually he or she introduces an inclusion dependency of the form $[A1] \subseteq [A]$ at the level of a universal relation scheme.

Each attribute specification also includes: a reference to a user defined domain, default value and check condition. Check condition, or the attribute check expression is a regular expression that further constrains possible values of an attribute. It is defined and used in a similar way as it is for domain check expressions. If the attribute check expression and domain check expression are both defined, they will be connected by the logical AND.

Both user defined domain and attribute specifications also provide for specifying a number of display properties of screen items that correspond to the attributes and their domains. Such display properties are used by the IIS*Case *Application Generator* aimed at generating executable application prototypes. Display properties of an attribute may inherit display properties of the associated domain or may override them.

Application Systems, Form Types, and Applications

Each application system may have many child application systems. In this way, a designer may create application system hierarchies in an IIS*Case project. An application system may comprise various kinds of IIS*Case repository objects. For PIM specifications, only two kinds of objects are important: a) form types and b) business applications, or applications, for short.

A form type is the main modeling concept in IIS*Case. It generalizes document types, i.e. screen forms or reports by means of users communicate with an IS (Mogin et al., 1994). It is a structure defined at the abstraction level of schema. Using the form type concept, a designer specifies a set of screen or report forms of transaction programs and, indirectly, specifies database schema attributes and constraints. Each particular business document is an instance of a form type.

Business applications are structures of form types. Each application must have one form type marked as the entry form type of the application. The execution of a generated application always starts from the entry form type. Form types in an application are related by form type calls. A form type call always relates two form types: a calling form type and a called form type. By a form type call, a designer specifies how values are passed between the forms during the call execution. *Business Application Designer* is a visually oriented tool for modeling business applications in IIS*Case.

Form types are classified as menus or programs. Menu form types are used to generate just menus without any data items. Program form types specify transaction programs with the UI. They have a complex structure and may be designated as (i) considered or (ii) not considered in database schema design. The first option is used for all form types aimed at updating database, as well as for some report form types. Only the form types that are "considered in database schema design" participate later on in generating database schema. The former option is used for report form types only.

Each program form type is a tree structure of component types. It must have at least one component type. The following two properties of a component type are distinguished: number of occurrences and operations allowed. Number of occurrences may be specified as (i) 0-N or (ii) 1-N. 0-N means that for each instance of the parent component type, zero or more instances of the subordinated component type are allowed. 1-N means that for each instance of the parent component type, we require the existence of at least one instance of the subordinated component type. By operations allowed a designer may specify the following "standard" database operations over the component types: read, insert, delete, and update instances of the component type.

Each component type has a set of attributes included from IIS*Case repository. An attribute may be included in a form type at most once. Each attribute included in a component type may be declared as: (i) mandatory or optional, and (ii) modifiable, query only or display only. Also, a set of allowed operations over an attribute in a component type is specified. It is a subset of the set of operations {query, insert, nullify, update}. Each component type must have at least one key, consisting of at least one component type attribute. Each component type key provides identification of each component instance, but only in the scope of its superordinated component instance. Also, a component type may have uniqueness constraints, each of them consisting of at least one component type attribute. A uniqueness constraint provides an identification of each component instance, but only if it has a non-null value. On the contrary to keys, attributes in a uniqueness constraint may be optional. Finally, a component type may have a check constraint defined. It is a logical expression constraining values of each component type instance. Like domain check expressions, they are specified and parsed by *Expression Editor*.

Both component type and form type attribute specifications provide for specifying a vast number of display properties of generated screen forms and their various UI elements. There is also the *Layout Manager* tool that assists designers in specifying component type display properties, and a tool *UI*Modeler* that is aimed at designing templates of various common UI models. All display properties combined with a selected common UI model are used by the *Application Generator* tool.

In the following example, we illustrate a form type created in an IIS*Case project named *FacultyIS*. Figure 1 presents a form type defined in the child application system *Student Service* of a parent application system *Faculty Organization*. It refers to information about student's grades (STG). In our simplified example, it has two component types: STUDENT representing instances of students, and GRADES, representing instances of grades for each student.

By the form type STG, we allow having students with zero or more grades. Component type attributes are presented in italic letters. *StudentId* is the key of the component type STUDENT, while *CourseShortName* is the key of GRADES. By this, each grade is uniquely identified by *CourseShortName* within the scope of a given student. Allowed database operation for STUDENT is only *read* (shown in a small rectangle on the top of the rectangle representing the component type), while the allowed database operations for GRADES are *read*, *insert*, *update* and *delete*.

Figure 2 presents a form type defined in the child application system *Courses and Study Programs* of a parent application system *Faculty Organization*. It refers to information about courses (CRS) and represents a model of a document used in a real system to create, update and delete faculty courses. In our simplified example, it has just one component type: COURSE representing instances of courses. *CourseId* and *CourseShortName* are the two equivalent keys of the component type COURSE. By this, each instance of a COURSE is uniquely identified by *CourseId* and *CourseShortName*, at the same time. Allowed database operations for COURSE are *read*, *insert*, *update* and *delete*.

It should be noticed that the attribute *CourseShortName*, which is a key of the component type COURSE from Figure 2, is included in the component type GRADES from Figure 1. With respect to that, a future transaction program generated to support form type STG from Figure 1 will provide users to insert new students' grades and reference just those course short names previously recorded in the database by means of a transaction program supporting form type CRS from Figure 2.

IIS*CASE META-MODEL AND MOTIVATION BEHIND IIS*CDESLANG

In Figure 3 we illustrate the four layered architecture of our IIS*Case Meta-model solution, which is tailored from OMG four-layered architecture standard. Level M3 comprises meta-meta-model MOF 2.0 that is used for implementation of

Figure 1. A form type in the application system student service

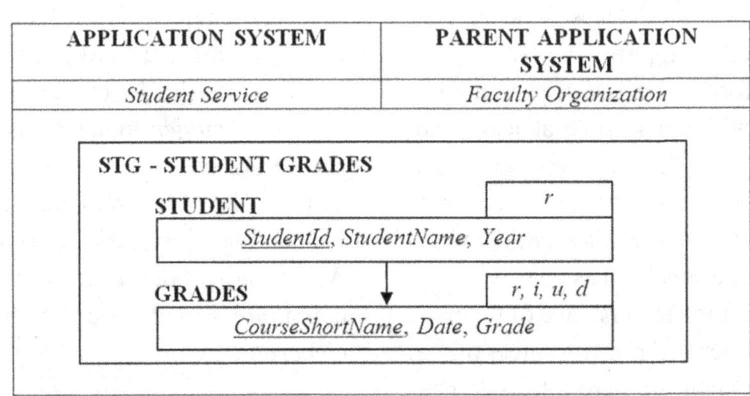

Figure 2. A form type in the application system courses and study programs

APPLICATION SYSTEM	PARENT APPLICATION SYSTEM
Courses and Study Programs	*Faculty Organization*

CRS – COURSE RECORDS

COURSE — *r, i, u, d*

CourseId, CourseShortName, CourseName, CurriculumId, CurriculumName, Lecturer, Prerequisite, Year, Semester

IIS*Case Meta-model. M2 abstraction level represents IIS*Case Meta-model specified by MOF and implemented in EMF. Using IIS*Case Meta-model, a designer may specify and implement a conceptual model of an IS that is placed at the M1 level. By using applications of an IS generated by IIS*Case, end-users manipulate real data, i.e. they create and use models of entities from real world (M0), using the conceptual model (M1).

EMF representation of our IIS*Case Meta-model is given in more details in Čeliković et al., (2011). Here we just present in a form of a diagram in Figure 4, a relatively small segment of meta-model of IIS*Case main PIM concepts with their properties and relationships. All classes presented in Figure 4 correspond to PIM concepts with the same names introduced in the section "IIS*Case PIM Concepts". All attributes of classes from Figure 4 represent the appropriate PIM concepts' properties. They may be mandatory or optional. To each attribute a data type is assigned. Lists of available values are also assigned to the appropriate attributes. Besides, by means of OCL language we specified all the necessary constraints to model various logical relationships between attribute values.

Our intention is not to discuss here all the details embedded into the model from Figure 4. In this paragraph, just as an illustration, we give a textual description of a part of the diagram from Figure 4. In accordance to the textual descriptions from "IIS*Case PIM Concepts" section, it follows from the class diagram from Figure 4 that each IIS*Project (represented by *Project* class) may include many application systems. The application system concept is represented by *ApplicationSystem* class. *ChildAppSystem* relationship from Figure 4 represents a hierarchy structure of application systems, where an application system may be a parent of many application systems, while an application system may be a child of just one parent application system. An application

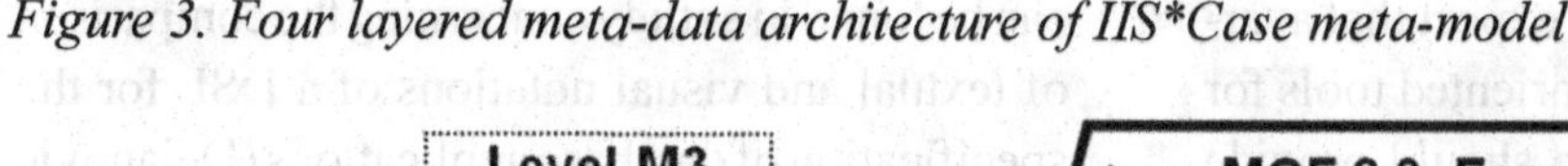
*Figure 3. Four layered meta-data architecture of IIS*Case meta-model*

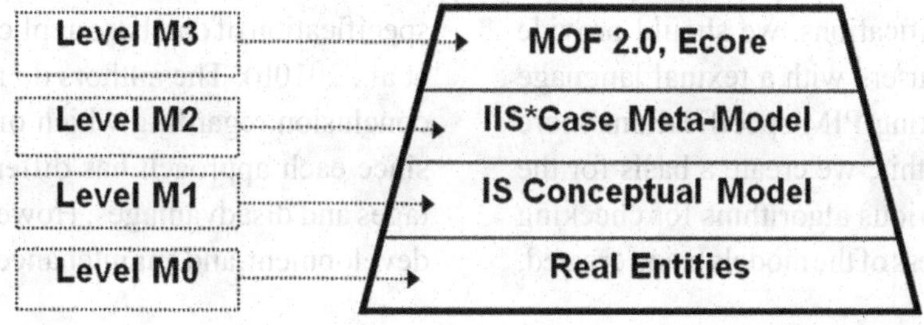

*Figure 4. A meta-model of IIS*Case main PIM concepts*

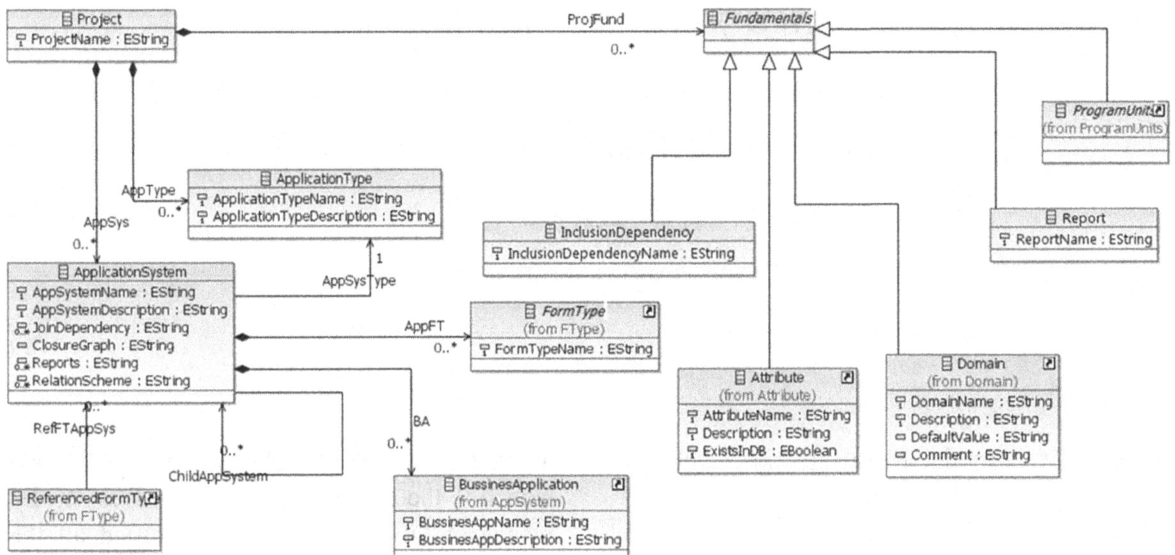

system may include many form types, while a form type belongs to exactly one application system. The form type concept is represented by *FormType* class in Figure 4, while the inclusion of form types into application systems is represented by *AppFT* relationship. *FormType* class from Figure 4 has the *FormTypeClass* attribute (not visible in Figure 4). It may have two possible values: one to represent a program form type, and the other to represent a menu form type, as it was discussed in the sub-section "Application Systems, Form Types and Applications".

Apart from having IIS*Case Meta-model expressed in a form of MOF specification and serving as a domain analysis specification, we need additionally a textual language representation of IIS*Case Meta-model, for the following reasons. (i) Despite that we may expect that average users prefer to use visually oriented tools for creating PIM specifications, we should provide more experienced users with a textual language and a tool for creating PIM specifications more efficiently. (ii) By this, we create a basis for the development of various algorithms for checking the formal correctness of the models being created, as well as for the implementation of some semantic analysis. A benefit of introducing IIS*CDesLang is to enable the creation of a parser aimed at checking the formal correctness of PIM project models under development. In this way, we may help designers in raising the quality of new IS specifications. A possibility to build two translators, IIS*Case repository-to-IIS*CDesLang specifications and IIS*CDesLang-to-IIS*Case repository definitions, is another value added by this approach. The benefit of the first one is to allow the correctness checking of PIM visual models without explicitly writing IIS*CDesLang specifications; and the benefit of the second one is a possibility of generating correct PIM repository specifications from IIS*CDesLang textual specifications. Further support for our decision can be found in a study concerning the comparison of textual and visual notations of a DSL for the specification of database applications (Dejanović et al., 2010b). The authors do not give a definite conclusion regarding which of the two is better, since each approach has different set of advantages and disadvantages. However, if the costs of development and maintenance do not present a problem, they recommend the use of both types of syntax but each for a distinct set of purposes.

AN OVERVIEW OF IIS*CDESLANG

In "IIS*Case and its Evolution" section we have already presented a development life-cycle of our IIS*Case tool, together with its repository-based modeling tools that implement IIS*Case Meta-model in a form of a visual DSL. We discussed there in brief all the development phases of our visual DSL: decision, analysis, design, implementation, deployment and maintenance. We may conclude that all these phases were present in our visual DSL development. During almost the two decades, they were completed mostly "by hand", without any support of specialized DSM or DSL development tools. We just used classical CASE tools to create repository specifications and general programming languages with the appropriate programming environments to develop the IIS*Case tool.

Apart from this history, our present research efforts are directed to the development of IIS*CDesLang – a textual DSL representation of IIS*Case Meta-model by applying DSM and DSL development tools. There are a number of meta-modeling approaches and tools suitable for that purpose. At present, we have decision, analysis and design phases completed. Deployment and maintenance phases are matters of our further research. Decision phase is common to all our research efforts and addressed in the previous sections of this chapter. Analysis is completed by creating a MOF based specification of IIS*Case Meta-model. Design phase is covered in two ways, by deploying: (i) a visual programming environment (VPE) for attribute grammar (AG) specifications, VisualLISA; and (ii) EMF with Eclipse plugin EMF text.

To create IIS*CDesLang, our first selection was a VPE for AG specifications, named VisualLISA (Varanda Pereira et al., 2008; Oliveira et al., 2010). We applied VisualLISA Syntactic and Semantic Validators to check the correctness of the specified grammar. In Luković et al. (2011) an AG specification of IIS*CDesLang, created by VisualLISA, together with a selection of generated productions, is described. The IIS*Case Meta-model concepts are mapped into IIS*CDesLang symbols establishing a correspondence between domain concepts and non-terminal or terminal grammar symbols in the systematic way described in Kosar et al., (2004).

Our recent efforts are to utilize Ecore IIS*Case Meta-model already created in EMF as an abstract syntax specification and generate concrete syntax with Eclipse plugin EMF text in the Human Usable Textual Notation (HUTN). Apart from using Ecore IIS*Case Meta-model as an abstract syntax specification, we experimented with EMF generators to automatically produce visual tools from Ecore IIS*Case Meta-model so as to compensate our "proprietary" IIS*Case tools. Technically speaking, experiment came to the success. However, as we expected according to our previous experience, such generated tools showed rather poor UI and were considerably far away from being efficiently used in practice.

Our intention is to present here just a fragment of an IIS*CDesLang program to illustrate the main idea of the IIS*Case Meta-model textual representation. In Listing 1 it is presented a selected fragment of IIS*CDesLang program that corresponds to the form type specification from Figure 1. The program from Listing 1 is organized in a way to cover the specification as a whole. Repeating segments of the specification, as well as a number of display and list-of-values (LOV) properties are omitted. To better explain various segments of the program, we have included in-line comments tagged with the symbol //. In the following text, we give a textual explanation of the presented program.

Firstly, the project *FacultyIS* with its two application systems is specified. The first one is a specification of the *Faculty Organization* applica-

*Listing 1. A fragment of IIS*CDesLang program that corresponds to the form type from Figure 1*

```
Project: Faculty IS
  Application System: Faculty Organization
    Description: "A unit of a Faculty IS"
    Type: ProjectSubsystem
  ... // Specification of the application system continues...
  ...
  Application System: Student Service is-child-of <<Faculty Organization>>
    Description: "A unit of Faculty Organization subsystem"
    Type: ProjectSubsystem
    ... // A list of form types is specified here
    ...
    // A specification of the form type STG begins
    FormType: "STG - Student Grades"
      Title: "Catalogue of student grades"
      UsageType: Program Considered-in-db-design: Yes
      ... // More form type properties are given here
      // A specification of the component type begins
      ComponentType: STUDENT
        Title: "Student Records"
        Allowed Operations: read
        Position: newWindow
        DataLayout: FieldLayout
        Window Position: Center
        Search Functionality: Yes
        Massive Delete Functionality: No
        Retain Last Inserted Record: No
        Component Type Attributes:
          Name: StudentID
            CTA_Title: "Student Id."
            CTA_Mandatory: Yes
            CTA_Behavior: queryOnly
            CTA_AllowedOperations: query
            CTA_DisplayType: textbox Height: 20 ...
            // More display properties are omitted ...
            CTA_LOV_FormType: <<STD - Student>> ...
            // More LOV properties are omitted ...
          Name: StudentName
            ...
          Name: Year
            ...
        Component Type KEY: StudentID
      // A specification of the component type ends
```

continued on following page

Listing 1. Continued

```
    // A specification of the component type begins
    ComponentType: GRADES is-child-of <<Student>>
      NoOfOccurrences: (0:N)
      Allowed Operations: read, insert, update, delete
      ... // More component type properties are given here
      ...
      Component Type Attributes:
        Name: CourseShortName
          CTA_Title: "Course Short Name"
          CTA_Mandatory: Yes
          CTA_Behavior: modifiable
          CTA_AllowedOperations: query, insert
          ... // Display and LOV properties are given here
        Name: Date
          ...
        Name: Grade
          ...
      Component Type KEY: CourseShortName
    // A specification of the component type ends
  // A specification of the form type STG ends
  ...
  ... // Specification of form types continues...
... // Specification of the project continues...
...
```

tion system and then a specification of its child application system *Student Service*. After specifying the application system properties *Description* and *Type*, a list of form type specifications included in *Student Service* is given. In Listing 1 it is presented a specification of the form type *STG – Student Grades* only. Each form type specification includes a list of properties including *Title* and *UsageType* that may be *program* or *menu*, and a list of component type specifications. A parent component type STUDENT and its child component type GRADES are specified in the form type *STG – Student Grades*.

The first, *Title* and *Allowed Operations* properties are specified for a component type. By this, *read* is the only allowed database operation for the component type STUDENT. After that, a list of display and other UI properties is specified. During the generation of UI of a transaction program of the form type *STG – Student Grades*, the component type STUDENT is to be positioned in a new window (*Position* property) and presented in a field layout style (*DataLayout* property). A window is to be centered to its parent window (*Window Position* property). Search functionality for student records is allowed (*Search Functionality* property), while multiple deletions (*Massive Delete Functionality* property) and retaining last inserted record in the screen form (*Retain Last Inserted Record* property) functionalities for student records are disabled. After the specifications of display and UI properties, a list of specifications of component type attributes follows.

For each component type attribute we specify its name (*Name* property), title (*CTA_Title* property), if it is mandatory or optional for entering values on the screen form (*CTA_Mandatory* property), behavior (*CTA_Behavior* property) and allowed operations on the screen form (*CTA_AllowedOperations* property). A set of display and LOV properties (preceded by *CTA_DisplayType* and *CTA_LOV_FormType* properties) may also be given.

After the list of component type attributes, the list of component type constraints is given. It may include the specifications of key, uniqueness and check constraints. In this example, only component type keys are specified for STUDENT and GRADES by the property *Component Type KEY*.

Just to illustrate the concrete syntax generated by Eclipse plugin EMF text, we present in Listing 2 a production for the *Project* concept in HUTN notation:

FUTURE RESEARCH DIRECTIONS

Our future research directions regarding the methodological approach to IS development, development of the IIS*Case tool and IIS*Case Meta-model may be organized into two large groups. (i) One concerns extending IIS*Case Meta-model with new concepts and IIS*Case with new functionalities so as to cover the IS development process more extensively. (ii) The other concerns improving IIS*Case Meta-model and IIS*Case to implement new tools for both visual and textual modeling of IS PIM specifications, as well as their formal correctness checking and semantics validation.

In the first group of future activities, we plan to research possibilities for better coverage of requirements specification phase in the IS development process. By this, we are going to investigate how to couple BPM formal languages and notations with our approach and IIS*Case. The main motivation for this research is in that business documents have its own life cycle with a flow and various states in a real system that may be formally modeled at the abstraction level of PIMs. Our form types represent business documents and therefore they are not identified and modeled in an isolated way, but in the context of business process and document flows that are to be modeled also at the abstraction level of PIMs. Another research issue is how to support modeling different system architectures at the abstraction level of PIMs. By this, we may provide by IIS*Case the deployment process of generated software applications. The third research issue is how to support modeling system security at the abstraction level of PIMs, according to the Role-based Access Control (RBAC) model, standardized by National Institute for Standards and Technology (NIST) and then to provide transformations for its embedding into the generated software applications and database scripts. The fourth research issue is how to support configuration management and dependency

Listing 2. A production for the project concept in HUTN notation

```
Project::= "Project" "{" ("ProjectName" ":"
ProjectName['"','"'] | "AppType" ":" AppType |
"ProjFund" ":" ProjFund | "AppSys" ":" AppSys)* "}";
It specifies a name of a project (ProjectName), possible types of application
systems (AppType), different fundamental concepts (ProjFund) and application
systems (AppSys) created in the context of the project.
```

management in IS development and deployment processes by IIS*Case.

In our current version of IIS*Case Meta-model, among other constraint types, we have concepts of a domain, attribute and component type check constraints. We have already provided their transformations in the relational data model and SQL scripts. One of the research activities we are already working on is how to provide algorithms for detecting formal collisions of check constraints modeled in different subschemas.

Our current research is also devoted to improving PIM specifications of functions by means of business application logic is specified. In this way, we may model not only "standard" database operations (read, insert, update, and delete), but also complex data processing operations. We are already developing the algorithms providing transformations of function specifications created at the level of PIMs, to the equivalent executable specifications expressed in a target programming environment and in the context of generated business applications.

Our intention is also to embed into IIS*Case transformations between different data models. Providing data model transformations may play an important role in the IS design process. In the course of data reengineering process, our plan is to provide the data integration from various sources based on different data models. Data transformation rules specified by QVT could be applied at the level of meta-models specified by various data-models, all expressed in a unified manner in MOF. One of the research issues is how to provide transformations of the models specified in IIS* Case to the UML models. Providing such transformations we allow designers to have models specified in UML with OCL constraints.

In the second group of our future activities, we plan to improve IIS*Case support for creating PIM specifications by introducing a completely new repository based tool for visual modeling of form type specifications. Besides, we are going to implement a new visual editor that will provide a guided way to create IIS*CDesLang textual specifications. Afterward, we plan to build the IIS*Case repository-to-IIS*CDesLang and IIS*CDesLang-to-IIS*Case repository translators. By means of all these tools, we will be able to experiment with different users having different levels of knowledge and habits so as to quantitatively measure their efficiency in creating IIS*Case PIM specifications by means of textual DSLs and visual DSLs, and then to compare and quantitatively analyze the obtained results. Another added value of these tools is to enable creation of a parser aimed at checking the formal correctness of PIM project models under development. Implementation of some semantics analyses is also possible. Two characteristic examples are domain compatibility analysis and check constraint equivalence analysis, necessary to provide detecting formal collisions between modeled check constrains. In this way, we plan to cover implementation and deployment phases in the DSL development life-cycle for IIS*CDesLang. Our plan is also to better formalize a domain analysis specification of our language by applying a selected formal method for this purpose, such as the Feature–Oriented Domain Analysis (FODA) method.

Our current experiences show that a MOF based representation of IIS*Case Meta-model, as a domain analysis specification is an important prerequisite to create a grammar specification of IIS*CDesLang, as a textual DSL. In our future research, apart from EMF, it is necessary to experiment with other technologies that rely on MOF. Current experiences presented in Djukić et al. (2011) lead to the usage of MetaEdit+ language workbench, for two reasons. One is to compare the strength of both DSM environments in creating MOF based representation of IIS*Case Meta-model, and the other to investigate possibilities for generating grammar specifications of IIS*CDesLang and the aforementioned IIS*Case tools for visual modeling of PIM specifications. The similar reasons lead to the selection of AMMA framework (Jouault et al., 2006), since we need to support bidirectional transformations between model-based end text-based PIM specifications.

CONCLUSION

In spite of having a vast number of references concerning various aspects of DSL applications in model driven approaches to software development, it seems that potentials for further research in this area are even more wider. We believe that it is particularly true for applied research in the area of IS development.

However, in recent years, various experiences from industry practice show an increasing level of investments into the development and deployment of "generic" ISs, instead of ISs customized to meet the requirements of a particular organization. These efforts are mostly directed just to unify common IS solutions so as to apply them in a greater number of organizations, and preserve a return of investments for a software company selling such software solutions. On the other hand, a room for real customizations of such generic IS solutions remains quite narrow and considerably expensive. As a consequence, such software solutions unfortunately not often (as it may be expected) meet real user requirements and business processes well. Instead, a reverse process is going on – an organization must change its processes and lower the strength of user requirements so as to meet a generic software solution being deployed. Finally, in such circumstances it appears that organizations in many cases cannot utilize fully all the power and capacities of their ISs, but the price they are paying for it would be much higher than it seemed to be at the time of introducing a generic IS solution.

To mitigate this problem bearing potentially serious consequences, a process of software development and its further customizations should be made more efficient and cheaper. This would be a good motivator for organizations to invest into the development of easily-customizable IS solutions, as well as for software companies to invest into the research of new methods, paradigms and development environments capable of supporting such a software development. We believe that a shifting to the arena of model driven approaches supported by application of DSLs may be a promising initiative. By this it is possible to contribute to narrowing ever-present gap between end-users and their viewpoints at one hand side, and system designers and their different viewpoints at the other side, and preserve their better understanding in the process of system design. Furthermore, such approaches followed by high quality software generators may considerably shorten the time between system specification and final software production. The intention of our research presented here is to contribute to these goals and ideas.

In this chapter, we offered a perspective on the recent history of IS development approaches. Some of the most important advances in this field include the emergence of MDA and a greater reliance on an ever increasing set of DSLs. We showed that these breakthroughs have not negated the benefits of preceding methods but helped solve, at least partially, several key problems which proved impenetrable to the prevailing methods of the time. The history of IS development does not consist of separate and isolated periods – these have actually been best coupled by the daring ideas promoted by the critical masses of researchers and practitioners who recognized prospective benefits of new approaches. This view was further substantiated by the included summary of IIS*Case, an IS development software which was first created more than two decades ago. The tool has evolved in many ways since its beginnings and adopted different ideas representative of the past periods. Its continuity, strong integration with MDSD principles and embracement of DSLs is demonstrative of the perspective given in the first part of the chapter.

Moreover, we presented two different approaches to create DSLs for IS specification.

One is based on attribute grammars (AGs) and visual programming environments (VPEs) for their specification, while the other on domain specific modeling and MOF. A question arises: Is it a waste of time, or a necessity to have two parallel approaches? Our experiences show that the latter is true, despite that such approach needs more time and efforts. From MOF based approach, we obtain a good domain analysis specification, necessary to precisely understand and present the application domain, and verify the structure of the IIS*Case repository being already developed. From AG and VPE approach we obtain a formal way to specify a grammar of the textual modeling language and later generate a parser for checking the formal correctness of the models being developed. The second important question is: Is there a way to relate and unify both approaches? In other words, could it be possible to create a MOF representation of our meta-model and then to generate an AG specification and the required IIS*Case tools automatically? We believe that further research will communicate better experiences and more definite answers. At the moment, it seems that a lot of work in that way should be done "by hand" if we intend to further develop IIS*Case as a MDSD environment that meets user expectations in a high quality manner.

From the point of our IIS*Case users, we believe that we should provide them at least two or more alternative ways how to model their PIM specifications and generate software applications of an IS. One is the usage of visual DSLs and visually guided tools, while the other is the usage of textual DSLs and the appropriate "smart" editors. Besides, we are convinced that deploying DSLs is a compulsory prerequisite for rising the IS development process to the level closer to the perception power and knowledge of average end-users and the system stakeholders.

REFERENCES

Aleksić, S., Luković, I., Mogin, P., & Govedarica, M. (2007). A generator of SQL schema specifications. *Computer Science and Information Systems*, *4*(2), 79–98. doi:10.2298/CSIS0702081A

Aleksić, S., Ristić, S., & Luković, I. (2011). An approach to generating server implementation of the inverse referential integrity constraints.In *Proceedings of the 5th International Conference on Information Technology* (pp. 1-7). Amman, Jordan: Al-Zaytoonah University of Jordan.

Banović, J. (2010). *An approach to generating executable software specifications of an information system*. Unpublished doctoral dissertation, University of Novi Sad, Faculty of Technical Sciences, Novi Sad, Serbia.

Bézivin, J. (2004). In search of a basic principle for model driven engineering. *UPGRADE - The European Journal for the Informatics Professional, 5*(2), 21-24.

Bicevskis, J., Cerina-Berzina, J., Karnitis, G., Lace, L., Medvedis, I., & Nesterovs, S. (2011). Practitioners view on domain specific business process modeling. In *Proceedings of the 2011 Conference on Databases and Information Systems VI: Selected Papers from the Ninth International Baltic Conference* (pp. 169-182). Amsterdam, The Netherlands: IOS Press.

Brinkkemper, S. (1996). Method engineering: Engineering of information systems development methods and tools. *Information and Software Technology*, *38*(4), 275–280. doi:10.1016/0950-5849(95)01059-9

Bureš, T., Malohlava, M., & Hnětynka, P. (2008). Using DSL for automatic generation of software connectors. In *Proceedings of the Seventh International Conference on Composition-Based Software Systems* (pp. 138-147). Washington, DC: IEEE Computer Society.

Čeliković, M., Luković, I., Aleksić, S., & Ivančević, V. (2011). A MOF based meta-model of IIS*Case PIM concepts. In *Proceedings of the Federated Conference on Computer Science and Information Systems* (pp. 833-840). Los Alamitos, CA: IEEE Computer Society Press.

Chen, P. P. S. (1976). The entity-relationship model – Toward a unified view of data. *ACM Transactions on Database Systems, 1*(1), 9–36. doi:10.1145/320434.320440

Choobineh, J., Mannino, M. V., Nunamaker, J. F., & Konsynski, B. R. (1988). An expert database design system based on analysis of forms. *IEEE Transactions on Software Engineering, 14*(2), 242–253. doi:10.1109/32.4641

Codd, E. F. (1970). A relational model of data for large shared data banks. *Communications of the ACM, 13*(6), 377–387. doi:10.1145/362384.362685

Dejanović, I., Milosavljević, G., Tumbas, M., & Perišić, B. (2010). A domain-specific language for defining static structure of database applications. *Computer Science and Information Systems, 7*(3), 409–440. doi:10.2298/CSIS090203002D

Dejanović, I., Tumbas, M., Milosavljević, G., & Perišić, B. (2010). Comparison of textual and visual notations of DOMMLite domain-specific language. In *Local Proceedings of the 14th East-European Conference on Advances in Databases and Information Systems* (pp. 131-136). Novi Sad, Serbia: University of Novi Sad, Faculty of Sciences.

Deursen van, A., Klint, P., & Visser, J. (2000). Domain-specific languages: An annotated bibliography. *ACM SIGPLAN Notices, 35*(6), 26-36.

Djukić, V., Luković, I., & Popović, A. (2011). Domain-specific modeling in document engineering. In *Proceedings of the Federated Conference on Computer Science and Information Systems* (pp. 825-832). Los Alamitos, CA: IEEE Computer Society Press.

EMF: Eclipse Modeling Framework. (n.d.). Retrieved October 6, 2011, from http://www.eclipse.org/modeling/emf/

France, R., & Rumpe, B. (2007). Model-driven development of complex software: A research roadmap. In *Future of Software Engineering* (pp. 37–54). Washington, DC: IEEE Computer Society. doi:10.1109/FOSE.2007.14

Frantz, R. Z., Corchuelo, R., & Gonzáles J. (2008). Advances in a DSL for application integration. *Actas de los Talleres de las Jornadas de Ingeniería del Software y Bases de Datos, 2*(2), 54-66.

Freudenthal, M. (2010a). Domain-specific languages in a customs information system. *IEEE Software, 27*(2), 65–71. doi:10.1109/MS.2010.41

Freudenthal, M. (2010b). Using DSLs for developing enterprise systems. In *Proceedings of the 10th Workshop on Language Descriptions, Tools and Applications*, article 11. New York, NY: ACM Press.

Fuentes-Fernández, L., & Vallecillo-Moreno, A. (2004). An introduction to UML profiles. *UPGRADE - The European Journal for the Informatics Professional, 5*(2), 6-13.

Giaglis, G. M. (2001). A taxonomy of business process modeling and information systems modeling techniques. *International Journal of Flexible Manufacturing Systems, 13*(2), 209–228. doi:10.1023/A:1011139719773

GME: Generic Modeling Environment. (2008, June 12). Retrieved October 6, 2011, from http://www.isis.vanderbilt.edu/Projects/gme/

Grundy, J., Hosking, J. G., Amor, R. W., Mugridge, W. B., & Li, Y. (2004). Domain-specific visual languages for specifying and generating data mapping systems. *Journal of Visual Languages and Computing*, *15*(3-4), 243–263. doi:10.1016/j.jvlc.2004.01.003

Gudas, S., & Lopata, A. (2007). Meta-model based development of use case model for business function. *Information Technology and Control, Kaunas. Technologija*, *36*(3), 302–309.

Hirschheim, R., & Klein, H. K. (1989). Four paradigms of information systems development. *Communications of the ACM*, *32*(10), 1199–1216. doi:10.1145/67933.67937

Irazábal, J., Pons, C., & Neil, C. (2010). Model transformation as a mechanism for the implementation of domain specific transformation languages. *SADIO Electronic Journal of Informatics and Operations Research*, *9*(1), 49–66.

Jouault, F., Bézivin, J., & Kurtev, I. (2006). TCS: A DSL for the specification of textual concrete syntaxes in model engineering. In *Proceedings of the 5th International Conference on Generative Programming and Component Engineering* (pp. 249-254). New York, NY: ACM Press.

Kelly, S. (2005). Improving developer productivity with domain-specific modeling languages. *Developer.* *. Retrieved September 23, 2011, from http://www.developerdotstar.com/mag/articles/domain_modeling_language.html

Kleppe, A., Warmer, J., & Bast, W. (2003). *MDA explained: The model driven architecture - practice and promise*. New York, NY: Addison-Wesley.

Kosar, T., Mernik, M., Henriques, P. R., Varanda Pereira, M. J., & Žumer, V. (2004). Software development with grammatical approach. *Informatica*, *28*(4), 39–404.

Kosar, T., Oliveira, N., Mernik, M., Varanda Pereira, M. J., Črepinšek, M., da Cruz, D., & Henriques, P. R. (2010). Comparing general-purpose and domain-specific languages: An empirical study. *Computer Science and Information Systems*, *7*(2), 247–264. doi:10.2298/CSIS1002247K

Kurtev, I., Bézivin, J., Jouault, F., & Valduriez, P. (2006). Model-based DSL frameworks. In *OOPSLA '06 Companion to the 21st ACM SIGPLAN Symposium on Object-oriented Programming Systems, Languages, and Applications* (pp. 602-615). New York, NY: ACM Press.

Luković, I. (2009). From the synthesis algorithm to the model driven transformations in database design. In *Proceedings of 10th International Scientific Conference on Informatics* (pp. 9-18). Košice, Slovakia: Slovak Society for Applied Cybernetics and Informatics and Technical University of Košice - Faculty of Electrical Engineering and Informatics.

Luković, I., Mogin, P., Pavićević, J., & Ristić, S. (2007). An approach to developing complex database schemas using form types. *Software, Practice & Experience*, *37*(15), 1621–1656. doi:10.1002/spe.820

Luković, I., Ristić, S., Aleksić, S., & Popović, A. (2008). An application of the MDSE principles in IIS*Case. In *Proceedings of the 3rd Workshop on Model Driven Software Engineering* (pp. 53-62). Berlin, Germany: TFH, University of Applied Sciences Berlin.

Luković, I., Ristić, S., & Mogin, P. (2003). A methodology of a database schema design using the subschemas. In *Proceedings of IEEE International Conference on Computational Cybernetics* (in CD ROM). Budapest, Hungary: Budapest Polytechnic.

Luković, I., Ristić, S., Mogin, P., & Pavićević, J. (2006). Database schema integration process – A methodology and aspects of its applying. *Novi Sad Journal of Mathematics*, *36*(1), 115–150.

Luković, I., Varanda Pereira, M. J., Oliveira, N., Cruz, D., & Henriques, P. R. (2011). A DSL for PIM specifications: Design and attribute grammar based implementation. *Computer Science and Information Systems*, *8*(2), 379–403. doi:10.2298/CSIS101229018L

Menezes, A. L., Cirilo, C. E., Moraes, J. L. C. D., Souza, W. L. D., & Prado, A. F. D. (2010). Using archetypes and domain specific languages on development of ubiquitous applications to pervasive healthcare. In *Proceedings of the 23rd IEEE International Symposium on Computer-Based Medical Systems* (pp. 395-400). Washington, DC: IEEE Computer Society Press.

Mernik, M., Heering, J., & Sloane, M. A. (2005). When and how to develop domain-specific languages. *ACM Computing Surveys*, *37*(4), 316–344. doi:10.1145/1118890.1118892

MetaCaseMetaEdit+. (n.d.). Retrieved October 6, 2011, from http://www.metacase.com/

Milanović, N., Cartsburg, M., Kutsche, R., Widiker, J., & Kschonsak, F. (2009). Model-based interoperability of heterogeneous information systems: An industrial case study. In Paige, R. F., Hartman, A., & Rensink, A. (Eds.), *Model Driven Architecture - Foundations and Applications* (*Vol. 5562*, pp. 325–336). Lecture Notes in Computer Science Berlin, Germany: Springer-Verlag. doi:10.1007/978-3-642-02674-4_24

MOF: Meta-object faculty. (2011, June 23). Retrieved October 6, 2011, from http://www.omg.org/mof/

Mogin, P., Luković, I., & Karadžić, Ž. (1994). Relational database schema design and application generating using IIS*CASE tool. In *Proceedings of International Conference on Technical Informatics* (pp. 49-58). Timisoara, Romania: 'Politehnica' University of Timisoara.

Nunes, D. A., & Schwabe, D. (2006). Rapid prototyping of web applications combining domain specific languages and model driven design. In *Proceedings of the 6th International Conference on Web engineering* (pp. 153-160). New York, NY: ACM Press.

Oliveira, N., Varanda Pereira, M. J., Henriques, P. R., Cruz, D., & Cramer, B. (2010). VisualLISA: A visual environment to develop attribute grammars. *Computer Science an Information Systems*, *7*(2), 265–289. doi:10.2298/CSIS1002265O

Pastor, O., Gómez, J., Insfrán, E., & Pelechano, V. (2001). The OO-Method approach for information systems modeling: From object-oriented conceptual modeling to automated programming. *Information Systems*, *26*(7), 507–534. doi:10.1016/S0306-4379(01)00035-7

Perišić, B., Milosavljević, G., Dejanović, I., & Milosavljević, B. (2011). UML profile for specifying user interfaces of business applications. *Computer Science and Information Systems*, *8*(2), 405–426. doi:10.2298/CSIS110112010P

Reiter, T., Kapsammer, E., Retschitzegger, W., Schwinger, W., & Stumptner, M. (2006). A generator framework for domain-specific model transformation languages. In *Proceedings of the Eighth International Conference on Enterprise Information Systems Databases and Information Systems Integration* (pp. 27-35). Paphos, Cyprus: ICEIS Press.

Ristić, S., Aleksić, S., Luković, I., & Banović, J. (2011). Form-driven application generating: A case study. In *Proceedings of 11th International Conference on Informatics* (pp. 115-120). Košice, Slovakia: Slovak Society for Applied Cybernetics and Informatics and Technical University of Košice - Faculty of Electrical Engineering and Informatics.

Ristić, S., Luković, I., Pavićević, J., & Mogin, P. (2007). Resolving database constraint collisions using IIS*case tool. *Journal of Information and Organizational Sciences, 31*(1), 187–206.

Ristić, S., Mogin, P., & Luković, I. (2003). Specifying database updates using a subschema. In *Proceedings of VII IEEE International Conference on Intelligent Engineering Systems* (pp. 203-212). Assiut-Luxor, Egypt: IEEE, Assiut University, Assiut, Egypt, and Budapest Polytechnic, Budapest, Hungary.

Schmidt, D. C. (2006). Model-driven engineering. *IEEE Computer, 39*(2), 25–31. doi:10.1109/MC.2006.58

Schuette, R., & Rotthowe, T. (1998). The guidelines of modeling - An approach to enhance the quality in information models. In *ER '98 Proceedings of the 17th International Conference on Conceptual Modeling* (pp. 240-254). London, UK: Springer-Verlag.

Shanks, G. (1997). Conceptual data modelling: An empirical study of expert and novice data modellers. *Australasian Journal of Information Systems, 4*(2), 63–73.

Sivonen, S. (2008). *Domain-specific modelling language and code generator for developing repository-based Eclipse plug-ins*. Espoo, Finland: VTT Publications.

Thomas, D. (2004). MDA: Revenge of the modelers or UML utopia? *IEEE Software, 21*(3), 22–24. doi:10.1109/MS.2004.1293067

Thomas, D., & Barry, B. M. (2003). Model driven development: The case for domain oriented programming. In *Companion of the 18th Annual ACM SIGPLAN Conference on Object-Oriented Programming, Systems, Languages, and Applications* (pp. 2-7). New York, NY: ACM Press.

Vara, J. M., Vela, B., Bollati, V., & Marcos, E. (2009). Supporting model-driven development of object-relational database schemas: A case study. In R. Paige (Ed.), *International Conference on Model Transformation, Lecture Notes in Computer Science, Vol. 5563* (pp. 181-196). Berlin, Germany: Springer-Verlag.

Varanda Pereira, M. J., Mernik, M., Cruz, D., & Henriques, P. R. (2008). VisualLISA: A visual interface for an attribute grammar based compiler-compiler. In *Proceedings of 2nd Conference on Compilers, Related Technologies and Applications* (pp. 265-289). Bragança, Portugal: IPB.

vom Brocke, J., & Buddendick, C. (2006). *Reusable conceptual models. Requirements based on the design science research paradigm.* Paper presented at the First International Conference on Design Science Research in Information Systems and Technology, Claremont, CA.

Wand, Y., & Weber, R. (1990). An ontological model of an information system. *IEEE Transactions on Software Engineering, 16*(11), 1282–1292. doi:10.1109/32.60316

Wand, Y., & Weber, R. (2002). Research commentary: Information systems and conceptual modeling – A research agenda. *Information Systems Research, 13*(4), 363–376. doi:10.1287/isre.13.4.363.69

Wendt, T., Häber, A., Brigl, B., & Winter, A. (2004). Modeling hospital information systems (Part 2): Using the 3LGM^2 tool for modeling patient record management. *Methods of Information in Medicine, 43*(3), 256–267.

Winter, A., Brigl, B., & Wendt, T. (2003). Modeling hospital information systems. Part 1: The revised three-layer graph-based meta model 3LGM². *Methods of Information in Medicine*, *42*(5), 544–551.

Živanov, Ž., Rakić, P., & Hajduković, M. (2008). Using code generation approach in developing kiosk applications. *Computer Science and Information Systems*, *5*(1), 41–59. doi:10.2298/CSIS0801041Z

ADDITIONAL READING

Bézivin, J. (2005). On the unification power of models. *Software & Systems Modeling*, *4*(2), 171–188. doi:10.1007/s10270-005-0079-0

Castro, J., Kolp, M., & Mylopoulos, J. (2002). Towards requirements-driven information systems engineering: The Tropos project. *Information Systems*, *27*, 365–389. doi:10.1016/S0306-4379(02)00012-1

Cook, S. (2004). Domain specific modeling and model driven architecture. *MDA Journal*. Retrieved October 8, 2011, from http://www.bptrends.com/publicationfiles/01-04%20COL%20Dom%20Spec%20Modeling%20Frankel-Cook.pdf

Dalgarno, M., & Fowler, M. (2008). UML versus domain specific languages. *EE Times*. Retrieved September 25, 2011, from http://www.eetimes.com/design/other/4026907/UML-versus-Domain-Specific-Languages

Demuth, B., & Wilke, C. (2009). Model and object verification by using Dresden OCL. In *Proceedings of the Russian-German Workshop Innovation Information Technologies: Theory and Practice* (pp. 1-9). Ufa, Russia: Ufa State Aviation Technical University.

Evans, E. (2003). *Domain-driven design: Tackling complexity in the heart of software*. Boston, MA: Addison Wesley Professional.

Fowler, M. (2010). *Domain-specific languages*. Upper Saddle River, NJ: Addison-Wesley.

Frankel, D. S. (2003). *Model driven architecture: Applying MDA to enterprise computing*. Indianapolis, IN: Wiley.

Gašević, D., Djurić, D., & Devedžić, V. (2009). *Model driven engineering and ontology development* (2nd ed.). Berlin, Germany: Springer-Verlag.

Ghosh, D. (2010). *DSLs in ACTION*. Stamford, CT: Manning Publications.

Gunasekaran, A. (Ed.). (2007). *Modeling and analysis of enterprise information systems*. Hershey, PA: IGI Publishing. doi:10.4018/978-1-59904-477-4

Gunasekaran, A. (Ed.). (2008). *Techniques and tools for the design and implementation of enterprise information systems*. Hershey, PA: IGI Publishing. doi:10.4018/978-1-59904-826-0

Guttman, M., & Parodi, J. (2007). *Real-life MDA: Solving business problems with model driven architecture*. San Francisco, CA: Morgan Kaufmann.

Halpin, T., & Morgan, T. (2008). *Information modeling and relational databases* (2nd ed.). San Francisco, CA: Morgan Kaufmann.

Hevner, A. R., March, S. T., Park, J., & Ram, S. (2004). Design science in information systems research. *Management Information Systems Quarterly*, *28*(1), 75–105.

Jouault, F., & Bézivin, J. (2006). KM3: A DSL for metamodel specification. In *Proceedings of 8th IFIP International Conference on Formal Methods for Open Object-Based Distributed Systems, Lecture Notes in Computer Science, Vol. 4037* (pp. 171-185). Berlin, Germany: Springer-Verlag.

Kelly, S., & Tolvanen, J. P. (2008). *Domain-specific modeling: Enabling full code generation*. Hoboken, NJ: John Wiley & Sons.

Krahn, H., Rumpe, B., & Völkel, S. (2006). Roles in software development using domain specific modelling languages. In *Proceedings of 6th OOPSLA Workshop on Domain-Specific Modeling* (pp. 150-158). Jyväskylä, Finland: University of Jyväskylä.

Medvidovic, N., & Rosenblum, D. S. (1997). Domains of concern in software architectures and architecture description languages. In *Proceedings of the Conference on Domain-Specific Languages* (pp. 199-212). Berkeley, CA: USENIX Association.

Smeets, G. J. W. M. (2010). *A domain specific language for web information systems: What about evolving data models?* Unpublished Master's thesis, Eindhoven University of Technology, Eindhoven, The Netherlands.

Stibe, A., & Bicevskis, J. (2009). Web site modeling and prototyping based on a domain-specific language. *Scientific Papers, University of Latvia. Computer Science and Information Technologies, 751*, 7–21.

Tolvanen, J. P., & Kelly, S. (2005). Defining domain-specific modeling languages to automate product derivation: Collected experiences. In H. Obbink & K. Pohl (Eds.), *The 9th International Software Product Line Conference, Lecture Notes in Computer Science, Vol. 3714* (pp. 198-209). Berlin, Germany: Springer-Verlag.

Vágó, D. (2006). *Simulation and transformation of domain-specific languages*. Unpublished Master's thesis, Budapest University of Technology and Economics, Budapest, Hungary.

Vanderdonckt, J. (2005). Amda-compliant environment for developing user interfaces of information systems. In Ó. Pastor & J. Falcão e Cunha (Eds.), *The 17th Conference on Advanced Information Systems Engineering, Lecture Notes in Computer Science, Vol. 3520* (pp. 16–31). Berlin, Germany: Springer-Verlag.

Yu, E. (2004). Information systems. In Singh, M. P. (Ed.), *The practical handbook of Internet computing* (pp. 33-1–33-19). Boca Raton, FL: Chapman & Hall/CRC. doi:10.1201/9780203507223.ch33

KEY TERMS AND DEFINITIONS

Conceptual Modeling (CM): System modeling based on a family of specification techniques that is expected to produce a representation of a system using technology independent concepts, closer to the end-users' perception of a system.

Domain Specific Application Development Environment (DSADE): A software environment that supports creation and evolution of different applications belonging to one application family by combining DSLs and MDSD approaches to create software specifications and generate executable applications.

Domain Specific Modeling (DSM): Modeling that relies on the use of a DSML. It provides creating models that are to be used as starting points for automatic code generation.

Domain Specific Modeling Language (DSML): A domain specific language created to provide a domain specific modeling technique covering all the necessary concepts, formal rules and semantics.

Model Driven Software Development (MDSD) Tool: A software (or CASE) tool that provides the software development process, including formal design, implementation and deployment activities. It provides necessary tools and languages for creating computational and platform independent model specifications, as well as for applying a chain of model transformations to the generated program code.

Model Transformation Language: A domain specific language that supports transformations between models belonging to the same or different abstraction levels.

Visual DSL: A visual and repository-based tool providing necessary domain specific concepts, aimed at modeling formal specifications.

Chapter 18
A Domain-Specific Language for High-Level Parallelization

Ritu Arora
Texas Advanced Computing Center, USA

Purushotham Bangalore
University of Alabama at Birmingham, USA

Marjan Mernik
University of Maribor, Slovenia

ABSTRACT

There are several ongoing research efforts in the High Performance Computing (HPC) domain that are employing Domain-Specific Languages (DSLs) as the means of augmenting end-user productivity. A discussion on some of the research efforts that can positively impact the end-user productivity without negatively impacting the application performance is presented in this chapter. An overview of the process of developing a DSL for specifying parallel computations, called High-Level Parallelization Language (Hi-PaL), is presented along with the metrics for measuring its impact. A discussion on the future directions in which the DSL-based approaches can be applied in the HPC domain is also included.

INTRODUCTION

The High Performance Computing (HPC) discipline has seen tremendous growth in the last decade in terms of the power and scale of computing platforms. By the next decade we might as well be into the exascale computing era. One of the key challenges on the path to exascale computing is to develop programming environments that would reduce the complexity associated with the process of developing HPC applications, especially in the light of heterogeneity in the computing platforms and multiple levels of memory hierarchies.

There are plenty of parallel programming models that are already in widespread usage or have the potential of being widely used - for example, MPI (MPI Forum, 2009), OpenMP (OpenMP, 2011), OpenCL (OpenCL, 2011), TBB (Threaded Building Blocks, 2011), Cilk Plus (Intel Cilk Plus, 2011), Coarray Fortran (Mellor-Crummey et al, 2009), and UPC (UPC, 2005). Each model is suitable for a particular architecture and has

DOI: 10.4018/978-1-4666-2092-6.ch018

a learning curve associated with it. Due to the rapidly evolving solution space for developing HPC applications, the programmers are caught in the "problem of plenty." Moreover, the exascale computing platforms are likely to use hybrid programming models – probably MPI for communication between different address spaces and a shared memory programming paradigm for communication within an address space. While programming in a single parallel paradigm is quite a challenge by itself (Arora et al, 2012), handling hybrid programming models could put additional burden on programmers.

With the increase in heterogeneity in the computing platforms, it is also a challenge to write portable applications that can run optimally on a variety of architectures. It is a tedious task to hand-tune the applications for every architecture that they are meant to run on. High-level parallel programming environments and abstractions that can assist in the rapid development of scalable and optimized HPC applications are, therefore, required.

Domain-Specific Languages (DSLs) that are written in a platform-independent manner can be helpful in capturing the description of algorithms at a high-level. The high-level description of an algorithm can then be used to generate low-level code for multiple HPC platforms (Sujeeth et al, 2011). The low-level code generated from the DSL code can be optimized automatically on the basis of the domain knowledge built in the compiler and run-time system. DSLs, therefore, not only have the potential of increasing the programmer productivity but can also help in squeezing maximum performance from the applications via domain-specific optimizations.

The key objectives of this chapter are to discuss some active research works that aim at increasing the productivity of HPC application developers through the usage of DSLs and abstractions, present a walk-through of the complete process of developing a DSL, and discuss ways to measure its impact.

BACKGROUND

DSLs are gradually gaining popularity in the HPC domain because DSL-based approaches have been shown to be helpful in developing parallel applications and algorithms at a high-level of abstraction. The low-level details related to the development and deployment of HPC applications (*viz.* managing the communication between processors, distribution of data on various processors, and load-balancing) can be hidden from the programmers. A key advantage of the DSL-based approaches is that the specifications of applications or algorithms need not be modified in the event of a change in the underlying architecture. Therefore, the application portability concerns are assuaged. DSLs are also helpful in the separation of concerns (Arora et al, 2011; Kiczales et al, 1997). Some of the DSLs that have the potential of reducing the adoption barriers to HPC are discussed in this section.

High-Level Parallelization Language (Hi-PaL) is an application-domain neutral, declarative and platform-independent DSL for expressing concurrency in existing sequential applications written in C/C++ (Arora et al, 2011). The existing sequential applications are analyzed for concurrency and data-dependencies by the programmers who then write Hi-PaL code to provide specifications about what to parallelize and where (in the sequential application). The Hi-PaL code is automatically translated into low-level C/C++/MPI code and woven into the existing applications with the help of a Source-to-Source Compiler (SSC). It is a multi-step process that involves generation of grammar-specific (C/C++ grammar-specific) rules so that the SSC can carry out automatic code transformation (Arora et al, 2011; Czarnecki et al, 2000). Without Hi-PaL, the end-users would have to write their own grammar-specific rules if they have to do automatic source-to-source transformation, or they would have to manually (and invasively) insert the C/C++/MPI code into the existing sequential application to make it parallel. Hi-PaL, therefore, raises the level of abstraction of parallelizing the existing sequential applications while separating sequential and parallel concerns. The performance of the parallel code generated by the system using Hi-PaL is comparable to that of the manually-written code. The complete transformation framework is called FraSPA (Arora et al, 2011). The design of Hi-PaL was influenced by the key-concepts in Aspect-Oriented Programming (AOP) languages (Kiczales et al, 1997). Like in AOP languages (*e.g.*, AspectC, and AspectC++), Hi-PaL has a notion of join-point model and pattern-matching for code transformation.

Another interesting work-in-progress is OptiML (Sujeeth et al, 2011). It is a DSL that helps in the implicit parallelization of problems in the machine learning domain. It is embedded in the Scala programming language and is built on the Delite runtime system (Sujeeth et al, 2011). OptiML can be used to express iterative statistical inference problems as dense or sparse linear algebra operations. These problems exhibit a combination of regular and irregular data parallelism. The OptiML code is translated into an intermediate representation of the program. Pattern-matching techniques are then applied on the intermediate representation for static optimization prior to the code generation (*e.g.*, the sequence of operations is optimized according to linear algebra simplification rules). Dynamic domain-specific optimizations are also done. The optimized intermediate code is then translated into the target languages which are C++, Scala, and CUDA. It is noted that not all OptiML operations can be translated into all the target languages (Sujeeth et al, 2011). Besides the code in the target language, the execution graph showing the program's operations and dependencies is also generated. The Delite runtime system runs the generated code with the execution graph. It also provides synchronization and communication between kernels.

Domain-Specific Language for Application-Level Checkpointing (DALC) helps in the non-invasive Application-Level Checkpointing (ALC) of legacy applications (Arora et al, 2010). ALC is useful for inserting the Checkpointing and Restart (CaR) mechanism directly into the applications, thus making them reliable. Only those application variables and data structures are saved to the disk during ALC that are critical for recreating the complete execution state of the application. The end-users provide the specifications for CaR – what to checkpoint/restart, where to checkpoint/restart, how often to checkpoint - by the means of DALC. These specifications are translated into the code that has the functionality of CaR. The generated CaR code is then inserted in the legacy application automatically. DALC was developed from scratch and, like Hi-PaL, has resemblance to AOP languages. Though DALC currently supports non-invasive ALC of applications written in C/C++ only, it can be extended to support legacy applications written in other high-level programming languages as well (*e.g.*, Java and FORTRAN).

Neptune (Bunch et al, 2011) is a DSL that automates the configuration and deployment of HPC applications over cloud computing platforms. It extends the open-source cloud computing platform, AppScale - AppScale Tools and AppController in particular (Chohan et al, 2009) - to support services like MPI (C/C++ bindings), X10 (Charles et al, 2005), and MapReduce (Dean et al, 2008). By using the Neptune interface and language, end-users can configure cloud resources and services for running HPC applications. As an example, to run MPI jobs in the cloud computing platforms, the end-users are required to specify the path to the executable, the number of machines on which the code should run, and the path to the output location. The Neptune language has been developed as an extension of the Ruby programming language.

The overview of the DSLs presented in this section indicates that both abstraction and performance can be achieved via DSL-based approaches. The HPC community has, for a long time, been skeptical about abstractions and high-level parallel programming paradigms and platforms (Basili et al, 2008). However, DSL-based approaches (*e.g.,* Hi-PaL, OptiML, DALC, and Neptune) are influencing the old school of thought and are receiving special attention due to their potential of allowing high-level of optimization in narrow domains. The DSL-based approaches (*viz.* Hi-PaL) could be helpful in leveraging from the years of software investment as they do not entail the complete algorithm or application rewrite. The specifications provided via DSLs could be used to generate code for multiple types of computing platforms (Sujeeth et al, 2011). Hence, two main issues related to the exascale computing era, the portability issues and issues related to the "problem of plenty," could be resolved to a great extent.

DESIGN AND DEVELOPMENT OF HIGH-LEVEL PARALLELIZATION LANGUAGE

MPI is the most widely used standard for developing parallel applications for distributed memory architectures. It involves explicit distribution of large tasks or data required for solving a problem amongst multiple *processes* such that the overall time required for finding a solution to the problem is reduced. Each *process* could be running on a different core or a processor and does the computation for its share of tasks. It should be noted that each *process* has a different address space and hence uses MPI routines for communicating with other *processes* for data exchange and synchronization purposes. Objects that are known as *communicators* and *groups* are used to set-up the communication between *processes*. *Communicators* are required by most MPI routines as an argument. A predefined communicator known as `MPI_COMM_WORLD` can be used to orchestrate the message-passing between all the *processes* in a particular *group*. The total number of *processes* that are associated with a particular *communicator* is usually referred to as the `size`. In a group of *processes*, each *process* has a unique identification number, an integer value ranging from 0 to (`size -1`), that is known as `rank`.

The speed, control, and scalability offered by MPI are the key reasons behind its widespread usage. However, there are several challenges associated with the process of developing parallel applications using the MPI paradigm. In order to develop a parallel program using MPI, the programmers usually start with a working sequential application. They identify the concurrency in the application and express the same by embedding the appropriate MPI-routines in the application. The MPI-routines can be broadly categorized as environment management routines (*e.g.,* `MPI_Init`, `MPI_Comm_size`, and `MPI_Comm_rank`) and communication routines (*e.g.,* `MPI_Send`, `MPI_Isend`, and `MPI_Bcast`).

The process of choosing the appropriate MPI-routine and communication pattern is usually ad-hoc (Skjellum et al, 2004). Besides choosing the type of MPI-routine, the programmers are also required to restructure their application to take care of data-distribution, synchronization, load-balancing, *etc.* (Arora et al, 2012). It is difficult to debug MPI applications as the error messages generated are not too informative. Once the programmers have a working parallel code, they are required to hand-tune it to obtain maximum performance.

Most of the aforementioned challenges associated with the process of parallelizing the applications using MPI can be reduced by developing high-level programming interfaces or DSLs. Hi-PaL is one such DSL that can be used by end-users (*e.g.,* computational biologists or chemists) for semi-automatically transforming their sequential applications into a parallel one. An overview of its design and implementation is presented in this section.

Hi-PaL is an extensible DSL that is helpful in capturing the specifications of parallelization at a high-level. The specifications provided in Hi-PaL are used to transform an existing sequential application into a performance-oriented MPI-based parallel application. A Source-to-Source Compiler (SSC) works in conjunction with Hi-PaL to achieve the transformation of a sequential application into a parallel one and this transformation is pictorially explained in Figure 1 (Arora et al, 2012). The end-user identifies concurrency in the existing *Sequential Code* and expresses the same using Hi-PaL. The *Rule Generator* parses the *Hi-PaL Code* and generates intermediate code. The intermediate code is a set of rules (*Generated Rules* in Figure 1) that the SSC can comprehend. These rules contain the precise information about the type of modifications desired by the end-user, and the place in the *Sequential Code* where these modifications should take effect. The SSC transforms the *Sequential Code* into *Parallel Code* by applying the *Generated Rules* and other code components (*e.g., Design Templates*).

Even though, all the steps that are involved in the transformation process are like a "black-box" to the end-user, they can understand the changes made to the sequential code by reading the generated parallel code (*Parallel Code* in Figure 1). Any performance analysis, if required, can be done on the transformed code like it can be done on a manually written code. In essence, the Hi-PaL based approach does not entail invasive manual-reengineering of existing applications, is platform-independent, and is application-domain neutral. While further details on the complete transformation framework called FraSPA can be found in (Arora et al, 2012), only the details related to the design and development of Hi-PaL are presented in this chapter.

Domain Analysis and Design

The first step in developing a DSL is analyzing the domain for which it is being developed. The domain of Hi-PaL is parallel processing. During the domain analysis phase, a survey of technical literature and existing implementations of high-level languages was done to get an overview of the terminologies and concepts related to the parallel processing domain. Commonly used terms and their relationships were utilized to develop the domain lexicon. Feature-Oriented Domain Analysis (FODA) (Czarnecki et al, 2000) was used for further domain analysis. Because the specifications for parallel processing can vary from application to application, different application-domains (*e.g.,* image processing, evolutionary algorithms, and stencil-based computations) were evaluated to build the key abstractions in the form of Hi-PaL. A production from the BNF of Hi-PaL is presented in Figure 2. This shows the general structure of Hi-PaL programs.

The mandatory keywords required for writing any syntactically correct Hi-PaL code are shown

Figure 1. Overview of parallel code generation using Hi-PaL code and existing sequential code

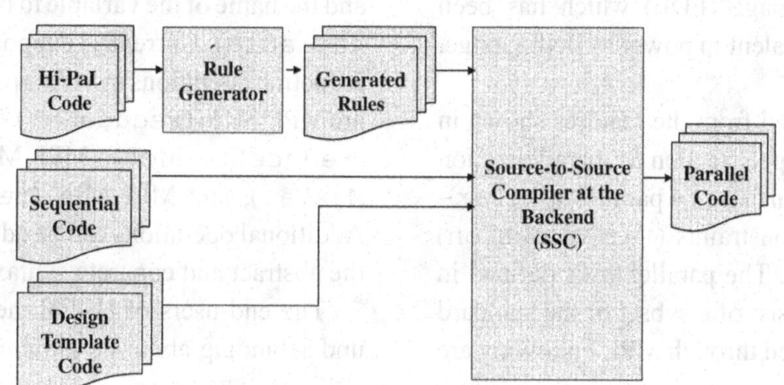

Figure 2. Structure of Hi-PaL programs

```
PROGRAM ::= 'Parallel section begins' HOOKTYPE, PATTERN 'mapping is' MAPPING
'{' , {PARSPECS}, '}'
```

Figure 3. Excerpt of the features and production rules in Hi-PaL

```
ParSpecs: all(ParTask, ParCondition)
ParCondition: {all(Hook, pattern)}+
Hook: all(HookType, HookElement)
HookType: one-of(before, after, around)
HookElement: one-of(statement, FCT)
FCT: one-of(function_call, function_execution)
ParTask: more-of(ParCompute, ParReduce, ParAllReduce, ParFor, ParGather,
        ParDistribute, ParExchange, ParBroadcast, ParWrite, ParRead)
ParReduce: all(RedType, redVariable)
RedType: all(one-of(reduceSum, reduceProduct, reduceMinVal, reduceMaxVal),DataType)
```

within single quotes in the EBNF definition in Figure 2 (*e.g.,* 'Parallel section begins'). The Hi-PaL code will not compile if any of these keywords are missing and appropriate error messages are generated. The words in boldface and without quotes are the variable features of Hi-PaL. Different data-distribution schemes can be specified by choosing different values for MAPPING. The feature PATTERN stands for search pattern. An excerpt of the features and production rules of Hi-PaL grammar are shown in Figure 3. These are described using Feature Description Language (FDL) which has been shown to be equivalent in power to BNF (Jonge, 2002).

It can be noticed from the features shown in Figure 3 that the specification for parallelization (ParSpecs) consists of a parallel task (ParTask) and the constraints (ParCondition) for parallelization. The parallel tasks defined in this grammar consist of a subset of the standard operations provided through MPI. Following are some examples: reducing the data or combining the value from multiple processes into a single value (ParReduce, ParAllReduce), gathering the data from the processes (ParGather), and distributing the data amongst the processes (ParDistribute). Each type of parallel task can be further broken down into the basic elements of the grammar. As an example, consider the rule for reducing the data. According to the Hi-PaL grammar, the specification of the reduction operation (ParReduce) consists of the specification of the type of reduction operation (RedType) and the name of the variable to be reduced (redVariable). Currently, support for a subset of reduction operations in MPI is provided and those are MPI_SUM (reduceSum), MPI_PRODUCT (reduceProduct), MPI_MAX (reduceMaxVal), and MPI_MIN (reduceMinVal). Additional operations can be added by extending the abstract and concrete syntax of Hi-PaL.

The end-users of Hi-PaL need not have any understanding about its grammar and its details

Figure 4. Excerpt of the Hi-PaL API

Hi-PaL API	Description
ReduceProductInt(<variable name>)	MPI_Reduce with product operation
ReduceSumInt(<variable name>)	MPI_Reduce with sum operation
ReduceMinValInt(<variable name>)	MPI_Reduce with min operation
AllReduceSumInt(<variable name>)	MPI_Allreduce with sum operation
ParDistributeVectorDouble(<vector name>, <num of rows>)	MPI_Scatterv to distribute the vector
ParGather2DArrayDouble(<array name>, <num of rows>, <num of columns>)	MPI_Gatherv to collect the data
ParBroadCast2DArrayDouble(<array name>, <num of rows>, <num of columns>)	MPI_Broadcast to broadcast the data
Parallelize_For_Loop where (<for_init_stmt>;<condition>;<stride>)	Parallelize for-loop with matching initialization statement, condition and stride

are only important for the programmers who wish to extend the language. With the help of Hi-PaL, the end-users can specify the tasks required for parallelizing the existing sequential applications at a very high-level, without having the knowledge about MPI API or its usage. A set of Hi-PaL API has been developed for the commonly used parallel tasks like data-distribution, data-collection, reading or writing the data in parallel, parallelizing a for-loop, *etc.* An excerpt of some of the Hi-PaL API and their brief description (type of MPI routine or the parallelization code associated with the API) is presented in Figure 4. To shorten the learning-curve, the API-names were chosen to be descriptive such that the end-user can understand the purpose of the API just by reading the name. As an example, the API, `ParDistributeVectorDouble(<vector name>, <num of rows>)`, means that the vector or a 1-dimensional array, specified by `<vector name>` is of type `double` and it needs to be distributed amongst the available processes. The length of the vector is specified by `<num of rows>`.

The end-user should specify the conditions or constraints (`ParCondition`) for parallelization by providing both a hook-definition and a search-pattern (`Hook` and `pattern` respectively in Figure 3). A hook-definition includes the specification of `HookType` and `HookElement`. An end-user can select one out of the three types of hooks (`HookType`) - *before*, *after*, and *around*. There are three choices available for `HookElement` as well - `statement`, `function_call`, and `function_execution`. It should be noted here that various language extensions for AOP (*e.g.*, AspectC++ and AspectC) do not allow loops to be specified as join-points (Kiczales et al, 1997). However, because in Hi-PaL, any syntactically correct program statement can qualify as a `HookElement`, loops can be specified directly for transformation (or parallelization) purposes. Specification of hook type and pattern is also required for specifying the point in the sequential application from where the parallelization should begin (`HOOKTYPE, PATTERN` in Figure 2) and because the pattern here is always a statement, the end-user need not specify the `HookElement` explicitly. Therefore, there are at least two hooks required for parallelization purposes – one for specifying the beginning of parallelization and the other for specifying the place where parallel operation should take effect.

The utility of `HookType`, `HookElement`, and search-pattern is explained with the help of

Figure 5. General structure of the Hi-PaL code

```
Parallel section begins <hook type> (<hook pattern>) mapping is <mapping type> {
    <operation along with the arguments> <hook> && in function (<function name>)
}
```

Figure 6. Sample Hi-PaL code showing the broadcast operation specification

```
Parallel section begins after ("SEED = atoi(argv[4]);") mapping is Linear{
  ParBroadCast2DArrayInt(life, M, N) after statement
  ("life = initMatrix<int>(life, M, N);") && in function ("main")
}
```

the following scenarios. If there is a statement in a sequential application *after* which the code for setting the MPI-environment should be inserted then the `HookType` in this case should be *after*, the `HookElement` should be `statement` (but it is implicit), and the statement itself must be specified as a search-pattern. If there is a statement in the sequential application that is not required in the parallel version of the code but should serve as an anchor for inserting a parallel task (`ParTask`), then the `HookType` in this case should be *around*, the `HookElement` should be `statement` (explicitly mentioned), and the statement itself must be specified as a search-pattern.

Apart from the hook-definition and search-pattern, an end-user is also required to specify the type of mapping, like Linear or Cyclic (Koelbel et al, 1994), which is desired in the parallel application. The general structure of the Hi-PaL code is shown in Figure 5 (and is similar to the EBNF program shown in Figure 2). The mandatory structural elements of the Hi-PaL code are shown in bold-face in Figure 5. The italicized elements inside angular brackets are the variable structural elements of the Hi-PaL code (*e.g.*, API for parallelization and statements for pattern matching). The "`&&`" operator is used for creating powerful match expressions. A sample program written in Hi-PaL is shown in Figure 6. This sample code demonstrates the method of specifying the broadcast operation on a matrix named `life` in function `main`. A one-to-one mapping of the structural elements of the Hi-PaL code (Figure 5) and the sample Hi-PaL code shown in Figure 6 is presented in Figure 7. This mapping illustrates the simplicity of Hi-PaL. The standard structural elements (*e.g.*, `Parallel section begins after` and `mapping is`) are going to remain the same in all the Hi-PaL programs.

Implementation of Hi-PaL

Hi-PaL was implemented using the Model-Driven Engineering (MDE) (Schmidt, 2006) platform called Atlas Model Management Architecture (AMMA, 2008). MDE is a software engineering paradigm that involves abstraction of real-world entities or concepts as models. With the help of a translator or an interpreter, the actual code can be automatically generated from the models. Hence, MDE raises the level of abstraction of programming in high-level languages and helps in expressing domain-specific concepts efficiently. Some of the MDE-concepts are defined below.

- **Model:** A model is a representation of a system and can be of three types - a terminal model, a metamodel or a metametamodel.
- **Terminal Model:** A model whose reference model is a metamodel.

Figure 7. One-to-one mapping of the Hi-PaL structural elements into the sample code

General Structure of Hi-PaL Code (Figure 5)	Sample Hi-PaL Code (Figure 6)
Parallel section begins	Parallel section begins
<hook type>	after
(<hook pattern>)	("SEED = atoi(argv[4]);")
mapping is	mapping is
<mapping type>	Linear
{	{
<operation along with the arguments>	ParBroadCast2DArrayInt(life, M, N)
<hook>	after statement
&& in function	&& in function
<function name>	("main")
}	}

- **MetaModel:** A model that defines a language for expressing other models. It describes different contained model elements and the relationship between them. It conforms to a metametamodel and the Meta-Object Facility (MOF) is an example of a metametamodel. The MOF metametamodel is self-defined.
- **MegaModel:** A megamodel is a model that records the global information on tools, services and other models.

AMMA provides a set of facilities for processing models and consists of the main blocks that are listed below.

- **Kernel MetaMetaModel (KM3):** It is an implementation-independent, textual domain-specific language for defining the abstract syntax of the DSLs in the form of metamodels (Jouault & Bézivin, 2006). KM3 uses concepts like package, class, attribute, reference, and primitive data type.
- **Textual Concrete Syntax (TCS):** TCS (Jouault, Bézivin & Kurtev, 2006) is itself a DSL and can be used to specify the textual concrete syntax of other DSLs by attaching syntactic information to metamodels. TCS-specifications are used to automatically generate tools for model-to-text (by generating ANTLR grammar) and text-to-model transformations (by using a Java-based extractor).
- **Atlas Transformation Language (ATL):** A model transformation language transforms a set of source models into a set of target models on the basis of the defined rules (Jouault & Kurtev, 2005). ATL has its abstract syntax defined as a metamodel and every ATL transformation is itself considered as a model. The language consists of rules and expressions that are based on OCL (OCL, 2006). Each rule consists of a source pattern on its left-hand side and a target pattern on the right-hand side. The source pattern consists of model element types from the source metamodels and the boolean expressions. The target pattern consists of the model element types from the target metamodel. A set of bindings is attached to each rule for specifying the way in which the properties of the target elements should be initialized.
- **Atlas MegaModel Management (AM3):** Provides support for global resource management in a model-engineering environment. The main features of AM3 are management of megamodels, management of

Figure 8. Excerpt of the KM3 code for modeling the grammar rule for `ParReduce`

```
1.  class ParSpecs extends LocatedElement {
2.    reference parTask [*] container : ParTask;
3.    reference parCond[*] container : ParCond;
4.  }

5.  abstract class ParTask extends LocatedElement { }

6.  class ParReduce extends ParTask {
7.    reference redVarType container : RedVar;
8.    reference varArgs[*] container : RedVarArg;
9.  }

10. class RedVarArg extends LocatedElement {
11.     attribute argument : String;
12. }

13. abstract class RedVar extends LocatedElement {}

14. class ReduceSumInt extends RedVar {}
```

various relations between artifacts (*e.g.,* models, metamodels, transformations, and semantic correspondences), sharing and exchanging of megamodel elements, and user interfaces for viewing megamodel elements (Bézivin et al, 2004; Kurtev et al, 2006). Because the AM3 supported megamodels allow the manipulation of other resources such as XML documents, database tables or flat files as well, the notion of artifacts is used in general.

In the case of Hi-PaL, KM3 and TCS were used for writing the abstract and concrete syntax. While KM3 itself is like a DSL for writing new DSLs, TCS is like a grammar-template that needs to be extended. Each production rule in Hi-PaL was coded as classes in KM3 and templates in TCS. A snippet of the KM3 code for modeling the grammar rule for `ParReduce` (refer to Figure 3) in Hi-PaL is shown in Figure 8 and line # 5 in Figure 8 shows that `ParTask` is defined as an abstract class. All the classes for specifying MPI tasks (*e.g.,* reduce, gather, and distribute) are required to extend this abstract class. The `ParReduce` class extends `ParTask` and contains references to other classes - `RedVar`, and `RedVarArg` (see lines 6-9 of Figure 8). Because there are multiple options available for the type of reduction operation, the class `RedVar` is modeled as an abstract class (line # 13 of Figure 8). Hence, the classes modeling the different types of reduction operations (*e.g.,* MPI_MAX or MPI_MIN) are required to extend the `RedVar` class. In essence, if there are multiple values possible for a particular element in a grammar rule, then that element is modeled as an abstract class and a separate class (which can be either abstract or concrete) extending this abstract class is written for every possible value that the element can take.

While the KM3 metamodel provides the abstract syntax of the language being developed, the concrete syntax of the language is specified in a separate model that is expressed using TCS. In a TCS model, the "Class templates" and the "Operator table" are of main interest to a language developer (Jouault, Bézivin & Kurtev, 2006). All classes in the KM3 specification require a cor-

Figure 9. Excerpt of the TCS code for modeling the grammar rule for `ParReduce`

```
1.    template ParSpecs
2.    : parTask parCond {separator = "&&"}
3.    ;

4.    template ParTask abstract;

5.    template ParReduce
6.    : redVarType "(" varArgs{separator = ","} ")"
7.    ;

8.    template RedVarArg
9.    : argument
10.   ;

11.   template RedVar abstract;

12.   template ReduceSumInt
13.   : "ReduceSumInt"
14.   ;
```

responding template definition in TCS. The "Operator table" is used for defining the syntax of DSL using operators. The terminal tokens, like separators and brackets, are a part of the TCS model. If the default lexer is not satisfactory, then the "Primitive template" in TCS can be modified as per the requirement. If additional symbols are required then the class for "Special symbols" should be modified. An excerpt of the concrete syntax of Hi-PaL, as defined in TCS, is shown in Figure 9. The keyword `template` is used as a part of the definition of all the KM3 classes as templates. The name of the KM3 class (`ParReduce`) is specified along with the name of the class elements (`redVarType` and `varArgs`) defined in the KM3 model. The, "," is to be used as a separator between the arguments and the same is specified as follows:

```
{separator = ","}
```

In the template definition of `ParReduce`, lines 5-7, note the specification of "(" and ")". These tokens could not be a part of KM3 model but are necessary for specifying the structure of the grammar rule and hence are a part of the TCS template definition.

The AMMA platform was not only used for developing Hi-PaL, but also for capturing the semantics of the transformation rules as a metamodel. This step was required for doing the metamodel-to-metamodel translation by using the ATL in the AMMA toolsuite. The metamodel for the Hi-PaL in the front-end is known as "source metamodel" whereas the metamodel for the rules to be used in the backend is called the "target metamodel." These transformation rules are specific to the SSC and are written in the Rules Specification Language (RSL) (Baxter et al, 2004).

The Hi-PaL specifications can be considered as a terminal model in the MDE terminology and are first injected into the source metamodel. The specifications are validated against the metamodel during the process of injection. With the help of the ATL transformations and Ant Scripts, the code injected in the Hi-PaL metamodel is translated into the terminal model for RSL rules. The process of obtaining the RSL terminal model from the RSL

Figure 10. Extraction and injection of models

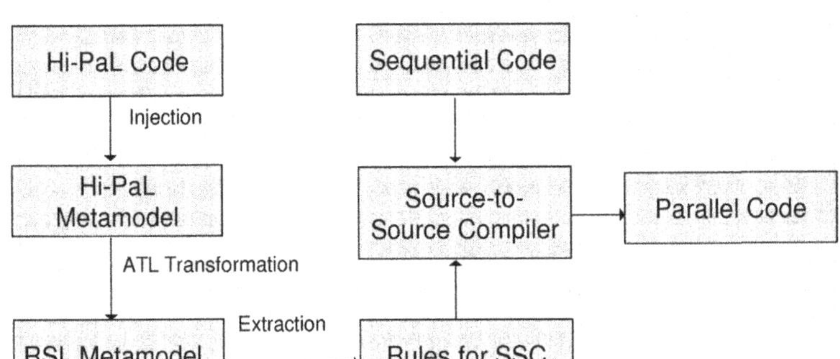

metamodel is called extraction. The RSL rules thus generated are used by the SSC for weaving the parallelization code into the existing application. All these steps result in the transformed code (parallel code), and the complete workflow of the process of transformation through models is pictorially shown in Figure 10.

The Rule Generator that was mentioned in Figure 1 is nothing but a combination of a set of ATL rules (ATL + OCL code), Ant Scripts, and RSL metamodel. A snippet of the ATL rule is shown in Figure 11, and shows that the rule consists of the description of the source metamodel (Hi-PaL) and the target metamodel (RSL) along with the mapping of the syntactic elements from the source metamodel to the target metamodel. The source and target metamodels are specified as `from` and `to` in the rule. Each type of RSL rule (*e.g.*, for modifying a for-loop, for setting up the MPI environment, and for performing the gather operation), is modeled as a separate ATL rule using the elements of ATL syntax and OCL expressions. For brevity, further details related to the ATL rules are not being provided in this chapter.

The ATL rule snippet that is shown in Figure 11 is meant for generating the RSL rule for automating the insertion of the MPI code for reduce operation in the existing sequential application. The compulsory elements of the RSL rule (*e.g.*, `statement_seq` and `add_var`) are hard-coded in the ATL rule. The variable parts that are application-specific are automatically derived from the terminal model (*i.e.*, the Hi-PaL code) provided by the end-user. It can be observed from the code snippet shown in Figure 11 that the OCL expressions are used for traversing the nodes of the terminal model to obtain the values of the variables in the ATL rule. The OCL expressions shown in Figure 11 are meant to derive the name of the variable to be reduced from the terminal model. The data type of the variable to be reduced is also derived from the terminal model. Both these derived values are used for declaring a variable in which the global value of the MPI operation (*e.g.*, MPI_SUM or MPI_MIN) is stored during the reduce operation.

The Ant Scripts are used in the transformation system for saving the KM3 model in the Ecore format, transforming the source model to target model on the basis of the specified ATL rule, serializing the target model into text, and for debugging. They are also used as the glue code for copying the files (RSL rules and sequential code) from AMMA platform to the required folders in the SSC installation, for invoking the SSC for code weaving, and for copying the generated parallel code back to AMMA platform. Therefore, the Ant Scripts are used for automating the complete workflow in this transformation system.

Figure 11. ATL code snippet

```
module HPAL2RSL;
create OUT : RSL from IN : HPAL;
rule HPAL2RSL {
   from
        s : HPAL!HPAL
   to
        t : RSL!RSL (
             domain <- dom,
             rslelems <- Sequence {pat1, expat1, rule1, pat2, pat3, expat2, rule2}, ruleset <- rs
        ),
        dom : RSL!Domain(
                dname <- 'Cpp'
         ),
         rs : RSL!RuleSet (
             rsname <- 'r',
             rname <- Sequence {'extend_decl', 'add_statements'}
        ),
        pat1 : RSL!Pattern(
             phead <- ph,
             ptoken <- 'statement_seq',
             ptext <- pt
        ),
        ph : RSL!PatternHead (
             name <- 'add_var'
        ),
        pt : RSL!SimplePatternText (
             ptext <- s.parSpecs->iterate(parSpec; c : String = ''| c +
                      if (parSpec.parTask->first().oclIsKindOf(PDSL!ParReduce))
                      then if(parSpec.parTask->first().redVarType.oclIsTypeOf(PDSL!ReduceMaxValInt)
                              or parSpec.parTask->first().redVarType.oclIsTypeOf(PDSL!ReduceSumInt)
                              or ...)
                         then
                        '\\>Cpp\\:[simple_declaration = decl_specifier_seq init_declarator_list\';\']
                          int
                          \\>Cpp\\:[declarator_id = id_expression]'+
                            parSpec.parTask->first().varArgs->first().argument + '…
                          \\<\\:declarator_id ;
                        \\<\\:simple_declaration'
                        else if (...
```

Example Showing the Usage of Hi-PaL

The Circuit Satisfiability application simulates the actual electronic circuit with logical gates and is adapted from the book "Parallel programming in C with MPI and OpenMP" (Quinn, 2004). The number of input bits, *N*, is specified and the application does an exhaustive search of the solution-space, which is 2^N, to find the relevant combination of input bits for which the circuit would produce an output of 1.

The sequential version of the application was implemented in C and a code snippet of the same is shown in Figure 12. The code snippet shows that this is an embarrassingly parallel application and the computation being done in the for-loop (line # 6-13) can be done in parallel as there are no data-dependencies. The results of partial computations done on multiple processes should be combined to produce a global result. With the MPI standard, the results of partial computations can be combined in multiple ways, but doing so via the MPI_Reduce routine would work best

Figure 12. Code snippet from the sequential circuit satisfiability application

```
1. //other code
2. start = 0;
3. end = pow(2, n);
4. num_solution= 0;
5. t1 = gettime();
6. for ( i = start; i < end; i++ ){
7.     //other code
8.     value = circuit_value ( n, bvec );
9.     if ( value == 1 ) {
10.        num_solution = num_solution + 1;
11.        //other code
12.    }
13. }
14. t2 = gettime();
```

here. The step in which the partial computations are combined to produce a global result will be referred to as "reducing the value" or "reducing the results" or "reducing the data" from this point on in this chapter.

The Hi-PaL code required for parallelizing the Circuit Satisfiability application is shown in Figure 13 and line # 1 of this code describes that the code for setting the MPI-environment should be inserted `after` the statement "`end = pow(2,n);`" found in the sequential application (line # 3 of Figure 12). The mapping is specified to be linear. The line # 2 of the code in Figure 13 describes that the for-loop which is `in function "main"` and has the conditions `(i = start; i < end; i++)` should be parallelized. There are two constraints specified for parallelizing the for-loop. The first constraint specifies that the for-loop is `after` the statement "`end = pow(2,n);`" and is `in function "main"`. This description of for-loop matches the for-loop on line # 6 of Figure 12. With line # 3 of the code in Figure 13, it is described that the results of computation done on multiple processes should be combined into a single value with the help of a reduce operation. The constraints specified on line # 3 mean that the reduce operation should be done before line # 14 of Figure 12.

On the basis of the specifications provided in Hi-PaL, any code-restructuring that might be required, is done. The generated parallel code will automatically have the required files included (*e.g.*, mpi.h and design templates for communication), variable declaration section extended, and MPI-routines inserted. A code snippet from the generated code for Circuit Satisfiability application is shown in Figure 14.

Results and Benefits of Using Hi-PaL

Over 90% reduction in the end-user effort has been seen in terms of the number of Lines of Code (LoC) written manually for all the test-cases that have been generated so far by using the Hi-PaL based framework (Arora et al, 2012). For the Circuit Satisfiability application, the transformation system generates 104 LoC to parallelize the sequential version of the application. The generated parallel application has the code that sets-up the parallel environment, terminates the MPI execution, and

Figure 13. Hi-PaL code for parallelizing the circuit satisfiability application

```
Parallel section begins after ("end = pow(2,n);") mapping is Linear {
Parallelize_For_Loop where (i = start; i < end; i++)
after statement ("end = pow(2,n);") && in function ("main");
ReduceSumInt(num_solution) before statement
("t2=gettime();") && in function ("main")
}
```

Figure 14. Code snippet from the generated parallel Circuit Satisfiability application

```
//other code. Files included & Variable declaration section extended.
start = 0;
end = pow(2, n);
MPI_Init(NULL, NULL);
MPI_Comm_size(MPI_COMM_WORLD, &size_Fraspa);
MPI_Comm_rank(MPI_COMM_WORLD, &rank_Fraspa);
lower_limit_Fraspa = rank_Fraspa *((end - start)…;
upper_limit_Fraspa=((rank_Fraspa==(size_Fraspa - 1))?...;
num_solution = 0;
t1 = MPI_Wtime();
for (i=lower_limit_Fraspa; i<=upper_limit_Fraspa;i++){
    value = circuit_value ( n, bvec );
    if ( value == 1 ) {
        num_solution = num_solution + 1;
        //other code
    }
}
MPI_Reduce(&num_solution,&num_solution_Fraspa,...)
num_solution = num_solution_Fraspa;
t2 = MPI_Wtime();
```

carries out the for-loop parallelization and reduces the desired value. The end-user had to write only 4 logical lines of Hi-PaL code in order to parallelize this application.

The process of code generation using Hi-PaL did not necessitate any explicit changes in the sequential application and the end-users did not have to adapt the application to any generic interfaces. The performance of the generated parallel code for all the test cases is within 5% of that of the manually written parallel code. The run-time comparison of the manually written and generated versions of the Circuit Satisfiability application is shown in Table 1 (Arora et al, 2012). The decrease in the end-user effort for making a sequential application parallel can be used as a measure of increase in end-user productivity. The number of LoC in the transformation system that were reused across various test-cases were also recorded. This gave an idea on the reusability of the components of the transformation system.

With the help of Hi-PaL, the end-users can specify the tasks required to parallelize the existing sequential applications at a very high-level without even knowing anything about MPI API or its usage. The end-users are, however, expected to be familiar with the logic of the sequential application and should be well acquainted with the concept of concurrency. A set of Hi-PaL API has been developed for the commonly used parallel tasks like data-distribution, data-collection, reading or writing the data in parallel, and parallelizing a for-loop.

Hi-PaL is useful for capturing the specifications related to parallel processing in an application-domain neutral manner. It also offers the desired flexibility to experiment with multiple communication patterns and algorithms without spending a lot of effort in manually writing the MPI/C/C++ code

Table 1. Runtime comparison of manually written and generated code - circuit satisfiability application

Number of Processes	Parallel Manual (runtime in seconds)	Parallel Generated (runtime in seconds)
30	7.706	7.718
40	6.073	6.075
50	5.077	5.097

for parallelization. Separation of sequential and parallel code concerns is achieved at a conceptual level, and hence, the process of developing HPC-applications can become a multi-person software development activity. The end-users can focus on the scientific contribution of their work instead of worrying about low-level MPI programming. On the other hand, the parallel programmers can develop optimized code components that can be exposed via Hi-PaL API.

There are some limitations that are associated with the current implementation of Hi-PaL. At present, Hi-PaL does not involve static code analysis for automatically detecting data-dependencies in a for-loop. Hence, the end-users are required to manually ascertain that the operations inside the for-loop are independent of the results in the previous iterations, and there are no data-dependencies in general in the code specified for parallelization. A mechanism to automatically detect a combination of incompatible API/functions is not yet in place. As an example, an end-user can provide specifications for combining multiple local values (reduce operation) but might forget to provide specifications for distributing the task for computing local values to multiple processors. Such limitations will be removed in future work.

FUTURE RESEARCH DIRECTIONS

With the advancement in science and technology, computational problems are growing in size and complexity, thereby, resulting in the increase in the demand for High Performance Computing (HPC) resources. To keep up with the competitive pressure, the demand for reduced time-to-solution is also increasing and simulations on high performance computers are being preferred over physical prototype development and testing. The rapid advancement in the HPC platforms has resulted in various programming challenges, especially for end-users who are not trained at developing and optimizing HPC applications for multiple computing platforms.

Several independent research efforts are geared towards building high-level user-interfaces, or languages for developing applications that give optimal performance on multiple architectures without burdening the programmers. Slowly, but steadily, the HPC community is realizing the potential of domain-specific optimizations and languages. This is evident from the growth in the number of workshops, conference keynotes, and publications where the need of performance, productivity, and portability via domain-specific languages is being discussed.

Investments are also being made towards developing high-productivity general-purpose languages like Coarray Fortran and X10. However, it is not clear whether DSLs or some high-productivity general-purpose language or a new parallel programming paradigm would be the ultimate solution to the challenges that HPC application programmers face. Finding a sweet-spot between performance, productivity, and portability is still an open research question.

The investment in legacy HPC applications is too huge to propose a complete application rewrite to the stakeholders. Therefore, solutions that can leverage from the existing applications are also needed. Hi-PaL based sequential to parallel application transformation is one such solution. However, currently, the Hi-PaL based application transformation framework only supports applications written in C/C++. FORTRAN is another popular language for which sequential to parallel application transformation support should be provided in the future.

CONCLUSION

This chapter presented a brief overview of the challenges and opportunities that the exascale computing era brings, along with a discussion on some of the DSL-based research efforts in the HPC domain. The design, implementation and impact of Hi-PaL were discussed through an example. With the help of Hi-PaL, the end-users can achieve performance and scalability without knowing low-level details associated with MPI programming. They are not required to do any manual invasive reengineering in the existing sequential application. The end-user effort is reduced in terms of the number of lines of code that are written for parallelizing an existing sequential application.

Approximately 14 KLoC were written to implement the Hi-PaL based application transformation framework. It was an effort well-spent because the framework can be used for parallelizing the sequential applications in an application-domain-neutral manner. Hi-PaL was shown to be helpful in reducing the effort and complexities associated with the process of MPI-based parallelization without any significant loss in performance. A brief discussion on the future of the DSL-based approaches and HPC was also included in this chapter.

REFERENCES

AMMA. (2008). *The AMMA platform.* Retrieved from from http://wiki.eclipse.org/AMMA

Arora, R., Bangalore, P., & Mernik, M. (2011). A technique for non-invasive application-level checkpointing. *The Journal of Supercomputing, 57*(3), 227–255. doi:10.1007/s11227-010-0383-5

Arora, R., Bangalore, P., & Mernik, M. (2012). Raising the level of abstraction for developing message passing applications. *The Journal of Supercomputing, 59*(2), 1079–1100. doi:10.1007/s11227-010-0490-3

Basili, V., Carver, J., Cruzes, D., Hochstein, L. M., Hollingsworth, J., Shull, F., & Zelkowitz, M. (2008). Understanding the high performance computing community: A software engineer's perspective. *IEEE Software, 25*(4), 29–36. doi:10.1109/MS.2008.103

Baxter, I., Pidgeon, C., & Mehlich, M. (2004). DMS: Program transformation for practical scalable software evolution. In the *Proceedings of the International Conference on Software Engineering* (pp. 625-634). Washington, DC: IEEE Computer Society.

Bézivin, J., Jouault, F., Rosenthal, P., & Valduriez, P. (2004). Modeling in the large and modeling in the small. In *Model Driven Architecture- Foundations and Application 2004* (*Vol. 3599*, pp. 33–46). Lecture Notes in Computer Science Springer-Verlag. doi:10.1007/11538097_3

Bunch, C., Chohan, N., Krintz, C., & Shams, K. (2011). Neptune: A domain specific language for deploying HPC software on cloud platforms. In the *Proceedings of the 2nd International Workshop on Scientific Cloud Computing ScienceCloud'11* (pp. 59-68).

Charles, P., Grothoff, C., Saraswat, V. A., Donawa, C., Kielstra, A., & Ebcioglu, K. (2005). X10: An object-oriented approach to non-uniform cluster computing. *SIGPLAN Notices, 40*(10), 519–538. doi:10.1145/1103845.1094852

Chohan, N., Bunch, C., Pang, S., Krintz, C., Mostafa, N., Soman, S., & Wolski, R. (2009). AppScale: Scalable and open AppEngine application development and deployment. In the *Proceedings of ICST International Conference on Cloud Computing, Lecture Notes of the Institute for Computer Sciences, Social Informatics and Telecommunications Engineering 34* (pp. 57-70). Springer.

CUDA. (2012). *CUDA API reference manual, version 4.1.* Retrieved from http://www.developer.nvidia.com/nvidia-gpu-computing-documentation

Czarnecki, K., & Eisenecker, U. (2000). *Generative programming: Methods, tools, and applications*. Addison-Wesley.

de Jonge, M., & Visser, J. (2002). Grammars as feature diagrams. In the *Proceedings of the Workshop on Generative Programming at the 7th International Conference on Software Reuse* (pp. 23-24).

Dean, J., & Ghemawat, S. (2008). MapReduce: Simplifed data processing on large clusters. *Communications of the ACM, 51*(1), 107–113. doi:10.1145/1327452.1327492

Forum, M. P. I. (2009). *MPI: A message-passing interface standard version 2.2.* Retrieved from http://mpi-forum.org

Intel Cilk Plus. (2011). *Intel cilk plus language extension specification version 1.1.* Retrieved from http://software.intel.com/file/40297

Jouault, F., & Bézivin, J. (2006). KM3: A DSL for metamodel specification. In *Formal Methods for Open Object-Based Distributed Systems, Lecture Notes in Computer Science Vol. 4037* (pp.171-185).

Jouault, F., Bézivin, J., & Kurtev, I. (2006). TCS: A DSL for the specification of textual concrete syntaxes in model engineering. In the *5th International conference on Generative Programming and Component Engineering* (pp. 249-254). Portland, Oregon.

Jouault, F., & Kurtev, I. (2005). Transforming models with ATL. In the *Proceedings of Model Transformations in Practice Workshop at International Conference on Model Driven Engineering Languages and Systems, Lecture Notes in Computer Science Vol. 3844* (pp. 128-138). Springer.

Kiczales, G., Lamping, J., Mendhekar, A., Maeda, C., Lopes, C., Loingtier, J., & Irwin, J. (1997). Aspect-oriented programming. In the *Proceedings of the European Conference on Object-Oriented Programming, Lecture Notes In Computer Science Vol. 1241,* (pp. 220-242). Springer.

Koelbel, C., Loveman, D. B., Steele, G. L., & Zosel, M. E. (1994). *High performance FORTRAN handbook.* MIT Press.

Kurtev, I., Bézivin, J., Jouault, F., & Valduriez, P. (2006). Model-based DSL frameworks. In *Companion to the 21st ACM SIGPLAN Symposium on Object-Oriented Programming Systems, Languages, and Applications* (pp. 602-616). New York, NY: ACM.

Mellor-Crummey, J., Adhianto, L., Jin, G., & Scherer, W. N., III. (2009). *A new vision for coarray Fortran.* Paper presented at the Third Conference on Partitioned Global Address Space Programming Models. Ashburn, Virginia.

Meta-Object Facility. (2006). *OMG's MetaObject facility.* Retrieved from http://www.omg.org/mof/

OCL. (2006). *Object constraint language specification.* Retrieved from http://www.omg.org/cgi-bin/apps/doc?formal/06-05-01.pdf

Open, C. L. (2011). *OpenCL - The open standard for parallel programming of heterogeneous systems.* Retrieved from http://www.khronos.org/opencl/

Open, M. P. (2011). *The OpenMP API specification for parallel programming.* Retrieved from http://openmp.org/wp/

Quinn, M. (2004). *Parallel programming in C with MPI and OpenMP*. McGraw-Hill.

Schmidt, M. (2006). Guest editor's introduction: Model-driven engineering. *IEEE Computer*, *39*(2), 25–31. doi:10.1109/MC.2006.58

Skjellum, A., Bangalore, P., Gray, J., & Bryant, B. (2004). *Reinventing explicit parallel programming for improved engineering of high performance computing software*. Paper presented at the International Workshop on Software Engineering for High Performance Computing System Applications. Scotland, U.K.

Sujeeth, A. K., Lee, H., Brown, K. J., Rompf, T., Chafi, H., & Wu, M. … Olukotun, K. (2011). OptiML: An implicitly parallel domain-specific language for machine learning. In the *Proceedings of the 28th International Conference on Machine Learning* (pp. 42-53). Bellevue, Washington.

Threaded Building Blocks. (2011). *Intel threaded building blocks for open source*. Retrieved from http://threadingbuildingblocks.org

UPC. (2005). *UPC language specifications V 1.2.* Retrieved from http://upc.lbl.gov/docs/user/upc_spec_1.2.pdf

ADDITIONAL READING

Apache Ant. (2010). Retrieved from http://ant.apache.org/

Bal, H. E., Kaashoek, M. F., & Tanenbaum, A. S. (1992). Orca: A language for parallel programming of distributed systems. *IEEE Transactions on Software Engineering, 18*(3), 190–205. doi:10.1109/32.126768

Catanzaro, B., Fox, A., Keutzer, K., Patterson, D., Su, B., & Snir, M. (2010). Ubiquitous parallel computing from Berkeley, Illinois, and Stanford. *IEEE Micro, 30*(2), 41–55. doi:10.1109/MM.2010.42

Chamberlain, B. L., Callahan, D., & Zima, H. P. (2007). Parallel programmability and the chapel language. *International Journal of High Performance Computing Applications, 21*(3), 291–312. doi:10.1177/1094342007078442

Cordy, J., Dean, T., Malton, A., & Schneider, K. (2002). Source transformation in software engineering using the TXL transformation system. *Journal of Information and Software Technology, 44*(13), 827–837. doi:10.1016/S0950-5849(02)00104-0

Dean, J., & Ghemawat, S. (2008). MapReduce: Simplifed data processing on large clusters. *Communications of the ACM, 51*(1), 107–113. doi:10.1145/1327452.1327492

Douglas, C. C., Haase, G., Hu, J., Kowarschik, M., Rüde, U., & Weiß, C. (2000). Portable memory hierarchy tehniques for PDE solvers. *SIAM News, 33*, 8–9.

Eclipse Modeling Framework (EMF). (2010). Retrieved from http://www.eclipse.org/modeling/emf/?project=emf

Fatahalian, K., Knight, T. J., Houston, M., Erez, M., Horn, D. R., & Leem, L. … Hanrahan, P. (2006). Sequoia: Programming the memory hierarchy. Paper presented at *ACM/IEEE SuperComputing 2006 Conference*, Article No. 83, Tampa Bay, Florida.

Feo, J. T., Cann, D. C., & Oldehoeft, R. R. (1990). A report on the Sisal language project. *Journal of Parallel and Distributed Computing, 10*(4), 349–366. doi:10.1016/0743-7315(90)90035-N

Freeh, V. W. (1996). A comparison of implicit and explicit parallel programming. *Journal of Parallel and Distributed Computing, 34*(1), 50–65. doi:10.1006/jpdc.1996.0045

Gropp, W., Lusk, E., & Skjellum, A. (1999). *Using MPI: Portable parallel programming with the message-passing interface*. MIT Press.

Hadoop MapReduce. (2011). Retrieved from http://hadoop.apache.org/common/docs/current/

Hi-PaL API. (2010). Retrieved from http://www.cis.uab.edu/ccl/index.php/Hi-PaL

Kale, L. V., & Krishnan, S. (1993). CHARM++: A portable concurrent object oriented system based on C++. *ACM SIGPLAN Notices, 28*(10), 91-108.

Liszt Hackathon. (2010). Retrieved from http://liszt.stanford.edu/

Mattson, T. G., Sanders, B. A., & Massingill, B. L. (2004). *A pattern language for parallel programming*. Addison Wesley.

Mehta, P., Amaral, N. A., & Szafron, D. (2006). Is MPI suitable for a generative design-pattern system? *Parallel Computing, 32*(7-8), 616–626. doi:10.1016/j.parco.2006.06.008

Mernik, M., Heering, J., & Sloane, A. M. (2005). When and how to develop domain-specific languages. *ACM Computing Surveys, 37*(4), 316–344. doi:10.1145/1118890.1118892

Püschel, M., Moura, J. M. F., Johnson, J., Padua, D., Veloso, M., & Singer, B. … Rizzolo, N. (2005). SPIRAL: Code generation for DSP transforms. *Proceedings of the IEEE, Special Issue on Program Generation, Optimization, and Adaptation, 93*(2), 232- 275.

ROSE homepage. (2012). Retrieved from http://www.rosecompiler.org/

van den Brand, M., Heering, J., Klint, P., & Olivier, P. (2002). Compiling rewrite systems: The ASF+SDF compiler. *ACM Transactions on Programming Languages and Systems, 24*(4), 334–336. doi:10.1145/567097.567099

Wile, D. (2004). Lessons learned from real DSL experiments. *Science of Computer Programming, 51*(3), 265–290. doi:10.1016/j.scico.2003.12.006

KEY TERMS AND DEFINITIONS

AMMA: Atlas Model Management Architecture is a model-driven engineering platform that can be used for developing domain-specific languages

Exascale Computing: Computations run on computing platforms that are capable of 1000 trillion FLOPS

Hi-PaL: High-Level Parallelization Language is a domain-specific language for specifying parallel computations

HPC: High Performance Computing involves the usage of parallel programming techniques on supercomputers or clusters for doing advanced computations in a small amount of time

Model: A model is a representation of a system and can be of three types - a terminal model, a metamodel or a metametamodel

MPI: Message Passing Interface is a parallel programming standard for distributed memory architectures

SSC: Source-to-Source Compiler helps in transforming the source code written in a high-level language into another high-level source code

Chapter 19
Design and Transformation of a Domain-Specific Language for Reconfigurable Conveyor Systems

Kyoungho An
Vanderbilt University, USA

Adam Trewyn
Vanderbilt University, USA

Aniruddha Gokhale
Vanderbilt University, USA

Shivakumar Sastry
The University of Akron, USA

ABSTRACT

Much of the existing literature on domain-specific modeling languages (DSMLs) focuses on either the DSML design and their use in developing complex software systems (e.g., in enterprise and web appli cations), or their use in physical systems (e.g., process control). With increasing focus on research and development of cyber-physical systems (CPS) such as autonomous automotive systems and process control systems, which are systems that tightly integrate cyber and physical artifacts, it becomes important to understand the need for and the roles played by DSMLs for such systems. One use of DSMLs for CPS systems is in the analysis and verification of different properties of the system. Many questions arise in this context: How are the cyber and physical artifacts represented in DSMLs? How can these DSMLs be used in analysis? This book chapter addresses these questions through a case study of reconfigurable conveyor systems used as a representative example.

INTRODUCTION

CPS are an emergent class of complex, distributed real-time and embedded systems gaining prominence in several application domains including intelligent transportation systems, automated warehouse management systems, advanced manufacturing systems, smart grids, and smart buildings, among others. These systems illustrate the tight integration of cyber artifacts, such as computing, communication and storage, with monitoring and control of physical objects in a reliable, secure and timely fashion. Emerging CPS

DOI: 10.4018/978-1-4666-2092-6.ch019

applications will be significantly complex than today's embedded systems. It is expected that in future people will interact with these engineered systems in very much the same way as they do with information systems using the Internet. In the USA, the National Science Foundation is at the forefront to support research and development in CPS. One of the key issues for which research is sought is in the core science required to build these systems. One of the issues that complicates CPS is the presence of both continuous and discrete system dynamics in the context of open and emergent environments.

Model-driven Engineering (MDE) plays a vital role in the design and development of CPS. DSMLs can capture the cyber and physical artifacts of the CPS domain, provide the mechanisms to capture the discrete and continuous dynamics of the system, and provide abstractions that are critical to realize CPS that are "correct-by-construction". Although these benefits of DSMLs are well-known, most prior work on DSMLs focuses on designing DSMLs that cater either to the physical or the cyber concepts in isolation but seldom integrate these in a way envisioned by CPS. Consequently, the integration of the two views in a holistic manner is hard, and requires complex mappings between the two for which automated transformations are needed but seldom exist. In this paper we focus on a case study from the domain of reconfigurable conveyor systems (RCS) and articulate the ideas behind designing DSMLs for CPS.

RCS are akin to Lego pieces wherein a desired layout of a conveyor system can be realized by simply connecting the appropriate building blocks. Realizing this vision of RCS is easier said than done. The intertwined relationships between the cyber-physical elements, *e.g.,* the logic embedded in individual micro-controllers of RCS that regulate the behavior of each physical unit, the wireless transceivers that provide communication links and protocols for messaging and coordination between micro-controllers in physically adjacent units, and the logic that processes sensor inputs for the physical transfer parts between the conveyor units present formidable challenges in finding answers to a number of design and operational issues. For example, a conveyor designer may want to understand if a particular layout will maximize the throughput of the system without actually having to deploy and test the system. Other questions could include understanding the resilience of the layout to one or more failures.

Answering the questions faced by the engineers and layout planners requires DSML support that can in tandem account for both the physical artifacts of a conveyor system (*e.g.*, speed of belts, inter-material spacing, size and type of the material being handled, response time of commands to control belt motor speeds, rate of flow of material into the input source of the system, and sensors that scan moving goods) and cyber artifacts (e.g., message formats and signaling protocols between the individual units of the reconfigurable system, timing of the messages, and synchronization policies among the highly concurrent executing software artifacts) (Lee, 2008, 2009). Many questions arise in this context of DSML for CPS (Karsai & Sztipanovits, 2008): Do the cyber and physical artifacts have separate DSMLs? If so, how are these integrated to represent the reality? How can these DSMLs be used in system analysis and code synthesis?

This chapter makes the following three contributions to demonstrate the role of DSMLs in CPS and how they help in analyzing different properties of CPS:

1. We describe how to develop a domain specific modeling language (Mernik, Heering & Sloane, 2005) for RCS CPS including how to define the intuitive abstractions available to engineers and layout planners to describe the proposed layouts of their system without unduly tightly coupling their intentions to any specific analysis capability. To that end we use the Generic Modeling Environment

(GME) (Ledeczi et al., 2001) as our DSML design tool.
2. We show how automated transformations from the level of abstractions provided at the DSML-level into an abstraction that has executable semantics can help conduct automated performance analysis of the system. We show transformations from our RCS domain-specific models to a MATLAB Simulink model to analyze the behavior of the conveyor units in the MATLAB Simulink/Stateflow simulation engine.
3. We show how generative programming (Czarnecki, Østerbye & Volter, 2002) helps to synthesize artifacts for the analysis engine, which helps to completely automate the design-time analysis process.

Our goal in describing these contributions is to use the case study and the decisions we made to highlight the general process in designing DSMLs for CPS. The research presented in this chapter complements and expands on our earlier work (An, Trewyn, Gokhale & Sastry, 2011) focusing on the design and implementation of an automated, design-time analysis tool for performance analysis of RCS. This prior work briefly highlighted the use of MDE including modeling and transformations to conduct performance analysis of an abstraction of reconfigurable conveyor system. However, the related effort did not focus primarily on DSMLs and did not provide the deeper insights needed to develop the multiple levels of DSMLs. In this chapter, we focus on that dimension and provide insights on how to develop DSMLs for CPS. Our additional prior work in the area of RCS has also focused on analyzing the reliability of the software controllers (Kuruvilla, Gokhale & Sastry, 2008) and providing efficient mechanisms for monitoring and diagnostics (Mamidisetty, Duan, Sastry & Sastry, 2009).

BACKGROUND AND RELATED WORK

This section presents background knowledge of RCS, explains the concepts of MDE and its usage of a DSML, and demonstrates usage of model transformation.

Reconfigurable Conveyor Systems

RCS offer significant advantages in a variety of industrial sectors such as manufacturing, automotive, and material handling because of their flexibility, ease of use, and dynamic reconfigurability. When faced with the task of using reconfigurable systems in businesses, such as a material handling system used in facilities like FedEx, UPS, and baggage handling in airport terminals, engineers and layout planners for the conveyor systems must often grapple with numerous questions including but not limited to: What is the maximum sustainable rate of flow of goods in the system? Can handling of certain types of goods be prioritized over others? Does a certain layout of the conveyor system lead to starvation of certain paths in the system? What is the impact of failures of certain sections of the conveyor system on the overall throughput and hence the economic efficiency? How should one plan the inter-material spacing on the conveyors such that the goods do not collide when they are switched through transfer elements?

There are diverse physical models of conveyor systems and they need to have different logics depending on their physical models. Therefore, we pick a typical package sorting conveyor system used in shipping service companies such as FedEx and UPS. The abstraction of reconfigurable conveyor systems we consider in this chapter move parts from one or more inputs, *I*, to the outputs, *O*. These systems are composed using two kinds of units, *Segments* and *Turns* (Figure 1), which have fixed behaviors (Archer, Sastry, Rowe & Rajkumar 2009; Hayslip, Sastry & Gerhardt, 2006). Each unit is autonomously regulated by a local microcontroller that interacts with microcontrollers in physically adjacent units over wireless links to coordinate the transfer of parts from one unit to another.

A Segment moves a part over a fixed distance, in one of two assigned directions. Input and Output units are halves of Segment units that can move parts in one direction only. S_u and S_d are, respectively, upstream and downstream sensors at each Segment that are activated as a part moves into its scanning range.

A Turn unit has four ports; each port can be configured either as an input port or as an output port. For each port there exists a sensor. In the figure, the suffixes denote the direction (east, west, north, south). To keep the presentation simple, we assume that a Turn can handle only one part at a time while a Segment may contain multiple parts spaced some distance apart as they flow from one end to the other. When two or more parts simultaneously arrive at different input ports of a Turn, it can accept only one of the parts.

A specific composition of instances of the above kinds of units is a conveyor system. Figure 2 shows an example of conveyor systems obtained by composition.

For the purposes of this chapter, we focus on reconfigurable conveyors employed in material handling facilities, such as those found in FedEx and UPS sorting facilities as well as baggage handling facilities in airport terminals. Thus, we classify goods (*i.e.*, a part) as belonging to a small (*e.g.*, envelopes), medium (*e.g.*, small boxes) or large category (*e.g.*, large boxes) that are sorted in a sorting facility.

Model-Driven Engineering

MDE (Kent, 2002) is an approach to develop software systems by creating models and applying automated transformations to them to ultimately generate the implementation for a target platform. The ability to create a software design and apply automated transformations to generate the implementation helps to avoid the complexity of systems.

Figure 1. Abstractions for segment and turn

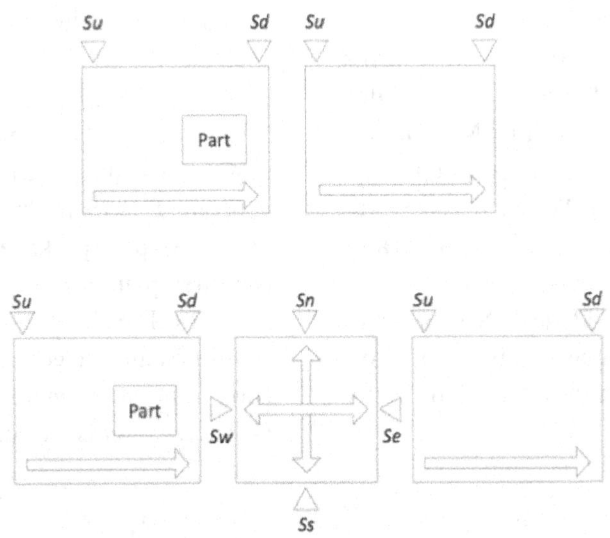

Figure 2. Sample layout of a reconfigurable conveyor system

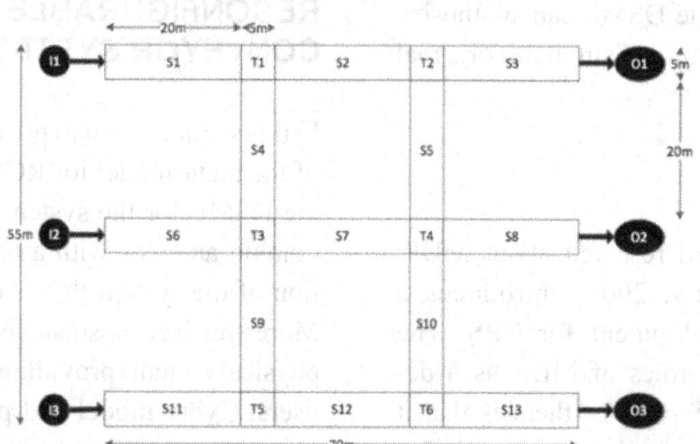

Although the reconfiguration features of RCS makes it feasible to change the layouts of the conveyors, yet it is infeasible to actually deploy the layout and understand whether that particular layout is able to satisfy the business objectives, which could include performance parameters, such as overall throughput of the system, maximum workload sustained by the layout, resilience to failures, among others. This is precisely where MDE plays a significant role. Applying the model-driven paradigm to the domain of a reconfigurable conveyor system has the following advantages. First, it helps to reduce the complexity of modification of the system by re-generating target codes for behavioral models based on modified structural models. Second, it supports transformations of a model to another; thus, models verified at design time can be transformed to actual deployed implementations. Use of MDE requires a modeling language. In particular, a DSML is ideal in contrast to a general-purpose language since a DSML can convey intuitive domain-specific abstractions that a general-purpose language cannot.

The usage of a DSML in the case of RCS development serves a crucial purpose of saving labor and reducing development time, as well as facilitating ease of communication with potential clients or customers whose familiarity with RCS machinery or traditional design techniques may be lacking. Especially during early design stages and brainstorming phases, the usage of a simplified DSML facilitates relatively quick considerations of RCS layout possibilities without getting bogged down into every low-level detail.

For our work, we have used the GME as a tool to design and visually represent a DSML describing the semantics of RCS topologies. By using our DSML within GME, one can develop and visualize potential layout designs of RCS facilities in the form of concrete models; these models may be further utilized for purposes of simulation and developmental refinement. The MATLAB Simulink scripts of cyber and physical behavioral models of conveyors are generated from a structural DSML-based model implemented in GME.

Clearly, for purposes of simulation, certification, and construction of RCS systems, a vague model alone will not suffice; detailed specifications and design drawings will be necessary. For these needs, a technique called model, facilitated within the GME toolkit, provides the ability to automatically generate a variety of additional artifacts; in our work on RCS systems, an especially important capability is the automated generation of digital files necessary for computer simulation of proposed RCS network topologies. This simulation is carried out in MATLAB/Simulink, however, there is no tight coupling of the models to MATLAB/Simulink; rather a different translator associated with the same DSML can synthesize artifacts for a different kind of simulator or a real system.

Related Work

There is various related research about MDE. (Karsai & Sztipanovits, 2008) introduces a model-integrated development for CPS. The paper explains critical roles of MDE as a development way of CPS. One of them is that it provides meta-modeling environment to define a DSML for diverse physical and cyber domains of systems. Additionally, design challenges and solutions for CPS are described by (Lee, 2008) and model-based design as a solution for CPS is suggested in the paper.

RCS are illustrated as an example domain of networked embedded systems in (Archer, Sastry, Rowe & Rajkumar, 2009; Hayslip, Sastry & Gerhardt, 2006). Based on the design suggested in the paper, our RCS DSML has been created. It shows components of RCS and it is called blocks, and divergent reconfigurable conveyer systems are possibly designed and deployed. When the systems need to be analyzed, many possible layouts of the systems demand different configurations and it is challenging for analyzers. Hence, model-based analysis for RCS is suggested in this chapter.

(Lamotte, Berruet & Philippe, 2006) describes a discrete event perspective of reconfigurable manufacturing systems. As in our case, it also utilizes MDE principles to layout of the system. Moreover, they also distinguish between the cyber and physical aspects of the system. This related research, however, focuses on developing mathematical models to conduct criticality analysis of different configurations (i.e., layouts) to determine the best configuration for a given set of product mix while also satisfying other constraints, such as cost. Overall, this research has similar goals to ours; the analysis approach used and metrics evaluated are different.

DESIGN OF DSMLS FOR RECONFIGURABLE CONVEYOR SYSTEMS

In this section, we will present the detailed design of the meta-model for RCS that is at the heart of the DSML for the system. The DSML provides domain analysts with a higher level of abstraction of the system that is easier to comprehend. Moreover, it encapsulates complexity of cyber and physical systems providing intuitive interfaces for users. Cyber model and physical model can be visually represented as an integrated component in the DSML. We focus on the design decisions we made in defining this DSML by incorporating CPS concepts. An additional modeling abstraction is presented that provides executable semantics and helps in the performance analysis.

Meta-Model for the DSML of Reconfigurable Conveyor Systems

CPS is an emerging and cross-disciplinary area with well-understood need for formal methods driven by challenges in system validation and verification by model-based design. It also needs convergence of different modeling layers such as system engineering, control engineering, and software engineering. Model-based approaches providing DSMLs help to reconcile and integrate the diverse modeling layers. In our system, the DSML developed in GME represents the structural models of system engineering for domain designers of RCS. Additionally, a DSML developed for MATLAB Simulink depicts behavioral models of control and software engineering for actual analysis business. MDE principles are used to reconcile the two views. For example, model-based analysis approach comes to the aid of representation of structural and behavioral semantics of the RCS system as well as integration of the different DSMLs.

Meta modeling is at the heart of a DSML that conveys the abstract and concrete syntax and semantics of the domain and is used to automatically generate a target domain-specific model. This concept is critical to perform the integration and transformation of divergent system domains or levels. The rest of the section describes how the meta-model of RCS is designed, and how the DSMLs defined by the meta-model are used. Subsequently, transformation of the DSMLs of RCS will be introduced in the next section.

When designing a DSML, the key idea is to identify the fundamental building blocks of the language and their relationships. For CPS such as reconfigurable conveyors, it is important that these building blocks capture both the physical and cyber artifacts. Figure 3 illustrates the meta-model of the structural building blocks, which is at the heart of the DSML for RCS. The meta-model of the system consists primarily of the building blocks found commonly in a conveyor system, such as input bins, output bins, and transportation element blocks. The meta-model also contains connection components used to link the building blocks.

The *block* model serves as a representation of the transportation elements within a conveyor system. A block may exist in the form of a Turn or a Segment; a Segment itself is either a *VSegment*, oriented vertically in the layout, or an *HSegment*, oriented horizontally. Within the GME meta-model, these "is a" relationships are indicated by the triangle connectors. Every block model, no matter which specific form it takes, possesses a list of attributes critical to future usage of the layout model. The length and speed parameters, for example, represent the physical belt size and transportation speed of the machines during later physical simulations; TX_WD, RX_WD, and COMM_WD represent timer settings within simulated machine controllers.

Related to the block model are the *input* and *output* models, which represent entry and exit bins by which objects enter and exit a conveyor system. The input and output models contain their own attributes that describe parameters utilized during DSML transformation into network simulations and other engineering artifacts.

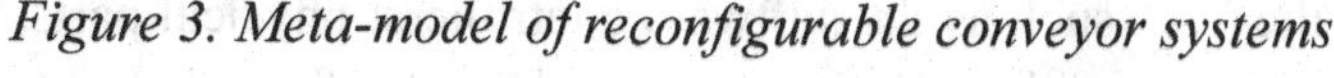

Figure 3. Meta-model of reconfigurable conveyor systems

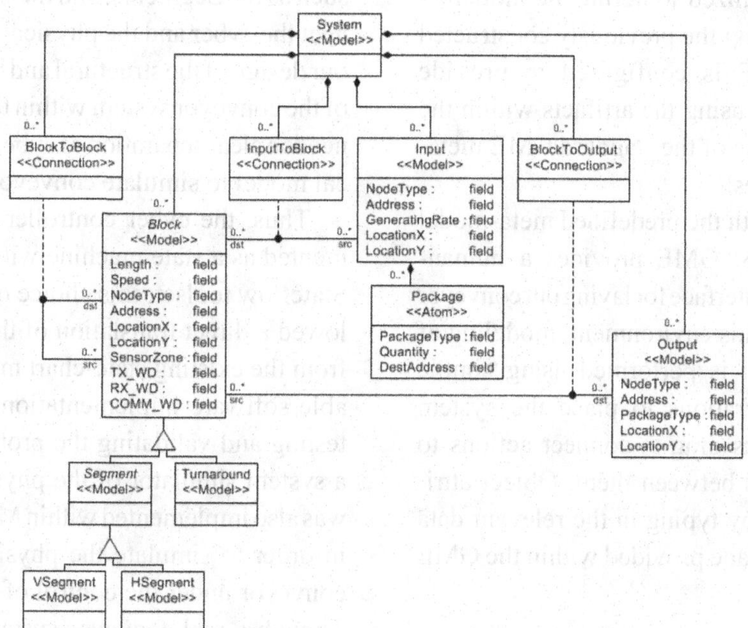

Within the meta-model, the connection objects *BlockToBlock, InputToBlock,* and *BlockToOutput* define the connections that may be made when modeling a conveyor system. In our meta-model, these definitions permit the connection of the various transportation blocks to each other as well as to input and output bin objects.

At the root of every conveyor network representation is the *System* model, which possesses a containment relationship with the relevant transportation blocks, input/output bins, and connections used to define a network. To enable an intuitive graphical modeling environment to the users, GME allows associating icons with the building blocks of the meta-model. For RCS therefore we associated icons with *Input, Output, HSegment, VSegment, and Turn.* These icons will appear in the part browser that becomes available when the DSML is used to build a concrete model of the RCS as explained below.

Creating a Model of a Reconfigurable Conveyor System

The process of modeling a reconfigurable conveyor system network takes place within the same GME tool utilized to define the modeling language. By loading the previously constructed meta-model, GME is configured to provide modeling capacity using the artifacts within the meta-model in place of the standard GME meta-modeling primitives.

Once loaded with the predefined meta-model paradigm for RCS, GME provides a human-friendly graphical interface for laying out conveyor networks. Within this environment, modeling of a conveyor system is performed using simple drag-and-drop operations to place the system artifacts, as well as drag-to-connect actions to define connections between them. Object attributes are defined by typing in the relevant data inside of a dialog pane provided within the GME environment.

Figure 4 illustrates the human-friendly graphical interface provided by GME for purposes of modeling RCS. The Part Browser pane (upper left) contains the RCS artifacts defined within the meta-model; instances of these artifacts may be dragged into the workspace pane (center) and arranged into a network. The Object Inspector pane (lower right) permits editing of object attributes once an object is selected.

DSML FOR EXECUTABLE SEMANTICS USED IN THE ANALYSIS ENGINE

This section covers the executable semantics of the RCS modeling language in detail. Executable models are needed to conduct various kinds of analysis for the end system. It is important that the executable model also comprise the rich cyber and physical artifacts of the domain, however, at an abstraction that is much closer to the physical realization as opposed to the more intuitive structural DSML used by RCS layout planners. Conveyor systems are composed of cyber parts, such as the software controllers; physical parts, such as the Segments; and the interfaces that connect the cyber and the physical world. Therefore, our design of the structural and behavioral models of the conveyor system within the analysis engine needs a clear separation of cyber model and physical model to simulate conveyor systems.

Thus, the cyber controller logic was implemented as a state machine within the MATLAB Stateflow toolset; this choice of environment allowed a direct translation of the controller logic from the existing state-chart model to an executable software implementation. For purposes of testing and validating the prototype controllers, a system simulator of the physical environment was also implemented within MATLAB Simulink in order to simulate the physical behavior of a conveyor under the control of block controllers. Though a real conveyor system will eventually

Figure 4. Graphical interface of GME

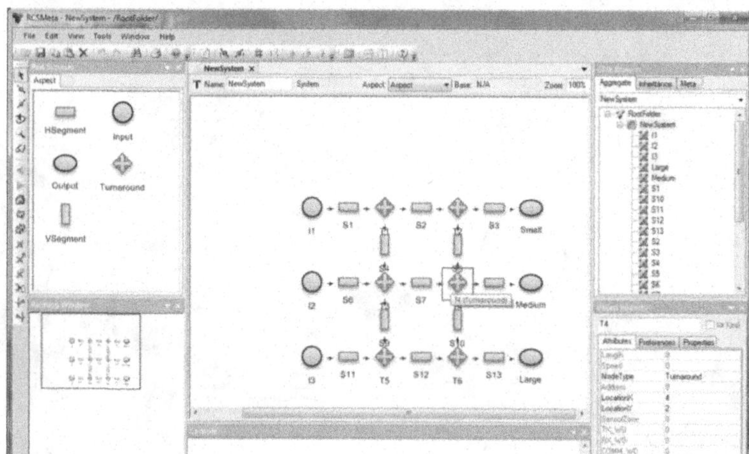

be needed to demonstrate the capabilities of controller logic, a software simulation is being relied upon in this paper in order to allow for maximum flexibility in unit testing, compositional testing, and architectural modifications.

We developed a modularized Simulink unit called a *Conveyor Skid*, which is implemented as a self-contained unit representing both the physical and cyber components of a single Segment for purposes of modeling a single conveyor block. Within a conveyor block, the Conveyor Skid exists as a single self-contained controller system as well as a single self-contained simulator block. As both the controller and simulator are intended to be self-contained, connections between these units are restricted to those intended to be present within the actual system; at this stage, these connections represent the motor control signal from controller to simulator and the sensor data feeds from simulator to controller. As such, the simulator block may eventually be removed and replaced with signal interfaces to a physical model without disrupting the implementation of the controller.

All remaining elements within the Conveyor Skid block consist solely of inputs/outputs to and from the outside of the block, as well as single-step signal delays necessary to break algebraic loops within Simulink. These input and output connections exist in order to provide for compositional simulation; that is, Conveyor Skid blocks may be connected together to form a conveyor network which may be simulated as a whole. The external connections represent external neighbor network connections between conveyor controllers, a diagnostic signal bus from the simulator, and a signal line for simulating package handoffs between simulator blocks.

Next we describe the details of the cyber and physical modeling artifacts in the Conveyor Skid.

Cyber Models in the Analysis Engine

The cyber model was implemented as a finite state machine using the Stateflow toolset in MATLAB. Each Segment and Turn has a receiver controller logic and transfer controller logic as well. Figure 5 shows finite state machines embedded in logic controllers of Segments and Turns. Figure 5-(a) shows a receiver state machine embedded in a controller of a Segment. Initially, a Segment waits until it receives a request message for transferring a part from an upstream block. When the Segment

Figure 5. State machines of segment and turn

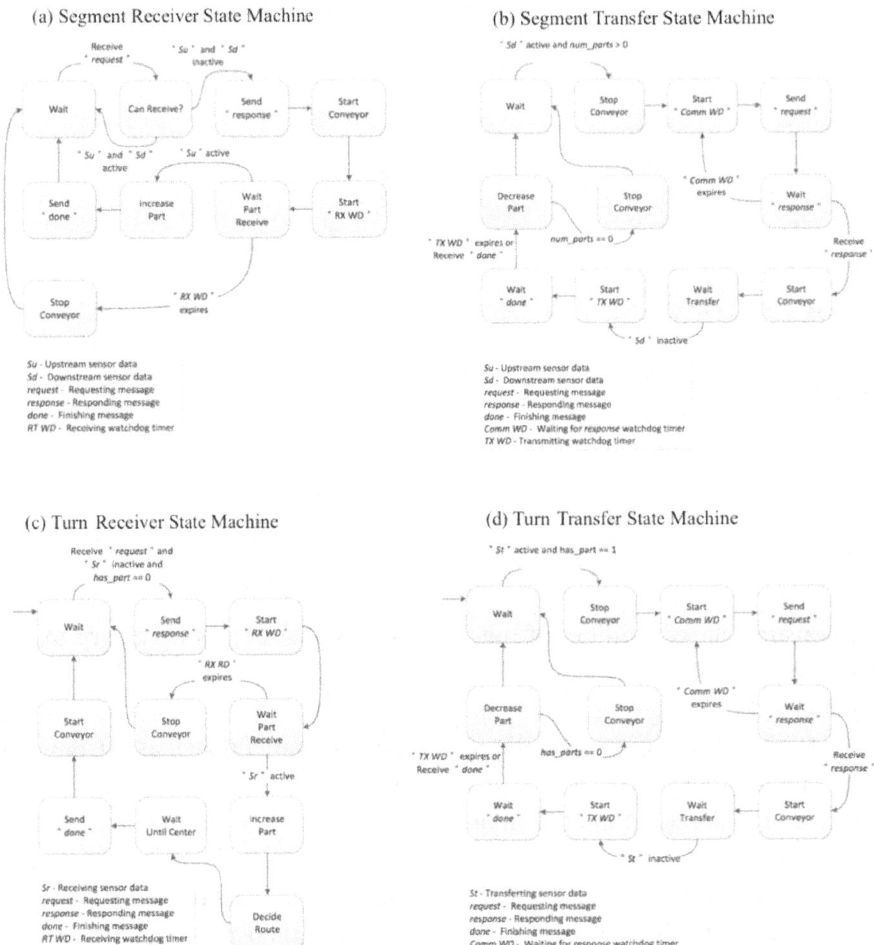

receives the request message from the upstream block, it checks if the upstream sensor is inactive which is for ensuring a space is available for a transferred part, and the downstream sensor is inactive in order to avoid a conflict between the receiver machine and the transfer machine in the same Segment.

If these conditions are all clear, it sends a response message back to the upstream block to notify that a part can be accepted and it actuates the conveyor belt at the configured speed. Then, it starts a watchdog timer to wait for the transferred part. If the watchdog timer is expired, that means the part has not arrived at the Segment and a problem occurred in the middle of the process of transferring the part between the blocks. If the upstream sensor is active, it indicates a part has safely arrived at the Segment. If a part has securely arrived at the Segment, it increases the number of packages on the Segment belt and sends a finishing message to inform transferring is done well.

A transfer state machine in a Segment, which coordinates with a receiver state machine in a next block, is depicted in Figure 5-(b). At first, the transfer state machine also waits until the downstream sensor is active and parts are on the belt. If both conditions are true, the Segment is ready for transferring a part to the next block. Therefore, it needs to be stopped until receiving permission from the next one, so it sends a request message to obtain the permission. Here, the receiver machine may not give the permission to the given request. In that case, Comm WD, which is used for waiting for the approval from receiver side, expires and the block sends a request again to the receiver machine. If the machine receives the response message, it energizes the conveyor belt of the Segment and waits for the part to successfully transfer to the next block. If the part is normally moved out, the transfer machine can get a successful done message from the receiver. If the message is acquired, the number of parts is decreased and the machine goes back to the initial state.

Controllers within Turns also incorporate a similar receiver state machine and a transfer state machine.. Figure 5-(c) represents a receiver state machine in a Turn. The processes of a receiver state machine of a Turn are similar to a receiver state machine in a Segment. A distinguishable difference of controllers between a Segment and a Turn is that a Turn has more incoming and outgoing ports than a Segment. Hence, state machines in a Turn should have logic to differentiate signals from varying ports.

A Turn owns 4 ports and accordingly holds four sensors for each direction. S_r in the receiver state machine stores a selected signal among a set of sensors called $S = \{S_w, S_s, S_e, S_n\}$ from an appropriate direction. Moreover, a Turn takes in functions to decide a direction for each package by the *Decide Route* state using a routing function determined and deployed by the GME interpreter. Accordingly it energizes a selected actuator among $A = \{A_{we}, A_{sn}\}$ and the direction of the actuator. After a route for a package is determined, a Turn should move the package to the center of the belt to avoid a physical collision which can occur by actuating the chosen belt before the package is centered in the Turn.

Lastly, a Turn accepts only one part to simplify its logic. After processing one part, it accepts another part to be processed. The rest of the logic in a receiver state machine in a Turn is basically the same as a Segment. A transfer state machine in a Turn shown in Figure 5-(d) is similar to a transfer state machine in a Segment excluding that it uses St as a sensor signal which is selected among $S = \{S_w, S_s, S_e, S_n\}$. Furthermore, it accepts only one part on a belt in the same way as the receiver machine. All receiver machines and transfer machines introduced above can seamlessly communicate with transfer machines and receiver machines of adjoining blocks (that are modeled in the layout model).

Figure 6. Simulation of the physics of segment and turn

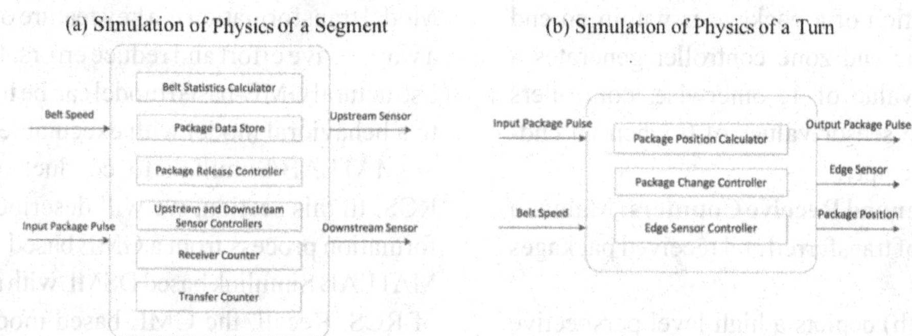

Physical Models in the Analysis Engine

Next we describe how we architected the physics of the different blocks of the conveyor system. Due to the complex nature of the simulation, we have given an abstract view of the pertinent details in our explanation while leaving out unnecessary low-level details of Simulink building blocks we used (Figure 6). Figure 6-(a) depicts a high level perspective of the physics of simulated Segment. It comprises the following building blocks:

1. **Belt Statistics Calculator:** Calculates belt odometer by continuously integrating belt speed input. It also maintains correct indices of head and tail cells in a rolling storage queue explained next.
2. **Package Data Store:** Stores package sizes and arrival odometer values within a queue. The queue is implemented as a rolling array. When a new package arrives, its size and the current odometer reading of the belt are recorded in the tail cell.
3. **Package Release Controller:** Continuously calculates position of head package on belt. When the rear edge of the head package falls past the end of the belt, it is removed from the queue and passed via a pulse to the downstream machine.
4. **Upstream and Downstream Sensor Controllers:** Continuously calculate positions of the head and tail packages. Whenever any portion of a package is within an end zone, the end zone controller generates a sensor value of 1; otherwise, controllers generate sensor values of 0 when an end-zone is empty.
5. **Transfer and Receive Counters:** Maintain counts of transferred and received packages

Figure 6-(b) depicts a high level perspective of the physics of simulated Turn. It comprises the following building blocks:

1. **Package Position Calculator:** Continuously integrates motor control signals for East-West and North-South axes in order to calculate and maintain position of package on belt.
2. **Package Change Controller:** Detects when packages enter or leave the Turn machine. Whenever a new package arrives (via pulse), this controller resets the Package Position Controller to the position and size of the newly arrived package. Note that if a package already exists on the belt when a new one arrives, the old package will be lost. When a package is determined to have moved completely off of the machine, a package pulse is generated on the appropriate directional output and the Package Position Controller is reset with a null package.
3. **Edge Sensor Controller:** Maintains sensor outputs for Edge Sensor Beams on all four sides of machine. Whenever any portion of a package is determined to reside within an edge beam, the appropriate edge sensor outputs the size of the package breaking the beam. Outputs for unbroken edge beams are set at zero.

RECONCILING DOMAIN-SPECIFIC MODELS WITH EXECUTABLE MODELS THROUGH MODEL TRANSFORMATIONS

Model transformation is a key feature of MDE and a way to save effort and reduce errors. In our case, a structural GME-based model can be transformed to a behavioral model with executable semantics in MATLAB/Simulink to conduct analysis of RCS. In this section, we will describe the transformation process from a GME based DSML to a MATLAB Simulink based DSML with an example of RCS. Recall, the GME based model itself is a structural model that does not contain business logic for systems. Note that it is easy to introduce a modeling language with executable semantics in GME and transform it to one of the many possible executables. Accordingly, the model needs to be transformed to another model to analyze or execute systems, and it is accomplished by the generative capabilities in GME. The generative capabilities within the GME DSML transform these models into appropriate models of another DSML of the whole system in the format recognized by the underlying analysis engine, such as a simulator.

Transformation Process

There are three steps to conduct transformations from GME-based DSML to MATLAB Simulink based DSML. The transformation is processed via the Universal Data Model (UDM) framework (Bakay & Magyari, 2001; Magyari et al., 2003), a feature of GME. The UDM framework includes the development process and set of supporting tools used to generate C++ interfaces from UML class diagrams of data structures. The generated interfaces provide handy programmatic access to traverse UML diagram models that are equivalent models defined by GME meta-modeling. In our system, the generated interfaces contain 955 lines of code in C++ and header, and the interpreter to parse GME models and generate MATLAB scripts has 359 lines of code in C++.

Step 1: Creating the UDM APIs in C++

The UDM APIs in C++ need to be generated from XML files created by the GME UML environment. There is a tool that automatically converts a MetaGME style RCS meta-model to a UML Class Diagram style RCS meta-model (Figure 7). When a user opens the RCS meta-model in GME, the user sees the interpreter shown in Figure 7-(a) that shows "Converts GME MATLAB to equivalent UML Class Diagram" at the top. The interpreter will create the UML Class Diagram style RCS meta-model when the user clicks the button. Once the user creates the UML Class Diagram style RCS meta-model, the user opens the generated UML Class Diagram style RCS meta-model in GME. Then, the user will see a button at the top shown in Figure 7-(b) saying "UML 2 UDM/XML Interpreter", and click the button to create the XML file for the RCS meta-model. Lastly, the user opens a command prompt and goes the directory where the user has saved the XML file and run the following command: *udm.exe RCSMeta.xml*. It will create a C++ source file, and a C++ header file that

Figure 7. Process for creating the UDM APIs for RCS

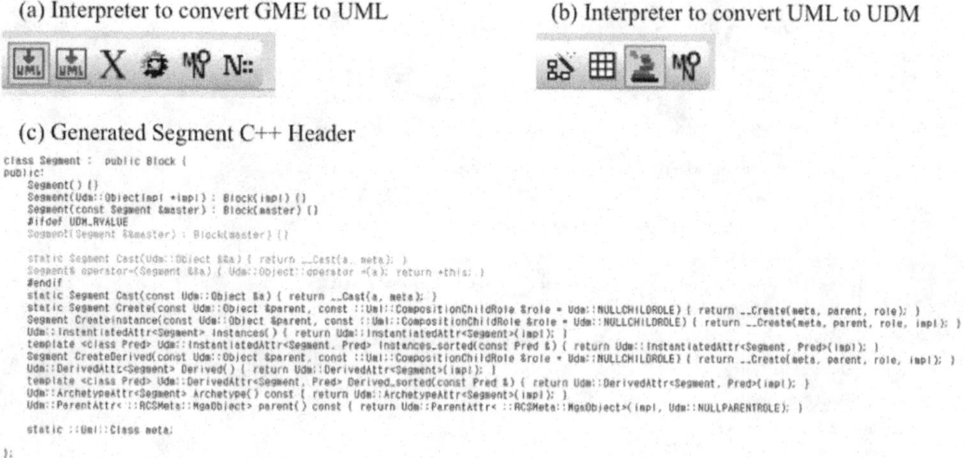


```
class Segment :  public Block {
public:
    Segment() {}
    Segment(Udm::ObjectImpl *impl) : Block(impl) {}
    Segment(const Segment &master) : Block(master) {}
    #ifdef UDM_RVALUE
    Segment(Segment &&master) : Block(master) {}

    static Segment Cast(Udm::Object &&a) { return __Cast(a, meta); }
    Segment& operator=(Segment &&a) { Udm::Object::operator =(a); return *this; }
    #endif
    static Segment Cast(const Udm::Object &a) { return __Cast(a, meta); }
    static Segment Create(const Udm::Object &parent, const ::Uml::CompositionChildRole &role = Udm::NULLCHILDROLE) { return __Create(meta, parent, role); }
    Segment CreateInstance(const Udm::Object &parent, const ::Uml::CompositionChildRole &role = Udm::NULLCHILDROLE) { return __Create(meta, parent, role, impl); }
    Udm::InstantiatedAttr&lt;Segment&gt; Instances() { return Udm::InstantiatedAttr&lt;Segment&gt;(impl); }
    template <class Pred> Udm::InstantiatedAttr&lt;Segment, Pred&gt; Instances_sorted(const Pred &) { return Udm::InstantiatedAttr&lt;Segment, Pred&gt;(impl); }
    Segment CreateDerived(const Udm::Object &parent, const ::Uml::CompositionChildRole &role = Udm::NULLCHILDROLE) { return __Create(meta, parent, role, impl); }
    Udm::DerivedAttr&lt;Segment&gt; Derived() { return Udm::DerivedAttr&lt;Segment&gt;(impl); }
    template <class Pred> Udm::DerivedAttr&lt;Segment, Pred&gt; Derived_sorted(const Pred &) { return Udm::DerivedAttr&lt;Segment, Pred&gt;(impl); }
    Udm::ArchetypeAttr&lt;Segment&gt; Archetype() const { return Udm::ArchetypeAttr&lt;Segment&gt;(impl); }
    Udm::ParentAttr< ::RCSMeta::MgaObject> parent() const { return Udm::ParentAttr< ::RCSMeta::MgaObject>(impl, Udm::NULLPARENTROLE); }

    static ::Uml::Class meta;

};
```

will be used to interpret components in the RCS meta-model. Figure 7-(c) represents the Segment class defined in the generated C++ header file.

Step 2: Transforming the GME Model to the Simulink Model via the GME Interpreter

The GME interpreter visits every component in the RCS DSML and builds a MATLAB Simulink script using the visitor pattern. There are two steps to make a script. First, the initialize function in the interpreter starts and opens a new system. Then, it also opens a library where all the components in RCS such as Segment, Turn, Input, and Output are implemented. Second, the traverse function starts to traverse components defined in the RCS meta-model. As we pointed out, the visitor pattern is used to traverse them. Therefore, each component has an *accept* function that accepts a visitor to stop by a component and a *visit* function that implements behavior when a

Figure 8. Implementation of GME interpreter using visitor pattern

(a) Horizontal Segment *visit* function

```
virtual void Visit_HSegment(const HSegment &s)
{

    name = s.name( );
    strAddress = IntToString((int)s.Address( ));
    nodeType = (string)s.NodeType( );
    length = (int) s.Length( );
    speed = (int) s.Speed( );

    xLocation = IntToString((int)s.LocationX( )*(X_SIZE + X_GAP));
    yLocation = IntToString((int)s.LocationY( )*(Y_SIZE + Y_GAP));
    xEndLocation = IntToString((int)s.LocationX( )*(X_SIZE + X_GAP)+X_SIZE);
    yEndLocation = IntToString((int)s.LocationY( )*(Y_SIZE + Y_GAP)+Y_SIZE);

    string str_location = "[" + xLocation +", " + yLocation + ", " + xEndLocation +", " + yEndLocation +"]";

    SaveFile << "add_block('Conveyor_Skids_Library/Segment_Skid', 'marc/";
    SaveFile << name << "', 'Position', ";
    SaveFile << str_location << ")" << endl;

}
```

(b) System accept function

```
void System::Accept(Visitor &v)
{
    v.Visit_System(*this);

    set<Input> input = this->Input_kind_children( );
    set<Output> output = this->Output_kind_children( );
    set<HSegment> hsegment = this->HSegment_kind_children( );
    set<VSegment> vsegment = this->VSegment_kind_children( );
    set<Turnaround> turnaround = this->Turnaround_kind_children( );
    set<BlockToBlock> conn = this->BlockToBlock_kind_children( );
    set<BlockToOutput> out = this->BlockToOutput_kind_children( );
    set<InputToBlock> in = this->InputToBlock_kind_children( );

    for(set<Input>::iterator it = input.begin( ); it != input.end( ); ++it)
    {
        (*it).Accept(v);
    }

    for(set<Output>::iterator it = output.begin( ); it != output.end( ); ++it)
    {
        (*it).Accept(v);
    }

    for(set<HSegment>::iterator it = hsegment.begin( ); it != hsegment.end( ); ++it)
    {
        (*it).Accept(v);
    }

    for(set<VSegment>::iterator it = vsegment.begin( ); it != vsegment.end( ); ++it)
    {
        (*it).Accept(v);
    }
    for(set<Turnaround>::iterator it = turnaround.begin( ); it != turnaround.end( ); ++it)
    {
        (*it).Accept(v);
    }
    for(set<BlockToBlock>::iterator l_it = conn.begin( ); l_it != conn.end( ); ++l_it)
    {
        (*l_it).Accept(v);
    }
    for(set<BlockToOutput>::iterator l_it = out.begin( ); l_it != out.end( ); ++l_it)
    {
        (*l_it).Accept(v);
    }
    for(set<InputToBlock>::iterator l_it = in.begin( ); l_it != in.end( ); ++l_it)
    {
        (*l_it).Accept(v);
    }
}
```

visitor visits a component. *Visit* functions in our interpreter contain the following implementations: setting a location of a block, adding a block from the opened library, and configuring attributes in a block. These steps implemented in the *visit* function are required for a behavioral model in MATLAB Simulink (Figure 8). Figure 8-(a) shows the *visit* function of horizontal Segment as an example, and Figure 8-(b) shows the *accept* function of the System component in the RCS meta-model that iterates over all *accept* functions of the containing components.

Step 3: Generating the Simulink Model from the MATLAB Script File

Once the MATLAB script file is created by the GME interpreter, the script will construct the actual behavioral model for analyzing performance (Moreno & Merson, 2008) of a reconfigurable conveyor system in MATLAB Simulink.

Analysis of Reconfigurable Conveyor Systems

Once model transformation has taken place using the GME interpreter, the resulting Simulink model may be utilized for purposes of simulation of conveyor network behavior in order to predict and analyze the performance and behavior of the proposed network under expected usage scenarios. In doing so, layout designers can obtain high confidence of design suitability for a given application according to such measures as package throughput rates and processing delays.

For all simulations, the set of expected usage patterns is application specific and determined through business case analysis by the ultimate end user. For example, a logistics provider may expect sorting network traffic to exhibit predictable patterns according to time of day (incoming truck cycle versus outgoing truck cycle) and time of year (February shipment patterns versus December shipment patterns). Business environment factors, for example medium-term expectations of economic growth, may also be considered when specifying usage scenarios, both in regard to the proposed layout and potential expanded reconfigurations.

Given a set of expected usage cases, the Simulink model may be configured accordingly with relevant input bin and routing settings in order to perform realistic simulations of traffic flow patterns. The resulting data may be analyzed to assess expected throughput rates and expectations of processing delays, among other statistics, as well as assess the suitability of proposed routing strategies.

It is expected that usage of the modeling and simulation tools will occur within an iterative design flow with regard to topological layouts, albeit one with short cycles. Inevitably, initial conveyor layout candidates will be rejected after simulation due to discovery of congested regions, inadequate throughput capacity, and/or excessive transport delays. Iterative refinement and simulation will allow designers to compile a set of layout candidates suitable for intended usage scenarios; ultimately, economic and business case analysis techniques beyond the scope of this work will be used to select the final design from this set.

Summary of Transformation Steps and Generalization of MDE in CPS

Transformation between DSMLs requires a meta-model or knowledge of source and target DSMLs. In our transformation process, a RCS structural DSML is defined by a GME-based meta-model, and transformation rules, which are based on a knowledge of a MATLAB-based behavioral model of RCS, are also defined by a UDM interpreter. There are three steps to accomplish the transformation process: creating the UDM APIs in C++, generating the Simulink script by the UDM interpreter, and generating the Simulink model by the created script. GME supports tools such as GME meta-modeling and

Figure 9. Model transformation steps

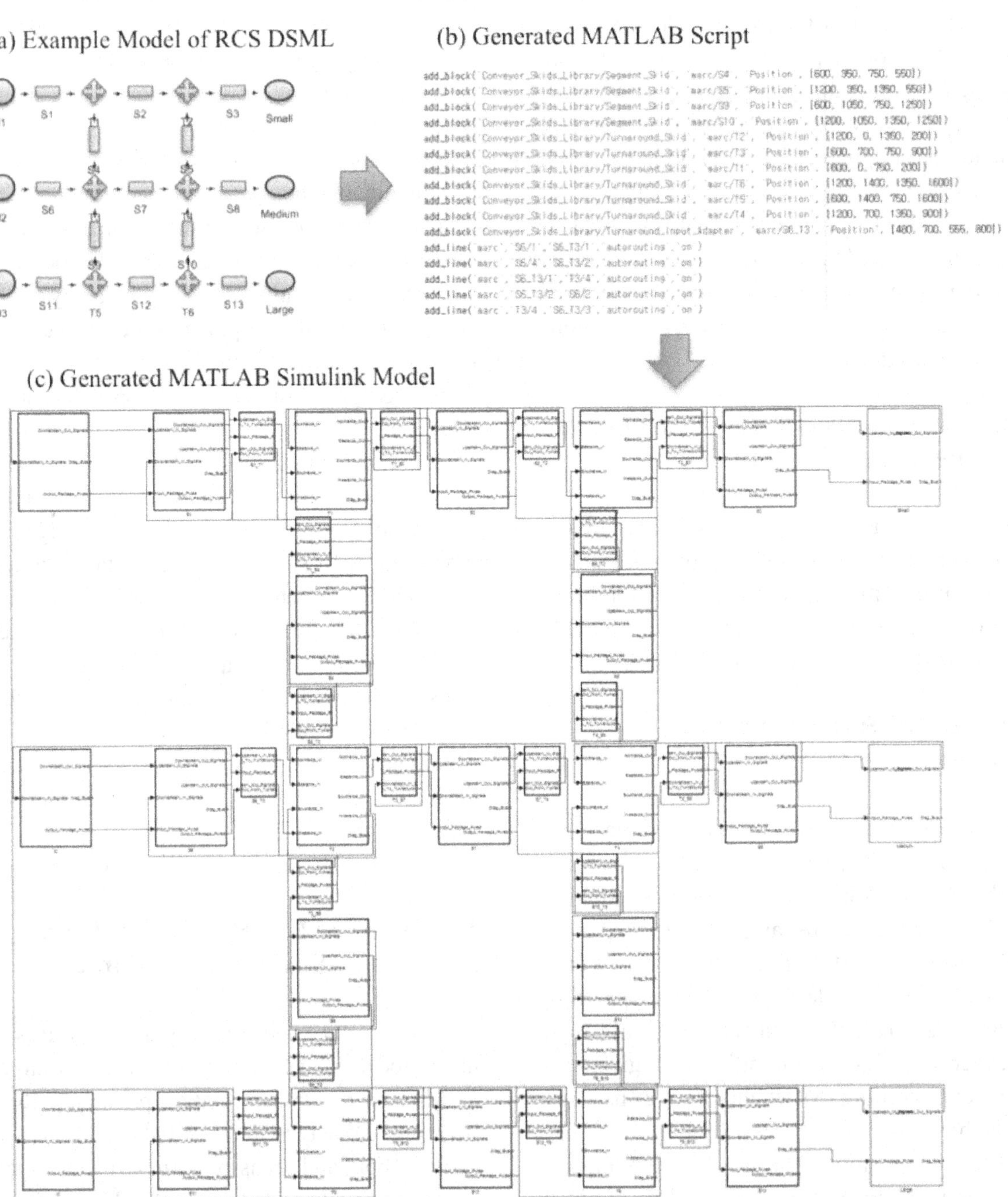

the UDM interpreter to achieve the entire process. Figure 9 shows the entire process of transformation from GME DSML to MATLAB Simulink model. Initially, blocks and connections in RCS are positioned by GME DSML environment. Then, as we just covered previously, the DSML will be interpreted to generate the MATLAB script file. Finally, the MATLAB script file will generate the executable model in MATLAB Simulink of the example RCS layout. Figure 9 partially presents generated products by the steps of transformation of an example RCS model we used.

Most CPS domains such as unmanned vehicles, medical monitoring, and process control systems are complex networked systems involving integration of physical and software components. It is not trivial to develop and evaluate the systems. Therefore, development of CPS needs to be component-based and there should be a need of a tool for integrating components. In our analysis application, physical and cyber behavioral model defined by Simulink for performance analysis of RCS is made and used, and it does not have features of simulating network. However, extending the analysis having features of network simulating is possible with using network simulators such as OMNeT++ and ns-3. In that case, integration process of different simulators is necessary and GME can be used to be in charge of integration of different simulators providing integration code. Additionally, CPS has various domains and each domain has different features. Accordingly, tools to define various DSMLs like GME are definitely required for CPS.

CONCLUSION

This chapter presented a MDE framework that can be used to conduct performance analysis of reconfigurable conveyor system. The primary artifacts of our MDE framework include a DSML, which allows a user to rapidly describe a layout of a RCS. The model transformation capability automates the conversion of high-level models into executable models based on MATLAB/Simulink. The executable models showed how the cyber and physical artifacts can be integrated to enable a wide range of performance analysis. This separation enables the model-driven framework to change the underlying analysis engine while also enabling the generative mechanisms to synthesize code artifacts when the system is actually fielded. As a result complete automation can be realized using a common framework.

Our future work in this area will explore analysis of failures in the system. We plan to target both the physical failures, such as motor failing, and cyber failures, such as the microcontroller logic failing. Our goal is to identify the impact on the system throughput due to failures, and also to understand how runtime adaptation by rerouting goods will help to maintain acceptable levels of performance in system operation. These are important dimensions to consider in CPS research. Naturally, a question we must answer is how DSMLs and MDE in general help with providing assurances for a variety of systemic properties of CPS.

REFERENCES

An, K., Trewyn, A., Gokhale, A., & Sastry, S. (2011). Model-driven performance analysis of reconfigurable conveyor systems used in material handling applications. In *Second IEEE/ACM International Conference on Cyber Physical Systems* (ICCPS 2011) (p. 141–150).

Archer, B., Sastry, S., Rowe, A., & Rajkumar, R. (2009). Profiling primitives of networked embedded automation. In *IEEE International Conference on Automation Science and Engineering* (CASE 2009) (pp. 531–536).

Bakay, A., & Magyari, E. (2001). *The UDM framework*. ISIS Vanderbilt University.

Czarnecki, K., Østerbye, K., & Volter, M. (2002). Generative programming. In *Object-Oriented Technology ECOOP 2002* (pp. 15–29). Workshop Reader. doi:10.1007/3-540-36208-8_2 de Lamotte, F., Berruet, P., & Philippe, J. (2006). Evaluation of reconfigurable manufacturing systems configurations using tolerance criteria. In *32nd Annual Conference on IEEE Industrial Electronics* (IECON 2006) (pp. 3715–3720).

Hayslip, N., Sastry, S., & Gerhardt, J. (2006). Networked embedded automation. *Assembly Automation, 26*(3), 235–241. doi:10.1108/01445150610679786

Karsai, G., & Sztipanovits, J. (2008). Model-integrated development of cyber-physical systems. *International Workshop on Software Technologies for Embedded and Ubiquitous Systems* (pp. 46–54).

Kent, S. (2002). Model driven engineering. In *Integrated formal methods* (pp. 286–298).

Kuruvilla, S., Gokhale, S., & Sastry, S. (2008). Reliability evaluation of reconfigurable conveyor systems. In *IEEE International Conference on Automation Science and Engineering* (CASE 2008) (pp. 929–934).

Ledeczi, A., Bakay, A., Maroti, M., Volgyesi, P., Nordstrom, G., & Sprinkle, J. (2001). Composing domain-specific design environments. *Computer, 34*(11), 44–51. doi:10.1109/2.963443

Lee, E. (2008). Cyber physical systems: Design challenges. In *11th IEEE Symposium on Object Oriented Real-Time Distributed Computing* (ISORC) (pp. 363–369).

Lee, E. (2009). Computing needs time. *Communications of the ACM, 52*(5), 70–79. doi:10.1145/1506409.1506426

Magyari, E., Bakay, A., Lang, A., Paka, T., Vizhanyo, A., Agrawal, A., et al. (2003). UDM: An infrastructure for implementing domain-specific modeling languages. In *3rd OOPSLA Workshop on Domain-Specific Modeling.*

Mamidisetty, K., Duan, M., Sastry, S., & Sastry, P. S. (2009). Multipath dissemination in regular mesh topologies. *IEEE Transactions on Parallel and Distributed Systems, 20*(8), 1188–1201. doi:10.1109/TPDS.2008.164

Mernik, M., Heering, J., & Sloane, A. (2005). When and how to develop domain-specific languages. *ACM Computing Surveys, 37*(4), 316–344. doi:10.1145/1118890.1118892

Moreno, G., & Merson, P. (2008). Model-driven performance analysis. In *4th International Conference on the Quality of Software Architectures* (pp. 135–151).

ADDITIONAL READING

Czarnecki, K., & Helsen, S. (2003). Classification of model transformation approaches. In *Proceedings of the 2nd OOPLSA Workshop on Generative Techniques in the Context of the Model Driven Architecture* (pp. 1–17).

Farid, A., & McFarlane, D. (2008). Production degrees of freedom as manufacturing system reconfiguration potential measures. *Proceedings of the Institution of Mechanical Engineers. Part B, Journal of Engineering Manufacture, 222*(10), 1301–1314. doi:10.1243/09544054JEM1056

Heilala, J., & Voho, P. (2001). Modular reconfigurable flexible final assembly systems. *Assembly Automation, 21*(1), 20–30. doi:10.1108/01445150110381646

Heragu, S., Meng, G., Zijm, W., & van Ommeren, J. (2001). *Design and analysis of reconfigurable layout systems. Internal Report.* University of Twente.

Kalita, D., & Khargonekar, P. (2002). Formal verification for analysis and design of logic controllers for reconfigurable machining systems. *IEEE Transactions on Robotics and Automation*, *18*(4), 463–474. doi:10.1109/TRA.2002.802206

Kolla, S., Michaloski, J., & Rippey, W. (2002). Evaluation of component-based reconfigurable machine controllers. In *Proceedings of the 5th Biannual World Automation Congress* (pp. 625–630).

Ledeczi, A., Maroti, M., Bakay, A., Karsai, G., Garrett, J., Thomason, C., et al. (2001). The generic modeling environment. In *Workshop on Intelligent Signal Processing*, Budapest, Hungary (Vol. 17).

Li, J., Dai, X., & Meng, Z. (2008). Improved net rewriting system-based approach to model reconfiguration of reconfigurable manufacturing systems. *International Journal of Advanced Manufacturing Technology*, *37*(11), 1168–1189. doi:10.1007/s00170-007-1037-5

Li, W., Yang, H., & Murata, T. (2010). An expandable petri net framework for method behavior evaluation of reconfigured equipment. In *Proceedings of the International MultiConference of Engineers and Computer Scientists*.

Mens, T., & Van Gorp, P. (2006). A taxonomy of model transformation. *Electronic Notes in Theoretical Computer Science*, *152*, 125–142. doi:10.1016/j.entcs.2005.10.021

KEY TERMS AND DEFINITIONS

Behavioral Model: An executable model that reproduces the required behavior of a system.

Cyber-Physical Systems (CPS): Systems featuring a tight combination between computational and physical elements.

Domain Specific Modeling Language (DSML): A graphical based language that illustrates components and connections in a particular domain.

Meta-Model: Construction and development of a collection of concepts which to form a model with a specific domain.

Model Transformation: A process of automatic converting source model to target model that can be defined as a set of transformation rules.

Model-Driven Engineering (MDE): A software development methodology that provides and leverages high-level abstraction for a particular domain.

Reconfigurable Conveyor Systems (RCS): Conveyor systems that offer significant flexibility in adapting to newer products and product lines by pluggable component blocks.

Chapter 20
MoDSEL:
Model-Driven Software Evolution Language

Ersin Er
Hacettepe University, Turkey

Bedir Tekinerdogan
Bilkent University, Turkey

ABSTRACT

Model-Driven Software Development (MDSD) aims to support the development and evolution of software intensive systems using the basic concepts of model, metamodel, and model transformation. In parallel with the ongoing academic research, MDSD is more and more applied in industrial practices. Like conventional non-MDSD practices, MDSD systems are also subject to changing requirements and have to cope with evolution. In this chapter, the authors provide a scenario-based approach for documenting and analyzing the impact of changes that apply to model-driven development systems. To model the composition and evolution of an MDSD system, they developed the so-called Model-Driven Software Evolution Language (MoDSEL) which is based on a megamodel for MDSD. MoDSEL includes explicit language abstractions to specify both the model elements of an MDSD system and the evolution scenarios that might apply to model elements. Based on MoDSEL specifications, an impact analysis is performed to assess the impact of evolution scenarios and the sensitivity of model elements. A case study is provided to show different kind of evolution scenarios and the required adaptations to model elements.

INTRODUCTION

In traditional, non-model-driven software development the link between the code and higher level design models is not formal but intentional. Required changes are usually addressed manually using the given modeling language. Because of the manual adaptation the maintenance effort is not optimal and as such sooner or later the design models become inconsistent with the code since changes are, in practice, defined at the code level. One of the key motivations for introducing

DOI: 10.4018/978-1-4666-2092-6.ch020

model-driven software development (MDSD) is the need to reduce the maintenance effort and as such support evolution. MDSD aims at achieving this goal through defining model elements as first class abstractions, and providing automated support using model transformations. For a given change requirement the code is not changed manually but automatically generated or regenerated, thereby substantially reducing maintenance effort. Further, because of the formal links between the models and the code the evolution of artefacts in the model-driven development process is synchronized. The link between the code and models is formal. In fact, there are only models, and as such, 'the documentation is the code'. Research on MDSD is continuing to improve the expressiveness of the three key abstractions of model, metamodel and transformation (Kleppe, 2008). As such even better and more automated support to cope with changing requirements and as such to provide reuse, portability, interoperability, and maintenance. Because of the promising benefits for development and evolution, MDSD is more and more applied in industrial projects (Hästbacka, 2011; Fieber, 2009; Maurmaier, 2008). Albeit, MDSD provides from one perspective better support for evolution, it also introduces new dimensions and challenges for software evolution (Visser, 2007; Briand, 2003). Like conventional code, models, metamodels and transformations might be subject to changing requirements and as such require to evolve in due time. Moreover, changes to the metamodels and transformations might render the terminal models invalid.

The software evolution problem in MDSD needs to address different challenges. One of the initial and key issues in considering evolution in MDSD is the impact of changes to the existing systems. To understand evolution in MDSD we have provided a *megamodel*, that consists of both a model for MDSD, the model for adapting model elements, and the model for scenarios that reflect the evolution process. Based on the megamodel we propose a scenario-based approach for analyzing the impact of changes that apply to model-driven development systems. For modeling the required changes we define the notion of so-called *evolution scenario,* which is defined as a description of the need for changes due to concerns of stakeholders. The concept *evolution scenario* has been inspired from the method called Scenario-based Analysis of Software Architecture that focuses on a more general use of scenarios (Kazman, 1996). Each evolution scenario will usually have an impact on the MDSD system and require changes to the models, metamodels or transformations.

To provide automated support for both documenting and analysis of evolution scenarios on MDSD projects we have developed the so-called domain-specific Model-Driven Software Evolution Language (MoDSEL). MoDSEL includes explicit language abstractions to specify model elements and evolution scenarios that apply to model elements. Based on MoDSEL specifications an impact analysis is provided to measure the impact of evolution scenarios and the sensitivity of model elements to the given evolution scenarios. We have supported the analysis process with a set of metrics (Fenton, 1997) that measure the impact of the defined scenarios as well as the sensitivity of each model element with respect to these scenarios. Once the system and the scenarios are modeled the metric values are automatically generated. The result of the measurement based on these metrics can support the decision in the design and refactoring of the system.

A case study for web-based conference management is used to show different kind of evolution scenarios and the required adaptations to model elements. The scope of our study includes the evolution in forward engineering that aims to derive concrete implementation from higher level abstractions. We do not consider evolution in reverse engineering projects.

The remainder of the chapter is organized as follows: In the second section we describe the example case of web-based conference management system. The third section defines the megamodel for modeling model-driven systems. The fourth section describes the design and implementation of MoDSEL. The fifth section presents the scenario-based impact analysis process. The sixth section describes the application of the process and the provided tool support. The seventh section provides the discussion of the proposed approach. The eight section provides the related work and finally we conclude in the last section.

CASE DESCRIPTION AND PROBLEM STATEMENT

In this section we describe the example case study: web-based conference chair system (MDChair) that is defined using model-driven development approach. The example will be used throughout the paper to explain the proposed approach. The system is inspired from existing conference chair application such as CyberChair (2001) and EasyChair (2010). A conference chair system supports the paper reviewing and selection process for scientific events such as conferences and workshops. The use case diagram for MDChair is shown in Figure 1. MDChair includes four different actors, *Maintainer, Author, PCChair* and *Reviewer. Maintainer* represents the person who configures which includes editing the files that contain the templates for forms and setting up the website (not shown in Figure 1). Further, *Maintainer* is also responsible for storing the files to database. *Author* is able to send their paper for review, view the review status of the paper, and send a camera-ready version of the paper in case it is accepted. *PCChair* can select and enter the reviewers' profiles into the system, assign papers to reviewers, send notification to authors and monitor the review process by generating overviews. *Reviewer* can access papers, bid for papers, submit reviews and check the complete reviews.

Paper reviews are based on an evaluation scheme and reviewers use these to assess the papers. The system includes functionality for automatic identification of possible conflicts which occur in case a paper received both the highest and lowest evaluation. In this case conflicting reviewers of the paper need to start a discussion to resolve the conflict.

The model-driven overview of this system is provided in Figure 2. The Conference Chair System is defined as an object-oriented class diagram in UML as defined by *Entities Model*. Entities are core application objects in most types of applications and they generally correspond to real world objects which the application addresses

Figure 1. Use case diagram of the conference chair system

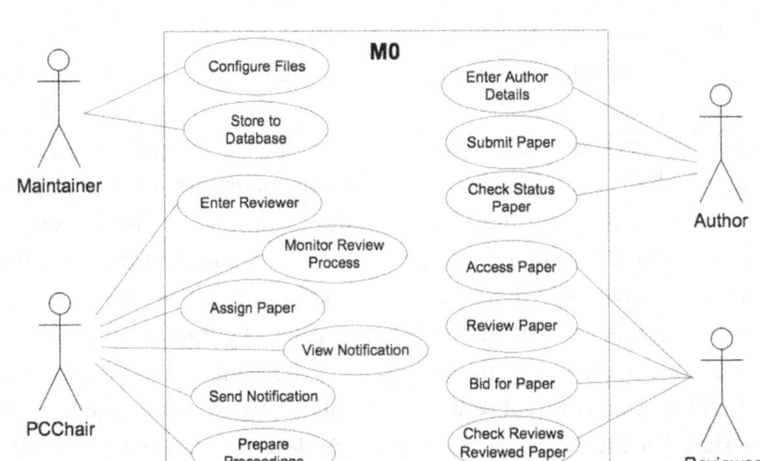

Figure 2. Model-driven design of the conference chair system example

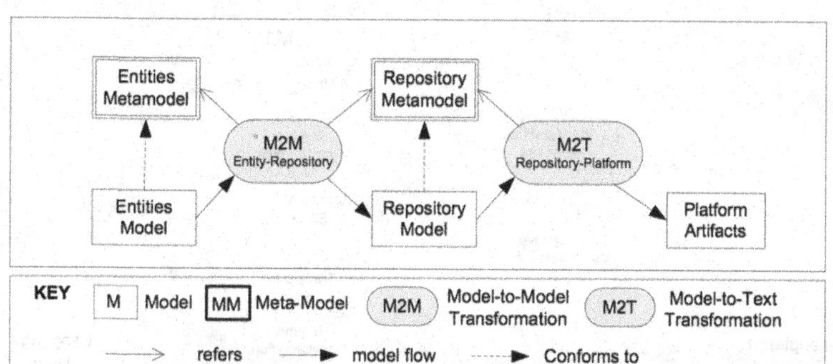

the issues of. Hereby, *Entities Model* includes model elements such as *Paper, Review, Notification* etc. Further, *Entities Model* conforms to the metamodel *Entities Metamodel* which serves as a language for defining the model for entities within predefined constraints. As our approach only addresses forward model-driven engineering, Model to Model (M2M) and Model to Text (M2T) types of transformations are used. M2M transformations take terminal models as source and output again terminal models. On the other hand, M2T transformations take terminal models as source and output text-based artifacts. For storing the entities to a persistent database an automatic model-to-model transformation *Entity-Repository M2M* is applied that is based on the source *Entities Metamodel* and target *Repository Metamodel*. The output of the *M2M* is *Repository Model*. A repository in an application defines abstractions for storage and retrieval of entity objects. The model-to-text transformation *Repository-Platform M2T* transforms *Repository Model* to *Platform Artefact*. Platform artifacts are the final products of this system which can be source codes, configuration files in a conventional software development environment. As such we can characterize this MDSD case as consisting of two metamodel elements (M2), two model transformation elements and three model elements (M1).

Obviously, like conventional software systems MDChair might soon or later cope with required changes for different stakeholders' concerns. For example Author might require that the personal information is stored in a secure manner. PCChair may require that a suitable access control is defined in case reviewers also submit papers and as such fulfill also the Author role. The maintainer might require that the system should not include too many retransformations. The reviewer might require an automatic detection of conflict etc. All of these changes will impact the model elements. Despite conventional system evolution the impact in this case might not be only required for M1 model elements but also require changes to metamodels and model transformations. As such we can observe here that evolution can be required at different levels in the metamodeling framework. Figure 3 shows the use case diagram that shows the possible evolution actions at the metamodeling level (M2) and modeling level (M1). To manage the evolution process in the different levels of MDSD process it is required that the changes and the corresponding rationale is documented. The explicit capturing, documentation and usage of the design rationale is important both for communication of the design decisions and the impact analysis.

At the highest abstraction level we can define software evolution in MDSD as the application of scenarios to model elements in the system. To define the possible changes to an MDSD system we use the notion of *evolution scenario*. Evolution scenarios, or usually called change scenarios have been widely discussed in the scenario-based ar-

Figure 3. Use case diagram for M2 level of the conference chair system

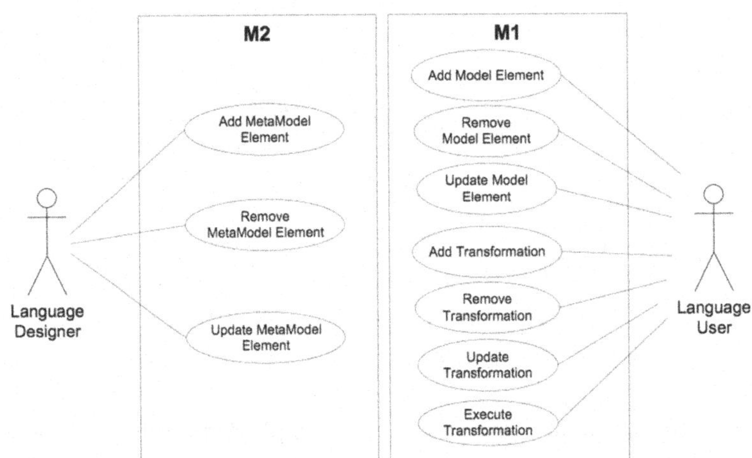

chitectural analysis domain. Dobrica & Niemela (2002) provide a comprehensive survey of the various software architecture design analysis methods that have been proposed so far. In the context of MDSD projects, each evolution scenario will relate to some model elements such as models, metamodel or transformations. An evolution scenario will typically require the realization of actions add, remove or update. For example introducing persistence (evolution scenario), might require adding a new metamodel to the MDSD system.

During the lifetime of the MDSD system different changes might be required. Documenting these changes with evolution scenarios will help to understand the MDSD system and also trace back the design decisions. In Table 1, for the given case we have provided a set of evolution scenarios. Each of these scenarios accesses the model elements as defined in the project. Scenario 1 relates to transitioning the current MDSD system to a web-based system and likewise will require the introduction of a new web-based user interface that can be integrated with existing platform. We can distinguish between the states of the system before a scenario is realized and after a scenario is realized. For scenario 1, the initial state of the system is as defined in Figure 2. The state after the realization of the scenario includes the addition of a new metamodel. The MDSD system is further enhanced with scenario S2 which requires generating the web based user interface, and as such the addition of the model-to-model transformation *Repository-to-Web*. In scenario S3 for automatic transformation of user interface model to platforms new model-model transformation *Web-to-Platform* is added. The result after realizing this scenario S3 would be like in Figure 4.

Scenario S4 requires the addition of functionality for storing and displaying all versions of the submitted paper by a user. The required actions for this scenario seem all to be at the level of Entities model. On the other hand scenario S5 and S6 again requires the addition of a new metamodel and update of model transformations for coping with the requirement to add security and access control to the system. Finally scenario S7 requires functionality for providing graphical statistics view for web chairs. This requires the update of metamodel *WebMM*. Obviously, as we can observe from this example different scenarios might require different changes at different modeling levels (M1, M2) of the MDSD system. We have adopted the similar usage of scenario as defined in the scenario-based architecture analysis approaches. Hereby, the

Table 1. Example evolution scenarios

Scenario	Description
S1	Introduce a language for Web based user interface and navigation modeling.
S2	Auto-generate essential web based user interface and page flow control models.
S3	Transform user interface model into platform artifacts.
S4	Store and display all versions of the submitted papers by a user.
S5	Introduce a language for declarative security and access control modeling.
S6	Realize security and access control requirements using the security language.
S7	Provide a graphical statistics view for conference chairs.
Etc.	

granularity is not explicitly defined but left to the stakeholders. The same holds for the causal relations among the scenarios. These can be related or not. The focus here is on the concerns of the stakeholders which are represented in the scenarios.

MEGAMODEL

To understand software evolution in model-driven software development we have developed a megamodel (Favre, 2004) as shown in Figure 5. The megamodel consists of two separate megamodels, the upper part represents the model for evolution while the lower part shows a model of model-driven software development. The key elements of the *Evolution* model are *Stakeholder*, *Concern*, *Scenario* and *Action*. The development and change is driven by *stakeholders* in the projects. A stakeholder is any person, group or organization who has interest in the given MDSD system. Typically, each stakeholder will have different *concerns* which could be functional or nonfunctional. A concern is generally defined as a general matter of interest that is held by some stakeholders. Concerns can be communicated by defining *scenarios*. A scenario is considered to be a brief description of some anticipated or desired use of the system. To realize each scenario a number of actions must be performed. An action in MDSD typically includes the basic actions of *Add, Remove*, and *Update* denoting the addition, removal and update of model elements, respectively. In addition we have defined the particular action *Execute* to denote the execution of transformations.

The lower part of the megamodel primarily describes model elements represented by *ModelElement*, which consists of four sub-elements: *Metamodel, TerminalModel, PlatformArtefact* and *Transformation*. *Metamodel* represents the metamodel for any *TerminalModel*. *TerminalModel* represents the model that is either edited by developers or generated by execution of a transformation. *PlatformArtifact* represents a generated artefact which does not explicitly conform to a Metamodel and is either generated by a model-to-text transformation or directly edited by developers. *Transformation* represents the

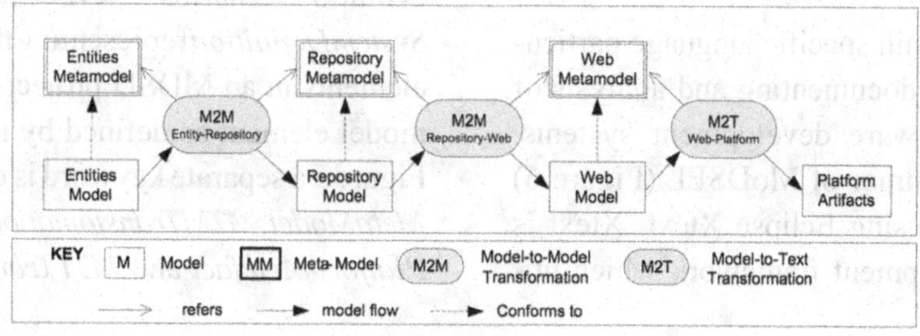

Figure 4. State of the MDChair after scenario S3

Figure 5. Adopted model for MDSD

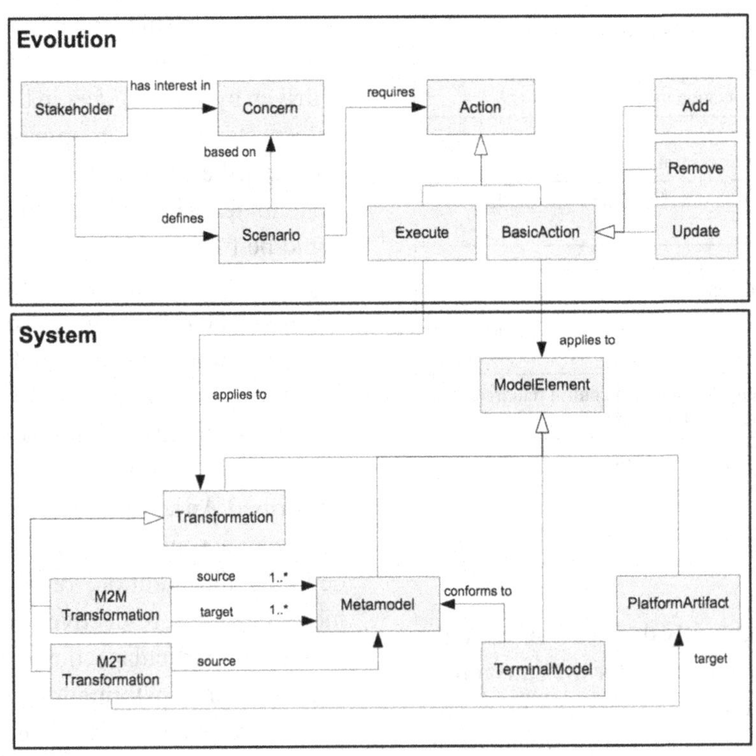

transformation definition for transforming a source model to a target element. We distinguish between model-to-model transformation (*M2M Transformation*) and model-to-text transformation *(M2T Transformation)* (Bezivin, 2005; Lanza, 2006) *M2M Transformation* transforms a model to another model conforming to the same or a different metamodel. In *M2T Transformation* a model is directly transformed to *PlatformArtifact* which are textual as usual.

MODSEL

MoDSEL is a domain specific language particularly designed for documenting and analysis of model-driven software development systems. The language grammar of MoDSEL (Figure 6) has been defined using Eclipse Xtext. Xtext is a language development framework which utilizes an EBNF like syntax language integrated with Eclipse Modelling Framework. Figure 6 shows the *System* part which corresponds to the lower part (System) of the model in Figure 5. Figure 6a shows the Ecore metamodel, whereas Figure 6b represents the grammar of MoDSEL. ECore is an implementation of OMG's EMOF (meta-metamodel) that has been defined in the Eclipse Modeling Framework (EMF, 2012). A close observation of MoDSEL grammar shows that it largely follows the megamodel as defined in Figure 5. The DSL includes mechanisms for specifying model elements as well as defining evolution scenarios. The root keyword starts with *SystemDefinition* representing the different model elements in an MDSD project. For each type of model element as defined by the megamodel in Figure 5 a separate keyword is defined, including *MetaModel*, *M2MTransfomation*, *TerminalModel*, *PlatformArtefact* and *M2TTransformation*.

Figure 6. MODSEL grammar – System part

```
modselSystem
  NamedElement
    name : EString
  SystemDefinition -> NamedElement
    metaModels : MetaModel
    m2mTransformations : M2MTransformation
    terminalModels : TerminalModel
    platformArtifacts : PlatformArtifact
    m2tTransformations : M2TTransformation
  MetaModel -> NamedElement
  M2MTransformation -> NamedElement
    sourceMetaModels : MetaModel
    targetMetaModels : MetaModel
  TerminalModel -> NamedElement
    metaModel : MetaModel
  PlatformArtifact -> NamedElement
  M2TTransformation -> NamedElement
    sourceMetaModels : MetaModel
    targetPlatformArtifacts : PlatformArtifact
```

a)

```
import 'classpath:/modselSystem.ecore' as modselSys

SystemDefinition returns modselSys::SystemDefinition:
    'SystemDefinition' name=ID
    '{'
        (metaModels+=MetaModel)*
        (m2mTransformations+=M2MTransformation)*
        (terminalModels+=TerminalModel)*
        (platformArtifacts+=PlatformArtifact)*
        (m2mTransformations+=M2MTransformation)*
    "}" ;

MetaModel returns modselSys::MetaModel:
    'metaModel' name=ID ;

M2MTransformation returns modselSys::M2MTransformation:
    'm2mTransformation' name=ID
        'from' '{' (sourceMetaModels+=[modselSys::MetaModel])+ '}'
        'to' '{' (targetMetaModels+=[modselSys::MetaModel])+ '}' ;

TerminalModel returns modselSys::TerminalModel:
    'terminalModel' name=ID
        'conformingTo' metaModel=[modselSys::MetaModel] ;

PlatformArtifact returns modselSys::PlatformArtifact:
    'platformArtifact' name=ID ;

M2TTransformation returns modselSys::M2TTransformation:
    'm2tTransformation' name=ID
        'from' '{' (sourceMetaModels+=[modselSys::MetaModel])+ '}'
        'to' '{' (targetPlatformArtifacts+=[modselSys::PlatformArtifact])+ '}' ;
```

b)

The part on evolution is defined in Figure 7. Hereby *EvolutionProcess* is defined as a root element which again contains a set of *Evolution-Scenarios*. *EvolutionScenario consists* of a set of *EvolutionActions*. Evolution actions relate to add, remove, update of model elements or execution of transformations. For each type of model element the corresponding keyword has been defined. Considering the model elements, and the possible actions, MoDSEL defines 17 evolution actions that can be used to describe the evolution of the system.

USING MODSEL FOR IMPACT ANALYSIS

In this section we provide the systematic overall process for documenting the evolution of scenarios and analyzing the impact of these changes on the existing model-driven system. The process is depicted in Figure 8.

While discussing the scenarios we have already implicitly described their impact on the system. The process in Figure 8 provides the systematic order of the steps which is as follows:

- *Analyze and Model the System*

First of all the MDSD system is analyzed and modeled as consisting of a set of models, metamodels and transformations. For this we use the system part of MoDSEL as given in Figure 6. The system to be analyzed could be already implemented or yet to be implemented. The provided model of the system is in principle an instance of the megamodel as defined in Figure 5. For example Figure 2 represents the model of the MDSD system for MDChair. Besides of a visual model the MDSD system is also modeled using MoDSEL, a domain specific language that we have developed for modeling model elements and scenarios in MDSD project.

- *Define Evolution Scenarios*

Based on the model of the MDSD system and the requirements artefacts, concrete scenarios are derived that define the required changes that will be made to the MDSD system over time. Again the scenarios are modeled using MoDSEL. Here, we use the evolution part of MoDSEL as given in Figure 7.

Figure 7. MODSEL grammar – Evolution part

```
import 'classpath:/modselEvolution.ecore' as modselEvol

EvolutionProcess returns modselEvol::EvolutionProcess:
        'EvolutionProcess' name=ID
        '{' (scenarios+=EvolutionScenario)+ '}' ;

EvolutionScenario returns modselEvol::EvolutionScenario:
        'EvolutionScenario' name=ID
        '{'    (actions+=EvolutionAction)+ '}' ;

EvolutionAction returns modselEvol::EvolutionAction:
        AddMetamodel | RemoveMetamodel | UpdateMetamodel |
        AddM2MTransformation | RemoveM2MTransformation | UpdateM2MTransformation |
        ExecuteM2MTransformation |
        AddTerminalModel | RemoveTerminalModel | UpdateTerminalModel |
        AddM2TTransformation | RemoveM2TTransformation | UpdateM2TTransformation |
        ExecuteM2TTransformation |
        AddPlatformArtifact | RemovePlatformArtifact | UpdatePlatformArtifact ;

AddMetamodel returns modselEvol::AddMetaModel:
        'add metaModel' metaModel=ID ;

RemoveMetamodel returns modselEvol::RemoveMetaModel:
        'remove metaModel' metaModel=ID ;

UpdateMetamodel returns modselEvol::UpdateMetaModel:
        'update metaModel' metaModel=ID ;

AddM2MTransformation returns modselEvol::AddM2MTransformation:
        'add m2mTransformation' transformation=ID
                'from' '{' (sourceMetaModels+=ID)+ '}'
                'to' '{' (targetMetaModels+=ID)+ '}' ;

RemoveM2MTransformation returns modselEvol::RemoveM2MTransformation:
        'remove m2mTransformation' transformation=ID ;

UpdateM2MTransformation returns modselEvol::UpdateM2MTransformation:
        'update m2mTransformation' transformation=ID ;

ExecuteM2MTransformation returns modselEvol::ExecuteM2MTransformation:
        'execute m2mTransformation' transformation=ID
                'from' '{' (sourceTerminalModels+=ID)+
                'to' '{' (targetTerminalModels+=ID)+ ;

AddTerminalModel returns modselEvol::AddTerminalModel:
        'add terminalModel' terminalModel=ID 'conformingTo' metaModel=ID ;

RemoveTerminalModel returns modselEvol::RemoveTerminalModel:
        'remove terminalModel' terminalModel=ID ;

UpdateTerminalModel returns modselEvol::UpdateTerminalModel:
        'update terminalModel' terminalModel=ID ;

AddM2TTransformation returns modselEvol::AddM2TTransformation:
        'add m2tTransformation' transformation=ID
                'from' '{' (sourceMetaModels+=ID)+ '}'
                'to' '{' (targetPlatformArtifacts+=ID)+ '}';

RemoveM2TTransformation returns modselEvol::RemoveM2TTransformation:
        'remove m2tTransformation' transformation=ID ;

UpdateM2TTransformation returns modselEvol::UpdateM2TTransformation:
        'update m2tTransformation' transformation=ID ;

ExecuteM2TTransformation returns modselEvol::ExecuteM2TTransformation:
        'execute m2tTransformation' transformation=ID
                'with' '{' (sourceTerminalModels+=ID)+ '}';

AddPlatformArtifact returns modselEvol::AddPlatformArtifact:
        'add platformArtifact' platformArtifact=ID;

RemovePlatformArtifact returns modselEvol::RemovePlatformArtifact:
        'remove platformArtifact' platformArtifact=ID;

UpdatePlatformArtifact returns modselEvol::UpdatePlatformArtifact:
        'update platformArtifact' platformArtifact=ID;
```

- *Define Impact Analysis*

Once the MDSD has been modeled and the corresponding scenarios are defined we can start the impact analysis of the scenarios on the MDSD system. Hereby, we will apply several metrics to measure the impact of scenarios on model elements, and to provide a global overview of the sensitivity of the elements in the MDSD system.

Figure 8. Impact analysis process using MoDSEL

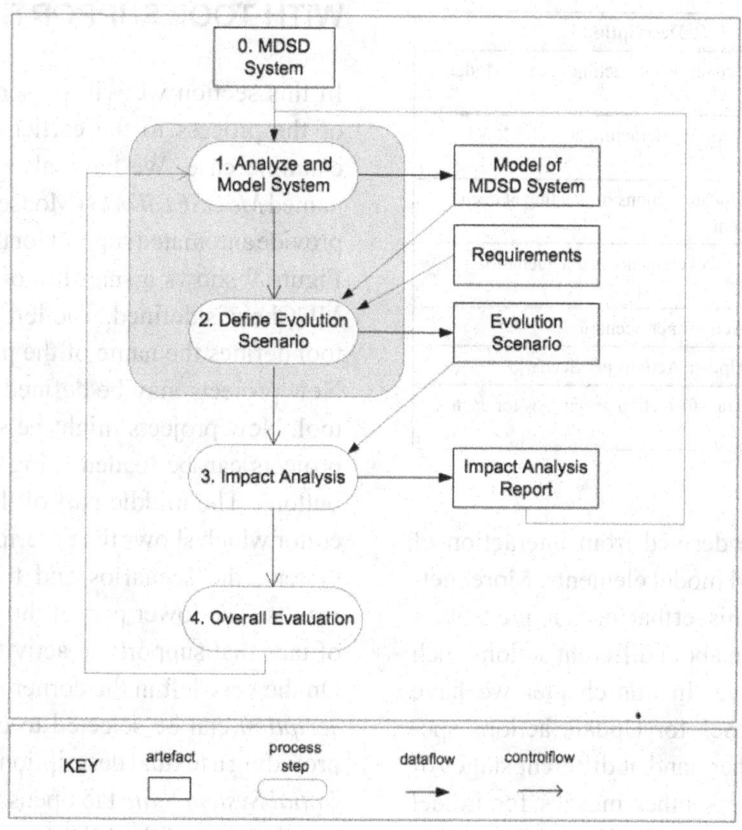

During the impact analysis process the metrics as defined in Table 2 are applied. The metrics NS_ME, NA_ME and NAU_ME regards the impact of scenarios from a model element perspective. NS_ME represents the scenarios that interact with a model element. Two scenarios interact at a same model element if they both require the change of the corresponding scenario to realize the needs of the scenario. Each scenario requires a set of actions to be fulfilled. The metric NA_ME counts the required number of actions for each model element. In this sense it is a finer grained metric than NS_ME which defines the impact based on the scenario only. Yet a more refined metric is NAU_ME which counts the number of updates required for a given model element. We have defined this particular metric since it appeared that the number of required updates has a substantial impact on the cost of evolution. The metrics NA_S, NAU_S and NT_S provide an evaluation from the scenario perspective. NA_S defines the required number of actions per scenario; NAU_S defines the required number of update actions per scenario. Finally, NT_S defines the required number of transformation executions for each scenario. In general we would like to minimize the number of scenarios that interact at each model element, minimize the number of model elements that scenarios impact and minimize the required number of transformation execution for each scenario. The impact analysis process results in a report in which the model elements, the scenarios and the impact of the scenarios on the MDSD system are summarized.

Table 2. Metrics to analyze impact of scenarios

Metric	Description
NS_ME	Number of Scenarios interacting at each Model Element
NA_ME	Number of Actions interacting at each Model Element
NAU_ME	Number of Update Actions interacting at each Model Element
NM_S	Number of Model elements that a Scenario impacts
NA_S	Number of Actions per Scenario
NAU_S	Number of Update Actions per Scenario
NT_S	Number of Transformation executions for each Scenario

The metrics are derived from interaction of scenario actions and model elements. More metrics can be added to this set that for example reflects detailed information about different actions such as Add and Remove. In this chapter we have provided only metrics for Update actions specifically. On the other hand at different stages of the evolution process other metrics for model elements could also be realized used for further analysis in the tool.

- *Overall evaluation*

Finally, the identified evolution scenarios might be weighted in terms of their relative importance and this weighting is used to determine an overall ranking and as such the required effort for evolving the MDSD system. The impact analysis report that is defined in the previous step will be used to communicate the impact and the cost of the required scenarios and to support the identification of alternative solutions that might optimize the cost.

APPLICATION OF THE PROCESS WITH TOOL SUPPORT

In this section we will presents the application of the process to the earlier defined MDChair example case. We have also developed a tool, named *MoDSEL Works* (Modsel, 2012), in order to provide automated support for the defined process. Figure 9 shows a snapshot of the tool in which MDChair is defined. The left corner field in the tool defines the name of the project (MDChair). New projects may be defined at any time in the tool. New projects might be saved and existing projects can be loaded using the corresponding buttons. The middle part of the tool defines the editor which shows the description of the MDSD system, the scenarios and the impact analysis results. The lower part of the tool includes a set of tabs that support the activities in the process. On the very left in the corner the tab *Project Description* can be selected to open the editor for providing a textual description of the project. The *Initial System State* tab opens the editor in which the elements of the MDSD system can be specified using MoDSEL. The specification in Figure 9 corresponds to the visual model as defined in Figure 2. Scenarios are documented in *Evolution Process Overview* and described in *MoDSEL Evolution Source*. The tab *Impact Analysis Results* shows the automatically generated overview of the values for the previously defined metrics in Table 2. The tab *Post Execution System* defines intermediate state of the MDSD system after execution of the scenarios. Similar to the initial system specification it is defined in MoDSEL. In the following we explain the application of the process steps and the related tool parts.

Figure 9. Initial system state represented in MoDSEL

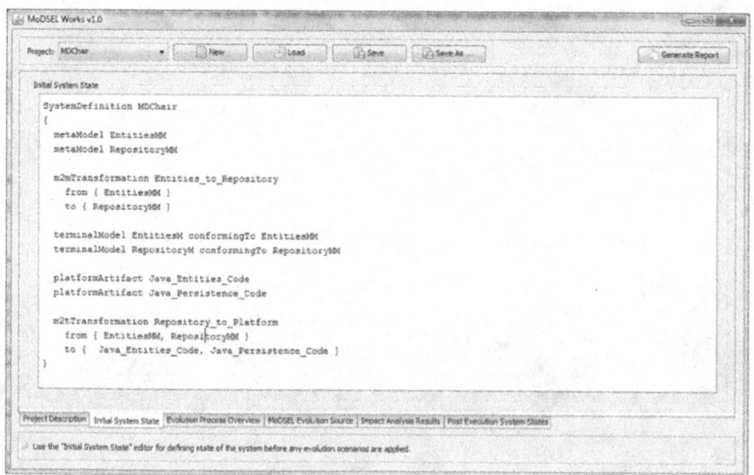

Model the System

The first step in the process is the modeling of the MDSD system. After describing the project textually in *Project Description* tab, the language engineer will open the tab *Initial System State* as shown in Figure 9. As it can be seen the specification of the MDSD system starts with keyword *SystemDefinition* and follows with the required metamodels and model transformations. The editor has also means to automatically validate the defined model with respect to the grammar of MoDSEL. As stated before the specification might refer either to an implemented MDSD system, or a system that still needs to be implemented.

Define Evolution Scenarios

The snapshot of the tool which shows the definition of scenarios is given in Figure 10. Evolution scenarios can be described in the system based on an evolution scenario template. Hereby the id of the scenario is given, a brief description, and the relevant stakeholders. In addition to the documentation part scenarios are also described in MoDSEL. The required actions for the scenarios are defined using (one of the 17) the actions of MoDSEL. For example, in Figure 11 we can see the specification of scenario S1 and S2 (and part of S3). The complete evolution is thus described in this process. This specification can be executed and result in a new state of the MDSD system (Figure 12, Figure 13, and Figure 14). This can be viewed by clicking on the tab *Post Execution System States*, resulting in the description as shown in Figure 15. The tools provide thus a useful instrument to view the impact of each scenario or a set of scenarios.

Impact Analysis

Once all the models and scenarios are defined we can derive the impact analysis of the defined scenarios on the MDSD system. Based on the model and scenario specifications the tool automatically generates the impact analysis results for the metrics in Table 2. For example, a snapshot of the tool showing the metric values for the number of scenarios interacting at each model element (*NS_ME*) is given in Figure 12. The tool

Figure 10. Tool editor for documenting evolution scenarios

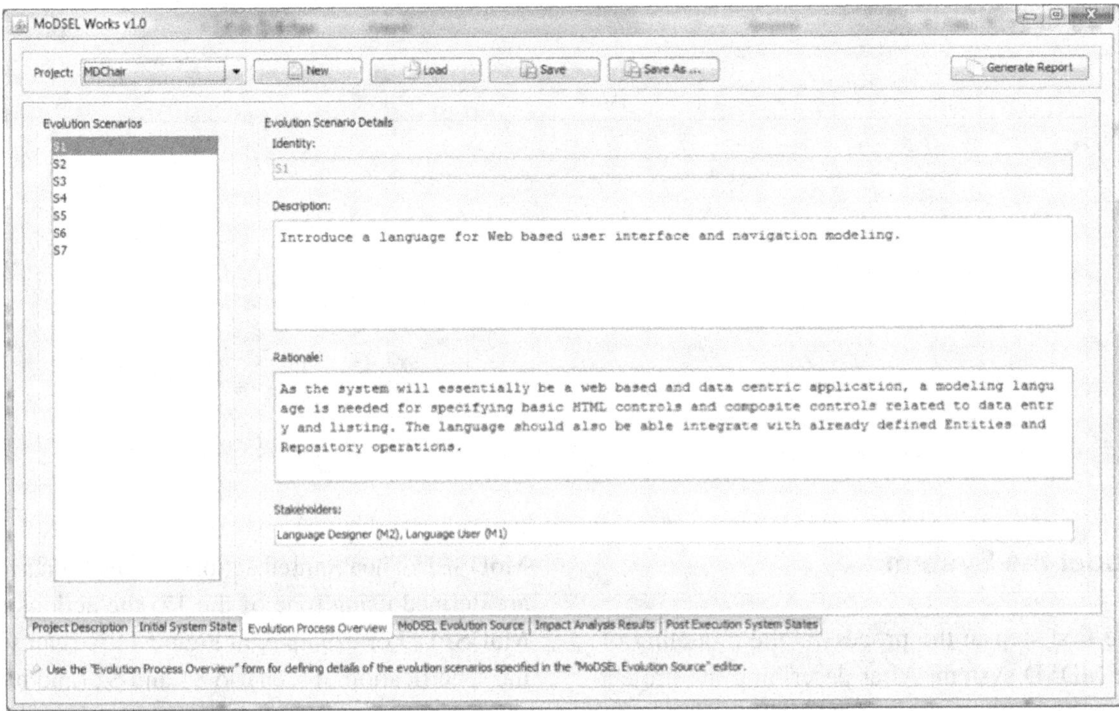

gives a direct insight in the impact of the defined evolution scenarios. In the figure we can observe that the model elements *WebM* and *WebMM* have the highest number of interacting scenarios. The transformation *Entities_to_Repository* seems to be impacted the least (1 scenario). In a similar sense other metric values can be viewed by clicking on the corresponding metrics in the left pane of the tool. We have provided all the results in Figure 13 and Figure 14. Figure 13 shows the results

Figure 11. Tool editor for specifying evolution scenarios

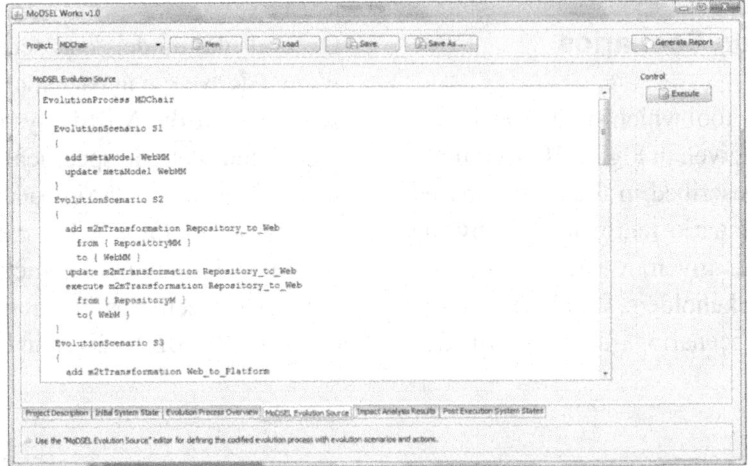

Figure 12. Part of the tool for viewing impact analysis

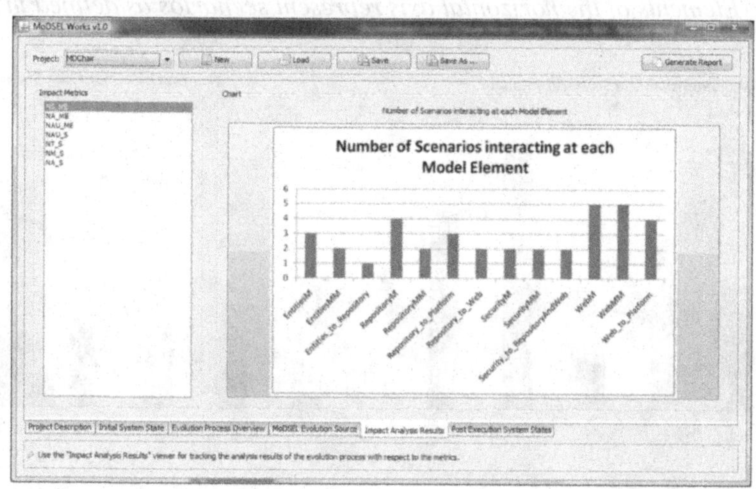

Figure 13. Automatically generated results of the impact analysis of scenarios for metrics NA_ME and NUA_ME

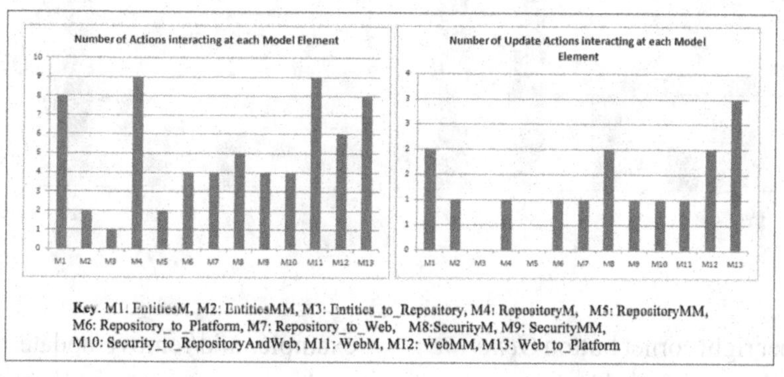

for the metrics *NA_ME* and *NUA_ME*. Figure 14 shows the results for the metrics *NM_S, NA_S, NUA_S,* and *NT_S.*

From Figure 13 we can observe that *RepositoryM* and *WebM* have the highest number of required actions. The difference stems from the fact that different scenarios may require different number of actions. The right part of Figure 13 shows the number of updates required for each model element, and it appears that *Web_to_Platform* requires the most update operations, and as such probably will be related with high costs.

Considering the metrics NM_S, NA_S, NUA_S Figure 14 shows that scenarios S6 (adding security) and S7 (adding graphical statistics) has the highest impact on the model elements. As such integrating these scenarios will not be easy given the initial MDSD system. The number of transformation execution per scenario (NT_S) is given in the last snapshot in Figure 14. Here scenario S4 (store and view versions of papers) leads to the highest value for NT_S. Scenarios S1 and S5 do not require any transformations.

The language designers and users might use the tool to model and analyze the impact of different scenarios on the MDSD system by browsing through the different tabs. However, the tool also provides the option to produce a final report by

Figure 14. Automatically generated results of the impact analysis of scenarios for metrics NM_S, NA_S, NUA_S, and NT_S (Elements of the horizontal axis represent scenarios as defined in Table 1)

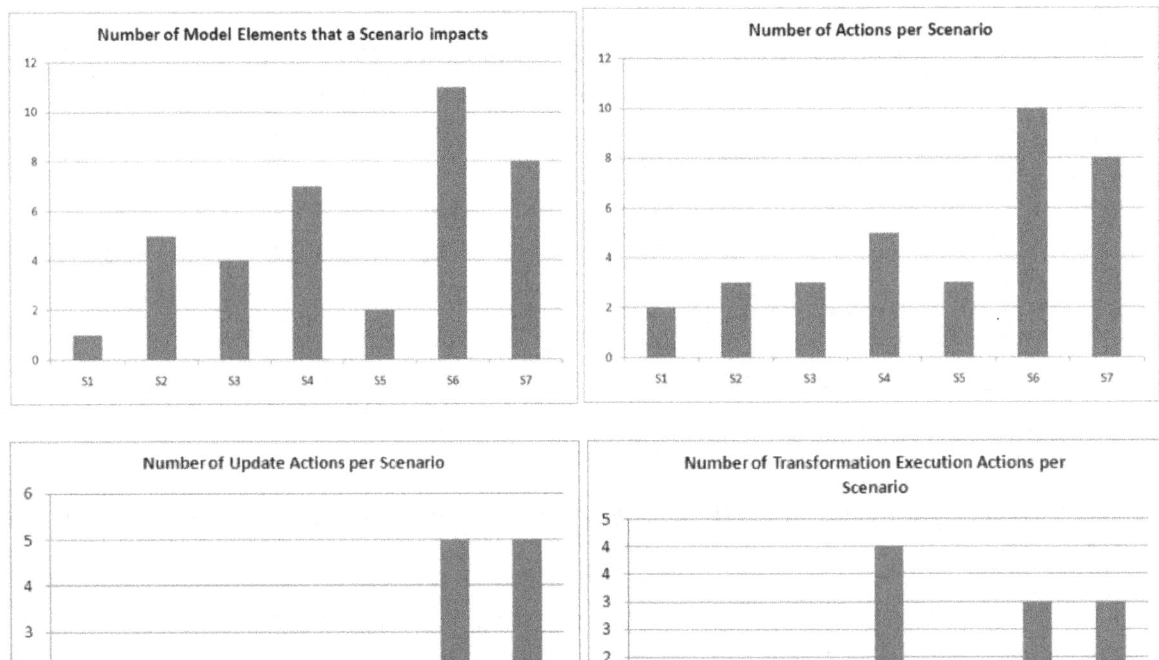

clicking on the upper right corner button *Generate Report*. The analysis report provides a complete overview of the system together with the overview of the metric values. The outline of the analysis report is given in the Table 3.

Overall Evaluation

After all the scenarios are executed the final design of the system would be as given in Figure 15. The impact analysis report shows the required changes and likewise the cost for realizing a given scenario. Currently the tool is defined for analysis purposes and does not provide guidelines for adapting or changing the MDSD system or the proposed scenarios. Hereby, the language designer can, for example, add/remove/update metamodels, while the language user can add/remove/update models.

DISCUSSION

In this chapter we have defined a DSL for supporting the impact analysis of evolution scenarios in a model-driven system. Our aim was to provide a practical tool that could be easily used to express both the evolution scenarios and the model elements. We have identified the following benefits of MoDSEL language and the process it supports:

Figure 15. End result of the given scenarios as defined as MoDSEL specification

```
SystemDefinition MDChair
{
 metaModel EntitiesMM
 metaModel RepositoryMM
 metaModel WebMM
 metaModel SecurityMM

 m2mTransformation Entities_to_Repository
  from { EntitiesMM }
  to { RepositoryMM }

 m2mTransformation Repository_to_Web
  from { RepositoryMM }
  to { WebMM }

 m2mTransformation Security_to_RepositoryAndWeb
  from { SecurityMM, EntitiesMM, RepositoryMM, WebMM }
  to { RepositoryMM, WebMM }

 terminalModel EntitiesM conformingTo EntitiesMM
 terminalModel RepositoryM conformingTo RepositoryMM
 terminalModel WebM conformingTo WebMM
 terminalModel SecurityM conformingTo SecurityMM

 platformArtifact Java_Entities_Code
 platformArtifact Java_Persistence_Code
 platformArtifact Java_Web_Framework_Code

 m2tTransformation Repository_to_Platform
  from { EntitiesMM, RepositoryMM }
  to { Java_Entities_Code, Java_Persistence_Code }

 m2tTransformation Web_to_Platform
  from { WebMM }
  to { Java_Web_Framework_Code }
}
```

Assessment of the Effort and Cost for Adapting the System and/or Introducing New Concerns

The basic motivation for the process and the tool is to analyze the existing or to-be developed MDSD system and highlight the required cost and effort. The tool provides the values for the metrics relatively easy. The results might be analyzed by MDSD engineers who can plan the required MDSD activities. They might decide to postpone or omit the required scenarios. For example, a scenario which requires too many model adaptations or retransformations could be reconsidered. For the given case study we could, for instance, state that scenario S6 (realize security and access control) requires too many update operations and as such will be an expensive scenario given the current model elements of the system.

Table 3. Outline of the generated impact analysis report

Section	Description
Project Description	Provides the textual description of the project
Model of the system	Provides a list of the model elements in natural language as well as the MoDSEL listing that was provided in the tool
Evolution Scenarios	Provides the list of evolution scenarios as described in the tool as well as the MoDSEL listing that was provided in the tool.
Impact Analysis	Provide the evaluation results for the given metrics

Supporting Design Decisions

The high effort and cost of the scenarios might also be related to the current quality of the MDSD system. An MDSD system which is defined as one huge metamodel will have a low impact for scenarios (at the most one module element) but on the other hand will have high number of scenario interactions and required transformation executions. In such case one might think to split up the metamodel, define new model transformations etc. For the given case study it appears that the metamodels EntitiesM, RepositoryM, WebM and Web_to_Platform require to many actions for the given scenarios. The designer as such can decide to refactor or redesign these model elements. Although in this paper we do not focus on defining guidelines for MDSD system design, the tool is a useful instrument to experiment with the different design alternatives.

Supporting the Alternative Space Analysis of Different Selections of Scenarios

Using the tool we can support the alternative space analysis for the MDSD project. Alternatives for the MDSD system stem from both the different selections of scenarios (concerns) and the selection of model elements. In addition, for a given set of scenarios we could even analyze the impact of different orderings which could result in a different impact analysis. For the given case, we could, for example, introduce new kind of evolution scenarios, or reorder existing evolution scenarios to check their impact. Alternatively, we could select different kind of model elements.

Supporting Decision on Selection of Model Elements

Since different alternatives can be defined using the tool, and the related impact analysis is provided relatively easily, the designer of the system can reason about the selection and/or elimination of various model elements. This will be beneficial in case, for example, a newer version of a metamodel is provided, a more advanced transformation is defined etc.

Guiding the MDSD Implementation Process

The tool can be used to experiment with defining various design alternatives. The impact analysis can be provided for each alternative and once an alternative is selected one can decide to implement the MDSD system. Figure 15 shows, for example, the final state of the system after realizing the scenarios as defined in Table 1. This specification can be used to manually implement the MDSD system. Also we might use this specification as a basis for automatic generation of the MDSD system. Since this is out of the scope of the paper we just state this as an idea for potential future work.

Support for Multiple Stakeholders

We have provided a general platform for modeling MDSD systems that could be of direct benefit for multiple stakeholders in the system. Given our tool and the mechanisms for impact analysis the designer can identify the "bad smells" in the MDSD system and, if needed, take action. The manager who is interested in the cost of a new release can get insight to support the high level management decisions. The maintenance engineer who is responsible for adapting the system, can get insight in the changes and decide on the required actions. Finally, the system can help guide the programmer who is concerned about the amount of code that should be manually written or integrated with existing generated code.

RELATED WORK

In this paper we observed the impact of several evolution scenarios on a model-driven system from a broad perspective using a megamodel. The notion of megamodel has been explained in detail in detail in (Favre, 2004; Favre & Nguyen, 2004). The authors also define megamodel to describe MDE concepts and their relationships. Similar to our work Favre et al. (2004) focus on *evolution-in-the-large*, that is the evolution of large-scale industrial software systems. Typically the evolution of these large scale systems often includes various technical spaces over time.

The notion of technical space has been defined in (Bezivin, 2005) and is defined as "a model management framework accompanied by a set of tools that operate on the models definable within the framework". Technical spaces as such denote a given technology at a more abstract level and as such allow reasoning about the similarities and differences and possibilities for integration with other technical spaces. Example technical spaces are programming languages (e.g. Java, C#), database systems, frameworks for markup languages (XML, SGML), knowledge representation techniques (e.g. ontologies), and modeling frameworks and languages (e.g. UML, Model Driven architecture (MDA). The megamodel perspective provides a suitable abstraction to reason about the different model elements in the megamodel. Favre et al. (2004) also provide a reasoning about model-driven software evolution in which they propose to model a model-driven system as a graph consisting of nodes that are connected using association links including decomposedIn (δ), RepresentationOf (μ), ElementOf (ε), ConformsTo (χ), and IsTransformedIn (τ). The evolution of the software system can be modelled by a composition of the corresponding graphs using τ links. In our approach we support both the notion of technical spaces and evolution-in-the-large. Actually the model elements in our approach can be of any technical space. We can also state that our approach is in particular useful for evolution-in-the-large that requires many model elements from various technical spaces. The difference with the megamodel of Favre et al. (2004) is that we integrate the notion of evolution scenario in the megamodel since our key objective is software evolution. Further our approach is targeted to a practical application and is supported by the corresponding tools. The megamodel from Favre et al. (2004) appears to be a theoretical framework that is generic and targets also other concerns than software evolution.

In (Deursen et al, 2007) the authors provide a research agenda for model-driven software evolution. They make a distinction between *regular evolution* that refers to traditional software evolution, and evolution dimensions in model-driven software development. In regular evolution, the modeling language is used to make the changes. In model-driven software development evolution they distinguish among *meta-model evolution*, *platform evolution* and *abstraction evolution.* Meta-model evolution refers to the changes in the modeling notation. Platform evolution refers to changes in the code generators and application framework to reflect new requirements on the target platform. Finally, abstraction evolution refers to adding new modeling languages or enhancing modeling languages to reflect increased understanding of a technical or business domain. According to the authors, one of the key premises for model-driven software evolution is that evolution should be a continuous process. This might require to continuously search for new patterns, richer meta-models and transformations. In our work we aimed to analyze the different dimensions of model-driven software evolution. Using the integrated view of evolution using scenarios and model elements expressed in the megamodel we can reason about meta-model evolution, platform evolution and abstraction evolution. Also our tool supports the continuous search and analysis of new model elements. It should be noted, though, that we focus on analysis and not on development. An interesting further direction is linking the model elements used in the analysis to the real elements (e.g., code in the system). We consider this as part of our future work.

In (Lange & Wijns, 2007) a tool called MetricViewEvolution is presented that aims to provide information on the evolution of model-driven systems and support model understanding, identification of quality problems and evolution trends. The tool provides six different views including *ContextView, MetaView, MetricView, UML-City View, Quality Tree View* and *Evolution View.* Each View is based on existing UML diagrams and combines structural model information with metrics data from inside the model and external sources. In our tool we have actually two basic views, a view from the evolution scenario perspective, and a view from the model element perspectives.

Scenario-based analysis approaches have been widely applied and validated over the past several years in the software architecture design community. Several scenario-based architecture analysis methods have been developed each focusing on particular quality attributes (Dobrica, 2002). In general, scenario-based analysis methods take as input a model of the architecture and measure the impact of the predefined scenarios on it in order to identify the potential risks and the sensitive points of the architecture. A scenario is generally considered to be a brief description of some anticipated or desired use of the system. Hereby, it is implicitly assumed that scenarios correspond to the particular quality attributes that need to be analyzed. The concept of Evolution Scenario Template as such builds on this existing work. Using the evolution scenario templates we do not only describe the scenarios but also define the impact on the model elements.

Model-driven software evolution has been very often addressed by considering the problem of metamodel evolution and model co-evolution (Garcés, 2009). For this model co-evolution problem it is necessary to include the notion of distance to express to what extent a model conforms to a metamodel (metamodel/model co-evolution), or a model is representation of code (model/code co-evolution) (Favre, 2004). Gruschko et al (2007) have presented a generic approach to addressing the model migration problem. They distinguish between so-called additive changes to M1 models, which do not break the corresponding M1 models, and invalidating changes that introduce incompatibilities and cross-version inconsistencies. They have implemented a transformation for M1 models, compensating for M2 model changes. Further, an early vertical prototype of the migrator for resolvable changes is implemented. Wachsmuth (2007) also distinguishes adaptations that ensure instance preservation from manipulations which induce co-evolutions. In their approach metamodel evolutions are specified by QVT relations, while co-adaptations are defined in terms of QVT transformations when resolvable changes occur. Our approach for model-driven software evolution analysis should be considered from a broader perspective than the co-evolution problem since we do not aim to provide a focused view on metamodel-model relation but depict the impact of evolution scenarios on the overall system. Likewise both perspectives could be seen as complementary approaches and it would be useful to consider the combination of both perspectives.

In (Briand, 2003) the authors propose a UML model-based approach to impact analysis that can be applied before any implementation of the changes, thus allowing an early decision-making and change planning process. For this they verify that the UML diagrams are consistent and changes between two different versions of a UML model are identified according to a change taxonomy. Using formally impact analysis rules expressed in the Object Constraint Language the model elements that are impacted by those changes are determined. The authors also present a prototype tool that provides automated support for the impact analysis strategy.

CONCLUSION

Software systems are rarely frozen and need to evolve continuously. From one important perspective, model-driven software development has been introduced as a paradigm to cope with the changes in software and likewise to support software evolution. The evolution is basically supported through automatic transformation of the enhanced source model to a target model. In parallel with the advantages for software evolution management, model-driven software development has also added new dimensions of evolution. Similar to conventional code, models, metamodels and transformations might be subject to changing requirements and as such require to evolve in due time. The notion of model-driven software evolution has been recognized by the model-driven software community and we can observe an ongoing research in this domain. In this chapter we have provided a systematic approach for analyzing the impact of evolution scenarios on a given MDSD system. For this we have first defined a megamodel that integrates both the concerns of software evolution and the elements in a model-driven software development system. Based on the megamodel we have defined the domain specific language MoDSEL that can be used to express both evolution scenarios and the model elements in an MDSD system. We have provided tool support with which we can model possible evolution scenarios and the model elements. Since each evolution scenario in a MoDSEL specification maps to a number of required evolution actions, the impact analysis of each scenario can be defined relatively easily. With the tool we provide two different perspectives of the impact analysis, the impact of evolution scenarios on model elements, and the sensitivity of each model element with respect to the interacting evolution scenarios. The impact analysis consisting of a set of recorded evolution scenarios is important from two perspectives. First of all, we have now a practical approach to document the evolution scenarios. Second, the impact analysis results can be used to guide the maintenance process because it defines the necessary actions for adapting the system. Our future work will focus on the refinement of the metrics for analyzing the impact of scenarios. Further we also aim to integrate the analysis results with the development of the model elements.

REFERENCES

Baroni, A., Braz, S., & Abreu, F. (2002). Using OCL to formalize object-oriented design metrics definitions. In *Workshop on Quantitative Approaches in Object-Oriented Software Engineering*.

Bézivin, J. (2005). On the unification power of models. *Software & Systems Modeling, 4*(2), 171–188. doi:10.1007/s10270-005-0079-0

Briand, L. C., Labiche, Y., & O'Sullivan, L. (2003). Impact analysis and change management of UML models. In *Proceedings of International Conference on Software Maintenance*, 2003 (pp. 256- 265): IEEE.

Deursen van, A., Klint, P., & Visser, J. (2000). Domain-specific languages: An annotated bibliography. *ACM SIGPLAN Notices, 35*(6), 26-36.

Deursen van. A., Visser, E., & Warmer, J. (2007). Model-driven software evolution: A research agenda. In D. Tamzalit (Ed.), *Workshop on ModelDriven Software Evolution at Conference on Software Maintenance and Reengineering* (pp. 41-49).

Dobrica, L., & Niemela, E. (2002). A survey on software architecture analysis methods. *IEEE Transactions on Software Engineering, 28*(7), 638–653. doi:10.1109/TSE.2002.1019479

EasyChair Conference System. (2010). Retrieved March 2010, from http://www.easychair.org

Eclipse Modeling Project – EMF. (2012). Retrieved February 2012, from http://www.eclipse.org/modeling/emf

Favre, J.-M. (2004). Foundations of model (driven) (reverse) engineering -- Episode I: Story of The Fidus Papyrus and the Solarus. *Post-Proceedings of Dagstuhl Seminar on Model Driven Reverse Engineering*.

Favre, J.-M., & Nguyen, T. (2004). Towards a megamodel to model software evolution through transformations. *Electronic Notes in Theoretical Computer Science*, *127*, 59–74. doi:10.1016/j.entcs.2004.08.034

Fenton, N. E., & Pfleeger, S. L. (1996). *Software metrics: A rigorous & practical approach* (2nd ed.). PWS Publishing Co.

Fieber, F., Regnat, N., & Rumpe, B. (2009). Assessing usability of model driven development in industrial projects. *From Code Centric to Model Centric Software Engineering: Practices Implications and ROI, Proceedings of the 4th European Workshop.*

Garcés, K., Jouault, F., Cointe, P., & Bézivin, J. (2009). Managing model adaptation by precise detection of metamodel changes. In Paige, R. F., Hartman, A., & Rensink, A. (Eds.), *Model driven architecture - Foundations and applications* (pp. 34–49). Berlin, Germany: Springer. doi:10.1007/978-3-642-02674-4_4

Gruschko, B., Kolovos, D., & Paige, R. (2007). Towards synchronizing models with evolving metamodels. In *Proceedings of Workshop of Model-Driven Software Evolution*.

Hästbacka, D., Vepsäläinen, T., & Kuikka, S. (2011). Model-driven development of industrial process control applications. *Journal of Systems and Software*, *84*(7), 1100–1113. doi:10.1016/j.jss.2011.01.063

Kazman, R., Abowd, G., Bass, L., & Clements, P. (1996). Scenario-based analysis of software architecture. *IEEE Software*, *13*(6), 47–55. doi:10.1109/52.542294

Kleppe, A. (2008). *Software language engineering: Creating domain-specific languages using metamodels* (1st ed.). Addison-Wesley Professional.

Kleppe, A. G., Warmer, J. B., & Bast, W. (2003). *MDA explained: The model driven architecture: Practice and promise*. Addison-Wesley Professional.

Lange, C. F. J., Wijns, M. A. M., & Chaudron, M. R. V. (2007). MetricViewEvolution: UML-based views for monitoring model evolution and quality. *11th European Conference on Software Maintenance and Reengineering* (pp. 327–328).

Lanza, M., Marinescu, R., & Ducasse, S. (2006). *Object-oriented metrics in practice: Using software metrics to characterize, evaluate, and improve the design of object-oriented systems*. Springer.

Maurmaier, M., & Göhner, P. (2008). Model-driven development in industrial automation. *Technology (Elmsford, N.Y.)*, 244–249.

Mens, T., Wermelinger, M., Ducasse, S., Demeyer, S., Hirschfeld, R., & Jazayeri, M. (2005). Challenges in software evolution. *Eighth International Workshop on Principles of Software Evolution* (pp. 13- 22): IEEE.

Modsel. (2012). Retrieved March 2012, from http://web.cs.hacettepe.edu.tr/~ersiner/modsel

Mohagheghi, P., & Dehlen, V. (2009). Existing model metrics and relations to model quality. *Workshop on Software Quality* (pp. 39–45).

Ramil, J. F. (2002). Laws of software evolution and their empirical support. *Proceedings of International Conference on Software Maintenance* (pp. 71- 71).

van de Stadt, R. (2001). *Cyberchair: A web-based groupware application to facilitate the paper reviewing process*. Retrieved from http://www.cyberchair.org

Wachsmuth, G. (2007). Metamodel adaptation and model co-adaptation. *European Conference on Object-Oriented Programming, Lecture Notes in Computer Science, Vol. 4609* (pp. 600-624). Springer.

ADDITIONAL READING

Breivold, H. P., & Crnkovic, I. (2010). A systematic review on architecting for software evolvability. *21st Australian Software Engineering Conference* (pp. 13-22). IEEE.

Cicchetti, A., Ruscio, D. D., Eramo, R., & Pierantonio, A. (2008). Automating co-evolution in model-driven engineering. *12th International IEEE Enterprise Distributed Object Computing Conference* (pp. 222-231).

Deng, G., Schmidt, D. C., Gokhale, A., Gray, J., Lin, Y., & Lenz, G. (2008). Evolution in model-driven software product-line architectures. In Tiako, P. F. (Ed.), *Designing software intensive systems: Methods and principles*. Hershey, PA: Information Science Reference. doi:10.4018/978-1-59904-699-0.ch005

Di Ruscio, D., Lämmel, R., & Pierantonio, A. (2010). Automated co-evolution of GMF editor models. In B. Malloy, S. Staab, & M. Van Den Brand (Eds.), *Proceedings of the Third International Conference on Software Language Engineering* (pp. 143-162).

Domínguez, E., Lloret, J., Rubio, Á. L., & Zapata, M. A. (2008). Model–driven, view–based evolution of relational databases. In Bhowmick, S. S., Küng, J., & Wagner, R. (Eds.), *Database and expert systems applications* (pp. 822–836). doi:10.1007/978-3-540-85654-2_74

Graaf, B. (2007). *Model-driven evolution of software architectures*. 11th European Conference on Software Maintenance and Reengineering.

Gray, J., Lin, Y., & Zhang, J. (2006). Automating change evolution in model-driven engineering. *IEEE Computer*, *39*(2), 51–58. doi:10.1109/MC.2006.45

Herrmannsdoerfer, M., Ratiu, D., & Wachsmuth, G. (2010). Language evolution in practice: The history of GMF. *International Conference on Software Language Engineering* (pp. 3-22).

Karaila, M. (2009). *Evolution of a domain specific language and its engineering environment - Lehman's laws revisited*. Workshop on Domain-Specific Modeling.

Lehman, M., Ramil, J., Wernick, P., Perry, D., & Turski, W. M. (1997). Metrics and laws of software evolution. *Proceedings of the 4th International Symposium on Software Metrics* (pp. 20-32).

Pizka, M., & Jurgens, E. (2007). Automating language evolution. *First Joint IEEE/IFIP Symposium on Theoretical Aspects of Software Engineering* (pp. 305-315).

Sneed, H. (2007). The drawbacks of model-driven software evolution. *Workshop on Model Driven Software Evolution* (pp. 130-140).

Sprinkle, J., Gray, J., & Mernik, M. (2009). *Fundamental limitations in domain-specific modeling language evolution*. Technical report TR-090831, University of Arizona.

Ulrich, W. M., & Newcomb, P. (2010). *Information systems transformation: Architecture-driven modernization case studies*. Morgan Kaufmann.

Zschaler, S., Kolovos, D., Drivalos, N., Paige, R. F., & Rashid, A. (2010). Domain-specific metamodelling languages for software language engineering. *International Conference on Software Language Engineering* (pp. 334–353).

KEY TERMS AND DEFINITIONS

Domain-Specific Language: A computer language that provides abstractions to define concepts and relations in a particular domain. Such a language is generally readable/writable by human experts of the domain.

Megamodel: A specific sophisticated model, which represents a system of modeling abstractions.

Meta-Model: Construction and development of a collection of concepts which to form a model with a specific domain.

Model Transformation: A process of automatic converting source model to target model that can be defined as a set of transformation rules.

Model-Driven Software Development (MDSD): A software development approach in which higher level abstractions of model, meta-model and transformations are used to define and realize a software system.

Software Evolution: Process of initial development and updating of a software system.

Compilation of References

Abadi, M., & Cardelli, L. (1996). *A theory of objects*. New-York, NY: Springer. doi:10.1007/978-1-4419-8598-9

Abdelzaher, T., Blum, B., Cao, Q., Chen, Y., Evans, D., & George, J. … Krishnamurthy, S. (2004). Envirotrack: Towards an environmental computing paradigm for distributed sensor networks. In *Proceedings of the 24th International Conference on Distributed Computing Systems* (pp. 582-589). IEEE.

Abelson, H., Allen, D., Coore, D., Hanson, C., Homsy, G., & Knight, T. Jr (2000). Amorphous computing. *Communications of the ACM*, *43*(5), 74–82. doi:10.1145/332833.332842

Ablonskis, L., & Nemuraite, L. (2010). Discovery of complex model implementation patterns in source code. *Information Technology and Control*, *39*(4), 291–300.

Abrahams, D., & Gurtovoy, A. (2004). *C++ template metaprogramming: Concepts, tools, and techniques from Boost and beyond*. Boston, MA: Addison-Wesley.

Ada. (1982). *Reference manual for the Ada programming language*. MIL-STD 1815 edition, U.S. Department of Defense.

Agosta, G., & Pelosi, G. (2007). A domain specific language for cryptography. In *Proceedings of the Forum on specification and Design Languages (FDL)* (pp. 159–164). Gières, France: ECSI.

Aho, A. V., & Ullman, J. D. (1977). *Principles of compiler design*. Boston, MA: Addison-Wesley Longman Publishing Co., Inc.

Aho, A., Sethi, R., & Ullman, J. (1986). *Compilers: Principles, techniques & tools*. Boston, MA: Addison-Wesley.

Ahonen, H., Mannila, H., & Nikunen, E. (1994). Forming grammars for structured documents: An application of grammatical inference. *Proceedings of the Second International Colloquium on Grammatical Inference and Applications* (pp. 153-167). Springer-Verlag.

Ahson, S. I., & Lamba, S. S. (1985). The use of Forth language in process control. *Computer Languages*, *10*(3), 179–187. doi:10.1016/0096-0551(85)90015-3

Akehurst, D., Bordbar, B., Evans, M., Howells, W., & McDonald-Maier, K. (2007). SiTra: Simple transformations in Java. In *10th International Conference on Model Driven Engineering Languages and Systems, Lecture Notes in Computer Science, Vol. 4735,* (pp. 351-364). Springer.

Aleksić, S., Ristić, S., & Luković, I. (2011). An approach to generating server implementation of the inverse referential integrity constraints.In *Proceedings of the 5th International Conference on Information Technology* (pp. 1-7). Amman, Jordan: Al-Zaytoonah University of Jordan.

Aleksić, S., Luković, I., Mogin, P., & Govedarica, M. (2007). A generator of SQL schema specifications. *Computer Science and Information Systems*, *4*(2), 79–98. doi:10.2298/CSIS0702081A

Alexandrescu, A. (2001). *Modern C++ design: Generic programming and design patterns applied*. Addison-Wesley.

Allen, E., Chase, D., Hallett, J., Luchangco, V., Maessen, J.-W., Ryu, S., Jr., G. L. S., … Tobin-Hochstadt, S. (2008). *The Fortress language specification version 1.0*. Sun Microsystems.

Allison, M., Allen, A. A., Yang, Z., & Clarke, P. J. (2011). A software engineering approach to user-driven control of the microgrid. In *Proceedings of the 23rd International Conference on Software Engineering and Knowledge Engineering (SEKE 2011)* (pp. 59-64).

Altmanninger, K., Seidl, M., & Wimmer, M. (2009). A survey on model versioning approaches. *International Journal of Web Information Systems*, *5*(3), 271–304. doi:10.1108/17440080910983556

Alur, R., & Henzinger, T. (1999). Reactive modules. *Formal Methods in System Design*, *15*(1), 7–48. doi:10.1023/A:1008739929481

Alvaro, P. (2009). *Dedalus: Datalog in time and space. Technical report*. DTIC Document.

AMMA. (2008). *The AMMA platform*. Retrieved from from http://wiki.eclipse.org/AMMA

Amrani, M., & Lúcio, L. Selim. G., Combemale, B., Dingel, J., Vangheluwe, H., Le Traon, Y., & Cordy, J. (2012). A tridimensional approach for studying the formal verification of model transformations. In *Proceedings of the First Workshop on Verification and Validation of Model Transformations* (Volt). (to appear)

Amrani, M., & Amàlio, N. (2011). *A set-theoretic formal specification of the semantics of Kermeta (Technical Report No. Tr-Lassy-11-03)*. Luxembourg: University of Luxembourg.

An, K., Trewyn, A., Gokhale, A., & Sastry, S. (2011). Model-driven performance analysis of reconfigurable conveyor systems used in material handling applications. In *Second IEEE/ACM International Conference on Cyber Physical Systems* (ICCPS 2011) (p. 141–150).

Andersson, L. (2001). *Parsing with Haskell*. Retrieved from http://www.cs.lth.se/eda120/assignment4/parser.pdf

Anlauff, M. (2000). XASM - An extensible, component-based ASM language. *Proceedings of the International Workshop on Abstract State Machines, Theory and Applications* (pp. 69-90). Springer-Verlag.

Annaratone, M., Arnould, E., Gross, T., Kung, H. T., Lam, M., Menzilcioglu, O., & Webb, J. A. (1987). The warp computer: Architecture, implementation, and performance. *IEEE Transactions on Computers C*, *36*(12), 1523–1538. doi:10.1109/TC.1987.5009502

Apache Software Foundation. (2011). *Apache logging services*. Retrieved from http://logging.apache.org/

Arango, G. (1989). Domain analysis: From art form to engineering discipline. In *Proceedings of the 5th International Workshop on Software Specification and Design (WSSD)* (pp. 152–159). New York, NY: ACM.

Arcaini, P., Gargantini, A., & Riccobene, E. (2010). AsmetaSMV: A way to link high-level ASM models to low-level NuSMV. In M. Frappier, U. Glässer, S. Khurshid, R. Laleau, & S. Reeves (Eds.), *Proceedings of the Second International Conference on Abstract State Machines, Alloy, B and Z (ABZ 2010)*. *5977*, (pp. 61-74). Berlin, Germany: Springer.

Arcaini, P., Gargantini, A., & Riccobene, E. (2010). Automatic review of abstract state machines by meta property verification. In C. A. Muñoz (Ed.), *Proceedings of the Second NASA Formal Methods Symposium (NFM 2010)* (pp. 4-13).

Arcaini, P., Gargantini, A., Riccobene, E., & Scandurra, P. (2011). A model-driven process for engineering a toolset for a formal method. *Software, Practice & Experience*, *41*(2), 155–166. doi:10.1002/spe.1019

Archer, B., Sastry, S., Rowe, A., & Rajkumar, R. (2009). Profiling primitives of networked embedded automation. In *IEEE International Conference on Automation Science and Engineering* (CASE 2009) (pp. 531–536).

Arendt, T., Biermann, E., Jurack, S., Krause, C., & Taentzer, G. (2010). Henshin: Advanced concepts and tools for in-place EMF model transformations. In Petriu, D. C., Rouquette, N., & Haugen, Ø. (Eds.), *Model Driven Engineering Languages and Systems (MoDELS)* (*Vol. 6394*, pp. 121–135). Lecture Notes in Computer ScienceBerlin, Germany: Springer. doi:10.1007/978-3-642-16145-2_9

Armstrong, J. (2007). A history of Erlang. In *HOPL III Proceedings of the Third ACM SIGPLAN Conference on History of Programming Languages* (pp. 6-1 - 6-26).

Arora, R., Bangalore, P., & Mernik, M. (2011). A technique for non-invasive application-level checkpointing. *The Journal of Supercomputing, 57*(3), 227–255. doi:10.1007/s11227-010-0383-5

Arora, R., Bangalore, P., & Mernik, M. (2012). Raising the level of abstraction for developing message passing applications. *The Journal of Supercomputing, 59*(2), 1079–1100. doi:10.1007/s11227-010-0490-3

Arpaia, P., Buzio, M., Fiscarelli, L., Inglese, V., La Commara, G., & Walckiers, L. (2009). Measurement-domain specific language for magnetic test specifications at CERN. In *IEEE International Instrumentation and Measurement Technology Conference* (pp. 1716 –1720). Washington, DC: IEEE.

ASCAPE. (2011). *Ascape guide*. Retrieved from http://ascape.sourceforge.net/

Ashley-Rollman, M. P., Lee, P., Goldstein, S. C., Pillai, P., & Campbell, J. D. (2009). Language for large ensembles of independently executing nodes. In *Proceedings of the International Conference on Logic Programming (ICLP '09)* (pp. 265-280).

Ashley-Rollman, M., Goldstein, S., Lee, P., Mowry, T., & Pillai, P. (2007). Meld: A declarative approach to programming ensembles. In *Proceedings of the IEEE/RSJ International Conference on Intelligent Robots and Systems* (pp. 2794-2800).

Atkins, D., Ball, T., Bruns, G., & Cox, K. (1999). Mawl: A domain-specific language for form-based services. *IEEE Transactions on Software Engineering, 25*(3), 334–346. doi:10.1109/32.798323

Atkinson, C., & Kühne, T. (2003). Model-driven development: A metamodeling foundation. *IEEE Software, 20*(5), 36–41. doi:10.1109/MS.2003.1231149

Augustsson, L., Mansell, H., & Sittenpalam, G. (2008). Paradise: A two-stage DSL embedded in Haskell. *ACM SIGPLAN Notices, 43*(9), 225–228. doi:10.1145/1411203.1411236

Avgeriou, P., & Zdun, U. (2005). Architectural patterns revisited - A pattern language. In A. Longshaw & U. Zdun (Ed.), *Proceedings of the 10th European Conference on Pattern Languages of Programs (EuroPLoP)* (pp. 431–469). Konstanz, Germany: Universitätsverlag Konstanz.

Ayala, C., Hauge, O., Conradi, R., Franch, X., & Li, J. (2011). Selection of third party software in off-the-shelf-based software development-An interview study with industrial practitioners. *Journal of Systems and Software, 84*(4), 620–637. doi:10.1016/j.jss.2010.10.019

Bachrach, J., & Beal, J. (2007). *Building spatial computers*. Technical Report MIT-CSAIL-TR-2007-017, MIT.

Bachrach, J. (2009). *Programming chained robotics in the gas programming language. Technical report.* Makani Power.

Bachrach, J., Beal, J., & McLurkin, J. (2010). Composable continuous space programs for robotic swarms. *Neural Computing & Applications, 19*(6), 825–847. doi:10.1007/s00521-010-0382-8

Bahlke, R., & Snelting, G. (1985). The PSG - Programming system generator. *ACM SIGPLAN Notices, 20*(7), 28–33. doi:10.1145/17919.806824

Bahlke, R., & Snelting, G. (1986). The PSG system: From formal language definitions to interactive programming environments. *ACM Transactions on Programming Languages and Systems, 8*(4), 547–576. doi:10.1145/6465.20890

Bakay, A., & Magyari, E. (2001). *The UDM framework*. ISIS Vanderbilt University.

Bakern, J., & Hsieh, W. (2002). Maya: Multiple-dispatch syntax extension in Java. *Proceedings of the ACM SIGPLAN 2002 Conference on Programming Language Design and Implementation* (pp. 270-281).

Baker, P., Loh, S., & Weil, F. (2005). Model-driven engineering in a large industrial context - Motorola case study. In Briand, L., & Williams, C. (Eds.), *Model Driven Engineering Languages and Systems* (*Vol. 3713*, pp. 476–491). Lecture Notes in Computer Science. doi:10.1007/11557432_36

Ballance, R. A., Graham, S. L., & de Vanter, M. L. V. (1990). The pan language-based editing system for integrated development environments. *ACM SIGSOFT Software Engineering Notes*, *15*(6), 77–93. doi:10.1145/99278.99286

Banović, J. (2010). *An approach to generating executable software specifications of an information system.* Unpublished doctoral dissertation, University of Novi Sad, Faculty of Technical Sciences, Novi Sad, Serbia.

Barišić, A., Amaral, V., Goulão, M., & Barroca, B. (2011). Quality in use of domain specific languages: A case study. In *3rd ACM SIGPLAN Workshop on Evaluation and Usability of Programming Languages and Tools (PLATEAU 2011)* (pp. 65-72). Portland, USA.

Barišić, A., Amaral, V., Goulão, M., & Barroca, B. (2011c). Quality in use of DSLs: Current evaluation methods. In *3rd INForum - Simpósio de Informática (INForum2011)*, Coimbra, Portugal.

Barišić, A., Amaral, V., Goulão, M., & Barroca, B. (2011a). *How to reach a usable DSL? Moving toward a systematic evaluation. Electronic Communications of the EASST*. MPM.

Barney, B. (Retrieved Feb. 20, 2012). *Introduction to parallel computing.* Retrieved from https://computing.llnl.gov/tutorials/parallel_comp/

Baroni, A., Braz, S., & Abreu, F. (2002). Using OCL to formalize object-oriented design metrics definitions. In *Workshop on Quantitative Approaches in Object-Oriented Software Engineering.*

Barreto, L. P., Douence, R., Muller, G., & Südholt, M. (2002). Programming OS schedulers with domain-specific languages and aspects: New approaches for OS kernel engineering. In *Proceedings of the 1st AOSD Workshop on Aspects, Components, and Patterns for Infrastructure Software* (pp. 1–6). Vancouver, Canada: University of British Columbia.

Basili, V. R. (1996). The role of experimentation in software engineering: past, current, and future. In *18th International Conference on Software Engineering (ICSE 1996)* (pp. 442-449).

Basili, V. R. (2007). The role of controlled experiments in software engineering research. In V. R. Basili, D. Rombach, K. Schneider, B. Kitchenham, D. Pfahl, & R. Selby (Eds.), *Empirical software engineering issues:Critical assessment and future directions* (pp. 33-37). Berlin, Germany: Springer.

Basili, V., Carver, J., Cruzes, D., Hochstein, L. M., Hollingsworth, J., Shull, F., & Zelkowitz, M. (2008). Understanding the high performance computing community: A software engineer's perspective. *IEEE Software*, *25*(4), 29–36. doi:10.1109/MS.2008.103

Batory, D., Sarvela, J., & Rauschmayer, A. (2003). Scaling step-wise refinement. *Proceedings of the 25th International Conference on Software Engineering (ICSE 2003)* (pp. 187-197).

Batory, D., Johnson, C., MacDonald, B., & Von Heeder, D. (2002). Achieving extensibility through product-lines and domain-specific languages: A case study. [TOSEM]. *ACM Transactions on Software Engineering and Methodology*, *11*(2), 191–214. doi:10.1145/505145.505147

Bauer, B., Müller, J., & Odell, J. (2001). Agent UML: A formalism for specifying multiagent interaction. In *Agent-Oriented Software Engineering, Volume 1957*, (pp. 91-103).

Baxter, I., Pidgeon, C., & Mehlich, M. (2004). DMS: Program transformation for practical scalable software evolution. In the *Proceedings of the International Conference on Software Engineering* (pp. 625-634). Washington, DC: IEEE Computer Society.

Beal, J. (2004). Programming an amorphous computational medium. In *Unconventional Programming Paradigms International Workshop, volume 3566 of Lecture Notes in Computer Science*, (pp. 121-136). Springer Berlin.

Beal, J. (2009). Dynamically defined processes for spatial computers. In *Spatial Computing Workshop* (pp. 206-211).

Beal, J. (2010). A basis set of operators for space-time computations. In *Spatial Computing Workshop* (pp. 91-97).

Beal, J., & Usbeck, K. (2011). On the evaluation of space-time functions. In *Self-Organizing Self-Adaptive Spatial Computing Workshop* (pp. 49-54).

Beal, J., & Bachrach, J. (2006). Infrastructure for engineered emergence on sensor/actuator networks. *IEEE Intelligent Systems*, *21*(2), 10–19. doi:10.1109/MIS.2006.29

Beal, J., Lu, T., & Weiss, R. (2011). Automatic compilation from high-level languages to genetic regulatory networks. *PLoS ONE*, *6*(8), E22490. doi:10.1371/journal.pone.0022490

Beck, K., & Andres, C. (2004). *Extreme programming explained: Embrace change* (2nd ed.). Boston, MA: Addison-Wesley Professional.

Bellamy, R., John, B., Richards, J., & Thomas, J. (2010). *Using CogTool to model programming tasks*. In *2nd ACM SIGPLAN Workshop on Evaluation and Usability of Programming Languages and Tools (PLATEAU 2010)*, Reno, Nevada, USA.

Bennett, M., Borgen, R., Havelund, K., Ingham, M., & Wagner, D. (2008). Development of a prototype domain-specific language for monitor and control systems. In *Aerospace Conference* (pp. 1–18). Washington, DC: IEEE Computer Society.

Bentley, J. (1986). Programming pearls: Little languages. *Communications of the ACM*, *29*(8), 711–721. doi:10.1145/6424.315691

Berkeley Software 2009 iGem Team (October 2009, Retrieved May 10, 2010.). *Eugene*. Retrieved from http://2009.igem.org/Team:Berkeley_Software/Eugene.

Bevan, N. (2009). Extending quality in use to provide a framework for usability measurement. *Human Centered Design*, 13-22.

Bevan, N. (1999). Quality in use: Meeting user needs for quality. *Journal of Systems and Software*, *49*(1), 89–96. doi:10.1016/S0164-1212(99)00070-9

Bevan, N. (2005). Cost benefits framework and case studies. In *Cost-justifying usability: An update for the internet age*. Morgan Kaufmann. doi:10.1016/B978-012095811-5/50020-1

Bex, G. J., Neven, F., & Vansummeren, S. (2007). Inferring XML schema definitions from XML data. *Proceedings of the 33rd International Conference on Very Large Data Bases* (pp. 998-1009). VLDB Endowment.

Beydoun, G., Low, G., Henderson-Sellers, B., Mouratidis, H., Gomez-Sanz, J., Pavon, J., & Gonzalez-Perez, C. (2009). FAML: A generic metamodel for MAS development. *IEEE Transactions on Software Engineering*, *35*(6), 841–863. doi:10.1109/TSE.2009.34

Bézivin, J. (2004). In search of a basic principle for model driven engineering. *UPGRADE - The European Journal for the Informatics Professional, 5*(2), 21-24.

Bézivin, J. (2005). On the unification power of models. *Software & Systems Modeling*, *4*(2), 171–188. doi:10.1007/s10270-005-0079-0

Bézivin, J., Jouault, F., Rosenthal, P., & Valduriez, P. (2004). Modeling in the large and modeling in the small. In *Model Driven Architecture- Foundations and Application 2004* (*Vol. 3599*, pp. 33–46). Lecture Notes in Computer ScienceSpringer-Verlag. doi:10.1007/11538097_3

Bicevskis, J., Cerina-Berzina, J., Karnitis, G., Lace, L., Medvedis, I., & Nesterovs, S. (2011). Practitioners view on domain specific business process modeling. In *Proceedings of the 2011 Conference on Databases and Information Systems VI: Selected Papers from the Ninth International Baltic Conference* (pp. 169-182). Amsterdam, The Netherlands: IOS Press.

Biermann, E., Ermel, C., & Taentzer, G. (2008). Precise semantics of EMF model transformations by graph transformation. In Czarnecki, K., Ober, I., Bruel, J.-M., Uhl, A., & Völter, M. (Eds.), *Model Driven Engineering Languages and Systems (MoDELS)* (*Vol. 5301*, pp. 53–67). Lecture Notes in Computer ScienceBerlin, Germany: Springer-Verlag. doi:10.1007/978-3-540-87875-9_4

Blumofe, R. D., Joerg, C. F., Kuszmaul, B. C., Leiserson, C. E., Randall, K. H., & Zhou, Y. (1995). CILK: An efficient multithreaded runtime system. In *Proceedings of the Fifth ACM SIGPLAN Symposium on Principles and Practice of Parallel Programming (PPoPP)* (pp. 207-216).

Bobrow, D. G., DeMichiel, L. G., Gabriel, R. P., Keene, S. E., Kiczales, G., & Moon, D. A. (1988). Common Lisp object system specification. *ACM SIGPLAN Notices*, *23*(SI), 1-142.

Bohm, C., & Jacopini, G. (1966). Flow diagrams, Turing Machines and languages with only two formation rules. *Communications of the ACM*, *9*(5), 366–371. doi:10.1145/355592.365646

Booch, G. A. (1994). *Object-oriented analysis and design with applications* (2nd ed.). Redwood City, CA: Addison-Wesley Longman.

Booch, G., Rumbaugh, J., & Jacobson, I. (2005). *Unified modeling language user guide*. Reading, MA, USA: Addison-Wesley Professional Object Technology Series.

Boost.Mpl. (2011). *The Boost metaprogram libraries*. Retrieved from http://www.boost.org/doc/libs/1_46_0/libs/mpl/doc

Boost.Preprocessor. (2011). *The Boost preprocessor library*. Retrieved from http://www.boost.org/doc/libs/1_46_0/libs/preprocessor/doc

Boost.Proto. (2011). *The Boost proto library*. Retrieved from http://www.boost.org/doc/libs/1_46_0/doc/html/proto.html

Boost.Xpressive. (2011). *The Boost xpressive regular library*. Available at http://www.boost.org/doc/libs/1_46_0/doc/html/xpressive.html

Borcea, C., Intanagonwiwat, C., Kang, P., Kremer, U., & Iftode, L. (2004). Spatial programming using smart messages: Design and implementation. In *Proceedings of 24th International Conference on Distributed Computing Systems* (pp. 690-699). IEEE.

Bordignon, M., Stoy, K., & Schultz, U. P. (2011a). Generalized programming of modular robots through kinematic configurations. In *2011 IEEE/RSJ International Conference on Intelligent Robots and Systems (IROS)* (pp. 3659-3666).

Bordignon, M., Stoy, K., & Schultz, U. P. (2011b). Robust and reversible execution of self-reconfiguration sequences. *Robotica*, *29*(1), 35–57. doi:10.1017/S0263574710000664

Börger, E., & Stärk, R. (2003). *Abstract state machines: A method for high-level system design and analysis*. Springer Verlag. doi:10.1007/978-1-84882-736-3_3

Borók-Nagy, Z., Májer, V., Mihalicza, J., Pataki, P., & Porkoláb, Z. (2010). Visualization of C++ template metaprograms. *10th IEEE Working Conference on Source Code Analysis and Manipulation* (pp. 167-176).

Boronat, A. (2007). *MoMent: A formal framework for MOdel manageMENT* (Ph.D. Doctoral Dissertation), University of Valencia, Spain.

Boronat, A., & Meseguer, J. (2008). An algebraic semantics for Mof. In Fiadeiro, J. L., & Inverardi, P. (Eds.), *Fundamental Approaches to Software Engineering (Fase)* (*Vol. 4961*, pp. 377–391). Lecture Notes in Computer ScienceBerlin, Germany: Springer-Verlag. doi:10.1007/978-3-540-78743-3_28

Borras, P., Clement, D., Despeyrouz, T., Incerpi, J., Kahn, G., Lang, B., & Pascual, V. (1989). Centaur: The system. In *Proceedings of the ACM SIGSOFT/SIGPLAN Software Engineering Symposium on Practical Software Development Environments (PSDE)*, Vol. 24, (pp. 14–24). New York, NY: ACM.

Boulis, A., Han, C., Shea, R., & Srivastava, M. (2007). Sensorware: Programming sensor networks beyond code update and querying. *Pervasive and Mobile Computing*, *3*(4), 386–412. doi:10.1016/j.pmcj.2007.04.007

Brabrand, C., & Schwartzbach, M. (2002). Growing languages with metamorphic syntax macros. *SIGPLAN Workshop on Partial Evaluation and Semantics-Based Program Manipulation*, (pp. 31-40).

Braem, M., Joncheere, N., Vanderperren, W., Van der Straeten, R., & Jonckers, V. (2006). Guiding service composition in a visual service creation environment. *In Proceedings of the 4th European Conference on Web Services (ECOWS '06)* (pp. 13-22).

Bravenboer, M. (2008). *Exercises in free syntax. Syntax definition, parsing, and assimilation of language conglomerates*. PhD. Thesis, Utrecht University.

Bravenboer, M., & Visser, E. (2008). Designing syntax embeddings and assimilations. In *Models in Software Engineering* (pp. 34-46).

Bravenboer, M., & Visser, E. (2008). Parse table composition. In *Software Language Engineering* (pp. 74-94).

Bravenboer, M., Kalleberg, K., Vermaas, R., & Visser, E. (2006). *Stratego/XT 0.16: Components for transformation systems*. Paper presented at the Workshop on Partial Evaluation and Program Manipulation, Charleston, SC.

Bravenboer, M., Kalleberg, K., Vermaas, R., & Visser, E. (2008). Stratego/XT 0.17. A language and toolset for program transformation. *Science of Computer Programming, 72*(1-2), 52–70. doi:10.1016/j.scico.2007.11.003

Bravenboer, M., van Dam, A., Olmos, K., & Visser, E. (2005). Program transformation with scoped dynamic rewrite rules. *Fundamenta Informaticae, 69*, 1–56.

Briand, L. C., Labiche, Y., & O'Sullivan, L. (2003). Impact analysis and change management of UML models. In *Proceedings of International Conference on Software Maintenance*, 2003 (pp. 256- 265): IEEE.

Brinkkemper, S. (1996). Method engineering: Engineering of information systems development methods and tools. *Information and Software Technology, 38*(4), 275–280. doi:10.1016/0950-5849(95)01059-9

Brooks, A. (1997). Meta analysis -A silver bullet for meta-analysts. *Empirical Software Engineering, 2*(4), 333–338. doi:10.1023/A:1009793700999

Bruce, D. (1997). What makes a good domain-specific language? APOSTLE, and its approach to parallel discrete event simulation. In S. Kamin (Ed.), *First ACM SIGPLAN Workshop on Domain-Specific Languages (DSL)* (pp. 17–35). University of Illinois.

Brun, C., Goubet, L., Musset, J., & Eysholdt, M. (2011). *EMF compare project*. Retrieved from http://wiki.eclipse.org/EMF_Compare

Bryant, B., Gray, J., Mernik, M., Clarke, P., France, R., & Karsai, G. (2011). Challenges and directions in formalizing the semantics of modeling languages. *Journal of Computer Science and Information Systems, 8*(2), 225–253. doi:10.2298/CSIS110114012B

Buchwalder, O., & Petitpierre, C. (2008). MEtaGile: A pragmatic domain-specific modeling environment. In *20th International Conference on Software Engineering and Knowledge Engineering (SEKE)* (pp. 764–768). Chicago, IL: Knowledge Systems Institute Graduate School.

Bunch, C., Chohan, N., Krintz, C., & Shams, K. (2011). Neptune: A domain specific language for deploying HPC software on cloud platforms. In the *Proceedings of the 2nd International Workshop on Scientific Cloud Computing ScienceCloud'11* (pp. 59-68).

Bureš, T., Malohlava, M., & Hnětynka, P. (2008). Using DSL for automatic generation of software connectors. In *Proceedings of the Seventh International Conference on Composition-Based Software Systems* (pp. 138-147). Washington, DC: IEEE Computer Society.

Burstall, R. (2000). Christopher Strachey — Understanding programming languages. *Higher Order Symbolic Computation, 13*(1-2), 51–55. doi:10.1023/A:1010052305354

Butcher, P., & Zedan, H. (1991). Lucinda – An overview. *ACM SIGPLAN Notices, 26*(8), 90–100. doi:10.1145/122598.122608

Butera, W. (2002). *Programming a paintable computer*. PhD thesis, MIT, Cambridge, MA, USA.

Butera, W. (2007). Text display and graphics control on a paintable computer. In *International Conference on Self-Adaptive and Self-Organizing Systems* (pp. 45-54).

C++. (2011). *International standard: Programming language*. ISO/IEC 14882:2011 (E).

Calcagno, C., Taha, W., Huang, L., & Leroy, X. (2003). *Implementing multi-stage languages using ASTs, gensym, and reflection*. Paper presented at the of the Second International Conference on Generative Programming and Component Engineering, Erfurt, Germany.

Calcagno, C., Taha, W., Huang, L., & Leroy, X. (2003). *Implementing multi-stage languages using asts, gensym, and reflection. Generative Programming and Component Engineering* (pp. 57–76). GPCE.

Calidonna, C., & Furnari, M. (2004). The cellular automata network compiler system: Modules and features. In *International Conference on Parallel Computing in Electrical Engineering* (pp. 271-276).

Cannon, B., & Wohlstadter, E. (2007). Controlling access to resources within the Python Interpreter. In B. Cannon, J. Hilliker, M. N. Razavi, & R. Werlinge (Eds.), *Proceedings of the Second EECE Mini-Conference on Computer Security* (pp. 1–8). Vancouver, Canada: University of British Columbia.

Cánovas, J. L., & García-Molina, J. (2009). A domain specific language for extracting models in software modernization. In R. F. Paige, A. Hartman, & A. Rensink (Eds.), *5th European Conference on Model Driven Architecture - Foundations and Applications, Lecture Notes in Computer Science, Vol. 5562,* (pp. 82-97). Springer.

Cardelli, L. (2005). Brane calculi. In V. Danos & V. Schächter (Eds.), *International Conference on Computational Methods in Systems Biology (CMSB 2004), Revised Selected Papers, volume 3082 of Lecture Notes in Computer Science*, (pp. 257-278). Springer.

Cardelli, L., & Gardner, P. (2010). Processes in space. In F. Ferreira, B. Löwe, E. Mayordomo, & L. M. Gomes (Eds.), *Programs, Proofs, Processes, 6th Conference on Computability in Europe, CiE 2010, volume 6158 of Lecture Notes in Computer Science*, (pp. 78-87). Springer.

Cardelli, L., Ma, F., & Abadi, M. (1993). Extensible grammars for language specialization. In *Proceedings of the Fourth International Workshop on Database Programming Languages* (pp. 11-31).

Cardelli, L. (2004). Type systems. In Tucker, A. B. (Ed.), *The computer science and engineering handbook.* Boca Raton, FL: CRC Press.

Cardelli, L., & Gordon, A. D. (2000). Mobile ambients. *Theoretical Computer Science, 240*(1), 177–213. doi:10.1016/S0304-3975(99)00231-5

Carette, J., Kiselyov, O., & Shan, C. C. (2009). Finally tagless, partially evaluated: Tagless staged interpreters for simpler typed languages. *Journal of Functional Programming, 19*(5), 509–543. doi:10.1017/S0956796809007205

Carioni, A., Gargantini, A., Riccobene, E., & Scandurra, P. (2008). A scenario-based validation language for ASMs. *Proceedings of the First International Conference on Abstract State Machines, B and Z (ABZ 2008)* (pp. 71-84): Springer-Verlag.

Caspi, E., Chu, M., Huang, R., Yeh, J., Wawrzynek, J., & DeHon, A. (2000). Stream computations organized for reconfigurable execution (score). In *Conference on Field Programmable Logic and Applications (FPL)*, (pp. 605-614).

Castagna, G., & Xu, Z. (2011). *Set-theoretic foundation of parametric polymorphism and subtyping.* In 16th ACM SigPlan International Conference on Functional Programming. Tokyo, Japan.

Catarci, T. (2000). What happened when database researchers met usability. *Information Systems, 25*(3), 177–212. doi:10.1016/S0306-4379(00)00015-6

Cazzola, W., & Speziale, I. (2009). Sectional domain specific languages. *In Proceedings of the Fourth Workshop on Domain-Specific Aspect Languages* (pp. 11-14).

CDO. (2011). *CDO framework.* Retrieved March 23, 2012, from http://www.eclipse.org/cdo/

Čeh, I., Črepinšek, M., Kosar, T., & Mernik, M. (2011). Ontology driven development of domain-specific languages. *Computer Science and Information Systems, 8*(2), 317–342. doi:10.2298/CSIS101231019C

Čeliković, M., Luković, I., Aleksić, S., & Ivančević, V. (2011). A MOF based meta-model of IIS*Case PIM concepts. In *Proceedings of the Federated Conference on Computer Science and Information Systems* (pp. 833-840). Los Alamitos, CA: IEEE Computer Society Press.

Centre for Policy Modelling. (2011). *Strictly declarative modelling language.* Retrieved from http://cfpm.org/sdml/

Chapel. (2011). *Chapel language specification version 0.82.* Cray, Inc.

Charles, P., Grothoff, C., Saraswat, V. A., Donawa, C., Kielstra, A., & Ebcioglu, K. (2005). X10: An object-oriented approach to non-uniform cluster computing. *SIGPLAN Notices, 40*(10), 519–538. doi:10.1145/1103845.1094852

Cheatham, T. E. (1977). Programming language design issues. In J. H. Williams & D. A. Fisher (Eds.), *Lecture Notes in Computer Science: Vol. 54, Design and Implementation of Programming Languages – Proceedings of a DoD Sponsored Workshop* (pp. 399–435). Berlin, Germany: Springer-Verlag.

Chedeau, C., & Verna, D. (2012). *JSPP: Morphing C++ into JavaScript*. Unpublished technical report 201201-TR, EPITA Research and Development Laboratory, France.

Chelimsky, D., Astels, D., Dennis, Z., Hellesoy, A., Helmkamp, B., & North, D. (2010). *The RSpec book: Behaviour driven development with RSpec, Cucumber, and friends*. Raleigh, NC: The Pragmatic Bookshelf.

Chen, J., Mundy, J., Bai, Y., Chan, S.-M. C., Petrica, P., & Bahar, R. I. (2003). A probabilistic approach to nano-computing. In *Workshop on Non-Silicon Computation*, (pp. 1-8).

Chen, K., Sztipanovits, J., & Neema, S. (2005). Toward a semantic anchoring infrastructure for domain-specific modeling languages. *Proceedings of the 5th ACM International Conference on Embedded Software* (pp. 35-43). ACM.

Chen, K., Sztipanovits, J., & Neema, S. (2007). Compositional specification of behavioral semantics. *Proceedings of Design Automation and Test in Europe Conference (DATE 07)* (pp. 906-911). EDA Consortium.

Chen, K., Sztipanovits, J., Abdelwahed, S., & Jackson, E. (2005). Semantic anchoring with model transformation. In *Proceedings of Model-Driven Architecture* (*Vol. 3748*, pp. 115–129). Nuremberg, Germany: Foundations and Applications.

Chen, P. P. S. (1976). The entity-relationship model – Toward a unified view of data. *ACM Transactions on Database Systems*, *1*(1), 9–36. doi:10.1145/320434.320440

Chidlovskii, B. (2001). Schema extraction from XML data: A grammatical inference approach. *Proceedings of the Eighth International Workshop on Knowledge Representation Meets Databases, CEUR Workshop Proceedings*.

Chiprianov, V., Alloush, I., Kermarrec, Y., & Rouvrais, S. (2011). Telecommunications service creation: Towards extensions for enterprise architecture modeling languages. In *Proceedings of the 6th International Conference on Software and Data Technologies* (pp. 23–29). Seville, Spain.

Chiprianov, V., Kermarrec, Y., & Rouvrais, S. (2011a). On the extensibility of plug-ins. In *Proceedings of the 6th International Conference on Software Engineering Advances* (pp. 557–562), Barcelona, Spain.

Chiprianov, V., Kermarrec, Y., & Rouvrais, S. (2011b). Practical model extension for modeling language profiles: An enterprise architecture modeling language extension for telecommunications service creation. In *Proceedings of Journées nationales Ingénierie Dirigée par les Modèles, Conférence francophone sur les Architectures Logicielles, et du Groupe De Recherche Génie de la Programmation et du Logiciel* (pp. 85–91). Lille, France.

Chiprianov, V., Kermarrec, Y., & Rouvrais, S. (2011c). Towards semantic interoperability of graphical domain specific modeling languages for telecommunications service design. In *Proceedings of the 2nd International Conference on Models and Ontology-based Design of Protocols, Architectures and Services* (pp. 21–24). Budapest, Hungary.

Chiprianov, V., Kermarrec, Y., & Rouvrais, S. (2012). Extending enterprise architecture modeling languages: Application to telecommunications service creation. In *Proceedings of the 27th Symposium on Applied Computing* (pp. 810–816). Trento, Italy.

Chohan, N., Bunch, C., Pang, S., Krintz, C., Mostafa, N., Soman, S., & Wolski, R. (2009). AppScale: Scalable and open AppEngine application development and deployment. In the *Proceedings of ICST International Conference on Cloud Computing, Lecture Notes of the Institute for Computer Sciences, Social Informatics and Telecommunications Engineering 34* (pp. 57-70). Springer.

Choobineh, J., Mannino, M. V., Nunamaker, J. F., & Konsynski, B. R. (1988). An expert database design system based on analysis of forms. *IEEE Transactions on Software Engineering*, *14*(2), 242–253. doi:10.1109/32.4641

Chou, H.-H., Huang, W., & Reggia, J. A. (2002). The trend cellular automata programming environment. *Simulation*, *78*(2), 59–75. doi:10.1177/0037549702078002204

Christensen, D. J., Schultz, U. P., & Moghadam, M. (2011). The assemble and animate control framework for modular reconfigurable robots. In *IROS Workshop on Reconfigurable Modular Robotics* (pp. 1-6).

Christensen, A., O'Grady, R., & Dorigo, M. (2007). Morphology control in a multirobot system. *IEEE Robotics & Automation Magazine*, *14*(4), 18–25. doi:10.1109/MRA.2007.908970

Chu, D., Tavakoli, A., Popa, L., & Hellerstein, J. (2006). Entirely declarative sensor network systems. In *Proceedings of the 32nd International Conference on Very Large Data Bases*, (pp.1203-1206). VLDB Endowment.

Ciciriello, P., Mottola, L., & Picco, G. (2006). Building virtual sensors and actuators over logical neighborhoods. In *Proceedings of the International Workshop on Middleware for Sensor Networks*, (pp. 19-24). ACM.

Cimatti, A., Clarke, E., Giunchiglia, E., Giunchiglia, F., Pistore, M., Roveri, M., et al. (2002). Nusmv 2: An opensource tool for symbolic model checking. In E. Brinksma, & K. Larsen (Eds.), *Proceedings of the 14th International Conference on Computer Aided Verification* (pp. 359-364): Springer-Verlag.

Clark, T., & Tratt, L. (2009). Language factories. *SIGPLAN Conference Companion on Object Oriented Programming Systems Languages and Applications* (pp. 949-955).

Clark, T., Evans, A., Kent, S., & Sammut, P. (2001). *The MMF approach to engineering object-oriented design languages.* Paper presented at Workshop on Language Descriptions, Tools and Applications.

Clark, T., Sammut, P., & Willans, J. (2008). *Applied Metamodelling: A foundation for language driven development.* Retrieved from http://bit.ly/He29h7

Clark, T., Sammut, P., & Willans, J. (2008). *Superlanguages: Developing languages and applications with XMF.* Retrieved from http://bit.ly/HiTOKp

Clarke, P. J., Hristidis, V., Wang, Y., Prabakar, N., & Deng, Y. (2006). A declarative approach for specifying user-centric communication. In *Proceedings of the International Symposium on Collaborative Technologies and Systems (CTS '06)* (pp. 89-98). Washington, DC: IEEE Computer Society.

Clark, R., & Wilson, L. (2001). *Comparative programming languages* (3rd ed.). Boston, MA: Addison-Wesley.

Clark, T., Evans, A., Sammut, P., & Willans, J. (2004). *Transformation language design: A metamodelling foundation* (pp. 223–226). Graph Transformations.

Clark, T., Evans, A., Sammut, P., & Willans, J. (2008). *Applied metamodelling – A foundation for language-driven development.* Sheffield, UK: Ceteva.

Clark, T., Sammut, P., & Willans, J. (2008). *Applied metamodelling: A foundation for language driven development* (2nd ed.). Ceteva.

Clark, T., & Tratt, L. (2010). Formalizing homogeneous language embeddings. *Electronic Notes in Theoretical Computer Science*, *253*(7), 75–88. doi:10.1016/j.entcs.2010.08.033

Clavel, M., Duran, F., Eker, S., Lincoln, P., Marti-Oliet, N., & Meseguer, J. (2007). *All about Maude. A high-performance logical framework.* Berlin, Germany: Springer.

Clojure. (2012). *Clojure language.* Retrieved March 23, 2012, from http://www.clojure.org

Codd, E. F. (1970). A relational model of data for large shared data banks. *Communications of the ACM*, *13*(6), 377–387. doi:10.1145/362384.362685

Cointe, P. (1987). Metaclasses are first class: The ObjVlisp model. *SIGPLAN Notices*, *22*(12), 156–162. doi:10.1145/38807.38822

Collier, N., & North, M. (2011). Repast SC++: A platform for large-scale agent-based modeling. *Large-Scale Computing Techniques for Complex System Simulations*, *80*, 81–109.

Collins, R. L. (2011). *Data-driven programming abstractions and optimization for multi-core platforms.* PhD thesis, Columbia University.

Combemale, B., Crégut, X., Garoche, P.-L., & Thirioux, X. (2009, November). Essay on semantics definition in MDE: An instrumented approach for model verification. *Journal of Software*, *4*(9), 943–958. doi:10.4304/jsw.4.9.943-958

Common Lisp. (1994). *American national standard: Programming language.* ANSI X3.226:1994 (R1999).

Consel, C., & Marlet, R. (1998). Architecturing software using a methodology for language development. *Lecture Notes in Computer Science: Vol. 1490, Proceedings of the 10th International Symposium on Programming Language Implementation and Logic Programming (PLILP)* (pp. 170–194). Berlin, Germany: Springer-Verlag.

Cook, S., Jones, G., Kent, S., & Wills, A. C. (2007). *Domain-specific development with visual studio DSL tools.* Boston, MA: Pearson Education, Inc.

Coore, D. (1999). *Botanical computing: A developmental approach to generating interconnect topologies on an amorphous computer*. PhD thesis, MIT.

Coplien, J. O. (1999). *Multi-paradigm design for C*. Boston, MA: Addison-Wesley.

Coplien, J., Hoffman, D., & Weiss, D. (1998). Commonality and variability in software engineering. *IEEE Software*, *15*(6), 37–45. doi:10.1109/52.730836

Cordy, J. R. (2006). The TXL source transformation language. *Science of Computer Programming*, *61*(3), 190–210. doi:10.1016/j.scico.2006.04.002

Correia, F. F., Ferreira, H. S., Flores, N., & Aguiar, A. (2009). Patterns for consistent software documentation. In *Proceedings of the 16th Conference for Pattern Languages of Programs*. New York, NY: ACM.

Correll, N., & Martinoli, A. (2011). Modeling self-organized aggregation in a swarm of miniature robots. *The International Journal of Robotics Research. Special Issue on Stochasticity in Robotics and Biological Systems*, *30*(5), 615–626.

Costa, P., Mottola, L., Murphy, A., & Picco, G. (2006). Teenylime: Transiently shared tuple space middleware for wireless sensor networks. In *Proceedings of the International Workshop on Middleware for Sensor Networks* (pp. 43-48). ACM.

Costagliola, G., Delucia, A., Orefice, S., & Polese, G. (2002). A classification framework to support the design of visual languages. *Journal of Visual Languages and Computing*, *13*(6), 573–600. doi:10.1006/jvlc.2002.0234

Couderc, P., & Banatre, M. (2003). Ambient computing applications: an experience with the spread approach. In *Hawaii International Conference on System Sciences (HICSS' 03)* (pp. 9-17).

Črepinšek, M., Kosar, T., Mernik, M., Cervelle, J., Forax, R., & Roussel, G. (2010). On automata and language based grammar metrics. *Journal on Computer Science and Information Systems*, *7*(2), 310–329.

Črepinšek, M., Mernik, M., Bryant, B. R., Javed, F., & Sprague, A. (2005a). Inferring context-free grammars for domain-specific languages. *Electronic Notes in Theoretical Computer Science*, *141*, 99–116. doi:10.1016/j.entcs.2005.02.055

Črepinšek, M., Mernik, M., Javed, F., Bryant, B. R., & Sprague, A. (2005b). Extracting grammar from programs: Evolutionary approach. *ACM SIGPLAN Notices*, *40*(4), 39–46.

Črepinšek, M., Mernik, M., & Žumer, V. (2005c). Extracting grammar from programs: Brute force approach. *ACM SIGPLAN Notices*, *40*(4), 29–38.

Cuadrado, J. S., & Molina, J. G. (2009). A model-based approach to families of embedded domain-specific languages. *IEEE Transactions on Software Engineering*, *35*(6), 825–840. doi:10.1109/TSE.2009.14

Cuaresma, M. J. E., & Koch, N. (2004). Requirements engineering for Web applications - A comparative study. *Journal of Web Engineering*, *2*(3), 193–212.

CUDA. (2012). *CUDA API reference manual, version 4.1*. Retrieved from http://www.developer.nvidia.com/nvidia-gpu-computing-documentation

Cunningham, H. C. (2008). A little language for surveys: Constructing an internal DSL in Ruby. In *Proceedings of the 46th Annual Southeast Regional Conference* (pp. 282–287). New York, NY: ACM.

Czar, M., Cai, Y., & Peccoud, J. (2009). Writing DNA with genocad. *Nucleic Acids Research*, *37*(W), W40-W47.

Czarnecki, K., Eisenecker, U., Glück, R., Vandevoorde, D., & Veldhuizen, T. (1998). Generative programming and active libraries. In M. Jazayeri, R. Loos, & D. Musser (Eds.), *Selected Papers from the International Seminar on Generic Programming* (pp. 25-39). London, UK: Springer-Verlag.

Czarnecki, K., & Eisenecker, U. W. (2000). *Generative programming: Methods, tools, and applications*. Boston, MA: Addison-Wesley.

Czarnecki, K., & Helsen, S. (2006). Feature-based survey of model transformation approaches. *IBM Systems Journal*, *45*(3), 621–645. doi:10.1147/sj.453.0621

Czarnecki, K., Østerbye, K., & Volter, M. (2002). Generative programming. In *Object-Oriented Technology ECOOP 2002* (pp. 15–29). Workshop Reader. doi:10.1007/3-540-36208-8_2

Czech Technical Institute Agent Technology Center. (2011). *Aglobe*. Retrieved from http://agents.felk.cvut.cz/aglobe/

David, V. (2009). *Language constructs for C++-like languages - Tools and extensions*. Ph.D. Thesis. Bergen, Norway: University of Bergen.

de Jonge, M., & Visser, J. (2002). Grammars as feature diagrams. In the *Proceedings of the Workshop on Generative Programming at the 7th International Conference on Software Reuse* (pp. 23-24).

de Lamotte, F., Berruet, P., & Philippe, J. (2006). Evaluation of reconfigurable manufacturing systems configurations using tolerance criteria. In *32nd Annual Conference on IEEE Industrial Electronics* (IECON 2006) (pp. 3715–3720).

de Lara, J., & Vangheluwe, H. (2010). Automating the transformation-based analysis of visual languages. *Formal Aspects of Computing, 22*(3–4), 297–326. doi:10.1007/s00165-009-0114-y

Dean, J., & Ghemawat, S. (2008). MapReduce: Simplifed data processing on large clusters. *Communications of the ACM, 51*(1), 107–113. doi:10.1145/1327452.1327492

DeHon, A., & Wawrzynek, J. (1999). Recon□gurable computing: What, why, and implications for design automation. In *Design Automation Conference (DAC)*, (pp. 610-615).

DeHon, A. (2002). Very large scale spatial computing. In *Unconventional Models of Computation*. In *Lecture Notes in Computer Science* (*Vol. 2509*, pp. 27–37). Springer.

Dejanović, I., Tumbas, M., Milosavljević, G., & Perišić, B. (2010). Comparison of textual and visual notations of DOMMLite domain-specific language. In *Local Proceedings of the 14th East-European Conference on Advances in Databases and Information Systems* (pp. 131-136). Novi Sad, Serbia: University of Novi Sad, Faculty of Sciences.

Dejanović, I., Milosavljević, G., Tumbas, M., & Perišić, B. (2010). A domain-specific language for defining static structure of database applications. *Computer Science and Information Systems, 7*(3), 409–440. doi:10.2298/CSIS090203002D

deLara, J., & Vangheluwe, H. (2002). Using Atom[3] as a meta-case tool. In *Proceedings of Fourth International Conference on Enterprise Information Systems* (Iceis): Vol. 2. (pp. 642 – 649). Berlin, Germany: Springer.

deLorimier, M., Kapre, N., Mehta, N., & DeHon, A. (2011). Spatial hardware implementation for sparse graph algorithms in graphstep. *ACM Transactions on Autonomous and Adaptive Systems, 6*(3), 17:1-17:20.

den Haan, J. (2012). *Model driven development: Code generation or model interpretation?* Retrieved February 1, 2012, from http://www.theenterprisearchitect.eu/archive/2010/06/28/model-driven-development-code-generation-or-model-interpretation

Denert, E., Ernst, G., & Wetzel, H. (1975). GRAPHEX68 graphical language features in Algol 68. *Computers & Graphics, 1*(2-3), 195–202. doi:10.1016/0097-8493(75)90007-2

Deng, Y., Sadjadi, S. M., Clarke, P. J., Hristidis, V., Rangaswami, R., & Wang, Y. (2008). CVM - A communication virtual machine. *Journal of Systems and Software, 81*(10), 1640–1662. doi:10.1016/j.jss.2008.02.020

Deursen van, A., & Klint, P. (1998). Little languages: Little maintenance? *Journal of Software Maintenance: Research and Practice, 10*(2), 75–92. doi:10.1002/(SICI)1096-908X(199803/04)10:2<75::AID-SMR168>3.0.CO;2-5

Deursen van, A., Klint, P., & Visser, J. (2000). Domain-specific languages: An annotated bibliography. *SIGPLAN Notices, 35*(6), 26-36.

Deursen van. A., Visser, E., & Warmer, J. (2007). Model-driven software evolution: A research agenda. In D. Tamzalit (Ed.), *Workshop on ModelDriven Software Evolution at Conference on Software Maintenance and Reengineering* (pp. 41-49).

Dewey, D., Ashley-Rollman, M., Rosa, M. D., Goldstein, S., Mowry, T., & Srinivasa, S. ... Campbell, J. (2008). Generalizing metamodules to simplify planning in modular robotic systems. In *Proceedings of the IEEE/RSJ International Conference on Intelligent Robots and Systems*, (pp. 1338-1345).

D'Hondt, E., & D'Hondt, T. (2001a). Amorphous geometry. In *European Conference on Artificial Life 2001*, (pp. 645-648).

D'Hondt, E., & D'Hondt, T. (2001b). Experiments in amorphous geometry. In *2001 International Conference on Artificial Intelligence* (pp. 285-290).

Di Ruscio, D., Jouault, F., Kurtev, I., Bézivin, J., & Pierantonio, A. (2006). *Extending AMMA for supporting dynamic semantics specifications of DSLs. Laboratoire d'Informatique de Nantes-Atlantique*. LINA.

Diaz, O., Puente, G., Cánovas, J. L., & García Molina, J. (in press). Harvesting models from web 2.0 databases. *Software and Systems Modeling*, in press. DOI: 10.1007/s10270-011-0194-z

Dietrich, C. (2011). *Pymorphous: Python language extensions for spatial computing*. Retrieved from http://pymorphous.googlecode.com

Dinkelaker, T., & Mezini, M. (2008). Dynamically linked domain-specific extensions for advice languages. In *Proceedings of the 2008 AOSD Workshop on Domain-Specific Aspect Languages* (pp. 1–7). New York, NY: ACM.

Djukić, V., Luković, I., & Popović, A. (2011). Domain-specific modeling in document engineering. In *Proceedings of the Federated Conference on Computer Science and Information Systems* (pp. 825-832). Los Alamitos, CA: IEEE Computer Society Press.

Dmitriev, S. (2004). *Language oriented programming: The next programming paradigm*. Retrieved October 5, 2011, from http://www.omg.org/cgi-bin/doc?omg/03-06-01

Dobrica, L., & Niemela, E. (2002). A survey on software architecture analysis methods. *IEEE Transactions on Software Engineering*, *28*(7), 638–653. doi:10.1109/TSE.2002.1019479

Dos Reis, G. Stroustrup, & B. Maurer, J. (2007). *Generalized constant expressions -Revision 5*. N2235=07-0095. Retrieved from http://www.open-std.org/jtc1/sc22/wg21/docs/papers/2007/n2235.pdf

Drey, Z., Faucher, C., Fleurey, F., Mahé, V., & Vojtisek, D. (2009). *The Kermeta language — Reference manual*. (Technical Report) University of Rennes, France. Retrieved from http://kermeta.org/documents/user_doc/manual/

Drossopoulou, S., Eisenbach, S., & Khurshid, S. (1999). Is the Java type system sound? *Journal of Theory and Practice of Object Systems (Tapos)*, *5*(1), 3–24. doi:10.1002/(SICI)1096-9942(199901/03)5:1<3::AID-TAPO2>3.0.CO;2-T

Duckham, M., Nittel, S., & Worboys, M. (2005). Monitoring dynamic spatial fields using responsive geosensor networks. In *Proceedings of the 13th Annual ACM International Workshop on Geographic Information Systems (GIS '05)* (pp. 51-60). New York, NY: ACM.

Dunkels, A., Gronvall, B., & Voigt, T. (2004). Contiki-a lightweight and flexible operating system for tiny networked sensors. In *29th Annual IEEE International Conference on Local Computer Networks*, (pp. 455-462). IEEE.

Dupont, P. (1994). Regular grammatical inference from positive and negative samples by genetic search: The GIG method. *Proceedings of the Second International Colloquium on Grammatical Inference and Applications* (pp. 236-245). Springer-Verlag.

Dutoit, A. H., McCall, R., Mistrík, I., & Paech, B. (2006). Rationale management in software engineering: Concepts and techniques. In *Rationale Management in Software Engineering* (pp. 1–48). Springer. doi:10.1007/978-3-540-30998-7_1

Earley, J. (1970). An efficient context-free parsing algorithm. *Communications of the ACM, 13*(2), 94–102. doi:10.1145/362007.362035

Easy Chair Conference System. (2010). Retrieved March 2010, from http://www.easychair.org

Eckart, J. D. (1997). *Cellang: Language reference manual*. Radford University.

Eclipse Modeling Project – EMF. (2012). Retrieved February 2012, from http://www.eclipse.org/modeling/emf

Eclipse Modelling Project. (2011). *Eclipse modeling project*. Retrieved from http://www.eclipse.org/modeling/

Eclipse XText Framework. (2011). *Eclipse XText framework*. Retrieved from http://www.eclipse.org/XText/

Eclipse, E. M. F. Project. (2011). *Eclipse modeling framework project*. Retrieved from http://www.eclipse.org/modeling/emf/

Eclipse, G. M. F. Framework. (2011). *Eclipse graphical modelingframework*. Retrieved from http://www.eclipse.org/modeling/gmp/

Edwards, G., Seo, C., & Medvidovic, N. (2008). Model interpreter frameworks: A foundation for the analysis of domain-specific software architectures. *Journal of Universal Computer Science*, *14*(8), 1182–1206.

Ehrig, H., Ehrig, K., Prange, U., & Taentzer, G. (2006). *Fundamentals of algebraic graph transformation (Monographs in Theoretical Computer Science. an EATCS Series)*. Secaucus, NJ: Springer-Verlag New York, Inc.

Ehrig, H., & Mahr, B. (1985). Fundamentals of algebraic specifications. In Brauer, W., Rozenberg, G., & Salomaa, A. (Eds.), *Monographs in Theoretical Computer Science: An EATCS Series* (*Vol. 6*). Berlin, Germany: Springer-Verlag.

Elliott, C. (1999). An embedded modeling language approach to interactive 3D and multimedia animation. *IEEE Transactions on Software Engineering*, *25*(3), 291–308. doi:10.1109/32.798320

Elliott, C. (2003). Functional images. In Gibbons, J., & de Moor, O. (Eds.), *The fun of programming* (pp. 131–150). Palgrave MacMillan.

Ellison, C. M., & Rosu, G. (2012). An Executable Formal Semantics of C with Applications. In J. Field & M. Hicks (Eds.), *Proceedings of the 39th Acm Sigplan-Sigact Symposium on Principles of Programming Languages (POPL)* (pp. 533–544). New York, NY: Association for Computing Machinery.

EMF: Eclipse Modeling Framework. (n.d.). Retrieved October 6, 2011, from http://www.eclipse.org/modeling/emf/

Engelen, L., & van den Brand, M. (2010). Integrating textual and graphical modelling languages. *Electronic Notes in Theoretical Computer Science*, *253*(7), 105–120. doi:10.1016/j.entcs.2010.08.035

Engels, G., Hausmann, J. H., Heckel, R., & Sauer, S. (2000). Dynamic meta modeling: A graphical approach to the operational semantics of behavioral diagrams in UML. In A. Evans, S. Kent, & B. Selic (Eds.), *Proceedings of the Third International Conference on The unified modeling language: advancing the standard (UML 2000)* (pp. 323-337). Springer-Verlag.

Engstrom, B. R., & Cappello, P. R. (1989). The SDEF programming system. *Journal of Parallel and Distributed Computing*, *7*(2), 201–231. doi:10.1016/0743-7315(89)90018-X

Erlang. (2011). *Erlang reference manual user's guide version 5.9*. Ericsson AB.

Ermel, C. H. (2005). Animated simulation of integrated UML behavioral models based on graph transformation. *Proceedings of the 2005 IEEE Symposium on Visual Languages and Human-Centric Computing* (pp. 125-133). IEEE Computer Society.

Erwig, M., & Walkingshaw, E. (2011). Semantics first! Rethinking the language design process. In *International Conference on Software Language Engineering*. To appear.

Erwig, M., & Kollmansberger, S. (2006). Probabilistic functional programming in Haskell. *Journal of Functional Programming*, *16*(1), 21–34. doi:10.1017/S0956796805005721

Evans, E. (2003). *Domain-driven design: Tackling complexity in the heart of software*. Addison-Wesley Professional.

Eysholdt, M., & Behrens, H. (2010). XText: Implement your language faster than the quick and dirty way. *SIGPLAN Conference Companion on Object Oriented Programming Systems Languages and Applications* (pp. 307-309).

Favre, J.-M. (2004). Foundations of model (driven) (reverse) engineering -- Episode I: Story of The Fidus Papyrus and the Solarus. *Post-Proceedings of Dagstuhl Seminar on Model Driven Reverse Engineering*.

Favre, J.-M., & Nguyen, T. (2004). Towards a megamodel to model software evolution through transformations. *Electronic Notes in Theoretical Computer Science, 127*, 59–74. doi:10.1016/j.entcs.2004.08.034

Felleisen, M., Findler, R. B., & Flatt, M. (2009). *Semantics engineering with PLT Redex*. Cambridge, MA: MIT Press.

Fenton, N. E., & Pfleeger, S. L. (1996). *Software metrics: A rigorous & practical approach* (2nd ed.). PWS Publishing Co.

Fernando, T. (1993). Comparative transition system semantics. In Börger, E., Jäger, G., Kleine Büning, H., Martini, S., & Richter, M. (Eds.), *Computer Science Logic* (*Vol. 702*, pp. 149–166). Lecture Notes in Computer ScienceBerlin, Germany: Springer. doi:10.1007/3-540-56992-8_11

Ferscha, A., Hechinger, M., Riener, A., dos Santos Rocha, M., Zeidler, A., Franz, M., & Mayrhofer, R. (2008). Peer-it: Stick-on solutions for networks of things. *Pervasive and Mobile Computing, 4*(3), 448–479. doi:10.1016/j.pmcj.2008.01.003

Fieber, F., Regnat, N., & Rumpe, B. (2009). Assessing usability of model driven development in industrial projects. *From Code Centric to Model Centric Software Engineering: Practices Implications and ROI, Proceedings of the 4th European Workshop.*

Finin, T., Fritzson, R., McKay, D., & McEntire, R. (1994). Kqml as an agent communication language. In *Proceedings of the Third International Conference on Information and Knowledge Management (CIKM '94)* (pp. 456-463). New York, NY: ACM.

Finkel, R. A. (1996). *Advanced programming language design*. Menlo Park, CA: Addison-Wesley.

Flake, S., & Müller, W. (2004). An ASM definition of the dynamic OCL 2.0 semantics. In T. Baar, A. Strohmeier, A. Moreira, & S. Mellor (Ed.), *Proceedings of the Seventh International Conference on UML Modeling Languages and Applications (UML 2004).* (pp. 226-240). Springer.

Flanagan, D., & Matsumoto, Y. (2008). *The Ruby programming language*. Sebastopol, CA, USA: O-Reilly Media.

Fleurey, F. (2006). *Langage et methode pour une ingenierie des modeles fiable* [Language and Method for Trustable Modelling Engineering]. (Ph.D. Doctoral Dissertation) University of Rennes, France.

Fleutot, F., & Tratt, L. (2007). *Contrasting compile-time meta-programming in Metalua and Converge*. Paper presented at the workshop on Dynamic Languages and Applications, Berlin, Germany.

Foderaro, J. (1991). Lisp: Introduction. *Communications of the ACM - Special Issue on Lisp, 34*(9), 27-28.

Fok, C., Roman, G., & Lu, C. (2005). Rapid development and flexible deployment of adaptive wireless sensor network applications. In *Proceedings of the 25th IEEE International Conference on Distributed Computing Systems*, (pp. 653-662). IEEE.

Forrest, S., & Jones, T. (1994). Modeling complex adaptive systems with echo. *Complex systems: Mechanisms of adaptation* (pp. 3-21).

Forum, D. S. M. (2010). *Domain-specific modeling*. Retrieved from http://www.dsmforum.org/

Forum, M. P. I. (2009). *MPI: A message-passing interface standard version 2.2.* Retrieved from http://mpi-forum.org

Fowler, M. (2005). Language workbenches: The killer-app for domain specific languages? Retrieved from www.martinfowler.com/articles/languageWorkbench.html

Fowler, M. (2003). *Patterns of enterprise application architecture*. Boston, MA: Addison-Wesley.

Fowler, M., & Parsons, R. (2010). *Domain specific languages*. Addison-Wesley Professional.

France, R., & Rumpe, B. (2007). Model-driven development of complex software: A research roadmap. In *Future of Software Engineering* (pp. 37–54). Washington, DC: IEEE Computer Society. doi:10.1109/FOSE.2007.14

Frank, C., & Romer, K. (2005). Algorithms for generic role assignment in wireless sensor networks. In *Proceedings of the 3rd International Conference on Embedded Networked Sensor Systems* (pp. 230-242). ACM.

Frantz, R. Z., Corchuelo, R., & Gonzáles J. (2008). Advances in a DSL for application integration. *Actas de los Talleres de las Jornadas de Ingeniería del Software y Bases de Datos, 2*(2), 54-66.

Frege, G. (1884). *Die Grundlagen der Arithmetik: Eine logisch-mathematische Untersuchung über den Begriff der Zahl*. Breslau.

Freiwald, U., & Weimar, J. (2002). The java based cellular automata simulation system Jcasim. *Future Generation Computer Systems, 18*, 995–1004. doi:10.1016/S0167-739X(02)00078-X

Freudenthal, M. (2010b). Using DSLs for developing enterprise systems. In *Proceedings of the 10th Workshop on Language Descriptions, Tools and Applications*, article 11. New York, NY: ACM Press.

Freudenthal, M. (2010a). Domain-specific languages in a customs information system. *IEEE Software, 27*(2), 65–71. doi:10.1109/MS.2010.41

Friedman-Hill, E. (2008). *JESS, the rule engine for the Java platform*. Retrieved from http://herzberg.ca.sandia.gov/jess/

Fuentes-Fernández, L., & Vallecillo-Moreno, A. (2004). An introduction to UML profiles. *UPGRADE - The European Journal for the Informatics Professional, 5*(2), 6-13.

Gabriel, P., Goulão, M., & Amaral, V. (2010). Do software languages engineers evaluate their languages? In *XIII Congreso Iberoamericano en "Software Engineering" (CIbSE'2010)* (pp. 149-162). Cuenca, Ecuador.

Gamma, E., Helm, R., Johnson, R., & Vlissides, J. M. (1994). *Design patterns: Elements of reusable object-oriented software*. Addison-Wesley Professional.

Garcés, K., Jouault, F., Cointe, P., & Bézivin, J. (2009). Managing model adaptation by precise detection of metamodel changes. In Paige, R. F., Hartman, A., & Rensink, A. (Eds.), *Model driven architecture - Foundations and applications* (pp. 34–49). Berlin, Germany: Springer. doi:10.1007/978-3-642-02674-4_4

Gargantini, A., Riccobene, E., & Scandurra, P. (2007). A metamodel-based simulator for ASMs. In A. Prinz (Ed.), *Proceedings of the 14th International ASM Workshop* (pp. 1-21).

Gargantini, A., Riccobene, E., & Scandurra, P. (2008). Model-driven language engineering: The ASMETA case study. In *Proceedings of the Third International Conference on Software Engineering Advances(ICSEA)* (pp. 373–378). Washington, DC: IEEE Computer Society.

Gargantini, A., Riccobene, E., & Scandurra, P. (2010). Combining formal methods and MDE techniques for model-driven system design and analysis. *International Journal on Advances in Software, 1&2*, 1-18.

Gargantini, A., Riccobene, E., & Scandurra, P. (2008). A metamodel-based language and a simulation engine for abstract state machines. *Journal of Universal Computer Science, 14*(12), 1949–1983.

Gargantini, A., Riccobene, E., & Scandurra, P. (2009). A semantic framework for metamodel-based languages. *Journal of Automated Software Engineering, 16*(3-4), 415–454. doi:10.1007/s10515-009-0053-0

Garofalakis, M., Gionis, A., Rastogi, R., Seshadri, S., & Shim, K. (2003). XTRACT: Learning document type descriptors from XML document collections. *Data Mining and Knowledge Discovery, 7*, 23–56. doi:10.1023/A:1021560618289

Gay, D., Levis, P., Von Behren, R., Welsh, M., Brewer, E., & Culler, D. (2003). The NesC language: A holistic approach to networked embedded systems. *ACM Sigplan Notices, 38*(5), 1–11. doi:10.1145/780822.781133

Gayle, O., & Coore, D. (2006). Self-organizing text in an amorphous environment. In *International Conference on Complex Systems*, (pp. 1-10).

Gelernter, D., & Carriero, N. (1992). Coordination languages and their significance. *Communications of the ACM, 35*(2), 97–107. doi:10.1145/129630.129635

Georgalas, N., Azmoodeh, M., & Ou, S. (2005). *Model driven integration of standard based OSS components*. EURESCOM Summit 2005-Ubiquitous Services and Applications.

Georgalas, N., Azmoodeh, M., Clark, T., Evans, A., Sammut, P., & Willans, J. (2004). MDA-driven development of standard-compliant OSS components: The OSS/J inventory case-study. *In Proceedings of the Second European Workshop on Model Driven Architecture (MDA)*.

George Mason University Evolutionary Computation Laboratory and Center for Social Complexity. (2011). *MASON multiagent simulation*. Retrieved from http://cs.gmu.edu/~eclab/projects/mason/

Ghosh, D. (2010). *DSLs in action*. Manning Publications.

Ghosh, D. (2011). DSL for the uninitiated - Domain-specific languages bridge the semantic gap in programming. *Communications of the ACM*, *54*(7), 44–50. doi:10.1145/1965724.1965740

Giaglis, G. M. (2001). A taxonomy of business process modeling and information systems modeling techniques. *International Journal of Flexible Manufacturing Systems*, *13*(2), 209–228. doi:10.1023/A:1011139719773

Giavitto, J.-L., Godin, C., Michel, O., & Zemyslaw Prusinkiewicz, P. (2002). *Computational models for integrative and developmental biology*. Technical Report 72-2002, Univerite d'Evry, LaMI.

Giavitto, J.-L., Michel, O., Cohen, J., & Spicher, A. (2004). *Computation in space and space in computation*. Technical Report 103-2004, Univerite d'Evry, LaMI.

Giavitto, J.-L., & Spicher, A. (2008). Topological rewriting and the geometrization of programming. *Physica D. Nonlinear Phenomena*, *237*(9), 1302–1314. doi:10.1016/j.physd.2008.03.039

Gil, Y., & Lenz, K. (2007). Simple and Safe SQL queries with C++ templates. In C. Consel & J. L. Lawall (Eds.), *6th International Conference Generative Programming and Component Engineering (GPCE 2007)* (pp. 13-24).

Gillespie, D. T. (1977). Exact stochastic simulation of coupled chemical reactions. *Journal of Physical Chemistry*, *81*(25), 2340–2361. doi:10.1021/j100540a008

Gilpin, K., Kotay, K., Rus, D., & Vasilescu, I. (2008). Miche: Modular shape formation by self-disassembly. *The International Journal of Robotics Research*, *27*, 345–372. doi:10.1177/0278364907085557

GME: Generic Modeling Environment. (2008, June 12). Retrieved October 6, 2011, from http://www.isis.vanderbilt.edu/Projects/gme/

Goncalves, M. K., de Souza, C. R. B., & Gonzalez, V. M. (2009). Initial findings from an observational study of software engineers. In *Proceedings of the 13th International Conference on Computer Supported Cooperative Work in Design* (pp. 498–503).

Gosling, J., Joy, B., Steele, G., & Bracha, G. (2005). *The Java language specification* (3rd ed.). Boston, MA: Addison-Wesley.

Goulão, M. (2008). *Component-based software engineering: A quantitative approach*. PhD Dissertation, Faculdade de Ciências e Tecnologia, Universidade Nova de Lisboa, Lisboa, Portugal.

Goulão, M., & Abreu, F. B. (2007). Modeling the experimental software engineering process. In *6th International Conference on the Quality of Information and Communications Technology (QUATIC'2007)* (pp. 77-90). Lisbon, Portugal.

Govett, M., Middlecoff, J., Hart, L., Henderson, T., & Schaffer, D. (2003). The scalable modeling system: Directive-based code parallelization for distributed and shared memory computers. *Parallel Computing*, *29*(8), 995–1020. doi:10.1016/S0167-8191(03)00084-X

Graham, P. (1993b). *Programming bottom-up*. Retrieved April 2, 2012, from http://www.paulgraham.com/progbot.html.

Graham, P. (1993a). *On Lisp*. Prentice Hall.

Granicz, A., & Hickey, J. (2003). Phobos: A front-end approach to extensible compilers. *In Proceedings of the 36th Annual Hawaii International Conference on System Sciences*.

Greenfield, J., Short, K., Cook, S., & Kent, S. (2004). *Software factories: Assembling applications with patterns, models, frameworks, and tools*. Indianapolis, IN: Wiley Publishing.

Gregor, D., & Järvi, J. (2009). Variadic templates for C++. Symposium on Applied Computing, *Proceedings of the 2007 ACM Symposium on Applied computing* (pp. 1101-1108).

Gregor, D., Järvi, J., Kulkarni, M., Lumsdaine, A., Musser, M., & Schupp, S. (2005). Generic programming and high-performance libraries. *International Journal of Parallel Programming*, *33*(2), 145–164. doi:10.1007/s10766-005-3580-8

Grelck, C., Penczek, F., & Trojahner, K. (2007). Caos: A domain-specific language for the parallel simulation of cellular automata. In *Parallel Computing Technologies, 9th International Conference (PaCT'07)* (pp. 410-417). Springer-Verlag.

Grimm, R. (2006). Better extensibility through modular syntax. *ACM SIGPLAN Conference on Programming Language Design and Implementation* (pp. 38-51).

Groote, J. F., Van Vlijmen, S. F. M., & Koorn, J. W. C. (1995). The safety guaranteeing system at station Hoorn-Kersenboogerd. In *Proceedings of the Tenth Annual Conference on Computer Assurance Systems Integrity, Software Safety and Process Security* (pp. 57–68). Washington, DC: IEEE.

Gropp, W., Lusk, E., & Skjellum, A. (1994). *Using MPI: Portable parallel programming with the message passing interface*. Cambridge, MA: MIT Press.

Grumbach, S., & Wang, F. (2010). *Netlog, a rule-based language for distributed programming* (pp. 88–103). Practical Aspects of Declarative Languages. doi:10.1007/978-3-642-11503-5_9

Grundy, J., Hosking, J. G., Amor, R. W., Mugridge, W. B., & Li, Y. (2004). Domain-specific visual languages for specifying and generating data mapping systems. *Journal of Visual Languages and Computing*, *15*(3-4), 243–263. doi:10.1016/j.jvlc.2004.01.003

Gruschko, B., Kolovos, D., & Paige, R. (2007). Towards synchronizing models with evolving metamodels. In *Proceedings of Workshop of Model-Driven Software Evolution*.

Gudas, S., & Lopata, A. (2007). Meta-model based development of use case model for business function. *Information Technology and Control, Kaunas. Technologija*, *36*(3), 302–309.

Guerra, E., Souza, J., & Fernandes, C. (2009). A pattern language for metadata-based frameworks. In *Proceedings of the 16th Conference on Pattern Languages of Programs*. New York, NY: ACM.

Gulyás, L., Kozsik, T., & Fazekas, S. (2011). *Multi-agent modeling language MAML*. Retrieved from http://www.maml.hu/

Gulyás, L., Kozsik, T., & Corliss, J. (1999). The multi-agent modelling language and the model design interface. *Journal of Artificial Societies and Social Simulation*, *2*(3), 8.

Gummadi, R., Gnawali, O., & Govindan, R. (2005). *Macro-programming wireless sensor networks using kairos* (pp. 466–466). Distributed Computing in Sensor Systems.

Günther, S. (2008). *Die Sprachbestandteile von Domänenspezifischen Sprachen: Eine Ableitung aus den sprachphilosophischen und linguistischen Wurzeln der Informatik.* Technical Report FIN-03-2008. Magdeburg, Germany: Otto-von- Guericke-Universität Magdeburg.

Günther, S. (2011, in press). PyQL: Introducing a SQL-like DSL for Python. In H.-K. Arndt & H. Krcmar (Ed.), *4th Workshop des Centers for Very Large Business Applications (CVLBA)*. Aachen, Germany: Shaker.

Günther, S., & Cleenewerck, T. (2010). Design principles for internal domain-specific languages: A pattern catalog illustrated by Ruby. In *Proceedings of the 7th Conference on Pattern Languages of Programs (PLoP)*.

Günther, S., & Sunkle, S. (2009). Feature-oriented programming with Ruby. In *Proceedings of the First International Workshop on Feature-Oriented Software Development (FOSD)* (pp. 11–18). New York, NY: ACM.

Günther, S., Haupt, M., & Splieth, M. (2010). *Utilizing internal domain-specific languages for deployment and maintenance of IT infrastructures. Technical report (Internet) FIN-004-2010.* Magdeburg, Germany: Otto-von-Guericke-Universität.

Günther, S., & Sunkle, S. (2011). rbFeatures: Feature-oriented programming with Ruby. *Science of Computer Programming, 77*(3), 52–173.

Gupta, G., & Pontelli, E. (2002). Specification, implementation, and verification of domain specific languages: A logic programming-based approach. *Computational Logic: Logic Programming and Beyond, Essays in Honour of Robert A. Kowalski, Part I,* (pp. 211 – 239).

Haase, A. (2007). Patterns for the definition of programming languages. In *Proceedings of 12th European Conference on Pattern Languages of Programs.*

Habermann, A. N., & Notkin, D. (1986). Gandalf: Software development environments. *IEEE Transactions on Software Engineering, 12*(12), 1117–1127.

Hahn, C. (2008). A domain specific modeling language for multiagent systems. *Proceedings of the 7th International Joint Conference on Autonomous Agents and Multiagent Systems (AAMAS 2008)* (pp. 233-240). International Foundation for Autonomous Agents and Multiagent Systems.

Halloway, S. (2009). *Programming Clojure.* Pragmatic Bookshelf.

Hamann, H., Stradner, J., Schmickl, T., & Crailsheim, K. (2010). A hormone-based controller for evolutionary multi-modular robotics: from single modules to gait learning. In *IEEE Congress on Evolutionary Computation (CEC'10)* (pp. 244-251).

Hamey, L. G. C. (2007). Efficient image processing with the Apply language. *Proceedings of International Conference on Digital Image Computing: Techniques and Applications* (pp. 533-540). IEEE Computer Society Press.

Hamey, L. G. C., & Goldrei, S. N. (2008). Implementing a domain-specific language using Stratego/XT: An experience paper. *Electronic Notes in Theoretical Computer Science, 203*(2), 37–51. doi:10.1016/j.entcs.2008.03.043

Hamey, L. G. C., Webb, J. A., & Wu, I.-C. (1987). Low-level vision on Warp and the Apply programming model. In Kowalik, J. (Ed.), *Parallel computation and computers for artificial intelligence* (pp. 185–199). Kluwer Academic Publishers. doi:10.1007/978-1-4613-1989-4_10

Hamey, L. G. C., Webb, J. A., & Wu, I.-C. (1989). An architecture independent programming language for low-level vision. *Computer Vision Graphics and Image Processing, 48*, 246–264. doi:10.1016/S0734-189X(89)80040-4

Harel, D., & Rumpe, B. (2004). Meaningful modelling: What's the semantics of "semantics"? *IEEE Computer, 37*(1), 64–72. doi:10.1109/MC.2004.172

Hästbacka, D., Vepsäläinen, T., & Kuikka, S. (2011). Model-driven development of industrial process control applications. *Journal of Systems and Software, 84*(7), 1100–1113. doi:10.1016/j.jss.2011.01.063

Havelund, K., Ingham, M., & Wagner, D. (2010). A case study in DSL development – An experiment with Python and Scala. In *Scala Days.* Lausanne, Switzerland: Ecole polytechnique federale de Lausanne.

Hayslip, N., Sastry, S., & Gerhardt, J. (2006). Networked embedded automation. *Assembly Automation, 26*(3), 235–241. doi:10.1108/01445150610679786

Heering, J. (2000). *Application software, domain-specific languages, and language design assistants. Technical report sen-r0010.* Amsterdam, Netherlands: Center for Mathematic and Computer Science, University of Amsterdam.

Heinzelman, W., Murphy, A., Carvalho, H., & Perillo, M. (2004). Middleware to support sensor network applications. *IEEE Network, 18*(1), 6–14. doi:10.1109/MNET.2004.1265828

Hejlsberg, A., Torgersen, M., Wiltamuth, S., & Golde, P. (2010). *The C# programming language.* Addison Wesley.

Helsen, S., Ryman, A., & Spinellis, D. (2008). Where's my jetpack? *IEEE Software, 25*(5), 18–21. doi:10.1109/MS.2008.138

Helsinger, A., Thome, M., & Wright, T. (2004). Cougaar: A scalable, distributed multi-agent architecture. In *IEEE International Conference on Systems, Man and Cybernetics, Volume 2,* (pp. 1910-1917). IEEE.

Henriques, P. R., Varando Pereira, M. J., Mernik, M., Lenič, M., Gray, J. G., & Wu, H. (2005). Automatic generation of language-based tools using the LISA system. *IEE Proceedings. Software, 152*(2), 54–69. doi:10.1049/ip-sen:20041317

Hermans, F., Pinzger, M., & Deursen, A. (2009). Domain-specific languages in practice: A user study on the success factors. In *Proceedings of the 12th International Conference on Model Driven Engineering Languages and System (MODELS '09)* (pp. 423–437), Berlin, Germany, Springer-Verlag.

Hirschheim, R., & Klein, H. K. (1989). Four paradigms of information systems development. *Communications of the ACM, 32*(10), 1199–1216. doi:10.1145/67933.67937

Hnat, T., Sookoor, T., Hooimeijer, P., Weimer, W., & Whitehouse, K. (2008). Macrolab: A vector-based macroprogramming framework for cyber-physical systems. In *Proceedings of the 6th ACM Conference on Embedded Network Sensor Systems* (pp. 225-238). ACM.

Hoare, C. A. R. (1973). *Hints on programming language design. Computer Science Department report no.stan-cs-73-403*. Stanford, CA: Stanford Artificial Intelligence Laboratory, Stanford University.

Holzmann, C., & Ferscha, A. (2010). A framework for utilizing qualitative spatial relations between networked embedded systems. *Pervasive and Mobile Computing, 6*(3), 362–381. doi:10.1016/j.pmcj.2010.03.001

Holzmann, G. J. (2004). *The SPIN model checker: Primer and reference manual*. Addison-Wesley.

HPF. (1997). *High performance Fortran language specification, Version 2.0*. High Performance Fortran Forum.

Hrnčič, D., Mernik, M., & Bryant, B. R. (2011). Embedding DSLS into GPLS: A grammatical inference approach. *Information Technology and Control, 40*(4), 307–315. doi:10.5755/j01.itc.40.4.980

Hrnčič, D., Mernik, M., Bryant, B. R., & Javed, F. (2012). A memetic grammar inference algorithm for language learning. *Applied Soft Computing, 12*(3), 1006–1020. doi:10.1016/j.asoc.2011.11.024

Hudak, P. (1998). Modular domain specific languages and tools. In P. Davenbu & J. Poulin (Eds.), *Proceedings of the Fifth International Conference on Software Reuse (ICSR)* (pp. 134–142). Washington, DC: IEEE.

Hudak, P. (1996). Building domain-specific embedded languages. *ACM Computing Surveys, 28*(4). doi:10.1145/242224.242477

Hudak, P. (2004). An algebraic theory of polymorphic temporal media. In Jayaraman, B. (Ed.), *Practical Aspects of Declarative Languages* (*Vol. 3057*, pp. 1–15). Lecture Notes in Computer ScienceBerlin, Germany: Springer-Verlag. doi:10.1007/978-3-540-24836-1_1

Huget, M. (2005). Modeling languages for multiagent systems. *Agent-Oriented Software Engineering (AOSE-2005)* (pp. 1-12).

Huzita, H., & Scimemi, B. (1989). The algebra of paper-folding. In *First International Meeting of Origami Science and Technology* (pp. 215-222).

Icon. (2010). The Icon Programming Language http://www.cs.arizona.edu/icon

IEEE. Computer Society. (2011). *Foundation for intelligent physical agents*. Retrieved from http://www.fipa.org/

Igarashi, A., Pierce, B. C., & Wadler, P. (2001). Featherweight Java: A minimal core calculus for Java and GJ. *ACM Transactions on Programming Languages and Systems, 23*(3), 396–450. doi:10.1145/503502.503505

Ignite Realtime. (2010). *Smack API 3.1.0*. Retrieved from http://www.igniterealtime.org/

Inchiosa, M., & Parker, M. (2002). Overcoming design and development challenges in agent-based modeling using ASCAPE. *Proceedings of the National Academy of Sciences of the United States of America, 99*(Suppl 3), 7304–7310. doi:10.1073/pnas.082081199

Information-Technology Promotion Agency. (2009). *Programming languages – Ruby*. Retrieved March 16, 2011, http://ruby-std.netlab.jp/draft-spec/draft-ruby-spec-20091201.pdf

Intel Cilk Plus. (2011). *Intel cilk plus language extension specification version 1.1*. Retrieved from http://software.intel.com/file/40297

International Telecommunication Union. (1999). *Specification and description language*. (Technical Report No. Z-100). Geneva, Switzerland: International Telecommunication Union.

Ioannidis, A., Priggouris, I., Marias, I., Hadjiefthymiades, S., Faist-Kassapoglou, C., Hernandez, J., & Merakos, L. (2003). PoLoS: Integrated platform for location-based services. In *Proceedings of the IST Mobile & Wireless Communications Summit,* Portugal.

Irazábal, J., Pons, C., & Neil, C. (2010). Model transformation as a mechanism for the implementation of domain specific transformation languages. *SADIO Electronic Journal of Informatics and Operations Research, 9*(1), 49–66.

ISO. (2001a). *ISO/IEC 9126-1 Quality model.*

ISO. (2001b). *ISO/IEC 9241-11 Ergonomic requirements for office work with visual display terminals (VDTs) -- Part 11: Guidance on usability.*

ISO/IEC 42010. (2007). *Systems and software engineering – Architecture description.*

ISO9126. (2001). *ISO/IEC 9126: Information technology - Software product evaluation - Software quality characteristics and metrics*. Geneva, Switzerland: International Organization for Standardization.

Javed, F., Mernik, M., Bryant, B. R., & Sprague, A. (2008b). An unsupervised incremental learning algorithm for domain-specific language development. *Applied Artificial Intelligence, 22*(7), 707–729. doi:10.1080/08839510802164127

Javed, F., Mernik, M., Gray, J., & Bryant, B. R. (2008a). MARS: A metamodel recovery system using grammar inference. *Information and Software Technology, 50*(9-10), 948–968. doi:10.1016/j.infsof.2007.08.003

Jedlitschka, A., Ciolkowski, M., & Pfahl, D. (2008). Reporting experiments in software engineering. In F. Shull, J. Singer, & D. I. K. Sjøberg (Eds.), *Guide to advanced empirical software engineering, Vol. 5971.* London, UK: Springer-Verlag.

Jesshope, C., Lankamp, M., & Zhang, L. (2009). Evaluating cmps and their memory architecture. In *Proceedings the 22nd International Conference on Architecture of Computing Systems ARCS 2009, LNCS 5455*, (pp. 246-257).

JetBrains. (2011). *MPS*. Retrieved March, 28, 2012, from http://www.jetbrains.com/mps

Jones, T., & Forrest, S. (2011). *An introduction to SFI echo*. Retrieved from http://tuvalu.santafe.edu/ pth/echo/how-to/how-to.html

Josuttis, N. (1999). *The C++ standard library: A tutorial and reference*. Addison-Wesley.

Jouault, F., & Bézivin, J. (2006). KM3: A DSL for metamodel specification. In *Formal Methods for Open Object-Based Distributed Systems, Lecture Notes in Computer Science Vol. 4037* (pp.171-185).

Jouault, F., & Kurtev, I. (2005). Transforming models with ATL. In the *Proceedings of Model Transformations in Practice Workshop at International Conference on Model Driven Engineering Languages and Systems, Lecture Notes in Computer Science Vol. 3844* (pp. 128-138). Springer.

Jouault, F., Bézivin, J., & Kurtev, I. (2006). TCS: A DSL for the specification of textual concrete syntaxes in model engineering. In the *5th International conference on Generative Programming and Component Engineering* (pp. 249-254). Portland, Oregon.

Jouault, F., Allilaire, F., Bézivin, J., & Kurtev, I. (2008). ATL: A model transformation tool. *Science of Computer Programming, 72*(1), 31–39. doi:10.1016/j.scico.2007.08.002

Jozwiak, L., Nedjah, N., & Figueroa, M. (2010). Modern development methods and tools for embedded reconfigurable systems: A survey. *Integration, the VLSI Journal, 43*(1), 1-33.

JRuby. (2012). *JRuby*. Retrieved March, 28, 2012, from http://www.jruby.com

Juhász, Z., Ádám Sipos, Á., & Porkoláb, Z. (2007). Implementation of a finite state machine with active libraries in C++. In R. Lammel, J. Visser, & J. Saraiva (Eds.), *Generative and Transformational Techniques in Software Engineering II, GTTSE 2007, Lecture Notes in Computer Science, Vol. 5235,* International Summer School, (pp. 474—488). Springer.

Jurack, S., & Taentzer, G. (2010). A component concept for typed graphs with inheritance and containment structures. In Ehrig, H., Rensink, A., Rozenberg, G., & Schürr, A. (Eds.), *Graph Transformations (ICGT)* (*Vol. 6372*, pp. 187–202). Lecture Notes in Computer ScienceBerlin, Germany: Springer. doi:10.1007/978-3-642-15928-2_13

Kabanov, J., & Raudjärv, R. (2008). Embedded typesafe domain specific languages for Java. In *Proceedings of the 6th International Symposium on Principles and Practice of Programming in Java* (pp. 189–197). New York, NY: ACM.

Kamin, S. N. (1998). Research on domain-specific embedded languages and program generators. *Electronic Notes in Theoretical Computer Science, 14*(1), 149–168. doi:10.1016/S1571-0661(05)80235-X

Kang, K., Cohen, S., Hess, J., Novak, W., & Peterson, A. (1990). *Feature-oriented domain analysis (FODA) feasibility study.* Technical Report CMU/SEI-90-TR-21. Pittsburgh, PA: Software Engineering Institute, Carnegie Mellon University.

Kappel, G., Kapsammer, E., Kargl, H., Kramler, G., Reiter, T., Retschitzegger, W., & Wimmer, M. (2006). Lifting meta-models to ontologies - A step to the semantic integration of modeling languages. In *Proceedings of the ACM/IEEE 9th International Conference on Model Driven Engineering Languages and Systems* (pp. 528–542).

Karlsson, B. (205). *Beyond the C++ standard library: An introduction to Boost.* Addison-Wesley.

Karsai, G., & Sztipanovits, J. (2008). Model-integrated development of cyber-physical systems. *International Workshop on Software Technologies for Embedded and Ubiquitous Systems* (pp. 46–54).

Katahdin. (2010). *The Katahdin project*. Retrieved from http://www.chrisseaton.com/katahdin

Kats, L. C. L., & Visser, E. (2010). The Spoofax language workbench. *Proceedings of the 25th Annual ACM SIGPLAN Conference on Object-Oriented Programming, Systems, Languages, and Applications,* (pp. 444-463). ACM Press.

Kats, L., Visser, E., & Wachsmuth, G. (2010). Pure and declarative syntax definition: Paradise lost and regained. *ACM SIGPLAN Notices, 45*(10), 918–932. doi:10.1145/1932682.1869535

Kay, A. C. (1969). *The reactive engine*. Unpublished doctoral dissertation, University of Hamburg, Germany.

Kazman, R., Abowd, G., Bass, L., & Clements, P. (1996). Scenario-based analysis of software architecture. *IEEE Software, 13*(6), 47–55. doi:10.1109/52.542294

Keene, S. E. (1989). *Object-oriented programming in Common Lisp: A programmer's guide to CLOS.* Addison-Wesley.

Kelly, S. (2005). Improving developer productivity with domain-specific modeling languages. *Developer.* *. Retrieved September 23, 2011, from http://www.developerdotstar.com/mag/articles/ domain_modeling_language.html

Kelly, S., & Tolvanen, J.-P. (2000). *Visual domain-specific modelling: benefits and experiences of using metaCASE tools*. In International Workshop on Model Engineering, at ECOOP'2000.

Kelly, S., & Tolvanen, J. P. (2008). *Domain-Specific Modeling: Enabling full code generation.* Hoboken, NJ: John Wiley & Sons, Inc.

Kennedy Carter Ltd. (2000). *UML ASL reference guide, ASL language level 2.5" manual. Guilford.* UK: Kennedy Carter.

Kent, S. (2002). Model driven engineering. In *Integrated Formal Methods* (pp. 286–298).

Kernighan, B. W., & Ritchie, D. M. (1977). *The m4 macro processor*. Unpublished technical report, Bell Laboratories, NJ.

Kiczales, G., Lamping, J., Mendhekar, A., Maeda, C., Lopes, C., Loingtier, J., & Irwin, J. (1997). Aspect-oriented programming. In the *Proceedings of the European Conference on Object-Oriented Programming, Lecture Notes In Computer Science Vol. 1241,* (pp. 220-242). Springer.

Kiczales, G. J., des Rivières, J., & Bobrow, D. G. (1991). *The art of the metaobject protocol*. Cambridge, MA: MIT Press.

Kieburtz, R. B., McKinney, L., Bell, J. M., Hook, J., Kotov, A., & Lewis, J. … Walton, L. (1996). A software engineering experiment in software component generation. In *18th International Conference on Software Engineering (ICSE'1996)* (pp. 542-552). Berlin, Germany.

Kinny, D. (2002). The ψ calculus: An algebraic agent language. In J.-J. Meyer & M. Tambe (Eds.), *Intelligent Agents VIII, volume 2333 of Lecture Notes in Computer Science*, (pp. 32-50). Berlin, Germany: Springer.

Kiselyov, O., & Shan, C.-C. (2009). Embedded probabilistic programming. In Taha, W. (Ed.), *Domain-Specific Languages* (*Vol. 5658*, pp. 360–384). Lecture Notes in Computer ScienceBerlin, Germany: Springer Verlag. doi:10.1007/978-3-642-03034-5_17

Klavins, E., Ghrist, R., & Lipsky, D. (2006). A grammatical approach to self-organizing robotic systems. *IEEE Transactions on Automatic Control*, *51*(6), 949–962. doi:10.1109/TAC.2006.876950

Klein, P., & Schürr, A. (1997). Constructing SDEs with the IPSEN meta environment. In *Proceedings of the 8th International Conference on Software Engineering Environments (SEE)* (pp. 2–10).

Kleppe, A. (2007). Towards the generation of a text-based IDE from a language metamodel. *Proceedings of the 3rd European Conference on Model Driven Architecture-Foundations and Applications* (pp. 114-129). Springer-Verlag.

Kleppe, A. G. (2009). *Software language engineering: Creating domain-specific languages using metamodels*. Addison-Wesley.

Kleppe, A., Warmer, J., & Bast, W. (2003). *MDA explained: The model driven architecture - practice and promise*. New York, NY: Addison-Wesley.

Klint, P. (1993). A meta-environment for generating programming environments. *ACM Transactions on Software Engineering and Methodology*, *2*(2), 176–201. doi:10.1145/151257.151260

Klint, P., Laemmel, R., & Verhoef, C. (2005). Toward an engineering discipline for grammarware. *ACM Transactions on Software Engineering and Methodology*, *14*(3), 331–380. doi:10.1145/1072997.1073000

Knuth, D. E. (1984). *The TeXbook*. Addison-Wesley.

Ko, A. J., DeLine, R., & Venolia, G. (2007). Information needs in collocated software development teams. In *Proceedings of the 29th International Conference on Software Engineering* (pp. 344–353).

Kodaganallur, V. (2004). Incorporating language processing into java applications: A JavaCC tutorial. *IEEE Software*, *21*(4), 70–77. doi:10.1109/MS.2004.16

Koelbel, C., Loveman, D. B., Steele, G. L., & Zosel, M. E. (1994). *High performance FORTRAN handbook*. MIT Press.

Kolomvatsos, K., Valkanas, G., & Hadjiefthymiades, S. (2012). Debugging applications created by a domain specific language: The IPAC case. *Journal of Systems and Software*, *85*(4), 932–943. doi:10.1016/j.jss.2011.11.1009

Kondacs, A. (2003). Biologically-inspired self-assembly of 2D shapes, using global-to-local compilation. In *International Joint Conference on Artificial Intelligence*, (pp. 633-638).

Kosar, T., Martínez López, P. E., Barrientos, P. A., & Mernik, M. (2008). A preliminary study on various implementation approaches of domain-specific language. *Information and Software Technology*, *50*(5), 390–405. doi:10.1016/j.infsof.2007.04.002

Kosar, T., Mernik, M., & Carver, J. C. (2012). Program comprehension of domain-specific and general-purpose languages: Comparison using a family of experiments. *Empirical Software Engineering*, *17*(3), 276–304. doi:10.1007/s10664-011-9172-x

Kosar, T., Mernik, M., Henriques, P. R., Varanda Pereira, M. J., & Žumer, V. (2004). Software development with grammatical approach. *Informatica*, *28*(4), 39–404.

Kosar, T., Oliveira, N., Mernik, M., Varanda Pereira, M. J., Črepinšek, M., da Cruz, D., & Henriques, P. R. (2010). Comparing general-purpose and domain-specific languages: An empirical study. *Computer Science and Information Systems*, *7*(2), 247–264. doi:10.2298/CSIS1002247K

Kothari, N., Gummadi, R., Millstein, T., & Govindan, R. (2007). Reliable and efficient programming abstractions for wireless sensor networks. In *Proceedings of the 2007 ACM SIGPLAN Conference on Programming Language Design and Implementation*, (pp. 200-210). ACM.

Krahn, H., Rumpe, B., & Voelkel, S. (2008). Monticore: Modular development of textual domain specific languages. *In Proceedings of the 30th International Conference on Software Engineering* (pp. 925-926).

Krishnan, P. (2000). Consistency checks for UML. In *Proceedings of the Seventh Asia-Pacific Software Engineering Conference (APSEC)* (pp. 162–171). Washington, DC: IEEE Computer Society.

Kruchten, P. (2008). Controversy corner: What do software architects really do? *Journal of Systems and Software*, *81*(12), 2413–2416. doi:10.1016/j.jss.2008.08.025

Kulesza, U., Garcia, A., & Lucena, C. (2004). An aspect-oriented generative approach. In *Companion to the 19th Annual ACM SIGPLAN Conference on Object-Oriented Programming Systems, Languages, and Applications (OOPSLA '04)* (pp. 166-167). New York, NY: ACM.

Kulesza, U., Garcia, A., Lucena, C., & Alencar, P. (2005). A generative approach for multi-agent system development. *Software Engineering for Multi-Agent Systems*, *III*, 52–69. doi:10.1007/978-3-540-31846-0_4

Kurtev, I., Bézivin, J., & Aksit, M. (2002). Technological spaces: An initial appraisal. *Tenth International Conference on Cooperative Information Systems (CoopIS), International Symposium on Distributed Objects and Applications (DOA) - Federated Conferences, Industrial Track*, (pp. 1-6).

Kurtev, I., Bézivin, J., Jouault, F., & Valduriez, P. (2006). Model-based DSL frameworks. In *OOPSLA '06 Companion to the 21st ACM SIGPLAN Symposium on Object-oriented Programming Systems, Languages, and Applications* (pp. 602-615). New York, NY: ACM Press.

Kuruvilla, S., Gokhale, S., & Sastry, S. (2008). Reliability evaluation of reconfigurable conveyor systems. In *IEEE International Conference on Automation Science and Engineering* (CASE 2008) (pp. 929–934).

Kwiatkowska, M., Norman, G., & Parker, D. (2011). PRISM 4.0: Verification of probabilistic real-time systems. In G. Gopalakrishnan & S. Qadeer (Eds.), *Proc. 23rd International Conference on Computer Aided Verification (CAV'11), volume 6806 of LNCS*, (pp. 585-591). Springer.

Ladd, D. A., & Ramming, J. C. (1994). Two application languages in software production. In *Proceedings of the USENIX Very High Level Languages Symposium* (pp. 10–18). Berkeley, CA: USENIX Association.

Ladd, D., & Ramming, J. (1995). A*: A language for implementing language processors. *IEEE Transactions on Software Engineering*, *21*(11), 894–901. doi:10.1109/32.473218

Lakatoš, D., Porubän, J., & Sabo, M. (2011). Assisted software language creation using internal model. *Proceedings of the International Conference on Engineering of Modern Electric Systems* (pp. 1-5). ACM.

Lämmel, R. (2003). Typed generic traversal with term rewriting strategies. *Journal of Logic and Algebraic Programming*, *54*, 1–64. doi:10.1016/S1567-8326(02)00028-0

Lämmel, R., & Verhoef, C. (2001). Cracking the 500-language problem. *IEEE Software*, *18*(6), 78–88. doi:10.1109/52.965809

Lämmel, R., & Verhoef, C. (2001). Semi-automatic grammar recovery. *Software, Practice & Experience*, *31*(15), 1395–1448. doi:10.1002/spe.423

Landin, P. J. (1966). The next 700 programming languages. *Communications of the ACM*, *9*(3), 157–166. doi:10.1145/365230.365257

Lang, K. J., Pearlmutter, B. A., & Price, R. A. (1998). Results of the Abbadingo One DFA learning competition and a new evidence-driven state merging algorithm. *Proceedings of the 4th International Colloquium on Grammatical Inference* (pp. 1-12). Springer-Verlag.

Lange, C. F. J., Wijns, M. A. M., & Chaudron, M. R. V. (2007). MetricViewEvolution: UML-based views for monitoring model evolution and quality. *11th European Conference on Software Maintenance and Reengineering* (pp. 327–328).

Lanza, M., Marinescu, R., & Ducasse, S. (2006). *Object-oriented metrics in practice: Using software metrics to characterize, evaluate, and improve the design of object-oriented systems*. Springer.

Larman, C. (2002). *Applying UML and patterns – An introduction to object-oriented analysis and design and the unified process* (2nd ed.). Upper-Saddle River, NJ: Prentice Hall.

Lasser, C., Massar, J., Miney, J., & Dayton, L. (1988). *Starlisp reference manual*. Thinking Machines Corporation.

Latry, F., Mercadal, J., & Consel, C. (2007). Staging telephony service creation: A language approach. In *Proceedings of the 1st International Conference on Principles, Systems and Applications of IP Telecommunications* (pp. 99–110). New York, NY: ACM.

Ledeczi, A., Bakay, A., Maroti, M., Volgyesi, P., Nordstrom, G., & Sprinkle, J. (2001). Composing domain-specific design environments. *Computer*, *34*(11), 44–51. doi:10.1109/2.963443

Lee, E. (2008). Cyber physical systems: Design challenges. In *11th IEEE Symposium on Object Oriented Real-Time Distributed Computing* (ISORC) (pp. 363–369).

Lee, E. (2009). Computing needs time. *Communications of the ACM*, *52*(5), 70–79. doi:10.1145/1506409.1506426

Lee, M.-H., Kim, Y.-S., & Lee, K.-H. (2007). Logical structure analysis: From HTML to XML. *Computer Standards & Interfaces*, *29*(1), 109–124. doi:10.1016/j.csi.2006.02.001

Lehmann, P. (2001). *Meta-Datenmanagement in Data-Warehouse-Systemen - Rekonstruierte Fachbegriffe als Grundlage einer konstruktiven, konzeptionellen Modellierung*. Ph.D. thesis, Magdeburg, Germany: Otto-von-Guericke-Universität Magdeburg.

Leijen, D., & Meijer, E. (2001). *Parsec: Direct style monadic parser combinators for the real world. Technical Report*. Utrecht, Netherlands: Utrecht University.

Levis, P., & Culler, D. (2002). Mate: a tiny virtual machine for sensor networks. In *ACM Sigplan Notices*, *37*(10), 85-95.

Levis, P., Madden, S., Polastre, J., Szewczyk, R., Whitehouse, K., & Woo, A. ... Brewer, E. (2005). Tinyos: An operating system for sensor networks. In *Ambient Intelligence*, (pp. 115-148).

Liang, S., & Bracha, G. (1998). Dynamic class loading in the Java virtual machine. *ACM SIGPLAN Notices*, *33*(10), 36–44. doi:10.1145/286942.286945

Lieberherr, K. J., & Holland, I. (1989). Formulations and benefits of the law of Demeter. *ACM SIGPLAN Notices*, *24*(3), 67–78. doi:10.1145/66083.66089

Lin, Y., Gray, J., & Jouault, F. (2007). DSMDiff: A differentiation tool for domain-specific models. *European Journal of Information Systems. Special Issue on Model-Driven Systems Development*, *16*(4), 349–361.

Li, S., Lin, Y., Son, S., Stankovic, J., & Wei, Y. (2004). Event detection services using data service middleware in distributed sensor networks. *Telecommunication Systems*, *26*(2), 351–368. doi:10.1023/B:TELS.0000029046.79337.8f

Litovsky, I., Métivier, Y., & Zielonka, W. (1992). The power and the limitations of local computations on graphs. In *Workshop on Graph-Theoretic Concepts in Computer Science* (pp. 333-345).

Liu, J., Chu, M., Liu, J., Reich, J., & Zhao, F. (2003). State-centric programming for sensor-actuator network systems. *IEEE Pervasive Computing / IEEE Computer Society [and] IEEE Communications Society*, *2*(4), 50–62. doi:10.1109/MPRV.2003.1251169

Loo, B., Condie, T., Garofalakis, M., Gay, D., Hellerstein, J., & Maniatis, P. ... Stoica, I. (2006). Declarative networking: Language, execution and optimization. In *Proceedings of the 2006 ACM SIGMOD International Conference on Management of Data* (pp. 97-108). ACM.

Lopes, N., Navarro, J., Rybalchenko, A., & Singh, A. (2010). Applying prolog to develop distributed systems. *Theory and Practice of Logic Programming*, *10*(4-6), 691–707. doi:10.1017/S1471068410000360

Luke, S., Cioffi-Revilla, C., Panait, L., & Sullivan, K. (2004). Mason: A new multi-agent simulation toolkit. In *Proceedings of the 2004 SwarmFest Workshop* (pp. 1-8).

Luković, I. (2009). From the synthesis algorithm to the model driven transformations in database design. In *Proceedings of 10th International Scientific Conference on Informatics* (pp. 9-18). Košice, Slovakia: Slovak Society for Applied Cybernetics and Informatics and Technical University of Košice - Faculty of Electrical Engineering and Informatics.

Luković, I., Ristić, S., & Mogin, P. (2003). A methodology of a database schema design using the subschemas. In *Proceedings of IEEE International Conference on Computational Cybernetics* (in CD ROM). Budapest, Hungary: Budapest Polytechnic.

Luković, I., Ristić, S., Aleksić, S., & Popović, A. (2008). An application of the MDSE principles in IIS*Case. In *Proceedings of the 3rd Workshop on Model Driven Software Engineering* (pp. 53-62). Berlin, Germany: TFH, University of Applied Sciences Berlin.

Luković, I., Mogin, P., Pavićević, J., & Ristić, S. (2007). An approach to developing complex database schemas using form types. *Software, Practice & Experience*, *37*(15), 1621–1656. doi:10.1002/spe.820

Luković, I., Ristić, S., Mogin, P., & Pavićević, J. (2006). Database schema integration process – A methodology and aspects of its applying. *Novi Sad Journal of Mathematics*, *36*(1), 115–150.

Luković, I., Varanda Pereira, M. J., Oliveira, N., Cruz, D., & Henriques, P. R. (2011). A DSL for PIM specifications: Design and attribute grammar based implementation. *Computer Science and Information Systems*, *8*(2), 379–403. doi:10.2298/CSIS101229018L

Lutz, M. (2009). *Learning Python* (4th ed.). Sebastopol, CA: O'Reilly Media.

Macal, C., & North, M. (2010). Tutorial on agent-based modelling and simulation. *Journal of Simulation*, *4*(3), 151–162. doi:10.1057/jos.2010.3

MacLean, A., Young, R. M., Bellotti, V. M. E., & Moran, T. P. (1991). Questions, options, and criteria: Elements of design space analysis. *Human-Computer Interaction*, *6*(3), 201–250. doi:10.1207/s15327051hci0603&4_2

MacLennan, B. (1990). *Continuous spatial automata*. Technical Report Department of Computer Science Technical Report CS-90-121, University of Tennessee, Knoxville.

Madden, S. R., Szewczyk, R., Franklin, M. J., & Culler, D. (2002). Supporting aggregate queries over ad-hoc wireless sensor networks. In *Workshop on Mobile Computing and Systems Applications*, (pp. 49 – 58).

Maes, P. (1987). *Concepts and experiments in computational reflection*. Paper presented at the conference on Object-Oriented Programming Systems, Languages and Applications, Orlando, FL.

Magyari, E., Bakay, A., Lang, A., Paka, T., Vizhanyo, A., Agrawal, A., et al. (2003). UDM: An infrastructure for implementing domain-specific modeling languages. In *3rd OOPSLA Workshop on Domain-Specific Modeling*.

Mallavarapu, A., Thomson, M., Ullian, B., & Gunawardena, J. (2009). Programming with models: Modularity and abstraction provide powerful capabilities for systems biology. *Journal of the Royal Society, Interface*, *6*(32), 257–270. doi:10.1098/rsif.2008.0205

Mamei, M., & Zambonelli, F. (2008). Programming pervasive and mobile computing applications: The TOTA approach. *ACM Transactions on Software Engineering and Methodology*, *18*(4), 15:1-15:56.

Mamidisetty, K., Duan, M., Sastry, S., & Sastry, P. S. (2009). Multipath dissemination in regular mesh topologies. *IEEE Transactions on Parallel and Distributed Systems*, *20*(8), 1188–1201. doi:10.1109/TPDS.2008.164

Mannucci, S., Mojana, B., Navazio, M. C., Romano, V., Terzi, M. C., & Torrigiani, P. (1989). Graspin: A structural development environment for analysis and design. *IEEE Software*, *6*(6), 35–43. doi:10.1109/52.41645

Marcus, A. (2004). The ROI of usability. In R. G. Bias & D. J. Mayhew (Eds.), *Cost-justifying usability*. North-Holland: Elsevier.

Margolus, N. (1993). CAM-8: A computer architecture based on cellular automata. In *American Mathematical Society*, *6*(1) 167-187.

Marlow, S. (2010). *Haskell 2010 language report*. Retrieved April 2, 2012, from http://www.haskell.org/onlinereport/haskell2010

Maroco, J. (2003). *Análise Estatística - Com Utilização do SPSS* (2nd ed.). Lisbon, Portugal: Edições Sílabo.

Martel, S., & Mohammadi, M. (2010). Using a swarm of self-propelled natural microrobots in the form of flagellated bacteria to perform complex micro-assembly tasks. In *Proceedings of the International Conference on Robotics and Automation (ICRA)* (pp. 500-505).

Martinoli, A., Easton, K., & Agassounon, W. (2004). Modeling of swarm robotic systems: A case study in collaborative distributed manipulation. *The International Journal of Robotics Research*, *23*(4), 415–436. doi:10.1177/0278364904042197

Martinoli, A., Ijspeert, A. J., & Mondada, F. (1999). Understanding collective aggregation mechanisms: From probabilistic modelling to experiments with real robots. *Robotics & Autonomous Systems. Special Issue on Distributed Autonomous Robotic Systems*, *29*, 51–63. doi:10.1016/S0921-8890(99)00038-X

Maurmaier, M., & Göhner, P. (2008). Model-driven development in industrial automation. *Technology (Elmsford, N.Y.)*, 244–249.

McIlroy, M. D. (1960). Macro instruction extensions of compiler languages. *Communications of the ACM*, *3*(4), 214–220. doi:10.1145/367177.367223

McKeeman, W. (1974). Programming language design. In F. L. Brauer, J. Eickel, F. L. D. Remer, M. Griffiths, U. Hill, J. J. Horning, …W. M. Waite (Eds.), *Lecture Notes in Computer Science: Vol. 21, Compiler Construction – An Advanced Course* (pp. 514–524). Berlin, Germany: Springer-Verlag.

McNamara, B., & Smaragdakis, Y. (2000). Functional programming in C++. *SIGPLAN Notices*, *35*(9), 118-129.

McNamara, B., & Smaragdakis, Y. (2000). Static interfaces in C. In *First C*. Template Programming Workshop.

Mellor-Crummey, J., Adhianto, L., Jin, G., & Scherer, W. N., III. (2009). *A new vision for coarray Fortran*. Paper presented at the Third Conference on Partitioned Global Address Space Programming Models. Ashburn, Virginia.

Menezes, A. L., Cirilo, C. E., Moraes, J. L. C. D., Souza, W. L. D., & Prado, A. F. D. (2010). Using archetypes and domain specific languages on development of ubiquitous applications to pervasive healthcare. In *Proceedings of the 23rd IEEE International Symposium on Computer-Based Medical Systems* (pp. 395-400). Washington, DC: IEEE Computer Society Press.

Mens, T., Wermelinger, M., Ducasse, S., Demeyer, S., Hirschfeld, R., & Jazayeri, M. (2005). Challenges in software evolution. *Eighth International Workshop on Principles of Software Evolution* (pp. 13- 22): IEEE.

Mernik, M., Heering, J., & Sloane, A. (2005). When and how to develop domain-specific languages. *ACM Computing Surveys*, *37*(4), 316–344. doi:10.1145/1118890.1118892

Mernik, M., Hrnčič, D., Bryant, B., Sprague, A., Gray, J., Liu, Q., & Javed, F. (2009). *Grammar inference algorithms and applications in software engineering. ICAT 2009 Information* (pp. 1–7). Communication and Automation Technologies.

Mernik, M., Lenič, M., Avdičaušević, E., & Žumer, V. (2000). Multiple attribute grammar inheritance. *Informatica*, *24*(2), 319–328.

Mernik, M., & Žumer, V. (2005). Incremental programming language development. [Elsevier.]. *Computer Languages, Systems & Structures*, *31*(1), 1–16. doi:10.1016/j.cl.2004.02.001

MetaCase. (2007a). EADS case study. Retrieved from http://www.metacase.com/papers/MetaEditinEADS.pdf.

MetaCase. (2007b). Nokia case study. Retrieved from http://www.metacase.com/papers/MetaEditinNokia.pdf

MetaCaseMetaEdit +. (n.d.). Retrieved October 6, 2011, from http://www.metacase.com/

Meta-Object Facility. (2006). *OMG's MetaObject facility*. Retrieved from http://www.omg.org/mof/

Meyer, B. (1997). *Object-oriented software construction* (2nd ed.). Upper Saddle River, NJ: Prentice Hall.

Meyers, B., & Vangheluwe, H. (2011). A framework for evolution of modelling languages. *Science of Computer Programming, Special Issue on Software Evolution. Adaptability and Variability*, *76*(12), 1223–1246.

Michalakes, J. (1994). *RSL: A parallel runtime system library for regular grid finite difference models using multiple nests.* Technical Report ANL/MCS-TM-197, Argonne National Laboratory.

Michalakes, J. (1997). *FLIC: A translator for same-source parallel implementation of regular grid applications.* Technical Report ANL/MCS-TM-223, Argonne National Laboratory.

Microsoft Research Team. (2012). *AsmL: Abstract state machine language*. Retrieved from http://research.microsoft.com/en-us/projects/asml/

Milanović, N., Cartsburg, M., Kutsche, R., Widiker, J., & Kschonsak, F. (2009). Model-based interoperability of heterogeneous information systems: An industrial case study. In Paige, R. F., Hartman, A., & Rensink, A. (Eds.), *Model Driven Architecture - Foundations and Applications* (*Vol. 5562*, pp. 325–336). Lecture Notes in Computer ScienceBerlin, Germany: Springer-Verlag. doi:10.1007/978-3-642-02674-4_24

Miller, G. (1956). The magical number seven, plus or minus two: Some limits on our capacity for processing information. *Psychological Review*, *63*(2), 81–97. doi:10.1037/h0043158

Miller, J. (2000). Applying meta-analytical procedures to software engineering experiments. *Journal of Systems and Software*, *54*(11), 29–39. doi:10.1016/S0164-1212(00)00024-8

Milner, R. (1999). *Communicating and mobile systems: The Pi-calculus*. Cambridge University Press.

Milner, R., Tofte, M., Harper, R., & MacQueen, D. (1997). *The definition of standard ML*. MIT Press.

Minar, N., Burkhart, R., Langton, C., & Askenazi, M. (1996). *The swarm simulation system, a toolkit for building multi-agent simulations.* Technical Report Working Paper 96-06-042, Santa Fe Institute.

Mirschel, S., Steinmetz, K., Rempel, M., Ginkel, M., & Gilles, E. D. (2009). Promot: Modular modeling for systems biology. *Bioinformatics (Oxford, England)*, *25*(5), 687–689. doi:10.1093/bioinformatics/btp029

Mishra, M., Callahan, T., Chelcea, T., Venkataramani, G., Budiu, M., & Goldstein, S. (2006). Tartan: Evaluating spatial computation for whole program execution. In *Proceedings of 12th ACM International Conference on Architecture Support for Programming Languages and Operating Systems (ASPLOS 2006)* (pp. 163-174).

MIT Media Lab and Schellar Teacher Education Program. (2011). *Starlogo*. Retrieved from http://education.mit.edu/starlogo/

Mitchell, J. C. (1998). *Foundations for programming languages*. Cambridge, MA: MIT Press.

Modsel. (2012). Retrieved March 2012, from http://web.cs.hacettepe.edu.tr/~ersiner/modsel

MOF: Meta-object faculty. (2011, June 23). Retrieved October 6, 2011, from http://www.omg.org/mof/

Moggi, E., Taha, W., Benaissa, Z., & Sheard, T. (1999). An idealized MetaML: Simpler, and more expressive. In *Proceedings of the 8th European Symposium on Programming Languages and Systems* (pp. 640-641).

Mogin, P., Luković, I., & Karadžić, Ž. (1994). Relational database schema design and application generating using IIS*CASE tool. In *Proceedings of International Conference on Technical Informatics* (pp. 49-58). Timisoara, Romania: 'Politehnica' University of Timisoara.

Moh, C. H., Lim, E. P., & Ng, W. K. (2000). Re-engineering structures from Web documents. *Proceedings of the Fifth ACM Conference on Digital Libraries* (pp. 67-76). New York, NY: ACM.

Mohagheghi, P., & Dehlen, V. (2009). Existing model metrics and relations to model quality. *Workshop on Software Quality* (pp. 39–45).

Montagna, S., Viroli, M., Risoldi, M., Pianini, D., & Di Marzo Serugendo, G. (2011). Self-organising pervasive ecosystems: A crowd evacuation example. In *3rd International Workshop on Software Engineering for Resilient Systems, volume 6968 of Lecture Notes in Computer Science*, (pp. 115-129). Springer.

Montague, R. (1970). Universal grammar. *Theoria*, *36*, 373–398. doi:10.1111/j.1755-2567.1970.tb00434.x

Moody, D. L. (2009). The "physics" of notations: Toward a scientific basis for constructing visual notations in software engineering. *IEEE Transactions on Software Engineering*, *35*(6), 756–779. doi:10.1109/TSE.2009.67

Moore, C. H. (1974). Forth: A new way to program a mini computer. *Astronomy and Astrophysics Supplement*, *15*(3), 497–511.

Moreno, G., & Merson, P. (2008). Model-driven performance analysis. In *4th International Conference on the Quality of Software Architectures* (pp. 135–151).

Morisio, M., Seaman, C. B., Basili, V. R., Parra, A. T., Kraft, S. E., & Condon, S. E. (2002). COTS-based software development: processes and open issues. *Journal of Systems and Software*, *61*(3), 189–200. doi:10.1016/S0164-1212(01)00147-9

Moss, S., Gaylard, H., Wallis, S., & Edmonds, B. (1998). SDML: A multi-agent language for organizational modelling. *Computational & Mathematical Organization Theory*, *4*, 43–69. doi:10.1023/A:1009600530279

Mottola, L., & Picco, G. (2006). *Logical neighborhoods: A programming abstraction for wireless sensor networks* (pp. 150–168). Distributed Computing in Sensor Systems. doi:10.1007/11776178_10

Mottola, L., & Picco, G. (2011). Programming wireless sensor networks: Fundamental concepts and state of the art. *ACM Computing Surveys*, *43*(3), 19–75. doi:10.1145/1922649.1922656

MPI2. (2009). *MPI: A message-passing interface standard version 2.2*. Message Passing Interface Forum.

Mucci, C., Campi, F., Brunelli, C., & Nurmi, J. (2007). Programming tools for reconfigurable processors. In Nurmi, J. (Ed.), *System-On-Chip Computing for ASICs and FPGAs on Processor Design* (pp. 427–446). Springer.

Muller, P.-A., Fleurey, F., & Jézéquel, J.-M. (2005). Weaving executability into object-oriented meta-languages. In Briand, L. C., & Williams, C. (Eds.), *Model Driven Engineering Languages and Systems (MoDELS)* (*Vol. 3713*, pp. 264–278). Lecture Notes in Computer ScienceBerlin, Germany: Springer. doi:10.1007/11557432_19

Munnelly, J., & Clarke, S. (2007). ALPH: A domain-specific language for crosscutting pervasive healthcare concerns. In *Proceedings of the 2nd Workshop on Domain Specific Aspect Languages*. New York, NY: ACM.

Murata, T. (1989). Petri nets: Properties, analysis and applications. *Proceedings of the IEEE*, *77*(4), 541–580. doi:10.1109/5.24143

Murray, N. S., Paton, N. W., Goble, C. A., & Bryce, J. (2000). Kaleidoquery--A flow-based visual language and its evaluation. *Journal of Visual Languages and Computing*, *11*(2), 151–189. doi:10.1006/jvlc.1999.0150

Musser, D., & Stepanov, A. (1994). Algorithm-oriented generic libraries. *Software, Practice & Experience*, *24*(7), 623–642. doi:10.1002/spe.4380240703

Myers, C., Barker, N., Jones, K., Kuwahara, H., Madsen, C., & Nguyen, N. (2009). iBioSim: A tool for the analysis and design of genetic circuits. *Bioinformatics (Oxford, England)*, *25*, 2848–2849. doi:10.1093/bioinformatics/btp457

Myers, G. J., & Sandler, C. (2004). *The art of software testing* (2nd ed.). Hoboken, NJ: John Wiley & Sons, Inc.

Nagpal, R. (2001). *Programmable self-assembly: Constructing global shape using biologically-inspired local interactions and origami mathematics*. PhD thesis, MIT.

Nain, G., Daubert, E., Barais, O., & Jézéquel, J.-M. (2008). Using MDE to build a schizophrenic middleware for home/building automation. *Towards a Service-Based Internet*. *Lecture Notes in Computer Science*, *5377*, 49–61. doi:10.1007/978-3-540-89897-9_5

Neighbors, J. (1980). *Software construction using components*. Ph.D. thesis, University of California, Berkeley.

Newton, R., & Welsh, M. (2004). Region streams: Functional macroprogramming for sensor networks. In *First International Workshop on Data Management for Sensor Networks (DMSN)* (pp. 78-87).

Newton, R., Morrisett, G., & Welsh, M. (2007). The regiment macroprogramming system. In *Proceedings of the 6th International Conference on Information Processing in Sensor Networks* (pp. 489-498). ACM.

Nguyen, D. N., Usbeck, K., Mongan, W. M., Cannon, C. T., Lass, R. N., Salvage, J., & Regli, W. C. (2010). A methodology for developing an agent systems reference architecture. In *11th International Workshop on Agent-Oriented Software Engineering* (pp. 177-188).

Nielsen, J., & Molich, R. (1990). Heuristic evaluation of user interfaces. In *SIGCHI Conference on Human Factors in Computing Systems: Empowering People (CHI'90)* (pp. 249-256). Seattle, WA, USA.

Nielsen, J. (1993). *Usability engineering*. Academic Press.

Nielsen, J., & Gilutz, S. (2003). *Usability return on investment* (4th ed.). Nielsen Norman Group.

Nomikos, V., & Kolomvatsos, K. (2009). *Documentation of the IPAC application description language*. Technical Report, Department of Informatics and Telecommunications, National and Kapodistrian University of Athens.

Norman, D. A. (2005). Human-centered design considered harmful. *Interactions (New York, N.Y.)*, *12*(4), 14–19. doi:10.1145/1070960.1070976

Norman, D. A., & Draper, S. W. (1986). *User-centered system design: New perspectives on human- computer interaction*. Erlbaum Associates.

North, M., Howe, T., Collier, N., & Vos, J. (2007). A declarative model assembly infrastructure for verification and validation. In *The First World Congress on Advancing Social Simulation* (pp. 129-140). Springer Japan.

Nunes, D. A., & Schwabe, D. (2006). Rapid prototyping of web applications combining domain specific languages and model driven design. In *Proceedings of the 6th International Conference on Web engineering* (pp. 153-160). New York, NY: ACM Press.

Ober, I., Dib, A. A., Féraud, L., & Percebois, C. (2008). Towards interoperability in component based development with a family of DSLs. In *Proceedings of the 2nd European Conference on Software Architecture* (pp. 148–163). Paphos, Cyprus.

Object Management Group (OMG). (2010). *Unified modeling language: Superstructure*, version 2. Retrieved from http://www.omg.org/spec/UML/2.3

Object Management Group. (2001). *MDA guide*. Retrieved October 5, 2011, from http://www.omg.org/cgi-bin/doc?omg/03-06-01

Object Management Group. (2006). *Meta-object facility (Mof) v2.0 core specification. (OMG Document No. formal/2006-01-01)*. Object Management Group.

Object Management Group. (2010). *Object constraint language (OCL) v2.0 specification. (OMG Document No. formal/2006-05-01)*. Object Management Group.

OCL. (2006). *Object constraint language specification*. Retrieved from http://www.omg.org/cgi-bin/apps/doc?formal/06-05-01.pdf

Odell, J., Parunak, H., & Bauer, B. (1999). Extending UML for agents. In *Agent-Oriented Systems Workshop at the 17th National Conference on Artificial Intelligence* (pp. 3-17). AAAI Press.

Odersky, M., Spoon, L., & Venners, B. (2008). *Programming in Scala*. Artima Press.

Okasaki, C. (2002). Techniques for embedding postfix languages in Haskell. In *ACM SIGPLAN Workshop on Haskell* (pp. 105–113).

Oliveira, N., Pereira, M., Henriques, P., & Cruz, D. (2009). Domain specific languages: A theoretical survey. In *INFORUM Simposio de Informatica*. Lisboa, Portugal: University of Lisboa.

Oliveira, N., Varanda Pereira, M. J., Henriques, P. R., Cruz, D., & Cramer, B. (2010). VisualLISA: A visual environment to develop attribute grammars. *Computer Science an Information Systems*, *7*(2), 265–289. doi:10.2298/CSIS1002265O

OMG Meta Object Facility (MOF), Core Specification v2.0, formal/2006-01-01. (2006). *OMG. Meta Object Facility (MOF), Core Specification v2.0, formal/2006-01-01*.

OMG MOF Specification. (2011). *Meta object facility specification*. Retrieved September 9th, 2011, from http://www.omg.org/spec/MOF/2.0/PDF/

OMG Object Constraint Language (OCL), v2.0 formal/2006-05-01. (2006). *OMG. Object Constraint Language (OCL), v2.0 formal/2006-05-01*.

OMG QVT Specification. (2011). *Query/view/transformation specification.* Retrieved September 9th, 2011, from http://www.omg.org/spec/QVT/1.1/PDF/

Oncina, J., & Garcia, P. (1992). Inferring regular languages in polynomial update time. [World Scientific Publishing.]. *Pattern Recognition and Image Analysis*, 49–61. doi:10.1142/9789812797902_0004

Open Group. (2009). *ArchiMate 1.0 specification.*

Open, C. L. (2011). *OpenCL - The open standard for parallel programming of heterogeneous systems.* Retrieved from http://www.khronos.org/opencl/

Open, M. P. (2011). *The OpenMP API specification for parallel programming.* Retrieved from http://openmp.org/wp/

Open, C. L. (2011). *The OpenCL specification, version 1.2.* Khronos OpenCL Working Group.

Open, M. P. (2011). *OpenMP application program interface version 3.1.* OpenMP Architecture Review Board.

Oracle Corp. (2011). *BPEL process manager*. Retrieved from http://www.oracle.com/technology/products/ias/bpel/index.html

OSGi Alliance. (2011). *OSGi service platform specification.* Retrieved from http://www.osgi.org/Release4/Download

Pactolus. (2011). *Guide to the RapidFLEX service creation environment: Product manual.* Retrieved September 9th, 2011 from http://radisys.custhelp.com/ci/fattach/get/128/

Paepcke, A. (1993). User-level language crafting - Introducing the CLOS metaobject protocol. In Paepcke, A. (Ed.), *Object-oriented programming: The CLOS perspective* (pp. 65–99). Cambridge, MA: MIT Press.

Pagan, F. (1979). Algol 68 as a meta-language for denotational semantics. *The Computer Journal, 22*(1), 63–66. doi:10.1093/comjnl/22.1.63

Paige, R., Kolovos, D., & Polack, F. (2006). An action semantics for MOF 2.0. In H. Haddad (Ed.), *ACM Symposium on Applied Computing* (SAC) (pp. 1304–1305). New York, NY: Association for Computing Machinery.

Palmer, J., & Steele, J. G. L. (1992). Connection machine model cm-5 system overview. In *Fourth Symposium on the Frontiers of Massively Parallel Computation* (pp. 474-483). IEEE Press.

Parr, T., & Quong, R. (1994). Antlr: A predicated-ll(k) parser generator. *Software, Practice & Experience, 25*(7), 789–810. doi:10.1002/spe.4380250705

Pastor, O., Gómez, J., Insfrán, E., & Pelechano, V. (2001). The OO-Method approach for information systems modeling: From object-oriented conceptual modeling to automated programming. *Information Systems, 26*(7), 507–534. doi:10.1016/S0306-4379(01)00035-7

Pathak, A., Mottola, L., Bakshi, A., Prasanna, V., & Picco, G. (2007). Expressing sensor network interaction patterns using data-driven macroprogramming. In *Proceedings of the Fifth IEEE International Conference on Pervasive Computing and Communications Workshops* (pp. 255-260). IEEE Computer Society.

Paun, G. (2000). Computing with membranes. *Journal of Computer and System Sciences, 61*(1), 108–143. doi:10.1006/jcss.1999.1693

Paun, G. (2002). *Membrane computing: An introduction.* Springer.

Pauty, J., Couderc, P., Banatre, M., & Berbers, Y. (2007). Geo-linda: a geometry aware distributed tuple space. In *IEEE 21st International Conference on Advanced Networking and Applications (AINA '07)* (pp. 370-377).

Pedersen, M., & Phillips, A. (2009). Towards programming languages for genetic engineering of living cells. *Journal of the Royal Society, Interface, 6*, S437–S450. doi:10.1098/rsif.2008.0516.focus

Perišić, B., Milosavljević, G., Dejanović, I., & Milosavljević, B. (2011). UML profile for specifying user interfaces of business applications. *Computer Science and Information Systems, 8*(2), 405–426. doi:10.2298/CSIS110112010P

Peristeras, V., & Tarabanis, K. (2006). The connection, communication, consolidation, collaboration interoperability framework (C4IF) for information systems interoperability. *International Journal of Interoperability in Business Information Systems, 1*(1), 61–72.

Perrotta, P. (2010). *Metaprogramming Ruby*. Raleigh, NC: The Pragmatic Bookshelf.

Petrascu, V., & Chiorean, D. (2010). Towards improving the static semantics of XCore. *Studia Universitatis Babes-Bolyai. Informatica*, *55*(3), 61–70.

Petrie, H., & Bevan, N. (2009). The evaluation of accessibility, usability and user experience. In Stephanidis, C. (Ed.), *The universal access handbook*. CRC Press. doi:10.1201/9781420064995-c20

Peyton Jones, S. L. (2003). *Haskell 98 language and libraries: The revised report*. Cambridge, UK: Cambridge University Press.

Pfeiffer, M., & Pichler, J. (2008). A comparison of tool support for textual domain-specific languages. In *OOPSLA Workshop on Domain-Specific Modeling* (pp. 1–7).

Phang, K. Y., Foster, J. S., Hicks, M., & Sazawal, V. (2009). Triaging checklists: A substitute for a PhD in static analysis. In *1st ACM SIGPLAN Workshop on Evaluation and Usability of Programming Languages and Tools (PLATEAU 2009)*.

Pierce, B. C. (2002). *Types and programming languages*. Cambridge, MA: MIT Press.

Pierce, B. C., & Turner, D. N. (2000). Pict: a programming language based on the pi-calculus. In Plotkin, G. D., Stirling, C., & Tofte, M. (Eds.), *Proof, language, and interaction, essays in honour of Robin Milner* (pp. 455–494). The MIT Press.

Pierro, A. D., Hankin, C., & Wiklicky, H. (2005). Continuous-time probabilistic klaim. *Electronic Notes in Theoretical Computer Science*, *128*(5), 27–38. doi:10.1016/j.entcs.2004.11.040

Plotkin, G. D. (1981). *A structural approach to operational semantics. DAIMI FN-19*. Computer Science Department, Aarhus University.

Poernomo, I. (2006). The meta-object facility (MOF) typed. In H. Haddad (Ed.), *Proceedings of the ACM Symposium on Applied Computing* (SAC) (pp. 1845–1849). New York, NY: Association for Computing Machinery.

Pokahr, A., Braubach, L., & Lamersdorf, W. (2003). Jadex: Implementing a BDI-infrastructure for jade agents. *EXP-in Search of Innovation*, *3*(3), 76–85.

Pollet, I. (2004). *Towards a generic framework for the abstract interpretation of Java*. (Ph.D. Doctoral Dissertation), Catholic University of Louvain, Belgium.

Porkoláb, Z. (2010). Domain-specific language integration with compile-time parser generator library. In E. Visser & J. Järvi (Eds.), *9th International Conference Generative Programming and Component Engineering (GPCE 2010)* (pp. 137-146).

Porkoláb, Z., Mihalicza, J., & Sipos, A. (2006). Debugging C++ template metaprograms. In S. Jarzabek, D. C. Schmidt, & T. L. Veldhuizen (Eds.), *5th International Conference Generative Programming and Component Engineering (GPCE 2006)* (pp. 255—264).

Porubän, J., Sabo, M., Kollár, J., & Mernik, M. (2010). Abstract syntax driven language development: Defining language semantics through aspects. *Proceedings of the International Workshop on Formalization of Modeling Languages* (pp. 21-25). ACM.

Porubän, J., Forgáč, M., Sabo, M., & Běhálek, M. (2010). Annotation Based Parser Generator. *Computer Science and Information Systems*, *7*(2), 291–307. doi:10.2298/CSIS1002291P

Pösch, R. (1997). Design by contract for Python. In *4th Asia-Pacific Software Engineering and International Computer Science Conference (APSEC)* (pp. 213–219). Washington, DC: IEEE Computer Society.

Power, J. F., & Malloy, J. F. (2004). A metrics suite for grammar-based software. *Journal of Software Maintenance and Evolution: Research and Practice*, *16*(6), 405–426. doi:10.1002/smr.293

Pratt, T. W., & Zelkowitz, M. V. (2000). *Programming languages – Design and implementation*. Upper Saddle River, NJ: Prentice Hall.

Prechelt, L. (2000). An empirical comparison of seven programming languages. *IEEE Computer*, *33*(10), 23–29. doi:10.1109/2.876288

Premaratne, S. (2011). *Strategic programming approaches to tree processing*. Master's thesis, Macquarie University.

Pressey, C. (Retrieved Feb 20, 2012). *The alpaca meta-language*. Retrieved from http://catseye.tc/projects/alpaca/

Priami, C. (1995). Stochastic pi-calculus. *The Computer Journal, 38*(7), 578–589. doi:10.1093/comjnl/38.7.578

Printf. (2011). *The printf grammar*. Retrieved from http://www.cplusplus.com/reference/clibrary/cstdio/printf

Prolog. (1995). *International standard: Programming language*. ISO/IEC 13211.1.

Prorok, A., Correll, N., & Martinoli, A. (2011). Multi-level spatial models for swarm-robotic systems. *The International Journal of Robotics Research. Special Issue on Stochasticity in Robotics and Biological Systems, 30*(5), 574–589.

Proto, M. I. T. (Retrieved November 22, 2010). *MIT Proto*. Retrieved from http://proto.bbn.com/

Prud'homme, C. (2006). A domain specific embedded language in C++ for automatic differentiation, projection, integration and variational formulations. *Journal of Scientific Programming, 14*(2), 81–110.

Prusinkiewicz, P., & Lindenmayer, A. (1990). *The algorithmic beauty of plants*. New York, NY: Springer-Verlag. doi:10.1007/978-1-4613-8476-2

Python Software Foundation. (2011). *Python reference documentation*. Retrieved March 16, 2011, from http://docs.python.org/release/2.6.6/

Quinn, M. (2004). *Parallel programming in C with MPI and OpenMP*. McGraw-Hill.

Raimbault, F., & Lavenier, D. (1993). Relacs for systolic programming. In *International Conference on Application-Specific Array Processors* (pp. 132-135).

Ramil, J. F. (2002). Laws of software evolution and their empirical support. *Proceedings of International Conference on Software Maintenance* (pp. 71- 71).

Rao, A., & Georgeff, M. (1995). BDI agents: From theory to practice. In *Proceedings of the First International Conference on Multi-Agent Systems (ICMAS-95)* (pp. 312-319).

Reggio, G., Cerioli, M., & Astesiano, E. (2001). Towards a rigorous semantics of UML supporting its multiview approach. In Hußmann, H. (Ed.), *Fundamental Approaches to Software Engineering (FASE)* (*Vol. 2029*, pp. 171–186). Lecture Notes in Computer ScienceBerlin, Germany: Springer-Verlag. doi:10.1007/3-540-45314-8_13

Regli, W. C., Mayk, I., Dugan, C. J., Kopena, J. B., Lass, R. N., & Modi, P. J. (2009). Development and specification of a reference model for agent-based systems. *Transactions on Systems Man and Cybernetics, 39*(Part C), 572–596. doi:10.1109/TSMCC.2009.2020507

Reinhartz-Berger, I. (2010). Towards automatization of domain modeling. *Data & Knowledge Engineering, 69*(5), 491–515. doi:10.1016/j.datak.2010.01.002

Reisner, P. (1988). Query languages. In *Handbook of human-computer interaction* (pp. 257–280). Amsterdam, The Netherlands: North-Holland.

Reiter, T., Kapsammer, E., Retschitzegger, W., Schwinger, W., & Stumptner, M. (2006). A generator framework for domain-specific model transformation languages. In *Proceedings of the Eighth International Conference on Enterprise Information Systems Databases and Information Systems Integration* (pp. 27-35). Paphos, Cyprus: ICEIS Press.

Rejimon, T., & Bhanja, S. (2005). Scalable probabilistic computing models using bayesian networks. In *48th Midwest Symposium on Circuits and Systems* (pp. 712-715).

Repast Team. (2011). *The repast suite*. Retrieved from http://repast.sourceforge.net/index.html

Repenning, A., & Ioannidou, A. (2007). *X-expressions in XMLisp: S-expressions and extensible markup language unite*. Paper presented at the International Lisp Conference, Cambridge, MA.

Resnick, M. (1996). Starlogo: An environment for decentralized modeling and decentralized thinking. In *Conference Companion on Human Factors in Computing Systems: Common Ground* (pp. 11-12). ACM.

Riccobene, E., & Scandurra, P. (2009). Weaving executability into UML class models at PIM level. *Proceedings of the 1st Workshop on Behavior Modeling in Model-Driven Architecture (BM-MDA 2009)* (pp. 1-9). ACM.

Riccobene, E., & Scandurra, P. (2010). An executable semantics of the SystemC UML profile. In M. Frappier, U. Glässer, S. Khurshid, R. Laleau, & S. Reeves (Eds.), *Proceedings of the Second International Conference on Abstract State Machines, Alloy, B and Z (ABZ 2010)* (pp. 75-90). Berlin, Germany: Springer.

Richters, M. (2001). *A precise approach to validating UML models and OCL constraints*. PhD thesis, Universität Bremen, Germany.

Ristić, S., Aleksić, S., Luković, I., & Banović, J. (2011). Form-driven application generating: A case study. In *Proceedings of 11th International Conference on Informatics* (pp. 115-120). Košice, Slovakia: Slovak Society for Applied Cybernetics and Informatics and Technical University of Košice - Faculty of Electrical Engineering and Informatics.

Ristić, S., Mogin, P., & Luković, I. (2003). Specifying database updates using a subschema. In *Proceedings of VII IEEE International Conference on Intelligent Engineering Systems* (pp. 203-212). Assiut-Luxor, Egypt: IEEE, Assiut University, Assiut, Egypt, and Budapest Polytechnic, Budapest, Hungary.

Ristić, S., Luković, I., Pavićević, J., & Mogin, P. (2007). Resolving database constraint collisions using IIS*case tool. *Journal of Information and Organizational Sciences*, *31*(1), 187–206.

Rivera, J. E. (2010). *On the semantics of real-time domain-specific modeling of languages*. (Ph.D. Doctoral Dissertation). University of Malaga, Spain.

Rivera, J. E., & Vallecillo, A. (2007). Adding behavioral semantics to models. In *Proceedings of the Eleven IEEE International Enterprise Distributed Object Computing Conference* (EDOC) (pp. 169–180). Washington, DC: Ieee Computer Society.

Rivera, J. E., Durán, F., & Vallecillo, A. (2009). Formal specification and analysis of domain specific models using Maude. *Simulation*, *85*(11-12), 778–792. doi:10.1177/0037549709341635

Romero, J., Rivera, J., Durán, F., & Vallecillo, A. (2007). Formal and tool support for model driven engineering with Maude (J. Bézivin, & B. Meyer, Eds.). *Journal of Object Technology*, *6*(9), 187-207.

Rompf, T., Sujeeth, A. K., Lee, H., Brown, K. J., Chafi, H., Odersky, M., & Olukotun, K. (2011). *Building-blocks for performance oriented DSLs*. Paper presented at the Working Conference on Domain-Specific Languages, Algarve, Portugal.

Rus, D., Butler, Z. J., Kotay, K., & Vona, M. (2002). Self-reconfiguring robots. *Communications of the ACM*, *45*(3), 39–45. doi:10.1145/504729.504752

Rus, D., & Vona, M. (2001). Crystalline robots: Self-reconfiguration with compressible unit modules. *Autonomous Robots*, *10*(1), 107–124. doi:10.1023/A:1026504804984

Russell, S., Norvig, P., Canny, J., Malik, J., & Edwards, D. (1995). *Artificial intelligence: A modern approach*. Englewood Cliffs, NJ: Prentice Hall.

Sabo, M. (2011). *Computer language patterns: The inference of textual notation for domain-specific languages*. Ph.D. Dissertation, Technical University of Košice.

Sadilek, D. A. (2007). Prototyping domain-specific languages for wireless sensor networks. In *Proceedings of the 4th International Workshop on Software Language Engineering* (pp. 76–91).

Sadilek, D. A. (2008). Prototyping domain-speci□c language semantics. *Companion to the 23rd ACM SIGPLAN conference on Object-oriented programming systems languages and applications* (pp. 895-896). Nashville, TN, USA: ACM.

Sadilek, D. A., & Wachsmuth, G. (2008). Prototyping visual interpreters and debuggers for domain-specific modelling languages. *In Proceedings of the 4th European Conference on Model Driven Architecture: Foundations and Applications* (pp. 63 – 78). Berlin, Germany.

Sadilek, D. A., & Wachsmuth, G. (2009). Using grammarware languages to define operational semantics of modelled languages. *47th International Conference Objects, Models, Components, Patterns (TOOLS Europe 2009)* (pp. 348-356).

Sánchez Cuadrado, J., García Molina, J., & Menárguez, M. (2006). RubyTL: A practical, extensible transformation language. In A. Rensink & J. Warmer (Eds.), *Second European Conference Model Driven Architecture - Foundations and Applications, Lecture Notes in Computer Science, vol. 4066*, (pp. 158-172). Springer.

Sánchez Cuadrado, J., & García Molina, J. (2007). Building domain-specific languages for model-driven development. *IEEE Software, 24*(5), 48–56. doi:10.1109/MS.2007.135

Sánchez Cuadrado, J., & García Molina, J. (2009). A model-based approach to families of embedded domain specific languages. *IEEE Transactions on Software Engineering, 25*(6), 825–840. doi:10.1109/TSE.2009.14

Sánchez Cuadrado, J., & García Molina, J. (2010). Modularization of model transformations through a phasing mechanism. *Software & Systems Modeling, 8*(3), 325–345. doi:10.1007/s10270-008-0093-0

Saraswat, V., Bloom, B., Peshansky, I., Tardieu, O., & Grove, D. (2012). *X10 language specification version 2.2*. Yorktown Heights, NY: IBM.

Scala. (2012). *Scala language*. Retrieved March, 28, 2012, from http://www.scala-lang.com

Scheidgen, M., & Fischer, J. (2007). Human comprehensible and machine processable specifications of operational semantics. *Proceedings of the Third European Conference on Model Driven Architecture- Foundations and Applications (ECMDA-FA 2007)* (pp. 157-171). Haifa, Israel: Springer-Verlag.

Schmidt, D. (2006). Model-driven engineering. *IEEE Computer, 39*(2), 25–31. doi:10.1109/MC.2006.58

Schmidt, D. A. (1986). *Denotational semantics*. Newton, MA: Allyn and Bacon.

Schmidt, D. C. (2006). Model-driven engineering. *IEEE Computer, 39*(2), 25–31. doi:10.1109/MC.2006.58

Schuette, R., & Rotthowe, T. (1998). The guidelines of modeling - An approach to enhance the quality in information models. In *ER '98 Proceedings of the 17th International Conference on Conceptual Modeling* (pp. 240-254). London, UK: Springer-Verlag.

Schultz, U. P., Christensen, D. J., & Stoy, K. (2007). A domain-specific language for programming self-reconfigurable robots. In *Workshop on Automatic Program Generation for Embedded Systems (APGES)* (pp. 28-36).

Schultz, U., Bordignon, M., Christensen, D., & Stoy, K. (2008). Spatial computing with labels. In *Spatial Computing Workshop* (pp. 326 – 331).

Schwerdfeger, A., & Van Wyk, E. (2009). Verifiable composition of deterministic grammars. *ACM SIGPLAN Conference on Programming Language Design and Implementation* (pp. 199-210).

Sebesta, R. W. (1999). *Concepts of programming languages*. Reading, UK: Addison-Wesley.

Sedigh-Ali, S., Ghafoor, A., & Paul, R. A. (2001). Software engineering metrics for COTS-based systems. *Computer, 34*(5), 44–50. doi:10.1109/2.920611

SEI. (2010). *CMMI for development*, version 1.3. Retrieved October 10, 2011, from http://www.sei.cmu.edu/library/abstracts/reports/10tr033.cfm

Seibel, P. (2005). *Practical Common Lisp*. Berkeley, CA: Apress. doi:10.1007/978-1-4302-0017-8

SGR. (1991). *International standard: Select graphic rendition*. ISO/IEC 6429 SGR / ECMA-48.

Shanks, G. (1997). Conceptual data modelling: An empirical study of expert and novice data modellers. *Australasian Journal of Information Systems, 4*(2), 63–73.

Sheard, T. (2001). Accomplishments and research challenges in meta-programming. In Taha, W. (Ed.), *Semantics, Applications, and Implementation of Program Generation* (*Vol. 2196*, pp. 2–44). Lecture Notes in Computer ScienceBerlin, Germany: Springer Verlag. doi:10.1007/3-540-44806-3_2

Sheard, T., Benaissa, Z., & Pasalic, E. (2000). DSL implementation using staging and monads. *ACM SIGPLAN Notices*, *35*(1), 81–94. doi:10.1145/331963.331975

Sheard, T., & Peyton-Jones, S. (2002). Template metaprogramming for Haskell. *SIGPLAN Notices*, *37*(12), 60–75. doi:10.1145/636517.636528

Shen, C., Srisathapornphat, C., & Jaikaeo, C. (2001). Sensor information networking architecture and applications. *IEEE Personal Communications*, *8*(4), 52–59. doi:10.1109/98.944004

Shen, W.-M., Will, P., Galstyan, A., & Chuong, C. (2004). Hormone-inspired self-organization and distributed control of robotic swarms. *Autonomous Robots*, *17*(1), 93–105. doi:10.1023/B:AURO.0000032940.08116.f1

Siek, G., & Lumsdaine, L. (2005). Essential language support for generic programming. *ACM SIGPLAN Notices*, *40*(6), 73–84. doi:10.1145/1064978.1065021

Siek, J., & Lumsdaine, A. (2000). Concept checking: Binding parametric polymorphism in C. In *First C*. Template Programming Workshop.

Simos, M. (1997). Organization domain modeling and OO analysis and design: Distinctions, integration, new directions. In *Proceedings of the 3rd Conference on Smalltalk and Java in Industry and Education (STJA)* (pp. 126–132).

Sinkovics, Á. (2010). Functional extensions to the Boost metaprogram library. In P. Porkoláb (Ed.), *The 3rd Workshop on Generative Technologies (WGT2010)* (pp. 56-66).

Sinkovics, Á. (2011). Nested lamda expressions with let expressions in C++ template metaprorgams. In P. Porkoláb, et al., (Eds.), *The 3rd Workshop on Generative Technologies*, Vol. III, (pp. 63-76).

Sinkovics, Á. (2011). *The source code of mpllibs. metaparse*. Retrieved from http://github.com/sabel83/mpllibs

Sivonen, S. (2008). *Domain-specific modelling language and code generator for developing repository-based Eclipse plug-ins*. Espoo, Finland: VTT Publications.

Sjøberg, D. I. K., Hannay, J. E., Hansen, O., Kampenes, V. B., Karahasanovic, A., Liborg, N.-K., & Rekdal, A. (2005). A survey of controlled experiments in software engineering. *IEEE Transactions on Software Engineering*, *31*(9), 733–753. doi:10.1109/TSE.2005.97

Skalski, K., Moskal, M., & Olszta, P. (2004). *Metaprogramming in Nemerle*. Unpublished technical report, University of Wroclaw, Poland.

Skeen, D. (1981). Nonblocking commit protocols. In *Proceedings of the ACM SIGMOD International Conference on Management of Data (SIGMOD '81)* (pp. 133-142). New York, NY: ACM.

Skjellum, A., Bangalore, P., Gray, J., & Bryant, B. (2004). *Reinventing explicit parallel programming for improved engineering of high performance computing software*. Paper presented at the International Workshop on Software Engineering for High Performance Computing System Applications. Scotland, U.K.

Sklar, E. (2007). Netlogo, a multi-agent simulation environment. *Artificial Life*, *13*(3), 303–311. doi:10.1162/artl.2007.13.3.303

Skype Limited. (2007). *Skype developer zone*. Retrieved from https://developer.skype.com/

Sloane, A. M. (2008). Experiences with domain-specific language embedding in Scala. In *2nd International Workshop on Domain-Specific Program Development*. Nashville, TN: ACM.

Sloane, A. M. (2011). Lecture Notes in Computer Science: *Vol. 6491. Lightweight language processing in Kiama. Generative and Transformational Techniques in Software Engineering III* (pp. 408–425). Springer-Verlag. doi:10.1007/978-3-642-18023-1_12

Sloane, A. M., Kats, L. C. L., & Visser, E. (2010). A pure object-oriented embedding of attribute grammars. *Electronic Notes in Theoretical Computer Science*, *253*(7), 205–219. doi:10.1016/j.entcs.2010.08.043

Smalltalk (1998). *American national standard: Programming language*. ANSI INCITS.319:1998 (R2002).

Smith, B. C. (1984). *Reflection and semantics in Lisp*. Paper presented at the Symposium on Principles of Programming Languages, Salt Lake City, UT.

Smith, L. P., Bergmann, F. T., Chandran, D., & Sauro, H. M. (2009). Antimony: A modular model definition language. *Bioinformatics (Oxford, England)*, *25*(18), 2452–2454. doi:10.1093/bioinformatics/btp401

Soden, M., & Eichler, H. (2009). Towards a model execution framework for Eclipse. *Proceedings of the First Workshop on Behavior Modeling in Model-Driven Architecture (BM-MDA 2009)* (pp. 1-7). ACM.

Sommerville, I. (2010). *Software engineering* (9th ed.). Boston, MA: Addison-Wesley.

Song, D., He, K., Liang, P., & Liu, W. (2005). A formal language for model transformation specification. In C. S. Chen, J. Filipe, I. Seruca, & J. Cordeiro (Eds.), *Proceedings of Seventh International Conference on Enterprise Information Systems* (ICEIS): Vol. 3, (pp. 429–433). Berlin, Germany: Springer.

Soon-Kyeong, K., & Carrington, D. (1999). Formalizing the UML class diagram using object-Z. In R. France & B. Rumpe (Eds.), *Lecture Notes in Computer Science: Vol. 1723, Second Conference on the Unified Modelling Language: Beyond the Standard* (pp. 83–98). Berlin, Germany: Springer-Verlag.

Sperber, M., Dybvig, R., Flatt, M., Straaten, A., Findler, R., & Matthews, J. (2009). Revised report on the algorithmic language Scheme. *Functional Programming*, *19*, 1–301. doi:10.1017/S0956796809990074

Spezzano, G., & Talia, D. (1997). A high-level cellular programming model for massively parallel processing. In *2nd Int'l Workshop on High-Level Programming Models and Supportive Environments (HIPS'97)* (pp. 55-63).

Spiewak, D., & Zhao, T. (2009). ScalaQL: Language-integrated database queries for Scala. In M. van den Brand, D. Gašević, & J. Gray (Eds.), *Lecture Notes in Computer Science: vol. 5966, Proceedings of the 2nd International Conference on Software Language Engineering* (pp. 154–163). Berlin, Germany: Springer-Verlag.

Spinellis, D. (2001). Notable design patterns for domain-specific languages. *Journal of Systems and Software*, *56*(1), 91–99. doi:10.1016/S0164-1212(00)00089-3

Spivey, J. M. (1992). *The Z notation: A reference manual*. Upper Saddle River, NJ: Prentice-Hall.

Sprinkle, J., Gray, J., & Mernik, M. (2009). *Fundamental limitations in domain-specific language evolution*. (Report No. TR-090831). Electrical and Computer Engineering, University of Arizona.

Sprinkle, J., Mernik, M., Tolvanen, J.-P., & Spinellis, D. (2009). Guest editors' introduction: What kinds of nails need a domain-specific hammer? *IEEE Software*, *26*(4), 15–18. doi:10.1109/MS.2009.92

Srinivas, Y. (1991). *Algebraic specification of domains. Domain Analysis and Software Systems Modeling* (pp. 90–124). New York, NY: IEEE.

Stahl, T., Volter, M., Bettin, J., Haase, A., Helsen, S., & Czarnecki, K. (2003). *Model-driven software development: Technology, engineering, management*. John Wiley & Sons.

Stanek, J., Kothari, S., & Kang, G. (2008). Method of comparing graph differencing algorithms for software differencing. In *Proceedings of the Electro/Information Technology (EIT 2008)* (pp.482-487).

Stark, R. F., Borger, E., & Schmid, J. (2001). *Java and the Java virtual machine: Definition, verification, validation*. Berlin, Germany: Springer-Verlag.

Steele, G. Jr. (1990). *Common LISP: The language* (2nd ed.). Digital Press.

Stehr, M.-O., Meseguer, J., & Ölveczky, P. C. (2001). *Rewriting logic as a unifying framework for Petri nets. Unifying Petri Nets, Advances in Petri Nets* (pp. 250–303). Berlin, Germany: Springer-Verlag.

Steinberg, D., Budinsky, F., Paternostro, M., & Merks, E. (2009). *EMF: Eclipse modeling framework 2.0*. Upper Saddle River, NJ: Addison-Wesley.

Stoy, K., & Nagpal, R. (2004). Self-repair through scale independent self-reconfiguration. In *Proceedings of the IEEE/RSJ International Conference on Intelligent Robots and Systems* (pp. 2062-2067).

Stoy, J., & Strachey, C. (1972). OS6 - An experimental operating system for a small computer. part 2: Input/output and filing system. *The Computer Journal*, *15*(3), 195–203. doi:10.1093/comjnl/15.3.195

Stratego (2010). The Stratego program transformation language. Retrieved from http://strategoxt.org/

Strembeck, M., & Zdun, U. (2009). An approach for the systematic development of domain-specific languages. *Software, Practice & Experience*, *39*(15), 1253–1292. doi:10.1002/spe.936

Stroustrup, B. (2007). Evolving a language in and for the real world: C++ 1991-2006. In *Proceedings of the Third ACM SIGPLAN Conference on History of Programming Languages (HOPL III)* (pp. 1-59).

Stroustrup, B. (2010). *C++0x FAQ*. Retrieved from http://www.research.att.com/~bs/C++0xFAQ.html

Stroustrup, B. (2000). *The C++ programming language* (special edition). Addison-Wesley.

Sugihara, R., & Gupta, R. (2008). Programming models for sensor networks: A survey. *ACM Transactions on Sensor Networks, 4*(2), 8:1-8:29.

Summerfield, M. (2010). *Programming in Python 3: A complete introduction to the Python Programming Language* (2nd ed.). Upper Saddle River, Boston, USA: Addison-Wesley.

Sunyé, G., Pennaneac'h, F., Ho, W.-M., Le Guennec, A., & Jézéquel, J.-M. (2001). Using UML action semantics for executable modeling and beyond. In K. R. Dittrich, A. Geppert, & M. C. Norrie (Ed.), *Proceedings of the 13th Conference on Advanced Information Systems Engineering (CAiSE 2001)* (pp. 433-447). Berlin, Germany: Springer.

Swanson, S., Schwerin, A., Mercaldi, M., Petersen, A., Putnam, A., Michelson, K., … Eggers, S. J. (2007). The wavescalar architecture. *ACM Transactions on Computing Systems, 25*(2), 4:1-4:54.

Szűgyi, Z., Sinkovics, Á., Pataki, N., & Porkoláb, Z. (2009). C++ metastring library and its applications. In M. Fernandes, J. Saraiva, R. Lammel, & J. Visser (Eds.), *Proceedings of the 3rd International Summer School Conference on Generative and Transformational Techniques in Software Engineering III (GTTSE'09)* (pp. 461-480).

Szymanski, M., & Woern, H. (2007). JaMOS - A MDL2ε based operating system for swarm micro robotics. In *Proceedings of the 2007 IEEE Swarm Intelligence Symposium* (pp. 324 – 331).

Taha, W., & Sheard, T. (1997). *Multi-stage programming with explicit annotations*. Paper presented at the symposium on Partial Evaluation and Semantics-Based Program Manipulation, Amsterdam, Netherlands.

Tambe, S., & Gokhale, A. (2009). LEESA: Embedding strategic and XPath-like object structure traversals in C. In Taha, W. (Ed.), *Domain-Specific Languages* (*Vol. 5658*, pp. 100–124). Lecture Notes in Computer ScienceBerlin, Germany: Springer-Verlag. doi:10.1007/978-3-642-03034-5_6

Tanter, E. (2008). Contextual values. In *Proceedings of the 2008 Symposium on Dynamic Languages*. Washington, DC, USA: IEEE.

Tatsubori, M., Chiba, S., Killijian, M., & Itano, K. (2000). OpenJava: A class-based macro system for Java. In *Proceedings of the 1st OOPSLA Workshop in Reflection and Software Engineering: Reflection* (pp. 117-133).

Taylor, M. B., Kim, J., Miller, J., Wentzlaff, D., Ghodrat, F., & Greenwald, B. (2002). The raw microprocessor: A computational fabric for software circuits and general purpose programs. *IEEE Micro, 22*(2), 25–35. doi:10.1109/MM.2002.997877

Technologies, B. B. N. (2011). *Cougaar: The cognitive agent architecture*. Retrieved from http://cougaar.org

Telecom Italia Lab. (2011). *JADE - Java Agent DEvelopment framework*. Retrieved from http://jade.tilab.com/

The Klavins Lab. (2012). *Gro: The cell programming language*. University of Washington. Retrieved from http://depts.washington.edu/soslab/gro/

The Xactium XMF Mosaic. (2007). *The Xactium XMF Mosaic*.

Thibault, S., Marlet, R., & Consel, C. (1997). A domain-specific language for video device drivers: From design to implementation. In *Proceedings of the Conference on Domain-Specific* (pp. 11–26).

Thielemann, H. (2004). Audio processing using Haskell. In *Proceedings of the 7th International Conference on Digital Audio Processing* (pp. 201–206).

Thies, W., Karczmarek, M., Gordon, M., Maze, D., Wong, J., Hoffmann, H., & Brown, M. (2001). *Streamit: A compiler for streaming applications*. Technical Report MIT-LCS Technical Memo TM-622, Massachusetts Institute of Technology.

Thomas, D., & Barry, B. M. (2003). Model driven development: The case for domain oriented programming. In *Companion of the 18th Annual ACM SIGPLAN Conference on Object-Oriented Programming, Systems, Languages, and Applications* (pp. 2-7). New York, NY: ACM Press.

Thomas, D. (2004). MDA: Revenge of the modelers or UML utopia? *IEEE Software*, *21*(3), 22–24. doi:10.1109/MS.2004.1293067

Thomas, D., Fowler, C., & Hunt, A. (2009). *Programming Ruby*. Pragmatic Bookshelf.

Thompson, S. (2011). *Haskell – The craft of functional programming* (3rd ed.). Harlow, UK: Addison-Wesley.

Threaded Building Blocks. (2011). *Intel threaded building blocks for open source*. Retrieved from http://threadingbuildingblocks.org

Tobin-Hochstadt, S., St-Amour, V., Culpepper, R., Flatt, M., & Felleisen, M. (2011). *Languages as libraries*. Paper presented at the Conference on Programming Language Design and Implementation, San Jose, CA.

Tobis, M. (2005). Pynsol: Objects as scaffolding. *Computing in Science & Engineering*, *7*(4), 84–91. doi:10.1109/MCSE.2005.78

Toffoli, T., & Margolus, N. (1987). *Cellular Automata Machines: A new environment for modeling*. MIT Press.

Tomita, M. (1985). *Efficient parsing for natural language: A fast algorithm for practical systems*. Kluwer Academic Publishing.

Torchiano, M., & Morisio, M. (2004). Overlooked aspects of COTS-based development. *IEEE Software*, *21*(2), 88–93. doi:10.1109/MS.2004.1270770

Tratt, L. (2005). *Compile-time meta-programming in a dynamically typed OO language*. Paper presented at the symposium on Dynamic Languages, San Diego, CA.

Tratt, L. (2008). Domain specific language implementation via compile-time metaprogramming. *ACM Transactions on Programming Languages and Systems*, *30*(31), 131–140.

Trencansky, I., & Cervenka, R. (2005). Agent modeling language (AML): A comprehensive approach to modeling MAS. *Informatica Ljubljana*, *29*(4), 391.

Tsetsos, V., Papataxiarhis, V., Kontos, T., Seneclauze, M., Hadjiefthymiades, S., & Fytros, E. (2010). An advanced sensor platform for autonomic computing: The IPAC approach. In *7th European Conference on Wireless Sensor Networks (EWSN)*, Coimbra, Portugal.

Turner, K. J. (1994). *Exploiting the m4 macro language*. Unpublished technical report, University of Stirling, Scotland.

University of Michigan Center for the Study of Complex Systems. (2011). *Swarm development wiki*. Retrieved from http://www.swarm.org/index.php/Main_Page

Unruh, E. (1994). *Prime number computation*. ANSI X3J16-94-0075/ISO WG21-462.

UPC. (2005). *UPC language specifications V 1.2*. Retrieved from http://upc.lbl.gov/docs/user/upc_spec_1.2.pdf

Usbeck, K., & Beal, J. (2011). An agent framework for agent societies. In *Proceedings of the Compilation of the Co-Located Workshops on DSM'11, TMC'11, AGERE!'11 at Systems, Programming, Languages and Applications: Software for Humanity* (pp. 201-212).

Vallecillo, A. (2010). On the combination of domain specific modeling languages. In *Proceedings of the 6th European Conference on Modelling Foundations and Applications, Lecture Notes in Computer Science 6138*, Paris, France (pp. 305–320).

van de Stadt, R. (2001). *Cyberchair: A web-based groupware application to facilitate the paper reviewing process*. Retrieved from http://www.cyberchair.org

van den Brand, M. G. J., de Jong, H. A., Klint, P., & Oliver, P. A. (2000). Efficient annotated terms. *Software, Practice & Experience*, *30*(3), 259–291. doi:10.1002/(SICI)1097-024X(200003)30:3<259::AID-SPE298>3.0.CO;2-Y van den Brand, M. G. J., & Klint, P. (2007). ATerms for manipulation and exchange of structured data: It's all about sharing. *Journal of Information and Software Technology, 49*(1), 55–64. doi:10.1016/j.infsof.2006.08.009

van Deursen, A., Klint, P., & Visser, J. (2000). Domain-specific languages: An annotated bibliography. *SIGPLAN Notices, 35*(6), 26–36. doi:10.1145/352029.352035

van Wijngaarden, A. (1981). Revised report of the algorithmic language Algol 68. *ALGOL Bulletin, 47*(Supplement), 1–119.

Van Wyk, E., & Schwerdfeger, A. (2007). Context-aware scanning for parsing extensible languages. In *Proceedings of the 6th International Conference on Generative Programming and Component Engineering (GPCE '07)* (pp. 63-72).

Van Wyk, E., Bodin, D., Gao, J., & Krishnan, L. (2008). Silver: An extensible attribute grammar system. *Electronic Notes in Theoretical Computer Science, 203*(12), 103–116. doi:10.1016/j.entcs.2008.03.047

Vanderbauwhede, W., Margala, M., Chalamalasetti, S. R., & Purohit, S. (2010). A C++-Embedded domain-specific language for programming the MORA soft processor array. In *Proceedings of the 21st IEEE International Conference on Application-Specific Systems Architectures and Processors* (pp. 141–148).

Vandevoorde, D., & Josuttis, N. (2002). *C++ templates: The complete guide*. Addison-Wesley.

Vara, J. M., Vela, B., Bollati, V., & Marcos, E. (2009). Supporting model-driven development of object-relational database schemas: A case study. In R. Paige (Ed.), *International Conference on Model Transformation, Lecture Notes in Computer Science, Vol. 5563* (pp. 181-196). Berlin, Germany: Springer-Verlag.

Varanda Pereira, M. J., Mernik, M., Cruz, D., & Henriques, P. R. (2008). VisualLISA: A visual interface for an attribute grammar based compiler-compiler. In *Proceedings of 2nd Conference on Compilers, Related Technologies and Applications* (pp. 265-289). Bragança, Portugal: IPB.

Varró, D. (2002). A formal semantics of UML statecharts by model transition systems. *Graph Transformation: First International Conference (ICGT 2002)* (pp. 378-392). Barcelona, Spain: Springer-Verlag.

Vasudevan, N., & Tratt, L. (2011). Comparative study of DSL tools. *Electronic Notes in Theoretical Computer Science, 264*(5), 103–121. doi:10.1016/j.entcs.2011.06.007

Veldhuizen, T. (1995). Expression templates. *C++ Report, 7*(5), 26-31.

Veldhuizen, T. (1996). Using C++ template metaprograms. *C++ Report, 7*(4), 459-473.

Veldhuizen, T. (1999). C++ templates as partial evaluation. In O. Danvy (Ed.), *Proceedings of the 1999 ACM SIGPLAN Workshop on Partial Evaluation and Semantics-Based Program Manipulation* (pp. 13-18).

Veldhuizen, T. (2005). Software libraries and their reuse: Entropy, Kolmogorov complexity, and Zipf's law. In *OOPSLA 2005 Workshop on Library-Centric Software Design (LCSD'05)*.

Veldhuizen, T. (2006). Tradeoffs in metaprogramming. In *Proceedings of the 2006 ACM SIGPLAN Symposium on Partial Evaluation and Semantics-Based Program Manipulation (PEPM '06)* (pp. 150-159).

Veldhuizen, T. (2007). Parsimony principles for software components and metalanguages. In *Proceedings of the 6th international conference on Generative programming and component engineering (GPCE '07)* (pp. 115-122).

Veldhuizen, T. L. (2003). *C++ templates are turing complete*. Unpublished technical report, University of Indiana, IN.

Veldhuizen, T., & Gannon, D. (1998). Active libraries: Rethinking the roles of compilers and libraries. In *Proceedings of the SIAM Workshop on Object Oriented Methods for Inter-operable Scientific and Engineering Computing (OO'98)* (pp. 21-23).

Verna, D. (2006). *Beating C in scientific computing applications*. Paper presented at the European Lisp Workshop, Nantes, France.

Verna, D. (2009). *Clos efficiency: Instantiation*. Paper presented at the International Lisp Conference, Cambridge, MA.

Verna, D. (2010). *Clon: The command-line options nuker library*. Retrieved April 2, 2012, from http://www.lrde.epita.fr/~didier/software/lisp/clon.php.

Viroli, M., Casadei, M., Montagna, S., & Zambonelli, F. (2011a). Spatial coordination of pervasive services through chemical-inspired tuple spaces. *ACM Transactions on Autonomous and Adaptive Systems, 6*(2), 14:1 - 14:24.

Viroli, M., Nardini, E., Castelli, G., Mamei, M., & Zambonelli, F. (2011b). A coordination approach to spatially-situated pervasive service ecosystems. In G. Fortino, A. Garro, L. Palopoli, W. Russo, & G. Spezzano (Eds.), *WOA 2011 - XII Workshop Nazionale "Dagli Oggetti agli Agenti", volume 741 of CEUR Workshop Proceedings*, (pp. 19-27). Sun SITE Central Europe, RWTH Aachen University.

Visser, E. (2006). Stratego/XT 0.16: components for transformation systems. *Proceedings of the 2006 ACM SIGPLAN Symposium on Partial Evaluation and Semantic-Based Program Manipulation* (pp. 95-99). ACM Press.

Visser, E. (2004). Program transformation with Stratego/XT: Rules, strategies, tools, and systems in StrategoXT-0.9. In Lengauer, C. (Eds.), *Domain-Specific Program Generation* (*Vol. 3016*, pp. 216–238). Lecture Notes in Computer Science. doi:10.1007/978-3-540-25935-0_13

Visser, E. (2005). A survey of strategies in rule-based program transformation systems. *Journal of Symbolic Computation, 40*, 831–873. doi:10.1016/j.jsc.2004.12.011

Voelter, M., & Solomatov, K. (2010). Language modularization and composition with projectional language workbenches illustrated with MPS. In *Proceedings of the 3rd International Conference on Software Language Engineering*.

Voelter, M. (2008). MD* best practices. *Journal of Object Technology, 8*(6), 79–102. doi:10.5381/jot.2009.8.6.c6

Völter, M. (2011). MPS, the Meta Programming System. Retrieved from http://www.jetbrains.com/mps/

vom Brocke, J., & Buddendick, C. (2006). *Reusable conceptual models. Requirements based on the design science research paradigm.* Paper presented at the First International Conference on Design Science Research in Information Systems and Technology, Claremont, CA.

von Kutschera, F. (1975). *Sprachphilosophie*. (2nd ed.). München, Germany: Wilhelm Fink Verlag.

Wachsmuth, G. (2007). Metamodel adaptation and model co-adaptation. *European Conference on Object-Oriented Programming, Lecture Notes in Computer Science, Vol. 4609* (pp. 600-624). Springer.

Wada, H. (2005). Modeling turnpike: A model-driven framework for domain-specific software development. In *Companion to the 20th Annual ACM SIGPLAN Conference on Object-Oriented Programming, Systems, Languages, and Applications (OOPSLA)* (pp. 128–129). New York, NY: ACM

Walkingshaw, E., & Erwig, M. (2009). A domain-specific language for experimental game theory. *Journal of Functional Programming, 19*(6), 645–661. doi:10.1017/S0956796809990220

Wallace, M., & Runciman, C. (1999). Haskell and XML: Generic combinators or type-based translation? In *4th ACM International Conference on Functional Programming* (pp. 148–159).

Walter, J., Welch, J., & Amato, N. (2004). Distributed reconfiguration of metamorphic robot chains. *Distributed Computing, 17*, 171–189. doi:10.1007/s00446-003-0103-y

Wampler, D., & Payne, A. (2009). *Programming Scala*. Sebastopol, CA: O'Reilly Media.

Wand, Y., & Weber, R. (1990). An ontological model of an information system. *IEEE Transactions on Software Engineering, 16*(11), 1282–1292. doi:10.1109/32.60316

Wand, Y., & Weber, R. (2002). Research commentary: Information systems and conceptual modeling–A research agenda. *Information Systems Research, 13*(4), 363–376. doi:10.1287/isre.13.4.363.69

Ward, M. (1994). Language-oriented programming. *Software — Concepts and Tools, 15*(4), 147-161.

Watt, D. A. (1991). *Programming languages syntax and semantics*. Cambridge, UK: Prentice Hall.

Weinberg, G. M. (1971). *The philosophy of programming languages*. New York, NY: John Wiley & Sons.

Weiss, R. (2001). *Cellular computation and communications using engineered genetic regular networks*. PhD thesis, MIT.

Weiss, D. M., & Lai, C. T. R. (1999). *Software product-line engineering: A family-based software development process*. Boston, MA: Addison-Wesley Longman Publishing Co., Inc.

Welsh, M., & Mainland, G. (2004). Programming sensor networks using abstract regions. In *Proceedings of the First USENIX/ACM Symposium on Networked Systems Design and Implementation (NSDI '04)* (pp. 3-17).

Welty, C. (2003). Ontology research. *AI Magazine*, *24*(3), 11–12.

Wende, C., Thieme, N., & Zschaler, S. (2010). A role-based approach towards modular language engineering. In *Proceedings of the 3rd International Conference on Software Language Engineering* (pp. 254-273).

Wendt, T., Häber, A., Brigl, B., & Winter, A. (2004). Modeling hospital information systems (Part 2): Using the 3LGM² tool for modeling patient record management. *Methods of Information in Medicine*, *43*(3), 256–267.

Werfel, J. (2006). *Anthills built to order: Automating construction with artificial swarms*. PhD thesis. Cambridge, MA: MIT Press.

Werfel, J., & Nagpal, R. (2007). Collective construction of environmentally-adaptive structures. In *2007 IEEE/RSJ International Conference on Intelligent Robots and Systems (IROS 2007)* (pp. 2345 – 2352). IEEE.

Werfel, J., Bar-Yam, Y., & Nagpal, R. (2005). Building patterned structures with robot swarms. In *International Joint Conference on Artificial Intelligence* (pp. 1495—1502).

Whitehouse, K., Sharp, C., Brewer, E., & Culler, D. (2004). Hood: A neighborhood abstraction for sensor networks. In *Proceedings of the 2nd International Conference on Mobile Systems, Applications, and Services* (pp. 99-110). ACM Press.

White, J., Hill, J. H., Gray, J., Tambe, S., Gokhale, A. S., & Schmidt, D. C. (2009). Improving domain-specific language reuse with software product line techniques. *IEEE Software*, *26*(4), 47–53. doi:10.1109/MS.2009.95

Wilensky, U. (2011). *Netlogo*. Retrieved from http://ccl.northwestern.edu/netlogo/

Wimmer, M., & Kramler, G. (2005). Bridging grammarware and modelware. *MoDELS Satellite Events* (pp. 159-168).

Winskel, G. (1993). *The formal semantics of programming languages: An introduction*. Cambridge, MA: Mit Press.

Winter, A., Brigl, B., & Wendt, T. (2003). Modeling hospital information systems. Part 1: The revised three-layer graph-based meta model 3LGM². *Methods of Information in Medicine*, *42*(5), 544–551.

Wirth, N. (1974). On the design of programming languages. In J. L. Rosenfeld (Ed.), *Proceedings of the 6th International Federation for Information Processing Congress* (pp. 386–393). Stockholm, Sweden: University of Stockholm.

Wirth, N. (1977). What can we do about the unnecessary diversity of notation for syntactic definitions? *Communications of the ACM*, *20*(11), 822–823. doi:10.1145/359863.359883

Withey, J. (1996). *Investment analysis of software assets for product lines*. Technical Report CMU/SEI96-TR-010. Pittsburgh, PA: Software Engineering Institute, Carnegie Mellon University.

Wohlin, C., Runeson, P., Höst, M., Ohlsson, M. C., Regnell, B., & Wesslén, A. (1999). *Experimentation in software engineering: An introduction* (*Vol. 6*). Kluwer Academic Publishers.

Wolf, T. (2007). *Rationale-based uni□ed software engineering model*. PhD thesis, TU Munchen, Germany.

Wu, H., & Gray, J. (2005). Testing domain-specific languages in Eclipse. In *Proceedings of the Conference on Object Oriented Programming Systems Languages and Applications, Companion to the 20th Annual ACM SIGPLAN Conference on Object-Oriented Programming, Systems, Languages and Applications* (pp. 173-174). San Diego, USA.

Wu, H., Gray, J., & Mernik, M. (2004). *Debugging domain-specific languages*. In Object Oriented Programming Systems, Languages, and Applications, Eclipse Technology Poster Session, Vancouver, Canada.

Wu, H., Gray, J., Roychoudhury, S., & Mernik, M. (2005). Weaving a debugging aspect into domain-specific language grammars. In *Proceedings of the 2005 ACM Symposium on Applied Computing* (pp. 1370 – 1374). Santa Fe, New Mexico.

Wu, Y., Hernandez, F., France, R., & Clarke, P. J. (2011b). A DSML for coordinating user-centric communication services. In *Proceedings of the 35th IEEE International Computer Software and Applications Conference (COMPSAC 11)* (pp. 93-102). IEEE Computer Society.

Wu, H., Gray, J., & Mernik, M. (2008). Grammar-driven generation of domain-specific language debuggers. *Software, Practice & Experience*, *38*(10), 1073–1103. doi:10.1002/spe.863

Wu, Y., Allen, A. A., Hernandez, F., France, R., & Clarke, P. J. (2011a). A domain-specific modeling approach to realizing user-centric communication. *Journal of Software Practice and Experience*, *42*(3), 357–390. doi:10.1002/spe.1081

Wyk, E. V., Bodin, D., Krishnan, L., & Gao, J. (2008). Silver: An extensible attribute grammar system. *Electronic Notes in Theoretical Computer Science*, *203*(2), 103–116. doi:10.1016/j.entcs.2008.03.047

Wyk, V. E., Bodin, D., & Gao, J. (2010). Silver: An extensible attribute grammar system. *Science of Computer Programming*, *75*(2), 39–54. doi:10.1016/j.scico.2009.07.004

XMF. (2010). *The XMF programming language*. Retrieved from http://itcentre.tvu.ac.uk/~clark/xmf.html

XPath. (2012). *XML path language (XPath) 2.0*. Retrieved March 28, 2012, from http://www.w3.org/TR/xpath20/

xText. (2011). *xText 2.0*. Retrieved March, 28, 2012, from http://www.xtext.org

Yamins, D. (2007). *A theory of local-to-global algorithms for one-dimensional spatial multi-agent systems*. PhD thesis, Harvard, Cambridge, MA, USA.

Yang, C., Wu, H., Huang, Q., Li, Z., & Li, J. (2011). Using spatial principles to optimize distributed computing for enabling the physical science discoveries. [PNAS]. *Proceedings of the National Academy of Sciences of the United States of America*, *108*(14), 5498–5503. doi:10.1073/pnas.0909315108

Yang, M., Michaelson, G., & Pooley, R. (2008). Formal action semantics for a UML action language. *Journal of Universal Computer Science*, *14*(21), 3608–3624.

Yao, Y., & Gehrke, J. (2002). The cougar approach to in-network query processing in sensor networks. *SIGMOD Record*, *31*(3), 9–18. doi:10.1145/601858.601861

Yim, M., Shen, W., Salemi, B., Rus, D., Moll, M., & Lipson, H. (2007). Modular self-reconfigurable robot systems: Grand challenges of robotics. *Robotics & Automation Magazine, IEEE*, *14*(1), 43–52. doi:10.1109/MRA.2007.339623

YourKit. (2011). Retrieved from http://www.yourkit.com/

Zambonelli, F., & Viroli, M. (2011). A survey on nature-inspired metaphors for pervasive service ecosystems. *International Journal of Pervasive Computing and Communications*, *7*(3), 186–204. doi:10.1108/17427371111172997

Zdun, U., & Strembeck, M. (2009). Reusable architectural decisions for DSL design: Foundational decisions in DSL projects. In A. Kelly & M. Weiss (Eds.), *Proceedings of the 14th Annual European Conference on Pattern Languages of Programming*. Aachen, Germany: CEUR, RWTH Aachen.

ZigBee Alliance. (2012). *ZigBee smart energy overview*. Retrieved from http://www.zigbee.org/Standards/ZigBeeSmartEnergy /Overview.aspx

Zimmermann, H. (1980). OSI reference model-the ISO model of architecture for open systems interconnection. *IEEE Transactions on Communications*, *28*(4), 425–432. doi:10.1109/TCOM.1980.1094702

Živanov, Ž., Rakić, P., & Hajduković, M. (2008). Using code generation approach in developing kiosk applications. *Computer Science and Information Systems*, *5*(1), 41–59. doi:10.2298/CSIS0801041Z

About the Contributors

Mernik Marjan received his MSc and PhD degrees in Computer Science from the University of Maribor in 1994 and 1998, respectively. He is currently a Professor at the University of Maribor, Faculty of Electrical Engineering and Computer Science. He is also a visiting Professor at the University of Alabama at Birmingham, Department of Computer and Information Sciences, and at the University of Novi Sad, Faculty of Technical Sciences. His research interests include programming languages, compilers, domain-specific (modeling) languages, grammar-based systems, grammatical inference, and evolutionary computations.

* * *

Slavica Aleksić received her MSc (5 year, former Diploma) degree from Faculty of Technical Sciences in Novi Sad. She completed her Mr (2 year) degree at the University of Novi Sad, Faculty of Technical Sciences. Currently, she works as a Teaching Assistant at the Faculty of Technical Sciences at the University of Novi Sad, where she assists in teaching several Computer Science and Informatics courses. Her research interests are related to Information Systems, Database Systems and Software Engineering.

Andrew A. Allen is a Visiting Assistant Professor in the Department of Computer Science at Georgia Southern University. He earned his BSc, MSc, and PhD degrees in Computer Science from the School of Computing and Information Sciences at Florida International University. His research interests are the areas of model-driven software development, autonomic computing, middleware for communication intensive collaboration, distributed systems and computer science education. He is a member of the ACM, IEEE Computer Society, and UPE.

Mark Allison is currently a PhD candidate in Computer Science at the Florida International University with research interests in Software Engineering emphasizing in Model Driven Software Development, energy managements systems and merging Artificial Intelligence methods. Mark received a BS and a MS degree from the City College of New York in Computer Science and Information Systems, respectively. Mark has worked in engineering and facilities management within the telecom industry for close to a decade. He is an active member in MENSA International and the Association for Computing Machinery (ACM).

Vasco Amaral is an Assistant Professor at FCT/UNL and Researcher at CITI (Research Center for Informatics and Information Technologies). He is Senior member at IEEE and Ordem dos Engenheiros (elected representative of the Portuguese Software Engineers), and holds a PhD. by the University of Mannheim in Germany. He has worked in High Energy Physics Computing at CERN (Switzerland), DESY (Germany), and LIP (Portugal). He presently researches on Software Languages Engineering and Model-Driven Development (MDD) at both the Foundations and Application level. He organizes several events like the international Summer School DSM-TP and workshops at MODELS, MPM@MODELS, INFORUM, besides steering PPPJ and serving in the scientific committee of several events.

Moussa Amrani is currently a PhD Student at University of Luxembourg (Luxembourg). He is currently working on the formal verification of modelling frameworks. The project is to build a complete framework for academics as well as practitioners, addressing the formal verification of Kermeta transformations by using model-checking and abstract interpretation techniques.

Kyoungho An is a PhD student in the Department of Electrical Engineering and Computer Science at Vanderbilt University, Nashville, TN, USA. He received his B.S. in Computer Science from Handong Global University, South Korea in 2009; and M.S. in Computer Science from Vanderbilt University, Nashville, TN, USA in 2011. He is currently investigating fault-tolerant and real-time mechanisms in cloud infrastructures for mission critical systems and model-driven engineering (MDE) for cloud services.

Paolo Arcaini graduated in Computer Science in 2009 at the University of Milan. He is currently a PhD student in Computer Science at the University of Milan, under the supervision of Professor Elvinia Riccobene. His research interests include software engineering and formal methods. In particular he has worked on formal verification and runtime monitoring by means of Abstract State Machines (ASMs), and validation of ASM and NuSMV specifications.

Ritu Arora received her PhD degree from the Department of Computer and Information Sciences at the University of Alabama at Birmingham. She works as a Research Associate at the Texas Advanced Computing Center (TACC) and is an adjunct faculty member in the Division of Statistics and Scientific Computation at the University of Texas at Austin. She provides consultancy to domain-specialists so that they can achieve their scientific goals through HPC resources while working at a high-level of abstraction. Her research interests include exploration of generative programming techniques for developing parallel programming environments, fault-tolerant systems, predictive analytics, and parallel benchmarks.

Ankica Barišić was born in Zagreb in 1983. She is a PhD student at FCT/UNL and researcher at CITI. She obtained an MSc degree in Mathematics, specializing in Computer Science, from University of Zagreb in 2010. From 2007 till 2010, she worked as designer of an information system for the financial industry. Her Master's thesis covered the topic of risk management with focus on modeling portfolio optimization using VaR. Her current research focus is a conceptual framework that supports software language engineering development process concerning the issue of domain-specific language usability evaluation reusing best practices from the human-computer interaction area.

Bruno F. Barroca is a PhD student and scientific researcher at FCT/UNL. He obtained his BSc. degree in Software Engineering from FCT/UNL in 2003. From 2003 to 2008, he worked in a medium sized software house, developing on a software scripting language. In 2007, he received his MSc degree in Software Engineering from FCT/UNL, in the topic of Languages for Rapid Design and Prototyping of Graphical User Interfaces. His current research interests are Domain Specific (Modeling) Languages Engineering, and Domain Specific Modeling, User-Centric Design, Model-based Development of UIs, DS(M)L's Quality, Model Driven Development, Model Transformations, Model-based Testing, and Model Checking.

Jacob Beal is a Scientist at Raytheon BBN Technologies, a research affiliate of MIT CSAIL, and a science Commons Fellow. His research interests center on the engineering of robust adaptive systems, with a focus on problems of modelling and control for spatially-distributed systems like sensor networks, robotic swarms, and natural or engineered biological cells. Dr. Beal completed his PhD in 2007 under Prof. Gerald Jay Sussman at the MIT Computer Science and Artificial Intelligence Laboratory.

Javier Luis Cánovas Izquierdo received a PhD in computer science from the University of Murcia, Spain in 2010 and a MSc from the University of Murcia in 2006. Since October 2011, he is a post-doctoral researcher in the AtlanMod team at INRIA Rennes Bretagne Atlantique. His research interests are domain-specific languages, model-driven development, and model-driven modernization.

Milan Čeliković graduated in 2009 at the Faculty of Technical Sciences, Novi Sad, at the Department of Computing and Control. Since 2009 he has worked as a Teaching Assistant at the Faculty of Technical Sciences, Novi Sad, at the Chair for Applied Computer Science. In 2010, he started his PhD studies at the Faculty of Technical Sciences, Novi Sad. His main research interests are focused on: domain specific modeling, domain specific languages, databases, and database management systems.

Vanea Chiprianov received his PhD in Computer Science jointly from University of Bretagne Sud and Telecom Bretagne, France, in 2012. His research interests include software and systems engineering, focusing on the design and architecture phases of developing large, complex systems. He has applied modeling (Model Driven Engineering) concepts and techniques to a variety of systems, spanning telecommunications services, the CDIO educational framework and the Multiple Criteria Decision Aid process. During his PhD, he was also a Teaching Assistant in disciplines like Software Engineering, Algorithms, Distributed Systems, and Databases.

Tony Clark is Professor of Informatics and Head of the Business Information systems Department in the School of Engineering and Information Sciences at Middlesex University. As an academic at King's College London he worked on languages for object-oriented specification and design including contributing to a range of industry standards (UML 2.0, MDA, QVT, MOF) through participation in the Object Management Group (OMG). Tony co-founded Xactium Ltd. in 2003 and served as Technical Director 2003-2008. The company sold UML-based meta-tools and acted as consultant to a number of blue-chip companies. Tony has published widely on language driven development, has developed many software tools, is an editorial board member of the SoSyM Journal, has edited several journal special issues including *IEEE Software* and *SoSyM*, and was co-chair of the MODELS conference in 2011.

Peter J. Clarke received his BSc degree in Computer Science and Mathematics from the University of the West Indies (Cave Hill) in 1987, MS degree from SUNY Binghamton University in 1996 and PhD in Computer Science from Clemson University in 2003. His research interests are in the areas of domain-specific modeling languages, model-driven software development, software testing, and software metrics. He is currently Associate Professor of Computing and Information Sciences at Florida International University. He is a member of the ACM (SIGSOFT, SIGCSE, and SIGAPP); IEEE Computer Society; and the Association for Software Testing (AST).

Nikolaus Correll is an Assistant Professor at the Department of Computer Science at the University of Colorado at Boulder. He obtained a PhD from EPFL in 2007, and spent was a post-doc at MIT CSAIL till 2009. Nikolaus' research interests are modeling, analysis, and synthesis of large-scale distributed swarming systems from robots to smart materials.

Stefan Dulman is an Assistant Professor at the Delft University of Technology, in the Embedded Software Chair. His current research interests include self-adaptive aspects of large-scale embedded systems (wireless sensor networks, robotic swarms, mobile ad-hoc networks), spatial computing, interactive distributed systems. His research has been integrated in the products of the Ambient Systems BV, a Dutch SME specialized in providing wireless solutions for the transport and logistics scenarios, where he acted as founding member and senior researcher between 2004-2010, and he is currently pursuing applications in interactive architecture. Dr. Dulman completed his PhD in 2005 at the University of Twente, the Netherlands, and is an author of more than 50 research papers in peer-reviewed publications.

Ersin Er received his BSc and MSc degrees in 2003 and 2006 in Computer Science and Engineering from Hacettepe University, Turkey. From 2003 to 2011 he worked as a research assistant in the same university where he is currently a PhD student. He has been working as a software architect since March 2011 at Peak Games, the largest and fastest-growing social gaming company in Turkey and Middle East and North Africa and a top 10 player globally. His research interests include Software Architecture Design and Model-Driven Software Development.

Martin Erwig is Professor of Computer Science at Oregon State University where he has been teaching since 2000. He received his PhD and Habilitation in Computer Science from the University of Hagen in Germany. He is the author or co-author of two books and over 100 peer-reviewed publications, for which he received several best paper awards. His research interests are in language design, functional programming, and visual languages.

Robert France is a Full Professor in the Department of Computer Science at Colorado State University. His research interests are in the area of software engineering, in particular formal specification techniques, software modeling techniques, software product lines, and domain-specific modeling languages. He is an Editor-in-Chief of the Springer journal on *Software and System Modeling* (SoSyM), and is on the editorial board of *IEEE Computer* and the *Journal on Software Testing, Verification, and Reliability.* He is a past Steering Committee Chair of the MoDELS/UML conference series, and is the PC Chair for MODELS 2012. He was also a member of the revision task forces for the UML 1.x standards. He was awarded the Ten Year Most Influential Paper award at MODELS in 2008.

Angelo Gargantini is Assistant Professor at the Faculty of Engineering of the University of Bergamo, where he teaches basic and advanced courses of Computer Science. He holds a PhD in Software Engineering from the Politecnico di Milano and a PhD in Computer Science from the University of Catania. He has been Assistant Professor at the University of Bergamo since 2005. His research topics include verification by theorem proving, test generation by model checking, and validation and verifications of (embedded) systems by abstract state machines. In these areas, he collaborates with the University of Milano, Saarbruecken University, and Naval Research Laboratory (USA).

Aniruddha S. Gokhale is an Associate Professor in the Department of Electrical Engineering and Computer Science at Vanderbilt University, Nashville, TN, USA. He has over 100 technical articles to his credit focusing on topics pertaining to model-driven engineering (MDE), middleware solutions for quality of service (QoS) assurance, and correct-by-construction design and development of distributed real-time and embedded systems. Dr. Gokhale obtained his B.E (Computer Engineering) from University of Pune, India, 1989; MS (Computer Science) from Arizona State University, 1992; and D.Sc (Computer Science) from Washington University in St. Louis, 1998. Prior to joining Vanderbilt, Dr. Gokhale was a member of technical staff at Lucent Bell Laboratories, NJ. Dr. Gokhale is a senior member of IEEE and a member of ACM.

Miguel Goulão was born in Lisbon in 1972. He received his PhD degree in Informatics from FCT/UNL in 2008. He is Assistant Professor at FCT/UNL and researcher in CITI, since 2000. His main research interests revolve around Experimental Software Engineering (ESE) and its applications to validate claims in several Software Engineering areas, including software languages engineering, software architecture and evolution. He has published over 30 peer-reviewed papers in international journals, conferences, and workshops, and serves as program committee member in several international events. He is also a member of the QUATIC conference series steering committee.

Sebastian Günther is a Postdoc Researcher with the Software Languages Lab at the Vrije Universiteit Brussel in Belgium. He received his PhD in Computer Science and Diploma (MSc equivalent) in Business Information Systems from the University of Magdeburg in Germany. His research interests are domain-specific languages, feature-oriented programming, context-oriented programming, and software variability.

Frank Hernandez is a PhD candidate in Computer Science in the School of Computing and Information Sciences at Florida International University (FIU). His research interests are in domain-specific modeling languages (DSML) and model-driven engineering. He has developed several DSMLs including a DSML for modeling BlackBerry applications called the Blackberry User Interface Modeling Language (BUIML), and is the lead designer for the Eberos Game Modeling Language (EberosGML) a DSML for creating 2d games. He is currently the President of the Special Interest Group of Gaming at FIU.

Stathes Hadjiefthymiades received his BSc, MSc and PhD in Informatics and Telecommunications from the Department of Informatics & Telecommunications (DIT) of the University of Athens (UoA), Athens, Greece. He also received a joint engineering-economics MSc degree from the National Technical University of Athens. In 1992 he joined the Greek consulting firm Advanced Services Group, Ltd., as an analyst/developer of telematic applications and systems. In 1995 he became a member of the Communication Networks Laboratory of UoA. From 2001 to 2002, he served as a visiting Assistant Professor at the University of Aegean, Department of Information and Communication Systems Engineering. In 2002 he joined the faculty of the Hellenic Open University (Department of Informatics), Patras, Greece, as an assistant professor. Since the beginning of 2004, he has been a member of the faculty of UoA, DIT where he is presently an Assistant Professor. He has participated in numerous projects realized in the context of EU and National Research Programmes. His research interests are in the areas of mobile, pervasive computing, web systems engineering, and networked multimedia applications. He is the author of over 150 publications in these areas.

Vladimir Ivančević is a PhD student in Applied Computer Science and Informatics and a teaching assistant at the Faculty of Technical Sciences, University of Novi Sad (Serbia), where he also gained his BSc and MSc in Electrical Engineering and Computing. His research interests include domain specific languages (DSLs), data mining (DM), and databases. At the moment, he is involved in several projects concerning application of DSLs and DM in the fields of software engineering, education, and public health.

Yvon Kermarrec is Professor of Computer Science at Institut Mines-Télécom / Télécom Bretagne in Brest, France. He currently chairs an R&D department of 30 faculty members and more than 35 PhD students. His research interests are related to software engineering applied to distributed and complex systems. He has a long term experience in teaching distributed systems at graduate level.

Ján Kollár is full Professor of Informatics at Department of Computers and Informatics, Technical university of Košice, Slovakia. He received his MSc summa cum laude in 1978 and his PhD in Computer Science in 1991. Since 1992 he is with the Department of Computer and Informatics at the Technical University of Košice. He was involved in research projects dealing with real-time systems, the design of microprogramming languages, image processing and remote sensing, dataflow systems, implementation of programming languages, and high performance computing. He is the author of process functional programming paradigm. Currently his research area covers formal languages and automata, programming paradigms, implementation of programming languages, functional programming, and adaptive software and language evolution.

Kostas Kolomvatsos received his B.Sc. in Informatics from the Department of Informatics at the Athens University of Economics and Business (AUEB) in 1995 and his M.Sc. in Computer Science from the Department of Informatics and Telecommunications at the National and Kapodistrian University of Athens (UoA) in 2005. He is currently a Ph.D. candidate in the National and Kapodistrian University of Athens – Department of Informatics and Telecommunications. His research interests are in the areas of Semantic Web Technologies, Ontological Engineering, Distributed Computing and Pervasive Computing. He has authored 20 publications in the above areas.

Ivan Luković received his MSc (5 year) degree in Informatics from the Faculty of Military and Technical Sciences in Zagreb in 1990. He completed his Mr (2 year) degree at the University of Belgrade, Faculty of Electrical Engineering in 1993, and his PhD at the University of Novi Sad, Faculty of Technical Sciences in 1996. Currently, he works as a Full Professor at the University of Novi Sad, where he lectures in several Computer Science and Informatics courses. His research interests are related to database systems and software engineering. He is the author or coauthor of over 80 research papers, 4 books, and 30 industry projects and software solutions.

Jesús García Molina is a full Professor in the Department of Informatics and Systems at the University of Murcia (Spain), where he leads the Modelum group, a R&D group with focus on Model-Driven Engineering and close partnership with industry. His research interests include model-driven development, domain-specific languages, and model-driven modernization. He received his PhD in Physical Chemistry from the University of Murcia.

Elvinia Riccobene is Associate Professor in Computer Science at the University of Milan. She received degree in Mathematics and PhD degree from the University of Catania. She holds visiting positions at the Center for High Assurance Computer System (Washington DC), at the Univ. of Bristol and Karlsruhe. Her research interests include formal methods, with particular expertise in the Abstract State Machine formalism, integration between formal modeling and MDE, formal semantics of metamodel-based languages, model-driven design, and model analysis techniques for software systems. She is member of the program committee of international conferences. She published several papers in international journals and in proceedings of international conferences.

Petros Patelis studied Computer Engineering at the Department of Electronic and Computer Engineering, Technical University of Crete. He received his Diploma in 2005 and his MSc in 2008 from the same Department. His research interests are in the areas of pervasive computing and knowledge management.

Zoltán Porkoláb, PhD. is a software developer at Ericsson and an Associate Professor at Eötvös Loránd University, Budapest, Hungary, where he is teaching programming languages, project tools, and advanced C++ programming. His research interests include programming paradigms, C++ template metaprogramming, software metrics, and software comprehension.

Shirren Premaratne is a Senior Research Officer in the Department of Computing at Macquarie University. His research interests are in programming-language design, programming principles and methods, data visualization, and interactive visual media.

Siegfried Rouvrais received his PhD in Computer Science from the University of Rennes in 2002, France. His dissertation focused on the construction process of complex software services by considering functional as well as extra-functional properties (e.g. performance, security, dependability). He is now Associate Professor in the Computer Engineering Department at Telecom Bretagne, France. On the one hand, Dr. Rouvrais is a researcher in software architecture. His current research interests are in large software and system design, architecture frameworks, business processes, and enterprise architectures. One the other hand, he has been involved in educational program design and reform since 2002. His current scholarly interests are in engineering education research and development, educational frameworks, quality assurance and continuous improvement, and international accreditations.

Miroslav Sabo is working for an IT company as a Consultant and an Architect. He received his MSc. 2008 and his PhD in Computer Science in 2011 at the Department of Computers and Informatics,

Technical University of Košice, Slovakia. He defended his PhD thesis about domain-specific languages and inference of concrete textual syntax in September, 2011.

Jesús Sánchez Cuadrado is an Assistant Professor at the Computer Science Department of the Universidad Autónoma of Madrid. He received his PhD in Computer Science from the University of Murcia. His research interests are model-driven development, model transformation languages, and dynamic languages. About these topics he has published several papers in referred journals such as *IEEE Transactions in Software Engineering* and *IEEE Software*, and he often attends conferences related to modeling and model transformation, such as ICMT and MoDELS. Besides, he has released some open source tools, notably the RubyTL transformation language.

Shivakumar Sastry is an Associate Professor with the Department of Electrical and Computer Engineering, The University of Akron. He received his PhD degree in Computer Engineering and Science from Case Western Reserve University and holds Masters Degrees in Computer Science from University of Central Florida and in Electrical Engineering from the Indian Institute of Science. His research interests are in Networked Embedded Systems, Real-time systems, and Graph algorithms. Prior to joining Akron, he was a Senior Research Scientist with Rockwell Automation.

Patrizia Scandurra is Assistant Professor at the Engineering Faculty of the University of Bergamo (Italy). Her research interests includes: integration of formal and semi-formal modeling languages; formal methods and functional analysis techniques; Component-based Development; Service-oriented Computing; Model-driven Engineering; design and analysis techniques for adaptive pervasive systems and embedded systems. She is a member of the Abstract State Machines (ASM) formal method community. She participated to several Italian and European research projects. She collaborated with companies such as STMicroelectronics, Opera21, and Atego, and with Italian universities (Milan, Pisa, and Politecnico di Milano) and the Simula Research Laboratory in Oslo (Norway).

Ábel Sinkovics is a Software Developer and a PhD student at Eötvös Loránd University, Budapest, Hungary. His research is about C++ template metaprogramming, functional programming, and domain-specific languages. He is building libraries supporting domain-specific language embedding based on template metaprogramming and libraries supporting template metaprogrammers.

Bedir Tekinerdogan received his MSc degree in Computer Science in 1994, and a PhD degree in Computer Science in 2000, both from the University of Twente, The Netherlands. From September 2003 until September 2008 he served as an Assistant Professor at University of Twente. Currently he is an Assistant Professor at Bilkent University in Turkey. He has more than 16 years of professional experience in software engineering research and education. His key research topic is software architecture design and related to this aspect-oriented software development, model-driven software development, software product line engineering, global software development, and service-oriented computing. He has been the organizer of around 50 workshops and served on the program committees and organising committees for conferences and workshops.

Adam Trewyn is a PhD student and Research Assistant in the Department of Electrical Engineering and Computer Science, Vanderbilt University. He obtained his Bachelor of Science Degree in Mathematics and in Computer Science at Florida Southern College in Lakeland, Florida, USA in 2009. Adam currently is researching software engineering practices relating to the complexities of real-time Cyber Physical Systems (CPS) as well as advanced manufacturing technologies and space-based cloud computing systems.

Kyle Usbeck works at Raytheon BBN Technologies as a Software Engineer and Scientist in the distributed systems group. There, he has contributed to projects involving Quality of Service (QoS) over airborne networks, spatial computing, information management systems, and electro-mechanical system design modification. His research interests include distributed systems, automated planning, agent-based systems, and spatial computing. Mr. Usbeck has a M.S. and B.S. in Computer Science from Drexel University.

George Valkanas studied Informatics at the Department of Informatics and Telecommunications, University of Athens, Greece, where he concluded his BSc studies in 2007. He received his MSc (honours) from the Department of Informatics, Aristotle University of Thessaloniki, Greece, in 2009. Since April 2009, he has been a PhD Candidate at the Dept. of Informatics and Telecommunications of the Univ. of Athens. His research interest include data and knowledge mining, data management and query processing in distributed domains, including wireless sensor networks and the WWW. He is a member of the Pervasive Computing group (http://p-comp.di.uoa.gr) and the KDDLab group (http://kddlab.di.uoa.gr).

Didier Verna has a PhD in Computer Science and works as an Assistant Professor at EPITA, a private computer science university located in Paris. Didier Verna is a member of the European Lisp Symposium steering committee and serves as a program committee member in various conferences (International Lisp Conference, European Lisp Symposium, Dynamic Languages Symposium, Context-Oriented Programming workshop, ACM Symposium on Applied Computing). Didier Verna is also involved in free software. He has been one of the core developers of XEmacs for more than 10 years, he maintains several LaTeX packages, and occasionally contributes to other Free Software projects.

Mirko Viroli is Associate Professor at the DEIS, Department of Electronics, Informatics and Systems of the Alma Mater Studiorum Universite di Bologna, Italy. He is an expert in computational models, in the areas of agent-based systems, coordination infrastructures, self-organising systems, and pervasive computing. He has written over 150 articles on such topics, with more than 30 in international refereed journals. He was Program Chair of the 2008 and 2009 ACM Symposium on Applied Computing (SAC), is a member of the Editorial Board of *The Knowledge Engineering Review* journal, and leads of the Bologna Unit of the FP7 STREP project "SAPERE" - Self-Aware Pervasive Service Ecosystems.

Eric Walkingshaw is a PhD student at Oregon State University studying language design with advisor Dr. Martin Erwig. He is interested in domain-specific languages, strongly-typed functional programming, and visual languages. He has developed languages for representing and typing variational software, explaining probabilistic reasoning problems, supporting philosophical research on causation, and supporting and explaining research in experimental game theory. He is originally from greater Seattle and shares the occasional affection of two cats with his wife Allison.

James Willans works for HSBC leading global distributed teams that help architect and implement the integration of systems using model-driven technology. In the past James has worked for companies in senior technical roles, architecting and leading the development of complex products. James has actively contributed to core industry standards for software development including UML 2.0, MOF 2.0, and QVT and has written and edited several books and articles on advanced software engineering techniques. James holds a BSc from Keele University and a PhD from the University of York.

Yali Wu is an Assistant Professor in the Department of Math, Computer Science, and Software Engineering, University of Detroit Mercy (UDM). Yali received her MSc and PhD degrees in Computer Sciences from Florida International University (FIU) in 2009 and 2011, respectively. She earned her BE degree in Software Engineering from Beihang University, China, in 2006. Her research interests include model-driven software development, domain-specific modeling languages, and computer science education. She has published several articles on software engineering research in peer reviewed conferences and journals. She is a member of the ACM and IEEE Computer Society.

Index

A

B

C

D

M

N

O

P

R

S

T

U

V

W

X